The Oxford

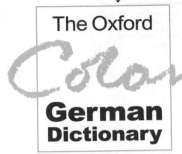

German Dictionary

Revised Edition

GERMAN–ENGLISH
ENGLISH–GERMAN

DEUTSCH–ENGLISCH
ENGLISCH–DEUTSCH

Gunhild Prowe

Jill Schneider

*Word games prepared by
Neil and Roswitha Morris*

Oxford   New York

OXFORD UNIVERSITY PRESS

1998

Oxford University Press, Great Clarendon Street, Oxford, OX2 6DP
Oxford New York
Athens Auckland Bangkok Bogota Bombay Buenos Aires
Calcutta Cape Town Dar es Salaam Delhi
Florence Hong Kong Istanbul Karachi
Kuala Lumpur Madras Madrid Melbourne
Mexico City Nairobi Paris Singapore
Taipei Tokyo Toronto Warsaw
and associated companies in
Berlin Ibadan

Oxford is a trade mark of Oxford University Press

© Oxford University Press 1998

First published 1997 as The Oxford–Duden Paperback
German dictionary
First published 1998 as The Oxford Color German Dictionary

British Library Cataloguing in Publication Data
Data available

Library of Congress Cataloging in Publication Data
Prowe, Gunhild.
The Oxford color German dictionary : German-English,
English-German = Deutsch-Englisch, Englisch-Deutsch / Gunhild Prowe,
Jill Schneider. — Rev. ed.
Originally published as: The Oxford German minidictionary : 1993.
1. German language—Dictionaries—English. 2. English language–
Dictionaries—German. I. Schneider, Jill. II. Title.
PF3640.P76   1998   433' .21—dc21   97–32054

ISBN 0-19-860189-1
10 9 8 7 6 5 4 3 2 1

Printed in Spain by
Mateu Cromo Artes Graficas S.A.
Madrid

Contents

Preface

The Oxford Color German Dictionary is a dictionary designed for begin-
ners of German. Its clear presentation and use of color headwords
make it easily accessible. This new edition includes word games
which are specifically designed to build key skills in using your dictionary more effectively, and to improve knowledge of German
vocabulary and usage in a fun and entertaining way. You will find
answers to all puzzles and games at the end of the section.

Introduction

As an aid to easy reference all main headwords, compounds, and derivatives appear in blue. The text of this new edition reflects recent changes to the spelling of German ratified in July 1996. The symbol (NEW) has been introduced to refer from the old spelling to the new, preferred one:

> **As** *nt* -ses, -se (NEW) **Ass**
> **Diät** *f* -,-en (*Med*) diet; **D~ leben** be on a diet. **d~** *adv* **d~ leben** (NEW) **D~ leben**, *s*. **Diät**.
> **absein**† *vi sep* (*sein*) (NEW) **ab sein**, *s*. **ab**
> **schneuzen (sich)** *vr* (NEW) **schnäuzen (sich)**
> **Rolladen** *m* (NEW) **Rollladen**

When the two forms follow each other alphabetically or are used in phrases, the old form is shown in brackets after the new, preferred one:

> **Abfluss** (**Abfluß**) *m* drainage; (*Öffnung*) drain. **A~rohr** *nt* drain-pipe
> **arm** *a* (**ärmer, ärmst**) poor; **Arm und Reich** (**arm und reich**) rich and poor

Where both the old and new forms are valid, an equals sign = is used to refer to the preferred form:

> **aufwändig** *a* = **aufwendig**
> **Tunfisch** *m* = **Thunfisch**
> **Rand** *m* . . . **zu R~e kommen mit** = **zurande kommen mit**, *s*. **zurande**
> **Stand** *m* . . . **in S~ halten/setzen** = **instand halten/setzen**, *s*. **instand**

When such forms follow each other alphabetically, they are given with commas, with the preferred form in first place:

> **Panther, Panter** *m* -s, - panther

In phrases, *od* (oder) is used:

> . . . **d~e(r,s)** *poss pron* yours; **die D~en** *od* **d~en** *pl* your family *sg*.
> . . . **s~e(r,s)** *poss pron* his; **das S~e** *od* **seine tun** do one's share

On the English–German side, only the preferred German form is given.

- A swung dash ∼ represents the headword or that part of the headword preceding a vertical bar |. The initial letter of a German headword is given to show whether or not it is a capital.
- The vertical bar | follows the part of the headword which is not repeated in compounds or derivatives.
- Square brackets [ ] are used for optional material.
- Angled brackets < > are used after a verb translation to indicate the object; before a verb translation to indicate the subject; before an adjective to indicate a typical noun which it qualifies.
- Round brackets ( ) are used for field or style labels (see list on page vii) and for explanatory matter.
- A box □ indicates a new part of speech within an entry.
- *od* (oder) and *or* denote that words or portions of a phrase are synonymous. An oblique stroke / is used where there is a difference in usage or meaning.
- ≈ is used where no exact equivalent exists in the other language.
- A dagger † indicates that a German verb is irregular and that the parts can be found in the verb table on page 503. Compound verbs are not listed there as they follow the pattern of the basic verb.
- The stressed vowel is marked in a German headword by ‗ (long) or ˌ (short). A phonetic transcription is only given for words which do not follow the normal rules of pronunciation. These rules can be found on page 501.
- Phonetics are given for all English headwords and for derivatives where there is a change of pronunciation or stress. In blocks of compounds, if no stress is shown, it falls on the first element.
- A change in pronunciation or stress shown within a block of compounds applies only to that particular word (subsequent entries revert to the pronunciation and stress of the headword).
- German headword nouns are followed by the gender and, with the exception of compound nouns, by the genitive and plural. These are only given at compound nouns if they

present some difficulty. Otherwise the user should refer to the final element.

- Nouns that decline like adjectives are entered as follows: -e(r) *m/f*, -e(s) *nt*.
- Adjectives which have no undeclined form are entered in the feminine form with the masculine and neuter in brackets -e(r,s).
- The reflexive pronoun **sich** is accusative unless marked (*dat*).

Proprietary terms

This dictionary includes some words which are, or are asserted to be, proprietary names or trademarks. Their inclusion does not imply that they have acquired for legal purposes a non-proprietary or general significance, nor is any other judgement implied concerning their legal status. In cases where the editor has some evidence that a word is used as a proprietary name or trademark this is indicated by the letter (P), but no judgement concerning the legal status of such words is made or implied thereby.

Abbreviations • Abkürzungen

adjective	a	Adjektiv
abbreviation	abbr	Abkürzung
accusative	acc	Akkusativ
Administration	Admin	Administration
adverb	adv	Adverb
American	Amer	amerikanisch
Anatomy	Anat	Anatomie
Archaeology	Archaeol	Archäologie
Architecture	Archit	Architektur
Astronomy	Astr	Astronomie
attributive	attrib	attributiv
Austrian	Aust	österreichisch
Motor vehicles	Auto	Automobil
Aviation	Aviat	Luftfahrt
Biology	Biol	Biologie
Botany	Bot	Botanik
Chemistry	Chem	Chemie
collective	coll	Kollektivum
Commerce	Comm	Handel
conjunction	conj	Konjunktion
Cookery	Culin	Kochkunst
dative	dat	Dativ
definite article	def art	bestimmter Artikel
demonstrative	dem	Demonstrativ-
dialect	dial	Dialekt
Electricity	Electr	Elektrizität
something	etw	etwas
feminine	f	Femininum
familiar	fam	familiär
figurative	fig	figurativ
genitive	gen	Genitiv
Geography	Geog	Geographie
Geology	Geol	Geologie
Geometry	Geom	Geometrie
Grammar	Gram	Grammatik
Horticulture	Hort	Gartenbau
impersonal	impers	unpersönlich
indefinite article	indef art	unbestimmter Artikel

indefinite pronoun	indef pron	unbestimmtes Pronomen
infinitive	inf	Infinitiv
inseparable	insep	untrennbar
interjection	int	Interjektion
invariable	inv	unveränderlich
irregular	irreg	unregelmäßig
someone	jd	jemand
someone	jdm	jemandem
someone	jdn	jemanden
someone's	jds	jemandes
Journalism	Journ	Journalismus
Law	Jur	Jura
Language	Lang	Sprache
literary	liter	dichterisch
masculine	m	Maskulinum
Mathematics	Math	Mathematik
Medicine	Med	Medizin
Meteorology	Meteorol	Meteorologie
Military	Mil	Militär
Mineralogy	Miner	Mineralogie
Music	Mus	Musik
noun	n	Substantiv
Nautical	Naut	nautisch
North German	N Ger	Norddeutsch
nominative	nom	Nominativ
neuter	nt	Neutrum
or	od	oder
Proprietary term	P	Warenzeichen
pejorative	pej	abwertend
Photography	Phot	Fotografie
Physics	Phys	Physik
plural	pl	Plural
Politics	Pol	Politik
possessive	poss	Possessiv-
past participle	pp	zweites Partizip
predicative	pred	prädikativ
prefix	pref	Präfix
preposition	prep	Präposition
present	pres	Präsens
present participle	pres p	erstes Partizip
pronoun	pron	Pronomen
Psychology	Psych	Psychologie

past tense	pt	Präteritum
Railway	Rail	Eisenbahn
reflexive	refl	reflexiv
regular	reg	regelmäßig
relative	rel	Relativ-
Religion	Relig	Religion
see	s.	siehe
School	Sch	Schule
separable	sep	trennbar
singular	sg	Singular
South German	S Ger	Süddeutsch
slang	sl	salopp
someone	s.o.	jemand
something	sth	etwas
Technical	Techn	Technik
Telephone	Teleph	Telefon
Textiles	Tex	Textilien
Theater	Theat	Theater
Television	TV	Fernsehen
Typography	Typ	Typographie
University	Univ	Universität
auxiliary verb	v aux	Hilfsverb
intransitive verb	vi	intransitives Verb
reflexive verb	vr	reflexives Verb
transitive verb	vt	transitives Verb
vulgar	vulg	vulgär
Zoology	Zool	Zoologie

Pronunciation of the alphabet • Aussprache des Alphabets

English/Englisch		German/Deutsch
eɪ	a	a:
bi:	b	be:
si:	c	tse:
di:	d	de:
i:	e	e:
ef	f	ɛf
dʒi:	g	ge:
eɪtʃ	h	ha:
aɪ	i	i:
dʒeɪ	j	jɔt
keɪ	k	ka:
el	l	ɛl
em	m	ɛm
en	n	ɛn
əʊ	o	o:
pi:	p	pe:
kju:	q	ku:
ɑ:(r)	r	ɛr
es	s	ɛs
ti:	t	te:
ju:	u	u:
vi:	v	faʊ
'dʌblju:	w	ve:
eks	x	ɪks
waɪ	y	'ʏpsilɔn
zed	z	tsɛt
eɪ umlaut	ä	ɛ:
əʊ umlaut	ö	ø:
ju: umlaut	ü	y:
es'zed	ß	ɛs'tsɛt

A

Aal *m* -[e]s,-e eel. a~en (sich) *vr* laze; *(ausgestreckt)* stretch out

Aas *nt* -es carrion; *(sl)* swine

ab *prep* (+ *dat*) from; ab Montag from Monday □ *adv* off; *(weg)* away; *(auf Fahrplan)* departs; ab sein *(fam)* have come off; *(erschöpft)* be worn out; von jetzt ab from now on; ab und zu now and then; auf und ab up and down

abändern *vt sep* alter; *(abwandeln)* modify

abarbeiten *vt sep* work off; sich a~ slave away

Abart *f* variety. a~ig *a* abnormal

Abbau *m* dismantling; *(Kohlen-)* mining; *(fig)* reduction. a~en *vt sep* dismantle; mine ⟨*Kohle*⟩; *(fig)* reduce, cut

abbeißen† *vt sep* bite off

abbeizen *vt sep* strip

abberufen† *vt sep* recall

abbestellen *vt sep* cancel; jdn a~ put s.o. off

abbiegen† *vi sep* (sein) turn off; [nach] links a~ turn left

Abbild *nt* image. a~en *vt sep* depict, portray. A~ung *f* -,-en illustration

Abbitte *f* A~ leisten apologize

abblättern *vi sep* (sein) flake off

abblend|en *vt/i sep* (haben) [die Scheinwerfer] a~en dip one's headlights. A~licht *nt* dipped headlights *pl*

abbrechen† *v sep* □ *vt* break off; *(abreißen)* demolish □ *vi* (sein/haben) break off

abbrennen† *v sep* □ *vt* burn off; *(niederbrennen)* burn down; let off ⟨*Feuerwerkskörper*⟩ □ *vi* (sein) burn down

abbringen† *vt sep* dissuade (von from)

Abbruch *m* demolition; *(Beenden)* breaking off; etw ⟨*dat*⟩ keinen A~ tun do no harm to sth

abbuchen *vt sep* debit

abbürsten *vt sep* brush down; *(entfernen)* brush off

abdank|en *vi sep* (haben) resign; ⟨*Herrscher:*⟩ abdicate. A~ung *f* -,-en resignation; abdication

abdecken *vt sep* uncover; *(abnehmen)* take off; *(zudecken)* cover; den Tisch a~ clear the table

abdichten *vt sep* seal

abdrehen *vt sep* turn off

Abdruck *m* (*pl* -e) impression; *(Finger-)* print; *(Nachdruck)* reprint. a~en *vt sep* print

abdrücken *vt/i sep* (haben) fire; sich a~ leave an impression

Abend *m* -s,-e evening; am A~ in the evening; heute A~ this evening, tonight; gestern A~ yesterday evening, last night. a~ *adv* heute/gestern a~ ⟨NEW⟩ heute/gestern A~, *s.* Abend. A~brot *nt* supper. A~essen *nt* dinner; *(einfacher)* supper. A~kurs[us] *m* evening class. A~mahl *nt* (*Relig*) [Holy] Communion. a~s *adv* in the evening

Abenteuer *nt* -s,- adventure; *(Liebes-)* affair. a~lich *a* fantastic; *(gefährlich)* hazardous

Abenteurer *m* -s,- adventurer

aber *conj* but; oder a~ or else □ *adv* (*wirklich*) really; a~ ja! but of course! Tausende und a~ Tausende thousands upon thousands

Aber|glaube *m* superstition. a~gläubisch *a* superstitious

aber|mals *adv* once again. A~tausende, a~tausende *pl* thousands upon thousands

abfahr|en† *v sep* □ *vi* (sein) leave; ⟨*Auto:*⟩ drive off □ *vt* take away; *(entlangfahren)* drive along; use ⟨*Fahrkarte*⟩; abgefahrene Reifen worn tyres. A~t *f* departure; *(Talfahrt)* descent; *(Piste)* run; *(Ausfahrt)* exit

Abfall *m* refuse, rubbish, *(Amer)* garbage; *(auf der Straße)* litter; *(Industrie-)* waste. A~eimer *m* rubbish-bin; litter-bin

abfallen† *vi sep* (sein) drop, fall; *(übrig bleiben)* be left (für for); *(sich neigen)* slope away; *(fig)* compare badly (gegen with); vom Glauben a~ renounce one's faith. a~d *a* sloping

Abfallhaufen *m* rubbish-dump

abfällig *a* disparaging, *adv* -ly

abfangen† *vt sep* intercept; *(beherrschen)* bring under control

abfärben *vi sep* (haben) ⟨*Farbe:*⟩ run; ⟨*Stoff:*⟩ not be colour-fast; a~ auf (+ *acc*) *(fig)* rub off on

abfassen *vt sep* draft

abfertigen *vt sep* attend to; *(zollamtlich)* clear; jdn kurz a~ *(fam)* give s.o. short shrift

abfeuern *vt sep* fire

abfind|en *vt sep* pay off; *(entschädigen)* compensate; **sich a~en mit** come to terms with. **A~ung** *f* -,-en compensation

abflauen *vi sep (sein)* decrease

abfliegen† *vi sep (sein)* fly off; *(Aviat)* take off

abfließen† *vi sep (sein)* drain *or* run away

Abflug *m (Aviat)* departure

Abfluss (Abfluß) *m* drainage; *(Öffnung)* drain. **A~rohr** *nt* drain-pipe

abfragen *vt sep* jdn *od* jdm Vokabeln a~ test s.o. on vocabulary

Abfuhr *f* - removal; *(fig)* rebuff

abführ|en *vt sep* take *or* lead away. **a~end** *a* laxative. **A~mittel** *nt* laxative

abfüllen *vt sep* auf *od* in Flaschen a~ bottle

Abgabe *f* handing in; *(Verkauf)* sale; *(Fußball)* pass; *(Steuer)* tax

Abgang *m* departure; *(Theat)* exit; *(Schul-)* leaving

Abgase *ntpl* exhaust fumes

abgeben† *vt sep* hand in; *(abliefern)* deliver; *(verkaufen)* sell; *(zur Aufbewahrung)* leave; *(Fußball)* pass; *(ausströmen)* give off; *(abfeuern)* fire; *(verlauten lassen)* give; cast *(Stimme)*; jdm etw a~ give s.o. a share of sth; **sich a~ mit** occupy oneself with

abgedroschen *a* hackneyed

abgeh|en† *v sep a vi (sein)* leave; *(Theat)* exit; *(sich lösen)* come off; *(abgezogen werden)* be deducted; *(abbiegen)* turn off; *(verlaufen)* go off; **ihr geht jeglicher Humor** she has totally lacks a sense of humour a *vt* walk along

abgehetzt *a* harassed. **abgelegen** *a* remote. **abgeneigt** *a* etw *(dat)* nicht abgeneigt sein not be averse to sth. **abgenutzt** *a* worn. **Abgeordnete(r)** *m/f* deputy; *(Pol)* Member of Parliament. **abgepackt** *a* pre-packed. **abgerissen** *a* ragged

abgeschieden *a* secluded. **A~heit** *f* - seclusion

abgeschlossen *a (fig)* complete; *(Wohnung)* self-contained. **abgeschmackt** *a (fig)* tasteless. **abgesehen** *prep* apart (from von). **abgespannt** *a* exhausted. **abgestanden** *a* stale. **abgestorben** *a* dead; *(Glied)* numb. **abgetragen** *a* worn. **abgewetzt** *a* threadbare

abgewinnen† *vt sep* win (jdm from s.o.); etw *(dat)* Geschmack a~ get a taste for sth

abgewöhnen *vt sep* jdm/sich das Rauchen a~ cure s.o. of/ give up smoking

abgezehrt *a* emaciated

abgießen† *vt sep* pour off; drain *(Gemüse)*

abgleiten† *vi sep (sein)* slip

Abgott *m* idol

abgöttisch *adv* a~ lieben idolize

abgrenz|en *vt sep* divide off; *(fig)* define. **A~ung** *f* - demarcation

Abgrund *m* abyss; *(fig)* depths *pl*

abgucken *vt sep (fam)* copy

Abguss (Abguß) *m* cast

abhacken *vt sep* chop off

abhaken *vt sep* tick off

abhalten† *vt sep* keep off; *(hindern)* keep, prevent (von from); *(veranstalten)* hold

abhanden *adv* a~ kommen get lost

Abhandlung *f* treatise

Abhang *m* slope

abhängen¹ *vt sep (reg)* take down; *(abkuppeln)* uncouple

abhäng|en²† *vi sep (haben)* depend (von on). **a~ig** *a* dependent (von on). **A~igkeit** *f* - dependence

abhärten *vt sep* toughen up

abhauen† *v sep a vt* chop off a *vi (sein) (fam)* clear off

abheben† *v sep a vt* take off; *(vom Konto)* withdraw; **sich a~** stand out (gegen against) a *vi (haben) (Cards)* cut [the cards]; *(Aviat)* take off; *(Rakete:)* lift off

abheften *vt sep* file

abhelfen† *vt sep* (+ *dat*) remedy

Abhilfe *f* remedy; **A~ schaffen** take [remedial] action

abholen *vt sep* collect; call for *(Person)*; jdn am Bahnhof a~ meet s.o. at the station

abhorchen *vt sep (Med)* sound

abhör|en *vt sep* listen to; *(überwachen)* tap; jdn *od* jdm Vokabeln a~en test s.o. on vocabulary. **A~gerät** *nt* bugging device

Abitur *nt* -s ≈ A levels *pl.* **A~ient(in)** *m* -en,-en *(f* -,-nen) pupil taking the 'Abitur'

abkanzeln *vt sep (fam)* reprimand

abkaufen *vt sep* buy (dat from)

abkehren (sich) *vr sep* turn away

abkette[l]n *vt/i sep (haben)* cast off

abklingen† *vi sep (sein)* die away; *(nachlassen)* subside

abkochen *vt sep* boil

abkommen† *vi sep (sein)* a~ von stray from; *(aufgeben)* give up; vom Thema a~ digress. **A~** *nt* -s,- agreement

abkömmlich *a* available

Abkömmling *m* -s,-e descendant

abkratzen *v sep a vt* scrape off a *vi (sein) (sl)* die

abkühlen *vt/i sep (sein)* cool; **sich a~** cool [down]; *(Wetter:)* turn cooler

Abkunft f - origin

abkuppeln vt sep uncouple

abkürz|en vt sep shorten; abbreviate ⟨Wort⟩. A~ung f short cut; ⟨Wort⟩ abbreviation

abladen† vt sep unload

Ablage f shelf; ⟨für Akten⟩ tray

ablager|n vt sep deposit; sich a~n be deposited. A~ung f -,-en deposit

ablassen† v sep □ vt drain [off]; let off ⟨Dampf⟩; ⟨vom Preis⟩ knock off □ vi ⟨haben⟩ a~ von give up; von jdm a~ leave s.o. alone

Ablauf m drain; ⟨Verlauf⟩ course; ⟨Ende⟩ end; ⟨einer Frist⟩ expiry. a~en† v sep □ vi ⟨sein⟩ run or drain off; ⟨verlaufen⟩ go off; ⟨enden⟩ expire; ⟨Zeit:⟩ run out; ⟨Uhrwerk:⟩ run down □ vt walk along; ⟨absuchen⟩ scour (nach for); ⟨abnutzen⟩ wear down

ableg|en v sep □ vt put down; discard ⟨Karte⟩; ⟨abheften⟩ file; ⟨ausziehen⟩ take off; ⟨aufgeben⟩ give up; sit, take ⟨Prüfung⟩; abgelegte Kleidung cast-offs pl □ vi ⟨haben⟩ take off one's coat; ⟨Naut⟩ cast off. A~er m -s,- ⟨Bot⟩ cutting; ⟨Schössling⟩ shoot

ablehn|en vt sep refuse; ⟨missbilligen⟩ reject. A~ung f -,-en refusal; rejection

ableit|en vt sep divert; sich a~en be derived (von/aus from). A~ung f derivation; ⟨Wort⟩ derivative

ablenk|en vt sep deflect; divert ⟨Aufmerksamkeit⟩; ⟨zerstreuen⟩ distract. A~ung f -,-en distraction

ablesen† vt sep read; ⟨absuchen⟩ pick off

ableugnen vt sep deny

ablicht|en vt sep photocopy. A~ung f photocopy

abliefern vt sep deliver

ablös|en vt sep detach; ⟨abwechseln⟩ relieve; sich a~en come off; ⟨sich abwechseln⟩ take turns. A~ung f relief

abmach|en vt sep remove; ⟨ausmachen⟩ arrange; ⟨vereinbaren⟩ agree; abgemacht! agreed! A~ung f -,-en agreement

abmager|n vi sep ⟨sein⟩ lose weight. A~ungskur f slimming diet

abmarschieren vi sep ⟨sein⟩ march off

abmelden vt sep cancel ⟨Zeitung⟩; sich a~ report that one is leaving; ⟨im Hotel⟩ check out

abmess|en† vt sep measure. A~ungen fpl measurements

abmühen (sich) vr sep struggle

abnäh|en vt sep take in. A~er m -s,- dart

Abnahme f - removal; ⟨Kauf⟩ purchase; ⟨Verminderung⟩ decrease

abnehm|en v sep □ vt take off, remove; pick up ⟨Hörer⟩; jdm etw a~en take/

⟨kaufen⟩ buy sth from s.o. □ vi ⟨haben⟩ decrease; ⟨nachlassen⟩ decline; ⟨Person:⟩ lose weight; ⟨Mond:⟩ wane. A~er m -s,- buyer

Abneigung f dislike (gegen of)

abnorm a abnormal, adv -ly

abnutz|en vt sep wear out; sich a~en wear out. A~ung f - wear [and tear]

Abon|nement /abɔnə'mã:/ nt -s,-s subscription. a~nent m -en,-en subscriber. a~nieren vt take out a subscription to

Abordnung f -,-en deputation

abpassen vt sep wait for; gut a~ time well

abprallen vi sep ⟨sein⟩ rebound; ⟨Geschoss:⟩ ricochet

abraten† vi sep ⟨haben⟩ jdm von etw a~ advise s.o. against sth

abräumen vt/i ⟨haben⟩ clear away; clear ⟨Tisch⟩

abrechn|en v sep □ vt deduct □ vi ⟨haben⟩ settle up; ⟨fig⟩ get even. A~ung f settlement [of accounts]; ⟨Rechnung⟩ account

Abreise f departure. a~n vi sep ⟨sein⟩ leave

abreißen† v sep □ vt tear off; ⟨demolieren⟩ pull down □ vi ⟨sein⟩ come off; ⟨fig⟩ break off

abrichten vt sep train

abriegeln vt sep bolt; ⟨absperren⟩ seal off

Abriss (Abriß) m demolition; ⟨Übersicht⟩ summary

abrufen† vt sep call away; ⟨Computer⟩ retrieve

abrunden vt sep round off; nach unten/oben a~ round down/up

abrupt a abrupt, adv -ly

abrüst|en vi sep ⟨haben⟩ disarm. A~ung f disarmament

abrutschen vi sep ⟨sein⟩ slip

Absage f -,-n cancellation; ⟨Ablehnung⟩ refusal. a~n v sep □ vt cancel □ vi ⟨haben⟩ [jdm] a~n cancel an appointment [with s.o.]; ⟨auf Einladung⟩ refuse [s.o.'s invitation]

absägen vt sep saw off; ⟨fam⟩ sack

Absatz m heel; ⟨Abschnitt⟩ paragraph; ⟨Verkauf⟩ sale

abschaff|en vt sep abolish; get rid of ⟨Auto, Hund⟩. A~ung f abolition

abschalten vt/i sep ⟨haben⟩ switch off

abschätzig a disparaging, adv -ly

Abschaum m ⟨fig⟩ scum

Abscheu m - revulsion

abscheulich a revolting; ⟨fam⟩ horrible, adv -bly

abschicken vt sep send off

Abschied m -[e]s,-e farewell; ⟨Trennung⟩ parting; A~ nehmen say goodbye (von to)

abschießen† *vt sep* shoot down; *(abtrennen)* shoot off; *(abfeuern)* fire; launch *(Rakete)*

abschirmen *vt sep* shield

abschlagen† *vt sep* knock off; *(verweigern)* refuse; *(abwehren)* repel

abschlägig *a* negative; a~e Antwort refusal

Abschlepp|dienst *m* breakdown service. a~en *vt sep* tow away. A~seil *nt* tow-rope. A~wagen *m* breakdown vehicle

abschließen† *v sep* □ *vt* lock; *(beenden, abmachen)* conclude; make *(Wette)*; balance *(Bücher)*; sich a~ *(fig)* cut oneself off □ *vi (haben)* lock up; *(enden)* end. a~d *adv* in conclusion

Abschluss (Abschluß) *m* conclusion. A~prüfung *f* final examination. A~zeugnis *nt* diploma

abschmecken *vt sep* season

abschmieren *vt sep* lubricate

abschneiden† *v sep* □ *vt* cut off; den Weg a~ take a short cut □ *vi (haben)* gut/schlecht a~ do well/badly

Abschnitt *m* section; *(Stadium)* stage; *(Absatz)* paragraph; *(Kontroll-)* counterfoil

abschöpfen *vt sep* skim off

abschrauben *vt sep* unscrew

abschreck|en *vt sep* deter; *(Culin)* put in cold water *(Ei)*. a~end *a* repulsive, *adv* -ly; a~endes Beispiel warning. A~ungsmittel *nt* deterrent

abschreib|en† *v sep* □ *vt* copy; *(Comm & fig)* write off □ *vi (haben)* copy. A~ung *f* *(Comm)* depreciation

Abschrift *f* copy

Abschuss (Abschuß) *m* shooting down; *(Abfeuern)* firing; *(Raketen-)* launch

abschüssig *a* sloping; *(steil)* steep

abschwächen *vt sep* lessen; sich a~ lessen; *(schwächer werden)* weaken

abschweifen *vi sep (sein)* digress

abschwellen† *vi sep (sein)* go down

abschwören† *vi sep (haben)* (+ *dat*) renounce

abseh|bar *a* in a~barer Zeit in the foreseeable future. a~en† *vt/i sep (haben)* copy; *(voraussehen)* foresee; a~en von disregard; *(aufgeben)* refrain from; es abgesehen haben auf (+ *acc*) have one's eye on; *(schikanieren)* have it in for

absein† *vi sep (sein)* NEW ab sein, *s.* ab

abseits *adv* apart; *(Sport)* offside □ *prep* (+ *gen*) away from. A~*nt* - *(Sport)* offside

absend|en† *vt sep* send off. A~er *m* sender

absetzen *v sep* □ *vt* put *or* set down; *(ablagern)* deposit; *(abnehmen)* take off; *(absagen)* cancel; *(abbrechen)* stop; *(entlassen)* dismiss; *(verkaufen)* sell; *(abziehen)* deduct; sich a~ be deposited; *(fliehen)* flee □ *vi (haben)* pause

Absicht *f* -,-en intention; mit A~ intentionally, on purpose

absichtlich *a* intentional, *adv* -ly, deliberate, *adv* -ly

absitzen† *v sep* □ *vi (sein)* dismount □ *vt* *(fam)* serve *(Strafe)*

absolut *a* absolute, *adv* -ly

Absolution /-'tsjo:n/ *f* - absolution

absolvieren *vt* complete; *(bestehen)* pass

absonderlich *a* odd

absonder|n *vt sep* separate; *(ausscheiden)* secrete; sich a~n keep apart *(von* from). A~ung *f* -,-en secretion

absorb|ieren *vt* absorb. A~ption /-'tsjo:n/ *f* - absorption

abspeisen *vt sep* fob off *(mit* with)

abspenstig *a* a~ machen take *(jdm* from s.o.)

absperr|en *vt sep* cordon off; *(abstellen)* turn off; *(SGer)* lock. A~ung *f* -,-en barrier

abspielen *vt sep* play; *(Fußball)* pass; sich a~ take place

Absprache *f* agreement

absprechen† *vt sep* arrange; sich a~ agree; jdm etw a~ deny s.o. sth

abspringen† *vi sep (sein)* jump off; *(mit Fallschirm)* parachute; *(abgehen)* come off; *(fam: zurücktreten)* back out

Absprung *m* jump

abspülen *vt sep* rinse; *(entfernen)* rinse off

abstamm|en *vi sep (haben)* be descended *(von* from). A~ung *f* - descent

Abstand *m* distance; *(zeitlich)* interval; A~ halten keep one's distance; A~ nehmen von *(fig)* refrain from

abstatten *vt sep* jdm einen Besuch a~ pay s.o. a visit

abstauben *vt sep* dust

abstech|en† *vi sep (haben)* stand out. A~er *m* -s,- detour

abstehen† *vi sep (haben)* stick out; a~ von be away from

absteigen† *vi sep (sein)* dismount; *(niedersteigen)* descend; *(Fußball)* be relegated

abstell|en *vt sep* put down; *(lagern)* store; *(parken)* park; *(abschalten)* turn off; *(fig: beheben)* remedy. A~gleis *nt* siding. A~raum *m* box-room

absterben† *vi sep (sein)* die; *(gefühllos werden)* go numb

Abstieg *m* -[e]s,-e descent; *(Fußball)* relegation

abstimm|en v sep □ vi (haben) vote (über + acc on); □ vt coordinate (auf + acc with). A∼ung f vote

Abstinenz /-st-/ f - abstinence. A∼ler m -s,- teetotaller

abstoßen† vt sep knock off; (abschieben) push off; (verkaufen) sell; (fig: ekeln) repel. a∼d a repulsive, adv -ly

abstrakt /-st-/ a abstract

abstreifen vt sep remove; slip off (Kleidungsstück, Schuhe)

abstreiten† vt sep deny

Abstrich m (Med) smear; (Kürzung) cut

abstufen vt sep grade

Absturz m fall; (Aviat) crash

abstürzen vi sep (sein) fall; (Aviat) crash

absuchen vt sep search; (ablesen) pick off

absurd a absurd

Abszess m -es,-e (Abszeß m -sses,-sse) abscess

Abt m -[e]s,-e abbot

abtasten vt sep feel; (Techn) scan

abtauen vt/i sep (sein) thaw; (entfrosten) defrost

Abtei f -,-en abbey

Abteil nt compartment

abteilen vt sep divide off

Abteilung f -,-en section; (Admin, Comm) department

abtragen† vt sep clear; (einebnen) level; (abnutzen) wear out; (abzahlen) pay off

abträglich a detrimental (dat to)

abtreib|en† v sep □ vt (Naut) drive off course; ein Kind a∼en lassen have an abortion □ vi (sein) drift off course. A∼ung f -,-en abortion

abtrennen vt sep detach; (abteilen) divide off

abtret|en† v sep □ vt cede (an + acc to); sich (dat) die Füße a∼en wipe one's feet □ vi (sein) (Theat) exit; (fig) resign. A∼er m -s,- doormat

abtrocknen vt/i sep (haben) dry; sich a∼ dry oneself

abtropfen vi sep (sein) drain

abtrünnig a renegade; a∼ werden (+ dat) desert

abtun† vt sep (fig) dismiss

abverlangen vt sep demand (dat from)

abwägen† vt sep (fig) weigh

abwandeln vt sep modify

abwandern vi sep (sein) move away

abwarten v sep □ vt wait for □ vi (haben) wait [and see]

abwärts adv down[wards]

Abwasch m -[e]s washing-up; (Geschirr) dirty dishes pl. a∼en† v sep □ vt wash;

wash up (Geschirr); (entfernen) wash off □ vi (haben) wash up. A∼lappen m dishcloth

Abwasser nt -s,⁻ sewage. A∼kanal m sewer

abwechseln vi/r sep (haben) [sich] a∼ alternate; (Personen.) take turns. a∼d a alternate, adv -ly

Abwechslung f -,-en change; zur A∼ for a change. a∼sreich a varied

Abweg m auf A∼e geraten (fig) go astray. a∼ig a absurd

Abwehr f - defence; (Widerstand) resistance; (Pol) counter-espionage. a∼en vt sep ward off; (Mil) repel; (zurückweisen) dismiss. A∼system nt immune system

abweich|en† vi sep (sein) deviate/(von Regel) depart (von from); (sich unterscheiden) differ (von from). a∼end a divergent; (verschieden) different. A∼ung f -,-en deviation; difference

abweis|en† vt sep turn down; turn away (Person); (abwehren) repel. a∼end a unfriendly. A∼ung f rejection; (Abfuhr) rebuff

abwenden† vt sep turn away; (verhindern) avert; sich a∼ turn away; den Blick a∼ look away

abwerfen† vt sep throw off; throw (Reiter); (Aviat) drop; (Kartenspiel) discard; shed (Haut, Blätter); yield (Gewinn)

abwert|en vt sep devalue. a∼end a pejorative, adv -ly. A∼ung f -,-en devaluation

abwesen|d a absent; (zerstreut) absentminded. A∼heit f - absence; absent-mindedness

abwickeln vt sep unwind; (erledigen) settle

abwischen vt sep wipe; (entfernen) wipe off

abwürgen vt sep stall (Motor)

abzahlen vt sep pay off

abzählen vt sep count

Abzahlung f instalment

abzapfen vt sep draw

Abzeichen nt badge

abzeichnen vt sep copy; (unterzeichnen) initial; sich a∼ stand out

Abzieh|bild nt transfer. a∼en† v sep □ vt pull off; take off (Laken); strip (Bett); (häuten) skin; (Phot) print; run off (Kopien); (zurückziehen) withdraw; (abrechnen) deduct □ vi (sein) go away; (Rauch:) escape

abzielen vi sep (haben) a∼ auf (+ acc) (fig) be aimed at

Abzug m withdrawal; (Abrechnung) deduction; (Phot) print; (Korrektur-) proof;

(*am Gewehr*) trigger; (*A~söffnung*) vent; A~*e pl* deductions

abzüglich *prep* (+ *gen*) less

Abzugshaube *f* [cooker] hood

abzweig|en *v sep* □ *vi* (*sein*) branch off □ *vt* divert. A~ung *f* -,-en junction; (*Gabelung*) fork

ach *int* oh; a~ je! oh dear! a~ so I see; mit A~ und Krach (*fam*) by the skin of one's teeth

Achse *f* -,-n axis; (*Rad*-) axle

Achsel *f* -,-n shoulder; die A~n zucken shrug one's shoulders. A~höhle *f* armpit. A~zucken *nt* -s shrug

acht[1] *inv a*, A~*f* -,-en eight; heute in a~ Tagen a week today

acht[2] außer a~ lassen/sich in a~ nehmen (NEW) außer Acht lassen/sich in Acht nehmen, s. Acht[2]

Acht[2] *f* A~ geben be careful; A~ geben auf (+ *acc*) look after; außer A~ lassen disregard; sich in A~ nehmen be careful

acht|e(r,s) *a* eighth. a~eckig *a* octagonal. a~el *inv a* eighth. A~el *nt* -s,- eighth. A~elnote *f* quaver, (*Amer*) eighth note

achten *vt* respect □ *vi* (*haben*) a~ auf (+ *acc*) pay attention to; (*aufpassen*) look after; darauf a~, dass take care that

ächten *vt* ban; ostracize (*Person*)

Achter|bahn *f* roller-coaster. a~n *adv* (*Naut*) aft

achtgeben† *vi sep* (*haben*) (NEW) Acht geben, s. Acht[2]

achtlos *a* careless, *adv* -ly

achtsam *a* careful, *adv* -ly

Achtung *f* - respect (vor + *dat* for); A~! look out! (*Mil*) attention! 'A~ Stufe' 'mind the step'

acht|zehn *inv a* eighteen. a~zehnte(r,s) *a* eighteenth. a~zig *a inv* eighty. a~zigste(r,s) *a* eightieth

ächzen *vi* (*haben*) groan

Acker *m* -s,- field. A~bau *m* agriculture. A~land *nt* arable land

addieren *vt/i* (*haben*) add; (*zusammenzählen*) add up

Addition /-'tsǐo:n/ *f* -,-en addition

ade *int* goodbye

Adel *m* -s nobility

Ader *f* -,-n vein; künstlerische A~ artistic bent

Adjektiv *nt* -s,-e adjective

Adler *m* -s,- eagle

adlig *a* noble. A~e(r) *m* nobleman

Administration /-'tsǐo:n/ *f* - administration

Admiral *m* -s,-e admiral

adop|tieren *vt* adopt. A~tion /-'tsǐo:n/ *f* -,-en adoption. A~tiveltern *pl* adoptive parents. A~tivkind *nt* adopted child

Adrenalin *nt* -s adrenalin

Adres|se *f* -,-n address. a~sieren *vt* address

adrett *a* neat, *adv* -ly

Adria *f* - Adriatic

Advent *m* -s Advent. A~skranz *m* Advent wreath

Adverb *nt* -s,-ien /-ǐə:n/ adverb

Affäre *f* -,-n affair

Affe *m* -n,-n monkey; (*Menschen*-) ape

Affekt *m* -[e]s,-e im A~ in the heat of the moment

affektiert *a* affected. A~heit *f* - affectation

affig *a* affected; (*eitel*) vain

Afrika *nt* -s Africa

Afrikan|er(in) *m* -s,- (*f* -,-nen) African. a~isch *a* African

After *m* -s,- anus

Agen|t(in) *m* -en,-en (*f* -,-nen) agent. A~tur *f* -,-en agency

Aggres|sion /-'sǐo:n/ *f* -,-en aggression. a~siv *a* aggressive, *adv* -ly. A~sivität *f* - aggressiveness

Agitation /-'tsǐo:n/ *f* - agitation

Agnostiker *m* -s,- agnostic

Ägypt|en /ɛ'gʏptn/ *nt* -s Egypt. A~er(in) *m* -s,- (*f* -,-nen) Egyptian. ä~isch *a* Egyptian

ähneln *vi* (*haben*) (+ *dat*) resemble; sich ä~ be alike

ahnen *vt* have a presentiment of; (*vermuten*) suspect

Ahnen *mpl* ancestors. A~forschung *f* genealogy. A~tafel *f* family tree

ähnlich *a* similar, *adv* -ly; jdm ä~ sehen resemble s.o.; (*typisch sein*) be just like s.o. Ä~keit *f* -,-en similarity; resemblance

Ahnung *f* -,-en premonition; (*Vermutung*) idea, hunch; keine A~ (*fam*) no idea. a~slos *a* unsuspecting

Ahorn *m* -s,-e maple

Ähre *f* -,-n ear [of corn]

Aids /e:ts/ *nt* - Aids

Akademie *f* -,-n academy

Akadem|iker(in) *m* -s,- (*f* -,-nen) university graduate. a~isch *a* academic, *adv* -ally

akklimatisieren (sich) *vr* become acclimatized

Akkord *m* -[e]s,-e (*Mus*) chord; im A~ arbeiten be on piece-work. A~arbeit *f* piece-work

Akkordeon *nt* -s,-s accordion

Akkumul_a_tor *m* -s,-en /-'to:rən/ (*Electr*) accumulator

Akkus_a_tiv *m* -s,-e accusative. A∼objekt *nt* direct object

Akr_o_bat|(in) *m* -en,-en (*f* , nen) acrobat. a∼isch *a* acrobatic

Akt *m* -[e]s,-e act; (*Kunst*) nude

Akte *f* -,-n file; A∼n documents. A∼ndeckel *m* folder. A∼nkoffer *m* attaché case. A∼nschrank *m* filing cabinet. A∼ntasche *f* briefcase

Aktie /'aktsjə/ *f* -,-n (*Comm*) share. A∼ngesellschaft *f* joint-stock company

Akti_o_n /ak'tsjo:n/ *f* -,-en action; (*Kampagne*) campaign. A∼är *m* -s,-e shareholder

akt_i_v *a* active,*adv* -ly. a∼_ie_ren *vt* activate. A∼it_ä_t *f* -,-en activity

Aktualit_ä_t *f* -,-en topicality; A∼en current events

aktu_e_ll *a* topical; (*gegenwärtig*) current; nicht mehr a∼ no longer relevant

Akupunkt_u_r *f* - acupuncture

Akust|ik *f* - acoustics *pl.* a∼isch *a* acoustic, *adv* -ally

ak_u_t *a* acute

Akz_e_nt *m* -[e]s,-e accent

akzept|_a_bel *a* acceptable. a∼_ie_ren *vt* accept

Al_a_rm *m* -s alarm; (*Mil*) alert; A∼schlagen raise the alarm. a∼_ie_ren *vt* alert; (*beunruhigen*) alarm. a∼_ie_rend *a* alarming

_A_lbdruck *m* = Alpdruck

_a_lbern *a* silly □ *adv* in a silly way □ *vi* (*haben*) play the fool

_A_lbtraum *m* = Alptraum

_A_lbum *nt* -s,-ben album

Algebra *f* - algebra

_A_lgen *fpl* algae

Alg_e_rien /-jən/ *nt* -s Algeria

_A_libi *nt* -s,-s alibi

Aliment_e_ *pl* maintenance *sg*

_A_lkohol *m* -s alcohol. a∼frei *a* non-alcoholic

Alkohol|iker(in) *m* -s,- (*f* -,-nen) alcoholic. a∼isch *a* alcoholic. A∼ismus *m* - alcoholism

all *inv pron* all das/mein Geld all the/my money; all dies all this

All *nt* -s universe

_a_lle *pred a* finished, (*fam*) all gone; a∼ machen finish up

_a_lle(r,s) *pron* all; (*jeder*) every; a∼es everything, all; (*alle Leute*) everyone; a∼e *pl* all; a∼es Geld all the money; a∼e meine Freunde all my friends; a∼e beide both [of them/us]; wir a∼e we all;

a∼e Tage every day; a∼e drei Jahre every three years; in a∼er Unschuld in all innocence; ohne a∼en Grund without any reason; vor a∼em above all; a∼es in a∼em all in all; a∼es aussteigen! all change! a∼edem *pron* bei/trotz a∼edem with/despite all that

All_ee_ *f* -,-n avenue

Alleg_o_rie *f* -,-n allegory. a∼_o_risch *a* allegorical

all_ei_n *adv* alone; (*nur*) only; a∼ stehend single; a∼ der Gedanke the mere thought; von a∼[e] of its/(*Person*) one's own accord; (*automatisch*) automatically; einzig und a∼ solely □ *conj* but. A∼erziehende(r) *m/f* single parent. a∼ig *a* sole. a∼stehend *a* (NEW) a∼ stehend, *s.* allein. A∼stehende *pl* single people

allemal *adv* every time; (*gewiss*) certainly; ein für a∼ (NEW) ein für alle Mal, *s.* Mal[1]

allenfalls *adv* at most; (*eventuell*) possibly

aller|beste(r,s) *a* very best; am a∼ besten best of all. a∼dings *adv* indeed; (*zwar*) admittedly. a∼erste(r,s) *a* very first

Allergie *f* -,-n allergy

allergisch *a* allergic (gegen to)

aller|hand *inv a* all sorts of □ *pron* all sorts of things; das ist a∼hand! that's quite something! (*empört*) that's a bit much! A∼heiligen *nt* -s All Saints Day. a∼höchstens *adv* at the very most. a∼lei *inv a* all sorts of □ *pron* all sorts of things. a∼letzte(r,s) *a* very last. a∼liebst *a* enchanting. a∼liebste(r,s) *a* favourite □ *adv* am a∼liebsten for preference; am a∼liebsten haben like best of all. a∼meiste(r,s) *a* most □ *adv* am a∼meisten most of all. A∼seelen *nt* -s All Souls Day. a∼seits *adv* generally; guten Morgen a∼seits! good morning everyone! a∼ wenigste(r,s) *a* very least □ *adv* am a∼ wenigsten least of all

alle|s *s.* alle(r,s). a∼samt *adv* all. A∼swisser *m* -s,- (*fam*) know-all

allgem_ei_n *a* general, *adv* -ly; im A∼en (a∼en) in general. A∼heit *f* - community; (*Öffentlichkeit*) general public

Allh_ei_lmittel *nt* panacea

Alli_a_nz *f* -,-en alliance

Alligator *m* -s,-en /-'to:rən/ alligator

alli_ie_rt *a* allied; die A∼en *pl* the Allies

all|j_ä_hrlich *a* annual, *adv* -ly. a∼m_ä_chtig *a* almighty; der A∼mächtige the Almighty. a∼m_ä_hlich *a* gradual, *adv* -ly

_A_lltag *m* working day; der A∼ (*flg*) everyday life

allt_ä_glich *a* daily; (*gewöhnlich*) everyday; (*Mensch*) ordinary □ *adv* daily

_a_lltags *adv* on weekdays

allzu *adv* [far] too; a∼ bald/oft all too soon/often; a∼ sehr/viel far too much; a∼ vorsichtig over-cautious. a∼bald *adv* NEW a∼ bald, *s.* allzu. a∼oft *adv* NEW a∼ oft, *s.* allzu. a∼sehr *adv* NEW a∼ sehr, *s.* allzu. a∼viel *adv* NEW a∼ viel, *s.* allzu

Alm *f* -,-en alpine pasture

Almosen *ntpl* alms

Alpdruck *m* nightmare

Alpen *pl* Alps. A∼veilchen *nt* cyclamen

Alphabet *nt* -[e]s,-e alphabet. a∼isch *a* alphabetical, *adv* -ly

Alptraum *m* nightmare

als *conj* as; (*zeitlich*) when; (*mit Kompara-tiv*) than; nichts als nothing but; als ob as if or though; so tun als ob (*fam*) pretend

also *adv & conj* so; a∼ gut all right then; na a∼! there you are!

alt *a* (älter, ältest) old; (*gebraucht*) second-hand; (*ehemalig*) former; alt werden grow old; alles beim A∼en (a∼en) lassen leave things as they are

Alt *m* -s (*Mus*) contralto

Altar *m* -s,⸗e altar

Alt|e(r) *m/f* old man/woman; die A∼en old people. A∼eisen *nt* scrap iron. A∼enheim *nt* old people's home

Alter *nt* -s,- age; (*Bejahrtheit*) old age; im A∼ von at the age of; im A∼ in old age

älter *a* older; mein ä∼er Bruder my elder brother

altern *vi* (*sein*) age

Alternative *f* -,-n alternative

Alters|grenze *f* age limit. A∼heim *nt* old people's home. A∼rente *f* old-age pension. a∼schwach *a* old and infirm; ⟨*Ding*⟩ decrepit

Alter|tum *nt* -s,⸗er antiquity. a∼tümlich *a* old; (*altmodisch*) old-fashioned

ältest|e(r,s) *a* oldest; der ä∼e Sohn the eldest son

althergebracht *a* traditional

altklug *a* precocious, *adv* -ly

ältlich *a* elderly

alt|modisch *a* old-fashioned ▫ *adv* in an old-fashioned way. A∼papier *nt* waste paper. A∼stadt *f* old [part of a] town. A∼warenhändler *m* second-hand dealer. A∼weibermärchen *nt* old wives' tale. A∼weibersommer *m* Indian summer; (*Spinnfäden*) gossamer

Alufolie *f* [aluminium] foil

Aluminium *nt* -s aluminium, (*Amer*) aluminum

am *prep* = an dem; am Montag on Monday; am Morgen in the morning; am besten/meisten [the] best/most; am teuersten sein be the most expensive

Amateur /-'tø:ɐ̯/ *m* -s,-e amateur

Ambition /-'tsjo:n/ *f* -,-en ambition

Amboss *m* -es,-e (Amboß *m* -sses,-sse) anvil

ambulan|t *a* out-patient . . . ▫ *adv* a∼t behandeln treat as an out-patient. A∼z *f* -,-en out-patients' department; (*Kran-kenwagen*) ambulance

Ameise *f* -,-n ant

amen *int*, A∼ *nt* -s amen

Amerika *nt* -s America

Amerikan|er(in) *m* -s,- (*f* -,-nen) American. a∼isch *a* American

Ami *m* -s,-s (*fam*) Yank

Ammoniak *nt* -s ammonia

Amnestie *f* -,-n amnesty

amoralisch *a* amoral

Ampel *f* -,-n traffic lights *pl*; (*Blumen-*) hanging basket

Amphib|ie /-jə/ *f* -,-n amphibian. a∼isch *a* amphibious

Amphitheater *nt* amphitheatre

Amput|ation /-'tsjo:n/ *f* -,-en amputation. a∼ieren *vt* amputate

Amsel *f* -,-n blackbird

Amt *nt* -[e]s,⸗er office; (*Aufgabe*) task; (*Te-leph*) exchange. a∼ieren *vi* (*haben*) hold office; a∼ierend acting. a∼lich *a* official, *adv* -ly. A∼szeichen *nt* dialling tone

Amulett *nt* -[e]s,-e [lucky] charm

amüs|ant *a* amusing, *adv* -ly. a∼ieren *vt* amuse; sich a∼ieren be amused (über + *acc* at); (*sich vergnügen*) enjoy oneself

an *prep* (+ *dat/acc*) at; (*haftend, berührend*) on; (*gegen*) against; (+ *acc*) ⟨*schicken*⟩ to; an der/die Universität at/to university; am Tag darauf that day; es ist an mir it is up to me; an [und für] sich actually; die Arbeit an sich the work as such ▫ *adv* (*angeschaltet*) on; (*auf Fahrplan*) arriving; an die zwanzig Mark/Leute about twenty marks/people; von heute an from today

analog *a* analogous; (*Computer*) analog. A∼ie *f* -,-n analogy

Analphabet *m* -en,-en illiterate person. A∼entum *nt* -s illiteracy

Analy|se *f* -,-n analysis. a∼sieren *vt* analyse. A∼tiker *m* -s,- analyst. a∼tisch *a* analytical

Anämie *f* - anaemia

Ananas *f* -,-[se] pineapple

Anarch|ie *f* - anarchy. A∼ist *m* -en,-en anarchist

Anat|omie *f* - anatomy. a∼omisch *a* anatomical, *adv* -ly

anbahnen (sich) *vr sep* develop

Anbau m cultivation; (Gebäude) extension. a~en vt sep build on; (anpflanzen) cultivate, grow

anbehalten† vt sep keep on

anbei adv enclosed

anbeißen† v sep □ vt take a bite of □ vi (haben) ⟨Fisch:⟩ bite; (fig) take the bait

anbelangen vt sep = anbetreffen

anbellen vt sep bark at

anbeten vt sep worship

Anbetracht m in A~ (+ gen) in view of

anbetreffen† vt sep was mich/das anbetrifft as far as I am/that is concerned

Anbetung f - worship

anbiedern (sich) vr sep ingratiate oneself (bei with)

anbieten† vt sep offer; sich a~ offer (zu to)

anbinden† vt sep tie up

Anblick m sight. a~en vt sep look at

anbrechen† v sep □ vt start on; break into ⟨Vorräte⟩ □ vi (sein) begin; ⟨Tag:⟩ break; ⟨Nacht:⟩ fall

anbrennen† v sep □ vt light □ vi (sein) burn; (Feuer fangen) catch fire

anbringen† vt sep bring [along]; (befestigen) fix

Anbruch m (fig) dawn; bei A~ des Tages/der Nacht at daybreak/nightfall

anbrüllen vt sep (fam) bellow at

Andacht f -,-en reverence; (Gottesdienst) prayers pl

andächtig a reverent, adv -ly; (fig) rapt, adv -ly

andauern vi sep (haben) last; (anhalten) continue. a~d a persistent, adv -ly; (ständig) constant, adv -ly

Andenken nt -s,- memory; (Souvenir) souvenir; zum A~ an (+ acc) in memory of

ander|e(r,s) a other; (verschieden) different; (nächste) next; ein a~er, eine a~e another □ pron der a~e/die a~en the other/others; ein a~er another [one]; (Person) someone else; kein a~er no one else; einer nach dem a~en one after the other; alles a~e/nichts a~es everything/nothing else; etwas ganz a~es something quite different; alles a~e als anything but; unter a~em among other things. a~enfalls adv otherwise. a~erseits adv on the other hand. a~mal adv ein a~mal another time

ändern vt alter; (wechseln) change; sich ä~ change

andernfalls adv otherwise

anders pred a different; a~ werden change □ adv differently; ⟨riechen, schmecken⟩ different; (sonst) else; jemand/niemand/irgendwo a~ someone/no one/somewhere else

anderseits adv on the other hand

anders|herum adv the other way round. a~wo adv (fam) somewhere else

anderthalb inv a one and a half; a~ Stunden an hour and a half

Änderung f -,-en alteration; (Wechsel) change

anderweitig a other □ adv otherwise; (anderswo) elsewhere

andeut|en vt sep indicate; (anspielen) hint at. A~ung f -,-en indication; hint

andicken vt sep (Culin) thicken

Andrang m rush (nach for); (Gedränge) crush

andre a & pron = andere

andrehen vt sep turn on; jdm etw a~ (fam) palm sth off on s.o.

andrerseits adv = andererseits

androhen vt sep jdm etw a~ threaten s.o. with sth

aneignen vt sep sich (dat) a~ appropriate; (lernen) learn

aneinander adv & pref together; ⟨denken⟩ of one another; a~ vorbei past one another; a~ geraten quarrel. a~geraten† vi sep (sein) (NEW) a~ geraten, s. aneinander

Anekdote f -,-n anecdote

anekeln vt sep nauseate

anerkannt a acknowledged

anerkenn|en† vt sep acknowledge, recognize; (würdigen) appreciate. a~end a approving, adv -ly. A~ung f - acknowledgement, recognition; appreciation

anfahren† v sep □ vt deliver; (streifen) hit; (schimpfen) snap at □ vi (sein) start; angefahren kommen drive up

Anfall m fit, attack. a~en† v sep □ vt attack □ vi (sein) arise; ⟨Zinsen:⟩ accrue

anfällig a susceptible (für to); (zart) delicate. A~keit f - susceptibility (für to)

Anfang m -s,-e beginning, start; zu od am A~ at the beginning; (anfangs) at first. a~en† vt/i sep (haben) begin, start; (tun) do

Anfäng|er(in) m -s,- (f -,-nen) beginner. a~lich a initial, adv -ly

anfangs adv at first. A~buchstabe m initial letter. A~laut nt starting salary. A~gründe mpl rudiments

anfassen v sep □ vt touch; (behandeln) treat; tackle ⟨Arbeit⟩; jdn a~ take s.o.'s hand; sich a~ hold hands; sich weich a~

feel soft □ *vi* (*haben*) mit a~ lend a hand

anfechten† *vt sep* contest; (*fig: beunruhigen*) trouble

anfeinden *vt sep* be hostile to

anfertigen *vt sep* make

anfeuchten *vt sep* moisten

anfeuern *vt sep* spur on

anflehen *vt sep* implore, beg

Anflug *m* (*Aviat*) approach; (*fig: Spur*) trace

anforder|n *vt sep* demand; (*Comm*) order. A~ung *f* demand

Anfrage *f* enquiry. a~n *vi sep* (*haben*) enquire, ask

anfreunden (sich) *vr sep* make friends (mit with); (*miteinander*) become friends

anfügen *vt sep* add

anfühlen *vt sep* feel; sich weich a~ feel soft

anführ|en *vt sep* lead; (*zitieren*) quote; (*angeben*) give; jdn a~en (*fam*) have s.o. on. A~er *m* leader. A~ungszeichen *ntpl* quotation marks

Angabe *f* statement; (*Anweisung*) instruction; (*Tennis*) service; (*fam: Angeberei*) showing-off; nähere A~n particulars

angeb|en† *v sep* □ *vt* state; give (*Namen, Grund*); (*anzeigen*) indicate; set (*Tempo*) □ *vi* (*haben*) (*Tennis*) serve; (*fam: protzen*) show off. A~er(in) *m* -s,- (*f* -,-nen) (*fam*) show-off. A~erei *f* - (*fam*) showing-off

angeblich *a* alleged, *adv* -ly

angeboren *a* innate; (*Med*) congenital

Angebot *nt* offer; (*Auswahl*) range; A~ und Nachfrage supply and demand

angebracht *a* appropriate

angebunden *a* kurz a~ curt

angegriffen *a* worn out; (*Gesundheit*) poor

angeheiratet *a* (*Onkel, Tante*) by marriage

angeheitert *a* (*fam*) tipsy

angehen† *v sep* □ *vi* (*sein*) begin, start; (*Licht, Radio:*) come on; (*anwachsen*) take root; a~ gegen fight □ *vt* attack; tackle (*Arbeit*); (*bitten*) ask (um for); (*betreffen*) concern; das geht dich nichts an it's none of your business. a~d *a* future; (*Künstler*) budding

angehör|en *vi sep* (*haben*) (+ *dat*) belong to. A~ige(r) *m/f* relative; (*Mitglied*) member

Angeklagte(r) *m/f* accused

Angel *f* -,-n fishing-rod; (*Tür-*) hinge

Angelegenheit *f* matter; auswärtige A~en foreign affairs

Angel|haken *m* fish-hook. a~n *vi* (*haben*) fish (nach for); a~n gehen go

fishing □ *vt* (*fangen*) catch. A~rute *f* fishing-rod

angelsächsisch *a* Anglo-Saxon

angemessen *a* commensurate (*dat* with); (*passend*) appropriate, *adv* -ly

angenehm *a* pleasant, *adv* -ly; (*bei Vorstellung*) a~! delighted to meet you!

angenommen *a* (*Kind*) adopted; (*Name*) assumed

angeregt *a* animated, *adv* -ly

angesehen *a* respected; (*Firma*) reputable

angesichts *prep* (+ *gen*) in view of

angespannt *a* intent, *adv* -ly; (*Lage*) tense

Angestellte(r) *m/f* employee

angetan *a* a~ sein von be taken with

angetrunken *a* slightly drunk

angewandt *a* applied

angewiesen *a* dependent (auf + *acc* on); auf sich selbst a~ on one's own

angewöhnen *vt sep* jdm etw a~ get s.o. used to sth; sich (*dat*) etw a~ get into the habit of doing sth

Angewohnheit *f* habit

Angina *f* - tonsilitis

angleichen† *vt sep* adjust (*dat* to)

Angler *m* -s,- angler

anglikanisch *a* Anglican

Anglistik *f* - English [language and literature]

Angorakatze *f* Persian cat

angreif|en† *vt sep* attack; tackle (*Arbeit*); (*schädigen*) damage; (*anbrechen*) break into; (*anfassen*) touch. A~er *m* -s,- attacker; (*Pol*) aggressor

angrenzen *vi sep* (*haben*) adjoin (an etw *acc* sth). a~d *a* adjoining

Angriff *m* attack; in A~ nehmen tackle. a~slustig *a* aggressive

Angst *f* -,-e fear; (*Psych*) anxiety; (*Sorge*) worry (um about); A~ haben be afraid (vor + *dat* of); (*sich sorgen*) be worried (um about); jdm A~ machen frighten s.o. □ mir ist a~ I am frightened; I am worried (um about); jdm a~ machen (NEW) jdm A~ machen

ängstigen *vt* frighten; (*Sorge machen*) worry; sich ä~ be frightened; be worried (um about)

ängstlich *a* nervous, *adv* -ly; (*scheu*) timid, *adv* -ly; (*verängstigt*) frightened, scared; (*besorgt*) anxious, *adv* -ly. Ä~keit *f* - nervousness; timidity; anxiety

angstvoll *a* anxious, *adv* -ly; (*verängstigt*) frightened

angucken *vt sep* (*fam*) look at

angurten (sich) *vr sep* fasten one's seatbelt

anhaben† *vt sep* have on; er/es kann mir nichts a~ *(fig)* he/it cannot hurt me

anhalt|en† *v sep* □ *vt* stop; hold ⟨Atem⟩; jdn zur Arbeit/Ordnung a~en urge s.o. to work; be tidy □ *vi* ⟨haben⟩ stop, *(andauern)* continue. a~end *a* persistent, *adv* -ly; ⟨Beifall⟩ prolonged. A~er(in) *m* -s,- *(f* -,-nen) hitchhiker; per A~er fahren hitchhike. A~spunkt *m* clue

anhand *prep* (+ *gen*) with the aid of

Anhang *m* appendix; *(fam: Angehörige)* family

anhängen¹ *vt sep* ⟨reg⟩ hang up; *(befestigen)* attach; *(hinzufügen)* add

anhäng|en²† *vi* ⟨haben⟩ be a follower *(dat)*. A~er *m* -s,- follower; ⟨Auto⟩ trailer; ⟨Schild⟩ [tie-on] label; ⟨Schmuck⟩ pendant; ⟨Aufhänger⟩ loop. A~erin *f* -,-nen follower. A~erschaft *f* following, followers *pl.* a~lich *a* affectionate. A~sel *nt* -s,- appendage

anhäufen *vt sep* pile up; sich a~ pile up, accumulate

anheben† *vt sep* lift; *(erhöhen)* raise

Anhieb *m* auf A~ straight away

Anhöhe *f* hill

anhören *vt sep* listen to; mit a~ overhear; sich gut a~ sound good

animieren *vt* encourage (zu to)

Anis *m* -es aniseed

Anker *m* -s,- anchor; vor A~ gehen drop anchor. a~n *vi* ⟨haben⟩ anchor; *(liegen)* be anchored

anketten *vt sep* chain up

Anklage *f* accusation; ⟨Jur⟩ charge; *(Ankläger)* prosecution. A~bank *f* dock. a~n *vt sep* accuse ⟨gen⟩ of; ⟨Jur⟩ charge *(gen* with)

Ankläger *m* accuser; ⟨Jur⟩ prosecutor

anklammern *vt sep* clip on; peg on the line ⟨Wäsche⟩; sich a~ cling (an + *acc* to)

Anklang *m* bei jdm A~ finden meet with s.o.'s approval

ankleben *v sep* □ *vt* stick on □ *vi* ⟨sein⟩ stick (an + *dat* to)

Ankleide|kabine *f* changing cubicle; *(zur Anprobe)* fitting-room. a~n *vt sep* dress; sich a~n dress

anklopfen *vt sep* ⟨haben⟩ knock

anknipsen *vt sep* ⟨fam⟩ switch on

anknüpfen *v sep* □ *vt* tie on; *(fig)* enter into ⟨Gespräch, Beziehung⟩ □ *vi* ⟨haben⟩ refer (an + *acc* to)

ankommen† *vi sep* ⟨sein⟩ arrive; *(sich nähern)* approach; gut a~ arrive safely; *(fig)* go down well (bei with); nicht a~ gegen *(fig)* be no match for; a~ auf (+ *acc*) depend on; es a~ lassen auf (+ *acc*) risk; das kommt darauf an it [all] depends

ankreuzen *vt sep* mark with a cross

ankündig|en *vt sep* announce. A~ung *f* announcement

Ankunft *f* - arrival

ankurbeln *vt sep* *(fig)* boost

anlächeln *vt sep* smile at

anlachen *vt sep* smile at

Anlage *f* -,-n installation; *(Industrie-)* plant; *(Komplex)* complex; *(Geld-)* investment; *(Plan)* layout; *(Beilage)* enclosure; *(Veranlagung)* aptitude; *(Neigung)* predisposition; [öffentliche] A~n [public] gardens; als A~ enclosed

Anlass *m* -es,-̈e ⟨Anlaß *m* -sses,-̈sse⟩ reason; *(Gelegenheit)* occasion; A~ geben zu give cause for

anlass|en† *vt sep* ⟨Auto⟩ start; ⟨fam⟩ leave on ⟨Licht⟩; keep on ⟨Mantel⟩; sich gut/ schlecht a~en start off well/badly. A~er *m* -s,- starter

anlässlich ⟨anläßlich⟩ *prep* (+ *gen*) on the occasion of

Anlauf *m* ⟨Sport⟩ run-up; *(fig)* attempt. a~en† *v sep* □ *vi* ⟨sein⟩ start; *(beschlagen)* mist up; ⟨Metall:⟩ tarnish; rot a~en go red; *(erröten)* blush; angelaufen kommen come running up □ *vt* ⟨Naut⟩ call at

anlegen *v sep* □ *vt* put (an + *acc* against); put on ⟨Kleidung, Verband⟩; lay back ⟨Ohren⟩; aim ⟨Gewehr⟩; *(investieren)* invest; *(ausgeben)* spend (für on); *(erstellen)* build; *(gestalten)* lay out; draw up ⟨Liste⟩; [mit] Hand a~ lend a hand; es darauf a~ *(fig)* aim (zu to); sich a~ mit quarrel with □ *vi* ⟨haben⟩ ⟨Schiff:⟩ moor; a~ auf (+ *acc*) aim at

anlehnen *vt sep* lean (an + *acc* against); sich a~ lean (an + *acc* on); eine Tür angelehnt lassen leave a door ajar

Anleihe *f* -,-n loan

anleinen *vt sep* put on a lead

anleit|en *vt sep* instruct. A~ung *f* instructions *pl*

anlernen *vt sep* train

Anliegen *nt* -s,- request; *(Wunsch)* desire

anlieg|en† *vi sep* ⟨haben⟩ ⟨eng⟩ a~en fit closely; [eng] a~end close-fitting. A~er *mpl* residents; 'A~er frei' "access for residents only"

anlocken *vt sep* attract

anlügen† *vt sep* lie to

anmachen *vt sep* ⟨fam⟩ fix; *(anschalten)* turn on; *(anzünden)* light; ⟨Culin⟩ dress ⟨Salat⟩

anmalen *vt sep* paint

Anmarsch *m* ⟨Mil⟩ approach

anmaßen vt sep sich (dat) a~en presume (zu to); sich (dat) ein Recht a~en claim a right. a~end a presumptuous, adv -ly; (arrogant) arrogant, adv -ly. A~ung f - presumption; arrogance

anmeld|en vt sep announce; (Admin) register; sich a~en say that one is coming; (Admin) register; (Sch) enrol; (im Hotel) check in; (beim Arzt) make an appointment. A~ung f announcement; (Admin) registration; (Sch) enrolment; (Termin) appointment

anmerk|en vt sep mark; sich (dat) etw a~en lassen show sth. A~ung f -,-en note

Anmut f - grace; (Charme) charm

anmuten vt sep es mutet mich seltsam/ vertraut an it seems odd/familiar to me

anmutig a graceful, adv -ly; (lieblich) charming, adv -ly

annähen vt sep sew on

annäher|nd a approximate, adv -ly. A~ungsversuche mpl advances

Annahme f -,-n acceptance; (Adoption) adoption; (Vermutung) assumption

annehm|bar a acceptable. a~en† vt sep accept; (adoptieren) adopt; acquire ⟨Gewohnheit⟩; (sich zulegen, vermuten) assume; sich a~en (+ gen) take care of; angenommen, dass assuming that. A~lichkeiten fpl comforts

annektieren vt annex

Anno adv A~ 1920 in the year 1920

Annon|ce /a'nõːsə/ f -,-n advertisement. a~cieren /-'siː-/ vt/i (haben) advertise

annullieren vt annul; cancel ⟨Flug⟩

anöden vt sep (fam) bore

Anomalie f -,-n anomaly

anonym a anonymous, adv -ly

Anorak m -s,-s anorak

anordn|en vt sep arrange; (befehlen) order. A~ung f arrangement; order

anorganisch a inorganic

anormal a abnormal

anpacken v sep □ vt grasp; tackle ⟨Arbeit, Problem⟩ □ vi (haben) mit a~ lend a hand

anpass|en vt sep try on; (angleichen) adapt (dat to); sich a~ adapt (dat to). A~ung f - adaptation. a~ungsfähig a adaptable. A~ungsfähigkeit f adaptability

Anpfiff m (Sport) kick-off; (fam: Rüge) reprimand

anpflanzen vt sep plant; (anbauen) grow

Anprall m -[e]s impact. a~en vi sep (sein) strike (an etw acc sth)

anprangern vt sep denounce

anpreisen† vt sep commend

Anprob|e f fitting. a~ieren vt sep try on

anrechnen vt sep count (als as); (berechnen) charge for; (verrechnen) allow ⟨Summe⟩; ich rechne ihm seine Hilfe hoch an I very much appreciate his help

Anrecht nt right (auf + acc to)

Anrede f [form of] address. a~n vt sep address; (ansprechen) speak to

anreg|en vt sep stimulate; (ermuntern) encourage (zu to); (vorschlagen) suggest. a~end a stimulating. A~ung f stimulation; (Vorschlag) suggestion

anreichern vt sep enrich

Anreise f journey; (Ankunft) arrival. a~n vi sep (sein) arrive

Anreiz m incentive

anrempeln vt sep jostle

Anrichte f -,-n sideboard. a~n vt sep (Culin) prepare; (garnieren) garnish (mit with); (verursachen) cause

anrüchig a disreputable

Anruf m call. A~beantworter m -s,- answering machine. a~en† v sep □ vt call to; (bitten) call on (um for); (Teleph) ring □ vi (haben) ring (bei jdm s.o.)

anrühren vt sep touch; (verrühren) mix

ans prep = an das

Ansage f announcement. a~n vt sep announce; sich a~n say that one is coming. A~r(in) m -s,- (f -,-nen) announcer

ansamm|eln vt sep collect; (anhäufen) accumulate; sich a~eln collect; (sich häufen) accumulate; ⟨Leute:⟩ gather. A~lung f collection; (Menschen-) crowd

ansässig a resident

Ansatz m beginning; (Haar-) hairline; (Versuch) attempt; (Techn) extension

anschaff|en vt sep [sich dat] etw a~en acquire/(kaufen) buy sth. A~ung f -,-en acquisition; (Kauf) purchase

anschalten vt sep switch on

anschau|en vt sep look at. a~lich a vivid, adv -ly. A~ung f -,-en (fig) view

Anschein m appearance; den A~ haben seem. a~end adv apparently

anschicken (sich) vr sep be about (zu to)

anschirren vt sep harness

Anschlag m notice; (Vor-) estimate; (Überfall) attack (auf + acc on); (Mus) touch; (Techn) stop; 240 A~e in der Minute ≈ 50 words per minute. A~brett nt notice board. a~en† v sep □ vt put up ⟨Aushang⟩; strike ⟨Note, Taste⟩; cast on ⟨Masche⟩; (beschädigen) chip □ vi (haben) strike/(stoßen) knock (an + acc against); ⟨Hund:⟩ bark; (wirken) be effective □ vi (sein) knock (an + acc against); mit dem Kopf a~en hit one's head. A~zettel m notice anschließen† v sep □ vt connect (an + acc to); (zufügen) add; sich a~ an (+ acc) (anstoßen) adjoin; (folgen) follow; (sich anfreunden) become friendly with; sich jdm a~ join s.o. □ vi (haben) a~ an (+ acc) adjoin; (folgen) follow. a~d a adjoining; (zeitlich) following □ adv afterwards; a~d an (+ acc) after

Anschluss (Anschluß) m connection; (Kontakt) contact; A~ finden make friends; im A~ an (+ acc) after

anschmieg|en (sich) vr sep snuggle up/ ⟨Kleid:⟩ cling (an + acc to). a~sam a affectionate

anschmieren vt sep smear; (fam: täuschen) cheat

anschnallen vt sep strap on; sich a~ fasten one's seat-belt

anschneiden† vt sep cut into; broach ⟨Thema⟩

anschreiben† vt sep write (an + acc on); (Comm) put on s.o.'s account; (sich wenden) write to; bei jdm gut/schlecht angeschrieben sein be in s.o.'s good/bad books

anschreien† vt sep shout at

Anschrift f address

anschuldig|en vt sep accuse. A~ung f -,-en accusation

anschwellen† vi sep (sein) swell

anschwemmen vt sep wash up

anschwindeln vt sep (fam) lie to

ansehen† vt sep look at; (einschätzen) regard (als as); [sich dat] etw a~ look at sth; (TV) watch sth. A~ nt -s respect; (Ruf) reputation

ansehnlich a considerable

ansetzen v sep □ vt join (an + acc); (festsetzen) fix; (veranschlagen) estimate; Rost a~ get rusty; sich a~ form □ vi (haben) (anbrennen) burn; zum Sprung a~ get ready to jump

Ansicht f view; meiner A~ nach in my view; zur A~ (Comm) on approval. A~s[post]karte f picture postcard. A~ssache f matter of opinion

ansiedeln (sich) vr sep settle

ansonsten adv apart from that

anspannen vt sep hitch up; (anstrengen) strain; tense ⟨Muskel⟩

anspiel|en vi sep (haben) a~en auf (+ acc) allude to; (versteckt) hint at. A~ung f -,-en allusion; hint

Anspitzer m -s,- pencil-sharpener

Ansporn m (fig) incentive. a~en vt sep spur on

Ansprache f address

ansprechen† v sep □ vt speak to; (fig) appeal to □ vi (haben) respond (auf + acc to). a~d a attractive

anspringen† v sep □ vt jump at □ vi (sein) (Auto) start

Anspruch m claim/(Recht) right (auf + acc to); A~ haben be entitled (auf + acc to); in A~ nehmen make use of; (erfordern) demand; take up ⟨Zeit⟩; occupy ⟨Person⟩; hohe A~e stellen be very demanding. a~slos a undemanding; (bescheiden) unpretentious. a~svoll a demanding; (kritisch) discriminating; (vornehm) up-market

anspucken vt sep spit at

anstacheln vt sep (fig) spur on

Anstalt f -,-en institution; A~en/keine A~en machen prepare/make no move (zu to)

Anstand m decency; (Benehmen) [good] manners pl

anständig a decent, adv -ly; (ehrbar) respectable, adv -bly; (fam: beträchtlich) considerable, adv -bly; (richtig) proper, adv -ly

Anstands|dame f chaperon. a~los adv without any trouble; (bedenkenlos) without hesitation

anstarren vt sep stare at

anstatt conj & prep (+ gen) instead of; a~ zu arbeiten instead of working

anstechen† vt sep tap ⟨Fass⟩

ansteck|en v sep □ vt pin (an + acc to/on); put on ⟨Ring⟩; (anzünden) light; (in Brand stecken) set fire to; (Med) infect; sich a~en catch an infection (bei from) □ vi (haben) be infectious. a~end a infectious, (fam) catching. A~ung f -,-en infection

anstehen† vi sep (haben) queue, (Amer) stand in line

ansteigen† vi sep (sein) climb; ⟨Gelände, Preise:⟩ rise

anstelle prep (+ gen) instead of

anstell|en vt sep put, stand (an + acc against); (einstellen) employ; (anschalten) turn on; (tun) do; sich a~en queue [up], (Amer) stand in line; (sich haben) make a fuss. A~ung f employment; (Stelle) job

Anstieg m -[e]s,-e climb; (fig) rise

anstift|en vt sep cause; (anzetteln) instigate; jdn a~n put s.o. up (zu to). A~r m instigator

Anstoß m (Anregung) impetus; (Stoß) knock; (Fußball) kick off; A~ erregen/ nehmen give/take offence (an + dat at). a~en† v sep □ vt knock; (mit dem Ellbogen) nudge □ vi (sein) knock (an + acc against) □ vi (haben) adjoin (an etw acc sth); [mit den Gläsern] a~en clink glasses; a~en auf (+ *acc*) drink to; mit der Zunge a~en lisp

anstößig *a* offensive, *adv* -ly

anstrahlen *vt sep* floodlight; (*anlachen*) beam at

anstreiche|n† *vt sep* paint; (*anmerken*) mark. A~r *m* -s,- painter

anstreng|en *vt sep* strain; (*ermüden*) tire; sich a~en exert oneself; (*sich bemühen*) make an effort (zu to). a~end *a* strenuous; (*ermüdend*) tiring. A~ung *f* -,-en strain; (*Mühe*) effort

Anstrich *m* coat [of paint]

Ansturm *m* rush; (*Mil*) assault

Ansuchen *nt* -s,- request

Antagonismus *m* - antagonism

Antarktis *f* - Antarctic

Anteil *m* share; A~ nehmen take an interest (an + *dat* in); (*mitfühlen*) sympathize. A~nahme *f* - interest (an + *dat* in); (*Mitgefühl*) sympathy

Antenne *f* -,-n aerial

Anthologie *f* -,-n anthology

Anthropologie *f* - anthropology

Anti|alkoholiker *m* teetotaller. A~biotikum *nt* -s,-ka antibiotic

antik *a* antique. A~e *f* - [classical] antiquity

Antikörper *m* antibody

Antilope *f* -,-n antelope

Antipathie *f* - antipathy

Anti|quariat *nt* -[e]s,-e antiquarian bookshop. a~quarisch *a* & *adv* secondhand

Antiquitäten *fpl* antiques. A~händler *m* antique dealer

Antisemitismus *m* - anti-Semitism

Antisept|ikum *nt* -s,-ka antiseptic. a~isch *a* antiseptic

Antrag *m* -[e]s,-e proposal; (*Pol*) motion; (*Gesuch*) application. A~steller *m* -s,- applicant

antreffen† *vt sep* find

antreiben† *v sep* □ *vt* urge on; (*Techn*) drive; (*anschwemmen*) wash up □ *vi* (*sein*) be washed up

antreten† *v sep* □ *vt* start; take up (*Amt*) □ *vi* (*sein*) line up; (*Mil*) fall in

Antrieb *m* urge; (*Techn*) drive; aus eigenem A~ of one's own accord

antrinken† *vt sep* sich (*dat*) einen Rausch a~ get drunk; sich (*dat*) Mut a~ give oneself Dutch courage

Antritt *m* start; bei A~ eines Amtes when taking office. A~srede *f* inaugural address

antun† *vt sep* jdm etw a~ do sth to s.o.; sich (*dat*) etwas a~ take one's own life; es jdm angetan haben appeal to s.o.

Antwort *f* -,-en answer, reply (auf + *acc* to). a~en *vt/i* (*haben*) answer (jdm s.o.)

anvertrauen *vt sep* entrust/(*mitteilen*) confide (jdm to s.o.); sich jdm a~ confide in s.o.

anwachsen† *vi sep* (*sein*) take root; (*zunehmen*) grow

Anwalt *m* -[e]s,-e, **Anwältin** *f* -,-nen lawyer; (*vor Gericht*) counsel

Anwandlung *f* -,-en fit (von of)

Anwärter(in) *m(f)* candidate

anweis|en† *vt sep* assign (*dat* to); (*beauftragen*) instruct. A~ung *f* instruction; (*Geld-*) money order

anwend|en *vt sep* apply (auf + *acc* to); (*gebrauchen*) use. A~ung *f* application; use

anwerben† *vt sep* recruit

Anwesen *nt* -s,- property

anwesen|d *a* present (bei at); die A~den those present. A~heit *f* - presence

anwidern *vt sep* disgust

Anwohner *mpl* residents

Anzahl *f* number

anzahl|en *vt sep* pay a deposit on; pay on account (*Summe*). A~ung *f* deposit

anzapfen *vt sep* tap

Anzeichen *nt* sign

Anzeige *f* -,-n announcement; (*Inserat*) advertisement; A~ erstatten gegen jdn report s.o. to the police. a~n *vt sep* announce; (*inserieren*) advertise; (*melden*) report [to the police]; (*angeben*) indicate, show. A~r *m* indicator

anzieh|en† *vt sep* □ *vt* attract; (*festziehen*) tighten; put on (*Kleider, Bremse*); draw up (*Beine*); (*ankleiden*) dress; sich a~en get dressed; was soll ich a~en? what shall I wear? gut angezogen well-dressed □ *vi* (*haben*) start pulling; (*Preise:*) go up. a~end *a* attractive. A~ung *f* -attraction. A~ungskraft *f* attraction; (*Phys*) gravity

Anzug *m* suit; im A~ sein (*fig*) be imminent

anzüglich *a* suggestive; (*Bemerkung*) personal

anzünden *vt sep* light; (*in Brand stecken*) set fire to

anzweifeln *vt sep* question

apart *a* striking, *adv* -ly

Apathie *f* - apathy

apathisch *a* apathetic, *adv* -ally

Aperitif *m* -s,-s aperitif

Apfel *m* -s,- apple. A~mus *nt* apple purée

Apfelsine *f* -,-n orange

Apostel *m* -s,- apostle

Apostroph *m* -s,-e apostrophe

Apothek|e *f* -,-n pharmacy. A∼er(in) *m* -s,- (*f* -,-nen) pharmacist, [dispensing] chemist

Apparat *m* -[e]s,-e device; (*Phot*) camera; (*Radio, TV*) set; (*Teleph*) telephone; am A∼! speaking! A∼ur *f* -,-en apparatus

Appell *m* -s,-e appeal; (*Mil*) roll-call. a∼ieren *vi* (*haben*) appeal (an + *acc* to)

Appetit *m* -s appetite; guten A∼! enjoy your meal! a∼lich *a* appetizing, *adv* -ly

applaudieren *vi* (*haben*) applaud

Applaus *m* -es applause

Aprikose *f* -,-n apricot

April *m* -[s] April; in den A∼ schicken (*fam*) make an April fool of

Aquarell *nt* -s,-e water-colour

Aquarium *nt* -s,-ien aquarium

Äquator *m* -s equator

Ära *f* - era

Araber(in) *m* -s,- (*f* -,-nen) Arab

arabisch *a* Arab; (*Geog*) Arabian; (*Ziffer*) Arabic

Arbeit *f* -,-en work; (*Anstellung*) employment, job; (*Aufgabe*) task; (*Sch*) [written] test; (*Abhandlung*) treatise; (*Qualität*) workmanship; bei der A∼ at work; zur A∼ gehen go to work; an die A∼ gehen, sich an die A∼ machen set to work; sich (*dat*) viel A∼ machen go to a lot of trouble. a∼en *v sep* □ *vi* (*haben*) work (an + *dat* on) □ *vt* make; einen Anzug a∼en lassen have a suit made; sich durch etw a∼en work one's way through sth. A∼er(in) *m* -s,- (*f* -,-nen) worker; (*Land-, Hilfs-*) labourer. A∼erklasse *f* working class

Arbeit|geber *m* -s,- employer. A∼nehmer *m* -s,- employee. a∼sam *a* industrious

Arbeits|amt *nt* employment exchange. A∼erlaubnis, A∼genehmigung *f* work permit. A∼kraft *f* worker; Mangel an A∼kräften shortage of labour. a∼los *a* unemployed; a∼los sein be out of work. A∼lose(r) *m/f* unemployed person; die A∼losen the unemployed *pl*. A∼losenunterstützung *f* unemployment benefit. A∼losigkeit *f* unemployment

arbeitsparend *a* labour-saving

Arbeits|platz *m* job. A∼tag *m* working day. A∼zimmer *nt* study

Archäo|loge *m* -n,-n archaeologist. A∼logie *f* - archaeology. a∼logisch *a* archaeological

Arche *f* - die A∼ Noah Noah's Ark

Architek|t(in) *m* -en,-en (*f* -,-nen) architect. a∼tonisch *a* architectural. A∼tur *f* - architecture

Archiv *nt* -s,-e archives *pl*

Arena *f* -,-nen arena

arg *a* (ärger, ärgst) bad; (*groß*) terrible; sein ärgster Feind his worst enemy □ *adv* badly; (*sehr*) terribly

Argentin|ien /-jən/ *nt* -s Argentina. a∼isch *a* Argentinian

Ärger *m* -s annoyance; (*Unannehmlichkeit*) trouble. ä∼lich *a* annoyed; (*leidig*) annoying; ä∼lich sein be annoyed. ä∼n *vt* annoy; (*necken*) tease; sich ä∼n get annoyed (über jdn/etw with s.o./ about sth). Ä∼nis *nt* -ses, -se annoyance; öffentliches Ä∼nis public nuisance

Arglist *f* - malice. a∼ig *a* malicious, *adv* -ly

arglos *a* unsuspecting; (*unschuldig*) innocent, *adv* -ly

Argument *nt* -[e]s,-e argument. a∼ieren *vi* (*haben*) argue (dass that)

Argwohn *m* -s suspicion

argwöhn|en *vt* suspect. a∼isch *a* suspicious, *adv* -ly

Arie /'aːrjə/ *f* -,-n aria

Aristo|krat *m* -en,-en aristocrat. A∼kratie *f* - aristocracy. a∼kratisch *a* aristocratic

Arithmetik *f* - arithmetic

Arkt|is *f* - Arctic. a∼isch *a* Arctic

arm *a* (ärmer, ärmst) poor; Arm und Reich (arm und reich) rich and poor

Arm *m* -[e]s,-e arm; jdn auf den Arm nehmen (*fam*) pull s.o.'s leg

Armaturenbrett *nt* instrument panel; (*Auto*) dashboard

Armband *nt* (*pl* -bänder) bracelet; (*Uhr-*) watch-strap. A∼uhr *f* wrist-watch

Arm|e(r) *m/f* poor man/woman; die A∼en the poor *pl*; du A∼e *od* Ärmste! you poor thing!

Armee *f* -,-n army

Ärmel *m* -s,- sleeve. Ä∼kanal *m* [English] Channel. a∼los *a* sleeveless

Arm|lehne *f* arm. A∼leuchter *m* candelabra

ärmlich *a* poor, *adv* -ly; (*elend*) miserable, *adv* -bly

armselig *a* miserable, *adv* -bly

Armut *f* - poverty

Arom|a *nt* -s,-men & -mas aroma; (*Culin*) essence. a∼atisch *a* aromatic

Arran|gement /arãʒə'mãː/ *nt* -s,-s arrangement. a∼gieren /-'ʒiːrən/ *vt* arrange, sich a∼gieren come to an arrangement

Arrest *m* -[e]s (*Mil*) detention

arrogan|t *a* arrogant, *adv* -ly. A∼z *f* - arrogance

Arsch *m* -[e]s,-̈e (*vulg*) arse

Ars̱en *nt* -s arsenic

Art *f* -,-en manner; (*Weise*) way; (*Natur*) nature; (*Sorte*) kind; (*Biol*) species; auf diese Art in this way. a~en *vi* (*sein*) a~en nach take after

Arterie /-jə/ *f* -,-n artery

Arthṟitis *f* - arthritis

artig *a* well-behaved; (*höflich*) polite, *adv* -ly; sei a~! be good!

Artikel *m* -s,- article

Artillerie *f* - artillery

Artischocke *f* -,-n artichoke

Artist(in) *m* -en,-en (*f* -,-nen) [circus] artiste

Arzṉei *f* -,-en medicine. A~mittel *nt* drug

Arzt *m* -[e]s,ˑe doctor

Ärzt|in *f* -,-nen [woman] doctor. ä~lich *a* medical

As *nt* -ses,-se (NEW) Ass

Asbest *m* -[e]s asbestos

Asche *f* - ash. A~nbecher *m* ashtray. A~rmittwoch *m* Ash Wednesday

Asiat|(in) *m* -en,-en (*f* -,-nen) Asian. a~isch *a* Asian

Asien /ˈaːzjən/ *nt* -s Asia

asozial *a* antisocial

Aspekt *m* -[e]s,-e aspect

Asphalt *m* -[e]s asphalt. a~ieren *vt* asphalt

Ass *nt* -es,-e ace

Assistent(in) *m* -en,-en (*f* -,-nen) assistant

Ast *m* -[e]s,ˑe branch

ästhetisch *a* aesthetic

Astẖ|ma *nt* -s asthma. a~matisch *a* asthmatic

Astro|loge *m* -n,-n astrologer. A~logie *f* - astrology. A~naut *m* -en,-en astronaut. A~nom *m* -en,-en astronomer. A~nomie *f* - astronomy. a~nomisch *a* astronomical

Asyl *nt* -s,-e home; (*Pol*) asylum. A~ant *m* -en,-en asylum-seeker

Atelier /-ˈlje:/ *nt* -s studio

Atem *m* -s breath; tief A~ holen take a deep breath. a~beraubend *a* breath-taking. a~los *a* breathless, *adv* -ly. A~pause *f* breather. A~zug *m* breath

Atheist *m* -en,-en atheist

Äther *m* -s ether

Äthiopien /-jən/ *nt* -s Ethiopia

Athlet|(in) *m* -en,-en (*f* -,-nen) athlete. a~isch *a* athletic

Atlant|ik *m* -s Atlantic. a~isch *a* Atlantic; der A~ische Ozean the Atlantic Ocean

Atlas *m* -lasses,-lanten atlas

atmen *vt*/*i* (*haben*) breathe

Atmosphär|e *f* -,-n atmosphere. a~isch *a* atmospheric

Atmung *f* - breathing

Atom *nt* -s,-e atom. a~ar *a* atomic. A~bombe *f* atom bomb. A~krieg *m* nuclear war

Atten|tat *nt* -[e]s,-e assassination attempt. A~täter *m* [would-be] assassin

Attest *nt* -[e]s,-e certificate

Attrak|tion /-ˈtsjoːn/ *f* -,-en attraction. a~tiv *a* attractive, *adv* -ly

Attrappe *f* -,-n dummy

Attribut *nt* -[e]s,-e attribute. a~iv *a* attributive, *adv* -ly

ätzen *vt* corrode; (*Med*) cauterize; (*Kunst*) etch. ä~d *a* corrosive; (*Spott*) caustic

au *int* ouch; au fein! oh good!

Aubergine /oberˈʒiːnə/ *f* -,-n aubergine

auch *adv* & *conj* also, too; (*außerdem*) what's more; (*selbst*) even; a~ wenn even if; ich mag ihn—ich a~ I like him—so do I; ich bin nicht müde—ich a~ nicht I'm not tired—nor *or* neither am I; sie weiß es a~ nicht she doesn't know either; wer/wie/was a~ immer whoever/however/whatever; ist das a~ wahr? is that really true?

Audienz *f* -,-en audience

audiovisuell *a* audiovisual

Auditorium *nt* -s,-ien (*Univ*) lecture hall

auf *prep* (+ *dat*) on; (+ *acc*) on [to]; (*bis*) until, till; (*Proportion*) to; auf Deutsch/Englisch in German/English; auf einer/eine Party at/to a party; auf der Straße in the street; auf seinem Zimmer in one's room; auf einem Ohr taub deaf in one ear; auf einen Stuhl steigen climb on [to] a chair; auf die Toilette gehen go to the toilet; auf ein paar Tage verreisen go away for a few days; auf 10 Kilometer zu sehen visible for 10 kilometres □ *adv* open; (*in die Höhe*) up; auf sein be open; ⟨*Person:*⟩ be up; auf und ab up and down; sich auf und davon machen make off; Tür auf! open the door!

aufarbeiten *vt sep* do up; (*Rückstände*) a~ clear arrears [of work]

aufatmen *vi sep* (*haben*) heave a sigh of relief

aufbahren *vt sep* lay out

Aufbau *m* construction; (*Struktur*) structure. a~en *v sep* □ *vt* construct, build; (*errichten*) erect; (*schaffen*) build up; (*arrangieren*) arrange; wieder a~en reconstruct; sich a~en (*fig*) be based (auf + *dat* on) □ *vi* (*haben*) be based (auf + *dat* on)

aufbäumen (sich) *vr sep* rear [up]; (*fig*) rebel

aufbauschen vt sep puff out; (fig) exaggerate

aufbehalten† vt sep keep on

aufbekommen† vt sep get open; (Sch) be given [as homework]

aufbessern vt sep improve; (erhöhen) increase

aufbewahr|en vt sep keep; (lagern) store. A~ung f - safe keeping; storage; (Gepäck-) left-luggage office

aufbieten† vt sep mobilize; (fig) summon up

aufblas|bar a inflatable. a~en† vt sep inflate; sich a~en (fig) give oneself airs

aufbleiben† vi sep (sein) stay open; (Person.) stay up

aufblenden vt/i sep (haben) (Auto) switch to full beam

aufblicken vi sep (haben) look up (zu at/(fig) to)

aufblühen vi sep (sein) flower; (Knospe:) open

aufbocken vt sep jack up

aufbraten† vt sep fry up

aufbrauchen vt sep use up

aufbrausen vi sep (sein) (fig) flare up. a~d a quick-tempered

aufbrechen† v sep □ vt break open □ vi (sein) (Knospe:) open; (sich aufmachen) set out, start

aufbringen† vt sep raise (Geld); find (Kraft); (wütend machen) infuriate

Aufbruch m start, departure

aufbrühen vt sep make (Tee)

aufbürden vt sep jdm etw a~ (fig) burden s.o. with sth

aufdecken vt sep (auflegen) put on; (abdecken) uncover; (fig) expose

aufdrängen vt sep force (dat on); sich jdm a~ force one's company on s.o.

aufdrehen vt sep turn on

aufdringlich a persistent

aufeinander adv one on top of the other; (schießen) at each other; (warten) for each other; a~ folgen follow one another; a~ folgend successive; (Tage) consecutive. a~folgen vi sep (sein) NEW a~ folgen, s. aufeinander. a~folgend a NEW a~ folgend, s. aufeinander

Aufenthalt m stay; 10 Minuten A~ haben (Zug:) stop for 10 minutes. A~serlaubnis, A~sgenehmigung f residence permit. A~sraum m recreation room; (im Hotel) lounge

auferlegen vt sep impose (dat on)

aufersteh|en† vi sep (sein) rise from the dead. A~ung f - resurrection

aufessen† vt sep eat up

auffahr|en† vi sep (sein) drive up; (aufprallen) crash, run (auf + acc into); (aufschrecken) start up; (aufbrausen) flare up. A~t f drive; (Autobahn-) access road, slip road; (Bergfahrt) ascent

auffallen† vi sep (sein) be conspicuous; unangenehm a~ make a bad impression; jdm a~ strike s.o. a~d a striking, adv -ly

auffällig a conspicuous, adv -ly; (grell) gaudy, adv -ily

auffangen† vt sep catch; pick up (Funkspruch)

auffass|en vt sep understand; (deuten) take; falsch a~en misunderstand. A~ung f understanding; (Ansicht) view. A~ungsgabe f grasp

aufforder|n vt sep ask; (einladen) invite; jdn zum Tanz a~n ask s.o. to dance. A~ung f request; invitation

auffrischen v sep □ vt freshen up; revive (Erinnerung); seine Englischkenntnisse a~ brush up one's English

aufführ|en vt sep perform; (angeben) list; sich a~en behave. A~ung f performance

auffüllen vt sep fill up; [wieder] a~ replenish

Aufgabe f task; (Rechen-) problem; (Verzicht) giving up; A~n (Sch) homework sg

Aufgang m way up; (Treppe) stairs pl; (Astr) rise

aufgeben† v sep □ vt give up; post (Brief); send (Telegramm); place (Bestellung); register (Gepäck); put in the paper (Annonce); jdm eine Aufgabe/ein Rätsel a~ set s.o. a task/a riddle; jdm Suppe a~ serve s.o. with soup □ vi (haben) give up

aufgeblasen a (fig) conceited

Aufgebot nt contingent (an + dat of); (Relig) banns pl; unter A~ aller Kräfte with all one's strength

aufgebracht a (fam) angry

aufgedunsen a bloated

aufgehen† vi sep (sein) open; (sich lösen) come undone; (Teig, Sonne:) rise; (Saat:) come up; (Math) come out exactly; in Flammen a~ go up in flames; in etw (dat) a~ (fig) be wrapped up in sth; ihm ging auf (fam) he realized (dass that)

aufgelegt a a~ sein zu be in the mood for; gut/schlecht a~ sein be in a good/bad mood

aufgelöst a (fig) distraught; in Tränen a~ in floods of tears

aufgeregt a excited, adv -ly; (erregt) agitated, adv -ly

aufgeschlossen a (fig) openminded

aufgesprungen a chapped

aufgeweckt *a* *(fig)* bright

aufgießen† *vt sep* pour on; *(aufbrühen)* make *(Tee)*

aufgreifen† *vt sep* pick up; take up *(Vorschlag, Thema)*

aufgrund *prep* (+ *gen*) on the strength of

Aufguss (Aufguß) *m* infusion

aufhaben† *v sep* □ *vt* have on; den Mund a~ have one's mouth open; viel a~ *(Sch)* have a lot of homework □ *vi* *(haben)* be open

aufhalsen *vt sep* *(fam)* saddle with

aufhalten† *vt sep* hold up; *(anhalten)* stop; *(abhalten)* keep, detain; *(offen halten)* hold open; hold out *(Hand)*; sich a~ stay; *(sich befassen)* spend one's time (mit on)

aufhäng|en *vt/i sep* *(haben)* hang up; *(henken)* hang; sich a~en hang oneself. A~er *m* -s,- loop. A~ung *f* - *(Auto)* suspension

aufheben† *vt sep* pick up; *(hochheben)* raise; *(aufbewahren)* keep; *(beenden)* end; *(rückgängig machen)* lift; *(abschaffen)* abolish; *(Jur)* quash *(Urteil)*; repeal *(Gesetz)*; *(ausgleichen)* cancel out; sich a~ cancel each other out; gut aufgehoben sein be well looked after. A~ *nt* -s viel A~s machen make a great fuss (von about)

aufheitern *vt sep* cheer up; sich a~ *(Wetter:)* brighten up

aufhellen *vt sep* lighten; sich a~ *(Himmel:)* brighten

aufhetzen *vt sep* incite

aufholen *v sep* □ *vt* make up □ *vi* *(haben)* catch up; *(zeitlich)* make up time

aufhorchen *vi sep* *(haben)* prick up one's ears

aufhören *vi sep* *(haben)* stop; mit der Arbeit a~, a~ zu arbeiten stop working

aufklappen *vt/i sep* *(sein)* open

aufklär|en *vt sep* solve; jdn a~en enlighten s.o.; *(sexuell)* tell s.o. the facts of life; sich a~en be solved; *(Wetter:)* clear up. A~ung *f* solution; enlightenment; *(Mil)* reconnaissance; sexuelle A~ung sex education

aufkleb|en *vt sep* stick on. A~er *m* -s,- sticker

aufknöpfen *vt sep* unbutton

aufkochen *v sep* □ *vt* bring to the boil □ *vi* *(sein)* come to the boil

aufkommen† *vi sep* *(sein)* start; *(Wind:)* spring up; *(Mode:)* come in; a~ für pay for

aufkrempeln *vt sep* roll up

aufladen† *vt sep* load; *(Electr)* charge

Auflage *f* impression; *(Ausgabe)* edition; *(Zeitungs-)* circulation; *(Bedingung)* condition; *(Überzug)* coating

auflassen† *vt sep* leave open; leave on *(Hut)*

auflauern *vi sep* *(haben)* jdm a~ lie in wait for s.o.

Auflauf *m* crowd; *(Culin)* ≈ soufflé. a~en† *vi sep* *(sein)* *(Naut)* run aground

auflegen *v sep* □ *vt* apply (auf + *acc* to); put down *(Hörer)*; neu a~ reprint □ *vi* *(haben)* ring off

auflehn|en (sich) *vr sep* *(fig)* rebel. A~ung *f* - rebellion

auflesen† *vt sep* pick up

aufleuchten *vi sep* *(haben)* light up

aufliegen† *vi sep* *(haben)* rest (auf + *dat* on)

auflisten *vt sep* list

auflockern *vt sep* break up; *(entspannen)* relax; *(fig)* liven up

auflös|en *vt sep* dissolve; close *(Konto)*; sich a~en dissolve; *(Nebel:)* clear. A~ung *f* dissolution; *(Lösung)* solution

aufmach|en *v sep* □ *vt* open; *(lösen)* undo; sich a~en set out (nach for); *(sich schminken)* make oneself up □ *vi* *(haben)* open; jdm a~en open the door to s.o. A~ung *f* -,-en get-up; *(Comm)* presentation

aufmerksam *a* attentive, *adv* -ly; a~ werden auf (+ *acc*) notice; jdn a~ machen auf (+ *acc*) draw s.o.'s attention to. A~keit *f* -,-en attention; *(Höflichkeit)* courtesy

aufmucken *vi sep* *(haben)* rebel

aufmuntern *vt sep* cheer up

Aufnahme *f* -,-n acceptance; *(Empfang)* reception; *(in Klub, Krankenhaus)* admission; *(Einbeziehung)* inclusion; *(Beginn)* start; *(Foto)* photograph; *(Film-)* shot; *(Mus)* recording; *(Band-)* tape recording. a~fähig *a* receptive. A~prüfung *f* entrance examination

aufnehmen† *vt sep* pick up; *(absorbieren)* absorb; take *(Nahrung, Foto)*; *(fassen)* hold; *(annehmen)* accept; *(leihen)* borrow; *(empfangen)* receive; *(in Klub, Krankenhaus)* admit; *(beherbergen, geistig erfassen)* take in; *(einbeziehen)* include; *(beginnen)* take up; *(niederschreiben)* take down; *(filmen)* film, shoot; *(Mus)* record; auf Band a~ tape-[record]; etw gelassen a~ take sth calmly; es a~ können mit *(fig)* be a match for

aufopfer|n *vt sep* sacrifice; sich a~n sacrifice oneself. a~nd *a* devoted, *adv* -ly. A~ung *f* self-sacrifice

aufpassen *vi sep* *(haben)* pay attention; *(sich vorsehen)* take care; a~ auf (+ *acc*) look after

aufpflanzen (sich) *vr sep* *(fam)* plant oneself

aufplatzen vi sep (sein) split open

aufplustern (sich) vr sep (Vogel:) ruffle up its feathers

Aufprall m -[e]s impact. a~en vi sep (sein) a~en auf (+ acc) hit

aufpumpen vt sep pump up, inflate

aufputsch|en vt sep incite; sich a~en take stimulants. A~mittel nt stimulant

aufquellen† vi sep (sein) swell

aufraffen vt sep pick up; sich a~ pick oneself up; (fig) pull oneself together; (sich aufschwingen) find the energy (zu for)

aufragen vi sep (sein) rise [up]

aufräumen vt/i sep (haben) tidy up; (wegräumen) put away; a~ mit (fig) get rid of

aufrecht a & adv upright. a~erhalten† vt sep (fig) maintain

aufreg|en vt excite; (beunruhigen) upset; (ärgern) annoy; sich a~en get excited; (sich erregen) get worked up. a~end a exciting. A~ung f excitement

aufreiben† vt sep chafe; (fig) wear down; sich a~ wear oneself out. a~d a trying, wearing

aufreißen† v sep □ vt tear open; dig up (Straße); open wide (Augen, Mund). □ vi (sein) split open

aufreizend a provocative, adv -ly

aufrichten vt sep erect; (fig: trösten) comfort; sich a~ straighten up; (sich setzen) sit up

aufrichtig a sincere, adv -ly. A~keit f -sincerity

aufriegeln vt sep unbolt

aufrollen vt sep roll up; (entrollen) unroll

aufrücken vi sep (sein) move up; (fig) be promoted

Aufruf m appeal (an + dat to). a~en† vt sep call out (Namen); jdn a~en call s.o.'s name; (fig) call on s.o. (zu to)

Aufruhr m -s,-e turmoil; (Empörung) revolt

aufrühr|en vt sep stir up. A~er m -s,- rebel. a~erisch a inflammatory; (rebellisch) rebellious

aufrunden vt sep round up

aufrüsten vi sep (haben) arm

aufs prep = auf das

aufsagen vt sep recite

aufsammeln vt sep gather up

aufsässig a rebellious

Aufsatz m top; (Sch) essay

aufsaugen† vt sep soak up

aufschauen vi sep (haben) look up (zu at/(fig) to)

aufschichten vt sep stack up

aufschieben† vt sep slide open; (verschieben) put off, postpone

Aufschlag m impact; (Tennis) service; (Hosen-) turn-up; (Ärmel-) upturned cuff; (Revers) lapel; (Comm) surcharge. a~en† v sep □ vt open; crack (Ei); (hochschlagen) turn up; (errichten) put up; (erhöhen) increase; cast on (Masche); sich (dat) das Knie a~en cut [open] one's knee. □ vi (haben) hit (auf etw acc/dat sth); (Tennis) serve; (teurer werden) go up

aufschließen† v sep □ vt unlock. □ vi (haben) unlock the door

aufschlitzen vt sep slit open

Aufschluss (Aufschluß) m A~ geben give information (über + acc on). a~reich a revealing; (lehrreich) informative

aufschneid|en† v sep □ vt cut open; (in Scheiben) slice; carve (Braten). □ vi (haben) (fam) exaggerate. A~er m -s,-(fam) showoff

Aufschnitt m sliced sausage, cold meat [and cheese]

aufschrauben vt sep screw on; (abschrauben) unscrew

aufschrecken v sep □ vt startle. □ vi† (sein) start up; aus dem Schlaf a~ wake up with a start

Aufschrei m [sudden] cry

aufschreiben† vt sep write down; (fam: verschreiben) prescribe; jdn a~ (Polizist:) book s.o.

aufschreien† vi sep (haben) cry out

Aufschrift f inscription; (Etikett) label

Aufschub m delay; (Frist) grace

aufschürfen vt sep sich (dat) das Knie a~ graze one's knee

aufschwatzen vt sep jdm etw a~ talk s.o. into buying sth

aufschwingen† (sich) vr sep find the energy (zu to)

Aufschwung m (fig) upturn

aufsehen† vi sep (haben) look up (zu at/(fig) to). A~ nt -s A~ erregen cause a sensation; A~ erregend sensational. a~erregend a (NEW)A~ erregend, s. Aufsehen

Aufseher(in) m -s,- (f -,-nen) supervisor; (Gefängnis-) warder

aufsein† vi sep (sein) (NEW)auf sein, s. auf

aufsetzen vt sep put on; (verfassen) draw up; (entwerfen) draft; sich a~ sit up

Aufsicht f supervision; (Person) supervisor. A~srat m board of directors

aufsitzen† vi sep (sein) mount

aufspannen vt sep put up

aufsparen vt sep save, keep

aufsperren vt sep open wide

aufspielen v sep □ vi (haben) play. □ vr sich a~ show off; sich als Held a~ play the hero

aufspießen *vt sep* spear

aufspringen† *vi sep* ⟨*sein*⟩ jump up; ⟨*aufprallen*⟩ bounce; ⟨*sich öffnen*⟩ burst open; ⟨*Haut:*⟩ become chapped; a∼ auf (+ *acc*) jump on

aufspüren *vt sep* track down

aufstacheln *vt sep* incite

aufstampfen *vi sep* ⟨*haben*⟩ mit dem Fuß a∼ stamp one's foot

Aufstand *m* uprising, rebellion

aufständisch *a* rebellious. A∼e(r) *m* rebel, insurgent

aufstapeln *vt sep* stack up

aufstauen *vt sep* dam [up]

aufstehen† *vi sep* ⟨*sein*⟩ get up; ⟨*offen sein*⟩ be open; ⟨*fig*⟩ rise up

aufsteigen† *vi sep* ⟨*sein*⟩ get on; ⟨*Reiter:*⟩ mount; ⟨*Bergsteiger:*⟩ climb up; ⟨*hochsteigen*⟩ rise [up]; ⟨*fig: befördert werden*⟩ rise (zu to); ⟨*Sport*⟩ be promoted

aufstell|en *vt sep* put up; ⟨*Culin*⟩ put on; ⟨*postieren*⟩ post; ⟨*in einer Reihe*⟩ line up; ⟨*nominieren*⟩ nominate; ⟨*Sport*⟩ select ⟨*Mannschaft*⟩; make out ⟨*Liste*⟩; lay down ⟨*Regel*⟩; make ⟨*Behauptung*⟩; set up ⟨*Rekord*⟩; sich a∼en rise [up]; ⟨*in einer Reihe*⟩ line up. A∼ung *f* nomination; ⟨*Liste*⟩ list

Aufstieg *m* -[e]s, -e ascent; ⟨*fig*⟩ rise; ⟨*Sport*⟩ promotion

aufstöbern *vt sep* flush out; ⟨*fig*⟩ track down

aufstoßen† *v sep* □ *vt* push open □ *vi* ⟨*haben*⟩ burp; a∼ auf (+ *acc*) strike. A∼ *nt* -s burping

aufstrebend *a* ⟨*fig*⟩ ambitious

Aufstrich *m* [sandwich] spread

aufstützen *vt sep* rest (auf + *acc* on); sich a∼ lean (auf + *acc* on)

aufsuchen *vt sep* look for; ⟨*besuchen*⟩ go to see

Auftakt *m* ⟨*fig*⟩ start

auftauchen *vi sep* ⟨*sein*⟩ emerge; ⟨*U-Boot:*⟩ surface; ⟨*fig*⟩ turn up; ⟨*Frage:*⟩ crop up

auftauen *v sep* ⟨*sein*⟩ thaw

aufteil|en *vt sep* divide [up]. A∼ung *f* division

auftischen *vt sep* serve [up]

Auftrag *m* -[e]s,⁓e task; ⟨*Kunst*⟩ commission; ⟨*Comm*⟩ order; im A∼ (+ *gen*) on behalf of. a∼en† *v sep* □ *vt* apply; ⟨*servieren*⟩ serve; ⟨*abtragen*⟩ wear out; jdm a∼en instruct s.o. (zu to) □ *vi* ⟨*haben*⟩ dick a∼en ⟨*fam*⟩ exaggerate. A∼ geber *m* -s,- client

auftreiben† *vt sep* distend; ⟨*fam: beschaffen*⟩ get hold of

auftrennen *vt sep* unpick, undo

auftreten† *v sep* □ *vi* ⟨*sein*⟩ tread; ⟨*sich benehmen*⟩ behave, act; ⟨*Theat*⟩ appear; ⟨die

Bühne betreten⟩ enter; ⟨*vorkommen*⟩ occur □ *vt* kick open. A∼ *nt* -s occurrence; ⟨*Benehmen*⟩ manner

Auftrieb *m* buoyancy; ⟨*fig*⟩ boost

Auftritt *m* ⟨*Theat*⟩ appearance; ⟨*auf die Bühne*⟩ entrance; ⟨*Szene*⟩ scene

auftun† *vt sep* jdm Suppe a∼ serve s.o. with soup; sich ⟨*dat*⟩ etw a∼ help oneself to sth; sich a∼ open

aufwachen *vi sep* ⟨*sein*⟩ wake up

aufwachsen† *vi sep* ⟨*sein*⟩ grow up

Aufwand *m* -[e]s expenditure; ⟨*Luxus*⟩ extravagance; ⟨*Mühe*⟩ trouble; A∼ treiben be extravagant

aufwändig *a* = aufwendig

aufwärmen *vt sep* heat up; ⟨*fig*⟩ rake up; sich a∼ warm oneself; ⟨*Sport*⟩ warm up

Aufwartefrau *f* cleaner

aufwärts *adv* upwards; ⟨*bergauf*⟩ uphill; es geht a∼ mit jdm/etw s.o./sth is improving. a∼gehen† *vi sep* ⟨*sein*⟩ NEW a∼ gehen, s. aufwärts

Aufwartung *f* - cleaner; jdm seine A∼ machen call on s.o.

aufwaschen† *vt/i sep* ⟨*haben*⟩ wash up

aufwecken *vt sep* wake up

aufweichen *v sep* □ *vt* soften □ *vi* ⟨*sein*⟩ become soft

aufweisen† *vt sep* have, show

aufwend|en† *vt sep* spend; Mühe a∼en take pains. a∼ig *a* lavish, *adv* -ly; ⟨*teuer*⟩ expensive, *adv* -ly

aufwerfen† *vt sep* ⟨*fig*⟩ raise

aufwert|en *vt sep* revalue. A∼ung *f* revaluation

aufwickeln *vt sep* roll up; ⟨*auswickeln*⟩ unwrap

aufwiegeln *vt sep* stir up

aufwiegen† *vt sep* compensate for

Aufwiegler *m* -s,- agitator

aufwirbeln *vt sep* Staub a∼ stir up dust; ⟨*fig*⟩ cause a stir

aufwisch|en *vt sep* wipe up; wash ⟨*Fußboden*⟩. A∼lappen *m* floorcloth

aufwühlen *vt sep* churn up; ⟨*fig*⟩ stir up

aufzähl|en *vt sep* enumerate, list. A∼ung *f* list

aufzeichn|en *vt sep* record; ⟨*zeichnen*⟩ draw. A∼ung *f* recording; A∼ungen notes

aufziehen† *v sep* □ *vt* pull up; hoist ⟨*Segel*⟩; ⟨*öffnen*⟩ open; draw ⟨*Vorhang*⟩; ⟨*auftrennen*⟩ undo; ⟨*großziehen*⟩ bring up; rear ⟨*Tier*⟩; mount ⟨*Bild*⟩; thread ⟨*Perlen*⟩; wind up ⟨*Uhr*⟩; ⟨*arrangieren*⟩ organize; ⟨*fam: necken*⟩ tease □ *vi* ⟨*sein*⟩ approach

Aufzucht *f* rearing

Aufzug _m_ hoist; (_Fahrstuhl_) lift, (_Amer_) elevator; (_Prozession_) procession; (_Theat_) act; (_fam: Aufmachung_) get-up

Augapfel _m_ eyeball

Auge _nt_ -s,-n eye; (_Punkt_) spot; vier A∼n werfen throw a four; gute A∼n good eyesight; unter vier A∼n in private; aus den A∼n verlieren lose sight of; im A∼ behalten keep in sight; (_fig_) bear in mind

Augenblick _m_ moment; im/jeden A∼ at the/at any moment; A∼! just a moment! a∼lich _a_ immediate; (_derzeitig_) present □ _adv_ immediately; (_derzeit_) at present

Augen|braue _f_ eyebrow. A∼höhle _f_ eye socket. A∼licht _nt_ sight. A∼lid _nt_ eyelid. A∼schein _m_ in A∼schein nehmen inspect. A∼zeuge _m_ eyewitness

August _m_ -[s] August

Auktion /ˈtsjoːn/ _f_ -,-en auction. A∼ator _m_ -s,-en /-ˈtoːrən/ auctioneer

Aula _f_ -,-len (_Sch_) [assembly] hall

Aupairmädchen /oˈpɛːr-/ _nt_ au pair

aus _prep_ (+ _dat_) out of; (_von_) from; (_bestehend_) [made] of; aus Angst from _or_ out of fear; aus Spaß for fun □ _adv_ out; (_Licht, Radio_) off; aus sein be out; (_Licht, Radio:_) be off; (_zu Ende sein_) be over; aus sein auf (+ _acc_) be after; mit ihm ist es aus he's had it; aus und ein in and out; nicht mehr aus noch ein wissen be at one's wits' end; von … aus from …; von sich aus of one's own accord; von mir aus as far as I'm concerned

ausarbeiten _vt sep_ work out

ausarten _vi sep_ (_sein_) degenerate (in + _acc_ into)

ausatmen _vt/i sep_ (_haben_) breathe out

ausbaggern _vt sep_ excavate; dredge (_Fluss_)

ausbauen _vt sep_ remove; (_vergrößern_) extend; (_fig_) expand

ausbedingen† _vt sep_ sich (_dat_) a∼ insist on; (_zur Bedingung machen_) stipulate

ausbessern _vt sep_ mend, repair. A∼ung _f_ repair

ausbeulen _vt sep_ remove the dents from; (_dehnen_) make baggy

Ausbeut|e _f_ yield. a∼en _vt sep_ exploit. A∼ung _f_ - exploitation

ausbild|en _vt sep_ train; (_formen_) form; (_entwickeln_) develop; sich a∼en train (als/zu as); (_entstehen_) develop. A∼er _m_ -s,- instructor. A∼ung _f_ training; (_Sch_) education

ausbitten† _vt sep_ sich (_dat_) a∼ ask for; (_verlangen_) insist on

ausblasen† _vt sep_ blow out

ausbleiben† _vi sep_ (_sein_) fail to appear/ (_Erfolg:_) materialize; (_nicht heimkommen_)

stay out; es konnte nicht a∼ it was inevitable. A∼ _nt_ -s absence

Ausblick _m_ view

ausbrech|en† _vi sep_ (_sein_) break out; (_Vulkan:_) erupt; (_fliehen_) escape; in Tränen a∼en burst into tears. A∼er _m_ runaway

ausbreit|en _vt sep_ spread [out]; sich a∼en spread. A∼ung _f_ spread

ausbrennen† _v sep_ □ _vt_ cauterize □ _vi_ (_sein_) burn out; (_Haus:_) be gutted [by fire]

Ausbruch _m_ outbreak; (_Vulkan-_) eruption; (_Wut-_) outburst; (_Flucht_) escape, break-out

ausbrüten _vt sep_ hatch

Ausbund _m_ A∼ der Tugend paragon of virtue

ausbürsten _vt sep_ brush; (_entfernen_) brush out

Ausdauer _f_ perseverance; (_körperlich_) stamina. a∼nd _a_ persevering; (_unermüdlich_) untiring; (_Bot_) perennial □ _adv_ with perseverance; untiringly

ausdehn|en _vt sep_ stretch; (_fig_) extend; sich a∼en stretch; (_Phys & fig_) expand; (_dauern_) last. A∼ung _f_ expansion; (_Umfang_) extent

ausdenken† _vt sep_ sich (_dat_) a∼ think up; (_sich vorstellen_) imagine

ausdrehen _vt sep_ turn off

Ausdruck _m_ expression; (_Fach-_) term; (_Computer_) printout. a∼en _vt sep_ print

ausdrück|en _vt sep_ squeeze out; squeeze (_Zitrone_); stub out (_Zigarette_); (_äußern_) express; sich a∼en express oneself. a∼lich _a_ express, _adv_ -ly

ausdrucks|los _a_ expressionless. a∼voll _a_ expressive, _adv_ -ly

auseinander _adv_ apart; (_entzwei_) in pieces; a∼ falten unfold; a∼ gehen part; (_Linien, Meinungen:_) diverge; (_Menge:_) disperse; (_Ehe:_) break up; (_entzweigehen_) come apart; a∼ halten tell apart; a∼ nehmen take apart _or_ to pieces; a∼ setzen place apart; (_erklären_) explain (jdm to s.o.); sich a∼ setzen sit apart; (_sich aussprechen_) have it out (mit jdm with s.o.); come to grips (mit einem Problem with a problem). a∼falten _vt sep_ NEW a∼ falten, s. auseinander. a∼gehen† _vi sep_ (_sein_) NEW a∼ gehen, s. auseinander. a∼halten† _vt sep_ NEW a∼ halten, s. auseinander. a∼nehmen† _vt sep_ NEW a∼ nehmen, s. auseinander. a∼setzen _vt sep_ NEW a∼ setzen, s. auseinander. A∼setzung _f_ -,-en discussion; (_Streit_) argument

auserlesen _a_ select, choice

ausfahr|en _v sep_ □ _vt_ take for a drive; take out (_Baby_) [in the pram] □ _vi_ (_sein_) go for a drive. A∼t *f* drive; *(Autobahn-, Garagen-)* exit

Ausfall *m* failure; *(Absage)* cancellation; *(Comm)* loss. a∼en† *vi sep (sein)* fall out; *(versagen)* fail; *(abgesagt werden)* be cancelled; gut/schlecht a∼en turn out to be good/poor

ausfallend, **ausfällig** *a* abusive

ausfertig|en *vt sep* make out. A∼ung *f* -,-en in doppelter/dreifacher A∼ung in duplicate/triplicate

ausfindig *a* a∼ machen find

ausflippen *vi (sein)* freak out

Ausflucht *f* -,-̈e excuse

Ausflug *m* excursion, outing

Ausflügler *m* -s,- [day-]tripper

Ausfluss (**Ausfluß**) *m* outlet; *(Abfluss)* drain; *(Med)* discharge

ausfragen *vt sep* question

ausfransen *vi sep (sein)* fray

Ausfuhr *f* -,-en *(Comm)* export

ausführ|en *vt sep (Comm)* export; *(durchführen)* carry out; *(erklären)* explain. a∼lich *a* detailed □ *adv* in detail. A∼ung *f* execution; *(Comm)* version; *(äußere)* finish; *(Qualität)* workmanship; *(Erklärung)* explanation

Ausgabe *f* issue; *(Buch-)* edition; *(Comm)* version

Ausgang *m* way out, exit; *(Flugsteig)* gate; *(Ende)* end; *(Ergebnis)* outcome, result; A∼ haben have time off. A∼spunkt *m* starting-point. A∼ssperre *f* curfew

ausgeben† *vt sep* hand out; issue *(Fahrkarten)*; spend *(Geld)*; buy *(Runde Bier)*; sich a∼ als pretend to be

ausgebeult *a* baggy

ausgebildet *a* trained

ausgebucht *a* fully booked; *(Vorstellung)* sold out

ausgedehnt *a* extensive; *(lang)* long

ausgedient *a* worn out; *(Person)* retired

ausgefallen *a* unusual

ausgefranst *a* frayed

ausgeglichen *a* [well-]balanced; *(gelassen)* even-tempered

ausgeh|en *vi sep (sein)* go out; *(Haare:)* fall out; *(Vorräte, Geld:)* run out; *(verblassen)* fade; *(herrühren)* come (von from); *(abzielen)* aim (auf + *acc* at); gut/schlecht a∼en end well/badly; leer a∼en come away empty-handed; davon a∼en, dass assume that. A∼verbot *nt* curfew

ausgelassen *a* high-spirited; a∼ sein be in high spirits

ausgelernt *a* [fully] trained

ausgemacht *a* agreed; *(fam: vollkommen)* utter

ausgenommen *conj* except; a∼ wenn unless

ausgeprägt *a* marked

ausgerechnet *adv* a∼ heute today of all days; a∼er/Rom he of all people/Rome of all places

ausgeschlossen *pred a* out of the question

ausgeschnitten *a* low-cut

ausgesprochen *a* marked □ *adv* decidedly

ausgestorben *a* extinct; [wie] a∼ ⟨Straße:⟩ deserted

Ausgestoßene(r) *m/f* outcast

ausgewachsen *a* fully-grown

ausgewogen *a* [well-]balanced

ausgezeichnet *a* excellent, *adv* -ly

ausgiebig *a* extensive, *adv* -ly; *(ausgedehnt)* long; a∼ Gebrauch machen von make full use of; a∼ frühstücken have a really good breakfast

ausgießen† *vt sep* pour out; *(leeren)* empty

Ausgleich *m* -[e]s balance; *(Entschädigung)* compensation. a∼en† *v sep* □ *vt* balance; even out *(Höhe)*; *(wettmachen)* compensate for; sich a∼en balance out □ *vi (haben) (Sport)* equalize. A∼snastik *f* keep-fit exercises *pl*. A∼streffer *m* equalizer

ausgleiten† *vi sep (sein)* slip

ausgrab|en† *vt sep* dig up; *(Archaeol)* excavate. A∼ung *f* -,-en excavation

Ausguck *m* -[e]s,-e look-out post; *(Person)* look-out

Ausguss (**Ausguß**) *m* [kitchen] sink

aushaben† *vt sep* have finished *(Buch)*; wann habt ihr Schule aus? when do you finish school?

aushalten† *v sep* □ *vt* bear, stand; hold *(Note)*; *(Unterhalt zahlen für)* keep; nicht auszuhalten, nicht zum A∼ unbearable □ *vi (haben)* hold out

aushandeln *vt sep* negotiate

aushändigen *vt sep* hand over

Aushang *m* [public] notice

aushängen¹ *vt sep (reg)* display; take off its hinges *(Tür)*

aushäng|en²† *vi sep (haben)* be displayed. A∼eschild *nt* sign

ausharren *vi sep (haben)* hold out

ausheben† *vt sep* excavate; take off its hinges *(Tür)*

aushecken *vt sep (fig)* hatch

aushelfen† *vi sep (haben)* help out (jdm s.o.)

Aushilfe *f* [temporary] assistant; zur A∼e to help out. A∼skraft *f* temporary worker. a∼sweise *adv* temporarily

<u>aus</u>höhlen *vt sep* hollow out

<u>aus</u>holen *vi sep (haben)* [zum Schlag] a∼ raise one's arm [ready to strike]

<u>aus</u>horchen *vt sep* sound out

<u>aus</u>kennen† (sich) *vr sep* know one's way around; sich mit/in etw *(dat)* a∼ know all about sth

<u>aus</u>kleiden *vt sep* undress; *(Techn)* line; sich a∼ undress

<u>aus</u>knipsen *vi sep* switch off

<u>aus</u>komment *vi sep (sein)* manage (mit/ohne with/without); *(sich vertragen)* get on (gut well). A∼ *nt* -s sein A∼/ ein gutes A∼haben get by/be well off

<u>aus</u>kosten *vt sep* enjoy [to the full]

<u>aus</u>kugeln *vt sep* sich *(dat)* den Arm a∼ dislocate one's shoulder

<u>aus</u>kühlen *vt/i sep (sein)* cool

<u>aus</u>kundschaften *vt sep* spy out; *(erfahren)* find out

<u>Aus</u>kunft *f* -,-ͤe information; *(A∼sstelle)* information desk/ *(Büro)* bureau; *(Teleph)* enquiries *pl*; eine A∼ a piece of information. A∼sbüro *nt* information bureau

<u>aus</u>lachen *vt sep* laugh at

<u>aus</u>ladent *vt sep* unload; *(fam: absagen)* put off *(Gast)*. a∼d *a* projecting

<u>Aus</u>lage *f* [window] display; A∼n expenses

<u>Aus</u>land *nt* im/ins A∼ abroad

<u>Aus</u>länd|er(in) *m* -s,- *(f* -,-nen) foreigner. a∼isch *a* foreign

<u>Aus</u>landsgespräch *nt* international call

<u>aus</u>lass|en *vt sep* let out; let down *(Saum)*; *(weglassen)* leave out; *(versäumen)* miss; *(Culin)* melt; *(fig)* vent *(Ärger)* (an + *dat* on); sich a∼en über (+ *acc)* go on about. A∼ungszeichen *nt* apostrophe

<u>Aus</u>lauf *m* run. a∼ent *vi sep (sein)* run out; *(Farbe:)* run; *(Naut)* put to sea; *(leer laufen)* run dry; *(enden)* end; *(Modell:)* be discontinued

<u>Aus</u>läufer *m (Geog)* spur; *(Bot)* runner, sucker

<u>aus</u>leeren *vt sep* empty [out]

<u>aus</u>leg|en *vt sep* lay out; display *(Waren)*; *(bedecken)* cover/ *(auskleiden)* line (mit with); *(bezahlen)* pay; *(deuten)* interpret. A∼ung *f* -,-en interpretation

<u>aus</u>leihent *vt sep* lend; sich *(dat)* a∼ borrow

<u>aus</u>lernen *vi sep (haben)* finish one's training

<u>Aus</u>lese *f* - selection; *(fig)* pick; *(Elite)* élite. a∼nt *vt sep* finish reading *(Buch)*; *(auswählen)* pick out, select

<u>aus</u>liefer|n *vt sep* hand over; *(Jur)* extradite; ausgeliefert sein (+ *dat)* be at the mercy of. A∼ung *f* handing over; *(Jur)* extradition; *(Comm)* distribution

<u>aus</u>liegent *vi sep (haben)* be on display

<u>aus</u>löschen *vt sep* extinguish; *(abwischen)* wipe off; *(fig)* erase

<u>aus</u>losen *vt sep* draw lots for

<u>aus</u>lös|en *vt sep* set off, trigger; *(fig)* cause; arouse *(Begeisterung)*; *(einlösen)* redeem; pay a ransom for *(Gefangene)*. A∼er *m* -s,- trigger; *(Phot)* shutter release

<u>Aus</u>losung *f* draw

<u>aus</u>lüften *vt/i sep (haben)* air

<u>aus</u>machen *vt sep* put out; *(abschalten)* turn off; *(abmachen)* arrange; *(erkennen)* make out; *(betragen)* amount to; *(darstellen)* represent; *(wichtig sein)* matter; das macht mir nichts aus I don't mind

<u>aus</u>malen *vt sep* paint; *(fig)* describe; sich *(dat)* a∼ imagine

<u>Aus</u>maß *nt* extent; A∼e dimensions

<u>aus</u>merzen *vt sep* eliminate

<u>aus</u>messent *vt sep* measure

<u>Aus</u>nahm|e *f* -,-n exception. A∼ezustand *m* state of emergency. a∼slos *adv* without exception. a∼sweise *adv* as an exception

<u>aus</u>nehment *vt sep* take out; gut *(Fisch)*; draw *(Huhn)*; *(ausschließen)* exclude; *(fam: schröpfen)* fleece; sich gut a∼ look good. a∼d *adv* exceptionally

<u>aus</u>nutz|en, <u>aus</u>nütz|en *vt sep* exploit; make the most of *(Gelegenheit)*. A∼ung *f* exploitation

<u>aus</u>packen *v sep* □ *vt* unpack; *(auswickeln)* unwrap □ *vi (haben) (fam)* talk

<u>aus</u>peitschen *vt sep* flog

<u>aus</u>pfeifen *vt sep* whistle and boo

<u>aus</u>plaudern *vt sep* let out, blab

<u>aus</u>plündern *vt sep* loot; rob *(Person)*

<u>aus</u>probieren *vt sep* try out

<u>Aus</u>puff *m* -s exhaust [system]. A∼gase *ntpl* exhaust fumes. A∼rohr *nt* exhaust pipe

<u>aus</u>pusten *vt sep* blow out

<u>aus</u>radieren *vt sep* rub out

<u>aus</u>rangieren *vt sep (fam)* discard

<u>aus</u>rauben *vt sep* rob

<u>aus</u>räuchern *vt sep* smoke out; fumigate *(Zimmer)*

<u>aus</u>räumen *vt sep* clear out

<u>aus</u>rechnen *vt sep* work out, calculate

<u>Aus</u>rede *f* excuse. a∼n *v sep* □ *vi (haben)* finish speaking; lass mich a∼n! let me finish! □ *vt* jdm etw a∼n talk s.o. out of sth

ausreichen vi sep (haben) be enough; a~ mit have enough. a~d a adequate, adv -ly; (Sch) ≈ pass

Ausreise f departure [from a country]. a~n vi sep (sein) leave the country. A~visum nt exit visa

ausreiß|en† v sep □ vt pull or tear out □ vi (sein) (fam) run away. A~er m (fam) runaway

ausrenken vt sep dislocate; sich (dat) den Arm a~ dislocate one's shoulder

ausrichten vt sep align; (bestellen) deliver; (erreichen) achieve; jdm a~ tell s.o. (dass that); kann ich etwas a~? can I take a message? ich soll Ihnen Grüße von X a~ X sends [you] his regards

ausrotten vt sep exterminate; (fig) eradicate

ausrücken vi sep (sein) (Mil) march off; (fam) run away

Ausruf m exclamation. a~en† vt sep exclaim; call out (Namen); (verkünden) proclaim; call (Streik); jdn a~en lassen have s.o. paged. A~ezeichen nt exclamation mark

ausruhen vt/i sep (haben) rest; sich a~ have a rest

ausrüst|en vt sep equip. A~ung f equipment; (Mil) kit

ausrutschen vi sep (sein) slip

Aussage f -,-n statement; (Jur) testimony, evidence; (Gram) predicate. a~n vt/i sep (haben) state; (Jur) give evidence, testify

Aussatz m leprosy

Aussätzige(r) m/f leper

ausschachten vt sep excavate

ausschalten vt sep switch or turn off; (fig) eliminate

Ausschank m sale of alcoholic drinks; (Bar) bar

Ausschau f - A~ halten nach look out for. a~en vi sep (haben) (SGer) look; a~en nach look out for

ausscheiden† v sep □ vi (sein) leave; (Sport) drop out; (nicht in Frage kommen) be excluded; aus dem Dienst a~ retire □ vt eliminate; (Med) excrete

ausschenken vt sep pour out; (verkaufen) sell

ausscheren vi sep (sein) (Auto) pull out

ausschildern vt sep signpost

ausschimpfen vt sep tell off

ausschlachten vt sep (fig) exploit

ausschlafen† v sep □ vi/r (haben) [sich] a~ get enough sleep; (morgens) sleep late; nicht ausgeschlafen haben od sein be still tired □ vt sleep off (Rausch)

Ausschlag m (Med) rash; den A~ geben (fig) tip the balance. a~en† v sep □ vi

(haben) kick [out]; (Bot) sprout; (Baum:) come into leaf □ vt knock out; (auskleiden) line; (ablehnen) refuse. a~gebend a decisive

ausschließ|en† vt sep lock out; (fig) exclude; (entfernen) expel. a~lich a exclusive, adv -ly

ausschlüpfen vi sep (sein) hatch

Ausschluss (Ausschluß) m exclusion; expulsion; unter A~ der Öffentlichkeit in camera

ausschmücken vt sep decorate; (fig) embellish

ausschneiden† vt sep cut out

Ausschnitt m excerpt, extract; (Zeitungs-) cutting; (Hals-) neckline

ausschöpfen vt sep ladle out; (Naut) bail out; exhaust (Möglichkeiten)

ausschreiben† vt sep write out; (ausstellen) make out; (bekanntgeben) announce; put out to tender (Auftrag)

Ausschreitungen fpl riots; (Exzesse) excesses

Ausschuss (Ausschuß) m committee; (Comm) rejects pl

ausschütten vt sep tip out; (verschütten) spill; (leeren) empty; sich vor Lachen a~ (fam) be in stitches

ausschweif|end a dissolute. A~ung f -,-en debauchery; A~ungen excesses

ausschwenken vt sep rinse [out]

aussehen† vi sep (haben) look; es sieht nach Regen aus it looks like rain; wie sieht er/es aus? what does he/it look like? ein gut a~der Mann a good-looking man. A~ nt -s appearance

aussein† vi sep (sein) (NEW) aus sein, s. aus

außen adv [on the] outside; nach a~ outwards. A~bordmotor m outboard motor. A~handel m foreign trade. A~minister m Foreign Minister. A~politik f foreign policy. A~seite f outside. A~seiter m -s,- outsider; (fig) misfit. A~stände mpl outstanding debts. A~stehende(r) m/f outsider

außer prep (+ dat) except [for], apart from; (außerhalb) out of; a~ Atem/Sicht out of breath/sight; a~ sich (fig) beside oneself □ conj except; a~ wenn unless. a~dem adv in addition, as well □ conj moreover

äußer|e(r,s) a external; (Teil, Schicht) outer. Ä~e(s) nt exterior; (Aussehen) appearance

außer|ehelich a extramarital. a~gewöhnlich a exceptional, adv -ly. a~halb prep (+ gen) outside □ adv a~halb wohnen live outside town

äußer|lich a external, adv -ly; (fig) outward, adv -ly. ä~n vt express; sich ä~n comment; (sich zeigen) manifest itself

außerordentlich *a* extraordinary, *adv* -ily; *(außergewöhnlich)* exceptional, *adv* -ly

äußerst *adv* extremely

außerstande *pred a* unable (zu to)

äußerste(r,s) *a* outermost; *(weiteste)* furthest; *(höchste)* utmost, extreme; *(letzte)* last; *(schlimmste)* worst; am ä~n Ende at the very end; aufs ä~ = aufs Ä~, s. Äußerste(s). Ä~(s) *nt* das Ä~ the limit; *(Schlimmste)* the worst; sein Ä~s tun do one's utmost; aufs Ä~ extremely

Äußerung *f* -,-en comment; *(Bemerkung)* remark

aussetzen *v sep* □ *vt* expose *(dat* to); abandon *(Kind, Hund)*; launch *(Boot)*; offer *(Belohnung)*; etwas auszusetzen haben an (+ *dat)* find fault with □ *vi (haben)* stop; *(Motor:)* cut out

Aussicht *f* -,-en view/*(fig)* prospect *(auf* + *acc* of); in A~ stellen promise; weitere A~en *(Meteorol)* further outlook *sg.* a~slos *a* hopeless, *adv* -ly. a~sreich *a* promising

aussöhnen *vt sep* reconcile; sich a~ become reconciled

aussortieren *vt sep* pick out; *(ausscheiden)* eliminate

ausspann|en *v sep* □ *vt* spread out; unhitch *(Pferd)*; *(fam: wegnehmen)* take *(dat* from) □ *vi (haben)* rest. A~ung *f* rest

aussperr|en *vt sep* lock out. A~ung *f* -,-en lock-out

ausspielen *v sep* □ *vt* play *(Karte)*; *(fig)* play off *(gegen* against) □ *vi (haben)* *(Kartenspiel)* lead

Aussprache *f* pronunciation; *(Sprechweise)* diction; *(Gespräch)* talk

aussprechen† *v sep* □ *vt* pronounce; *(äußern)* express; sich a~ talk; come out *(für/gegen* in favour of/against) □ *vi (haben)* finish [speaking]

Ausspruch *m* saying

ausspucken *v sep* □ *vt* spit out □ *vi (haben)* spit

ausspülen *vt sep* rinse out

ausstaffieren *vt sep (fam)* kit out

Ausstand *m* strike; in den A~ treten go on strike

ausstatt|en *vt sep* equip; mit Möbeln a~en furnish. A~ung *f* -,-en equipment; *(Innen-)* furnishings *pl*; *(Theat)* scenery and costumes *pl*; *(Aufmachung)* get-up

ausstehen† *v sep* □ *vt* suffer; Angst a~ be frightened; ich kann sie nicht a~ I can't stand her □ *vi (haben)* be outstanding

aussteig|en† *vi sep (sein)* get out; *(aus Bus, Zug)* get off; *(fam: ausscheiden)* opt out;

(aus einem Geschäft) back out; alles a~en! all change! A~er(in) *m* -s,- *(f* -,-nen) *(fam)* drop-out

ausstell|en *vt sep* exhibit; *(Comm)* display; *(ausfertigen)* make out; issue *(Pass)*. A~er *m* -s,- exhibitor. A~ung *f* exhibition; *(Comm)* display. A~ungsstück *nt* exhibit

aussterben† *vi sep (sein)* die out; *(Biol)* become extinct. A~ *nt* -s extinction

Aussteuer *f* trousseau

Ausstieg *m* -[e]s,-e exit

ausstopfen *vt sep* stuff

ausstoßen† *vt sep* emit; utter *(Fluch)*; heave *(Seufzer)*; *(ausschließen)* expel

ausstrahl|en *vt/i sep (sein)* radiate, emit; *(Radio, TV)* broadcast. A~ung *f* radiation; *(fig)* charisma

ausstrecken *vt sep* stretch out; put out *(Hand)*; sich a~ stretch out

ausstreichen† *vt sep* cross out

ausstreuen *vt sep* scatter; spread *(Gerüchte)*

ausströmen *v sep* □ *vi (sein)* pour out; *(entweichen)* escape □ *vt* emit; *(ausstrahlen)* radiate

aussuchen *vt sep* pick, choose

Austausch *m* exchange. a~bar *a* interchangeable. a~en *vt sep* exchange; *(auswechseln)* replace

austeilen *vt sep* distribute; *(ausgeben)* hand out

Auster *f* -,-n oyster

austoben (sich) *vr sep (Sturm:)* rage; *(Person:)* let off steam; *(Kinder:)* romp about

austragen† *vt sep* deliver; hold *(Wettkampf)*; play *(Spiel)*

Austral|ien /-jən/ *nt* -s Australia. A~ier(in) *m* -s,- *(f* -,-nen) Australian. a~isch *a* Australian

austreiben† *v sep* □ *vt* drive out; *(Relig)* exorcize □ *vi (haben)* *(Bot)* sprout

austreten† *v sep* □ *vt* stamp out; *(abnutzen)* wear down □ *vi (sein)* come out; *(ausscheiden)* leave (aus etw sth); [mal] a~ *(fam)* go to the loo; *(Sch)* be excused

austrinken† *vt/i sep (haben)* drink up; *(leeren)* drain

Austritt *m* resignation

austrocknen *vt/i sep (sein)* dry out

ausüben *vt sep* practise; carry on *(Handwerk)*; exercise *(Recht)*; exert *(Druck, Einfluss)*; have *(Wirkung)*

Ausverkauf *m* [clearance] sale. a~t *a* sold out; a~tes Haus full house

auswachsen† *vt sep* outgrow

Auswahl *f* choice, selection; *(Comm)* range; *(Sport)* team

auswählen vt sep choose, select

Auswander|er m emigrant. a∼n vi sep (sein) emigrate. A∼ung f emigration

auswärt|ig a non-local; (ausländisch) foreign. a∼s adv outwards; (Sport) away; a∼s essen eat out; a∼s arbeiten not work locally. A∼ sspiel nt away game

auswaschen† vt sep wash out

auswechseln vt sep change; (ersetzen) replace; (Sport) substitute

Ausweg m (fig) way out. a∼los a (fig) hopeless

ausweich|en† vi sep (sein) get out of the way; jdm/etw a∼en avoid/ (sich entziehen) evade s.o./sth. a∼end a evasive, adv -ly

ausweinen vt sep sich (dat) die Augen a∼ cry one's eyes out; sich a∼ have a good cry

Ausweis m -es,-e pass; (Mitglieds-, Studenten-) card. a∼en† vt sep deport; sich a∼en prove one's identity. A∼papiere ntpl identification papers. A∼ung f deportation

ausweiten vt sep stretch; (fig) expand

auswendig adv by heart

auswerten vt sep evaluate; (nutzen) utilize

auswickeln vt sep unwrap

auswirk|en (sich) vr sep have an effect (auf + acc on). A∼ung f effect; (Folge) consequence

auswischen vt sep wipe out; jdm eins a∼ (fam) play a nasty trick on s.o.

auswringen vt sep wring out

Auswuchs m excrescence; Auswüchse (fig) excesses

auszahlen vt sep pay out; (entlohnen) pay off; (abfinden) buy out; sich a∼ (fig) pay off

auszählen vt sep count; (Boxen) count out

Auszahlung f payment

auszeichn|en vt sep (Comm) price; (ehren) honour; (mit einem Preis) award a prize to; (Mil) decorate; sich a∼en distinguish oneself. A∼ung f honour; (Preis) award; (Mil) decoration; (Sch) distinction

ausziehen† v sep □ vt pull out; (auskleiden) undress; take off (Mantel, Schuhe); sich a∼ take off one's coat; (sich entkleiden) undress □ vi (sein) move out; (sich aufmachen) set out

Auszubildende(r) m/f trainee

Auszug m departure; (Umzug) move; (Ausschnitt) extract, excerpt; (Bank-) statement

authentisch a authentic

Auto nt -s,-s car; A∼ fahren drive; (mitfahren) go in the car. A∼bahn f motorway, (Amer) freeway

Autobiographie f autobiography

Auto|bus m bus. A∼fähre f car ferry. A∼fahrer(in) m(f) driver, motorist. A∼fahrt f drive

Autogramm nt -s,-e autograph

autokratisch a autocratic

Automat m -en,-en automatic device; (Münz-) slot-machine; (Verkaufs-) vending-machine; (Fahrkarten-) machine; (Techn) robot. A∼ik f - automatic mechanism; (Auto) automatic transmission

Auto|mation /-'tsjo:n/ f - automation. a∼matisch a automatic, adv -ally

autonom a autonomous. A∼ie f - autonomy

Autonummer f registration number

Autopsie f -,-n autopsy

Autor m -s,-en /-'to:rən/ author

Auto|reisezug m Motorail. A∼rennen nt motor race

Autorin f -,-nen author[ess]

Autori|sation /-'tsjo:n/ f - authorization. a∼sieren vt authorize. a∼tär a authoritarian. A∼tät f -,-en authority

Auto|schlosser m motor mechanic. A∼skooter /-sku:te/ m -s,- dodgem. A∼stopp m -s per A∼stopp fahren hitchhike. A∼verleih m car hire [firm]. A∼waschanlage f car wash

autsch int ouch

Aversion f -,-en aversion (gegen to)

Axt f -,-̈e axe

B

B, b /be:/ nt - (Mus) B flat

Baby /'be:bi/ nt -s,-s baby. B∼ausstattung f layette. B∼-sitter /-sɪtɐ/ m -s,- babysitter

Bach m -[e]s,-̈e stream

Backbord nt -[e]s port [side]

Backe f -,-n cheek

backen v □ vt/i† (haben) bake; (braten) fry □ vi (reg) (haben) (kleben) stick (an + dat to)

Backenzahn m molar

Bäcker m -s,- baker. B∼ei f -,-en, B∼laden m baker's shop.

Back|form f baking tin. B∼obst nt dried fruit. B∼ofen m oven. B∼pfeife f (fam) slap in the face. B∼pflaume f prune.

B∼pulver nt baking-powder. B∼rohr nt oven. B∼stein m brick. B∼work nt cakes and pastries pl

Bad nt -[e]s,¨er bath; (im Meer) bathe; (Zimmer) bathroom; (Schwimm-) pool; (Ort) spa

Bade|anstalt f swimming baths pl. B∼anzug m swim-suit. B∼hose f swimming trunks pl. B∼kappe f bathing-cap. B∼mantel m bathrobe. B∼matte f bath-mat. B∼mütze f bathing-cap. b∼n vi (haben) have a bath; (im Meer) bathe □ vt bath; (waschen) bathe. B∼ort m seaside resort; (Kurort) spa. B∼tuch nt bathtowel. B∼wanne f bath. B∼zimmer nt bathroom

Bagatelle f -,-n trifle; (Mus) bagatelle

Bagger m -s,- excavator; (Nass-) dredger. b∼n vt/i (haben) excavate; dredge. B∼see m flooded gravel-pit

Bahn f -,-en path; (Astr) orbit; (Sport) track; (einzelne) lane; (Rodel-) run; (Stoff-, Papier-) width; (Rock-) panel; (Eisen-) railway; (Zug) train; (Straßen-) tram; auf die schiefe B∼ kommen (fig) get into bad ways. b∼brechend a (fig) pioneering. b∼en vt sich (dat) einen Weg b∼en clear a way (durch through). B∼hof m [railway] station. B∼steig m -[e]s,-e platform. B∼übergang m level crossing, (Amer) grade crossing

Bahre f -,-n stretcher; (Toten-) bier

Baiser /bɛˈzeː/ nt -s,-s meringue

Bajonett nt -[e]s,-e bayonet

Bake f -,-n (Naut, Aviat) beacon

Bakterien /-jən/ fpl bacteria

Balance /baˈlãːsə/ f - balance; die B∼e halten/verlieren keep/lose one's balance. b∼ieren vt/i (haben/sein) balance

bald adv soon; (fast) almost; b∼ ... b∼ ... now ... then ...

Baldachin /-xiːn/ m -s,-e canopy

bald|ig a early; (Besserung) speedy. b∼möglichst adv as soon as possible

Balg m & nt -[e]s,¨er (fam) brat. b∼en (sich) vr tussle. B∼erei f -,-en tussle

Balkan m -s Balkans pl

Balken m -s,- beam

Balkon /balˈkõː/ m -s,-s balcony; (Theat) circle

Ball¹ m -[e]s,¨e ball

Ball² m -[e]s,¨e (Tanz) ball

Ballade f -,-n ballad

Ballast m -[e]s ballast. B∼stoffe mpl roughage sg

ballen vt die [Hand zur] Faust b∼ clench one's fist; sich b∼ gather, mass. B∼ m -s,- bale; (Anat) ball of the hand/(Fuß-) foot; (Med) bunion

Ballerina f -,-nen ballerina

Ballett nt -s,-e ballet

Balletttänzer(in) (Ballettänzer(in)) m(f) ballet dancer

ballistisch a ballistic

Ballon /baˈlõː/ m -s,-s balloon

Ball|saal m ballroom. B∼ungsgebiet nt conurbation. B∼wechsel m (Tennis) rally

Balsam m -s balm

Baltikum nt -s Baltic States pl. b∼isch a Baltic

Balustrade f -,-n balustrade

Bambus m -ses,-se bamboo

banal a banal. B∼ität f -,-en banality

Banane f -,-n banana

Banause m -n,-n philistine

Band¹ nt -[e]s,¨er ribbon; (Naht-, Ton-, Ziel-) tape; (Anat) ligament; auf B∼ aufnehmen tape; laufendes B∼ conveyor belt; am laufenden B∼ (fam) non-stop

Band² nt -[e]s,¨e volume

Band³ nt -[e]s,-e (fig) bond; B∼e der Freundschaft bonds of friendship

Band⁴ /bɛnt/ f -,-s [jazz] band

Bandage /banˈdaːʒə/ f -,-n bandage. b∼ieren vt bandage

Bande f -,-n gang

bändigen vt control, restrain; (zähmen) tame

Bandit m -en,-en bandit

Band|maß nt tape-measure. B∼nudeln fpl noodles. B∼scheibe f (Anat) disc. B∼scheibenvorfall m slipped disc. B∼wurm m tapeworm

bang[e] a (bänger, bängst) anxious; jdm b∼e machen (NEW) jdm B∼e machen, s. Bange. B∼e f B∼e haben be afraid; jdm B∼e machen frighten s.o. b∼en vi (haben) fear (um for); mir b∼t davor I dread it

Banjo nt -s,-s banjo

Bank¹ f -,¨e bench

Bank² f -,-en (Comm) bank. B∼einzug m direct debit

Bankett nt -s,-e banquet

Bankier /banˈkjeː/ m -s,-s banker

Bank|konto nt bank account. B∼note f banknote

Bankrott m -s,-s bankruptcy; B∼ machen od gehen go bankrupt. b∼ a bankrupt

Bankwesen nt banking

Bann m -[e]s,-e (fig) spell; in jds D∼ under s.o.'s spell. b∼en vt exorcize; (abwenden) avert; [wie] gebannt spellbound

Banner nt -s,- banner

Baptist(in) m -en,-en (f -,-nen) Baptist

bar a (rein) sheer; (Gold) pure; b~es Geld cash; [in] bar bezahlen pay cash; etw für b~e Münze nehmen (fig) take sth as gospel

Bar f -,-s bar

Bär m -en,-en bear; jdm einen B~en aufbinden (fam) pull s.o.'s leg

Baracke f -,-n (Mil) hut

Barb|ar m -en,-en barbarian. b~arisch a barbaric

bar|fuß adv barefoot. B~geld nt cash

Bariton m -s,-e /-'to:nə/ baritone

Barkasse f -,-n launch

Barmann m (pl -männer) barman

barmherzig a merciful. B~keit f - mercy

barock a baroque. B~ nt & m -[s] baroque

Barometer nt -s,- barometer

Baron m -s,-e baron. B~in f -,-nen baroness

Barren m -s,- (Gold-) bar, ingot; (Sport) parallel bars pl. B~gold nt gold bullion

Barriere f -,-n barrier

Barrikade f -,-n barricade

barsch a gruff, adv -ly; (kurz) curt, adv -ly

Barsch m -[e]s,-e (Zool) perch

Barschaft f - meine ganze B~ all I have/had on me

Bart m -[e]s,̈e beard; (der Katze) whiskers pl

bärtig a bearded

Barzahlung f cash payment

Basar m -s,-e bazaar

Base¹ f -,-n [female] cousin

Base² f -,-n (Chem) alkali, base

Basel nt -s Basle

basieren vi (haben) be based (auf + dat on)

Basilikum nt -s basil

Basis f -,Basen base; (fig) basis

basisch a (Chem) alkaline

Bask|enmütze f beret. b~isch a Basque

Bass m -es,̈e (Baß m -sses,̈sse) bass; (Kontra-) double-bass

Bassin /ba'sɛ:/ nt -s,-s pond; (Brunnen-) basin; (Schwimm-) pool

Bassist m -en,-en bass player; (Sänger) bass

Bassstimme (Baßstimme) f bass voice

Bast m -[e]s raffia

basta int [und damit] b~! and that's that!

bast|eln vt make □ vi (haben) do handicrafts; (herum-) tinker (an + dat with). B~ler m -s,- amateur craftsman; (Heim-) do-it-yourselfer

Bataillon /batal'jo:n/ nt -s,-e battalion

Batterie f -,-n battery

Bau¹ m -[e]s,-e burrow; (Fuchs-) earth

Bau² m -[e]s,-ten construction; (Gebäude) building; (Auf-) structure; (Körper-) build; (B~stelle) building site; im Bau under construction. B~arbeiten fpl building work sg; (Straßen-) road-works. B~art f design; (Stil) style

Bauch m -[e]s, Bäuche abdomen, belly; (Magen) stomach; (Schmer-) paunch; (Bauchung) bulge. b~ig a bulbous. B~nabel m navel. B~redner m ventriloquist. B~schmerzen mpl stomach-ache sg. B~speicheldrüse f pancreas. B~weh nt stomach-ache

bauen vt build; (konstruieren) construct; (an-) grow; einen Unfall b~ (fam) have an accident □ vi (haben) build (an etw dat sth); b~ auf (+ acc) (fig) rely on

Bauer¹ m -s,-n farmer; (Schach) pawn

Bauer² nt -s,- [bird]cage

Bäuer|in f -,-nen farmer's wife. b~lich a rustic

Bauern|haus nt farmhouse. B~hof m farm

bau|fällig a dilapidated. B~genehmigung f planning permission. B~gerüst nt scaffolding. B~jahr nt year of construction; B~jahr 1985 (Auto) 1985 model. B~kasten m box of building bricks; (Modell-) model kit. B~klotz m building brick. B~kunst f architecture. b~lich a structural, adv -ly. B~lichkeiten fpl buildings

Baum m -[e]s, Bäume tree

baumeln vi (haben) dangle; die Beine b~ lassen dangle one's legs

bäumen (sich) vr rear [up]

Baum|schule f [tree] nursery. B~stamm m tree-trunk. B~wolle f cotton. b~wollen a cotton

Bauplatz m building plot

bäurisch a rustic; (plump) uncouth

Bausch m -[e]s, Bäusche wad; in B~ und Bogen (fig) wholesale. b~en vt (und) sich b~en billow [out]. b~ig a puffed [out]; (Ärmel) full

Bau|sparkasse f building society. B~stein m building brick; (fig) element. B~stelle f building site; (Straßen-) roadworks pl. B~unternehmer m building contractor. B~werk nt building. B~zaun m hoarding

Bayer|(in) m -s,-n (f -,-nen) Bavarian. B~n nt -s Bavaria

bay[e]risch a Bavarian

Bazillus m -,-len bacillus; (fam: Keim) germ

beabsichtig|en vt intend. b~t a intended; (absichtlich) intentional beacht|en vt take notice of; (einhalten) observe; (folgen) follow; nicht b~en ignore. b~lich a considerable. B~ung f -observance; etw (dat) keine B~ung schenken take no notice of sth

Beamte(r) m, Beamtin f -,-nen official; (Staats-) civil servant; (Schalter-) clerk

beängstigend a alarming

beanspruchen vt claim; (erfordern) demand; (brauchen) take up; (Techn) stress; die Arbeit beansprucht ihn sehr his work is very demanding

beanstand|en vt find fault with; (Comm) make a complaint about. B~ung f -,-en complaint

beantragen vt apply for

beantworten vt answer

bearbeiten vt work; (weiter-) process; (behandeln) treat (mit with); (Admin) deal with; (redigieren) edit; (Theat) adapt; (Mus) arrange; (fam: bedrängen) pester; (fam: schlagen) pummel

Beatmung f künstliche B~ artificial respiration. B~sgerät nt ventilator

beaufsichtig|en vt supervise. B~ung f - supervision

beauftrag|en vt instruct; commission (Künstler); jdn mit einer Arbeit b~en assign a task to s.o. B~te(r) m/f representative

bebauen vt build on; (bestellen) cultivate

beben vi (haben) tremble

bebildert a illustrated

Becher m -s,- beaker; (Henkel-) mug; (Joghurt-, Sahne-) carton

Becken nt -s,- basin; (Schwimm-) pool; (Mus) cymbals pl; (Anat) pelvis

bedacht a careful; b~ auf (+ acc) concerned about; darauf b~ anxious (zu to)

bedächtig a careful, adv -ly; (langsam) slow, adv -ly

bedanken (sich) vr thank (bei jdm s.o.)

Bedarf m -s need/(Comm) demand (an + dat for); bei B~ if required. B~sartikel mpl requisites. B~shaltestelle f request stop

bedauer|lich a regrettable. b~licherweise adv unfortunately. b~n vt regret; (bemitleiden) feel sorry for; bedaure! sorry! B~n nt -s regret; (Mitgefühl) sympathy. b~nswert a pitiful; (bedauerlich) regrettable

bedeck|en vt cover; sich b~en (Himmel:) cloud over. b~t a covered; (Himmel) overcast

bedenken† vt consider; (überlegen) think over; jdn b~ give s.o. a present; sich b~ consider. B~ pl misgivings; ohne B~

without hesitation. b~los a unhesitating, adv -ly

bedenklich a doubtful; (verdächtig) dubious; (bedrohlich) worrying; (ernst) serious

bedeut|en vi (haben) mean; jdm viel/ nichts b~en mean a lot/nothing to s.o.; es hat nichts zu b~en it is of no significance. b~end a important; (beträchtlich) considerable. b~sam a = b~ungsvoll. B~ung f -,-en meaning; (Wichtigkeit) importance. b~ungslos a meaningless; (unwichtig) unimportant. b~ungsvoll a significant; (vielsagend) meaningful, adv -ly

bedien|en vt serve; (betätigen) operate; sich [selbst] b~en help oneself. B~ung f -,-en service; (Betätigung) operation; (Kellner) waiter; (Kellnerin) waitress. B~ungsgeld nt, B~ungszuschlag m service charge

bedingt a conditional; (eingeschränkt) qualified

Bedingung f -,-en condition; B~en conditions; (Comm) terms. b~slos a unconditional, adv -ly; (unbedingt) unquestioning, adv -ly

bedräng|en vt press; (belästigen) pester

bedroh|en vt threaten. b~lich a threatening. B~ung f threat

bedrück|en vt depress. b~end a depressing. b~t a depressed

bedruckt a printed

bedürf|en† vi (haben) (+ gen) need. B~nis nt -ses,-se need. B~nisanstalt f public convenience. b~tig a needy

Beefsteak /'bi:fste:k/ nt -s,-s steak; deutsches B~ hamburger

beeilen (sich) vr hurry; hasten (zu to); beeilt euch! hurry up!

beeindrucken vt impress

beeinflussen vt influence

beeinträchtigen vt mar; (schädigen) impair

beend|ig|en vt end

beengen vt restrict; beengt wohnen live in cramped conditions

beerben vt jdn b~ inherit s.o.'s property

beerdig|en vt bury. B~ung f -,-en funeral

Beere f -,-n berry

Beet nt -[e]s,-e (Hort) bed

Beete f -,-n rote B~ beetroot

befähig|en vt enable; (qualifizieren) qualify. B~ung f - qualification; (Fähigkeit) ability

befahr|bar a passable. b~en† vt drive along; stark b~ene Straße busy road

befallen† vt attack; (Angst:) seize

befangen *a* shy; (*gehemmt*) self-conscious; (*Jur*) biased. B~heit *f* - shyness; self-consciousness; bias

befassen (sich) *vr* concern oneself/ (*behandeln*) deal (mit with)

Befehl *m* -[e]s,-e order; (*Leitung*) command (über + *acc* of). b~en† *vt* jdm etw b~en order s.o. to do sth □ *vi* (*haben*) give the orders. b~igen *vt* (*Mil*) command. B~sform *f* (*Gram*) imperative. B~shaber *m* -s,- commander

befestig|en *vt* fasten (an + *dat* to); (*stärken*) strengthen; (*Mil*) fortify. B~ung *f* -,-en fastening; (*Mil*) fortification

befeuchten *vt* moisten

befinden† (sich) *vr* be. B~ *nt* -s [state of] health

beflecken *vt* stain

beflissen *a* assiduous, *adv* -ly

befolgen *vt* follow

beförder|n *vt* transport; (*im Rang*) promote. B~ung *f* -,-en transport; promotion

befragen *vt* question

befrei|en *vt* free; (*räumen*) clear (von of); (*freistellen*) exempt (von from); sich b~en free oneself. B~er *m* -s,- liberator. b~t *a* (*erleichtert*) relieved. B~ung *f* - liberation; exemption

befremd|en *vt* disconcert. B~en *nt* -s surprise. b~lich *a* strange

befreunden (sich) *vr* make friends; befreundet sein be friends

befriedig|en *vt* satisfy. b~end *a* satisfying; (*zufrieden stellend*) satisfactory. B~ung *f* - satisfaction

befrucht|en *vt* fertilize. B~ung *f* - fertilization; künstliche B~ung artificial insemination

Befug|nis *f* -,-se authority. b~t *a* authorized

Befund *m* result

befürcht|en *vt* fear. B~ung *f* -,-en fear

befürworten *vt* support

begab|t *a* gifted. B~ung *f* -,-en gift, talent

begatten (sich) *vr* mate

begeben† (sich) *vr* go; (*liter: geschehen*) happen; sich in Gefahr b~ expose oneself to danger. B~heit *f* -,-en incident

begegn|en *vi* (*sein*) jdm/etw b~en meet s.o./sth; sich b~en meet. B~ung *f* -,-en meeting; (*Sport*) encounter

begehen† *vt* walk along; (*verüben*) commit; (*feiern*) celebrate

begehr|en *vt* desire. b~enswert *a* desirable. b~t *a* sought-after

begeister|n *vt* jdn b~n arouse s.o.'s enthusiasm; sich b~n be enthusiastic (für

about). b~t *a* enthusiastic, *adv* -ally; (*eifrig*) keen. B~ung *f* - enthusiasm

Begier|de *f* -,-n desire. b~ig *a* eager (auf + *acc* for)

begießen† *vt* water; (*Culin*) baste; (*fam: feiern*) celebrate

Beginn *m* -s beginning; zu B~ at the beginning. b~en† *vt/i* (*haben*) start, begin; (*anstellen*) do

beglaubigen *vt* authenticate

begleichen† *vt* settle

begleit|en *vt* accompany. B~er *m* -s,- B~erin *f* -,-nen companion; (*Mus*) accompanist. B~ung *f* -,-en company; (*Gefolge*) entourage; (*Mus*) accompaniment

beglück|en *vt* make happy. b~t *a* happy. b~wünschen *vt* congratulate (zu on)

begnadig|en *vt* (*Jur*) pardon. B~ung *f* -,-en (*Jur*) pardon

begnügen (sich) *vr* content oneself (mit with)

Begonie /-iə/ *f* -,-n begonia

begraben† *vt* bury

Begräbnis *n* -ses,-se burial; (*Feier*) funeral

begreif|en† *vt* understand; nicht zu b~en incomprehensible. b~lich *a* understandable; jdm etw b~lich machen make s.o. understand sth. b~licherweise *adv* understandably

begrenz|en *vt* form the boundary of; (*beschränken*) restrict. b~t *a* limited. B~ung *f* -,-en restriction; (*Grenze*) boundary

Begriff *m* -[e]s,-e concept; (*Ausdruck*) term; (*Vorstellung*) idea; für meine B~e to my mind; im B~ sein *od* stehen be about (zu to); schwer von B~ (*fam*) slow on the uptake. B~sstutzig *a* obtuse

begründ|en *vt* give one's reason for; (*gründen*) establish. b~et *a* justified. B~ung *f* -,-en reason

begrüß|en *vt* greet; (*billigen*) welcome. b~enswert *a* welcome. B~ung *f* - greeting; welcome

begünstigen *vt* favour; (*fördern*) encourage

begutachten *vt* give an opinion on; (*fam: ansehen*) look at

begütert *a* wealthy

begütigen *vt* placate

behaart *a* hairy

behäbig *a* portly; (*gemütlich*) comfortable, *adv* -bly

behagen *vi* (*haben*) please (jdm s.o.). B~en *nt* -s contentment; (*Genuss*) enjoyment. b~lich *a* comfortable, *adv* -bly. B~lichkeit *f* - comfort

behalten† *vt* keep; (*sich merken*) remember; etw für sich b~ (*verschweigen*) keep sth to oneself

Behälter *m* -s,- container

behände *a* nimble, *adv* -bly

behandeln *vt* treat; (*sich befassen*) deal with. B~lung *f* treatment

beharr|en *vi* (*haben*) persist (auf + *dat* in). b~lich *a* persistent, *adv* -ly; (*hartnäckig*) dogged, *adv* -ly. B~lichkeit *f* - persistence

behaupt|en *vt* maintain; (*vorgeben*) claim; (*sagen*) say; (*bewahren*) retain; sich b~en hold one's own. B~ung *f* -,-en assertion; claim; (*Äußerung*) statement

beheben† *vt* remedy; (*beseitigen*) remove

behelf|en† (sich) *vr* make do (mit with). b~smäßig *a* make-shift □ *adv* provisionally

behelligen *vt* bother

behende *a* (NEW) behände

beherbergen *vt* put up

beherrsch|en *vt* rule over; (*dominieren*) dominate; (*meistern, zügeln*) control; (*können*) know; sich b~en control oneself. b~t *a* self-controlled. B~ung *f* -control; (*Selbst-*) self-control; (*Können*) mastery

beherz|igen *vt* heed. b~t *a* courageous, *adv* -ly

behilflich *a* jdm b~ sein help s.o.

behinder|n *vt* hinder; (*blockieren*) obstruct. b~t *a* handicapped; (*schwer*) disabled. B~te(r) *m/f* handicapped/disabled person. B~ung *f* -,-en obstruction; (*Med*) handicap; disability

Behörde *f* -,-n [public] authority

behüte|n *vt* protect; Gott behüte! heaven forbid! b~t *a* sheltered

behutsam *a* careful, *adv* -ly; (*zart*) gentle, *adv* -ly

bei *prep* (+ *dat*) near; (*dicht*) by; at (*Firma, Veranstaltung*); bei der Hand nehmen take by the hand; bei sich haben have with one; bei mir at my place; (*in meinem Fall*) in my case; Herr X bei Meyer Mr X c/o Meyer; bei Regen when/(*falls*) if it rains; bei Feuer in case of fire; bei Tag/Nacht by day/night; bei der Ankunft on arrival; bei Tisch/der Arbeit at table/work; bei guter Gesundheit in good health; bei der hohen Miete [what] with the high rent; bei all seiner Klugheit for all his cleverness

beibehalten† *vt sep* keep

beibringen† *vt sep* jdm etw b~ teach s.o. sth; (*mitteilen*) break sth to s.o.; (*zufügen*) inflict sth on s.o.

Beicht|e *f* -,-n confession. b~en *vt/i* (*haben*) confess. B~stuhl *m* confessional

beide *a & pron* both; die b~n Brüder the two brothers; b~s both; dreißig b~ (*Tennis*) thirty all. b~rseitig *a* mutual. b~rseits *adv & prep* (+ *gen*) on both sides (of)

beidrehen *vi sep* (*haben*) heave to

beieinander *adv* together

Beifahrer|(in) *m(f)* [front-seat] passenger; (*Lkw*) driver's mate; (*Motorrad*) pillion passenger. B~sitz *m* passenger seat

Beifall *m* -[e]s applause; (*Billigung*) approval; B~ klatschen applaud

beifällig *a* approving, *adv* -ly

beifügen *vt sep* add; (*beilegen*) enclose

beige /bɛːʒ/ *inv a* beige

beigeben† *v sep* □ *vt* add □ *vi* (*haben*) klein b~ give in

Beigeschmack *m* [slight] taste

Beihilfe *f* financial aid; (*Studien-*) grant; (*Jur*) aiding and abetting

beikommen† *vi sep* (*sein*) jdm b~ get the better of s.o.

Beil *nt* -[e]s,-e hatchet, axe

Beilage *f* supplement; (*Gemüse*) vegetable; als B~ Reis (*Culin*) served with rice

beiläufig *a* casual, *adv* -ly

beilegen *vt sep* enclose; (*schlichten*) settle

Beileibe *adv* b~ nicht by no means

Beileid *nt* condolences *pl.* B~sbrief *m* letter of condolence

beiliegend *a* enclosed

beim *prep* = bei dem; b~ Militär in the army; b~ Frühstück at breakfast; b~ Lesen when reading; b~ Lesen sein be reading

beimessen† *vt sep* (*fig*) attach (*dat* to)

Bein *nt* -[e]s,-e leg; jdm ein B~ stellen trip s.o. up

beinah[e] *adv* nearly, almost

Beiname *m* epithet

beipflichten *vi sep* (*haben*) agree (*dat* with)

Beirat *m* advisory committee

beirren *vt* sich nicht b~ lassen not let oneself be put off

beisammen *adv* together; b~ sein be together. b~seint *vi sep* (*sein*) (NEW) b~ sein, s. beisammen. B~sein *nt* -s get-together

Beisein *nt* presence

beiseite *adv* aside; (*abseits*) apart; b~ legen put aside; (*sparen*) put by; Spaß *od* Scherz b~ joking apart

beisetz|en *vt sep* bury. B~ung *f* -,-en funeral

Beispiel *nt* example; zum B~ for example. b~haft *a* exemplary. b~los *a* unprecedented. b~sweise *adv* for example

beispringen† *vi sep* (*sein*) jdm b∼ come to s.o.'s aid

beißen† *vt/i* (*haben*) bite; (*brennen*) sting; sich b∼en (*Farben:*) clash. b∼end *a* (*fig*) biting; (*Bemerkung*) caustic. B∼zange *f* pliers *pl*

Beistand *m* -[e]s help; jdm b∼stand leisten help s.o. b∼stehen† *vi sep* (*haben*) jdm b∼stehen help s.o.

beisteuern *vt sep* contribute

beistimmen *vi sep* (*haben*) agree

Beistrich *m* comma

Beitrag *m* -[e]s,ⁱe contribution; (*Mitglieds-*) subscription; (*Versicherungs-*) premium; (*Zeitungs-*) article. b∼en† *vt/i sep* (*haben*) contribute

beitreten† *vi sep* (*sein*) (+ *dat*) join. B∼tritt *m* joining

beiwohnen *vi sep* (*haben*) (+ *dat*) be present at

Beize *f* -,-n (*Holz-*) stain; (*Culin*) marinade

beizeiten *adv* in good time

beizen *vt* stain (*Holz*)

bejahen *vt* answer in the affirmative; (*billigen*) approve of

bejahrt *a* aged, old

bejubeln *vt* cheer

bekämpf|en *vt* fight. B∼ung *f* - fight (*gen* against)

bekannt *a* well-known; (*vertraut*) familiar; jdm b∼ sein be known to s.o.; jdn b∼ machen introduce s.o.; etw b∼ machen *od* geben announce sth; b∼ werden become known. B∼e(r) *m/f* acquaintance; (*Freund*) friend. B∼gabe *f* announcement. b∼geben† *vt sep* ⟨NEW⟩ b∼ geben, *s.* bekannt. b∼lich *adv* as is well known. b∼machen *vt sep* ⟨NEW⟩b∼ machen, *s.* bekannt. B∼machung *f* -,-en announcement; (*Anschlag*) notice. B∼schaft *f* - acquaintance; (*Leute*) acquaintances *pl*; (*Freunde*) friends *pl*. b∼werden† *vi sep* (*sein*) ⟨NEW⟩b∼ werden, *s.* bekannt

bekehr|en *vt* convert; sich b∼en become converted. B∼ung *f* -,-en conversion

bekenn|en† *vt* confess, profess (*Glauben*); sich [für] schuldig b∼en admit one's guilt; sich b∼en zu confess to (*Tat*); profess (*Glauben*); (*stehen zu*) stand by. B∼tnis *nt* -ses,-se confession; (*Konfession*) denomination

beklag|en *vt* lament; (*bedauern*) deplore; sich b∼en complain. b∼enswert *a* unfortunate. B∼te(r) *m/f* (*Jur*) defendant

beklatschen *vt* applaud

bekleid|en *vt* hold (*Amt*). b∼et *a* dressed (mit in). B∼ung *f* clothing

Beklemmung *f* -,-en feeling of oppression

beklommen *a* uneasy; (*ängstlich*) anxious, *adv* -ly

bekommen† *vt* get; have (*Baby*); catch (*Erkältung*); Angst/Hunger b∼ get frightened/hungry; etw geliehen b∼ be lent sth □ *vi* (*sein*) jdm gut b∼ do s.o. good; (*Essen:*) agree with s.o.

bekömmlich *a* digestible

beköstig|en *vt* feed; sich selbst b∼en cater for oneself. B∼ung *f*- board; (*Essen*) food

bekräftigen *vt* reaffirm; (*bestätigen*) confirm

bekreuzigen (sich) *vr* cross oneself

bekümmert *a* troubled; (*besorgt*) worried

bekunden *vt* show; (*bezeugen*) testify

belächeln *vt* laugh at

beladen† *vt* load □ *a* laden

Belag *m* -[e]s,ⁱe coating; (*Fußboden-*) covering; (*Brot-*) topping; (*Zahn-*) tartar; (*Brems-*) lining

belager|n *vt* besiege. B∼ung *f* -,-en siege

Belang *m* von/ohne B∼ of/of no importance; B∼e *pl* interests. b∼en *vt* (*Jur*) sue. b∼los *a* irrelevant; (*unwichtig*) trivial. B∼losigkeit *f* -,-en triviality

belassen† *vt* leave; es dabei b∼ leave it at that

belasten *vt* load; (*fig*) burden; (*beanspruchen*) put a strain on; (*Comm*) debit; (*Jur*) incriminate

belästigen *vt* bother; (*bedrängen*) pester; (*unsittlich*) molest

Belastung *f* -,-en load; (*fig*) strain; (*Last*) burden; (*Comm*) debit. B∼smaterial *nt* incriminating evidence. B∼szeuge *m* prosecution witness

belaufen† (sich) *vr* amount (auf + *acc* to)

belauschen *vt* eavesdrop on

beleb|en *vt* (*fig*) revive; (*lebhaft machen*) enliven; wieder b∼en (*Med*) revive, resuscitate; (*fig*) revive (*Handel*); sich b∼en revive; (*Stadt:*) come to life. b∼t *a* lively; (*Straße*) busy

Beleg *m* -[e]s,-e evidence; (*Beispiel*) instance (für of); (*Quittung*) receipt. b∼en *vt* cover/(*garnieren*) garnish (mit with); (*besetzen*) reserve; (*Univ*) enrol for; (*nachweisen*) provide evidence for; den ersten Platz b∼en (*Sport*) take first place. B∼schaft *f* -,-en work-force. b∼t *a* occupied; (*Zunge*) coated; (*Stimme*) husky; b∼te Brote open sandwiches; der Platz ist b∼t this seat is taken

belehren *vt* instruct; (*aufklären*) inform

beleibt *a* corpulent

beleidig|en *vt* offend; *(absichtlich)* insult. B~ung *f* -,-en insult

belesen *a* well-read

beleucht|en *vt* light; *(anleuchten)* illuminate. B~ung *f* -,-en illumination; *(elektrisch)* lighting; *(Licht)* light

Belg|ien /-jən/ *nt* -s Belgium. B~ier(in) *m* -s,- *(f* -,-nen) Belgian. b~isch *a* Belgian

belicht|en *vt (Phot)* expose. B~ung *f* - exposure

Belieb|en *nt* -s nach B~en [just] as one likes; *(Culin)* if liked. b~ig *a* eine b~ige Zahl/Farbe any number/colour you like □ *adv* b~ig lange/oft as long/often as one likes. b~t *a* popular. B~theit *f* - popularity

beliefern *vt* supply (mit with)

bellen *vi (haben)* bark

belohn|en *vt* reward. B~ung *f* -,-en reward

belüften *vt* ventilate

belügen† *vt* lie to; sich [selbst] b~ deceive oneself

belustig|en *vt* amuse. B~ung *f* -,-en amusement

bemächtigen (sich) *vr* (+ *gen*) seize

bemalen *vt* paint

bemängeln *vt* criticize

bemannt *a* manned

bemerk|bar *a* sich b~bar machen attract attention; *(Ding:)* become noticeable. b~en *vt* notice; *(äußern)* remark. b~ enswert *a* remarkable, *adv* -bly. B~ung *f* -,-en remark

bemitleiden *vt* pity

bemittelt *a* well-to-do

bemüh|en *vt* trouble; sich b~en try (zu to; um etw to get sth); *(sich kümmern)* attend (um to); b~t sein endeavour (zu to). B~ung *f* -,-en effort; *(Mühe)* trouble

bemuttern *vt* mother

benachbart *a* neighbouring

benachrichtig|en *vt* inform; *(amtlich)* notify. B~ung *f* -,-en notification

benachteilig|en *vt* discriminate against; *(ungerecht sein)* treat unfairly. B~ung *f* -,-en discrimination (gen against)

benehmen† (sich) *vr* behave. B~ *nt* -s behaviour

beneiden *vt* envy (um etw sth). b~swert *a* enviable

Bengel *m* -s,- boy; *(Rüpel)* lout

benommen *a* dazed

benötigen *vt* need

benutz|en, *(SGer)* benütz|en *vt* use; take *(Bahn)*. B~er *m* -s,- user. b~erfreundlich *a* user-friendly. B~ung *f* use

Benzin *nt* -s petrol, *(Amer)* gasoline. B~tank *m* petrol tank

beobacht|en *vt* observe. B~er *m* -s,- observer. B~ung *f* -,-en observation

bepacken *vt* load (mit with)

bepflanzen *vt* plant (mit with)

bequem *a* comfortable, *adv* -bly; *(mühelos)* easy, *adv* -ily; *(faul)* lazy. b~en (sich) *vr* deign (zu to). B~lichkeit *f* -,-en comfort; *(Faulheit)* laziness

berat|en† *vt* advise; *(überlegen)* discuss; sich b~en confer; sich b~en lassen get advice □ *vi (haben)* discuss (über etw *acc* sth); *(beratschlagen)* confer. B~er(in) *m* -s,- *(f* -,-nen) adviser. b~schlagen *vi (haben)* confer. B~ung *f* -,-en guidance; *(Rat)* advice; *(Besprechung)* discussion; *(Med, Jur)* consultation. B~ungsstelle *f* advice centre

berauben *vt* rob (gen of)

berauschen *vt* intoxicate. b~d *a* intoxicating, heady

berechn|en *vt* calculate; *(anrechnen)* charge for; *(abfordern)* charge. b~end *a* *(fig)* calculating. B~ung *f* calculation

berechtig|en *vt* entitle; *(befugen)* authorize; *(fig)* justify. b~t *a* justified, justifiable. B~ung *f* -,-en authorization; *(Recht)* right; *(Rechtmäßigkeit)* justification

bered|en *vt* talk about; *(klatschen)* gossip about; *(überreden)* talk round; sich b~en talk. B~samkeit *f* - eloquence

beredt *a* eloquent, *adv* -ly

Bereich *m* -[e]s,-e area; *(fig)* realm; *(Fach)* field

bereichern *vt* enrich; sich b~ grow rich (an + *dat* on)

Bereifung *f* - tyres *pl*

bereinigen *vt (fig)* settle

bereit *a* ready. b~en *vt* prepare; *(verursachen)* cause; give *(Überraschung)*. b~halten† *vt sep* have/*(ständig)* keep ready. b~legen *vt sep* put out [ready]. b~machen *vt sep* get ready; sich b~machen get ready. b~s *adv* already

Bereitschaft *f* -,-en readiness; *(Einheit)* squad. B~sdienst *m* B~sdienst haben *(Mil)* be on stand-by; *(Arzt:)* be on call; *(Apotheke:)* be open for out-of-hours dispensing. B~spolizei *f* riot police

bereit|stehen† *vi sep (haben)* be ready. b~stellen *vt sep* put out ready; *(verfügbar machen)* make available. B~ung *f* - preparation b~willig *a* willing, *adv* -ly. B~willigkeit *f* - willingness

bereuen *vt* regret

Berg *m* -[e]s,-e mountain; *(Anhöhe)* hill; in den B~en in the mountains. b~ab *adv* downhill. b~an *adv* uphill. B~arbeiter *m* miner. b~**auf** *adv* uphill; es geht b~auf (*fig*) things are looking up. B~bau *m* -[e]s mining

bergen† *vt* recover; (*Naut*) salvage; (*retten*) rescue

Berg|führer *m* mountain guide. b~ig *a* mountainous. B~kette *f* mountain range. B~mann *m* (*pl* -leute) miner. B~steigen *nt* -s mountaineering. B~steiger(in) *m* -s,- (*f* -,-nen) mountaineer, climber. B~und-T albahn *f* roller-coaster

Bergung *f* - recovery; (*Naut*) salvage; (*Rettung*) rescue

Berg|wacht *f* mountain rescue service. B~werk *nt* mine

Bericht *m* -[e]s,-e report; (*Reise-*) account; B~ erstatten report (über + *acc* on). b~en *vt/i* (*haben*) report; (*erzählen*) tell (von of). B~erstatter(in) *m* -s,- (*f* -,-nen) reporter; (*Korrespondent*) correspondent

berichtig|en *vt* correct. B~ung *f* -,-en correction

beriesel|n *vt* irrigate. B~ungsanlage *f* sprinkler system

beritten *a* (*Polizei*) mounted

Berlin *nt* -s Berlin. B~er *m* -s,- Berliner; (*Culin*) doughnut □ *a* Berlin ...

Bernhardiner *m* -s,- St Bernard

Bernstein *m* amber

bersten *vi* (*sein*) burst

berüchtigt *a* notorious

berückend *a* entrancing

berücksichtig|en *vt* take into consideration. B~ung *f* - consideration

Beruf *m* profession; (*Tätigkeit*) occupation; (*Handwerk*) trade. b~en† *vt* appoint; sich b~en refer (auf + *acc* to); (*vorgeben*) plead (auf etw *acc* sth) □ *a* competent; b~en sein be destined (zu to). b~lich *a* professional; (*Ausbildung*) vocational □ *adv* professionally; b~lich tätig sein work, have a job. B~saussichten *fpl* career prospects. B~sberater(in) *m*(*f*) careers officer. B~sberatung *f* vocational guidance. b~smäßig *adv* professionally. B~sschule *f* vocational school. B~ssoldat *m* regular soldier. b~stätig *a* working; b~stätig sein work, have a job. B~stätige(r) *m*/*f* working man/woman. B~sverkehr *m* rush-hour traffic. B~ung *f* -,-en appointment; (*Bestimmung*) vocation; (*Jur*) appeal; B~ung einlegen appeal. B~ungsgericht *nt* appeal court

beruhen *vi* (*haben*) be based (auf + *dat* on); eine Sache auf sich b~ lassen let a matter rest

beruhig|en *vt* calm [down]; (*zuversichtlich machen*) reassure; sich b~en calm

down. b~end *a* calming; (*tröstend*) reassuring; (*Med*) sedative. B~ung *f* - calming; reassurance; (*Med*) sedation. B~ungsmittel *nt* sedative; (*bei Psychosen*) tranquillizer

berühmt *a* famous. B~heit *f* -,-en fame; (*Person*) celebrity

berühr|en *vt* touch; (*erwähnen*) touch on; (*beeindrucken*) affect; sich b~en touch. B~ung *f* -,-en touch; (*Kontakt*) contact

besag|en *vt* say; (*bedeuten*) mean. b~t *a* [afore]said

besänftigen *vt* soothe; sich b~ calm down

Besatz *m* -es,-̈e trimming

Besatzung *f* -,-en crew; (*Mil*) occupying force

besaufen† (sich) *vr* (*sl*) get drunk

beschädig|en *vt* damage. B~ung *f* -,-en damage

beschaffen *vt* obtain, get □ *a* so b~ sein, dass be such that; wie ist es b~ mit? what about? B~heit *f* - consistency; (*Art*) nature

beschäftig|en *vt* occupy; (*Arbeitgeber:*) employ; sich b~en occupy oneself. b~t *a* busy; (*angestellt*) employed (bei at). B~te(r) *m*/*f* employee. B~ung *f* -,-en occupation; (*Anstellung*) employment. b~ungslos *a* unemployed. B~ungstherapie *f* occupational therapy

beschäm|en *vt* make ashamed. b~end *a* shameful; (*demütigend*) humiliating. b~t *a* ashamed; (*verlegen*) embarrassed

beschatten *vt* shade; (*überwachen*) shadow

beschau|en *vt* (*SGer*) [sich (*dat*)] etw b~en look at sth. b~lich *a* tranquil; (*Relig*) contemplative

Bescheid *m* -[e]s information; jdm B~ sagen *od* geben let s.o. know; B~ wissen know

bescheiden *a* modest, *adv* -ly. B~heit *f* - modesty

bescheinen† *vt* shine on; von der Sonne beschienen sunlit

bescheinig|en *vt* certify. B~ung *f* -,-en [written] confirmation; (*Schein*) certificate

beschenken *vt* give a present/presents to

bescher|en *vt* jdn b~en give s.o. presents; jdm etw b~en give s.o. sth. B~ung *f* -,-en distribution of Christmas presents; (*fam: Schlamassel*) mess

beschießen† *vt* fire at; (*mit Artillerie*) shell, bombard

beschildern *vt* signpost

beschimpf|en *vt* abuse, swear at. B~ung *f* -,-en abuse

beschirmen *vt* protect

Beschlag *m* in B∼ nehmen, mit B∼ belegen monopolize. b∼en† *vt* shoe □ *vi* (*sein*) steam or mist up □ a steamed or misted up; (*erfahren*) knowledgeable (in + *dat* about). B∼nahme *f* -,-n confiscation; (*Jur*) seizure. b∼nahmen *vt* confiscate; (*Jur*) seize; (*fam*) monopolize

beschleunig|en *vt* hasten; (*schneller machen*) speed up; quicken (*Schritt, Tempo*); sich b∼en speed up; quicken □ *vi* (*haben*) accelerate. B∼ung *f* - acceleration

beschließen† *vt* decide; (*beenden*) end □ *vi* (*haben*) decide (über + *acc* about)

Beschluss (Beschluß) *m* decision

beschmieren *vt* smear/(*bestreichen*) spread (mit with)

beschmutzen *vt* make dirty; sich b∼ get [oneself] dirty

beschneid|en† *vt* trim; (*Hort*) prune; (*fig: kürzen*) cut back; (*Relig*) circumcise. B∼ung *f* - circumcision

beschneit *a* snow-covered

beschnüffeln, beschnuppern *vt* sniff at

beschönigen *vt* (*fig*) gloss over

beschränken *vt* limit, restrict; sich b∼ auf (+ *acc*) confine oneself to; (*Sache:*) be limited to

beschrankt *a* (*Bahnübergang*) with barrier[s]

beschränk|t *a* limited; (*geistig*) dull-witted; (*borniert*) narrow-minded. B∼ung *f* -,-en limitation, restriction

beschreib|en† *vt* describe; (*schreiben*) write on. B∼ung *f* -,-en description

beschuldig|en *vt* accuse. B∼ung *f* -,-en accusation

beschummeln *vt* (*fam*) cheat

Beschuss (Beschuß) *m* (*Mil*) fire; (*Artillerie-*) shelling

beschütz|en *vt* protect. B∼er *m* -s,- protector

Beschwer|de *f* -,-n complaint; B∼den (*Med*) trouble *sg*. b∼en *vt* weight down; sich b∼en complain. b∼lich *a* difficult

beschwichtigen *vt* placate

beschwindeln *vt* cheat (um out of); (*belügen*) lie to

beschwingt *a* elated; (*munter*) lively

beschwipst *a* (*fam*) tipsy

beschwören† *vt* swear to; (*anflehen*) implore; (*herauf-*) invoke

beseehen *vt* look at

beseitig|en *vt* remove. B∼ung *f* - removal

Besen *m* -s,- broom. B∼ginster *m* (*Bot*) broom. B∼stiel *m* broomstick

besessen *a* obsessed (von by)

besetz|en *vt* occupy; fill (*Posten*); (*Theat*) cast (*Rolle*); (*verzieren*) trim (mit with). b∼t *a* occupied; (*Toilette, Leitung*) engaged; (*Zug, Bus*) full up; der Platz ist b∼t this seat is taken; mit Perlen b∼t set with pearls. B∼tzeichen *nt* engaged tone. B∼ung *f* -,-en occupation; (*Theat*) cast

besichtig|en *vt* look round (*Stadt, Museum*); (*prüfen*) inspect; (*besuchen*) visit. B∼ung *f* -,-en visit; (*Prüfung*) inspection; (*Stadt-*) sightseeing

besiedelt *a* dünn/dicht b∼ sparsely/densely populated

besiegeln *vt* (*fig*) seal

besieg|en *vt* defeat; (*fig*) overcome. B∼te(r) *m/f* loser

besinn|en† (sich) *vr* think, reflect; (*sich erinnern*) remember (auf jdn/etw s.o./sth); sich anders b∼en change one's mind. b∼lich *a* contemplative; (*nachdenklich*) thoughtful. B∼ung *f* - reflection; (*Bewusstsein*) consciousness; bei/ohne B∼ung conscious/unconscious; zur B∼ung kommen regain consciousness; (*fig*) come to one's senses. b∼ungslos *a* unconscious

Besitz *m* possession; (*Eigentum, Land-*) property; (*Gut*) estate. b∼anzeigend *a* (*Gram*) possessive. b∼en† *vt* own, possess; (*haben*) have. B∼er(in) *m* -s,- (*f* -,-nen) owner; (*Comm*) proprietor. B∼ung *f* -,-en [landed] property; (*Gut*) estate

besoffen *a* (*sl*) drunken; b∼ sein be drunk

besohlen *vt* sole

besold|en *vt* pay. B∼ung *f* - pay

besonder|e(r,s) *a* special; (*bestimmt*) particular; (*gesondert*) separate; nichts B∼es nothing special. B∼heit *f* -,-en peculiarity. b∼s *adv* [e]specially, particularly; (*gesondert*) separately

besonnen *a* calm, *adv* -ly

besorg|en *vt* get; (*kaufen*) buy; (*erledigen*) attend to; (*versorgen*) look after. B∼nis *f* -,-nisse anxiety; (*Sorge*) worry. b∼niserregend *a* worrying. b∼t *a* worried/(*bedacht*) concerned (um about). B∼ung *f* -,-en errand; B∼ungen machen do shopping

bespielt *a* recorded

bespitzeln *vt* spy on

besprech|en† *vt* discuss; (*rezensieren*) review; sich b∼en confer; ein Tonband b∼en make a tape recording. B∼ung *f* -,-en discussion; review; (*Konferenz*) meeting

bespritzen *vt* splash

besser _a_ & _adv_ better. b∼n _vt_ improve;
sich b∼n get better, improve. B∼ung _f_ -
improvement; gute B∼ung! get well
soon! B∼wisser _m_ -s,- know-all

Bestand _m_ -[e]s,-̈e existence; (_Vorrat_)
stock (an + _dat_ of); B∼haben, von B∼
sein last

beständig _a_ constant, _adv_ -ly; (_Wetter_)
settled; b∼ gegen resistant to

Bestand|saufnahme _f_ stocktaking.
B∼teil _m_ part

bestärken _vt_ (_fig_) strengthen

bestätig|en _vt_ confirm; acknowledge
(_Empfang_); sich b∼en prove to be true.
B∼ung _f_ -,-en confirmation

bestatt|en _vt_ bury. B∼ung _f_ -,-en funeral.
B∼ungsinstitut _nt_ [firm of] undertakers
_pl_, (_Amer_) funeral home

bestäuben _vt_ pollinate

bestaubt _a_ dusty

Bestäubung _f_ - pollination

bestaunen _vt_ gaze at in amazement; (_be-
wundern_) admire

best|e(r,s) _a_ best; b∼en Dank! many
thanks! am b∼en sein be best; zum b∼en
geben/halten (NEW) zum B∼en geben/
halten, _s._ Beste(r,s). B∼e(r,s) _m_/_f_/_nt_
best; sein B∼es tun do one's best; zum
B∼en der Armen for the benefit of the
poor; zum B∼en geben recite (_Gedicht_);
tell (_Geschichte, Witz_); sing (_Lied_); jdn
zum B∼n halten (_fam_) pull s.o.'s leg

bestech|en† _vt_ bribe; (_bezaubern_) captiv-
ate. b∼end _a_ captivating. b∼lich _a_ corruptible. B∼ung _f_ - bribery.
B∼ungsgeld _nt_ bribe

Besteck _nt_ -[e]s,-e [set of] knife, fork and
spoon; (_coll_) cutlery

besteh|en† _vi_ (_haben_) exist; (_fortdauern_)
last; (_bei Prüfung_) pass; ∼ aus consist/(_ge-
macht sein_) be made of; ∼ auf (+ _dat_)
insist on □ _vt_ pass (_Prüfung_). B∼ _nt_ -s
existence

bestehlen† _vt_ rob

besteig|en† _vt_ climb; (_einsteigen_) board;
(_aufsteigen_) mount; ascend (_Thron_).
B∼ung _f_ ascent

bestell|en _vt_ order; (_vor-_) book; (_ernennen_)
appoint; (_bebauen_) cultivate; (_ausrichten_)
tell; zu sich b∼en send for; b∼t sein have
an appointment; kann ich etwas b∼en?
can I take a message? b∼en Sie Ihrer
Frau Grüße von mir give my regards
to your wife. B∼schein _m_ order form.
B∼ung _f_ order; (_Botschaft_) message; (_Be-
bauung_) cultivation

besten|falls _adv_ at best. b∼s _adv_ very
well

besteuer|n _vt_ tax. B∼ung _f_ - taxation

bestialisch /-st-/ _a_ bestial

Bestie /'bɛstjə/ _f_ -,-n beast

bestimm|en _vt_ fix; (_entscheiden_) decide;
(_vorsehen_) intend; (_ernennen_) appoint; (_er-
mitteln_) determine; (_definieren_) define;
(_Gram_) qualify □ _vi_ (_haben_) be in charge
(über + _acc_ of). ∼t _a_ definite, _adv_ -ly;
(_gewiss_) certain, _adv_ -ly; (_fest_) firm, _adv_
-ly. B∼theit _f_ - firmness; mit B∼theit
for certain. B∼ung _f_ fixing; (_Vorschrift_)
regulation; (_Ermittlung_) determination;
(_Definition_) definition; (_Zweck_) purpose;
(_Schicksal_) destiny. B∼ungsort _m_ destination

Bestleistung _f_ (_Sport_) record

bestraf|en _vt_ punish. B∼ung _f_ -,-en pun-
ishment

bestrahl|en _vt_ shine on; (_Med_) treat with
radiotherapy; irradiate (_Lebensmittel_).
B∼ung _f_ radiotherapy

Bestreb|en _nt_ -s endeavour; (_Absicht_)
aim. b∼t _a_ b∼t sein endeavour (zu to).
B∼ung _f_ -,-en effort

bestreichen† _vt_ spread (mit with)

bestreikt _a_ strike-hit

bestreiten† _vt_ dispute; (_leugnen_) deny;
(_bezahlen_) pay for

bestreuen _vt_ sprinkle (mit with)

bestürmen _vt_ (_fig_) besiege

bestürz|t _a_ dismayed; (_erschüttert_)
stunned. B∼ung _f_ - dismay, consternation

Bestzeit _f_ (_Sport_) record [time]

Besuch _m_ -[e]s,-e visit; (_kurz_) call; (_Schul-_)
attendance; (_Gast_) visitor; (_Gäste_) visitors
_pl_; B∼ haben have a visitor/visitors; bei
jdm zu od auf B∼ sein be staying with
s.o. b∼en _vt_ visit; (_kurz_) call on; (_teil-
nehmen_) attend; go to (_Schule, Ausstel-
lung_); gut b∼t well attended. B∼er(in)
_m_ -s,- (_f_ -,-nen) visitor; caller; (_Theat_) patron. B∼szeit _f_ visiting hours _pl_

betagt _a_ aged, old

betasten _vt_ feel

betätig|en _vt_ operate; sich b∼en work
(als as); sich politisch b∼en engage in
politics. B∼ung _f_ -,-en operation; (_Tätig-
keit_) activity

betäub|en _vt_ stun; (_Lärm:_) deafen; (_Med_)
anaesthetize; (_lindern_) ease; deaden
(_Schmerz_); wie b∼t dazed. B∼ung _f_ -
daze; (_Med_) anaesthesia; unter örtlicher
B∼ung under local anaesthetic.
B∼ungsmittel _nt_ anaesthetic

Bete _f_ -,-n rote B∼ beetroot

beteilig|en _vt_ give a share to; sich b∼en
take part (an + _dat_ in); (_beitragen_) contribute (an + _dat_ to). b∼t _a_ b∼t sein take
part/(_an Unfall_) be involved/(_Comm_)
have a share (an + _dat_ in); alle B∼ten

all those involved. B~ung f -,-en participation; involvement; (*Anteil*) share

beten vi (*haben*) pray; (*bei Tisch*) say grace □ vt say

beteuer|n vt protest. B~ung f -,-en protestation

Beton /be'tɔŋ/ m -s concrete

betonen vt stressed, emphasize

betonieren vt concrete

beton|t a stressed; (*fig*) pointed, adv -ly. B~ung f -,-en stress, emphasis

betören vt bewitch

betr., Betr. abbr (betreffs) re

Betracht m in B~ ziehen consider; außer B~ lassen disregard; nicht in B~ kommen be out of the question. b~en vt look at; (*fig*) regard (als as)

beträchtlich a considerable, adv -bly

Betrachtung f -,-en contemplation; (*Überlegung*) reflection

Betrag m -[e]s,ˬe amount. b~en† vt amount to; sich b~en behave. B~en nt -s behaviour; (*Sch*) conduct

betrauen vt entrust (mit with)

betrauern vt mourn

betreff|en† vt affect; (*angehen*) concern; was mich betrifft as far as I am concerned. b~end a relevant; der b~ende Brief the letter in question. b~s prep (+ gen) concerning

betreiben† vt (*leiten*) run; (*ausüben*) carry on; (*vorantreiben*) pursue; (*antreiben*) run (mit on)

betreten† vt step on; (*eintreten*) enter; 'B~ verboten' 'no entry'; (*bei Rasen*) 'keep off [the grass]' □ a embarrassed □ adv in embarrassment

betreu|en vt look after. B~er(in) m -s,- (f -,-nen) helper; (*Kranken-*) nurse. B~ung f - care

Betrieb m business; (*Firma*) firm; (*Treiben*) activity; (*Verkehr*) traffic; in B~ working; (*in Gebrauch*) in use; außer B~ not in use; (*defekt*) out of order

Betriebs|anleitung f operating instructions pl. B~ferien pl firm's holiday; 'B~ferien' 'closed for the holidays'. B~leitung f management. B~rat m works committee. B~ruhe f 'montags B~ruhe' 'closed on Mondays'. B~störung f breakdown

betrinken† (sich) vr get drunk

betroffen a disconcerted; b~ sein be affected (von by); die B~en those affected □ adv in consternation

betrüb|en vt sadden. b~lich a sad. b~t a sad, adv -ly

Betrug m -[e]s deception; (*Jur*) fraud

betrüg|en† vt cheat, swindle; (*Jur*) defraud; (*in der Ehe*) be unfaithful to; sich selbst b~en deceive oneself. B~er(in) m -s,- (f -,-nen) swindler. B~erei f -,-en fraud b~erisch a fraudulent; (*Person*) deceitful

betrunken a drunken; b~ sein be drunk. B~e(r) m drunk

Bett nt -[e]s,-en bed; im B~ in bed; ins od zu B~ gehen go to bed. B~couch f sofa-bed. B~decke f blanket; (*Tages-*) bedspread

bettel|arm a destitute. B~ei f - begging. b~n vi (*haben*) beg

bett|en vt lay, put; sich b~en lie down. b~lägerig a bedridden. B~laken nt sheet

Bettler(in) m -s,- (f -,-nen) beggar

Bettpfanne f bedpan

Betttuch (Bettuch) nt sheet

Bett|vorleger m bedside rug. B~wäsche f bed linen. B~zeug nt bedding

betupfen vt dab (mit with)

beug|en vt bend; (*Gram*) decline; conjugate (*Verb*); sich b~en bend; (*lehnen*) lean; (*sich fügen*) submit (dat to). B~ung f -,-en (*Gram*) declension; conjugation

Beule f -,-n bump; (*Delle*) dent

beunruhig|en vt worry; sich b~en worry. B~ung f - worry

beurlauben vt give leave to; (*des Dienstes entheben*) suspend

beurteil|en vt judge. B~ung f -,-en judgement; (*Ansicht*) opinion

Beute f - booty, haul; (*Jagd-*) bag; (*B~tier*) quarry; (*eines Raubtiers*) prey

Beutel m -s,- bag; (*Geld-*) purse; (*Tabak- & Zool*) pouch. B~tier nt marsupial

bevölker|n vt populate. B~ung f -,-en population

bevollmächtig|en vt authorize. B~te(r) m/f [authorized] agent

bevor conj before; b~ nicht until

bevormunden vt treat like a child

bevorstehen† vi sep (*haben*) approach; (*unmittelbar*) be imminent; jdm b~ be in store for s.o. b~d a approaching, forthcoming; unmittelbar b~d imminent

bevorzug|en vt prefer; (*begünstigen*) favour. b~t a privileged; (*Behandlung*) preferential; (*beliebt*) favoured

bewachen vt guard; bewachter Parkplatz car park with an attendant

bewachsen a covered (mit with)

Bewachung f - guard; unter B~ under guard

bewaffn|en vt arm. b~et a armed. B~ung f - armament; (*Waffen*) arms pl

bewahren vt protect (vor + dat from); (behalten) keep; die Ruhe b~ keep calm; Gott bewahre! heaven forbid!

bewähren (sich) vr prove one's/⟨Ding:⟩ its worth; (erfolgreich sein) prove a success

bewahrheiten (sich) vr prove to be true

bewähr|t a reliable; (erprobt) proven. B~ung f - (Jur) probation. B~ungsfrist f [period of] probation. B~ungsprobe f (fig) test

bewaldet a wooded

bewältigen vt cope with; (überwinden) overcome; (schaffen) manage

bewandert a knowledgeable

bewässer|n vt irrigate. B~ung f - irrigation

bewegen[1] vt (reg) move; sich b~ move; (körperlich) take exercise

bewegen[2] vt jdn dazu b~, etw zu tun induce s.o. to do sth

Beweg|grund m motive. b~lich a movable, mobile; (wendig) agile. B~lichkeit f - mobility; agility. b~t a moved; (ereignisreich) eventful; ⟨See⟩ rough. B~ung f -,-en movement; (Phys) motion; (Rührung) emotion; (Gruppe) movement; körperliche B~ung physical exercise; sich in B~ung setzen [start to] move. B~ungsfreiheit f freedom of movement/(fig) of action. b~ungslos a motionless

beweinen vt mourn

Beweis m -es,-e proof; (Zeichen) token; B~e evidence sg. b~en† vt prove; (zeigen) show; sich b~en prove oneself/⟨Ding:⟩ itself. B~material nt evidence

bewenden vi es dabei b~lassen leave it at that

bewerb|en (sich) vr apply (um for; bei to). B~er(in) m -s,- (f -,-nen) applicant. B~ung f -,-en application

bewerkstelligen vt manage

bewerten vt value; (einschätzen) rate; (Sch) mark, grade

bewilligen vt grant

bewirken vt cause; (herbeiführen) bring about; (erreichen) achieve

bewirt|en vt entertain. B~ung f - hospitality

bewohn|bar a habitable. b~en vt inhabit, live in. B~er(in) m -s,- (f -,-nen) resident, occupant; (Einwohner) inhabitant

bewölk|en (sich) vr cloud over; b~t cloudy. B~ung f - clouds pl

bewunder|n vt admire. b~nswert a admirable. B~ung f - admiration

bewusst (bewußt) a conscious (gen of); (absichtlich) deliberate, adv -ly; (besagt) said; sich (dat) etw (gen) b~ sein/ werden be/become aware of sth. b~los a unconscious. B~losigkeit f - unconsciousness; B~sein n -s consciousness; (Gewissheit) awareness; bei [vollem] B~sein [fully] conscious; mir kam zum B~sein I realized (dass that)

bez. abbr (bezahlt) paid; (bezüglich) re

bezahl|en vt/i (haben) pay; pay for ⟨Ware, Essen⟩; gut b~te Arbeit well-paid work; sich b~t machen (fig) pay off. B~ung f - payment; (Lohn) pay

bezähmen vt control; (zügeln) restrain; sich b~ restrain oneself

bezaubern vt enchant. b~d a enchanting

bezeichn|en vt mark; (bedeuten) denote; (beschreiben, nennen) describe (als as). b~end a typical. B~ung f marking; (Beschreibung) description (als as); (Ausdruck) term; (Name) name

bezeugen vt testify to

bezichtigen vt accuse (gen of)

bezieh|en† vt cover; (einziehen) move into; (beschaffen) obtain; (erhalten) get, receive; take ⟨Zeitung⟩; (in Verbindung bringen) relate (auf + acc to); sich b~en (bewölken) cloud over; sich b~en auf (+ acc) refer to; das Bett frisch b~en put clean sheets on the bed. B~ung f -,-en relation; (Verhältnis) relationship; (Bezug) respect; in dieser B~ung in this respect; [gute] B~ungen haben have [good] connections. b~ungsweise adv respectively; (vielmehr) or rather

beziffern (sich) vr amount (auf + acc to)

Bezirk m -[e]s,-e district

Bezug m cover; (Kissen~) case; (Beschaffung) obtaining; (Kauf) purchase; (Zusammenhang) reference; B~e pl earnings; B~ nehmen refer (auf + acc to); in B~ (b~) auf (+ acc) regarding, concerning

bezüglich prep (+ gen) regarding, concerning □ a relating (auf + acc to); (Gram) relative

bezwecken vt (fig) aim at

bezweifeln vt doubt

bezwingen† vt conquer

BH /beː'haː/ m -[s],-[s] bra

bibbern vi (haben) tremble; (vor Kälte) shiver

Bibel f -,-n Bible

Biber[1] m -s,- beaver

Biber[2] m & nt -s flannelette

Biblio|graphie, B~grafie f -,-n bibliography. B~thek f -,-en library. B~thekar(in) m -s,- (f -,-nen) librarian

bib̲lisch *a* biblical

bie̲der *a* honest, upright; (*ehrenwert*) worthy; (*einfach*) simple

bie̲g|en† *vt* bend; sich b∼en bend; sich vor Lachen b∼en (*fam*) double up with laughter □ *vi* (*sein*) curve (nach to); um die Ecke b∼en turn the corner. b∼sam *a* flexible, supple. B∼ung *f* -,-en bend

Bie̲ne *f* -,-n bee. B∼nhonig *m* natural honey. B∼nstock *m* beehive. B∼nwabe *f* honeycomb

Bie̲r *nt* -s,-e beer. B∼deckel *m* beer-mat. B∼krug *m* beer-mug

Bie̲st *nt* -[e]s,-er (*fam*) beast

bie̲ten† *vt* offer; (*bei Auktion*) bid; (*zeigen*) present; das lasse ich mir nicht b∼ I won't stand for that

Bifoka̲lbrille *f* bifocals *pl*

Biga̲|mie *f* - bigamy. b∼ mist *m* -en,-en bigamist

bigo̲tt *a* over-pious

Biki̲ni *m* -s,-s bikini

Bila̲nz *f* -,-en balance sheet; (*fig*) result; die B∼ ziehen (*fig*) draw conclusions (aus from)

Bi̲ld *nt* -[e]s,-er picture; (*Theat*) scene; jdn ins B∼ setzen put s.o. in the picture

bi̲lden *vt* form; (*sein*) be; (*erziehen*) educate; sich b∼ form; (*geistig*) educate oneself

Bi̲ld|erbuch *nt* picture-book. B∼ergalerie *f* picture gallery. B∼fläche *f* screen; von der B∼fläche verschwinden disappear from the scene. B∼hauer *m* -s,- sculptor. B∼hauerei *f* - sculpture. b∼hübsch *a* very pretty. b∼lich *a* pictorial; (*figurativ*) figurative, *adv* -ly. B∼nis *nt* -ses,-se portrait. B∼schirm *m* (*TV*) screen. B∼schirmgerät *nt* visual display unit, VDU. b∼schön *a* very beautiful

Bi̲ldung *f* - formation; (*Erziehung*) education; (*Kultur*) culture

Billa̲rd /'bɪljart/ *nt* -s billiards *sg.* B∼tisch *m* billiard table

Bille̲tt /bɪl'jɛt/ *nt* -[e]s,-e & -s ticket

Billia̲rde *f* -,-n thousand million million

bi̲llig *a* cheap, *adv* -ly; (*dürftig*) poor; (*gerecht*) just; recht und b∼ right and proper. b∼en *vt* approve. B∼ung *f* - approval

Billio̲n /bɪljo:n/ *f* -,-en million million, billion

hi̲mmeln *vi* (*haben*) tinkle

Bi̲msstein *m* pumice stone

bi̲n *s.* sein; ich bin I am

Bi̲nde *f* -,-n band; (*Verband*) bandage; (*Damen-*) sanitary towel. B∼hautentzündung *f* conjunctivitis. b∼n† *vt* tie

(an + *acc* to); make ⟨*Strauß*⟩; bind ⟨*Buch*⟩; (*fesseln*) tie up; (*Culin*) thicken; sich b∼n commit oneself. b∼nd *a* (*fig*) binding. B∼strich *m* hyphen. B∼wort *nt* (*pl* -wörter) (*Gram*) conjunction

Bi̲nd|faden *m* string; ein B∼faden a piece of string. B∼ung *f* -,-en (*fig*) tie, bond; (*Beziehung*) relationship; (*Verpflichtung*) commitment; (*Ski-*) binding; (*Tex*) weave

bi̲nnen *prep* (+ *dat*) within; b∼ kurzem shortly. B∼handel *m* home trade

Bi̲nse *f* -,-n (*Bot*) rush. B∼nwahrheit, B∼nweisheit *f* truism

Bi̲o- *pref* organic

Bi̲o|chemie *f* biochemistry. b∼dynamisch *m* organic. B∼graphie̲, B∼grafie̲ *f* -,-n biography

Bi̲o|hof *m* organic farm. B∼laden *m* health-food store

Biolo̲g|e *m* -n,-n biologist. B∼ie̲ *f* - biology. b∼isch *a* biological, *adv* -ly; b∼ischer Anbau organic farming; b∼isch angebaut organically grown

Bi̲rke *f* -,-n birch [tree]

Bi̲rm|a *nt* -s Burma. B∼anisch *a* Burmese

Bi̲rn|baum *m* pear-tree. B∼e *f* -,-n pear; (*Electr*) bulb

bi̲s *prep* (+ *acc*) as far as, [up] to; (*zeitlich*) until, till; (*spätestens*) by; bis zu up to; bis jetzt up to now, so far; bis dahin until/ (*spätestens*) by then; bis auf (+ *acc*) (*einschließlich*) [down] to; (*ausgenommen*) except [for]; drei bis vier Mark three to four marks; bis morgen! see you tomorrow! □ *conj* until

Bi̲schof *m* -s,ⁿe bishop

bi̲sher *adv* so far, up to now. b∼ig *attrib a* ⟨*Präsident*⟩ outgoing; meine b∼igen Erfahrungen my experiences so far

Biskui̲t|rolle /bɪs'kviːt-/ *f* Swiss roll. B∼teig *m* sponge mixture

bisla̲ng *adv* so far, up to now

Bi̲ss *m* -es,-e (Biß *m* -sses,-sse) bite

bi̲sschen (bißchen) *inv pron* ein b∼ a bit, a little; ein b∼ Brot a bit of bread; kein b∼ not a bit

Bi̲ss|en *m* -s,- bite, mouthful. b∼ig *a* vicious; (*fig*) caustic

bi̲st *s.* sein; du b∼ you are

Bi̲stum *nt* -s,ⁿer diocese, see

biswei̲len *adv* from time to time

bi̲tt|e *adv* please; (*nach Klopfen*) come in; (*als Antwort auf 'danke'*) don't mention it, you're welcome; wie b∼e? pardon? (*empört*) I beg your pardon? möchten Sie Kaffee?—ja b∼e would you like some coffee?—yes please. B∼e *f* -,-n request/(*dringend*) plea (um for). b∼en† *vt/i* (*haben*) ask/(dringend) beg (um for); (einladen) invite, ask; ich b~e dich! I beg [of] you! (empört) I ask you! b~end a pleading, adv -ly

bitter a bitter, adv -ly. B~keit f - bitterness. b~lich adv bitterly

Bittschrift f petition

bizarr a bizarre, adv -ly

bläh|en vt swell; puff out (Vorhang); sich b~en swell; (Vorhang, Segel.) billow □ vi (haben) cause flatulence. B~ungen fpl flatulence sg, (fam) wind sg

Blamage /bla'ma:ʒə/ f -,-n humiliation; (Schande) disgrace

blamieren vt disgrace; sich b~ disgrace oneself; (sich lächerlich machen) make a fool of oneself

blanchieren /blã'ʃi:rən/ vt (Culin) blanch

blank a shiny; (nackt) bare; b~ sein (fam) be broke. B~oscheck m blank cheque

Blase f -,-n bubble; (Med) blister; (Anat) bladder. B~balg m -[e]s,-̈e bellows pl. b~n† vt/i (haben) blow; play (Flöte). B~nentzündung f cystitis

Bläser m -s,- (Mus) wind player; die B~ the wind section sg

blasiert a blasé

Blas|instrument nt wind instrument. B~kapelle f brass band

Blasphemie f - blasphemy

blass (blaß) a (blasser, blassest) pale; (schwach) faint; b~ werden turn pale

Blässe f - pallor

Blatt nt -[e]s,-̈er (Bot) leaf; (Papier) sheet; (Zeitung) paper; kein B~ vor den Mund nehmen (fig) not mince one's words

blätter|n vi (haben) b~n in (+ dat) leaf through. B~teig m puff pastry

Blattlaus f greenfly

blau a,B~ nt -s,- blue; b~er Fleck bruise; b~es Auge black eye; b~ sein (fam) be tight; Fahrt ins B~e mystery tour. B~beere f bilberry. B~licht nt blue flashing light. b~machen vi sep (haben) (fam) skive off work

Blech nt -[e]s,-e sheet metal; (Weiß-) tin; (Platte) metal sheet; (Back-) baking sheet; (Mus) brass; (fam: Unsinn) rubbish. b~en vt/i (haben) (fam) pay. B~[blas]instrument nt brass instrument. B~schaden m (Auto) damage to the bodywork

Blei nt -[e]s lead

Bleibe f - place to stay. b~n† vi (sein) remain, stay; (übrig-) be left; ruhig b~n keep calm; bei etw b~n (fig) stick to sth; b~n Sie am Apparat hold the line; etw b~n lassen not do sth; (aufhören) stop

doing sth. b~nd a permanent; (anhaltend) lasting. b~nlassen† vt sep (NEW) b~n lassen, s. bleiben

bleich a pale. b~en† vi (sein) bleach; (ver-) fade □ vt (reg) bleach. B~mittel nt bleach

blei|ern a leaden. b~frei a unleaded. B~stift m pencil. B~stiftabsatz m stiletto heel. B~stiftspitzer m -s,- pencil-sharpener

Blende f -,-n shade, shield; (Sonnen-) [sun] visor; (Phot) diaphragm; (Kleidung) aperture; (an Kleid) facing. b~n vt dazzle, blind. b~nd a (fig) dazzling; (prima) marvellous, adv -ly

Blick m -[e]s,-e look; (kurz) glance; (Aussicht) view; auf den ersten B~ at first sight; einen B~ für etw haben (fig) have an eye for sth. b~en vi (haben) look; (kurz) glance (auf + acc at). B~punkt m (fig) point of view

blind a blind; (trübe) dull; b~er Alarm false alarm; b~er Passagier stowaway. B~darm m appendix. B~darmentzündung f appendicitis. B~e(r) m/f blind man/woman; die B~en the blind. B~enhund m guidedog. B~enschrift f braille. B~gänger m -s,- (Mil) dud. B~heit f - blindness. b~lings adv (fig) blindly

blink|en vi (haben) flash; (funkeln) gleam; (Auto) indicate. B~er m -s,- (Auto) indicator. B~licht nt flashing light

blinzeln vi (haben) blink

Blitz m -es,-e [flash of] lightning; (Phot) flash; ein B~ aus heiterem Himmel (fig) a bolt from the blue. B~ableiter m lightning-conductor. b~artig a lightning . . . □ adv like lightning. B~birne f flashbulb. b~en vi (haben) flash; (funkeln) sparkle; es hat geblitzt there was a flash of lightning. B~gerät nt flash [unit]. B~licht nt (Phot) flash. b~sauber a spick and span. b~schnell a lightning . . . □ adv like lightning. B~strahl m flash of lightning

Block m -[e]s,-e block □-[e]s,-s & -̈e (Schreib-) [note-]pad; (Häuser-) block; (Pol) bloc

Blockade f -,-n blockade

Blockflöte f recorder

blockieren vt block; (Mil) blockade

Blockschrift f block letters pl

blöd[e] a feeble-minded; (dumm) stupid, adv -ly

Blödsinn m -[e]s idiocy; (Unsinn) nonsense. b~ig a feeble-minded; (verrückt) idiotic

blöken vi (haben) bleat

blond a fair-haired; (Haar) fair. B~ine f -,-n blonde

bloß a bare; (alleinig) mere; mit b~em Auge with the naked eye □ adv only, just; was mache ich b~? whatever shall I do?

Blöße f -,-n nakedness; sich (dat) eine B~ geben (fig) show a weakness

bloß|legen vt sep uncover. b~stellen vt sep compromise; sich b~stellen show oneself up

Bluff m -s,-s bluff. b~en vt/i (haben) bluff

blühen vi (haben) flower; (fig) flourish. b~d a flowering; (fig) flourishing, thriving; (Phantasie) fertile

Blume f -,-n flower; (vom Wein) bouquet. B~nbeet n flower-bed. B~ngeschäft nt flower-shop, florist's [shop]. B~nkohl m cauliflower. B~nmuster nt floral design. B~nstrauß m bunch of flowers. B~ntopf m flowerpot; (Pflanze) [flowering] pot plant. B~nzwiebel f bulb

blumig a (fig) flowery

Bluse f -,-n blouse

Blut nt -[e]s blood. b~arm a anaemic. B~bahn f blood-stream. b~befleckt a blood-stained. B~bild nt blood count. B~buche f copper beech. B~druck m blood pressure. b~dürstig a bloodthirsty

Blüte f -,-n flower, bloom; (vom Baum) blossom; (B~zeit) flowering period; (Baum-) blossom time; (fig) flowering; (Höhepunkt) peak, prime; (fam: Banknote) forged note, (fam) dud

Blut|egel m -s,- leech. b~en vi (haben) bleed

Blüten|blatt nt petal. B~staub m pollen

Blut|er m -s,- haemophiliac. B~erguss (B~erguß) m bruise. B~gefäß nt blood-vessel. B~gruppe f blood group. B~hund m bloodhound. b~ig a bloody. b~jung a very young. B~körperchen nt -s,- [blood] corpuscle. B~probe f blood test. b~rünstig a (fig) bloody, gory; (Person) blood-thirsty. B~schande f incest. B~spender m blood donor. B~sturz m haemorrhage. B~sverwandte(r) m/f blood relation. B~transfusion, B~übertragung f blood transfusion. B~ung f -,-en bleeding; (Med) haemorrhage; (Regel-) period. b~unterlaufen a bruised; (Auge) bloodshot. B~vergießen nt -s bloodshed. B~vergiftung f blood-poisoning. B~wurst f black pudding

Bö f -,-en gust; (Regen-) squall

Bob m -s,-s bob[-sleigh]

Bock m -[e]s,¨e buck; (Ziege) billy goat; (Schaf) ram; (Gestell) support; einen B~ schießen (fam) make a blunder. b~en vi (haben) (Pferd:) buck; (Kind:) be stubborn. b~ig a (fam) stubborn. B~springen nt leap-frog

Boden m -s,¨ ground; (Erde) soil; (Fuß-) floor; (Grundfläche) bottom; (Dach-) loft, attic. B~kammer f attic [room]. b~los a bottomless; (fam) incredible. B~satz m sediment. B~schätze mpl mineral deposits. B~see (der) Lake Constance

Bogen m -s,- & ¨- curve; (Geom) arc; (beim Skilauf) turn; (Archit) arch; (Waffe, Geigen-) bow; (Papier) sheet; einen großen B~ um jdn/etw machen (fam) give s.o./sth a wide berth. B~gang m arcade. B~schießen nt archery

Bohle f -,-n [thick] plank

Böhm|en nt -s Bohemia. b~isch a Bohemian

Bohne f -,-n bean; grüne B~n French beans. B~nkaffee m real coffee

bohnern vt polish. B~wachs nt floor-polish

bohr|en vt/i (haben) drill (nach for); drive (Tunnel); sink (Brunnen); (Insekt:) bore; in der Nase b~en pick one's nose. B~er m -s,- drill. B~insel f [offshore] drilling rig. B~maschine f electric drill. B~turm m derrick

Boje f -,-n buoy

Böllerschuss m gun salute

Bolzen m -s,- bolt; (Stift) pin

bombardieren vt bomb; (fig) bombard (mit with)

bombastisch a bombastic

Bombe f -,-n bomb. B~nangriff m bombing raid. B~nerfolg m huge success. B~r m -s,- (Aviat) bomber

Bon /boŋ/ m -s,-s voucher; (Kassen-) receipt

Bonbon /boŋ'boŋ/ m & nt -s,-s sweet

Bonus m -[sses],-[sse] bonus

Boot nt -[e]s,-e boat. B~ssteg m landing-stage

Bord¹ nt -[e]s,-e shelf

Bord² m (Naut) an B~ aboard, on board; über B~ overboard. B~buch nt log [-book]

Bordell nt -s,-e brothel

Bord|karte f boarding-pass. B~stein m kerb

borgen vt borrow; jdm etw b~ lend s.o. sth

Borke f -,-n bark

borniert a narrow-minded

Börse f -,-n purse; (Comm) stock exchange. B~nmakler m stockbroker

Borst|e f -,-n bristle. b~ig a bristly

Borte f -,-n braid

bösartig a vicious; (Med) malignant

Böschung f -,-en embankment; (Hang) slope

böse a wicked, evil; (*unartig*) naughty; (*schlimm*) bad, adv -ly; (*zornig*) cross; jdm od auf jdn b~ sein be cross with s.o. B~wicht m -[e]s,-e villain; (*Schlingel*) rascal

bos|haft a malicious, adv -ly; (*gehässig*) spiteful, adv -ly. B~heit f -,-en malice; spite; (*Handlung*) spiteful act/(*Bemerkung*) remark

böswillig a malicious, adv -ly. B~keit f - malice

Botani|k f - botany. B~ker(in) m -s,- (f -,-nen) botanist. b~sch a botanical

Bot|e m -n,-n messenger. B~engang m errand. B~schaft f -,-en message; (*Pol*) embassy. B~schafter m -s,- ambassador

Bottich m -[e]s,-e vat; (*Wasch-*) tub

Bouillon /'bulˈjõ/ f -,-s clear soup. B~würfel m stock cube

Bowle /'boːlə/ f -,-n punch

box|en vi (haben) box ▫ vt punch. B~en nt -s boxing. B~er m -s,- boxer. B~kampf m boxing match; (*Boxen*) boxing

Boykott m -[e]s,-s boycott. b~ieren vt boycott; (*Comm*) black

brachliegen† vi sep (haben) lie fallow

Branche /'brãːʃə/ f -,-n [line of] business. B~nverzeichnis nt (*Teleph*) classified directory

Brand m -[e]s,-e fire; (*Med*) gangrene; (*Bot*) blight; in B~ geraten catch fire; in B~ setzen od stecken set on fire. B~bombe f incendiary bomb

branden vi (haben) surge; (*sich brechen*) break

Brand|geruch m smell of burning. b~marken vt (fig) brand. B~stifter m arsonist. B~stiftung f arson

Brandung f - surf. B~sreiten nt surfing

Brand|wunde f burn. B~zeichen nt brand

Branntwein m spirit; (coll) spirits pl. B~brennerei f distillery

bras|ilianisch a Brazilian. B~ilien /-jən/ nt -s Brazil

Brat|apfel m baked apple. b~en† vt/i (haben) roast; (in der Pfanne) fry. B~en m -s,- roast; (B~stück) joint. B~ensoße f gravy. b~fertig a oven-ready. B~hähnchen, B~huhn nt roast/(zum Braten) roasting chicken. B~kartoffeln fpl fried potatoes. B~klops m rissole. B~pfanne f frying-pan

Bratsche f -,-n (Mus) viola

Brat|spieß m spit. B~wurst f sausage for frying; (gebraten) fried sausage

Brauch m -[e]s,Bräuche custom. b~bar a usable; (nützlich) useful. b~en vt need; (ge-, verbrauchen) use; take (Zeit); er b~t

es nur zu sagen he only has to say; du b~st nicht zu gehen you needn't go

Braue f -,-n eyebrow

brau|en vt brew. B~er m -s,- brewer. B~erei f -,-en brewery

braun a, B~ nt -s,- brown; b~ werden (*Person:*) get a tan; b~ [gebrannt] sein be [sun-]tanned

Bräune f - [sun-]tan. b~n vt/i (haben) brown; (in der Sonne) tan

braungebrannt a (NEW) braun gebrannt, s. braun

Braunschweig nt -s Brunswick

Brause f -,-n (Dusche) shower; (an Gießkanne) rose; (B~limonade) fizzy drink. b~n vi (haben) roar; (duschen) shower ▫ vi (sein) rush [along] ▫ vr sich b~n shower. b~nd a roaring; (sprudelnd) effervescent

Braut f -,-e bride; (Verlobte) fiancée

Bräutigam m -s,-e bridegroom; (Verlobter) fiancé

Brautkleid nt wedding dress

bräutlich a bridal

Brautpaar nt bridal couple; (Verlobte) engaged couple

brav a good, well-behaved; (redlich) honest ▫ adv dutifully; (redlich) honestly

bravo int bravo!

BRD abbr (Bundesrepublik Deutschland) FRG

Brech|eisen nt jemmy; (B~stange) crowbar. b~en† vt break; (Phys) refract ⟨Licht⟩; (erbrechen) vomit; sich b~en ⟨Wellen:⟩ break; ⟨Licht:⟩ be refracted; sich (dat) den Arm b~en break one's arm ▫ vi (sein) break ▫ vi (haben) vomit, be sick; mit jdm b~en (fig) break with s.o. B~er m -s,- breaker. B~reiz m nausea. B~stange f crowbar

Brei m -[e]s,-e paste; (Culin) purée; (Grieß-) pudding; (Hafer-) porridge. b~ig a mushy

breit a wide; (Schultern, Grinsen) broad ▫ adv b~ grinsen grin broadly. b~beinig a & adv with legs apart. B~e f -,-n width; breadth; (Geog) latitude. b~en vt spread (über + acc over). B~engrad m [degree of] latitude. B~enkreis m parallel. B~ seite f long side; (Naut) broadside

Bremse¹ f -,-n horsefly

Bremse² f -,-n brake. b~n vt slow down; (fig) restrain ▫ vi (haben) brake

Bremslicht nt brake-light

brenn|bar a combustible; leicht b~bar highly [in]flammable. b~en† vi/(haben) burn; ⟨Licht:⟩ be on; ⟨Zigarette:⟩ be alight; (weh tun) smart, sting; es b~t in X there's a fire in X; darauf b~en, etw zu tun be dying to do sth ▫ vt burn; (rösten) roast;

(im Brennofen) fire; (destillieren) distil. b~end a burning; (angezündet) lighted; (fig) fervent □ adv ich würde b~end gern ... I'd love to ... B~erei f -,-en distillery

Brennessel f (NEW) Brennnessel

Brenn|holz nt firewood. B~nessel f stinging nettle. B~ofen m kiln. B~punkt m (Phys) focus; im B~punkt des Interesses stehen be the focus of attention. B~spiritus m methylated spirits. B~stoff m fuel

brenzlig a (fam) risky; b~er Geruch smell of burning

Bresche f -,-n (fig) breach

Bretagne /bre'tanjə/ (die) - Brittany

Brett nt -[e]s,-er board; (im Regal) shelf; schwarzes B~ notice board. B~chen nt -s,- slat; (Frühstücks-) small board (used as plate). B~spiel nt board game

Brezel f -,-n pretzel

Bridge /brɪtʃ/ nt - (Spiel) bridge

Brief m -[e]s,-e letter. B~beschwerer m -s,- paperweight. B~block m writing pad. B~freund(in) m(f) pen-friend. B~kasten m letter-box, (Amer) mailbox. B~kopf m letter-head. b~lich a & adv by letter. B~marke f [postage] stamp. B~öffner m paper-knife. B~papier nt notepaper. B~porto nt letter rate. B~tasche f wallet. B~träger m postman, (Amer) mailman. B~umschlag m envelope. B~wahl f postal vote. B~wechsel m correspondence

Brigade f -,-n brigade

Brikett nt -s,-s briquette

brillan|t /brɪl'jant/ a brilliant, adv -ly. B~t m -en,-en [cut] diamond. B~z f - brilliance

Brille f -,-n glasses pl, spectacles pl; (Schutz-) goggles pl; (Klosett-) toilet seat

bringen† vt bring; (fort-) take; (ein-) yield; (veröffentlichen) publish; (im Radio) broadcast; show (Film); ins Bett b~ put to bed; jdn nach Hause b~ take/(begleiten) see s.o. home; an sich (acc) b~ get possession of; mit sich b~ entail; um etw b~ deprive of sth; etw hinter sich (acc) b~ get sth over [and done] with; jdn dazu b~, etw zu tun get s.o. to do sth; es weit b~ (fig) go far

brisant a explosive

Brise f -,-n breeze

Brit|e m -n,-n, B~in f -,-nen Briton. b~isch a British

Bröckchen nt -s,- (Culin) crouton. b~elig a crumbly; (Gestein) friable. b~eln vt/i (haben/sein) crumble

Brocken m -s,- chunk; (Erde, Kohle) lump; ein paar B~ Englisch (fam) a smattering of English

Brokat m -[e]s,-e brocade

Brokkoli pl broccoli sg

Brombeer|e f blackberry. B~strauch m bramble [bush]

Bronchitis f - bronchitis

Bronze /'brõːsə/ f -,-n bronze

Brosch|e f -,-n brooch. b~iert a paperback. B~üre f -,-n brochure; (Heft) booklet

Brösel mpl (Culin) breadcrumbs

Brot n -[e]s,-e bread; ein B~ a loaf [of bread]; (Scheibe) a slice of bread; sein B~ verdienen (fig) earn one's living (mit by)

Brötchen n -s,- [bread] roll

Brot|krümel m breadcrumb. B~verdiener m breadwinner

Bruch m -[e]s,-e break; (Brechen) breaking; (Rohr-) burst; (Med) fracture; (Eingeweide-) rupture, hernia; (Math) fraction; (fig) breach; (in Beziehung) break-up

brüchig a brittle

Bruch|landung f crash-landing. B~rechnung f fractions pl. B~stück nt fragment. b~stückhaft a fragmentary. B~teil m fraction

Brücke f -,-n bridge; (Teppich) rug

Bruder m -s,- brother

brüderlich a brotherly, fraternal

Brügge nt -s Bruges

Brüh|e f -,-n broth; (Knochen-) stock; klare B~e clear soup. b~en vt scald; (auf-) make (Kaffee). B~würfel m stock cube

brüllen vt/i (haben) roar; (Kuh:) moo; (fam: schreien) bawl

brumm|eln vt/i (haben) mumble. b~en vi (haben) (Insekt:) buzz; (Bär:) growl; (Motor:) hum; (murren) grumble □ vt mutter. B~er m -s,- (fam) bluebottle. b~ig a (fam) grumpy, adv -ily

brünett a dark-haired. B~e f -,-n brunette

Brunnen m -s,- well; (Spring-) fountain; (Heil-) spa water. B~kresse f watercress

brüsk a brusque, adv -ly. b~ieren vt snub

Brüssel nt -s Brussels

Brust f -,-e chest; (weibliche, Culin: B~stück) breast. B~bein nt breastbone. B~beutel m purse worn round the neck

brusten (sich) vr boast

Brust|fellentzündung f pleurisy. B~schwimmen nt breaststroke

Brüstung f -,-en parapet

Brustwarze f nipple

Brut *f* -,-en incubation; (*Junge*) brood; (*Fisch-*) fry

brutal *a* brutal, *adv* -ly. B∼ität *f* -,-en brutality

brüten *vi* (*haben*) sit (*on eggs*); (*fig*) ponder (über + *dat* over); b∼de Hitze oppressive heat

Brutkasten *m* (*Med*) incubator

brutto *adv,* B∼ *pref* gross

brutzeln *vi* (*haben*) sizzle □ *vt* fry

Bub *m* -en,-en (*SGer*) boy. B∼e *m* -n,-n (*Karte*) jack, knave

Bubikopf *m* bob

Buch *nt* -[e]s,¨er book; B∼ führen keep a record (über + *acc* of); die B∼er führen keep the accounts. B∼drucker *m* printer

Buche *f* -,-n beech

buchen *vt* book; (*Comm*) enter

Bücher|bord, B∼brett *nt* bookshelf. B∼ei *f* -,-en library. B∼regal *nt* bookcase, bookshelves *pl.* B∼schrank *m* bookcase. B∼wurm *m* bookworm

Buchfink *m* chaffinch

Buch|führung *f* bookkeeping. B∼halter(in) *m* -s,- (*f* -,-nen) bookkeeper, accountant. B∼haltung *f* bookkeeping, accountancy; (*Abteilung*) accounts department. B∼händler(in) *m(f)* bookseller. B∼handlung *f* bookshop. B∼macher *m* -s,- bookmaker. B∼prüfer *m* auditor

Büchse *f* -,-n box; (*Konserven-*) tin, can; (*Gewehr*) [sporting] gun. B∼nmilch *f* evaporated milk. B∼nöffner *m* tin *or* can opener

Buch|stabe *m* -n,-n letter. b∼stabieren *vt* spell [out]. b∼stäblich *adv* literally

Buchstützen *fpl* book-ends

Bucht *f* -,-en (*Geog*) bay

Buchung *f* -,-en booking, reservation; (*Comm*) entry

Buckel *m* -s,-hump; (*Beule*) bump; (*Hügel*) hillock; einen B∼ machen (*Katze:*) arch its back

bücken (sich) *vr* bend down

bucklig *a* hunchbacked. B∼e(r) *m/f* hunchback

Bückling *m* -s,-e smoked herring; (*fam: Verbeugung*) bow

buddeln *vt/i* (*haben*) (*fam*) dig

Buddhis|mus *m* - Buddhism. B∼t(in) *m* -en,-en (*f* -,-nen) Buddhist. b∼tisch *a* Buddhist

Bude *f* -,-n hut; (*Kiosk*) kiosk; (*Markt-*) stall; (*fam: Zimmer*) room; (*Studenten-*) digs *pl*

Budget /by'dʒe:/ *nt* -s,-s budget

Büfett *nt* -[e]s,-e sideboard; (*Theke*) bar; kaltes B∼ cold buffet

Büffel *m* -s,- buffalo. b∼n *vt/i* (*haben*) (*fam*) swot

Bug *m* -[e]s,-e (*Naut*) bow[s *pl*]

Bügel *m* -s,- frame; (*Kleider-*) coathanger; (*Steig-*) stirrup; (*Brillen-*) sidepiece. B∼brett *nt* ironing-board. B∼eisen *nt* iron. B∼falte *f* crease. b∼frei *a* noniron. b∼n *vt/i* (*haben*) iron

bugsieren *vt* (*fam*) manœuvre

buhen *vi* (*haben*) (*fam*) boo

Buhne *f* -,-n breakwater

Bühne *f* -,-n stage. B∼nbild *nt* set. B∼neingang *m* stage door

Buhrufe *mpl* boos

Bukett *nt* -[e]s,-e bouquet

Bulette *f* -,-n [meat] rissole

Bulgarien /-jən/ *nt* -s Bulgaria

Bull|auge *nt* (*Naut*) porthole. B∼dogge *f* bulldog. B∼dozer /-do:zə/ *m* -s,- bulldozer. B∼e *m* -n,-n bull; (*sl: Polizist*) cop

Bummel *m* -s,- (*fam*) stroll. B∼lant *m* -en,-en (*fam*) dawdler; (*Faulenzer*) loafer. B∼lei *f* - (*fam*) dawdling; (*Nachlässigkeit*) carelessness

bummel|ig *a* (*fam*) slow; (*nachlässig*) careless. b∼n *vi* (*sein*) (*fam*) stroll □ *vi* (*haben*) (*fam*) dawdle. B∼streik *m* goslow. B∼zug *m* (*fam*) slow train

Bums *m* -es,-e (*fam*) bump, thump

Bund[1] *nt* -[e]s,-e bunch; (*Stroh-*) bundle

Bund[2] *m* -[e]s,¨e association; (*Bündnis*) alliance; (*Pol*) federation; (*Rock-, Hosen-*) waistband; im B∼e sein be in league (mit with); der B∼ the Federal Government; (*fam: Bundeswehr*) the [German] Army

Bündel *nt* -s,- bundle. b∼n *vt* bundle [up]

Bundes|-*pref*Federal. B∼genosse *m* ally. B∼kanzler *m* Federal Chancellor. B∼land *nt* [federal] state; (*Aust*) province. B∼liga *f* German national league. B∼rat *m* Upper House of Parliament. B∼regierung *f* Federal Government. B∼republik *f* die B∼republik Deutschland the Federal Republic of Germany. B∼straße *f* ≈ A road. B∼tag *m* Lower House of Parliament. B∼wehr *f* [Federal German] Army

bünd|ig *a & adv* kurz und b∼ig short and to the point. B∼nis *nt* -sses,-sse alliance

Bunker *m* -s,- bunker; (*Luftschutz-*) shelter

bunt *a* coloured; (*farbenfroh*) colourful; (*grell*) gaudy; (*gemischt*) varied; (*wirr*) confused; b∼er Abend social evening; b∼e Platte assorted cold meats □ *adv* b∼ durcheinander higgledy-piggledy; es zu b∼ treiben (*fam*) go too far. B∼stift *m* crayon

Bürde *f* -,-n (*fig*) burden

Burg *f* -,-en castle

Bürge *m* -n,-n guarantor. b~n *vi* (*haben*) b~n für vouch for; (*fig*) guarantee

Bürger|(in) *m* -s,- (*f* -,-nen) citizen. B~krieg *m* civil war. b~lich *a* civil; (*Pflicht*) civic; (*mittelständisch*) middle-class; b~liche Küche plain cooking. B~liche(r) *m/f* commoner. B~meister *m* mayor. B~rechte *npl* civil rights. B~steig *m* -[e]s, -e pavement, (*Amer*) sidewalk

Burggraben *m* moat

Bürgschaft *f* -,-en surety; B~ leisten stand surety

Burgunder *m* -s,- (*Wein*) Burgundy

Burleske *f* -,-n burlesque

Büro *nt* -s,-s office. B~angestellte(r) *m/f* office-worker. B~klammer *f* paper-clip. B~krat *m*-en,-en bureaucrat. B~kratie *f* -,-n bureaucracy. b~kratisch *a* bureaucratic

Bursch|e *m* -n,-n lad, youth; (*fam: Kerl*) fellow. b~ikos *a* hearty; (*männlich*) mannish

Bürste *f* -,-n brush. b~n *vt* brush. B~nschnitt *m* crew cut

Bus *m* -ses,-se bus; (*Reise-*) coach. B~bahnhof *m* bus and coach station

Busch *m* -[e]s,-e bush

Büschel *nt* -s,- tuft

buschig *a* bushy

Busen *m* -s,- bosom

Bussard *m* -s,-e buzzard

Buße *f* -,-n penance; (*Jur*) fine

büßen *vt/i* (*haben*) [für] etw b~ atone for sth; (*fig: bezahlen*) pay for sth

buß|fertig *a* penitent. B~geld *nt* (*Jur*) fine

Büste *f* -,-n bust; (*Schneider-*) dummy. B~nhalter *m* -s,- bra

Butter *f* - butter. B~blume *f* buttercup. B~brot *nt* slice of bread and butter. B~brotpapier *nt* grease-proof paper. B~fass (B~faß) *nt* churn. B~milch *f* buttermilk. b~n *vi* (*haben*) make butter □ *vt* butter

b.w. *abbr* (bitte wenden) P.T.O.

bzgl. *abbr* s. bezüglich

bzw. *abbr* s. beziehungsweise

C

ca. *abbr* (circa) about

Café /ka'fe:/ *nt* -s,-s café

Cafeteria /kafete'ri:a/ *f* -,-s cafeteria

camp|en /'kɛmpən/ *vi* (*haben*) go camping. C~ing *nt* -s camping. C~ingplatz *m* campsite

Cape /ke:p/ *nt* -s,-s cape

Caravan /'ka[:]ravan/ *m* -s,-s (*Auto*) caravan; (*Kombi*) estate car

Cassette /ka'sɛtə/ *f* -,-n cassette. C~nrecorder /-rekɔrdɐ/ *m* -s,- cassette recorder

CD /tse:'de:/ *f* -,-s compact disc, CD

Cell|ist(in) /tʃɛ'lıst(ın)/ *m* -en, -en (*f* -,-nen) cellist. C~o /'tʃɛlo/ *nt* -,-los & -li cello

Celsius /'tsɛlzjʊs/ *inv* Celsius, centigrade

Cembalo /'tʃɛmbalo/ *nt* -s,-los & -li harpsichord

Champagner /ʃam'panjɐ/ *m* -s champagne

Champignon /'ʃampınjɔŋ/ *m* -s,-s [field] mushroom

Chance /'ʃã:sə/ *f* -,-n chance

Chaos /'ka:ɔs/ *nt* - chaos

chaotisch /ka'o:tıʃ/ *a* chaotic

Charakter /ka'raktɐ/ *m* -s,-e /-'te:rə/ character. c~isieren *vt* characterize. c~istisch *a* characteristic (für of), *adv* -ally

Charism|a /ka'rısma/ *nt* -s charisma. c~atisch *a* charismatic

charm|ant /ʃar'mant/ *a* charming, *adv* -ly. C~e /ʃarm/ *m* -s charm

Charter|flug /'tʃ-, 'ʃartɐ-/ *m* charter flight. c~n *vt* charter

Chassis /ʃa'si:/ *nt* -,- /-'si:[s], -'si:s/ chassis

Chauffeur /ʃɔ'føːɐ/ *m* -s,-e chauffeur; (*Taxi-*) driver

Chauvinis|mus /ʃovi'nısmʊs/ *m* - chauvinism. C~t *m* -en,-en chauvinist

Chef /ʃɛf/ *m* -s,-s head; (*fam*) boss

Chem|ie /çe'mi:/ *f* - chemistry. C~ikalien /-jən/ *fpl* chemicals

Chem|iker(in) /'çe:-/ *m* -s,- (*f* -,-nen) chemist. c~isch *a* chemical, *adv* -ly; c~ische Reinigung dry-cleaning; (*Geschäft*) dry-cleaner's

Chicorée /'ʃikore:/ *m* -s chicory

Chiffr|e /'ʃıfɐ, 'ʃıfrə/ *f* -,-n cipher; (*bei Annonce*) box number. c~iert *a* coded

Chile /'çi:le/ *nt* -s Chile

Chin|a /'çi:na/ *nt* -s China. C~ese *m* -n, -n, C~esin *f* -,-nen Chinese. c~esisch *a* Chinese. C~esisch *nt* -[s] (*Lang*) Chinese

Chip /tʃıp/ *m* -s, ɛ [micro]chip. C~s *pl* crisps, (*Amer*) chips

Chirurg /çi'rʊrk/ *m* -en,-en surgeon. C~ie /-'gi:/ *f* - surgery. c~isch *a* /-g-/ *a* surgical, *adv* -ly

D

Chlor /klo:ɐ̯/ *nt* -s chlorine. C∼oform /kloro'fɔrm/ *nt* -s chloroform

Choke /tʃo:k/ *m* -s,-s (*Auto*) choke

Cholera /'ko:lera/ *f* - cholera

cholerisch /ko'le:rɪʃ/ *a* irascible

Cholesterin /ço-, koleste'ri:n/ *nt* -s cholesterol

Chor /ko:ɐ̯/ *m* -[e]s,⁻e choir; (*Theat*) chorus; im C∼ in chorus

Choral /ko'ra:l/ *m* -[e]s,⁻e chorale

Choreographie, Choreografie /koreogra'fi:/ *f* -,-n choreography

Chor|knabe /'ko:ɐ̯-/ *m* choirboy. C∼musik *f* choral music

Christ /krɪst/ *m* -en,-en Christian. C∼baum *m* Christmas tree. C∼entum *nt* -s Christianity. C∼in *f* -,-nen Christian. C∼kind *nt* Christ-child; (*als Geschenkbringer*) ≈ Father Christmas. c∼lich *a* Christian

Christus /'krɪstʊs/ *m* -ti Christ

Chrom /kro:m/ *nt* -s chromium

Chromosom /kromo'zo:m/ *nt* -s,-en chromosome

Chronik /'kro:nɪk/ *f* -,-en chronicle

chron|isch /'kro:nɪʃ/ *a* chronic, *adv* -ally. c∼ologisch *a* chronological, *adv* -ly

Chrysantheme /kryzan'te:mə/ *f* -,-n chrysanthemum

circa /'tsɪrka/ *adv* about

Clique /'klɪkə/ *f* -,-n clique

Clou /klu:/ *m* -s,-s highlight, (*fam*) high spot

Clown /klaʊn/ *m* -s,-s clown. c∼en *vi* (*haben*) clown

Club /klʊp/ *m* -s,-s club

Cocktail /'kɔkte:l/ *m* -s,-s cocktail

Code /ko:t/ *m* -s,-s code

Cola /'ko:la/ *f* -,- (*fam*) Coke (P)

Comic-Heft /'kɔmɪk-/ *nt* comic

Computer /kɔm'pju:tɐ/ *m* -s,- computer. c∼isieren *vt* computerize

Conférencier /kõ'ferã'sje:/ *m* -s,- compère

Cord /kɔrt/ *m* -s, C∼samt *m* corduroy. C∼[samt]hose *f* cords *pl*

Couch /kaʊtʃ/ *f* -,-es settee. C∼tisch *m* coffee-table

Coupon /ku'põ:/ *m* -s,-s = Kupon

Cousin /ku'zɛ̃:/ *m* -s,-s [male] cousin. C∼e /-'zi:nə/ *f* -,-n [female] cousin

Crem|e /kre:m/ *f* -s,-s cream; (*Speise*) cream dessert. c∼efarben *a* cream. c∼ig *a* creamy

Curry /'kari, 'kœri/ *nt & m* -s curry powder. ◻ *nt* -s,-s (*Gericht*) curry

da *adv* there; (*hier*) here; (*zeitlich*) then; (*in dem Fall*) in that case; von da an from then on; da sein be there/(*hier*) here; (*existieren*) exist; wieder da sein be back; noch nie da gewesen unprecedented ◻ *conj* as, since

dabehalten† *vt sep* keep there

dabei (*emphatic*: dabei) *adv* nearby; (*daran*) with it; (*eingeschlossen*) included; (*hinsichtlich*) about it; (*währenddem*) during this; (*gleichzeitig*) at the same time; (*doch*) and yet; dicht d∼ close by; d∼ sein be present; (*mitmachen*) be involved; d∼ sein, etw zu tun be just doing sth; d∼ bleiben (*fig*) remain adamant; was ist denn d∼? (*fam*) so what? d∼sein† *vi sep* (*sein*) NEW d∼ sein, s. dabei

dableiben† *vi sep* (*sein*) stay there

Dach *nt* -[e]s,⁻er roof. D∼boden *m* loft. D∼gepäckträger *m* roof-rack. D∼kammer *f* attic room. D∼luke *f* skylight. D∼rinne *f* gutter

Dachs *m* -es,-e badger

Dach|sparren *m* -s,- rafter. D∼ziegel *m* [roofing] tile

Dackel *m* -s,- dachshund

dadurch (*emphatic*: dadurch) *adv* through it/them; (*Ursache*) by it; (*deshalb*) because of that; d∼, dass because

dafür (*emphatic*: dafür) *adv* for it/them; (*anstatt*) instead; (*als Ausgleich*) but [on the other hand]; d∼, dass considering that; ich kann nichts dafür it's not my fault. d∼können† *vi sep* (*haben*) NEW d∼ können, s. dafür

dagegen (*emphatic*: dagegen) *adv* against it/them; (*Mittel, Tausch*) for it; (*verglichen damit*) by comparison; (*jedoch*) however; hast du was d∼? do you mind? d∼halten† *vt sep* argue (dass that)

daheim *adv* at home

daher (*emphatic*: daher) *adv* from there; (*deshalb*) for that reason; das kommt d∼, weil that's because; d∼ meine Eile hence my hurry ◻ *conj* that is why

dahin (*emphatic*: dahin) *adv* there; bis d∼ up to there; (*bis dann*) until/(*Zukunft*) by then; jdn d∼ bringen, dass er etw tut get s.o. to do sth; d∼ sein (*fam*) be gone. d∼gehen† *vi sep* (*sein*) walk along; (*Zeit*:) pass. d∼gestellt *a* d∼gestellt lassen (*fig*) leave open; das bleibt d∼gestellt that remains to be seen dahinten *adv* back there

dahinter *(emphatic:* dahinter) *adv* behind it/them; d~ kommen *(fig)* get to the bottom of lt. d~kommen† *vi sep* (sein) NEW d~ kommen, *s.* dahinter

Dahlie /-ja/ *f* -,-n dahlia

dalassen† *vt sep* leave there

daliegen† *vi sep* (haben) lie there

damalig *a* at that time; der d~e Minister the then minister

damals *adv* at that time

Damast *m* -es,-e damask

Dame *f* -,-n lady; *(Karte, Schach)* queen; *(D~spiel)* draughts *sg*, *(Amer)* checkers *sg*; *(Doppelstein)* king. D~n- *pref* ladies'/lady's ... d~nhaft *a* ladylike

damit *(emphatic:* damit) *adv* with it/them; *(dadurch)* by it; hör auf d~! stop it! □ *conj* so that

dämlich *a (fam)* stupid, *adv* -ly

Damm *m* -[e]s,-e dam; *(Insel-)* causeway; nicht auf dem D~ *(fam)* under the weather

dämmer|ig *a* dim; es wird d~ig dusk is falling. D~licht *nt* twilight. d~n *vi (haben) (Morgen:)* dawn; der Abend d~t dusk is falling; es d~t it is getting light/ *(abends)* dark. D~ung *f* dawn; *(Abend-)* dusk

Dämon *m* -s,-en /-'mo:nən/ demon

Dampf *m* -es,-e steam; *(Chem)* vapour. d~en *vi (haben)* steam

dämpfen *vt (Culin)* steam; *(fig)* muffle *(Ton)*; lower *(Stimme)*; dampen *(Enthusiasmus)*

Dampf|er *m* -s,- steamer. D~kochtopf *m* pressure-cooker. D~maschine *f* steam engine. D~walze *f* steamroller

Damwild *nt* fallow deer *pl*

danach *(emphatic:* danach) *adv* after it/ them; *(suchen)* for it/them; *(riechen)* of it; *(später)* afterwards; *(entsprechend)* accordingly; es sieht d~ aus it looks like it

Däne *m* -n,-n Dane

daneben *(emphatic:* daneben) *adv* beside it/them; *(außerdem)* in addition; *(verglichen damit)* by comparison. d~gehen† *vi sep (sein)* miss; *(scheitern)* fail

Dän|emark *nt* -s Denmark. D~in *f* -,-nen Dane. d~isch *a* Danish

Dank *m* -es thanks *pl*; vielen D~! thank you very much! d~ *prep (+ dat or gen)* thanks to. d~bar *a* grateful, *adv* -ly; *(erleichtert)* thankful, *adv* -ly; *(lohnend)* rewarding. D~barkeit *f* - gratitude. d~e *adv* d~e [schön *od* sehr]! thank you [very much]! [nein] d~e! no thank you! d~en *vi (haben)* thank (jdm s.o.); *(ablehnen)* decline; ich d~e! no thank you! nichts zu d~en! don't mention it!

dann *adv* then; d~ und wann now and then; nur/selbst d~, wenn only/even if

daran *(emphatic:* daran) *adv* on it/them; at it/them; *(denken)* of it; nahe d~ on the point (etw zu tun of doing sth); denkt d~! remember! d~gehen† *vi sep (sein)*, d~machen (sich) *vr sep* set about (etw zu tun doing sth). d~setzen *vt sep* alles d~setzen do one's utmost (zu to)

darauf *(emphatic:* darauf) *adv* on it/them; at it/them; *(danach)* after that; *(d~hin)* as a result; am Tag d~ the day after; am d~folgenden Tag the following *or* next day. d~folgend *a* NEW d~ folgend, *s.* darauf. d~hin *adv* as a result

daraus *(emphatic:* daraus) *adv* out of *or* from it/them; er macht sich nichts d~ he doesn't care for it; was ist d~ geworden? what has become of it?

Darbietung *f* -,-en performance; *(Nummer)* item

darin *(emphatic:* darin) *adv* in it/them

darlegen *vt sep* expound; *(erklären)* explain

Darlehen *nt* -s,- loan

Darm *m* -[e]s,-e intestine; *(Wurst-)* skin. D~grippe *f* gastric flu

darstell|en *vt sep* represent; *(bildlich)* portray; *(Theat)* interpret; *(spielen)* play; *(schildern)* describe. D~er *m* -s,- actor. D~erin *f* -,-nen actress. D~ung *f* representation; interpretation; description; *(Bericht)* account

darüber *(emphatic:* darüber) *adv* over it/ them; *(höher)* above it/them; *(sprechen, lachen, sich freuen)* about it; *(mehr)* more; *(inzwischen)* in the meantime; d~ hinaus beyond [it]; *(dazu)* on top of that

darum *(emphatic:* darum) *adv* round it/ them; *(bitten, kämpfen)* for it; *(deshalb)* that is why; d~, weil because

darunter *(emphatic:* darunter) *adv* under it/them; *(tiefer)* below it/them; *(weniger)* less; *(dazwischen)* among them

das *def art & pron s.* der

dasein† *vi sep* (sein) NEW da sein, *s.* da. D~ *nt* -s existence

dasitzen† *vi sep* (haben) sit there

dasjenige *pron s.* derjenige

dass (daß) *conj* that; d~ du nicht fällst! mind you don't fall!

dasselbe *pron s.* derselbe

dastehen† *vi sep* (haben) stand there; allein d~ *(fig)* be on one's own

Daten|sichtgerät *nt* visual display unit, VDU. D~verarbeitung *f* data processing

datieren *vt/i (haben)* date

Dativ *m* -s,-e dative. D~objekt *nt* indirect object

Dattel *f* -,-n date

Datum *nt* s,-ten date; Daten dates; *(Angaben)* data

Dauer f -duration, length; (*Jur*) term; von D~ lasting; auf die D~ in the long run. D~auftrag m standing order. d~haft a lasting, enduring; (*fest*) durable. D~karte f season ticket. D~lauf m im D~lauf at a jog. D~milch f long-life milk. d~n vi (haben) last; lange d~ntake a long time. d~nd a lasting; (*ständig*) constant, adv -ly; d~nd fragen keep asking. D~stellung f permanent position. D~welle f perm. D~wurst f salami-type sausage

Daumen m -s,- thumb; jdm den D~ drücken od halten keep one's fingers crossed for s.o.

Daunen fpl down sg. D~decke f [down-filled] duvet

davon (*emphatic:* davon) adv from it/ them; (*dadurch*) by it; (*damit*) with it/ them; (*darüber*) about it; (*Menge*) of it/ them; die Hälfte d~ half of it/them; das kommt d~! it serves you right! d~kommen† vi sep (sein) escape (mit dem Leben with one's life). d~laufen† vi sep (sein) run away. d~machen (sich) vr sep (fam) make off. d~tragen† vt sep carry off; (*erleiden*) suffer; (*gewinnen*) win

davor (*emphatic:* davor) adv in front of it/them; (*sich fürchten*) of it; (*zeitlich*) before it/them

dazu (*emphatic:* dazu) adv to it/them; (*damit*) with it/them; (*dafür*) for it; noch d~ in addition to that; jdn d~ bringen, etw zu tun get s.o. to do sth; ich kam nicht d~ I didn't get round to [doing] it. d~gehören vi sep (haben) belong to it/them; alles, was d~gehört everything that goes with it. d~kommen† vi sep (sein) arrive [on the scene]; (*hinzukommen*) be added; d~ kommt, dass er krank ist on top of that he is ill. d~rechnen vt sep add to it/them

dazwischen (*emphatic:* dazwischen) adv between them; in between; (*darunter*) among them. d~fahren† vi sep (sein) (fig) intervene. d~kommen† vi sep (sein) (fig) crop up; wenn nichts d~kommt if all goes well. d~reden vi sep (haben) interrupt. d~treten† vi sep (sein) (fig) intervene

DDR f - abbr (Deutsche Demokratische Republik) GDR

Debatte f -,-n debate; zur D~te stehen be at issue. d~ieren vt/i (haben) debate

Debüt /de'by:/ nt -s,-s début

dechiffrieren /deʃi'fri:rən/ vt decipher

Deck nt -[e]s,-s (Naut) deck; an D~ on deck. D~bett nt duvet

Decke f -,-n cover; (Tisch-) table-cloth; (Bett-) blanket; (Reise-) rug; (Zimmer-) ceiling; unter einer D~stecken (fam) be in league

Deckel m -s,- lid; (Flaschen-) top; (Buch-) cover

decken vt cover; tile (Dach); lay (Tisch); (schützen) shield; (Sport) mark; meet (Bedarf); jdn d~ (fig) cover up for s.o.; sich d~ (fig) cover oneself (gegen against); (übereinstimmen) coincide

Deck|mantel m (fig) pretence. D~name m pseudonym

Deckung f -(Mil) cover; (Sport) defence; (Mann-) marking; (Boxen) guard; (Sicherheit) security; in D~ gehen take cover

Defekt m -[e]s,-e defect. d~ a defective

defensiv a defensive. D~e f - defensive

defilieren vi (sein/haben) file past

defin|ieren vt define. D~ition /-'tsjo:n/ f -,-en definition. d~itiv a definite, adv -ly

Defizit nt -s,-e deficit

Deflation /-'tsjo:n/ f - deflation

deformiert a deformed

deftig a (fam) (Mahlzeit) hearty; (Witz) coarse

Degen m -s,- sword; (Fecht-) épée

degenerier|en vi (sein) degenerate. d~t a (fig) degenerate

degradieren vt (Mil) demote; (fig) degrade

dehn|bar a elastic. d~en vt stretch; lengthen (Vokal); sich d~en stretch

Deich m -[e]s,-e dike

Deichsel f -,-n pole; (Gabel-) shafts pl

dein poss pron your. d~e(r,s) poss pron yours; die D~en od d~en pl your family sg. d~erseits adv for your part. d~etwegen adv for your sake; (wegen dir) because of you, on your account. d~etwillen adv um d~etwillen for your sake. d~ige poss pron der/die/das d~ige yours. d~s poss pron yours

Deka nt -[s],- (Aust) = Dekagramm

dekaden|t a decadent. D~z f - decadence

Dekagramm nt (Aust) 10 grams; 10 D~ 100 grams

Dekan m -s,-e dean

Deklin|ation /-'tsjo:n/ f -,-en declension. d~ieren vt decline

Dekolleté, Dekolletee /dekɔl'te:/ nt -s,-s low neckline

Dekor m & nt -s decoration. D~ateur /-'tø:ɐ/ m -s,-e interior decorator; (Schaufenster-) window-dresser. D~ation /-'tsjo:n/ f -,-en decoration; (Schaufenster-) window-dressing; (Auslage) display; D~ationen (Theat) scenery sg. d~ativ a decorative. d~ieren vt decorate; dress (Schaufenster)

Delegation /-'tsjo:n/ f -,-en delegation. d~ieren vt delegate. D~ierte(r) m/f delegate

Delfin *m* -s,-e = Delphin

delikat *a* delicate; (*lecker*) delicious; (*taktvoll*) tactful, *adv* -ly. D~esse *f* -,-n delicacy. D~essengeschäft *nt* delicatessen

Delikt *nt* -[e]s,-e offence

Delinquent *m* -en,-en offender

Delirium *nt* -s delirium

Delle *f* -,-n dent

Delphin *m* -s,-e dolphin

Delta *nt* -s,-s delta

dem *def art & pron s.* der

Dement|i *nt* -s,-s denial. d~ieren *vt* deny

dem|**entsprechend** *a* corresponding; (*passend*) appropriate □ *adv* accordingly; (*passend*) appropriately. d~gemäß *adv* accordingly. d~nach *adv* according to that; (*folglich*) consequently. d~nächst *adv* soon; (*in Kürze*) shortly

Demokrat *m* -en,-en democrat. D~ie *f* -,-n democracy. d~isch *a* democratic, -ally

demolieren *vt* wreck

Demonstr|**ant** *m* -en,-en demonstrator. D~ation /-'tsio:n/ *f* -,-en demonstration. d~ativ *a* pointed, *adv* -ly; (*Gram*) demonstrative. D~ativpronomen *nt* demonstrative pronoun. d~ieren *vt/i* (*haben*) demonstrate

demontieren *vt* dismantle

demoralisieren *vt* demoralize

Demoskopie *f* - opinion research

Demut *f* - humility

demütig *a* humble, *adv* -bly. d~en *vt* humiliate, sich d~en humble oneself. D~ung *f* -,-en humiliation

demzufolge *adv* = demnach

den *def art & pron s.* der. d~en *pron s.* der

denk|**bar** *a* conceivable. d~en† *vt/i* (*haben*) think (an + *acc* of); (*sich erinnern*) remember (an etw *acc* sth); für jdn gedacht meant for s.o.; das kann ich mir d~en I can imagine [that]; ich d~e nicht daran I have no intention of doing it; d~t daran! don't forget! D~mal *nt* memorial; (*Monument*) monument. d~würdig *a* memorable. D~zettel *m* jdm einen D~zettel geben (*fam*) teach s.o. a lesson

denn *conj* for; besser/mehr d~ je better/more than ever □ *adv* wie/wo d~? but how/where? warum d~ nicht? why ever not? es sei d~ [, dass] unless

dennoch *adv* nevertheless

Denunz|**iant** *m* -en,-en informer. d~ieren *vt* denounce

Deodorant *nt* -s,-s deodorant

deplaciert, deplatziert (**deplaziert**) /-'tsi:ɐt/ *a* (*fig*) out of place

Deponie *f* -,-n dump. d~ren *vt* deposit

deportieren *vt* deport

Depot /de'po:/ *nt* -s,-s depot; (*Lager*) warehouse; (*Bank-*) safe deposit

Depression *f* -,-en depression

deprim|**ieren** *vt* depress. d~d *a* depressing

Deputation /-'tsio:n/ *f* -,-en deputation

der, die, das, *pl* **die** *def art* (*acc* den, die, das, *pl* die; *gen* des, der, des, *pl* der; *dat* dem, der, dem, *pl* den) the; der Mensch man; die Natur nature; das Leben life; das Lesen/Tanzen reading/dancing; sich (*dat*) das Gesicht/die Hände waschen wash one's face/hands; 5 Mark das Pfund 5 marks a pound □ *pron* (*acc* den, die, das, *pl* die; *gen* dessen, deren, dessen, *pl* deren; *dat* dem, der, dem, *pl* denen) □ *dem pron* that; (*substantivisch*) he, she, it; (*Ding*) it; (*betont*) that; (*d~jenige*) the one; (*pl*) they, those; (*Dinge*) those; (*diejenigen*) the ones; der und der such and such; um die und die Zeit at such and such a time; das waren Zeiten! those were the days! □ *rel pron* who; (*Ding*) which, that

derart *adv* so; (*so sehr*) so much. d~ig *a* such □ *adv* = derart

derb *a* tough; (*kräftig*) strong; (*grob*) coarse, *adv* -ly; (*unsanft*) rough, *adv* -ly

deren *pron s.* der

dergleichen *inv a* such □ *pron* such a thing/such things; nichts d~ nothing of the kind; und d~ and the like

der-/die-/dasjenige, *pl* **diejenigen** *pron* the one; (*Person*) he, she; (*Ding*) it; (*pl*) those, the ones

dermaßen *adv* = derart

der-/die-/dasselbe, *pl* **dieselben** *pron* the same; ein- und dasselbe one and the same thing

derzeit *adv* at present

des *def art s.* der

Desert|**eur** /-'tø:ɐ̯/ *m* -s,-e deserter. d~ieren *vi* (*sein/haben*) desert

desgleichen *adv* likewise □ *pron* the like

deshalb *adv* for this reason; (*also*) therefore

Designer(in) /di'zainɐ, -nərin/ *m* -s,- (*f* -,-nen) designer

Desin|**fektion** /dɛs'ʔɪnfɛk'tsio:n/ *f* disinfecting. D~fektionsmittel *nt* disinfectant. d~fizieren *vt* disinfect

Despot *m* -en,-en despot

dessen *pron s.* der

Dessert /dɛ'se:ɐ̯/ *nt* -s,-s dessert, sweet. D~löffel *m* dessertspoon

Destill|**ation** /-'tsio:n/ *f* - distillation. d~ieren *vt* distil desto *adv* je mehr/eher, d∼ besser the more/sooner the better

destruktiv *a* (*fig*) destructive

deswegen *adv* = deshalb

Detail /de'tai/ *nt* -s,-s detail

Detektiv *m* -s,-e detective. D∼roman *m* detective story

Detonation *f* -,-en explosion. d∼ieren *vi* (*sein*) explode

deuten *vt* interpret; predict (*Zukunft*) □ *vi* (*haben*) point (auf + *acc* at/(*fig*) to). d∼lich *a* clear, *adv* -ly; (*eindeutig*) plain, *adv* -ly. D∼lichkeit *f* - clarity

deutsch *a* German; auf d∼ NEW auf D∼, s. Deutsch. D∼ *nt* -[s] (*Lang*) German; auf D∼ in German. D∼e(r) *m/f* German. D∼land *nt* -s Germany

Deutung *f* -,-en interpretation

Devise *f* -,-n motto. D∼n *pl* foreign currency *or* exchange *sg*

Dezember *m* -s,- December

dezent *a* unobtrusive, *adv* -ly; (*diskret*) discreet, *adv* -ly

Dezernat *nt* -[e]s,-e department

Dezimal|system *nt* decimal system. D∼zahl *f* decimal

dezimieren *vt* decimate

dgl. *abbr* s. dergleichen

d.h. *abbr* (*das heißt*) i.e.

Dia *nt* -s,-s (*Phot*) slide

Diabet|es *m* - diabetes. D∼iker *m* -s,- diabetic

Diadem *nt* -s,-e tiara

Diagnos|e *f* -,-n diagnosis. d∼tizieren *vt* diagnose

diagonal *a* diagonal, *adv* -ly. D∼e *f* -,-n diagonal

Diagramm *nt* -s,-e diagram; (*Kurven-*) graph

Diakon *m* -s,-e deacon

Dialekt *m* -[e]s,-e dialect

Dialog *m* -[e]s,-e dialogue

Diamant *m* -en,-en diamond

Diameter *m* -s,- diameter

Diapositiv *nt* -s,-e (*Phot*) slide

Diaprojektor *m* slide projector

Diät *f* -,-en (*Med*) diet; D∼ leben be on a diet. d∼ *adv* d∼ leben NEW D∼ leben, s. Diät. D∼assistent(in) *m(f)* dietician

dich *pron* (*acc of* du) you; (*refl*) yourself

dicht *a* dense; (*dick*) thick; (*undurchlässig*) airtight; (*wasser-*) watertight □ *adv* densely; thickly; (*nahe*) close (bei to). D∼e *f* - density. d∼en¹ *vt* make watertight; (*ab-*) seal

dicht|en² *vi* (*haben*) write poetry □ *vt* write, compose. D∼er(in) *m* -s,- (*f* -,-en)

poet. d∼erisch *a* poetic. D∼ung¹ *f* -,-en poetry; (*Gedicht*) poem

Dichtung² *f* -,-en seal; (*Ring*) washer; (*Auto*) gasket

dick *a* thick, *adv* -ly; (*beleibt*) fat; (*geschwollen*) swollen; (*fam; eng*) close; d∼ werden get fat; d∼ machen be fattening. ein d∼es Fell haben (*fam*) be thick-skinned. D∼e *f* -,-n thickness; (*D∼leibigkeit*) fatness. d∼fellig *a* (*fam*) thick-skinned. d∼flüssig *a* thick; (*Phys*) viscous. D∼kopf *m* (*fam*) stubborn person; einen D∼kopf haben be stubborn. d∼köpfig *a* (*fam*) stubborn

didaktisch *a* didactic

die *def art & pron s.* der

Dieb|(in) *m* -[e]s,-e (*f* -,-nen) thief. d∼isch *a* thieving; (*Freude*) malicious. D∼stahl *m* -[e]s,-e theft; (*geistig*) plagiarism

diejenige *pron s.* derjenige

Diele *f* -,-n floorboard; (*Flur*) hall

dien|en *vi* (*haben*) serve. D∼er *m* -s,- servant; (*Verbeugung*) bow. D∼erin *f* -,-nen maid, servant. d∼lich *a* helpful

Dienst *m* -[e]s,-e service; (*Arbeit*) work; (*Amtsausübung*) duty; außer D∼ off duty; (*pensioniert*) retired; D∼ haben work; (*Soldat, Arzt:*) be on duty; der D∼ habende Arzt the duty doctor; jdm einen schlechten D∼ erweisen do s.o. a disservice

Dienstag *m* Tuesday. d∼s *adv* on Tuesdays

Dienst|alter *nt* seniority. d∼bereit *a* obliging; (*Apotheke*) open. D∼bote *m* servant. d∼eifrig *a* zealous, *adv* -ly. d∼frei *a* d∼freier Tag day off; d∼frei haben have time off; (*Soldat, Arzt:*) be off duty. D∼grad *m* rank. d∼habend *a* NEW D∼ habend, s. Dienst. D∼leistung *f* service. d∼lich *a* official □ *adv* d∼lich verreist away on business. D∼mädchen *nt* maid. D∼reise *f* business trip. D∼stelle *f* office. D∼stunden *fpl* office hours. D∼weg *m* official channels *pl*

dies *inv pron* this. d∼bezüglich *a* relevant □ *adv* regarding this matter. d∼e(r,s) *pron* this; (*pl*) these; (*substantivisch*) this [one]; (*pl*) these; d∼e Nacht tonight; (*letzte*) last night

Diesel *m* -[s],- (*fam*) diesel

dieselbe *pron s.* derselbe

Diesel|kraftstoff *m* diesel [oil]. D∼motor *m* diesel engine

diesig *a* hazy, misty

dies|mal *adv* this time. d∼seits *adv & prep* (+ *gen*) this side (of)

Dietrich *m* -s,-e skeleton key

Diffam|ation /-'tsi̯o:n/ f - defamation. **d~ierend** a defamatory

Differential /-'tsi̯a:l/ nt -s,-e (NEW) Differenzial

Differenz f -,-en difference. **D~ial** nt -s,-e differential. **d~ieren** vt/i (haben) differentiate (zwischen + dat between)

Digital- pref digital. **D~uhr** f digital clock/watch

Dikt|at nt -[e]s,-e dictation. **D~ator** m -s,-en /-'to:rən/ dictator. **d~atorisch** a dictatorial. **D~atur** f -,-en dictatorship. **d~ieren** vt/i (haben) dictate

Dilemma nt -s,-s dilemma

Dilettant|(in) m -en,-en (f -,-nen) dilettante. **d~isch** a amateurish

Dill m -s dill

Dimension f -,-en dimension

Ding nt -[e]s,-e & (fam) -er thing; guter **D~e** sein be cheerful; vor allen **D~en** above all

Dinghi /'dɪŋi/ nt -s,-s dinghy

Dinosaurier /-i̯ɐ/ m -s,- dinosaur

Diözese f -,-n diocese

Diphtherie f - diphtheria

Diplom nt -s,-e diploma; (Univ) degree

Diplomat m -en,-en diplomat. **D~ie** f - diplomacy. **d~isch** a diplomatic, adv -ally

dir pron (dat of du) [to] you; (refl) yourself; ein Freund von dir a friend of yours

direkt a adv directly; (wirklich) really. **D~ion** /-'tsi̯o:n/ f - management; (Vorstand) board of directors. **D~or** m -s,-en /-'to:rən/, **D~orin** f -,-nen director; (Bank-, Theater-) manager; (Sch) head; (Gefängnis) governor. **D~übertragung** f live transmission

Dirig|ent m -en,-en (Mus) conductor. **d~ieren** vt direct; (Mus) conduct

Dirndl nt -s,- dirndl [dress]

Dirne f -,-n prostitute

Diskant m -s,-e (Mus) treble

Diskette f -,-n floppy disk

Disko f -,-s (fam) disco. **D~thek** f -,-en discothèque

Diskrepanz f -,-en discrepancy

diskret a discreet, adv -ly. **D~ion** /-'tsi̯o:n/ f - discretion

diskriminier|en vt discriminate against. **D~ung** f - discrimination

Diskus m -,-se & Disken discus

Disku|ssion f -,-en discussion. **d~tieren** vt/i (haben) discuss

disponieren vi (haben) make arrangements; **d~** [können] über (+ acc) have at one's disposal

Disput m -[e]s,-e dispute

Disqualifi|kation /-'tsi̯o:n/ f disqualification. **d~zieren** vt disqualify

Dissertation /-'tsi̯o:n/ f -,-en dissertation

Dissident m -en,-en dissident

Dissonanz f -,-en dissonance

Distanz f -,-en distance. **d~ieren (sich)** vr dissociate oneself (von from). **d~iert** a aloof

Distel f -,-n thistle

distinguiert /dɪstɪŋ'gi:ɐt/ a distinguished

Disziplin f -,-en discipline. **d~arisch** a disciplinary. **d~iert** a disciplined

dito adv ditto

diverse attrib a pl various

Divid|ende f -,-en dividend. **d~ieren** vt divide (durch by)

Division f -,-en division

DJH abbr (Deutsche Jugendherberge) [German] youth hostel

DM abbr (Deutsche Mark) DM

doch conj & adv but; (dennoch) yet; (trotzdem) after all; wenn d~ ...! if only ...! nicht d~! don't [do that]! er kommt d~? he is coming, isn't he? kommst du nicht? —d~! aren't you coming?—yes, I am!

Docht m -[e]s,-e wick

Dock nt -s,-s dock. **d~en** vt/i (haben) dock

Dogge f -,-n Great Dane

Dogma nt -s,-men dogma. **d~atisch** a dogmatic, adv -ally

Dohle f -,-n jackdaw

Doktor m -s,-en /-'to:rən/ doctor. **D~arbeit** f [doctoral] thesis. **D~würde** f doctorate

Doktrin f -,-en doctrine

Dokument nt -[e]s,-e document. **D~arbericht** m documentary. **D~arfilm** m documentary film

Dolch m -[e]s,-e dagger

doll a (fam) fantastic; (schlimm) awful □ adv beautifully; (sehr) very; (schlimm) badly

Dollar m -s,- dollar

dolmetsch|en vt/i (haben) interpret. **D~er(in)** m -s,- (f -,-nen) interpreter

Dom m -[e]s,-e cathedral

domin|ant a dominant. **d~ieren** vi (haben) dominate; (vorherrschen) predominate

Domino nt -s,-s dominoes sg. **D~stein** m domino

Dompfaff m -en,-en bullfinch

Donau f - Danube

Donner m -s thunder. **d~n** vi (haben) thunder

Donnerstag *m* Thursday. d~s *adv* on Thursdays

Donnerwetter *nt* (*fam*) telling-off; (*Krach*) row ◻ *int* /'--'--/ wow! (*Fluch*) damn it!

doof *a* (*fam*) stupid, *adv* -ly

Doppel *nt* -s,- duplicate; (*Tennis*) doubles *pl*. D~bett *nt* double bed. D~decker *m* -s,- doubledecker [bus]. d~deutig *a* ambiguous. D~gänger *m* -s,- double. D~kinn *nt* double chin. D~name *m* double-barrelled name. D~punkt *m* (*Gram*) colon. D~schnitte *f* sandwich. d~sinnig *a* ambiguous. D~stecker *m* two-way adaptor. d~t *a* double; (*Boden*) false; in d~ter Ausfertigung in duplicate; die d~te Menge twice the amount ◻ *adv* doubly; (*zweimal*) twice; d~t so viel twice as much. D~zimmer *nt* double room

Dorf *nt* -[e]s,¨er village. D~bewohner *m* villager

dörflich *a* rural

Dorn *m* -[e]s,-en thorn. d~ig *a* thorny

Dörrobst *nt* dried fruit

Dorsch *m* -[e]s,-e cod

dort *adv* there; d~ drüben over there. d~her *adv* [von] d~her from there. d~hin *adv* there. d~ig *a* local

Dose *f* -,-n tin, can; (*Schmuck-*) box

dösen *vi* (*haben*) doze

Dosen|milch *f* evaporated milk. D~öffner *m* tin *or* can opener

dosieren *vt* measure out

Dosis *f* -, Dosen dose

Dotter *m* & *nt* -s,- [egg] yolk

Dozent(in) *m* -en,-en (*f* -,-nen) (*Univ*) lecturer

Dr. *abbr* (Doktor) Dr

Drache *m* -n,-n dragon. D~n *m* -s,- kite; (*fam: Frau*) dragon. D~nfliegen *nt* hanggliding. D~nflieger *m* hang-glider

Draht *m* -[e]s,¨e wire; auf D~ (*fam*) on the ball. d~ig *a* (*fig*) wiry. D~seilbahn *f* cable railway

drall *a* plump; (*Frau*) buxom

Dram|a *nt* -s,-men drama. D~atik *f* - drama. D~atiker *m* -s,- dramatist. d~atisch *a* dramatic, *adv* -ally. d~atisieren *vt* dramatize

dran *adv* (*fam*) = daran; gut/schlecht d~ sein be well off/in a bad way; ich bin d~ it's my turn

Dränage /-'na:ʒə/ *f* - drainage

Drang *m* -[e]s urge; (*Druck*) pressure

dräng|eln *vt/i* (*haben*) push; (*bedrängen*) pester. d~en *vt* push; (*bedrängen*) urge; sich d~en crowd (um round) ◻ *vi* (*haben*)

push; (*eilen*) be urgent; (*Zeit:*) press; d~en auf (+ *acc*) press for

dran|halten† (sich) *vr sep* hurry. d~kommen† *vi sep* (*sein*) have one's turn; wer kommt dran? whose turn is it?

drapieren *vt* drape

drastisch *a* drastic, *adv* -ally

drauf *adv* (*fam*) = darauf; d~ und dran sein be on the point (etw zu tun of doing sth). D~gänger *m* -s,- daredevil. d~gängerisch *a* reckless

draus *adv* (*fam*) = daraus

draußen *adv* outside; (*im Freien*) out of doors

drechseln *vt* (*Techn*) turn

Dreck *m* -s dirt; (*Morast*) mud; (*fam: Kleinigkeit*) trifle; in den D~ ziehen (*fig*) denigrate. d~ig *a* dirty; muddy

Dreh *m* -s (*fam*) knack; den D~ heraushaben have got the hang of it. D~bank *f* lathe. D~bleistift *m* propelling pencil. D~buch *nt* screenplay, script. D~en *vt* turn; (*im Kreis*) rotate; (*verschlingen*) twist; roll (*Zigarette*); shoot (*Film*); lauter/ leiser d~en turn up/down; sich d~en turn; (*im Kreis*) rotate; (*schnell*) spin; (*Wind:*) change; sich d~en um revolve around; (*sich handeln*) be about ◻ *vi* (*haben*) turn; (*Wind:*) change; an etw (*dat*) d~en turn sth. D~orgel *f* barrel organ. D~stuhl *m* swivel chair. D~tür *f* revolving door. D~ung *f* -,-en turn; (*im Kreis*) rotation. D~zahl *f* number of revolutions

drei *inv a*, D~ *f* -,-en three; (*Sch*) ≈ pass. D~eck *nt* -[e]s,-e triangle. d~eckig *a* triangular. D~einigkeit *f* - die [Heilige] D~einigkeit the [Holy] Trinity. d~erlei *inv a* three kinds of ◻ *pron* three things. d~fach *a* triple; in d~facher Ausfertigung in triplicate. D~faltigkeit *f* - = D~einigkeit. d~mal *adv* three times. D~rad *nt* tricycle

dreißig *inv a* thirty. d~ste(r,s) *a* thirtieth

dreist *a* impudent, *adv* -ly; (*verwegen*) audacious, *adv* -ly. D~igkeit *f* - impudence; audacity

dreiviertel *inv a* (NEW) drei viertel, s. viertel. D~stunde *f* three-quarters of an hour

dreizehn *inv a* thirteen. d~te(r,s) *a* thirteenth

dreschen† *vt* thresh

dress|ieren *vt* train. D~ur *f* - training

dribbeln *vi* (*haben*) dribble

Drill *m* -[e]s (*Mil*) drill. d~en *vt* drill

Drillinge *mpl* triplets

drin *adv* (*fam*) = darin; (*drinnen*) inside

dring|en† *vi* (*sein*) penetrate (in + *acc* into; durch etw sth); (*heraus-*) come (aus out of); d~en auf (+ acc) insist on. d~end a urgent, adv -ly. d~lich a urgent. D~lichkeit f -. urgency

Drink m -[s],-s [alcoholic] drink

drinnen adv inside; (im Haus) indoors

dritt adv zu d~ in threes; wir waren zu d~ there were three of us. d~e(r,s) a third; ein D~er a third person. d~el inv a third; ein d~el Apfel a third of an apple. D~el nt -s,- third. d~ens adv thirdly. d~rangig a third-rate

Droge f -,-n drug. D~enabhängige(r) m/f drug addict. D~erie f -,-n chemist's shop, (Amer) drugstore. D~ist m -en,-en chemist

drohen vi (haben) threaten (jdm s.o.). d~d a threatening; (Gefahr) imminent

dröhnen vi (haben) resound; (tönen) boom

Drohung f -,-en threat

drollig a funny; (seltsam) odd

Drops m -,- [fruit] drop

Droschke f -,-n cab

Drossel f -,-n thrush

drosseln vt (Techn) throttle; (fig) cut back

drüb|en adv over there. d~er adv (fam) = darüber

Druck[1] m -[s],-e pressure; unter D~ setzen (fig) pressurize

Druck[2] m -[e]s,-e printing; (Schrift, Reproduktion) print. D~buchstabe m block letter

Drückeberger m -s,- shirker

drucken vt print

drücken vt/i (haben) press; (aus-) squeeze; (Schuh:) pinch; (umarmen) hug; (fig: belasten) weigh down; Preise d~ force down prices; (an Tür) d~ push; sich d~ (fam) make oneself scarce; sich d~ vor (+ dat) (fam) shirk. d~d a heavy; (schwül) oppressive

Drucker m -s,- printer

Drücker m -s,- push-button; (Tür-) door knob

Druckerei f -,-en printing works

Druck|fehler m misprint. D~knopf m press-stud; (Drücker) push-button. D~luft f compressed air. D~sache f printed matter. D~schrift f type; (Veröffentlichung) publication; in D~schrift in block letters pl

drucksen vi (haben) hum and haw

Druck|stelle f bruise. D~taste f push-button. D~topf m pressure-cooker

drum adv (fam) = darum

drunter adv (fam) = darunter; alles geht d~ und drüber (fam) everything is topsy-turvy

Drüse f -,-n (Anat) gland

Dschungel m -s,- jungle

du pron (familiar address) you; auf Du und Du (auf du und du) on familiar terms

Dübel m -s,- plug

duck|en vt duck; (fig: demütigen) humiliate; sich d~en duck; (fig) cringe. D~mäuser m -s,- moral coward

Dudelsack m bagpipes pl

Duell nt -s,-e duel

Duett nt -s,-e [vocal] duet

Duft m -[e]s,-e fragrance, scent; (Aroma) aroma. d~en vi (haben) smell (nach of). d~ig a fine; (zart) delicate

duld|en vt tolerate; (erleiden) suffer ◻ vi (haben) suffer. d~sam a tolerant

dumm a (dümmer, dümmst) stupid, adv -ly; (unklug) foolish, adv -ly; (fam: lästig) awkward; wie d~! what a nuisance! der D~e sein (fig) be the loser. d~erweise adv stupidly; (leider) unfortunately. D~heit f -,-en stupidity; (Torheit) foolishness; (Handlung) folly. D~kopf m (fam) fool.

dumpf a dull, adv -y; (muffig) musty. d~ig a musty

Düne f -,-n dune

Dung m -s manure

Düng|emittel nt fertilizer. d~en vt fertilize. D~er m -s,- fertilizer

dunk|el a dark; (vage) vague, adv -ly; (fragwürdig) shady; d~les Bier brown ale; im D~eln in the dark

Dünkel m -s conceit

dunkel|blau a dark blue. d~braun a dark brown

dünkelhaft a conceited

Dunkel|heit f -. darkness. D~kammer f dark-room. d~n vi (haben) get dark. d~rot a dark red

dünn a thin, adv -ly; (Buch) slim; (spärlich) sparse; (schwach) weak

Dunst m -es,-e mist, haze; (Dampf) vapour

dünsten vt steam

dunstig a misty, hazy

Dünung f -. swell

Duo nt -s,-s [instrumental] duet

Duplikat nt -[e]s,-e duplicate

Dur nt -. (Mus) major [key]; in A-Dur in A major

durch prep (+ acc) through; (mittels) by; [geteilt] d~ (Math) divided by ◻ adv die Nacht d~ throughout the night; sechs Uhr d~ (fam) gone six o'clock; d~ und d~ nass wet through

durcharbeiten vt sep work through; sich d~ work one's way through

durchaus adv absolutely; d~ nicht by no means

durchbeißen† vt sep bite through

durchblättern vt sep leaf through

durchblicken vi sep (haben) look through; d∼ lassen (fig) hint at

Durchblutung f circulation

durchbohren vt insep pierce

durchbrechen†[1] vt/i sep (haben) break [in two]

durchbrechen†[2] vt insep break through; break (Schallmauer)

durchbrennen† vi sep (sein) burn through; (Sicherung:) blow; (fam: weglaufen) run away

durchbringen† vt sep get through; (verschwenden) squander; (versorgen) support; sich d∼ mit make a living by

Durchbruch m breakthrough

durchdacht a gut d∼ well thought out

durchdrehen v sep ◻ vt mince ◻ vi (haben/sein) d∼ (fam) go crazy

durchdringen†[1] vt insep penetrate

durchdringen†[2] vi sep (sein) penetrate; (sich durchsetzen) get one's way. d∼d a penetrating; (Schrei) piercing

durcheinander adv in a muddle; (Person) confused; d∼ bringen muddle [up]; confuse (Person); d∼ geraten get mixed up; d∼ reden all talk at once. D∼ nt -s muddle. d∼bringen† vt sep (NEW) d∼ bringen, s. durcheinander. d∼geraten† vi sep (sein) (NEW) d∼ geraten, s. durcheinander. d∼reden vi sep (haben) (NEW) d∼ reden, s. durcheinander

durchfahren†[1] vi sep (sein) drive through; (Zug:) go through

durchfahren†[2] vt insep drive/go through; jdn d∼ (Gedanke:) flash through s.o.'s mind

Durchfahrt f journey/drive through; auf der D∼ passing through; 'D∼ verboten' 'no thoroughfare'

Durchfall m diarrhoea; (fam: Versagen) flop. d∼en/vi sep (sein) fall through; (fam: versagen) flop; (bei Prüfung) fail

durchfliegen†[1] vi sep (sein) fly through; (fam: durchfallen) fail

durchfliegen†[2] vt insep fly through; (lesen) skim through

durchfroren a frozen

Durchfuhr f - (Comm) transit

durchführ|bar a feasible. d∼en vt sep carry out

Durchgang m passage; (Sport) round; 'D∼ verboten' 'no entry'. D∼sverkehr m through traffic

durchgeben† vt sep pass through; (übermitteln) transmit; (Radio, TV) broadcast

durchgebraten a gut d∼ well done

durchgehen† v sep ◻ vi (sein) go through; (davonlaufen) run away; (Pferd:) bolt; jdm etw d∼ lassen let s.o. get away with sth ◻ vt go through. d∼d a continuous, adv -ly; d∼d geöffnet open all day; d∼der Wagen/Zug through carriage/train

durchgreifen† vi sep (haben) reach through; (vorgehen) take drastic action. d∼d a drastic

durchhalte|n† v sep (fig) ◻ vi (haben) hold out ◻ vt keep up. D∼vermögen nt stamina

durchhängen† vi sep (haben) sag

durchkommen† vi sep (sein) come through; (gelangen, am Telefon) get through; (bestehen) pass; (überleben) pull through; (finanziell) get by (mit on)

durchkreuzen vt insep thwart

durchlassen† vt sep let through

durchlässig a permeable; (undicht) leaky

durchlaufen†[1] v sep ◻ vi (sein) run through ◻ vt wear out

durchlaufen†[2] vt insep pass through

Durchlauferhitzer m -s,- geyser

durchleben vt insep live through

durchlesen† vt sep read through

durchleuchten vt insep X-ray

durchlöchert a riddled with holes

durchmachen vt sep go through; (erleiden) undergo; have (Krankheit)

Durchmesser m -s,- diameter

durchnässt (durchnäßt) a wet through

durchnehmen† vt sep (Sch) do

durchnummeriert (durchnumeriert) a numbered consecutively

durchpausen vt sep trace

durchqueren vt insep cross

Durchreiche f -,-n (serving) hatch. d∼n vt sep pass through

Durchreise f journey through; auf der D∼ passing through. d∼n vi sep (sein) pass through

durchreißen† vt/i sep (sein) tear

durchs adv = durch das

Durchsage f -,-n announcement. d∼n vt sep announce

durchschauen vt insep (fig) see through

durchscheinend a translucent

Durchschlag m carbon copy; (Culin) colander. d∼en†[1] v sep ◻ vt (Culin) rub through a sieve; sich d∼en (fig) struggle through ◻ vi (sein) (Sicherung:) blow

durchschlagen†[2] vt insep smash

durchschlagend a (fig) effective; (Erfolg) resounding

durchschneiden† vt sep cut

Durchschnitt *m* average; im D∼ on average. d∼lich *a* average □ *adv* on average. D∼s- *pref* average

Durchschrift *f* carbon copy

durchsehen† *v sep* □ *vi (haben)* see through □ *vt* look through

durchseihen *vt sep* strain

durchsetzen¹ *vt sep* force through; sich d∼ assert oneself; ⟨*Mode:*⟩ catch on

durchsetzen² *vt insep* intersperse; ⟨*in-filtrieren*⟩ infiltrate

Durchsicht *f* check

durchsichtig *a* transparent

durchsickern *vi sep (sein)* seep through; ⟨*Neuigkeit:*⟩ leak out

durchsprechen† *vt sep* discuss

durchstehen† *vt sep (fig)* come through

durchstreichen† *vt sep* cross out

durchsuch|en *vt insep* search. D∼ung *f* -,-en search

durchtrieben *a* cunning

durchwachsen *a* ⟨*Speck:*⟩ streaky; ⟨*fam: gemischt*⟩ mixed

durchwacht *a* sleepless ⟨*Nacht*⟩

durchwählen *vi sep (haben)* ⟨*Teleph*⟩ dial direct

durchweg *adv* without exception

durchweicht *a* soggy

durchwühlen *vt insep* rummage through; ransack ⟨*Haus*⟩

durchziehen† *v sep* □ *vt* pull through □ *vi (sein)* pass through

durchzucken *vt insep (fig)* shoot through; jdn d∼ ⟨*Gedanke:*⟩ flash through s.o.'s mind

Durchzug *m* through draught

dürfen† *vt & v aux* etw [tun] d∼ be allowed to do sth; darf ich? may I? sie darf es nicht sehen she must not see it; ich hätte es nicht tun/sagen d∼ I ought not to have done/said it; das dürfte nicht allzu schwer sein that should not be too difficult

dürftig *a* poor; ⟨*Mahlzeit*⟩ scanty

dürr *a* dry; ⟨*Boden*⟩ arid; ⟨*mager*⟩ skinny. D∼e *f* -,-n drought

Durst *m* -[e]s thirst; D∼ haben be thirsty. d∼en *vi (haben)* be thirsty. d∼ig *a* thirsty

Dusche *f* -,-n shower. d∼n *vi/r (haben)* [sich] d∼n have a shower

Düse *f* -,-n nozzle. D∼nflugzeug *nt* jet

düster *a* gloomy, *adv* -ily; ⟨*dunkel*⟩ dark

Dutzend *nt* -s,-e dozen. d∼weise *adv* by the dozen

duzen *vt* jdn d∼ call s.o. 'du'

Dynam|ik *f* - dynamics *sg*; ⟨*fig*⟩ dynamism. d∼isch *a* dynamic; ⟨*Rente*⟩ index-linked

Dynamit *nt* -es dynamite

Dynamo *m* -s,-s dynamo

Dynastie *f* -,-n dynasty

D-Zug /'de:-/ *m* express [train]

E

Ebbe *f* -,-n low tide

eben *a* level; ⟨*glatt*⟩ smooth; zu e∼er Erde on the ground floor □ *adv* just; ⟨*genau*⟩ exactly; e∼ noch only just; ⟨*gerade vorhin*⟩ just now; das ist es e∼! that's just it! [na] e∼ exactly! E∼bild *nt* image. e∼bürtig *a* equal; jdm e∼bürtig sein be s.o.'s equal

Ebene *f* -,-n ⟨*Geog*⟩ plain; ⟨*Geom*⟩ plane; ⟨*fig: Niveau*⟩ level

eben|falls *adv* also; danke, e∼falls thank you, [the] same to you. E∼holz *nt* ebony. e∼mäßig *a* regular, *adv* -ly. e∼so *adv* just the same; ⟨*ebenso sehr*⟩ just as much; e∼so schön/teuer just as beautiful/expensive; e∼so gut just as good; *adv* just as well; e∼so sehr just as much; e∼so viel just as much/many; e∼so wenig just as little/few; ⟨*noch*⟩ no more. e∼sogut *adv* NEW e∼so gut, *s.* ebenso. e∼sosehr *adv* NEW e∼so sehr, *s.* ebenso. e∼soviel *adv* NEW e∼so viel, *s.* ebenso. e∼sowenig *adv* NEW e∼so wenig, *s.* ebenso

Eber *m* -s,- boar. E∼esche *f* rowan

ebnen *vt* level; ⟨*fig*⟩ smooth

Echo *nt* -s,-s echo. e∼en *vt/i (haben)* echo

echt *a* genuine, real; ⟨*authentisch*⟩ authentic; ⟨*Farbe*⟩ fast; ⟨*typisch*⟩ typical □ *adv* ⟨*fam*⟩ really; typically. E∼heit *f* - authenticity

Eck|ball *m* ⟨*Sport*⟩ corner. E∼e *f* -,-n corner; um die E∼e bringen ⟨*fam*⟩ bump off. e∼ig *a* angular; ⟨*Klammern*⟩ square; ⟨*unbeholfen*⟩ awkward. E∼stein *m* corner-stone. E∼stoß *m* = E∼ball. E∼zahn *m* canine tooth

Ecu,ECU /e'ky:/ *m* -[s],-[s] ecu

edel *a* noble, *adv* -bly; ⟨*wertvoll*⟩ precious; ⟨*fein*⟩ fine. E∼mann *m* (*pl* -leute) nobleman. E∼mut *m* magnanimity. e∼mütig *a* magnanimous, *adv* -ly. E∼stahl *m* stainless steel. E∼stein *m* precious stone

Efeu *m* -s ivy

Effekt *m* -[e]s,-e effect. E∼en *pl* securities. e∼iv *a* actual, *adv* -ly; ⟨*wirksam*⟩ effective, *adv* -ly. e∼voll *a* effective

EG f - *abbr* (Europäische Gemeinschaft) EC

egal *a* das ist mir e~ (*fam*) it's all the same to me □ *adv* e~ wie/wo no matter how/where. e~itär *a* egalitarian

Egge f -,-n harrow

Ego|ismus m - selfishness. E~ist(in) m -en,-en (f -,-nen) egoist. e~istisch *a* selfish, *adv* -ly. e~zentrisch *a* egocentric

eh *adv* (*Aust fam*) anyway; seit eh und je from time immemorial

ehe *conj* before; ehe nicht until

Ehe f -,-n marriage. E~bett *nt* double bed. E~bruch *m* adultery. E~frau f wife. E~leute *pl* married couple *sg*. e~lich *a* marital; (*Recht*) conjugal; (*Kind*) legitimate

ehemal|ig *a* former. e~s *adv* formerly

Ehe|mann m (*pl* -männer) husband. E~paar *nt* married couple

eher *adv* earlier, sooner; (*lieber, vielmehr*) rather; (*mehr*) more

Ehering m wedding ring

ehr|bar *a* respectable. E~e f -,-n honour; jdm E~e machen do credit to s.o. e~en *vt* honour. e~enamtlich *a* honorary □ *adv* in an honorary capacity. E~endoktorat *nt* honorary doctorate. E~engast *m* guest of honour. e~enhaft *a* honourable, *adv* -bly. e~enmann *m* (*pl* -männer) man of honour. E~enmitglied *nt* honorary member. e~enrührig *a* defamatory. E~enrunde f lap of honour. E~ensache f point of honour. e~enwert *a* honourable. E~enwort *nt* word of honour. e~erbietig *a* deferential, *adv* -ly. E~erbietung f - deference. E~furcht f reverence; (*Scheu*) awe. e~fürchtig *a* reverent, *adv* -ly. E~gefühl *nt* sense of honour. E~geiz *m* ambition. e~geizig *a* ambitious. e~lich *a* honest, *adv* -ly; e~lich gesagt to be honest. E~lichkeit f - honesty. e~los *a* dishonourable. e~sam *a* respectable. e~würdig *a* venerable; (*als Anrede*) Reverend

Ei *nt* -[e]s,-er egg

Eibe f -,-n yew

Eiche f -,-n oak. E~l f -,-n acorn. E~lhäher *m* -s,- jay

eichen *vt* standardize

Eichhörnchen *nt* -s,- squirrel

Eid m -[e]s,-e oath

Eidechse f -,-n lizard

eidlich *a* sworn □ *adv* on oath

Eidotter *m* & *nt* egg yolk

Eier|becher m egg-cup. E~kuchen m pancake; (*Omelett*) omelette. E~schale f eggshell. E~schnee *m* beaten egg-white. E~stock *m* ovary. E~uhr f egg-timer

Eifer m -s eagerness; (*Streben*) zeal. E~sucht f jealousy. e~süchtig *a* jealous, *adv* -ly

eiförmig *a* egg-shaped; (*oval*) oval

eifrig *a* eager, *adv* -ly; (*begeistert*) keen, *adv* -ly

Eigelb *nt* -[e]s,-e [egg] yolk

eigen *a* own; (*typisch*) characteristic (*dat* of); (*seltsam*) odd, *adv* -ly; (*genau*) particular. E~art f peculiarity. e~artig *a* peculiar, *adv* -ly; (*seltsam*) odd. E~brötler m -s,- crank. e~händig *a* personal, *adv* -ly; (*Unterschrift*) own. E~heit f -,-en peculiarity. e~mächtig *a* high-handed; (*unbefugt*) unauthorized □ *adv* high-handedly; without authority. E~name *m* proper name. E~nutz *m* self-interest. e~nützig *a* selfish, *adv* -ly. e~s *adv* specially. E~schaft f -,-en quality; (*Phys*) property; (*Merkmal*) characteristic; (*Funktion*) capacity. E~schaftswort *nt* (*pl* -wörter) adjective. E~sinn *m* obstinacy. e~sinnig *a* obstinate, *adv* -ly

eigentlich *a* actual, real; (*wahr*) true □ *adv* actually, really; (*streng genommen*) strictly speaking; wie geht es ihm e~? by the way, how is he?

Eigen|tor *nt* own goal. E~tum *nt* -s property. E~tümer(in) m -s,- (f -,-nen) owner. e~tümlich *a* odd, *adv* -ly; (*typisch*) characteristic. E~tumswohnung f freehold flat. e~willig *a* self-willed; (*Stil*) highly individual

eign|en (sich) *vr* be suitable. E~ung f - suitability

Eil|brief m express letter. E~e f - hurry; E~e haben be in a hurry; (*Sache:*) be urgent. e~en *vi* (*sein*) hurry □ (*haben*) (*drängen*) be urgent. e~ends *adv* hurriedly. e~ig *a* hurried, *adv* -ly; (*dringend*) urgent, *adv* -ly; es e~ig haben be in a hurry. E~zug *m* semi-fast train

Eimer m -s,- bucket; (*Abfall-*) bin

ein¹ *adj* one; e~es Tages/Abends one day/evening; mit jdm in einem Zimmer schlafen sleep in the same room as s.o. □ *indef art* a, (*vor Vokal*) an; so ein such a; was für ein (*Frage*) what kind of a? (*Ausruf*) what a!

ein² *adv* ein und aus in and out; nicht mehr ein noch aus wissen (*fam*) be at one's wits' end

einander *pron* one another

einarbeiten *vt sep* train

einäscher|n *vt sep* reduce to ashes; cremate (*Leiche*). E~ung f -,-en cremation

einatmen *vt/i sep* (*haben*) inhale, breathe in

ein|äugig *a* one-eyed. E~bahnstraße f one-way street

einbalsamieren vt sep embalm

Einband m binding

Einbau m installation; (Montage) fitting. e~en vt sep install; (montieren) fit. E~küche f fitted kitchen

einbegriffen pred a included

einberuf|en† vt sep convene; (Mil) call up, (Amer) draft. E~ung f call-up, (Amer) draft

Einbettzimmer nt single room

einbeulen vt sep dent

einbeziehen† vt sep [mit] e~ include; (berücksichtigen) take into account

einbiegen† vi sep (sein) turn

einbild|en vt sep sich (dat) etw e~en imagine sth; sich (dat) viel e~en be conceited. E~ung f imagination; (Dünkel) conceit. E~ungskraft f imagination

einbläuen vt sep jdm etw e~ (fam) drum sth into s.o.

einblenden vt sep fade in

einbleuen vt sep (NEW) einbläuen

Einblick m insight

einbrech|en vi sep (haben/sein) break in; bei uns ist eingebrochen worden we have been burgled □ (sein) set in; (Nacht:) fall. E~er m burglar

einbring|en† vt sep get in; bring in ⟨Geld⟩; das bringt nichts ein it's not worth while. e~lich a profitable

Einbruch m burglary; bei E~ der Nacht at nightfall

einbürger|n vt sep naturalize; sich e~n become established. E~ung f - naturalization

Ein|buße f loss (an + dat of). e~büßen vt sep lose

einchecken /-tʃɛkən/ vt/i sep (haben) check in

eindecken (sich) vr sep stock up

eindeutig a unambiguous; (deutlich) clear, adv -ly

eindicken vt sep (Culin) thicken

eindring|en† vi sep (sein) e~en in (+ acc) penetrate into; (mit Gewalt) force one's/ ⟨Wasser:⟩ its way into; (Mil) invade; auf jdn e~en (fig) press s.o.; (bittend) plead with s.o. e~lich a urgent, adv -ly. E~ling m -s,-e intruder

Eindruck m impression; E~ machen impress (auf jdn s.o.)

eindrücken vt sep crush

eindrucksvoll a impressive

ein|e(r,s) pron one; (jemand) someone; (man) one, you; e~er von uns one of us; es macht e~en müde it makes you tired

einebnen vt sep level

eineiig a ⟨Zwillinge⟩ identical

eineinhalb inv a one and a half; e~ Stunden an hour and a half

Einelternfamilie f one-parent family

einengen vt sep restrict

Einer m -s,- (Math) unit. e~ pron s. eine(r,s). e~lei inv a □ attrib a one kind of; (eintönig, einheitlich) the same □ pred a (fam) immaterial; es ist mir e~lei it's all the same to me. E~lei nt -s monotony. e~seits adv on the one hand

einfach a simple, adv -ly; (Essen) plain; ⟨Faden, Fahrt, Fahrkarte⟩ single; e~er Soldat private. E~heit f - simplicity

einfädeln vt sep thread; (fig: arrangieren) arrange; sich e~ (Auto) filter in

einfahr|en v sep □ vi (sein) arrive; (Zug:) pull in □ vt (Auto) run in; die Ernte e~en get in the harvest. E~t f arrival; (Eingang) entrance, way in; (Auffahrt) drive; (Autobahn-) access road; keine E~t no entry

Einfall m idea; (Mil) invasion. e~en† vt sep (sein) collapse; (eindringen) invade; (einstimmen) join in; jdm e~en occur to s.o.; sein Name fällt mir nicht ein I can't think of his name; was fällt ihm ein! what does he think he is doing! e~sreich a imaginative

Einfalt f - naïvety

einfältig a simple; (naiv) naïve

Einfaltspinsel m simpleton

einfangen† vt sep catch

einfarbig a of one colour; ⟨Stoff, Kleid⟩ plain

einfass|en vt sep edge; set ⟨Edelstein⟩. E~ung f border, edging

einfetten vt sep grease

einfinden† (sich) vr sep turn up

einfließen† vi sep (sein) flow in

einflößen vt sep jdm etw e~ give s.o. sips of sth; jdm Angst e~ (fig) frighten s.o.

Einfluss (Einfluß) m influence. e~reich a influential

einförmig a monotonous, adv -ly. E~keit f - monotony

einfried[ig]|en vt sep enclose. E~ung f -,-en enclosure

einfrieren† vt/i sep (sein) freeze

einfügen vt sep insert; (einschieben) interpolate; sich e~ fit in

einfühl|en (sich) vr sep empathize (in + acc with). e~sam a sensitive

Einfuhr f -,-en import

einführ|en vt sep introduce; (einstecken) insert; (einweisen) initiate; (Comm) import. e~end a introductory. E~ung f introduction; (Einweisung) initiation

Eingabe f petition; (Computer) input

Eingang *m* entrance, way in; (*Ankunft*) arrival

eingebaut *a* built-in; ⟨*Schrank*⟩ fitted

eingeben† *vt sep* hand in; (*einflößen*) give (jdm s.o.); ⟨*Computer*⟩ feed in

eingebildet *a* imaginary; (*überheblich*) conceited

Eingeborene(r) *m/f* native

Eingebung *f* -,-en inspiration

eingedenk *prep* (+ *gen*) mindful of

eingefleischt *a* e~er Junggeselle confirmed bachelor

eingehakt *adv* arm in arm

eingehen† *v sep* □ *vi* (*sein*) come in; (*ankommen*) arrive; (*einlaufen*) shrink; ⟨*sterben*⟩ die; ⟨*Zeitung, Firma:*⟩ fold; auf etw⟨*acc*⟩ e~ go into sth; (*annehmen*) agree to sth □ *vt* enter into; contract ⟨*Ehe*⟩; make ⟨*Wette*⟩; take ⟨*Risiko*⟩. e~d *a* detailed; (*gründlich*) thorough, *adv* -ly

eingelegt *a* inlaid; (*Culin*) pickled; (*mariniert*) marinaded

eingemacht *a* (*Culin*) bottled

eingenommen *pred a* (*fig*) taken (von with); prejudiced (gegen against); von sich e~ conceited

eingeschneit *a* snowbound

eingeschrieben *a* registered

Einge|ständnis *nt* admission. e~**stehen†** *vt sep* admit

eingetragen *a* registered

Eingeweide *pl* bowels, entrails

eingewöhnen (sich) *vr sep* settle in

eingießen† *vt sep* pour in; (*einschenken*) pour

eingleisig *a* single-track

einglieder|n *vt sep* integrate. E~**ung** *f* integration

eingraben† *vt sep* bury

eingravieren *vt sep* engrave

eingreifen† *vi sep* (*haben*) intervene. E~**nt** -s intervention

Eingriff *m* intervention; (*Med*) operation

einhaken *vt/r sep* jdn e~ *od* sich bei jdm e~ take s.o.'s arm

einhalten† *v sep* □ *vt* keep; (*befolgen*) observe □ *vi* (*haben*) stop

einhändigen *vt sep* hand in

einhängen *v sep* □ *vt* hang; put down ⟨*Hörer*⟩; sich bei jdm e~ take s.o.'s arm □ *vi* (*haben*) hang up

einheimisch *a* local; (*eines Landes*) native; (*Comm*) home-produced. E~e(r) *m/f* local; native

Einheit *f* -,-en unity (*Maß-, Mil*) unit. e~lich *a* uniform, *adv* -ly; (*vereinheitlicht*) standard. E~spreis *m* standard price; (*Fahrpreis*) flat fare

einhellig *a* unanimous, *adv* -ly

einholen *vt sep* catch up with; (*aufholen*) make up for; (*erbitten*) seek; (*einkaufen*) buy; e~ gehen go shopping

einhüllen *vt sep* wrap

einhundert *inv a* one hundred

einig *a* united; [sich (*dat*)] e~ werden/sein come to an/be in agreement

einig|e(r,s) *pron* some; (*ziemlich viel*) quite a lot of; (*substantivisch*) e~e *pl* some; (*mehrere*) several; (*ziemlich viele*) quite a lot; e~es sg some things; vor e~er Zeit some time ago. e~emal *adv* (NEW) e~e Mal, s. Mal[1]

einigen *vt* unite; unify ⟨*Land*⟩; sich e~ come to an agreement; (*ausmachen*) agree (auf + *acc* on)

einigermaßen *adv* to some extent; (*ziemlich*) fairly; (*ziemlich gut*) fairly well

Einig|keit *f* - unity; (*Übereinstimmung*) agreement. E~**ung** *f* - unification; (*Übereinkunft*) agreement

einjährig *a* one-year-old; (*ein Jahr dauernd*) one year's . . .; e~e Pflanze annual

einkalkulieren *vt sep* take into account

einkassieren *vt sep* collect

Einkauf *m* purchase; (*Einkaufen*) shopping; Einkäufe machen do some shopping. e~en *vt sep* buy; e~en gehen go shopping. E~skorb *m* shopping/(*im Geschäft*) wire basket. E~stasche *f* shopping bag. E~swagen *m* shopping trolley. E~szentrum *nt* shopping centre

einkehren *vi sep* (*sein*) [in einem Lokal] e~ stop for a meal/drink [at an inn]

einklammern *vt sep* bracket

Einklang *m* harmony; in E~ stehen be in accord (mit with)

einkleben *vt sep* stick in

einkleiden *vt sep* fit out

einklemmen *vt sep* clamp; sich (*dat*) den Finger in der Tür e~ catch one's finger in the door

einkochen *v sep* □ *vi* (*sein*) boil down □ *vt* preserve, bottle

Einkommen *nt* -s income. E~[s]steuer *f* income tax

einkreisen *vt sep* encircle; rot e~ ring in red

Einkünfte *pl* income *sg*; (*Einnahmen*) revenue *sg*

einlad|en† *vt sep* load; (*auffordern*) invite; (*bezahlen für*) treat. e~end *a* inviting. E~ung *f* invitation

Einlage *f* enclosure; (*Schuh-*) arch support; (*Zahn-*) temporary filling;

(*Programm-*) interlude; (*Comm*) investment; (*Bank-*) deposit; Suppe mit E~ soup with noodles/dumplings

Ein|lass *m* -es (**Einlaß** *m* -sses) admittance. e~lassen† *vt sep* let in; run ⟨*Bad, Wasser*⟩; sich auf etw (*acc*)/mit jdm e~lassen get involved in sth/with s.o.

einlaufen† *vi sep* (*sein*) (*ankommen*) arrive; ⟨*Wasser:*⟩ run in; (*schrumpfen*) shrink; [in den Hafen] e~ enter port

einleben (sich) *vr sep* settle in

Einlege|arbeit *f* inlaid work. e~n *vt sep* put in; lay in ⟨*Vorrat*⟩; lodge ⟨*Protest, Berufung*⟩; (*einfügen*) insert; ⟨*Auto*⟩ engage ⟨*Gang*⟩; (*verzieren*) inlay; (*Culin*) pickle; (*marinieren*) marinade; eine Pause e~n have a break. E~sohle *f* insole

einleit|en *vt sep* initiate; (*eröffnen*) begin. e~end *a* introductory. E~ung *f* introduction

einlenken *vi sep* (*haben*) (*fig*) relent

einleuchten *vi sep* (*haben*) be clear (*dat* to). e~d *a* convincing

einliefer|n *vt sep* take (ins Krankenhaus to hospital). E~ung *f* admission

einlösen *vt sep* cash ⟨*Scheck*⟩; redeem ⟨*Pfand*⟩; (*fig*) keep

einmachen *vt sep* preserve

einmal *adv* once; (*eines Tages*) one *or* some day; noch/schon e~ again/before; noch e~ so teuer twice as expensive; auf e~ at the same time; (*plötzlich*) suddenly; nicht e~ not even; es geht nun e~ nicht it's just not possible. E~eins *nt* - [multiplication] tables *pl*. e~ig *a* single; (*einzigartig*) unique; (*fam: großartig*) fantastic, *adv* -ally

einmarschieren *vi sep* (*sein*) march in

einmisch|en (sich) *vr sep* interfere. E~ung *f* interference

einmütig *a* unanimous, *adv* -ly

Einnahme *f* -,-n taking; (*Mil*) capture; E~n *npl* income *sg*; (*Einkünfte*) revenue *sg*; (*Comm*) receipts; (*eines Ladens*) takings

einnehmen† *vt sep* take; have ⟨*Mahlzeit*⟩; (*Mil*) capture; take up ⟨*Platz*⟩; (*fig*) prejudice (gegen against); jdn für sich e~ win s.o. over. e~d *a* engaging

einnicken *vi sep* (*sein*) nod off

Einöde *f* wilderness

einordnen *vt sep* put in its proper place; (*klassifizieren*) classify; sich e~ fit in; (*Auto*) get in lane

einpacken *vt sep* pack; (*einhüllen*) wrap

einparken *vt sep* park

einpauken *vt sep* jdm etw e~ (*fam*) drum sth into s.o.

einpflanzen *vt sep* plant; implant ⟨*Organ*⟩

einplanen *vt sep* allow for

einpräg|en *vt sep* impress ⟨jdm [up]on s.o.); sich (*dat*) etw e~en memorize sth. e~sam *a* easy to remember; ⟨*Melodie*⟩ catchy

einquartieren *vt sep* (*Mil*) billet (bei on); sich in einem Hotel e~ put up at a hotel

einrahmen *vt sep* frame

einrasten *vi sep* (*sein*) engage

einräumen *vt sep* put away; (*zugeben*) admit; (*zugestehen*) grant

einrechnen *vt sep* include

einreden *v sep* □ *vt* jdm/sich (*dat*) etw e~ persuade s.o./oneself of sth □ *vi* (*haben*) auf jdn e~ talk insistently to s.o.

einreib|en† *vt sep* rub (mit with). E~mittel *nt* liniment

einreichen *vt sep* submit; die Scheidung e~ file for divorce

Einreih|er *m* -s,- single-breasted suit. e~ig *a* single-breasted

Einreise *f* entry. e~n *vi sep* (*sein*) enter (nach Irland Ireland). E~visum *nt* entry visa

einreißen† *v sep* □ *vt* tear; (*abreißen*) pull down □ *vi* (*sein*) tear; ⟨*Sitte:*⟩ become a habit

einrenken *vt sep* (*Med*) set

einricht|en *vt sep* fit out; (*möblieren*) furnish; (*anordnen*) arrange; (*Med*) set ⟨*Bruch*⟩; (*eröffnen*) set up; sich e~en furnish one's home; (*sich einschränken*) economize; (*sich vorbereiten*) prepare (auf + *acc* for). E~ung *f* furnishing; (*Möbel*) furnishings *pl*; (*Techn*) equipment; (*Vorrichtung*) device; (*Eröffnung*) setting up; (*Institution*) institution; (*Gewohnheit*) practice. E~ungsgegenstand *m* piece of equipment/(*Möbelstück*) furniture

einrollen *vt sep* roll up; put in rollers ⟨*Haare*⟩

einrosten *vi sep* (*sein*) rust; (*fig*) get rusty

einrücken *v sep* □ *vi* (*sein*) (*Mil*) be called up; (*einmarschieren*) move in □ *vt* indent

eins *inv a & pron* one; noch e~ one other thing; mir ist alles e~ (*fam*) it's all the same to me. E~ *f* -,-en one; (*Sch*) ≈ A

einsam *a* lonely; (*allein*) solitary; (*abgelegen*) isolated. E~keit *f* -loneliness; solitude; isolation

einsammeln *vt sep* collect

Einsatz *m* use; (*Mil*) mission; (*Wett-*) stake; (*E~teil*) insert; im E~ in action. e~bereit *a* ready for action

einschalt|en *vt sep* switch on; (*einschieben*) interpolate; (*fig: beteiligen*) call in; sich e~en (*fig*) intervene. E~quote *f* (*TV*) viewing figures *pl*; ≈ ratings *pl* einschärfen *vt sep* jdm etw e~ impress sth [up]on s.o.

einschätz|en *vt sep* assess; (*bewerten*) rate. E~ung *f* assessment; estimation

einschenken *vt sep* pour

einscheren *vi sep* (*sein*) pull in

einschicken *vt sep* send in

einschieben† *vt sep* push in; (*einfügen*) insert; (*fig*) interpolate

einschiff|en (sich) *vr sep* embark. E~ung *f* - embarkation

einschlafen† *vi sep* (*sein*) go to sleep; (*aufhören*) peter out

einschläfern *vt sep* lull to sleep; (*betäuben*) put out; (*töten*) put to sleep. e~d *a* soporific

Einschlag *m* impact; (*fig: Beimischung*) element. e~en† *v sep* □ *vt* knock in; (*zerschlagen*) smash; (*einwickeln*) wrap; (*falten*) turn up; (*drehen*) turn; take (*Weg*); take up (*Laufbahn*) □ *vi* (*haben*) hit/ (*Blitz:*) strike (in etw *acc* sth); (*zustimmen*) shake hands [on a deal]; (*Erfolg haben*) be a hit; auf jdn e~en beat s.o.

einschlägig *a* relevant

einschleusen *vt sep* infiltrate

einschließ|en† *vt sep* lock in; (*umgeben*) enclose; (*einkreisen*) surround; (*einbeziehen*) include; sich e~en lock oneself in; Bedienung eingeschlossen service included. e~lich *adv* inclusive □ *prep* (+ *gen*) including

einschmeicheln (sich) *vr sep* ingratiate oneself (bei with)

einschnappen *vi sep* (*sein*) click shut; eingeschnappt sein (*fam*) be in a huff

einschneiden† *vt/i sep* (*haben*) [in] etw *acc* e~ cut into sth. e~d *a* (*fig*) drastic, *adv* -ally

Einschnitt *m* cut; (*Med*) incision; (*Lücke*) gap; (*fig*) decisive event

einschränk|en *vt sep* restrict; (*reduzieren*) cut back; sich e~en economize. E~ung *f* -,-en restriction; (*Reduzierung*) reduction; (*Vorbehalt*) reservation

Einschreib|[e]brief *m* registered letter. e~en† *vt sep* enter; register (*Brief*); sich e~en put one's name down; (*sich anmelden*) enrol. E~en *nt* registered letter/packet; als *od* per E~en by registered post

einschreiten† *vi sep* (*sein*) intervene

einschüchter|n *vt sep* intimidate. E~ung *f* - intimidation

einsegn|en *vt sep* (*Relig*) confirm. E~ung *f* -,-en confirmation

einsehen† *vt sep* inspect; (*lesen*) consult; (*begreifen*) see. E~ *nt* -s ein E~ haben show some understanding; (*vernünftig sein*) see reason

einseitig *a* one-sided; (*Pol*) unilateral □ *adv* on one side; (*fig*) one-sidedly; (*Pol*) unilaterally

einsenden† *vt sep* send in

einsetzen *v sep* □ *vt* put in; (*einfügen*) insert; (*verwenden*) use; put on (*Zug*); call out (*Truppen*); (*Mil*) deploy; (*ernennen*) appoint; (*wetten*) stake; (*riskieren*) risk; sich e~ für support □ *vi* (*haben*) start; (*Winter, Regen:*) set in

Einsicht *f* insight; (*Verständnis*) understanding; (*Vernunft*) reason; zur E~ kommen see reason. e~ig *a* understanding; (*vernünftig*) sensible

Einsiedler *m* hermit

einsilbig *a* monosyllabic; (*Person*) taciturn

einsinken† *vi sep* (*sein*) sink in

einspannen *vt sep* harness; jdn e~ (*fam*) rope s.o. in; sehr eingespannt (*fam*) very busy

einsparen *vt sep* save

einsperren *vt sep* shut/(*im Gefängnis*) lock up

einspielen (sich) *vr sep* warm up; gut aufeinander eingespielt sein work well together

einsprachig *a* monolingual

einspringen† *vi sep* (*sein*) step in (für for)

einspritzen *vt sep* inject

Einspruch *m* objection; E~ erheben object; (*Jur*) appeal

einspurig *a* single-track; (*Auto*) single-lane

einst *adv* once; (*Zukunft*) one day

Einstand *m* (*Tennis*) deuce

einstecken *vt sep* put in; post (*Brief*); (*Electr*) plug in; (*fam: behalten*) pocket; (*fam: hinnehmen*) take; suffer (*Niederlage*); etw e~ put sth in one's pocket

einstehen† *vi sep* (*haben*) e~ für vouch for; answer for (*Folgen*)

einsteigen† *vi sep* (*sein*) get in; (*in Bus/Zug*) get on

einstell|en *vt sep* put in; (*anstellen*) employ; (*aufhören*) stop; (*regulieren*) adjust, set; (*Optik*) focus; tune (*Motor, Zündung*); tune to (*Sender*); sich e~en turn up; (*ankommen*) arrive; (*eintreten*) occur; (*Schwierigkeiten:*) arise; sich e~en auf (+ *acc*) adjust to; (*sich vorbereiten*) prepare for. E~ung *f* employment; (*Aufhören*) cessation; (*Regulierung*) adjustment; (*Optik*) focusing; (*TV, Auto*) tuning; (*Haltung*) attitude

Einstieg *m* -[e]s,-e entrance

einstig *a* former

einstimmen *vi sep* ⟨*haben*⟩ join in

einstimmig *a* unanimous, *adv* -ly. E∼keit *f* - unanimity

einstöckig *a* single-storey

einstudieren *vt sep* rehearse

einstufen *vt sep* classify

Ein|sturz *m* collapse. e∼stürzen *vi sep* ⟨*sein*⟩ collapse

einstweil|en *adv* for the time being; (*inzwischen*) meanwhile. e∼ig *a* temporary

eintasten *vt sep* key in

eintauchen *vt/i sep* ⟨*sein*⟩ dip in; (*heftiger*) plunge in

eintauschen *vt sep* exchange

eintausend *inv a* one thousand

einteil|en *vt sep* divide (in + *acc* into); (*Biol*) classify; sich (*dat*) seine Zeit gut e∼en organize one's time well. e∼ig *a* one-piece. E∼ung *f* division; classification

eintönig *a* monotonous, *adv* -ly. E∼keit *f* - monotony

Eintopf *m*, E∼gericht *nt* stew

Ein|tracht *f* - harmony. e∼trächtig *a* harmonious ❑ *adv* in harmony

Eintrag *m* -[e]s, ̈e entry. e∼en† *vt sep* enter; (*Admin*) register; (*einbringen*) bring in; sich e∼en put one's name down

einträglich *a* profitable

Eintragung *f* -,-en registration; (*Eintrag*) entry

eintreffen† *vi sep* ⟨*sein*⟩ arrive; (*fig*) come true; (*geschehen*) happen. E∼ *nt* -s arrival

eintreiben† *vt sep* drive in; (*einziehen*) collect

eintreten† *vi sep* ⟨*sein*⟩ enter; (*geschehen*) occur; in einen Klub e∼ join a club; e∼ für (*fig*) stand up for ❑ *vt* kick in

Eintritt *m* entrance; (*zu Veranstaltung*) admission; (*Beitritt*) joining; (*Beginn*) beginning. E∼skarte *f* [admission] ticket

eintrocknen *vi sep* ⟨*sein*⟩ dry up

einüben *vt sep* practise

einundachtzig *inv a* eighty-one

einverleiben *vt sep* incorporate (*dat* into); sich (*dat*) etw e∼ (*fam*) consume sth

Einvernehmen *nt* -s understanding; (*Übereinstimmung*) agreement; in bestem E∼ on the best of terms

einverstanden *a* e∼ sein agree

Einverständnis *nt* agreement; (*Zustimmung*) consent

Einwand *m* -[e]s, ̈e objection

Einwander|er *m* immigrant. e∼n *vi sep* ⟨*sein*⟩ immigrate. E∼ung *f* immigration

einwandfrei *a* perfect, *adv* -ly, (*untadelig*) impeccable, *adv* -bly; (*eindeutig*) indisputable, *adv* -bly

einwärts *adv* inwards

einwechseln *vt sep* change

einwecken *vt sep* preserve, bottle

Einweg- *pref* non-returnable; ⟨*Feuerzeug*⟩ throw-away

einweichen *vt sep* soak

einweih|en *vt sep* inaugurate; (*Relig*) consecrate; (*einführen*) initiate; (*fam*) use for the first time; in ein Geheimnis e∼en let into a secret. E∼ung *f* -,-en inauguration; consecration; initiation

einweisen† *vt sep* direct; (*einführen*) initiate; ins Krankenhaus e∼ send to hospital

einwenden† *vt sep* etwas e∼ object (gegen to); dagegen hätte ich nichts einzuwenden (*fam*) I wouldn't say no

einwerfen† *vt sep* insert; post ⟨*Brief*⟩; (*Sport*) throw in; (*vorbringen*) interject; (*zertrümmern*) smash

einwickeln *vt sep* wrap [up]

einwillig|en *vi sep* ⟨*haben*⟩ consent, agree (in + *acc* to). E∼ung *f* - consent

einwirken *vi sep* ⟨*haben*⟩ e∼ auf (+ *acc*) have an effect on; (*beeinflussen*) influence

Einwohner|in *m* -s,- /*f* -,-nen inhabitant. E∼zahl *f* population

Einwurf *m* interjection; (*Einwand*) objection; (*Sport*) throw-in; (*Münz-*) slot

Einzahl *f* (*Gram*) singular

einzahl|en *vt sep* pay in. E∼ung *f* payment; (*Einlage*) deposit

einzäunen *vt sep* fence in

Einzel *nt* -s,- (*Tennis*) singles *pl*. E∼bett *nt* single bed. E∼fall *m* individual/(*Sonderfall*) isolated case. E∼gänger *m* -s,- loner. E∼haft *f* solitary confinement. E∼handel *m* retail trade. E∼händler *m* retailer. E∼haus *nt* detached house. E∼heit *f* -,-en detail. E∼karte *f* single ticket. E∼kind *nt* only child

einzeln *a* single, *adv* -ly; (*individuell*) individual, *adv* -ly; (*gesondert*) separate, *adv* -ly; odd ⟨*Handschuh, Socken*⟩; e∼e Fälle some cases. E∼e(r,s) (e∼e(r,s)) *pron* der/die E∼e (e∼e) the individual; ein E∼er (e∼er) a single one; (*Person*) one individual; jeder E∼e (e∼e) every single one; (*Person*) each individual; E∼e (e∼e) *pl* some; im E∼en (e∼en) in detail; ins E∼e (e∼e) gehen go into detail

Einzel|person *f* single person. E∼teil *nt* [component] part E∼zimmer *nt* single room

einziehen† *v sep* ❑ *vt* pull in; draw i ⟨*Atem, Krallen*⟩; (*Zool, Techn*) retract; dent ⟨*Zeile*⟩; (*aus dem Verkehr zie* withdraw; *(beschlagnahmen)* confiscate; *(eintreiben)* collect; *(Erkundigungen)* *(Mil)* call up; *(einfügen)* insert; *(einbauen)* put in; den Kopf e~ duck [one's head] □ *vi* *(sein)* enter; *(umziehen)* move in; *(eindringen)* penetrate

einzig *a* *(einmalig)* unique; *(eine/ keine* e~e Frage a/not a single question; ein e~es Mal only once □ *adv* only; e~ und allein solely. e~artig *a* unique *(unvergleichlich)* unparalleled. e~e(r,s) *(e~e(r,s)) pron* der/die/das E~e (e~e) the only one; ein/kein E~er (e~er) a/not a single one; das E~e (e~e), was mich stört the only thing that bothers me

Einzug *m* entry; *(Umzug)* move (in + *acc* into). E~sgebiet *nt* catchment area

Eis *nt* -es ice; *(Speise-)* ice-cream; Eis am Stiel ice lolly; Eis laufen skate. E~bahn *f* ice rink. E~bär *m* polar bear. E~becher *m* ice-cream sundae. E~bein *nt* *(Culin)* knuckle of pork. E~berg *m* iceberg. E~diele *f* ice-cream parlour

Eisen *nt* -s,- iron. E~bahn *f* railway. E~bahner *m* -s,- railwayman

eisern *a* iron; *(fest)* resolute, *adv* -ly; e~er Vorhang *(Theat)* safety curtain; *(Pol)* Iron Curtain

Eis|fach *nt* freezer compartment. e~gekühlt *a* chilled. e~ig *a* icy. E~kaffee *m* iced coffee. e~kalt *a* ice cold; *(fig)* icy, *adv* -ily. E~kunstlauf *m* figure skating. E~lauf *m* skating. e~laufen† *vi sep* *(sein)* NEW Eis laufen, s. Eis. E~läufer(in) *m(f)* skater. E~pickel *m* ice-axe. E~scholle *f* ice-floe. E~schrank *m* refrigerator. E~vogel *m* kingfisher. E~würfel *m* icecube. E~zapfen *m* icicle. E~zeit *f* ice age

eitel *a* vain; *(rein)* pure. E~keit *f* - vanity

Eiter *m* -s pus. e~n *vi* *(haben)* discharge pus

Eiweiß *nt* -es,-e egg-white; *(Chem)* protein

Ekel[1] *m* -s disgust; *(Widerwille)* revulsion

Ekel[2] *nt* -s,- *(fam)* beast

ekel|erregend *a* nauseating. e~haft *a* nauseating; *(widerlich)* repulsive. e~n *vt/i* *(haben)* mich *od* mir e~t [es] davor it makes me feel sick □ *vr* sich e~n vor (+ *dat*) find repulsive

eklig *a* disgusting, repulsive

Eksta|se *f* - ecstasy. e~tisch *a* ecstatic, *adv* -ally

Ekzem *nt* -s,-e eczema

elasti|sch *a* elastic; *(federnd)* springy; *(fig)* flexible. E~zität *f* - elasticity; flexibility

Elch *m* -[e]s,-e elk

Elefant *m* -en,-en elephant

elegan|t *a* elegant, *adv* -ly. E~z *f* - elegance

elektrifizieren *vt* electrify

Elektri|ker *m* -s,- electrician. e~sch *a* electric, *adv* -ally

elektrisieren *vt* electrify; sich e~ get an electric shock

Elektrizität *f* - electricity. E~swerk *nt* power station

Elektro|artikel *mpl* electrical appliances. E~ode *f* -,-n electrode. E~oherd *m* electric cooker. E~on *nt* -s,-en /-'tro:nən/ electron. E~onik *f* - electronics *sg*. e~onisch *a* electronic

Element *nt* -[e]s,-e element; *(Anbau-)* unit. e~ar *a* elementary

Elend *nt* -s misery; *(Armut)* poverty. e~ *a* miserable, *adv* -bly, wretched, *adv* -ly; *(krank)* poorly; *(gemein)* contemptible; *(fam: schrecklich)* dreadful, *adv* -ly. E~sviertel *nt* slum

elf *inv a*, E~ *f* -,-en eleven

Elfe *f* -,-n fairy

Elfenbein *nt* ivory

Elfmeter *m* *(Fußball)* penalty

elfte(r,s) *a* eleventh

eliminieren *vt* eliminate

Elite *f* -,-n élite

Elixier *nt* -s,-e elixir

Ell[en]bogen *m* elbow

Ellip|se *f* -,-n ellipse. e~tisch *a* elliptical

Elsass (Elsaß) *nt* - Alsace

elsässisch *a* Alsatian

Elster *f* -,-n magpie

elter|lich *a* parental. E~n *pl* parents. E~nhaus *nt* [parental] home. e~nlos *a* orphaned. E~nteil *m* parent

Email /e'maj/ *nt* -s,-s, E~le /e'maljə/ *f* -,-n enamel. e~lieren /ema[l]'ji:rən/ *vt* enamel

Emanzi|pation /-'tsio:n/ *f* - emancipation. e~piert *a* emancipated

Embargo *nt* -s,-s embargo

Emblem *nt* -s,-e emblem

Embryo *m* -s,-s embryo

Emigr|ant(in) *m* -en,-en *(f* -,-nen) emigrant. E~ation /-'tsio:n/ *f* - emigration. e~ieren *vi* *(sein)* emigrate

eminent *a* eminent, *adv* -ly

Emission *f* -,-en emission; *(Comm)* issue

Emotion /-'tsio:n/ *f* -,-en emotion. e~al *a* emotional

Empfang *m* -[e]s,:e reception; *(Erhalt)* receipt; in E~ nehmen receive; *(annehmen)* accept. e~en† *vt* receive; *(Biol)* conceive

Empfäng|er *m* -s,- recipient; *(Post-)* addressee; *(Zahlungs-)* payee; *(Radio, TV)*

receiver. e~lich a receptive/(Med) susceptible (für to). E~nis f - (Biol) conception

Empfängnisverhütung f contraception. E~smittel nt contraceptive

Empfangs|bestätigung f receipt. E~chef m reception manager. E~dame f receptionist. E~halle f [hotel] foyer

empfehl|en† vt recommend; sich e~en be (an)sable; (verabschieden) take one's leave. e~nswert a to be recommended; (ratsam) advisable. E~ung f -,-en recommendation; (Gruß) regards pl

empfind|en† vt feel. ~lich a sensitive (gegen to); (zart) delicate; (Wund) tender; (reizbar) touchy; (hart) severe, adv -ly. E~lichkeit f - sensitivity; delicacy; tenderness; touchiness. e~sam a sensitive; (sentimental) sentimental. E~ung f -,-en sensation; (Regung) feeling

emphatisch a emphatic, adv -ally

empor adv (liter) up[wards]

empören vt incense; sich e~ be indignant; (sich auflehnen) rebel. e~d a outrageous

Empor|kömmling m -s,-e upstart. e~ragen vi sep (haben) rise [up]

empör|t a indignant, adv -ly. E~ung f - indignation; (Auflehnung) rebellion

emsig a busy, adv -ily

Ende nt -s,-n end; (eines Films, Romans) ending; (fam: Stück) bit; E~ Mai at the end of May; zu E~sein/gehen be finished/come to an end; etw zu E~ schreiben finish writing sth; am E~ at the end; (schließlich) in the end; (fam: vielleicht) perhaps; (fam: erschöpft) at the end of one's tether

end|en vi (haben) end. e~gültig a final, adv -ly; (bestimmt) definite, adv -ly

Endivie /-jə/ f -,-n endive

end|lich adv at last, finally; (schließlich) in the end. e~los a endless, adv -ly. E~resultat nt final result. E~spiel nt final. E~spurt m -[e]s final spurt. E~station f terminus. E~ung f -,-en (Gram) ending

Energie f - energy

energisch a resolute, adv -ly; (nachdrücklich) vigorous, adv -ly; e~ werden put one's foot down

eng a narrow; (beengt) cramped; (anliegend) tight; (nah) close, adv -ly; e~ anliegend tight-fitting

Enga|gement /ãgaʒə'mã:/ nt -s,-s (Theat) engagement; (fig) commitment. e~gieren /-'ʒiːrən/ vt (Theat) engage; sich e~gieren become involved; e~giert committed

eng|anliegend a (NEW) e~ anliegend, s. eng. E~e f - narrowness; in die E~e treiben (fig) drive into a corner

Engel m -s,- angel. e~haft a angelic

engherzig a petty

England nt -s England

Engländer m -s,- Englishman; (Techn) monkey-wrench; die E~ the English pl. E~in f -,-nen Englishwoman

englisch a English; auf e~ (NEW) auf E~, s. Englisch. E~ nt -[s] (Lang) English; auf E~ in English

Engpass (Engpaß) m (fig) bottle-neck

en gros /ã'gro:/ adv wholesale

engstirnig a narrowminded

Enkel m -s,- grandson; E~ pl grandchildren. E~in f -,-nen granddaughter. E~kind nt grandchild. E~sohn m grandson. E~tochter f granddaughter

enorm a enormous, adv -ly; (fam: großartig) fantastic

Ensemble /ã'bəl/ nt -s,-s ensemble; (Theat) company

entart|en vi (sein) degenerate. e~et a degenerate

entbehr|en vt do without; (missen) miss. e~lich a dispensable; (überflüssig) superfluous. E~ung f -,-en privation

entbind|en† vt release (von from); (Med) deliver (von of) □ vi (haben) give birth. E~ung f delivery. E~ungsstation f maternity ward

entblöß|en vt bare. e~t a bare

entdeck|en vt discover. E~er m -s,- discoverer; (Forscher) explorer. E~ung f -,-en discovery

Ente f -,-n duck

entehren vt dishonour

enteignen vt dispossess; expropriate ⟨Eigentum⟩

enterben vt disinherit

Enterich m -s,-e drake

entfachen vt kindle

entfallen† vi (sein) not apply; jdm e~ slip from s.o.'s hand; (aus dem Gedächtnis) slip s.o.'s mind; auf jdn e~ be s.o.'s share

entfalt|en vt unfold; (entwickeln) develop; (zeigen) display; sich e~en unfold; develop. E~ung f - development

entfern|en vt remove; sich e~en leave. e~t a distant; (schwach) vague, adv -ly; 2 Kilometer e~t 2 kilometres away; e~t verwandt distantly related; nicht im E~testen (e~testen) not in the least. E~ung f -,-en removal; (Abstand) distance; (Reichweite) range. E~ungsmesser m range-finder

entfesseln vt (fig) unleash

entfliehen† vi (sein) escape

entfremd|en *vt* alienate. E~ung *f* - alienation

entfrosten *vt* defrost

entführ|en *vt* abduct, kidnap; hijack ⟨*Flugzeug*⟩. E~er *m* abductor, kidnapper; hijacker. E~ung *f* abduction, kidnapping; hijacking

entgegen *adv* towards □ *prep* (+ *dat*) contrary to. e~gehen† *vi sep* (*sein*) (+ *dat*) go to meet; ⟨*fig*⟩ be heading for. e~gesetzt *a* opposite; ⟨*gegensätzlich*⟩ opposing. e~halten† *vt sep* ⟨*fig*⟩ object. e~kommen† *vi sep* (*sein*) (+ *dat*) come to meet; ⟨*zukommen auf*⟩ come towards; ⟨*fig*⟩ oblige. E~kommen *nt* -s helpfulness; ⟨*Zugeständnis*⟩ concession. e~kommend *a* approaching; ⟨*Verkehr*⟩ oncoming; ⟨*fig*⟩ obliging. e~nehmen† *vt sep* accept. e~sehen† *vi sep* (*haben*) (+ *dat*) ⟨*fig*⟩ await; ⟨*freudig*⟩ look forward to. e~setzen *vt sep* Widerstand e~setzen (+ *dat*) resist. e~treten† *vi sep* (*sein*) (+ *dat*) ⟨*fig*⟩ confront; ⟨*bekämpfen*⟩ fight. e~wirken *vi sep* (*haben*) (+ *dat*) counteract; ⟨*fig*⟩ oppose

entgegn|en *vt* reply (auf + *acc* to). E~ung *f* -,-en reply

entgehen† *vi sep* (*sein*) (+ *dat*) escape; jdm e~ ⟨*unbemerkt bleiben*⟩ escape s.o.'s notice; sich (*dat*) etw e~ lassen miss sth

entgeistert *a* flabbergasted

Entgelt *nt* -[e]s payment; gegen E~ for money. e~en *vt* jdn etw e~en lassen ⟨*fig*⟩ make s.o. pay for sth

entgleis|en *vi* (*sein*) be derailed; ⟨*fig*⟩ make a gaffe. E~ung *f* -,-en derailment; ⟨*fig*⟩ gaffe

entgleiten† *vi* (*sein*) jdm e~ slip from s.o.'s grasp

entgräten *vt* fillet, bone

Enthaarungsmittel *nt* depilatory

enthalt|en† *vt* contain; in etw (*dat*) e~en sein be contained/ ⟨*eingeschlossen*⟩ included in sth; sich der Stimme e~en ⟨*Pol*⟩ abstain. e~sam *a* abstemious. E~samkeit *f* - abstinence. E~ung *f* ⟨*Pol*⟩ abstention

enthaupten *vt* behead

entheben† *vt* jdn seines Amtes e~ relieve s.o. of his post

enthüll|en *vt* unveil; ⟨*fig*⟩ reveal. E~ung *f* -,-en revelation

Enthusias|mus *m* - enthusiast. E~t *m* -en,-en enthusiast. e~tisch *a* enthusiastic, *adv* -ally

entkernen *vt* stone; core ⟨*Apfel*⟩

entkleid|en *vt* undress; sich e~en undress. E~ungsnummer *f* strip-tease [act]

entkommen† *vi* (*sein*) escape

entkorken *vt* uncork

entkräft|en *vt* weaken; ⟨*fig*⟩ invalidate. E~ung *f* - debility

entkrampfen *vt* relax; sich e~ relax

entladen† *vt* unload; ⟨*Electr*⟩ discharge; sich e~ discharge; ⟨*Gewitter:*⟩ break; ⟨*Zorn:*⟩ explode

entlang *adv* & *prep* (+ *preceding acc or following dat*) along; die Straße e~, der Straße along the road; an etw (*dat*) e~ along sth. e~fahren† *vi sep* (*sein*) drive along. e~gehen† *vi sep* (*sein*) walk along

entlarven *vt* unmask

entlass|en† *vt* dismiss; ⟨*aus Krankenhaus*⟩ discharge; ⟨*aus der Haft*⟩ release; aus der Schule e~en werden leave school. E~ung *f* -,-en dismissal; discharge; release

entlast|en† *vt* relieve the strain on; ease ⟨*Gewissen, Verkehr*⟩; relieve (von of); ⟨*Jur*⟩ exonerate. E~ung *f* - relief; exoneration. E~ungszug *m* relief train

entlaufen† *vi* (*sein*) run away

entledigen (sich) *vr* (+ *gen*) rid oneself of; ⟨*ausziehen*⟩ take off; ⟨*erfüllen*⟩ discharge

entleeren *vt* empty

entlegen *a* remote

entleihen† *vt* borrow (von from)

entlocken *vt* coax (*dat* from)

entlohnen *vt* pay

entlüft|en *vt* ventilate. E~er *m* -s,- extractor fan. E~ung *f* ventilation

entmündigen *vt* declare incapable of managing his own affairs

entmutigen *vt* discourage

entnehmen† *vt* take (*dat* from); ⟨*schließen*⟩ gather (*dat* from)

Entomologie *f* - entomology

entpuppen (sich) *vr* ⟨*fig*⟩ turn out (als etw to be sth)

entrahmt *a* skimmed

entreißen† *vt* snatch (*dat* from)

entrichten *vt* pay

entrinnen† *vi* (*sein*) escape

entrollen *vt* unroll; unfurl ⟨*Fahne*⟩; sich e~ unroll; unfurl

entrüst|en *vt* fill with indignation; sich e~en be indignant (über + *acc* at). e~et *a* indignant, *adv* -ly. E~ung *f* - indignation

entsaft|en *vt* extract the juice from. E~er *m* -s,- juice extractor

entsag|en *vi* (*haben*) (+ *dat*) renounce. E~ung *f* - renunciation

entschädig|en *vt* compensate. E~ung *f* -,-en compensation

entschärfen *vt* defuse

entscheid|en† vt/i (haben) decide; sich e~en decide; (Sache:) be decided. e~end a decisive, adv -ly; (kritisch) crucial. E~ung f decision

entschieden a decided, adv -ly; (fest) firm, adv -ly

entschlafen† vi (sein) (liter) pass away

entschließen† (sich) vr decide, make up one's mind; sich anders e~ change one's mind

entschlossen a determined; (energisch) resolute, adv -ly; kurz e~ without hesitation; (spontan) on the spur of the moment. E~heit f - determination

Entschluss (Entschluß) m decision; einen E~ fassen make a decision

entschlüsseln vt decode

entschuld|bar a excusable. e~igen vt excuse; sich e~igen apologize (bei to); e~igen Sie [bitte]! sorry! (bei Frage) excuse me. E~igung f -,-en apology; (Ausrede) excuse; [jdn] um E~igung bitten apologize [to s.o.]; E~igung! sorry! (bei Frage) excuse me

entsetz|en vt horrify. E~en nt -s horror. e~lich a horrible, adv -bly, (schrecklich) terrible, adv -bly. e~t a horrified

entsinnen† (sich) vr (+ gen) remember

Entsorgung f - waste disposal

entspann|en vt relax; sich e~en relax; (Lage:) ease. E~ung f - relaxation; easing; (Pol) détente

entsprech|en† vi (haben) (+ dat) correspond to; (übereinstimmen) agree with; (nachkommen) comply with. e~end a corresponding; (angemessen) appropriate; (zuständig) relevant □ adv correspondingly; appropriately; (demgemäß) accordingly □ prep (+ dat) in accordance with. E~ung f -,-en equivalent

entspringen† vi (sein) (Fluss:) rise; (fig) arise, spring (dat from); (entfliehen) escape

entstammen vi (sein) come/(abstammen) be descended (dat from)

entsteh|en† vi (sein) come into being; (sich bilden) form; (sich entwickeln) develop; (Brand:) start; (stammen) originate/(sich ergeben) result (aus from). E~ung f - origin; formation; development; (fig) birth

entsteinen vt stone

entstell|en vt disfigure; (verzerren) distort. E~ung f disfigurement; distortion

entstört a (Electr) suppressed

enttäusch|en vt disappoint. E~ung f disappointment

entvölkern vt depopulate

entwaffnen vt disarm. e~d a (fig) disarming

Entwarnung f all-clear [signal]

entwässer|n vt drain. E~ung f - drainage

entweder conj & adv either

entweichen† vi (sein) escape

entweih|en vt desecrate. E~ung f - desecration

entwenden vt steal (dat from)

entwerfen† vt design; (aufsetzen) draft; (skizzieren) sketch

entwert|en vt devalue; (ungültig machen) cancel. E~er m -s,- ticket-cancelling machine. E~ung f devaluation; cancelling

entwick|eln vt develop; sich e~eln develop. E~lung f -,-en development; (Biol) evolution. E~lungsland nt developing country

entwinden† vt wrench (dat from)

entwirren vt disentangle; (fig) unravel

entwischen vi (sein) jdm e~ (fam) give s.o. the slip

entwöhnen vt wean (gen from); cure (Süchtige)

entwürdigend a degrading

Entwurf m design; (Konzept) draft; (Skizze) sketch

entwurzeln vt uproot

entzie|hen† vt take away (dat from); jdm den Führerschein e~hen disqualify s.o. from driving; sich e~hen (+ dat) withdraw from; (entgehen) evade. E~hungskur f treatment for drug/alcohol addiction

entziffern vt decipher

entzück|en vt delight. E~ nt -s delight. e~d a delightful

Entzug m withdrawal; (Vorenthaltung) deprivation. E~serscheinungen fpl withdrawal symptoms

entzünd|en vt ignite; (anstecken) light; (fig: erregen) inflame; sich e~en ignite; (Med) become inflamed. e~et a (Med) inflamed. e~lich a inflammable. E~ung f (Med) inflammation

entzwei a broken. e~en (sich) vr quarrel. e~gehen† vi sep (sein) break

Enzian m -s,-e gentian

Enzyklo|pädie f -,-en encyclopaedia. e~pädisch a encyclopaedic

Enzym nt -s,-e enzyme

Epidemie f -,-n epidemic

Epi|lepsie f - epilepsy. E~leptiker(in) m -s,- (f -,-nen) epileptic. e~leptisch a epileptic

Epilog m -s,-e epilogue

episch a epic

Episode f -,-n episode

Epit**a**ph *nt* -s,-e epitaph

Ep**o**che *f* -,-n epoch. e~machend *a* epoch-making

Epos *nt* -/Epen epic

er *pron* he; ⟨*Ding, Tier*⟩ it

erachten *vt* consider (für nötig necessary). E~ *nt* -s meines E~s in my opinion

erbarmen (sich) *vr* have pity/⟨*Gott:*⟩ mercy ⟨*gen* on). E~ *nt* -s pity; mercy

erb**ä**rmlich *a* wretched, *adv* -ly; ⟨*stark*⟩ terrible, *adv* -bly

erbarmungslos *a* merciless, *adv* -ly

erb**au**|en *vt* build; ⟨*fig*⟩ edify; sich e~en be edified (an + *dat* by); nicht e~t von ⟨*fam*⟩ not pleased about. e~lich *a* edifying

Erbe[1] *m* -n,-n heir

Erbe[2] *nt* -s inheritance; ⟨*fig*⟩ heritage. e~n *vt* inherit

erb**eu**ten *vt* get; ⟨*Mil*⟩ capture

Erbfolge *f* ⟨*Jur*⟩ succession

erb**ie**ten† (sich) *vr* offer (zu to)

Erbin *f* -,-nen heiress

erb**i**tten† *vt* ask for

erb**i**ttert *a* bitter; ⟨*heftig*⟩ fierce, *adv* -ly

erblassen *vi* (sein) turn pale

erblich *a* hereditary

erbl**i**cken *vt* catch sight of

erbl**i**nden *vi* (sein) go blind

erb**o**st *a* angry, *adv* -ily

erbr**e**chen† *vt* vomit □ *vi/r* [sich] e~. vomit. E~ *nt* -s vomiting

Erbschaft *f* -,-en inheritance

Erbse *f* -,-n pea

Erb|stück *nt* heirloom. E~teil *nt* inheritance

Erd|apfel *m* (Aust) potato. E~beben *nt* -s,- earthquake. E~beere *f* strawberry. E~boden *m* ground

Erde *f* -,-n earth; ⟨*Erdboden*⟩ ground; ⟨*Fußboden*⟩ floor; auf der E~ on earth; ⟨*auf dem Boden*⟩ on the ground/floor. e~n *vt* ⟨*Electr*⟩ earth

erd**e**nklich *a* imaginable

Erd|gas *nt* natural gas. E~geschoss (E~geschoß) *nt* ground floor, (Amer) first floor. e~ig *a* earthy. E~kugel *f* globe. E~kunde *f* geography. E~nuss (E~nuß) *f* peanut. E~öl *nt* [mineral] oil. E~reich *nt* soil

erdr**ei**sten (sich) *vr* have the audacity (zu to)

erdr**o**sseln *vt* strangle

erdr**ü**cken *vt* crush to death. e~d *a* ⟨*fig*⟩ overwhelming

Erd|rutsch *m* landslide. E~teil *m* continent

erd**u**lden *vt* endure

er**ei**fern (sich) *vr* get worked up

er**ei**gnen (sich) *vr* happen

Er**ei**gnis *nt* -ses,-se event. e~los *a* uneventful. e~reich *a* eventful

Erem**i**t *m* -en,-en hermit

ererbt *a* inherited

erf**a**hr|en† *vt* learn, hear; ⟨*erleben*⟩ experience □ *a* experienced. E~ung *f* -,-en experience; in E~ung bringen find out

erf**a**ssen *vt* seize; ⟨*begreifen*⟩ grasp; ⟨*einbeziehen*⟩ include; ⟨*aufzeichnen*⟩ record; von einem Auto erfasst werden be struck by a car

erf**i**nd|en† *vt* invent. E~er *m* -s,- inventor. e~erisch *a* inventive. E~ung *f* -,-en invention

Erf**o**lg *m* -[e]s,-e success; ⟨*Folge*⟩ result; E~ haben be successful; E~ versprechend promising. e~en *vi* (sein) take place; ⟨*geschehen*⟩ happen. e~los *a* unsuccessful, *adv* -ly. e~reich *a* successful, *adv* -ly. e~versprechend *a* ⟨NEW⟩E~ versprechend, s. Erfolg

erf**o**rder|lich *a* required, necessary. e~n *vt* require, demand. E~nis *nt* -ses,-se requirement

erf**o**rsch|en *vt* explore; ⟨*untersuchen*⟩ investigate. E~ung *f* exploration; investigation

erfr**eu**|en *vt* please; sich guter Gesundheit e~en enjoy good health. e~lich *a* pleasing, gratifying; ⟨*willkommen*⟩ welcome. e~licherweise *adv* happily. e~t *a* pleased

erfr**ie**r|en† *vi* (sein) freeze to death; ⟨*Glied:*⟩ become frostbitten; ⟨*Pflanze:*⟩ be killed by the frost. E~ung *f* -,-en frostbite

erfr**i**sch|en *vt* refresh; sich e~en refresh oneself. e~end *a* refreshing. E~ung *f* -,-en refreshment

erf**ü**ll|en *vt* fill; ⟨*nachkommen*⟩ fulfil; serve ⟨*Zweck*⟩; discharge ⟨*Pflicht:*⟩; sich e~en come true. E~ung *f* fulfilment; in E~ung gehen come true

erf**u**nden invented; ⟨*fiktiv*⟩ fictitious

erg**ä**nz|en *vt* complement; ⟨*nachtragen*⟩ supplement; ⟨*auffüllen*⟩ replenish; ⟨*vervollständigen*⟩ complete; ⟨*hinzufügen*⟩ add; sich e~en complement each other. E~ung *f* complement; supplement; ⟨*Zusatz*⟩ addition. E~ungsband *m* supplement

erg**e**b|en† *vt* produce; ⟨*zeigen*⟩ show, establish; sich e~en result; ⟨*Schwierigkeit:*⟩ arise; ⟨*kapitulieren*⟩ surrender; ⟨*sich fügen*⟩ submit; es ergab sich it turned out (dass that) □ *a* devoted, *adv* -ly; ⟨*resigniert*⟩ resigned, *adv* -ly. E~enheit *f* - devotion

Ergebnis nt -ses,-se result. e~los a fruitless, adv -ly

ergehen† vi (sein) be issued; etw über sich (acc) e~ lassen submit to sth; wie ist es dir ergangen? how did you get on? □ vr sich e~ in (+ dat) indulge in

ergiebig a productive; (fig) rich

ergötzen vt amuse

ergreifen† vt seize; take ⟨Maßnahme, Gelegenheit;⟩ take up ⟨Beruf⟩; (rühren) move; die Flucht e~ flee. e~d a moving

ergriffen a deeply moved. E~heit f - emotion

ergründen vt (fig) get to the bottom of

erhaben a raised; (fig) sublime; über etw (acc) e~ sein (fig) be above sth

Erhalt m -[e]s receipt. e~en† vt receive, get; (gewinnen) obtain; (bewahren) preserve, keep; (instand halten) maintain; (unterhalten) support; am Leben e~en keep alive □ a gut/schlecht e~en in good/bad condition; e~en bleiben survive

erhältlich a obtainable

Erhaltung f - (s. erhalten) preservation; maintenance

erhängen (sich) vr hang oneself

erhärten vt (fig) substantiate

erheb|en† vt raise; levy ⟨Steuer⟩; charge ⟨Gebühr⟩; Anspruch e~en lay claim (auf + acc to); Protest e~en protest; sich e~en rise; ⟨Frage:⟩ arise; (sich empören) rise up. e~lich a considerable, adv -bly. E~ung f -,-en elevation; (Anhöhe) rise; (Aufstand) uprising; (Ermittlung) survey

erheiter|n vt amuse. E~ung f - amusement

erhitzen vt heat; sich e~ get hot; (fig) get heated

erhoffen vt sich (dat) etw e~ hope for sth

erhöh|en vt raise; (fig) increase; sich e~en rise, increase. E~ung f -,-en increase. E~ungszeichen nt (Mus) sharp

erhol|en (sich) vr recover (von from); (nach Krankheit) convalesce, recuperate; (sich ausruhen) have a rest. e~sam a restful. E~ung f - recovery; convalescence; (Ruhe) rest. E~ungsheim nt convalescent home

erhören vt (fig) answer

erinner|n vt remind (an + acc of); sich e~n remember (an jdn/etw s.o./sth). E~ung f -,-en memory; (Andenken) souvenir

erkält|en (sich) vr catch a cold; e~et sein have a cold. E~ung f -,-en cold

erkenn|bar a recognizable; (sichtbar) visible. e~en† vt recognize; (wahrnehmen) distinguish; (einsehen) realize. e~tlich a

sich e~tlich zeigen show one's appreciation. E~tnis f -,-se recognition; realization; (Wissen) knowledge; die neuesten E~tnisse the latest findings

Erker m -s,- bay

erklär|en vt declare; (erläutern) explain; sich bereit e~en agree (zu to); ich kann es mir nicht e~en I can't explain it. e~end a explanatory. e~lich a explicable; (verständlich) understandable. e~licherweise adv understandably. e~t attrib a declared. E~ung f -,-en declaration; explanation; öffentliche E~ung public statement

erklingen† vi (sein) ring out

erkrank|en vi (sein) fall ill; be taken ill (an + dat with). E~ung f -,-en illness

erkunden vt explore; (Mil) reconnoitre

erkundig|en (sich) vr enquire (nach jdm/etw after s.o./about sth). E~ung f -,-en enquiry

erlahmen vi (sein) tire; ⟨Kraft, Eifer:⟩ flag

erlangen vt attain, get

Erlass m -es,-̈e (Erlaß m -sses,-̈sse) (Admin) decree; (Befreiung) exemption; (Straf-) remission

erlassen† vt (Admin) issue; jdm etw e~ exempt s.o. from sth; let s.o. off ⟨Strafe⟩

erlauben vt allow, permit; sich e~, etw zu tun take the liberty of doing sth; ich kann es mir nicht e~ I can't afford it

Erlaubnis f - permission. E~schein m permit

erläuter|n vt explain. E~ung f -,-en explanation

Erle f -,-n alder

erleb|en vt experience; (mit-) see; have ⟨Überraschung, Enttäuschung⟩; etw nicht mehr e~en not live to see sth. E~nis nt -ses,-se experience

erledig|en vt do; (sich befassen mit) deal with; (beenden) finish; (entscheiden) settle; (töten) kill; e~t sein be done/settled/⟨fam: müde⟩ worn out/⟨fam: ruiniert⟩ finished

erleichter|n vt lighten; (vereinfachen) make easier; (befreien) relieve; (lindern) ease; sich e~n (fig) unburden oneself. e~t a relieved. E~ung f - relief

erleiden† vt suffer

erlernen vt learn

erlesen a exquisite; (auserlesen) choice, select

erleuchten vt illuminate; hell e~et brightly lit. E~ung f -,-en (fig) inspiration

erliegen† vi (sein) succumb (dat to); seinen Verletzungen e~ die of one's injuries

erlogen a untrue, false

Erlös m -es proceeds pl

erlöschen† vi (sein) go out; (vergehen) die; (aussterben) die out; (ungültig werden) expire; erloschener Vulkan extinct volcano

erlös|en vt save; (befreien) release (von from); (Relig) redeem. e∼t a relieved. E∼ung f release; (Erleichterung) relief; (Relig) redemption

ermächtig|en vt authorize. E∼ung f -,-en authorization

ermahn|en vt exhort; (zurechtweisen) admonish. E∼ung f exhortation; admonition

ermäßig|en vt reduce. E∼ung f -,-en reduction

ermatt|en vi (sein) grow weary □ vt weary. E∼ung f - weariness

ermessen† vt judge; (begreifen) appreciate. E∼ nt -s discretion; (Urteil) judgement; nach eigenem E∼ at one's own discretion

ermitt|eln vt establish; (herausfinden) find out □ vi (haben) investigate (gegen jdn s.o.). E∼lungen fpl investigations. E∼lungsverfahren nt (Jur) preliminary inquiry

ermöglichen vt make possible

ermord|en vt murder. E∼ung f -,-en murder

ermüd|en vt tire □ vi (sein) get tired. E∼ung f - tiredness

ermunter|n vt encourage; sich e∼n rouse oneself. E∼ung f - encouragement

ermutigen vt encourage. e∼d a encouraging

ernähr|en vt feed; (unterhalten) support, keep; sich e∼en von live/(Tier:) feed on. E∼er m -s,- breadwinner. E∼ung f - nourishment; nutrition; (Kost) diet

ernenn|en† vt appoint. E∼ung f -,-en appointment

erneu|ern vt renew; (auswechseln) replace; change (Verband); (renovieren) renovate. E∼erung f renewal; replacement; renovation. e∼t a renewed; (neu) new □ adv again

erniedrig|en vt degrade; sich e∼en lower oneself. e∼end a degrading. E∼ungszeichen nt (Mus) flat

ernst a serious, adv -ly; e∼ nehmen take seriously. E∼ m -es seriousness; im E∼ seriously; mit einer Drohung E∼ machen carry out a threat; ist das dein E∼? are you serious? E∼fall m im E∼fall when the real thing happens. e∼haft a serious, adv -ly. e∼lich a serious, adv -ly

Ernte f -,-n harvest; (Ertrag) crop. E∼dankfest nt harvest festival. e∼n vt harvest; (fig) reap, win

ernüchter|n vt sober up; (fig) bring down to earth; (enttäuschen) disillusion. e∼nd a (fig) sobering. E∼ung f - disillusionment

Erober|er m -s,- conqueror. e∼n vt conquer. E∼ung f -,-en conquest

eröffn|en vt open; jdm etw e∼en announce sth to s.o.; sich jdm e∼en (Aussicht:) present itself to s.o. E∼ung f opening; (Mitteilung) announcement. E∼ungsansprache f opening address

erörter|n vt discuss. E∼ung f -,-en discussion

Erosion f -,-en erosion

Erot|ik f - eroticism. e∼isch a erotic

Erpel m -s,- drake

erpicht a e∼ auf (+ acc) keen on

erpress|en vt extort; blackmail (Person). E∼er m -s,- blackmailer. E∼ung f - extortion; blackmail

erprob|en vt test. e∼t a proven

erquicken vt refresh

errat|en† vt guess

erreg|bar a excitable. e∼en vt excite; (hervorrufen) arouse; sich e∼en get worked up. e∼end a exciting. E∼er m -s,- (Med) germ. e∼t a agitated; (hitzig) heated. E∼ung f - excitement; (Erregtheit) agitation

erreich|bar a within reach; (Ziel) attainable; (Person) available. e∼en vt reach; catch (Zug); live to (Alter:) (durchsetzen) achieve

erretten vt save

errichten vt erect

erringen† vt gain, win

erröten vi (sein) blush

Errungenschaft f -,-en achievement; (fam: Anschaffung) acquisition; E∼en der Technik technical advances

Ersatz m -es replacement, substitute; (Entschädigung) compensation. E∼dienst m = Zivildienst. E∼reifen m spare tyre. E∼spieler(in) m(f) substitute. E∼teil nt spare part

ersäufen vt drown

erschaffen† vt create

erschallen† vi (sein) ring out

erschein|en† vi (sein) appear; (Buch:) be published; jdm merkwürdig e∼en seem odd to s.o. E∼en nt -s appearance; publication. E∼ung f -,-en appearance; (Person) figure; (Phänomen) phenomenon; (Symptom) symptom; (Geist) apparition

erschießen† vt shoot [dead]. E∼ungskommando nt firing squad erschlaffen *vi* (*sein*) go limp; ⟨*Haut, Muskeln:*⟩ become flabby

erschlagen† *vt* beat to death; (*tödlich treffen*) strike dead; vom Blitz e~ werden be killed by lightning □ *a* (*fam*) (*erschöpft*) worn out; (*fassungslos*) stunned

erschließen† *vt* develop; (*zugänglich machen*) open up; (*nutzbar machen*) tap

erschöpf|en *vt* exhaust. e~end *a* exhausting; (*fig: vollständig*) exhaustive. e~t *a* exhausted. E~ung *f* - exhaustion

erschreck|en† *vi* (*sein*) get a fright □ *vt* (*reg*) startle; (*beunruhigen*) alarm; du hast mich e~t you gave me a fright □ *vr* (*reg & irreg*) sich e~en get a fright. e~end *a* alarming, *adv* -ly

erschrocken *a* frightened; (*erschreckt*) startled; (*bestürzt*) dismayed

erschütter|n *vt* shake; (*ergreifen*) upset deeply. E~ung *f* -,-en shock

erschweren *vt* make more difficult

erschwinglich *a* affordable

ersehen† *vt* (*fig*) see (aus from)

ersetzen *vt* replace; make good ⟨*Schaden*⟩; refund ⟨*Kosten*⟩; jdm etw e~ compensate s.o. for sth

ersichtlich *a* obvious, apparent

erspar|en *vt* save; jdm etw e~en save/(*fern halten*) spare s.o. sth. E~nis *f* -,-se saving; (*Geld*) e~nisse savings

erst *adv* (*zuerst*) first; (*noch nicht mehr als*) only; (*nicht vor*) not until; e~ dann only then; eben *od* gerade e~ [only] just; das machte ihn e~ recht wütend it made him all the more angry

erstarren *vi* (*sein*) solidify; (*gefrieren*) freeze; (*steif werden*) go stiff; (*vor Schreck*) be paralysed

erstatten *vt* (*zurück-*) refund; Bericht e~ report (jdm to s.o.)

Erstaufführung *f* first performance, première

erstaun|en *vt* amaze, astonish. E~en *nt* amazement, astonishment. e~lich *a* amazing, *adv* -ly. e~licherweise *adv* amazingly

Erst|ausgabe *f* first edition. e~e(r,s) *a* first; (*beste*) best; e~e (E~e) Hilfe first aid; der e~e Beste (beste) the first one to come along; (*fam*) any Tom, Dick or Harry; als e~es/fürs e~e ⟨NEW⟩als E~es/fürs E~e, s. Erste(r,s). E~e(r) *m/f* first; (*Beste*) best; fürs E~e for the time being; als E~es first of all; er kam als E~er he arrived first; er ist der/sie ist die E~e in Latein he/she is top in Latin

erstechen† *vt* stab to death

erstehen† *vt* buy

ersteigern *vt* buy at an auction

erst|emal *adv* das e~emal/zum e~enmal ⟨NEW⟩das erste Mal/zum ersten Mal, s. Mal[1]. e~ere(r,s) *a* the former; der/die/das e~ere (e~ere) the former

ersticken *vt* suffocate; smother ⟨*Flammen*⟩; (*unterdrücken*) suppress □ *vi* (*sein*) suffocate. E~ *nt* -s suffocation; zum E~ stifling

erst|klassig *a* first-class. e~mals *adv* for the first time

erstreben *vt* strive for. e~swert *a* desirable

erstrecken (sich) *vr* stretch; sich e~ auf (+ *acc*) (*fig*) apply to

ersuchen *vt* ask, request. E~ *nt* -s request

ertappen *vt* (*fam*) catch

erteilen *vt* give (jdm s.o.)

ertönen *vi* (*sein*) sound; (*erschallen*) ring out

Ertrag *m* -[e]s,-e yield. e~en† *vt* bear

erträglich *a* bearable; (*leidlich*) tolerable

ertränken *vt* drown

ertrinken† *vi* (*sein*) drown

erübrigen (sich) *vr* be unnecessary

erwachen *vi* (*sein*) awake

erwachsen *a* grown-up. E~e(r) *m/f* adult, grown-up

erwäg|en† *vt* consider. E~ung *f* -,-en consideration; in E~ung ziehen consider

erwähn|en *vt* mention. E~ung *f* -,-en mention

erwärmen *vt* warm; sich e~ warm up; (*fig*) warm (für to)

erwart|en *vt* expect; (*warten auf*) wait for. E~ung *f* -,-en expectation. e~ungsvoll *a* expectant, *adv* -ly

erwecken *vt* (*fig*) arouse; give ⟨*Anschein*⟩

erweichen *vt* soften; (*fig*) move; sich e~ lassen (*fig*) relent

erweisen† *vt* prove; (*bezeigen*) do ⟨*Gefallen, Dienst, Ehre*⟩; sich e~ als prove to be

erweitern *vt* widen; dilate ⟨*Pupille*⟩; (*fig*) extend, expand

Erwerb *m* -[e]s acquisition; (*Kauf*) purchase; (*Brot-*) livelihood; (*Verdienst*) earnings *pl*. e~en† *vt* acquire; (*kaufen*) purchase; (*fig: erlangen*) gain. e~slos *a* unemployed. e~stätig *a* [gainfully] employed. E~ung *f* -,-en acquisition

erwider|n *vt* reply; return ⟨*Besuch, Gruß*⟩. E~ung *f* -,-en reply

erwirken *vt* obtain

erwischen *vt* (*fam*) catch

erwünscht *a* desired

erwürgen *vt* strangle

Erz nt -es,-e ore

erzähl|en vt tell (jdm s.o.) □ vi (haben) talk (von about). E~er m -s,- narrator. E~ung f -,-en story, tale

Erzbischof m archbishop

erzeug|en vt produce; (Electr) generate; (fig) create. E~er m -s,- producer; (Vater) father. E~nis nt -ses,-se product; landwirtschaftliche E~nisse farm produce sg. E~ung f - production; generation

Erz|feind m arch-enemy. E~herzog m archduke

erzieh|en† vt bring up; (Sch) educate. E~er m -s,- [private] tutor. E~erin f -,-nen governess. E~ung f - upbringing; education

erzielen vt achieve; score ⟨Tor⟩

erzogen a gut/schlecht e~ well/badly brought up

erzürnt a angry

erzwingen† vt force

es pron it; (Mädchen) she; (acc) her; impers es regnet it is raining; es gibt there is/(pl) are; ich hoffe es I hope so

Esche f -,-n ash

Esel m -s,- donkey; (fam: Person) ass. E~sohr nt E~sohren haben (Buch:) be dog-eared

Eskal|ation /-'tsio:n/ f - escalation. e~ieren vt/i (haben) escalate

Eskimo m -[s],-[s] Eskimo

Eskort|e f -,-n (Mil) escort. e~ieren vt escort

essbar (eßbar) a edible. Essecke (Eßecke) f dining area

essen† vt/i (haben) eat; zu Mittag/Abend e~ have lunch/supper; [auswärts] e~ gehen eat out; chinesisch e~ have a Chinese meal. E~ nt -s,- food; (Mahl) meal; (festlich) dinner

Essenz f -,-en essence

Esser(in) m -s,- (f -,-nen) eater

Essig m -s vinegar. E~gurke f [pickled] gherkin

Esskastanie (Eßkastanie) f sweet chestnut. Esslöffel (Eßlöffel) m ≈ dessertspoon. Essstäbchen (Eßstäbchen) ntpl chopsticks. Esstisch (Eßtisch) m dining-table. Esswaren (Eßwaren) fpl food sg; (Vorräte) provisions. Esszimmer (Eßzimmer) nt diningroom

Estland nt -s Estonia

Estragon m -s tarragon

etablieren (sich) vr establish oneself/ ⟨Geschäft:⟩ itself

Etage /e'ta:ʒə/ f -,-n storey. E~nbett nt bunk-beds pl. E~nwohnung f flat, (Amer) apartment

Etappe f -,-n stage

Etat /e'ta:/ m -s,-s budget

etepetete a (fam) fussy

Eth|ik f - ethic; (Sittenlehre) ethics sg. e~isch a ethical

Etikett nt -[e]s,-e[n] label; (Preis-) tag. E~e f -,-n etiquette; (Aust) = Etikett. e~ieren vt label

etlich|e(r,s) pron some; (mehrere) several; e~e Mal several times; e~es a number of things; (ziemlich viel) quite a lot. e~emal adv (NEW) e~e Mal, s. etliche(r,s)

Etui /e'tvi:/ nt -s,-s case

etwa adv (ungefähr) about; (zum Beispiel) for instance; (womöglich) perhaps; nicht e~, dass ... not that ...; denkt nicht e~ ... don't imagine ...; du hast doch nicht e~ Angst? you're not afraid, are you? e~ig a possible

etwas pron something; (fragend/verneint) anything; (ein bisschen) some, a little; ohne e~ zu sagen without saying anything; sonst noch e~? anything else? noch e~ Tee? some more tea? so e~ Ärgerliches! what a nuisance! □ adv a bit

Etymologie f - etymology

euch pron (acc of ihr pl) you; (dat) [to] you; (refl) yourselves; (einander) each other; ein Freund von e~ a friend of yours

euer poss pron pl your. e~e, e~t- s. eure, euret-

Eule f -,-n owl

Euphorie f - euphoria

eur|e poss pron pl your. e~e(r,s) poss pron yours. e~erseits adv for your part. e~etwegen adv for your sake; (wegen euch) because of you, on your account. e~etwillen adv um e~etwillen for your sake. e~ige poss pron der/die/das e~ige yours

Euro m -[s]/-[s] Euro. E~ pref Euro-

Europa nt -s Europe. E~ pref European

Europä|er(in) m -s,- (f -,-nen) European. e~isch a European; E~ische Gemeinschaft European Community

Euro|paß m Europasport. E~scheck m Eurocheque

Euter nt -s,- udder

evakuier|en vt evacuate. E~ung f - evacuation

evangelisch a Protestant. E~gelist m -en,-en evangelist. E~gelium nt -s,-ien gospel

evaporieren vt/i (sein) evaporate

Eventualität f -,-en eventuality. e~ell a possible □ adv possibly; (vielleicht) perhaps

Evolution /-'tsio:n/ f - evolution

evtl. *abbr s.* eventuell

ewig *a* eternal, *adv* -ly; (*fam: ständig*) constant, *adv* -ly; (*endlos*) never-ending; e~
dauern (*fam*) take ages. E~keit *f* - eternity; eine E~keit (*fam*) ages

exakt *a* exact, *adv* -ly. E~heit *f* - exactitude

Examen *nt* -s,-& -mina (*Sch*) examination

Exekutive *f* - (*Pol*) executive

Exempel *nt* -s,- example; ein E~ an jdm
statuieren make an example of s.o.

Exemplar *nt* -s,-e specimen; (*Buch*) copy.
e~isch *a* exemplary

ex·er·zieren *vt/i* (*haben*) (*Mil*) drill; (*üben*)
practi...

exhumier·e... *vt* exhume

Exil *nt* -s exile

Existenz *f* -,-en existe... (*Lebensgrundlage*) livelihood; (*pej: Person*) ...dividual

existieren *vi* (*haben*) exist

exklusiv *a* exclusive. e~e *prep* (+ *gen*)
excluding

exkommunizieren *vt* excommunicate

Exkremente *npl* excrement *sg*

exotisch *a* exotic

expan·dieren *vt/i* (*haben*) expand. E~
sion *f* - expansion

Expedition /-'tsio:n/ *f* -,-en expedition

Experiment *nt* -[e]s,-e experiment.
e~ell *a* experimental. e~ieren *vi* (*haben*)
experiment

Experte *m* -n,-n expert

explo·dieren *vi* (*sein*) explode. E~sion *f*
-,-en explosion. e~siv *a* explosive

Expor|t *m* -[e]s,-e export. E~teur
/-'tø:r/ *m* -s,-e exporter. e~tieren *vt* export

Express *m* -es,-e (Expreß *m* -sses,-sse)
express

extra *adv* separately; (*zusätzlich*) extra;
(*eigens*) specially; (*fam: absichtlich*) on
purpose

Extrakt *m* -[e]s,-e extract

Extras *npl* (*Auto*) extras

extravagan|t *a* flamboyant, *adv* -ly;
(*übertrieben*) extravagant. E~z *f* -,-en
flamboyance; extravagance; (*Überspanntheit*) folly

extravertiert *a* extrovert

extrem *a* extreme, *adv* -ly. E~ *nt* -s,-e extreme. E~ist *m* -en,-en extremist. E~itäten *fpl* extremities

Exzellenz *f* - (*title*) Excellency

Exzen|triker *m* -s,- eccentric. e~isch *a*
eccentric

Exzess *m* -es,-e (Exzeß *m* -sses, -sse) excess

F

Fabel *f* -,-n fable. f~haft *a* (*fam*) fantastic,
adv -ally

Fabrik *f* -,-en factory. F~ant *m* -en,-en
manufacturer. F~at *nt* -[e]s,-e product;
(*Marke*) make. F~ation /-'tsio:n/ *f* -
manufacture

Facette /fa'sɛtə/ *f* -,-n facet

Fach *nt* -[e]s,-er compartment; (*Schub*)
drawer; (*Gebiet*) field; (*Sch*) subject.
F~arbeiter *m* skilled worker. F~arzt *m*,
F~ärztin *f* specialist. F~ausdruck *m*
technical term

fäch|eln (sich) *vr* fan oneself. F~er *m* -s,-
fan

Fach|gebiet *nt* field. f~gemäß,
f~gerecht *a* expert, *adv* -ly. F~hochschule *f* ≈ technical university. f~kundig...expert, *adv* -ly. f~lich *a* technical,
adv -ly; (*...nftlich*) professional. F~mann
m (*pl* -leute & ...nert. f~männisch *a* expert, *adv* -ly. F~s... *le f* technical college. f~simpeln *vi* (*hül... n*) (*fam*) talk
shop. F~werkhaus *nt* hal... timbered
house. F~wort *nt* (*pl* -wörter) tecl... *nal*
term

Fackel *f* -,-n torch. F~zug *m* torchlight
procession

fade *a* insipid; (*langweilig*) dull

Faden *m* -s,- thread; (*Bohnen-*) string;
(*Naut*) fathom. f~scheinig *a* threadbare;
(*Grund*) flimsy

Fagott *nt* -[e]s,-e bassoon

fähig *a* capable (zu/gen of); (*tüchtig*) able,
competent. F~keit *f* -,-en ability; competence

fahl *a* pale

fahnd|en *vi* (*haben*) search (nach for).
F~ung *f* -,-en search

Fahne *f* -,-n flag; (*Druck-*) galley [proof];
eine F~ haben (*fam*) reek of alcohol.
F~nflucht *f* desertion. f~nflüchtig *a*
f~nflüchtig werden desert

Fahr|ausweis *m* ticket. F~bahn *f* carriageway; (*Straße*) road. f~bar *a* mobile

Fähre *f* -,-n ferry

fahr|en *vi* (*sein*) go, travel; (*Fahrer:*)
drive; (*Radfahrer:*) ride; (*verkehren*) run,
(*ab-*) leave; (*Schiff:*) sail; mit dem Auto/
Zug f~en go by car/train; in die Höhe
f~en start up; in die Kleider f~en throw
on one's clothes; mit der Hand über etw
(*acc*) f~en run one's hand over sth; was
ist in ihn gefahren? (*fam*) what has got
into him? □ *vt* drive; ride (*Fahrrad*); take

⟨Kurve⟩. f∼end a moving; (f∼bar) mobile; (nicht sesshaft) travelling, itinerant. F∼er m -s,- driver. F∼erflucht f failure to stop after an accident. F∼erhaus nt driver's cab. F∼erin f -,-nen woman driver. F∼gast m passenger; (im Taxi) fare. F∼geld nt fare. F∼gestell nt chassis; (Aviat) undercarriage. f∼ig a nervy; (zerstreut) distracted. F∼karte f ticket. F∼kartenausgabe f, F∼kartenschalter m ticket office. f∼lässig a negligent, adv -ly. F∼lässigkeit f - negligence. F∼lehrer m driving instructor. F∼plan m timetable. f∼planmäßig a scheduled □ adv according to/(pünktlich) on schedule. F∼preis m fare. F∼prüfung f driving test. F∼rad nt bicycle. F∼schein m ticket

Fährschiff nt ferry

Fahr|schule f driving school. F∼schüler(in) m(f) learner driver. F∼spur f [traffic] lane. F∼stuhl m lift, (Amer) elevator. F∼stunde f driving lesson

Fahrt f -,-en journey; (Auto) drive; (Ausflug) trip; (Tempo) speed; in voller F∼ at full speed. F∼ausweis m ticket

Fährte f -,-n track; (Witterung) scent; auf der falschen F∼ (fig) on the wrong track

Fahr|tkosten pl travelling expenses. F∼werk nt undercarriage. F∼zeug nt -[e]s,-e vehicle; (Wasser-) craft, vessel

fair /fɛ:ɐ̯/ a fair, adv -ly. F∼ness (F∼neß) f - fairness

Fakten pl facts

Faktor m -s,-en /-'to:rən/ factor

Fakul|tät f -,-en faculty. f∼tativ a optional

Falke m -n,-n falcon

Fall m -[e]s,ⁿe fall; (Jur, Med, Gram) case; im F∼[e] in case (gen of); auf jeden F∼, auf alle F∼e in any case; (bestimmt) definitely; für alle F∼e just in case; auf keinen F∼ on no account

Falle f -,-n trap; eine F∼ stellen set a trap (dat for)

fallen† vi (sein) fall; (sinken) go down; [im Krieg] f∼ be killed in the war; f∼ lassen drop (etw, fig: Plan, jdn); make (Bemerkung)

fällen vt fell; (fig) pass (Urteil); make (Entscheidung)

fallenlassen† vt sep NEW fallen lassen, s. fallen

fällig a due; (Wechsel) mature; längst f∼ long overdue. F∼keit f - (Comm) maturity

Fallobst nt windfalls pl

falls conj in case; (wenn) if

Fallschirm m parachute. F∼jäger m paratrooper. F∼springer m parachutist

Falltür f trapdoor

falsch a wrong; (nicht echt, unaufrichtig) false; (gefälscht) forged; ⟨Geld⟩ counterfeit; ⟨Schmuck⟩ fake □ adv wrongly; falsely; ⟨singen⟩ out of tune; f∼ gehen ⟨Uhr:⟩ be wrong

fälsch|en vt forge, fake. F∼er m -s,- forger

Falsch|geld nt counterfeit money. F∼heit f - falseness

fälschlich a wrong, adv -ly; (irrtümlich) mistaken, adv -ly. f∼erweise adv by mistake

Falsch|meldung f false report; (absichtlich) hoax report. F∼münzer m -s,- counterfeiter

Fälschung f -,-en forgery, fake; (Fälschen) forging

Falte f -,-n fold; (Rock-) pleat; (Knitter-) crease; (im Gesicht) line; (Runzel) wrinkle

falten vt fold; sich f∼ ⟨Haut:⟩ wrinkle. F∼rock m pleated skirt

Falter m -s,- butterfly; (Nacht-) moth

faltig a creased; ⟨Gesicht⟩ lined; (runzlig) wrinkled

familiär a family …; (vertraut, zudringlich) familiar; (zwanglos) informal

Familie /-jə/ f -,-n family. F∼nanschluss (F∼nanschluß) m F∼nanschluss haben live as one of the family. F∼nforschung f genealogy. F∼nleben nt family life. F∼nname m surname. F∼nplanung f family planning. F∼nstand m marital status

Fan /fɛn/ m -s,-s fan

Fana|tiker m -s,- fanatic. f∼tisch a fanatical, adv -ly. F∼tismus m - fanaticism

Fanfare f -,-n trumpet; (Signal) fanfare

Fang m -[e]s,ⁿe capture; (Beute) catch; F∼e (Krallen) talons; (Zähne) fangs. F∼arm m tentacle. f∼en† vt catch; (ein-) capture; sich f∼en get caught (in + dat in); (fig) regain one's balance/(seelisch) composure; gefangen nehmen take prisoner; gefangen halten hold prisoner; keep in captivity ⟨Tier⟩. F∼en nt -s F∼en spielen play tag. F∼frage f catch question. F∼zahn m fang

Fantasie f -,-n = Phantasie

fantastisch a = phantastisch

Farb|aufnahme f colour photograph. F∼band nt (pl -bänder) typewriter ribbon. F∼e f -,-n colour; (Maler-) paint; (zum Färben) dye; (Karten) suit. f∼echt a colour-fast

färben vt colour; dye (Textilien, Haare); (fig) slant ⟨Bericht⟩; sich [rot] f∼ turn [red] □ vi (haben) not be colour-fast

farb|enblind a colour-blind. f∼enfroh a colourful. F∼fernsehen nt colour television. F∼film m colour film. F∼foto nt colour photo. f~ig *a* coloured □ *adv* in colour. F~ige(r) *m/f* coloured man/woman. F~kasten *m* box of paints. f~los *a* colourless. F~stift *m* crayon. F~stoff *m* dye; (*Lebensmittel-*) colouring. F~ton *m* shade

Färbung *f* -,-en colouring; (*fig: Anstrich*) bias

Farce /'farsə/ *f* -,-n farce; (*Culin*) stuffing

Farn *m* -[e]s,-e, F~kraut *nt* fern

Färse *f* -,-n heifer

Fasan *m* -[e]s,-e[n] pheasant

Faschierte(s) *nt* (*Aust*) mince

Fasching *m* -s (*SGer*) carnival

Faschis|mus *m* - fascism. F~t *m* -en,-en fascist. f~tisch *a* fascist

faseln *vt/i* (*haben*) (*fam*) [Unsinn] f~ talk nonsense

Faser *f* -,-n fibre. f~n *vi* (*haben*) fray

Fass *nt* -es,¨er (Faß *nt* -sses,¨sser) barrel, cask; Bier vom F~ draught beer; F~ ohne Boden (*fig*) bottomless pit

Fassade *f* -,-n façade

fassbar (faßbar) *a* comprehensible; (*greifbar*) tangible

fassen *vt* take [hold of], grasp; (*ergreifen*) seize; (*fangen*) catch; (*ein-*) set; (*enthalten*) hold; (*fig: begreifen*) take in, grasp; conceive (*Plan*); make (*Entschluss*); sich f~ compose oneself; sich kurz/in Geduld f~ be brief/patient; in Worte f~ put into words; nicht zu f~ (*fig*) unbelievable □ *vi* (*haben*) f~ an (+ *acc*) touch; f~ nach reach for

fasslich (faßlich) *a* comprehensible

Fasson /fa'sõ:/ *f* - style; (*Form*) shape; (*Weise*) way

Fassung *f* -,-en mount; (*Edelstein-*) setting; (*Electr*) socket; (*Version*) version; (*Beherrschung*) composure; aus der F~ bringen disconcert. f~slos *a* shaken; (*erstaunt*) flabbergasted. F~svermögen *nt* capacity

fast *adv* almost, nearly; f~ nie hardly ever

fast|en *vi* (*haben*) fast. F~enzeit *f* Lent. F~nacht *f* Shrovetide; (*Karneval*) carnival. F~nachtsdienstag *m* Shrove Tuesday. F~tag *m* fast-day

Faszin|ation /-'tsio:n/ *f* - fascination. f~ieren *vt* fascinate; f~ierend fascinating

fatal *a* fatal; (*peinlich*) embarrassing. F~ismus *m* - fatalism. F~ist *m* -en,-en fatalist

Fata Morgana *f* -,- -nen mirage

fauchen *vi* (*haben*) spit, hiss □ *vt* snarl

faul *a* lazy; (*verdorben*) rotten, bad; (*Ausrede*) lame; (*zweifelhaft*) bad; (*verdächtig*) fishy

Fäule *f* - decay

faul|en *vi* (*sein*) rot; (*Zahn:*) decay; (*verwesen*) putrefy. f~enzen *vi* (*haben*) be lazy. F~enzer *m* -s,- lazy-bones *sg*. F~heit *f* - laziness. f~ig *a* rotting; (*Geruch*) putrid

Fäulnis *f* - decay

Faulpelz *m* (*fam*) lazy-bones *sg*

Fauna *f* - fauna

Faust *f* -,Fäuste fist; auf eigene F~ (*fig*) off one's own bat. F~handschuh *m* mitten. F~schlag *m* punch

Fauxpas /fo'pa/ *m* -,- /-[s],-s/ gaffe

Favorit(in) /favo'ri:t(in)/ *m* -en, -en (*f* -,-nen) (*Sport*) favourite

Fax *nt* -,-[e] fax. f~en *vt* fax

Faxen *fpl* (*fam*) antics; F~ machen fool about; F~ schneiden pull faces

Faxgerät *nt* fax machine

Feber *m* -s,- (*Aust*) February

Februar *m* -s,-e February

fecht|en *vi* (*haben*) fence. F~er *m* -s,- fencer

Feder *f* -,-n feather; (*Schreib-*) pen; (*Spitze*) nib; (*Techn*) spring. F~ball *m* shuttlecock; (*Spiel*) badminton. F~busch *m* plume. f~leicht *a* as light as a feather. F~messer *nt* penknife. f~nd *vi* (*haben*) be springy; (*nachgeben*) give; (*hoch-*) bounce. f~nd *a* springy; (*elastisch*) elastic. F~ung *f* - (*Techn*) springs *pl*; (*Auto*) suspension

Fee *f* -,-n fairy

Fegefeuer *nt* purgatory

fegen *vt* sweep □ *vi* (*sein*) (*rasen*) tear

Fehde *f* -,-n feud

fehl *a* f~ am Platze out of place. F~betrag *m* deficit. f~en *vi* (*haben*) be missing/(*Sch*) absent; (*mangeln*) be lacking; es f~t an (+ *dat*) there is a shortage of; mir f~t die Zeit I haven't got the time; sie/es f~t mir sehr I miss her/it very much; was f~t ihm? what's the matter with him? es f~te nicht viel und er ... he very nearly ...; das hat uns noch gefehlt! that's all we need! f~end *a* missing; (*Sch*) absent

Fehler *m* -s,- mistake, error; (*Sport & fig*) fault; (*Makel*) flaw. f~frei *a* faultless, *adv* -ly. f~haft *a* faulty. f~los *a* flawless, *adv* -ly

Fehl|geburt *f* miscarriage. f~gehen† *vi* *sep* (*sein*) go wrong; (*Schuss:*) miss; (*fig*) be mistaken. F~griff *m* mistake. F~kalkulation *f* miscalculation. F~schlag *m* failure. f~schlagen† *vi* *sep* (*sein*) fail. F~start *m* (*Sport*) false start. F~tritt *m* false step; (*fig*) [moral] lapse. F~zündung *f* (*Auto*) misfire

Feier f -,-n celebration; (*Zeremonie*) ceremony; (*Party*) party. F~abend m end of the working day; F~abend machen stop work, (*fam*) knock off; nach F~abend after work. f~lich a solemn, adv -ly; (*förmlich*) formal, adv -ly. F~lichkeit f -,-en solemnity; F~lichkeiten festivities. f~n vt celebrate; hold (*Fest*); (*ehren*) fête □ vi (*haben*) celebrate; (*lustig sein*) make merry. F~tag m [public] holiday; (*kirchlicher*) feast-day; erster/zweiter F~tag Christmas Day / Boxing Day. f~tags adv on public holidays

feige a cowardly; f~ sein be a coward □ adv in a cowardly way

Feige f -,-n fig. F~nbaum m fig tree

Feigheit f - cowardice. F~ling m -s,-e coward

Feile f -,-n file. f~n vt/i (*haben*) file

feilschen vi (*haben*) haggle

Feilspäne mpl filings

fein a fine, adv -ly; (*zart*) delicate, adv -ly; (*Strümpfe*) sheer; (*Unterschied*) subtle; (*scharf*) keen; (*vornehm*) refined; (*elegant*) elegant; (*prima*) great; sich f~ machen dress up. F~arbeit f precision work

feind a jdm f~ sein NEW jdm F~ sein, s. Feind. F~(in) m -es,-e (f -,-nen) enemy; jdm F~ sein be hostile towards s.o. f~lich a enemy; (*f~selig*) hostile. F~schaft f -,-en enmity. f~selig a hostile. F~seligkeit f -,-en hostility

fein|fühlig a sensitive. F~gefühl nt sensitivity; (*Takt*) delicacy. F~heit f -,-en (s. fein) fineness; delicacy; subtlety; keenness; refinement; F~heiten subtleties. F~kostgeschäft nt delicatessen [shop]. F~schmecker m -s,- gourmet

feist a fat

feixen vi (*haben*) smirk

Feld nt -[e]s,-er field; (*Fläche*) ground; (*Sport*) pitch; (*Schach-*) square; (*auf Formular*) box. F~bau m agriculture. F~bett nt camp-bed, (*Amer*) cot. F~forschung f fieldwork. F~herr m commander. F~marschall m Field Marshal. F~stecher m -s,- field-glasses pl. F~webel m -s,- (*Mil*) sergeant. F~zug m campaign

Felge f -,-n [wheel] rim

Fell nt -[e]s,-e (*Zool*) coat; (*Pelz*) fur; (*abgezogen*) skin, pelt; ein dickes F~ haben (*fam*) be thick-skinned

Fels m -en,-en rock. F~block m boulder. F~en m -s,- rock. f~enfest a (*fig*) firm, adv -ly. f~ig a rocky

feminin a feminine; (*weibisch*) effeminate

Femininum nt -s,-na (*Gram*) feminine

Feminist|(in) m -en,-en (f -,-nen) feminist. f~isch a feminist

Fenchel m -s fennel

Fenster nt -s,- window. F~brett nt window-sill. F~laden m [window] shutter. F~leder nt chamois[-leather]. F~putzer m -s,- window-cleaner. F~scheibe f [window-]pane

Ferien /'fe:rjən/ pl holidays; (*Univ*) vacation sg; F~ haben be on holiday. F~ort m holiday resort

Ferkel nt -s,- piglet

fern a distant; der F~e Osten the Far East; f~ halten keep away; sich f~ halten keep away □ adv far away; von f~ from a distance □ prep (+ dat) far [away] from. F~bedienung f remote control. f~bleiben† vi sep (*sein*) stay away (*dat* from). F~e f - distance; in/aus der F~e in the/from a distance; in weiter F~e far away; (*zeitlich*) in the distant future. f~er a further □ adv (*außerdem*) furthermore; (*in Zukunft*) in future. f~gelenkt a remote-controlled; (*Rakete*) guided. F~gespräch nt long-distance call. f~gesteuert a = f~gelenkt. F~glas nt binoculars pl. f~halten† vt sep (+ haben) f~ halten, s. fern. F~kopierer m -s,- fax machine. F~kurs[us] m correspondence course. F~lenkung f remote control. F~licht nt (*Auto*) full beam. F~meldewesen nt telecommunications pl. F~rohr nt telescope. F~schreiben nt telex. F~schreiber m -s,- telex [machine]

Fernseh|apparat m television set. f~en† vi sep (*haben*) watch television. F~en nt -s television. F~er m -s,- [television] viewer; (*Gerät*) television set. F~gerät nt television set

Fernsprech|amt nt telephone exchange, (*Amer*) central. F~er m telephone. F~nummer f telephone number. F~zelle f telephone box

Fernsteuerung f remote control

Ferse f -,-n heel. F~ngeld nt F~ngeld geben (*fam*) take to one's heels

fertig a finished; (*bereit*) ready; (*Comm*) ready-made; (*Gericht*) ready-to-serve; f~ werden mit finish; (*bewältigen*) cope with; f~ sein have finished; (*fig*) be through (mit jdm with s.o.); (*fam: erschöpft*) be all in; (*seelisch*) shattered; etw f~ bringen od (*fam*) kriegen manage to do sth; (*beenden*) finish sth; ich bringe od (*fam*) kriege es nicht f~ I can't bring myself to do it; etw/jdn f~ machen finish sth; (*bereitmachen*) get sth/s.o. ready; (*fam: erschöpfen*) wear s.o. out; (*seelisch*) shatter s.o.; (*fam: abkanzeln*) carpet s.o.; sich f~ machen get ready; etw f~ stellen complete sth □ adv f~ essen/lesen finish eating/reading. F~bau m (pl -bauten) prefabricated building.

f~bringen† vt sep (NEW) f~ bringen, s.
fertig. f~en vt make. F~gericht nt
ready-to-serve meal. F~haus nt prefabricated house. F~keit f -,-en skill. f~
kriegen vt sep (fam) (NEW) f~ kriegen,
s. fertig. f~machen vt sep (NEW) f~
machen, s. fertig. f~stellen vt sep
(NEW) f~ stellen, s. fertig. F~stellung
f completion. F~ung f - manufacture

fesch a (fam) attractive; (flott) smart;
(Aust: nett) kind

Fessel f -,-n ankle

fesseln vt tie up; tie (an + acc to); (fig)
fascinate; ans Bett gefesselt confined to
bed. F~ fpl bonds. f~d a (fig) fascin-
ating; (packend) absorbing

fest a firm; (nicht flüssig) solid; (erstarrt)
set; (haltbar) strong; (nicht locker) tight;
(feststehend) fixed; (ständig) steady; (Anstellung) permanent; (Schlaf) sound;
(Blick, Stimme) steady; f~ werden
harden; (Gelee:) set; f~e Nahrung solids
pl a adv firmly; (tightly; steadily; soundly;
(kräftig, tüchtig) hard; f~ schlafen be fast
asleep; f~ angestellt permanent

Fest nt -[e]s,-e celebration; (Party) party;
(Relig) festival; frohes F~! happy
Christmas!

fest|angestellt a (NEW) f~ angestellt, s.
fest. f~binden† vt sep tie (an + dat to).
f~bleiben† vi sep (sein) (fig) remain firm.
f~e adv (fam) hard. F~essen nt =
F~mahl. f~fahren vi/r sep (sein) [sich]
f~fahren get stuck; (Verhandlungen:)
reach deadlock. f~halten† v sep □ vt hold
on to; (aufzeichnen) record; sich
f~halten hold on □ vi (haben) f~halten
an (+ dat) (fig) stick to; cling to (Tradition). f~igen vt strengthen; sich f~igen
grow stronger. F~iger m -s,- styling
lotion/(Schaum-) mousse. F~igkeit f - (s.
fest) firmness; solidity; strength; stead-
iness. f~klammern vt sep clip (an + dat
to); sich f~klammern cling (an + dat
to). F~land nt mainland; (Kontinent) continent. f~legen vt sep (fig) fix, settle; lay
down (Regeln); tie up (Geld); sich f~legen
commit oneself

festlich a festive, adv -ly. F~keiten fpl
festivities

fest|liegen† vi sep (haben) be fixed,
settled. f~machen v sep □ vt fasten/
(binden) tie (an + dat to); (f~legen) fix,
settle □ vi (haben) (Naut) moor. F~mahl
nt feast; (Bankett) banquet. F~nahme f
-,-n arrest. f~nehmen† vt sep arrest.
F~ordner m steward. f~setzen vt sep fix,
settle; (inhaftieren) gaol; f~setzen
collect. f~sitzen† vi sep (haben) be
firm/(Schraube:) tight; (haften) stick;
(nicht weiterkommen) be stuck. F~spiele

npl festival sg. f~stehen† vi sep (haben)
be certain. f~stellen vt sep fix; (ermitteln)
establish; (bemerken) notice; (sagen) state.
F~stellung f establishment; (Aussage)
statement; (Erkenntnis) realization.
F~tag m special day

Festung f -,-en fortress

Fest|zelt nt marquee. f~ziehen† vt sep
pull tight. F~zug m [grand] procession

Fete /'fe:tə, 'fɛ:tə/ f -,-n party

fett a fat; (f~reich) fatty; (fettig) greasy;
(üppig) rich; (Druck) bold; f~ gedruckt
bold. F~ nt -[e]s,-e fat; (flüssig) grease.
f~arm a low-fat. f~en vt grease □ vi
(haben) be greasy. F~fleck m grease
mark. f~ig a greasy. F~leibig a obese.
F~näpfchen nt ins F~näpfchen treten
(fam) put one's foot in it

Fetzen m -s,- scrap; (Stoff) rag; in F~ in
shreds

feucht a damp, moist; (Luft) humid.
f~heiß a humid. F~igkeit f - dampness;
(Nässe) moisture; (Luft-) humidity.
F~igkeitscreme f moisturizer

feudal a (fam: vornehm) sumptuous, adv
-ly. F~ismus m - feudalism

Feuer nt -s,- fire; (für Zigarette) light; (Begeisterung) passion; F~ machen light a
fire; F~ fangen catch fire; (fam: sich verlieben) be smitten; jdm F~ geben give
s.o. a light; F~ speiender Berg volcano.
F~alarm m fire alarm. F~bestattung f
cremation. f~gefährlich a [in]flam-
mable. F~leiter f fire-escape. F~löscher
m -s,- fire extinguisher. F~melder m -s,-
fire alarm. F~n vi (haben) fire (auf + acc
on) □ vt (fam) (schleudern) fling;
(entlassen) fire. F~probe f (fig) test.
f~rot a crimson. f~speiend a (NEW) F~
speiend, s. Feuer. F~stein m flint.
F~stelle f hearth. F~treppe f fire-escape. F~wache f fire station. F~waffe
f firearm. F~wehr f -,-en fire brigade.
F~wehrauto nt fire-engine. F~wehr-
mann m (pl -männer & -leute) fireman.
F~werk nt firework display,
fireworks pl. F~werkskörper m firework. F~zeug nt lighter

feurig a fiery; (fig) passionate

Fiaker m -s,- (Aust) horse-drawn cab

Fichte f -,-n spruce

fidel a cheerful

Fieber nt -s [raised] temperature; F~
haben have a temperature. f~haft a (fig)
feverish, adv -ly. f~n vi (haben) be feverish. F~thermometer nt thermometer

fiebrig a feverish

fies a (fam) nasty, adv -ily

Figur f -,-en figure; (Roman-, Film-)
character; (Schach-) piece

Fik|tion /-'tsi̯o:n/ f -,-en fiction. f~tiv a fictitious

Filet /fi'le:/ nt -s,-s fillet

Filia|le f -,-n, F~geschäft nt (Comm) branch

Filigran nt -s filigree

Film m -[e]s,-e film; (Kino-) film, (Amer) movie; (Schicht) coating. f~en vt/i (haben) film. F~kamera f cine/(für Kinofilm) film camera

Filt|er m & (Techn) nt filter; (Zigaretten-) filter-tip. f~ern vt filter. F~erzigarette f filter-tipped cigarette. f~rieren vt filter

Filz m -es felt. f~en vi (haben) become matted □ vt (fam) (durchsuchen) frisk; (stehlen) steal. F~schreiber m -s,-, F~stift m felt-tipped pen

Fimmel m -s,- (fam) obsession

Fina|le nt -s,- (Mus) finale; (Sport) final. F~list(in) m -en,-en (f -,-nen) finalist

Finanz f -,-en finance. F~amt nt tax office. f~iell a financial, adv -ly. f~ieren vt finance. F~minister m minister of finance

find|en† vt find; (meinen) think; den Tod f~en meet one's death; wie f~est du das? what do you think of that? f~est du? do you think so? es wird sich f~en it'll turn up; (fig) it'll be all right □ vi (haben) find one's way. F~er m -s,- finder. F~erlohn m reward. f~ig a resourceful. F~ling m -s,-e boulder

Finesse f -,-n (Kniff) trick; F~n (Techn) refinements

Finger m -s,- finger; die F~ lassen von (fam) leave alone; etw im kleinen F~ haben (fam) have sth at one's fingertips. F~abdruck m finger-mark; (Admin) fingerprint. F~hut m thimble. F~nagel m finger-nail. F~ring m ring. F~spitze f finger-tip. F~zeig m -[e]s,-e hint

fingier|en vt fake. f~t a fictitious

Fink m -en,-en finch

Finn|e m -n,-n, F~in f -,-nen Finn. f~isch a Finnish. F~land nt -s Finland

finster a dark; (düster) gloomy; (unheildrohend) sinister; im F~n in the dark. F~nis f - darkness; (Astr) eclipse

Finte f -,-n trick; (Boxen) feint

Firma f -,-men firm, company

firmen vt (Relig) confirm

Firmen|wagen m company car. F~zeichen nt trade mark, logo

Firmung f -,-en (Relig) confirmation

Firnis m -ses,-se varnish. f~sen vt varnish

First m -[e]s,-e [roof] ridge

Fisch m -[e]s,-e fish; F~e (Astr) Pisces. F~dampfer m trawler. f~en vt/i (haben) fish; aus dem Wasser f~en (fam) fish out of the water. F~er m -s,- fisherman. F~erei f -, F~fang m fishing. F~gräte f fishbone. F~händler m fishmonger. F~otter m otter. F~reiher m heron. F~stäbchen nt -s,- fish finger. F~teich m fish-pond

Fiskus m - der F~ the Treasury

Fisole f -,-n (Aust) French bean

fit a fit. Fitness (Fitneß) f - fitness

fix a (fam) quick, adv -ly; (geistig) sharp; f~e Idee obsession; fix und fertig all finished; (bereit) all ready; (fam: erschöpft) shattered. F~er m -s,- (sl) junkie

fixier|en vt stare at; (Phot) fix

Fjord m -[e]s,-e fiord

FKK abbr (Freikörperkultur) naturism

flach a flat; (eben) level; (niedrig) low; (nicht tief) shallow; f~er Teller dinner plate; die f~e Hand the flat of the hand

Fläche f -,-n area; (Ober-) surface; (Seite) face. F~nmaß nt square measure

Flachs m -es flax. f~blond a flaxen-haired; (Haar) flaxen

flackern vi (haben) flicker

Flagge f -,-n flag

flagrant a flagrant

Flair /flɛːɐ̯/ nt -s air, aura

Flak f -,-[s] anti-aircraft artillery/(Geschütz) gun

flämisch a Flemish

Flamme f -,-n flame; (Koch-) burner; in F~n in flames

Flanell m -s (Tex) flannel

Flank|e f -,-n flank. f~ieren vt flank

Flasche f -,-n bottle. F~nbier nt bottled beer. F~nöffner m bottle-opener

flatter|haft a fickle. f~n vi (sein/haben) flutter; (Segel:) flap

flau a (schwach) faint; (Comm) slack; mir ist f~ I feel faint

Flaum m -[e]s down. f~ig a downy; f~ig rühren (Aust Culin) cream

flauschig a fleecy; (Spielzeug) fluffy

Flausen fpl (fam) silly ideas; (Ausflüchte) silly excuses

Flaute f -,-n (Naut) calm; (Comm) slack period; (Schwäche) low

fläzen (sich) vr (fam) sprawl

Flechte f -,-n (Med) eczema; (Bot) lichen; (Zopf) plait. f~n† vt plait; weave (Korb)

Fleck m -[e]s,-e[n] spot; (größer) patch; (Schmutz-) stain, mark; blauer F~ bruise; nicht vom F~ kommen (fam) make no progress. f~en vi (haben) stain. F~en m -s,- = Fleck; (Ortschaft) small town. f~enlos a spotless. F~entferner m -s,- stain remover. f~ig a stained; ⟨Haut⟩ blotchy

Fledermaus f bat

Flegel m -s,- lout. f~haft a loutish. F~jahre npl ⟨fam⟩ awkward age sg. f~n (sich) vr loll

flehen vi (haben) beg (um for). f~tlich a pleading, adv -ly

Fleisch nt -[e]s flesh; ⟨Culin⟩ meat; ⟨Frucht-⟩ pulp; F~ fressend carnivorous. F~er m -s,- butcher. F~erei f -,-en, F~erladen m butcher's shop. f~fressend a ⟨NEW⟩ F~ fressend, s. Fleisch. F~fresser m -s,- carnivore. F~hauer m -s,- ⟨Aust⟩ butcher. f~ig a fleshy. f~lich a carnal. F~wolf m mincer. F~wunde f flesh-wound

Fleiß m -es diligence; mit F~ diligently; ⟨absichtlich⟩ on purpose. f~ig a diligent, adv -ly; ⟨arbeitsam⟩ industrious, adv -ly

flektieren vt ⟨Gram⟩ inflect

fletschen vt die Zähne f~ ⟨Tier:⟩ bare its teeth

flex|ibel a flexible; ⟨Einband⟩ limp. F~ibilität f - flexibility. F~ion f -,-en ⟨Gram⟩ inflexion

flicken vt mend; ⟨mit Flicken⟩ patch. F~ m -s,- patch

Flieder m -s lilac. f~farben a lilac

Fliege f -,-n fly; ⟨Schleife⟩ bow-tie; zwei F~n mit einer Klappe schlagen kill two birds with one stone. f~n† vi (sein) fly; ⟨geworfen werden⟩ be thrown; ⟨fam: fallen⟩ fall; ⟨fam: entlassen werden⟩ be fired/⟨von der Schule⟩ expelled; in die Luft f~n blow up □ vt fly. f~nd a flying; ⟨Händler⟩ itinerant; in f~nder Eile in great haste. F~r m -s,- airman; ⟨Pilot⟩ pilot; ⟨fam: Flugzeug⟩ plane. F~rangriff m air raid

flieh|en vi (sein) flee (vor + dat from); ⟨entweichen⟩ escape □ vt shun. f~end a fleeing; ⟨Kinn, Stirn⟩ receding. F~kraft f centrifugal force

Fliese f -,-n tile

Fließ|band nt assembly line. f~en† vi (sein) flow; ⟨aus Wasserhahn⟩ run. f~end a flowing; ⟨Wasser⟩ running; ⟨Verkehr⟩ moving; ⟨geläufig⟩ fluent, adv -ly. F~heck nt fastback. F~wasser nt running water

flimmern vi (haben) shimmer; ⟨TV⟩ flicker; es flimmert mir vor den Augen everything is dancing in front of my eyes

flink a nimble, adv -bly; ⟨schnell⟩ quick, adv -ly

Flinte f -,-n shotgun

Flirt /flœrt/ m -s,-s flirtation. f~en vi (haben) flirt

Flitter m -s sequins pl; ⟨F~schmuck⟩ tinsel. F~wochen fpl honeymoon sg

flitzen vi (sein) ⟨fam⟩ dash; ⟨Auto:⟩ whizz

Flock|e f -,-n flake; ⟨Wolle⟩ tuft. f~ig a fluffy

Floh m -[e]s,⸚e flea. F~markt m flea market. F~spiel nt tiddly-winks sg

Flor m -s gauze; ⟨Trauer-⟩ crape; ⟨Samt-, Teppich-⟩ pile

Flora f - flora

Florett nt -[e]s,-e foil

florieren vi (haben) flourish

Floskel f -,-n [empty] phrase

Floß nt -es,⸚e raft

Flosse f -,-n fin; ⟨Seehund-, Gummi-⟩ flipper; ⟨sl: Hand⟩ paw

Flöt|e f -,-n flute; ⟨Block-⟩ recorder. f~en vi (haben) play the flute/recorder; ⟨fam: pfeifen⟩ whistle □ vt play on the flute/recorder. F~ist(in) m -en,-en (f -,-nen) flautist

flott a quick, adv -ly; ⟨lebhaft⟩ lively; ⟨schick⟩ smart, adv -ly; f~ leben live it up

Flotte f -,-n fleet

flottmachen vt sep wieder f~ ⟨Naut⟩ refloat; get going again ⟨Auto⟩; put back on its feet ⟨Unternehmen⟩

Flöz nt -es,-e [coal] seam

Fluch m -[e]s,⸚e curse. f~en vi (haben) curse, swear

Flucht[1] f -,-en ⟨Reihe⟩ line; ⟨Zimmer-⟩ suite

Flucht[2]† f - flight; ⟨Entweichen⟩ escape; die F~ ergreifen take flight. f~artig a hasty, adv -ily

flücht|en vi (sein) flee (vor + dat from); ⟨entweichen⟩ escape □ vr sich f~en take refuge. f~ig a fugitive; ⟨kurz⟩ brief, adv -ly; ⟨Blick, Gedanke⟩ fleeting; ⟨Bekanntschaft⟩ passing; ⟨oberflächlich⟩ cursory, adv -ily; ⟨nicht sorgfältig⟩ careless, adv -ly; ⟨Chem⟩ volatile; f~ig sein be on the run; f~ig kennen know slightly. F~igkeitsfehler m slip. F~ling m -s,-e fugitive; ⟨Pol⟩ refugee

Fluchwort nt (pl -wörter) swear-word

Flug m -[e]s,⸚e flight. F~abwehr f anti-aircraft defence. F~ball m ⟨Tennis⟩ volley. F~blatt nt pamphlet

Flügel m -s,- wing; ⟨Fenster-⟩ casement; ⟨Mus⟩ grand piano

Fluggast m [air] passenger

flügge a fully-fledged

Flug|gesellschaft f airline. F~hafen m airport. F~lotse m air traffic controller. F~platz m airport, ⟨klein⟩ airfield. F~preis m air fare. F~schein m air ticket. F~schneise f flight path. F~schreiber m -s,- flight recorder. F~

schrift *f* pamphlet. F~steig *m* -[e]s,-e gate. F~wesen *nt* aviation. F~zeug *nt* -[e]s,-e aircraft, plane

Fluidum *nt* -s aura

Flunder *f* -,-n flounder

flunkern *vi* (*haben*) (*fam*) tell fibs; (*aufschneiden*) tell tall stories

Flunsch *m* -[e]s,-e pout

fluoreszierend *a* fluorescent

Flur *m* -[e]s,-e [entrance] hall; (*Gang*) corridor

Flur *f* -,-en field

Flusen *fpl* fluff *sg*

Fluss *m* -es,-e (Fluß *m* -sses,-sse) river; (*Fließen*) flow; im F~ (*fig*) in a state of flux. f~abwärts *adv* down-stream. f~aufwärts *adv* up-stream. F~bett *nt* river-bed

flüssig *a* liquid; (*Lava*) molten; (*fließend*) fluent, *adv* -ly; (*Verkehr*) freely moving. F~keit *f* -,-en liquid; (*Anat*) fluid

Flusspferd (Flußpferd) *nt* hippopotamus

flüstern *vt/i* (*haben*) whisper

Flut *f* -,-en high tide; (*fig*) flood; F~en waters. F~licht *nt* flood-light. F~welle *f* tidal wave

Föderation /-'tsjo:n/ *f* -,-en federation

Fohlen *nt* -s,- foal

Föhn *m* -s föhn [wind]; (*Haartrockner*) hair-drier. f~en *vt* [blow-]dry

Folge *f* -,-n consequence; (*Reihe*) succession; (*Fortsetzung*) instalment; (*Teil*) part; F~e leisten (+ *dat*) accept (*Einladung*); obey (*Befehl*). f~en *vi* (*sein*) follow (jdm/etw s.o./sth); (*zuhören*) listen (*dat* to); daraus f~t, dass it follows that; wie f~t as follows □ (*haben*) (*gehorchen*) obey (jdm s.o.). f~end *a* following; F~endes (f~endes) the following. f~endermaßen *adv* as follows

folgern *vt* conclude (aus from). F~ung *f* -,-en conclusion

folglich *adv* consequently. f~sam *a* obedient, *adv* -ly

Folie /'fo:ljə/ *f* -,-n foil; (*Plastik-*) film

Folklore *f* - folklore

Folter *f* -,-n torture; auf die F~ spannen (*fig*) keep on tenterhooks. f~n *vt* torture

Fön (P) *m* -s,-e hair-drier

Fonds /fõ:/ *m* -,- // -[s],-s// fund

fönen *vt* (NEW) föhnen

Fontäne *f* -,-n jet; (*Brunnen*) fountain

Förderband *nt* (*pl* -bänder) conveyor belt. f~lich *a* beneficial

fordern *vt* demand; (*beanspruchen*) claim; (*zum Kampf*) challenge; gefordert werden (*fig*) be stretched

fördern *vt* promote; (*unterstützen*) encourage; (*finanziell*) sponsor; (*gewinnen*) extract

Forderung *f* -,-en demand; (*Anspruch*) claim

Förderung *f* -(s. fördern) promotion; encouragement; (*Techn*) production

Forelle *f* -,-n trout

Form *f* -,-en form; (*Gestalt*) shape; (*Culin, Techn*) mould; (*Back-*) tin; [gut] in F~ in good form

Formalität *f* -,-en formality

Format *nt* -[e]s,-e format; (*Größe*) size; (*fig: Bedeutung*) stature

Formation /-'tsjo:n/ *f* -,-en formation

Formel *f* -,-n formula

formell *a* formal, *adv* -ly

formen *vt* shape, mould; (*bilden*) form; sich f~ take shape

förmlich *a* formal, *adv* -ly; (*regelrecht*) virtual, *adv* -ly. F~keit *f* -,-en formality

formlos *a* shapeless; (*zwanglos*) informal, *adv* -ly. F~sache *f* formality

Formular *nt* -s,-e [printed] form

formulieren *vt* formulate, word. F~ung *f* -,-en wording

forsch *a* brisk, *adv* -ly; (*schneidig*) dashing, *adv* -ly

forschen *vi* (*haben*) search (nach for). f~end *a* searching. F~er *m* -s,- research scientist; (*Reisender*) explorer. F~ung *f* -,-en research. F~ungsreisende(r) *m* explorer

Forst *m* -[e]s,-e forest

Förster *m* -s,- forester

Forstwirtschaft *f* forestry

Forsythie /-tsjə/ *f* -,-n forsythia

Fort *nt* -s,-s (*Mil*) fort

fort *adv* away; f~ sein be away; (*gegangen/verschwunden*) have gone; und so f~ and so on; in einem f~ continuously. f~bewegen *vt sep* move. f~bewegen move. F~bewegung *f* locomotion. F~bildung *f* further education/training. f~bleiben† *vi sep* (*sein*) stay away. f~bringen† *vt sep* take away. f~fahren† *vi sep* (*sein*) go away □ (*haben/sein*) continue (zu to). f~fallen† *vi sep* (*sein*) be dropped/ (*ausgelassen*) omitted; (*entfallen*) no longer apply; (*aufhören*) cease. f~führen *vt sep* continue. F~gang *m* departure; (*Verlauf*) progress. f~gehen† *vi sep* (*sein*) leave, go away; (*ausgehen*) go out; (*andauern*) go on. f~geschritten *a* advanced; (*spät*) late. F~geschrittene(r) *m/f* advanced student. f~gesetzt *a* constant, *adv* -ly. f~jagen *vt sep* chase away. f~lassen† *vt* sep let go; (*auslassen*) omit. f~laufen† *vi sep* (*sein*) run away; (*sich f~setzen*) continue. f~laufend *a* consecutive, *adv* -ly. f~nehmen† *vt sep* take away. f~pflanzen (*sich*) *vr sep* reproduce; ⟨*Ton, Licht:*⟩ travel. F~pflanzung *f* - reproduction. F~pflanzungsorgan *nt* reproductive organ. f~reißen† *vt sep* carry away; (*entreißen*) tear away. f~schaffen *vt sep* take away. f~schicken *vt sep* send away; (*abschicken*) send off. f~schreiten† *vi sep* (*sein*) continue; (*Fortschritte machen*) progress, advance. f~schreitend *a* progressive; ⟨*Alter*⟩ advancing. F~schritt *m* progress; F~schritte machen make progress. f~schrittlich *a* progressive. f~setzen *vt sep* continue; sich f~setzen continue. F~setzung *f* -,-en continuation; (*Folge*) instalment; F~setzung folgt to be continued. F~setzungsroman *m* serialized novel, serial. f~während *a* constant, *adv* -ly. f~werfen† *vt sep* throw away. f~ziehen† *v sep* □ *vt* pull away □ *vi* (*sein*) move away

Fossil *nt* -,-ien /-jən/ fossil

Foto *nt* -s,-s photo. F~apparat *m* camera. f~gen *a* photogenic

Fotograf|(in) *m* -en,-en (*f* -,-nen) photographer. F~ie *f* -,-n photography; (*Bild*) photograph. f~ieren *vt* take a photo [graph] of; sich f~ieren lassen have one's photo[graph] taken □ *vi* (*haben*) take photographs. f~isch *a* photographic

Fotokopie *f* photocopy. F~ren *vt* photocopy. F~rgerät *nt* photocopier

Fötus *m* -,-ten foetus

Foul /faul/ *nt* -s,-s (*Sport*) foul. f~en *vt* foul

Foyer /foaˈjeː/ *nt* -s,-s foyer

Fracht *f* -,-en freight. F~er *m* -s,- freighter. F~gut *nt* freight. F~schiff *nt* cargo boat

Frack *m* -[e]s,-̈e & -s tailcoat; im F~ in tails *pl*

Frage *f* -,-n question; ohne F~ undoubtedly; eine F~ stellen ask a question; etw in F~ stellen = etw infrage stellen, *s.* infrage; nicht in F~ kommen = nicht infrage kommen, *s.* infrage. F~bogen *m* questionnaire. F~n *vt* (*haben*) ask; sich f~n wonder (ob whether). f~nd *a* questioning, *adv* -ly; (*Gram*) interrogative. F~zeichen *nt* question mark

frag|lich *a* doubtful; (*Person, Sache*) in question. f~los *adv* undoubtedly

Fragment *nt* -[e]s,-e fragment. f~arisch *a* fragmentary

fragwürdig *a* questionable; (*verdächtig*) dubious

fraisefarben /ˈfrɛːs-/ *a* strawberry-pink

Fraktion /-ˈtsi̯oːn/ *f* -,-en parliamentary party

Franken[1] *m* -s,- (*Swiss*) franc

Franken[2] *nt* -s Franconia

Frankfurter *f* -,- frankfurter

frankieren *vt* stamp, frank

Frankreich *nt* -s France

Fransen *fpl* fringe *sg*

Franz|ose *m* -n,-n Frenchman; die F~osen the French *pl*. F~ösin *f* -,-nen Frenchwoman. f~ösisch *a* French. F~ösisch *nt* -[s] (*Lang*) French

frapp|ant *a* striking. f~ieren *vt* (*fig*) strike; f~ierend striking

fräsen *vt* (*Techn*) mill

Fraß *m* -es feed; (*pej: Essen*) muck

Fratze *f* -,-n grotesque face; (*Grimasse*) grimace; (*pej: Gesicht*) face; F~n schneiden pull faces

Frau *f* -,-en woman; (*Ehe-*) wife; F~ Thomas Mrs/(*unverheiratet*) Miss/ (*Admin*) Ms Thomas; Unsere Liebe F~ (*Relig*) Our Lady. F~chen *nt* -s,- mistress

Frauen|arzt *m*, F~ärztin *f* gynaecologist. F~rechtlerin *f* -,-nen feminist. F~zimmer *nt* woman

Fräulein *nt* -s,- single woman; (*jung*) young lady; (*Anrede*) Miss

fraulich *a* womanly

frech *a* cheeky, *adv* -ily; (*unverschämt*) impudent, *adv* -ly. F~dachs *m* (*fam*) cheeky monkey. F~heit *f* -,-en cheekiness; impudence; (*Äußerung, Handlung*) impertinence

frei *a* free; (*freischaffend*) freelance; ⟨*Künstler*⟩ independent; (*nicht besetzt*) vacant; (*offen*) open; (*bloß*) bare; f~er Tag day off; sich (*dat*) f~ nehmen take time off; f~ machen (*räumen*) clear; vacate (*Platz*); (*befreien*) liberate; f~ lassen leave free; jdm f~e Hand lassen give s.o. a free hand; ist dieser Platz f~? is this seat taken? 'Zimmer f~' 'vacancies' □ *adv* freely; (*ohne Notizen*) without notes; (*umsonst*) free

Frei|bad *nt* open-air swimming pool. f~bekommen† *vt sep* get released; einen Tag f~bekommen get a day off. f~beruflich *a* & *adv* freelance. F~e *nt* im F~en in the open air, out of doors. F~frau *f* baroness. F~gabe *f* release. f~geben† *v sep* □ *vt* release; (*eröffnen*) open; jdm einen Tag f~geben give s.o. a day off □ *vi* (*haben*) jdm f~geben give s.o. time off. f~gebig *a* generous, *adv* -ly. F~gebigkeit *f* - generosity. f~haben† *v sep* □ *vt* eine Stunde f~haben have an hour off; (*Sch*) have a free period □ *vi* (*haben*) be off work/(*Sch*) school; (*beurlaubt sein*) have time off. f~halten† *vt sep* keep clear;

(*belegen*) keep; einen Tag/sich f~halten keep a day/oneself free; jdn f~halten treat s.o. [to a meal/drink]. F~handelszone *f* free-trade area. f~händig *adv* without holding on

Freiheit *f* -,-en freedom, liberty; sich (*dat*) F~en erlauben take liberties. F~sstrafe *f* prison sentence

freiheraus *adv* frankly

Frei|herr *m* baron. F~karte *f* free ticket. F~körperkultur *f* naturism. f~lassen† *vt sep* release, set free. F~lassung *f* - release. F~lauf *m* free-wheel. f~legen *vt sep* expose. f~lich *adv* admittedly; (*natürlich*) of course. F~lichttheater *nt* open-air theatre. f~machen *v sep* □ *vt* (*frankieren*) frank; (*entkleiden*) bare; einen Tag f~machen take a day off □ *vi/r* (*haben*) [sich] f~machen take time off. F~marke *f* [postage] stamp. F~maurer *m* Freemason. f~mütig *a* candid, *adv* -ly. F~platz *m* free seat; (*Sch*) free place. f~schaffend *a* freelance. f~schwimmen† (sich) *v sep* pass one's swimming test. f~setzen *vt sep* release; (*entlassen*) make redundant. f~sprechen† *vt sep* acquit. F~spruch *m* acquittal. f~stehen† *vi sep* (*haben*) stand empty; es steht ihm f~ (*fig*) he is free (zu to). f~stellen *vt sep* exempt (von from); jdm etw f~stellen leave sth up to s.o. f~stempeln *vt sep* frank. F~stil *m* freestyle. F~stoß *m* free kick. f~stunde *f* (*Sch*) free period

Freitag *m* Friday. f~s *adv* on Fridays

Frei|tod *m* suicide. F~übungen *fpl* [physical] exercises. F~umschlag *m* stamped envelope. f~weg *adv* freely; (*offen*) openly. f~willig *a* voluntary, *adv* -ly. F~willige(r) *m/f* volunteer. F~zeichen *nt* ringing tone; (*Rufzeichen*) dialling tone. F~zeit *f* free or spare time; (*Muße*) leisure; (*Tagung*) [weekend/holiday] course. F~zeit- *pref* leisure ... F~zeitbekleidung *f* casual wear. f~zügig *a* unrestricted; (*großzügig*) liberal; (*moralisch*) permissive

fremd *a* foreign; (*unbekannt, ungewohnt*) strange; (*nicht das eigene*) other people's; ein f~er Mann a stranger; f~e Leute strangers; unter f~em Namen under an assumed name; jdm f~ sein be unknown/(*wesens-*) alien to s.o.; ich bin hier f~ I'm a stranger here. f~artig *a* strange, *adv* -ly; (*exotisch*) exotic. F~e *f* - in der F~e away from home; (*im Ausland*) in a foreign country. F~e(r) *m/f* stranger; (*Ausländer*) foreigner; (*Tourist*) tourist. F~enführer *m* [tourist] guide. F~enverkehr *m* tourism. F~enzimmer *nt* room [to let]; (*Gäste-*) guest room.

f~gehen† *vi sep* (*sein*) (*fam*) be unfaithful. F~körper *m* foreign body. f~ländisch *a* foreign; (*exotisch*) exotic. F~ling *m* -s,-e stranger. F~sprache *f* foreign language. F~wort *nt* (*pl* -wörter) foreign word

frenetisch *a* frenzied

frequ|entieren *vt* frequent. F~enz *f* -,-en frequency

Freske *f* -,-n, **Fresko** *nt* -s,-ken fresco

Fresse *f* -,-n (*sl*) (*Mund*) gob; (*Gesicht*) mug; halt die F~! shut your trap! f~n† *vt/i* (*haben*) eat. F~n *nt* -s feed; (*sl: Essen*) grub

Fressnapf (Freßnapf) *m* feeding bowl

Freud|e *f* -,-n pleasure; (*innere*) joy; mit F~en with pleasure; jdm eine F~e machen please s.o. f~ig *a* joyful, *adv* -ly; f~iges Ereignis (*fig*) happy event. f~los *a* cheerless; (*traurig*) sad

freuen *vt* please; sich f~ be pleased (über + *acc* about); sich f~ auf (+ *acc*) look forward to; es freut mich, ich freue mich I'm glad *or* pleased (dass that)

Freund *m* -es,-e friend; (*Verehrer*) boyfriend; (*Anhänger*) lover (*gen* of). F~in *f* -,-nen friend; (*Liebste*) girlfriend; (*Anhängerin*) lover (*gen* of). f~lich *a* kind, *adv* -ly; (*umgänglich*) friendly; (*angenehm*) pleasant; wären Sie so f~lich? would you be so kind? f~licherweise *adv* kindly. F~lichkeit *f* -,-en kindness; friendliness; pleasantness

Freundschaft *f* -,-en friendship; F~ schließen become friends. f~lich *a* friendly

Frevel /'fre:fəl/ *m* -s,- (*liter*) outrage. f~haft *a* (*liter*) wicked

Frieden *m* -s peace; F~ schließen make peace; im F~ in peace-time; laß mich in F~! leave me alone! F~srichter *m* ≈ magistrate. F~svertrag *m* peace treaty

fried|fertig *a* peaceable. F~hof *m* cemetery. f~lich *a* peaceful, *adv* -ly; (*verträglich*) peaceable. f~liebend *a* peace-loving

frieren† *vi* (*haben*) (*Person:*) be cold; *impers* es friert/hat gefroren it is freezing/ there has been a frost; frierst du? friert [es] dich? are you cold? □ (*sein*) (*gefrieren*) freeze

Fries *m* -es,-e frieze

Frikadelle *f* -,-n [meat] rissole

frisch *a* fresh; (*sauber*) clean; (*leuchtend*) bright; (*munter*) lively; (*rüstig*) fit; sich f~machen freshen up □ *adv* freshly, newly; f~ gelegte Eier new-laid eggs; ein Bett f~ beziehen put clean sheets on a bed; f~ gestrichen! wet paint! F~e *f* - freshness; brightness; liveliness; fitness. F~haltepackung *f* vacuum pack.

F∼käse m ≈ cottage cheese. f∼weg adv freely

Fri|seur /fri'zøːɐ̯/ m -s,-e hairdresser; (Herren-) barber. F∼seursalon m hairdressing salon. F∼seuse /-'zøːzə/ f -,-n hairdresser

frisier|en vt jdn/sich f∼en do s.o.'s/one's hair; die Bilanz/einen Motor f∼en (fam) fiddle the accounts/soup up an engine. F∼kommode f dressing-table. F∼salon m = Friseursalon. F∼tisch m dressing-table

Frisör m -s,-e = Friseur

Frist f -,-en period; (Termin) deadline; (Aufschub) time; drei Tage F∼ three days' grace. f∼en vt sein Leben f∼en eke out an existence. f∼los a instant, adv -ly

Frisur f -,-en hairstyle

frittieren (fritieren) vt deep-fry

frivol /fri'voːl/ a frivolous, adv -ly; (schlüpfrig) smutty

froh a happy; (freudig) joyful; (erleichtert) glad; f∼e Ostern! happy Easter!

fröhlich a cheerful, adv -ly; (vergnügt) merry, adv -ily; f∼e Weihnachten! merry Christmas! F∼keit f - cheerfulness; merriment

frohlocken vi (haben) rejoice; (schadenfroh) gloat

Frohsinn m - cheerfulness

fromm a (frömmer, frömmst) devout, adv -ly; (gutartig) docile, adv -ly; f∼er Wunsch idle wish

Frömm|igkeit f - devoutness, piety. f∼lerisch a sanctimonious, adv -ly

frönen vi (haben) indulge (dat in)

Fronleichnam m Corpus Christi

Front f -,-en front. F∼al a frontal; (Zusammenstoß) head-on □ adv from the front; (zusammenstoßen) head-on. F∼alzusammenstoß m head-on collision

Frosch m -[e]s,-̈e frog. F∼laich m frogspawn. F∼mann m (pl -männer) frogman

Frost m -[e]s,-̈e frost. F∼beule f chilblain

frösteln vi (haben) shiver; mich fröstelte [es] I shivered/(fror) felt chilly

frost|ig a frosty, adv -ily. F∼schutzmittel nt antifreeze

Frottee nt & m -s towelling

frottier|en vt rub down. F∼[hand]tuch nt terry towel

frotzeln vt/i (haben) [über] jdn f∼ make fun of s.o.

Frucht f -,-̈e fruit; F∼ tragen bear fruit. f∼bar a fertile; (fig) fruitful. F∼barkeit f - fertility. f∼en vi (haben) wenig/nichts f∼en have little/no effect. f∼ig a fruity.

f∼los a fruitless, adv -ly. F∼saft m fruit juice

frugal a frugal, adv -ly

früh a early □ adv early; (morgens) in the morning; heute/gestern/morgen f∼ this/yesterday/tomorrow morning; von f∼ an od auf from an early age. f∼auf adv von f∼auf (NEW) von f∼ auf, s. früh. F∼aufsteher m -s,- early riser. F∼e f - in aller F∼e bright and early; in der F∼e (SGer) in the morning. f∼er adv earlier; (eher) sooner; (ehemals) formerly; (vor langer Zeit) in the old days; f∼er oder später sooner or later; ich wohnte f∼er in X I used to live in X. f∼ere(r,s) a earlier; (ehemalig) former; (vorige) previous; in f∼eren Zeiten in former times. f∼estens adv at the earliest. F∼geburt f premature birth/(Kind) baby. F∼jahr nt spring. F∼jahrsputz m spring-cleaning. F∼kartoffeln fpl new potatoes. F∼ling m -s,-e spring. f∼morgens adv early in the morning. f∼reif a precocious

Frühstück nt breakfast. f∼en vi (haben) have breakfast

frühzeitig a & adv early; (vorzeitig) premature, adv -ly

Frustr|ation /-'tsi̯oːn/ f -,-en frustration. f∼ieren vt frustrate; f∼ierend frustrating

Fuchs m -es,-̈e fox; (Pferd) chestnut. f∼en vt (fam) annoy

Füchsin f -,-nen vixen

fuchteln vi (haben) mit etw f∼ (fam) wave sth about

Fuder nt -s,- cart-load

Fuge¹ f -,-n joint; aus den F∼n gehen fall apart

Fuge² f -,-n (Mus) fugue

füg|en vt fit (in + acc into); (an-) join (an + acc on to); (dazu-) add (zu to); (fig: bewirken) ordain; sich f∼en fit (in + acc into); adjoin/(folgen) follow (an etw acc sth); (fig: gehorchen) submit (dat to); sich in sein Schicksal f∼en resign oneself to one's fate; es f∼te sich it so happened (dass that). f∼sam a obedient, adv -ly. F∼ung f -,-en eine F∼ung des Schicksals a stroke of fate

fühl|bar a noticeable. f∼en vt/i (haben) feel; sich f∼en feel (krank/einsam ill/lonely); (fam: stolz sein) fancy oneself; sich [nicht] wohl f∼en [not] feel well. F∼er m -s,- feeler. F∼ung f - contact; F∼ung aufnehmen get in touch

Fuhre f -,-n load

führ|en vt lead; guide (Tourist); (geleiten) take; (leiten) run; (befehligen) command; (verkaufen) stock; bear (Namen, Titel); keep (Liste, Bücher, Tagebuch); bei od mit sich f~en carry; sich gut/schlecht f~en conduct oneself well/badly □ vi (haben) lead; (verlaufen) go, run; zu etw f~en lead to sth. f~end a leading. F~er m -s,- leader; (Fremden-) guide; (Buch) guide[book]. F~erhaus nt driver's cab. F~erschein m driving licence; den F~erschein machen take one's driving test. F~erscheinentzug m disqualification from driving. F~ung f -,-en leadership; (Leitung) management; (Mil) command; (Betragen) conduct; (Besichtigung) guided tour; (Vorsprung) lead; in F~ung gehen go into the lead

Fuhr|unternehmer m haulage contractor. F~werk nt cart

Fülle f -,-n abundance, wealth (an + dat of); (Körper-) plumpness. f~n vt fill; (Culin) stuff; sich f~n fill [up]

Füllen nt -s,- foal

Füll|er m -s,- (fam), F~federhalter m fountain pen. f~ig a plump; (Busen) ample. F~ung f -,-en filling; (Kissen-, Braten-) stuffing; (Pralinen-) centre

fummeln vi (haben) fumble (an + dat with)

Fund m -[e]s,-e find

Fundament nt -[e]s,-e foundations pl. f~al a fundamental

Fund|büro nt lost-property office. F~grube f (fig) treasure trove. F~sachen fpl lost property sg

fünf inv a, F~ f -,-en five; (Sch) ≈ fail mark. F~linge mpl quintuplets. f~te(r,s) a fifth. f~zehn inv a fifteen. f~zehnte(r,s) a fifteenth. f~zig inv a fifty. F~ziger m -s,- man in his fifties; (Münze) 50-pfennig piece. f~zigste(r,s) a fiftieth

fungieren vi (haben) act (als as)

Funk m -s radio; über F~ over the radio. F~e m -n,-n spark. f~eln vi (haben) sparkle; ⟨Stern:⟩ twinkle. F~elnagelneu a (fam) brand-new. F~en m -s,- spark. f~en vt radio. F~er m -s,- radio operator. F~sprechgerät nt walkie-talkie. F~spruch m radio message. F~streife f [police] radio patrol

Funktion f -'tsjo:n/ f -,-en function; (Stellung) position; (Funktionieren) working; außer F~ out of action. F~är m -s,-e official. f~ieren vi (haben) work

für prep (+ acc) for; Schritt für Schritt step by step; was für [ein] what [a]! (fragend) what sort of [a]? für sich by oneself/⟨Ding:⟩ itself. Für nt das Für und Wider the pros and cons pl. F~bitte f intercession

Furche f -,-n furrow

Furcht f - fear (vor + dat of); F~ erregend terrifying. f~bar a terrible, adv -bly

fürcht|en vt/i (haben) fear; sich f~en be afraid (vor + dat of); ich f~e, das geht nicht I'm afraid that's impossible. f~erlich a dreadful, adv -ly

furcht|erregend a NEW F~ erregend s. Furcht. F~los a fearless, adv -ly. f~sam a timid, adv -ly

füreinander adv for each other

Furnier nt -s,-e veneer. f~t a veneered

fürs prep = für das

Fürsorg|e f care; (Admin) welfare; (fam: Geld) ≈ social security. F~er(in) m -s,- (f -,-nen) social worker. f~lich a solicitous

Fürsprache f intercession; f~ einlegen intercede

Fürsprecher m (fig) advocate

Fürst m -en,-en prince. F~entum nt -s, ¨-er principality. F~in f -,-nen princess. f~lich a princely; (üppig) lavish, adv -ly

Furt f -,-en ford

Furunkel m -s,- (Med) boil

Fürwort nt (pl -wörter) pronoun

Furz m -es,-e (vulg) fart. f~en vi (haben) (vulg) fart

Fusion f -,-en fusion; (Comm) merger. f~ieren vi (haben) (Comm) merge

Fuß m -es,-e foot; (Aust: Bein) leg; (Lampen-) base; (von Weinglas) stem; zu Fuß on foot; zu Fuß gehen walk; auf freiem Fuß free; auf freundschaftlichem/großem Fuß on friendly terms/in grand style. F~abdruck m footprint. F~abtreter m -s,- doormat. F~bad nt footbath. F~ball m football. F~ball-spieler m footballer. F~balltoto nt football pools pl. F~bank f footstool. F~boden m floor. F~bremse f footbrake

Fussel f -,-n & m -s,-[n] piece of fluff; F~n fluff sg. f~n vi (haben) shed fluff

fuß|en vi (haben) be based (auf + dat on). F~ende nt foot

Fußgänger|(in) m -s,- (f -,-nen) pedestrian. F~brücke f footbridge. F~überweg m pedestrian crossing. F~zone f pedestrian precinct

Fuß|geher m -s,- (Aust) = F~gänger. F~gelenk nt ankle. F~hebel m pedal. F~nagel m toenail. F~note f footnote. F~pflege f chiropody. F~pfleger(in) m(f) chiropodist. F~rücken m instep. F~sohle f sole of the foot. F~stapfen pl in jds F~stapfen treten (fig) follow in s.o.'s footsteps. F~tritt m kick. F~weg m footpath; eine Stunde F~weg an hour's walk

futsch pred a (fam) gone

Futter¹ nt -s feed; (Trocken-) fodder

Futter² *nt* -s,- (*Kleider-*) lining
Futteral *nt* -s,-e case
füttern¹ *vt* feed
füttern² *vt* line
Futur *nt* -s (*Gram*) future; zweites F~ future perfect. f~istisch *a* futuristic

G

Gabe *f* -,-n gift; (*Dosis*) dose
Gabel *f* -,-n fork. g~n (sich) *vr* fork. G~stapler *m* -s,- fork-lift truck. G~ung *f* -,-en fork
gackern *vi* (*haben*) cackle
gaffen *vi* (*haben*) gape, stare
Gag /gɛk/ *m* -s,-s (*Theat*) gag
Gage /'gaːʒə/ *f* -,-n (*Theat*) fee
gähnen *vi* (*haben*) yawn. G~ *nt* -s yawn; (*wiederholt*) yawning
Gala *f* - ceremonial dress
galant *a* gallant, *adv* -ly
Galavorstellung *f* gala performance
Galerie *f* -,-n gallery
Galgen *m* -s,- gallows *f* (*fam*) reprieve
Galionsfigur *f* figurehead
Galle *f* - bile; (*G~nblase*) gall-bladder. G~nblase *f* gall-bladder. G~nstein *m* gallstone
Gallert *nt* -[e]s,-e, **Gallerte** *f* -,-n [meat] jelly
Galopp *m* -s gallop; im G~ at a gallop. g~ieren *vi* (*sein*) gallop
galvanisieren *vt* galvanize
gammeln *vi* (*haben*) (*fam*) loaf around. G~ler(in) *m* -s,- (*f* -,-nen) drop-out
Gams *f* -,-en (*Aust*) chamois
Gämse *f* -,-n chamois
gang *pred a* g~ und gäbe quite usual
Gang *m* -[e]s,ˉe walk; (*G~art*) gait; (*Boten-*) errand; (*Funktionieren*) running; (*Verlauf, Culin*) course; (*Durch-*) passage; (*Korridor*) corridor; (*zwischen Sitzreihen*) aisle, gangway; (*Anat*) duct; (*Auto*) gear; in G~ bringen/halten get/keep going; in G~ kommen get going/(*fig*) under way; im G~e/in vollem G~e sein be in progress/in full swing; Essen mit vier G~en four-course meal. G~art *f* gait
gängig *a* common; (*Comm*) popular
Gangschaltung *f* gear change
Gangster /'gɛŋstɐ/ *m* -s,- gangster
Gangway /'gɛŋweː/ *f* -,-s gangway
Ganove *m* -n,-n (*fam*) crook

Gans *f* -,ˉe goose
Gänse|blümchen *nt* -s,- daisy. G~füßchen *ntpl* inverted commas. G~haut *f* goose pimples *pl*. G~marsch *m* im G~marsch in single file. G~rich *m* -s,-e gander
ganz *a* whole, entire; (*vollständig*) complete; (*fam: heil*) undamaged, intact; die g~e Zeit all the time, the whole time; eine g~e Weile/Menge quite a while/lot; g~e zehn Mark all of ten marks; meine g~en Bücher all my books; *inv* g~ Deutschland the whole of Germany; g~ bleiben (*fam*) remain intact; wieder g~ machen (*fam*) mend; im G~en (g~en) in all, altogether; im Großen und G~en (im großen und g~en) on the whole □ *adv* quite; (*völlig*) completely, entirely; (*sehr*) very; nicht g~ not quite; g~ allein all on one's own; ein g~ alter Mann a very old man; g~ wie du willst just as you like; es war g~ nett it was quite nice; g~ und gar completely, totally; g~ und gar nicht not at all. G~e(s) *nt* whole; es geht ums G~e it's all or nothing. g~jährig *adv* all the year round
gänzlich *adv* completely, entirely
ganz|tägig *a & adv* full-time; (*geöffnet*) all day. g~tags *adv* all day; (*arbeiten*) full-time
gar¹ *a* done, cooked
gar² *adv* gar nicht/nichts/niemand not/nothing/no one at all; oder gar or even
Garage /ɡaˈraːʒə/ *f* -,-n garage
Garantie *f* -,-n guarantee. g~ren *vt/i* (*haben*) [für] etw g~ren guarantee sth; er kommt g~rt zu spät (*fam*) he's sure to be late. G~schein *m* guarantee
Garbe *f* -,-n sheaf
Garderobe *f* -,-n (*Kleider*) wardrobe; (*Ablage*) cloakroom, (*Amer*) checkroom; (*Flur-*) coat-rack; (*Künstler-*) dressing-room. G~nfrau *f* cloakroom attendant
Gardine *f* -,-n curtain. G~nstange *f* curtain rail
garen *vt/i* (*haben*) cook
gären† *vi* (*haben*) ferment; (*fig*) seethe
Garn *nt* -[e]s,-e yarn; (*Näh-*) cotton
Garnele *f* -,-n shrimp; (*rote*) prawn
garnieren *vt* decorate; (*Culin*) garnish
Garnison *f* -,-en garrison
Garnitur *f* -,-en set; (*Wäsche*) set of matching underwear; (*Möbel-*) suite; erste/zweite G~ sein (*fam*) be first-rate/second-best
garstig *a* nasty
Garten *m* -s,ˉ garden; botanischer G~ botanical gardens *pl*. G~arbeit *f* gardening. G~bau *m* horticulture. G~haus *nt*, G~laube *f* summerhouse. G~lokal

nt open-air café. G∼schere *f* secateurs *pl*

Gärtner|(in) *m* -s,- (*f* -,-nen) gardener. G∼ei *f* -,-en nursery; (*fam: Gartenarbeit*) gardening

Gärung *f* - fermentation

Gas *nt* -es,-e gas; Gas geben (*fam*) accelerate. G∼herd *m* gas cooker. G∼maske *f* gas mask. G∼pedal *nt* (*Auto*) accelerator

Gasse *f* -,-n alley; (*Aust*) street

Gast *m* -[e]s,-e guest; (*Hotel-, Urlaubs-*) visitor; (*im Lokal*) patron; zum Mittag G∼e haben have people to lunch; bei jdm zu G∼ sein be staying with s.o. G∼arbeiter *m* foreign worker. G∼bett *nt* spare bed

Gäste|bett *nt* spare bed. G∼buch *nt* visitors' book. G∼zimmer *nt* (*Hotel*) room; (*privat*) spare room; (*Aufenthaltsraum*) residents' lounge

gast|frei, g∼freundlich *a* hospitable, *adv* -bly. G∼freundschaft *f* hospitality. G∼geber *m* -s,- host. G∼geberin *f* -,-nen hostess. G∼haus *nt*, G∼hof *m* inn, hotel

gastieren *vi* (*haben*) make a guest appearance; (*Truppe, Zirkus:*) perform (in + *dat* in)

gastlich *a* hospitable, *adv* -bly. G∼keit *f* - hospitality

Gastro|nomie *f* - gastronomy. g∼nomisch *a* gastronomic

Gast|spiel *nt* guest performance. G∼spielreise *f* (*Theat*) tour. G∼stätte *f* restaurant. G∼stube *f* bar; (*Restaurant*) restaurant. G∼wirt *m* landlord. G∼wirtin *f* landlady. G∼wirtschaft *f* restaurant

Gas|werk *nt* gasworks *sg*. G∼zähler *m* gas-meter

Gatte *m* -n,-n husband

Gatter *nt* -s,- gate; (*Gehege*) pen

Gattin *f* -,-nen wife

Gattung *f* -,-en kind; (*Biol*) genus; (*Kunst*) genre. G∼sbegriff *m* generic term

Gaudi *f* - (*Aust, fam*) fun

Gaul *m* -[e]s, Gäule [old] nag

Gaumen *m* -s,- palate

Gauner *m* -s,- crook, swindler. G∼ei *f* -,-en swindle

Gaze /'ga:zə/ *f* - gauze

Gazelle *f* -,-n gazelle

geachtet *a* respected

geädert *a* veined

geartet *a* gut g∼ good-natured; anders g∼ different

Gebäck *nt* -s [cakes and] pastries *pl*; (*Kekse*) biscuits *pl*

Gebälk *nt* -s timbers *pl*

geballt *a* (*Faust*) clenched

Gebärde *f* -,-n gesture. g∼n (sich) *vr* behave (wie like)

Gebaren *nt* -s behaviour

gebär|en† *vt* give birth to, bear; geboren werden be born. G∼mutter *f* womb, uterus

Gebäude *nt* -s,- building

Gebeine *ntpl* [mortal] remains

Gebell *nt* -s barking

geben† *vt* give; (*tun, bringen*) put; (*Karten*) deal; (*aufführen*) perform; (*unterrichten*) teach; etw verloren g∼ give sth up as lost; von sich g∼ utter; (*fam: erbrechen*) bring up; viel/wenig g∼ auf (+ *acc*) set great/little store by; sich g∼ (*nachlassen*) wear off; (*besser werden*) get better; (*sich verhalten*) behave; sich geschlagen g∼ admit defeat □ *impers* es gibt there is/are; was gibt es Neues/zum Mittag/im Kino? what's the news/for lunch/on at the cinema? es wird Regen g∼ it's going to rain; das gibt es nicht there's no such thing □ *vi* (*haben*) (*Karten*) deal

Gebet *nt* -[e]s,-e prayer

Gebiet *nt* -[e]s,-e area; (*Hoheits-*) territory; (*Sach-*) field

gebiet|en† *vt* command; (*erfordern*) demand □ *vi* (*haben*) rule. G∼er *m* -s,- master; (*Herrscher*) ruler. g∼erisch *a* imperious, *adv* -ly; (*Ton*) peremptory

Gebilde *nt* -s,- structure

gebildet *a* educated; (*kultiviert*) cultured

Gebirg|e *nt* -s,- mountains *pl*. g∼ig *a* mountainous

Gebiss *nt* -es,-e (Gebiß *nt* -sses, -sse) teeth *pl*; (*künstliches*) false teeth *pl*, dentures *pl*; (*des Zaumes*) bit

geblümt *a* floral, flowered

gebogen *a* curved

geboren *a* born; g∼er Deutscher German by birth; Frau X, g∼e Y Mrs X, née Y

geborgen *a* safe, secure. G∼heit *f* - security

Gebot *nt* -[e]s,-e rule; (*Relig*) commandment; (*bei Auktion*) bid

gebraten *a* fried

Gebrauch *m* use; (*Sprach-*) usage; Gebräuche customs; in G∼ in use; G∼ machen von make use of. g∼en *vt* use; ich kann es nicht/gut g∼en I have no use for/can make good use of it; zu nichts zu g∼en useless

gebräuchlich *a* common; (*Wort*) in common use

Gebrauch|sanleitung, G∼sanweisung *f* directions *pl* for use. g∼t *a* used; (*Comm*) secondhand. G∼twagen *m* used car

gebrechlich *a* frail, infirm

gebrochen *a* broken □ *adv* g~ Englisch sprechen speak broken English

Gebrüll *nt* -s roaring; ⟨*fam. Schreien*⟩ bawling

Gebrumm *nt* -s buzzing; ⟨*Motoren-*⟩ humming

Gebühr *f* -,-en charge, fee; über G~ excessively. g~en *vi* (*haben*) ihm g~t Respekt he deserves respect; wie es sich g~t as is right and proper. g~end *a* due, *adv* duly; (*geziemend*) proper, *adv* -ly. g~enfrei *a* free □ *adv* free of charge. g~enpflichtig *a* & *adv* subject to a charge; g~enpflichtige Straße toll road

gebunden *a* bound; ⟨*Suppe*⟩ thickened

Geburt *f* -,-en birth; von G~ by birth. G~enkontrolle, G~enregelung *f* birth-control. G~enziffer *f* birth-rate

gebürtig *a* native (aus of); g~er Deutscher German by birth

Geburts|datum *nt* date of birth. G~helfer *m* obstetrician. G~hilfe *f* obstetrics *sg*. G~ort *m* place of birth. G~tag *m* birthday. G~urkunde *f* birth certificate

Gebüsch *nt* -[e]s,-e bushes *pl*

Gedächtnis *nt* -ses memory; aus dem G~ from memory

gedämpft *a* ⟨*Ton*⟩ muffled; ⟨*Stimme*⟩ hushed; ⟨*Musik*⟩ soft; ⟨*Licht, Stimmung*⟩ subdued

Gedanke *m* -ns,-n thought (an + *acc* of); (*Idee*) idea; sich (*dat*) G~n machen worry (über + *acc* about). G~nblitz *m* brainwave. g~nlos *a* thoughtless, *adv*-ly; (*zerstreut*) absent-minded, *adv* -ly. G~nstrich *m* dash. G~nübertragung *f* telepathy. g~nvoll *a* pensive, *adv* -ly

Gedärme *ntpl* intestines; ⟨*Tier-*⟩ entrails

Gedeck *nt* -[e]s,-e place setting; ⟨*auf Speisekarte*⟩ set meal; ein G~ auflegen set a place. g~t *a* covered; ⟨*Farbe*⟩ muted

gedeihen† *vi* (*sein*) thrive, flourish

gedenken† *vi* (*haben*) propose (etw zu tun to do sth); jds/etw g~ remember s.o./sth. G~ *nt* -s memory; zum G~ an (+ *acc*) in memory of

Gedenk|feier *f* commemoration. G~gottesdienst *m* memorial service. G~stätte *f* memorial. G~tafel *f* commemorative plaque. G~tag *m* day of remembrance; (*Jahrestag*) anniversary

Gedicht *nt* -[e]s, e poem

gediegen *a* quality . . .; ⟨*solide*⟩ well-made; ⟨*Charakter*⟩ upright; ⟨*Gold*⟩ pure □ *adv* g~ gebaut well built

Gedräng|e *nt* -s crush, crowd. g~t *a* ⟨*knapp*⟩ concise □ *adv* g~t voll packed

gedrückt *a* depressed

gedrungen *a* stocky

Geduld *f* - patience; G~ haben be patient. g~en (sich) *vr* be patient. g~ig *a* patient, *adv* -ly. G~[s]spiel *nt* puzzle

gedunsen *a* bloated

geehrt *a* honoured; Sehr g~er Herr X Dear Mr X

geeignet *a* suitable; im g~en Moment at the right moment

Gefahr *f* -,-en danger; in/außer G~ in/ out of danger; auf eigene G~ at one's own risk; G~ laufen run the risk (etw zu tun of doing sth)

gefähr|den *vt* endanger; ⟨*fig*⟩ jeopardize. g~lich *a* dangerous, *adv* -ly; ⟨*riskant*⟩ risky

gefahrlos *a* safe

Gefährt *nt* -[e]s,-e vehicle

Gefährte *m* -n,-n, Gefährtin *f* -,-nen companion

gefahrvoll *a* dangerous, perilous

Gefälle *nt* -s,- slope; ⟨*Straßen-*⟩ gradient

gefallen† *vi* (*haben*) jdm g~ please s.o.; er/es gefällt mir I like him/it; sich (*dat*) etw g~ lassen put up with sth

Gefallen[1] *m* -s,- favour

Gefallen[2] *nt* -s pleasure (an + *dat* in); G~ finden an (+ *dat*) like; dir zu G~ to please you

Gefallene(r) *m* soldier killed in the war

gefällig *a* pleasing; (*hübsch*) attractive, *adv*-ly; (*hilfsbereit*) obliging; jdm g~ sein do s.o. a good turn; [sonst] noch etwas g~? will there be anything else? G~keit *f* -,-en favour; (*Freundlichkeit*) kindness. g~st *adv* (*fam*) kindly

Gefangen|e(r) *m*/*f* prisoner. g~halten† *vt sep* NEW g~ halten, *s.* fangen. G~nahme *f* - capture. g~nehmen† *vt sep* NEW g~ nehmen, *s.* fangen. G~schaft *f* - captivity; in G~schaft geraten be taken prisoner

Gefängnis *nt* -ses,-se prison; ⟨*Strafe*⟩ imprisonment. G~strafe *f* imprisonment; ⟨*Urteil*⟩ prison sentence. G~wärter *m* [prison] warder; (*Amer*) guard

Gefäß *nt* -es,-e container, receptacle; (*Blut-*) vessel

gefasst (gefaßt) *a* composed; (*ruhig*) calm, *adv* -ly; g~ sein auf (+ *acc*) be prepared for

Gefecht *nt* -[e]s,-e fight; (*Mil*) engagement; außer G~ setzen put out of action

gefedert *a* sprung

gefeiert *a* celebrated

Gefieder *nt* -s plumage. g~t *a* feathered

Geflecht *nt* -[e]s,-e network; (*Gewirr*) tangle; (*Korb-*) wicker-work

gefleckt *a* spotted

geflissentlich adv studiously

Geflügel nt -s poultry. G~klein nt -s giblets pl. g~t a winged; g~tes Wort familiar quotation

Geflüster nt -s whispering

Gefolge nt -s retinue, entourage. G~schaft f - followers pl, following; (Treue) allegiance

gefragt a popular; g~ sein be in demand

gefräßig a voracious; (Mensch) greedy

Gefreite(r) m lance-corporal

gefrier|en† vi (sein) freeze. G~fach nt freezer compartment. G~punkt m freezing point. G~schrank m upright freezer. G~truhe f chest freezer

gefroren a frozen. G~e(s) nt (Aust) ice-cream

Gefüge nt -s,- structure; (fig) fabric

gefügig a compliant; (gehorsam) obedient

Gefühl nt -[e]s,-e feeling; (Empfindung) sensation; (G~sregung) emotion; im G~ haben know instinctively. g~los a insensitive; (herzlos) unfeeling; (taub) numb. g~sbetont a emotional. g~skalt a (fig) cold. g~smäßig a emotional, adv -ly; (instinktiv) instinctive, adv -ly. G~sregung f emotion. g~voll a sensitive, adv -ly; (sentimental) sentimental, adv -ly

gefüllt a filled; (voll) full; (Bot) double; (Culin) stuffed; (Schokolade) with a filling

gefürchtet a feared, dreaded

gefüttert a lined

gegeben a given; (bestehend) present; (passend) appropriate; zu g~er Zeit at the proper time. g~enfalls adv if need be. G~heiten fpl realities, facts

gegen prep (+ acc) against; (Sport) versus; (g~über) to[wards]; (Vergleich) compared with; (Richtung, Zeit) towards; (ungefähr) around; ein Mittel g~ a remedy for □ adv g~ 100 Leute about 100 people. G~angriff m counter-attack

Gegend f -,-en area, region; (Umgebung) neighbourhood

gegeneinander adv against/(gegenüber) towards one another

Gegen|fahrbahn f opposite carriageway. G~gift nt antidote. G~leistung f als G~leistung in return. G~maßnahme f countermeasure. G~satz m contrast; (Widerspruch) contradiction; (G~teil) opposite; im G~satz zu unlike. g~sätzlich a contrasting; (widersprüchlich) opposing. g~seitig a mutual, adv -ly; sich g~seitig hassen hate one another. G~spieler m opponent. G~sprechanlage f intercom. G~stand m object; (Gram, Gesprächs-) subject. g~standslos a unfounded; (überflüssig)

irrelevant; (abstrakt) abstract. G~stück nt counterpart; (G~teil) opposite. G~teil nt opposite, contrary; im G~teil on the contrary. g~teilig a opposite

gegenüber prep (+ dat) opposite; (Vergleich) compared with; jdm g~ höflich sein be polite to s.o. □ adv opposite. G~ nt -s person opposite. g~liegen† vi sep (haben) be opposite (etw dat sth). g~liegend a opposite. g~stehen† vi sep (haben) (+ dat) face; feindlich g~stehen (+ dat) be hostile to. g~stellen vt sep confront; (vergleichen) compare. g~treten† vi sep (sein) (+ dat) face

Gegen|verkehr m oncoming traffic. G~vorschlag m counter-proposal. G~wart f - present; (Anwesenheit) presence. g~wärtig a present □ adv at present. G~wehr f - resistance. G~wert m equivalent. G~wind m head wind. g~zeichnen vt sep countersign

geglückt a successful

Gegner|(in) m -s,- (f -,-nen) opponent. g~isch a opposing

Gehabe nt -s affected behaviour

Gehackte(s) nt mince, (Amer) ground meat

Gehalt¹ m -[e]s content

Gehalt² nt -[e]s,-̈er salary. G~serhöhung f rise, (Amer) raise

gehaltvoll a nourishing

gehässig a spiteful, adv -ly

gehäuft a heaped

Gehäuse nt -s,- case; (TV, Radio) cabinet; (Schnecken-) shell; (Kern-) core

Gehege nt -s,- enclosure

geheim a secret; g~ halten keep secret; im G~en (g~en) secretly. G~dienst m Secret Service. g~halten† vt sep (NEW) g~ halten, s. geheim. G~nis nt -ses,-se secret. g~nisvoll a mysterious, adv -ly. G~polizei f secret police

gehemmt a (fig) inhibited

gehen† vi (sein) go; (zu Fuß) walk; (fort-) leave; (funktionieren) work; (Teig:) rise; tanzen/einkaufen g~ go dancing/shopping; an die Arbeit g~ set to work; in Schwarz [gekleidet] g~ dress in black; nach Norden g~ (Fenster:) face north; wenn es nach mir ginge if I had my way; über die Straße g~ cross the road; was geht hier vor sich? what is going on here? das geht zu weit (fam) that's going too far; impers wie geht es [Ihnen]? how are you? es geht ihm gut/besser/schlecht he is well/better/not well; (geschäftlich) he is doing well/better/badly; ein gut g~des Geschäft a flourishing or thriving business; es geht nicht/nicht anders it's impossible/there is no other way; **es ging ganz schnell** it was very quick; **es geht um** it concerns; **es geht ihr nur ums Geld** she is only interested in the money; **es geht** [so] (*fam*) not too bad; **sich g~ lassen** lose one's self-control; (*sich vernachlässigen*) let oneself go □ *vi* walk. **g~lassen†** (*sich*) *vr sep* NEW~ lassen (sich), s. gehen

geheuer *a* **nicht g~** eerie; (*verdächtig*) suspicious; **mir ist nicht g~** I feel uneasy

Geheul *nt* -s howling

Gehife *m* -n,-n, **Gehilfin** *f* -,-nen trainee; (*Helfer*) assistant

Gehirn *nt* -s brain; (*Verstand*) brains *pl*. **G~erschütterung** *f* concussion. **G~hautentzündung** *f* meningitis. **G~wäsche** *f* brainwashing

gehoben *a* (*fig*) superior; (*Sprache*) elevated

Gehöft *nt* -[e]s,-e farm

Gehölz *nt* -es,-e coppice, copse

Gehör *nt* -s hearing; **G~ schenken** (+ *dat*) listen to

gehorchen *vi* (*haben*) (+ *dat*) obey

gehören *vi* (*haben*) belong (*dat* to); **zu den Besten g~** be one of the best; **dazu gehört Mut** that takes courage; **sich g~** be [right and] proper; **es gehört sich nicht** it isn't done

gehörig *a* proper, *adv* -ly; **jdn g~ verprügeln** give s.o. a good hiding

gehörlos *a* deaf

Gehörn *nt* -s,-e horns *pl*; (*Geweih*) antlers *pl*

gehorsam *a* obedient, *adv* -ly. **G~** *m* -s obedience

Gehisteig *m* -[e]s,-e pavement, (*Amer*) sidewalk. **G~weg** *m* = Gehsteig; (*Fußweg*) footpath

Geier *m* -s,- vulture

Geigle *f* -,-n violin. **g~en** *vi* (*haben*) play the violin □ *vt* play on the violin. **G~er(in)** *m* -s,- (*f* -,-nen) violinist

geil *a* lecherous; (*fam*) randy; (*fam: toll*) great

Geisel *f* -,-n hostage

Geiß *f* -,-en (*SGer*) [nanny-]goat. **G~blatt** *nt* honeysuckle

Geißel *f* -,-n scourge

Geist *m* -[e]s,-er mind; (*Witz*) wit; (*Gesinnung*) spirit; (*Gespenst*) ghost; **der Heilige G~** the Holy Ghost *or* Spirit; **im G~** in one's mind. **g~erhaft** *a* ghostly

geistesabwesend *a* absent-minded, *adv* -ly. **G~blitz** *m* brainwave. **G~gegenwart** *f* presence of mind. **g~gegenwärtig** *adv* with great presence of mind. **g~gestört** *a* [mentally] deranged. **g~krank** *a* mentally ill. **G~krankheit** *f* mental illness. **G~wissenschaften** *fpl* arts. **G~zustand** *m* mental state

geistlig *a* mental, *adv* -ly; (*intellektuell*) intellectual, *adv* -ly; **g~ige Getränke** spirits. **g~lich** *a* spiritual, *adv* -ly; (*religiös*) religious; (*Musik*) sacred; (*Tracht*) clerical. **G~liche(r)** *m* clergyman. **G~lichkeit** *f* clergy. **g~los** *a* uninspired. **g~reich** *a* clever; (*witzig*) witty

Geiz *m* -es meanness. **g~en** *vi* (*haben*) be mean (mit with). **G~hals** *m* (*fam*) miser. **g~ig** *a* mean, miserly. **G~kragen** *m* (*fam*) miser

Gekicher *nt* -s giggling

geknickt *a* (*fam*) dejected, *adv* -ly

gekonnt *a* accomplished □ *adv* expertly

Gekrakel *nt* -s scrawl

gekränkt *a* offended, hurt

Gekritzel *nt* -s scribble

gekünstelt *a* affected, *adv* -ly

Gelächter *nt* -s laughter

geladen *a* loaded; (*fam: wütend*) furious

Gelage *nt* -s,- feast

gelähmt *a* paralysed

Gelände *nt* -s,- terrain; (*Grundstück*) site. **G~lauf** *m* cross-country run

Geländer *nt* -s,- railings *pl*; (*Treppen-*) banisters *pl*; (*Brücken-*) parapet

gelangen *vi* (*sein*) reach/(*fig*) attain (**zu etw/an etw** *acc* sth); **in jds Besitz g~** come into s.o.'s possession

gelassen *a* composed; (*ruhig*) calm, *adv* -ly. **G~heit** *f* - equanimity; (*Fassung*) composure

Gelatine /ʒela-/ *f* - gelatine

geläufig *a* common, current; (*fließend*) fluent, *adv* -ly; **jdm g~ sein** be familiar to s.o.

gelaunt *a* **gut/schlecht g~e Leute** good-humoured/bad-tempered people; **gut/schlecht g~ sein** be in a good/bad mood

gelb *a* yellow; (*bei Ampel*) amber; **g~e Rübe** (*SGer*) carrot; **das G~e vom Ei** the yolk of the egg. **G~** *nt* -s,- yellow; **bei G~** (*Auto*) on [the] amber. **g~lich** *a* yellowish. **G~sucht** *f* jaundice

Geld *nt* -es,-er money; **öffentliche G~er** public funds. **G~börse** *f* purse. **G~beutel** *m*, **G~börse** *f* purse. **G~geber** *m* -s,- backer. **g~lich** *a* financial, *adv* -ly. **G~mittel** *ntpl* funds. **G~schein** *m* banknote. **G~schrank** *m* safe. **G~strafe** *f* fine. **G~stück** *nt* coin

Gelee /ʒe'le:/ *nt* -s,-s jelly

gelegen *a* situated; (*passend*) convenient; **jdm sehr g~ sein** *od* **kommen** suit s.o. well; **mir ist viel/wenig daran g~** I'm very/not keen on it; (*es ist wichtig*) it matters a lot/little to me

Gelegenheit f -,-en opportunity, chance; (Anlass) occasion; (Comm) bargain; bei G~ some time. G~sarbeit f casual work. G~sarbeiter m casual worker. G~skauf m bargain

gelegentlich a occasional □ adv occasionally; (bei Gelegenheit) some time □ prep (+ gen) on the occasion of

gelehrt a learned. G~e(r) m/f scholar

Geleise nt -s,- = Gleis

Geleit nt -[e]s escort; freies G~ safe conduct. g~en vt escort. G~zug m (Naut) convoy

Gelenk nt -[e]s,-e joint. g~ig a supple; (Techn) flexible

gelernt a skilled

Geliebte(r) m/f lover; (liter) beloved

gelieren /ʒe-/ vi (haben) set

gelinde a mild, adv -ly; g~ gesagt to put it mildly

gelingent vi (sein) succeed, be successful; es gelang ihm, zu entkommen he succeeded in escaping. G~ nt -s success

gell int (SGer) = gelt

gellend a shrill, adv -y

geloben vt promise [solemnly]; sich (dat) g~ vow (zu to); das Gelobte Land the Promised Land

Gelöbnis nt -ses,-se vow

gelöst a (fig) relaxed

Gelse f -,-n (Aust) mosquito

gelt nt (SGer) das ist schön, g~? it's nice, isn't it? ihr kommt doch, g~? you are coming, aren't you?

geltent vi (haben) be valid; (Regel:) apply; g~ als be regarded as; etw nicht g~ lassen not accept sth; wenig/viel g~ be worth/(fig) count for little/a lot; jdm g~ be meant for s.o.; das gilt nicht that doesn't count. g~d a valid; (Preise) current; (Meinung) prevailing; g~d machen assert (Recht, Forderung); bring to bear (Einfluss)

Geltung f - validity; (Ansehen) prestige; G~ haben be valid; zur G~ bringen/ kommen set off/show to advantage

Gelübde nt -s,- vow

gelungen a successful

Gelüst nt -[e]s,-e desire/(stark) craving (nach for)

gemächlich a leisurely □ adv in a leisurely manner

Gemahl m -s,-e husband. G~in f -,-nen wife

Gemälde nt -s,- painting. G~galerie f picture gallery

gemäß prep (+ dat) in accordance with □ a etw (dat) g~ sein be in keeping with sth

gemäßigt a moderate; (Klima) temperate

gemein a common; (unanständig) vulgar; (niederträchtig) mean; g~er Soldat private; etw g~ haben have sth in common □ adv shabbily; (fam:schrecklich) terribly

Gemeinde f -,-n [local] community; (Admin) borough; (Pfarr-) parish; (bei Gottesdienst) congregation. G~rat m local council/(Person) councillor. G~wahlen fpl local elections

gemein|gefährlich a dangerous. G~heit f -,-en (s. gemein) commonness; vulgarity; meanness; (Bemerkung, Handlung) mean thing [to say/do]; so eine G~heit! how mean! (wie ärgerlich) what a nuisance! g~kosten pl overheads. g~nützig a charitable. G~platz m platitude. g~sam a common; etw g~sam haben have sth in common □ adv together

Gemeinschaft f -,-en community. g~lich a joint; (Besitz) communal □ adv jointly; (zusammen) together. G~sarbeit f team-work

Gemenge nt -s,- mixture

gemessen a measured; (würdevoll) dignified

Gemetzel nt -s,- carnage

Gemisch nt -[e]s,-e mixture. g~t a mixed

Gemme f -,-n engraved gem

Gemse f -,-n NEW Gämse

Gemurmel nt -s murmuring

Gemüse nt -s,- vegetable; (coll) vegetables pl. G~händler m greengrocer

gemustert a patterned

Gemüt nt -[e]s,-er nature, disposition; (Gefühl) feelings pl; (Person) soul

gemütlich a cosy; (gemächlich) leisurely; (zwanglos) informal; (Person) genial; es sich (dat) g~ machen make oneself comfortable □ adv cosily; in a leisurely manner; informally. G~keit f - cosiness; leisureliness

Gemüts|art f nature, disposition. G~mensch m (fam) placid person. G~ruhe f in aller G~ruhe (fam) calmly. G~verfassung f frame of mind

Gen nt -s,-e gene

genau a exact, adv -ly, precise, adv -ly; (Waage, Messung) accurate, adv -ly; (sorgfältig) meticulous, adv -ly; (ausführlich) detailed; nichts G~es wissen not know any details; es nicht so g~ nehmen not be too particular; g~ genommen strictly speaking; g~! exactly! g~genommen adv NEW g~ genommen, s. genau. G~igkeit f - exactitude; precision; accuracy; meticulousness

genauso adv just the same; (g~ sehr) just as much; g~ schön/teuer just as beautiful/expensive; g~ gut just as good; adv just as well; g~ sehr just as much; g~ viel just as much/many; g~ wenig just as little/few; (noch) no more. g~gut adv (NEW)g~ gut, s. genauso. g~sehr adv (NEW)g~ sehr, s. genauso. g~viel adv (NEW)g~ viel, s. genauso. g~wenig adv (NEW)g~ wenig, s. genauso

Gendarm /ʒã'darm/ m -en,-en (Aust) policeman

Genealogie f - genealogy

genehmig|en vt grant; approve ⟨Plan⟩. G~ung f -,-en permission; (Schein) permit

geneigt a sloping, inclined; (fig) well-disposed (dat towards); [nicht] g~ sein (fig) [not] feel inclined (zu to)

General m -s,-e general. G~direktor m managing director. g~isieren vi (haben) generalize. G~probe f dress rehearsal. G~streik m general strike. g~überholen vt insep (inf & pp only) completely overhaul

Generation /-'tsjoːn/ f -,-en generation

Generator m -s,-en /-'toːrən/ generator

generell a general, adv -ly

genes|en† vi (sein) recover. G~ung f - recovery; (Erholung) convalescence

Genet|ik f - genetics sg. g~isch a genetic, adv -ally

Genf nt -s Geneva. G~er a Geneva ...; G~er See Lake Geneva

genial a brilliant, adv -ly; ein g~er Mann a man of genius. G~ität f - genius

Genick nt -s,-e [back of the] neck; sich (dat) das G~ brechen break one's neck

Genie /ʒe'niː/ nt -s,-s genius

genieren /ʒe'niːrən/ vt embarrass; sich g~ feel or be embarrassed

genieß|bar a fit to eat/drink. g~en† vt enjoy; (verzehren) eat/drink. G~er m -s,- gourmet. g~erisch a appreciative ▢ adv with relish

Genitiv m -s,-e genitive

Genosse m -n,-n (Pol) comrade. G~nschaft f -,-en cooperative

Genre /'ʒã:rə/ nt -s,-s genre

Gentechnologie f genetic engineering

genug inv a & adv enough

Genüge f zur G~ sufficiently. g~n vi (haben) be enough; jds Anforderungen g~n meet s.o.'s requirements. g~nd inv a sufficient, enough; (Sch) fair ▢ adv sufficiently, enough

genügsam a frugal, adv -ly; (bescheiden) modest, adv -ly

Genugtuung f - satisfaction

Genuss m -es,˙-e (Genuß m -sses,˙-sse) enjoyment; (Vergnügen) pleasure; (Verzehr) consumption. genüsslich (genüßlich) a pleasurable ▢ adv with relish

geöffnet a open

Geo|graphie, G~grafie f - geography. g~graphisch, g~grafisch a geographical, adv -ly. G~loge m -n,-n geologist. G~logie f - geology. g~logisch a geological. adv -ly. G~meter m -s,- surveyor. G~metrie f - geometry. g~metrisch a geometric[al]

geordnet a well-ordered; (stabil) stable; alphabetisch g~ in alphabetical order

Gepäck nt -s luggage, baggage. G~ablage f luggage-rack. G~aufbewahrung f left-luggage office. G~schalter m luggage office. G~schein m left-luggage ticket; (Aviat) baggage check. G~stück nt piece of luggage. G~träger m porter; (Fahrrad-) luggage carrier; (Dach-) roofrack. G~wagen m luggage-van

Gepard m -s,-e cheetah

gepflegt a well-kept; ⟨Person⟩ well-groomed; ⟨Hotel⟩ first-class

Gepflogenheit f -,-en practice; (Brauch) custom

Gepolter nt -s [loud] noise

gepunktet a spotted

gerade a straight; (direkt) direct; (aufrecht) upright; (aufrichtig) straightforward; ⟨Zahl⟩ even; etw g~ biegen straighten sth; sich g~ halten hold oneself straight ▢ adv directly; (eben) just; (genau) exactly; (besonders) especially; g~ sitzen/stehen sit/stand [up] straight; nicht g~ billig not exactly cheap; g~ erst only just; g~ an dem Tag on that very day. G~ f -,-n straight line. g~aus adv straight ahead/on

gerade|biegen† vt sep (NEW)g~ biegen, s. gerade. g~halten† (sich) vr sep (NEW) sich g~ halten, s. gerade. g~heraus adv (fig) straight out. g~sitzen† vi sep (haben) (NEW)g~ sitzen, s. gerade. g~so adv just the same; g~so gut just as good; adv just as well. g~sogut adv (NEW)g~so gut, s. geradeso. g~stehen† vi sep (haben) (fig) accept responsibility (für for); (aufrecht stehen) (NEW)g~ stehen, s. gerade. g~wegs adv directly, straight. g~zu adv virtually; (wirklich) absolutely

Geranie /-jə/ f -,-n geranium

Gerät nt -[e]s,-e tool; (Acker-) implement; (Küchen-) utensil; (Elektro-) appliance; (Radio-, Fernseh-) set; (Turn-) piece of apparatus; (coll) equipment

geraten† vi (sein) get; in Brand g~ catch fire; in Wut g~ get angry; in Streit g~ start quarrelling; gut/schlecht g~ turn out well/badly; nach jdm g∼ take after s.o.

Geratewohl nt aufs G∼ at random

geräuchert a smoked

geräumig a spacious, roomy

Geräusch nt -[e]s,-e noise. g∼los a noiseless, adv -ly. g∼voll a noisy, adv -ily

gerben vt tan

gerecht a just, adv -ly; (fair) fair, adv -ly; g∼ werden (+ dat) do justice to. g∼fertigt a justified. G∼igkeit f - justice; fairness

Gerede nt -s talk; (Klatsch) gossip

geregelt a regular

gereift a mature

gereizt a irritable, adv -bly. G∼heit f - irritability

gereuen vt es gereut mich nicht I don't regret it

Geriatrie f - geriatrics sg

Gericht[1] nt -[e]s,-e (Culin) dish

Gericht[2] nt -[e]s,-e court [of law]; vor G∼ in court; das Jüngste ∼ the Last Judgement; mit jdm ins G∼ gehen take s.o. to task. g∼lich a judicial; (Verfahren) legal □ adv g∼lich vorgehen take legal action. G∼sbarkeit f - jurisdiction. G∼shof m court of justice. G∼smedizin f forensic medicine. G∼ssaal m court-room. G∼svollzieher m -s,- bailiff

gerieben a grated; (fam: schlau) crafty

gering a small; (niedrig) low; (g∼fügig) slight; jdn/etw g∼ achten have little regard for s.o./sth; (verachten) despise s.o./sth. g∼achten vt sep (NEW) g∼ achten, s. gering. g∼fügig a slight, adv -ly. g∼schätzig a contemptuous, adv -ly; (Bemerkung) disparaging. g∼ste(r,s) a least; nicht im G∼sten (g∼sten) not in the least

gerinnen† vi (sein) curdle; ⟨Blut:⟩ clot

Gerippe nt -s,- skeleton; (fig) framework

gerissen a (fam) crafty

Germ m -[e]s & (Aust) f - yeast

German|e m -n,-n [ancient] German. g∼isch a Germanic. G∼ist(in) m -en,-en (f -,-nen) Germanist. G∼istik f - German [language and literature]

gern[e] adv gladly; g∼ haben like; (lieben) be fond of; ich tanze/schwimme g∼ I like dancing/swimming; das kannst du g∼ tun you're welcome to do that; willst du mit?—g∼! do you want to come?—I'd love to!

gerötet a red

Gerste f - barley. G∼nkorn nt (Med) stye

Geruch m -[e]s,∸e smell (von/nach of). g∼los a odourless. G∼ssinn m sense of smell

Gerücht nt -[e]s,-e rumour

geruhen vi (haben) deign (zu to)

gerührt a (fig) moved, touched

Gerümpel nt -s lumber, junk

Gerüst nt -[e]s,-e scaffolding; (fig) framework

gesalzen a salted; (fam: hoch) steep

gesammelt a collected; (gefasst) composed

gesamt a entire, whole. G∼ausgabe f complete edition. G∼betrag m total amount. G∼eindruck m overall impression. G∼heit f - whole. G∼schule f comprehensive school. G∼summe f total

Gesandte(r) m/f envoy

Gesang m -[e]s,∸e singing; (Lied) song; (Kirchen-) hymn. G∼buch nt hymn-book. G∼verein m choral society

Gesäß nt -es buttocks pl. G∼tasche f hip pocket

Geschäft nt -[e]s,-e business; (Laden) shop, (Amer) store; (Transaktion) deal; (fam: Büro) office; schmutzige G∼e shady dealings; ein gutes G∼ machen do very well (mit out of); sein G∼ verstehen know one's job. g∼ehalber adv on business. g∼ig a busy, adv -ily; (Treiben) bustling. G∼igkeit f - activity. g∼lich a business . . . □ adv on business

Geschäfts|brief m business letter. G∼führer m manager; (Vereins-) secretary. G∼mann m (pl -leute) businessman. G∼reise f business trip. G∼stelle f office; (Zweigstelle) branch. g∼tüchtig a g∼tüchtig sein be a good businessman/ -woman. G∼viertel nt shopping area. G∼zeiten fpl hours of business

geschehen† vi (sein) happen (dat to); es ist ein Unglück g∼ there has been an accident; es ist um uns g∼ we are done for; das geschieht dir recht! it serves you right! gern g∼! you're welcome! G∼ nt -s events pl

gescheit a clever; daraus werde ich nicht g∼ I can't make head or tail of it

Geschenk nt -[e]s,-e present, gift. G∼korb m gift hamper

Geschicht|e f -,-n history; (Erzählung) story; (fam: Sache) business. g∼lich a historical, adv -ly

Geschick nt -[e]s fate; (Talent) skill; G∼ haben be good (zu at). G∼lichkeit f - skilfulness, skill. g∼t a skilful, adv -ly; (klug) clever, adv -ly

geschieden a divorced. G∼e(r) m/f divorcee

Geschirr nt -s,-e (coll) crockery; (Porzellan) china; (Service) service; (Pferde-) harness; schmutziges G∼ dirty dishes pl.

G~spülmaschine f dishwasher. G~tuch nt tea-towel

Geschlecht nt -[e]s,-er sex; (Gram) gender; (Familie) family, (Generation) generation. g~lich a sexual, adv -ly. G~skrankheit f venereal disease. G~steile ntpl genitals. G~sverkehr m sexual intercourse. G~swort nt (pl -wörter) article

geschliffen a (fig) polished

geschlossen a closed □adv unanimously; (vereint) in a body

Geschmack m -[e]s,-e taste; (Aroma) flavour; (g~ssinn) sense of taste; einen guten G~ haben (fig) have good taste; G~ finden an (+ dat) acquire a taste for. g~los a tasteless, adv -ly; g~los sein (fig) be in bad taste. G~ssache f matter of taste. g~voll a (fig) tasteful, adv -ly

geschmeidig a supple; (weich) soft

Geschöpf nt -[e]s,-e creature

Geschoss nt -es,-e(Geschoß nt -sses,-sse) missile; (Stockwerk) storey, floor

geschraubt a (fig) stilted

Geschrei nt -s screaming; (fig) fuss

Geschütz nt -es,-e gun, cannon

geschützt a protected; (Stelle) sheltered

Geschwader nt -s,- squadron

Geschwätz nt -es talk. g~ig a garrulous

geschweift a curved

geschweige conj g~ denn let alone

geschwind a quick, adv -ly

Geschwindigkeit f -,-en speed; (Phys) velocity. G~sbegrenzung, G~sbeschränkung f speed limit

Geschwister pl brother[s] and sister[s]; siblings

geschwollen a swollen; (fig) pompous, adv -ly

Geschworene|(r) m/f juror; die G~n the jury sg

Geschwulst f -,-e swelling; (Tumor) tumour

geschwungen a curved

Geschwür nt -s,-e ulcer

Geselle m -n,-n fellow; (Handwerks-) journeyman

gesellig a sociable; (Zool) gregarious; (unterhaltsam) convivial; g~er Abend social evening. G~keit f -,-en entertaining; die G~keit lieben love company

Gesellschaft f -,-en company; (Veranstaltung) party, die G~ society; jdm G~ leisten keep s.o. company. g~lich a social, adv -ly. G~sreise f group tour. G~sspiel nt party game

Gesetz nt -es,-e law. G~entwurf m bill. g~gebend a legislative. G~gebung f -legislation. g~lich a legal, adv -ly. g~los

a lawless. g~mäßig a lawful, adv -ly; (gesetzlich) legal, adv -ly

gesetzt a staid; (Sport) seeded □conj g~ den Fall supposing

gesetzwidrig a illegal, adv -ly

gesichert a secure

Gesicht nt -[e]s,-er face; (Aussehen) appearance; zu G~ bekommen set eyes on. G~sausdruck m [facial] expression. G~sfarbe f complexion. G~spunkt m point of view. G~szüge mpl features

Gesindel nt -s riff-raff

gesinnt a gut/übel g~ well/ill disposed (dat towards)

Gesinnungf -,-en mind; (Einstellung) attitude; politische G~ political convictions pl

gesittet a well-mannered; (zivilisiert) civilized

gesondert a separate, adv -ly

Gespann nt -[e]s,-e team; (Wagen) horse and cart/carriage

gespannt a taut; (fig) tense, adv -ly; (Beziehungen) strained; (neugierig) eager, adv -ly; (erwartungsvoll) expectant, adv -ly; g~ sein, do wonder whether; auf etw/jdn g~ sein look forward eagerly to sth/to seeing s.o.

Gespenst nt -[e]s,-er ghost. g~isch a ghostly; (unheimlich) eerie

Gespött nt -[e]s mockery; zum G~ werden become a laughing-stock

Gespräch nt -[e]s,-e conversation; (Telefon-) call; ins G~ kommen get talking; im G~ sein be under discussion. g~ig a talkative. G~sgegenstand m, G~sthema nt topic of conversation

gesprenkelt a speckled

Gespür nt -s feeling; (Instinkt) instinct

Gestalt f -,-en figure; (Form) shape, form; G~ annehmen (fig) take shape. g~en vt shape; (organisieren) arrange; (schaffen) create; (entwerfen) design; sich g~en turn out

geständig a confessed; g~ig sein have confessed. G~nis nt -ses,-se confession

Gestank m -s stench, [bad] smell

gestatten vt allow, permit; nicht gestattet prohibited; g~ Sie? may I?

Geste /'gɛ-, 'ge:stə/ f -,-en gesture

Gesteck nt -[e]s,-e flower arrangement

gestehen vt/i (haben) confess; confess to (Verbrechen); offen gestanden to tell the truth

Gestein nt -[e]s,-e rock

Gestell nt -[e]s,-e stand; (Flaschen-) rack; (Rahmen) frame

gestellt a gut/schlecht g∼ well/badly off; auf sich (acc) selbst g∼ sein be thrown on one's own resources

gestelzt a (fig) stilted

gesteppt a quilted

gestern adv yesterday; g∼ Nacht (nacht) last night

Gestik /'gɛstɪk/ f- gestures pl. g∼ulieren vi (haben) gesticulate

gestrandet a stranded

gestreift a striped

gestrichelt a (Linie) dotted

gestrichen a g∼er Teelöffel level teaspoon[ful]

gestrig /'gɛstrɪç/ a yesterday's; am g∼en Tag yesterday

Gestrüpp nt -s,-e undergrowth

Gestüt nt -[e]s,-e stud [farm]

Gesuch nt -[e]s,-e request; (Admin) application. g∼t a sought-after; (gekünstelt) contrived

gesund a healthy, adv -ily; g∼ sein be in good health; (Sport, Getränk) be good for one; wieder g∼ werden get well again

Gesundheit f- health; G∼! (bei Niesen) bless you! g∼lich a health ...; g∼licher Zustand state of health □ adv es geht ihm g∼lich gut/schlecht he is in good/poor health. g∼shalber adv for health reasons. g∼sschädlich a harmful. G∼szustand m state of health

getäfelt a panelled

getigert a tabby

Getöse nt -s racket, din

getragen a solemn, adv -ly

Getränk nt -[e]s,-e drink. G∼ekarte f wine-list

getrauen vt sich (dat) etw g∼ dare [to] do sth; sich g∼ dare

Getreide nt -s (coll) grain

getrennt a separate, adv -ly; g∼ leben live apart; g∼ schreiben write as two words. g∼schreiben† vt sep (NEW)g∼ schreiben, s. getrennt

getreu a faithful, adv -ly □ prep (+ dat) true to; der Wahrheit g∼ truthfully. g∼lich adv faithfully

Getriebe nt -s,- bustle; (Techn) gear; (Auto) transmission; (Gehäuse) gearbox

getrost adv with confidence

Getto nt -s,-s ghetto

Getue nt -s (fam) fuss

Getümmel nt -s tumult

getüpfelt a spotted

geübt a skilled; (Auge, Hand) practised

Gewächs nt -es,-e plant; (Med) growth

gewachsen a jdm/etw g∼ sein (fig) be a match for s.o./be equal to sth

Gewächshaus nt greenhouse; (Treibhaus) hothouse

gewagt a daring

gewählt a refined

gewahr a g∼ werden become aware (acc/gen of)

Gewähr f- guarantee

gewahren vt notice

gewähr|en vt grant; (geben) offer; jdn g∼en lassen let s.o. have his way. g∼leisten vt guarantee

Gewahrsam m -s safekeeping; (Haft) custody

Gewährsmann m (pl -männer &-leute) informant, source

Gewalt f-,-en power; (Kraft) force; (Brutalität) violence; mit G∼ by force; G∼ anwenden use force; sich in der G∼ haben be in control of oneself. G∼herrschaft f tyranny. g∼ig a powerful; (fam: groß) enormous, adv -ly; (stark) tremendous, adv -ly. g∼sam a forcible, adv -bly; (Tod) violent. g∼tätig a violent. G∼tätigkeit f-,-en violence; (Handlung) act of violence

Gewand nt -[e]s,ʺer robe

gewandt a skilful, adv -ly; (flink) nimble, adv -bly. G∼heit f- skill; nimbleness

Gewässer nt -s,- body of water; G∼ pl waters

Gewebe nt -s,- fabric; (Anat) tissue

Gewehr nt -s,-e rifle, gun

Geweih nt -[e]s,-e antlers pl

Gewerb|e nt -s,- trade. g∼lich a commercial, adv -ly. g∼smäßig a professional, adv -ly

Gewerkschaft f -,-en trade union. G∼ler(in) m -s,- (f-,-nen) trade unionist

Gewicht nt -[e]s,-e weight; (Bedeutung) importance. G∼heben nt -s weight-lifting. g∼ig a important

gewieft a (fam) crafty

gewillt a g∼ sein be willing

Gewinde nt -s,- [screw] thread

Gewinn m -[e]s,-e profit; (fig) gain, benefit; (beim Spiel) winnings pl; (Preis) prize; (Los) winning ticket; G∼ bringend profitable, adv -bly. G∼beteiligung f profit-sharing. g∼bringend a (NEW)G∼ bringend, s. Gewinn. g∼en† vt win; (erlangen) gain; (fördern) extract; jdn für sich g∼en win s.o. over □ vi (haben) win; g∼en an (+ dat) gain in. g∼end a engaging. G∼er(in) m -s,- (f-,-nen) winner

Gewirr nt -s,-e tangle; (Straßen-) maze; G∼ von Stimmen hubbub of voices

gewiss (gewiß) a (gewisser, gewissest) certain, adv -ly

Gewissen *nt* -s,- conscience. g~haft *a* conscientious, *adv* -ly. g~los *a* unscrupulous. G~sbisse *mpl* pangs of conscience

gewissermaßen *adv* to a certain extent; (*sozusagen*) as it were

Gewissheit (Gewißheit) *f* - certainty

Gewitter *nt* -s,- thunderstorm. g~ern *vi* (*haben*) es g~ert it is thundering. g~rig *a* thundery

gewogen *a* (*fig*) well-disposed (*dat* towards)

gewöhnen *vt* jdn/sich g~ an (+ *acc*) get s.o. used to/get used to; [an] jdn/etw gewöhnt sein be used to s.o./sth

Gewohnheit *f* -,-en habit. g~smäßig *a* habitual, *adv* -ly. G~srecht *nt* common law

gewöhnlich *a* ordinary, *adv* -ily; (*üblich*) usual, *adv* -ly; (*ordinär*) common

gewohnt *a* customary; (*vertraut*) familiar; (*üblich*) usual; etw (*acc*) g~ sein be used to sth

Gewöhnung *f* - getting used (an + *acc* to); (*Süchtigkeit*) addiction

Gewölb|e *nt* -s,- vault. g~t *a* curved; (*Archit*) vaulted

gewollt *a* forced

Gewühl *nt* -[e]s crush

gewunden *a* winding

gewürfelt *a* check[ed]

Gewürz *nt* -es,-e spice. G~nelke *f* clove

gezackt *a* serrated

gezähnt *a* serrated; (*Säge*) toothed

Gezeiten *fpl* tides

gezielt *a* specific; (*Frage*) pointed

geziemend *a* proper, *adv* -ly

geziert *a* affected, *adv* -ly

gezwungen *a* forced □ *adv* g~ lachen give a forced laugh. g~ermaßen *adv* of necessity; etw g~ermaßen tun be forced to do sth

Gicht *f* - gout

Giebel *m* -s,- gable

Gier *f* - greed (nach for). g~ig *a* greedy, *adv* -ily

gieß|en† *vt* pour; water (*Blumen, Garten*); (*Techn*) cast □ *v impers* es g~t it is pouring [with rain]. G~erei *f* -,-en foundry. G~kanne *f* watering-can

Gift *nt* -[e]s,-e poison; (*Schlangen-*) venom; (*Biol, Med*) toxin. g~ig *a* poisonous; (*Schlange*) venomous; (*Med, Chem*) toxic; (*fig*) spiteful, *adv* -ly. G~müll *m* toxic waste. G~pilz *m* poisonous fungus, toadstool. G~zahn *m* [poison] fang

gigantisch *a* gigantic

Gilde *f* -,-n guild

Gimpel *m* -s,- bullfinch; (*fam: Tölpel*) simpleton

Gin /dʒɪn/ *m* -s gin

Ginster *m* -s (*Bot*) broom

Gipfel *m* -s,- summit, top; (*fig*) peak. G~konferenz *f* summit conference. g~n *vi* (*haben*) culminate (in + *dat* in)

Gips *m* -es plaster. G~abguss (G~abguß) *m* plaster cast. G~er *m* -s,- plasterer. G~verband *m* (*Med*) plaster cast

Giraffe *f* -,-n giraffe

Girlande *f* -,-n garland

Girokonto /ˈʒiːro-/ *nt* current account

Gischt *m* -[e]s & *f* - spray

Gitar|re *f* -,-n guitar. G~rist(in) *m* -en, -en (*f* -,-nen) guitarist

Gitter *nt* -s,- bars *pl*; (*Rost*) grating, grid; (*Geländer, Zaun*) railings *pl*; (*Fenster-*) grille; (*Draht-*) wire screen; hinter G~n (*fam*) behind bars. G~netz *nt* grid

Glanz *m* -es shine; (*von Farbe, Papier*) gloss; (*Seiden-*) sheen; (*Politur*) polish; (*fig*) brilliance; (*Pracht*) splendour

glänzen *vi* (*haben*) shine. g~d *a* shining, bright; (*Papier, Haar*) glossy; (*fig*) brilliant, *adv* -ly

glanz|los *a* dull. G~stück *nt* masterpiece; (*einer Sammlung*) show-piece. g~voll *a* (*fig*) brilliant, *adv* -ly; (*prachtvoll*) splendid, *adv* -ly. G~zeit *f* heyday

Glas *nt* -es,¨er glass; (*Brillen-*) lens; (*Fern-*) binoculars *pl*; (*Marmeladen-*) [glass] jar. G~er *m* -s,- glazier

gläsern *a* glass ...

Glashaus *nt* greenhouse

glasieren *vt* glaze; ice (*Kuchen*)

glas|ig *a* glassy; (*durchsichtig*) transparent. G~scheibe *f* pane

Glasur *f* -,-en glaze; (*Culin*) icing

glatt *a* smooth; (*eben*) even; (*Haar*) straight; (*rutschig*) slippery; (*einfach*) straightforward; (*eindeutig*) downright; (*Absage*) flat; g~ streichen smooth out □ *adv* smoothly; evenly; (*fam: völlig*) completely; (*gerade*) straight; (*leicht*) easily; (*ablehnen*) flatly; g~ rasiert clean-shaven; g~ gehen *od* verlaufen go off smoothly; das ist g~ gelogen it's a downright lie

Glätte *f* - smoothness; (*Rutschigkeit*) slipperiness

Glatteis *nt* [black] ice; aufs G~ führen (*fam*) take for a ride

glätten *vt* smooth; sich g~ become smooth; (*Wellen:*) subside

glatt|gehen† *vi sep* (*sein*) ⟨NEW⟩ g~ gehen, s. glatt. g~rasiert *a* ⟨NEW⟩ g~ rasiert, s. glatt. g~streichen† *vt sep* ⟨NEW⟩ g~

streichen, s. glatt. g~weg adv (fam) out-
right

Glatz|e f -,-n bald patch; (Voll-) bald head;
eine G~e bekommen go bald. g~köpfig
a bald

Glaube m -ns belief (an + acc in); (Relig)
faith; in gutem G~n in good faith; G~n
schenken (+ dat) believe. g~n vt/i
(haben) believe (an + acc in); (vermuten)
think; jdm g~n believe s.o; nicht zu
g~n unbelievable, incredible. G~nsbe-
kenntnis nt creed

glaubhaft a credible; (überzeugend) convincing, adv -ly

gläubig a religious; (vertrauend) trusting,
adv -ly. G~e(r) m/f (Relig) believer; die
G~en the faithful. G~er m -s,- (Comm)
creditor

glaub|lich a kaum g~lich scarcely be-
lievable. g~würdig a credible; (Person)
reliable. G~würdigkeit f - credibility;
reliability

gleich a same; (identisch) identical;
(g~wertig) equal; g~ bleibend constant;
2 mal 5 [ist] g~ 10 two times 5 equals 10;
das ist mir g~ it's all the same to me;
ganz g~, wo/wer no matter where/who
□ adv equally; (übereinstimmend) identi-
cally, the same; (sofort) immediately; (in
Kürze) in a minute; (fast) nearly; (direkt)
right; g~ gesinnt like-minded; g~
alt/schwer sein be the same age/weight.
g~altrig a [of] the same age. g~artig
a similar. g~bedeutend a synonymous.
g~berechtigt a equal. G~berechtigung
f equality. g~bleibend a NEW g~ bleibend, s. gleich

gleichen† vi (haben) jdm/etw g~ be like
or resemble s.o/sth; sich g~ be alike

gleich|ermaßen adv equally. g~falls
adv also, likewise; danke g~falls thank
you, the same to you. g~förmig a uniform, adv -ly; (eintönig) monotonous, adv
-ly. G~förmigkeit f uniformity; monotony. g~gesinnt a NEW g~ gesinnt, s.
gleich. G~gewicht nt balance; (Phys &
fig) equilibrium. g~gültig a indifferent,
adv -ly; (unwichtig) unimportant. G~gül-
tigkeit f indifference. G~heit f -
equality; (Ähnlichkeit) similarity.
g~machen vt sep make equal; dem Erdboden g~machen raze to the ground.
g~mäßig a even, adv -ly, regular, adv -ly;
(beständig) constant, adv -ly. G~mäßig-
keit f - regularity. G~mut m equanimity.
g~mütig a calm, adv -ly

Gleichnis nt -ses,-se parable

gleich|sam adv as it were. G~schritt m
im G~schritt in step. g~sehen† vi sep
(haben) jdm g~sehen look like s.o.; (fam:
typisch sein) be just like s.o. g~setzen vt

sep equate/(g~stellen) place on a par (dat/
mit with). g~stellen vt sep place on a par
(dat with). G~strom m direct current.
g~tun† vi sep (haben) es jdm g~tun
emulate s.o.

Gleichung f -,-en equation

gleich|viel adv no matter (ob/wer
whether/who). g~wertig a of equal
value. g~zeitig a simultaneous, adv -ly

Gleis nt -es,-e track; (Bahnsteig) platform;
G~ 5 platform 5

gleiten† vi (sein) glide; (rutschen) slide.
g~d a sliding; g~de Arbeitszeit flexitime

Gleitzeit f flexitime

Gletscher m -s,- glacier. G~spalte f crevasse

Glied nt -[e]s,-er limb; (Teil) part; (Ketten-)
link; (Mitglied) member; (Mil) rank.
g~ern vt arrange; (einteilen) divide; sich
g~ern be divided (in + acc into).
G~maßen fpl limbs

glimmen† vi (haben) glimmer

glimpflich a lenient, adv -ly; g~ davonkommen get off lightly

glitschig a slippery

glitzern vi (haben) glitter

global a global, adv -ly

Globus m -& -busses,-ben & -busse globe

Glocke f -,-n bell. G~nturm m bell-tower,
belfry

glorifizieren vt glorify

glorreich a glorious

Glossar nt -s,-e glossary

Glosse f -,-n comment

glotzen vi (haben) stare

Glück nt -[e]s [good] luck; (Zufriedenheit)
happiness; G~ bringend lucky;
G~/kein G~ haben be lucky/unlucky;
zum G~ luckily, fortunately; auf gut G~
on the off chance; (wahllos) at random.
g~bringend a NEW G~ bringend, s.
Glück. g~en vi (sein) succeed; es ist mir
geglückt I succeeded

gluckern vi (haben) gurgle

glücklich a lucky, fortunate; (zufrieden)
happy; (sicher) safe □ adv happily; safely;
(fam: endlich) finally. g~erweise adv
luckily, fortunately

glückselig a blissfully happy. G~keit f
bliss

glucksen vi (haben) gurgle

Glücksspiel nt game of chance; (Spielen)
gambling

Glückwunsch m good wishes pl; (Gratu-
lation) congratulations pl; herzlichen
G~! congratulations! (zum Geburtstag)
happy birthday! G~karte f greetings
card

Glüh|birne f light-bulb. g~en vi (haben) glow. g~end a glowing; (rot-) red-hot; ⟨Hitze⟩ scorching; (leidenschaftlich) fervent, adv -ly. G~faden m filament. G~wein m mulled wine. G~würmchen nt -s,- glow-worm

Glukose f - glucose

Glut f - embers pl; (Röte) glow; (Hitze) heat; (fig) ardour

Glyzinie /-jə/ f -,-n wisteria

GmbH abbr (Gesellschaft mit beschränkter Haftung) ≈ plc

Gnade f - mercy; (Gunst) favour; (Relig) grace. G~nfrist f reprieve. g~nlos a merciless, adv -ly

gnädig a gracious, adv -ly; (mild) lenient, adv -ly; g~e Frau Madam

Gnom m -en,-en gnome

Gobelin /gobə'lɛ̃/ m -s,-s tapestry

Gold nt -[e]s gold. g~en a gold ...; (g~farben) golden; g~ene Hochzeit golden wedding. G~fisch m goldfish. G~grube f gold-mine. g~ig a sweet, lovely. G~lack m wallflower. G~regen m laburnum. G~schmied m goldsmith

Golf¹ m -[e]s,-e (Geog) gulf

Golf² nt -s golf. G~platz m golf-course. G~schläger m golf-club. G~spieler(in) m(f) golfer

Gondel f -,-n gondola; (Kabine) cabin

Gong m -s,-s gong

gönnen vt jdm etw g~ not begrudge s.o. sth; jdm etw nicht g~ begrudge s.o. sth; sie gönnte sich (dat) keine Ruhe she allowed herself no rest

Gönner m -s,- patron. g~haft a patronizing, adv -ly

Gör nt -s,-en, Göre f -,-n (fam) kid

Gorilla m -s,-s gorilla

Gosse f -,-n gutter

Got|ik f - Gothic. g~isch a Gothic

Gott m -[e]s,-er God; (Myth) god

Götterspeise f jelly

Gottes|dienst m service. g~lästerlich a blasphemous, adv -ly. G~lästerung f blasphemy

Gottheit f -,-en deity

Göttin f -,-nen goddess

göttlich a divine, adv -ly

gott|los a ungodly; (atheistisch) godless; g~ verlassen a God-forsaken

Götze m -n,-n, G~nbild nt idol

Gouver|nante /guvər'nantə/ f -,-n governess. G~neur /-'nø:ɐ̯/ m -s,-e governor

Grab nt -[e]s,-er grave

graben vi (haben) dig

Graben m -s,- ditch; (Mil) trench

Grab|mal nt tomb. G~stein m gravestone, tombstone

Grad m -[e]s,-e degree

Graf m -en,-en count

Grafik f -,-en graphics sg; (Kunst) graphic arts pl; (Druck) print

Gräfin f -,-nen countess

grafisch a graphic; g~e Darstellung diagram

Grafschaft f -,-en county

Gram m -s grief

grämen (sich) vr grieve

grämlich a morose, adv -ly

Gramm nt -s,-e gram

Gram|matik f -,-en grammar. g~matikalisch, g~matisch a grammatical, adv -ly

Granat m -[e]s,-e (Miner) garnet. G~apfel m pomegranate. G~e f -,-n shell; (Hand-) grenade

Granit m -s,-e granite

Graph|ik f, g~isch a = Grafik, grafisch

Gras nt -es,-er grass. g~en vi (haben) graze. G~hüpfer m -s,- grasshopper

grassieren vi (haben) be rife

grässlich (gräßlich) a dreadful, adv -ly

Grat m -[e]s,-e [mountain] ridge

Gräte f -,-n fishbone

Gratifikation /-'tsio:n/ f -,-en bonus

gratis adv free [of charge]. G~probe f free sample

Gratu|lant(in) m -en,-en (f -,-nen) wellwisher. G~lation /-'tsio:n/ f -,-en congratulations pl; (Glückwünsche) best wishes pl. g~lieren vi (haben) jdm g~lieren congratulate s.o. (zu on); (zum Geburtstag) wish s.o. happy birthday; [ich] g~liere! congratulations!

grau a, G~ nt -s,- grey. G~brot nt mixed rye and wheat bread

Gräuel m -s,- horror. G~tat f atrocity

grauen¹ vi (haben) der Morgen od es graut dawn is breaking

grauen² v impers mir graut [es] davor I dread it. G~ nt -s dread. g~haft, g~voll a gruesome; (grässlich) horrible, adv -bly

gräulich¹ a greyish

gräulich² a horrible, adv -bly

Graupeln fpl soft hail sg

grausam a cruel, adv -ly. G~keit f -,-en cruelty

graus|en v impers mir graust davor I dread it. G~en nt -s horror, dread. g~ig a gruesome

gravieren vt engrave. g~d a (fig) serious

Grazie /'gra:tsiə/ f - grace

graziös a graceful, adv -ly

greifbar a tangible; in g~er Nähe within reach

greifen† vt take hold of; ⟨fangen⟩ catch □ vi ⟨haben⟩ reach (nach for); g~ zu ⟨fig⟩ turn to; um sich g~ ⟨fig⟩ spread. G~ nt G~ spielen play tag

Greis m -es,-e old man. G~enalter nt extreme old age. g~enhaft a old. G~in f -,-nen old woman

grell a glaring; ⟨Farbe⟩ garish; ⟨schrill⟩ shrill, adv -y

Gremium nt -s,-ien committee

Grenz|e f -,-n border; ⟨Staats-⟩ frontier; ⟨Grundstücks-⟩ boundary; ⟨fig⟩ limit. g~en vi ⟨haben⟩ border (an + acc on). g~enlos a boundless; ⟨maßlos⟩ infinite, adv -ly. G~fall m borderline case

Greu|el m -s,-. NEW Gräuel. g~lich a NEW gräulich²

Griech|e m -n,-n Greek. G~enland nt -s Greece. G~in f -,-nen Greek woman. g~isch a Greek. G~isch nt -[s] ⟨Lang⟩ Greek

griesgrämig a ⟨fam⟩ grumpy

Grieß m -es semolina

Griff m -[e]s,-e grasp, hold; ⟨Hand-⟩ movement of the hand; ⟨Tür-, Messer-⟩ handle; ⟨Schwert-⟩ hilt. g~bereit a handy

Grill m -s,-s grill; ⟨Garten-⟩ barbecue

Grille f -,-n ⟨Zool⟩ cricket; ⟨fig: Laune⟩ whim

grill|en vt grill; ⟨im Freien⟩ barbecue □ vi ⟨haben⟩ have a barbecue. G~fest nt barbecue. G~gericht nt grill

Grimasse f -,-n grimace; G~n schneiden pull faces

grimmig a furious; ⟨Kälte⟩ bitter

grinsen vi ⟨haben⟩ grin. G~ nt -s grin

Grippe f -,-n influenza, ⟨fam⟩ flu

grob a ⟨gröber, gröbst⟩ coarse, adv -ly; ⟨unsanft, ungefähr⟩ rough, adv -ly; ⟨unhöflich⟩ rude, adv -ly; ⟨schwer⟩ gross, adv -ly; ⟨Fehler⟩ bad; g~e Arbeit rough work; g~ geschätzt roughly. G~ian m -s,-e brute

gröblich a gross, adv -ly

grölen vt/i ⟨haben⟩ bawl

Groll m -[e]s resentment; einen G~ gegen jdn hegen bear s.o. a grudge. g~en vi ⟨haben⟩ be angry ⟨dat with⟩; ⟨Donner:⟩ rumble

Grönland nt -s Greenland

Gros¹ nt -ses,- ⟨Maß⟩ gross

Gros² /groː/ nt - majority, bulk

Groschen m -s,- ⟨Aust⟩ groschen; ⟨fam⟩ ten-pfennig piece; der G~ ist gefallen ⟨fam⟩ the penny's dropped

groß a ⟨größer, größt⟩ big; ⟨Anzahl, Summe⟩ large; ⟨bedeutend, stark⟩ great;

⟨g~artig⟩ grand; ⟨Buchstabe⟩ capital; g~e Ferien summer holidays; g~e Angst haben be very frightened; der größte Teil the majority or bulk; g~ werden ⟨Person:⟩ grow up; g~ in etw ⟨dat⟩ sein be good at sth; g~ geschrieben werden ⟨fig⟩ be very important (bei jdm to s.o.); G~ und Klein (g~ und klein) young and old; im G~en und Ganzen (im g~en und ganzen) on the whole □ adv ⟨feiern⟩ in style; ⟨fam: viel⟩ much; jdn g~ ansehen look at s.o. in amazement

groß|artig a magnificent, adv -ly. G~aufnahme f close-up. G~britannien nt -s Great Britain. G~buchstabe m capital letter. G~e(r) m/f unser G~er our eldest; die G~en the grown-ups; ⟨fig⟩ the great pl

Größe f -,-n size; ⟨Ausmaß⟩ extent; ⟨Körper-⟩ height; ⟨Bedeutsamkeit⟩ greatness; ⟨Math⟩ quantity; ⟨Person⟩ great figure

Groß|eltern pl grandparents. g~enteils adv largely

Größenwahnsinn m megalomania

Groß|handel m wholesale trade. G~händler m wholesaler. g~herzig a magnanimous, adv -ly. G~macht f superpower. G~mut f - magnanimity. g~mütig a magnanimous, adv -ly. G~mutter f grandmother. G~onkel m great-uncle. G~reinemachen nt -s spring-clean. g~schreiben† vt sep write with a capital [initial] letter; g~geschrieben werden ⟨fig⟩ NEW g~ geschrieben werden, s. groß. G~schreibung f capitalization. g~sprecherisch a boastful. g~spurig a pompous, adv -ly; ⟨überheblich⟩ arrogant, adv -ly. G~stadt f [large] city. g~städtisch a city … G~tante f great-aunt. G~teil m large proportion; ⟨Hauptteil⟩ bulk

größtenteils adv for the most part

groß|tun† ⟨sich⟩ vr sep brag. G~vater m grandfather. g~ziehen† vt sep bring up; rear ⟨Tier⟩. g~zügig a generous, adv -ly; ⟨weiträumig⟩ spacious. G~zügigkeit f - generosity

grotesk a grotesque, adv -ly

Grotte f -,-n grotto

Grübchen nt -s,- dimple

Grube f -,-n pit

grübeln vi ⟨haben⟩ brood

Gruft f -,-̈e [burial] vault

grün a green; im G~en out in the country; die G~en the Greens. G~ nt -s,- green; ⟨Laub, Zweige⟩ greenery

Grund m -[e]s,-̈e ground; ⟨Boden⟩ bottom; ⟨Hinter-⟩ background; ⟨Ursache⟩ reason; aus diesem G~e for this reason; von G~

auf(*fig*) radically; im G∼e [genommen] basically; auf G∼ laufen (*Naut*) run aground; auf G∼ (+ *gen*) = aufgrund; zu G∼e richten/gehen/liegen = zugrunde richten/gehen/liegen, s. zugrunde. G∼begriffe *mpl* basics. G∼besitz *m* landed property. G∼besitzer *m* landowner

gründ|en *vt* found, set up; start (*Familie*); (*fig*) base (auf + *acc* on); sich g∼en be based (auf + *acc* on). G∼er(in) *m* -s,- (*f* -,-nen) founder

Grund|farbe *f* primary colour. G∼form *f* (*Gram*) infinitive. G∼gesetz *nt* (*Pol*) constitution. G∼lage *f* basis, foundation. g∼legend *a* fundamental, *adv* -ly

gründlich *a* thorough, *adv* -ly. G∼keit *f* - thoroughness

grund|los *a* bottomless; (*fig*) groundless □ *adv* without reason. G∼mauern *fpl* foundations

Gründonnerstag *m* Maundy Thursday

Grund|regel *f* basic rule. G∼riss (G∼riß) *m* ground-plan; (*fig*) outline. G∼satz *m* principle. g∼sätzlich *a* fundamental, *adv* -ly; (*im Allgemeinen*) in principle; (*prinzipiell*) on principle; G∼schule *f* primary school. G∼stein *m* foundation-stone. G∼stück *nt* plot [of land]

Gründung *f* -,-en foundation

grün|en *vi* (*haben*) become green. G∼gürtel *m* green belt. G∼span *m* verdigris. G∼streifen *m* grass verge; (*Mittel-*) central reservation, (*Amer*) median strip

grunzen *vi* (*haben*) grunt

Gruppe *f* -,-n group; (*Reise-*) party

gruppieren *vt* group; sich g∼ form a group/groups

Gruselgeschichte *f* horror story. g∼ig *a* creepy

Gruß *m* -es,-e greeting; (*Mil*) salute; einen schönen G∼ an X give my regards to X; viele/herzliche G∼e regards; Mit freundlichen G∼en Yours sincerely/(*Comm*) faithfully

grüßen *vt/i* (*haben*) say hallo (jdn to s.o.); (*Mil*) salute; g∼ Sie X von mir give my regards to X; jdn g∼ lassen send one's regards to s.o.; grüß Gott! (*SGer, Aust*) good morning/afternoon/evening!

guck|en *vi* (*haben*) (*fam*) look. G∼loch *nt* peep-hole

Guerilla /ge'rɪlja/ *f* - guerrilla warfare. G∼kämpfer *m* guerrilla

Gulasch *nt* & *m* -[e]s goulash

gültig *a* valid, *adv* -ly. G∼keit *f* - validity

Gummi *m* & *nt* -s,-[s] rubber; (*Harz*) gum. G∼band *nt* (*pl* -bänder) elastic *or* rubber band; (*G∼zug*) elastic

gummiert *a* gummed

Gummi|knüppel *m* truncheon. G∼stiefel *m* gumboot, wellington. G∼zug *m* elastic

Gunst *f* - favour; zu jds G∼en in s.o.'s favour; zu G∼ (+ *gen*) = zugunsten

günstig *a* favourable, *adv* -bly; (*passend*) convenient, *adv* -ly

Günstling *m* -s,-e favourite

Gurgel *f* -,-n throat. g∼n *vi* (*haben*) gargle. G∼wasser *nt* gargle

Gurke *f* -,-n cucumber; (*Essig-*) gherkin

gurren *vi* (*haben*) coo

Gurt *m* -[e]s,-e strap; (*Gürtel*) belt; (*Auto*) safety-belt. G∼band *nt* (*pl* -bänder) waistband

Gürtel *m* -s,- belt. G∼linie *f* waistline. G∼rose *f* shingles *sg*

GUS *abbr* (Gemeinschaft Unabhängiger Staaten) CIS

Guss *m* -es,-e (Guß *m* -sses,-sse) (*Techn*) casting; (*Strom*) stream; (*Regen-*) downpour; (*Torten-*) icing. G∼eisen *nt* cast iron. g∼eisern *a* cast-iron

gut *a* (besser, best) good; (*Gewissen*) clear; (*gütig*) kind (zu to); jdm gut sein be fond of s.o.; im G∼en (g∼en) amicably; zu g∼er Letzt in the end; schon gut that's all right □ *adv* well; (*schmecken, riechen*) good; (*leicht*) easily; es gut haben be well off; (*Glück haben*) be lucky; gut zu sehen clearly visible; gut drei Stunden a good three hours; du hast gut reden it's easy for you to talk

Gut *nt* -[e]s,-er possession, property; (*Land-*) estate; Gut und Böse good and evil; Güter (*Comm*) goods

Gutachten *nt* -s,- expert's report. G∼er *m* -s,- expert

gut|artig *a* good-natured; (*Med*) benign. g∼aussehend *a* (NEW) gut aussehend, s. aussehen. g∼bezahlt *a* (NEW) gut bezahlt, s. bezahlen. G∼dünken *nt* -s nach eigenem G∼dünken at one's own discretion

Gute|(s) *nt* etwas/nichts G∼s something/nothing good; G∼s tun do good; das G∼ daran the good thing about it all; alles G∼! all the best!

Güte *f* -,-n goodness, kindness; (*Qualität*) quality; du meine G∼! my goodness!

Güterzug *m* goods/(*Amer*) freight train

gut|gehen† *vi sep* (*sein*) (NEW) gut gehen, s. gehen. g∼gehend *a* (NEW) gut gehend, s. gehen. g∼gemeint *a* (NEW) gut gemeint, s. meinen. g∼gläubig *a* trusting. g∼haben† *vt sep* fünfzig Mark g∼haben have fifty marks credit (bei with). G∼haben *nt* -s,- [credit] balance;

(Kredit) credit. g~heißen† *vt sep* approve of

gütig *a* kind, *adv* -ly

gütlich *a* amicable, *adv* -bly

gut|machen *vt sep* make up for; make good *(Schaden)*. g~mütig *a* good-natured, *adv* -ly. G~mütigkeit *f* - good nature. G~schein *m* credit note; *(Bon)* voucher; *(Geschenk-)* gift token. g~schreiben† *vt sep* credit. G~schrift *f* credit

Guts|haus *nt* manor house. G~hof *m* manor

gut|situiert *a* (NEW) gut situiert, *s.* situiert. g~tun† *vi sep (haben)* (NEW) gut tun, *s.* tun. g~willig *a* willing, *adv* -ly

Gymnasium *nt* -s,-ien ≈ grammar school

Gymnast|ik *f* - [keep-fit] exercises *pl*; *(Turnen)* gymnastics *sg.* g~isch *a* g~i-sche Übung exercise

Gynäko|loge *m* -n,-n gynaecologist. G~logie *f* - gynaecology. g~logisch *a* gynaecological

H

H, h /ha:/ *nt*, -,- *(Mus)* B, b

Haar *nt* -[e]s,-e hair; sich *(dat)* die Haare *od* das H~ waschen wash one's hair; um ein H~ *(fam)* very nearly. H~bürste *f* hairbrush. h~en *vi (haben)* shed hairs; *(Tier:)* moult □ *vr* sich h~en moult. h~ig *a* hairy; *(fam)* tricky. H~klammer, H~klemme *f* hair-grip. H~nadel *f* hairpin. H~nadelkurve *f* hairpin bend. H~schleife *f* bow. H~schnitt *m* haircut. H~spange *f* slide. h~sträubend *a* hairraising; *(empörend)* shocking. H~trockner *m* -s,- hair-drier. H~waschmittel *nt* shampoo

Habe *f* - possessions *pl*

haben† *vt* have; Angst/Hunger/Durst h~ be frightened/hungry/thirsty; ich hätte gern I'd like; sich h~ *(fam)* make a fuss; es gut/schlecht h~ be well/badly off; etw gegen jdn h~ have sth against s.o.; was hat er? what's the matter with him? □ *v aux* have; ich habe/hatte geschrieben I have/had written; er hätte ihr geholfen he would have helped her

Habgier *f* - greed. h~ig *a* greedy

Habicht *m* -[e]s,-e hawk

Hab|seligkeiten *fpl* belongings. H~sucht *f* = Habgier

Hachse *f* -,-n *(Culin)* knuckle

Hack|beil *nt* chopper. H~braten *m* meat loaf

Hacke¹ *f* -,-n hoe; *(Spitz-)* pick

Hacke² *f* -,-n, Hacken *m* -s,- heel

hack|en *vt* hoe; *(schlagen, zerkleinern)* chop; *(Vogel:)* peck; gehacktes Rindfleisch minced/ *(Amer)* ground beef. H~fleisch *nt* mince, *(Amer)* ground meat

Hafen *m* -s,: harbour; *(See-)* port. H~arbeiter *m* docker. H~damm *m* mole. H~stadt *f* port

Hafer *m* -s oats *pl*. H~flocken *fpl* [rolled] oats. H~mehl *nt* oatmeal

Haft *f* - *(Jur)* custody; *(H~strafe)* imprisonment. h~bar *a* *(Jur)* liable. H~befehl *m* warrant [for arrest]

haften *vi (haben)* cling; *(kleben)* stick; *(bürgen)* vouch/(*Jur*) be liable (für for)

Häftling *m* -s,-e detainee

Haftpflicht *f* *(Jur)* liability. H~versicherung *f* *(Auto)* third-party insurance

Haftstrafe *f* imprisonment

Haftung *f* - *(Jur)* liability

Hagebutte *f* -,-n rose-hip

Hagel *m* -s hail. H~korn *nt* hailstone. h~n *vi (haben)* hail

hager *a* gaunt

Hahn *m* -[e]s,:-e cock; *(Techn)* tap, *(Amer)* faucet

Hähnchen *nt* -s,- *(Culin)* chicken

Hai[fisch] *m* -[e]s,-e shark

Häkchen *nt* -s,- tick

häkel|n *vt/i (haben)* crochet. H~nadel *f* crochet-hook

Haken *m* -s,- hook; *(Häkchen)* tick; *(fam: Schwierigkeit)* snag. h~ *vt* hook (an + *acc* to). H~kreuz *nt* swastika. H~nase *f* hooked nose

halb *a* half; eine h~e Stunde half an hour; zum h~en Preis at half price; auf h~em Weg half-way □ *adv* half; h~ drei half past two; fünf [Minuten] vor/nach h~ vier twenty-five [minutes] past three/to four; h~ und h~ half and half; *(fast ganz)* more or less. H~blut *nt* halfbreed. H~dunkel *nt* semi-darkness. H~e(r,s) *f/m/nt* half [a litre]

halber *prep* (+ *gen*) for the sake of; Geschäfte h~ on business

Halb|finale *nt* semifinal. H~heit *f* -,-en *(fig)* half-measure

halbieren *vt* halve, divide in half; *(Geom)* bisect

Halb|insel *f* peninsula. H~kreis *m* semicircle. H~kugel *f* hemisphere. h~laut *a* low □ *adv* in an undertone. h~mast *adv* at half-mast. H~messer *m* -s,- radius. H~mond *m* half moon. H~pension *f* half-board. h~rund *a* semicircular.

H~schuh *m* [flat] shoe. h~stündlich *a* & *adv* half-hourly. h~tags *adv* [for] half a day; h~tags arbeiten ≈ work part-time. H- ton *m* semitone. h~wegs *adv* halfway; (*ziemlich*) more or less. h~wüchsig *a* adolescent. H~zeit *f* (*Sport*) half-time; (*Spielzeit*) half

Halde *f* -,-n dump, tip

Hälfte *f* -,-n half; zur H~ half

Halfter[1] *m* & *nt* -s,- halter

Halfter[2] *f* -,-n & *nt* -s,- holster

Hall *m* -[e]s,-e sound

Halle *f* -,-n hall; (*Hotel*-) lobby; (*Bahnhofs*-) station concourse

hallen *vi* (*haben*) resound; (*wider*-) echo

Hallen- *pref* indoor

hallo *int* hallo

Halluzination /-'tsio:n/ *f* -,-en hallucination

Halm *m* -[e]s,-e stalk; (*Gras*-) blade

Hals *m* -es,-̈e neck; (*Kehle*) throat; aus vollem H~e at the top of one's voice; (*lachen*) out loud. H~ausschnitt *m* neckline. H~band *nt* (*pl* -bänder) collar. H~kette *f* necklace. H~schmerzen *mpl* sore throat *sg*. h~starrig *a* stubborn. H~tuch *nt* scarf

halt[1] *adv* (*SGer*) just; es geht h~ nicht it's just not possible

halt[2] *int* stop! (*Mil*) halt! (*fam*) wait a minute!

Halt *m* -[e]s,-e hold; (*Stütze*) support; (*innerer*) stability; (*Anhalten*) stop; H~ machen stop. h~bar *a* durable; (*Tex*) hard-wearing; (*fig*) tenable; h~bar bis ... (*Comm*) use by ...

halten† *vt* hold; make 〈*Rede*〉; give 〈*Vortrag*〉; (*einhalten, bewahren*) keep; 〈*sich (dat)*〉 etw h~ keep 〈*Hund*〉; take 〈*Zeitung*〉; run 〈*Auto*〉; warm h~ keep warm; h~ für regard as; viel/nicht viel h~ von think highly/little of; sich h~ hold on (an + *dat* to); (*fig*) hold out; 〈*Geschäft*:〉 keep going; (*haltbar sein*) keep; 〈*Wetter*:〉 hold; 〈*Blumen*:〉 last; sich links h~ keep left; sich gerade h~ hold oneself upright; sich h~ an (+ *acc*) (*fig*) keep to □ *vi* (*haben*) hold; (*haltbar sein, bestehen bleiben*) keep; 〈*Freundschaft, Blumen*:〉 last; (*Halt machen*) stop; h~ auf (+ *acc*) (*fig*) set great store by; auf sich (*acc*) h~ take pride in oneself; an sich (*acc*) h~ contain oneself; zu jdm h~ be loyal to s.o.

~~Holter m s.~~ holder

Halte|stelle *f* stop. H~verbot *nt* waiting restriction; 'H~verbot' 'no waiting'

halt|los *a* (*fig*) unstable; (*unbegründet*) unfounded. h~machen *vi sep* (*haben*) ⟨NEW⟩ H~ machen, s. Halt

Haltung *f* -,-en (*Körper*-) posture; (*Verhalten*) manner; (*Einstellung*) attitude; (*Fassung*) composure; (*Halten*) keeping; H~ annehmen (*Mil*) stand to attention

Halunke *m* -n,-n scoundrel

Hamburger *m* -s,- hamburger

hämisch *a* malicious, *adv* -ly

Hammel *m* -s,-̈ ram; (*Culin*) mutton. H~fleisch *nt* mutton

Hammer *m* -s,-̈ hammer

hämmern *vt/i* (*haben*) hammer; 〈*Herz*:〉 pound

Hämorrhoiden /hɛmɔro'iːdən/, **Hämorriden** /hɛmɔ'riːdən/ *fpl* haemorrhoids

Hamster *m* -s,- hamster. h~n *vt/i* (*fam*) hoard

Hand *f* -,-̈e hand; eine H~ voll Kirschen a handful of cherries; jdm die H~ geben shake hands with s.o.; rechter/linker H~ on the right/left; [aus] zweiter H~ second-hand; unter der H~ unofficially; (*geheim*) secretly; an H~ (+ *gen*) = anhand; H~ und Fuß haben (*fig*) be sound. H~arbeit *f* manual work; (*handwerklich*) handicraft; (*Nadelarbeit*) needlework; (*Gegenstand*) hand-made article. H~ball *m* [German] handball. H~besen *m* brush. H~bewegung *f* gesture. H~bremse *f* handbrake. H~buch *nt* handbook, manual

Händedruck *m* handshake

Handel *m* -s trade, commerce; (*Unternehmen*) business; (*Geschäft*) deal; H~ treiben trade. h~n *vi* (*haben*) act; (*Handel treiben*) trade (mit in); von etw *od* über etw (*acc*) h~n deal with sth; sich h~n um be about, concern. H~smarine *f* merchant navy. H~sschiff *nt* merchant vessel. H~sschule *f* commercial college. h~süblich *a* customary. H~sware *f* merchandise

Hand|feger *m* -s,- brush. H~fertigkeit *f* dexterity. h~fest *a* sturdy; (*fig*) solid. H~fläche *f* palm. h~gearbeitet *a* handmade. H~gelenk *nt* wrist. h~gemacht *a* handmade. H~gemenge *nt* -s,- scuffle. H~gepäck *nt* hand-luggage. h~geschrieben *a* hand-written. H~granate *f* hand-grenade. h~greiflich *a* tangible; h~greiflich werden become violent. H~griff *m* handle; mit einem H~griff with a flick of the wrist

handhaben *vt insep* (*reg*) handle

Handikap /'hɛndikɛp/ *nt* -s,-s handicap

Hand|kuss (Handkuß) *m* kiss on the hand. H~lauf *m* handrail

Händler *m* -s,- dealer, trader

handlich *a* handy

Handlung f -,-en act; (Handeln) action; (Roman-) plot; (Geschäft) shop. H~sweise f conduct

Hand|schellen fpl handcuffs. H~schlag m handshake. H~schrift f handwriting; (Text) manuscript. H~schuh m glove. H~schuhfach nt glove compartment. H~stand m handstand. H~tasche f handbag. H~tuch nt towel. H~voll f -,-. eine H~voll (NEW) eine H~ voll, s. Hand

Handwerk nt craft, trade; sein H~ verstehen know one's job. H~er m -s,- craftsman; (Arbeiter) workman

Handy /'hɛndi/ nt -s,-s mobile phone

Hanf m -[e]s hemp

Hang m -[e]s,-e slope; (fig) inclination, tendency

Hänge|brücke f suspension bridge. H~lampe f [light] pendant. H~matte f hammock

hängen[1] vt (reg) hang

hängen[2] vi (haben) hang; h~ an (+ dat) (fig) be attached to; h~ bleiben stick (an + dat to); (Kleid:) catch (an + dat on); h~ lassen leave; den Kopf h~ lassen be downcast. h~bleiben† vi sep (sein) (NEW) h~ bleiben, s. hängen. h~lassen† vt sep (NEW) h~ lassen, s. hängen

Hannover nt -s Hanover

hänseln vt tease

hantieren vi (haben) busy oneself

hapern vi (haben) es hapert there's a lack (an + dat of)

Happen m -s,- mouthful; einen H~ essen have a bite to eat

Harfe f -,-n harp

Harke f -,-n rake. h~n vt/i (haben) rake

harmlos a harmless; (arglos) innocent, adv -ly. H~igkeit f - harmlessness; innocence

Harmonie f -,-n harmony. h~ren vi (haben) harmonize; (gut auskommen) get on well

Harmonika f -,-s accordion; (Mund-) mouth-organ

harmonisch a harmonious, adv -ly

Harn m -[e]s urine. H~blase f bladder

Harpune f -,-n harpoon

hart (härter, härtest) a hard; (heftig) violent; (streng) harsh □ adv hard; (streng) harshly

Härte f -,-n hardness; (Strenge) harshness; (Not) hardship. h~n vt harden

Hart|faserplatte f hardboard. h~gekocht a (NEW) h~ gekocht, s. kochen. h~herzig a hard-hearted. h~näckig a

stubborn, adv -ly; (ausdauernd) persistent, adv -ly. H~näckigkeit f - stubbornness; persistence

Harz nt -es,-e resin

Haschee nt -s,-s (Culin) hash

haschen vi (haben) h~ nach try to catch

Haschisch nt & m -[s] hashish

Hase m -n,-n hare; falscher H~ meat loaf

Hasel f -,-n hazel. H~maus f dormouse. H~nuss (H~nuß) f hazel-nut

Hasenfuß m (fam) coward

Hass m -es (Haß m -sses) hatred

hassen vt hate

hässlich (häßlich) a ugly; (unfreundlich) nasty, adv -ily. H~keit f - ugliness; nastiness

Hast f - haste. h~en vi (sein) hasten, hurry. h~ig a hasty, adv -ily, hurried, adv -ly

hast, hat, hatte, hätte s. haben

Haube f -,-n cap; (Trocken-) drier; (Kühler-) bonnet; (Amer) hood

Hauch m -[e]s breath; (Luft-) breeze; (Duft) whiff; (Spur) tinge. h~dünn a very thin; (Strümpfe) sheer. h~en vt/i (haben) breathe

Haue f -,-n pick; (fam: Prügel) beating. h~n† vt beat; (hämmern) knock; (meißeln) hew; sich h~n fight; übers Ohr h~n (fam) cheat □ vi (haben) bang (auf + acc on); jdm ins Gesicht h~n hit s.o. in the face

Haufen m -s,- heap, pile; (Leute) crowd

häufen vt heap or pile [up]; sich h~ pile up; (zunehmen) increase

haufenweise adv in large numbers; h~ Geld pots of money

häufig a frequent, adv -ly. H~keit f - frequency

Haupt nt -[e]s, Häupter head. H~bahnhof m main station. H~darsteller m, H~darstellerin f male/female lead. H~fach nt main subject. H~gericht nt main course. H~hahn m mains tap; (Wasser-) stopcock

Häuptling m -s,-e chief

Haupt|mahlzeit f main meal. H~mann m (pl -leute) captain. H~person f most important person; (Theat) principal character. H~post f main post office. H~quartier nt headquarters pl. H~rolle f lead; (fig) leading role. H~sache f main thing; in der H~sache in the main. h~sächlich a main, adv -ly. H~satz m main clause. H~schlüssel m master key. H~stadt f capital. H~straße f main street. H~verkehrsstraße f main road. H~verkehrszeit f rush-hour. H~wort nt (pl -wörter) noun

Haus nt -es, Häuser house; (*Gebäude*) building; (*Schnecken-*) shell; zu H~e at home; nach H~e home; H~ halten = haushalten. H~angestellte(r) m/f domestic servant. H~arbeit f housework; (*Sch*) homework. H~arzt m family doctor. H~aufgaben fpl homework sg. H~besetzer m -s,- squatter. H~besuch m house-call

hausen vi (*haben*) live; (*wüten*) wreak havoc

Haus|frau f housewife. H~gehilfin f domestic help. h~gemacht a homemade. H~halt m -[e]s,-e household; (*Pol*) budget. H~halten† vi sep (*haben*) h~halten mit manage carefully; conserve (*Kraft*). H~hälterin f -,-nen housekeeper. H~haltsgeld nt housekeeping [money]. H~haltsplan m budget. H~herr m head of the household; (*Gastgeber*) host. h~hoch a huge; (*fam*) big □ adv (*fam*) vastly; (*verlieren*) by a wide margin

hausier|en vi (*haben*) h~en mit hawk. H~er m -s,- hawker

Hauslehrer m [private] tutor. H~in f governess

häuslich a domestic, (*Person*) domesticated

Haus|meister m caretaker. H~nummer f house number. H~ordnung f house rules pl. H~putz m cleaning. H~rat m -[e]s household effects pl. H~schlüssel m front-door key. H~schuh m slipper. H~stand m household. H~suchung f [police] search. H~suchungsbefehl m search-warrant. H~tier nt domestic animal; (*Hund, Katze*) pet. H~tür f front door. H~wart m -[e]s,-e caretaker. H~wirt m landlord. H~wirtin f landlady

Haut f -,Häute skin; (*Tier-*) hide; aus der H~ fahren (*fam*) fly off the handle. H~arzt m dermatologist

häuten vt skin; sich h~ moult

haut|eng a skin-tight. H~farbe f colour; (*Teint*) complexion

Haxe f -,-n = Hachse

Hbf. abbr s. Hauptbahnhof

Hebamme f -,-n midwife

Hebel m -s,- lever. H~kraft, H~wirkung f leverage

heben† vt lift; (*hoch-, steigern*) raise; sich h~ rise; (*Nebel:*) lift; (*sich verbessern*) improve

hebräisch a Hebrew

hecheln vi (*haben*) pant

Hecht m -[e]s,-e pike

Heck nt -s,-s (*Naut*) stern; (*Aviat*) tail; (*Auto*) rear

Hecke f -,-n hedge. H~nschütze m sniper

Heck|fenster nt rear window. H~motor m rear engine. H~tür f hatchback

Heer nt -[e]s,-e army

Hefe f - yeast. H~teig m yeast dough

Heft nt -[e]s,-e haft, handle

Heft² nt -[e]s,-e booklet; (*Sch*) exercise book; (*Zeitschrift*) issue. h~en vt (*nähen*) tack; (*stecken*) pin/(*klammern*) clip/(*mit Heftmaschine*) staple (an + acc to). H~er m -s,- file

heftig a fierce, adv -ly, violent, adv -ly; (*Schlag, Regen*) heavy, adv -ily; (*Schmerz, Gefühl*) intense, adv -ly; (*Person*) quick-tempered. H~keit f -fierceness, violence; intensity

Heft|klammer f staple; (*Büro-*) paper-clip. H~maschine f stapler. H~pflaster nt sticking plaster. H~zwecke f -,-n drawing-pin

hegen vt care for; (*fig*) cherish (*Hoffnung*); harbour (*Verdacht*)

Hehl nt & m kein[en] H~ machen aus make no secret of. H~er m -s,- receiver, fence

Heide¹ m -n,-n heathen

Heide² f -,-n heath; (*Bot*) heather. H~kraut nt heather

Heidelbeere f bilberry, (*Amer*) blueberry

Heid|in f -,-nen heathen. h~nisch a heathen

heikel a difficult, tricky; (*delikat*) delicate; (*dial*) (*Person*) fussy

heil a undamaged, intact; (*Person*) unhurt; (*gesund*) well; mit h~er Haut (*fam*) unscathed

Heil nt -s salvation; sein H~ versuchen try one's luck

Heiland m -s (*Relig*) Saviour

Heil|anstalt f sanatorium; (*Nerven-*) mental hospital. H~bad nt spa. h~bar a curable

Heilbutt m -[e]s,-e halibut

heilen vt cure; heal (*Wunde*) □ vi (*sein*) heal

heilfroh a (*fam*) very relieved

Heilgymnastik f physiotherapy

heilig a holy; (*geweiht*) sacred; der H~e Abend Christmas Eve; die h~e Anna Saint Anne; h~ halten hold sacred; keep (*Feiertag*); h~ sprechen canonize. H~abend m Christmas Eve. H~e(r) m/f saint. h~en vt keep, observe. H~enschein m halo. h~halten† vt sep (NEW) h~ halten, s. halten. H~keit f - sanctity holiness. h~sprechen† vt sep (NEW) h~ sprechen, s. heilig. H~tum nt -s,-er shrine

heil|kräftig a medicinal. H~kräuter ntpl medicinal herbs. h~los a unholy.

H~mittel *nt* remedy. H~praktiker *m* -s,- practitioner of alternative medicine. h~sam *a* (*fig*) salutary. H~sarmee *f* Salvation Army. H~ung *f* - cure

Heim *nt* -[e]s,-e home; (*Studenten-*) hostel. h~ *adv* home

Heimat *f* -,-en home; (*Land*) native land. H~abend *m* folk evening. h~los *a* homeless. H~stadt *f* home town

heim|begleiten *vt sep* see home. h~bringen† *vt sep* bring home; (*begleiten*) see home. H~computer *m* home computer. h~fahren† *v sep □ vi* (*sein*) go/drive home. □ *vt* take/drive home. H~fahrt *f* way home. h~gehen† *vi sep* (*sein*) go home; (*sterben*) die

heimisch *a* native, indigenous; (*Pol*) domestic; h~ sein/sich h~fühlen be/ feel at home

Heim|kehr *f* - return [home]. h~kehren *vi sep* (*sein*) return home. h~kommen† *vi sep* (*sein*) come home

heimlich *a* secret, *adv* -ly; h~ tun be secretive; etw h~ tun do sth secretly *or* in secret. H~keit *f* -,-en secrecy; H~keiten secrets. H~tuerei *f* - secretiveness

Heim|reise *f* journey home. h~reisen *vi sep* (*sein*) go home. H~spiel *nt* home game. h~suchen *vt sep* afflict. h~tückisch *a* treacherous; (*Krankheit*) insidious. h~wärts *adv* home. H~weg *m* way home. H~weh *nt* -s homesickness; H~weh haben be homesick. H~werker *m* -s,- [home] handyman. h~zahlen *vt sep* jdm etw h~zahlen (*fig*) pay s.o. back for sth

Heirat *f* -,-en marriage. h~en *vt/i* (*haben*) marry. H~santrag *m* proposal; jdm einen H~santrag machen propose to s.o. h~sfähig *a* marriageable

heiser *a* hoarse, *adv* -ly. H~keit *f* - hoarseness

heiß *a* hot, *adv* -ly; (*hitzig*) heated; (*leidenschaftlich*) fervent, *adv* -ly; mein h~ geliebter Sohn my beloved son; mir ist h~ I am hot

heißen† *vi* (*haben*) be called; (*bedeuten*) mean; ich heiße ... my name is ...; wie h~ Sie? what is your name? wie heißt ... auf Englisch? what's the English for ...? es heißt it says; (*man sagt*) it is said; das heißt that is [to say]; was soll das h~? what does it mean? (*empört*) what is the meaning of this? □ *vt* call; jdn etw tun h~ tell s.o. to do sth

heißgeliebt *a* (NEW) h~ geliebt, s. heiß. h~hungrig *a* ravenous. H~wasserbereiter *m* -s,- water heater

heiter *a* cheerful, *adv* -ly; (*Wetter*) bright; (*amüsant*) amusing; aus h~em Himmel

(*fig*) out of the blue. H~keit *f* - cheerfulness; (*Gelächter*) mirth

Heiz|anlage *f* heating; (*Auto*) heater. H~decke *f* electric blanket. h~en *vt* heat; (*Ofen*) □ *vi* (*haben*) put the heating on; (*Ofen:*) give out heat. H~gerät *nt* heater. H~kessel *m* boiler. H~körper *m* radiator. H~lüfter *m* -s,- fan heater. H~material *nt* fuel. H~ofen *m* heater. H~ung *f* -,-en heating; (*Heizkörper*) radiator

Hektar *nt & m* -s,- hectare

hektisch *a* hectic

Held *m* -en,-en hero. h~enhaft *a* heroic, *adv* -ally. H~enmut *m* heroism. h~enmütig *a* heroic, *adv* -ally. H~entum *nt* -s heroism. H~in *f* -,-nen heroine

helfen† *vi* (*haben*) help (jdm s.o.); (*nützen*) be effective; sich (*dat*) nicht zu h~en wissen not know what to do; es hilft nichts it's no use. H~er(in) *m* -s,- (*f* -,-nen) helper, assistant. H~ershelfer *m* accomplice

hell *a* light; (*Licht ausstrahlend, klug*) bright; (*Stimme*) clear; (*fam: völlig*) utter; h~es Bier ≈ lager □ *adv* brightly; h~ begeistert absolutely delighted. h~hörig *a* poorly soundproofed; h~hörig werden (*fig*) sit up and take notice

hellicht *a* (NEW) helllicht

Hell|igkeit *f* - brightness. h~licht *a* h~lichter Tag broad daylight. H~seher(in) *m* -s,- (*f* -,-nen) clairvoyant. h~wach *a* wide awake

Helm *m* -[e]s,-e helmet

Hemd *nt* -[e]s,-e vest, (*Amer*) undershirt; (*Ober-*) shirt. H~bluse *f* shirt

Hemisphäre *f* -,-n hemisphere

hemm|en *vt* check; (*verzögern*) impede; (*fig*) inhibit. H~ung *f* -,-en (*fig*) inhibition; (*Skrupel*) scruple; H~ungen haben be inhibited. h~ungslos *a* unrestrained, *adv* -ly

Hendl *nt* -s,-[n] (*Aust*) chicken

Hengst *m* -[e]s,-e stallion. H~fohlen *nt* colt

Henkel *m* -s,- handle

henken *vt* hang

Henne *f* -,-n hen

her *adv* here; (*zeitlich*) ago; her mit ...! give me ...! von oben unten/Norden/weit her from above/below/the north/far away; von der Farbe/vom Thema her as far as the colour/subject is concerned; vor/hinter jdm/etw her in front of/behind s.o./sth; hinter jdm/etw her sein be after s.o./sth; her sein come (von/from); es ist schon lange/drei Tage her it was a long time/three days ago

herab *adv* down [here]; von oben h∼from above; *(fig)* condescending, *adv* -ly. h∼blicken *vi sep (haben)* = h∼sehen

herablass|en† *vt sep (haben)* let down; sich h∼en condescend (zu to). h∼end *a* condescending, *adv* -ly. H∼ung *f* - condescension

herab|setzen *vt sep (haben)* look down (auf + *acc* on). h∼setzen *vt sep* reduce, cut; *(fig)* belittle. h∼setzend *a* disparaging, *adv* -ly. h∼würdigen *vt sep* belittle, disparage

Heraldik *f* - heraldry

heran *adv* near; [bis] h∼ an (+ *acc*) up to. h∼bilden *vt sep* train. h∼gehen† *vi sep (sein)* h∼gehen an (+ *acc*) go up to; get down to ⟨*Arbeit*⟩. h∼kommen *vi sep (sein)* approach; h∼kommen an (+ *acc*) come up to; *(erreichen)* get at; *(fig)* measure up to. h∼machen (sich) *vr sep* sich h∼machen an (+ *acc*) approach; get down to ⟨*Arbeit*⟩. h∼reichen *vi sep (haben)* h∼reichen an (+ *acc*) reach; *(fig)* measure up to. h∼wachsen† *vi sep (sein)* grow up. h∼ziehen† *v sep* ◻ *vt* pull up (an + *acc* to); *(züchten)* raise; *(h∼bilden)* train; *(hinzuziehen)* call in ◻ *vi (sein)* approach

herauf *adv* up [here]; die Treppe h∼ up the stairs. h∼beschwören *vt sep* evoke; *(verursachen)* cause. h∼kommen† *vi sep (sein)* come up. h∼setzen *vt sep* raise, increase

heraus *adv* out (aus of); h∼ damit *od* mit der Sprache! out with it! h∼ sein be out; aus dem Gröbsten h∼ sein be over the worst; fein h∼ sein be sitting pretty. h∼bekommen† *vt sep* get out; *(ausfindig machen)* find out; *(lösen)* solve; Geld h∼bekommen get change. h∼bringen† *vt sep* bring out; *(fam)* get out. h∼finden† *v sep* ◻ *vt* find out ◻ *vi (haben)* find one's way out. H∼forderer *m* -s,- challenger. h∼fordern *vt sep* provoke; challenge ⟨*Person*⟩. H∼forderung *f* provocation; challenge. H∼gabe *f* handing over; *(Admin)* issue; *(Veröffentlichung)* publication. h∼geben† *vt sep* hand over; *(Admin)* issue; *(veröffentlichen)* publish; edit ⟨*Zeitschrift*⟩; jdm Geld h∼geben give s.o. change ◻ *vi (haben)* give change (auf + *acc* for). H∼geber *m* -s,- publisher; editor. h∼gehen† *vi sep (sein)* come out; aus sich h∼gehen *(fig)* come out of one's shell. h∼halten† (sich) *vr sep (fig)* keep out (aus of). h∼holen *vt sep* get out. h∼kommen† *vi sep (sein)* come out; *(aus Schwierigkeit, Takt)* get out; auf eins *od* dasselbe h∼kommen *(fam)* come to the same thing. h∼lassen† *vt sep* let out. h∼machen *vt sep* get out; sich gut

h∼machen *(fig)* do well. h∼nehmen† *vt sep* take out; sich zu viel h∼nehmen *(fig)* take liberties. h∼platzen *vi sep (haben) (fam)* burst out laughing. h∼putzen (sich) *vr sep* doll oneself up. h∼ragen *vi sep (haben)* jut out; *(fig)* stand out. h∼reden (sich) *vr sep* make excuses. h∼rücken *v sep* ◻ *vt* move out; *(hergeben)* hand over ◻ *vi (sein)* h∼rücken mit hand over; *(fig: sagen)* come out with. h∼rutschen *vi sep (sein)* slip out. h∼schlagen† *vt sep* knock out; *(fig)* gain. h∼stellen *vt sep* put out; sich h∼stellen turn out (als to be; daß that). h∼suchen *vt sep* pick out. h∼wollen† *vi sep (haben)* nicht mit der Sprache h∼wollen hum and haw. h∼ziehen† *vt sep* pull out

herb *a* sharp; ⟨*Wein*⟩ dry; ⟨*Landschaft*⟩ austere; *(fig)* harsh

herbei *adv* here. h∼führen *vt sep (fig)* bring about. h∼lassen† (sich) *vr sep* condescend (zu to). h∼schaffen *vt sep* get. h∼sehnen *vt sep* long for

Herberg|e *f* -,-n [youth] hostel; *(Unterkunft)* lodging. H∼svater *m* warden

herbestellen *vt sep* summon

herbitten† *vt sep* ask to come

herbringen† *vt sep* bring [here]

Herbst *m* -[e]s,-e autumn. h∼lich *a* autumnal

Herd *m* -[e]s,-e stove, cooker; *(fig)* focus

Herde *f* -,-n herd; ⟨*Schaf-*⟩ flock

herein *adv* in [here]; h∼! come in! h∼bitten† *vt sep* ask in. h∼brechen† *vi sep (sein)* burst in; *(fig)* set in; ⟨*Nacht:*⟩ fall; h∼brechen über (+ *acc*) *(fig)* overtake. h∼fallen† *vi sep (sein) (fam)* be taken in (auf + *acc* by). h∼kommen† *vi sep (sein)* come in. h∼lassen† *vt sep* let in. h∼legen *vt sep (fam)* take for a ride. h∼rufen† *vt sep* call in

Herfahrt *f* journey/drive here

herfallen† *vi sep (sein)* h∼ über (+ *acc*) attack; fall upon ⟨*Essen*⟩

hergeben† *vt sep* hand over; *(fig)* give up; sich h∼ zu *(fig)* be a party to

hergebracht *a* traditional

hergehen† *vi sep (sein)* h∼ vor/neben/hinter (+ *dat*) walk along in front of/beside/behind; es ging lustig her *(fam)* there was a lot of merriment

herhalten† *vi sep (haben)* hold out; h∼ müssen be the one to suffer

herholen *vt sep* fetch; weit hergeholt *(fig)* far fetched

Hering *m* -s,-e herring; *(Zeltpflock)* tentpeg

her|kommen *vi sep (sein)* come here; wo kommt das her? where does it come from? H~kömmlich *a* traditional. H~kunft *f* - origin

herlaufen† *vi sep* (*sein*) h~ vor/neben/hinter (+ *dat*) run/(*gehen*) walk along in front of/beside/behind

herleiten *vt sep* derive

hermachen *vt sep* viel/wenig h~ be impressive/unimpressive; (*wichtig nehmen*) make a lot of/little fuss (von of); sich h~ über (+ *acc*) fall upon; tackle 〈*Arbeit*〉

Hermelin¹ *nt* -s,-e (*Zool*) stoat

Hermelin² *m* -s,-e (*Pelz*) ermine

hermetisch *a* hermetic, *adv* -ally

Hernie /'hɛrnjə/ *f* -,-n hernia

Heroin *nt* -s heroin

heroisch *a* heroic, *adv* -ally

Herr *m* -n,-en gentleman; (*Gebieter*) master (über + *acc* of); [Gott,] der H~ the Lord [God]; H~ Meier Mr Meier; Sehr geehrte H~en Dear Sirs. H~chen *nt* -s,-master. H~enhaus *nt* manor [house]. h~enlos *a* ownerless; 〈*Tier*〉 stray. H~ensitz *m* manor

Herrgott *m* der H~ the Lord; H~ [nochmal]! damn it!

herrichten *vt sep* prepare; wieder h~ renovate

Herrin *f* -,-nen mistress

herrisch *a* imperious, *adv* -ly; 〈*Ton*〉 peremptory; (*herrschsüchtig*) overbearing

herrlich *a* marvellous, *adv* -ly; (*großartig*) magnificent, *adv* -ly. H~keit *f* -,-en splendour

Herrschaft *f* -,-en rule; (*Macht*) power; (*Kontrolle*) control; meine H~en! ladies and gentlemen!

herrsch|en *vi* (*haben*) rule; (*verbreitet sein*) prevail; es h~te Stille/große Aufregung there was silence/great excitement. H~er(in) *m* -s,- (*f* -,-nen) ruler. h~süchtig *a* domineering

herrühren *vi sep* (*haben*) stem (von from)

hersein† *vi sep* (*sein*) (NEW) her sein, s. her

herstammen *vi sep* (*haben*) come (aus/von from)

herstell|en *vt sep* establish; (*Comm*) manufacture, make. H~er *m* -s,- manufacturer, maker. H~ung *f* - establishment; manufacture

herüber *adv* over [here]. h~kommen† *vi sep* (*sein*) come over [here]

herum *adv* im Kreis h~ [round] in a circle; falsch h~ the wrong way round; um ... h~ round ...; (*ungefähr*) [round] about ...; h~ sein be over. h~albern *vi sep* (*haben*) fool around. h~drehen *vt sep* turn round/(*wenden*) over; turn 〈*Schlüssel*〉; sich h~drehen turn round/over. h~gehen† *vi sep* (*sein*) walk around;

〈*Zeit:*〉 pass; h~gehen um go round. h~kommen† *vi sep* (*sein*) get about; h~kommen um get round; come round 〈*Ecke*〉; um etw [nicht] h~kommen (*fig*) [not] get out of sth. h~kriegen *vt sep* jdn h~kriegen (*fam*) talk s.o. round. h~liegen† *vi sep* (*sein*) lie around. h~lungern *vi sep* (*haben*) loiter. h~schnüffeln *vi sep* (*haben*) (*fam*) nose about. h~sitzen† *vi sep* (*haben*) sit around; h~sitzen um sit round. h~sprechen† (sich) *vr sep* 〈*Gerücht:*〉 get about. h~stehen† *vi sep* (*haben*) stand around; h~stehen um stand round. h~treiben† (sich) *vr sep* hang around. h~ziehen† *vi sep* (*sein*) move around; (*ziellos*) wander about

herunter *adv* down [here]; die Treppe h~ down the stairs; h~ sein be down; (*körperlich*) be run down; h~fallen† *vi* fall off. h~gehen† *vi sep* (*sein*) come down; (*sinken*) go/come down. h~gekommen *a* (*fig*) run-down; (*Gebäude*) dilapidated; 〈*Person*〉 down-at-heel. h~kommen† *vi sep* (*sein*) come down; (*fig*) go to rack and ruin; 〈*Firma, Person:*〉 go downhill; (*gesundheitlich*) get run down. h~lassen† *vt sep* let down, lower. h~machen *vt sep* (*fam*) reprimand; (*herabsetzen*) run down. h~spielen *vt sep* (*fig*) play down. h~ziehen† *vt sep* pull down

hervor *adv* out (aus of). h~bringen† *vt sep* produce; utter (*Wort*). h~gehen† *vi sep* (*sein*) come/(*sich ergeben*) emerge/(*folgen*) follow (aus from). h~heben† *vt sep* (*fig*) stress, emphasize. h~quellen† *vi sep* (*sein*) stream out; (*h~treten*) bulge. h~ragen *vi sep* (*haben*) jut out; (*fig*) stand out. h~ragend *a* (*fig*) outstanding. h~rufen† *vt sep* (*fig*) cause. h~stehen† *vi sep* (*haben*) protrude. h~treten† *vi sep* (*sein*) protrude, bulge; (*fig*) stand out. h~tun† (sich) *vr sep* (*fig*) distinguish oneself; (*angeben*) show off

Herweg *m* way here

Herz *nt* -ens,-en heart; (*Kartenspiel*) hearts *pl*; sich (*dat*) ein H~ fassen pluck up courage. H~anfall *m* heart attack

herzeigen *vt sep* show

herz|en *vt* hug. H~enslust *f* nach H~enslust to one's heart's content. h~haft *a* hearty, *adv* -ily; (*würzig*) savoury

herziehen† *v sep* ▫ *vt* hinter sich (*dat*) h~ pull along [behind one] ▫ *vi* (*sein*) hinter jdm h~ follow along behind s.o.; über jdn h~ (*fam*) run s.o. down

herz|ig *a* sweet, adorable. H~infarkt *m* heart attack. H~klopfen *nt* -s palpitations *pl*; ich hatte H~klopfen my heart was pounding

herzlich *a* cordial, *adv* -ly; (*warm*) warm, *adv* -ly; (*aufrichtig*) sincere, *adv* -ly; h~en Dank! many thanks! h~e Grüße kind regards; h~ wenig precious little. H~keit *f* - cordiality; warmth; sincerity

herzlos *a* heartless

Herzog *m* -s,̈-e duke. H~in *f* -,-nen duchess. H~tum *nt* -s,̈-er duchy

Herz|schlag *m* heartbeat; (*Med*) heart failure. h~zerreißend *a* heart-breaking

Hessen *nt* -s Hesse

heterosexuell *a* heterosexual

Hetze *f* - rush; (*Kampagne*) virulent campaign (gegen against). h~n *vt* chase; sich h~n hurry □ *vi* (*haben*) agitate; (*sich beeilen*) hurry □ *vi* (*sein*) rush

Heu *nt* -s hay; Geld wie Heu haben (*fam*) have pots of money

Heuchelei *f* - hypocrisy

heuch|eln *vt* feign □ *vi* (*haben*) pretend. H~ler(in) *m* -s,- (*f* -,-nen) hypocrite. h~lerisch *a* hypocritical, *adv* -ly

heuer *adv* (*Aust*) this year

Heuer *f* -,-n (*Naut*) pay. h~n *vt* hire; sign on (*Matrosen*)

heulen *vi* (*haben*) howl; (*fam: weinen*) cry; (*Sirene:*) wail

Heurige(r) *m* (*Aust*) new wine

Heu|schnupfen *m* hay fever. H~schober *m* -s,- haystack. H~schrecke *f* -,-n grasshopper; (*Wander-*) locust

heute *adv* today; (*heutzutage*) nowadays; h~e früh od Morgen (morgen) this morning; von h~e auf morgen from one day to the next. h~ig *a* today's ...; (*gegenwärtig*) present; der h~ige Tag today. h~zutage *adv* nowadays

Hexe *f* -,-n witch. h~n *vi* (*haben*) work magic; ich kann nicht h~n (I can't perform miracles. H~njagd *f* witchhunt. H~nschuss (H~nschuß) *m* lumbago. H~rei *f* - witchcraft

Hieb *m* -[e]s,-e blow; (*Peitschen-*) lash; H~e hiding *pl*

hier *adv* here; h~ sein/bleiben/lassen/behalten be/stay/leave/keep here; h~ und da here and there; (*zeitlich*) now and again

Hierarchie /hjerar'çi:/ *f* -,-n hierarchy

hier|auf *adv* on this/these; (*antworten*) to this; (*zeitlich*) after this. h~aus *adv* out of *or* from this/these. h~behalten† *vt sep* (NEW) h~ behalten, s. hier. h~bleiben† *vi sep* (*sein*) (NEW) h~ bleiben, s. hier. h~durch *adv* through this/these; (*Ursache*) as a result of this. h~für *adv* for this/these. h~her *adv* here. h~hin *adv* here. h~in *adv* in this/these. h~lassen† *vt sep* (NEW) h~ lassen, s. hier.

h~mit *adv* with this/these; (*Comm*) herewith; (*Admin*) hereby. h~nach *adv* after this/these; (*demgemäß*) according to this/these. h~sein† *vi sep* (*sein*) (NEW) h~ sein, s. hier. h~über *adv* over/(*höher*) above this/these; (*sprechen, streiten*) about this/these. h~unter *adv* under/(*tiefer*) below this/these; (*dazwischen*) among these. h~von *adv* from this/these; (*h~über*) about this/these; (*Menge*) of this/these. h~zu *adv* to this/these; (*h~für*) for this/these. h~zulande *adv* here

hiesig *a* local. H~e(r) *m/f* local

Hilfe *f* -,-n help, aid; um H~e rufen call for help; jdm zu H~e kommen come to s.o.'s aid; mit H~e (+ *gen*) (NEW) mithilfe. h~los *a* helpless, *adv* -ly. H~losigkeit *f* - helplessness. h~reich *a* helpful

Hilfs|arbeiter *m* unskilled labourer. h~bedürftig *a* needy; h~bedürftig sein be in need of help. h~bereit *a* helpful, *adv* -ly. H~kraft *f* helper. H~mittel *nt* aid. H~verb, H~zeitwort *nt* auxiliary verb

Himbeere *f* raspberry

Himmel *m* -s,- sky; (*Relig & fig*) heaven; (*Bett-*) canopy; am H~ in the sky; unter freiem H~ in the open air. H~bett *nt* four-poster [bed]. H~fahrt *f* Ascension; Mariä H~fahrt Assumption. h~schreiend *a* scandalous. H~srichtung *f* compass point; in alle H~srichtungen in all directions. h~weit *a* (*fam*) vast

himmlisch *a* heavenly

hin *adv* there; hin und her to and fro; hin und zurück there and back; (*Rail*) return; hin und wieder now and again; an (+ *dat*) ... hin along; auf (+ *acc*) ... hin in reply to (*Brief, Anzeige*); on (*jds Rat*); zu od nach ... hin towards; vor sich hin reden talk to oneself; hin sein (*fam*) be gone; (*kaputt, tot*) have had it; [ganz] hin sein to be overwhelmed by; es ist noch/nicht mehr lange hin it's a long time yet/not long to go

hinab *adv* down [there]

hinauf *adv* up [there]; die Treppe/Straße h~ up the stairs/road. h~gehen† *vi sep* (*sein*) go up. h~setzen *vt sep* raise

hinaus *adv* out [there]; (*nach draußen*) outside; zur Tür h~ out of the door; auf Jahre h~ for years to come; über etw (*acc*) h~ beyond sth; (*Menge*) [over and] above sth; über etw (*acc*) h~ sein (*fig*) be past sth. h~fliegen† *vi sep* (*sein*) fly out; (*fam*) get the sack □ *vt sep* (*sein*) fly out. h~gehen† *vi sep* (*sein*) go out; (*Zimmer:*) face (nach Norden north); h~gehen über (+ *acc*) go beyond, exceed. h~kommen† *vi sep* (*sein*) get out; h~kommen über (+ *acc*) get beyond. h~laufen† *vi* *sep* (sein) run out; h~laufen auf (+ *acc*) (*fig*) amount to. h~lehnen (sich) *vr sep* lean out. h~ragen *vi sep* (haben) h~ragen über (+ *acc*) project beyond; (*in der Höhe*) rise above; (*fig*) stand out above. h~schicken *vt sep* send out. h~schieben† *vt sep* push out; (*fig*) put off. h~sehen† *vi sep* (haben) look out. h~sein† *vi sep* (sein) (NEW) h~ sein, s. hinaus. h~werfen† *vt sep* throw out; (*fam: entlassen*) fire. h~wollen† *vi sep* (haben) want to go out; h~wollen auf (+ *acc*) (*fig*) aim at; hoch h~wollen (*fig*) be ambitious. h~ziehen† *v sep* □ *vt* pull out; (*in die Länge ziehen*) drag out; (*verzögern*) delay; sich h~ziehen drag on; be delayed □ *vi* (sein) move out. h~zögern *vt* delay; sich h~zögern be delayed

Hinblick *m* im H~ auf (+ *acc*) in view of; (*hinsichtlich*) regarding

hinbringen† *vt sep* take there; (*verbringen*) spend

hinder|lich *a* awkward; jdm h~lich sein hamper s.o. h~n *vt* hamper; (*verhindern*) prevent. **H~nis** *nt* -ses,-se obstacle. **H~nisrennen** *nt* steeplechase

hindeuten *vi sep* (haben) point (auf + *acc* to)

Hindu *m* -s,-s Hindu. **H~ismus** *m* - Hinduism

hindurch *adv* through it/them; den Sommer h~ throughout the summer

hinein *adv* in [there]; (*nach drinnen*) inside; h~ in (+ *acc*) into. h~fallen† *vi sep* (sein) fall in. h~gehen† *vi sep* (sein) go in; h~gehen in (+ *acc*) go into. h~laufen† *vi sep* (sein) run in; h~laufen in (+ *acc*) run into. h~reden *vi sep* (haben) jdm h~reden interrupt s.o.; (*sich einmischen*) interfere in s.o.'s affairs. h~versetzen (sich) *vr sep* sich in jds Lage h~versetzen put oneself in s.o.'s position. h~ziehen† *vt sep* pull in; h~ziehen in (+ *acc*) pull into; in etw (*acc*) h~gezogen werden (*fig*) become involved in sth

hin|fahren† *v sep* □ *vi* (sein) go/drive there □ *vt* take/drive there. **H~fahrt** *f* journey/drive there; (*Rail*) outward journey. h~fallen† *vi sep* (sein) fall. h~fällig *a* (*gebrechlich*) frail; (*ungültig*) invalid. h~fliegen† *v sep* □ *vi* (sein) fly there; (*fam*) fall □ *vt* fly there. **H~flug** *m* flight there; (*Admin*) outward flight. **H~gabe** *f* - devotion; (*Eifer*) dedication

hingeb|en† *vt sep* give up; sich h~en (*fig*) devote oneself (*einer Aufgabe* to a task); abandon oneself (*dem Vergnügen* to pleasure). **H~ung** *f* - devotion. h~ungsvoll *a* devoted, *adv* -ly

hingegen *adv* on the other hand

hingehen† *vi sep* (sein) go/(*zu Fuß*) walk there; (*vergehen*) pass; h~ zu go up to; wo gehst du hin? where are you going? etw h~ lassen (*fig*) let sth pass

hingerissen *a* rapt, *adv* -ly; h~ sein be carried away (von by)

hin|halten† *vt sep* hold out; (*warten lassen*) keep waiting. h~hocken (sich) *vr sep* squat down. h~kauern (sich) *vr sep* crouch down

hinken *vi* (haben/sein) limp

hin|knien (sich) *vr sep* kneel down. h~kommen† *vi sep* (sein) get there; (*h~gehören*) belong, go; (*fam: auskommen*) manage (mit with); (*fam: stimmen*) be right. h~länglich *a* adequate, *adv* -ly. h~laufen† *vi sep* (sein) run/(*gehen*) walk there. h~legen *vt sep* lay or put down; sich h~legen lie down. h~nehmen† *vt sep* (*fig*) accept

hinreichen *v sep* □ *vt* hand (*dat* to) □ *vi* (haben) extend (bis to); (*ausreichen*) be adequate. h~d *a* adequate, *adv* -ly

Hinreise *f* journey there; (*Rail*) outward journey

hinreißen† *vt sep* (*fig*) carry away; sich h~ lassen get carried away. h~d *a* ravishing, *adv* -ly

hinricht|en *vt sep* execute. **H~ung** *f* execution

hinschicken *vt sep* send there

hinschleppen *vt sep* drag there; (*fig*) drag out; sich h~ drag oneself along; (*fig*) drag on

hinschreiben† *vt sep* write there; (*aufschreiben*) write down

hinsehen† *vi sep* (haben) look

hinsein† *vi sep* (sein) (fam) (NEW) hin sein, s. hin

hinsetzen *vt sep* put down; sich h~ sit down

Hinsicht *f* - in dieser/gewisser H~ in this respect/in a certain sense; in finanzieller H~ financially. h~lich *prep* (+ *gen*) regarding

hinstellen *vt sep* put *or* set down; park ⟨*Auto*⟩; (*fig*) make out (als to be); sich h~ stand

hinstrecken *vt sep* hold out; sich h~ extend

hintan|setzen, h~stellen *vt sep* ignore; (*vernachlässigen*) neglect

hinten *adv* at the back; dort h~ back there; nach/von h~ to the back/from behind. h~herum *adv* round the back; (*fam*) by devious means; ⟨*erfahren*⟩ in a roundabout way

hinter *prep* (+ *dat/acc*) behind; (*nach*) after; h~ jdm/etw herlaufen run after s.o./sth; h~ etw (*dat*) stecken (*fig*) be

behind sth; h~ etw (*acc*) kommen (*fig*)
get to the bottom of sth; etw h~ sich (*acc*)
bringen get sth over [and done] with.
H~*bein* *nt* hind log

Hinterbliebene *pl* (*Admin*) surviving
dependants; die H~n the bereaved family
sg

hinterbringen† *vt* tell (jdm s.o.)

hintere|(r,s) *a* back, rear; h~s Ende far
end

hintereinander *adv* one behind/(*zeitlich*) after the other; dreimal h~ three
times in succession *or* (*fam*) in a row

Hintergedanke *m* ulterior motive

hintergehen† *vt* deceive

Hinter|grund *m* background. H~halt *m*
-[e]s,-e ambush; aus dem H~halt überfallen ambush. h~hältig *a* underhand

hinterher *adv* behind, after; (*zeitlich*)
afterwards. h~gehen† *vi sep* (*sein*) follow
(jdm s.o.). h~kommen† *vi sep* (*sein*) follow [behind]. h~laufen† *vi sep* (*sein*) run
after (jdm s.o.)

Hinter|hof *m* back yard. H~kopf *m* back
of the head

hinterlassen† *vt* leave [behind]; (*Jur*)
leave, bequeath (*dat* to). H~schaft *f*-,-en
(*Jur*) estate

hinterlegen *vt* deposit

Hinter|leib *m* (*Zool*) abdomen. H~list *f*
deceit. h~listig *a* deceitful, *adv* -ly. h~m
prep = hinter dem. H~mann *m* (*pl*
-männer) person behind. h~n *prep* =
hinter den. H~n *m* -s,- (*fam*) bottom,
backside. H~rad *nt* rear *or* back wheel.
h~rücks *adv* from behind. h~s *prep* =
hinter das. h~ste(r,s) *a* last; h~ste
Reihe back row. H~teil *nt* (*fam*) behind

hintertreiben† *vt* (*fig*) block

Hinter|treppe *f* back stairs *pl*. H~tür *f*
back door; (*fig*) loophole

hinterziehen† *vt* (*Admin*) evade

Hinterzimmer *nt* back room

hinüber *adv* over *or* across [there]; h~
sein (*fam: unbrauchbar, tot*) have had it;
(*betrunken*) be gone. h~gehen† *vi sep*
(*sein*) go over *or* across; h~gehen über
(+ *acc*) cross

hinunter *adv* down [there]; die Treppe/
Straße h~ down the stairs/road.
h~gehen† *vi sep* (*sein*) go down.
h~schlucken *vt sep* swallow

Hinweg *m* way there

hinweg *adv* away, off, h~ über (+ *acc*)
over; über eine Zeit h~ over a period
h~gehen† *vi sep* (*sein*) h~gehen über
(+ *acc*) (*fig*) pass over. h~kommen† *vi
sep* (*sein*) h~kommen über (+ *acc*) (*fig*)
get over. h~sehen† *vi sep* (*haben*)
h~sehen über (+ *acc*) see over; (*fig*)

overlook. h~setzen (sich) *vr sep* sich
h~setzen über (+ *acc*) ignore

Hinweis *m* -es,-e reference; (*Andeutung*)
hint; (*Anzeigen*) indication; unter H~
auf (+ *acc*) with reference to. h~en† *v
sep* □ *vi* (*haben*) point (auf + *acc* to). □ *vt*
jdn auf etw (*acc*) h~en point sth out to
s.o. h~end *a* (*Gram*) demonstrative

hin|wenden† *vt sep* turn; sich
h~wenden turn (zu to). h~werfen† *vt
sep* throw down; drop (*Bemerkung*);
(*schreiben*) jot down; (*zeichnen*) sketch;
(*fam: aufgeben*) pack in

hinwieder *adv* on the other hand

hin|zeigen *vi sep* (*haben*) point (auf +
acc to). h~ziehen† *vt sep* pull; (*fig: in die
Länge ziehen*) drag out; (*verzögern*) delay;
sich h~ziehen drag on; be delayed; sich
h~gezogen fühlen zu (*fig*) feel drawn to

hinzu *adv* in addition. h~fügen *vt sep* add.
h~kommen† *vt sep* (*sein*) be added; (*ankommen*) arrive [on the scene]; join (zu
s.o.). h~rechnen *vt sep* add. h~zie-
hen† *vt sep* call in

Hiobsbotschaft *f* bad news *sg*

Hirn *nt* -s brain; (*Culin*) brains *pl*. H~ge-
spinst *nt* -[e]s,-e figment of the imagination. H~hautentzündung *f* meningitis. h~verbrannt *a* (*fam*) crazy

Hirsch *m* -[e]s,-e deer; (*männlich*) stag;
(*Culin*) venison

Hirse *f* - millet

Hirt *m* -en,-en, Hirte *m* -n,-n shepherd

hissen *vt* hoist

Histor|iker *m* -s,- historian. h~isch *a*
historical; (*bedeutend*) historic

Hit *m* -s,-s (*Mus*) hit

Hitze *f* - heat. H~ewelle *f* heatwave.
h~ig *a* (*fig*) heated, *adv* -ly; (*Person*) hot-
headed; (*jähzornig*) hot-tempered.
H~kopf *m* hothead. H~schlag *m* heat-
stroke

H-Milch /'haː-/ *f* long-life milk

Hobby *nt* -s,-s hobby

Hobel *m* -s,- (*Techn*) plane; (*Culin*) slicer.
h~n *vt/i* (*haben*) plane; (*Culin*) slice.
H~späne *mpl* shavings

hoch *a* (höher, höchst; *attrib* hohe(r,s))
high; (*Baum, Mast*) tall; (*Offizier*) high-
ranking; (*Alter*) great; (*Summe*) large;
(*Strafe*) heavy; hohe Schuhe ankle boots
□ *adv* high; (*sehr*) highly; h~ gewachsen
tall; h~ begabt highly gifted; h~ ge-
stellte Persönlichkeit important person; die Treppe/den Berg h~ up the
stairs/hill; sechs Mann h~ six of us/
them. H~ *nt* -s,-s cheer; (*Meteorol*) high

Hoch|achtung *f* high esteem. H~ach-
tungsvoll *adv* Yours faithfully. H~amt
nt High Mass. h~arbeiten (sich) *vr sep*

work one's way up. h~begabt *attrib a* ⟨NEW⟩ h~ begabt, *s.* hoch. H~betrieb *m* great activity; in den Geschäften herrscht H~betrieb the shops are terribly busy. H~burg *f* ⟨*fig*⟩ stronghold. H~deutsch *nt* High German. H~druck *m* high pressure. H~ebene *f* plateau. h~fahren† *vi sep* (*sein*) go up; (*auffahren*) start up; (*aufbrausen*) flare up. h~fliegend *a* ⟨*fig*⟩ ambitious. h~gehen† *vi sep* (*sein*) go up; (*explodieren*) blow up; (*aufbrausen*) flare up. h~gestellt *attrib a* ⟨*Zahl*⟩ superior; ⟨*fig*⟩ ⟨NEW⟩ h~ gestellt, *s.* hoch. h~gewachsen *a* ⟨NEW⟩ h~ gewachsen, *s.* hoch. H~glanz *m* high gloss. h~gradig *a* extreme, *adv* -ly. h~hackig *a* high-heeled. h~halten† *vt sep* hold up; ⟨*fig*⟩ uphold. H~haus *nt* high-rise building. h~heben† *vt sep* lift up; raise ⟨*Kopf, Hand*⟩. h~herzig *a* magnanimous, *adv* -ly. h~kant *adv* on end. h~kommen† *vi sep* (*sein*) come up; (*aufstehen*) get up; ⟨*fig*⟩ get on [in the world]. H~konjunktur *f* boom. h~leben *vi sep* (*haben*) h~leben lassen give three cheers for; … lebe hoch! three cheers for …! H~mut *m* pride, arrogance. h~mütig *a* arrogant, *adv* -ly. h~näsig *a* ⟨*fam*⟩ snooty. h~nehmen† *vt sep* pick up; ⟨*fam*⟩ tease. H~ofen *m* blast-furnace. h~ragen *vi sep* rise [up]; ⟨*Turm*⟩ soar. H~ruf *m* cheer. H~saison *f* high season. H~schätzung *f* high esteem. h~schlagen† *vt sep* turn up ⟨*Kragen*⟩. h~schrecken† *vi sep* (*sein*) start up. H~schule *f* university; (*Musik-, Kunst-*) academy. h~sehen† *vi sep* (*haben*) look up. H~sommer *m* midsummer. H~spannung *f* high/⟨*fig*⟩ great tension. h~spielen *vt sep* ⟨*fig*⟩ magnify. H~sprache *f* standard language. H~sprung *m* high jump

höchst *adv* extremely, most

Hochstapler *m* -s,- confidence trickster

höchst|e(r,s) *a* highest; ⟨*Baum, Turm*⟩ tallest; (*oberste, größte*) top; es ist h~e Zeit it is high time. h~ens *adv* at most; (*es sei denn*) except perhaps. H~fall *m* im H~fall at most. H~geschwindigkeit *f* top *or* maximum speed. H~maß *nt* maximum. h~persönlich *adv* in person. H~preis *m* top price. H~temperatur *f* maximum temperature. h~wahrscheinlich *adv* most probably

hoch|trabend *a* pompous, *adv* -ly. h~treiben† *vt sep* push up ⟨*Preis*⟩. H~verrat *m* high treason. H~wasser *nt* high tide; (*Überschwemmung*) floods *pl.* H~würden *m* -s Reverend; (*Anrede*) Father

Hochzeit *f* -,-en wedding; H~ feiern get married. H~skleid *nt* wedding dress.

H~sreise *f* honeymoon [trip]. H~stag *m* wedding day/(*Jahrestag*) anniversary

hochziehen† *vt sep* pull up; (*hissen*) hoist; raise ⟨*Augenbrauen*⟩

Hocke *f* - in der H~ sitzen squat; in die H~ gehen squat down. h~n *vi* (*haben*) squat □ *vr* sich h~n squat down

Hocker *m* -s,- stool

Höcker *m* -s,- bump; (*Kamel-*) hump

Hockey /ˈhɔki/ *nt* -s hockey

Hode *f* -,-n, **Hoden** *m* -s,- testicle

Hof *m* -[e]s,¨e [court]yard; (*Bauern-*) farm; (*Königs-*) court; (*Schul-*) playground; (*Astr*) halo; Hof halten hold court

hoffen *vt/i* (*haben*) hope (auf + *acc* for). h~tlich *adv* I hope, let us hope; (*als Antwort*) h~tlich/h~tlich nicht let's hope so/not

Hoffnung *f* -,-en hope. h~slos *a* hopeless, *adv* -ly. h~svoll *a* hopeful, *adv* -ly

höflich *a* polite, *adv* -ly, courteous, *adv* -ly. H~keit *f* -,-en politeness, courtesy; (*Äußerung*) civility

hohe(r,s) *a s.* hoch

Höhe *f* -,-n height; (*Aviat, Geog*) altitude; (*Niveau*) level; (*einer Summe*) size; (*An-*) hill; in die H~ gehen rise, go up; nicht auf der H~ (*fam*) under the weather; das ist die H~! (*fam*) that's the limit!

Hoheit *f* -,-en (*Staats-*) sovereignty; (*Titel*) Highness. H~sgebiet *nt* [sovereign] territory. H~szeichen *nt* national emblem

Höhe|nlinie *f* contour line. H~nsonne *f* sun-lamp. H~nzug *m* mountain range. H~punkt *m* ⟨*fig*⟩ climax, peak; (*einer Vorstellung*) highlight. h~r *a & adv* higher; h~re Schule secondary school

hohl *a* hollow; (*leer*) empty

Höhle *f* -,-n cave; (*Tier-*) den; (*Hohlraum*) cavity; (*Augen-*) socket

Hohl|maß *nt* measure of capacity. H~raum *m* cavity

Hohn *m* -s scorn, derision

höhn|en *vt* deride □ *vi* (*haben*) jeer. h~isch *a* scornful, *adv* -ly

holen *vt* fetch, get; (*kaufen*) buy; (*nehmen*) take (aus from); h~ lassen send for; [tief] Atem *od* Luft h~ take a [deep] breath; sich (*dat*) etw h~ get sth; catch ⟨*Erkältung*⟩

Holland *nt* -s Holland

Holländ|er *m* -s,- Dutchman; die H~er the Dutch *pl.* H~erin *f* -,-nen Dutchwoman. h~isch *a* Dutch

Höll|e *f* -hell. h~isch *a* infernal; (*schrecklich*) terrible, *adv* -bly

holpern *vi* (*sein*) jolt *or* bump along □ *vi* (*haben*) be bumpy

holp[e]rig *a* bumpy

Holunder m -s (Bot) elder

Holz nt -es, ̈er wood; (Nutz-) timber.
H∼blasinstrument nt woodwind instrument

hölzern a wooden

Holz|hammer m mallet. h∼ig a woody.
H∼kohle f charcoal. H∼schnitt m woodcut. H∼schuh m [wooden] clog. H∼wolle
f wood shavings pl. H∼wurm m woodworm

homogen a homogeneous

Homöopathie f - homoeopathy

homosexuell a homosexual. H∼e(r) m/f
homosexual

Honig m -s honey. H∼wabe f honeycomb

Hono|rar nt -s,-e fee. h∼rieren vt remunerate; (fig) reward

Hopfen m -s hops pl; (Bot) hop

hopsen vi (sein) jump

Hör|apparat m hearing-aid. h∼bar a
audible, adv -bly

horchen vi (haben) listen (auf + acc to);
(heimlich) eavesdrop

Horde f -,-n horde; (Gestell) rack

hören vt hear; (an-) listen to ○ vi (haben)
hear; (horchen) listen; (gehorchen) obey;
h∼auf (+ acc) listen to. H∼sagen nt vom
H∼sagen from hearsay

Hör|er m -s,- listener; (Teleph) receiver.
H∼funk m radio. H∼gerät nt hearingaid

Horizon|t m -[e]s horizon. h∼tal a horizontal, adv -ly

Hormon nt -s,-e hormone

Horn nt -s, ̈er horn. H∼haut f hard skin;
(Augen-) cornea

Hornisse f -,-n hornet

Horoskop nt -[e]s,-e horoscope

Hörrohr nt stethoscope

Horrorfilm m horror film

Hör|saal m (Univ) lecture hall. H∼spiel
nt radio play

Hort m -[e]s,-e (Schatz) hoard; (fig) refuge.
h∼en vt hoard

Hortensie /-jə/ f -,-n hydrangea

Hörweite f in/außer H∼ within/out of
earshot

Hose f -,-n, Hosen pl trousers pl. H∼nrock m culottes pl. H∼nschlitz m fly,
flies pl. H∼nträger mpl braces, (Amer)
suspenders

Hostess (Hosteß) f -,-tessen hostess;
(Aviat) air hostess

Hostie /'hɔstjə/ f -,-n (Relig) host

Hotel nt -s,-s hotel; H∼ garni / ∼ gar'ni:/
bed-and-breakfast hotel. H∼ier /-'lje:/ m
-s,-s hotelier

hübsch a pretty, adv -ily; (nett) nice, adv
-ly; ⟨Summe⟩ tidy

Hubschrauber m -s,- helicopter

huckepack adv jdn h∼ tragen give s.o.
a piggyback

Huf m -[e]s,-e hoof. H∼eisen nt horseshoe

Hüft|e f -,-n hip. H∼gürtel, H∼halter m
-s,- girdle

Hügel m -s,- hill. h∼ig a hilly

Huhn nt -s, ̈er chicken; ⟨Henne⟩ hen

Hühn|chen nt -s,- chicken. H∼erauge nt
corn. H∼erbrühe f chicken broth.
H∼erstall m henhouse, chicken-coop

huldig|en vi (haben) pay homage (dat to).
H∼ung f - homage

Hülle f -,-n cover; (Verpackung) wrapping;
(Platten-) sleeve; in H∼ und Fülle in
abundance. h∼n vt wrap

Hülse f -,-n (Bot) pod; (Etui) case.
H∼nfrüchte fpl pulses

human a humane, adv -ly. h∼itär a humanitarian. H∼ität f - humanity

Hummel f -,-n bumble-bee

Hummer m -s,- lobster

Hum|or m -s humour; H∼or haben have
a sense of humour. h∼oristisch a humorous. h∼orvoll a humorous, adv -ly

humpeln vi (sein/haben) hobble

Humpen m -s,- tankard

Hund m -[e]s,-e dog; (Jagd-) hound. H∼ehalsband nt dog-collar. H∼ehütte f kennel. H∼eleine f dog lead

hundert inv a one/a hundred. H∼ nt
-s,-e hundred; H∼e od h∼e von hundreds
of. H∼jahrfeier f centenary, (Amer) centennial. h∼prozentig a & adv one hundred per cent. h∼ste(r,s) a hundredth.
H∼stel nt -s,- hundredth

Hündin f -,-nen bitch

Hüne m -n,-n giant

Hunger m -s hunger; H∼ haben be hungry. h∼n vi (haben) starve; h∼n nach
(fig) hunger for. H∼snot f famine

hungrig a hungry, adv -ily

Hupe f -,-n (Auto) horn. h∼n vi (haben)
sound one's horn

hüpf|en vi (sein) skip; ⟨Vogel, Frosch:⟩ hop;
⟨Grashüpfer:⟩ jump. H∼er m -s,- skip, hop

Hürde f -,-n (Sport & fig) hurdle; (Schaf-)
pen, fold

Hure f -,-n whore

hurra int hurray. H∼ nt -s,-s hurray;
(Beifallsruf) cheer

Husche f -,-n [short] shower. h∼n vi (sein)
slip; ⟨Eidechse:⟩ dart; ⟨Maus:⟩ scurry; ⟨Lächeln:⟩ flit

hüsteln vi (haben) give a slight cough

husten *vi* (*haben*) cough. H∼ *m* -s cough. H∼saft *m* cough mixture

Hut¹ *m* -[e]s,-̈e hat; (*Pilz-*) cap

Hut² *f* - auf der H∼ sein be on one's guard (vor + *dat* against)

hüten *vt* watch over; tend 〈*Tiere*〉; (*aufpassen*) look after; das Bett h∼ müssen be confined to bed; sich h∼ be on one's guard (vor + *dat* against); sich h∼, etw zu tun take care not to do sth

Hütte *f* -,-n hut; (*Hunde-*) kennel; (*Techn*) iron and steel works. H∼nkäse *m* cottage cheese. H∼nkunde *f* metallurgy

Hyäne *f* -,-n hyena

Hybride *f* -,-n hybrid

Hydrant *m* -en,-en hydrant

hydraulisch *a* hydraulic, *adv* -ally

hydroelektrisch /hydro'e'lɛktrɪʃ/ *a* hydroelectric

Hygien|e /hy'gie:nə/ *f* - hygiene. h∼isch *a* hygienic, *adv* -ally

hypermodern *a* ultra-modern

Hypno|se *f* - hypnosis. h∼tisch *a* hypnotic. H∼tiseur /-'zø:ɐ/ *m* -s,-e hypnotist. h∼tisieren *vt* hypnotize

Hypochonder /hypo'xɔndɐ/ *m* -s,- hypochondriac

Hypothek *f* -,-en mortgage

Hypothe|se *f* -,-n hypothesis. h∼tisch *a* hypothetical, *adv* -ly

Hys|terie *f* - hysteria. h∼terisch *a* hysterical, *adv* -ly

I

ich *pron* I; ich bin's it's me. Ich *nt* -[s],-[s] self; (*Psych*) ego

IC-Zug /i'tse:-/ *m* inter-city train

ideal *a* ideal. I∼ *nt* -s,-e ideal. i∼isieren *vt* idealize. I∼ismus *m* - idealism. I∼ist(in) *m* -en, -en (*f* -,-nen) idealist. i∼istisch *a* idealistic

Idee *f* -,-n idea; fixe I∼ obsession; eine I∼ (*fam: wenig*) a tiny bit

identifizieren *vt* identify

identi|sch *a* identical. I∼tät *f* -,-en identity

Ideo|logie *f* -,-n ideology. i∼logisch *a* ideological

idiomatisch *a* idiomatic

Idiot *m* -en,-en idiot. i∼isch *a* idiotic, *adv* -ally

Idol *nt* -s,-e idol

idyllisch /i'dylɪʃ/ *a* idyllic

Igel *m* -s,- hedgehog

ignorieren *vt* ignore

ihm *pron* (*dat of* er, es) [to] him; (*Ding, Tier*) [to] it; Freunde von ihm friends of his

ihn *pron* (*acc of* er) him; (*Ding, Tier*) it. i∼en *pron* (*dat of* sie *pl*) [to] them; Freunde von i∼en friends of theirs. I∼en *pron* (*dat of* Sie) [to] you; Freunde von I∼en friends of yours

ihr *pron* (*2nd pers pl*) you □ (*dat of* sie *sg*) [to] her; (*Ding, Tier*) [to] it; Freunde von ihr friends of hers □ *poss pron* her; (*Ding, Tier*) its; (*pl*) their. i∼e(r,s) *poss pron* yours. i∼erseits *adv* for her/(*pl*) their part. I∼erseits *adv* on your part. i∼etwegen *adv* for her/(*Ding, Tier*) its/(*pl*) their sake; (*wegen*) because of her/it/them, on her/its/their account. I∼etwegen *adv* for your sake; (*wegen*) because of you, on your account. i∼etwillen *adv* um i∼etwillen for her/(*Ding, Tier*) its/(*pl*) their sake. I∼etwillen *adv* um I∼etwillen for your sake. i∼ige *poss pron* der/die/das i∼ige hers; (*pl*) theirs. I∼ige *poss pron* der/die/das I∼ige yours. i∼s *poss pron* hers; (*pl*) theirs. I∼s *poss pron* yours

Ikone *f* -,-n icon

illegal *a* illegal, *adv* -ly

Illus|ion *f* -,-en illusion; sich (*dat*) I∼ionen machen delude oneself. i∼orisch *a* illusory

Illustr|ation /-'tsjo:n/ *f* -,-en illustration. i∼ieren *vt* illustrate. I∼ierte *f* -n,-[n] [illustrated] magazine

Iltis *m* -ses,-se polecat

im *prep* = in dem; im Mai in May; im Kino at the cinema

Image /'ɪmɪdʒ/ *nt* -[s],-s /-ɪs/ [public] image

Imbiss (*Imbiß*) *m* snack. I∼halle, I∼stube *f* snack-bar

Imit|ation /-'tsjo:n/ *f* -,-en imitation. i∼ieren *vt* imitate

Imker *m* -s,- bee-keeper

Immatrikul|ation /-'tsjo:n/ *f* - (*Univ*) enrolment. i∼ieren *vt* (*Univ*) enrol; sich i∼ieren enrol

immer *adv* always; für i∼ for ever; (*endgültig*) for good; i∼ noch still; i∼ mehr/weniger/wieder more and more/less and less/again and again; wer/was [auch] i∼ whoever/whatever. i∼fort *adv* = i∼zu. i∼grün *a* evergreen. i∼hin *adv* (*wenigstens*) at least; (*trotzdem*) all the same; (*schließlich*) after all. i∼zu *adv* all the time

Immobilien /-jən/ *pl* real estate *sg*. I∼händler, I∼makler *m* estate agent, (*Amer*) realtor

immun *a* immune (gegen to). i∼isieren *vt* immunize. I∼ität *f* - immunity

Imperativ *m* -s,-e imperative

Imperfekt *nt* -s,-e imperfect

Imperialismus *m* - imperialism

impf|en *vt* vaccinate, inoculate. I∼stoff *m* vaccine. I∼ung *f* -,-en vaccination, inoculation

Implantat *nt* -[e]s,-e implant

imponieren *vi* (*haben*) impress (jdm s.o.)

Impor|t *m* -[e]s,-e import. I∼teur /-'tø:ɐ/ *m* -s,-e importer. i∼tieren *vt* import

imposant *a* imposing

impoten|t *a* (*Med*) impotent. I∼z *f* - (*Med*) impotence

imprägnieren *vt* waterproof

Impressionismus *m* - impressionism

improvisieren *vt/i* (*haben*) improvise

Impuls *m* -es,-e impulse. i∼iv *a* impulsive, *adv* -ly

imstande *pred a* able (zu to); capable (etw zu tun of doing sth)

in *prep* (+ *dat*) in; (+ *acc*) into, in; (*bei Bus, Zug*) on; in der Schule/Oper at school/ the opera; in die Schule to school □ *a* in sein be in

Inbegriff *m* embodiment. i∼en *pred a* included

Inbrunst *f* - fervour

inbrünstig *a* fervent, *adv* -ly

indem *conj* (*während*) while; (*dadurch*) by (+ -ing)

Inder(in) *m* -s,- (*f* -,-nen) Indian

indessen *conj* while □ *adv* (*unterdessen*) meanwhile; (*jedoch*) however

Indian *m* -s,-e (*Aust*) turkey

Indian|er(in) *m* -s,- (*f* -,-nen) (American) Indian. i∼isch *a* Indian

Indien /-'ɪndjən/ *nt* -s India

indigniert *a* indignant, *adv* -ly

Indikativ *m* -s,-e indicative

indirekt *a* indirect, *adv* -ly

indisch *a* Indian

indiskre|t *a* indiscreet. I∼tion /-'tsjo:n/ *f* -,-en indiscretion

indiskutabel *a* out of the question

indisponiert *a* indisposed

Individu|alist *m* -en,-en individualist. I∼alität *f* - individuality. i∼ell *a* individual, *adv* -ly. I∼um /-'vi:duʊm/ *nt* -s,-duen individual

Indizienbeweis /ɪn'di:tsjən-/ *m* circumstantial evidence

indoktrinieren *vt* indoctrinate

industr|ialisiert *a* industrialized. I∼ie *f* -,-n industry. i∼iell *a* industrial. I∼ielle(r) *m* industrialist

ineinander *adv* in/into one another

Infanterie *f* - infantry

Infektion /-'tsjo:n/ *f* -,-en infection. I∼skrankheit *f* infectious disease

Infinitiv *m* -s,-e infinitive

infizieren *vt* infect; sich i∼ become/(*Person:*) be infected

Inflation /-'tsjo:n/ *f* - inflation. i∼är *a* inflationary

infolge *prep* (+ *gen*) as a result of. i∼dessen *adv* consequently

Inform|atik *f* - information science. I∼ation /-'tsjo:n/ *f* -,-en information; I∼ationen information *sg*. i∼ieren *vt* inform; sich i∼ieren find out (über + *acc* about)

infrage *adv* etw i∼ stellen question sth; (*ungewiss machen*) make sth doubtful; nicht i∼ kommen be out of the question

infrarot *a* infra-red

Ingenieur /ɪnʒe'njø:ɐ/ *m* -s,-e engineer

Ingwer *m* -s ginger

Inhaber(in) *m* -s,- (*f* -,-nen) holder; (*Besitzer*) proprietor; (*Scheck-*) bearer

inhaftieren *vt* take into custody

inhalieren *vt/i* (*haben*) inhale

Inhalt *m* -[e]s,-e contents *pl*; (*Bedeutung, Gehalt*) content; (*Geschichte*) story. I∼sangabe *f* summary. I∼sverzeichnis *nt* list/(*in Buch*) table of contents

Initiale /-'tsja:lə/ *f* -,-n initial

Initiative /-iniʦia'ti:və/ *f* -,-n initiative

Injektion /-'tsjo:n/ *f* -,-en injection.

injizieren *vt* inject

inklusive *prep* (+ *gen*) including □ *adv* inclusive

inkognito *adv* incognito

inkonsequen|t *a* inconsistent, *adv* -ly. I∼z *f* -,-en inconsistency

inkorrekt *a* incorrect, *adv* -ly

Inkubationszeit /-'tsjo:ns-/ *f* (*Med*) incubation period

Inland *nt* -[e]s home country; (*Binnenland*) interior. I∼sgespräch *nt* inland call

inmitten *prep* (+ *gen*) in the middle of; (*unter*) amongst □ *adv* i∼ von amongst, amidst

inne|haben† *vt sep* hold, have. i∼halten† *vi* (*haben*) pause

innen *adv* inside; nach i∼ inwards. I∼architekt(in) *m(f)* interior designer. I∼minister *m* Minister of the Interior; (*in UK*) Home Secretary. I∼politik *f* domestic policy. I∼stadt *f* town centre inner|e(r,s) a inner; (Med, Pol) internal. I~e(s) nt interior; (Mitte) centre; (fig: Seele) inner being. I~eien fpl (Culin) offal sg. i~halb prep (+ gen) inside; (zeitlich & fig) within; (während) during □ adv i~halb von within. i~lich a internal; (see-lisch) inner; (besinnlich) introspective □ adv internally; (im Inneren) inwardly. i~ste(r,s) a innermost; im I~sten (fig) deep down

innig a sincere, adv -ly; (tief) deep, adv -ly; (eng) intimate, adv -ly

Innung f -,-en guild

inoffiziell a unofficial, adv -ly

ins prep = in das; ins Kino/Büro to the cinema/office

Insasse m -n,-n inmate; (im Auto) occu-pant; (Passagier) passenger

insbesondere adv especially

Inschrift f inscription

Insekt nt -[e]s,-en insect. I~envertil-gungsmittel nt insecticide

Insel f -,-n island

Inser|at nt -[e]s,-e [newspaper] advertise-ment. I~ent m -en,-en advertiser. i~ieren vt/i (haben) advertise

insgeheim adv secretly. i~samt adv [all] in all

Insignien /-jən/ pl insignia

insofern, insoweit adv /-'zo:-/ in this re-spect; i~ als in as much as □ conj /-zo-'fern, -'vait/ i~ als in so far as

Insp|ektion /ɪnspɛk'tsjoːn/ f -,-en inspec-tion. I~ektor m -en,-en /-'toːrən/ inspector

Inspir|ation /ɪnspira'tsjoːn/ f -,-en in-spiration. i~ieren vt inspire

inspizieren /-sp-/ vt inspect

Install|ateur /ɪnstalaˈtøːɐ̯/ m -s,-e fitter; (Klempner) plumber. i~ieren vt install

instand adv i~ halten maintain; (pflegen) look after; i~ setzen restore; (reparieren) repair. I~haltung f - maintenance, up-keep

inständig a urgent, adv -ly

Instandsetzung f - repair

Instant- /'ɪnstant-/ pref instant

Instanz f -st-/ f -,-en authority

Instinkt /-st-/ m -[e]s,-e instinct. i~iv a instinctive, adv -ly

Institu|t /-st-/ nt -[e]s,-e institute. I~tion /-'tsjoːn/ f -,-en institution

Instrument /-st-/ nt -[e]s,-e instrument. I~almusik f instrumental music

Insulin nt -s insulin

inszenier|en vt (Theat) produce. I~ung f -,-en production

Integr|ation /-'tsjoːn/ f - integration. i~ieren vt integrate; sich i~ieren integrate. I~ität f - integrity

Intellekt m -[e]s intellect. i~uell a intel-lectual

intelligen|t a intelligent, adv -ly. I~z f - intelligence; (Leute) intelligentsia

Intendant m -en,-en director

Intens|ität f - intensity. i~iv a intensive, adv -ly. i~ivieren vt intensify. I~iv-station f intensive-care unit

inter|essant a interesting. I~esse nt -s,-n interest; I~esse haben be interested (an + dat in). I~essengruppe f pressure group. I~essent m -en,-en interested party; (Käufer) prospective buyer. i~essieren vt interest; sich i~essie-ren be interested (für in)

intern a (fig) internal, adv -ly

Inter|nat nt -[e]s,-e boarding school. i~national a international, adv -ly. i~nie-ren vt intern. I~nierung f - internment. I~nist m -en,-en specialist in internal diseases. I~pretation /-'tsjoːn/ f -,-en in-terpretation. i~pretieren vt interpret. I~punktion /-'tsjoːn/ f - punctuation. I~rogativpronomen nt interrogative pronoun. I~vall nt -s,-e interval. I~ven-tion /-'tsjoːn/ f -,-en intervention

Interview /'ɪntɐvjuː/ nt -s,-s interview. i~en /-'vjuːən/ vt interview

intim a intimate, adv -ly. I~ität f -,-en intimacy

intoleran|t a intolerant. I~z f - intoler-ance

intransitiv a intransitive, adv -ly

intravenös a intravenous, adv -ly

Intrig|e f -,-n intrigue. i~ieren vi (haben) plot

introvertiert a introverted

Intui|tion /-'tsjoːn/ f -,-en intuition. i~tiv a intuitive, adv -ly

Invalidenrente f disability pension

Invasion f -,-en invasion

Inven|tar nt -s,-e furnishings and fittings pl; (Techn) equipment; (Bestand) stock; (Liste) inventory. I~tur f -,-en stock-tak-ing

investieren vt invest

inwendig a & adv inside

inwiefern adv in what way. i~weit adv how far, to what extent

Inzest m -[e]s incest

inzwischen adv in the meantime

Irak (der) -[s] Iraq. i~isch a Iraqi

Iran (der) -[s] Iran. i~isch a Iranian

irdisch a earthly

Ire m -n,-n Irishman; die I~n the Irish pl

irgend *adv* wer/was/wann i~ whoever/
whatever/whenever; wenn i~ möglich
if at all possible; i~ etwas (NEW) i~etwas;
i~ jemand (NEW) i~jemand. i~ein *indef
art* some/any; i~ein anderer some-
one/anyone else. i~eine(r,s) *pron* any
one; (*jemand*) someone/anyone. i~etwas
pron something; (*fragend, verneint*) anything. i~jemand *pron* someone;
(*fragend, verneint*) anyone. i~wann *pron*
at some time [or other]/at any time.
i~was *pron* (*fam*) something [or other]/
anything. i~welche(r,s) *pron* any.
i~wer *pron* someone/anyone. i~wie *adv*
somehow [or other]. i~wo *adv* some-
where/anywhere; i~wo anders somewhere else

Irin *f* -,-nen Irishwoman

Iris *f* -,- (*Anat, Bot*) iris

irisch *a* Irish

Irland *nt* -s Ireland

Ironie *f* - irony

ironisch *a* ironic, *adv* -ally

irr *a* = irre

irrational *a* irrational

irre *a* mad, crazy; (*fam: gewaltig*) incredible, *adv* -bly; i~ werden (NEW)
i~werden. I~(r) *m/f* lunatic. i~führen
vt sep (*fig*) mislead. i~gehen† *vi sep* (*sein*)
lose one's way; (*sich täuschen*) be wrong

irrelevant *a* irrelevant

irre|machen *vt sep* confuse. i~n *vi/r*
(*haben*) [nicht] i~n be mistaken; wenn
ich mich nicht i~ if I am not mistaken
□ *vi* (*sein*) wander. I~nanstalt *f*,
I~nhaus *nt* lunatic asylum. i~reden *vi
sep* (*haben*) ramble. i~werden† *vi sep*
(*sein*) get confused

Irr|garten *m* maze. i~ig *a* erroneous

irritieren *vt* irritate

Irr|sinn *m* madness, lunacy. i~sinnig *a*
mad; (*fam: gewaltig*) incredible, *adv* -bly.
I~tum *m* -s,-er mistake. i~tümlich *a*
mistaken, *adv* -ly

Ischias *m* & *nt* - sciatica

Islam (der)- [s] Islam. is**lämisch** *a* Islamic

Island *nt* -s Iceland

Isolier|band *nt* insulating tape. i~en *vt*
isolate; (*Phys, Electr*) insulate; (*gegen
Schall*) soundproof. I~ung *f* - isolation;
insulation; soundproofing

Israel /'israɛl/ *nt* -s Israel. I~li *m* [s],
-s & *f* -,-[s] Israeli. i~elisch *a* Israeli

ist *s* sein; er ist he is

Italien /-jən/ *nt* -s Italy. I~iener(in) *m*
-s,- (*f* -,-nen) Italian. i~ienisch *a* Italian.
I~ienisch *nt* -[s] (*Lang*) Italian

J

ja *adv*, **Ja** *nt* -[s] yes; ich glaube ja I think
so; ja nicht! not on any account! seid ja
vorsichtig! whatever you do, be careful!
da seid ihr ja! there you are! das ist es
ja that's just it; das mag ja wahr sein
that may well be true

Jacht *f* -,-en yacht

Jacke *f* -,-n jacket; (*Strick-*) cardigan

Jackett /ʒa'kɛt/ *nt* -s,-s jacket

Jade *m* -[s] & *f* - jade

Jagd *f* -,-en hunt; (*Schießen*) shoot; (*Jagen*)
hunting; shooting; (*fig*) pursuit (nach of);
auf die J~ gehen go hunting/shooting.
J~flugzeug *nt* fighter aircraft.
J~gewehr *nt* sporting gun. J~hund *m*
gun-dog; (*Hetzhund*) hound

jagen *vt* hunt; (*schießen*) shoot; (*verfolgen,
wegjagen*) chase; (*treiben*) drive; sich j~
chase each other; in der Luft j~ blow up
□ *vi* (*haben*) hunt, go hunting/shooting;
(*fig*) chase (nach after) □ *vi* (*sein*) race,
dash

Jäger *m* -s,- hunter

jäh *a* sudden, *adv* -ly; (*steil*) steep, *adv* -ly

Jahr *nt* -[e]s,-e year. J~buch *nt* year-book.
j~elang *adv* for years. J~estag *m* anniversary. J~eszahl *f* year. J~eszeit *f* season. J~gang *m* year; (*Wein*) vintage.
J~hundert *nt* century. J~hundertfeier
f centenary, (*Amer*) centennial

jährlich *a* annual, yearly □ *adv* annually,
yearly

Jahr|markt *m* fair. J~tausend *nt* mil-
lenium. J~zehnt *nt* -[e]s,-e decade

Jähzorn *m* violent temper. j~ig *a* a hot-
tempered

Jalousie /ʒalu'zi:/ *f* -,-n venetian blind

Jammer *m* -s misery; (*Klagen*) lamenting;
es ist ein J~ it is a shame

jämmerlich *a* miserable, *adv* -bly; (*Mitleid erregend*) pitiful, *adv* -ly

jammer|n *vi* (*haben*) lament □ *vt* jdn j~n
arouse s.o.'s pity. j~schade *a* j~schade
sein (*fam*) be a terrible shame

Jänner *m* -s,- (*Aust*) January

Januar *m* -s,-e January

Jap|an *nt* -s Japan. J~aner(in) *m* -s,- (*f*
-,-nen) Japanese. j~anisch *a* Japanese.
J~anisch *nt* -[s] (*Lang*) Japanese

Jargon /ʒar'gõ:/ *m* -s jargon

jäten *vt/i* (*haben*) weed

jauchzen *vi* (*haben*) (*liter*) exult

jaulen *vi* (*haben*) yelp

Jause *f* -,-n (*Aust*) snack

jawohl *adv* yes

Jawort *nt* jdm sein J~ geben accept s.o.'s proposal [of marriage]

Jazz /jats, dʒɛs/ *m* - jazz

je *adv* (*jemals*) ever; (*jeweils*) each; (*pro*) per; je nach according to; seit eh und je always; besser denn je better than ever □ *conj* je mehr, desto od umso besser the more the better □ *prep* (+ *acc*) per

Jeans /dʒiːns/ *pl* jeans

jed|e(r,s) *pron* every; (*j~er Einzelne*) each; (*j~er Beliebige*) everyone; (*substantivisch*) everyone; each one; anyone; ohne j~en Grund without any reason. j~enfalls *adv* in any case; (*wenigstens*) at least. j~ermann *pron* everyone. j~erzeit *adv* at any time. j~esmal *adv* (NEW) jedes Mal, s. Mal¹

jedoch *adv & conj* however

jeher *adv* von od seit j~ always

jemals *adv* ever

jemand *pron* someone, somebody; (*fragend, verneint*) anyone, anybody

jen|e(r,s) *pron* those; (*substantivisch*) that one; (*pl*) those. j~seits *prep* (+ *gen*) [on] the other side of

jetzig *a* present; (*Preis*) current

jetzt *adv* now. J~zeit *f* present

jeweilig *a* respective. j~s *adv* at a time

jiddisch *a*, J~ *nt* -[s] Yiddish

Job /dʒɔp/ *m* -s,-s job. j~ben *vi* (*haben*) (*fam*) work

Joch *nt* -[e]s,-e yoke

Jockei, Jockey /'dʒɔki/ *m* -s,-s jockey

Jod *nt* -[e]s iodine

jodeln *vi* (*haben*) yodel

Joga *m & nt* -[s] yoga

jogg|en /'dʒɔgən/ *vi* (*haben/sein*) jog. J~ing *nt* -[s] jogging

Joghurt, Jogurt *m & nt* -[s] yoghurt

Johannisbeere *f* redcurrant; schwarze J~ blackcurrant

johlen *vi* (*haben*) yell; (*empört*) jeer

Joker *m* -s,- (*Karte*) joker

Jolle *f* -,-n dinghy

Jongl|eur /ʒõ'gløːɐ̯/ *m* -s,-e juggler. j~ieren *vi* (*haben*) juggle

Joppe *f* -,-n [thick] jacket

Jordanien /-jən/ *nt* -s Jordan

Journalis|mus /ʒurna'lɪsmʊs/ *m* - journalism. J~t(in) *m* -en,-en (*f* -,-nen) journalist

Jubel *m* -s rejoicing, jubilation. j~n *vi* (*haben*) rejoice

Jubil|ar(in) *m* -s,-e (*f* -,-nen) person celebrating an anniversary. J~äum *nt* -s,-äen jubilee; (*Jahrestag*) anniversary

juck|en *vi* (*haben*) itch; sich j~en scratch; es j~t mich I have an itch; (*fam: möchte*) I'm itching (zu to). J~reiz *m* itch[ing]

Jude *m* -n,-n Jew. J~ntum *nt* -s Judaism; (*Juden*) Jewry

Jüd|in *f* -,-nen Jewess. j~isch *a* Jewish

Judo *nt* -[s] judo

Jugend *f* - youth; (*junge Leute*) young people *pl*. J~herberge *f* youth hostel. J~klub *m* youth club. J~kriminalität *f* juvenile delinquency. j~lich *a* youthful. J~liche(r) *m/f* young man/woman; (*Admin*) juvenile; J~liche *pl* young people. J~stil *m* art nouveau. J~zeit *f* youth

Jugoslaw|ien /-jən/ *nt* -s Yugoslavia. j~isch *a* Yugoslav

Juli *m* -[s],-s July

jung *a* (jünger, jüngst) young; (*Wein*) new □ *pron* J~ und Alt (ju~ and old) young and old. J~e *m* -n,-n boy. J~e(s) *nt* young animal/bird; (*Katzen-*) kitten; (*Bären-, Löwen-*) cub; (*Hunde-, Seehund-*) pup; die J~en the young *pl*. j~enhaft *a* boyish

Jünger *m* -s,- disciple

Jungfer *f* -,-n alte J~ old maid. J~nfahrt *f* maiden voyage

Jung|frau *f* virgin; (*Astr*) Virgo. j~fräulich *a* virginal. J~geselle *m* bachelor

Jüngling *m* -s,-e youth

jüngst|e(r,s) *a* youngest; (*neueste*) latest; in j~er Zeit recently

Juni *m* -[s],-s June

Junior *m* -s,-en /-'oːrən/ junior

Jura *pl* law *sg*

Jurist|(in) *m* -en,-en (*f* -,-nen) lawyer. j~isch *a* legal, *adv* -ly

Jury /ʒy'riː/ *f* -,-s jury; (*Sport*) judges *pl*

justieren *vt* adjust

Justiz *f* - die J~ justice. J~irrtum *m* miscarriage of justice. J~minister *m* Minister of Justice

Juwel *nt* -s,-en & (*fig*) -e jewel. J~ier *m* -s,-e jeweller

Jux *m* -es,-e (*fam*) joke; aus Jux for fun

K

Kabarett *nt* -s,-s & -e cabaret

kabbelig *a* choppy

Kabel *nt* -s,- cable. K~fernsehen *nt* cable television

Kabeljau *m* -s,-e & -s cod

Kabine *f* -,-n cabin; (*Umkleide-*) cubicle; (*Telefon-*) booth; (*einer K~nbahn*) car. K~nbahn *f* cable-car

Kabinett *nt* -s,-e (*Pol*) Cabinet

Kabriolett *nt* -s,-s convertible

Kachel *f* -,-n tile. k~n *vt* tile

Kadaver *m* -s,- carcass

Kadenz *f* -,-en (*Mus*) cadence; (*für Solisten*) cadenza

Kadett *m* -en,-en cadet

Käfer *m* -s,- beetle

Kaff *nt* -s,-s (*fam*) dump

Kaffee /ˈkafeː, kaˈfeː/ *m* -s,-s coffee; (*Mahlzeit*) afternoon coffee. K~grund *m* = K~satz. K~kanne *f* coffee-pot. K~maschine *f* coffee-maker. K~mühle *f* coffee-grinder. K~satz *m* coffee-grounds *pl*

Käfig *m* -s,-e cage

kahl *a* bare; (*haarlos*) bald; k~ geschoren shaven. k~geschoren *a* (NEW) k~ geschoren, s. kahl. k~köpfig *a* bald-headed

Kahn *m* -s,-e boat; (*Last-*) barge

Kai *m* -s,-s quay

Kaiser *m* -s,- emperor. K~in *f* -,-nen empress. k~lich *a* imperial. K~reich *nt* empire. K~schnitt *m* Caesarean [section]

Kajüte *f* -,-n (*Naut*) cabin

Kakao /kaˈkau/ *m* -s cocoa

Kakerlak *m* -s & -en,-en cockroach

Kaktee /kakˈteːə/ *f* -,-n, **Kaktus** *m* -,-teen /-ˈteːən/ cactus

Kalb *nt* -[e]s,-er calf. K~fleisch *nt* veal

Kalender *m* -s,- calendar; (*Taschen-, Termin-*) diary

Kaliber *nt* -s,- calibre; (*Gewehr-*) bore

Kalium *nt* -s potassium

Kalk *m* -[e]s,-e lime; (*Kalzium*) calcium. k~en *vt* whitewash. K~stein *m* limestone

Kalkulation /-ˈtsjoːn/ *f* -,-en calculation. k~ieren *vt/i* (*haben*) calculate

Kalorie *f* -,-n calorie

kalt *a* (kälter, kältest) cold; es ist k~ it is cold; mir ist k~ I am cold. K~blütig *a* cold-blooded, *adv* -ly; (*ruhig*) cool, *adv* -ly

Kälte *f* - cold; (*Gefühls-*) coldness; 10 Grad K~ 10 degrees below zero. K~welle *f* cold spell

kalt|herzig *a* cold-hearted. k~schnäuzig *a* (*fam*) cold, *adv* -ly

Kalzium *nt* -s calcium

Kamel *nt* -s,-e camel; (*fam: Idiot*) fool

Kamera *f* -,-s camera

Kamerad|(in) *m* -en,-en (*f* -,-nen) companion; (*Freund*) mate; (*Mil, Pol*) comrade. K~schaft *f* - comradeship

Kameramann *m* (*pl* -männer & -leute) cameraman

Kamille *f* - camomile

Kamin *m* -s,-e fireplace; (*SGer: Schornstein*) chimney. K~feger *m* -s,- (*SGer*) chimney-sweep

Kamm *m* -[e]s,-e comb; (*Berg-*) ridge, (*Zool, Wellen-*) crest

kämmen *vt* comb; jdn/sich k~ comb s.o.'s/one's hair

Kammer *f* -,-n small room; (*Techn, Biol, Pol*) chamber. K~diener *m* valet. K~musik *f* chamber music

Kammgarn *nt* (*Tex*) worsted

Kampagne /kamˈpanjə/ *f* -,-n (*Pol, Comm*) campaign

Kampf *m* -es,-e fight; (*Schlacht*) battle; (*Wett-*) contest; (*fig*) struggle; schwere K~e heavy fighting *sg*; den K~ ansagen (+ *dat*) (*fig*) declare war on

kämpf|en *vi* (*haben*) fight; sich k~en durch fight one's way through. K~er(in) *m* -s,- (*f* -,-nen) fighter

kampf|los *adv* without a fight. K~richter *m* (*Sport*) judge

kampieren *vi* (*haben*) camp

Kanada *nt* -s Canada

Kanad|ier(in) /-jɐ, -jərɪn/ *m* -s,- (*f* -,-nen) Canadian. k~isch *a* Canadian

Kanal *m* -s,-e canal; (*Abfluss-*) drain, sewer; (*Radio, TV*) channel; der K~ the [English] Channel

Kanalis|ation /-ˈtsjoːn/ *f* - sewerage system, drains *pl*. k~ieren *vt* canalize; (*fig: lenken*) channel

Kanarienvogel /-jən-/ *m* canary

Kanarisch *a* K~e Inseln Canaries

Kandi|dat(in) *m* -en,-en (*f* -,-nen) candidate. k~dieren *vi* (*haben*) stand (für for)

kandiert *a* candied

Känguru (Känguruh) *nt* -s,-s kangaroo

Kaninchen *nt* -s,- rabbit

Kanister *m* -s,- canister; (*Benzin-*) can

Kännchen *nt* -s,- [small] jug; (*Kaffee-*) pot

Kanne *f* -,-n jug; (*Kaffee-, Tee-*) pot; (*Öl-*) can; (*große Milch-*) churn; (*Gieß-*) watering-can

Kannibal|e *m* -n,-n cannibal. K~ismus *m* - cannibalism

Kanon *m* -s,-s canon; (*Lied*) round

Kanone *f* -,-n cannon, gun; (*fig: Könner*) ace

kanonisieren *vt* canonize

Kantate *f* -,-n cantata

Kante *f* -,-n edge, auf die hohe K~ legen (*fam*) put by

Kanten *m* -s,- crust [of bread]

Kanter *m* -s,- canter

kantig *a* angular

Kantine *f* -,-n canteen

Kanton m -s,-e (Swiss) canton

Kantor m -s,-en /-'to:rən/ choir-master and organist

Kanu nt -s,-s canoe

Kanzel f -,-n pulpit; (Aviat) cockpit

Kanzleistil m officialese

Kanzler m -s,- chancellor

Kap nt -s,-s (Geog) cape

Kapazität f -,-en capacity; (Experte) authority

Kapelle f -,-n chapel; (Mus) band

Kaper f -,-n (Culin) caper

kapern vt (Naut) seize

kapieren vt (fam) understand, (fam) get

Kapital nt -s capital; K~ schlagen aus (fig) capitalize on. K~ismus m - capitalism. K~ist m -en,-en capitalist. K~istisch a capitalist

Kapitän m -s,-e captain

Kapitel nt -s,- chapter

Kapitul|ation f -'tsjo:n/ f - capitulation. k~ieren vi (haben) capitulate

Kaplan m -s,-e curate

Kappe f -,-n cap. k~n vt cut

Kapsel f -,-n capsule; (Flaschen-) top

kaputt a (fam) broken; (zerrissen) torn; (defekt) out of order; (ruiniert) ruined; (erschöpft) worn out. k~gehen† vi sep (sein) (fam) break; (zerreißen) tear; (defekt werden) pack up; (Ehe, Freundschaft:) break up. k~lachen (sich) vr sep (fam) be in stitches. k~machen vt sep (fam) break; (zerreißen) tear; (erschöpfen) put out of order; (erschöpfen) wear out; sich k~machen wear oneself out

Kapuze f -,-n hood

Kapuzinerkresse f nasturtium

Karaffe f -,-n carafe; (mit Stöpsel) decanter

Karambolage /karambo'la:ʒə/ f -,-n collision

Karamell (Karamel) m -s caramel. K~bonbon m & nt ≈ toffee

Karat nt -[e]s,-e carat

Karawane f -,-n caravan

Kardinal m -s,-e cardinal. K~zahl f cardinal number

Karfiol m (Aust) cauliflower

Karfreitag m Good Friday

karg a (kärger, kärgst) meagre; (frugal) frugal; (spärlich) sparse; (unfruchtbar) barren; (gering) scant. k~en vi (haben) be sparing (mit with)

kärglich a poor, meagre; (gering) scant

Karibik f - Caribbean

kariert a check[ed]; (Papier) squared; schottisch k~ tartan

Karikatur f -,-en caricature; (Journ) cartoon. k~ieren vt caricature

karitativ a charitable

Karneval m -s,-e & -s carnival

Karnickel nt -s,- (dial) rabbit

Kärnten nt -s Carinthia

Karo nt -s,-s (Raute) diamond; (Viereck) square; (Muster) check; (Kartenspiel) diamonds pl. K~muster nt check

Karosserie f -,-n bodywork

Karotte f -,-n carrot

Karpfen m -s,- carp

Karre f -,-n = Karren

Karree nt -s,-s square; ums K~ round the block

Karren m -s,- cart; (Hand-) barrow. k~ vt cart

Karriere /ka'rje:rə/ f -,-n career; K~ machen get to the top

Karte f -,-n card; (Eintritts-, Fahr-) ticket; (Speise-) menu; (Land-) map

Kartei f -,-en card index. K~karte f index card

Karten|spiel nt card-game; (Spielkarten) pack/(Amer) deck of cards. K~vorverkauf m advance booking

Kartoffel f -,-n potato. K~brei m, K~püree nt mashed potatoes pl. K~salat m potato salad

Karton /kar'tɔŋ/ m -s,-s cardboard; (Schachtel) carton, cardboard box

Karussell nt -s,-s & -e roundabout

Karwoche f Holy Week

Käse m -s,- cheese. K~kuchen m cheesecake

Kaserne f -,-n barracks pl

Kasino nt -s,-s casino

Kasperle nt & m -s,- Punch. K~theater nt Punch and Judy show

Kasse f -,-n till; (Registrier-) cash register; (Zahlstelle) cash desk; (im Supermarkt) check-out; (Theater-) box-office; (Geld) pool [of money], (fam) kitty; (Kranken-) health insurance scheme; (Spar-) savings bank; knapp/gut bei K~ sein (fam) be short of cash/be flush. K~npatient m ≈ NHS patient. K~nschlager m box-office hit. K~nwart m -[e]s,-e treasurer. K~nzettel m receipt

Kasserolle f -,-n saucepan [with one handle]

Kassette f -,-n cassette; (Film-, Farbband-) cartridge; (Geld-) money-box; (Schmuck-) case. K~nrecorder /-rəkɔrdɐ/ m -s,- cassette recorder

kassier|en vi (haben) collect the money/(im Bus) the fares □ vt collect. K~er(in) m -s,- (f -,-nen) cashier

Kastagnetten /kastan'jɛtən/ *pl* castanets

Kastanie /kas'ta:njə/ *f* -,-n [horse] chestnut; *(fam)* conker. **k∼nbraun** *a* chestnut

Kaste *f* -,-n caste

Kasten *m* -s,: box; *(Brot-)* bin; *(Flaschen-)* crate; *(Brief-)* letter-box; *(Aust: Schrank)* cupboard; *(Kleider-)* wardrobe

kastrieren *vt* castrate; neuter ⟨*Tier*⟩

Kasus *m* -,- /-u:s/ *(Gram)* case

Katalog *m* -[e]s,-e catalogue. **k∼isieren** *vt* catalogue

Katalysator *m* -s,-en /-'to:rən/ catalyst; *(Auto)* catalytic converter

Katapult *nt* -[e]s,-e catapult. **k∼ieren** *vt* catapult

Katarrh, Katarr *m* -s,-e catarrh

katastr|ophal *a* catastrophic. **K∼ophe** *f* -,-n catastrophe

Katechismus *m* - catechism

Kategor|ie *f* -,-n category. **k∼orisch** *a* categorical, *adv* -ly

Kater *m* -s,- tom-cat; *(fam: Katzenjammer)* hangover

Katheder *nt* -s,- [teacher's] desk

Kathedrale *f* -,-n cathedral

Kath|olik(in) *m* -en,-en *(f* -,-nen) Catholic. **k∼olisch** *a* Catholic. **K∼olizismus** *m* - Catholicism

Kätzchen *nt* -s,- kitten; *(Bot)* catkin

Katze *f* -,-n cat. **K∼njammer** *m (fam)* hangover. **K∼nsprung** *m* ein **K∼nsprung** *(fam)* a stone's throw

Kauderwelsch *nt* -[s] gibberish

kauen *vt/i (haben)* chew; bite ⟨*Nägel*⟩

kauern *vi (haben)* crouch; sich k∼ crouch down

Kauf *m* -[e]s, Käufe purchase; guter K∼ bargain; in K∼ nehmen *(fig)* put up with. **k∼en** *vt/i (haben)* buy; **k∼en bei** shop at

Käufer(in) *m* -s,- *(f* -,-nen) buyer; *(im Geschäft)* shopper

Kauf|haus *nt* department store. **K∼kraft** *f* purchasing power. **K∼laden** *m* shop

käuflich *a* saleable; *(bestechlich)* corruptible; **k∼ sein** be for sale; **k∼ erwerben** buy

Kauf|mann *m (pl* -leute) businessman; *(Händler)* dealer; *(dial)* grocer. **k∼männisch** *a* commercial. **K∼preis** *m* purchase price

Kaugummi *m* chewing-gum

Kaulquappe *f* -,-n tadpole

kaum *adv* hardly; **k∼ glaublich** *od* zu glauben hard to believe

kauterisieren *vt* cauterize

Kaution /-'tsjo:n/ *f* -,-en surety; *(Jur)* bail; *(Miet-)* deposit

Kautschuk *m* -s rubber

Kauz *m* -es, Käuze owl; **komischer K∼** *(fam)* odd fellow

Kavalier *m* -s,-e gentleman

Kavallerie *f* - cavalry

Kaviar *m* -s caviare

keck *a* bold; *(frech)* cheeky

Kegel *m* -s,- skittle; *(Geom)* cone; **mit Kind und K∼** *(fam)* with all the family. **K∼bahn** *f* skittle-alley. **k∼förmig** *a* conical. **k∼n** *vi (haben)* play skittles

Kehl|e *f* -,-n throat; aus voller K∼e at the top of one's voice; etw in die falsche K∼e bekommen *(fam)* take sth the wrong way. **K∼kopf** *m* larynx. **K∼kopfentzündung** *f* laryngitis

Kehr|e *f* -,-n [hairpin] bend. **k∼en** *vi (haben) (fegen)* sweep □ *vt* sweep; *(wenden)* turn; den Rücken k∼en turn one's back *(dat* on); sich k∼en an (+ *acc)* not take notice of. **K∼icht** *m* -[e]s sweepings *pl.* **K∼reim** *m* refrain. **K∼seite** *f (fig)* drawback; die K∼seite der Medaille the other side of the coin. **k∼tmachen** *vi sep (haben)* turn back; *(sich umdrehen)* turn round. **K∼twendung** *f* about-turn; *(fig)* U-turn

keifen *vi (haben)* scold

Keil *m* -[e]s,-e wedge

Keile *f* - *(fam)* hiding. **k∼n (sich)** *vr (fam)* fight. **K∼rei** *f* -,-en *(fam)* punch-up

Keil|kissen *nt* [wedge-shaped] bolster. **K∼riemen** *m* fan belt

Keim *m* -[e]s,-e *(Bot)* sprout; *(Med)* germ; im K∼ ersticken *(fig)* nip in the bud. **k∼en** *vi (haben)* germinate; *(austreiben)* sprout. **k∼frei** *a* sterile

kein *pron* no; not a; auf k∼en Fall on no account; k∼e fünf Minuten less than five minutes. **k∼e(r,s)** *pron* no one, nobody; *(Ding)* none, not one. **k∼esfalls** *adv* on no account. **k∼eswegs** *adv* by no means. **k∼mal** *adv* not once. **k∼s** *pron* none, not one

Keks *m* -[es],-[e] biscuit, *(Amer)* cookie

Kelch *m* -[e]s,-e goblet, cup; *(Relig)* chalice; *(Bot)* calyx

Kelle *f* -,-n ladle; *(Maurer-, Pflanz-)* trowel

Keller *m* -s,- cellar. **K∼ei** *f* -,-en winery. **K∼geschoss (K∼geschoß)** *nt* cellar; *(bewohnbar)* basement. **K∼wohnung** *f* basement flat

Kellner *m* -s,- waiter. **K∼in** *f* -,-nen waitress

keltern *vt* press

keltisch *a* Celtic

Kenia *nt* -s Kenya

kenn|en *vt* know; **k∼en lernen** get to know; *(treffen)* meet; sich k∼en lernen

meet; (*näher*) get to know one another.
k~enlernen *vt sep* (NEW) k~en lernen,
s. kennen. K~er *m* -s,-, K~erin *f* -,-nen
connoisseur; (*Experte*) expert. K~melodie *f* signature tune. k~tlich *a* recognizable; k~tlich machen mark. K~tnis *f*
-,-se knowledge; zur K~tnis nehmen
take note of; in K~tnis setzen inform
(von of). K~wort *nt* (*pl* -wörter) reference; (*geheimes*) password. K~zeichen *nt*
distinguishing mark or feature; (*Merkmal*) characteristic, (*Markierung*) mark,
marking; (*Abzeichen*) badge; (*Auto*)
registration. k~zeichnen *vt* distinguish;
(*markieren*) mark. K~zeichnend *a* typical (für of). K~ziffer *f* reference number

kentern *vi* (*sein*) capsize

Keramik *f* -,-en pottery, ceramics *sg*;
(*Gegenstand*) piece of pottery

Kerbe *f* -,-n notch

Kerbholz *nt* etwas auf dem K~ haben
(*fam*) have a record

Kerker *m* -s,- dungeon; (*Gefängnis*) prison

Kerl *m* -s,-e & -s (*fam*) fellow, bloke

Kern *m* -s,-e pip; (*Kirsch-*) stone; (*Nuss-*)
kernel; (*Techn*) core; (*Atom-, Zell-* & *fig*)
nucleus; (*Stadt-*) centre; (*einer Sache*)
heart. K~energie *f* nuclear energy.
K~gehäuse *nt* core. k~gesund *a* perfectly healthy. k~ig *a* robust; (*Ausspruch*)
pithy. K~los *a* seedless. K~physik *f* nuclear physics *sg*

Kerze *f* -,-n candle. K~ngerade *a* & *adv*
straight. K~nhalter *m* -s,- candlestick

kess (keß) *a* (kesser, kessest) pert

Kessel *m* -s,- kettle; (*Heiz-*) boiler.
K~stein *m* fur

Ketschup (Ketchup) /'ketʃap/ *m* -[s],-s
ketchup

Kette *f* -,-n chain; (*Hals-*) necklace. k~n
vt chain (an + *acc* to). K~nladen *m* chain
store. K~nraucher *m* chain-smoker.
K~nreaktion *f* chain reaction

Ketze|r(in) *m* -s,- (*f* -,-nen) heretic.
K~rei *f* -heresy

keuch|en *vi* (*haben*) pant. K~husten *m*
whooping cough

Keule *f* -,-n club; (*Culin*) leg; (*Hühner-*)
drumstick

keusch *a* chaste. K~heit *f* -chastity

Kfz *abbr s.* Kraftfahrzeug

Khaki *nt* -khaki. k~farben *a* khaki

kichern *vi* (*haben*) giggle

Kiefer¹ *f* -,-n pine[-tree]

Kiefer² *m* -s,- jaw

Kiel *m* -s,-e (*Naut*) keel. K~wasser *nt*
wake

Kiemen *fpl* gills

Kies *m* -es gravel. K~el *m* -s,-, K~elstein
m pebble. K~grube *f* gravel pit

Kilo *nt* -s,-[s] kilo. K~gramm *nt* kilogram.
K~hertz *nt* kilohertz. K~meter *m* kilometre. k~meterstand *m* ≈ mileage.
K~watt *nt* kilowatt

Kind *nt* -es,-er child; von K~ auf from
childhood

Kinder|arzt *m*, K~ärztin *f* paediatrician. K~bett *nt* child's cot. K~ei *f*
-,-en childish prank. K~garten *m* nursery school. K~gärtnerin *f* nursery-school teacher. K~geld *nt* child benefit.
K~gottesdienst *m* Sunday school.
K~lähmung *f* polio. k~leicht *a* very
easy. k~los *a* childless. K~mädchen *nt*
nanny. k~reich *a* k~reiche Familie
large family. K~reim *m* nursery rhyme.
K~spiel *nt* children's game; das ist
ein/kein K~spiel that is dead easy/not
easy. K~tagesstätte *f* day nursery.
K~teller *m* children's menu. K~wagen
m pram, (*Amer*) baby carriage.
K~zimmer *nt* child's/children's room;
(*für Baby*) nursery

Kind|heit *f* -childhood. k~isch *a* childish, puerile. k~lich *a* childlike

kinetisch *a* kinetic

Kinn *nt* -[e]s,-e chin. K~lade *f* jaw

Kino *nt* -s,-s cinema

Kiosk *m* -[e]s,-e kiosk

Kippe *f* -,-n (*Müll-*) dump; (*fam:
Zigaretten-*) fag-end; auf der K~ stehen
(*fam*) be in a precarious position; (*unsicher sein*) hang in the balance. k~lig *a*
wobbly. k~ln *vi* (*haben*) wobble. k~n *vt*
tilt; (*schütten*) tip (in + *acc* into) □ *vi* (*sein*)
topple

Kirche *f* -,-n church. K~nbank *f* pew.
K~ndiener *m* verger. K~nlied *nt*
hymn. K~nschiff *nt* nave. K~hof *m*
churchyard. k~lich *a* church ... □ *adv*
k~lich getraut werden be married in
church. K~turm *m* church tower,
steeple. K~weih *f* -,-en [village] fair

Kirmes *f* -,-sen = Kirchweih

Kirsch|e *f* -,-n cherry. K~wasser *nt*
kirsch

Kissen *nt* -s,- cushion; (*Kopf-*) pillow

Kiste *f* -,-n crate; (*Zigarren-*) box

Kitsch *m* -es sentimental rubbish; (*Kunst*)
kitsch. k~ig *a* slushy; (*Kunst*) kitschy

Kitt *m* -s [adhesive] cement; (*Fenster-*) putty

Kittel *m* -s,- overall, smock; (*Arzt-, Labor-*)
white coat

kitten *vt* stick; (*fig*) cement

Kitz *nt* -es,-e (*Zool*) kid

Kitz|el *m* -s,- tickle; (*Nerven-*) thrill. k~eln
vt/i (*haben*) tickle. k~lig *a* ticklish

Kladde f -,-n notebook

klaffen vi (haben) gape

kläffen vi (haben) yap

Klage f -,-n lament, (Beschwerde) complaint; (Jur) action. k~n vi (haben) lament; (sich beklagen) complain; (Jur) sue

Kläger(in) m -s,- (f -,-nen) (Jur) plaintiff

kläglich a pitiful, adv -ly; (erbärmlich) miserable, adv -bly

klamm a cold and damp; (steif) stiff. K~ f -,-en (Geog) gorge

Klammer f -,-n (Wäsche-) peg; (Büro-) paper-clip; (Heft-) staple; (Haar-) grip; (für Zähne) brace; (Techn) clamp; (Typ) bracket. k~n (sich) vr cling (an + acc to)

Klang m -[e]s,·e sound; (K~farbe) tone. k~voll a resonant; (Stimme) sonorous

Klapp|bett nt folding bed. K~e f -,-n flap; (fam: Mund) trap. k~en vt fold; (hoch-) tip up □ vi (haben) (fam) work out. K~entext m blurb

Klapper f -,-n rattle. k~n vi (haben) rattle. K~schlange f rattlesnake

klapp|rig a rickety; (schwach) decrepit. K~stuhl m folding chair. K~tisch m folding table

Klaps m -es,·e pat; (strafend) smack. k~en vt smack

klar a clear; k~ werden clear; (fig) become clear (dat to); sich (dat) k~ werden make up one's mind; (erkennen) realize (dass that); sich (dat) k~ od im k~en (k~en) sein realize (dass that) □ adv clearly; (fam: natürlich) of course. K~e(r) m (fam) schnapps

klären vt clarify; sich k~ clear; (fig: sich lösen) resolve itself

Klarheit f -clarity

Klarinette f -,-n clarinet

klar|machen vt sep make clear (dat to); sich (dat) etw k~machen understand sth. K~sichtfolie f transparent/(haftend) cling film. k~stellen vt sep clarify

Klärung f -clarification

klarwerden† vi sep (sein) (NEW) klar werden, s. klar

Klasse f -,-n class; (Sch) class, form, (Amer) grade; (Zimmer) classroom; erster/zweiter K~ reisen travel first/second class. k~ inv a (fam) super. K~narbeit f (written) test. K~nbuch nt ≈ register. K~nkamerad(in) m(f) classmate. K~nkampf m class struggle. K~nzimmer nt classroom

Klassifikation f -,-en classification

Klass|ik f -classicism; (Epoche) classical period. K~iker m -s,- classical author/(Mus) composer. k~isch a classical; (mustergültig, typisch) classic

---

Klatsch m -[e]s gossip. K~base f (fam) gossip. k~en vt slap; Beifall k~en applaud □ vi (haben) make a slapping sound; (im Wasser) splash; (tratschen) gossip; (applaudieren) clap; [in die Hände] k~en clap one's hands □ vi (haben/sein) slap (gegen against). K~maul nt gossip. k~nass (k~naß) a (fam) soaking wet

klauben vt pick

Klaue f -,-n claw; (fam: Schrift) scrawl. k~n vt/i (haben) (fam) steal

Klausel f -,-n clause

Klaustrophobie f -claustrophobia

Klausur f -,-en (Univ) [examination] paper; (Sch) written test

Klaviatur f -,-en keyboard

Klavier nt -s,-e piano. K~spieler(in) m(f) pianist

kleb|en vt stick/(mit Klebstoff) glue (an + acc to) □ vi (haben) stick (an + dat to). k~rig a sticky. K~stoff m adhesive, glue. K~streifen m adhesive tape

kleckern vi (haben) (fam) = klecksen

Klecks m -es,-e stain; (Tinten-) blot; (kleine Menge) dab. k~en vi (haben) make a mess

Klee m -s clover. K~blatt nt clover leaf

Kleid nt -[e]s,-er dress; K~er dresses; (Kleidung) clothes. k~en vt dress; (gut stehen) suit; sich k~en dress. K~erbügel m coat-hanger. K~erbürste f clothesbrush. K~erhaken m coat-hook. K~errock m pinafore dress. K~erschrank m wardrobe, (Amer) clothes closet. k~sam a becoming. K~ung f clothes pl, clothing. K~ungsstück nt garment

Kleie f -bran

klein a small, little; (von kleinem Wuchs) short; k~ hacken/schneiden chop/cut up small or into small pieces; k~ geschrieben werden (fig) count for very little (bei jdm with s.o.); von k~ auf from childhood. K~arbeit f painstaking work. K~bus m minibus. K~e(r,s) m/f/nt little one. K~geld nt [small] change. k~hacken vt sep (NEW) k~ hacken, s. klein. K~handel m retail trade. K~heit f -smallness; (Wuchs) short stature. K~holz nt firewood. K~igkeit f -,-en trifle; (Mahl) snack. K~kind nt infant. K~kram m (fam) odds and ends pl; (Angelegenheiten) trivia pl. k~laut a subdued. k~lich a petty. K~lichkeit f -pettiness. k~mütig a faint-hearted

Kleinod nt -[e]s,-e jewel

klein|schneiden† vt sep (NEW) k~ schneiden, s. klein. k~schreiben† vt sep write with a small [initial] letter; k~geschrieben werden (fig) (NEW) k~ geschrieben werden, s. klein. K~stadt

f small town. **k~städtisch** *a* provincial.
K~wagen *m* small car

Kleister *m* -s paste. **k~n** *vt* paste

Klemme *f* -,-n [hair-]grip; in der
K~sitzen (*fam*) be in a fix. **k~n** *vt*
jam; sich (*dat*) den Finger **k~n** get one's
finger caught □ *vi* (*haben*) jam, stick

Klempner *m* -s,- plumber

Klerus (der) - the clergy

Klette *f* -,-n burr; **wie eine K~** (*fig*) like
a limpet

kletter|n *vi* (*sein*) climb. **K~pflanze** *f*
climber. **K~rose** *f* climbing rose

Klettverschluss (**Klettverschluß**) *m*
Velcro (P) fastening

klicken *vi* (*haben*) click

Klient(in) /kli'ɛnt(ɪn)/ *m* -en,-en (*f*
-,-nen) (*Jur*) client

Kliff *nt* -[e]s,-e cliff

Klima *nt* -s climate. **K~anlage** *f* air-con-
ditioning

klimat|isch *a* climatic. **k~isiert** *a* air-
conditioned

klimpern *vi* (*haben*) jingle; **k~ auf** (+
dat) tinkle on ⟨*Klavier*⟩; strum ⟨*Gitarre*⟩

Klinge *f* -,-n blade

Klingel *f* -,-n bell. **k~n** *vi* (*haben*) ring;
es **k~t** there's a ring at the door

klingen† *vi* (*haben*) sound

Klini|k *f* -,-en clinic. **k~sch** *a* clinical,
adv -ly

Klinke *f* -,-n [door] handle

klipp *pred a* **k~ und klar** quite plain, *adv*
-ly

Klipp *m* -s,-s = Klips

Klippe *f* -,-n [submerged] rock

Klips *m* -es,-e clip; (*Ohr*-) clip-on ear-ring

klirren *vi* (*haben*) rattle; ⟨*Geschirr, Glas:*⟩
chink

Klischee *nt* -s,-s cliché

Klo *nt* -s,-s (*fam*) loo, (*Amer*) john

klobig *a* clumsy

klönen *vi* (*haben*) (*NGer fam*) chat

klopf|en *vi* (*haben*) knock; (*leicht*) tap;
⟨*Herz:*⟩ pound; es **k~te** there was a knock
at the door □ *vt* beat; (*ein*-) knock

Klops *m* -es,-e meatball; (*Brat*-) rissole

Klosett *nt* -s,-s lavatory

Kloß *m* -es,ˉe dumpling; **ein K~ im** Hals
(*fam*) a lump in one's throat

Kloster *nt* -s,ˉ monastery; (*Nonnen*-) convent

klösterlich *a* monastic

Klotz *m* -es,ˉe block

Klub *m* -s,-s club

Kluft[1] *f* -,ˉe cleft; (*fig: Gegensatz*) gulf

Kluft[2] *f* -,-en outfit; (*Uniform*) uniform

klug *a* (klüger, klügst) intelligent, *adv* -ly;
(*schlau*) clever, *adv* -ly; **nicht k~ werden**
aus not understand. **K~heit** *f* - cleverness

Klump|en *m* -s,- lump. **k~en** *vi* (*haben*)
go lumpy

knabbern *vt/i* (*haben*) nibble

Knabe *m* -n,-n boy. **k~nhaft** *a* boyish

Knäckebrot *nt* crispbread

knack|en *vt/i* (*haben*) crack. **K~s** *m*
-es,-e crack; einen **K~s** haben be
cracked/(*fam: verrückt sein*) crackers

Knall *m* -[e]s,-e bang. **K~bonbon** *m* cracker. **k~en** *vi* (*haben*) go bang; ⟨*Peitsche:*⟩
crack □ *vt* (*fam: werfen*) chuck; jdm eine
k~en (*fam*) clout s.o. **k~ig** *a* (*fam*)
gaudy. **k~rot** *a* bright red

knapp *a* (*gering*) scant; (*kurz*) short; (*man-
gelnd*) scarce; (*gerade ausreichend*) bare;
(*eng*) tight; **ein k~es** Pfund just under a
pound; jdn **k~ halten** (*fam*) keep s.o.
short (mit of). **k~halten†** *vt sep* NEW **k~**
halten, s. knapp. **K~heit** *f* - scarcity

Knarre *f* -,-n rattle. **k~n** *vi* (*haben*) creak

Knast *m* -[e]s (*fam*) prison

knattern *vi* (*haben*) crackle; ⟨*Gewehr:*⟩
stutter

Knäuel *m & nt* -s,- ball

Knauf *m* -[e]s, Knäufe knob

knauser|ig *a* (*fam*) stingy. **k~n** *vi*
(*haben*) (*fam*) be stingy

knautschen *vt* (*fam*) crumple □ *vi*
(*haben*) crease

Knebel *m* -s,- gag. **k~n** *vt* gag

Knecht *m* -[e]s,-e farm-hand; (*fig*) slave.
k~en *vt* (*fig*) enslave. **K~schaft** *f* - (*fig*)
slavery

kneif|en† *vt* pinch □ *vi* (*haben*) pinch;
(*fam: sich drücken*) chicken out.
K~zange *f* pincers *pl*

Kneipe *f* -,-n (*fam*) pub, (*Amer*) bar

knet|en *vt* knead; (*formen*) mould.
K~masse *f* Plasticine (P)

Knick *m* -[e]s,-e bend; (*im Draht*) kink;
(*Kniff*) crease. **k~en** *vt* bend; (*kniffen*)
fold; geknickt sein (*fam*) be dejected.
k~[e]rig *a* (*fam*) stingy

Knicks *m* -es,-e curtsy. **k~en** *vi* (*haben*)
curtsy

Knie *nt* -s,- /'kni:ə/ knee. **K~bundhose** *f*
knee-breeches *pl*. **K~kehle** *f* hollow of
the knee

knien /'kni:ən/ *vi* (*haben*) kneel □ *vr* **sich
k~** kneel [down]

Knie|scheibe *f* kneecap. **K~strumpf** *m*
knee-length sock

Kniff *m* -[e]s,-e pinch; (*Falte*) crease; (*fam:
Trick*) trick. **k~en** *vt* fold. **k~[e]lig** *a*
(*fam*) tricky

knipsen vt (lochen) punch; (Phot) photograph □ vi (haben) take a photograph/ photographs

Knirps m -es,-e (fam) little chap; (P) (Schirm) telescopic umbrella

knirschen vi (haben) grate; (Schnee, Kies:) crunch; mit den Zähnen k~ grind one's teeth

knistern vi (haben) crackle; (Papier:) rustle

Knitter|falte f crease. k~frei a crease-resistant. k~n vi (haben) crease

knobeln vi (haben) toss (um for); (fam: überlegen) puzzle

Knoblauch m -s garlic

Knöchel m -s,- ankle; (Finger-) knuckle

Knochen m -s,- bone. K~mark nt bone marrow. k~trocken a bone-dry

knochig a bony

Knödel m -s,- (SGer) dumpling

Knolle f -,-n tuber. k~ig a bulbous

Knopf m -[e]s,"e button; (Kragen-) stud; (Griff) knob

knöpfen vt button

Knopfloch nt buttonhole

Knorpel m -s gristle; (Anat) cartilage

knorrig a gnarled

Knospe f -,-n bud

Knötchen nt -s,- nodule

Knoten m -s,- knot; (Med) lump; (Haar-) bun, chignon. k~ vt knot. K~punkt m junction

knotig a knotty; (Hände:) gnarled

knuffen vt poke

knüll|en vt crumple □ vi (haben) crease. K~er m -s,- (fam) sensation

knüpfen vt knot; (verbinden) attach (an + acc to)

Knüppel m -s,- club; (Gummi-) truncheon

knurr|en vi (haben) growl; (Magen:) rumble; (fam: schimpfen) grumble. k~ig a grumpy

knusprig a crunchy, crisp

knutschen vi (haben) (fam) smooch

k.o. /ka'?o:/ a k.o. schlagen knock out; k.o. sein (fam) be worn out. K.o. m -s,-s knock-out

Koalition /koali'tsio:n/ f -,-en coalition

Kobold m -[e]s,-e goblin, imp

Koch m -[e]s,"e cook; (im Restaurant) chef. K~buch nt cookery book, (Amer) cookbook. k~en vt cook; (sieden) boil, make (Kaffee, Tee); hart gekochtes Ei hard-boiled egg □ vi (haben) cook; (sieden) boil; (fam) seethe (vor + dat with). K~en nt -s cooking; (Sieden) boiling; zum K~n bringen/kommen bring/come to the boil. k~end a boiling □ adv k~end heiß

boiling hot. K~er m -s,- cooker. K~gelegenheit f cooking facilities pl. K~herd m cooker, stove

Köchin f -,-nen [woman] cook

Koch|kunst f cookery. K~löffel m wooden spoon. K~nische f kitchenette. K~platte f hotplate. K~topf m saucepan

Kode /ko:t/ m -s,-s code

Köder m -s,- bait

Koexist|enz /'ko:?eksistɛnts/ f coexistence. k~ieren vi (haben) coexist

Koffein /kofe'i:n/ nt -s caffeine. k~frei a decaffeinated

Koffer m -s,- suitcase. K~kuli m luggage trolley. K~radio nt portable radio. K~raum m (Auto) boot, (Amer) trunk

Kognak /'kɔnjak/ m -s,-s brandy

Kohl m -[e]s cabbage

Kohle f -,-n coal. K~[n]hydrat nt -[e]s, -e carbohydrate. K~nbergwerk nt coalmine, colliery. K~ndioxid nt carbon dioxide. K~ngrube f = K~nbergwerk. K~nherd m [kitchen] range. K~nsäure f carbon dioxide. K~nstoff m carbon. K~papier nt carbon paper

Kohl|kopf m cabbage. K~rabi m -[s],-[s] kohlrabi. K~rübe f swede

Koje f -,-n (Naut) bunk

Kokain /koka'i:n/ nt -s cocaine

kokett a flirtatious. k~ieren vi (haben) flirt

Kokon /ko'kõ:/ m -s,-s cocoon

Kokosnuss (Kokosnuß) f coconut

Koks m -es coke

Kolben m -s,- (Gewehr-) butt; (Mais-) cob; (Techn) piston; (Chem) flask

Kolibri m -s,-s humming-bird

Kolik f -,-en colic

Kollabora|teur /-'tø:ɐ̯/ m -s,-e collaborator. K~tion /-'tsio:n/ f - collaboration

Kolleg nt -s,-s & -ien /-jən/ (Univ) course of lectures

Kolleg|e m -n,-n, K~in f -,-nen colleague. K~ium nt -s,-ien staff

Kollek|te f -,-n (Relig) collection. K~tion /-'tsio:n/ f -,-en collection. k~tiv a collective. K~tivum nt -s,-va collective noun

kolli|dieren vi (sein) collide. K~sion f -,-en collision

Köln nt -s Cologne. K~ischwasser, K~isch Wasser nt eau-de-Cologne

Kolonialwaren fpl groceries

Kolon|ie f -,-n colony. k~isieren vt colonize

Kolonne f -,-n column; (Mil) convoy

Koloss m -es,-e (Koloß m -sses,-sse) giant

kolossal a enormous, adv -ly

Kolumne f -,-n (Journ) column

Koma nt -s,-s coma

Kombi m -s,-s = K~wagen. K~nation /-'tsjo:n/ f -,-en combination; (Folgerung) deduction; (Kleidung) co-ordinating outfit. k~nieren vt combine; (fig) reason; (folgern) deduce. K~wagen m estate car, (Amer) station-wagon

Kombüse f -,-n (Naut) galley

Komet m -en,-en comet. k~enhaft a (fig) meteoric

Komfort /kɔm'fo:ɐ̯/ m -s comfort; (Luxus) luxury. k~abel /-'ta:bəl/ a comfortable, adv -bly; (luxuriös) luxurious, adv -ly

Komik f - humour. K~er m -s,- comic, comedian

komisch a funny; (Oper) comic; (sonderbar) odd, funny □ adv funnily; oddly. k~erweise adv funnily enough

Komitee nt -s,-s committee

Komma nt -s,-s & -ta comma; (Dezimal-) decimal point; drei K~ fünf three point five

Komman|dant m -en,-en commanding officer. K~deur /-'dø:ɐ̯/ m -s,-e commander. k~dieren vt command; (befehlen) order; (fam: herum-) order about □ vi (haben) give the orders

Kommando nt -s,-s order; (Befehlsgewalt) command; (Einheit) detachment. K~brücke f bridge

kommen† vi (sein) come; (eintreffen) arrive; (gelangen) get (nach to); k~ lassen send for; auf/hinter etw (acc) k~ think of/find out about sth; um/zu etw k~ lose/acquire sth; wieder zu sich k~ come round; wie kommt das? why is that? K~ nt -s coming; K~ und Gehen coming and going. k~d a coming; k~den Montag next Monday

Kommen|tar m -s,-e commentary; (Bemerkung) comment. K~tator m -s,-en /-'to:rən/ commentator. k~tieren vt comment on

kommer|zialisieren vt commercialize. k~ziell a commercial, adv -ly

Kommili|tone m -n,-n, K~tonin f -,-nen fellow student

Kommiss m -es (Kommiß m -sses) (fam) army

Kommissar m -s,-e commissioner; (Polizei-) superintendent

Kommission f -,-en commission; (Gremium) committee

Kommode f -,-n chest of drawers

Kommunalwahlen fpl local elections

Kommunikation /-'tsjo:n/ f -,-en communication

Kommunikee /kɔmyni'ke:/ nt -s,-s = Kommuniqué

Kommunion f -,-en [Holy] Communion

Kommuniqué /kɔmyni'ke:/ nt -s,-s communiqué

Kommun|ismus m - Communism. K~ist(in) m -en,-en (f -,-nen) Communist. k~istisch a Communist

kommunizieren vi (haben) receive [Holy] Communion

Komödie /ko'mø:djə/ f -,-n comedy

Kompagnon /'kɔmpanjõ:/ m -s,-s (Comm) partner

kompakt a compact. K~schallplatte f compact disc

Kompanie f -,-n (Mil) company

Komparativ m -s,-e comparative

Komparse m -n,-n (Theat) extra

Kompass m -es,-e (Kompaß m -sses,-sse) compass

kompatibel a compatible

kompeten|t a competent. K~z f -,-en competence

komplett a complete, adv -ly

Komplex m -es,-e complex. k~ a complex

Komplikation /-'tsjo:n/ f -,-en complication

Kompliment nt -[e]s,-e compliment

Komplize m -n,-n accomplice

komplizier|en vt complicate. k~t a complicated

Komplott nt -[e]s,-e plot

kompo|nieren vt/i (haben) compose. K~nist m -en,-en composer. K~sition /-'tsjo:n/ f -,-en composition

Kompositum nt -s,-ta compound

Kompost m -[e]s compost

Kompott nt -[e]s,-e stewed fruit

Kompresse f -,-n compress

komprimieren vt compress

Kompromiss m -es,-e (Kompromiß m -sses,-sse) compromise; einen K~ schließen compromise. k~los a uncompromising

kompromittieren vt compromise

Konden|sation /-'tsjo:n/ f - condensation. k~sieren vt condense

Kondensmilch f evaporated/(gesüßt) condensed milk

Kondition /-'tsjo:n/ f - (Sport) fitness; in K~ in form. K~al m -s,-e (Gram) conditional

Konditor m -s,-en /-'to:rən/ confectioner. K~ei f -,-en patisserie

Kondo|lenzbrief m letter of condolence. k~lieren vi (haben) express one's condolences

Kondom nt & m -s,-e condom

Konfekt nt -[e]s confectionery; (*Pralinen*) chocolates pl

Konfektion /-'tsjo:n/ f - ready to-wear clothes pl

Konferenz f -,-en conference; (*Besprechung*) meeting

Konfession f -,-en [religious] denomination. k~ell a denominational. k~slos a non-denominational

Konfetti nt -s confetti

Konfirm|and(in) m -en,-en (f -,-nen) candidate for confirmation. K~ation /-'tsjo:n/ f -,-en (*Relig*) confirmation. k~ieren vt (*Relig*) confirm

Konfitüre f -,-n jam

Konflikt m -[e]s,-e conflict

Konföderation /-'tsjo:n/ f confederation

Konfront|ation /-'tsjo:n/ f -,-en confrontation. k~ieren vt confront

konfus a confused

Kongress m -es,-e (Kongreß m -sses,-sse) congress

König m -s,-e king. K~in f -,-nen queen. k~lich a royal, adv -ly; (*hoheitsvoll*) regal, adv -ly; (*großzügig*) handsome, adv -ly; (*fam: groß*) tremendous, adv -ly. K~reich nt kingdom

konisch a conical

Konjug|ation /-'tsjo:n/ f -,-en conjugation. k~ieren vt conjugate

Konjunktion /-'tsjo:n/ f -,-en (*Gram*) conjunction

Konjunktiv m -s,-e subjunctive

Konjunktur f - economic situation; (*Hoch-*) boom

konkav a concave

konkret a concrete

Konkurren|t(in) m -en,-en (f -,-nen) competitor, rival. K~z f - competition; jdm K~z machen compete with s.o. k~zfähig a (*Comm*) competitive. K~zkampf m competition, rivalry

konkurrieren vi (*haben*) compete

Konkurs m -es,-e bankruptcy; K~ machen go bankrupt

können† vt/i (*haben*) etw k~ be able to do sth; (*beherrschen*) know sth; k~ Sie Deutsch? do you know any German? das kann ich nicht I can't do that; er kann nicht mehr he can't go on; für etw nichts k~ not be to blame; **[...]** sen/schwimmen k~ be able to read/ swim; er kann/konnte es tun he can/ could do it; das kann od könnte [gut] sein that may [well] be. K~ nt -s ability; (*Wissen*) knowledge.

Könner(in) m -s,- (f -,-nen) expert

konsequen|t a consistent, adv -ly; (*logisch*) logical, adv -ly. K~z f -,-en consequence

konservativ a conservative

Konserv|en fpl tinned or canned food sg. K~enbüchse, K~endose f tin, can. k~ieren vt preserve; (*in Dosen*) tin, can. K~ierungsmittel nt preservative

Konsistenz f - consistency

konsolidieren vt consolidate

Konsonant m -en,-en consonant

konsterniert a dismayed

Konstitution /-'tsjo:n/ f -,-en constitution. k~ell a constitutional

konstru|ieren vt construct; (*entwerfen*) design

Konstruk|tion /-'tsjo:n/ f -,-en construction; (*Entwurf*) design. k~tiv a constructive

Konsul m -s,-n consul. K~at nt -[e]s,-e consulate

Konsult|ation /-'tsjo:n/ f -,-en consultation. k~ieren vt consult

Konsum m -s consumption. K~ent m -en,-en consumer. K~güter ntpl consumer goods

Kontakt m -[e]s,-e contact. K~linsen fpl contact lenses. K~person f contact

Kontinent /'kɔn-, kɔnti'nɛnt/ m -[e]s,-e continent

Kontingent nt -[e]s,-e (*Comm*) quota; (*Mil*) contingent

Kontinuität f - continuity

Konto nt -s,-s account. K~auszug m [bank] statement. K~nummer f account number. K~stand m [bank] balance

Kontrabass (Kontrabaß) m double-bass

Kontrast m -[e]s,-e contrast

Kontroll|abschnitt m counterfoil. K~e f -,-n control; (*Prüfung*) check. K~eur /-'lø:ɐ/ m -s,-e [ticket] inspector. k~ieren vt check; inspect (*Fahrkarten*); (*beherrschen*) control

Kontroverse f -,-n controversy

Kontur f -,-en contour

Konvention /-'tsjo:n/ f -,-en convention. k~ell a conventional, adv -ly

Konversation /-'tsjo:n/ f -,-en conversation. K~slexikon nt encyclopaedia

konvert|ieren vi (*haben*) (*Relig*) convert. K~it m -en,-en convert

Konvoi /kɔn'vɔy/ m -s,-s convoy

Konzentration /-'tsjo:n/ f -,-en concentration. K~slager nt concentration camp

konzentrieren vt concentrate; sich k~ concentrate (auf + acc on)

Konzept *nt* -[e]s,-e [rough] draft; jdn aus dem K~ bringen put s.o. off his stroke. K~papier *nt* rough paper

Konzern *m* -s,-e (*Comm*) group [of companies]

Konzert *nt* -[e]s,-e concert; (*Klavier-, Geigen-*) concerto. K~meister *m* leader, (*Amer*) concertmaster

Konzession *f* -,-en licence; (*Zugeständnis*) concession

Konzil *nt* -s,-e (*Relig*) council

Kooperation /ko'ɔpera'tsǐoːn/ *f* cooperation

Koordin|ation /ko'ɔrdina'tsǐoːn/ *f* - co-ordination. k~ieren *vt* co-ordinate

Kopf *m* -[e]s,ᵉe head; ein K~ Kohl/Salat a cabbage/lettuce; aus dem K~ from memory; (*auswendig*) by heart; auf dem K~ (*verkehrt*) upside down; K~ an K~ neck and neck; (*stehen*) shoulder to shoulder; K~ stehen stand on one's head; sich (*dat*) den K~ waschen wash one's hair; sich (*dat*) den K~ zerbrechen rack one's brains. K~ball *m* header. K~bedeckung *f* head-covering

Köpf|chen *nt* -s,- little head; K~chen haben (*fam*) be clever. k~en *vt* behead; (*Fußball*) head

Kopf|ende *nt* head. K~haut *f* scalp. K~hörer *m* headphones *pl*. K~kissen *nt* pillow. K~kissenbezug *m* pillow-case. k~los *a* panic-stricken. K~nicken *nt* -s nod. K~rechnen *nt* mental arithmetic. K~salat *m* lettuce. K~schmerzen *mpl* headache *sg*. K~schütteln *nt* -s shake of the head. K~sprung *m* header, dive. K~stand *m* headstand. K~steinpflaster *nt* cobble-stones *pl*. K~stütze *f* head-rest. K~tuch *nt* headscarf. k~über *adv* head first; (*fig*) headlong. K~wäsche *f* shampoo. K~weh *nt* headache. K~zerbrechen *nt* -s K~zerbrechen machen rack one's brains; (*sich sorgen*) worry

Kopie *f* -,-n copy. k~ren *vt* copy

Koppel¹ *f* -,-n enclosure; (*Pferde-*) paddock

Koppel² *nt* -s,- (*Mil*) belt. k~n *vt* couple

Koralle *f* -,-n coral

Korb *m* -[e]s,ᵉe basket; jdm einen K~ geben (*fig*) turn s.o. down. K~ball *m* [kind of] netball. K~stuhl *m* wicker chair

Kord *m* -s (*Tex*) corduroy

Kordel *f* -,-n cord

Korinthe *f* -,-n currant

Kork *m* -s,-e cork. K~en *m* -s,- cork. K~enzieher *m* -s,- corkscrew

Korn¹ *nt* -[e]s,ᵉer grain, (*Samen-*) seed; (*coll: Getreide*) grain, corn; (*am Visier*) front sight

Korn² *m* -[e]s,- (*fam*) grain schnapps

Körn|chen *nt* -s,- granule. k~ig *a* granular

Körper *m* -s,- body; (*Geom*) solid. K~bau *m* build, physique. k~behindert *a* physically disabled. K~lich *a* physical, *adv* -ly; (*Strafe*) corporal. K~pflege *f* personal hygiene. K~puder *m* talcum powder. K~schaft *f* -,-en corporation, body. K~strafe *f* corporal punishment. K~teil *m* part of the body

Korps /koːɐ̯/ *nt* -,- /-[s],-s/ corps

korpulent *a* corpulent

korrekt *a* correct, *adv* -ly. K~or *m* -s,-en /-'toːrən/ proof-reader. K~ur *f* -,-en correction. K~urabzug, K~urbogen *m* proof

Korrespon|dent(in) *m* -en,-en (*f* -,-nen) correspondent. K~denz *f* -,-en correspondence. k~dieren *vi* (*haben*) correspond

Korridor *m* -s,-e corridor

korrigieren *vt* correct

Korrosion *f* - corrosion

korrumpieren *vt* corrupt

korrup|t *a* corrupt. K~tion /-'tsǐoːn/ *f* - corruption

Korsett *nt* -[e]s,-e corset

koscher *a* kosher

Kose|name *m* pet name. K~wort *nt* (*pl* -wörter) term of endearment

Kosmet|ik *f* - beauty culture. K~ika *ntpl* cosmetics. K~ikerin *f* -,-nen beautician. k~isch *a* cosmetic; (*Chirurgie*) plastic

kosm|isch *a* cosmic. K~onaut(in) *m* -en,-en (*f* -,-nen) cosmonaut. k~opolitisch *a* cosmopolitan

Kosmos *m* - cosmos

Kost *f* - food; (*Ernährung*) diet; (*Verpflegung*) board

kostbar *a* precious. K~keit *f* -,-en treasure

kosten¹ *vt/i* (*haben*) [von] etw k~ taste sth

kosten² *vt* cost; (*brauchen*) take; wie viel kostet es? how much is it? K~ *pl* expense *sg*, cost *sg*; (*Jur*) costs; auf meine K~ at my expense. K~[vor]anschlag *m* estimate. k~los *a* free □ *adv* free [of charge]

Kosthappen *m* taste

köstlich *a* delicious; (*entzückend*) delightful. K~keit *f* -,-en (*fig*) gem; (*Culin*) delicacy

Kost|probe *f* taste; (*fig*) sample. k~spielig *a* expensive, costly

Kostüm *nt* -s,-e (*Theat*) costume; (*Verkleidung*) fancy dress; (*Schneider-*) suit. K~fest *nt* fancy-dress party. k~iert *a* k~iert sein be in fancy dress

Kot m -[e]s excrement; (Schmutz) dirt

Kotelett /ˈkɔtˈlet/ nt -s,-s chop, cutlet.
K~en pl sideburns

Köter m -s,· (pej) dog

Kotflügel m (Auto) wing, (Amer) fender

kotzen vi (haben) (sl) throw up; es ist zum
K~ it makes you sick

Krabbe f -,-n crab; (Garnele) shrimp;
(rote) prawn

krabbeln vi (sein) crawl

Krach m -[e]s,ˉe din, racket; (Knall) crash;
(fam: Streit) row; (fam: Ruin) crash.
k~en vi (haben) crash; es hat gekracht
there was a bang/(fam: Unfall) a crash
□ (sein) break, crack; (auftreffen) crash
(gegen into)

krächzen vi (haben) croak

Kraft f -,ˉe strength; (Gewalt) force;
(Arbeits-) worker; in/außer K~ in/no
longer in force; in K~ treten come into
force. k~ prep (+ gen) by virtue of.
K~ausdruck m swear-word. K~fahrer
m driver. K~fahrzeug nt motor vehicle.
K~fahrzeugbrief m [vehicle] registration document

kräftig a strong; (gut entwickelt) sturdy;
(nahrhaft) nutritious; (heftig) hard ▪ adv
strongly; (heftig) hard. k~en vt strength-
en

kraft|los a weak. K~post f post bus ser-
vice. K~probe f trial of strength. K~rad
nt motorcycle. K~stoff m (Auto) fuel.
k~voll a strong, powerful. K~wagen m
motor car. K~werk nt power station

Kragen m -s,· collar

Krähe f -,-n crow

krähen vi (haben) crow

krakeln vt/i (haben) scrawl

Kralle f -,-nclaw. k~n (sich)vr clutch (an
jdn/etws.o./sth); (Katze:) dig its claws (in
+ acc into)

Kram m -s (fam) things pl, (fam) stuff;
(Angelegenheiten) business; wertloser
K~ junk. k~en vi (haben) rummage
about (in + dat in; nach for). K~laden
m [small] general store

Krampf m -[e]s,ˉe cramp. K~adern fpl
varicose veins. k~haft a convulsive, adv
-ly; (verbissen) desperate, adv -ly

Kran m -[e]s,ˉe (Techn) crane

Kranich m -s,-e (Zool) crane

krank a (kränker, kränkst) sick; (Knie,
Herz) bad; k~ sein/werden/machen be/
fall/make ill; jdn k~ melden/schrei-
ben ⟨NEW⟩ jdn k~melden/krankschrei-
ben, s. krankmelden, krankschreiben.
K~e(r) m/f sick man/woman, invalid;
die K~en the sick pl

kränkeln vi (haben) be in poor health.
k~d a ailing

kranken vi (haben) (fig) suffer (an + dat
from)

kränken vt offend, hurt

Kranken|bett nt sick-bed. K~geld nt
sickness benefit. K~gymnast(in) m
-en,-(en (f -,-nen) physiotherapist. K~
gymnastik f physiotherapy. K~haus nt
hospital. K~kasse f health insurance
scheme/(Amt) office. K~pflege f nursing. K~pfleger(in) m(f) nurse. K~saal
m [hospital] ward. K~schein m certificate of entitlement to medical treatment.
K~schwester f nurse. K~urlaub m
sick-leave. K~versicherung f health
insurance. K~wagen m ambulance.
K~zimmer nt sick-room

krank|haft a morbid; (pathologisch)
pathological. K~heit f -,-en illness,
disease

kränklich a sickly

krank|melden vt sep jdn k~melden re-
port s.o. sick; sich k~melden report sick.
k~schreiben† vt sep jdn k~schreiben
give s.o. a medical certificate; sich
k~schreiben lassen get a medical certificate

Kränkung f -,-en slight

Kranz m -es,ˉe wreath; (Ring) ring

Krapfen m -s,· doughnut

krass (kraß) a (krasser, krassest) glaring; (offensichtlich) blatant; (stark) gross;
rank (Außenseiter)

Krater m -s,· crater

kratz|bürstig a (fam) prickly. k~en vt/i
(haben) scratch; sich k~en scratch one-
self/(Tier:) itself. K~er m -s,· scratch;
(Werkzeug) scraper

Kraul nt -s (Sport) crawl. k~en¹ vi (ha-
ben/sein) (Sport) do the crawl

kraulen vt tickle; sich am Kopf k~
scratch one's head

kraus a wrinkled; (Haar) frizzy; (verworren) muddled; k~ ziehen wrinkle.
K~e f -,-n frill, ruffle; (Haar-) frizziness

kräuseln vt wrinkle; frizz (Haar); gather
(Stoff); ripple (Wasser); sich k~wrinkle;
(sich kringeln) curl; (Haar:) go frizzy;
(Wasser:) ripple

krausen vt wrinkle; frizz (Haar); gather
(Stoff); sich k~wrinkle; (Haar:) go frizzy

Kraut nt -[e]s, Kräuter herb; (SGer) cabbage, (Sauer-) sauerkraut; wie K~ und
Rüben (fam) higgledy-piggledy

Krawall m -s,-e riot; (Lärm) row

Krawatte f -,-n [neck]tie

kraxeln vi (sein) (fam) clamber

krea|tiv /krea'ti:f/ *a* creative. K~tür *f* -,-en creature

Krebs *m* -es,-e crayfish; (*Med*) cancer; (*Astr*) Cancer. k~ig *a* cancerous

Kredit *m* -s,-e credit; (*Darlehen*) loan; auf K~ on credit. K~karte *f* credit card

Kreid|e *f* - chalk. k~ebleich *a* deathly pale. k~ig *a* chalky

kreieren /kre'i:rən/ *vt* create

Kreis *m* -es,-e circle; (*Admin*) district

kreischen *vt/i* (*haben*) screech; (*schreien*) shriek

Kreisel *m* -s,- [spinning] top; (*fam: Kreisverkehr*) roundabout

kreis|en *vi* (*haben*) circle; revolve (um around). k~förmig *a* circular. K~lauf *m* cycle; (*Med*) circulation. k~rund *a* circular. K~säge *f* circular saw. K~verkehr *m* [traffic] roundabout, (*Amer*) traffic circle

Krem *f* -,-s & *m* -s,-e cream

Krematorium *nt* -s,-ien crematorium

Krempe *f* -,-n [hat] brim

Krempel *m* -s (*fam*) junk

krempeln *vt* turn (nach oben up)

Kren *m* -[e]s (*Aust*) horseradish

krepieren *vi* (*sein*) explode; (*sl: sterben*) die

Krepp *m* -s,-s & -e crêpe

Krepppapier (**Kreppapier**) *nt* crêpe paper

Kresse *f* -,-n cress; (*Kapuziner-*) nasturtium

Kreta *nt* -s Crete

Kreuz *nt* -es,-e cross; (*Kreuzung*) intersection; (*Mus*) sharp; (*Kartenspiel*) clubs *pl*; (*Anat*) small of the back; über K~ crosswise; das K~ schlagen cross oneself. k~ *adv* k~ und quer in all directions. k~en *vt* cross; sich k~en cross; (*Straßen:*) intersect; (*Meinungen:*) clash □ *vi* (*haben/sein*) cruise; (*Segelschiff:*) tack. K~er *m* -s,- cruiser. K~fahrt *f* (*Naut*) cruise; (*K~zug*) crusade. K~feuer *nt* crossfire. K~gang *m* cloister

kreuzig|en *vt* crucify. K~ung *f* -,-en crucifixion

Kreuz|otter *f* adder, common viper. K~ung *f* -,-en intersection; (*Straßen-*) crossroads *sg*; (*Hybride*) cross. K~verhör *nt* cross-examination; ins K~verhör nehmen cross-examine. K~weg *m* crossroads *sg*; (*Relig*) Way of the Cross. K~weise *adv* crosswise. K~worträtsel *nt* crossword [puzzle]. K~zug *m* crusade

kribbel|ig *a* (*fam*) edgy. k~n *vi* (*haben*) tingle; (*kitzeln*) tickle

kriech|en† *vi* (*sein*) crawl; (*fig*) grovel (vor + *dat* to). k~erisch *a* grovelling. K~spur *f* (*Auto*) crawler lane. K~tier *nt* reptile

Krieg *m* -[e]s,-e war; K~ führen wage war (gegen on)

kriegen *vt* (*fam*) get; ein Kind k~ have a baby

Krieger|denkmal *nt* war memorial. k~isch *a* warlike; (*militärisch*) military

kriegs|beschädigt *a* war-disabled. K~dienstverweigerer *m* -s,- conscientious objector. K~gefangene(r) *m* prisoner of war. K~gefangenschaft *f* captivity. K~gericht *nt* court martial. K~list *f* stratagem. K~rat *m* council of war. K~recht *nt* martial law. K~schiff *nt* warship. K~verbrechen *nt* war crime

Krimi *m* -s,-s (*fam*) crime story/film. K~nalität *f* - crime; (*Vorkommen*) crime rate. K~nalpolizei *f* criminal investigation department. K~nalroman *m* crime novel. k~nell *a* criminal. K~nelle(r) *m* criminal

kringeln (sich) *vr* curl [up]; (*vor Lachen*) fall about

Kripo *f* - = Kriminalpolizei

Krippe *f* -,-n manger; (*Weihnachts-*) crib; (*Kinder-*) crèche. K~nspiel *nt* Nativity play

Krise *f* -,-n crisis

Kristall¹ *nt* -s (*Glas*) crystal; (*geschliffen*) cut glass

Kristall² *m* -s,-e crystal. k~isieren *vi/r* (*haben*) [sich] k~isieren crystallize

Kriterium *nt* -s,-ien criterion

Kritik *f* -,-en criticism; (*Rezension*) review; unter aller K~ (*fam*) abysmal

Kriti|ker *m* -s,- critic; (*Rezensent*) reviewer. k~sch *a* critical, *adv* -ly. k~sieren *vt* criticize; review

kritteln *vi* (*haben*) find fault (an + *acc* with)

kritzeln *vt/i* (*haben*) scribble

Krokette *f* -,-n (*Culin*) croquette

Krokodil *nt* -s,-e crocodile

Krokus *m* -,-[se] crocus

Krone *f* -,-n crown; (*Baum-*) top

krönen *vt* crown

Kronleuchter *m* chandelier. K~prinz *m* crown prince

Krönung *f* -,-en coronation; (*fig: Höhepunkt*) crowning event/(*Leistung*) achievement

Kropf *m* -[e]s,-e (*Zool*) crop; (*Med*) goitre

Kröte *f* -,-n toad

Krücke *f* -,-n crutch; (*Stock-*) handle; an K~n on crutches

Krug *m* -[e]s,-e jug; (*Bier-*) tankard

Krume *f* -,-n soft part [of loaf]; (*Krümel*) crumb; (*Acker-*) topsoil

Krümel *m* -s,- crumb. **k~ig** *a* crumbly. **k~n** *vt* crumble □ *vi* (*haben*) be crumbly; ⟨*Person:*⟩ drop crumbs

krumm *a* crooked; (*gebogen*) curved; (*verbogen*) bent; **etw k~ nehmen** (*fam*) take sth amiss. **k~beinig** *a* bow-legged

krümmen *vt* bend; crook ⟨*Finger*⟩; **sich k~** bend; (*sich winden*) writhe; (*vor Schmerzen/Lachen*) double up

krummnehmen† *vt sep* (NEW) **krumm nehmen**, *s.* **krumm**

Krümmung *f* -,-en bend; (*Kurve*) curve

Krüppel *m* -s,- cripple

Kruste *f* -,-n crust; (*Schorf*) scab

Kruzifix *nt* -es,-e crucifix

Krypta /ˈkrʏpta/ *f* -,-ten crypt

Kub|a *nt* -s Cuba. **k~anisch** *a* Cuban

Kübel *m* -s,- tub; (*Eimer*) bucket; (*Techn*) skip

Kubik- *pref* cubic. **K~meter** *m & nt* cubic metre

Küche *f* -,-n kitchen; (*Kochkunst*) cooking; **kalte/warme K~** cold/hot food; **französische K~** French cuisine

Kuchen *m* -s,- cake

Küchen|herd *m* cooker, stove. **K~maschine** *f* food processor, mixer. **K~schabe** *f* -,-n cockroach. **K~zettel** *m* menu

Kuckuck *m* -s,-e cuckoo; **zum K~!** (*fam*) hang it! **K~suhr** *f* cuckoo clock

Kufe *f* -,-n [sledge] runner

Kugel *f* -,-n ball; (*Geom*) sphere; (*Gewehr-*) bullet; (*Sport*) shot. **k~förmig** *a* spherical. **K~lager** *nt* ball-bearing. **k~n** *vt/i* (*haben*) roll; **sich k~n** roll/(*vor Lachen*) fall about. **k~rund** *a* spherical; (*fam: dick*) tubby. **K~schreiber** *m* -s,-, ballpoint [pen]. **k~sicher** *a* bullet-proof. **K~stoßen** *nt* -s shot-putting

Kuh *f* -,¨e cow

kühl *a* cool, *adv* -ly; (*kalt*) chilly. **K~box** *f* -,-en cool-box. **K~e** *f* - coolness; chilliness. **k~en** *vt* cool; refrigerate ⟨*Lebensmittel*⟩; chill ⟨*Wein*⟩. **K~er** *m* -s,- icebucket; (*Auto*) radiator. **K~erhaube** *f* bonnet, (*Amer*) hood. **K~fach** *nt* frozen-food compartment. **K~raum** *m* cold store. **K~schrank** *m* refrigerator. **K~truhe** *f* freezer. **K~ung** *f* - cooling; (*Frische*) coolness. **K~wasser** *nt* [radi- ator] water

Kuhmilch *f* cow's milk

kühn *a* bold, *adv* -ly; (*wagemutig*) daring. **K~heit** *f* - boldness

Kuhstall *m* cowshed

Küken *nt* -s,- chick; (*Enten-*) duckling

Kukuruz *m* -[es] (*Aust*) maize

kulant *a* obliging

Kuli *m* -s,- (*fam: Kugelschreiber*) ballpoint [pen], Biro (P)

kulinarisch *a* culinary

Kulissen *fpl* (*Theat*) scenery *sg;* (*seitlich*) wings; **hinter den K~** (*fig*) behind the scenes

kullern *vt/i* (*sein*) (*fam*) roll

Kult *m* -[e]s,-e cult

kultivier|en *vt* cultivate. **k~t** *a* cultured

Kultur *f* -,-en culture; **K~en** plantations. **K~beutel** *m* toiletbag. **k~ell** *a* cultural. **K~film** *m* documentary film

Kultusminister *m* Minister of Education and Arts

Kümmel *m* -s caraway; (*Getränk*) kümmel

Kummer *m* -s sorrow, grief; (*Sorge*) worry; (*Ärger*) trouble

kümmer|lich *a* puny; (*dürftig*) meagre; (*armselig*) wretched. **k~n** *vt* concern; **sich k~n um** look after; (*sich befassen*) concern oneself with; (*beachten*) take notice of; **ich werde mich darum k~n** I shall see to it; **k~e dich um deine eigenen Angelegenheiten!** mind your own business!

kummervoll *a* sorrowful

Kumpel *m* -s,- (*fam*) mate

Kunde *m* -n,-n customer. **K~ndienst** *m* [after-sales] service

Kund|gebung *f* -,-en (*Pol*) rally. **k~ig** *a* knowledgeable; (*sach-*) expert

kündig|en *vt* cancel ⟨*Vertrag*⟩; give notice of withdrawal for ⟨*Geld*⟩; give notice to quit ⟨*Wohnung*⟩; **seine Stellung k~en** give [in one's] notice □ *vi* (*haben*) give [in one's] notice; **jdm k~en** give s.o. notice [of dismissal/⟨*Vermieter:*⟩ to quit]. **K~ung** *f* -,-en cancellation; notice [of withdrawal/dismissal/to quit]; (*Entlassung*) dismissal. **K~ungsfrist** *f* period of notice

Kund|in *f* -,-nen [woman] customer. **K~machung** *f* -,-en (*Aust*) [public] notice. **K~schaft** *f* - clientele, customers *pl*

künftig *a* future □ *adv* in future

Kunst *f* -,¨e art; (*Können*) skill. **K~dünger** *m* artificial fertilizer. **K~faser** *f* synthetic fibre. **k~fertig** *a* skilful. **K~fertigkeit** *f* skill. **K~galerie** *f* art gallery. **k~gerecht** *a* expert, *adv* -ly. **K~geschichte** *f* history of art. **K~gewerbe** *nt* [illegible] **K~griff** *m* trick. **K~händler** *m* art dealer

Künstler *m* -s,- artist; (*Könner*) master. **K~in** *f* -,-nen [woman] artist. **k~isch** *a* artistic, *adv* -ally. **K~name** *m* pseudonym; (*Theat*) stage name

künstlich a artificial, adv -ly

kunst|los a simple. K~maler m painter. K~stoff m plastic. K~stopfen nt invisible mending. K~stück nt trick; (große Leistung) feat. k~voll a artistic; (geschickt) skilful, adv -ly; (kompliziert) elaborate, adv -ly. K~werk nt work of art

kunterbunt a multicoloured; (gemischt) mixed □ adv k~ durcheinander higgledy-piggledy

Kupfer nt -s copper. k~n a copper

kupieren vt crop

Kupon /ku'põ:/ m -s,-s voucher; (Zins-) coupon; (Stoff-) length

Kuppe f -,-n [rounded] top; (Finger-) end, tip

Kuppel f -,-n dome

kupp|eln vt couple (an + acc to) □ vi (haben) (Auto) operate the clutch. K~lung f -,-en coupling; (Auto) clutch

Kur f -,-en course of treatment; (im Kurort) cure

Kür f -,-en (Sport) free exercise; (Eislauf) free programme

Kurbel f -,-n crank. k~n vt wind (nach oben/unten up/down). K~welle f crankshaft

Kürbis m -ses,-se pumpkin; (Flaschen-) marrow

Kurgast m health-resort visitor

Kurier m -s,-e courier

kurieren vt cure

kurios a curious, odd. K~ität f -,-en oddness; (Objekt) curiosity; (Kunst) curio

Kur|ort m health resort; (Badeort) spa. K~pfuscher m quack

Kurs m -es,-e course; (Aktien-) price. K~buch nt timetable

kursieren vi (haben) circulate

kursiv a italic □ adv in italics. K~schrift f italics pl

Kursus m -,Kurse course

Kurswagen m through carriage

Kurtaxe f visitors' tax

Kurve f -,-n curve; (Straßen-) bend

kurz a (kürzer, kürzest) short; (knapp) brief; (rasch) quick; (schroff) curt; k~e Hosen shorts; vor k~em a short time ago; seit k~em lately; binnen k~em shortly; den Kürzeren (kürzeren) ziehen get the worst of it □ adv briefly; quickly; curtly; k~ vor/nach a little way/ (zeitlich) shortly before/after; sich k~ fassen be brief; k~ und gut in short; über k~ oder lang sooner or later; zu k~ kommen get less than one's fair share. K~arbeit f short-time working. k~ärmelig a short-sleeved. k~atmig a k~atmig sein be short of breath

Kürze f - shortness; (Knappheit) brevity; in K~ shortly. k~n vt shorten; (verringern) cut

kurz|erhand adv without further ado. k~fristig a short-term □ adv at short notice. K~geschichte f short story. k~lebig a short-lived

kürzlich adv recently

Kurz|meldung f newsflash. K~nachrichten fpl news headlines. K~schluss (K~schluß) m short circuit; (fig) brainstorm. K~schrift f shorthand. k~sichtig a short-sighted. K~sichtigkeit f short-sightedness. K~streckenrakete f short-range missile. k~um adv in short

Kürzung f -,-en shortening; (Verringerung) cut (gen in)

Kurz|waren fpl haberdashery sg, (Amer) notions. k~weilig a amusing. K~welle f short wave

kuscheln (sich) vr snuggle (an + acc up to)

Kusine f -,-n [female] cousin

Kuss m -es,ːe (Kuß m -sses,-sse) kiss

küssen vt/i (haben) kiss; sich k~ kiss

Küste f -,-n coast. K~nwache, K~nwacht f coastguard

Küster m -s,- verger

Kustos m -,-toden /-'to:-/ curator

Kutsch|e f -,-n [horse-drawn] carriage/ (geschlossen) coach. K~er m -s,- coachman, driver. k~ieren vt/i (haben) drive

Kutte f -,-n (Relig) habit

Kutter m -s,- (Naut) cutter

Kuvert /ku'veːɐ̯/ nt -s,-s envelope

KZ /kaːˈt͡sɛt/ nt -[s],-[s] concentration camp

L

labil a unstable

Labor nt -s,-s and -e laboratory. L~ant(in) m -en,-en (f -,-nen) laboratory assistant. L~atorium nt -s,-ien laboratory

Labyrinth nt -[e]s,-e maze, labyrinth

Lache f -,-n puddle; (Blut-) pool

lächeln vi (haben) smile. L~ nt -s smile. l~d a smiling

lachen vi (haben) laugh. L~ nt -s laugh; (Gelächter) laughter

lächerlich a ridiculous, adv -ly; sich l~ machen make a fool of oneself. L~keit f -,-en ridiculousness; (Kleinigkeit) triviality

lachhaft a laughable

Lachs m -es,-e salmon. l~farben, l~rosa a salmon-pink

Lack m -[e]s,-e varnish; (Japan-) lacquer; (Auto) paint. l~en vt varnish. l~ieren vt varnish; (spritzen) spray. L~schuhe mpl patent-leather shoes

Lade f -,-n drawer

laden† vt load; (Electr) charge; (Jur: vor-) summons

Laden m -s,- shop, (Amer) store; (Fenster-) shutter. L~dieb m shop-lifter. L~diebstahl m shop-lifting. L~schluss (L~schluß) m [shop] closing-time. L~tisch m counter

Laderaum m (Naut) hold

lädieren vt damage

Ladung f -,-en load; (Naut, Aviat) cargo; (elektrische, Spreng-) charge; (Jur: Vor-) summons

Lage f -,-n position; (Situation) situation; (Schicht) layer; (fam: Runde) round; nicht in der L~ sein not be in a position (zu to)

Lager nt -s,- camp; (L~haus) warehouse; (Vorrat) stock; (Techn) bearing; (Erz-, Ruhe-) bed; (eines Tieres) lair; [nicht] auf L~[not] in stock. L~haus nt warehouse. l~n vt store; (legen) lay; sich l~n settle; (sich legen) lie down □ vi (haben) camp; (liegen) lie; (Waren:) be stored. L~raum m store-room. L~stätte f (Geol) deposit. L~ung f -storage

Lagune f -,-n lagoon

lahm a lame; l~ legen (fig) paralyse. l~en vi (haben) be lame

lähmen vt paralyse

lahmlegen vt sep (NEW) lahm legen, s. lahm

Lähmung f -,-en paralysis

Laib m -[e]s,-e loaf

Laich m -[e]s (Zool) spawn. l~en vi (haben) spawn

Laie m -n,-n layman; (Theat) amateur. l~nhaft a amateurish. L~nprediger m lay preacher

Lake f -,-n brine

Laken nt -s,- sheet

lakonisch a laconic, adv -ally

Lakritze f -liquorice

lallen vt/i (haben) mumble; (Baby:) babble

Lametta nt -s tinsel

Lamm nt -[e]s,-er lamb

Lampe f -,-n lamp; (Decken-, Wand-) light; (Glüh-) bulb. L~nfieber nt stage fright. L~nschirm m lampshade

Lampion /lamˈpjɔŋ/ m -s,-s Chinese lantern

lancieren /lãˈsiːrən/ vt (Comm) launch

Land nt -[e]s,-er country; (Fest-) land; (Bundes-) state, Land; (Aust) province; Stück L~ piece of land; auf dem L~e in the country; an L~ gehen (Naut) go ashore, hier zu L~e = hierzulande. L~arbeiter m agricultural worker. L~ebahn f runway. l~einwärts adv inland. l~en vt/i (sein) land; (fam: gelangen) end up

Länderei|en pl estates

Länderspiel nt international

Landesteg m landing-stage

Landesverrat m treason

Land|karte f map. l~läufig a popular

ländlich a rural

Land|maschinen fpl agricultural machinery sg. L~schaft f -,-en scenery; (Geog, Kunst) landscape; (Gegend) country[side]. l~schaftlich a scenic; (regional) regional. L~smann m (pl -leute) fellow countryman, compatriot. L~männin f -,-nen fellow countrywoman. L~straße f country road; (Admin) ≈ B road. L~streicher m -s,- tramp. L~tag m state/(Aust) provincial parliament

Landung f -,-en landing. L~sbrücke f landing-stage

Land|vermesser m -s,- surveyor. L~weg m country lane; auf dem L~weg overland. L~wirt m farmer. L~wirtschaft f agriculture; (Hof) farm. l~wirtschaftlich a agricultural

lang¹ adv & prep (+ preceding acc or preceding an + dat) along; den od am Fluss l~ along the river

lang² a (länger, längst) long; (groß) tall; seit l~em for a long time □ adv eine Stunde/Woche l~ for an hour/a week; mein Leben l~ all my life. l~ärmelig a long-sleeved. l~atmig a long-winded. l~e adv a long time; (schlafen) late; wie/zu l~e how/too long; schon l~e [for] a long time ago; (zurückliegend) a long time ago; so l~e wie möglich as long as possible; l~e nicht not for a long time; (bei weitem nicht) nowhere near

Länge f -,-n length; (Geog) longitude; der L~ nach lengthways; (liegen, fallen) full length

langen vt hand (dat to) □ vi (haben) reach (an etw acc sth; nach for); (genügen) be enough

Längengrad m degree of longitude. L~enmaß nt linear measure. l~er a & adv longer; (längere Zeit) [for] some time

Langeweile f - boredom; L~ haben be bored

lang|fristig a long-term; ⟨Vorhersage⟩ long-range. l∼jährig a long-standing; ⟨Erfahrung⟩ long. l∼lebig a long-lived

länglich a oblong; l∼ rund oval

langmütig a long-suffering

längs adv & prep (+ gen/dat) along; ⟨der Länge nach⟩ lengthways

lang|sam a slow, adv -ly. L∼samkeit f - slowness. L∼schläfer(in) m(f) ⟨fam⟩ late riser. L∼schrift f longhand

längst adv [schon] l∼ for a long time; ⟨zurückliegend⟩ a long time ago; l∼ nicht nowhere near

Lang|strecken- pref long-distance; ⟨Mil, Aviat⟩ long-range. l∼weilen vt bore; sich l∼weilen be bored. l∼weilig a boring, adv -ly. L∼welle f long wave. l∼wierig a lengthy

Lanze f -,-n lance

Lappalie /la'pa:ljə/ f -,-n trifle

Lappen m -s,- cloth; ⟨Anat⟩ lobe

läppisch a silly

Lapsus m -,- slip

Lärche f -,-n larch

Lärm m -s noise. l∼en vi ⟨haben⟩ make a noise. l∼end a noisy

Larve /'larfə/ f -,-n larva; ⟨Maske⟩ mask

lasch a listless; ⟨schlaff⟩ limp; ⟨fade⟩ insipid

Lasche f -,-n tab; ⟨Verschluss-⟩ flap; ⟨Zunge⟩ tongue

Laser /'le:-, 'la:zɐ/ m -s,- laser

lassen† vt leave; ⟨zulassen⟩ let; jdm etw l∼ let s.o. keep sth; sein Leben l∼ lose one's life; etw [sein od bleiben] l∼ not do sth; ⟨aufhören⟩ stop [doing] sth; lass das! stop it! jdn schlafen/gewinnen l∼ let s.o. sleep/win; jdn warten l∼ keep s.o. waiting; etw machen/reparieren l∼ have sth done/repaired; etw verschwinden l∼ make sth disappear; sich [leicht] biegen/öffnen l∼ bend/open [easily]; sich gut waschen l∼ wash well; es lässt sich nicht leugnen it is undeniable; lasst uns gehen! let's go!

lässig a casual, adv -ly. L∼keit f - casualness

Lasso nt -s,-s lasso

Last f -,-en load; ⟨Gewicht⟩ weight; ⟨fig⟩ burden; l∼en charges; ⟨Steuern⟩ taxes; jdm zur L∼ fallen be a burden on s.o. L∼auto nt lorry. l∼en vi ⟨haben⟩ weigh heavily/⟨liegen⟩ rest (auf + dat on). L∼enaufzug m goods lift

Laster¹ m -s,- ⟨fam⟩ lorry, ⟨Amer⟩ truck

Laster² nt -s,- vice. l∼haft a depraved; ⟨zügellos⟩ dissolute

läster|lich a blasphemous. l∼n vt blaspheme □ vi ⟨haben⟩ make disparaging remarks (über + acc about). L∼ung f -,-en blasphemy

lästig a troublesome; l∼ sein/werden be/ become a nuisance

Last|kahn m barge. L∼[kraft]wagen m lorry, ⟨Amer⟩ truck. L∼zug m lorry with trailer[s]

Latein nt -[s] Latin. L∼amerika nt Latin America. l∼isch a Latin

latent a latent

Laterne f -,-n lantern; ⟨Straßen-⟩ street lamp. L∼npfahl m lamp-post

latschen vi ⟨sein⟩ ⟨fam⟩ traipse; ⟨schlurfen⟩ shuffle

Latte f -,-n slat; ⟨Tor-, Hoch- sprung-⟩ bar

Latz m -es,ˆe bib

Lätzchen nt -s,- [baby's] bib

Latzhose f dungarees pl

lau a lukewarm; ⟨mild⟩ mild

Laub nt -[e]s leaves pl; ⟨L∼werk⟩ foliage. L∼baum m deciduous tree

Laube f -,-n summer-house; ⟨gewachsen⟩ arbour. L∼ngang m pergola; ⟨Archit⟩ arcades pl

Laub|säge f fretsaw. L∼wald m deciduous forest

Lauch m -[e]s leeks pl

Lauer f auf der L∼ liegen lie in wait. l∼n vi ⟨haben⟩ lurk; l∼n auf (+ acc) lie in wait for

Lauf m -[e]s, Läufe run; ⟨Laufen⟩ running; ⟨Verlauf⟩ course; ⟨Wett-⟩ race; ⟨Sport: Durchgang⟩ heat; ⟨Gewehr-⟩ barrel; im L∼[e] (+ gen) in the course of. L∼bahn f career. l∼en† vi ⟨sein⟩ run; ⟨zu Fuß gehen⟩ walk; ⟨gelten⟩ be valid; Ski/Schlittschuh l∼en ski/skate; jdn l∼en lassen ⟨fam⟩ let s.o. go. l∼end a running; ⟨gegenwärtig⟩ current; ⟨regelmäßig⟩ regular; l∼ende Nummer serial number; auf dem L∼enden (l∼enden) sein/jdn auf dem L∼enden (l∼enden) halten be/keep s.o. up to date □ adv continually. l∼enlassen† vt sep ⟨NEW⟩ l∼en lassen, s. laufen

Läufer m -s,- ⟨Person, Teppich⟩ runner; ⟨Schach⟩ bishop

Lauf|gitter nt play-pen. L∼masche f ladder. L∼rolle f castor. L∼schritt m im L∼schritt at a run; ⟨Mil⟩ at the double. L∼stall m play-pen. L∼zettel m circular

Lauge f -,-n soapy water

Laun|e f -,-n mood; ⟨Einfall⟩ whim; guter L∼e sein, gute L∼e haben be in a good mood. l∼enhaft a capricious. l∼isch a moody

Laus f -,Läuse louse; (Blatt-) greenfly. L~bub m (fam) rascal

lauschen vi (haben) listen; (heimlich) eavesdrop

lausig a (fam) lousy □ adv terribly

laut a loud, adv -ly; (geräuschvoll) noisy, adv -ily; l~ lesen read aloud; l~er stellen turn up □ prep (+ gen/dat) according to. L~ m -es,-e sound

Laute f -,-n (Mus) lute

lauten vi (haben) ⟨Text:⟩ run, read; auf jds Namen l~ be in s.o.'s name

läuten vt/i (haben) ring

lauter a pure; (ehrlich) honest; ⟨Wahrheit⟩ plain □ a inv sheer; (nichts als) nothing but. L~keit f - integrity

läutern vt purify

laut|hals adv at the top of one's voice; ⟨lachen⟩ out loud. l~los a silent, adv -ly; ⟨Stille⟩ hushed. L~schrift f phonetics pl. L~sprecher m loudspeaker. l~stark a vociferous, adv -ly. L~stärke f volume

lauwarm a lukewarm

Lava f -,-ven lava

Lavendel m -s lavender

lavieren vi (haben) manœuvre

Lawine f -,-n avalanche

lax a lax. L~heit f - laxity

Lazarett nt -[e]s,-e military hospital

leasen /'li:sən/ vt rent

Lebehoch nt cheer

leben vt/i (haben) live (von on); leb wohl! farewell! L~ nt -s,- life, (Treiben) bustle; am L~ alive. l~d a living

lebendig a live; (lebhaft) lively; (anschaulich) vivid, adv -ly; l~ sein be alive. L~keit f - liveliness; vividness

Lebens|abend m old age. L~alter nt age. L~art f manners pl. l~fähig a viable. L~gefahr f mortal danger; in L~gefahr in mortal danger; ⟨Patient⟩ critically ill. l~gefährlich a extremely dangerous; ⟨Verletzung⟩ critical □ adv critically. L~größe f in L~größe life-sized. L~haltungskosten pl cost of living sg. l~lang a lifelong. l~länglich a life ... □ adv for life. L~lauf m curriculum vitae. L~mittel ntpl food sg. L~mittelgeschäft nt food shop. L~mittelhändler m grocer. l~notwendig a vital. L~retter m rescuer; (beim Schwimmen) life-guard. L~standard m standard of living. L~unterhalt m livelihood; seinen L~unterhalt verdienen earn one's living. L~versicherung f life assurance. L~wandel m conduct. l~wichtig a vital. L~zeichen nt sign of life. L~zeit f auf L~zeit for life

Leber f -,-n liver. L~fleck m mole. L~wurst f liver sausage

Lebe|wesen nt living being. L~wohl nt -s,-s & -e farewell

leb|haft a lively; ⟨Farbe⟩ vivid. L~haftigkeit f - liveliness. L~kuchen m gingerbread. l~los a lifeless. L~tag m mein/dein L~tag all my/your life. L~zeiten fpl zu jds L~zeiten in s.o.'s lifetime

leck a leaking. L~ nt -s,-s leak. l~en¹ vi (haben) leak

lecken² vt/i (haben) lick

lecker a tasty. L~bissen m delicacy. L~ei f -,-en sweet

Leder nt -s,- leather. l~n a leather; (wie Leder) leathery

ledig a single. l~lich adv merely

Lee f & nt - nach Lee (Naut) to leeward

leer a empty; (unbesetzt) vacant; l~ laufen (Auto) idle. L~e f - emptiness; (leerer Raum) void. l~en vt empty; sich l~en empty. L~lauf m (Auto) neutral. L~ung f -,-en (Post) collection

legal a legal, adv -ly. l~isieren vt legalize. L~ität f - legality

Legas|thenie f - dyslexia. L~theniker m -s,- dyslexic

legen vt put; ⟨hin-, ver-⟩ lay; set ⟨Haare⟩; Eier l~ lay eggs; sich l~ lie down; ⟨Staub:⟩ settle; (nachlassen) subside

legendär a legendary

Legende f -,-n legend

leger /le'ʒe:ɐ̯/ a casual, adv -ly

legier|en vt alloy; (Culin) thicken. L~ung f -,-en alloy

Legion f -,-en legion

Legislative f - legislature

legitim a legitimate, adv -ly. l~ieren (sich) vr prove one's identity. L~ität f - legitimacy

Lehm m -s clay. l~ig a clayey

Lehn|e f -,-n (Rücken-) back; (Arm-) arm. l~en vt lean (an + acc against); sich l~en lean (an + acc against) □ vi (haben) be leaning (an + dat against). L~sessel, L~stuhl m armchair

Lehr|buch nt textbook. L~e f -,-n apprenticeship; (Anschauung) doctrine; (Theorie) theory; (Wissenschaft) science; (Ratschlag) advice; (Erfahrung) lesson; jdm eine L~e erteilen (fig) teach s.o. a lesson. l~en vt/i (haben) teach. L~er m -s,- teacher; (Fahr-, Ski-) instructor. L~erin f -,-nen teacher. L~erzimmer nt staff-room. L~fach nt (Sch) subject. L~gang m course. L~kraft f teacher. L~ling m -s,-e apprentice; (Auszubildender) trainee. L~plan m syllabus. l~

reich *a* instructive. L∼stelle *f* apprenticeship. L∼stuhl *m* (*Univ*) chair. L∼zeit *f* apprenticeship

Leib *m* -es,-er body; (*Bauch*) belly. L∼eserziehung *f* (*Sch*) physical education. L∼eskraft *f* aus L∼eskräften as hard/⟨schreien⟩ loud as one can. L∼gericht *nt* favourite dish. l∼haftig *a* der l∼haftige Satan the devil incarnate □ *adv* in the flesh. l∼lich *a* physical; (*blutsverwandt*) real, natural. L∼speise *f* = L∼gericht. L∼wache *f* (*coll*) bodyguard. L∼wächter *m* bodyguard. L∼wäsche *f* underwear

Leiche *f* -,-n [dead] body; corpse. L∼nbegängnis *nt* -ses,-se funeral. L∼nbestatter *m* -s,- undertaker. l∼nblass (l∼nblaß) *a* deathly pale. L∼nhalle *f* mortuary. L∼nwagen *m* hearse. L∼nzug *m* funeral procession, cortège

Leichnam *m* -s,-e [dead] body

leicht *a* light, *adv* -ly; ⟨Stoff, Anzug⟩ lightweight; (*gering*) slight, *adv* -ly; (*mühelos*) easy, *adv* -ily; jdm l∼ fallen be easy for s.o.; etw l∼ machen make sth easy (dat for); es sich (dat) l∼ machen take the easy way out; etw l∼ nehmen (*fig*) take sth lightly. L∼athletik *f* [track and field] athletics *sg*. l∼fallen† *vi sep* (*sein*) NEW l∼ fallen, s. leicht. l∼fertig *a* thoughtless, *adv* -ly; (*vorschnell*) rash, *adv* -ly; (*frivol*) frivolous, *adv* -ly. L∼gewicht *nt* (*Boxen*) lightweight. l∼gläubig *a* gullible. l∼hin *adv* casually. L∼igkeit *f* -lightness; (*Mühelosigkeit*) ease; (L∼sein) easiness; mit L∼igkeit with ease. l∼lebig *a* happy-go-lucky. l∼machen *vt sep* NEW l∼ machen, s. leicht. l∼nehmen† *vt sep* NEW l∼ nehmen, s. leicht. L∼sinn *m* carelessness; recklessness; (*Frivolität*) frivolity. l∼sinnig *a* careless, *adv* -ly; (*unvorsichtig*) reckless, *adv* -ly; (*frivol*) frivolous, *adv* -ly

Leid *nt* -[es] sorrow, grief; (*Böses*) harm; es tut mir L∼ I am sorry; er tut mir L∼ I feel sorry for him; jdm etw zu L∼e tun = jdm etw zuleide tun, s. zuleide. l∼ *a* jdn/etw l∼ sein/werden be/get tired of s.o./sth; jdm l∼ tun NEW jdm L∼ tun, s. Leid

Leide|form *f* passive. l∼n† *vt/i* (*haben*) suffer (an + *dat* from); jdn [gut] l∼n können like s.o.; jdn/etw nicht l∼n können dislike s.o./sth. L∼n *nt* -s,- suffering; (*Med*) complaint; (*Krankheit*) disease. l∼nd *a* suffering; l∼nd sein be in poor health. L∼nschaft *f* -,-en passion. l∼nschaftlich *a* passionate, *adv* -ly

leid|er *adv* unfortunately; l∼er ja/nicht I'm afraid so/not. l∼ig *a* wretched.

l∼lich *a* tolerable, *adv* -bly. L∼tragende(r) *m/f* person who suffers; (*Trauernde*) mourner. L∼wesen *nt* zu meinem L∼wesen to my regret

Leier *f* -,-n die alte L∼ (*fam*) the same old story. L∼kasten *m* barrel-organ. l∼n *vt/i* (*haben*) wind; (*herunter-*) drone out

Leih|bibliothek *f* lending library. L∼e *f* -,-n loan. l∼en† *vt* lend; sich (dat) etw l∼en borrow sth. L∼gabe *f* loan. L∼gebühr *f* rental; (*für Bücher*) lending charge. L∼haus *nt* pawnshop. L∼wagen *m* hire-car. l∼weise *adv* on loan

Leim *m* -s glue. l∼en *vt* glue

Leine *f* -,-n rope; (*Wäsche-*) line; (*Hunde-*) lead, leash

Lein|en *nt* -s linen. l∼en *a* linen. L∼tuch *nt* sheet. L∼wand *f* linen; (*Kunst*) canvas; (*Film-*) screen

leise *a* quiet, *adv* -ly; ⟨Stimme, Musik, Berührung⟩ soft, *adv* -ly; (*schwach*) faint, *adv* -ly; (*leicht*) light, *adv* -ly; l∼r stellen turn down

Leiste *f* -,-n strip; (*Holz-*) batten; (*Zier-*) moulding; (*Anat*) groin

leisten *vt* achieve, accomplish; sich (dat) etw l∼en treat oneself to sth; (*fam: anstellen*) get up to sth; ich kann es mir nicht l∼en I can't afford it. L∼ung *f* -,-en achievement; (*Sport, Techn*) performance; (*Produktion*) output; (*Zahlung*) payment. l∼ungsfähig *a* efficient. L∼ungsfähigkeit *f* efficiency

Leit|artikel *m* leader, editorial. L∼bild *nt* (*fig*) model. l∼en *vt* run, manage; (*an-/hinführen*) lead; (*Mus, Techn, Phys*) conduct; (*lenken, schicken*) direct. l∼end *a* leading; ⟨Posten⟩ executive

Leiter¹ *f* -,-n ladder

Leit|er² *m* -s,- director; (*Comm*) manager; (*Führer*) leader; (*Sch*) head; (*Mus, Phys*) conductor. L∼erin *f* -,-nen director; manageress; leader; head. L∼faden *m* manual. L∼kegel *m* [traffic] cone. L∼planke *f* crash barrier. L∼spruch *m* motto. L∼ung *f* -,-en (*Führung*) direction; (*Comm*) management; (*Aufsicht*) control; (*Electr: Schnur*) lead, flex; (*Kabel*) cable; (*Telefon-*) line; (*Rohr-*) pipe; (*Haupt-*) main. L∼ungswasser *nt* tap water

Lektion /-'tsjo:n/ *f* -,-en lesson

Lekt|or *m* -s,-en /-'to:rən/, L∼orin *f* -,-nen (*Univ*) assistant lecturer; (*Verlags-*) editor. L∼üre *f* -,-n reading matter; (*Lesen*) reading

Lende *f* -,-n loin

lenk|bar *a* steerable; (*fügsam*) tractable. l∼en *vt* guide; (*steuern*) steer; (*Aust*) drive; (regeln) control; jds Aufmerksamkeit ziehen auf (acc) l~en attract s.o.'s attention. L~er m -s,- driver; (L~stange) handlebars pl. L~rad nt steering-wheel. L~stange f handlebars pl. L~ung f - steering

Leopard m -en,-en leopard

Lepra f - leprosy

Lerche f -,-n lark

lernen vt/i (haben) learn; (für die Schule) study; schwimmen l~ learn to swim

lesbar a readable; (leserlich) legible

Lesbierin /'lɛsbjərın/ f -,-nen lesbian. l~isch a lesbian

Lese f -,-n harvest. L~buch nt reader. l~n† vt/i (haben) read; (Univ) lecture □ vt pick, gather. L~n nt -s reading. L~r(in) m -s,- (f -,-nen) reader. L~ratte f (fam) bookworm. l~rlich a legible, adv -bly. L~zeichen nt bookmark

Lesung f -,-en reading

lethargisch a lethargic, adv -ally

Lettland nt -s Latvia

letzt|e(r,s) a last; (neueste) latest; in l~er Zeit recently; l~en Endes in the end; er kam als L~er (l~er) he arrived last. l~emal adv das l~emal/zum l~enmal NEW das l~e Mal/zum l~en Mal, s. Mal¹. l~ens adv recently; (zuletzt) lastly. l~ere(r,s) a the latter; der/die/das L~ere (l~ere) the latter

Leucht|e f -,-n light. l~en vi (haben) shine. L~end a shining. L~er m -s,- candlestick. L~feuer nt beacon. L~kugel, L~rakete f flare. L~reklame f neon sign. L~[stoff]röhre f fluorescent tube. L~turm m lighthouse. L~ziffer-blatt nt luminous dial

leugnen vt deny

Leukämie f - leukaemia

Leumund m -s reputation

Leute pl people; (Mil) men; (Arbeiter) workers

Leutnant m -s,-s second lieutenant

leutselig a affable, adv -bly

Levkoje /lɛf'ko:jə/ f -,-n stock

Lexikon nt -s,-ka encyclopaedia; (Wörterbuch) dictionary

Libanon (der) -s Lebanon

Libelle f -,-n dragonfly; (Techn) spirit-level; (Haarspange) slide

liberal a (Pol) Liberal

Libyen nt -s Libya

Licht nt -[e]s,-er light; (Kerze) candle; L~ machen turn on the light; hinters L~ führen (fam) dupe. l~ a bright; (Med) lucid; (spärlich) sparse. L~bild nt [passport] photograph; (Dia) slide. L~bilder-vortrag m slide lecture. L~blick m (fig)

ray of hope. l~en vt thin out; den Anker l~en (Naut) weigh anchor; sich l~en become less dense; (Haare:) thin. L~hupe f headlight flasher; die L~hupe betätigen flash one's headlights. L~maschine f dynamo. L~schalter m light-switch. L~ung f -,-en clearing

Lid nt -[e]s,-er [eye]lid. L~schatten m eye-shadow

lieb a dear; (nett) nice; (artig) good; jdn l~ haben be fond of s.o.; (lieben) love s.o.; jdn l~ gewinnen grow fond of s.o.; es ist mir l~ I'm glad (dass that); es wäre mir l~er I should prefer it (wenn if). l~äu-geln vi (haben) l~äugeln mit fancy; toy with (Gedanken)

Liebe f -,-n love. l~lei f -,-en flirtation. l~n vt love; (mögen) like; sich l~n love each other; (körperlich) make love. l~nd a loving □ adv etw l~nd gern tun love to do sth. l~nswert a lovable. l~nswür-dig a kind. l~nswürdigerweise adv very kindly. L~nswürdigkeit f -,-en kindness

lieber adv rather; (besser) better; l~ mögen like better; ich trinke l~ Tee I prefer tea

Liebes|brief m love letter. L~dienst m favour. L~geschichte f love story. L~kummer m heartache; L~kummer haben be depressed over an unhappy love-affair. L~paar nt [pair of] lovers pl

lieb|evoll a loving, adv -ly, (zärtlich) affectionate, adv -ly. l~gewinnen† vt sep NEW l~ gewinnen, s. lieb. l~haben† vt sep NEW l~ haben, s. lieb. L~haber m -s,- lover; (Sammler) collector. L~habe-rei f -,-en hobby. l~kosen vt caress. L~kosung f -,-en caress. l~lich a lovely; (sanft) gentle; (süß) sweet. L~ling m -s,-e darling; (Bevorzugte) favourite. L~lings-pref favourite. l~los a loveless; (Eltern) uncaring; (unfreundlich) unkind □ adv unkindly; (ohne Sorgfalt) without care. L~schaft f -,-en [love] affair. l~ste(r,s) a dearest; (bevorzugt) favourite □ adv am l~sten best [of all]; jdn/etw am l~sten mögen like s.o./sth best [of all]; ich hätte am l~sten geweint I felt like crying. L~ste(r) m/f beloved; (Schatz) sweet-heart

Lied nt -[e]s,-er song

liederlich a slovenly; (unordentlich) untidy; (ausschweifend) dissolute. L~keit f - slovenliness; untidiness; dissoluteness

Lieferant m -en,-en supplier

lieferbar a (Comm) available. L~frist f sup-ply; (zustellen) deliver; (hervorbringen) yield. L~ung f -,-en delivery; (Sendung) consignment; (per Schiff) shipment. L~wagen m delivery van

Liege f -,-n couch. l~n† vi (haben) lie; (gelegen sein) be situated; l~n bleiben remain lying [there]; (im Bett) stay in bed;
⟨Ding:⟩ be left; ⟨Schnee:⟩ settle; ⟨Arbeit:⟩ remain undone; (zurückgelassen werden) be
left behind; (Panne haben) break down;
l~n lassen leave [lying there]; (zurücklassen) leave behind; (nicht fortführen)
leave undone; l~n an (+ dat) (fig) be due
to; (abhängen) depend on; jdm [nicht]
l~n [not] suit s.o.; (ansprechen) [not] appeal to s.o.; mir liegt viel/nicht daran it
is very/ not important to me. l~nblei-
ben† vi sep (sein) NEW l~n bleiben, s.
liegen. l~nlassen† vt sep NEW l~n
lassen, s. liegen. L~sitz m reclining seat.
L~stuhl m deck-chair. L~stütz m -es,-e
press-up, (Amer) push-up. L~wagen m
couchette car. L~wiese f lawn for sun-
bathing

Lift m -[e]s,-e & -s lift, (Amer) elevator

Liga f -,-gen league

Likör m -s,-e liqueur

lila inv a mauve; (dunkel) purple

Lilie /'li:li̯ə/ f -,-n lily

Liliputaner(in) m -s,- (f -,-nen) dwarf

Limo f -,-[s] (fam), L~nade f -,-n fizzy
drink, (Amer) soda; (Zitronen-) lemonade

Limousine /limu'zi:nə/ f -,-n saloon,
(Amer) sedan; (mit Trennscheibe) limousine

lind a mild; (sanft) gentle

Linde f -,-n lime tree

linder|n vt relieve, ease. L~ung f - relief

Line|al nt -s,-e ruler. l~ar a linear

Linguistik f - linguistics sg

Linie /-ji̯ə/ f -,-n line; (Zweig) branch;
(Bus-) route; L~ 4 number 4 [bus/tram];
in erster L~ primarily. L~nflug m
scheduled flight. L~nrichter m linesman

lin[i]iert a lined, ruled

Link|e f -n,-n left side; (Hand) left hand;
(Boxen) left; die L~e (Pol) the left; zu
meiner L~en on my left. l~e(r,s) a left;
(Pol) left-wing; l~e Seite left[-hand] side;
(von Stoff) wrong side; l~e Masche purl.
l~isch a awkward, adv -ly

links adv on the left; (bei Stoff) on the
wrong side; (verkehrt) inside out; von/
nach l~ from/to the left; l~ stricken
purl. L~händer(in) m -s,- (f -,-nen) left-
hander. l~händig a & adv left-handed.
L~verkehr m driving on the left

Linoleum /-leʊm/ nt -s lino, linoleum

Linse f -,-n lens; (Bot) lentil

Lippe f -,-n lip. L~nstift m lipstick

Liquid|ation /-'tsi̯o:n/ f -,-en
liquidation. l~ieren vt liquidate

lispeln vt/i (haben) lisp

List f -,-en trick, ruse; (Listigkeit) cunning

Liste f -,-n list

listig a cunning, adv -ly, crafty, adv -ily

Litanei f -,-en litany

Litauen nt -s Lithuania

Liter m & nt -s,- litre

liter|arisch a literary. L~atur f - litera-
ture

Litfaßsäule f advertising pillar

Liturgie f -,-n liturgy

Litze f -,-n braid; (Electr) flex

live /laif/ adv (Radio, TV) live

Lizenz f -,-en licence

Lkw /ɛlka've:/ m -[s],-s = Lastkraftwa-
gen

Lob nt -[e]s praise

Lobby /'lɔbi/ f - (Pol) lobby

loben vt praise. l~swert a praiseworthy,
laudable

löblich a praiseworthy

Lobrede f eulogy

Loch nt -[e]s,-̈er hole. l~en vt punch a
hole/holes in; punch ⟨Fahrkarte⟩. L~er
m -s,- punch

löcher|ig a full of holes. l~n vt (fam) pes-
ter

Locke f -,-n curl. l~n¹ vt curl; sich l~n
curl

locken² vt lure, entice; (reizen) tempt. l~d
a tempting

Lockenwickler m -s,- curler; (Rolle)
roller

locker a loose, adv -ly; ⟨Seil⟩ slack; ⟨Erde,
Kuchen⟩ light; (zwanglos) casual; (zu frei)
lax; (unmoralisch) loose. l~n vt loosen;
slacken ⟨Seil, Zügel⟩; break up ⟨Boden⟩; relax ⟨Griff⟩; sich l~n become loose; ⟨Seil:⟩
slacken; (sich entspannen) relax. L~ungs-
übungen fpl limbering-up exercises

lockig a curly

Lock|mittel nt bait. L~ung f -,-en lure;
(Versuchung) temptation. L~vogel m de-
coy

Loden m -s (Tex) loden

lodern vi (haben) blaze

Löffel m -s,- spoon; (L~ voll) spoonful.
l~n vt spoon up

Logarithmus m -,-men logarithm

Logbuch nt (Naut) log-book

Loge /'lo:ʒə/ f -,-n lodge; (Theat) box

Logierbesuch /lo'ʒi:ɐ̯-/ m house
guest/guests pl

Log|ik f - logic. l~isch a logical, adv -ly

Logo nt -s,-s logo

Lohn m -[e]s,-̈e wages pl, pay; (fig) reward.
L~empfänger m wage-earner. l~en vt/r
(haben) [sich] l~en be worth it or worth

while □ *vt* be worth; jdm etw l~en reward s.o. for sth. l~end *a* worthwhile; (*befriedigend*) rewarding. L~erhöhung *f* [pay] rise; (*Amer*) raise. L~steuer *f* income tax

Lok *f* -,-s (*fam*) = Lokomotive

Lokal *nt* -s,-e restaurant; (*Trink-*) bar. l~ *a* local. l~sieren *vt* locate; (*begrenzen*) localize

Lokomotiv|e *f* -,-n engine, locomotive. L~führer *m* engine driver

London *nt* -s London. L~er *a* London … □ *m* -s,- Londoner

Lorbeer *m* -s,-en laurel; echter L~ bay. L~blatt *nt* (*Culin*) bay-leaf

Lore *f* -,-n (*Rail*) truck

Los *nt* -es,-e lot; (*Lotterie-*) ticket; (*Schicksal*) fate; das große Los ziehen hit the jackpot

los *pred a* los sein be loose; jdn/etw los sein be rid of s.o./sth; was ist [mit ihm] los? what's the matter [with him]? □ *adv* los! go on! Achtung, fertig, los! ready, steady, go!

lösbar *a* soluble

losbinden† *vt sep* untie

Lösch|blatt *nt* sheet of blotting-paper. l~¹ *vt* put out, extinguish; quench (*Durst*); blot (*Tinte*); (*tilgen*) cancel; (*streichen*) delete; erase (*Aufnahme*)

löschen² *vt* (*Naut*) unload

Lösch|fahrzeug *nt* fire-engine. L~gerät *nt* fire extinguisher. L~papier *nt* blotting-paper

lose *a* loose, *adv* -ly

Lösegeld *nt* ransom

losen *vi* (*haben*) draw lots (um for)

lösen *vt* undo; (*lockern*) loosen; (*entfernen*) detach; (*klären*) solve; (*auflösen*) dissolve; cancel (*Vertrag*); break off (*Beziehung, Verlobung*); (*kaufen*) buy; sich l~ come off; (*sich trennen*) detach oneself/itself; (*lose werden*) come undone; (*sich entspannen*) relax; (*sich klären*) resolve itself; (*sich auflösen*) dissolve

los|fahren† *vi sep* (*sein*) start; (*Auto:*) drive off; l~fahren auf (+ *acc*) head for; (*fig: angreifen*) go for. l~gehen† *vi sep* (*sein*) set off; (*fam: anfangen*) start; (*fam: abgehen*) come off; (*Bombe, Gewehr:*) go off; l~gehen auf (+ *acc*) head for; (*fig: angreifen*) go for. l~kommen† *vi sep* (*sein*) get away (von from); l~kommen auf (+ *acc*) come towards you. l~lachen *vi sep* (*haben*) burst out laughing. l~lassen† *vt sep* let go of; (*freilassen*) release

löslich *a* soluble

los|lösen *vt sep* detach; sich l~lösen become detached; (*fig*) break away (von

from). l~machen *vt sep* detach; (*losbinden*) untie; sich l~machen free oneself/itself. l~platzen *vi sep* (*sein*) (*fam*) burst out laughing. l~reißen† *vt sep* tear off; sich l~reißen break free; (*fig*) tear oneself away. l~sagen (*sich*) *vr* renounce (von etw sth). l~schicken *vt sep* send off. l~sprechen† *vt sep* absolve (von from). l~steuern *vi sep* (*sein*) head (auf + *acc* for)

Losung *f* -,-en (*Pol*) slogan; (*Mil*) password

Lösung *f* -,-en solution. L~smittel *nt* solvent

los|werden† *vt sep* get rid of. l~ziehen† *vi sep* (*sein*) set off; l~ziehen gegen *od* über (+ *acc*) (*beschimpfen*) run down

Lot *nt* -[e]s,-e perpendicular; (*Blei-*) plumb[-bob]; im Lot sein (*fig*) be all right. l~en *vt* plumb

löt|en *vt* solder. L~lampe *f* blow-lamp, (*Amer*) blowtorch. L~metall *nt* solder

lotrecht *a* perpendicular, *adv* -ly

Lotse *m* -n,-n (*Naut*) pilot. l~n *vt* (*Naut*) pilot; (*fig*) guide

Lotterie *f* -,-n lottery

Lotto *nt* -s,-s lotto; (*Lotterie*) lottery

Löw|e *m* -n,-n lion; (*Astr*) Leo. L~enanteil *m* (*fig*) lion's share. L~enzahn *m* (*Bot*) dandelion. L~in *f* -,-nen lioness

loyal /loa'ja:l/ *a* loyal. L~ität *f* - loyalty

Luchs *m* -es,-e lynx

Lücke *f* -,-n gap. L~nbüßer *m* -s,- stopgap. l~nhaft *a* incomplete; (*Wissen*) patchy. l~nlos *a* complete; (*Folge*) unbroken

Luder *nt* -s,- (*sl*) (*Frau*) bitch; armes L~ poor wretch

Luft *f* -,÷e air; tief L~ holen take a deep breath; in die L~ gehen explode. L~angriff *m* air raid. L~aufnahme *f* aerial photograph. L~ballon *m* balloon. L~bild *nt* aerial photograph. L~blase *f* air bubble

Lüftchen *nt* -s,- breeze

luft|dicht *a* airtight. L~druck *m* atmospheric pressure

lüften *vt* air; raise (*Hut*); reveal (*Geheimnis*)

Luft|fahrt *f* aviation. L~fahrtgesellschaft *f* airline. L~gewehr *nt* airgun. L~hauch *m* breath of air. L~ig *a* airy; (*Kleid*) light. L~kissenfahrzeug *nt* hovercraft. L~krieg *m* aerial warfare. L~kurort *m* climatic health resort. L~leere *f* vacuum. L~linie *f* 100 km L~linie 100 km as the crow flies. L~loch *nt* air-hole; (*Aviat*) air pocket. L~matratze *f* air-bed, inflatable mattress. L~pirat *m* [aircraft] hijacker. L~post *f* airmail. L~pumpe *f* air pump;

(Fahrrad-) bicycle-pump. L~röhre *f* windpipe. L~schiff *nt* airship. L~schlange *f* [paper] streamer. L~schlösser *ntpl* castles in the air. L~schutzbunker *m* air-raid shelter

Lüftung *f* - ventilation

Luft|veränderung *f* change of air. L~waffe *f* air force. L~weg *m* auf dem L~weg by air. L~zug *m* draught

Lüg|e *f* -,-n lie. l~en† *vt/i (haben)* lie. L~ner(in) *m* -s,- *(f* -,-nen) liar. l~nerisch *a* untrue; *(Person)* untruthful

Luke *f* -,-n hatch; *(Dach-)* skylight

Lümmel *m* -s,- lout; *(fam: Schelm)* rascal. l~n *(sich) vr* loll

Lump *m* -en,-en scoundrel. L~en *m* -s,- rag; in L~en in rags. l~en *vt* sich nicht l~en lassen be generous. L~engesindel, L~enpack *nt* riff-raff. L~ensammler *m* rag-and-bone man. l~ig *a* mean, shabby; *(gering)* measley

Lunchpacket /'lan[t]ʃ-/ *nt* packed lunch

Lunge *f* -,-n lungs *pl*; *(L~nflügel)* lung. L~nentzündung *f* pneumonia

lungern *vi (haben)* loiter

Lunte *f* L~ riechen *(fam)* smell a rat

Lupe *f* -,-n magnifying glass

Lurch *m* -[e]s,-e amphibian

Lust *f* -,-̈e pleasure; *(Verlangen)* desire; *(sinnliche Begierde)* lust; L~ haben feel like *(auf etw acc* sth); ich habe keine L~ I don't feel like it; *(will nicht)* I don't want to

Lüster *m* -s,- lustre; *(Kronleuchter)* chandelier

lüstern *a* greedy *(auf + acc* for); *(sinnlich)* lascivious; *(geil)* lecherous

lustig *a* jolly; *(komisch)* funny; sich l~ machen über *(+ acc)* make fun of

Lüstling *m* -s,-e lecher

lust|los *a* listless, *adv* -ly. L~mörder *m* sex killer. L~spiel *nt* comedy

lutherisch *a* Lutheran

lutsch|en *vt/i (haben)* suck. L~er *m* -s,- lollipop; *(Schnuller)* dummy, *(Amer)* pacifier

lütt *a (NGer)* little

Lüttich *nt* -s Liège

Luv *f & nt* - nach Luv *(Naut)* to windward

luxuriös *a* luxurious, *adv* -ly

Luxus *m* - luxury. L~artikel *m* luxury article. L~ausgabe *f* de luxe edition. L~hotel *nt* luxury hotel

Lymph|drüse /'lymf-/ *f*, L~knoten *m* lymph gland

lynchen /'lynçən/ *vt* lynch

Lyr|ik *f* - lyric poetry. L~iker *m* -s,- lyric poet. l~isch *a* lyrical; *(Dichtung)* lyric

M

Mach|art *f* style. m~bar *a* feasible. m~en *vt* make; get *(Mahlzeit)*; take *(Foto)*; *(ausführen, tun, in Ordnung bringen)* do; *(Math: ergeben)* be; *(kosten)* come to; sich *(dat)* etw m~en lassen have sth made; was m~st du da? what are you doing? was m~t die Arbeit? how is work? das m~t 6 Mark [zusammen] that's 6 marks [altogether]; das m~t nichts it doesn't matter; sich *(dat)* wenig/nichts m~en aus care little/ nothing for □ *vr* sich m~en do well; sich an die Arbeit m~en get down to work □ *vi (haben)* m~en *(fam)* wet the bed; schnell m~en hurry. M~enschaften *fpl* machinations

Macht *f* -,-̈e power; mit aller M~ with all one's might. M~haber *m* -s,- ruler

mächtig *a* powerful; *(groß)* enormous □ *adv (fam)* terribly

macht|los *a* powerless. M~wort *nt* ein M~wort sprechen put one's foot down

Mädchen *nt* -s,- girl; *(Dienst-)* maid. m~haft *a* girlish. M~name *m* girl's name; *(vor der Ehe)* maiden name

Made *f* -,-n maggot

Mädel *nt* -s,- girl

madig *a* maggoty; jdn m~ machen *(fam)* run s.o. down

Madonna *f* -,-nen madonna

Magazin *nt* -s,-e magazine; *(Lager)* warehouse; *(Raum)* store-room

Magd *f* -,-̈e maid

Magen *m* -s,-̈ stomach. M~schmerzen *mpl* stomachache *sg.* M~verstimmung *f* stomach upset

mager *a* thin; *(Fleisch)* lean; *(Boden)* poor; *(dürftig)* meagre. M~keit *f* - thinness; leanness. M~sucht *f* anorexia

Magie *f* - magic

Mag|ier /'ma:giə/ *m* -s,- magician. m~isch *a* magic; *(geheimnisvoll)* magical

Magistrat *m* -s,-e city council

Magnesia *f* - magnesia

Magnet *m* -en & -[e]s,-e magnet. m~isch *a* magnetic. m~isieren *vt* magnetize. M~ismus *m* - magnetism

Mahagoni *nt* -s mahogany

Mäh|drescher *m* -s,- combine harvester. m~en *vt/i (haben)* mow

Mahl *nt* -[e]s,-̈er & -e meal

mahlen† *vt* grind

Mahlzeit *f* meal; M~! enjoy your meal!

Mähne *f* -,-n mane

mahn|en vt/i (haben) remind (wegen about); (ermahnen) admonish; (auffordern) urge (zu to); zur Vorsicht/Eile m~en urge caution/haste. M~ung f -,-en reminder; admonition; (Aufforderung) exhortation

Mai m -[e]s,-e May; der Erste Mai May Day. M~glöckchen nt -s,- lily of the valley. M~käfer m cockchafer

Mailand nt -s Milan

Mais m -es maize, (Amer) corn; (Culin) sweet corn. M~kolben m corn-cob

Majestät f -,-en majesty. m~isch a majestic, adv -ally

Major m -s,-e major

Majoran m -s marjoram

Majorität f -,-en majority

makaber a macabre

Makel m -s,- blemish; (Defekt) flaw; (fig) stain. m~los a flawless; (fig) unblemished

mäkeln vi (haben) grumble

Makkaroni pl macaroni sg

Makler m -s,- (Comm) broker

Makrele f -,-n mackerel

Makrone f -,-n macaroon

mal adv (Math) times; (bei Maßen) by; (fam: einmal) once; (eines Tages) one day; schon mal once before; (jemals) ever; nicht mal not even; hört/seht mal! listen!/look!

Mal¹ nt -[e]s,-e time; das erste/zweite/letzte/nächste Mal the first/second/last/next time; zum ersten/letzten Mal for the first/last time; mit einem Mal all at once; ein für alle Mal once and for all; jedes Mal every time; jedes Mal, wenn whenever; einige/mehrere Mal a few/several times

Mal² nt -[e]s,-e mark; (auf der Haut) mole; (Mutter-) birthmark

Mal|buch nt colouring book. m~en vt/i (haben) paint. M~er m -s,- painter. M~erei f -,-en painting. M~erin f -,-en painter. m~erisch a picturesque

Malheur /ma'løː(ɐ)/ nt -s,-e & -s (fam) mishap; (Ärger) trouble

Mallorca /ma'lɔrka, -'jɔrka/ nt -s Majorca

malnehmen† vt sep multiply (mit by)

Malz nt -es malt. M~bier nt malt beer

Mama /'mama, ma'ma:/ f -s,-s mummy

Mammut nt -s,-e & -s mammoth

mampfen vt (fam) munch

man pron one, you; (die Leute) people, they; man sagt they say, it is said

Manager /'mɛnidʒɐ/ m -s,- manager

manch inv pron m~ ein(er) many a; m~ einer/eine many a man/woman. m~e(r,s) pron many a; [so] m~es Mal

many a time; m~e Leute some people □ (substantivisch) m~er/m~e many a man/woman; m~e pl some; (Leute) some people; (viele) many [people]; m~es some things; (vieles) many things m~erlei inv a various □ pron various things

manchmal adv sometimes

Mandant(in) m -en,-en (f -,-nen) (Jur) client

Mandarine f -,-n mandarin

Mandat nt -[e]s,-e mandate; (Jur) brief; (Pol) seat

Mandel f -,-n almond; (Anat) tonsil. M~entzündung f tonsillitis

Manege /ma'neːʒə/ f -,-n ring; (Reit-) arena

Mangel¹ m -s,- lack; (Knappheit) shortage; (Med) deficiency; (Fehler) defect; M~ leiden go short

Mangel² f -,-n mangle

mangel|haft a faulty, defective; (Sch) unsatisfactory. m~n¹ vi (haben) es m~t an (+ dat) there is a lack/(Knappheit) shortage of

mangeln² vt put through the mangle

mangels prep (+ gen) for lack of

Mango f -,-s mango

Manie f -,-n mania; (Sucht) obsession

Manier f -,-en manner; M~en manners. m~lich a well-mannered □ adv properly

Manifest nt -[e]s,-e manifesto. m~ieren (sich) vr manifest itself

Maniküre f -,-n manicure; (Person) manicurist. m~n vt manicure

Manipul|ation /-'tsjoːn/ f -,-en manipulation. m~ieren vt manipulate

Manko nt -s,-s disadvantage; (Fehlbetrag) deficit

Mann m -[e]s,-er man; (Ehe-) husband

Männchen nt -s,- little man; (Zool) male; M~ machen (Hund:) sit up

Mannequin /'manəkɛ̃/ nt -s,-s model

Männerchor m male voice choir

Mannes|alter nt manhood. M~kraft f virility

mannhaft a manful, adv -ly

mannigfaltig a manifold; (verschieden) diverse

männlich a male; (Gram & fig) masculine; (mannhaft) manly; (Frau) mannish. M~keit f -masculinity; (fig) manhood

Mannschaft f -,-en team; (Naut) crew. M~sgeist m team spirit

Manöv|er nt -s,- manœuvre; (Winkelzug) trick. m~rieren vt/i (haben) manœuvre

Mansarde f -,-n attic room; (Wohnung) attic flat

Manschette f -,-n cuff; (*Blumentopf-*) paper frill. M~nknopf m cuff-link

Mantel m -s,: coat; (*dick*) overcoat; (*Reifen-*) outer tyre

Manuskript nt -[e]s,-e manuscript

Mappe f -,-n folder; (*Akten-*) briefcase; (*Schul-*) bag

Marathon m -s,-s marathon

Märchen nt -s,- fairy-tale. m~haft a fairy-tale …; (*phantastisch*) fabulous

Margarine f - margarine

Marienkäfer /ma'ri:ən-/ m lady-bird, (*Amer*) ladybug

Marihuana nt -s marijuana

Marille f -,-n (*Aust*) apricot

Marine f marine; (*Kriegs-*) navy. m~blau a navy [blue]. M~infanterist m marine

marinieren vt marinade

Marionette f -,-n puppet, marionette

Mark¹ f -,- mark; drei M~ three marks

Mark² nt -[e]s (*Knochen-*) marrow; (*Bot*) pith; (*Frucht-*) pulp; bis ins M~ getroffen (*fig*) cut to the quick

markant a striking

Marke f -,-n token; (*rund*) disc; (*Erkennungs-*) tag; (*Brief-*) stamp; (*Lebensmittel-*) coupon; (*Spiel-*) counter; (*Markierung*) mark; (*Fabrikat*) make; (*Tabak-*) brand. M~nartikel m branded article

markier|en vt mark; (*fam: vortäuschen*) fake. M~ung f -,-en marking

Markise f -,-n awning

Markstück nt one-mark piece

Markt m -[e]s,:e market; (*M~platz*) market-place. M~forschung f market research. M~platz m market-place

Marmelade f -,-n jam; (*Orangen-*) marmalade

Marmor m -s marble

Marokko nt -s Morocco

Marone f -,-n [sweet] chestnut

Marotte f -,-n whim

Marsch¹ f -,-en marsh

Marsch² m -[e]s,:e march. m~ int (*Mil*) march! m~ ins Bett! off to bed!

Marschall m -s,:e marshal

marschieren vi (*sein*) march

Marter f -,-n torture. m~n vt torture

Martinshorn nt [police] siren

Märtyrer(in) m -s,- (f -,-nen) martyr

Martyrium nt -s martyrdom

Mar|xismus m - Marxism. m~xistisch a Marxist

März m -,-e March

Marzipan nt -s marzipan

Masche f -,-n stitch; (*im Netz*) mesh; (*fam: Trick*) dodge. M~ndraht m wire netting

Maschin|e f -,-n machine; (*Flugzeug*) plane; (*Schreib-*) typewriter; M~e schreiben type. m~egeschrieben a typewritten, typed. m~ell a machine … □ adv by machine. M~enbau m mechanical engineering. M~engewehr nt machine-gun. M~enpistole f submachine-gun. M~erie f - machinery. M~eschreiben nt typing. M~ist m -en,-en machinist; (*Naut*) engineer

Masern pl measles sg

Maserung f -,-en [wood] grain

Maske f -,-n mask; (*Theat*) make-up. M~rade f -,-n disguise; (*fig: Heuchelei*) masquerade

maskieren vt mask; sich m~ dress up (als as)

Maskottchen nt -s,- mascot

maskulin a masculine

Maskulinum nt -s,-na (*Gram*) masculine

Masochis|mus /mazo'xɪsmus/ m - masochism. M~t m -en,-en masochist

Maß¹ nt -es,-e measure; (*Abmessung*) measurement; (*Grad*) degree; (*Mäßigung*) moderation; Maß halten exercise moderation; in od mit Maß[en] in moderation; in hohem Maße to a high degree

Maß² f -,- (*SGer*) litre [of beer]

Massage /ma'sa:ʒə/ f -,-n massage

Massaker nt -s,- massacre

Maß|anzug m made-to-measure suit. M~band nt (pl -bänder) tape-measure

Masse f -,-n mass; (*Culin*) mixture; (*Menschen-*) crowd; eine M~ Arbeit (*fam*) masses of work. M~nartikel m mass-produced article. m~nhaft adv in huge quantities. M~nmedien pl mass media. M~nproduktion f mass production. m~nweise adv in huge numbers

Masseu|r /ma'sø:ɐ̯/ m -s,-e masseur. M~rin f -,-nen, M~se /-'sø:zə/ f -,-n masseuse

maß|gebend a authoritative; (*einflussreich*) influential. m~geblich a decisive, adv -ly. m~geschneidert a made-to-measure. m~halten† vi sep (*haben*) (NEW) Maß halten, s. Maß¹

massieren¹ vt massage

massieren² (sich) vr mass

massig a massive

mäßig a moderate, adv -ly; (*mittelmäßig*) indifferent. m~en vt moderate; sich m~en moderate; (*sich beherrschen*) restrain oneself. M~keit f - moderation. M~ung f - moderation

massiv a solid; (*stark*) heavy

Maß|krug *m* beer mug. m∼los *a* excessive; (*grenzenlos*) boundless; (*äußerst*) extreme, *adv* -ly. M∼nahme *f* -,-n measure. m∼regeln *nt* reprimand

Maßstab *m* scale; (*Norm & fig*) standard. m∼sgerecht, m∼sgetreu *a* scale ... □ *adv* to scale

maßvoll *a* moderate

Mast[1] *m* -[e]s,-en pole; (*Überland-*) pylon; (*Naut*) mast

Mast[2] *f* - fattening. M∼darm *m* rectum

mästen *vt* fatten

Masturb|ation /-'tsjo:n/ *f* - masturbation. m∼ieren *vi* (*haben*) masturbate

Material *nt* -s,-ien /-jən/ material; (*coll*) materials *pl*. M∼ismus *m* - materialism. m∼istisch *a* materialistic

Mater|ie /ma'te:rjə/ *f*-,-n matter; (*Thema*) subject. m∼iell *a* material

Mathe *f* - (*fam*) maths *sg*

Mathe|matik *f* - mathematics *sg*. M∼matiker *m* -s,- mathematician. m∼matisch *a* mathematical

Matinee *f* -,-n (*Theat*) morning performance

Matratze *f* -,-n mattress

Mätresse *f* -,-n mistress

Matrose *m* -n,-n sailor

Matsch *m* -[e]s mud; (*Schnee-*) slush. m∼ig *a* muddy; slushy; (*weich*) mushy

matt *a* weak; (*gedämpft*) dim; (*glanzlos*) dull; (*Politur, Farbe*) matt; jdn m∼ setzen checkmate s.o. M∼ *nt* -s (*Schach*) mate

Matte *f* -,-n mat

Mattglas *nt* frosted glass

Matt|igkeit *f* - weakness; (*Müdigkeit*) weariness. M∼scheibe *f* (*fam*) television screen

Matura *f* - (*Aust*) ≈ A levels *pl*

Mauer *f* -,-n wall. m∼n *vt* build □ *vi* (*haben*) lay bricks. M∼werk *nt* masonry

Maul *nt* -[e]s, Mäuler (*Zool*) mouth; halt's M∼! (*fam*) shut up! m∼en *vi* (*haben*) (*fam*) grumble. M∼korb *m* muzzle. M∼tier *nt* mule. M∼wurf *m* mole. M∼wurfshaufen, M∼wurfshügel *m* molehill

Maurer *m* -s,- bricklayer

Maus *f* -,Mäuse mouse. M∼efalle *f* mousetrap

mausern (sich) *vr* moult; (*fam*) turn (zu into)

Maut *f* -,-en (*Aust*) toll. M∼straße *f* toll road

maximal *a* maximum

Maximum *nt* -s,-ma maximum

Mayonnaise /majo'nɛ:zə/ *f* -,-n mayonnaise

Mäzen *m* -s,-e patron

Mechan|ik /me'ça:nɪk/ *f* - mechanics *sg*; (*Mechanismus*) mechanism. M∼iker *m* -s,- mechanic. m∼isch *a* mechanical, *adv* -ly. m∼isieren *vt* mechanize. M∼ismus *m* -,-men mechanism

meckern *vi* (*haben*) bleat; (*fam: nörgeln*) grumble

Medaill|e /me'daljə/ *f* -,-n medal. M∼on /-'jõ:/ *nt* -s,-s medallion; (*Schmuck*) locket

Medikament *nt* -[e]s,-e medicine

Medit|ation /-'tsjo:n/ *f* -,-en meditation. m∼ieren *vi* (*haben*) meditate

Medium *nt* -s,-ien medium; die Medien the media

Medizin *f* -,-en medicine. M∼er *m* -s,- doctor; (*Student*) medical student. m∼isch *a* medical; (*heilkräftig*) medicinal

Meer *nt* -[e]s,-e sea. M∼busen *m* gulf. M∼enge *f* strait. M∼esspiegel *m* sea-level. M∼jungfrau *f* mermaid. M∼rettich *m* horseradish. M∼schweinchen *nt* -s,- guinea-pig

Megaphon, Megafon *nt* -s,-e megaphone

Mehl *nt* -[e]s flour. m∼ig *a* floury. M∼schwitze *f* (*Culin*) roux. M∼speise *f* (*Aust*) dessert; (*Kuchen*) pastry. M∼tau *m* (*Bot*) mildew

mehr *pron & adv* more; nicht m∼ no more; (*zeitlich*) no longer; nichts m∼ no more; (*nichts weiter*) nothing else; nie m∼ never again. m∼deutig *a* ambiguous. m∼en *vt* increase; sich m∼en increase. m∼ere *pron* several. m∼eremal *adv* (NEW) m∼ere Mal, s. Mal[1]. m∼eres *pron* several things *pl*. m∼fach *a* multiple; (*mehrmalig*) repeated □ *adv* several times. M∼fahrtenkarte *f* book of tickets. m∼farbig *a* [multi]coloured. M∼heit *f* -,-en majority. m∼malig *a* repeated. m∼mals *adv* several times. m∼sprachig *a* multilingual. m∼stimmig *a* (*Mus*) for several voices □ *adv* m∼stimmig singen sing in harmony. M∼wertsteuer *f* value-added tax, VAT. M∼zahl *f* majority; (*Gram*) plural. M∼zweck- *pref* multi-purpose

meiden† *vt* avoid, shun

Meierei *f* -,-en (*dial*) dairy

Meile *f* -,-n mile. M∼nstein *m* milestone. m∼nweit *adv* [for] miles

mein *poss pron* my. m∼e(r,s) *poss pron* mine; die M∼en *od* m∼en *pl* my family *sg*

Meineid *m* perjury, einen M∼ leisten perjure oneself

meinen *vt* mean; (*glauben*) think; (*sagen*) say; gut gemeinter Rat wel-meant advice; es gut m∼ mean well

mein|erseits *adv* for my part.
m~etwegen*adv* for my sake; (*wegen mir*)
because of me, on my account; (*fam: von
mir aus*) as far as I'm concerned. m~et-
willen*adv* um m~etwillen for my sake.
m~ige *poss pron* der/die/das m~ige
mine. m~s *poss pron* mine

Meinung *f* -,-en opinion; jdm die M~
sagen give s.o. a piece of one's mind.
M~sumfrage *f* opinion poll

Meise *f* -,-n (*Zool*) tit

Meißel *m* -s,- chisel. m~n *vt/i* (*haben*)
chisel

meist *adv* mostly; (*gewöhnlich*) usually.
m~e *a* der/die/das m~e most; die
m~en Leute most people; die m~e Zeit
most of the time; am m~en [the] most
□ *pron* das m~e most [of it]; die m~en
most. m~ens *adv* mostly; (*gewöhnlich*)
usually

Meister *m* -s,- master craftsman; (*Könner*)
master; (*Sport*) champion. m~haft *a* masterly □ *adv* in masterly fashion. m~n *vt*
master. M~schaft *f* -,-en mastery;
(*Sport*) championship. M~stück,
M~werk *nt* masterpiece

Melanch|olie /melaŋko'li:/ *f* - melan-
choly. m~olisch *a* melancholy

meld|en *vt* report; (*anmelden*) register;
(*ankündigen*) announce; sich m~en report (bei to); (*zum Militär*) enlist;
(*freiwillig*) volunteer; (*Teleph*) answer;
(*Sch*) put up one's hand; (*von sich hören
lassen*) get in touch (bei with); sich krank
m~en (NEW) sich krankmelden. M~ung
f -,-en report; (*Anmeldung*) registration

meliert *a* mottled; grau m~es Haar hair
flecked with grey

melken† *vt* milk

Melod|ie *f* -,-n tune, melody. m~iös *a*
melodious

melodisch *a* melodic; (*melodiös*) melodious, tuneful

melodramatisch *a* melodramatic, *adv*
-ally

Melone *f* -,-n melon; [schwarze] M~
(*fam*) bowler [hat]

Membran *f* -,-en membrane

Memoiren /me'mŋaːrən/ *pl* memoirs

Menge *f* -,-n amount, quantity; (*Menschen*) crowd; (*Math*) set; eine M~ Geld
a lot of money. m~n *vt* mix

Mensa *f* -,-sen (*Univ*) refectory

Mensch *m* -en,-en human being; der M~
man; die M~en people; jeder/kein M~
everybody/nobody. M~enaffe *m* ape.
M~enfeind *m* misanthropist. M~en-
feindlich *a* antisocial. M~enfresser *m*
-s,-cannibal; (*Zool*) man-eater; (*fam*) ogre.
m~enfreundlich *a* philanthropic.

M~enleben *nt* human life; (*Lebenszeit*)
lifetime. m~enleer *a* deserted. M~en-
menge *f* crowd. M~enraub *m* kidnap-
ping. M~enrechte *ntpl* human rights.
m~enscheu *a* unsociable. M~enskind
int (*fam*) good heavens! M~enverstand
m gesunder M~enverstand common
sense. m~enwürdig *a* humane, *adv* -ly.
M~heit *f* - die M~heit mankind, humanity. m~lich *a* human; (*human*) humane, *adv* -ly. M~lichkeit *f* - humanity

Menstru|ation /-'tsjoːn/ *f* - menstru-
ation. m~ieren *vi* (*haben*) menstruate

Mentalität *f* -,-en mentality

Menü *nt* -s,-s menu; (*festes M~*) set meal

Menuett *nt* -[e]s,-e minuet

Meridian *m* -s,-e meridian

merk|bar *a* noticeable. M~blatt *nt* [ex-
planatory] leaflet. m~en *vt* notice; sich
(*dat*) etw m~en remember sth. m~lich
a noticeable, *adv* -bly. M~mal *nt* feature

merkwürdig *a* odd, *adv* -ly, strange, *adv*
-ly. m~erweise *adv* oddly enough

meß|bar (meßbar) *a* measurable.
M~becher *m* (*Culin*) measure

Messe¹ *f* -,-n (*Relig*) mass; (*Comm*) [trade]
fair

Messe² *f* -,-n (*Mil*) mess

messen *vt/i* (*haben*) measure; (*ansehen*)
look at; [bei jdm] Fieber m~ take s.o.'s
temperature; sich m~ compete (mit
with); sich mit jdm m~/nicht m~
können be a/no match for s.o.

Messer *nt* -s,- knife

Messias *m* - Messiah

Messing *nt* -s brass

Messung *f* -,-en measurement

Metabolismus *m* - metabolism

Metall *nt* -s,-e metal. m~en *a* metal;
(*metallisch*) metallic. m~isch *a* metallic

Metallurgie *f* - metallurgy

Metamorphose *f* -,-n metamorphosis

Metaph|er *f* -,-n metaphor. m~orisch *a*
metaphorical, *adv* -ly

Meteor *m* -s,-e meteor. M~ologe *m* -n,-n
meteorologist. M~ologie *f* -meteorology.
m~ologisch *a* meteorological

Meter *m & nt* -s,- metre, (*Amer*) meter.
M~maß *nt* tape-measure

Method|e *f* -,-n method. m~isch *a* meth-
odical

metrisch *a* metric

Metropole *f* -,-n metropolis

metzeln *vt* (*fig*) massacre

Metzger *m* -s,- butcher. M~ei *f* -,-en butcher's shop

Meute *f* -,-n pack [of hounds]; (*fig: Menge*)
mob

Meuterei f -,-en mutiny

meutern vi (haben) mutiny; (fam: schimpfen) grumble

Mexikan|er(in) m -s,- (f -,-nen) Mexican. m~isch a Mexican

Mexiko nt -s Mexico

miauen vi (haben) mew, miaow

mich pron (acc of ich) me; (refl) myself

Mieder nt -s,- bodice; (Korsett) corset

Miene f -,-n expression; M~ machen make as if (zu to)

mies a (fam) lousy; mir ist m~ I feel rotten

Miet|e f -,-n rent; (Mietgebühr) hire charge; zur M~e wohnen live in rented accommodation. m~en vt rent (Haus, Zimmer); hire (Auto, Boot, Fernseher). M~er(in) m -s,- (f -,-nen) tenant. m~frei a & adv rent-free. M~shaus nt block of rented flats. M~vertrag m lease. M~wagen m hire-car. M~wohnung f rented flat; (zu vermieten) flat to let

Mieze f -,-n (fam) puss[y]

Migräne f -,-n migraine

Mikrobe f -,-n microbe

Mikro|chip m microchip. M~computer m microcomputer. M~film m microfilm

Mikro|fon, M~phon nt -s,-e microphone. M~prozessor m -s,-en /-'so:rən/ microprocessor. M~skop nt -s,-e microscope. m~skopisch a microscopic

Mikrowelle f microwave. M~ngerät nt, M~nherd m microwave oven

Milbe f -,-n mite

Milch f - milk. M~bar f milk bar. M~geschäft nt dairy. M~glas nt opal glass. m~ig a milky. M~kuh f dairy cow. M~mann m (pl -männer) milkman. M~mixgetränk nt milk shake. M~straße f Milky Way. M~zahn m milk tooth

mild a mild; (nachsichtig) lenient; m~e Gaben alms. M~e f - mildness; leniency. m~ern vt make milder; (mäßigen) moderate; (lindern) alleviate, ease; sich m~ern become milder; (sich mäßigen) moderate; (nachlassen) abate; (Schmerz:) ease; m~ernde Umstände mitigating circumstances. m~tätig a charitable

Milieu /mi'ljø:/ nt -s,-s [social] environment

militant a militant

Militär nt -s army; (Soldaten) troops pl; beim M~ in the army. m~isch a military

Miliz f -,-en militia

Milliarde /mr'ljardə/ f -,-n thousand million, billion

Milli|gramm nt milligram. M~meter m & nt millimetre. M~meterpapier nt graph paper

Million /mr'ljo:n/ f -,-en million. M~är m -s,-e millionaire. M~ärin f -,-nen millionairess

Milz f (Anat) spleen

mim|en vt (fam: vortäuschen) act. M~ik f- [expressive] gestures and facial expressions pl

Mimose f -,-n mimosa

minder a lesser ☐ adv less; mehr oder m~ more or less. M~heit f -,-en minority

minderjährig a (Jur) under-age; m~ sein be under age. M~e(r) m/f (Jur) minor. M~keit f- (Jur) minority

minder|n vt diminish; decrease (Tempo). M~ung f- decrease

minderwertig a inferior. M~keit f- inferiority. M~keitskomplex m inferiority complex

Mindest- pref minimum. m~e a & pron der/die/das M~e od m~e the least; zum M~en od m~en at least; nicht im M~en od m~en not in the least. M~ens adv at least. M~lohn m minimum wage. M~maß nt minimum

Mine f -,-n mine; (Bleistift-) lead; (Kugelschreiber-) refill. M~nfeld nt minefield. M~nräumboot nt minesweeper

Mineral nt -s,-e & -ien /-jən/ mineral. m~isch a mineral. M~ogie f - mineralogy. M~wasser nt mineral water

Miniatur f -,-en miniature

Minigolf nt miniature golf

minimal a minimal

Minimum nt -s,-ma minimum

Minirock m miniskirt

Mini|ster m -s,- minister. m~steriell a ministerial. M~sterium nt -s,-ien ministry

Minorität f -,-en minority

minus conj, adv & prep (+ gen) minus. M~ nt - deficit; (Nachteil) disadvantage. M~zeichen nt minus [sign]

Minute f -,-n minute

mir pron (dat of ich) [to] me; (refl) myself; mir nichts, dir nichts without so much as a 'by your leave'

Misch|ehe f mixed marriage. m~en vt mix; blend (Tee, Kaffee); toss (Salat); shuffle (Karten); sich m~en mix; (Person:) mingle (unter + acc with); sich m~en in (+ acc) join in (Gespräch); meddle in (Angelegenheit) ☐ vi (haben) shuffle the cards. M~ling m -s,-e halfcaste; (Hund) cross. M~masch m -[e]s,-e (fam) hotchpotch. M~ung f -,-en mixture; blend

miserabel a abominable; (erbärmlich) wretched

missachten (miß achten) *vt* disregard

Miss|achtung (Miß|achtung) *f* disregard. **M∼behagen** *nt* [feeling of] unease. **M∼bildung** *f* deformity

missbilligen (mißbilligen) *vt* disapprove of

Miss|billigung (Miß|billigung) *f* disapproval. **M∼brauch** *m* abuse; **M∼brauch** treiben mit abuse

miss|brauchen (miß|brauchen) *vt* abuse; ⟨*vergewaltigen*⟩ rape. **m∼deuten** *vt* misinterpret

missen *vt* do without; ich möchte es nicht **m∼** I should not like to be without it

Miss|erfolg (Miß|erfolg) *m* failure. **M∼ernte** *f* crop failure

Misse|tat *f* misdeed. **M∼täter** *m* ⟨*fam*⟩ culprit

missfallen† (mißfallen†) *vi* (haben) displease; ⟨jdm s.o.⟩

Miss|fallen (Miß|fallen) *nt* -s displeasure; ⟨*Missbilligung*⟩ disapproval. **m∼gebildet** *a* deformed. **M∼geburt** *f* freak; ⟨*fig*⟩ monstrosity. **M∼geschick** *nt* mishap; ⟨*Unglück*⟩ misfortune. **m∼gestimmt** *a* **m∼gestimmt** sein be in a bad mood

miss|glücken (miß|glücken) *vi* (sein) fail. **m∼gönnen** *vt* begrudge

Miss|griff (Miß|griff) *m* mistake. **M∼gunst** *f* resentment. **m∼günstig** *a* resentful

misshandeln (mißhandeln) *vt* ill-treat

Miss|handlung (Miß|handlung) *f* ill-treatment. **M∼helligkeit** *f* -,-en disagreement

Mission *f* -,-en mission

Missionar(in) *m* -s,-e (*f* -,-nen) missionary

Miss|klang (Miß|klang) *m* discord. **M∼kredit** *m* discredit; in **M∼kredit** bringen discredit. **m∼lich** *a* awkward. **m∼liebig** *a* unpopular

misslingen† (mißlingen†) *vi* (sein) fail; es misslang ihr she failed. **M∼** *nt* -s failure

Missmut (Mißmut) *m* ill humour. **m∼ig** *a* morose, *adv* -ly

missraten† (mißraten†) *vi* (sein) turn out badly

Miss|stand (Miß|stand) *m* abuse; ⟨*Zustand*⟩ undesirable state of affairs. **M∼stimmung** *f* discord; ⟨*Laune*⟩ bad mood. **M∼ton** *m* discordant note

misstrauen (mißtrauen) *vi* (haben) jdm/etw **m∼** mistrust s.o./sth; ⟨*Argwohn hegen*⟩ distrust s.o./sth

Misstrau|en (Mißtrau|en) *nt* -s mistrust; ⟨*Argwohn*⟩ distrust. **M∼ensvotum** *nt*

vote of no confidence. **m∼isch** *a* distrustful; ⟨*argwöhnisch*⟩ suspicious

Miss|verhältnis (Miß|verhältnis) *nt* disproportion. **M∼verständnis** *nt* misunderstanding. **m∼verstehen†** *vt* misunderstand. **M∼wirtschaft** *f* mismanagement

Mist *m* -[e]s manure; ⟨*fam*⟩ rubbish

Mistel *f* -,-n mistletoe

Misthaufen *m* dungheap

mit *prep* (+ *dat*) with; ⟨*sprechen*⟩ to; ⟨*mittels*⟩ by; ⟨*inklusive*⟩ including; ⟨*bei*⟩ at; mit Bleistift in pencil; mit lauter Stimme in a loud voice; mit drei Jahren at the age of three □ *adv* ⟨*auch*⟩ as well; mit anfassen ⟨*fig*⟩ lend a hand; es ist mit das ärmste Land der Welt it is among the poorest countries in the world

Mitarbeit *f* collaboration. **m∼en** *vi sep* collaborate (an + *dat* on). **M∼er(in)** *m(f)* collaborator; ⟨*Kollege*⟩ colleague; ⟨*Betriebsangehörige*⟩ employee

Mitbestimmung *f* co-determination

mitbring|en† *vt sep* bring [along]; jdm Blumen **m∼en** bring/⟨*hinbringen*⟩ take s.o. flowers. **M∼sel** *nt* -s,- present ⟨*brought back from holiday etc*⟩

Mitbürger *m* fellow citizen

miteinander *adv* with each other

miterleben *vt sep* witness

Mitesser *m* ⟨*Med*⟩ blackhead

mitfahren† *vi sep* (sein) go/come along; mit jdm **m∼** go with s.o.; ⟨*mitgenommen werden*⟩ be given a lift by s.o.

mitfühlen *vi sep* (haben) sympathize. **m∼d** *a* sympathetic; ⟨*mitleidig*⟩ compassionate

mitgeben† *vt sep* jdm etw **m∼** give s.o. sth to take with him

Mitgefühl *nt* sympathy

mitgehen† *vi sep* (sein) mit jdm **m∼** go with s.o.; etw **m∼** lassen ⟨*fam*⟩ pinch sth

mitgenommen *a* worn; **m∼** sein be in a sorry state; ⟨*erschöpft*⟩ be exhausted

Mitgift *f* -,-en dowry

Mitglied *nt* member. **M∼schaft** *f* - membership

mithalten† *vi sep* (haben) join in; mit jdm nicht **m∼** können not be able to keep up with s.o.

Mithilfe *f* assistance

mithilfe *prep* (+ *gen*) with the aid of

mitkommen† *vi sep* (sein) come [along] too; ⟨*fig: folgen können*⟩ keep up; ⟨*verstehen*⟩ follow

Mitlaut *m* consonant

Mitleid *nt* pity, compassion; **M∼** erregend pitiful. **M∼enschaft** *f* in **M∼enschaft** ziehen affect. **m∼erregend** *a* =

M∼ erregend, s. Mitleid. m∼ig a pitying; (mitfühlend) compassionate. m∼slos a pitiless

mitmachen v sep □ vt take part in; (erleben) go through □ vi (haben) join in

Mitmensch m fellow man

mitnehmen† vt sep take along; (mitfahren lassen) give a lift to; (fig: schädigen) affect badly; (erschöpfen) exhaust; 'zum M∼' 'to take away', (Amer) 'to go'

mitnichten adv not at all

mitreden vi sep (haben) join in [the conversation]; (mit entscheiden) have a say (bei in)

mitreißen† vt sep sweep along; (fig: begeistern) carry away; m∼d rousing

mitsamt prep (+ dat) together with

mitschneiden† vt sep record

mitschreiben† vt sep (haben) take down

Mitschuld f partial blame. m∼ig a m∼ig sein be partly to blame

Mitschüler(in) m(f) fellow pupil

mitspiel|en vi sep (haben) join in; (Theat) be in the cast; (beitragen) play a part; jdm übel m∼en treat s.o. badly. M∼er m fellow player; (Mitwirkender) participant

Mittag m midday, noon; (Mahlzeit) lunch; (Pause) lunch-break; heute/gestern M∼ at lunch-time today/yesterday; [zu] M∼ essen have lunch. m∼ adv heute/gestern m∼ (NEW) heute/gestern M∼, s. Mittag. M∼essen nt lunch. m∼s adv at noon; (als Mahlzeit) for lunch; um 12 Uhr m∼s at noon. M∼spause f lunchhour; (Pause) lunch-break. M∼schlaf m after-lunch nap. M∼stisch m lunch table; (Essen) lunch. M∼szeit f lunch-time

Mittäter|(in) m(f) accomplice. M∼schaft f complicity

Mitte f -,-n middle; (Zentrum) centre; die goldene M∼ the golden mean; M∼ Mai in mid-May; in unserer M∼ in our midst

mitteil|en vt sep jdm etw m∼en tell s.o. sth; (amtlich) inform s.o. of sth. m∼sam a communicative. M∼ung f -,-en communication; (Nachricht) piece of news

Mittel nt -s,- means sg; (Heil) remedy; (Medikament) medicine; (M∼wert) mean; (Durchschnitt) average; M∼ pl (Geld-) funds, resources. m∼ pred a medium; (m∼mäßig) middling. M∼alter nt Middle Ages pl. m∼alterlich a medieval. m∼bar a indirect, adv -ly. M∼ding nt (fig) cross. m∼europäisch a Central European. M∼finger m middle finger. m∼groß a medium-sized; (Person) of medium height. M∼klasse f middle range. m∼los a destitute. m∼mäßig a middling; [nur] m∼mäßig mediocre.

M∼meer nt Mediterranean. M∼punkt m centre; (fig) centre of attention

mittels prep (+ gen) by means of

Mittel|schule f = Realschule. M∼smann m (pl -männer), M∼sperson f intermediary, go-between. M∼stand m middle class. m∼ste(r,s) a middle. M∼streifen m (Auto) central reservation, (Amer) median strip. M∼stürmer m centre-forward. M∼weg m (fig) middle course; goldener M∼weg happy medium. M∼welle f medium wave. M∼wort nt (pl -wörter) participle

mitten adv m∼ in/auf (dat/acc) in the middle of; m∼ unter (dat/acc) amidst. m∼durch adv [right] through the middle

Mitternacht f midnight

mittler|e(r,s) a middle; (Größe, Qualität) medium; (durchschnittlich) mean, average. m∼weile adv meanwhile; (seitdem) by now

Mittwoch m -s,-e Wednesday. m∼s adv on Wednesdays

mitunter adv now and again

mitwirk|en vi sep (haben) take part; (helfen) contribute. M∼ung f participation

mix|en vt mix. M∼er m -s,- (Culin) liquidizer, blender. M∼tur f -,-en (Med) mixture

Möbel pl furniture sg. M∼stück nt piece of furniture. M∼tischler m cabinet-maker. M∼wagen m removal van

mobil a mobile; (fam: munter) lively; (nach Krankheit) fit [and well]; m∼ machen mobilize

Mobile nt -s,-s mobile

Mobiliar nt -s furniture

mobilisier|en vt mobilize. M∼ung f mobilization

Mobil|machung f - mobilization. M∼telefon nt mobile phone

möblier|en vt furnish; m∼tes Zimmer furnished room

mochte, möchte s. mögen

Modalverb nt modal auxiliary

Mode f -,-n fashion; M∼ sein be fashionable

Modell nt -s,-e model; M∼ stehen pose (jdm for s.o.). m∼ieren vt model

Modenschau f fashion show

Modera|tor m -s,-en /-'to:rən/, M∼torin f -,-nen (TV) presenter

modern¹ vi (haben) decay

modern² a modern; (modisch) fashionable. m∼isieren vt modernize

Mode|schmuck m costume jewellery. M∼schöpfer m fashion designer

Modifi|kation /-'tsjo:n/ f -,-en modifica-
tion. m~zieren vt modify

modisch a fashionable

Modistin f -,-nen milliner

modrig a musty

modulieren vt modulate

Mofa nt -s,-s moped

mogeln vi (haben) (fam) cheat

mögen† vt like; lieber m~ prefer □ v aux
ich möchte I'd like; möchtest du nach
Hause? do you want to go home? ich mag
nicht mehr I've had enough; ich hätte
weinen m~ I could have cried; ich mag
mich irren I may be wrong; wer/was
mag das sein? whoever/whatever can it
be? wie mag es ihm ergangen sein? I
wonder how he got on; [das] mag sein
that may well be; mag kommen, was da
will come what may

möglich a possible; alle m~en all sorts
of; über alles M~e (m~e) sprechen talk
about all sorts of things; sein M~stes
(m~stes) tun do one's utmost. m~er-
weise adv possibly. M~keit f -,-en possibility. M~keitsform f subjunctive.
m~st adv if possible; m~st viel/früh as
much/early as possible

Mohammedan|er(in) m -s,- (f -,-nen)
Muslim. m~isch a Muslim

Mohn m -s poppy; (Culin) poppyseed.
M~blume f poppy

Möhre, Mohrrübe f -,-n carrot

mokieren (sich) vr make fun (über + acc
of)

Mokka m -s mocha; (Geschmack) coffee

Molch m -[e]s,-e newt

Mole f -,-n (Naut) mole

Molekül nt -s,-e molecule

Molkerei f -,-en dairy

Moll nt - (Mus) minor

mollig a cosy; (warm) warm; (rundlich)
plump

Moment m -s,-e moment; im/jeden M~
at the/any moment; M~ [mal]! just a
moment! m~an a momentary, adv -ily;
(gegenwärtig) at the moment

Momentaufnahme f snapshot

Monarch m -en,-en monarch. M~ie f
-,-n monarchy

Monat m -s,-e month. m~elang adv for
months. m~lich a & adv monthly.
M~skarte f monthly season ticket

Mönch m -[e]s,-e monk

Mond m -[e]s,-e moon

mondän a fashionable, adv -bly

Mond|finsternis f lunar eclipse.
m~hell a moonlit. M~sichel f crescent
moon. M~schein m moonlight

monieren vt criticize

Monitor m -s,-en /-'to:rən/ (Techn) monitor

Monogramm nt -s,-e monogram

Mono|log m -s,-e monologue. M~pol nt
-s,-e monopoly. m~polisieren vt monopolize. m~ton a monotonous, adv -ly.
M~tonie f - monotony

Monster nt -s,- monster

monstr|ös a monstrous M~osität f
-,-en monstrosity

Monstrum nt -s,-stren monster

Monsun m -s,-e monsoon

Montag m Monday

Montage /mɔn'ta:ʒə/ f -,-n fitting; (Zu-
sammenbau) assembly; (Film-) editing;
(Kunst) montage

montags adv on Mondays

Montanindustrie f coal and steel indus-
try

Monteur /mɔn'tø:ɐ/ m -s,-e fitter.
M~anzug m overalls pl

montieren vt fit; (zusammenbauen) assemble

Monument nt -[e]s,-e monument. m~al
a monumental

Moor nt -[e]s,-e bog; (Heide-) moor

Moos nt es,-e moss. m~ig a mossy

Mop m -s,-s (NEW) Mopp

Moped nt -s,-s moped

Mopp m -s,-s mop

Mops m -s,-ͤe pug [dog]

Moral f -morals pl; (Selbstvertrauen) morale; (Lehre) moral. m~isch a moral, adv
-ly. m~isieren vi (haben) moralize

Morast m -[e]s,-e morass; (Schlamm) mud

Mord m -[e]s,-e murder, (Pol) as-
sassination. M~anschlag m murder/as-
sassination attempt. m~en vt/i (haben)
murder, kill

Mörder m -s,- murderer, (Pol) assassin.
M~in f -,-nen murderess. m~isch a
murderous; (fam: schlimm) dreadful

Mords- pref (fam) terrific. m~mäßig a
(fam) frightful, adv -ly

morgen adv tomorrow; m~ Abend
(abend)/Nachmittag (nachmittag)
tomorrow evening/afternoon; heute/
gestern/Montag m~ (NEW) heute/
gestern/Montag M~, s. Morgen

Morgen m -s,- morning; (Maß) ≈ acre; am
M~ in the morning; heute/ges-
tern/Montag M~ this/yesterday/Mon-
day morning. M~dämmerung f dawn.
m~dlich a morning ... M~grauen nt -s
dawn; im M~grauen at dawn. M~man-
tel, M~rock m dressing-gown. M~rot nt
red sky in the morning. m~s a in the
morning

morgig a tomorrow's; der m∼e Tag tomorrow

Morphium nt-s morphine

morsch a rotten

Morsealphabet nt Morse code

Mörtel m-s mortar

Mosaik /moza'i:k/ nt-s,-e[n] mosaic

Moschee f-,-n mosque

Mosel f- Moselle. M∼wein m Moselle [wine]

Moskau nt-s Moscow

Moskito m-s,-s mosquito

Mos|lem m-s,-s Muslim. m∼lemisch a Muslim

Most m-[e]s must; (Apfel-) ≈ cider

Mostrich m-s (NGer) mustard

Motel m-s,-s motel

Motiv nt-s,-e motive; (Kunst) motif. M∼ation /-'tsio:n/ f - motivation. m∼ieren vt motivate

Motor /'mo:tor,mo'to:g/ m-s,-en /-'to:rən/ engine; (Elektro-) motor. M∼boot nt motor boat

motorisieren vt motorize

Motor|rad nt motor cycle. M∼radfahrer m motor-cyclist. M∼roller m motor scooter

Motte f-,-n moth. M∼nkugel f mothball

Motto nt-s,-s motto

Möwe f-,-n gull

Mücke f-,-n gnat; (kleine) midge; (Stech-) mosquito

mucksen (sich) vr sich nicht m∼ (fam) keep quiet

müd|e a tired; nicht m∼e werden/es m∼e sein not tire/be tired (etw zu tun of doing sth). M∼igkeit f- tiredness

Muff m-s,-e muff

muffig a musty; (fam: mürrisch) grumpy

Mühe f-,-n effort; (Aufwand) trouble; sich (dat) M∼ geben make an effort; (sich bemühen) try; nicht der M∼ wert not worth while; mit M∼ und Not with great difficulty; (gerade noch) only just. m∼los a effortless, adv -ly

muhen vi (haben) moo

mühe|n (sich) vr struggle. m∼voll a laborious; (anstrengend) arduous

Mühl|e f -,-n mill; (Kaffee-) grinder. M∼stein m millstone

Müh|sal f-,-e (liter) toil; (Mühe) trouble. m∼sam a laborious, adv -ly; (beschwerlich) difficult, adv with difficulty. m∼selig a laborious, adv -ly

Mulde f-,-n hollow

Müll m-s refuse, (Amer) garbage. M∼abfuhr f refuse collection

Mullbinde f gauze bandage

Mülleimer m waste bin; (Mülltonne) dustbin, (Amer) garbage can

Müller m-s,- miller

Müll|halde f [rubbish] dump. M∼schlucker m refuse chute. M∼tonne f dustbin, (Amer) garbage can. M∼wagen m dustcart, (Amer) garbage truck

mulmig a (fam) dodgy; (Gefühl) uneasy; ihm war m∼ zumute he felt uneasy/ (übel) queasy

multi|national a multinational. M∼plikation /-'tsio:n/ f-,-en multiplication. m∼plizieren vt multiply

Mumie /'mu:mjə/ f-,-n mummy

mumifiziert a mummified

Mumm m-s (fam) energy

Mumps m- mumps

Mund m-[e]s,¨er mouth; ein M∼ voll Suppe a mouthful of soup; halt den M∼! be quiet! (sl) shut up! M∼art f dialect. m∼artlich a dialect

Mündel nt & m-s,- (Jur) ward. m∼sicher a gilt-edged

münden vi (sein) flow/(Straße:) lead (in + acc into)

mund|faul a taciturn. M∼geruch m bad breath. M∼harmonika f mouth-organ

mündig a m∼ sein/werden (Jur) be/ come of age. M∼keit f- (Jur) majority

mündlich a verbal, adv -ly; m∼e Prüfung oral

Mund|stück nt mouthpiece; (Zigaretten-) tip. m∼tot a m∼tot machen (fig) gag

Mündung f -,-en (Fluss-) mouth; (Gewehr-) muzzle

Mund|voll m-,- ein M∼voll (NEW)ein M∼ voll, s. Mund. M∼wasser nt mouthwash. M∼werk nt ein gutes M∼werk haben (fam) be very talkative. M∼winkel m corner of the mouth

Munition /-'tsio:n/ f- ammunition

munkeln vt/i (haben) talk (von of); es wird gemunkelt rumour has it (dass that)

Münster nt-s,- cathedral

munter a lively; (heiter) merry; m∼ sein (wach) be wide awake/(aufgestanden, gesund) up and about; gesund und m∼ fit and well □ adv [immer] m∼ merrily

Münz|e f -,-n coin; (M∼stätte) mint. m∼en vt mint; das war auf mich gemünzt (fam) that was aimed at you. M∼fernsprecher m coin-box telephone, payphone. M∼wäscherei f launderette

mürbe a crumbly; (Obst) mellow; (Fleisch) tender; jdn m∼ machen (fig) wear s.o. down. M∼teig m short pastry

Murmel f-,-n marble

murmeln *vt/i* (*haben*) murmur; (*undeutlich*) mumble, mutter. M~ *nt* -s murmur

Murmeltier *nt* marmot

murren *vt/i* (*haben*) grumble

mürrisch *a* surly

Mus *nt* -es purée

Muschel *f* -,-n mussel; (*Schale*) [sea] shell

Museum /mu'ze:ʊm/ *nt* -s,-seen /-'ze:ən/ museum

Musik *f* - music. M~alien /-jən/ *pl* [printed] music *sg.* m~alisch *a* musical

Musikbox *f* juke-box

Musiker(in) *m* -s,- (*f* -,-nen) musician

Musik|instrument *nt* musical instrument. M~kapelle *f* band. M~pavillon *m* bandstand

musisch *a* artistic

musizieren *vi* (*haben*) make music

Muskat *m* -[e]s nutmeg

Muskel *m* -s,-n muscle. M~kater *m* stiff and aching muscles *pl*

Musku|latur *f* - muscles *pl.* m~lös *a* muscular

Müsli *nt* -s muesli

muss (muß) *s.* müssen. Muss (Muß) *nt* - ein M~ a must

Muße *f* - leisure; mit M~ at leisure

müssen *v aux* etw tun m~ have to/(*fam*) have got to do sth; ich muss jetzt gehen I have to *or* must go now; ich musste lachen I had to laugh; ich muss es wissen I need to know; du müsstest es mal versuchen you ought to *or* should try it; muss das sein? is that necessary?

müßig *a* idle; (*unnütz*) futile. M~gang *m* - idleness

musste (mußte), **müsste** (müßte) *s.* müssen

Muster *nt* -s,- pattern; (*Probe*) sample; (*Vorbild*) model. M~beispiel *nt* typical example; (*Vorbild*) perfect example. M~betrieb *m* model factory. m~gültig, m~haft *a* exemplary. m~n *vt* eye; (*inspizieren*) inspect. M~schüler(in) *m*(*f*) model pupil. M~ung *f* -,-en inspection; (*Mil*) medical; (*Muster*) pattern

Mut *m* -[e]s courage; jdm Mut machen encourage s.o.; zu M~e sein = zumute sein, *s.* zumute

Mutation /-'tsio:n/ *f* -,-en (*Biol*) mutation

mut|ig *a* courageous, *adv* -ly. m~los *a* despondent; (*entmutigt*) disheartened

mutmaß|en *vt* presume; (*Vermutungen anstellen*) speculate. m~lich *a* probable, *adv* -bly; der m~liche Täter the suspect. M~ung *f* -,-en speculation, conjecture

Mutprobe *f* test of courage

Mutter¹ *f* -,- mother; werdende M~ mother-to-be

Mutter² *f* -,-n (*Techn*) nut

Muttergottes *f* -,- madonna

Mutter|land *nt* motherland. M~leib *m* womb

mütterlich *a* maternal; (*fürsorglich*) motherly. m~erseits *adv* on one's/the mother's side

Mutter|mal *nt* birthmark; (*dunkel*) mole. M~schaft *f* - motherhood. m~seelenallein *a & adv* all alone. M~sprache *f* mother tongue. M~tag *m* Mother's Day

Mutti *f* -,-s (*fam*) mummy

Mutwill|e *m* wantonness. m~ig *a* wanton, *adv* -ly

Mütze *f* -,-n cap; wollene M~ woolly hat

MwSt. *abbr* (Mehrwertsteuer) VAT

mysteriös *a* mysterious, *adv* -ly

Myst|ik /'mʏstɪk/ *f* - mysticism. m~isch *a* mystical

myth|isch *a* mythical. M~ologie *f* - mythology. M~os *m* -,-then myth

N

na *int* well; na gut all right then; na ja oh well; na und? so what?

Nabe *f* -,-n hub

Nabel *m* -s,- navel. N~schnur *f* umbilical cord

nach *prep* (+ *dat*) after; (*Uhrzeit*) past; (*Richtung*) to; (*greifen, rufen, sich sehnen*) for; (*gemäß*) according to; meiner Meinung n~ in my opinion; n~ oben upwards □ *adv* n~ und n~ gradually, bit by bit; n~ wie vor still

nachäffen *vt sep* mimic

nachahm|en *vt sep* imitate. N~ung *f* -,-en imitation

nacharbeiten *vt sep* make up for

nacharten *vi sep* (*sein*) jdm n~ take after s.o.

Nachbar|(in) *m* -n,-n (*f* -,-nen) neighbour. N~haus *nt* house next door. N~land *nt* neighbouring country. n~lich *a* neighbourly; (*Nachbar-*) neighbouring. N~schaft *f* - neighbourhood; gute N~schaft neighbourliness

nachbestell|en *vt sep* reorder. N~ung *f* repeat order

nachbild|en *vt sep* copy, reproduce. N~ung *f* copy, reproduction

nachdatieren *vt sep* backdate

nachdem *conj* after; je n~ it depends

nachdenk|en† *vi sep* (*haben*) think (über + *acc* about). N~en *nt* -s reflection, thought. n~lich *a* thoughtful, *adv* -ly

Nachdruck *m* (*pl* -e) reproduction; (*unveränderter*) reprint; (*Betonung*) emphasis

nachdrücklich *a* emphatic, *adv* -ally

nacheifern *vi sep* (*haben*) jdm n~ emulate s.o.

nacheilen *vi sep* (*sein*) (+ *dat*) hurry after

nacheinander *adv* one after the other

Nachfahre *m* -n,-n descendant

Nachfolg|e *f* succession. n~en *vi sep* (*sein*) (+ *dat*) follow; (*im Amt*) succeed. N~er(in) *m* -s,- (*f* -,-nen) successor

nachforsch|en *vi sep* (*haben*) make enquiries. N~ung *f* enquiry; N~ungen anstellen make enquiries

Nachfrage *f* (*Comm*) demand. n~n *vi sep* (*haben*) enquire

nachfüllen *vt sep* refill (*Behälter*); Wasser n~ fill up with water

nachgeben† *v sep* □ *vi* (*haben*) give way; (*sich fügen*) give in, yield □ *vt* jdm Suppe n~ give s.o. more soup

Nachgebühr *f* surcharge

nachgehen† *vi sep* (*sein*) (*Uhr:*) be slow; jdm/etw n~ follow s.o./sth; follow up (*Spur, Angelegenheit*); pursue (*Angelegenheit, Tätigkeit*); go about (*Arbeit*)

nachgeraten† *vi sep* (*sein*) jdm n~ take after s.o.

Nachgeschmack *m* after-taste

nachgiebig *a* indulgent; (*gefällig*) compliant. N~keit *f* - indulgence; compliance

nachgrübeln *vi sep* (*haben*) ponder (über + *acc* on)

nachhallen *vi sep* (*haben*) reverberate

nachhaltig *a* lasting

nachhause *adv* = nach Hause, *s.* Haus

nachhelfen† *vi sep* (*haben*) help

nachher *adv* later; (*danach*) afterwards; bis n~! see you later!

Nachhilfeunterricht *m* coaching

Nachhinein (nachhinein) *adv* im N~ (n~) afterwards

nachhinken *vi sep* (*sein*) (*fig*) lag behind

nachholen *vt sep* (*später holen*) fetch later; (*mehr holen*) get more; (*später machen*) do later; (*aufholen*) catch up on; make up for (*Zeit*)

nachjagen *vi sep* (*haben*) (+ *dat*) chase after

Nachkomme *m* -n,-n descendant. n~n† *vi sep* (*sein*) follow [later], come later; (*Schritt halten*) keep up; etw (*dat*) n~n (*fig*) comply with (*Bitte, Wunsch*); carry out (*Versprechen, Pflicht*). N~nschaft *f* - descendants *pl*, progeny

Nachkriegszeit *f* post-war period

Nachlass *m* -es,¨e (Nachlaß *m* -sses,¨sse) discount; (*Jur*) [deceased's] estate

nachlassen† *v sep* □ *vi* (*haben*) decrease; (*Regen, Hitze:*) let up; (*Schmerz:*) ease; (*Sturm:*) abate; (*Augen, Kräfte, Leistungen:*) deteriorate; er ließ nicht nach [mit Fragen] he persisted [with his questions] □ *vt* etw vom Preis n~ take sth off the price

nachlässig *a* careless, *adv* -ly; (*leger*) casual, *adv* -ly; (*unordentlich*) sloppy, *adv* -ily. N~keit *f* - carelessness; sloppiness

nachlaufen† *vi sep* (*sein*) (+ *dat*) run after

nachlegen *vt sep* Holz/Kohlen n~ put more wood/coal on the fire

nachlesen† *vt sep* look up

nachlöse|n *vi sep* (*haben*) pay one's fare on the train/on arrival. N~schalter *m* excess-fare office

nachmachen *vt sep* (*später machen*) do later; (*imitieren*) imitate, copy; (*fälschen*) forge; jdm etw n~ copy sth from s.o.; repeat (*Übung*) after s.o.

Nachmittag *m* afternoon; heute/gestern N~ this/yesterday afternoon. n~ *adv* heute/gestern n~ (NEW) heute/gestern N~, *s.* Nachmittag. n~s *adv* in the afternoon

Nachnahme *f* etw per N~ schicken send sth cash on delivery *or* COD

Nachname *m* surname

Nachporto *nt* excess postage

nachprüfen *vt sep* check, verify

nachrechnen *vt sep* work out; (*prüfen*) check

Nachrede *f* üble N~ defamation

Nachricht *f* -,-en [piece of] news *sg*; N~en news *sg*; eine N~ hinterlassen leave a message; jdm N~ geben inform, notify s.o. N~endienst *m* (*Mil*) intelligence service. N~ensendung *f* news bulletin. N~enwesen *nt* communications *pl*

nachrücken *vi sep* (*sein*) move up

Nachruf *m* obituary

nachsagen *vt sep* repeat (jdm after s.o.); jdm Schlechtes/Gutes n~ speak ill/well of s.o.; man sagt ihm nach, dass er geizig ist he is said to be stingy

Nachsaison *f* late season

Nachsatz *m* postscript

nachschicken *vt sep* (*später schicken*) send later; (*hinterher-*) send after (jdm s.o.); send on (*Post*) (jdm to s.o.)

nachschlag|en† *v sep* □ *vt* look up □ *vi* (*haben*) in einem Wörterbuch n~en consult a dictionary; jdm n~en take after s.o. N~ewerk *nt* reference book

Nachschlüssel *m* duplicate key

Nachschrift f transcript; (*Nachsatz*) postscript

Nachschub m (*Mil*) supplies pl

nachsehen† v sep □ vt (*prüfen*) check; (*nachschlagen*) look up; (*hinwegsehen über*) overlook □ vi (*haben*) have a look; (*prüfen*) check; im Wörterbuch n~ consult a dictionary; jdm/etw n~ gaze after s.o./sth. N~ nt das N~ haben (*fam*) go empty-handed

nachsenden† vt sep forward ⟨Post⟩ (jdm to s.o.); 'bitte n~' 'please forward'

Nachsicht f forbearance; (*Milde*) leniency; (*Nachgiebigkeit*) indulgence. n~ig a forbearing; lenient; indulgent

Nachsilbe f suffix

nachsitzen† vi sep (*haben*) n~ müssen be kept in [after school]; jdn n~ lassen give s.o. detention. N~ nt -s (*Sch*) detention

Nachspeise f dessert, sweet

Nachspiel nt (*fig*) sequel

nachspionieren vi sep (*haben*) jdm n~ spy on s.o.

nachsprechen† vt sep repeat (jdm after s.o.)

nachspülen vt sep rinse

nächst /-çst/ prep (+ *dat*) next to. n~beste(r,s) a first [available]; (*zweitbeste*) next best. n~e(r,s) a next; (*nächstgelegene*) nearest; (*Verwandte*) closest; n~e Woche next week; in n~er Nähe close by; am n~en sein be nearest or closest □ pron der/die/das N~e (n~e) the next; der N~e (n~e) bitte next please; als N~es (n~es) nächst; fürs N~e (n~e) for the time being. N~e(r) m fellow man

nachstehen† a following □ adv below

nachstellen v sep □ vt readjust; put back ⟨Uhr⟩ □ vi (*haben*) (+ *dat*) pursue

nächst|emal adv das n~emal □~emal (NEW) das nächste Mal, s. Mal[1]. N~enliebe f charity. n~ens adv shortly. n~gelegen a nearest. n~liegend a most obvious

nachstreben vi sep (*haben*) jdm n~ emulate s.o.

nachsuchen vi sep (*haben*) search; n~ um request

Nacht f -,¨e night; über/bei N~ overnight/at night; Montag/morgen N~ Monday/tomorrow night; heute N~ tonight; (*letzte Nacht*) last night; gestern N~ last night; (*vorletzte Nacht*) the night before last. n~ adv morgen/heute/gestern n~ (NEW) morgen/heute/gestern N~, s. Nacht. N~dienst m night duty

Nachteil m disadvantage; zum N~ to the detriment (*gen* of). n~ig a adverse, adv -ly

Nacht|essen nt (*SGer*) supper. N~falter m moth. N~hemd nt night-dress; (*Männer-*) night-shirt

Nachtigall f -,-en nightingale

Nachtisch m dessert

Nacht|klub m night-club. N~leben nt night-life

nächtlich a nocturnal, night ...

Nacht|lokal nt night-club. N~mahl nt (*Aust*) supper

Nachtrag m postscript; (*Ergänzung*) supplement. n~en† vt sep add; jdm etw n~en show/walk behind s.o. carrying sth; (*fig*) bear a grudge against s.o. for sth. n~end a vindictive; n~end sein bear grudges

nachträglich a subsequent, later; (*verspätet*) belated □ adv later; (*nachher*) afterwards; (*verspätet*) belatedly

nachtrauern vi sep (*haben*) (+ *dat*) mourn the loss of

Nacht|ruhe f night's rest; angenehme N~ruhe! sleep well! n~s adv at night; 2 Uhr n~s 2 o'clock in the morning. N~schicht f night-shift. N~tisch m bedside table. N~tischlampe f bedside lamp. N~topf m chamber-pot. N~wächter m night-watchman. N~zeit f night-time

Nachuntersuchung f check-up

nachwachsen† vi sep (*sein*) grow again

Nachwahl f by-election

Nachweis m -es,-e proof. n~bar a demonstrable. n~en† vt sep prove; (*aufzeigen*) show; (*vermitteln*) give details of; jdm nichts n~en können have no proof against s.o. n~lich a demonstrable, adv -bly

Nachwelt f posterity

Nachwirkung f after-effect

Nachwort nt ⟨pl -e⟩ epilogue

Nachwuchs m new generation; (*fam: Kinder*) offspring. N~spieler m young player

nachzahlen vt/i sep (*haben*) pay extra; (*später zahlen*) pay later; Steuern n~ pay tax arrears

nachzählen vt/i sep (*haben*) count again; (*prüfen*) check

Nachzahlung f extra/later payment; (*Gehalts-*) back-payment

nachzeichnen vt sep copy

Nachzügler m -s,- late-comer; (*Zurückgebliebener*) straggler

Nacken m -s,- nape or back of the neck

nackt a naked; (*bloß, kahl*) bare; (*Wahrheit*) plain. N~baden nt nude bathing. N~heit f - nakedness, nudity. N~kultur f nudism. N~schnecke f slug

Nadel f -,-n needle; (Häkel-) hook; (Schmuck-, Hut-) pin. N~arbeit f needlework. N~baum m conifer. N~kissen nt pincushion. N~stich m stitch; (fig) pinprick. N~wald m coniferous forest

Nagel m -s,- nail. N~bürste f nail-brush. N~feile f nail-file. N~haut f cuticle. N~lack m nail varnish. n~n vt nail. n~neu a brand-new. N~schere f nail scissors pl

nagen vt/i (haben) gnaw (an + dat at); n~d (fig) nagging

Nagetier nt rodent

nah a, adv & prep = nahe; von nah und fern from far and wide

Näharbeit f sewing; eine N~ a piece of sewing

Nahaufnahme f close-up

nahe a (näher, nächst) nearby; (zeitlich) imminent; (eng) close; der N~ Osten the Middle East; in n~r Zukunft in the near future; von n~m [from] close to; n~ sein be close (dat to); den Tränen n~ close to tears (dat to); (verwandt) closely; n~ an (+ acc/dat) near [to], close to; n~ daran sein, etw zu tun nearly do sth; n~ liegen be close; (fig) be highly likely; n~ liegende Lösung obvious solution; n~ legen (fig) recommend (dat to); jdm n~ legen, etw zu tun urge s.o. to do sth; jdm n~ stehen (fig) be close to s.o.; etw (dat) n~ kommen (fig) come close to sth; jdm n~ kommen (fig) get close to s.o.; jdm n~ gehen (fig) affect s.o. deeply; jdm zu n~ treten (fig) offend s.o. ❑ prep (+ dat) near [to], close to

Nähe f - nearness, proximity; aus der N~ [from] close to; in der N~ near or close by; in der N~ der Kirche near the church

nahebei adv near or close by

nahe|gehen† vi sep (sein) NEW n~ gehen, s. nahe. n~kommen† vi sep (sein) NEW n~ kommen, s. nahe. n~legen vt sep NEW n~ legen, s. nahe. n~liegen† vi sep (sein) NEW n~ liegen, s. nahe. n~liegend a NEW n~ liegend, s. nahe

nahen vi (sein) (liter) approach

nähen vt/i (haben) sew; (anfertigen) make; (Med) stitch [up]

näher a closer; (Weg) shorter; (Einzelheiten) further □ adv closer; (genauer) more cloosly; n~ kommen come closer, approach; (fig) get closer (dat to); sich n~ erkundigen make further enquiries; n~an (+ acc/dat) nearer [to], closer to □ prep (+ dat) nearer [to], closer to. N~e[s] nt [further] details pl. n~kommen† vi sep (sein) NEW n~ kommen, s. näher. n~n (sich) vr approach

nahestehen† vi sep (haben) NEW nahe stehen, s. nahe

nahezu adv almost

Nähgarn nt [sewing] cotton

Nahkampf m close combat

Näh|maschine f sewing machine. N~nadel f sewing-needle

nähren vt feed; (fig) nurture; sich n~ von live on □ vi (haben) be nutritious

nahrhaft a nutritious

Nährstoff m nutrient

Nahrung f - food, nourishment. N~smittel nt food

Nährwert m nutritional value

Naht f -,-e seam; (Med) suture. n~los a seamless

Nahverkehr m local service. N~szug m local train

Nähzeug nt sewing; (Zubehör) sewing kit

naiv /na'i:f/ a naïve, adv -ly. N~ität /-vi'tε:t/ f - naïvety

Name m -ns,-n name; im N~n (+ gen) in the name of; (handeln) on behalf of; das Kind beim rechten N~n nennen (fam) call a spade a spade. n~nlos a nameless; (unbekannt) unknown, anonymous. n~ns adv by the name of □ prep (+ gen) on behalf of. N~nstag m name-day. N~nsvetter m namesake. N~nszug m signature. n~ntlich adv by name; (besonders) especially

namhaft a noted; (ansehnlich) considerable; n~ machen name

nämlich adv (und zwar) namely; (denn) because

nanu int hallo

Napf m -[e]s,-e bowl

Narbe f -,-n scar

Narkose f -,-n general anaesthetic. N~arzt m anaesthetist. N~mittel nt anaesthetic

Narkot|ikum nt -s,-ka narcotic; (Narkosemittel) anaesthetic. n~isieren vt anaesthetize

Narr m -en,-en fool; zum N~en haben od halten make a fool of. n~en vt fool. n~ensicher a foolproof. N~heit f -,-en folly

Närr|in f -,-nen fool. n~isch a foolish; (fam: verrückt) crazy (auf + acc about)

Narzisse f -,-n narcissus; gelbe N~ daffodil

nasal a nasal

nasch|en vt/i (haben) nibble (an + dat at); wer hat von Kuchen genascht? who's been at the cake? n~haft a sweet-toothed

Nase f -,-n nose; an der N~ herumführen (fam) dupe

näseln vi (haben) speak through one's nose; n~d nasal

Nasen|bluten nt -s nosebleed. N~loch nt nostril. N~rücken m bridge of the nose

Naseweis m -es,-e (fam) know-all

Nashorn nt rhinoceros

nass (naß) a (nasser, nassest) wet

Nässe f - wet; (Nasssein) wetness. n~n vt wet

nasskalt (naßkalt) a cold and wet

Nation /na'tsjo:n/ f -,-en nation. n~al a national. N~alhymne f national anthem. N~alismus m - nationalism. N~alität f -,-en nationality. N~alsozialismus m National Socialism. N~alspieler m international

Natrium nt -s sodium

Natron nt -s doppeltkohlensaures N~ bicarbonate of soda

Natter f -,-n snake; (Gift-) viper

Natur f -,-en nature; von N~ aus by nature. N~alien /-jon/ pl natural produce sg. n~alisieren vt naturalize. N~alisierung f -,-en naturalization

Naturell nt -s,-e disposition

Natur|erscheinung f natural phenomenon. n~farben a natural[-coloured]. N~forscher m naturalist. N~kunde f natural history. N~lehrpfad m nature trail

natürlich a □ adv naturally; (selbstverständlich) of course. N~keit f - naturalness

natur|rein a pure. N~schutz m nature conservation; unter N~schutz stehen be protected. N~schutzgebiet nt nature reserve. N~wissenschaft f [natural] science. N~wissenschaftler m scientist. n~wissenschaftlich a scientific; (Sch) science ...

nautisch a nautical

Navigation /-'tsjo:n/ f - navigation

Nazi m -s,-s Nazi

n.Chr. abbr (nach Christus) AD

Nebel m -s,- fog; (leicht) mist. n~haft a hazy. N~horn nt foghorn. n~ig a = neblig

neben prep (+ dat/acc) next to, beside; (+ dat) (außer) apart from; n~ mir next to me. n~an adv next door

Neben|anschluss (Nebenanschluß) m (Teleph) extension. N~ausgaben fpl incidental expenses

nebenbei adv in addition; (beiläufig) casually; n~ bemerkt incidentally

Neben|bemerkung f passing remark. N~beruf m second job. N~beschäftigung f spare-time occupation. N~buhler(in) m -s,- (f -,-nen) rival

nebeneinander adv next to each other, side by side

Neben|eingang m side entrance. N~fach nt (Univ) subsidiary subject. N~fluss (N~fluß) m tributary. N~gleis nt siding. N~haus nt house next door

nebenher adv in addition. n~gehen† vi sep (sein) walk alongside

nebenhin adv casually

Neben|höhle f sinus. N~kosten pl additional costs. N~mann m (pl -männer) person next to one. N~produkt nt by-product. N~rolle f supporting role; (kleine) minor role; eine N~rolle spielen (fig) be unimportant. N~sache f unimportant matter. n~sächlich a unimportant. N~satz m subordinate clause. N~straße f minor road; (Seiten-) side street. N~verdienst m additional earnings pl. N~wirkung f side-effect. N~zimmer nt room next door

neblig a foggy; (leicht) misty

nebst prep (+ dat) [together] with

Necessaire /nesε'sε:ɐ/ nt -s,-s toilet bag; (Näh-, Nagel-) set

neck|en vt tease. N~erei f - teasing. n~isch a teasing; (kess) saucy

nee adv (fam) no

Neffe m -n,-n nephew

negativ a negative. N~ nt -s,-e (Phot) negative

Neger m -s,- Negro

nehmen† vt take (dat from); sich (dat) etw n~ take sth; help oneself to (Essen); jdn zu sich n~ have s.o. to live with one

Neid m -[e]s envy, jealousy. n~en vt jdm den Erfolg n~en be jealous of s.o.'s success. n~isch a envious, jealous (auf + acc of); auf jdn n~isch sein envy s.o.

neig|en vt incline; (zur Seite) tilt; (beugen) bend; sich n~en incline; (Boden:) slope; (Person:) bend (über + acc over) □ vi (haben) n~en zu (fig) have a tendency towards; be prone to (Krankheit); incline towards (Ansicht); dazu n~en, etw zu tun tend to do sth. N~ung f -,-en inclination; (Gefälle) slope; (fig) tendency; (Hang) leaning; (Herzens-) affection

nein adv, N~ nt -s no

Nektar m -s nectar

Nelke f -,-n carnation; (Feder-) pink; (Culin) clove

nenn|en† vt call; (taufen) name; (angeben) give; (erwähnen) mention; sich n~en call oneself. n~enswert a significant. N~ung f -,-en mention; (Sport) entry. N~wert m face value

Neofaschismus m neofascism

Neon nt -s neon. N~beleuchtung f fluorescent lighting

neppen *vt* (*fam*) rip off

Nerv *m* -s,-en /-fan/ nerve; **die N~en verlieren** lose control of oneself. **n~en** *vt* **jdn n~en** (*sl*) get on s.o.'s nerves. **N~enarzt** *m* neurologist. **n~enaufreibend** *a* nerve-racking. **N~enbündel** *nt* (*fam*) bundle of nerves. **N~enkitzel** *m* (*fam*) thrill. **N~ensystem** *nt* nervous system. **N~enzusammenbruch** *m* nervous breakdown

nervös *a* nervy, edgy; (*Med*) nervous; **n~ sein** be on edge

Nervosität *f* - nerviness, edginess

Nerz *m* -es,-e mink

Nessel *f* -,-n nettle

Nessessär *nt* -s,-s = Necessaire

Nest *nt* -[e]s,-er nest; (*fam: Ort*) small place

nesteln *vi* (*haben*) fumble (**an** + *dat* with)

Nesthäkchen *nt* -s,- (*fam*) baby of the family

nett *a* nice, *adv* -ly; (*freundlich*) kind, *adv* -ly

netto *adv* net. **N~gewicht** *nt* net weight

Netz *nt* -es,-e net; (*Einkaufs-*) string bag; (*Spinnen-*) web; (*auf Landkarte*) grid; (*System*) network; (*Electr*) mains *pl*. **N~haut** *f* retina. **N~karte** *f* area season ticket. **N~werk** *nt* network

neu *a* new; (*modern*) modern; **wie neu** as good as new; **das ist mir neu** it's news to me; **aufs N~e** (**n~e**) [once] again; **von n~em** all over again *□ adv* newly; (*gerade erst*) only just; (*erneut*) again; **etw neu schreiben/streichen** rewrite/repaint sth; **neu vermähltes Paar** newly-weds *pl*. **N~ankömmling** *m* -s,-e newcomer. **N~anschaffung** *f* recent acquisition. **n~artig** *a* new [kind of]. **N~auflage** *f* new edition; (*unverändert*) reprint. **N~bau** *m* (*pl* -ten) new house/building

Neu|e(r) *m/f* new person, newcomer; (*Schüler*) new boy/girl. **N~e(s)** *nt* das **N~e** the new; etwas **N~es** something new; (*Neuigkeit*) a piece of news; was gibt's **N~es**? what's the news?

neuer|dings *adv* [just] recently. **n~lich** *a* renewed, new *□ adv* again. **N~ung** *f* -,-en innovation

neuest|e(r,s) *a* newest; (*letzte*) latest; seit **n~em** just recently. **N~e** *nt* das **N~e** the latest thing; (*Neuigkeit*) the latest news *sg*

neugeboren *a* newborn

Neugier, Neugierde *f* - curiosity; (*Wissbegierde*) inquisitiveness

neugierig *a* curious (*auf* + *acc* about) *adv* -ly; (*wissbegierig*) inquisitive, *adv* -ly

Neuheit *f* -,-en novelty; (*Neusein*) newness; die letzte **N~** the latest thing

Neuigkeit *f* -,-en piece of news; **N~en** news *sg*

Neujahr *nt* New Year's Day; **über N~** over the New Year

neulich *adv* the other day

Neu|ling *m* -s,-e novice. **n~modisch** *a* newfangled. **N~mond** *m* new moon

neun *inv a*, **N~** *f* -,-en nine. **N~malkluge(r)** *m* (*fam*) clever Dick. **n~te(r,s)** *a* ninth. **n~zehn** *inv a* nineteen. **n~zehnte(r,s)** *a* nineteenth. **n~zig** *inv a* ninety. **n~zigste(r,s)** *a* ninetieth

Neuralgie *f* -,-n neuralgia

neureich *a* nouveau riche

Neurologe *m* -n,-n neurologist

Neuro|se *f* -,-n neurosis. **n~tisch** *a* neurotic

Neuschnee *m* fresh snow

Neuseeland *nt* -s New Zealand

neuste(r,s) *a* = neueste(r,s)

neutral *a* neutral. **n~isieren** *vt* neutralize. **N~ität** *f* - neutrality

Neutrum *nt* -s,-tra neuter noun

neu|vermählt *a* ⟨NEW⟩ **n~ vermählt, s. neu**. **N~zeit** *f* modern times *pl*

nicht *adv* not; **ich kann n~** I cannot *or* can't; **er ist n~ gekommen** he hasn't come; **n~ mehr/besser als** no more/better than; **bitte n~!** please don't! **n~ berühren!** do not touch! **du kommst doch auch, ~ [wahr]?** you are coming too, aren't you? **du kennst ihn doch, n~?** you know him, don't you?

Nichtachtung *f* disregard; (*Geringschätzung*) disdain

Nichte *f* -,-n niece

nichtig *a* trivial; (*Jur*) [null and] void

Nichtraucher *m* non-smoker. **N~abteil** *nt* non-smoking compartment

nichts *pron* & *a* nothing; **n~ anderes/Besseres** nothing else/better; **n~ mehr** no more; **ich weiß n~** I know nothing *or* don't know anything; **n~ ahnend** unsuspecting; **n~ sagend** meaningless; (*uninteressant*) nondescript. **N~** *nt* - nothingness; (*fig: Leere*) void; (*Person*) nonentity. **n~ahnend** *a* ⟨NEW⟩ **n~ ahnend, s. nichts**

Nichtschwimmer *m* non-swimmer

nichtsdesto|trotz *adv* all the same. **n~weniger** *adv* nevertheless

nichts|nutzig *a* good-for-nothing; (*fam: unartig*) naughty. **n~sagend** *a* ⟨NEW⟩ **n~ sagend, s. nichts**. **N~tun** *nt* -s idleness

Nickel *nt* -s nickel

nicken *vi* (*haben*) nod. **N~** *nt* -s nod

Nickerchen *nt* -s,- (*fam*) nap; **ein N~ machen** have forty winks

nie *adv* never

nieder *a* low *□ adv* down. **n~brennen†** *vt/i sep* (*sein*) burn down. **N~deutsch** *nt*

Low German. N~gang *m* (*fig*) decline. n~gedrückt *a* (*fig*) depressed. n~gehen† *vi sep* (*sein*) come down. n~geschlagen *a* dejected, despondent. N~geschlagenheit *f* - dejection, despondency. N~kunft *f* -,-̈e confinement. N~lage *f* defeat

Niederlande (die) *pl* the Netherlands

Niederländ|er *m* -s,- Dutchman; die N~er the Dutch *pl*. N~erin *f* -,-nen Dutchwoman. n~isch *a* Dutch

nieder|lassen† *vt sep* let down; sich n~lassen settle; (*sich setzen*) sit down. N~lassung *f* -,-en settlement; (*Zweigstelle*) branch. n~legen *vt sep* put *or* lay down; resign (*Amt*); die Arbeit n~legen go on strike; sich n~legen lie down. n~machen, n~metzeln *vt sep* massacre. n~reißen† *vt sep* tear down. N~sachsen *nt* Lower Saxony. N~schlag *m* precipitation; (*Regen*) rainfall; (*radioaktiver*) fallout; (*Boxen*) knock-down; n~schlagen† *vt sep* knock down; lower (*Augen*); (*unterdrücken*) crush. n~schmettern *vt sep* (*fig*) shatter. n~schreiben† *vt sep* write down. n~schreien† *vt sep* shout down. n~setzen *vt sep* put *or* set down; sich n~setzen sit down. n~strecken *vt sep* fell; (*durch Schuss*) gun down

niederträchtig *a* base, vile

Niederung *f* -,-en low ground

nieder|walzen *vt sep* flatten. n~werfen† *vt sep* throw down; (*unterdrücken*) crush; sich n~werfen prostrate oneself

niedlich *a* pretty; (*goldig*) sweet; (*Amer*) cute

niedrig *a* low; (*fig: gemein*) base □ *adv* low

niemals *adv* never

niemand *pron* nobody, no one

Niere *f* -,-n kidney; künstliche N~ kidney machine

nieseln *vi* (*haben*) drizzle; es n~t it is drizzling. N~regen *m* drizzle

niesen *vi* (*haben*) sneeze. N~ *nt* -s sneezing; (*Nieser*) sneeze

Niet *m & nt* -[e]s,e, **Niete¹** *f* -,-n rivet; (*an Jeans*) stud

Niete² *f* -,-n blank; (*fam*) failure

nieten *vt* rivet

Nikotin *nt* -s nicotine

Nil *m* -[s] Nile. N~pferd *nt* hippopotamus

nimmer *adv* (*SGer*) not any more; nie und n~ never. n~müde *a* tireless. n~satt *a* insatiable. N~wiedersehen *nt* auf N~wiedersehen (*fam*) for good

nippen *vi* (*haben*) take a sip (an + *dat* of)

nirgends, nirgendwo *adv* nowhere

Nische *f* -,-n recess, niche

nisten *vi* (*haben*) nest

Nitrat *nt* -[e]s,-e nitrate

Niveau /ni'voː/ *nt* -s,-s level; (*geistig, künstlerisch*) standard

nix *adv* (*fam*) nothing

Nixe *f* -,-n mermaid

nobel *a* noble; (*fam: luxuriös*) luxurious; (*fam: großzügig*) generous

noch *adv* still; (*zusätzlich*) as well; (*mit Komparativ*) even; n~ nicht not yet; gerade n~ only just; n~ immer *od* immer n~ still; n~ letzte Woche only last week; es ist n~ viel Zeit there's plenty of time yet; wer/was/wo n~? who/what/where else? n~ jemand/etwas someone/something else; (*Frage*) anyone/anything else? n~ einmal again; n~ einmal so viel as much again; n~ ein Bier another beer; n~ größer even bigger; n~ so sehr/schön however much/beautiful □ *conj* weder . . . n~ neither . . . nor

nochmal|ig *a* further. n~s *adv* again

Nomad|e *m* -n,-n nomad. n~isch *a* nomadic

Nominativ *m* -s,-e nominative

nominell *a* nominal, *adv* -ly

nominier|en *vt* nominate. N~ung *f* -,-en nomination

nonchalant /nõʃa'lãː/ *a* nonchalant, *adv* -ly

Nonne *f* -,-n nun. N~nkloster *nt* convent

Nonstopflug *m* direct flight

Nord *m* -[e]s north. N~amerika *nt* North America. n~deutsch *a* North German

Norden *m* -s north; nach N~ north

nordisch *a* Nordic

nördlich *a* northern; (*Richtung*) northerly □ *adv & prep* (+ *gen*) n~ [von] der Stadt [to the] north of the town

Nordosten *m* north-east

Nord|pol *m* North Pole. N~see *f* - North Sea. n~wärts *adv* northwards. N~westen *m* north-west

Nörgelei *f* -,-en grumbling

nörgeln *vi* (*haben*) grumble

Norm *f* -,-en norm; (*Techn*) standard; (*Soll*) quota

normal *a* normal, *adv* -ly. n~erweise *adv* normally. n~isieren *vt* normalize; sich n~isieren return to normal

normen, normieren *vt* standardize

Norwe|gen *nt* -s Norway. N~ger(in) *m* -s,- (*f* -,-nen) Norwegian. n~gisch *a* Norwegian

Nostalgie *f* -nostalgia. n~algisch *a* nostalgic

Not f -,˖e need; (*Notwendigkeit*) necessity; (*Entbehrung*) hardship; (*seelisch*) trouble; Not leiden be in need, suffer hardship; Not leidende Menschen needy people; mit knapper Not only just; zur Not if need be; (*äußerstenfalls*) at a pinch

Notar m -s,-e notary public

Not|arzt m emergency doctor. N∼ausgang m emergency exit. N∼behelf m -[e]s,-e makeshift. N∼bremse f emergency brake. N∼dienst m N∼dienst haben be on call. n∼dürftig a scant; (*behelfsmäßig*) makeshift

Note f -,-n note; (*Zensur*) mark; ganze/halbe N∼ (*Mus*) semi-breve/minim, (*Amer*) whole/half note; N∼n lesen read music; persönliche N∼ personal touch. N∼nblatt nt sheet of music. N∼nschlüssel m clef. N∼nständer m music-stand

Notfall m emergency; im N∼ in an emergency; (*notfalls*) if need be; für den N∼ just in case. n∼s adv if need be

not|gedrungen adv of necessity. N∼groschen m nest-egg

notieren vt note down; (*Comm*) quote; sich (*dat*) etw n∼ make a note of sth

nötig a necessary; n∼ haben need; das N∼ste the essentials pl □ adv urgently. n∼en vt force; (*auffordern*) press; laßt euch nicht n∼en help yourselves. n∼enfalls adv if need be. N∼ung f -coercion

Notiz f -,-en note; (*Zeitungs-*) item; [keine] N∼ nehmen von take [no] notice of. N∼buch nt notebook. N∼kalender m diary

Not|lage f plight. n∼landen vi (*sein*) make a forced landing. N∼landung f forced landing. n∼leidend a ⟨NEW⟩Not leidend, s. Not. N∼lösung f stopgap. N∼lüge f white lie

notorisch a notorious

Not|ruf m emergency call; (*Naut, Aviat*) distress call; (*Nummer*) emergency services number. N∼signal nt distress signal. N∼stand m state of emergency. N∼unterkunft f emergency accommodation. N∼wehr f - (*Jur*) self-defence

notwendig a necessary; (*unerlässlich*) essential □ adv urgently. N∼keit f -,-en necessity

Notzucht f - (*Jur*) rape

Nougat /'nu:gat/ m & nt -s nougat

Novelle f -,-n novella; (*Pol*) amendment

November m -s,- November

Novität f -,-en novelty

Novize m -n,-n, **Novizin** f -,-nen (*Relig*) novice

Nu m im Nu (*fam*) in a flash

Nuance /'nyã:sə/ f -,-n nuance; (*Spur*) shade

nüchtern a sober; (*sachlich*) matter-of-fact; (*schmucklos*) bare; (*ohne Würze*) bland; auf n∼en Magen on an empty stomach □ adv soberly

Nudel f -,-n piece of pasta; N∼n pasta sg; (*Band-*) noodles. N∼holz nt rolling-pin

Nudist m -en,-en nudist

nuklear a nuclear

null inv a zero, nought; (*Teleph*) O; (*Sport*) nil; (*Tennis*) love; n∼ Fehler no mistakes; n∼ und nichtig (*Jur*) null and void. N∼ f -,-en nought, zero; (*fig: Person*) nonentity; drei Grad unter N∼ three degrees below zero. N∼punkt m zero

numerieren vt ⟨NEW⟩nummerieren

numerisch a numerical

Nummer f -,-n number; (*Ausgabe*) issue; (*Darbietung*) item; (*Zirkus-*) act; (*Größe*) size. n∼ieren vt number. N∼nschild nt number-/(*Amer*) license-plate

nun adv now; (*na*) well; (*halt*) just; von nun an from now on; nun gut! very well then! das Leben ist nun mal so life's like that

nur adv only, just; wo kann sie nur sein? wherever can she be? alles, was ich nur will everything I could possibly want; er soll es nur versuchen! (*drohend*) just let him try! könnte/hätte ich nur ...! if only I could/had ...! nur Geduld! just be patient!

Nürnberg nt -s Nuremberg

nuscheln vt/i (*haben*) mumble

Nuss f -;̈e (Nuß f -; :sse) nut. N∼baum m walnut tree. N∼knacker m -s,- nutcrackers pl. N∼schale f nutshell

Nüstern fpl nostrils

Nut f -,-en, **Nute** f -,-n groove

Nutte f -,-n (*Sl*) tart (*sl*)

Nutz zu N∼e machen = zunutze machen, s. zunutze. n∼bar a usable; n∼bar machen utilize; cultivate (*Boden*). n∼bringend a profitable, adv -bly

nütze a zu etwas/nichts n∼ sein be useful/useless

nutzen vt use, utilize; (*aus-*) take advantage of □ vi (*haben*) = nützen. N∼ m -s benefit; (*Comm*) profit; N∼ ziehen aus benefit from; von N∼ sein be useful

nützen vi (*haben*) be useful or of use (*dat* to); (*Mittel:*) be effective; nichts n∼ be useless or no use; was nützt mir das? what good is that to me? □ vt = nutzen

Nutzholz nt timber

nützlich a useful; sich n∼ machen make oneself useful. N∼keit f - usefulness

nutz|los a useless; *(vergeblich)* vain. N~losigkeit f - uselessness. N~nießer m -s,- beneficiary. N~ung f - use, utilization

Nylon /'naɪlɔn/ nt -s nylon

Nymphe /'nʏmfə/ f -,-n nymph

O

o int o ja/nein! oh yes/no! o weh! oh dear!

Oase f -,-n oasis

ob conj whether; ob reich, ob arm rich or poor; ob sie wohl krank ist? I wonder whether she is ill; und ob! *(fam)* you bet!

Obacht f O~ geben pay attention; O~ geben auf (+ acc) look after; O~! look out!

Obdach nt -[e]s shelter. o~los a homeless. O~lose(r) m/f homeless person; die O~losen the homeless pl

Obduktion /-'tsi̯o:n/ f -,-en post-mortem

O-Beine ntpl *(fam)* bow-legs, bandy legs. O~beinig, o-beinig a bandy-legged

oben adv at the top; *(auf der Oberseite)* on top; *(eine Treppe hoch)* upstairs; *(im Text)* above; da o~ up there; o~ im Norden up in the north; siehe o~ see above; o~ auf (+ acc/dat) on top of; nach o~ up[wards]; *(die Treppe hinauf)* upstairs; von o~ from above/upstairs; von o~ bis unten from top to bottom/⟨Person⟩ to toe; jdn von o~ bis unten mustern look s.o. up and down; o~ erwähnt od genannt above-mentioned. o~an adv at the top. o~auf on top; o~auf sein *(fig)* be cheerful. o~drein adv on top of that. o~erwähnt, o~genannt a (NEW) o~ erwähnt od genannt, s. oben. o~hin adv casually

Ober m -s,- waiter

Ober|arm m upper arm. O~arzt m ≈ senior registrar. O~befehlshaber m commander-in-chief. O~begriff m generic term. O~deck nt upper deck. o~e(r,s) a upper; *(höhere)* higher. O~fläche f surface. o~flächlich a superficial, adv -ly. O~geschoss (O~geschoß) nt upper storey. o~halb adv & prep (+ gen) above; o~halb vom Dorf od des Dorfes above the village. O~hand f die O~hand gewinnen gain the upper hand. O~haupt nt *(fig)* head. O~haus nt *(Pol)* upper house; *(in UK)* House of Lords. O~hemd nt [man's] shirt

Oberin f -,-nen matron; *(Relig)* mother superior

ober|irdisch a surface ... □ adv above ground. O~kellner m head waiter. O~kiefer m upper jaw. O~körper m upper part of the body. O~leutnant m lieutenant. O~licht nt overhead light; *(Fenster)* skylight; *(über Tür)* fanlight. O~lippe f upper lip

Obers nt - *(Aust)* cream

Ober|schenkel m thigh. O~schicht f upper class. O~schule f grammar school. O~schwester f *(Med)* sister. O~seite f upper/*(rechte Seite)* right side

Oberst m -en & -s,-en colonel

oberste(r,s) a top; *(höchste)* highest; *(Befehlshaber, Gerichtshof)* supreme; *(wichtigste)* first

Ober|stimme f treble. O~stufe f upper school. O~teil nt top. O~weite f chest/*(der Frau)* bust size

obgleich conj although

Obhut f - care; in guter O~ sein be well looked after

obig a above

Objekt nt -[e]s,-e object; *(Haus, Grundstück)* property; O~ der Forschung subject of research

Objektiv nt -s,-e lens. O~ a objective, adv -ly. O~ität f - objectivity

Oblate f -,-n *(Relig)* wafer

obliga|t a *(fam)* inevitable. O~tion /-'tsi̯o:n/ f -,-en obligation; *(Comm)* bond. o~torisch a obligatory

Obmann m *(pl* -männer*)* [jury] foreman; *(Sport)* referee

Oboe /o'bo:ə/ f -,-n oboe

Obrigkeit f - authorities pl

obschon conj although

Observatorium nt -s,-ien observatory

obskur a obscure; *(zweifelhaft)* dubious

Obst nt -es *(coll)* fruit. O~baum m fruit-tree. O~garten m orchard. O~händler m fruiterer. O~kuchen m fruit flan. O~salat m fruit salad

obszön a obscene. O~ität f -,-en obscenity

O-Bus m trolley bus

obwohl conj although

Ochse m -n,-n ox. o~n vi *(haben)* *(fam)* swot. O~nschwanzsuppe f oxtail soup

öde a desolate; *(unfruchtbar)* barren; *(langweilig)* dull. Öde f - desolation; barrenness; dullness; *(Gegend)* waste

oder conj or; du kennst ihn doch, o~? you know him, don't you?

Ofen m -s,- stove; *(Heiz-)* heater; *(Back-)* oven; *(Techn)* furnace

offen a open, adv -ly; *(Haar)* loose; *(Flamme)* naked; *(o~herzig)* frank, adv

-ly; (o~ *gezeigt*) overt, *adv* -ly; (*unentschieden*) unsettled; o~e Stelle vacancy; Tag der o~en Tür open day; Wein o~ verkaufen sell wine by the glass; o~ bleiben remain open; o~ halten hold open 〈Tür〉; keep open 〈Mund, Augen〉; o~ lassen leave open; leave vacant 〈Stelle〉; o~ stehen be open; 〈Rechnung:〉 be outstanding; jdm o~ stehen (*fig*) be open to s.o.; *adv* o~ gesagt *od* gestanden to be honest. o~bar *a* obvious □ *adv* apparently. o~baren *vt* reveal. O~barung *f* -,-en revelation. o~bleiben† *vi sep* (sein) NEW o~ bleiben, s. offen. o~halten† *vt sep* NEW o~ halten, s. offen. O~heit *f* - frankness, openness. o~herzig *a* frank, *adv* -ly. O~herzigkeit *f* - frankness. o~kundig *a* manifest, *adv* -ly. o~lassen† *vt sep* NEW o~ lassen, s. offen. o~sichtlich *a* obvious, *adv* -ly

offensiv *a* offensive. O~e *f* -,-n offensive

offenstehen† *vi sep* (haben) NEW offen stehen, s. offen

öffentlich *a* public, *adv* -ly. Ö~keit *f* - public; an die Ö~keit gelangen become public; in aller Ö~keit in public, publicly

Offerte *f* -,-n (*Comm*) offer

offiziell *a* official, *adv* -ly

Offizier *m* -s,-e (*Mil*) officer

öffn|en *vt/i* (haben) open; sich ö~en open. Ö~er *m* -s,- opener. Ö~ung *f* -,-en opening. Ö~ungszeiten *fpl* opening hours

oft *adv* often

öfter *a* quite often. ö~e(r,s) *a* frequent; des Ö~en (ö~en) frequently. ö~s *adv* (*fam*) quite often

oftmals *adv* often

oh *int* oh!

ohne *prep* (+ *acc*) without; o~ mich! count me out! oben o~ topless; nicht o~ sein (*fam*) be not bad; (*nicht harmlos*) be quite nasty □ *conj* o~ zu überlegen without thinking; o~ dass ich es merkte without my noticing it. o~dies *adv* anyway. o~gleichen *pred* *a* unparalleled; eine Frechheit o~gleichen a piece of unprecedented insolence. o~hin *adv* anyway

Ohn|macht *f* -,-en faint; (*fig*) powerlessness; in O~macht fallen faint. o~mächtig *a* unconscious; (*fig*) powerless; o~mächtig werden faint

Ohr *nt* -[e]s,-en ear; übers Ohr hauen (*fam*) cheat

Öhr *nt* -[e]s,-e eye

ohren|betäubend *a* deafening. O~schmalz *nt* ear-wax. O~schmerzen *mpl* earache *sg*. O~sessel *m* wing-chair. O~tropfen *mpl* ear drops

Ohrfeige *f* slap in the face; jdm eine O~ geben slap s.o.'s face. o~n *vt* jdn o~n slap s.o.'s face

Ohr|läppchen *nt* -s,- ear-lobe. O~ring *m* ear-ring. O~wurm *m* earwig

oje *int* oh dear!

okay /o'ke:/ *a* & *adv* (*fam*) OK

okkult *a* occult

Öko|logie *f* - ecology. ö~logisch *a* ecological. Ö~nomie *f* - economy; (*Wissenschaft*) economics *sg*. ö~nomisch *a* economic; (*sparsam*) economical

Oktave *f* -,-n octave

Oktober *m* -s,- October

Okular *nt* -s,-e eyepiece

okulieren *vt* graft

ökumenisch *a* ecumenical

Öl *nt* -[e]s,-e oil; in Öl malen paint in oils. Ölbaum *m* olivetree. ölen *vt* oil; wie ein geölter Blitz (*fam*) like greased lightning. Ölfarbe *f* oil-paint. Ölfeld *nt* oilfield. Ölgemälde *nt* oil-painting. ölig *a* oily

Oliv|e *f* -,-n olive. O~enöl *nt* olive oil. o~grün *a* olive[-green]

oll *a* (*fam*) old; (*fam: hässlich*) nasty

Ölmessstab (Ölmeßstab) *m* dip-stick. Ölsardinen *fpl* sardines in oil. Ölstand *m* oil-level. Öltanker *m* oil-tanker. Ölteppich *m* oil-slick

Olympiade *f* -,-n Olympic Games *pl*, Olympics *pl*

Olymp|iasieger(in) /o'lvmpia-/ *m(f)* Olympic champion. o~isch *a* Olympic; O~ische Spiele Olympic Games

Ölzeug *nt* oilskins *pl*

Oma *f* -,-s (*fam*) granny

Omelett *nt* -[e]s,-e & -s omelette

Omen *nt* -s,- omen

ominös *a* ominous

Omnibus *m* bus; (*Reise-*) coach

onanieren *vi* (haben) masturbate

Onkel *m* -s,- uncle

Opa *m* -s,-s (*fam*) grandad

Opal *m* -s,-e opal

Oper *f* -,-n opera

Operation /-'tsio:n/ *f* -,-en operation. O~ssaal *m* operating theatre

Operette *f* -,-n operetta

operieren *vt* operate on (*Patient, Herz*); sich o~ lassen have an operation □ *vi* (haben) operate

Opern|glas *nt* opera-glasses *pl*. O~haus *nt* opera-house. O~sänger(in) *m(f)* opera-singer

Opfer *nt* -s,- sacrifice; (*eines Unglücks*) victim; ein O~ bringen make a sacrifice; jdm/etw zum O~ fallen fall victim to s.o./sth. o~n *vt* sacrifice. O~ung *f* -,-en sacrifice

Opium *nt* -s opium

opponieren *vi (haben)* o~ gegen oppose

Opportunist *m* -en,-en opportunist. o~isch *a* opportunist

Opposition /-'tsjo:n/ *f* -. opposition. O~spartei *f* opposition party

Optik *f* - optics *sg (fam: Objektiv)* lens. O~er *m* -s,- optician

optimal *a* optimum

Optimis|mus *m* - optimism. O~t *m* -en, -en optimist. o~tisch *a* optimistic, *adv* -ally

Optimum *nt* -s,-ma optimum

Option /ɔp'tsjo:n/ *f* -,-en option

optisch *a* optical; *(Eindruck)* visual

Orakel *nt* -s,- oracle

Orange /o'rã:ʒə/ *f* -,-n orange. o~ *inv a* orange. O~ade /orã'ʒa:də/ *f* -,-n orangeade. O~nmarmelade *f* [orange] marmalade. O~nsaft *m* orange juice

Oratorium *nt* -s,-ien oratorio

Orchester /ɔr'kɛstɐ/ *nt* -s,- orchestra. o~rieren *vt* orchestrate

Orchidee /ɔrçi'de:ə/ *f* -,-n orchid

Orden *m* -s,- *(Ritter-, Kloster-)* order; *(Auszeichnung)* medal, decoration; jdm einen O~ verleihen decorate s.o. O~stracht *f (Relig)* habit

ordentlich *a* neat, tidy; *(anständig)* respectable; *(ordnungsgemäß, fam: richtig)* proper; *(Mitglied, Versammlung)* ordinary; *(fam: gut)* decent; *(fam: gehörig)* good ◻ *adv* neatly, tidily; respectably; properly; *(fam: gut, gehörig)* well; *(sehr)* very; *(regelrecht)* really

Order *f* -,-s & -n order

ordinär *a* common

Ordination /-'tsjo:n/ *f* -,-en *(Relig)* ordination; *(Aust)* surgery. o~ieren *vt (Relig)* ordain

ordnen *vt* put in order; *(aufräumen)* tidy; *(an-)* arrange; sich zum Zug o~en form a procession. O~er *m* -s,- steward; *(Akten-)* file

Ordnung *f* - order; O~ halten keep order; O~ machen tidy up; in O~ bringen put in order; *(aufräumen)* tidy; *(reparieren)* mend; *(fig)* put right; in O~ sein be in order; *(ordentlich sein)* be tidy; *(fig)* be all right; ich bin mit dem Magen *od* mein Magen ist nicht ganz in O~ I have a slight stomach upset; [geht] in O~! OK! o~sgemäß *a* proper, *adv* -ly. O~sstrafe *f (Jur)* fine. o~swidrig *a* improper, *adv* -ly

Ordonnanz Ordonanz *f* -,-en *(Mil)* orderly

Organ *nt* -s,-e organ; *(fam: Stimme)* voice

Organi|sation /-'tsjo:n/ *f* -,-en organization. O~sator *m* -s,-en /-'to:rən/ organizer

organisch *a* organic, *adv* -ally

organisieren *vt* organize; *(fam: beschaffen)* get [hold of]

Organis|mus *m* -,-men organism; *(System)* system. O~t *m* -en,-en organist

Organspenderkarte *f* donor card

Orgasmus *m* -,-men orgasm

Orgel *f* -,-n *(Mus)* organ. O~pfeife *f* organ-pipe

Orgie /'ɔrgjə/ *f* -,-n orgy

Orient /'o:rjɛnt/ *m* -s Orient. o~talisch *a* Oriental

orientier|en /orjɛn'ti:rən/ *vt* inform *(über + acc* about); sich o~en get one's bearings, orientate oneself; *(unterrichten)* inform oneself *(über + acc* about). O~ung *f* - orientation; die O~ung verlieren lose one's bearings

original *a* original. O~ *nt* -s,-e original; *(Person)* character. O~ität *f* - originality. O~übertragung *f* live transmission

originell *a* original; *(eigenartig)* unusual

Orkan *m* -s,-e hurricane

Ornament *nt* -[e]s,-e ornament

Ornat *m* -[e]s,-e robes *pl*

Ornithologie *f* - ornithology

Ort *m* -[e]s,-e place; *(Ortschaft)* [small] town; am Ort locally; am Ort des Verbrechens at the scene of the crime; an Ort und Stelle in the right place; *(sofort)* on the spot. o~en *vt* locate

ortho|dox *a* orthodox. O~graphie, O~-grafie *f* - spelling. o~graphisch, o~-grafisch *a* spelling ... O~päde *m* -n,-n orthopaedic specialist. o~pädisch *a* orthopaedic

örtlich *a* local, *adv* -ly. Ö~keit *f* -,-en locality

Ortschaft *f* -,-en [small] town; *(Dorf)* village; geschlossene O~ *(Auto)* built-up area

orts|fremd *a* o~fremd sein be a stranger. O~gespräch *nt (Teleph)* local call. O~name *m* place-name. O~sinn *m* sense of direction. O~verkehr *m* local traffic. O~zeit *f* local time

Öse *f* -,-n eyelet; *(Schlinge)* loop; Haken und Öse hook and eye

Ost *m* -[e]s east. o~deutsch *a* Eastern/(Pol) East German

Osten *m* -s east; nach O~ east

ostentativ *a* pointed, *adv* -ly

Osteopath *m* -en,-en osteopath

Oster|ei /'o:stɐʔaɪ/ nt Easter egg. O~fest nt Easter. O~glocke f daffodil. O~montag m Easter Monday. O~n nt -·- Easter; frohe O~n! happy Easter!

Österreich nt -s Austria. Ö~er m, -s,-, Ö~erin f -,-nen Austrian. ö~isch a Austrian

östlich a eastern; (Richtung) easterly □ adv & prep (+ gen) ö~ [von] der Stadt [to the] east of the town

Ost|see f Baltic [Sea]. o~wärts adv eastwards

oszillieren vi (haben) oscillate

Otter¹ m -s,- otter

Otter² f -,-n adder

Ouverture /uver'ty:rə/ f -,-n overture

oval a oval. O~ nt -s,-e oval

Ovation /-'tsjo:n/ f -,-en ovation

Ovulation /-'tsjo:n/ f -,-en ovulation

Oxid, Oxyd nt -[e]s,-e oxide

Ozean m -s,-e ocean

Ozon nt -s ozone. O~loch nt hole in the ozone layer. O~schicht f ozone layer

P

paar pron inv ein p~ a few; ein p~ Mal a few times; alle p~ Tage every few days. P~ nt -[e]s,-e pair; (Ehe-, Liebes-, Tanz-) couple. p~en vt mate; (verbinden) combine; sich p~en mate. p~mal adv ein p~mal a few times; ein p~ Mal, s. paar. P~ung f -,-en mating. p~weise adv in pairs, in twos

Pacht f -,-en lease; (P~summe) rent. p~en vt lease

Pächter m -s,- lessee; (eines Hofes) tenant

Pachtvertrag m lease

Pack¹ m -[e]s,-e bundle

Pack² nt -[e]s (sl) rabble

Päckchen nt -s,- package, small packet

pack|en vt/i (haben) pack; (ergreifen) seize; (fig:fesseln) grip; p~ dich! (sl) beat it! P~en m -s,- bundle. p~end a (fig) gripping. P~papier nt [strong] wrapping paper. P~ung f -,-en packet; (Med) pack

Pädagog|e m -n,-n educationalist; (Lehrer) teacher. P~ik f - educational science. p~isch a educational

Paddel nt -s,- paddle. P~boot nt canoe. p~n vt/i (haben/sein) paddle. P~sport m canoeing

Page /'pa:ʒə/ m -n,-n page

Paillette /paj'jɛtə/ f -,-n sequin

Paket nt -[e]s,-e packet; (Post-) parcel

Pakist|an nt -s Pakistan. P~aner(in) m -s,-,(f-,-nen) Pakistani. p~anisch a Pakistani

Pakt m -[e]s,-e pact

Palast m -[e]s,-̈e palace

Palästin|a nt -s Palestine. P~enser(in) m -s,-,(f-,-nen) Palestinian. p~ensisch a Palestinian

Palette f -,-n palette

Palm|e f -,-n palm[-tree]; jdn auf die P~e bringen (fam) drive s.o. up the wall. P~sonntag m Palm Sunday

Pampelmuse f -,-n grapefruit

Panier|mehl nt (Culin) breadcrumbs pl. p~t a (Culin) breaded

Panik f - panic; in P~ geraten panic

panisch a p~e Angst panic

Panne f -,-n breakdown; (Reifen-) flat tyre; (Missgeschick) mishap. P~ndienst m breakdown service

Panorama nt -s panorama

panschen vt adulterate □ vi (haben) splash about

Panther, Panter m -s,- panther

Pantine f -,-n [wooden] clog

Pantoffel m -s,-n slipper; (ohne Ferse) mule. P~held m (fam) henpecked husband

Pantomime¹ f -,-n mime

Pantomime² m -n,-n mime artist

pantschen vt/i = panschen

Panzer m -s,- armour; (Mil) tank; (Zool) shell. p~n vt armourplate. P~schrank m safe

Papa m -s,-s daddy

Papagei m -s & -en,-en parrot

Papier nt -[e]s,-e paper. P~korb m wastepaper basket. P~schlange f streamer. P~waren fpl stationery sg

Pappe f - cardboard; (dial: Kleister) glue

Pappel f -,-n poplar

pappen vt/i (haben) (fam) stick

pappig a (fam) sticky

Papp|karton m, P~schachtel f cardboard box

Paprika m -s,-[s] [sweet] pepper; (Gewürz) paprika □ f -,-[s] (P~schote) pepper

Papst m -[e]s,-̈e pope

päpstlich a papal

Parade f -,-n parade

Paradeiser m -s,- (Aust) tomato

Paradies nt -es,-e paradise. p~isch a heavenly

Paradox nt -es,-e paradox. p~ a paradoxical

Paraffin nt -s paraffin

Paragraph Paragraf m -en,-en section

parall**e**l a & adv parallel. P~ef f -,-n parallel

P**a**ranuss (P**a**ranuß) f Brazil nut

Paras**i**t m -en,-en parasite

par**a**t a ready

P**ä**rchen nt -s,- pair; (Liebes-) couple

Parc**ou**rs /par'ku:g/ m -,- /-[s],-s/ (Sport) course

Pard**o**n /par'dõ:/ int sorry!

Parf**ü**m nt -s,-e & -s perfume, scent. p~**i**ert a perfumed, scented

par**ie**ren¹ vt parry

par**ie**ren² vi (haben) (fam) obey

Parit**ä**t f - parity; (in Ausschuss) equal representation

Park m -s,-s park. p~en vt/i (haben) park. P~en nt -s parking; 'P~en verboten' 'no parking'

Park**e**tt nt -[e]s,-e parquet floor; (Theat) stalls pl

Park|haus nt multi-storey car park. P~lücke f parking space. P~platz m car park, (Amer) parking-lot; (für ein Auto) parking space; (Autobahn-) lay-by. P~scheibe f parking-disc. P~schein m car-park ticket. P~uhr f parking-meter. P~verbot nt parking ban; 'P~verbot' 'no parking'

Parlam**e**nt nt -[e]s,-e parliament. p~**a**risch a parliamentary

Parod**ie** f -,-n parody. p~ren vt parody

Par**o**le f -,-n slogan; (Mil) password

Part m -s,-s (Theat, Mus) part

Part**ei** f -,-en (Pol, Jur) party; (Miet-) tenant; für jdn P~ ergreifen take s.o.'s part. p~isch a biased. P~los a independent

Parterre /par'tcr/ nt -s,-s ground floor, (Amer) first floor; (Theat) rear stalls pl. p~ adv on the ground floor

Part**ie** f -,-n part; (Tennis, Schach) game; (Golf) round; (Comm) batch; eine gute P~ machen marry well

Part**i**kel¹ nt -s,- particle

Part**i**kel² f -,-n (Gram) particle

Partit**u**r f -,-en (Mus) full score

Partiz**i**p nt -s,-ien /-jən/ participle; erstes/zweites P~ present/past participle

Partner|(in) m -s,- (f -,-nen) partner. P~schaft f -,-en partnership. P~stadt f twin town

Party /'pa:gti/ f -,-s party

Parz**e**lle f -,-n plot [of ground]

Pass m -es,¨e (Paß m -sses,¨sse) passport; (Geog, Sport) pass

pass**a**bel a passable

Passage /pa'sa:ʒə/ f -,-n passage; (Einkaufs-) shopping arcade

Passag**ie**r /pasa'ʒi:g/ m -s,-e passenger

Pass**a**mt (Paßamt) nt passport office

Pass**a**nt(in) m -en,-en (f -,-nen) passerby

Passb**i**ld (Paßbild) nt passport photograph

P**a**sse f -,-n yoke

p**a**ssen vi (haben) fit; (geeignet sein) be right (für for); (Sport) pass the ball; (aufgeben) pass; p~ zu go [well] with; (übereinstimmen) match; jdm p~ fit s.o.; (gelegen sein) suit s.o.; seine Art passt mir nicht I don't like his manner; [ich] passe pass. p~d a suitable; (angemessen) appropriate; (günstig) convenient; (übereinstimmend) matching

p**a**ssier|bar a passable. p~en vt pass; cross (Grenze); (Culin) rub through a sieve □ vi (sein) happen (jdm to s.o.); es ist ein Unglück p~t there has been an accident. P~schein m pass

Passi**o**n f -,-en passion. p~**ie**rt a very keen (Jäger, Angler)

pass**i**v a passive. P~ nt -s,-e (Gram) passive

Pass|kontrolle (Paßkontrolle) f passport control. P~straße f pass

P**a**ste f -,-n paste

Past**e**ll nt -[e]s,-e pastel. P~farbe f pastel colour

Past**e**t|chen nt -s,- [individual] pie; (Königin-) vol-au-vent. P~e f -,-n pie; (Gänseleber-) pâté

pasteurisieren /pastøri'zi:rən/ vt pasteurize

Past**i**lle f -,-n pastille

Pastin**a**ke f -,-n parsnip

Past**o**r m -s,-en /-'to:rən/ pastor

P**a**te m -n,-n godfather; (fig) sponsor; P~n godparents. P~nkind nt godchild. P~nschaft f - sponsorship. P~nsohn m godson

Pat**e**nt nt -[e]s,-e patent; (Offiziers-) commission. p~ a (fam) clever, adv -ly; (Person) resourceful. p~**ie**ren vt patent

Pat**e**ntochter f god-daughter

P**a**ter m -s,- (Relig) Father

path**e**tisch a emotional □ adv with emotion

Pathol**o**g|e m -n,-n pathologist. p~isch a pathological, adv -ly

P**a**thos nt - emotion, feeling

P**a**tience /pa'sjã:s/ f -,-n patience

Pat**ie**nt(in) /pa'tsjɛnt(ɪn)/ m -en, -en (f -,-nen) patient

Pat**i**n f -,-nen godmother

Patri**o**t|(in) m -en,-en (f -,-nen) patriot. p~isch a patriotic. P~ismus m - patriotism

Patr**o**ne f -,-n cartridge

Patrouill|e /pa'truljə/ *f* -,-n patrol. p~ieren /-'ji:rən/ *vi* (*haben*/*sein*) patrol

Patsch|e *f* in der P~e sitzen (*fam*) be in a jam. p~en *vi* (*haben*/*sein*) splash □ *vt* slap. p~nass (p~naß) *a* (*fam*) soaking wet

Patt *nt* -s stalemate

Patz|er *m* -s,- (*fam*) slip. p~ig *a* (*fam*) insolent

Pauk|e *f* -,-n kettledrum; auf die P~e hauen (*fam*) have a good time; (*prahlen*) boast. p~en *vt*/*i* (*haben*) (*fam*) swot. P~er *m* -s,- (*fam*: *Lehrer*) teacher

pausbäckig *a* chubby-cheeked

pauschal *a* all-inclusive; (*einheitlich*) flat-rate; (*fig*) sweeping (*Urteil*); p~e Summe lump sum □ *adv* in a lump sum; (*fig*) wholesale. P~e *f* -,-n lump sum. P~reise *f* package tour. P~summe *f* lump sum

Pause¹ *f* -,-n break; (*beim Sprechen*) pause; (*Theat*) interval; (*im Kino*) intermission; (*Mus*) rest; P~ machen have a break

Pause² *f* -,-n tracing. p~n *vt* trace

pausenlos *a* incessant, *adv* -ly

pausieren *vi* (*haben*) have a break; (*ausruhen*) rest

Pauspapier *nt* tracing-paper

Pavian *m* -s,-e baboon

Pavillon /'pavɪljõ/ *m* -s,-s pavilion

Pazif|ik *m* -s Pacific [Ocean]. p~sch *a* Pacific

Pazifist *m* -en,-en pacifist

Pech *nt* -s pitch; (*Unglück*) bad luck; P~ haben be unlucky. p~schwarz *a* pitch-black; (*Haare, Augen*) jet-black. P~strähne *f* run of bad luck. P~vogel *m* (*fam*) unlucky devil

Pedal *nt* -s,-e pedal

Pedant *m* -en,-en pedant. p~isch *a* pedantic, *adv* -ally

Pediküre *f* -,-n pedicure

Pegel *m* -s,- level; (*Gerät*) water-level indicator. P~stand *m* [water] level

peilen *vt* take a bearing on; über den Daumen gepeilt (*fam*) at a rough guess

Pein *f* - (*liter*) torment. p~igen *vt* torment

peinlich *a* embarrassing, awkward; (*genau*) scrupulous, *adv* -ly; es war mir sehr p~ I was very embarrassed

Peitsche *f* -,-n whip. p~n *vt* whip; (*fig*) lash (*an* + *acc* against). P~nhieb *m* lash

pekuniär *a* financial, *adv* -ly

Pelikan *m* -s,-e pelican

Pell|e *f* -,-n skin. p~en *vt* peel; shell (*Ei*); sich p~en peel. P~kartoffeln *fpl* potatoes boiled in their skins

Pelz *m* -es,-e fur. P~mantel *m* fur coat

Pendel *nt* -s,- pendulum. p~n *vi* (*haben*) swing □ *vi* (*sein*) commute. P~verkehr *m* shuttle-service; (*für Pendler*) commuter traffic

Pendler *m* -s,- commuter

penetrant *a* penetrating; (*fig*) obtrusive, *adv* -ly

penibel *a* fastidious, fussy; (*pedantisch*) pedantic

Penis *m* -,-se penis

Penne *f* -,-n (*fam*) school. p~n *vi* (*haben*) (*fam*) sleep. P~r *m* -s,- (*sl*) tramp

Pension /pã'zjo:n/ *f* -,-en pension; (*Hotel*) . guest-house; bei voller/halber P~ with full/half board. P~är(in) *m* -s,-e (*f* -,-nen) pensioner. P~at *nt* -[e]s,-e boarding-school. p~ieren *vt* retire. p~iert *a* retired. P~ierung *f* - retirement

Pensum *nt* -s [allotted] work

Peperoni *f* -,- chilli

per *prep* (+ *acc*) by; per Luftpost by airmail

perfekt *a* perfect, *adv* -ly; p~ sein (*Vertrag*:) be settled

Perfekt *nt* -s (*Gram*) perfect

Perfektion /-'tsjo:n/ *f* - perfection

perforiert *a* perforated

Pergament *nt* -[e]s,-e parchment. P~papier *nt* grease-proof paper

Period|e *f* -,-n period. p~isch *a* periodic, *adv* -ally

Perl|e *f* -,-n pearl; (*Glas-, Holz-*) bead; (*Sekt-*) bubble; (*fam*: *Hilfe*) treasure. p~en *vi* (*haben*) bubble. P~mutt *nt* -s, P~mutter *f* - & *nt* -s mother-of-pearl

perplex *a* (*fam*) perplexed

Perserkatze *f* Persian cat

Pers|ien /-jən/ *nt* -s Persia. p~isch *a* Persian

Person *f* -,-en person; (*Theat*) character; ich für meine P~ [I] for my part; für vier P~en for four people

Personal *nt* -s personnel, staff. P~ausweis *m* identity card. P~chef *m* personnel manager. P~ien /-jən/ *pl* personal particulars. P~mangel *m* staff shortage. P~pronomen *nt* personal pronoun

Personen|kraftwagen *m* private car. P~zug *m* stopping train

personifizieren *vt* personify

persönlich *a* personal □ *adv* personally, in person. P~keit *f* -,-en personality

Perspektive *f* -,-n perspective; (*Zukunfts-*) prospect

Perücke *f* -,-n wig

pervers *a* [sexually] perverted. P~ion *f* -,-en perversion

Pessimis|mus *m* - pessimism. P~t *m* -en,-en pessimist. p~tisch *a* pessimistic, *adv* -ally

Pest *f* - plague

Petersilie /-jə/ *f* - parsley

Petroleum /-leʊm/ *nt* -s paraffin, (*Amer*) kerosene

Petze *f* -,-n (*fam*) sneak. p~n *vi* (*haben*) (*fam*) sneak

Pfad *m* -[e]s,-e path. P~finder *m* -s,- [Boy] Scout. P~finderin *f* -,-nen [Girl] Guide

Pfahl *m* -[e]s,-̈e stake, post

Pfalz (die) - the Palatinate

Pfand *nt* -[e]s,-̈er pledge; (*beim Spiel*) forfeit; (*Flaschen-*) deposit

pfänd|en *vt* (*Jur*) seize. P~erspiel *nt* game of forfeits

Pfand|haus *nt* pawnshop. P~leiher *m* -s,- pawnbroker

Pfändung *f* -,-en (*Jur*) seizure

Pfann|e *f* -,-n [frying-]pan. P~kuchen *m* pancake; Berliner P~kuchen doughnut

Pfarr|er *m* -s,- vicar, parson; (*katholischer*) priest. P~haus *nt* vicarage

Pfau *m* -s,-en peacock

Pfeffer *m* -s pepper. P~kuchen *m* gingerbread. P~minzbonbon *m* & *nt* [pepper-]mint. P~minze *f* - (*Bot*) peppermint. P~minztee *m* [pepper]mint tea. p~n *vt* pepper; (*fam: schmeißen*) chuck. P~streuer *m* -s,- pepperpot

Pfeif|e *f* -,-n whistle; (*Tabak-, Orgel-*) pipe. p~en† *vt/i* (*haben*) whistle; (*als Signal*) blow the whistle; ich p~e darauf! (*fam*) I couldn't care less [about it]!

Pfeil *m* -[e]s,-e arrow

Pfeiler *m* -s,- pillar; (*Brücken-*) pier

Pfennig *m* -s,-e pfennig; 10 P~ 10 pfennigs

Pferch *m* -[e]s,-e [sheep] pen. p~en *vt* (*fam*) cram (in + *acc* into)

Pferd *nt* -es,-e horse; zu P~e on horseback; das P~ beim Schwanz aufzäumen put the cart before the horse. P~erennen *nt* horse-race; (*als Sport*) [horse-]racing. P~eschwanz *m* horse's tail; (*Frisur*) pony-tail. P~estall *m* stable. P~estärke *f* horsepower. P~ewagen *m* horse-drawn cart

Pfiff *m* -[e]s,-e whistle. P~ haben (*fam*) have style

Pfifferling *m* -s,-e chanterelle

pfiffig *a* smart

Pfingst|en *nt* -s Whitsun. P~montag *m* Whit Monday. P~rose *f* peony

Pfirsich *m* -s,-e peach. p~farben *a* peach[-coloured]

Pflanz|e *f* -,-n plant. p~en *vt* plant. P~enfett *nt* vegetable fat. p~lich *a* vegetable; (*Mittel*) herbal. P~ung *f* -,-en plantation

Pflaster *nt* -s,- pavement; (*Heft-*) plaster. p~n *vt* pave. P~stein *m* paving-stone

Pflaume *f* -,-n plum

Pflege *f* - care; (*Kranken-*) nursing; in P~ nehmen look after; (*Admin*) foster (*Kind*). p~bedürftig *a* in need of care. P~eltern *pl* foster-parents. P~kind *nt* foster-child. p~leicht *a* easy-care. P~mutter *f* foster-mother. p~n *vt* look after, care for; nurse (*Kranke*); cultivate (*Künste, Freundschaft*). P~r(in) *m* -s,- (*f* -,-nen) nurse; (*Tier-*) keeper

Pflicht *f* -,-en duty; (*Sport*) compulsory exercise/routine. p~bewusst (p~bewußt) *a* conscientious, *adv* -ly. p~eifrig *a* zealous, *adv* -ly. P~fach *nt* (*Sch*) compulsory subject. P~gefühl *nt* sense of duty. p~gemäß *a* due □ *adv* duly

Pflock *m* -[e]s,-̈e peg

pflücken *vt* pick

Pflug *m* -[e]s,-̈e plough

pflügen *vt/i* (*haben*) plough

Pforte *f* -,-n gate

Pförtner *m* -s,- porter

Pfosten *m* -s,- post

Pfote *f* -,-n paw

Pfropfen *m* -s,- stopper; (*Korken*) cork. p~ *vt* graft (auf + *acc* on [to]); (*fam: pressen*) cram (in + *acc* into)

pfui *int* ugh; p~ schäm dich! you should be ashamed of yourself!

Pfund *nt* -[e]s,-e & - pound

Pfusch|arbeit *f* (*fam*) shoddy work. p~en *vi* (*haben*) botch one's work. P~er *m* -s,- (*fam*) shoddy worker. P~erei *f* -,-en (*fam*) botch-up

Pfütze *f* -,-n puddle

Phänomen *nt* -s,-e phenomenon. p~al *a* phenomenal

Phantasie *f* -,-n imagination; P~n fantasies; (*Fieber-*) hallucinations. p~los *a* unimaginative. p~ren *vi* (*haben*) fantasize; (*im Fieber*) be delirious. p~voll *a* imaginative, *adv* -ly

phant|astisch *a* fantastic, *adv* -ally. P~om *nt* -s,-e phantom

pharma|zeutisch *a* pharmaceutical. P~zie *f* - pharmacy

Phase *f* -,-n phase

Philanthrop *m* -en,-en philanthropist. p~isch *a* philanthropic

Philolo|ge *m* -n,-n teacher/student of language and literature. P~gie *f* - [study of] language and literature

Philosoph *m* -en,-en philosopher. P~ie *f* -,-n philosophy. p~ieren *vi* (*haben*) philosophize

philosophisch *a* philosophical, *adv* -ly

phlegmatisch *a* phlegmatic

Phobie f -,-n phobia

Phonet|ik f - phonetics sg. **p~isch** a phonetic, adv -ally

Phonotypistin f -,-nen audio typist

Phosphor m -s phosphorus

Photo nt, **Photo-** = Foto, Foto-

Phrase f -,-n empty phrase

Physik f - physics sg. **p~alisch** a physical; ⟨Experiment, Forschung⟩ physics ...

Physiker(in) m -s,- (f -,-nen) physicist

Physio|logie f -physiology. **P~therapie** f physiotherapy

physisch a physical, adv -ly

Pianist(in) m -en,-en (f -,-nen) pianist

Pickel m -s,- pimple, spot; ⟨Spitzhacke⟩ pick. **p~ig** a spotty

picken vt/i (haben) peck (nach at); ⟨fam: nehmen⟩ pick (aus out of); ⟨Aust fam: kleben⟩ stick

Picknick nt -s,-s picnic. **p~en** vi (haben) picnic

piep[s]|en vi (haben) ⟨Vogel:⟩ cheep; ⟨Maus:⟩ squeak; ⟨Techn⟩ bleep. **P~er** m -s,- bleeper

Pier m -s,-e [harbour] pier

Pietät /pie'tɛːt/ f -reverence. **p~los** a irr-everent, adv -ly

Pigment nt -[e]s,-e pigment. **P~ierung** f -pigmentation

Pik nt -s,-s ⟨Karten⟩ spades pl

pikant a piquant; ⟨gewagt⟩ racy

piken vt (fam) prick

pikiert a offended, hurt

piksen vt (fam) prick

Pilger|(in) m -s,- (f -,-nen) pilgrim. **P~fahrt** f pilgrimage. **p~n** vi (sein) make a pilgrimage

Pille f -,-n pill

Pilot m -en,-en pilot

Pilz m -es,-e fungus; ⟨essbarer⟩ mushroom; **wie P~e aus dem Boden schießen** (fig) mushroom

pingelig a (fam) fussy

Pinguin m -s,-e penguin

Pinie /-jə/ f -,-n stone-pine

pink pred a shocking pink

pinkeln vi (haben) (fam) pee

Pinsel m -s,- [paint]brush

Pinzette f -,-n tweezers pl

Pionier m -s,-e ⟨Mil⟩ sapper; (fig) pioneer. **P~arbeit** f pioneering work

Pirat m -en,-en pirate

pirschen vi (haben) **p~ auf** (+ acc) stalk □ vr sich **p~** creep (an + acc up to)

pissen vi (haben) (sl) piss

Piste f -,-n ⟨Ski⟩ run, piste; ⟨Renn-⟩ track; ⟨Aviat⟩ runway

Pistole f -,-n pistol

pitschnass (pitschnaß) a (fam) soaking wet

pittoresk a picturesque

Pizza f -,-s pizza

Pkw /'pe:kave:/ m -s,-s (= Personen-kraftwagen) [private] car

placieren /-'tsi:rən/ vt = platzieren

Plackerei f - (fam) drudgery

plädieren vi (haben) plead (für for); **auf Freispruch p~** ⟨Jur⟩ ask for an acquittal

Plädoyer /plɛdoa'je:/ nt -s,-s ⟨Jur⟩ closing speech; (fig) plea

Plage f -,-n [hard] labour; ⟨Mühe⟩ trouble; ⟨Belästigung⟩ nuisance. **P~n** vt torment, plague; ⟨bedrängen⟩ pester; **sich p~n** struggle; ⟨arbeiten⟩ work hard

Plagi|at nt -[e]s,-e plagiarism. **p~ieren** vt plagiarize

Plakat nt -[e]s,-e poster

Plakette f -,-n badge

Plan m -[e]s,-e plan

Plane f -,-n tarpaulin; ⟨Boden-⟩ ground-sheet

planen vt/i (haben) plan

Planet m -en,-en planet

planier|en vt level. **P~raupe** f bulldozer

Planke f -,-n plank

plan|los a unsystematic, adv -ally. **p~mäßig** a systematic; ⟨Ankunft⟩ sched-uled □ adv systematically; ⟨nach Plan⟩ ac-cording to plan; ⟨ankommen⟩ on schedule

Plansch|becken nt paddling pool. **p~en** vi (haben) splash about

Plantage /plan'taːʒə/ f -,-n plantation

Planung f - planning

Plapper|maul nt (fam) chatter-box. **p~n** vi (haben) chatter □ vt talk ⟨Unsinn⟩

plärren vi (haben) bawl; ⟨Radio:⟩ blare

Plasma nt -s plasma

Plastik¹ f -,-en sculpture

Plast|ik² nt -s plastic. **p~isch** a three-dimensional; ⟨formbar⟩ plastic; ⟨anschaulich⟩ graphic, adv -ally; **p~ische Chirurgie** plastic surgery

Platane f -,-n plane [tree]

Plateau /pla'to:/ nt -s,-s plateau

Platin nt -s platinum

Platitüde f -,-n (NEW) Plattitüde

platonisch a platonic

platschen vi (sein) splash

plätschern vi (haben) splash; ⟨Bach:⟩ babble □ vi (sein) ⟨Bach:⟩ babble along

platt a & adv flat; **p~ sein** (fam) be flab-bergasted. **P~nt** -[s]⟨Lang⟩ Low German

Plättbrett nt ironing-board

Platte f -,-n slab; (Druck-) plate; (Metall-, Glas-) sheet; (Fliese) tile; (Koch-) hotplate; (Tisch-) top; (Auszieh-) leaf; (Schall-) record, disc; (zum Servieren) [flat] dish, platter; kalte P~ assorted cold meats and cheeses pl

Plätt|eisen nt iron. p~en vt/i (haben) iron

Plattenspieler m record-player

Platt|form f -,-en platform. P~füße mpl flat feet. P~heit f -,-en platitude

Plattitüde f -,-n platitude

Platz m -es,⁻e place; (von Häusern umgeben) square; (Sitz-) seat; (Sport-) ground; (Fußball-) pitch; (Tennis-) court; (Golf-) course; (freier Raum) room, space; P~ nehmen take a seat; P~ machen/lassen make/leave room; vom P~ stellen (Sport) send off. P~angst f agoraphobia; (Klaustrophobie) claustrophobia. P~anweiserin f -,-nen usherette

Plätzchen nt -s,- spot; (Culin) biscuit

platzen vi (sein) burst; (auf-) split; (fam: scheitern) fall through; (Verlobung:) be off; vor Neugier p~ be bursting with curiosity

platzieren vt place, put; sich p~ (Sport) be placed

Platz|karte f seat reservation ticket. P~konzert nt open-air concert. P~mangel m lack of space. P~patrone f blank. P~regen m downpour. P~verweis m (Sport) sending off. P~wunde f laceration

Plauderei f -,-en chat

plaudern vi (haben) chat

Plausch m -[e]s,-e (SGer) chat. p~en vi (haben) (SGer) chat

plausibel a plausible

plazieren vt (NEW) platzieren

pleite a (fam) p~ sein be broke; (Firma:) be bankrupt; p~ gehen (NEW) p~ gehen, s. Pleite. P~ f -,-n (fam) bankruptcy; (Misserfolg) flop; P~ gehen od machen go bankrupt

plissiert a [finely] pleated

Plomb|e f -,-n seal; (Zahn-) filling. p~ieren vt seal; fill (Zahn)

plötzlich a sudden, adv -ly

plump a plump; (ungeschickt) clumsy, adv -ily

plumpsen vi (sein) (fam) fall

Plunder m -s (fam) junk, rubbish

plündern vt/i (haben) loot

Plunderstück nt Danish pastry

Plural m -s,-e plural

plus adv, conj & prep (+ dat) plus. P~ nt -surplus; (Gewinn) profit; (Vorteil) advantage, plus. P~punkt m (Sport) point; (fig)

plus. P~quamperfekt nt pluperfect. P~zeichen nt plus sign

Po m -s,-s (fam) bottom

Pöbel m -s mob, rabble. p~haft a loutish

pochen vi (haben) knock; (Herz:) pound; p~ auf (+ acc) (fig) insist on

pochieren /pɔ'ʃiːrən/ vt (Culin) poach

Pocken pl smallpox sg

Podest nt -[e]s,-e rostrum

Podium nt -s,-ien /-jən/ platform; (Podest) rostrum

Poesie /poe'ziː/ f - poetry

poetisch a poetic

Pointe /'pɔ̃ːtə/ f -,-n point (of a joke)

Pokal m -s,-e goblet; (Sport) cup

pökeln vt (Culin) salt

Poker nt -s poker

Pol m -s,-e pole. p~ar a polar

polarisieren vt polarize

Polarstern m pole-star

Pole m, -n,-n Pole. P~n nt -s Poland

Police /po'liːsə/ f -,-n policy

Polier m -s,-e foreman

polieren vt polish

Polin f -,-nen Pole

Politesse f -,-n [woman] traffic warden

Politik f - politics sg; (Vorgehen, Maßnahme) policy

Polit|iker(in) m -s,- (f,-,-nen) politician. p~isch a political, adv -ly

Politur f -,-en polish

Polizei f - police pl. P~beamte(r) m police officer. p~lich a police ... ; □ adv by the police; (sich anmelden) with the police. P~streife f police patrol. P~stunde f closing time. P~wache f police station

Polizist m -en,-en policeman. P~in f -,-nen policewoman

Pollen m -s pollen

polnisch a Polish

Polohemd nt polo shirt

Polster nt -s,- pad; (Kissen) cushion; (Möbel-) upholstery; (fam: Rücklage) reserves pl. P~er m -s,- upholsterer. P~möbel pl upholstered furniture sg. p~n vt pad; upholster (Möbel). P~ung f - padding; upholstery

Polter|abend m wedding-eve party. p~n vi (haben) thump, bang; (schelten) bawl □ vi (sein) crash down; (gehen) clump [along]; (fahren) rumble [along]

Polyäthylen nt -s polythene

Polyester m -s polyester

Polyp m -en,-en polyp; (sl: Polizist) copper; P~en adenoids pl

Pomeranze f -,-n Seville orange

Pommes *pl* (*fam*) French fries

Pommes frites /pɔm'fri:t/ *pl* chips; (*dünner*) French fries

Pomp *m* -s pomp

Pompon /põ'põ:/ *m* -s,-s pompon

pompös *a* ostentatious, *adv* -ly

Pony[1] *nt* -s,-s pony

Pony[2] *m* -s,-s fringe

Pop *m* -[s] pop. P~musik *f* pop music

Popo *m* -s,-s (*fam*) bottom

populär *a* popular. P~arität *f* - popularity

Pore *f* -,-n pore

Porno|graphie, Pornografie *f* - pornography. p~graphisch, p~grafisch *a* pornographic

porös *a* porous

Porree *m* -s leeks *pl*; eine Stange P~ a leek

Portal *nt* -s,-e portal

Portemonnaie /pɔrtmɔ'ne:/ *nt* -s,-s purse

Portier /pɔr'tje:/ *m* -s,-s doorman, porter

Portion /-'tsjo:n/ *f* -,-en helping, portion

Portmonee *nt* -s,-s = Portemonnaie

Porto *nt* -s postage. p~frei *adv* post free, post paid

Porträt /pɔr'trɛ:/ *nt* -s,-s portrait. p~tieren *vt* paint a portrait of

Portugal *nt* -s Portugal

Portugies|e *m* -n,-n, P~in *f* -,-nen Portuguese. p~isch *a* Portuguese

Portwein *m* port

Porzellan *nt* -s china, porcelain

Posaune *f* -,-n trombone

Pose *f* -,-n pose

posieren *vi* (*haben*) pose

Position /-'tsjo:n/ *f* -,-en position

positiv *a* positive, *adv* -ly. P~ *nt* -s,-e (*Phot*) positive

Posse *f* -,-n (*Theat*) farce. P~n *m* -s,- prank; P~n *pl* tomfoolery *sg*

Possessivpronomen *nt* possessive pronoun

possierlich *a* cute

Post *f* - post office; (*Briefe*) mail, post; mit der P~ by post

postalisch *a* postal

Post|amt *nt* post office. P~anweisung *f* postal money order, P~bote *m* postman

Postbaⁿⁿ ~~... ... ... (*Woche*) ...~~ *(Waren-)* batch; *(Rechnungs-)* item, ... ; P~ stehen stand guard; nicht auf dem P~ (*fam*) under the weather

Poster *nt & m* -s,- poster

Postfach *nt* post-office *or* PO box

postieren *vt* post, station; sich p~ station oneself

Post|karte *f* postcard. p~lagernd *adv* poste restante. P~leitzahl *f* postcode, *(Amer)* Zip code P~scheckkonto *nt* ≈ National Girobank account. P~stempel *m* postmark

postum *a* posthumous, *adv* -ly

post|wendend *adv* by return of post. P~wertzeichen *nt* [postage] stamp

Poten|tial /-'tsja:l/ *nt* -s,-e = Potenzial. p~tiell /-'tsjɛl/ *a* = potenziell

Potenz *f* -,-en potency; (*Math & fig*) power. P~ial *nt* -s,-e potential. p~iell *a* potential, *adv* -ly

Pracht *f* - magnificence, splendour. P~exemplar *nt* magnificent specimen

prächtig *a* magnificent, *adv* -ly; (*prima*) splendid, *adv* -ly

prachtvoll *a* magnificent, *adv* -ly

Prädikat *nt* -[e]s,-e rating; (*Comm*) grade; (*Gram*) predicate. p~iv *a* (*Gram*) predicative, *adv* -ly. P~swein *m* high-quality wine

präge|n *vt* stamp (auf + *acc* on); emboss (*Leder, Papier*); mint (*Münze*); coin (*Wort, Ausdruck*); (*fig*) shape. P~stempel *m* die

pragmatisch *a* pragmatic, *adv* -ally

prägnant *a* succinct, *adv* -ly

prähistorisch *a* prehistoric

prahl|en *vi* (*haben*) boast, brag (mit about). p~erisch *a* boastful, *adv* -ly

Prakti|k *f* -,-en practice. P~kant(in) *m* -en,-en (*f* -,-nen) trainee

Prakti|kum *nt* -s,-ka practical training. p~sch *a* practical; (*nützlich*) handy; (*tatsächlich*) virtual; p~scher Arzt general practitioner □ *adv* practically; virtually; (*in der Praxis*) in practice; p~sch arbeiten do practical work. p~zieren *vt/i* (*haben*) practise; (*anwenden*) put into practice; (*fam: bekommen*) get

Praline *f* -,-n chocolate; Schachtel P~n box of chocolates

prall *a* bulging; (*dick*) plump; (*Sonne*) blazing □ *adv* p~ gefüllt full to bursting. p~en *vi* (*sein*) p~ auf (+ *acc*)/gegen collide with, hit; (*Sonne:*) blaze down on

Prämie /-jə/ *f* -,-n premium; (*Preis*) award

prämi|ieren *vt* award a prize to

Pranger *m* -s,- pillory

Pranke *f* -,-n paw

Präpar|at *nt* -[e]s,-e preparation. p~ieren *vt* prepare; (*zerlegen*) dissect; ~~[präⁿⁿ⁾ⁿ⁾]~~ stutt

Präposition /-'tsjo:n/ ~~... ... ...~~ ...ⁿⁿⁿ

Präsens *nt* - (*Gram*) present

präsentieren *vt* present; sich p~ present itself/(*Person:*) oneself

Präsenz f -presence
Präservativ nt -s,-e condom
Präsident|(in) m -en,-en (f -,-nen) president. **P~schaft** f -presidency
Präsidium nt -s presidency; (Gremium) executive committee; (Polizei-) headquarters pl
prasseln vi (haben) (Regen:) beat down; (Feuer:) crackle □ vi (sein) p~ auf (+ acc)/gegen beat down on/beat against
prassen vi (haben) live extravagantly; (schmausen) feast
Präteritum nt -s imperfect
präventiv a preventive
Praxis f -,-xen practice; (Erfahrung) practical experience; (Arzt-) surgery; in der P~ in practice
Präzedenzfall m precedent
präzis[e] a precise, adv -ly
Präzision f -precision
predig|en vt/i (haben) preach. **P~er** m -s,-preacher. **P~t** f -,-en sermon
Preis m -es,-e price; (Belohnung) prize; um jeden/keinen P~ at any/not at any price. **P~ausschreiben** nt competition
Preiselbeere f (Bot) cowberry; (Culin) ≈ cranberry
preisen† vt praise; sich glücklich p~ count oneself lucky
preisgeben† vt sep abandon (dat to); reveal (Geheimnis)
preis|gekrönt a award-winning. **P~gericht** nt jury. **p~günstig** a reasonably priced □ adv at a reasonable price. **P~lage** f price range. **p~lich** a price ... □ adv in price. **P~richter** m judge. **P~schild** nt price-tag. **P~träger(in)** m(f) prize-winner. **p~wert** a reasonable, adv -bly; (billig) inexpensive, adv -ly
prekär a difficult; (heikel) delicate
Prell|bock m buffers pl. **p~en** vt bounce; (verletzen) bruise; (fam: betrügen) cheat. **P~ung** f -,-en bruise
Premiere /prə'mjeːrə/ f -,-n première
Premierminister(in) /prə'mjeː-/ m(f) Prime Minister
Presse f -,-n press. **p~n** vt press; sich p~n press (an + acc against)
pressieren vi (haben) (SGer) be urgent
Pressluft (Preßluft) f compressed air. **P~bohrer** m pneumatic drill
Prestige /prɛs'tiːʒə/ nt -s prestige
Preuß|en nt -s Prussia. **p~isch** a Prussian
prickeln vi (haben) tingle
Priester m -s,-priest
prima inv a first-class, first-rate; (fam: toll) fantastic, adv fantastically well

primär a primary, adv -ily
Primel f -,-n primula; (Garten-) polyanthus
primitiv a primitive
Prinz m -en,-en prince. **P~essin** f -,-nen princess
Prinzip nt -s,-ien/-jən/ principle; im/aus P~ in/on principle. **p~iell** a (Frage) of principle □ adv on principle; (im Prinzip) in principle
Priorität f -,-en priority
Prise f -,-n **P~ Salz** pinch of salt
Prisma nt -s men prism
privat a private, adv -ly; (persönlich) personal. **P~adresse** f home address. **p~isieren** vt privatize
Privat|leben nt private life. **P~lehrer** m private tutor. **P~lehrerin** f governess. **P~patient(in)** m(f) private patient
Privileg nt -[e]s,-ien /-jən/ privilege. **p~iert** a privileged
pro prep (+ dat) per. **Pro** nt - das Pro und Kontra the pros and cons pl
Probe f -,-n test, trial; (Menge, Muster) sample; (Theat) rehearsal; auf die P~ stellen put to the test; ein Auto P~ fahren test-drive a car. **P~fahrt** f test drive. **p~n** vt/i (haben) (Theat) rehearse. **p~weise** adv on a trial basis. **P~zeit** f probationary period
probieren vt/i (haben) try; (kosten) taste; (proben) rehearse
Problem nt -s,-e problem. **p~atisch** a problematic
problemlos a problem-free □ adv without any problems
Produkt nt -[e]s,-e product
Produk|tion /-'tsjoːn/ f -,-en production. **p~tiv** a productive. **P~tivität** f -productivity
Produ|zent m -en,-en producer. **p~zieren** vt produce; sich p~zieren (fam) show off
professionell a professional, adv -ly
Professor m -s,-en /-'soːrən/ professor
Profi m -s,-s (Sport) professional
Profil nt -s,-e profile; (Reifen-) tread; (fig) image. **p~iert** a (fig) distinguished
Profit m -[e]s,-e profit. **p~ieren** vi (haben) profit (von from)
Prognose f -,-n forecast; (Med) prognosis
Programm nt -s,-e programme; (Computer-) program; (TV) channel; (Comm: Sortiment) range. **p~ieren** vt/i (haben) (Computer) program. **P~ierer(in)** m -s,- (f -,-nen) [computer] programmer
progressiv a progressive
Projekt nt -[e]s,-e project

Projektor *m* -s,-en /-'toːrən/ projector

projizieren *vt* project

Proklam|ation /-'tsjoːn/ *f* -,-en proclamation. p~ieren *vt* proclaim

Prolet *m* -en,-en boor. P~ariat *nt* -[e]s proletariat. P~arier /-jɐ/ *m* -s,-, proletarian

Prolog *m* -s,-e prologue

Promenade *f* -,-n promenade. P~nmischung *f* (*fam*) mongrel

Promille *pl* (*fam*) alcohol level *sg* in the blood; zu viel P~ haben (*fam*) be over the limit

prominen|t *a* prominent. P~z *f*- prominent figures *pl*

Promiskuität *f* - promiscuity

promovieren *vi* (*haben*) obtain one's doctorate

prompt *a* prompt, *adv* -ly; (*fam: natürlich*) of course

Pronomen *nt* -s,- pronoun

Propag|anda *f* - propaganda; (*Reklame*) publicity. p~ieren *vt* propagate

Propeller *m* -s,- propeller

Prophet *m* -en,-en prophet. p~isch *a* prophetic

prophezei|en *vt* prophesy. P~ung *f* -,-en prophecy

Proportion /-'tsjoːn/ *f* -,-en proportion. p~al *a* proportional. p~iert *a* gut p~iert well proportioned

Prosa *f* - prose

prosaisch *a* prosaic, *adv* -ally

prosit *int* cheers!

Prospekt *m* -[e]s,-e brochure; (*Comm*) prospectus

prost *int* cheers!

Prostitu|ierte *f* -n,-n prostitute. P~tion /-'tsjoːn/ *f* - prostitution

Protest *m* -[e]s,-e protest

Protestant|(in) *m* -en,-en (*f* -,-nen) (*Relig*) Protestant. p~isch *a* (*Relig*) Protestant

protestieren *vi* (*haben*) protest

Prothese *f* -,-n artificial limb; (*Zahn-*) denture

Protokoll *nt* -s,-e record; (*Sitzungs-*) minutes *pl*; (*diplomatisches*) protocol; (*Strafzettel*) ticket

Prototyp *m* -s,-en prototype

protz|en *vi* (*haben*) show off (mit etw acc). p~ig *a* ostentatious

Proviant *m* -s provisions *pl*

Provinz *f* -,-en province. p~iell *a* provincial

Provision *f* -,-en (*Comm*) commission

provisorisch *a* provisional, *adv* -ly, temporary, *adv* -ily

Provokation /-'tsjoːn/ *f* -,-en provocation

provozieren *vt* provoke. p~d *a* provocative, *adv* -ly

Prozedur *f* -,-en [lengthy] business

Prozent *nt* -[e]s,-e & - per cent; 5 P~ 5 per cent. P~satz *m* percentage. p~ual *a* percentage ...

Prozess *m* -es,-e (Prozeß *m* -sses,-sse) process; (*Jur*) lawsuit; (*Kriminal-*) trial

Prozession *f* -,-en procession

prüde *a* prudish

prüf|en *vt* test/(*über-*) check (auf + acc for); audit (*Bücher*); (*Sch*) examine; p~ender Blick searching look. P~er *m* -s,- inspector; (*Buch-*) auditor; (*Sch*) examiner. P~ling *m* -s,-e examination candidate. P~ung *f* -,-en examination; (*Test*) test; (*Bücher-*) audit; (*fig*) trial

Prügel *m* -s,- cudgel; P~ *pl* hiding *sg*, beating *sg*. P~ei *f* -,-en brawl, fight. p~n *vt* beat, thrash; sich p~n fight, brawl

Prunk *m* -[e]s magnificence, splendour. p~en *vi* (*haben*) show off (mit etw sth). p~voll *a* magnificent, *adv* -ly

prusten *vi* (*haben*) splutter; (*schnauben*) snort

Psalm *m* -s,-en psalm

Pseudonym *nt* -s,-e pseudonym

pst *int* shush!

Psychi|ater *m* -s,- psychiatrist. P~atrie *f* - psychiatry. p~atrisch *a* psychiatric

psychisch *a* psychological, *adv* -ly; (*Med*) mental, *adv* -ly

Psycho|analyse *f* psychoanalysis. P~loge *m* -n,-n psychologist. P~logie *f* - psychology. p~logisch *a* psychological, *adv* -ly

Pubertät *f* - puberty

publik *a* p~ werden/machen become/ make public

Publi|kum *nt* -s public; (*Zuhörer*) audience; (*Zuschauer*) spectators *pl*. p~zieren *vt* publish

Pudding *m* -s,-s blancmange; (*im Wasserbad gekocht*) pudding

Pudel *m* -s,- poodle

Puder *m* & (*fam*) *nt* -s,- powder; (*Körper-*) talcum [powder]. P~dose *f* [powder] compact. p~n *vt* powder. P~zucker *m* icing sugar

Puff[1] *m* -[e]s,-̈e push, poke

Puff[2] *m* & *nt* -s,-s (*sl*) brothel

puffen *vt* (*fam*) poke □ *vi* (*sein*) puff along

Puffer *m* -s,- (*Rail*) buffer; (*Culin*) pancake. P~zone *f* buffer zone

Pull|i *m* -s,-s jumper. P~over *m* -s,- jumper; (*Herren-*) pullover

Puls m -es pulse. P~ader f artery. p~ieren vi (haben) pulsate

Pult nt -[e]s,-e desk; (Lese-) lectern

Pulver nt -s,- powder. p~ig a powdery. p~isieren vt pulverize

Pulver|kaffee m instant coffee. P~schnee m powder snow

pummelig a (fam) chubby

Pump m auf P~ (fam) on tick

Pumpe f -,-n pump. p~n vt/i (haben) pump; (fam: leihen) lend; [sich (dat)] etw p~n (fam: borgen) borrow sth

Pumps /pœmps/ pl court shoes

Punkt m -[e]s,-e dot; (Tex) spot; (Geom, Sport & fig) point; (Gram) full stop, period; P~ sechs Uhr at six o'clock sharp; nach P~en siegen win on points. p~iert a (Li-nie, Note) dotted

pünktlich a punctual, adv -ly. P~keit f - punctuality

Punsch m -[e]s,-e [hot] punch

Pupille f -,-n (Anat) pupil

Puppe f -,-n doll; (Marionette) puppet; (Schaufenster-, Schneider-) dummy; (Zool) chrysalis

pur a pure; (fam: bloß) sheer; Whisky pur neat whisky

Püree nt -s,-s purée; (Kartoffel-) mashed potatoes pl

puritanisch a puritanical

purpurrot a crimson

Purzel|baum m (fam) somersault. p~n vi (sein) (fam) tumble

pusseln vi (haben) (fam) potter

Puste f - (fam) breath; aus der P~ out of breath. p~n vt/i (haben) (fam) blow

Pute f -,-n turkey; (Henne) turkey hen. P~r m -s,- turkey cock

Putsch m -[e]s,-e coup

Putz m -es plaster; (Staat) finery. p~en vt clean; (Aust) dry-clean; (zieren) adorn; sich p~en dress up; sich (dat) die Zäh-ne/Nase p~en clean one's teeth/blow one's nose. P~frau f cleaner, char-woman. p~ig a (fam) amusing, cute; (seltsam) odd. P~macherin f -,-nen milliner

Puzzlespiel /'pazl-/ nt jigsaw

Pyramide f -,-n pyramid

Q

Quacksalber m -s,- quack

Quadrat nt -[e]s,-e square. q~isch a square. Q~meter m & nt square metre

quaken vi (haben) quack; (Frosch:) croak

quäken vi (haben) screech; (Baby:) whine

Quäker(in) m -s,- (f -,-nen) Quaker

Qual f -,-en torment; (Schmerz) agony

quälen vt torment; (foltern) torture; (be-drängen) pester; sich q~ torment oneself; (leiden) suffer; (sich mühen) struggle. q~d a agonizing

Quälerei f -,-en torture; (Qual) agony

Quälgeist m (fam) pest

Qualifi|kation f -/-'tsjo:n/ f -,-en qualifi-cation. q~zieren vt qualify; sich q~zieren qualify. q~ziert a qualified; (fähig) competent; (Arbeit) skilled

Qualität f -,-en quality

Qualle f -,-n jellyfish

Qualm m -s [thick] smoke. q~en vi (haben) smoke

qualvoll a agonizing

Quantität f -,-en quantity

Quantum nt -s,-ten quantity; (Anteil) share, quota

Quarantäne f - quarantine

Quark m -s quark, ≈ curd cheese; (fam: Unsinn) rubbish

Quartal nt -s,-e quarter

Quartett nt -[e]s,-e quartet

Quartier nt -s,-e accommodation; (Mil) quarters pl; ein Q~ suchen look for ac-commodation

Quarz m -es quartz

quasseln vi (haben) (fam) jabber

Quaste f -,-n tassel

Quatsch m -[e]s (fam) nonsense, rubbish; Q~ machen (Unfug machen) fool around; (etw falsch machen) do a silly thing. q~en (fam) vi (haben) talk; (schwatzen) natter; (Wasser, Schlamm:) squelch □ vt talk. q~nass (q~naß) a (fam) soaking wet

Quecksilber nt mercury

Quelle f -,-n spring; (Fluss- & fig) source. q~n† vi (sein) well [up]/(fließen) pour (aus from); (aufquellen) swell; (hervor-treten) bulge

quengeln vi (fam) whine; (Baby:) grizzle

quer adv across, crosswise; (schräg) diag-onally; q~ gestreift horizontally striped

Quere f - der Q~ nach across, crosswise; jdm in die Q~ kommen get in s.o.'s way

querfeldein adv across country

quer|gestreift a (NEW) q~ gestreift, s. quer. q~köpfig a (fam) awkward. Q~latte f crossbar. Q~schiff nt tran-sept. Q~schnitt m cross-section. q~schnittsgelähmt a paraplegic. Q~straße f side-street; die erste Q~straße links the first turning on the left. Q~verweis m cross-reference

quetsch|en vt squash; (drücken) squeeze; (zerdrücken) crush; (Culin) mash; sich q~en in (+ acc) squeeze into; sich (dat) den Arm q~en bruise one's arm. Q~ung f -,-en, Q~wunde f bruise

Queue /køː/ nt -s,-s cue

quicklebendig a very lively

quieken vi (haben) squeal; (Maus:) squeak

quietschen vi (haben) squeal; (Tür, Dielen:) creak

Quintett nt -[e]s,-e quintet

Quirl m -[e]s,-e blender with a star-shaped head. q~en vt mix

quitt a q~ sein (fam) be quits

Quitte f -,-n quince

quittieren vt receipt (Rechnung); sign for (Geldsumme, Sendung); (reagieren auf) greet (mit with); den Dienst q~ resign

Quittung f -,-en receipt

Quiz /kvɪs/ nt -,- quiz

Quote f -,-n proportion

R

Rabatt m -[e]s,-e discount

Rabatte f -,-n (Hort) border

Rabattmarke f trading stamp

Rabbiner m -s,- rabbi

Rabe m -n,-n raven. r~nschwarz a pitch-black

rabiat a violent, adv -ly; (wütend) furious, adv -ly

Rache f - revenge, vengeance

Rachen m -s,- pharynx; (Maul) jaws pl

rächen vt avenge; sich r~ take revenge (an + dat on); (Fehler, Leichtsinn:) cost s.o. dear

Racker m -s,- (fam) rascal

Rad nt -[e]s,-er wheel; (Fahr-) bicycle, (fam) bike; Rad fahren cycle

Radar m & nt -s radar

Radau m -s (fam) din, racket

radebrechen vt/i (haben) [Deutsch/Englisch] r~ speak broken German/English

radeln vi (sein) (fam) cycle

Rädelsführer m ringleader

radfahren vt sep (sein) (NEW) Rad fahren, s. Rad. R~er(in) m(f) -s,-(-,-nen) cyclist

radier|en vt/i (haben) rub out; (Kunst) etch. R~gummi m eraser, rubber. R~ung f -,-en etching

Radieschen /-ˈdiːsçən/ nt -s,- radish

radikal a radical, adv -ly; (drastisch) drastic, adv -ally. R~e(r) m/f (Pol) radical

Radio nt -s,-s radio

radioaktiv a radioactive, R~ität f - radioactivity

Radioapparat m radio [set]

Radius m -,-ien /-jən/ radius

Rad|kappe f hub-cap. R~ler m -s,- cyclist; (Getränk) shandy. R~weg m cycle track

raff|en vt grab; (kräuseln) gather; (kürzen) condense. r~gierig a avaricious

Raffin|ade f - refined sugar. R~erie f -,-n refinery. R~esse f -,-n refinement; (Schlauheit) cunning. r~ieren vt refine. r~iert a ingenious, adv -ly; (durchtrieben) crafty, adv -ily

Rage /ˈraːʒə/ f - (fam) fury

ragen vi (haben) rise [up]

Rahm m -s (SGer) cream

rahmen vt frame. R~ m -s,- frame; (fig) framework; (Grenze) limits pl; (einer Feier) setting

Rain m -[e]s,-e grass verge

räkeln v = rekeln

Rakete f -,-n rocket; (Mil) missile

Rallye /ˈrali/ nt -s,-s rally

rammen vt ram

Rampe f -,-n ramp; (Theat) front of the stage. R~nlicht nt im R~nlicht stehen (fig) be in the limelight

ramponier|en vt (fam) damage; (ruinieren) ruin; r~t battered

Ramsch m -[e]s junk. R~laden m junk-shop

ran adv = heran

Rand m -[e]s,-er edge; (Teller-, Gläser-, Brillen-) rim; (Zier-) border, edging; (Buch-, Brief-) margin; (Stadt-) outskirts pl; (Ring) ring; am R~e des Ruins on the brink of ruin; am R~e erwähnen mention in passing; zu R~e kommen mit = zurande kommen mit, s. zurande; außer R~ und Band (fam: ausgelassen) very boisterous

randalieren vi (haben) rampage

Rand|bemerkung f marginal note. R~streifen m (Auto) hard shoulder

Rang m -[e]s,-e rank; (Theat) tier; erster/zweiter R~ (Theat) dress/upper circle; ersten R~es first-class

rangieren /raŋˈʒiːrən/ vt shunt □ vi (haben) rank (vor + dat before); an erster Stelle r~ come first

Rangordnung f order of importance, (Hierarchie) hierarchy

Ranke f -,-n tendril; (Trieb) shoot

ranken (sich) vr (Bot) trail; (in die Höhe) climb; sich r~ um twine around

Ranzen *m* -s,- *(Sch)* satchel

ranzig *a* rancid

Rappe *m* -n,-n black horse

rappeln *v (fam)* ▫ *vi (haben)* rattle ▫ *vr* sich r~n pick oneself up; *(fig)* rally

Raps *m* -es *(Bot)* rape

rar *a* rare; er macht sich rar *(fam)* we don't see much of him. R~ität *f* -,-en rarity

rasant *a* fast; *(schnittig, schick)* stylish ▫ *adv* fast; stylishly

rasch *a* quick, *adv* -ly

rascheln *vi (haben)* rustle

Rasen *m* -s,- lawn

rasen *vi (sein)* tear [along]; ⟨*Puls:*⟩ race; ⟨*Zeit:*⟩ fly; gegen eine Mauer r~ career into a wall ▫ *vi (haben)* rave; ⟨*Sturm:*⟩ rage; vor Begeisterung r~ go wild with enthusiasm; r~d *a* furious; *(tobend)* raving; ⟨*Sturm, Durst*⟩ raging; ⟨*Schmerz*⟩ excruciating; *(Beifall)* tumultuous ▫ *adv* terribly

Rasenmäher *m* lawn-mower

Raserei *f* - speeding; *(Toben)* frenzy

Rasier|apparat *m* razor. r~en *vt* shave; sich r~en shave. R~klinge *f* razor blade. R~pinsel *m* shaving-brush. R~wasser *nt* aftershave [lotion]

Raspel *f* -,-n rasp; *(Culin)* grater. r~n *vt* grate

Rasse *f* -,-n race. R~hund *m* pedigree dog

Rassel *f* -,-n rattle. r~n *vi (haben)* rattle; ⟨*Schlüssel:*⟩ jangle; ⟨*Kette:*⟩ clank ▫ *vi (sein)* rattle [along]

Rassen|diskriminierung *f* racial discrimination. R~trennung *f* racial segregation

Rassepferd *nt* thoroughbred

rassisch *a* racial

Rassis|mus *m* - racism. r~tisch *a* racist

Rast *f* -,-en rest. r~en *vi (haben)* rest. R~haus *nt* motorway restaurant. r~los *a* restless, *adv* -ly; *(ununterbrochen)* ceaseless, *adv* -ly. R~platz *m* picnic area. R~stätte *f* motorway restaurant [and services]

Rasur *f* -,-en shave

Rat¹ *m* -[e]s [piece of] advice; guter Rat good advice; sich *(dat)* keinen Rat wissen not know what to do; zu Rat[e] ziehen = zurate ziehen, *s.* zurate

Rat² *m* -[e]s,-e *(Admin)* council; *(Person)* councillor

Rate *f* -,-n instalment

raten† *vt* guess; *(empfehlen)* advise ▫ *vi (haben)* guess; jdm r~ advise s.o.

Ratenzahlung *f* payment by instalments

Rat|geber *m* -s,- adviser; *(Buch)* guide. R~haus *nt* town hall

ratifizier|en *vt* ratify. R~ung *f* -,-en ratification

Ration /ra'tsi:o:n/ *f* -,-en ration; eiserne R~ iron rations *pl.* r~al *a* rational, *adv* -ly. r~alisieren *vt/i (haben)* rationalize. r~ell *a* efficient, *adv* -ly. r~ieren *vt* ration

rat|los *a* helpless, *adv* -ly; r~los sein not know what to do. r~sam *pred a* advisable; *(klug)* prudent. R~schlag *m* piece of advice; R~schläge advice *sg*

Rätsel *nt* -s,- riddle; *(Kreuzwort-)* puzzle; *(Geheimnis)* mystery. r~haft *a* puzzling, mysterious. r~n *vi (haben)* puzzle

Ratte *f* -,-n rat

rattern *vi (haben)* rattle ▫ *vi (sein)* rattle [along]

rau *a* rough, *adv* -ly; *(unfreundlich)* gruff, *adv* -ly; *(Klima, Wind)* harsh, raw; *(Landschaft)* rugged; *(heiser)* husky; *(Hals)* sore

Raub *m* -[e]s robbery; *(Menschen-)* abduction; *(Beute)* loot, booty. r~en *vt* steal; abduct ⟨*Menschen*⟩; jdm etw r~en rob s.o. of sth

Räuber *m* -s,- robber

Raub|mord *m* robbery with murder. R~tier *nt* predator. R~überfall *m* robbery. R~vogel *m* bird of prey

Rauch *m* -[e]s smoke. r~en *vt/i (haben)* smoke. R~en *nt* -s smoking; 'R~en verboten' 'no smoking'. R~er *m* -s,-smoker. R~erabteil *nt* smoking compartment

Räucher|lachs *m* smoked salmon. r~n *vt (Culin)* smoke

Rauch|fang *m (Aust)* chimney. r~ig *a* smoky. R~verbot *nt* smoking ban

räudig *a* mangy

rauf *adv* = herauf, hinauf

rauf|en *vt* pull; sich *(dat)* die Haare r~en *(fig)* tear one's hair ▫ *vr/i (haben)* [sich] r~en fight. R~erei *f* -,-en fight

rauh *a* (NEW)rau

rau|haarig *a* wire-haired. R~heit *f* - *(s.* rau) roughness; gruffness; harshness; ruggedness

rauh|haarig *a* (NEW)rauhaarig. R~reif *m* (NEW)Raureif

Raum *m* -[e]s, Räume room; *(Gebiet)* area; *(Welt-)* space

räumen *vt* clear; vacate ⟨*Wohnung*⟩; evacuate ⟨*Gebäude, Gebiet, (Mil) Stellung*⟩; *(bringen)* put (in/auf + *acc* into/on); *(holen)* get (aus out of); beiseite r~ move/put to one side; aus dem Weg r~ *(fam)* get rid of

Raum|fahrer *m* astronaut. R~fahrt *f* space travel. R~fahrzeug *nt* spacecraft.

R~flug m space flight. R~inhalt m volume

räumlich a spatial. R~keiten fpl rooms

Raum|pflegerin f cleaner. R~schiff nt spaceship

Räumung f -(s. räumen) clearing; vacating; evacuation. R~sverkauf m clearance/closing-down sale

raunen vt/i (haben) whisper

Raupe f -,-n caterpillar

Raureif m hoar-frost

raus adv = heraus, hinaus

Rausch m -[e]s, Räusche intoxication; (fig) exhilaration; einen R~ haben be drunk

rauschen vi (haben) ⟨Wasser, Wind:⟩ rush; ⟨Bäume Blätter:⟩ rustle □ vi (sein) rush [along]; aus dem Zimmer r~ sweep out of the room. r~d a rushing; rustling; ⟨Applaus⟩ tumultuous

Rauschgift nt [narcotic] drug; (coll) drugs pl. R~süchtige(r) m/f drug addict

räuspern (sich) vr clear one's throat

rausschmeiß|en vt sep (fam) throw out; (entlassen) sack. R~er m -s,- (fam) bouncer

Raute f -,-n diamond

Razzia f -,-ien /-jən/ [police] raid

Reagenzglas nt test-tube

reagieren vi (haben) react (auf + acc to)

Reaktion /-'tsjo:n/ f -,-en reaction. r~är a reactionary

Reaktor m -s,-en /-'to:rən/ reactor

real a real; (gegenständlich) tangible; (realistisch) realistic, adv -ally. r~isieren vt realize

Realis|mus m - realism. R~t m -en,-en realist. r~tisch a realistic, adv -ally

Realität f -,-en reality

Realschule f ≈ secondary modern school

Rebe f -,-n vine

Rebell m -en,-en rebel. r~ieren vi (haben) rebel. R~ion f -,-en rebellion

rebellisch a rebellious

Rebhuhn nt partridge

Rebstock m vine

Rechen m -s- rake. r~ vt/i (haben) rake

Rechen|aufgabe f arithmetical problem; (Sch) sum. R~fehler m arithmetical error. R~maschine f calculator

Rechenschaft f - R~ ablegen give account (über + acc of); jdn zur R~ ziehen call s.o. to account

recherchieren /reʃɛr'ʃiːrən/ vt/i (haben) investigate; (Journ) research

rechnen vi (haben) do arithmetic; (schätzen) reckon; (zählen) count (zu among; auf + acc on); r~ mit reckon with; (erwarten) expect; gut r~ können be good at figures □ vt calculate, work out; do ⟨Aufgabe⟩; (dazu-) add (zu to); (fig) count (zu among). R~ nt -s arithmetic

Rechner m -s,- calculator; (Computer) computer; ein guter R~ sein be good at figures

Rechnung f -,-en bill, (Amer) check; (Comm) invoice; (Berechnung) calculation; R~ führen über (+ acc) keep account of; etw (dat) R~ tragen (fig) take sth into account. R~sjahr nt financial year. R~sprüfer m auditor

Recht nt -[e]s,-e law; (Berechtigung) right (auf + acc to); im R~ sein be in the right; R~ haben/behalten be right; R~ bekommen be proved right; jdm R~ geben agree with s.o.; mit od zu R~rightly; von R~s wegen by right; (eigentlich) by rights

recht a right; (wirklich) real; ich habe keine r~e Lust I don't really feel like it; es jdm r~ machen please s.o.; jdm r~ sein be all right with s.o.; r~ haben/ behalten/bekommen (NEW) Recht haben/behalten/bekommen, s. Recht; jdm r~ geben (NEW) jdm Recht geben, s. Recht □ adv correctly; (ziemlich) quite; (sehr) very; r~ vielen Dankmany thanks

Rechte| f -n,-[n] right side; (Hand) right hand; (Boxen) right; die R~e (Pol) the right; zu meiner R~en on my right. r~e(r,s) a right; (Pol) right-wing; r~e Masche plain stitch. R~e(r) m/f der/die R~e the right man/woman; du bist mir der/die R~e! you're a fine one! R~e(s) nt das R~e the right thing; etwas R~es lernen learn something useful; nach dem R~en sehen see that everything is all right

Rechteck nt -[e]s,-e rectangle. r~ig a rectangular

rechtfertig|en vt justify; sich r~en justify oneself. R~ung f - justification

recht|haberisch a opinionated. r~lich a legal, adv -ly. r~mäßig a legitimate, adv -ly.

rechts adv on the right; (bei Stoff) on the right side; von/nach r~ from/to the right; zwei r~, zwei links stricken knit two, purl two. R~anwalt m, R~anwältin f lawyer

rechtschaffen a upright; (ehrlich) honest, adv -ly; r~ müde thoroughly tired

rechtschreib|en vi (inf only) spell correctly. R~fehler m spelling mistake. R~ung f - spelling

Rechts|händer(in) m -s,- (f -,-nen) right-hander. r~händig a & adv right-handed. r~kräftig a legal, adv -ly.

R~streit m law suit. R~verkehr m driving on the right. r~widrig a illegal, adv -ly. R~wissenschaft f jurisprudence

recht|winklig a right-angled. r~zeitig a & adv in time

Reck nt -[e]s,-e horizontal bar

recken vt stretch; sich r~ stretch; den Hals r~ crane one's neck

Redakteur /redak'tø:ɐ/ m -s,-e editor; (Radio, TV) producer

Redaktion /-'tsjo:n/ f -,-en editing; (Radio, TV) production; (Abteilung) editorial/production department. r~ell a editorial

Rede f -,-n speech; zur R~ stellen demand an explanation from; davon ist keine R~ there's no question of it; nicht der R~ wert not worth mentioning. r~gewandt a eloquent, adv -ly. r~n vi (haben) talk (von about; mit to); (eine Rede halten) speak □ vt talk; speak (Wahrheit); kein Wort r~ not say a word. R~sart f saying; (Phrase) phrase

Redewendung f idiom

redigieren vt edit

redlich a honest, adv -ly

Red|ner m -s,- speaker. r~selig a talkative

reduzieren vt reduce

Reeder m -s,- shipowner. R~ei f -,-en shipping company

reell a real; (ehrlich) honest, adv -ly; (Preis, Angebot) fair

Refer|at nt -[e]s,-e report; (Abhandlung) paper; (Abteilung) section. R~ent(in) m -en,-en (f -,-nen) speaker; (Sachbearbeiter) expert. R~enz f -,-en reference. r~ieren vi (haben) deliver a paper; (berichten) report (über + acc on)

reflektieren vt/i (haben) reflect (über + acc on)

Reflex m -es,-e reflex; (Widerschein) reflection. R~ion f -,-en reflection. r~iv a reflexive. R~ivpronomen nt reflexive pronoun

Reform f -,-en reform. R~ation /-'tsjo:n/ f - (Relig) Reformation

Reform|haus nt health-food shop. r~ieren vt reform

Refrain /rə'frɛ:/ m -s,-s refrain

Regal nt -s,-e [set of] shelves pl

Regatta f -,-ten regatta

rege a active; (lebhaft) lively; (geistig) alert; (Handel) brisk □ adv actively

Regel f -,-n rule; (Monats-) period; in der R~ as a rule. r~mäßig a regular, adv -ly. r~n vt regulate; direct (Verkehr); (erledigen) settle. r~recht a real, proper □ adv

really. R~ung f -,-en regulation; settlement. r~widrig a irregular, adv -ly

regen vt move; sich r~ move; (wach werden) stir

Regen m -s,- rain. R~bogen m rainbow. R~bogenhaut f iris

Regener|ation /-'tsjo:n/ f - regeneration. r~ieren vt regenerate; sich r~ieren regenerate

Regen|mantel m raincoat. R~schirm m umbrella. R~tag m rainy day. R~tropfen m raindrop. R~wetter nt wet weather. R~wurm m earthworm

Regie /re'ʒi:/ f - direction; R~ führen direct

regier|en vt/i (haben) govern, rule; (Monarch:) reign [over]; (Gram) take. r~end a ruling; reigning. R~ung f -,-en government; (Herrschaft) rule; (eines Monarchen) reign

Regime /re'ʒi:m/ nt -s,- /-mə/ regime

Regiment[1] nt -[e]s,-er regiment

Regiment[2] nt -[e]s,-e rule

Region f -,-en region. r~al a regional, adv -ly

Regisseur /reʒɪ'sø:ɐ/ m -s,-e director

Register nt -s,- register; (Inhaltsverzeichnis) index; (Orgel-) stop

registrier|en vt register; (Techn) record. R~kasse f cash register

Regler m -s,- regulator

reglos a & adv motionless

regn|en vi (haben) rain; es r~et it is raining. r~erisch a rainy

regulär a normal, adv -ly; (rechtmäßig) legitimate, adv -ly. r~ieren vt regulate

Regung f -,-en movement; (Gefühls-) emotion. r~slos a & adv motionless

Reh nt -[e]s,-e roe-deer; (Culin) venison

Rehabilit|ation /-'tsjo:n/ f - rehabilitation. r~ieren vt rehabilitate

Rehbock m roebuck

Reib|e f -,-n grater. r~en† vt rub; (Culin) grate; blank r~en polish □ vi (haben) rub. R~ereien fpl (fam) friction sg. R~ung f - friction. r~ungslos a (fig) smooth, adv -ly

reich a rich (an + dat in), adv -ly; (r~haltig) abundant; Arm und R~ (arm und r~) rich and poor

Reich nt -[e]s,-e empire; (König-) kingdom; (Bereich) realm

Reich|e(r) m/f rich man/woman; die R~en the rich pl

reichen vt hand; (anbieten) offer □ vi (haben) be enough; (in der Länge) be long enough; r~ bis zu reach [up to]; (sich erstrecken) extend to; mit dem Geld r~

have enough money; mir reicht's! I've had enough!

reich|haltig a extensive, large; ⟨Mahlzeit⟩ substantial. r~lich a ample; ⟨Vorrat⟩ abundant, plentiful; eine r~liche Stunde a good hour □ adv amply; abundantly; ⟨fam: sehr⟩ very. R~tum m -s,-tümer wealth (an + dat of); R~tümer riches. R~weite f reach; ⟨Techn, Mil⟩ range

Reif m -[e]s [hoar-]frost

reif a ripe; ⟨fig⟩ mature; r~ für ready for. R~e f - ripeness; ⟨fig⟩ maturity. r~en vi ⟨sein⟩ ripen; ⟨Wein, Käse & fig⟩ mature

Reifen m -s,- hoop; ⟨Arm-⟩ bangle; ⟨Auto-⟩ tyre. R~druck m tyre pressure. R~panne f puncture, flat tyre

Reifeprüfung f ≈ A levels pl

reiflich a careful, adv -ly

Reihe f -,-n row; ⟨Anzahl & Math⟩ series; der R~ nach in turn; außer der R~ out of turn; wer ist an der od kommt an die R~? whose turn is it? r~n ⟨sich⟩ vr sich r~n an (+ acc) follow. R~nfolge f order. R~nhaus nt terraced house. R~nweise adv in rows; ⟨fam⟩ in large numbers

Reiher m -s,- heron

Reim m -[e]s,-e rhyme. r~en vt rhyme; sich r~en rhyme

rein[1] a pure; ⟨sauber⟩ clean; ⟨Unsinn, Dummheit⟩ sheer; ins R~e (r~e) schreiben make a fair copy of; ins R~e (r~e) bringen ⟨fig⟩ sort out □ adv purely; ⟨fam⟩ absolutely

rein[2] adv = herein, hinein

Reineclaude /rɛːnɔˈkloːdə/ f -,-n greengage

Reinfall m ⟨fam⟩ let-down; ⟨Misserfolg⟩ flop. r~en† vi sep ⟨sein⟩ fall in; ⟨fam⟩ be taken in (auf + acc by)

Rein|gewinn m net profit. R~heit f - purity

reinig|en vt clean; ⟨chemisch⟩ dry-clean. R~ung f -,-en cleaning; ⟨chemische⟩ dry-cleaning; ⟨Geschäft⟩ dry cleaner's

Reinkarnation /reˈɪnkarnaˈtsɪoːn/ f -,-en reincarnation

rein|legen vt sep put in; ⟨fam⟩ dupe; ⟨betrügen⟩ take for a ride

reinlich a clean. R~keit f - cleanliness

Rein|machefrau f cleaner. R~schrift f fair copy. r~seiden a pure silk

Reis m -es rice

Reise f -,-n journey; ⟨See-⟩ voyage; ⟨Urlaubs-, Geschäfts-⟩ trip. R~andenken nt souvenir. R~büro nt travel agency. R~bus m coach. R~führer m tourist guide; ⟨Buch⟩ guide. R~gesellschaft f tourist group. R~leiter(in) m(f) courier.

r~n vi ⟨sein⟩ travel. R~nde(r) m/f traveller. R~pass (R~paß) m passport. R~scheck m traveller's cheque. R~unternehmer, R~veranstalter m -s,- tour operator. R~ziel nt destination

Reisig nt -s brushwood

Reißaus m R~ nehmen ⟨fam⟩ run away

Reißbrett nt drawing-board

reißen† vt tear; ⟨weg-⟩ snatch; ⟨töten⟩ kill; Witze r~ crack jokes; aus dem Schlaf r~ awaken rudely; an sich ⟨acc⟩ r~ snatch; seize ⟨Macht⟩; mit sich r~ sweep away; sich r~ um ⟨fam⟩ fight for; ⟨gern mögen⟩ be keen on; hin und her gerissen sein ⟨fig⟩ be torn □ vi ⟨sein⟩ tear; ⟨Seil, Faden:⟩ break □ vi ⟨haben⟩ r~ an (+ dat) pull at. r~d a raging; ⟨Tier⟩ ferocious; ⟨Schmerz⟩ violent

Reißer m -s,- ⟨fam⟩ thriller; ⟨Erfolg⟩ big hit. r~isch a ⟨fam⟩ sensational

Reiß|nagel m = R~zwecke. R~verschluss (R~verschluß) m zip [fastener]. R~wolf m shredder. R~zwecke f -,-n drawing-pin, ⟨Amer⟩ thumbtack

reit|en† vt/i ⟨sein⟩ ride. R~er(in) m -s,- ⟨f -,-nen⟩ rider. R~hose f riding breeches pl. R~pferd nt saddle-horse. R~schule f riding-school. R~weg m bridle-path

Reiz m -es,-e stimulus; ⟨Anziehungskraft⟩ attraction, appeal; ⟨Charme⟩ charm. r~bar a irritable. R~barkeit f - irritability. r~en vt provoke; ⟨Med⟩ irritate; ⟨interessieren, locken⟩ appeal to; attract; arouse ⟨Neugier⟩; ⟨beim Kartenspiel⟩ bid. r~end a charming, adv -ly; ⟨entzückend⟩ delightful. R~ung f -,-en ⟨Med⟩ irritation. r~voll a attractive

rekapitulieren vt/i ⟨haben⟩ recapitulate

rekeln ⟨sich⟩ vr stretch; ⟨lümmeln⟩ sprawl

Reklamation /-ˈtsɪoːn/ f -,-en ⟨Comm⟩ complaint

Reklam|e f -,-n advertising, publicity; ⟨Anzeige⟩ advertisement; ⟨TV, Radio⟩ commercial; R~e machen advertise (für etw sth). r~ieren vt complain about; ⟨fordern⟩ claim □ vi ⟨haben⟩ complain

rekonstruieren vt reconstruct. R~ktion /-ˈtsɪoːn/ f -,-en reconstruction

Rekonvaleszenz f - convalescence

Rekord m -[e]s,-e record

Rekrut m -en,-en recruit. r~ieren vt recruit

Rek|tor m -s,-en /-ˈtoːrən/ ⟨Sch⟩ head-|master; ⟨Univ⟩ vice-chancellor. R~torin f -,-nen head|mistress); vice-chancellor

Relais /rəˈlɛː/ nt -,- /-s,-s/ ⟨Electr⟩ relay

relativ a relative, adv -ly, R~pronomen nt relative pronoun

relevan|t a relevant (für to). R~z f - relevance

Relief /rə'li:ɛf/ nt -s,-s relief

Religi|on f -,-en religion; (Sch) religious education. r~ös a religious

Reling f -,-s (Naut) rail

Reliquie /re'li:kviə/ f -,-n relic

Remouladensoße /remu'la:dən-/ f ≈ tartar sauce

rempeln vt jostle; (stoßen) push

Ren nt -s,-s reindeer

Reneklode f -,-n greengage

Renn|auto nt racing car. R~bahn f racetrack; (Pferde-) racecourse. R~boot nt speed-boat. r~en vt/i (sein) run; um die Wette r~en have a race. R~en nt -s,- race. R~pferd nt racehorse. R~sport m racing. R~wagen m racing car

renommiert a renowned; (Hotel, Firma) of repute

renovier|en vt renovate; redecorate (Zimmer). R~ung f - renovation; redecoration

rentabel a profitable, adv -bly

Rente f -,-n pension; in R~ gehen (fam) retire. R~nversicherung f pension scheme

Rentier nt reindeer

rentieren (sich) vr be profitable; (sich lohnen) be worth while

Rentner(in) m -s,- (f -,-nen) [old-age] pensioner

Reparatur f -,-en repair. R~werkstatt f repair workshop; (Auto) garage

reparieren vt repair, mend

repatriieren vt repatriate

Repertoire /reper'toa:ɐ/ nt -s,-s repertoire

Reportage /-'ta:ʒə/ f -,-n report

Reporter(in) m -s,- (f -,-nen) reporter

repräsent|ativ a representative (für of); (eindrucksvoll) imposing; (Prestige verleihend) prestigious. r~ieren vt represent ◻ vi (haben) perform official/social duties

Repress|alie /-lja/ f -,-en reprisal. r~iv a repressive

Reprodu|ktion /-'tsjo:n/ f -,-en reproduction. r~zieren vt reproduce

Reptil nt -s,-ien /-jən/ reptile

Republik f -,-en republic. r~anisch a republican

requirieren vt (Mil) requisition

Requisiten pl (Theat) properties, (fam) props

Reservat nt -[e]s,-e reservation

Reserve f -,-n reserve; (Mil, Sport) reserves pl. R~rad nt spare wheel. R~spieler m reserve. R~tank m reserve tank

reservier|en vt reserve; r~en lassen book. r~t a reserved. R~ung f -,-en reservation

Reservoir /rezɛr'voa:ɐ/ nt -s,-s reservoir

Resid|enz f -,-en residence. r~ieren vi (haben) reside

Resign|ation /-'tsjo:n/ f - resignation. r~ieren vi (haben) (fig) give up. r~iert a resigned, adv -ly

resolut a resolute, adv -ly

Resolution /-'tsjo:n/ f -,-en resolution

Resonanz f -,-en resonance; (fig: Widerhall) response

Respekt /-sp-, -ʃp-/ m -[e]s respect (vor + dat for). r~abel a respectable. r~ieren vt respect

respekt|los a disrespectful, adv -ly. r~voll a respectful, adv -ly

Ressort /rɛ'so:ɐ/ nt -s,-s department

Rest m -[e]s,-e remainder, rest; R~e remains; (Essens-) leftovers

Restaurant /rɛsto'rã:/ nt -s,-s restaurant

Restaur|ation /rɛstaura'tsjo:n/ f -restoration. r~ieren vt restore

Rest|betrag m balance. r~lich a remaining. r~los a utter, adv -ly

Resultat nt -[e]s,-e result

Retorte f -,-n (Chem) retort. R~nbaby nt (fam) test-tube baby

rett|en vt save (vor + dat from); (aus Gefahr befreien) rescue; sich r~en save oneself; (flüchten) escape. R~er m -s,- rescuer; (fig) saviour

Rettich m -s,-e white radish

Rettung f -,-en rescue; (fig) salvation; jds letzte R~ s.o.'s last hope. R~sboot nt lifeboat. R~sdienst m rescue service. R~sgürtel m lifebelt. r~slos adv hopelessly. R~sring m lifebelt. R~swagen m ambulance

retuschieren vt (Phot) retouch

Reu|e f - remorse; (Relig) repentance. r~en vt fill with remorse; es reut mich nicht I don't regret it. r~ig a penitent. r~mütig a contrite, adv -ly

Revanch|e /re'vã:ʃə/ f -,-n revenge; R~e fordern (Sport) ask for a return match. r~ieren (sich) vr take revenge; (sich erkenntlich zeigen) reciprocate (mit with); sich für eine Einladung r~ieren return an invitation

Revers /re've:ɐ/ nt -,- /-[s],-s/lapel

revidieren vt revise; (prüfen) check

Revier nt -s,-e district; (Zool & fig) territory; (Polizei-) [police] station

Revision f -,-en revision; (Prüfung) check; (Bücher-) audit; (Jur) appeal

Revolte f -,-n revolt

Revolution /-'tsio:n/ f -,-en revolution. r~är a revolutionary. r~ieren vt revolutionize

Revolver m -s,- revolver

Revue /rə'vy:/ f -,-n revue

Rezen|sent m -en,-en reviewer. r~sieren vt review. R~sion f -,-en review

Rezept nt -[e]s,-e prescription; (Culin) recipe

Rezeption /-'tsio:n/ f -,-en reception

Rezession f -,-en recession

rezitieren vt recite

R-Gespräch nt reverse-charge call, (Amer) collect call

Rhabarber m -s rhubarb

Rhapsodie f -,-n rhapsody

Rhein m -s Rhine. R~land nt -s Rhineland. R~wein m hock

Rhetori|k f - rhetoric. r~sch a rhetorical

Rheum|a nt -s rheumatism. r~atisch a rheumatic. R~atismus m - rheumatism

Rhinozeros nt -[ses],-se rhinoceros

rhyth|misch /'rYt-/ a rhythmic[al], adv -ally. R~mus m -,-men rhythm

Ribisel f -,-n (Aust) redcurrant

richten vt direct (auf + acc at); address (Frage, Briefe) (an + acc to); aim, train (Waffe) (auf + acc at); (einstellen) set; (vorbereiten) prepare; (reparieren) mend; (hinrichten) execute; (SGer: ordentlich machen) tidy; in die Höhe r~ raise [up]; das Wort an jdn r~ address s.o.; sich r~ be directed (auf + acc at; gegen against); (Blick:) turn (auf + acc on); sich r~ nach comply with (Vorschrift, jds Wünschen); fit in with (jds Plänen); (befolgen) go by; (abhängen) depend on ◻ vi (haben) r~ über (+ acc) judge

Richter m -s,- judge

Richtfest nt topping-out ceremony

richtig a right, correct; (wirklich, echt) real; das R~e (r~e) the right thing ◻ adv correctly; really; r~ stellen put right (Uhr); (fig) correct (Irrtum); die Uhr geht r~ the clock is right. R~keit f - correctness. r~stellen vt sep (NEW) r~ stellen, s. richtig

Richt|linien fpl guidelines

Richtung f -,-en direction; (fig) trend

riechen vt/i (haben) smell (nach of; an etw dat sth)

Riegel m -s,- bolt; (Seife) bar

Riemen m -s,- strap; (Ruder) oar

Riese m -n,-n giant

rieseln vi (sein) trickle; (Schnee:) fall lightly

riesig a huge; (gewaltig) enormous ◻ adv (fam) terribly

Riff nt -[e]s,-e reef

rigoros a rigorous, adv -ly

Rille f -,-n groove

Rind nt -es,-er ox; (Kuh) cow; (Stier) bull; (R~fleisch) beef. R~er cattle pl

Rinde f -,-n bark; (Käse-) rind; (Brot-) crust

Rinderbraten m roast beef

Rind|fleisch nt beef. R~vieh nt cattle pl; (fam: Idiot) idiot

Ring m -[e]s,-e ring

ringeln (sich) vr curl; (Schlange:) coil itself (um round)

ring|en vi (haben) wrestle; (fig) struggle (um/nach for) ◻ vt wring (Hände). R~en nt -s wrestling. R~er m -s,- wrestler. R~kampf m wrestling match; (als Sport) wrestling. R~richter m referee

rings adv r~ im Kreis in a circle; r~ um jdn/etw all around s.o./sth. r~herum, r~um adv all around

Rinn|e f -,-n channel; (Dach-) gutter. r~en† vi (sein) run; (Sand:) trickle. R~stein m gutter

Rippe f -,-n rib. R~nfellentzündung f pleurisy. R~nstoß m dig in the ribs

Risiko nt -s,-s & -ken risk; ein R~ eingehen take a risk

risk|ant a risky. r~ieren vt risk

Riss m -es,-e (Riß m -sses,-sse) tear; (Mauer-) crack; (fig) rift

rissig a cracked; (Haut) chapped

Rist m -[e]s,-e instep

Ritt m -[e]s,-e ride

Ritter m -s,- knight. r~lich a chivalrous, adv -ly. R~lichkeit f - chivalry

rittlings adv astride

Ritu|al nt -s,-e ritual. r~ell a ritual

Ritz m -es,-e scratch. R~e f -,-n crack; (Fels-) cleft; (zwischen Betten, Vorhängen) gap. r~en vt scratch

Rival|e m -n,-n, R~in f -,-nen rival. r~isieren vi (haben) compete (mit with). r~isierend a rival . . R~ität f -,-en rivalry

Robbe f -,-n seal. r~n vi (sein) crawl

Robe f -,-n gown; (Talar) robe

Roboter m -s,- robot

robust a robust

röcheln vi (haben) breathe stertorously

Rochen m -s,- (Zool) ray

Rock[1] m -[e]s, :-e skirt; (Jacke) jacket

Rock[2] m -[s] (Mus) rock

Rodel|bahn f toboggan run. r~n nt (sein/ haben) toboggan. R~schlitten m toboggan

roden vt clear (Land); grub up (Stumpf)

Rogen m -s,- [hard] roe

Roggen m -s rye

roh a rough; (ungekocht) raw; (Holz) bare; (brutal) brutal; r~e Gewalt brute force ◻ adv roughly; brutally. R~bau m -[e]s, -ten shell. R~heit f -,-en brutality. R~kost f raw [vegetarian] food. R~ling m -s,-e brute. R~material nt raw material. R~öl nt crude oil

Rohr nt -[e]s,-e pipe; (Geschütz-) barrel; (Bot) reed; (Zucker-, Bambus-) cane

Röhr|chen nt -s,- [drinking] straw; (Auto, fam) breathalyser (P). R~e f -,-n tube; (Radio-) valve; (Back-) oven

Rohstoff m raw material

Rokoko nt -s rococo

Rolladen m (NEW)Rollladen

Rollbahn f taxiway; (Start-/Landebahn) runway

Rolle f -,-n roll; (Garn-) reel; (Draht-) coil; (Techn) roller; (Seil-) pulley; (Wäsche-) mangle; (Lauf-) castor; (Schrift-) scroll; (Theat) part, role; das spielt keine R~ (fig) that doesn't matter. r~n vt/i roll; (auf-) roll up; roll out (Teig); put through the mangle (Wäsche); sich r~n roll; (sich ein-) curl up r~n sich) roll; (Flugzeug:) taxi ◻ vi (haben) (Donner:) rumble. R~r m -s,- scooter

Roll|feld nt airfield. R~kragen m polo-neck. R~laden m roller shutter. R~mops m rollmop[s] sg

Rollo nt -s,-s [roller] blind

Roll|schuh m roller-skate; R~schuh laufen roller-skate. R~splitt m -s loose chippings pl. R~stuhl m wheelchair. R~treppe f escalator

Rom nt -s Rome

Roman m -s,-e novel. r~isch a Rom-anesque; (Sprache) Romance. R~schriftsteller(in) m(f) novelist

Romant|ik f -romanticism. r~isch a ro-mantic, adv -ally

Romanze f -,-n romance

Röm|er(in) m -s,- (f -,-nen) Roman. r~isch a Roman

Rommé, Rommee /'rɔme:/ nt -s rummy

röntgen vt X-ray. R~aufnahme f, R~bild nt X-ray. R~strahlen mpl X-rays

rosa inv a, R~ nt -[s],- pink

Rose f -,-n rose. R~nkohl m [Brussels] sprouts pl. R~nkranz m (Relig) rosary. R~nmontag m Monday before Shrove Tuesday

Rosette f -,-n rosette

rosig a rosy

Rosine f -,-n raisin

Rosmarin m -s rosemary

Ross nt -es,-̈er (Roß nt -sses,-̈sser) horse. R~kastanie f horse-chestnut

Rost[1] m -[e]s,-e grating; (Kamin-) grate; (Brat-) grill

Rost[2] m -[e]s rust. r~en vi (haben) rust; nicht r~end stainless

röst|en vt roast; toast (Brot). R~er m -s,- toaster

rostfrei a stainless

rostig a rusty

rot a (röter, rötest), Rot nt -s,- red; rot werden turn red; (erröten) go red, blush

Rotation /-'tsio:n/ f -,-en rotation

Röte f - redness; (Scham-) blush

Röteln pl German measles sg

röten vt redden; sich r~ turn red

rothaarig a red-haired

rotieren vi (haben) rotate

Rot|kehlchen nt -s,- robin. R~kohl m red cabbage

rötlich a reddish

Rot|licht nt red light. R~wein m red wine

Rou|lade /ru'la:də/ f -,-n beef olive. R~leau /-'lo:/ nt -s,-s [roller] blind

Route /'ru:tə/ f -,-n route

Routin|e /ru'ti:nə/ f -,-n routine; (Erfahrung) experience. r~emäßig a routine . . . ◻ adv routinely. r~iert a experienced

Rowdy /'raʊdi/ m -s,-s hooligan

Rübe f -,-n beet; rote R~ beetroot; gelbe R~ (SGer) carrot

rüber adv = herüber, hinüber

Rubin m -s,-e ruby

Rubrik f -,-en column; (Kategorie) cat-egory

Ruck m -[e]s,-e jerk

Rückantwort f reply

ruckartig a jerky, adv -ily

rück|bezüglich a (Gram) reflexive. R~blende f flashback. R~blick m (fig) review (auf + acc of). r~blickend adv in retrospect. r~datieren vt (inf & pp only) backdate

rücken vt/i (sein/haben) move; an etw (dat) r~ move sth

Rücken m -s,- back; (Buch-) spine; (Berg-) ridge. R~lehne f back. R~mark nt spi-nal cord. R~schwimmen nt backstroke. R~wind m following wind; (Aviat) tail wind

rückerstatten vt (inf & pp only) refund

Rückfahr|karte f return ticket. R~t f return journey

Rück|fall m relapse. r~fällig a r~fällig werden (Jur) re-offend. R~flug m return flight. R~frage f [further] query. r~fragen vi (haben) (inf & pp only) check (bei with). R~gabe f return. R~gang m decline; (Preis-) drop, fall. r~gängig a r~gängig machen cancel; break off ⟨*Verlobung*⟩. R~grat *nt* -[e]s, -e spine, backbone. R~halt *m* (*fig*) support. R~hand *f* backhand. R~kehr return. R~lagen *fpl* reserves. R~licht *nt* rear-light. r~lings *adv* backwards; ⟨*von hinten*⟩ from behind. R~reise *f* return journey

Rucksack *m* rucksack

Rück|schau *f* review. R~schlag *m* (*Sport*) return; (*fig*) set-back. R~schluss (R~schluß) *m* conclusion. R~schritt *m* (*fig*) retrograde step. r~schrittlich *a* retrograde. R~seite *f* back; ⟨*einer Münze*⟩ reverse

Rücksicht *f* -,-en consideration; R~ nehmen auf (+ *acc*) show consideration for; ⟨*berücksichtigen*⟩ take into consideration. R~nahme *f* - consideration. r~slos *a* inconsiderate, *adv* -ly; ⟨*schonungslos*⟩ ruthless, *adv* -ly. r~svoll *a* considerate, *adv* -ly

Rück|sitz *m* back seat; ⟨*Sozius*⟩ pillion. R~spiegel *m* rear-view mirror. R~spiel *nt* return match. R~sprache *f* consultation; R~sprache nehmen mit consult. R~stand *m* (*Chem*) residue; ⟨*Arbeits-*⟩ backlog; R~stände arrears; im R~stand sein be behind. r~ständig *a* (*fig*) backward. R~stau *m* (*Auto*) tailback. R~strahler *m* -s,- reflector. R~tritt *m* resignation; ⟨*Fahrrad*⟩ back pedalling. r~vergüten *vt* (*inf* & *pp only*) refund. R~wanderer *m* repatriate

rückwärt|ig *a* back ..., rear ... . r~s *adv* backwards. R~sgang *m* reverse [gear]

Rückweg *m* way back

ruckweise *adv* jerkily

rück|wirkend *a* retrospective, *adv* -ly. R~wirkung *f* retrospective force; mit R~wirkung vom backdated to. R~zahlung *f* repayment. R~zug *m* retreat

Rüde *m* -n,-n [male] dog

Rudel *nt* -s,- herd; ⟨*Wolfs-*⟩ pack; ⟨*Löwen-*⟩ pride

Ruder *nt* -s,- oar; ⟨*Steuer-*⟩ rudder; am R~ (*Naut* & *fig*) at the helm. R~boot *nt* rowing boat. R~er *m* -s,- oarsman. r~n *vt/i* ⟨*haben/sein*⟩ row

Ruf *m* -[e]s,-e call; ⟨*laut*⟩ shout; ⟨*Telefon*⟩ Telephone number; ⟨*Ansehen*⟩ reputation; Künstler ... von Ruf artist of repute. r~en† *vt/i* ⟨*haben*⟩ call ⟨*nach* for⟩; r~en lassen send for

Rüffel *m* -s,- ⟨*fam*⟩ telling-off. r~n *vt* ⟨*fam*⟩ tell off

Ruf|name *m* forename by which one is known. R~nummer *f* telephone number. R~zeichen *nt* dialling tone

Rüge *f* -,-n reprimand. r~n *vt* reprimand; ⟨*kritisieren*⟩ criticize

Ruhe *f* - rest; ⟨*Stille*⟩ quiet; ⟨*Frieden*⟩ peace; ⟨*innere*⟩ calm; ⟨*Gelassenheit*⟩ composure; die R~ bewahren keep calm; in R~ lassen leave in peace; sich zur R~ setzen retire; R~ [da]! quiet! R~gehalt *nt* [retirement] pension. r~los *a* restless, *adv* -ly. r~n *vi* ⟨*haben*⟩ rest (auf + *dat* on); ⟨*Arbeit, Verkehr:*⟩ have stopped; hier ruht ... here lies ... R~pause *f* rest, break. R~stand *m* retirement; in den R~stand treten retire; im R~stand retired. R~störung *f* disturbance of the peace. R~tag *m* day of rest; 'Montag R~tag' 'closed on Mondays'

ruhig *a* quiet, *adv* -ly; ⟨*erholsam*⟩ restful; ⟨*friedlich*⟩ peaceful, *adv* -ly; ⟨*unbewegt, gelassen*⟩ calm, *adv* -ly; r~ bleiben remain calm; sehen Sie sich r~ um you're welcome to look round; man kann r~ darüber sprechen there's no harm in talking about it

Ruhm *m* -[e]s fame; ⟨*Ehre*⟩ glory

rühmen *vt* praise; sich r~ boast ⟨*gen* about⟩

ruhmreich *a* glorious

Ruhr *f* - ⟨*Med*⟩ dysentery

Rühr|ei *nt* scrambled eggs *pl*. r~en *vt* move; ⟨*Culin*⟩ stir; sich r~en move; zu Tränen r~en move to tears; r~t euch! ⟨*Mil*⟩ at ease! □ *vi* ⟨*haben*⟩ stir; r~en an (+ *acc*) touch; ⟨*fig*⟩ touch on; r~en von ⟨*fig*⟩ come from. r~end *a* touching, *adv* -ly

rühr|ig *a* active. r~selig *a* sentimental. R~ung *f* - emotion

Ruin *m* -s ruin. R~e *f* -,-n ruin; ruins *pl* ⟨*gen* of⟩. r~ieren *vt* ruin

rülpsen *vi* ⟨*haben*⟩ ⟨*fam*⟩ belch

Rum *m* -s rum

rum *adv* = herum

Rumän|ien /-jən/ *nt* -s Romania. r~isch *a* Romanian

Rummel *m* -s ⟨*fam*⟩ hustle and bustle; ⟨*Jahrmarkt*⟩ funfair. R~platz *m* fairground

rumoren *vi* ⟨*haben*⟩ make a noise; ⟨*Magen:*⟩ rumble

Rumpel|kammer *f* junk-room. r~n *vi* ⟨*haben/sein*⟩ rumble

Rumpf *m* -[e]s,-e body, trunk; ⟨*Schiffs-*⟩ hull; ⟨*Aviat*⟩ fuselage

rümpfen *vt* die Nase r~ turn up one's nose (über + *acc* at)

rund *a* round □ *adv* approximately; r~ um [a]round. R~blick *m* panoramic view. R~brief *m* circular [letter]

Runde *f* -,-n round; ⟨*Kreis*⟩ circle; ⟨*eines Polizisten*⟩ beat; ⟨*beim Rennen*⟩ lap; eine R~ Bier a round of beer. r~n *vt* round; sich r~n become round; ⟨*Backen:*⟩ fill out

Rund|fahrt f tour. R~**frage** f poll

Rundfunk m radio; im R~ on the radio. R~**gerät** nt radio [set]

Rund|gang m round; (Spaziergang) walk (durch round). r~**heraus** adv straight out. r~**herum** adv all around. r~**lich** a rounded; (mollig) plump. R~**reise** f [circular] tour. R~**schreiben** nt circular. r~**um** adv all round. R~**ung** f -,-en curve. r~**weg** adv (ablehnen) flatly

runter adv = herunter, hinunter

Runzel f -,-n wrinkle. r~**n** vt die Stirn r~**n** frown

runzlig a wrinkled

Rüpel m -s,- (fam) lout. r~**haft** a (fam) loutish

rupfen vt pull out; pluck (Geflügel); (fam: schröpfen) fleece

ruppig a rude, adv -ly

Rüsche f -,-n frill

Ruß m -es soot

Russe m -n,-n Russian

Rüssel m -s,- (Zool) trunk

ruß|en vi (haben) smoke. r~**ig** a sooty

Russ|in f -,-nen Russian. r~**isch** a Russian. R~**isch** nt -[s] (Lang) Russian

Russland (Rußland) nt -s Russia

rüsten vi (haben) prepare (zu/für for) □ vr sich r~ get ready; gerüstet sein be ready

rüstig a sprightly

rustikal a rustic

Rüstung f -,-en armament; (Harnisch) armour. R~**skontrolle** f arms control

Rute f -,-n twig; (Angel-, Wünschel-) rod; (zur Züchtigung) birch; (Schwanz) tail

Rutsch m -[e]s,-e slide. R~**bahn** f slide. R~**e** f -,-n chute. r~**en** vt slide; (rücken) move □ vi (sein) slide; (aus-, rücken) slip; (Auto) skid; (rücken) move [along]. r~**ig** a slippery

rütteln vt shake □ vi (haben) r~ an (+ dat) rattle

S

Saal m -[e]s,Säle hall; (Theat) auditorium; (Kranken-) ward

Saat f -,-en seed; (Säen) sowing; (Gesätes) crop. S~**gut** nt seed

sabbern vi (haben) (fam) slobber; (Baby:) dribble; (reden) jabber

Säbel m -s,- sabre

Sabo|tage /zabo'taːʒə/ f - sabotage. S~**teur** /-'tøːɐ̯/ m -s,-e saboteur. s~**tieren** vt sabotage

Sach|bearbeiter m expert. S~**buch** nt non-fiction book. s~**dienlich** a relevant

Sache f -,-n matter, business; (Ding) thing; (fig) cause; zur S~ kommen come to the point

Sach|gebiet nt (fig) area, field. s~**gemäß** a proper, adv -ly. S~**kenntnis** f expertise. s~**kundig** a expert, adv -ly. s~**lich** a factual, adv -ly; (nüchtern) matter-of-fact, adv -ly; (objektiv) objective, adv -ly; (schmucklos) functional

sächlich a (Gram) neuter

Sachse m -n,-n Saxon. S~**n** nt -s Saxony

sächsisch a Saxon

sacht a gentle, adv -ly

Sach|verhalt m -[e]s facts pl. s~**verständig** a expert, adv -ly. S~**verständige(r)** mf expert

Sack m -[e]s,-̈e sack; mit S~ und Pack with all one's belongings

sacken vi (sein) sink; (zusammen-) go down; (Person:) slump

Sack|gasse f cul-de-sac; (fig) impasse. S~**leinen** nt sacking

Sadis|mus m - sadism. S~**t** m -en,-en sadist. s~**tisch** a sadistic, adv -ally

säen vt/i (haben) sow

Safe /zɛːf/ m -s,-s safe

Saft m -[e]s,-̈e juice; (Bot) sap. s~**ig** a juicy; (Wiese) lush; (Preis, Rechnung) hefty; (Witz) coarse. s~**los** a dry

Sage f -,-n legend

Säge f -,-n saw. S~**mehl** nt sawdust

sagen vt say; (mitteilen) tell; (bedeuten) mean; das hat nichts zu s~ it doesn't mean anything; ein viel s~der Blick a meaningful look

sägen vt/i (haben) saw

sagenhaft a legendary; (fam: unglaublich) fantastic, adv -ally

Säge|späne mpl wood shavings. S~**werk** nt sawmill

Sahn|e f - cream. S~**ebonbon** m & nt ≈ toffee. s~**ig** a creamy

Saison /zɛ'zõː/ f -,-s season

Saite f -,-n (Mus, Sport) string. S~**ninstrument** nt stringed instrument

Sakko m & nt -s,-s sports jacket

Sakrament nt -[e]s,-e sacrament

Sakrileg nt -s,-e sacrilege

Sakrist|an m -s,-e verger. S~**ei** f -,-en vestry

Salat m -[e]s,-e salad; ein Kopf S~ a lettuce. S~**soße** f salad-dressing

Salbe f -,-n ointment

Salbei m -s & f -sage

salben vt anoint

Saldo m -s,-dos & -den balance

Salon /za'lõː/ m -s,-s salon; (Naut) saloon

salopp *a* casual, *adv* -ly; ⟨*Benehmen*⟩ informal, *adv* -ly; ⟨*Ausdruck*⟩ slangy

Salto *m* -s,-s somersault

Salut *m* -[e]s,-e salute. s~ieren *vi* ⟨*haben*⟩ salute

Salve *f* -,-n volley; ⟨*Geschütz-*⟩ salvo; ⟨*von Gelächter*⟩ burst

Salz *nt* -es,-e salt. s~en† *vt* salt. S~fass ⟨S~faß⟩ *nt* salt-cellar. s~ig *a* salty. S~kartoffeln *fpl* boiled potatoes. S~säure *f* hydrochloric acid

Samen *m* -s,- seed; ⟨*Anat*⟩ semen, sperm

sämig *a* ⟨*Culin*⟩ thick

Sämling *m* -s,-e seedling

Sammel|becken *nt* reservoir. S~begriff *m* collective term. s~n *vt/i* ⟨*haben*⟩ collect; ⟨*suchen, versammeln*⟩ gather; sich s~n collect; ⟨*sich versammeln*⟩ gather; ⟨*sich fassen*⟩ collect oneself. S~name *m* collective noun

Samm|ler(in) *m* -s,- ⟨*f* -,-nen⟩ collector. S~lung *f* -,-en collection; ⟨*innere*⟩ composure

Samstag *m* -s,-e Saturday. s~s *adv* on Saturdays

samt *prep* (+ *dat*) together with □ *adv* s~ und sonders without exception

Samt *m* -[e]s velvet. s~ig *a* velvety

sämtlich *indef pron inv* all. s~e(r,s) *indef pron* all the; s~e Werke complete works; meine s~en Bücher all my books

Sanatorium *nt* -s,-ien sanatorium

Sand *m* -[e]s sand

Sandale *f* -,-n sandal. S~ette *f* -,-n high-heeled sandal

Sand|bank *f* sandbank. S~burg *f* sandcastle. s~ig *a* sandy. S~kasten *m* sandpit. S~kuchen *m* Madeira cake. S~papier *nt* sandpaper. S~stein *m* sandstone

sanft *a* gentle, *adv* -ly. s~mütig *a* meek

Sänger(in) *m* -s,- ⟨*f* -,-nen⟩ singer

sanieren *vt* clean up; redevelop ⟨*Gebiet*⟩; ⟨*modernisieren*⟩ modernize; make profitable ⟨*Industrie, Firma*⟩; sich s~ become profitable

sanitär *a* sanitary

Sanität|er *m* -s,- first-aid man; ⟨*Fahrer*⟩ ambulance man; ⟨*Mil*⟩ medical orderly. S~swagen *m* ambulance

Sanktion /zaŋk'tsio:n/ *f* -,-en sanction. s~ieren *vt* sanction

Saphir *m* -s,-e sapphire

Sardelle *f* -,-n anchovy

Sardine *f* -,-n sardine

Sarg *m* -[e]s,-e coffin

Sarkas|mus *m* - sarcasm. s~tisch *a* sarcastic, *adv* -ally

Sat|an *m* -s Satan; ⟨*fam: Teufel*⟩ devil. s~anisch *a* satanic

Satellit *m* -en,-en satellite. S~enfernsehen *nt* satellite television

Satin /za'tɛ̃/ *m* -s satin

Satir|e *f* -,-n satire. s~isch *a* satirical, *adv* -ly

satt *a* full; ⟨*Farbe*⟩ rich; s~ sein have had enough [to eat]; sich s~ essen eat as much as one wants; s~ machen feed; ⟨*Speise:*⟩ be filling; etw s~ haben ⟨*fam*⟩ be fed up with sth

Sattel *m* -s,- saddle. s~n *vt* saddle. S~schlepper *m* tractor unit. S~zug *m* articulated lorry

sättigen *vt* satisfy; ⟨*Chem & fig*⟩ saturate □ *vi* ⟨*haben*⟩ be filling. s~d *a* filling

Satz *m* -es,-e sentence; ⟨*Teil-*⟩ clause; ⟨*These*⟩ proposition; ⟨*Math*⟩ theorem; ⟨*Mus*⟩ movement; ⟨*Tennis, Zusammengehöriges*⟩ set; ⟨*Boden-*⟩ sediment; ⟨*Kaffee-*⟩ grounds *pl*; ⟨*Steuer-, Zins-*⟩ rate; ⟨*Druck-*⟩ setting; ⟨*Schrift-*⟩ type; ⟨*Sprung-*⟩ leap, bound. S~aussage *f* predicate. S~gegenstand *m* subject. S~zeichen *nt* punctuation mark

Sau *f* -,Säue sow; ⟨*sl: schmutziger Mensch*⟩ dirty pig

sauber *a* clean; ⟨*ordentlich*⟩ neat, *adv* -ly; ⟨*anständig*⟩ decent, *adv* -ly; ⟨*fam: nicht anständig*⟩ fine; s~ halten keep clean; s~ machen clean. s~halten† *vt sep* (NEW) halten, s. sauber. S~keit *f* - cleanliness; neatness; decency

säuberlich *a* neat, *adv* -ly

saubermachen *vt/i sep* ⟨*haben*⟩ (NEW) sauber machen, s. sauber

säuber|n *vt* clean; ⟨*befreien*⟩ rid/ ⟨*Pol*⟩ purge ⟨*von* of⟩. S~ungsaktion *f* ⟨*Pol*⟩ purge

Sauce /'zo:sə/ *f* -,-n sauce; ⟨*Braten-*⟩ gravy

Saudi-Arabien /-jən/ *nt* -s Saudi Arabia

sauer *a* sour; ⟨*Chem*⟩ acid; ⟨*eingelegt*⟩ pickled; ⟨*schwer*⟩ hard; saurer Regen acid rain; s~ sein ⟨*fam*⟩ be annoyed

Sauerei *f* -,-en = Schweinerei

Sauerkraut *nt* sauerkraut

säuerlich *a* slightly sour

Sauer|stoff *m* oxygen

saufen† *vt/i* ⟨*haben*⟩ drink; ⟨*sl*⟩ booze

Säufer *m* -s,- ⟨*sl*⟩ boozer

saugen† *vt/i* ⟨*haben*⟩ suck; ⟨*staub-*⟩ vacuum, hoover; sich voll Wasser s~ soak up water

säugen *vt* suckle

Sauger *m* -s,- [baby's] dummy; ⟨*Amer*⟩ pacifier; ⟨*Flaschen-*⟩ teat

Säugetier *nt* mammal

saugfähig *a* absorbent

Säugling m -s,-e infant

Säule f -,-n column

Saum m -[e]s,Säume hem; (Rand) edge

säumen[^1] vt hem; (fig) line

säum|en[^2] vi (haben) delay. s~ig a dilatory

Sauna f -,-nas & -nen sauna

Säure f -,-n acidity; (Chem) acid

säuseln vi (haben) rustle (softly)

sausen vi (haben) rush; (Ohren:) buzz □ vi (sein) rush [along]

Sauwetter nt (sl) lousy weather

Saxophon, **Saxofon** nt -s,-e saxophone

SB- /ɛs'be:-/ pref (= Selbstbedienung) self-service . . .

S-Bahn f city and suburban railway

sch int shush! (fort) shoo!

Schabe f -,-n cockroach

schaben vt/i (haben) scrape

schäbig a shabby, adv -ily

Schablone f -,-n stencil; (Muster) pattern; (fig) stereotype

Schach nt -s chess; S~! check! in S~ halten (fig) keep in check. S~brett nt chessboard

schachern vi (haben) haggle

Schachfigur f chess-man

schachmatt a s~ setzen checkmate; s~! checkmate!

Schachspiel nt game of chess

Schacht m -[e]s,:e shaft

Schachtel f -,-n box; (Zigaretten-) packet

Schachzug m move

schade a s~ sein be a pity or shame: zu s~ für too good for; [wie] s~! [what a] pity or shame!

Schädel m -s, skull. S~bruch m fractured skull

schaden vi (haben) (+ dat) damage; (nachteilig sein) hurt; das schadet nichts that doesn't matter. S~ m -s,- damage; (Defekt) defect; (Nachteil) disadvantage; zu S~ kommen be hurt. S~ersatz m damages pl. S~freude f malicious glee. s~froh a gloating

schadhaft a defective

schädig|en vt damage, harm. S~ung f -,-en damage

schädlich a harmful

Schädling m -s,-e pest. S~sbe-kämpfungsmittel nt pesticide

Schaf nt -[e]s,-e sheep; (fam: Idiot) idiot. S~bock m ram

Schäfchen nt -s,- lamb

Schäfer m -s,- shepherd. S~hund m sheepdog; Deutscher S~hund German shepherd, alsatian

Schaffell nt sheepskin

schaffen†[^1] vt create; (herstellen) establish; make (Platz); wie geschaffen für made for

schaffen[^2] v (reg) □ vt manage [to do]; pass (Prüfung); catch (Zug); (bringen) take; jdm zu s~ machen trouble s.o.; sich (dat) zu s~ machen busy oneself (an + dat with) □ vi (haben) (SGer: arbeiten) work. S~ nt -s work

Schaffner m -s,- conductor; (Zug-) ticket-inspector

Schaffung f - creation

Schaft m -[e]s,:e shaft; (Gewehr-) stock; (Stiefel-) leg. S~stiefel m high boot

Schal m -s,-s scarf

schal a insipid; (abgestanden) flat; (fig) stale

Schale f -,-n skin; (abgeschält) peel; (Eier-, Nuss-, Muschel-) shell; (Schüssel) dish

schälen vt peel; sich s~ peel

schalkhaft a mischievous, adv -ly

Schall m -[e]s sound. S~dämpfer m silencer. s~dicht a soundproof. s~en vi (haben) ring out; (nachhallen) resound; s~end lachen roar with laughter. S~mauer f sound barrier. S~platte f record, disc

schalt|en vt switch □ vi (haben) switch/ (Ampel:) turn (auf + acc to); (Auto) change gear; (fam: begreifen) catch on. S~er m -s,- switch; (Post-, Bank-) counter; (Fahrkarten-) ticket window. S~hebel m switch; (Auto) gear lever. S~jahr nt leap year. S~kreis m circuit. S~ung f -,-en circuit; (Auto) gear change

Scham f - shame; (Anat) private parts pl; falsche S~ false modesty

schämen (sich) vr be ashamed; schämt euch! you should be ashamed of yourselves!

scham|haft a modest, adv -ly; (schüchtern) bashful, adv -ly. s~los a shameless, adv -ly

Schampon nt -s shampoo. s~ieren vt shampoo

Schande f - disgrace, shame; S~ machen (+ dat) bring shame on; zu S~n machen/werden = zuschanden machen/werden, s. zuschanden

schänd|en vt dishonour; (fig) defile; (Relig) desecrate; (sexuell) violate. s~lich a disgraceful, adv -ly. S~ung f -,-en defilement, desecration; violation

Schänke f -,-n = Schenke

Schanktisch m bar

Schanze f -,-n [ski-]jump

Schar f -,-en crowd; (Vogel-) flock; in [hellen] S~en in droves

Scharade f -,-n charade

[^1]:
[^2]:

scharen vt um sich s~ gather round one; sich s~ um flock round s~weise adv in droves

scharf a (schärfer, schärfst) sharp; (stark) strong; (stark gewürzt) hot; (Geruch) pungent; (Frost, Wind, Augen, Verstand) keen; (streng) harsh; (Galopp, Ritt) hard; (Munition) live; (Hund) fierce; s~ einstellen (Phot) focus; s~ sein (Phot) be in focus; s~ sein auf (+ acc) (fam) be keen on □ adv sharply; (hinsehen, nachdenken, bremsen, reiten) hard; (streng) harshly; s~ schießen fire live ammunition

Scharfblick m perspicacity

Schärfe f -,-s (s. scharf) sharpness; strength; hotness; pungency; keenness; harshness. s~n vt sharpen

scharf|machen vt sep (fam) incite. S~richter m executioner. S~schütze m marksman. s~sichtig a perspicacious. S~sinn m astuteness. s~sinnig a astute, adv -ly

Scharlach m -s scarlet fever

Scharlatan m -s,-e charlatan

Scharnier nt -s,-e hinge

Schärpe f -,-n sash

scharren vi (haben) scrape; (Huhn) scratch; (Pferd:) paw the ground □ vt scrape

Schart|e f -,-n nick. s~ig a jagged

Schaschlik m & nt -s,-s kebab

Schatten m -s,- shadow; (schattige Stelle) shade; im S~ in the shade. s~haft a shadowy. S~riss (S~riß) m silhouette. S~seite f shady side; (fig) disadvantage

schattier|en vt shade. S~ung f -,-n shading; (fig: Variante) shade

schattig a shady

Schatz m -es,-ᵉe treasure; (Freund, Freundin) sweetheart; (Anrede) darling

schätzen vt estimate; (taxieren) value; (achten) esteem; (würdigen) appreciate; (fam: vermuten) reckon; sich glücklich s~ consider oneself lucky

Schätzung f -,-en estimate; (Taxierung) valuation. s~sweise adv approximately

Schau f -,-en show; zur S~ stellen display. S~bild nt diagram

Schauder m -s shiver; (vor Abscheu) shudder. s~haft a dreadful, adv -ly. s~n vi (haben) shiver; (vor Abscheu) shudder; mich s~te I shivered/shuddered

schauen vi (haben) (SGer, Aust) look; s~, dass make sure that

Schauer m -s,- shower; (Schauder) shiver. S~geschichte f horror story. s~lich a

ghastly. s~n vi (haben) shiver; mich s~te I shivered

Schaufel f -,-n shovel; (Kehr-) dustpan. s~n vt shovel; (graben) dig

Schaufenster nt shop-window. S~bummel m window-shopping. S~puppe f dummy

Schaukasten m display case

Schaukel f -,-n swing. s~n vt rock □ vi (haben) rock; (auf einer Schaukel) swing; (schwanken) sway. S~pferd nt rocking-horse. S~stuhl m rocking-chair

schaulustig a curious

Schaum m -[e]s foam; (Seifen-) lather; (auf Bier) froth; (als Frisier-, Rasiermittel) mousse

schäumen vi (haben) foam, froth; (Seife:) lather

Schaum|gummi m foam rubber. s~ig a frothy; s~ig rühren (Culin) cream. S~krone f white crest; (auf Bier) head. S~speise f mousse. S~stoff m [synthetic] foam. S~wein m sparkling wine

Schauplatz m scene

schaurig a dreadful, adv -ly; (unheimlich) eerie, adv eerily

Schauspiel nt play; (Anblick) spectacle. S~er m actor. S~erin f actress. S~ern vi (haben) act; (sich verstellen) play-act

Scheck m -s,-s cheque, (Amer) check. S~buch, S~heft nt cheque-book. S~karte f cheque card

Scheibe f -,-n disc; (Schieß-) target; (Glas-) pane; (Brot-, Wurst-) slice. S~nwaschanlage f windscreen washer. S~nwischer m -s,- windscreen-wiper

Scheich m -s,-e & -s sheikh

Scheide f -,-n sheath; (Anat) vagina

scheid|en† vt separate; (unterscheiden) distinguish; dissolve (Ehe); sich s~en lassen get divorced; sich s~en diverge; (Meinungen:) differ □ vi (sein) leave; (voneinander) part. S~ung f -,-en divorce

Schein m -[e]s,-e light; (Anschein) appearance; (Bescheinigung) certificate; (Geld-) note; etw nur zum S~ tun only pretend to do sth. s~bar a apparent, adv -ly. s~en† vi (haben) shine; (den Anschein haben) seem, appear; mir s~t it seems to me

scheinheilig a hypocritical, adv -ly. S~keit f hypocrisy

Scheinwerfer m -s,- floodlight; (Such-) searchlight; (Auto) headlight; (Theat) spotlight

Scheiß m, scheiß- pref (vulg) bloody. S~e f - (vulg) shit. s~en† vi (haben) (vulg) shit

Scheit nt -[e]s,-e log

Scheitel m -s,- parting. s~n vt part (Haar)

scheitern vi (sein) fail

Schelle f -,-n bell. s~n vi (haben) ring

Schellfisch m haddock

Schelm m -s,-e rogue. s~isch a mischievous, adv -ly

Schelte f - scolding. s~n† vi (haben) grumble (über + acc about); mit jdm s~n scold s.o. □ vt scold; (bezeichnen) call

Schema nt -s,-mata model, pattern; (Skizze) diagram

Schemel m -s,- stool

Schenke f -,-n tavern

Schenkel m -s,- thigh; (Geom) side

schenken vt give [as a present]; jdm Vertrauen/Glauben s~ trust/believe s.o.; sich (dat) etw s~ give sth a miss

scheppern vi (haben) clank

Scherbe f -,-n [broken] piece

Schere f -,-n scissors pl; (Techn) shears pl; (Hummer-) claw. s~n† vt shear; crop (Haar); clip (Hund)

scheren[2] vt (reg) (fam) bother; sich nicht s~ um not care about; scher dich zum Teufel! go to hell!

Scherenschnitt m silhouette

Schererei|en fpl (fam) trouble sg

Scherz m -es,-e a joke; im/zum S~ as a joke. s~en vi (haben) joke. S~frage f riddle. s~haft a humorous

scheu a shy, adv -ly; (Tier) timid; s~ werden (Pferd:) shy; s~ machen startle. S~ f - shyness; timidity; (Ehrfurcht) awe

scheuchen vt shoo

scheuen vt be afraid of; (meiden) shun; keine Mühe/Kosten s~ spare no effort/expense; sich s~ be afraid (vor + dat of); shrink (etw zu tun from doing sth) □ vi (haben) (Pferd:) shy

Scheuer|lappen m floor-cloth. s~n vt scrub; (mit Scheuerpulver) scour; (reiben) rub; [wund] s~n chafe □ vi (haben) rub, chafe. S~tuch nt floor-cloth

Scheuklappen fpl blinkers

Scheune f -,-n barn

Scheusal nt -s,-e monster

scheußlich a horrible, adv -bly

Schi m -s,-er ski; S~ fahren od laufen ski

Schicht f -,-en layer; (Geol) stratum; (Gesellschafts-) class; (Arbeits-) shift. S~arbeit f shift work. s~en vt stack [up]

schick a stylish, adv -ly; (Frau) chic; (fam: prima) great. S~ m -[e]s style

schicken vt/i (haben) send; s~ nach send for; sich s~ in (+ acc) resign oneself to

schicklich a fitting, proper

Schicksal nt -s,-e fate. s~haft a fateful. S~sschlag m misfortune

Schieb|edach nt (Auto) sun-roof. s~en†‡ vt push; (gleitend) slide; (fam: handeln mit) traffic in; etw s~en auf (+ acc) (fig) put sth down to; shift (Schuld, Verantwortung) on to □ vi (haben) push. S~er m -s,-slide; (Person) black marketeer. S~etür f sliding door. S~ung f -,-en (fam) illicit deal; (Betrug) rigging, fixing

Schieds|gericht nt panel of judges; (Jur) arbitration tribunal. S~richter m referee; (Tennis) umpire; (Jur) arbitrator

schief a crooked; (unsymmetrisch) lopsided; (geneigt) slanting, sloping; (nicht senkrecht) leaning; (Winkel) oblique; (fig) false; (misstrauisch) suspicious □ adv not straight; jdn s~ ansehen look at s.o. askance; s~ gehen (fig) go wrong

Schiefer m -s slate

schief|gehen† vi sep (sein) NEW s~ gehen, s. schief. s~lachen (sich) vr sep double up with laughter

schielen vi (haben) squint

Schienbein nt shin; (Knochen) shinbone

Schiene f -,-n rail; (Gleit-) runner; (Med) splint. s~n vt (Med) put in a splint

schier[1] adv almost

schier[2] a pure; (Fleisch) lean

Schieß|bude f shooting-gallery. s~en†‡ vt shoot; fire (Kugel); score (Tor) □ vi (haben) shoot, fire (auf + acc at) □ vi (sein) shoot [along]; (strömen) gush; in die Höhe s~en shoot up. S~erei f -,-en shooting. S~scheibe f target. S~stand m shooting-range

Schifahr|en nt skiing. S~er(in) m(f) skier

Schiff nt -[e]s,-e ship; (Kirchen-) nave; (Seiten-) aisle

Schiffahrt f NEW Schifffahrt

schiff|bar a navigable. S~bau m ship-building. S~bruch m shipwreck. s~brüchig a shipwrecked. S~chen nt -s,-small boat; (Tex) shuttle. S~er m -s,-skipper. S~fahrt f shipping

Schikan|e f -,-n harassment; mit allen S~en (fam) with every refinement. s~ieren vt harass; (tyrannisieren) bully

Schi|laufen nt -s skiing. S~läufer(in) m(f) -s,- (f -,-nen) skier

Schild[1] m -[e]s,-e shield; etw im S~e führen (fam) be up to sth

Schild[2] nt -[e]s,-er sign; (Namens-, Nummern-) plate; (Mützen-) badge; (Etikett) label

Schilddrüse f thyroid [gland]

schilder|n vt describe. S~ung f -,-en description

Schild|kröte f tortoise; (See-) turtle. S~patt nt -[e]s tortoiseshell

Schilf nt -[e]s reeds pl

schillern vi (haben) shimmer

Schimmel m -s,- mould; (Pferd) white horse. s~ig a mouldy. ∘~n vi (haben/sein) go mouldy

Schimmer m -s gleam; (Spur) glimmer. s~n vi (haben) gleam

Schimpanse m -n,-n chimpanzee

schimpf|en vi (haben) grumble (mit at; über + acc about); scold (mit jdm s.o.) □ vt call. S~name m term of abuse. S~wort nt (pl -wörter) swear-word; (Beleidigung) insult

schind|en† vt work or drive hard; (quälen) ill-treat; sich s~en slave [away]; Eindruck s~en (fam) try to impress. S~er m -s,- slave-driver. S~erei f - slave-driving; (Plackerei) hard slog

Schinken m -s,- ham. S~speck m bacon

Schippe f -,-n shovel. s~n vt shovel

Schirm m -[e]s,-e umbrella; (Sonnen-) sunshade; (Lampen-) shade; (Augen-) visor; (Mützen-) peak; (Ofen-, Bild-) screen; (fig: Schutz) shield. S~herr m patron. S~herrschaft f patronage. S~mütze f peaked cap

schizophren a schizophrenic. S~ie f - schizophrenia

Schlacht f -,-en battle

schlachten vt slaughter, kill

Schlachter, Schlächter m -s,- (NGer) butcher

Schlacht|feld nt battlefield. S~haus nt, S~hof m abattoir. S~platte f plate of assorted cooked meats and sausages. S~schiff nt battleship

Schlacke f -,-n slag

Schlaf m -[e]s sleep; im S~ in one's sleep. S~anzug m pyjamas pl, (Amer) pajamas pl. S~couch f sofa bed

Schläfe f -,-n (Anat) temple

schlafen† vi (haben) sleep; (fam: nicht aufpassen) be asleep; s~ gehen go to bed; er schläft noch he is still asleep. S~szeit f bedtime

Schläfer(in) m -s,- (f -,-nen) sleeper

schlaff a limp, adv -ly; (Seil) slack; (Muskel) flabby

Schlaf|lied nt lullaby. s~los a sleepless. S~losigkeit f - insomnia. S~mittel nt sleeping drug

schläfrig a sleepy, adv -ily

Schlaf|sack m sleeping-bag. S~tablette f sleeping-pill. s~trunken a [still] half asleep. S~wagen m sleeping-car, sleeper. s~wandeln vi (haben/sein) sleep-walk. S~zimmer nt bedroom

Schlag m -[e]s,⸗e blow; (Faust-) punch; (Herz-, Puls-, Trommel-) beat; (einer Uhr) chime; (Glocken-, Gong- & Med) stroke; (elektrischer) shock; (Portion) helping; (Art) type; (Aust) whipped cream; S~e bekommen get a beating; S~ auf S~ in rapid succession. S~ader f artery. S~anfall m stroke. S~artig a sudden, adv -ly. S~baum m barrier

Schlägel m -s,- mallet; (Trommel-) stick

schlagen† vt hit, strike; (fällen) fell; knock (Loch, Nagel) (in + acc into); (prügeln, besiegen) beat; (Culin) whisk (Eiweiß); whip (Sahne); (legen) throw; (wickeln) wrap; (hinzufügen) add (zu to); sich s~en fight; sich geschlagen geben admit defeat □ vi (haben) beat; (Tür:) bang; (Uhr:) strike; (melodisch) chime; mit den Flügeln s~ flap its wings; um sich s~ lash out; es schlug sechs the clock struck six □ vi (sein) in etw (acc) s~ (Blitz, Kugel:) strike sth; s~ an (+ acc) knock against; nach jdm s~ (fig) take after s.o. s~d a (fig) conclusive, adv -ly

Schlager m -s,- popular song; (Erfolg) hit

Schläger m -s,- racket; (Tischtennis-) bat; (Golf-) club; (Hockey-) stick; (fam: Raufbold) thug. S~ei f -,-en fight, brawl

schlag|fertig a quick-witted. S~instrument nt percussion instrument. S~loch nt pothole. S~sahne f whipped cream; (ungeschlagen) whipping cream. S~seite f (Naut) list. S~stock m truncheon. S~wort nt (pl -worte) slogan. S~zeile f headline. S~zeug nt (Mus) percussion. S~zeuger m -s,- percussionist; (in Band) drummer

schlaksig a gangling

Schlamassel m & nt -s (fam) mess

Schlamm m -[e]s mud. s~ig a muddy

Schlamp|e f -,-n (fam) slut. s~en vi (haben) (fam) be sloppy (bei in). S~erei f -,-en sloppiness; (Unordnung) mess. s~ig a slovenly; (Arbeit) sloppy □ adv in a slovenly way; (nachlässig)

Schlange f -,-n snake; (Menschen-, Auto-) queue; S~ stehen queue, (Amer) stand in line

schlängeln (sich) vr wind; (Person:) weave (durch through)

Schlangen|biss (Schlangenbiß) m snakebite. S~linie f wavy line

schlank a slim. S~heit f - slimness. S~heitskur f slimming diet

Schlappe f -,-n (fam) setback. S~hut m [floppy hat]. s~machen vi (haben) (fam) flag. S~en m -s,- slipper. S~heit f - exhaustion. S~ohr nt (fam) sly dog. S~e f -,-n (fam) setback

schlau a clever, adv -ly; (gerissen) crafty, adv -ily; ich werde nicht s~ daraus I can't make head or tail of it

Schl**au**ch *m* -[e]s,Schläuche tube; (*Wasser-*) hose[pipe]. S~boot *nt* rubber dinghy. s~en *vt* (*fam*) exhaust

Schl**au**fe *f* -,-n loop

schl**e**cht *a* bad; (*böse*) wicked; (*unzulänglich*) poor; s~ werden go bad; (*Wetter:*) turn bad; s~er werden get worse; s~ aussehen look bad/(*Person:*) unwell; mir ist s~ I feel sick; s~ machen (*fam*) run down □ *adv* badly; poorly; (*kaum*) not really. □~gehen† *vi sep* (*sein*) (NEW) s~ gehen, *s.* gehen. s~gelaunt *a* (NEW) s~ gelaunt, *s.* gelaunt. s~hin *adv* quite simply. S~igkeit *f* - wickedness. s~machen *vt sep* (NEW) s~ machen, *s.* schlecht

schl**e**cken *vt/i* (*haben*) lick (an etw *dat* sth); (*auf-*) lap up

Schl**e**gel *m* -s,-(SGer: Keule) leg; (*Hühner-*) drumstick; (*Techn, Mus*) (NEW) Schlägel

schl**ei**chen† *vi* (*sein*) creep; (*langsam gehen/fahren*) crawl □ *vr* sich s~ creep. s~d *a* creeping; (*Krankheit*) insidious

Schl**ei**er *m* -s,- veil; (*fig*) haze. s~haft *a* es ist mir s~haft (*fam*) it's a mystery to me

Schl**ei**fe *f* -,-n bow; (*Fliege*) bow-tie; (*Biegung*) loop

schl**ei**fen¹ *v* (*reg*) □ *vt* drag; (*zerstören*) raze to the ground □ *vi* (*haben*) trail, drag

schl**ei**fen†² *vt* grind; (*schärfen*) sharpen; cut (*Edelstein, Glas*); (*drillen*) drill

Schl**ei**m *m* -[e]s slime; (*Anat*) mucus; (*Med*) phlegm. s~ig *a* slimy

schl**e**mm|en *vi* (*haben*) feast □ *vt* feast on. S~er *m* -s,- gourmet

schl**e**ndern *vi* (*sein*) stroll

schl**e**nkern *vt/i* (*haben*) swing; s~ mit swing; dangle (*Beine*)

Schl**e**pp|dampfer *m* tug. S~e *f* -,-n train. S~en *vt* drag; (*tragen*) carry; (*ziehen*) tow; sich s~en drag oneself; (*sich hinziehen*) drag on; sich s~en mit carry. s~end *a* slow, *adv* -ly. S~er *m* -s,- tug; (*Traktor*) tractor. S~kahn *m* barge. S~lift *m* T-bar lift. S~tau *nt* tow-rope; ins S~tau nehmen take in tow

Schl**eu**der *f* -,-n catapult; (*Wäsche-*) spin-drier. s~n *vt* hurl; spin (*Wäsche*); extract (*Honig*) □ *vi* (*sein*) skid; ins S~n geraten skid. S~preise *mpl* knock-down prices. S~sitz *m* ejector seat

schl**eu**nigst *adv* hurriedly; (*sofort*) at once

Schl**eu**se *f* -,-n lock; (*Sperre*) sluice[-gate]. s~n *vt* steer

Schl**i**che *pl* tricks; jdm auf die S~ kommen (*fam*) get on to s.o.

schl**i**cht *a* plain, *adv* -ly; (*einfach*) simple, *adv* -ply

schl**i**cht|en *vt* settle □ *vi* arbitrate. S~ung *f* - settlement; (*Jur*) arbitration

Schl**i**ck *m* -[e]s silt

Schl**ie**ße *f* -,-n clasp; (*Schnalle*) buckle

schl**ie**ßen† *vt* close (*ab-*) lock; fasten (*Kleid, Verschluss*); (*stilllegen*) close down; (*beenden, folgern*) conclude; enter into (*Vertrag*); sich s~ close; in die Arme s~ embrace; etw s~ an (+ *acc*) connect sth to; sich s~ an (+ *acc*) follow on □ *vi* (*haben*) close, (*den Betrieb einstellen*) close down; (*den Schlüssel drehen*) turn the key; (*enden, folgern*) conclude; s~ lassen auf (+ *acc*) suggest

Schl**ie**ß|fach *nt* locker. s~lich *adv* finally, in the end; (*immerhin*) after all. S~ung *f* -,-en closure

Schl**i**ff *m* -[e]s cut; (*Schleifen*) cutting; (*fig*) polish; der letzte S~ the finishing touches *pl*

schl**i**mm *a* bad, *adv* -ly; s~er werden get worse; nicht so s~! it doesn't matter! s~stenfalls *adv* if the worst comes to the worst

Schl**i**nge *f* -,-n loop; (*Henkers-*) noose; (*Med*) sling; (*Falle*) snare

Schl**i**ngel *m* -s,- (*fam*) rascal

schl**i**ng|en† *vt* wind, wrap; tie (*Knoten*); sich s~en um coil around □ *vi* (*haben*) bolt one's food. S~pflanze *f* climber

Schl**i**ps *m* -es,-e tie

Schl**i**tten *m* -s,- sledge; (*Rodel-*) toboggan; (*Pferde-*) sleigh; S~ fahren toboggan

schl**i**ttern *vi* (*haben*/ *sein*) slide

Schl**i**ttschuh *m* skate; S~ laufen skate. S~läufer(in) *m(f)* -s,-/ -,-nen) skater

Schl**i**tz *m* -es,-e slit; (*für Münze*) slot; (*Jacken-*) vent; (*Hosen-*) flies *pl*. s~en *vt* slit

Schl**o**ss *nt* -es,-̈er (*Schloß nt* -sses,-̈sser) lock; (*Vorhänge-*) padlock; (*Verschluss*) clasp; (*Gebäude*) castle; (*Palast*) palace

Schl**o**sser *m* -s,- locksmith; (*Auto-*) mechanic; (*Maschinen-*) fitter

Schl**o**t *m* -[e]s,-e chimney

schl**o**ttern *vi* (*haben*) shake, tremble; (*Kleider:*) hang loose

Schl**u**cht *f* -,-en ravine, gorge

schl**u**chz|en *vi* (*haben*) sob. S~er *m* -s,- sob

Schl**u**ck *m* -[e]s,-e mouthful; (*klein*) sip

Schl**u**ckauf *m* -s hiccups *pl*

schl**u**cken *vt/i* (*haben*) swallow. S~ *m* -s hiccups *pl*

schl**u**d|ern *vi* (*haben*) be sloppy (bei in). s~rig *a* sloppy, *adv* -ily; (*Arbeit*) slipshod

Schl**u**mmer *m* -s slumber. s~n *vi* (*haben*) slumber

Schlund *m* -[e]s [back of the] throat; *(fig)* mouth

schlüpf|en *vi (sein)* slip; [aus dem Ei] s~en hatch. S~er *m* -s,- knickers *pl.* s~rig *a* slippery; *(anstößig)* smutty

schlurfen *vi (sein)* shuffle

schlürfen *vt/i (haben)* slurp

Schluss *m* -es,-̈e (Schluß *m* -sses,-̈sse) end; *(S~folgerung)* conclusion; zum S~ finally; S~ machen stop (mit etw sth); finish (mit jdm with s.o.)

Schlüssel *m* -s,- key; *(Schrauben-)* spanner; *(Geheim-)* code; *(Mus)* clef. S~bein *nt* collar-bone. S~bund *m* & *nt* bunch of keys. S~loch *nt* keyhole. S~ring *m* keyring

Schlussfolgerung (Schlußfolgerung) *f* conclusion

schlüssig *a* conclusive, *adv* -ly; sich *(dat)* s~ werden make up one's mind

Schluss|licht (Schluß|licht) *nt* rearlight. S~verkauf *m* [end of season] sale

Schmach *f* - disgrace

schmachten *vi (haben)* languish

schmächtig *a* slight

schmackhaft *a* tasty

schmal *a* narrow; *(dünn)* thin; *(schlank)* slender; *(karg)* meagre

schmälern *vt* diminish; *(herabsetzen)* belittle

Schmalz[1] *nt* -es lard; *(Ohren-)* wax

Schmalz[2] *m* -es *(fam)* schmaltz. s~ig *a* *(fam)* schmaltzy, slushy

schmarotz|en *vi (haben)* be parasitic (auf + *acc* on); *(Person:)* sponge (bei on). S~er *m* -s,- parasite; *(Person)* sponger

Schmarren *m* -s,- *(Aust)* pancake [torn into strips]; *(fam: Unsinn)* rubbish

schmatzen *vi (haben)* eat noisily

schmausen *vi (haben)* feast

schmecken *vi (haben)* taste (nach of); [gut] s~ taste good; hat es dir geschmeckt? did you enjoy it? □ *vt* taste

Schmeichelei *f* -,-en flattery; *(Kompliment)* compliment

schmeichel|haft *a* complimentary, flattering. s~n *vi (haben)* (+ *dat*) flatter

schmeißen† *vt/i (haben)* s~ [mit] *(fam)* chuck

Schmeißfliege *f* bluebottle

schmelz|en† *vt/i (sein)* melt, smelt *(Erze)*. S~wasser *nt* melted snow and ice

Schmerbauch *m* *(fam)* paunch

Schmerz *m* -es,-en pain; *(Kummer)* grief; S~en haben be in pain. s~en *vt* hurt; *(fig)* grieve □ *vi (haben)* hurt, be painful. S~ensgeld *nt* compensation for pain and suffering. s~haft *a* painful. s~lich *a (fig)*

painful; *(traurig)* sad, *adv* -ly. s~los *a* painless, *adv* -ly. s~stillend *a* pain-killing; s~stillendes Mittel analgesic, pain-killer. S~tablette *f* pain-killer

Schmetterball *m* *(Tennis)* smash

Schmetterling *m* -s,-e butterfly

schmettern *vt* hurl; *(Tennis)* smash; *(singen)* sing; *(spielen)* blare out □ *vi (haben)* sound; *(Trompeten:)* blare

Schmied *m* -[e]s,-e blacksmith

Schmiede *f* -,-n forge. S~eisen *nt* wrought iron. s~n *vt* forge; *(fig)* hatch; Pläne s~n make plans

schmieg|en *vt* press; sich s~en an (+ *acc*) nestle or snuggle up to; *(Kleid:)* cling to. s~sam *a* supple

Schmier|e *f* -,-n grease; *(Schmutz)* mess. s~en *vt* lubricate; *(streichen)* spread; *(schlecht schreiben)* scrawl; *(sl: bestechen)* bribe □ *vi (haben)* smudge; *(schreiben)* scrawl. S~fett *nt* grease. S~geld *nt (fam)* bribe. s~ig *a* greasy; *(schmutzig)* grubby; *(anstößig)* smutty; *(Person)* slimy. S~mittel *nt* lubricant

Schminke *f* -,-n make-up. s~n *vt* make up; sich s~n put on make-up; sich *(dat)* die Lippen s~n put on lipstick

schmirgel|n *vt* sand down. S~papier *nt* emery-paper

schmökern *vt/i (haben)* *(fam)* read

schmollen *vi (haben)* sulk; *(s~d den Mund verziehen)* pout

schmor|en *vt/i (haben)* braise; *(fam: schwitzen)* roast. S~topf *m* casserole

Schmuck *m* -[e]s jewellery; *(Verzierung)* ornament, decoration

schmücken *vt* decorate, adorn; sich s~ adorn oneself

schmuck|los *a* plain. S~stück *nt* piece of jewellery; *(fig)* jewel

schmuddelig *a* grubby

Schmuggel *m* -s smuggling. s~n *vt* smuggle. S~ware *f* contraband

Schmuggler *m* -s,- smuggler

schmunzeln *vi (haben)* smile

schmusen *vi (haben)* cuddle

Schmutz *m* -es dirt; in den S~ziehen *(fig)* denigrate. s~en *vi (haben)* get dirty. S~fleck *m* dirty mark. s~ig *a* dirty

Schnabel *m* -s,-̈ beak, bill; *(eines Kruges)* lip; *(Tülle)* spout

Schnake *f* -,-n mosquito; *(Kohl-)* daddy-long-legs

Schnalle *f* -,-n buckle. s~n *vt* strap; *(zu-)* buckle; den Gürtel enger s~n tighten one's belt

schnalzen *vi (haben)* mit der Zunge/den Fingern s~ click one's tongue/snap one's fingers

schnapp|en vi (haben) s~en nach snap at; gasp for (Luft) □ vt snatch, grab; (fam: festnehmen) nab. S~schloss (S~schloß) nt spring lock. S~schuss (S~schuß) m snapshot

Schnaps m -es,-̈e schnapps

schnarchen vi (haben) snore

schnarren vi (haben) rattle; ⟨Klingel:⟩ buzz

schnattern vi (haben) cackle

schnauben vi (haben) snort □ vt sich (dat) die Nase s~ blow one's nose

schnaufen vi (haben) puff, pant

Schnauze f -,-n muzzle; (eines Kruges) lip; (Tülle) spout

schnäuzen (sich) vr blow one's nose

Schnecke f -,-n snail; (Nackt-) slug; (Spirale) scroll; (Gebäck) ≈ Chelsea bun. S~nhaus nt snail-shell

Schnee m -s snow; (Eier-) beaten egg-white. S~ball m snowball. S~besen m whisk. S~brille f snow-goggles pl. S~fall m snow-fall. S~flocke f snow-flake. S~glöckchen nt -s,- snowdrop. S~kette f snow chain. S~mann m (pl -männer) snowman. S~pflug m snow-plough. S~schläger m whisk. S~sturm m snowstorm, blizzard. S~wehe f -,-n snowdrift

Schneid m -[e]s (SGer) courage

Schneide f -,-n (cutting) edge; (Klinge) blade

schneiden† vt cut; (in Scheiben) slice; (kreuzen) cross; (nicht beachten) cut dead; Gesichter s~ pull faces; sich s~ cut oneself; (über-) intersect; sich (dat/acc) in den Finger s~ cut one's finger. s~d a cutting; (kalt) biting

Schneider m -s,- tailor. S~in f -,-nen dressmaker. s~n vt make ⟨Anzug, Kostüm⟩

Schneidezahn m incisor

schneidig a dashing, adv -ly

schneien vi (haben) snow; es schneit it is snowing

Schneise f -,-n path; (Feuer-) firebreak

schnell a quick; ⟨Auto, Tempo⟩ fast □ adv quickly; (in s~em Tempo) fast; (bald) soon; mach s~! hurry up! s~en vi (sein) in die Höhe s~en shoot up. S~igkeit f - rapidity; (Tempo) speed. S~imbiss (S~imbiß) m snack-bar. S~kochtopf m pressure-cooker. S~reinigung f express cleaners. s~stens adv as quickly as possible. S~zug m express [train]

schnetzeln vt cut into thin strips

schneuzen (sich) vr (NEW) schnäuzen (sich)

schnippen vt flick

schnippisch a pert, adv -ly

Schnipsel m & nt -s,- scrap

Schnitt m -[e]s,-e cut; (Film-) cutting; (S~muster) [paper] pattern; im S~ (durchschnittlich) on average

Schnitte f -,-n slice [of bread]; (belegt) open sandwich

schnittig a stylish; (stromlinienförmig) streamlined

Schnitt|käse m hard cheese. S~lauch m chives pl. S~muster nt [paper] pattern. S~punkt m [point of] intersection. S~wunde f cut

Schnitzel nt -s,- scrap; (Culin) escalope. s~n vt shred

schnitz|en vt/i (haben) carve. S~er m -s,- carver; (fam: Fehler) blunder. S~erei f -,-en carving

schnodderig a (fam) brash

schnöde a despicable, adv -bly; (verächtlich) contemptuous, adv -ly

Schnorchel m -s,- snorkel

Schnörkel m -s,- flourish; (Kunst) scroll. s~ig a ornate

schnorren vt/i (haben) (fam) scrounge

schnüffeln vi (haben) sniff (an etw dat sth); (fam: spionieren) snoop [around]

Schnuller m -s,- [baby's] dummy, (Amer) pacifier

Schnupf|en vt sniff; Tabak s~en take snuff. S~en m -s,- [head] cold. S~tabak m snuff

schnuppern vt/i (haben) sniff (an etw dat sth)

Schnur f -,-̈e string; (Kordel) cord; (Besatz-) braid; (Electr) flex; eine S~ a piece of string

Schnür|chen nt -s,- wie am S~chen (fam) like clockwork. s~en vt tie; lace [up] ⟨Schuhe⟩

schnurgerade a & adv dead straight

Schnurr|bart m moustache. s~en vi (haben) hum; ⟨Katze:⟩ purr

Schnür|schuh m lace-up shoe. S~senkel m [shoe-]lace

schnurstracks adv straight

Schock m -[e]s,-s shock. s~en vt (fam) shock; geschockt sein be shocked. s~ieren vt shock; s~ierend shocking

Schöffe m -n,-n lay judge

Schokolade f - chocolate

Scholle f -,-n clod [of earth]; (Eis-) ice-floe; (Fisch) plaice

schon adv already; (allein) just; (sogar) even; (ohnehin) anyway; s~ einmal before; (jemals) ever; s~ immer/oft/wieder always/often/again; hast du ihn s~ gesehen? have you seen him yet? s~ der Gedanke daran the mere thought of it;

s~ deshalb for that reason alone; das ist s~ möglich that's quite possible; ja s~, aber well yes, but; nun geh/komm s~! go/come on then!

schön a beautiful; (*Wetter*) fine; (*angenehm, nett*) nice; (*gut*) good; (*fam: beträchtlich*) pretty; s~en Dank! thank you very much! na s~ all right then ◻ *adv* beautifully; nicely; (*gut*) well; s~ langsam nice and slowly

schonen *vt* spare; (*gut behandeln*) look after; sich s~ take things easy. s~d a gentle, *adv* -tly

Schönheit *f* -,-en beauty. S~sfehler *m* blemish. S~skonkurrenz *f*, S~swettbewerb *m* beauty contest

schönmachen *vt sep* smarten up; sich s~ make oneself look nice

Schonung *f* -,-en gentle care; (*nach Krankheit*) rest; (*Baum-*) plantation. s~slos a ruthless, *adv* -ly

Schonzeit *f* close season

schöpf|en *vt* scoop [up]; ladle ⟨*Suppe*⟩; Mut s~en take heart; frische Luft s~en get some fresh air. S~er *m* -s,- creator; ⟨*Kelle*⟩ ladle. s~erisch a creative. S~kelle *f*, S~löffel *m* ladle. S~ung *f* -,-en creation

Schoppen *m* -s,- (*SGer*) ≈ pint

Schorf *m* -[e]s scab

Schornstein *m* chimney. S~feger *m* -s,- chimney-sweep

Schoß *m* -es,⸚e lap; (*Frack-*) tail

Schössling (Schößling) *m* -s,-e (*Bot*) shoot

Schote *f* -,-n pod; (*Erbse*) pea

Schotte *m* -n,-n Scot, Scotsman

Schotter *m* -s gravel; (*für Gleise*) ballast

schott|isch a Scottish, Scots. S~land *nt* -s Scotland

schraffieren *vt* hatch

schräg a diagonal, *adv* -ly; (*geneigt*) sloping; s~ halten tilt. S~e *f* -,-n slope. S~strich *m* oblique stroke

Schramme *f* -,-n scratch. s~n *vt* scrape, scratch

Schrank *m* -[e]s,⸚e cupboard; (*Kleider-*) wardrobe; (*Akten-, Glas-*) cabinet

Schranke *f* -,-n barrier

Schraube *f* -,-n screw; (*Schiffs-*) propeller. s~n *vt* screw; (*ab-*) unscrew; (*drehen*) turn; sich in die Höhe s~n spiral upwards. S~nmutter *f* nut. S~nschlüssel *m* spanner. S~nzieher *m* -s,- screwdriver

Schraubstock *m* vice

Schrebergarten *m* ≈ allotment

Schreck *m* -[e]s,-e fright; jdm einen S~ einjagen give s.o. a fright. S~en *m* -s,- fright; (*Entsetzen*) horror. s~en *vt* (*reg*) frighten; (*auf-*) startle ◻ *vi*† (*sein*) in die Höhe s~en start up

Schreck|gespenst *nt* spectre. s~haft a easily frightened; (*nervös*) jumpy, s~lich a terrible, *adv* -bly. S~schuss (S~schuß) *m* warning shot

Schrei *m* -[e]s,-e cry, shout; (*gellend*) scream; der letzte S~ (*fam*) the latest thing

Schreib|block *m* writing-pad. s~en† *vt/i* (*haben*) write; (*auf der Maschine*) type; richtig/falsch s~en spell right/wrong; sich s~en ⟨*Wort:*⟩ be spelt; (*korrespondieren*) correspond; krank s~en (NEW) krankschreiben. S~en *nt* -s,- writing; (*Brief*) letter. S~fehler *m* spelling mistake. S~heft *nt* exercise book. S~kraft *f* clerical assistant; (*für Maschineschreiben*) typist. S~maschine *f* typewriter. S~papier *nt* writing-paper. S~schrift *f* script. S~tisch *m* desk. S~ung *f* -,-en spelling. S~waren *fpl* stationery *sg*. S~weise *f* spelling

schreien† *vt/i* (*haben*) cry; (*gellend*) scream; (*rufen, laut sprechen*) shout; zum S~ sein (*fam*) be a scream. s~d a (*fig*) glaring; (*grell*) garish

Schreiner *m* -s,- joiner

schreiten† *vi* (*sein*) walk

Schrift *f* -,-en writing; (*Druck-*) type; (*Abhandlung*) paper; die Heilige S~ the Scriptures *pl*. S~führer *m* secretary. s~lich a written ◻ *adv* in writing. S~sprache *f* written language. S~steller(in) *m* -s,- (*f* -,-nen) writer. S~stück *nt* document. S~zeichen *nt* character

schrill a shrill, *adv* -y

Schritt *m* -[e]s,-e step; (*Entfernung*) pace; (*Gangart*) walk; (*der Hose*) crotch; im S~ in step; (*langsam*) at walking pace; S~ halten mit (*fig*) keep pace with. S~macher *m* -s,- pace-maker. s~weise *adv* step by step

schroff a precipitous, *adv* -ly; (*abweisend*) brusque, *adv* -ly; (*unvermittelt*) abrupt, *adv* -ly; (*Gegensatz*) stark

schröpfen *vt* (*fam*) fleece

Schrot *m & nt* -[e]s coarse meal; (*Blei-*) small shot. s~en *vt* grind coarsely. S~flinte *f* shotgun

Schrott *m* -[e]s scrap[-metal]; zu S~ fahren (*fam*) write off. S~platz *m* scrapyard. s~reif a ready for the scrap-heap

schrubb|en *vt/i* (*haben*) scrub. S~er *m* -s, [long-handled] scrubbing-brush

Schrull|e *f* -,-n whim; alte S~e (*fam*) old crone. s~ig a cranky

schrumpfen *vi* (*sein*) shrink; (*Obst:*) shrivel

schrump[e]lig a wrinkled

Schrunde f -,-n crack; (*Spalte*) crevasse

Schub m -[e]s,-e (*Phys*) thrust; (S~*fach*) drawer; (*Menge*) batch. S~fach nt drawer. S~karre f, S~karren m wheelbarrow. S~lade f drawer

Schubs m -es,-e push, shove. s~en vt push, shove

schüchtern a shy, adv -ly; (*zaghaft*) tentative, adv -ly. S~heit f - shyness

Schuft m -[e]s,-e (*pej*) swine. s~en vi (*haben*) (*fam*) slave away

Schuh m -[e]s,-e shoe. S~anzieher m -s,- shoehorn. S~band nt (*pl* -bänder) shoelace. S~creme f shoe-polish. S~löffel m shoehorn. S~macher m -s,- shoemaker; (*zum Flicken*) [shoe] mender. S~werk nt shoes pl

Schul|abgänger m -s,- schoolleaver. S~arbeiten, S~aufgaben fpl homework sg. S~buch nt school-book

Schuld f -,-en guilt; (*Verantwortung*) blame; (*Geld-*) debt; S~en machen get into debt; S~ haben be to blame (an + dat for); jdm S~ geben blame s.o.; sich (dat) etwas zu S~en kommen lassen = sich etwas zuschulden kommen lassen, s. zuschulden ⟹ s~ sein be to blame (an + dat for); s~ haben/jdm s~ geben (NEW)S~ haben/jdm S~ geben, s. Schuld. s~en vt owe

schuldig a guilty (gen of); (*gebührend*) due; jdm etw s~ sein owe s.o. sth. S~keit f - duty

schuld|los a innocent. S~ner m -s,- debtor. S~spruch m guilty verdict

Schule f -,-n school; in der/die S~ at/to school. s~n vt train

Schüler|(in) m -s,- (f -,-nen) pupil. S~lotse m pupil acting as crossing warden

schul|frei a s~freier Tag day without school; wir haben morgen s~frei there's no school tomorrow. S~hof m [school] playground. S~jahr nt school year; (*Klasse*) form. S~junge m schoolboy. S~kind nt schoolchild. S~leiter(in) m(f) head [teacher]. S~mädchen nt schoolgirl. S~stunde f lesson

Schulter f -,-n shoulder. S~blatt nt shoulder-blade. s~n vt shoulder. S~tuch nt shawl

Schulung f - training

schummeln vi (*haben*) (*fam*) cheat

Schund m -[e]s trash. S~roman m trashy novel

Schuppe f -,-n scale; S~n pl dandruff sg. s~n (sich) vr flake [off]

Schuppen m -s,- shed

Schur f - shearing

Schür|eisen nt poker. s~en vt poke; (*fig*) stir up

schürf|en vt mine; sich (dat) das Knie s~en graze one's knee ⟹ vi (*haben*) s~en nach prospect for. S~wunde f abrasion, graze

Schürhaken m poker

Schurke m -n,-n villain

Schürze f -,-n apron. s~n vt (*raffen*) gather [up]; tie ⟨*Knoten*⟩; purse ⟨*Lippen*⟩. S~njäger m (*fam*) womanizer

Schuss m -es,¨e (*Schuß* m -sses,¨sse) shot; (*kleine Menge*) dash

Schüssel f -,-n bowl; (*TV*) dish

schusselig a (*fam*) scatter-brained

Schuss|fahrt (Schußfahrt) f (*Ski*) schuss. S~waffe f firearm

Schuster m -s,- = Schuhmacher

Schutt m -[e]s rubble. S~abladeplatz m rubbish dump

Schüttel|frost m shivering fit. s~n vt shake; sich s~n shake oneself/itself; (*vor Ekel*) shudder; jdm die Hand s~n shake s.o.'s hand

schütten vt pour; (*kippen*) tip; (*ver-*) spill ⟹ vi (*haben*) es schüttet it is pouring [with rain]

Schutthaufen m pile of rubble

Schutz m -es protection; (*Zuflucht*) shelter; (*Techn*) guard; S~ suchen take refuge; unter dem S~ der Dunkelheit under cover of darkness. S~anzug m protective suit. S~blech nt mudguard. S~brille goggles pl

Schütze m -n,-n marksman; (*Tor-*) scorer; (*Astr*) Sagittarius; guter S~ good shot

schützen vt protect/(*Zuflucht gewähren*) shelter (vor + dat from) ⟹ vi (*haben*) give protection/shelter (vor + dat from). s~d a protective, adv -ly

Schützenfest nt fair with shooting competition

Schutz|engel m guardian angel. S~heilige(r) m/f patron saint

Schützling m -s,-e charge; (*Protegé*) protégé

schutz|los a defenceless, helpless. S~mann m (*pl* -männer & -leute) policeman. S~umschlag m dust-jacket

Schwaben nt -s Swabia

schwäbisch a Swabian

schwach a (schwächer, schwächst) weak, adv -ly; (*nicht gut; gering*) poor, adv -ly; (*leicht*) faint, adv -ly

Schwäche f -,-n weakness. s~n vt weaken

Schwach|heit f - weakness. S~kopf m (*fam*) idiot

schwäch|lich a delicate. S~ling m -s,-e weakling

Schwachsinn m mental deficiency, s~ig a mentally deficient; (fam) idiotic

Schwächung f - weakening

schwafeln (fam) vi (haben) waffle □ vt talk

Schwager m -s,ᵉ brother-in-law

Schwägerin f -,-nen sister-in-law

Schwalbe f -,-n swallow

Schwall m -[e]s torrent

Schwamm m -[e]s,ᵉe sponge; (SGer: Pilz) fungus; (essbar) mushroom. s~ig a spongy; (aufgedunsen) bloated

Schwan m -[e]s,ᵉe swan

schwanen vi (haben) (fam) mir schwante, dass I had a nasty feeling that

schwanger a pregnant

schwängern vt make pregnant

Schwangerschaft f -,-en pregnancy

Schwank m -[e]s,ᵉe (Theat) farce

schwank|en vi (haben) sway; (Boot:) rock; (sich ändern) fluctuate; (unentschieden sein) be undecided □ (sein) stagger. S~ung f -,-en fluctuation

Schwanz m -es,ᵉe tail

schwänzen vt (fam) skip; die Schule s~ play truant

Schwarm m -[e]s,ᵉe swarm; (Fisch-) shoal; (fam: Liebe) idol

schwärmen vi (haben) swarm; s~ für (fam) adore; (verliebt sein) have a crush on; s~ von (fam) rave about

Schwarte f -,-n (Speck-) rind; (fam: Buch) tome

schwarz a (schwärzer, schwärzest) black; (fam: illegal) illegal, adv -ly; s~er Markt black market; s~ gekleidet dressed in black; s~ auf weiß in black and white; s~ sehen (fig) be pessimistic; ins S~e treffen score a bull's-eye. S~ nt -[e]s,- black. S~arbeit f moonlighting. s~arbeiten vi sep (haben) moonlight. S~brot nt black bread. S~e(r) m/f black

Schwärze f - blackness. s~n vt blacken

Schwarz|fahrer m fare-dodger. S~handel m black market (mit in). S~händler m black marketeer. S~markt m black market. s~sehen† vi sep (haben) watch television without a licence; (fig) (NEW) s~ sehen, s. schwarz. S~wald m Black Forest. s~weiß a black and white

Schwatz m -es (fam) chat

schwatzen, (SGer) schwätzen vi (haben) chat; (klatschen) gossip; (Sch) talk [in class] □ vt talk

schwatzhaft a garrulous

Schwebe f - in der S~ (fig) undecided. S~bahn f cable railway. S~n vi (haben) float; (fig) be undecided; (Verfahren:) be pending; in Gefahr s~n be in danger □ (sein) float

Schwed|e m -n,-n Swede. S~en nt -s Sweden. S~in f -,-nen Swede. s~isch a Swedish

Schwefel m -s sulphur. S~säure f sulphuric acid

schweigen† vi (haben) be silent; ganz zu s~ von to say nothing of, let alone. S~ nt -s silence; zum S~ bringen silence. s~d a silent, adv -ly

schweigsam a silent; (wortkarg) taciturn

Schwein nt -[e]s,-e pig; (Culin) pork; (sl) (schmutziger Mensch) dirty pig; (Schuft) swine; S~ haben (fam) be lucky. S~ebraten m roast pork. S~efleisch nt pork. S~ehund m (sl) swine. S~erei f -,-en (sl) [dirty] mess; (Gemeinheit) dirty trick. S~estall m pigsty. s~isch a lewd. S~sleder nt pigskin

Schweiß m -es sweat

Schweiß|en vt weld. S~er m -s,- welder

Schweiz (die) - Switzerland. S~er a & m -s,-, S~erin f -,-nen Swiss. s~erisch a Swiss

schwelen vi (haben) smoulder

schwelgen vi (haben) feast; s~ in (+ dat) wallow in

Schwelle f -,-n threshold; (Eisenbahn-) sleeper

schwell|en† vi (sein) swell. S~ung f -,-en swelling

Schwemme f -,-n watering-place; (fig: Überangebot) glut. s~n vt wash; an Land s~n wash up

Schwenk m -[e]s swing. s~en vt swing; (schwingen) wave; (spülen) rinse; in Butter s~en toss in butter □ vi (sein) swing

schwer a heavy; (schwierig) difficult; (mühsam, streng) hard; (ernst) serious; (schlimm) bad; 3 Pfund s~ sein weigh 3 pounds □ adv heavily; with difficulty; (mühsam, streng) hard; (schlimm, sehr) badly, seriously; s~ krank/verletzt seriously ill/injured; s~ arbeiten work hard; s~ hören be hard of hearing; etw s~ nehmen take sth seriously; jdm s~ fallen be hard for s.o.; es jdm s~ machen make it or things difficult for s.o.; sich s~ tun have difficulty (mit with); s~ zu sagen difficult or hard to say

Schwere f - heaviness; (Gewicht) weight; (Schwierigkeit) difficulty; (Ernst) gravity. S~losigkeit f - weightlessness

schwer|fallen† vi sep (sein) (NEW) s~ fallen, s. schwer. s~fällig a ponderous, adv -ly; (unbeholfen) clumsy, adv -ily. S~gewicht nt heavyweight. s~hörig a s~hörig sein be hard of hearing.

S~kraft f (Phys) gravity. s~krank a (NEW)s~ krank, s. schwer. s~lich adv hardly. s~machen vt sep (NEW)s~ machen, s. schwer. s~mütig a melancholic. s~nehmen† vt sep (NEW)s~ nehmen, s. schwer. S~punkt m centre of gravity; (fig) emphasis

Schwert nt -[e]s,-er sword. S~lilie f iris

schwer|tun† (sich) vr sep (NEW)s~ tun (sich), s. schwer. s~verbrecher m serious offender. s~verdaulich a (NEW)s~ verdaulich, s. verdaulich. s~verletzt a (NEW)s~ verletzt, s. schwer. s~wiegend a weighty

Schwester f -,-n sister; (Kranken-) nurse. s~lich a sisterly

Schwieger|eltern pl parents-in-law. S~mutter f mother-in-law. S~sohn m son-in-law. S~tochter f daughter-in-law. S~vater m father-in-law

Schwiele f -,-n callus

schwierig a difficult. S~keit f -,-en difficulty

Schwimm|bad nt swimming-baths pl. S~becken nt swimming-pool. s~en† vt/i (sein/haben) swim; (auf dem Wasser treiben) float. S~er m -s,- swimmer; (Techn) float. S~weste f life-jacket

Schwindel m -s dizziness, vertigo; (fam: Betrug) fraud; (Lüge) lie. S~anfall m dizzy spell. s~frei a s~frei sein have a good head for heights. s~n vi (haben) (lügen) lie; mir od mich s~t I feel dizzy

schwinden† vi (sein) dwindle; (vergehen) fade; (nachlassen) fail

Schwindl|er m -s,- liar; (Betrüger) fraud, con-man. s~ig a dizzy; mir ist od wird s~ig I feel dizzy

schwing|en† vi (haben) swing; (Phys) oscillate; (vibrieren) vibrate □ vt swing; wave (Fahne); (drohend) brandish. S~tür f swing-door. S~ung f -,-en oscillation; vibration

Schwips m -es,-e einen S~ haben (fam) be tipsy

schwirren vi (haben/sein) buzz; (surren) whirr

Schwitz|e f -,-n (Culin) roux. s~en vi (haben) sweat; ich s~e od mich s~t I am hot □ vt (Culin) sweat

schwör|en† vt/i (haben) swear (auf + acc by); Rache s~ swear revenge

schwul a (fam: homosexuell) gay

schwül a close. S~e f - closeness

schwülstig a bombastic, adv -ally

Schwung m -[e]s,-e swing; (Bogen) sweep; (Schnelligkeit) momentum; (Kraft) vigour; (Feuer) verve; (fam: Anzahl) batch; in S~ kommen gather momentum; (fig) get going. s~haft a brisk, adv -ly. s~los

a dull. s~voll a vigorous, adv -ly; (Bogen, Linie) sweeping; (mitreißend) spirited, lively

Schwur m -[e]s,-e vow; (Eid) oath. S~gericht nt jury [court]

sechs inv a, S~ f -,-en six; (Sch) ≈ fail mark. s~eckig a hexagonal. s~te(r,s) a sixth

sechzehn inv a sixteen. s~te(r,s) a sixteenth. s~zig inv a sixty. s~zigste(r,s) a sixtieth

sedieren vt sedate

See[1] m -s,-n ['ze:ɔn] lake

See[2] f - sea; an die/der See to/at the seaside; auf See at sea. S~bad nt seaside resort. S~fahrt f [sea] voyage; (Schifffahrt) navigation. S~gang m schwerer S~gang rough sea. S~hund m seal. s~krank a seasick

Seele f -,-n soul. s~nruhig a calm, adv -ly

seelisch a psychological, adv -ly; (geistig) mental, adv -ly

Seelsorger m -s,- pastor

See|luft f sea air. S~macht f maritime power. S~mann m (pl -leute) seaman, sailor. S~not f in S~not in distress. S~räuber m pirate. S~reise f [sea] voyage. S~rose f water-lily. S~sack m kitbag. S~stern m starfish. S~tang m seaweed. s~tüchtig a seaworthy. S~weg m sea route; auf dem S~weg by sea. S~zunge f sole

Segel nt -s,- sail. S~boot nt sailing-boat. S~fliegen nt gliding. S~flieger m glider pilot. S~flugzeug nt glider. s~n vt/i (sein/haben) sail. S~schiff nt sailing-ship. S~sport m sailing. S~tuch nt canvas

Segen m -s blessing. s~sreich a beneficial; (gesegnet) blessed

Segler m -s,- yachtsman

Segment nt -[e]s,-e segment

segnen vt bless; gesegnet mit blessed with

sehen† vt see; watch (Fernsehsendung); jdn/etw wieder s~ see s.o./sth again; sich s~ lassen show oneself □ vi (haben) see; (blicken) look (auf + acc at); (ragen) show (aus above); gut/schlecht s~ have good/bad eyesight; vom S~ kennen know by sight; s~ nach keep an eye on; (betreuen) look after; (suchen) look for; darauf s~, dass see [to it] that. s~swert, s~swürdig a worth seeing. S~swürdigkeit f -,-en sight

Sehkraft f sight, vision

Sehne f -,-n tendon; (eines Bogens) string

sehnen (sich) vr long (nach for)

sehnig a sinewy; (zäh) stringy

sehn|lich[st] a (Wunsch) dearest □ adv longingly. S~sucht f - longing (nach for).

s~süchtig *a* longing, *adv* -ly; ⟨*Wunsch*⟩ dearest

s̲e̲hr *adv* very; (*mit Verb*) very much; so s~, dass so much that

s̲e̲icht *a* shallow

s̲e̲id *s.* sein¹; ihr s~ you are

S̲e̲ide *f* -,-n silk

S̲e̲idel *nt* -s,- beer-mug

s̲e̲iden *a* silk ... S~papier *nt* tissue paper. S~raupe *f* silk-worm. s~weich *a* silky-soft

s̲e̲idig *a* silky

S̲e̲ife *f* -,-n soap. S~npulver *nt* soap powder. S~nschaum *m* lather

s̲e̲ifig *a* soapy

s̲e̲ihen *vi* strain

S̲e̲il *nt* -[e]s,-e rope; (*Draht-*) cable. S~bahn *f* cable railway. s~springen† *vi* (sein) (*inf* & *pp only*) skip. S~tänzer(in) *m(f)* tightrope walker

s̲e̲in†¹ *vi* (sein) be; er ist Lehrer he is a teacher; sei still! be quiet! mir ist kalt/schlecht I am cold/feel sick; wie dem auch sei be that as it may; etw s~ lassen leave sth; (*aufhören mit*) stop sth □ *v aux* have; angekommen/gestorben s~ have arrived/died; er war/wäre gefallen he had/would have fallen; es ist/war viel zu tun/nichts zu sehen there is/was a lot to be done/nothing to be seen

s̲e̲in² *poss pron* his; (*Ding, Tier*) its; (*nach man*) one's; sein Glück versuchen try one's luck. s~e(r,s) *poss pron* his; (*nach man*) one's own; das S~e *od* seine tun do one's share. s~erseits *adv* for his part. s~erzeit *adv* in those days. s~etwegen *adv* for his sake; (*wegen ihm*) because of him, on his account. s~etwillen *adv* um s~etwillen for his sake. s~ige *poss pron* der/die/das s~ige his

s̲e̲inlassen† *vt sep* (NEW) sein lassen, *s.* sein¹

s̲e̲ins *poss pron* his; (*nach man*) one's own

s̲e̲it *conj* & *prep* (+ *dat*) since; s~ wann? since when? s~ einiger Zeit for some time [past]; ich wohne s~ zehn Jahren hier I've lived here for ten years. s~d̲e̲m *conj* since □ *adv* since then

S̲e̲ite *f* -,-n side; (*Buch-*) page; S~ an S~ side by side; zur S~ legen/treten put/step aside; jds starke S~ s.o.'s strong point; auf der einen/anderen S~ (*fig*) on the one/other hand; von ... s~ (*+ gen*) = vonseiten

s̲e̲itens *prep* (+ *gen*) on the part of

S̲e̲iten|schiff *nt* [side] aisle. S~sprung *m* infidelity; einen S~sprung machen be unfaithful. S~stechen *nt* -s (*Med*) stitch.

S~straße *f* side-street. S~streifen *m* verge; (*Autobahn-*) hard shoulder

s̲e̲ither *adv* since then

s̲e̲it|lich *a* side ... □ *adv* at/on the side; s~lich von to one side of □ *prep* (+ *gen*) to one side of. s~wärts *adv* on/to one side; (*zur Seite*) sideways

Sekr̲e̲t *nt* -[e]s,-e secretion

Sekret|ä̲r *m* -s,-e secretary; (*Schrank*) bureau. S~ariat *nt* -[e]s,-e secretary's office. S~ä̲rin *f* -,-nen secretary

S̲e̲kt *m* -[e]s [German] sparkling wine

S̲e̲kte *f* -,-n sect

Sekti̲o̲n /'tsi̲o̲:n/ *f* -,-en section; (*Sezierung*) autopsy

S̲e̲ktor *m* -s,-en /-'to:rən/ sector

Sekund̲a̲nt *m* -en,-en (*Sport*) second

sekund̲ä̲r *a* secondary

Sek̲u̲nde *f* -,-n second

s̲e̲lber *pron* (*fam*) = selbst

s̲e̲lbst *pron* oneself; ich/du/er/sie s~ I myself /you yourself/ he himself/she herself; wir/ihr/sie s~ we ourselves/you yourselves/they themselves; ich schneide mein Haar s~ I cut my own hair; von s~ of one's own accord; (*automatisch*) automatically; s~ gemacht home-made □ *adv* even. S~achtung *f* self-esteem, self-respect

s̲e̲lbständig *a* = selbstständig. S~keit *f* - = Selbstständigkeit

S̲e̲lbstaufopferung *f* self-sacrifice

S̲e̲lbstbedienung *f* self-service. S~srestaurant *nt* self-service restaurant, cafeteria

S̲e̲lbst|befriedigung *f* masturbation. S~beherrschung *f* self-control. S~bestimmung *f* self-determination. s~bewusst (s~bewußt) *a* self-confident. S~bewusstsein (S~bewußtsein) *nt* self-confidence. S~bildnis *nt* self-portrait. S~erhaltung *f* self-preservation. s~gefällig *a* self-satisfied, smug, *adv* -ly. s~gemacht *a* (NEW) s~ gemacht, *s.* selbst. s~gerecht *a* self-righteous. S~gespräch *nt* soliloquy; S~gespräche führen talk to oneself. s~haftend *a* self-adhesive. s~herrlich *a* autocratic, *adv* -ally. S~hilfe *f* self-help. s~klebend *a* self-adhesive. S~kostenpreis *m* cost price. S~laut *m* vowel. s~los *a* selfless, *adv* -ly. S~mitleid *nt* self-pity. S~mord *m* suicide. S~mörder(in) *m(f)* suicide. s~mörderisch *a* suicidal. S~porträt *nt* self-portrait. s~sicher *a* self-assured. S~sicherheit *f* self-assurance. s~ständig *a* independent, self-employed; sich s~ständig machen set up on one's own. S~ständigkeit *f* - independence. s~süchtig *a* selfish, *adv*

-ly. S~tanken *nt* self-service (*for petrol*). s~tätig *a* automatic, *adv* -ally. S~versorgung *f* self-catering

selbstverständlich *a* natural, *adv* -ly; etw für s~ halten take sth for granted; das ist s~ that goes without saying; s~! of course! S~keit *f* - matter of course; das ist eine S~keit that goes without saying

Selbst|verteidigung *f* self-defence. S~vertrauen *nt* self-confidence. S~verwaltung *f* self-government. s~zufrieden *a* complacent, *adv* -ly

selig *a* blissfully happy; (*Relig*) blessed; (*verstorben*) late. S~keit *f* - bliss

Sellerie *m* -s,-s & *f* -,- celeriac; (*Stangen-*) celery

selten *a* rare □ *adv* rarely, seldom; (*besonders*) exceptionally. S~heit *f* -,-en rarity

Selterswasser *nt* seltzer [water]

seltsam *a* odd, *adv* -ly, strange, *adv* -ly. s~erweise *adv* oddly/strangely enough

Semester *nt* -s,- (*Univ*) semester

Semikolon *nt* -s,-s semicolon

Seminar *nt* -s,-e seminar; (*Institut*) department; (*Priester-*) seminary

Semmel *f* -,-n [bread] roll. S~brösel *pl* breadcrumbs

Senat *m* -[e]s,-e senate. S~or *m* -s,-en /-'to:rən/ senator

senden[1] *vt* send

senden[2] *vt* (*reg*) broadcast; (*über Funk*) transmit, send. S~r *m* -s,- [broadcasting] station; (*Anlage*) transmitter. S~reihe *f* series

Sendung *f* -,-en consignment, shipment; (*Auftrag*) mission; (*Radio, TV*) programme

Senf *m* -s mustard

sengend *a* scorching

senil *a* senile. S~ität *f* - senility

Senior *m* -s,-en /-'io:rən/ senior; S~en senior citizens. S~enheim *nt* old people's home. S~enteller *m* senior citizen's menu

Senke *f* -,-n dip, hollow

Senkel *m* -s,- [shoe-]lace

senken *vt* lower; bring down (*Fieber, Preise*); bow (*Kopf*); sich s~ come down, fall; (*absinken*) subside; (*abfallen*) slope down

senkrecht *a* vertical, *adv* -ly. S~e *f* -n,-n perpendicular

Sensation /-'tsjo:n/ *f* -,-en sensation. s~ell *a* sensational, *adv* -ly

Sense *f* -,-n scythe

sensib|el *a* sensitive, *adv* -ly. S~ilität *f* - sensitivity

sentimental *a* sentimental. S~ität *f* - sentimentality

separat *a* separate, *adv* -ly

September *m* -s,- September

Serenade *f* -,-n serenade

Serie /'ze:rjə/ *f* -,-n series; (*Briefmarken*) set; (*Comm*) range. S~nnummer *f* serial number

seriös *a* respectable, *adv* -bly; (*zuverlässig*) reliable, *adv* -bly; (*ernst gemeint*) serious

Serpentine *f* -,-n winding road; (*Kehre*) hairpin bend

Serum *nt* -s,Sera serum

Service[1] /zɛr'vi:s/ *nt* -[s],- /-'vi:s[əs], -'vi:-sə/ service, set

Service[2] /'zœ:ɛvis/ *m* & *nt* -s /-vis[əs]/ (*Comm, Tennis*) service

servier|en *vt/i* (*haben*) serve. S~erin *f* -,-nen waitress. S~wagen *m* trolley

Serviette *f* -,-n napkin, serviette

Servus *int* (*Aust*) cheerio; (*Begrüßung*) hallo

Sessel *m* -s,- armchair. S~bahn *f*, S~lift *m* chair-lift

sesshaft (**seßhaft**) *a* settled; s~ werden settle down

Set /zɛt/ *nt* & *m* -[s],-s set; (*Deckchen*) place-mat

setz|en *vt* put; (*abstellen*) set down; (*hin-*) sit down (*Kind*); move (*Spielstein*); (*pflanzen*) plant; (*schreiben, wetten*) put; sich s~en sit down; (*sinken*) settle □ *vi* (*sein*) leap □ *vi* (*haben*) s~en auf (+ *acc*) back. S~ling *m* -s,-e seedling

Seuche *f* -,-n epidemic

seufz|en *vi* (*haben*) sigh. S~er *m* -s,- sigh

Sex /zɛks/ *m* -[es] sex. s~istisch *a* sexist

Sexualität *f* - sexuality. s~ell *a* sexual, *adv* -ly

sexy /'zɛksi/ *inv a* sexy

sezieren *vt* dissect

Shampoo /ʃam'pu:/, **Shampoon** /ʃam'po:n/ *nt* -s shampoo

siamesisch *a* Siamese

sich *refl pron* oneself; (*mit er/sie/es*) himself/herself/itself; (*mit sie pl*) themselves; (*mit Sie*) yourself; (*pl*) yourselves; (*einander*) each other; s~ kennen know oneself/(*einander*) each other; s~ waschen have a wash; s~ (*dat*) die Zähne putzen/die Haare kämmen clean one's teeth/comb one's hair; s~ (*dat*) das Bein brechen break a leg; s~ wundern/schämen be surprised/ashamed; s~ gut lesen/verkaufen read/sell well; von s~ aus of one's own accord

Sichel *f* -,-n sickle

sicher *a* safe; (*gesichert*) secure; (*gewiss*) certain; (*zuverlässig*) reliable; sure (*Urteil, Geschmack*); steady (*Hand*); (*selbstbewusst*) self-confident; sich (*dat*) etw ⟨gen⟩ s~ sein be sure of sth; bist du s~? are you sure? □ adv safely; securely; certainly; reliably; self-confidently; (wahrscheinlich) most probably; er kommt s~ he is sure to come; s~! certainly! s~gehen† vi sep ⟨sein⟩ (fig) be sure

Sicherheit f - safety; ⟨Pol, Psych, Comm⟩ security; (Gewissheit) certainty; (Zuverlässigkeit) reliability; (des Urteils, Geschmacks) surety; (Selbstbewusstsein) self-confidence. S~gurt m safety-belt; ⟨Auto⟩ seat-belt. s~shalber adv to be on the safe side. S~snadel f safety-pin

sicherlich adv certainly; (wahrscheinlich) most probably

sicher|n vt secure; (garantieren) safeguard; (schützen) protect; put the safety-catch on ⟨Pistole⟩; sich ⟨dat⟩ etw s~n secure sth. s~stellen vt sep safeguard; (beschlagnahmen) seize. S~ung f -,-en safeguard, protection; (Gewehr-) safety-catch; ⟨Electr⟩ fuse

Sicht f - view; (S~weite) visibility; in S~ kommen come into view; auf lange S~ in the long term. s~bar a visible, adv -bly. s~en vt sight; (durchsehen) sift through. s~lich a obvious, adv -ly. S~vermerk m visa. S~weite f visibility; in/außer S~weite within/out of sight

sickern vi ⟨sein⟩ seep

sie pron ⟨nom⟩ ⟨sg⟩ she; ⟨Ding, Tier⟩ it; ⟨pl⟩ they; ⟨acc⟩ ⟨sg⟩ her; ⟨Ding, Tier⟩ it; ⟨pl⟩ them

Sie pron you; gehen/warten Sie! go/wait!

Sieb nt -[e]s,-e sieve; ⟨Tee-⟩ strainer. s~en¹ vt sieve, sift

sieben² inv a, S~ f -,-en seven. S~sachen fpl (fam) belongings. S~te(r,s) a seventh

sieb|te(r,s) a seventh. s~zehn inv a seventeen. s~zehnte(r,s) a seventeenth. s~zig inv a seventy. s~zigste(r,s) a seventieth

sied|en† vt/i ⟨haben⟩ boil; s~nd heiß boiling hot. S~punkt m boiling point

Siedl|er m -s,- settler. S~ung f -,-en [housing] estate; (Niederlassung) settlement

Sieg m -[e]s,-e victory

Siegel nt -s,- seal. S~ring m signet-ring

sieg|en vi ⟨haben⟩ win. S~er(in) m -s,- ⟨f -,-nen⟩ winner. s~reich a victorious

siezen vt jdn s~ call s.o. 'Sie'

Signal nt -s,-e signal. s~isieren vt signal

signieren vt sign

Silbe f -,-n syllable. S~ntrennung f word-division

Silber nt -s silver. S~hochzeit f silver wedding. s~n a silver. S~papier nt silver paper

Silhouette /zɪ'lɡɛta/ f -,-n silhouette

Silizium nt -s silicon

Silo m & nt -s,-s silo

Silvester nt -s New Year's Eve

simpel a simple, adv -ply; (einfältig) simple-minded

Simplex nt -,-e simplex

Sims m & nt -es,-e ledge; ⟨Kamin-⟩ mantelpiece

Simul|ant m -en,-en malingerer. s~ieren vt feign; ⟨Techn⟩ simulate □ vi ⟨haben⟩ pretend; (sich krank stellen) malinger

simultan a simultaneous, adv -ly

sind s. sein¹; wir/sie s~ we/they are

Sinfonie f -,-n symphony

singen† vt/i ⟨haben⟩ sing

Singular m -s,-e singular

Singvogel m songbird

sinken† vi ⟨sein⟩ sink; ⟨nieder-⟩ drop; (niedriger werden) go down, fall; den Mut s~ lassen lose courage

Sinn m -[e]s,-e sense; (Denken) mind; (Zweck) point; im S~ haben have in mind; in gewissem S~e in a sense; es hat keinen S~ it is pointless; nicht bei S~en sein be out of one's mind. S~bild nt symbol. s~en† vi ⟨haben⟩ think; auf Rache s~en plot one's revenge

sinnlich a sensory; (sexuell) sensual; ⟨Genüsse⟩ sensuous. S~keit f - sensuality; sensuousness

sinn|los a senseless, adv -ly; (zwecklos) pointless, adv -ly. s~voll a meaningful; (vernünftig) sensible, adv -bly

Sintflut f flood

Siphon /'zi:fõ/ m -s,-s siphon

Sipp|e f -,-n clan. S~schaft f - clan; ⟨Pack⟩ crowd

Sirene f -,-n siren

Sirup m -s,-e syrup; (schwarzer) treacle

Sitte f -,-n custom; S~n manners. s~nlos a immoral

sittlich a moral, adv -ly. S~keit f - morality. S~keitsverbrecher m sex offender

sittsam a well-behaved; (züchtig) demure, adv -ly

Situ|ation /-'tsjo:n/ f -,-en situation. s~iert a gut/schlecht s~iert well/badly off

Sitz m -es,-e seat; (Passform) fit

sitzen† vi ⟨haben⟩ sit; (sich befinden) be; (passen) fit; (fam: treffen) hit home; [im Gefängnis] s~ (fam) be in jail; s~ bleiben remain seated; (fam) ⟨Sch⟩ stay or be kept down; (nicht heiraten) be left on the shelf; s~ bleiben auf (+ dat) be left with; jdn s~ lassen let s.o. down; (fam) ⟨Sch⟩ keep s.o. down; (nicht heiraten) jilt s.o.; (im Stich lassen) leave s.o. in the lurch. s~bleiben† vi sep ⟨sein⟩ NEW s~ bleiben

s. sitzen. s~d a seated; ⟨Tätigkeit⟩ sedentary. s~lassen† vt sep (NEW) s~ lassen, s. sitzen

Sitz|gelegenheit f seat. **S~platz** m seat. **S~ung** f -,-en session

Sizilien /-jən/ nt -s Sicily

Skala f -,-len scale; ⟨Reihe⟩ range

Skalpell nt -s,-e scalpel

skalpieren vt scalp

Skandal m -s,-e scandal. **s~ös** a scandalous

skandieren vt scan ⟨Verse⟩; chant ⟨Parolen⟩

Skandinav|ien /-jən/ nt -s Scandinavia. **s~isch** a Scandinavian

Skat m -s skat

Skelett nt -[e]s,-e skeleton

Skep|sis f - scepticism. **s~tisch** a sceptical, adv -ly; ⟨misstrauisch⟩ doubtful, adv -ly

Ski /ʃiː/ m -s,-er ski; **Ski fahren od laufen** ski. **S~fahrer(in)**, **S~läufer(in)** m(f) -s,- (f -,-nen) skier. **S~sport** m skiing

Skizz|e f -,-n sketch. **s~enhaft** a sketchy, adv -ily. **s~ieren** vt sketch

Sklav|e m -n,-n slave. **S~erei** f - slavery. **S~in** f -,-nen slave. **s~isch** a slavish, adv -ly

Skorpion m -s,-e scorpion; ⟨Astr⟩ Scorpio

Skrupel m -s,- scruple. **s~los** a unscrupulous

Skulptur f -,-en sculpture

skurril a absurd, adv -ly

Slalom m -s,-s slalom

Slang /slɛŋ/ m -s slang

Slaw|e m -n,-n, **S~in** f -,-nen Slav. **s~isch** a Slav; ⟨Lang⟩ Slavonic

Slip m -s,-s briefs pl

Smaragd m -[e]s,-e emerald

Smoking m -s,-s dinner jacket, (Amer) tuxedo

Snob m -s,-s snob. **S~ismus** m - snobbery. **s~istisch** a snobbish

so adv so; ⟨so sehr⟩ so much; ⟨auf diese Weise⟩ like this/that; ⟨solch⟩ such; ⟨fam: sowieso⟩ anyway; ⟨fam: umsonst⟩ free; ⟨fam: ungefähr⟩ about; nicht so schnell/viel not so fast/much; so gut/bald wie as good/soon as; so ein Mann a man like that; so ein Zufall! what a coincidence! so nicht not like that; mir ist so, als ob I feel as if; so oder so in any case; eine Stunde oder so an hour or so; so um zehn Mark ⟨fam⟩ about ten marks; [es ist] gut so that's fine; so, das ist geschafft there, that's done; so? really? so kommt doch! come on then! □ conj ⟨also⟩ so; ⟨dann⟩ then; so gern ich auch käme as much as I would like to come; so dass ⟨daß⟩ = sodass

sobald conj as soon as

Söckchen nt -s,- [ankle] sock

Socke f -,-n sock

Sockel m -s,- plinth, pedestal

Socken m -s,- sock

Soda nt -s soda

sodass conj so that

Sodawasser nt soda water

Sodbrennen nt -s heartburn

soeben adv just [now]

Sofa nt -s,-s settee, sofa

sofern adv provided [that]

sofort adv at once, immediately; ⟨auf der Stelle⟩ instantly. **s~ig** a immediate

Software /ˈzɔftvɛːɐ̯/ f - software

sogar adv even

sogenannt a so-called

sogleich adv at once

Sohle f -,-n sole; ⟨Tal-⟩ bottom

Sohn m -[e]s,ːe son

Sojabohne f soya bean

solange conj as long as

solch inv pron such; **s~ ein(e)** such a; **s~ einer/eine/eins** one/⟨Person⟩ someone like that. **s~e(r,s)** pron such; ein **s~er Mann/eine s~e Frau** a man/woman like that; ich habe **s~e Angst** I am so afraid □ ⟨substantivisch⟩ ein **s~er/eine s~e/ ein s~es** one/⟨Person⟩ someone like that; **s~e** (pl) those; ⟨Leute⟩ people like that

Sold m -[e]s ⟨Mil⟩ pay

Soldat m -en,-en soldier

Söldner m -s,- mercenary

solidarisch a **s~e Handlung** act of solidarity; **sich s~ erklären** declare one's solidarity

Solidarität f - solidarity

solide a solid, adv -ly; ⟨haltbar⟩ sturdy, adv -ily; ⟨sicher⟩ sound, adv -ly; ⟨anständig⟩ respectable, adv -bly

Solist(in) m -en,-en (f -,-nen) soloist

Soll nt -s ⟨Comm⟩ debit; ⟨Produktions-⟩ quota

sollen† v aux er soll warten he is to wait; ⟨möge⟩ let him wait; was soll ich machen? what shall I do? du sollst nicht lügen you shouldn't tell lies; du sollst nicht töten ⟨liter⟩ thou shalt not kill; ihr sollt jetzt still sein! will you be quiet now! du solltest dich schämen you ought to or should be ashamed of yourself; es hat nicht sein s~ it was not to be; ich hätte es nicht tun s~ I ought not to or should not have done it; er soll sehr nett/ reich sein he is supposed to be very nice/rich; sollte es regnen, so ... if it should rain then ...; das soll man nicht [tun] you're not supposed to [do that]; soll ich [mal versuchen]? shall I [try]? soll er doch! let him! was soll's! so what!

Solo nt -s,-los & -li solo. s~ adv solo

somit adv therefore, so

Sommer m -s,- summer. S~ferien pl summer holidays. s~lich a summery; (Sommer-) summer ... □ adv s~lich warm as warm as summer. S~schlussverkauf (S~schlußverkauf) m summer sale. S~sprossen fpl freckles. s~sprossig a freckled

Sonate f -,-n sonata

Sonde f -,-n probe

Sonder|angebot nt special offer. s~bar a odd, adv -ly. S~fahrt f special excursion. S~fall m special case. s~gleichen adv eine Gemeinheit/Grausamkeit s~gleichen unparalleled meanness/cruelty. s~lich a particular, esp; (sonderbar) odd, adv -ly. S~ling m -s,-e crank. S~marke f special stamp

sondern conj but; nicht nur ... s~ auch not only ... but also

Sonder|preis m special price. S~schule f special school. S~zug m special train

sondieren vt sound out

Sonett nt -[e]s,-e sonnet

Sonnabend m -s,-e Saturday. s~s adv on Saturdays

Sonne f -,-n sun. s~n (sich) vr sun oneself; (fig) bask (in + dat in)

Sonnen|aufgang m sunrise. s~baden vi (haben) sunbathe. S~bank f sun-bed. S~blume f sunflower. S~brand m sunburn. S~brille f sun-glasses pl. S~energie f solar energy. S~finsternis f solar eclipse. S~milch f sun-tan lotion. S~öl nt sun-tan oil. S~schein m sunshine. S~schirm m sunshade. S~stich m sunstroke. S~uhr f sundial. S~untergang m sunset. S~wende f solstice

sonnig a sunny

Sonntag m -s,-e Sunday. s~s adv on Sundays

sonst adv (gewöhnlich) usually; (im Übrigen) apart from that; (andernfalls) otherwise, or [else]; wer/was/wie/wo s~? who/what/how/where else? s~ niemand/nichts no one/nothing else, s~ noch jemand/etwas? anyone/anything else? s~ noch Fragen? any more questions? s~ jemand od wer someone/(fragend, verneint) anyone else; (irgendjemand) [just] anyone; s~ wie some/(fragend, verneint) any other way; s~ wo somewhere/(fragend, verneint) anywhere else; (irgendwo) [just] anywhere. s~ig a other. s~jemand pron ⟨NEW⟩ s~ jemand, s. sonst. s~wer pron ⟨NEW⟩ s~ wer, s. sonst. s~wie

adv ⟨NEW⟩ s~ wie, s. sonst. s~wo adv ⟨NEW⟩ s~ wo, s. sonst

sooft conj whenever

Sopran m -s,-e soprano

Sorge f -,-n worry (um about); (Fürsorge) care; in S~ sein be worried; sich (dat) S~n machen worry; keine S~! don't worry! s~n vi (haben) s~n für look after, care for; (vorsorgen) provide for; (sich kümmern) see to; dafür s~n, dass see [to it] or make sure that □ vr sich s~n worry. s~nfrei a carefree. s~nvoll a worried, adv -ly. S~recht nt (Jur) custody

Sorg|falt f -. care. s~fältig a careful, adv -ly. s~los a careless, adv -ly; (unbekümmert) carefree. S~sam a careful, adv -ly

Sorte f -,-n kind, sort; (Comm) brand

sort|ieren vt sort [out]; (Comm) grade. S~iment nt -[e]s,-e range

sosehr conj however much

Soße f -,-n sauce; (Braten-) gravy; (Salat-) dressing

Souffl|eur /zu'flø:ɐ̯/ m -s,-e, S~euse /-ø:zə/ f -,-n prompter. s~ieren vi (haben) prompt

Souvenir /zuvə'ni:ɐ̯/ nt -s,-s souvenir

souverän /zuvə'rɛ:n/ a sovereign; (fig: überlegen) expert, adv -ly. S~ität f -sovereignty

soviel conj however much; s~ ich weiß as far as I know □ adv ⟨NEW⟩ so viel, s. viel

soweit conj as far as; (insoweit) [in] so far as □ adv ⟨NEW⟩ so weit, s. weit

sowenig conj however little □ adv ⟨NEW⟩ so wenig, s. wenig

sowie conj as well as; (sobald) as soon as

sowieso adv anyway, in any case

sowjet|isch a Soviet. S~union f -Soviet Union

sowohl adv s~ ... als od wie auch ...... as well as ...; s~ er als auch seine Frau both he and his wife

sozial a social, adv -ly; (Einstellung, Beruf) caring. S~arbeit f social work. S~arbeiter(in) m(f) social worker. S~demokrat m social democrat. S~hilfe f social security

Sozialis|mus m - socialism. S~t m -en, -en socialist. s~tisch a socialist

Sozial|versicherung f National Insurance. S~wohnung f ≈ council flat

Soziol|oge m -n,-n sociologist. S~ogie f -sociology

Sozius m -se (Comm) partner; (Beifahrersitz) pillion

sozusagen adv so to speak

Spachtel m -s,- & f -,-n spatula

Spagat m -[e]s,-e (Aus) string; S~ machen do the splits pl

Spaghetti. Spagetti pl spaghetti sg

spähen vi (haben) peer

Spalier nt -s,-e trellis; S~ stehen line the route

Spalt m -[e]s,-e crack; (im Vorhang) chink

Spalt|e f -,-n crack, crevice; (Gletscher-) crevasse; (Druck-) column; (Orangen-) segment. s~en† vt split; sich s~en split. S~ung f -,-en splitting; (Kluft) split; (Phys) fission

Span m -[e]s,-e [wood] chip; (Hobel-) shaving

Spange f -,-n clasp; (Haar-) slide; (Zahn-) brace; (Arm-) bangle

Span|ien /-jən/ nt -s Spain. S~ier m -s,-, S~ierin f -,-nen Spaniard. s~isch a Spanish. S~isch nt -[s] (Lang) Spanish

Spann m -[e]s instep

Spanne f -,-n span; (Zeit-) space; (Comm) margin

spann|en vt stretch; put up (Leine); (straffen) tighten; (an-) harness (an + acc to); den Hahn s~en cock the gun; sich s~en tighten □ vi (haben) be too tight. S~end a exciting. S~er m -s,- (fam) Peeping Tom. S~ung f -,-en tension; (Erwartung) suspense; (Electr) voltage

Spar|buch nt savings book. S~büchse f money-box. s~en vt/i (haben) save; (sparsam sein) economize (mit/an + dat on); sich (dat) die Mühe s~en save oneself the trouble. S~er m -s,- saver

Spargel m -s,- asparagus

Spar|kasse f savings bank. S~konto nt deposit account

spärlich a sparse, adv -ly; (dürftig) meagre; (knapp) scanty, adv -ily

Sparren m -s,- rafter

sparsam a economical, adv -ly; (Person) thrifty. S~keit f - economy; thrift

Sparschwein nt piggy bank

spartanisch a Spartan

Sparte f -,-n branch; (Zeitungs-) section; (Rubrik) column

Spaß m -es,-e fun; (Scherz) joke; im/aus/zum S~ for fun; S~ machen be fun; (Person:) be joking; es macht mir keinen S~ I don't enjoy it; viel S~! have a good time! s~en vi (haben) joke. s~ig a amusing, funny. S~vogel m joker

Spast|iker m -s,- spastic. s~isch a spastic

spät a & adv late; wie s~ ist es? what time is it? zu s~ too late; zu s~ kommen be late. s~abends adv late at night

Spatel m -s,- & f -,-n spatula

Spaten m -s,- spade

später a later; (zukünftig) future □ adv later

spätestens adv at the latest

Spatz m -en,-en sparrow

Spätzle pl (Culin) noodles

spazieren vi (sein) stroll; s~ gehen go for a walk. s~gehen† vi sep (sein) (NEW)s~ gehen, s. spazieren

Spazier|gang m walk; einen S~gang machen go for a walk. S~gänger(in) m -s,- (f -,-nen) walker. S~stock m walking-stick

Specht m -[e]s,-e woodpecker

Speck m -s bacon; (fam: Fettpolster) fat. s~ig a greasy

Spedi|teur /ʃpedi'tø:ɐ/ m -s,-e haulage/(für Umzüge) removals contractor. S~tion /-'tsjo:n/ f -,-en carriage, haulage; (Firma) haulage/(für Umzüge) removals firm

Speer m -[e]s,-e spear; (Sport) javelin

Speiche f -,-n spoke

Speichel m -s saliva

Speicher m -s,- warehouse; (dial: Dachboden) attic; (Computer) memory. s~n vt store

speien† vt spit; (erbrechen) vomit

Speise f -,-n food; (Gericht) dish; (Pudding) blancmange. S~eis nt ice-cream. S~kammer f larder. S~karte f menu. s~n vi (haben) eat; zu Abend s~n have dinner □ vt feed. S~röhre f oesophagus. S~saal m dining-room. S~wagen m dining-car

Spektakel m -s (fam) noise

spektakulär a spectacular

Spektrum nt -s,-tra spectrum

Spekul|ant m -en,-en speculator. S~ation /-'tsjo:n/ f -,-en speculation. s~ieren vi (haben) speculate; s~ieren auf (+ acc) (fam) hope to get

Spelze f -,-n husk

spendabel a generous

Spende f -,-n donation. s~n vt donate; give (Blut, Schatten); Beifall s~n applaud. S~r m -s,- donor; (Behälter) dispenser

spendieren vt pay for; jdm etw/ein Bier s~ treat s.o. to sth/stand s.o. a beer

Spengler m -s,- (SGer) plumber

Sperling m -s,-e sparrow

Sperre f -,-n barrier; (Verbot) ban; (Comm) embargo. s~n vt close; (ver-) block; (verbieten) ban; cut off (Strom, Telefon); stop (Scheck, Kredit); s~n in (+ acc) put in (Gefängnis, Käfig); sich s~n balk (gegen at); gesperrt gedruckt (Typ) spaced

Sperr|holz nt plywood. s~ig a bulky. S~müll m bulky refuse. S~stunde f closing-time

Spesen pl expenses

spezial|isieren (sich) *vr* specialize (auf + *acc* in). S~**ist** *m* -en,-en specialist. S~**ität** *f* -,-en speciality

speziell *a* special, *adv* -ly

spezifisch *a* specific, *adv* -ally

Sphäre /'sfɛːrə/ *f* -,-n sphere

spicken *vt* (Culin) lard; gespickt mit ⟨fig⟩ full of □ *vi* (haben) ⟨fam⟩ crib (bei from)

Spiegel *m* -s,- mirror; (Wasser-, Alkohol-) level. S~**bild** *nt* reflection. S~**ei** *nt* fried egg. s~**n** *vt* reflect; sich s~**n** be reflected □ *vi* (haben) reflect [the light]; ⟨glänzen⟩ gleam. S~**ung** *f* -,-en reflection

Spiel *nt* -[e]s,-e game; (Spielen) playing; (Glücks-) gambling; (Schau-) play; (Satz) set; ein S~ Karten a pack/(Amer) deck of cards; auf dem S~ stehen be at stake; aufs S~ setzen risk. S~**art** *f* variety. S~**automat** *m* fruit machine. S~**bank** *f* casino. S~**dose** *f* musical box. s~**en** *vt/i* (haben) play; (um Glücksspiel) gamble; (vortäuschen) act; ⟨Roman:⟩ be set (in + dat in); s~**en** mit ⟨fig⟩ toy with. s~**end** *a* (mühelos) effortless, *adv* -ly

Spieler|(in) *m* -s,- (*f* -,-nen) player; (Glücks-) gambler. S~**ei** *f* -,-en amusement; ⟨Kleinigkeit⟩ trifle

Spiel|feld *nt* field, pitch. S~**gefährte** *m*, S~**gefährtin** *f* playmate. S~**karte** *f* playing-card. S~**marke** *f* chip. S~**plan** *m* programme. S~**platz** *m* playground. S~**raum** *m* ⟨fig⟩ scope; (Techn) clearance. S~**regeln** *fpl* rules [of the game]. S~**sachen** *fpl* toys. S~**verderber** *m* -s,- spoilsport. S~**waren** *fpl* toys. S~**warengeschäft** *nt* toyshop. S~**zeug** *nt* toy; (S~sachen) toys *pl*

Spieß *m* -es,-e spear; (Brat-) spit; (für Schaschlik) skewer; (Fleisch-) kebab; den S~ umkehren turn the tables on s.o. S~**bürger** *m* [petit] bourgeois. s~**bürgerlich** *a* bourgeois. s~**en** *vt* etw auf etw (acc) s~**en** spear sth with sth. S~**er** *m* -s,- [petit] bourgeois. s~**ig** *a* bourgeois. S~**ruten** *fpl* S~**ruten** laufen run the gauntlet

Spike[s]reifen /'ʃpaik[s]-/ *m* studded tyre

Spinat *m* -s spinach

Spind *m* & *nt* -[e]s,-e locker

Spindel *f* -,-n spindle

Spinne *f* -,-n spider

spinn|en† *vt/i* (haben) spin; er spinnt ⟨fam⟩ he's crazy. S~**ennetz** *nt* spider's web. S~**[en]gewebe** *nt*, S~**webe** *f* -,-n cobweb

Spion *m* -s,-e spy

Spionage /ʃpio'naːʒə/ *f* - espionage, spying; S~ treiben spy. S~**abwehr** *f* counter-espionage

spionieren *vi* (haben) spy

Spionin *f* -,-nen [woman] spy

Spirale *f* -,-n spiral. s~**ig** *a* spiral

Spiritis|mus *m* - spiritualism. s~**tisch** *a* spiritualist

Spirituosen *pl* spirits

Spiritus *m* - alcohol; (Brenn-) methylated spirits *pl*. S~**kocher** *m* spirit stove

Spital *nt* -s,ˈer (Aust) hospital

spitz *a* pointed; (scharf) sharp; (schrill) shrill; (Winkel) acute; s~**e** Bemerkung dig. S~**bube** *m* scoundrel; (Schlingel) rascal. s~**bübisch** *a* mischievous, *adv* -ly

Spitze *f* -,-n point; (oberer Teil) top; (vorderer Teil) front; (Pfeil-, Finger-, Nasen-) tip; (Schuh-, Strumpf-) toe; (Zigarren-, Zigaretten-) holder; (Höchstleistung) maximum; (Tex) lace; (fam: Anspielung) dig; an der S~ liegen be in the lead

Spitzel *m* -s,- informer

spitzen *vt* sharpen; purse ⟨Lippen⟩; prick up ⟨Ohren⟩; sich s~ auf (+ acc) ⟨fam⟩ look forward to. S~**geschwindigkeit** *f* top speed

spitz|findig *a* over-subtle. S~**hacke** *f* pickaxe. S~**name** *m* nickname

Spleen /ʃpliːn/ *m* -s,-e obsession; einen S~ haben be crazy. s~**ig** *a* eccentric

Splitter *m* -s,- splinter. s~**n** *vi* (sein) shatter. s~**[faser]nackt** *a* (fam) stark naked

sponsern *vt* sponsor

spontan *a* spontaneous, *adv* -ly

sporadisch *a* sporadic, *adv* -ally

Spore *f* -,-n (Biol) spore

Sporn *m* -[e]s, Sporen spur; einem Pferd die Sporen geben spur a horse

Sport *m* -[e]s sport; (Hobby) hobby. S~**art** *f* sport. S~**fest** *nt* sports day. S~**ler** *m* -s,- sportsman. S~**lerin** *f* -,-nen sportswoman. s~**lich** *a* sports ...; (fair) sporting, *adv* -ly; (flott, schlank) sporty. S~**platz** *m* sports ground. S~**verein** *m* sports club. S~**wagen** *m* sports car; (Kinder-) push-chair, (Amer) stroller

Spott *m* -[e]s mockery. s~**billig** *a* & *adv* dirt cheap

spötteln *vi* (haben) mock; s~ über (+ acc) poke fun at

spotten *vi* (haben) mock; s~ über (+ acc) make fun of; (höhnend) ridicule

spöttisch *a* mocking, *adv* -ly

Sprach|e *f* -,-n language; (Sprechfähigkeit) speech; zur S~e bringen bring up. S~**fehler** *m* speech defect. S~**labor** *nt* language laboratory. s~**lich** *a* linguistic, *adv* -ally. s~**los** *a* speechless

Spray /ʃpreː/ *nt* & *m* -s,-s spray. S~**dose** *f* aerosol [can]

Sprech|anlage f intercom. S~chor m chorus; im S~chor rufen chant

sprechen† vi (haben) speak/(sich unterhalten) talk (über + acc/von about/of); Deutsch/Englisch s~ speak German/English □ vt speak; (sagen, aufsagen) say; pronounce ⟨Urteil⟩; schuldig s~ find guilty; jdn s~ speak to s.o.; Herr X ist nicht zu s~ Mr X is not available

Sprecher(in) m -s,- (f -,-nen) speaker; (Radio, TV) announcer; (Wortführer) spokesman; f spokeswoman

Sprechstunde f consulting hours pl; (Med) surgery. S~nhilfe f (Med) receptionist

Sprechzimmer nt consulting room

spreizen vt spread

Sprengel m -s,- parish

spreng|en vt blow up □ast (Felsen); (fig) burst; (begießen) water; (mit Sprenger) sprinkle; (über ⟨Wäsche⟩. S~er m -s,- sprink... S~kopf m warhead. S~körper m explosive device. S~stoff m explosive

Spreu f -chaff

Sprich|wort nt (pl -wörter) proverb. s~wörtlich a proverbial

sprießen† vi (sein) sprout

Springbrunnen m fountain

spring|en† vi (sein) jump; (Schwimmsport) dive; (Ball:) bounce; (spritzen) spurt; (zer-) break; (rissig werden) crack; (SGer: laufen) run. S~er m -s,- jumper; (Kunst-) diver; (Schach) knight. S~reiten nt show-jumping. S~seil nt skipping-rope

Sprint m -s,-s sprint

Sprit m -s (fam) petrol

Spritz|e f -,-n syringe; (Injektion) injection; (Feuer-) hose. s~en vt spray; (be-, ver-) splash; (Culin) pipe; (Med) inject □ vi (haben) splash; (Fett:) spit □ vi (sein) splash; (hervor-) spurt; (fam: laufen) dash. S~er m -s,- splash; (Schuss) dash. s~ig a lively; ⟨Wein, Komödie⟩ sparkling. S~tour f (fam) spin

spröde a brittle; (trocken) dry; (rissig) chapped; ⟨Stimme⟩ harsh; (abweisend) aloof

Spross m -es,-e (Sproß m -sses, -sse) shoot

Sprosse f -,-n rung. S~nkohl m (Aust) Brussels sprouts pl

Sprössling (Sprößling) m -s,-e (fam) offspring

Sprotte f -,-n sprat

Spruch m -[e]s,-̈e saying; (Denk-) motto; (Zitat) quotation. S~band nt (pl -bänder) banner

Sprudel m -s,- sparkling mineral water. s~n vi (haben/sein) bubble

Sprüh|dose f aerosol [can]. s~en vt spray □ vi (sein) ⟨Funken:⟩ fly; (fig) sparkle. S~regen m fine drizzle

Sprung m -[e]s,-̈e jump, leap; (Schwimmsport) dive; (fam: Katzen-) stone's throw; (Riss) crack; auf einen S~ (fam) for a moment. S~brett nt springboard. s~haft a erratic; (plötzlich) sudden, adv -ly. S~schanze f ski-jump. S~seil nt skipping-rope

Spuck|e f - spit. s~en vt/i (haben) spit; (sich übergeben) be sick

Spuk m -[e]s,-e [ghostly] apparition. s~en vi (haben) ⟨Geist:⟩ walk; in diesem Haus s~t es this house is haunted

Spülbecken nt sink

Spule f -,-n spool

Spüle f -,-n sink unit; (Becken) sink

spulen vt spool

spül|en vt rinse; (schwemmen) wash; Geschirr s~en wash up □ vi (haben) flush [the toilet]. S~kasten m cistern. S~mittel nt washing-up liquid. S~tuch nt dishcloth

Spur f -,-en track; (Fahr-) lane; (Fährte) trail; (Anzeichen) trace; (Hinweis) lead; keine od nicht die S~ (fam) not in the least

spürbar a noticeable, adv -bly

spuren vi (haben) (fam) toe the line

spür|en vt feel; (seelisch) sense. S~hund m tracker dog

spurlos adv without trace

spurten vi (sein) put on a spurt; (fam: laufen) sprint

sputen (sich) vr hurry

Staat m -[e]s,-en state; (Land) country; (Putz) finery. s~lich a state ... □ adv by the state

Staatsangehörig|e(r) m/f national. S~keit f - nationality

Staats|anwalt m state prosecutor. S~beamte(r) m civil servant. S~besuch m state visit. S~bürger(in) m(f) national. S~mann m (pl -männer) statesman. S~streich m coup

Stab m -[e]s,-̈e rod; (Gitter-) bar; (Sport) baton; (Mitarbeiter-) team; (Mil) staff

Stäbchen ntpl chopsticks

Stabhochsprung m pole-vault

stabil a stable; (gesund) robust; (solide) sturdy, adv -ily. s~isieren vt stabilize; sich s~isieren stabilize. S~ität f - stability

Stachel m -s,- spine; (Gift-) sting; (Spitze) spike. S~beere f goose-berry. S~draht *m* barbed wire. s~ig *a* prickly. S~schwein *nt* porcupine

Stadion *nt* -s,-ien stadium

Stadium *nt* -s,-ien stage

Stadt *f* -,-e town; (Groß-) city

Städt|chen *nt* -s,- small town. s~isch *a* urban; (kommunal) municipal

Stadt|mauer *f* city wall. S~mitte *f* town centre. S~plan *m* street map. S~teil *m* district. S~zentrum *nt* town centre

Staffel *f* -,-n team; (S~lauf) relay; (Mil) squadron

Staffelei *f* -,-en easel

Staffel|lauf *m* relay race. s~n *vt* stagger; (abstufen) grade

Stagnation /-'tsjo:n/ *f* - stagnation. s~ieren *vi* (haben) stagnate

Stahl *m* -s steel. S~beton *m* reinforced concrete

Stall *m* -[e]s,-e stable; (Kuh-) shed; (Schweine-) sty; (Hühner-) coop; (Kaninchen-) hutch

Stamm *m* -[e]s,-e trunk; (Sippe) tribe; (Kern) core; (Wort-) stem. S~baum *m* family tree; (eines Tieres) pedigree

stammeln *vt/i* (haben) stammer

stammen *vi* (haben) come/(zeitlich) date (von/aus from); das Zitat stammt von Goethe the quotation is from Goethe

Stamm|gast *m* regular. S~halter *m* son and heir

stämmig *a* sturdy

Stamm|kundschaft *f* regulars pl. S~lokal *nt* favourite pub. S~tisch *m* table reserved for the regulars; (Treffen) meeting of the regulars

stampf|en *vi* (haben) stamp; (Maschine:) pound; mit den Füßen s~en stamp one's feet □ *vi* (sein) tramp □ *vt* pound; mash (Kartoffeln). S~kartoffeln *fpl* mashed potatoes

Stand *m* -[e]s,-e standing position; (Zustand) state; (Spiel-) score; (Höhe) level; (gesellschaftlich) class; (Verkaufs-) stall; (Messe-) stand; (Taxi-) rank; auf den neuesten S~ bringen up-date; in S~ halten/setzen = instand halten/setzen, s. instand; im/außer S~e sein = imstande/außerstande sein, s. imstande, außerstande; zu S~e bringen/kommen = zustande bringen/kommen, s. zustande

Standard *m* -s,-s standard. s~isieren *vt* standardize

Standarte *f* -,-n standard

Standbild *nt* statue

Ständchen *nt* -s,- serenade; jdm ein S~ bringen serenade s.o.

Ständer *m* -s,- stand; (Geschirr-, Platten-) rack; (Kerzen-) holder

Standes|amt *nt* registry office. S~beamte(r) *m* registrar. S~unterschied *m* class distinction

stand|haft *a* steadfast, adv -ly. s~halten† *vi sep* (haben) stand firm; etw (dat) s~halten stand up to sth

ständig *a* constant, adv -ly; (fest) permanent, adv -ly

Stand|licht *nt* sidelights pl. S~ort *m* position; (Firmen-) location; (Mil) garrison. S~pauke *f* (fam) dressing-down. S~punkt *m* point of view. S~spur *f* hard shoulder. S~uhr *f* grandfather clock

Stange *f* -,-n bar; (Holz-) pole; (Gardinen-) rail; (Hühner-) perch; (Zimt-) stick; von der S~ (fam) off the peg

Stängel *m* -s,- stalk, stem

Stangen|bohne *f* runner bean. S~brot *nt* French bread

Stanniol *nt* -s tin foil. S~papier *nt* silver paper

stanzen *vt* stamp; (aus-) stamp out; punch (Loch)

Stapel *m* -s,- stack, pile; vom S~ laufen be launched. S~lauf *m* launch[ing]. s~n *vt* stack or pile up; sich s~n pile up

stapfen *vi* (sein) tramp, trudge

Star[1] *m* -[e]s,-e starling

Star[2] *m* -[e]s (Med) [grauer] S~ cataract; grüner S~ glaucoma

Star[3] *m* -s,-s (Theat, Sport) star

stark *a* (stärker, stärkst) strong; (Motor) powerful; (Verkehr, Regen) heavy; (Hitze, Kälte) severe; (groß) big; (schlimm) bad; (dick) thick; (korpulent) stout □ *adv* strongly; heavily; badly; (sehr) very much

Stärk|e *f* -,-n (s. stark) strength; power; thickness; stoutness; (Größe) size; (Mais-, Wäsche-) starch. S~emehl *nt* cornflour. s~en *vt* strengthen; starch (Wäsche); sich s~en fortify oneself. S~ung *f* -,-en strengthening; (Erfrischung) refreshment

starr *a* rigid, adv -ly; (steif) stiff, adv -ly; (Blick) fixed; (unbeugsam) inflexible, adv -bly

starren *vi* (haben) stare; vor Schmutz s~ be filthy

starr|köpfig *a* stubborn. S~sinn *m* obstinacy. s~sinnig *a* obstinate, adv -ly

Start *m* -s,-s start; (Aviat) take-off. S~bahn *f* runway. s~en *vi* (sein) start; (Aviat) take off; (aufbrechen) set off; (teilnehmen) compete □ *vt* start; (fig) launch

Station /-'tsjo:n/ *f* -,-en station; (Haltestelle) stop; (Abschnitt) stage; (Med) ward; S~ machen break one's journey; bei freier S~ all found. s~är *adv* as an in-patient. s~ieren *vt* station

statisch *a* static

Statist(in) *m* -en,-en (*f* -,-nen) (*Theat*) extra

Statisti|k *f* -,-en statistics *sg*; (*Aufstellung*) statistics *pl*. s∼sch *a* statistical, *adv* -ly

Stativ *nt* -s,-e (*Phot*) tripod

statt *prep* (+ *gen*) instead of; an seiner s∼ in his place; an Kindes∼ annehmen adopt; s∼ dessen (NEW)s∼dessen □ *conj* s∼ etw zu tun instead of doing sth. s∼dessen *adv* instead

Stätte *f* -,-n place

statt|finden† *vi sep* (*haben*) take place. s∼haft *a* permitted

stattlich *a* imposing; (*beträchtlich*) considerable

Statue /'ʃta:tuə/ *f* -,-n statue

Statur *f* - build, stature

Status *m* - status. S∼symbol *nt* status symbol

Statut *nt* -[e]s,-en statute

Stau *m* -[e]s,-s congestion; (*Auto*) [traffic] jam; (*Rück-*) tailback

Staub *m* -[e]s dust; S∼ wischen dust; S∼ saugen vacuum, hoover

Staubecken *nt* reservoir

stauben *vi* (*haben*) raise dust; es s∼t it's dusty. s∼ig *a* dusty. s∼saugen *vt/i* (*haben*) vacuum, hoover. S∼sauger *m* vacuum cleaner, Hoover (P). S∼tuch *nt* duster

Staudamm *m* dam

Staude *f* -,-n shrub

stauen *vt* dam up; sich s∼ accumulate; (*Autos:*) form a tailback

staunen *vi* (*haben*) be amazed *or* astonished. S∼ *nt* -s amazement, astonishment

Stausee *m* reservoir. S∼ung *f* -,-en congestion; (*Auto*) [traffic] jam

Steak /ʃte:k, ste:k/ *nt* -s,-s steak

stechen† *vt* stick (in + *acc* in); (*verletzen*) prick; (*mit Messer*) stab; (*Insekt:*) sting; (*Mücke:*) bite; (*gravieren*) engrave □ *vi* (*haben*) prick; (*Insekt:*) sting; (*Mücke:*) bite; (*mit Stechuhr*) clock in/out; in See s∼ put to sea. s∼d *a* stabbing; (*Geruch*) pungent

Stech|ginster *m* gorse. S∼kahn *m* punt. S∼mücke *f* mosquito. S∼palme *f* holly. S∼uhr *f* time clock

Steck|brief *m* 'wanted' poster. S∼dose *f* socket. s∼en *vt* put; (*mit Nadel, Reißzwecke*) pin; (*pflanzen*) plant □ *vi* (*haben*) be; (*fest-*) be stuck; s∼ bleiben get stuck; den Schlüssel s∼ lassen leave the key in the lock; hinter etw (*dat*) s∼en (*fig*) be behind sth

Stecken *m* -s,- (*SGer*) stick

stecken|bleiben† *vi sep* (*sein*) (NEW)s∼ bleiben, *s.* stecken. s∼lassen† *vt sep* (NEW)s∼ lassen, *s.* stecken. S∼pferd *nt* hobby-horse

Steck|er *m* -s,- (*Electr*) plug. S∼ling *m* -s,-e cutting. S∼nadel *f* pin. S∼rübe *f* swede

Steg *m* -[e]s,-e foot-bridge; (*Boots-*) landing-stage; (*Brillen-*) bridge. S∼reif *m* aus dem S∼reif extempore

stehen† *vi* (*haben*) stand; (*sich befinden*) be; (*still-*) be stationary; (*Maschine, Uhr:*) have stopped; s∼ bleiben remain standing; (*Gebäude:*) be left standing; (*anhalten*) stop; (*Motor:*) stall; (*Zeit:*) stand still; s∼ lassen leave [standing]; sich (*dat*) einen Bart s∼ lassen grow a beard; vor dem Ruin s∼ face ruin; zu jdm/etw s∼ (*fig*) stand by s.o./sth; gut s∼ (*Getreide, Aktien:*) be doing well; (*Chancen:*) be good; jdm [gut] s∼ suit s.o.; sich gut s∼ be on good terms; es steht 3 zu 1 the score is 3–1; es steht schlecht um ihn he is in a bad way. S∼ *nt* -s standing; zum S∼ bringen/kommen bring/come to a standstill. s∼bleiben† *vi sep* (*sein*) (NEW) s∼ bleiben, *s.* stehen. s∼d *a* standing; (*sich nicht bewegend*) stationary; (*Gewässer:*) stagnant. s∼lassen† *vt sep* (NEW) s∼ lassen, *s.* stehen

Steh|lampe *f* standard lamp. S∼leiter *f* step-ladder

stehlen† *vt/i* (*haben*) steal; sich s∼ steal, creep

Steh|platz *m* standing place. S∼vermögen *nt* stamina, staying-power

steif *a* stiff, *adv* -ly. S∼heit *f* - stiffness

Steig|bügel *m* stirrup. S∼eisen *nt* crampon

steigen† *vi* (*sein*) climb; (*hochgehen*) rise, go up; (*Schulden, Spannung:*) mount; s∼ auf (+ *acc*) climb on [to] (*Stuhl*); climb (*Berg, Leiter*); get on (*Pferd, Fahrrad*); s∼ in (+ *acc*) climb into; get in (*Auto*); get on (*Bus, Zug*); s∼ aus climb out of; get out of (*Bett, Auto*); get off (*Bus, Zug*); einen Drachen s∼ lassen fly a kite; s∼de Preise rising prices

steiger|n *vt* increase; sich s∼n increase; (*sich verbessern*) improve. S∼ung *f* -,-en increase; improvement; (*Gram*) comparison

Steigung *f* -,-en gradient; (*Hang*) slope

steil *a* steep, *adv* -ly. S∼küste *f* cliffs *pl*

Stein *m* -[e]s,-e stone; (*Ziegel-*) brick; (*Spiel-*) piece. s∼alt *a* ancient. S∼bock *m* ibex; (*Astr*) Capricorn. S∼bruch *m* quarry. S∼garten *m* rockery. S∼gut *nt* earthenware. s∼hart *a* rock-hard. s∼ig *a* stony. s∼igen *vt* stone. S∼kohle *f* [hard] coal. s~reich a (fam) very rich. S~schlag m rock fall

Stelle f -,-n place; (Fleck) spot; (Abschnitt) passage; (Stellung) job, post; (Büro) office; (Behörde) authority; kahle S~ bare patch; auf der S~ immediately; an deiner S~ in your place

stellen vt put; (aufrecht) stand; set (Wecker, Aufgabe); ask (Frage); make (Antrag, Forderung, Diagnose); zur Verfügung s~ provide; lauter/leiser s~ turn up/down; kalt/warm s~ chill/keep hot; sich s~ [go and] stand; give oneself up (der Polizei to the police); sich tot/schlafend s~ pretend to be dead/asleep; gut gestellt sein be well off

Stellen|anzeige f job advertisement. S~vermittlung f employment agency. s~weise adv in places

Stellung f -,-en position; (Arbeit) job; S~ nehmen make a statement (zu on). s~slos a jobless. S~suche f job-hunting

stellvertret|end a deputy ... □ adv as a deputy; s~end für jdn on s.o.'s behalf. S~er m deputy

Stellwerk nt signal-box

Stelzen fpl stilts. s~ vi (sein) stalk

stemmen vt press; lift (Gewicht); sich s~ gegen brace oneself against

Stempel m -s,- stamp; (Post-) post-mark; (Präge-) die; (Feingehalts-) hallmark. s~n vt stamp; hallmark (Silber); cancel (Marke)

Stengel m -s,- (NEW) Stängel

Steno f -(fam) shorthand

Steno|gramm nt -[e]s,-e shorthand text. S~graphie, S~grafie f - shorthand. s~graphieren, s~grafieren vt take down in shorthand □ vi (haben) do shorthand. S~typistin f -,-nen shorthand typist

Steppdecke f quilt

Steppe f -,-n steppe

Stepptanz (Steptanz) m tap-dance

sterben vi (sein) die (an + dat of); im S~ liegen be dying

sterblich a mortal. S~e(r) m/f mortal. S~keit f - mortality

stereo adv in stereo. S~anlage f stereo [system]

stereotyp a stereotyped

steril a sterile. s~isieren vt sterilize. S~ität f - sterility

Stern m -[e]s,-e star. S~bild nt constellation. S~chen nt -s,- asterisk. S~kunde f astronomy. S~schnuppe f -,-n shooting star. S~warte f -,-n observatory

stetig a steady, adv -ily

stets adv always

Steuer[1] nt -s,- steering-wheel; (Naut) helm; am S~ at the wheel

Steuer[2] f -,-n tax

Steuer|bord nt -[e]s starboard [side]. S~erklärung f tax return. s~frei a & adv tax-free. S~mann m (pl -leute) helmsman; (beim Rudern) cox. s~n vt steer; (Aviat) pilot; (Techn) control □ vi (haben) be at the wheel/(Naut) helm □ (sein) head (nach for). s~pflichtig a taxable. S~rad nt steering-wheel. S~ruder nt helm. S~ung f - steering; (Techn) controls pl. S~zahler m -s,- tax-payer

Stewardess /'stju:ɐdɛs/ f -,-en (Stewardeß f -,-ssen) air hostess, stewardess

Stich m -[e]s,-e prick; (Messer-) stab; (S~wunde) stab wound; (Bienen-) sting; (Mücken-) bite; (Schmerz) stabbing pain; (Näh-) stitch; (Kupfer-) engraving; (Kartenspiel) trick; S~ ins Rötliche tinge of red; jdn im S~ lassen leave s.o. in the lurch; (Gedächtnis:) fail s.o. s~eln vi (haben) make snide remarks

Stich|flamme f jet of flame. s~haltig a valid. S~probe f spot check. S~wort nt (pl -wörter) headword; (pl -worte) (Theat) cue; S~worte notes

sticken vt/i (haben) embroider. S~erei f - embroidery

stickig a stuffy

Stickstoff m nitrogen

Stiefbruder m stepbrother

Stiefel m -s,- boot

Stief|kind nt stepchild. S~mutter f stepmother. S~mütterchen nt -s,- pansy. S~schwester f stepsister. S~sohn m stepson. S~tochter f stepdaughter. S~vater m stepfather

Stiege f -,-n stairs pl

Stiel m -[e]s,-e handle; (Blumen-, Gläser-) stem; (Blatt-) stalk

Stier m -[e]s,-e bull; (Astr) Taurus

stieren vi (haben) stare

Stier|kampf m bullfight

Stift[1] m -[e]s,-e pin; (Nagel) tack; (Blei-) pencil; (Farb-) crayon

Stift[2] nt -[e]s,-e [endowed] foundation. s~en vt endow; (spenden) donate; create (Unheil, Verwirrung); bring about (Frieden). S~er m -s,- founder; (Spender) donor. S~ung f -,-en foundation; (Spende) donation

Stigma nt -s,(fig) stigma

Stil m -[e]s,-e style; in großem S~ in style. s~isiert a stylized. s~istisch a stylistic, adv -ally

still a quiet, adv -ly; (reglos; ohne Kohlensäure) still; (heimlich) secret, adv -ly; der

S~e Ozean the Pacific; im S~en (s~en) secretly; (bei sich) inwardly. S~e f - quiet; (Schweigen) silence

Stilleben nt (NEW) Stilleben

stillegen vt sep (NEW) stilllegen

stillen vt satisfy; quench (Durst); stop (Schmerzen, Blutung); breast-feed (Kind)

still|halten† vi sep (haben) keep still. S~leben nt still life. s~legen vt sep close down. S~legung f -, -en closure

Stillschweigen nt silence. s~d a silent, adv -ly; (fig) tacit, adv -ly

still|sitzen† vi sep (haben) sit still. S~stand m standstill; zum S~stand bringen/kommen stop. s~stehen† vi sep (haben) stand still; (anhalten) stop; (Verkehr:) be at a standstill

Stil|möbel pl reproduction furniture sg. s~voll a stylish, adv -ly

Stimm|bänder ntpl vocal cords. s~berechtigt a entitled to vote. S~bruch m er ist im S~bruch his voice is breaking

Stimme f -, -n voice; (Wahl-) vote

stimmen vi (haben) be right; (wählen) vote; stimmt das? is that right/(wahr) true? s~ vt tune; jdn traurig/fröhlich s~ make s.o. feel sad/happy

Stimm|enthaltung f abstention. S~recht nt right to vote

Stimmung f -, -en mood; (Atmosphäre) atmosphere. s~svoll a full of atmosphere

Stimmzettel m ballot-paper

stimulieren vt stimulate

stink|en† vi (haben) smell/(stark) stink (nach of). S~tier nt skunk

Stipendium nt -s, -ien scholarship; (Beihilfe) grant

Stirn f -, -en forehead; die S~ bieten (+ dat) (fig) defy. S~runzeln nt -s frown

stöbern vi (haben) rummage

stochern vi (haben) s~ in (+ dat) poke (Feuer); pick at (Essen); pick (Zähne)

Stock[1] m -[e]s, -̈e stick; (Ski-) pole; (Bienen-) hive; (Rosen-) bush; (Reb-) vine

Stock[2] m -[e]s, - storey, floor. S~bett nt bunk-beds pl. s~dunkel a (fam) pitch-dark

stock|en vi (haben) stop; (Verkehr:) come to a standstill; (Person:) falter. s~end a hesitant, adv -ly. s~taub a (fam) stone-deaf. S~ung f -, -en hold-up

Stockwerk nt storey, floor

Stoff m -[e]s, -e substance; (Tex) fabric, material; (Thema) subject [matter]; (Gesprächs-) topic. S~tier nt soft toy. S~wechsel m metabolism

stöhnen vi (haben) groan, moan. S~ nt -s groan, moan

stoisch a stoic, adv -ally

Stola f -, -len stole

Stollen m -s, - gallery; (Kuchen) stollen

stolpern vi (sein) stumble; s~ über (+ acc) trip over

stolz a proud (auf + acc of), adv -ly. S~ m -es pride

stolzieren vi (sein) strut

stopfen vt stuff; (stecken) put; (ausbessern) darn. □ vi (haben) be constipating; (fam: essen) guzzle

Stopp m -s, -s stop. s~ int stop!

stoppel|ig a stubbly. S~n fpl stubble sg

stopp|en vt stop; (Sport) time. □ vi (haben) stop. S~schild nt stop sign. S~uhr f stop-watch

Stöpsel m -s, - plug; (Flaschen-) stopper

Storch m -[e]s, -̈e stork

Store /ʃtoːɐ/ m -s, -s net curtain

stören vt disturb; disrupt (Rede, Sitzung); jam (Sender); (missfallen) bother; stört es Sie, wenn ich rauche? do you mind if I smoke? □ vi (haben) be a nuisance; entschuldigen Sie, dass ich störe I'm sorry to bother you

stornieren vt cancel

störrisch a stubborn, adv -ly

Störung f -, -en (s. stören) disturbance; disruption; (Med) trouble; (Radio) interference; technische S~ technical fault

Stoß m -es, -̈e push, knock; (mit Ellbogen) dig; (Hörner-) butt; (mit Waffe) thrust; (Schwimm-) stroke; (Ruck) jolt; (Erd-) shock; (Stapel) stack, pile. S~dämpfer m -s, - shock absorber

stoßen† vt push, knock; (mit Füßen) kick; (mit Kopf, Hörnern) butt; (an-) poke, nudge; (treiben) thrust; sich s~ knock oneself; sich (dat) den Kopf s~ hit one's head □ vi (haben) push; s~ an (+ acc) knock against; (angrenzen) adjoin □ vi (sein) s~ gegen knock against; bump into (Tür); s~ auf (+ acc) bump into; (entdecken) come across; strike (Öl); (fig) meet with (Ablehnung)

Stoß|stange f bumper. S~verkehr m rush-hour traffic. S~zahn m tusk. S~zeit f rush-hour

stottern vt/i (haben) stutter, stammer

Str. abbr (Straße) St

Straf|anstalt f prison. S~arbeit f (Sch) imposition. s~bar a punishable; sich s~bar machen commit an offence

Strafe f -, -n punishment; (Jur & fig) penalty; (Geld-) fine; (Freiheits-) sentence. s~n vt punish

straff a tight, taut. s~en vt tighten; sich s~en tighten

Strafgesetz nt criminal law

sträf|lich a criminal, adv -ly. S~ling m -s,-e prisoner

Straf|mandat nt (Auto) [parking/speeding] ticket. S~porto nt excess postage. S~predigt f (fam) lecture. S~raum m penalty area. S~stoss (S~stoß) m penalty. S~tat f crime. S~zettel m (fam) = S~mandat

Strahl m -[e]s,-en ray; (einer Taschenlampe) beam; (Wasser-) jet. s~en vi (haben) shine; (funkeln) sparkle; (lächeln) beam. S~enbehandlung f radiotherapy. s~end a shining; sparkling; beaming; radiant (Schönheit). S~entherapie f radiotherapy. S~ung f - radiation

Strähn|e f -,-n strand. s~ig a straggly

stramm a tight, adv -ly; (kräftig) sturdy; (gerade) upright

Strampel|höschen /-sç-/ nt -s,- rompers pl. s~n vi (haben) (Baby:) kick

Strand m -[e]s,-e beach. s~en vi (sein) run aground; (fig) fail. S~korb m wicker beach-chair. S~promenade f promenade

Strang m -[e]s,-e rope

Strapaz|e f -,-n strain. s~ieren vt be hard on; tax (Nerven, Geduld). s~ierfähig a hard-wearing. s~iös a exhausting

Strass m - & -es (Straß m - & -sses) paste

Straße f -,-n road; (in der Stadt auch) street; (Meeres-) strait; auf der S~ in the road/street. S~nbahn f tram, (Amer) streetcar. S~nkarte f road-map. S~nlaterne f street lamp. S~nsperre f road-block

Strat|egie f -,-n strategy. s~egisch a strategic, adv -ally

sträuben vt ruffle up (Federn); sich s~ (Fell, Haar:) stand on end; (fig) resist

Strauch m -[e]s, Sträucher bush

straucheln vi (sein) stumble

Strauß[1] m -es, Sträuße bunch [of flowers]; (Bukett) bouquet

Strauß[2] m -es,-e ostrich

Strebe f -,-n brace, strut

streben vi (haben) strive (nach for) □ vi (sein) head (nach/zu for)

Streber m -s,- pushy person; (Sch) swot. s~sam a industrious

Strecke f -,-n stretch, section; (Entfernung) distance; (Rail) line; (Route) route

strecken vt stretch; (aus-) stretch out; (gerade machen) straighten; (Culin) thin down; sich s~ stretch; (sich aus-) stretch out; den Kopf aus dem Fenster s~ put one's head out of the window

Streich m -[e]s,-e prank, trick; jdm einen S~ spielen play a trick on s.o.

streicheln vt stroke

streichen† vt spread; (weg-) smooth; (an-) paint; (aus-) delete, (kürzen) cut □ vi (haben) s~ über (+ acc) stroke

Streicher m -s,- string-player; die S~ the strings

Streichholz nt match. S~schachtel f matchbox

Streich|instrument nt stringed instrument. S~käse m cheese spread. S~orchester nt string orchestra. S~ung f -,-en deletion; (Kürzung) cut

Streife f -,-n patrol

streifen vt brush against; (berühren) touch; (verletzen) graze; (fig) touch on (Thema); (ziehen) slip (über + acc over); mit dem Blick s~ glance at □ vi (sein) roam

Streifen m -s,- stripe; (Licht-) streak; (auf der Fahrbahn) line; (schmales Stück) strip

Streif|enwagen m patrol car. s~ig a streaky. S~schuss (S~schuß) m glancing shot; (Wunde) graze

Streik m -s,-s strike; in den S~ treten go on strike. S~brecher m strike-breaker, (pej) scab. s~en vi (haben) strike; (fam) refuse; (versagen) pack up. S~ende(r) m striker. S~posten m picket

Streit m -[e]s,-e quarrel; (Auseinandersetzung) dispute. s~en† vr/i (haben) [sich] s~en quarrel. s~ig a jdm etw s~ig machen dispute s.o.'s right to sth. S~igkeiten fpl quarrels. S~kräfte fpl armed forces. s~süchtig a quarrelsome

streng a strict, adv -ly; (Blick, Ton) stern, adv -ly; (rau, nüchtern) severe, adv -ly; (Geschmack) sharp; s~ genommen strictly speaking. S~e f - strictness; sternness; severity. s~genommen adv (NEW) s~ genommen, s. streng. s~gläubig a strict; (orthodox) orthodox. s~stens adv strictly

Stress m -es,-e (Streß m -sses,-sse) stress

stressig a (fam) stressful

streuen vt spread; (ver-) scatter; sprinkle (Zucker, Salz); die Straßen s~ grit the roads

streunen vi (sein) roam; s~der Hund stray dog

Strich m -[e]s,-e line; (Feder-, Pinsel-) stroke; (Morse-, Gedanken-) dash; gegen den S~ the wrong way; (fig) against the grain. S~kode m bar code. S~punkt m semicolon

Strick m -[e]s,-e cord; (Seil) rope; (fam: Schlingel) rascal

strick|en vt/i (haben) knit. S~jacke f cardigan. S~leiter f rope-ladder. S~nadel f knitting-needle. S~waren fpl knitwear sg. S~zeug nt knitting

striegeln vt groom

strikt a strict, adv -ly

strittig a contentious

Stroh nt -[e]s straw. S~blumen fpl everlasting flowers. S~dach nt thatched roof. s~gedeckt a thatched. S~halm m straw

Strolch m -[e]s,-e (fam) rascal

Strom m -[e]s,-̈e river; (Menschen-, Auto-, Blut-) stream; (Tränen-) flood; (Schwall) torrent; (Electr) current, power; gegen den S~ (fig) against the tide; es regnet in Strömen it is pouring with rain. s~abwärts adv downstream. s~aufwärts adv upstream

strömen vi (sein) flow; (Menschen, Blut:) stream, pour; s~der Regen pouring rain

Strom|kreis m circuit. s~linienförmig a streamlined. S~sperre f power cut

Strömung f -,-en current

Strophe f -,-n verse

strotzen vi (haben) be full (vor + dat of); vor Gesundheit s~d bursting with health

Strudel m -s,- whirlpool; (SGer Culin) strudel

Struktur f -,-en structure; (Tex) texture

Strumpf m -[e]s,-̈e stocking; (Knie-) sock. S~band nt (pl -bänder) suspender, (Amer) garter. S~bandgürtel m suspender/(Amer) garter belt. S~halter m = S~band. S~hose f tights pl, (Amer) pantyhose

Strunk m -[e]s,-̈e stalk; (Baum-) stump

struppig a shaggy

Stube f -,-n room. s~nrein a house-trained

Stuck m -s stucco

Stück nt -[e]s,-e piece; (Zucker-) lump; (Seife) tablet; (Theater-) play; (Gegenstand) item; (Exemplar) specimen; 20 S~ Vieh 20 head of cattle; ein S~ (Entfernung) some way; aus freien S~en voluntarily. S~chen nt -s,- [little] bit. s~weise adv bit by bit; (einzeln) singly

Student|(in) m -en,-en (f -,-nen) student. s~isch a student ...

Studie /-jə/ f -,-n study

studier|en vt/i (haben) study. S~zimmer nt study

Studio nt -s,-s studio

Studium nt -s,-ien studies pl

Stufe f -,-n step; (Treppen-) stair; (Raketen-) stage; (Niveau) level. s~n vt terrace; (staffeln) grade

Stuhl m -[e]s,-̈e chair; (Med) stools pl. S~gang m bowel movement

stülpen vt put (über + acc over)

stumm a dumb; (schweigsam) silent, adv -ly

Stummel m -s,- stump; (Zigaretten-) butt; (Bleistift-) stub

Stümper m -s,- bungler. s~haft a incompetent, adv -ly

stumpf a blunt; (Winkel) obtuse; (glanzlos) dull; (fig) apathetic, adv -ally. S~ m -[e]s, -̈e stump

Stumpfsinn m apathy; (Langweiligkeit) tedium. s~ig a apathetic, adv -ally; (langweilig) tedious

Stunde f -,-n hour; (Sch) lesson

stunden vt jdm eine Schuld s~ give s.o. time to pay a debt

Stunden|kilometer mpl kilometres per hour. s~lang adv for hours. S~lohn m hourly rate. S~plan m timetable. s~weise adv by the hour

stündlich a & adv hourly

Stups m -es,-e nudge; (Schubs) push. s~en vt nudge; (schubsen) push. S~nase f snub nose

stur a pigheaded; (phlegmatisch) stolid, adv -ly; (unbeirrbar) dogged, adv -ly

Sturm m -[e]s,-̈e gale; (schwer) storm; (Mil) assault

stürm|en vi (haben) (Wind:) blow hard; es s~t it's blowing a gale ☐ vi (sein) rush ☐ vt storm; (bedrängen) besiege. S~er m -s,-forward. s~isch a stormy; (Überfahrt) rough; (fig) tumultuous, adv -ly; (ungestüm) tempestuous, adv -ly

Sturz m -es,-̈e [heavy] fall; (Preis-, Kurs-) sharp drop; (Pol) overthrow

stürzen vi (sein) fall [heavily]; (in die Tiefe) plunge; (Preise, Kurse:) drop sharply; (Regierung:) fall; (eilen) rush ☐ vt throw; (umkippen) turn upside down; turn out (Speise, Kuchen); (Pol) overthrow, topple; sich s~ throw oneself (aus/in + acc out of/into); sich s~ auf (+ acc) pounce on

Sturz|flug m (Aviat) dive. S~helm m crash-helmet

Stute f -,-n mare

Stütze f -,-n support; (Kopf-, Arm-) rest

stutzen vi (haben) stop short ☐ vt trim; (Hort) cut back; (kupieren) crop

stützen vt support; (auf-) rest; sich s~ auf (+ acc) lean on; (beruhen) be based on

Stutzer m -s,- dandy

stutzig a puzzled; (misstrauisch) suspicious

Stützpunkt m (Mil) base

Subjekt nt -[e]s,-e subject. s~iv a subjective, adv -ly

Subskription /-'tsjo:n/ f -,-en subscription

Substantiv nt -s,-e noun

Substanz f -,-en substance

subtil *a* subtle, *adv* -tly

subtra|hieren *vt* subtract. **S~ktion** /-'tsjo:n/ *f* -,-en subtraction

Subvention /-'tsjo:n/ *f* -,-en subsidy. **s~ieren** *vt* subsidize

subversiv *a* subversive

Such|e *f* - search; auf der S~e nach looking for. **s~en** *vt* look for; (*intensiv*) search for; seek ⟨*Hilfe, Rat*⟩; 'Zimmer gesucht' 'room wanted' □ *vi* (*haben*) look, search (nach for). **S~er** *m* -s,- (*Phot*) viewfinder

Sucht *f* -,-e addiction; (*fig*) mania

süchtig *a* addicted. **S~e(r)** *m/f* addict

Süd *m* -[e]s south. **S~afrika** *nt* South Africa. **S~amerika** *nt* South America. **s~deutsch** *a* South German

Süden *m* -s south; nach S~ south

Süd|frucht *f* tropical fruit. **s~lich** *a* southern; ⟨*Richtung*⟩ southerly □ *adv* & *prep* (+ *gen*) **s~lich** [von] der Stadt [to the] south of the town. **S~osten** *m* southeast. **S~pol** *m* South Pole. **s~wärts** *adv* southwards. **S~westen** *m* south-west

süffisant *a* smug, *adv* -ly

suggerieren *vt* suggest (*dat* to)

Suggest|ion /-'tjo:n/ *f* -,-en suggestion. **s~iv** *a* suggestive

Sühne *f* -,-n atonement; (*Strafe*) penalty. **s~n** *vt* atone for

Sultanine *f* -,-n sultana

Sülze *f* -,-n [meat] jelly; (*Schweinskopf-*) brawn

Summe *f* -,-n sum

summ|en *vi* (*haben*) hum; ⟨*Biene:*⟩ buzz □ *vt* hum. **S~er** *m* -s,- buzzer

summieren (sich) *vr* add up; (*sich häufen*) increase

Sumpf *m* -[e]s,-e marsh, swamp. **s~ig** *a* marshy

Sünd|e *f* -,-n sin. **S~enbock** *m* scapegoat. **S~er(in)** *m* -s,- (*f* -,-nen) sinner. **s~haft** *a* sinful. **s~igen** *vi* (*haben*) sin

super *inv* *a* (*fam*) great. **S~lativ** *m* -s,-e superlative. **S~markt** *m* supermarket

Suppe *f* -,-n soup. **S~nlöffel** *m* soupspoon. **S~nteller** *m* soup-plate. **S~nwürfel** *m* stock cube

Surf|brett /'sœpf-/ *nt* surfboard. **S~en** *nt* -s surfing

surren *vi* (*haben*) whirr

süß *a* sweet, *adv* -ly. **S~e** *f* - sweetness. **s~en** *vt* sweeten. **S~igkeit** *f* -,-en sweet. **s~lich** *a* sweetish; (*fig*) sugary. **S~speise** *f* sweet. **S~stoff** *m* sweetener. **S~waren** *fpl* confectionery *sg*, sweets *pl*. **S~wasser-** *pref* freshwater ...

Sylvester *nt* -s = Silvester

Symbol *nt* -s,-e symbol. **S~ik** *f* - symbolism. **s~isch** *a* symbolic, *adv* -ally. **s~isieren** *vt* symbolize

Sym|metrie *f* - symmetry. **s~metrisch** *a* symmetrical, *adv* -ly

Sympathie *f* -,-n sympathy

sympath|isch *a* agreeable; ⟨*Person*⟩ likeable. **s~isieren** *vi* (*haben*) be sympathetic (mit to)

Symphonie *f* -,-n = Sinfonie

Symptom *nt* -s,-e symptom. **s~atisch** *a* symptomatic

Synagoge *f* -,-n synagogue

synchronisieren /zynkroni'zi:rən/ *vt* synchronize; dub ⟨*Film*⟩

Syndikat *nt* -[e]s,-e syndicate

Syndrom *nt* -s,-e syndrome

synonym *a* synonymous, *adv* -ly. **S~** *nt* -s,-e synonym

Syntax /'zyntaks/ *f* - syntax

Synthe|se *f* -,-n synthesis. **S~tik** *nt* -s synthetic material. **s~tisch** *a* synthetic, *adv* -ally

Syrien /-jən/ *nt* -s Syria

System *nt* -s,-e system. **s~atisch** *a* systematic, *adv* -ally

Szene *f* -,-n scene. **S~rie** *f* - scenery

T

Tabak *m* -s,-e tobacco

Tabelle *f* -,-n table; (*Sport*) league table

Tablett *nt* -[e]s,-s tray

Tablette *f* -,-n tablet

tabu *a* taboo. **T~** *nt* -s,-s taboo

Tacho *m* -s,-s, **Tachometer** *m* & *nt* speedometer

Tadel *m* -s,- reprimand; (*Kritik*) censure; (*Sch*) black mark. **t~los** *a* impeccable, *adv* -bly. **t~n** *vt* reprimand; censure. **t~nswert** *a* reprehensible

Tafel *f* -,-n (*Tisch, Tabelle*) table; (*Platte*) slab; (*Anschlag-, Hinweis-*) board; (*Gedenk-*) plaque; (*Schiefer-*) slate; (*Wand-*) blackboard; (*Bild-*) plate; (*Schokolade*) bar. **t~n** *vi* (*haben*) feast

Täfelung *f* - panelling

Tag *m* -[e]s,-e day; Tag für Tag day by day; am [?~e] in the daytime; eines T~es one day; unter [?~e] underground; es wird Tag it is getting light; guten Tag! good morning/afternoon! zu T~e treten *od* kommen/bringen = zutage treten *od* kommen/bringen, s. zutage. **t~aus** *adv* t~aus, t~ein day in, day out

Tage|buch *nt* diary. t~**lang** *adv* for days

tagen *vi (haben)* meet; *(Gericht:)* sit; es tagt day is breaking

Tages|anbruch *m* daybreak. T~**ausflug** *m* day trip. T~**decke** *f* bedspread. T~**karte** *f* day ticket; *(Speise-)* menu of the day. T~**licht** *nt* daylight. T~**mutter** *f* child-minder. T~**ordnung** *f* agenda. T~**rückfahrkarte** *f* day return [ticket]. T~**zeit** *f* time of the day. T~**zeitung** *f* daily [news]paper

täglich *a & adv* daily; zweimal t~ twice a day

tags *adv* by day; t~ zuvor/darauf the day before/after

tagsüber *adv* during the day

tag|täglich *a* daily □ *adv* every single day. T~**traum** *m* day-dream. T~**undnachtgleiche** *f* -,-n equinox. T~**ung** *f* -,-en meeting; *(Konferenz)* conference

Taill|e /ˈtaljə/ *f* -,-n waist. t~**iert** /taˈjiːɐ̯t/ *a* fitted

Takt *m* -[e]s,-e tact; *(Mus)* bar; *(Tempo)* time; *(Rhythmus)* rhythm; im T~ in time [to the music]. T~**gefühl** *nt* tact

Takt|ik *f* - tactics *pl*. t~**isch** *a* tactical, *adv* -ly

takt|los *a* tactless, *adv* -ly. T~**losigkeit** *f* - tactlessness. T~**stock** *m* baton. t~**voll** *a* tactful, *adv* -ly

Tal *nt* -[e]s,-e valley

Talar *m* -s,-e robe; *(Univ)* gown

Talent *nt* -[e]s,-e talent. t~**iert** *a* talented

Talg *m* -s tallow; *(Culin)* suet

Talsperre *f* dam

Tampon /tamˈpõː/ *m* -s,-s tampon

Tang *m* -s seaweed

Tangente *f* -,-n tangent; *(Straße)* bypass

Tank *m* -s,-s tank. t~**en** *vt* fill up with *(Benzin)* □ *vi (haben)* fill up with petrol; *(Aviat)* refuel; ich muss t~en I need petrol. T~**er** *m* -s,- tanker. T~**stelle** *f* petrol/*(Amer)* gas station. T~**wart** *m* -[e]s,-e petrol-pump attendant

Tanne *f* -,-n fir [tree]. T~**nbaum** *m* fir tree; *(Weihnachtsbaum)* Christmas tree. T~**nzapfen** *m* fir cone

Tante *f* -,-n aunt

Tantiemen /tanˈtjeːmən/ *pl* royalties

Tanz *m* -es,-e dance. t~**en** *vt/i (haben)* dance

Tänzer(in) *m* -s,- (*f* -,-nen) dancer

Tanz|lokal *nt* dance-hall. T~**musik** *f* dance music

Tapete *f* -,-n wallpaper. T~**nwechsel** *m* *(fam)* change of scene

tapezier|en *vt* paper. T~**er** *m* -s,- paperhanger, decorator

tapfer *a* brave, *adv* -ly. T~**keit** *f* - bravery

tappen *vi (sein)* walk hesitantly; *(greifen)* grope (nach for)

Tarif *m* -s,-e rate; *(Verzeichnis)* tariff

tarn|en *vt* disguise; *(Mil)* camouflage; sich t~en disguise/camouflage oneself. T~**ung** *f* - disguise; camouflage

Tasche *f* -,-n bag; *(Hosen-, Mantel-)* pocket. T~**nbuch** *nt* paperback. T~**ndieb** *m* pickpocket. T~**ngeld** *nt* pocket-money. T~**nlampe** *f* torch, *(Amer)* flashlight. T~**nmesser** *nt* penknife. T~**ntuch** *nt* handkerchief

Tasse *f* -,-n cup

Tastatur *f* -,-en keyboard

tast|bar *a* palpable. T~**e** *f* -,-n key; *(Druck-)* push-button. t~**en** *vi (haben)* feel, grope (nach for) □ *vt* key in *(Daten)*; sich t~en feel one's way (zu to). t~**end** *a* tentative, *adv* -ly

Tat *f* -,-en action; *(Helden-)* deed; *(Straf-)* crime; in der Tat indeed; auf frischer Tat ertappt caught in the act. t~**enlos** *adv* passively

Täter(in) *m* -s,- (*f* -,-nen) culprit; *(Jur)* offender

tätig *a* active, *adv* -ly; t~ sein work. T~**keit** *f* -,-en activity; *(Funktionieren)* action; *(Arbeit)* work, job

Tatkraft *f* energy

tätlich *a* physical, *adv* -ly; t~ werden become violent. T~**keiten** *fpl* violence *sg*

Tatort *m* scene of the crime

tätowier|en *vt* tattoo. T~**ung** *f* -,-en tattooing; *(Bild)* tattoo

Tatsache *f* fact. T~**nbericht** *m* documentary

tatsächlich *a* actual, *adv* -ly

tätscheln *vt* pat

Tatze *f* -,-n paw

Tau¹ *m* -[e]s dew

Tau² *nt* -[e]s,-e rope

taub *a* deaf; *(gefühllos)* numb; *(Nuss)* empty; *(Gestein)* worthless

Taube *f* -,-n pigeon; *(Turtel- & fig)* dove. T~**nschlag** *m* pigeon-loft

Taub|heit *f* - deafness; *(Gefühllosigkeit)* numbness. t~**stumm** *a* deaf and dumb

tauch|en *vt* dip, plunge; *(unter-)* duck □ *vi (haben/sein)* dive/*(ein-)* plunge (in + *acc* into); *(auf-)* appear (aus out of). T~**er** *m* -s,- diver. T~**eranzug** *m* diving-suit. T~**sieder** *m* -s,- [small, portable] immersion heater

tauen *vi (sein)* melt, thaw □ *impers* es taut it is thawing

Tauf|becken *nt* font. T~**e** *f* -,-n christening, baptism. t~**en** *vt* christen, baptize. T~**pate** *m* godfather. T~**stein** *m* font

tauge|n vi (haben) etwas/nichts t~n be good/no good; zu etw t~n/nicht t~n be good/no good for sth. T~nichts m -es,-e good-for-nothing

tauglich a suitable; (Mil) fit. T~keit f - suitability; fitness

Taumel m -s daze; wie im T~ in a daze. t~n vi (sein) stagger

Tausch m -[e]s,-e exchange, (fam) swap. t~en vt exchange/(handeln) barter (gegen for); die Plätze t~en change places □ vi (haben) swap (mit etw sth; mit jdm with s.o.)

täuschen vt deceive, fool; betray (Vertrauen); sich t~ delude oneself; (sich irren) be mistaken □ vi (haben) be deceptive. t~d a deceptive; (Ähnlichkeit) striking

Tausch|geschäft nt exchange. T~handel m barter; (T~geschäft) exchange

Täuschung f -,-en deception; (Irrtum) mistake; (Illusion) delusion

tausend inv a one/a thousand. T~ nt -s, -e thousand; T~e od t~e von thousands of. T~füßler m -s,- centipede. t~ste(r, s) a thousandth. T~stel nt -s,- thousandth

Tau|tropfen m dewdrop. T~wetter nt thaw. T~ziehen nt -s tug of war

Taxe f -,-n charge; (Kur-) tax; (Taxi) taxi

Taxi nt -s,-s taxi, cab

taxieren vt estimate/value/(im Wert) value (auf + acc at); (fam: mustern) size up

Taxi|fahrer m taxi driver. T~stand m taxi rank

Teakholz /'ti:k-/ nt teak

Team /ti:m/ nt -s,-s team

Techni|k f -,-en technology; (Methode) technique. T~ker m -s,- technician. t~sch a technical, adv -ly; (technologisch) technological, adv -ly; T~sche Hochschule Technical University

Techno|logie f -,-n technology. t~logisch a technological

Teckel m -s,- dachshund

Teddybär m teddy bear

Tee m -s,-s tea. T~beutel m tea-bag. T~kanne f teapot. T~kessel m kettle. T~löffel m teaspoon

Teer m -s tar. t~en vt tar

Tee|sieb nt tea-strainer. T~tasse f teacup. T~wagen m [tea] trolley

Teich m -[e]s,-e pond

Teig m -[e]s,-e pastry; (Knet-) dough; (Rühr-) mixture; (Pfannkuchen-) batter. T~rolle f, T~roller m rolling-pin. T~waren fpl pasta sg

Teil m -[e]s,-e part; (Bestand-) component; (Jur) party; der vordere T~ the front part; zum T~ partly; zum großen/

größten T~ for the most part □ m & nt -[e]s (Anteil) share; sein[en] T~ beitragen do one's share; ich für mein[en] T~ for my part □ nt -[e]s,-e part; (Ersatz-) spare part; (Anbau-) unit

teil|bar a divisible. T~chen nt -s,- particle. t~en vt divide; (auf-) share out; (gemeinsam haben) share; (Pol) partition (Land); sich (dat) etw mit jdm t~en share sth [with s.o.]; sich t~en divide; (sich gabeln) fork; (Vorhang:) open; (Meinungen:) differ □ vi (haben) share

teilhab|en† vi sep (haben) share (an etw dat sth). T~er m -s,- (Comm) partner

Teilnahm|e f - participation; (innere) interest; (Mitgefühl) sympathy. t~slos a apathetic, adv -ally

teilnehm|en† vi sep (haben) t~en an (+ dat) take part in; (mitfühlen) share [in]. T~er(in) m -s,- (f-,-nen) participant; (an Wettbewerb) competitor

teil|s adv partly. T~ung f -,-en division; (Pol) partition. t~weise a partial □ adv partially, partly; (manchmal) in some cases. T~zahlung f part-payment; (Rate) instalment. T~zeitbeschäftigung f part-time job

Teint /tɛ:/ m -s,-s complexion

Telefax nt fax

Telefon nt -s,-e [tele]phone. T~anruf m, T~at nt -[e]s,-e [tele]phone call. T~buch nt [tele]phone book. t~ieren vi (haben) [tele]phone

telefon|isch a [tele]phone ... □ adv by [tele]phone. T~ist(in) m -en,-en (f -,-nen) telephonist. T~karte f phone card. T~nummer f [tele]phone number. T~zelle f [tele]phone box

Telegraf m -en,-en telegraph. T~enmast m telegraph pole. t~ieren vi (haben) send a telegram. t~isch a telegraphic □ adv by telegram

Telegramm nt -s,-e telegram

Telegraph m -en,-en = Telegraf

Teleobjektiv nt telephoto lens

Telepathie f - telepathy

Telephon nt -s,-e = Telefon

Teleskop nt -s,-e telescope. t~isch a telescopic

Telex nt -,-[e] telex. t~en vt telex

Teller m -s,- plate

Tempel m -s,- temple

Temperament nt -s,-e temperament; (Lebhaftigkeit) vivacity. t~los a dull. t~voll a vivacious; (Pferd) spirited

Temperatur f -,-en temperature

Tempo nt -s,-s speed; (Mus: pl -pi) tempo; T~ [T~]! hurry up!

Tend|enz f -,-en trend; (*Neigung*) tendency. t~**ieren** vi (*haben*) tend (zu towards)

Tennis nt - tennis. T~**platz** m tennis-court. T~**schläger** m tennis-racket

Tenor m -s,-̈e (*Mus*) tenor

Teppich m -s,-e carpet. T~**boden** m fitted carpet

Termin m -s,-e date; (*Arzt-*) appointment; [letzter] T~ deadline. T~**kalender** m [appointments] diary

Terminologie f -,-n terminology

Terpentin nt -s turpentine

Terrain /tɛ'rɛ̃ː/ nt -s,-s terrain

Terrasse f -,-n terrace

Terrier /'tɛriɐ/ m -s,- terrier

Terrine f -,-n tureen

Territorium nt -s,-ien territory

Terror m -s terror. t~**isieren** vt terrorize. T~**ismus** m -terrorism. T~**ist** m -en,-en terrorist

Terzett nt -[e]s,-e [vocal] trio

Tesafilm (P) m ≈ Sellotape (P)

Test m -[e]s,-s & -e test

Testament nt -[e]s,-e will; Altes/Neues T~ Old/New Testament. T~**svollstrecker** m -s,- executor

testen vt test

Tetanus m - tetanus

teuer a expensive, adv -ly; (*lieb*) dear; wie t~? how much? T~**ung** f -,-en rise in prices

Teufel m -s,- devil; zum T~! (*sl*) damn [it]! T~**skreis** m vicious circle

teuflisch a fiendish

Text m -[e]s,-e text; (*Passage*) passage; (*Bild-*) caption; (*Lied-*) lyrics pl, words pl; (*Opern-*) libretto. T~**er** m -s,- copy-writer; (*Schlager-*) lyricist

Textil|ien /-jən/ pl textiles; (*Textilwaren*) textile goods. T~**industrie** f textile industry

Textverarbeitungssystem nt word processor

TH abbr = Technische Hochschule

Theater nt -s,- theatre; (*fam: Getue*) fuss, to-do; T~ **spielen** act; (*fam*) put on an act. T~**kasse** f box-office. T~**stück** nt play

theatralisch a theatrical, adv -ly

Theke f -,-n ink. T~**nfisch** m squid

Thema nt -s,-men subject; (*Mus*) theme

Themse f - Thames

Theolo|ge m -n,-n theologian. T~**gie** f - theology

theor|etisch a theoretical, adv -ly. T~**ie** f -,-n theory

Therapeut|(in) m -en,-en (f -,-nen) therapist. t~**isch** a therapeutic

Therapie f -,-n therapy

Thermal|bad nt thermal bath; (*Ort*) thermal spa. T~**quelle** f thermal spring

Thermometer nt -s,- thermometer

Thermosflasche (P) f Thermos flask (P)

Thermostat m -[e]s,-e thermostat

These f -,-n thesis

Thrombose f -,-n thrombosis

Thron m -[e]s,-e throne. t~**en** vi (*haben*) sit [in state]. T~**folge** f succession. T~**folger** m -s,- heir to the throne

Thunfisch m tuna

Thymian m -s thyme

Tick m -s,-s (*fam*) quirk; einen T~ haben be crazy

ticken vi (*haben*) tick

tief a deep; (t~ *liegend*, *niedrig*) low; (t~*gründig*) profound; t~er Teller soup-plate; im t~sten Winter in the depths of winter □ adv deep; low; (*sehr*) deeply, profoundly; ⟨*schlafen*⟩ soundly; t~ greifend (*fig*) radical, adv -ly; t~ schürfend (*fig*) profound. T~ nt -s,-s (*Meteorol*) depression. T~**bau** m civil engineering. T~**e** f -,-n depth

Tief|ebene f [lowland] plain. T~**garage** f underground car park. t~**gekühlt** a [deep-]frozen. t~**greifend** a NEW t~ greifend, s. tief. t~**gründig** a (*fig*) profound

Tiefkühl|fach nt freezer compartment. T~**kost** f frozen food. T~**truhe** f deep-freeze

Tief|land nt lowlands pl. T~**punkt** m (*fig*) low. t~**schürfend** a NEW t~ schürfend, s. tief. t~**sinnig** (*fig*) profound; (*trübsinnig*) melancholy. T~**stand** m (*fig*) low

Tiefsttemperatur f minimum temperature

Tier nt -[e]s,-e animal. T~**arzt** m, T~**ärztin** f vet, veterinary surgeon. T~**garten** m zoo. t~**isch** a animal . . .; (*fig: roh*) bestial. T~**kreis** m zodiac. T~**kreiszeichen** nt sign of the zodiac. T~**kunde** f zoology. T~**quälerei** f cruelty to animals

Tiger m -s,- tiger

tilgen vt pay off ⟨*Schuld*⟩; (*streichen*) delete; (*fig: auslöschen*) wipe out

Tinte f -,-n ink. T~**nfisch** m squid

Tipp (Tip) m -s,-s (*fam*) tip

tipp|en vt (*fam*) type □ vi (*haben*) (*berühren*) touch (auf/an etw acc sth); (*fam: Maschine schreiben*) type; t~**en auf** (+ acc) (*fam: wetten*) bet on. T~**fehler** m (*fam*) typing error. T~**schein** m pools/lottery coupon

tipptopp a (*fam*) immaculate, adv -ly

Tirol nt -s [the] Tyrol

Tisch *m* -[e]s,-e table; (*Schreib-*) desk; nach T~ after the meal. T~decke *f* table-cloth. T~gebet *nt* grace. T~ler *m* -s,- joiner; (*Möbel-*) cabinet-maker. T~rede *f* after-dinner speech. T~tennis *nt* table tennis. T~tuch *nt* table-cloth

Titel *m* -s,- title. T~rolle *f* title-role

Toast /toːst/ *m* -[e]s,-e toast; (*Scheibe*) piece of toast; einen T~ ausbringen propose a toast (auf + *acc* to). T~er *m* -s,- toaster

tob|en *vi* (*haben*) rave; (*Sturm:*) rage; (*Kinder:*) play boisterously □ *vi* (*sein*) rush. t~süchtig *a* raving mad

Tochter *f* -,: daughter. T~gesellschaft *f* subsidiary

Tod *m* -es death. t~blass (t~blaß) *n* deathly pale. t~ernst *a* deadly serious, *adv* -ly

Todes|angst *f* mortal fear. T~anzeige *f* death announcement; (*Zeitungs-*) obituary. T~fall *m* death. T~opfer *nt* fatality, casualty. T~strafe *f* death penalty. T~urteil *nt* death sentence

Tod|feind *m* mortal enemy. t~krank *a* dangerously ill

tödlich *a* fatal, *adv* -ly; (*Gefahr*) mortal, *adv* -ly; (*groß*) deadly; t~ gelangweilt bored to death

tod|müde *a* dead tired. t~sicher *a* (*fam*) dead certain □ *adv* for sure. T~sünde *f* deadly sin. t~unglücklich *a* desperately unhappy

Toilette /tŏaˈlɛtə/ *f* -,-n toilet. T~npapier *nt* toilet paper

toler|ant *a* tolerant. T~anz *f* - tolerance. t~ieren *vt* tolerate

toll *a* crazy, mad; (*fam: prima*) fantastic; (*schlimm*) awful □ *adv* beautifully; (*sehr*) very; (*schlimm*) badly. t~en *vi* (*haben/sein*) romp. t~kühn *a* foolhardy. t~patschig *a* clumsy, *adv* -ily. T~wut *f* rabies. t~wütig *a* rabid

tolpatschig *a* (NEW)tollpatschig

Tölpel *m* -s,- fool

Tomate *f* -,-n tomato. T~nmark *nt* tomato purée

Tombola *f* -,-s raffle

Ton¹ *m* -[e]s clay

Ton² *m* -[e]s,-e tone; (*Klang*) sound; (*Note*) note; (*Betonung*) stress; (*Farb-*) shade; der gute Ton (*fig*) good form. T~abnehmer *m* -s,- pick-up. t~angebend *a* (*fig*) leading. T~art *f* tone [of voice]; (*Mus*) key. T~band *nt* (*pl* -bänder) tape. T~band-gerät *nt* tape recorder

tönen *vi* (*haben*) sound □ *vt* tint

Ton|fall *m* tone [of voice]; (*Akzent*) intonation. T~leiter *f* scale. t~los *a* toneless, *adv* -ly

Tonne *f* -,-n barrel, cask; (*Müll-*) bin; (*Maß*) tonne, metric ton

Topf *m* -[e]s,-e pot; (*Koch-*) pan

Topfen *m* -s (Aust) ≈ curd cheese

Töpfer|(in) *m* -s,- (*f* -,-nen) potter. T~ei *f* -,-en pottery

Töpferwaren *fpl* pottery *sg*

Topf|lappen *m* oven-cloth. T~pflanze *f* potted plant

Tor¹ *m* -en,-en fool

Tor² *nt* -[e]s,-e gate; (*Einfahrt*) gateway; (*Sport*) goal. T~bogen *m* archway

Torf *m* -s peat

Torheit *f* -,-en folly

Torhüter *m* -s,- goalkeeper

töricht *a* foolish, *adv* -ly

torkeln *vi* (*sein/habe*) stagger

Tornister *m* -s,- knapsack; (*Sch*) satchel

torp|edieren *vt* torpedo. T~edo *m* -s,-s torpedo

Torpfosten *m* goal-post

Torte *f* -,-n gateau; (*Obst-*) flan

Tortur *f* -,-en torture

Torwart *m* -s,-e goalkeeper

tosen *vi* (*haben*) roar; (*Sturm:*) rage

tot *a* dead; tot geboren stillborn; sich tot stellen pretend to be dead; einen t~en Punkt haben (*fig*) be at a low ebb

total *a* total, *adv* -ly. t~itär *a* totalitarian. T~schaden *m* ≈ write-off

Tote|(r) *m/f* dead man/woman; (*Todes-opfer*) fatality; die T~n the dead *pl*

töten *vt* kill

toten|blass (*totenblaß*) *a* deathly pale. T~gräber *m* -s,- grave-digger. T~kopf *m* skull. T~schein *m* death certificate. T~stille *f* deathly silence

tot|fahren† *vt sep* run over and kill. t~geboren *a* (NEW)tot geboren, *s.* tot. t~lachen (sich) *vt sep* (*fam*) be in stitches

Toto *nt & m* -s football pools *pl*. T~schein *m* pools coupon

tot|schießen† *vt sep* shoot dead. T~schlag *m* (*Jur*) manslaughter. t~schlagen† *vt sep* kill. t~schweigen† *vt sep* (*fig*) hush up. t~stellen (sich) *vr sep* (NEW)tot stellen (sich), *s.* tot

Tötung *f* -,-en killing; fahrlässige T~ (*Jur*) manslaughter

Toup|et /tuˈpeː/ *nt* -s,-s toupee. t~ieren *nt* back-comb

Tour /tuːɐ/ *f* -,-en tour; (*Ausflug*) trip; (*Auto-*) drive; (*Rad-*) ride; (*Strecke*) distance; (*Techn*) revolution, (*fam: Weise*) way; auf vollen T~en at full speed; (*fam*) flat out

Touris|mus /tuˈrɪsmʊs/ *m* - tourism. T~t *m* -en,-en tourist

Tournee /tur'ne:/ f -,-n tour

Trab m -[e]s trot

Trabant m -en,-en satellite

traben vi (haben/sein) trot

Tracht f -,-en [national] costume; eine T~ Prügel a good hiding

trachten vi (haben) strive (nach for); jdm nach dem Leben t~ be out to kill s.o

trächtig a pregnant

Tradition /-'tsio:n/ f -,-en tradition. t~ell a traditional, adv -ly

Trafik f -,-en (Aust) tobacconist's

Trag|bahre f stretcher. t~bar a portable; ⟨Kleidung⟩ wearable; ⟨erträglich⟩ bearable

träge a sluggish, adv -ly; ⟨faul⟩ lazy, adv -ily; (Phys) inert

tragen† vt carry; (an-/ aufhaben) wear; (fig) bear □ vi (haben) carry; gut t~ ⟨Baum:⟩ produce a good crop; schwer t~ carry a heavy load; (fig) be deeply affected (an + dat by). t~d a (Techn) load-bearing; ⟨trächtig⟩ pregnant

Träger m -s,- porter; (Inhaber) bearer; ⟨eines Ordens⟩ holder; (Bau-) beam; (Stahl-) girder; (Achsel-) [shoulder] strap. T~kleid nt pinafore dress

Trag|etasche f carrier bag. T~fläche f (Aviat) wing; (Naut) hydrofoil. T~flächenboot, T~flügelboot nt hydrofoil

Trägheit f - sluggishness; (Faulheit) laziness; (Phys) inertia

Trag|ik f - tragedy. t~isch a tragic, adv -ally

Tragödie /-jə/ f -,-n tragedy

Tragweite f range; (fig) consequence

Train|er /'trɛːnɐ/ m -s,- trainer; (Tennis-) coach. t~ieren vt/i (haben) train

Training /'trɛːnɪŋ/ nt -s training. T~anzug m tracksuit. T~s-schuhe mpl trainers

Trakt m -[e]s,-e section; (Flügel) wing

traktieren vi (haben) mit Schlägen/ Tritten t~ hit/kick

Traktor m -s,-en /-'to:rən/ tractor

trampeln vi (haben) stamp one's feet □ vi (sein) trample (auf + acc on) □ vt trample

trampen /'trɛmpən/ vi (sein) (fam) hitchhike

Trance /'trãːsə/ f -,-n trance

Tranchier|messer /trã'ʃiːɐ̯-/ nt carving-knife. t~en vt carve

Träne f -,-n tear. t~n vi (haben) water. T~ngas nt tear-gas

Tränke f -,-n watering-place; (Trog) drinking-trough. t~n vt water ⟨Pferd⟩; (nässen) soak (mit with)

Trans|aktion f transaction. T~fer m -s,-s transfer. T~formator m -s,-en /-'to:rən/ transformer. T~fusion f -,-en [blood] transfusion

Transistor m -,-en /-'to:rən/ transistor

Transit /tran'ziːt/ m -s transit

transitiv a transitive, adv -ly

Transparent nt -[e]s,-e banner; (Bild) transparency

transpirieren vi (haben) perspire

Transplantation /-'tsio:n/ f -,-en transplant

Transport m -[e]s,-e transport; (Güter-) consignment. t~ieren vt transport. T~mittel nt means of transport

Trapez nt -es,-e trapeze; (Geom) trapezium

Tratsch m -[e]s (fam) gossip. t~en vi (haben) (fam) gossip

Tratte f -,-n (Comm) draft

Traube f -,-n bunch of grapes; (Beere) grape; (fig) cluster. T~nzucker m glucose

trauen vi (haben) (+ dat) trust; ich traute kaum meinen Augen I could hardly believe my eyes □ vt marry; sich t~ dare (etw zu tun [to] do sth); venture (in + acc/aus into/out of)

Trauer f - mourning; (Schmerz) grief (um for); T~ tragen be [dressed] in mourning. T~fall m bereavement. T~feier f funeral service. T~marsch m funeral march. t~n vi (haben) grieve; t~n um mourn [for]. T~spiel nt tragedy. T~weide f weeping willow

traulich a cosy, adv -ily

Traum m -[e]s, Träume dream

Trau|ma nt -s,-men trauma. t~matisch a traumatic

träumen vt/i (haben) dream

traumhaft a dreamlike; (schön) fabulous, adv -ly

traurig a sad, adv -ly; (erbärmlich) sorry. T~keit f - sadness

Trau|ring m wedding-ring. T~schein m marriage certificate. T~ung f -,-en wedding [ceremony]

Treck m -s,-s trek

Trecker m -s,- tractor

Treff nt -s,-s (Karten) spades pl

treff|en† vt hit; (Blitz:) strike; (fig: verletzen) hurt; (zusammenkommen mit) meet; take ⟨Maßnahme⟩; sich t~en meet (mit jdm s.o.); sich gut t~en be convenient; es traf sich, dass it so happened that; es gut/schlecht t~en be lucky/unlucky □ vi (haben) hit the target; t~en auf (+ acc) meet; (fig) meet with. T~en nt -s,-meeting. t~end a apt, adv -ly; (Ähnlichkeit) striking. T~er m -s,- hit; (Los) winner. T~punkt m meeting-place

treiben† vt drive; (sich befassen mit) do; carry on ⟨Gewerbe⟩; indulge in ⟨Luxus⟩; get up to ⟨Unfug⟩; Handel t∼ trade; Blüten/Blätter t∼ come into flower/leaf; zur Eile t∼ hurry [up]; was treibt ihr da? (fam) what are you up to? □ vi (sein) drift; (schwimmen) float □ vi (haben) (Bot) sprout. T∼ nt -s activity; (Getriebe) bustle

Treib|haus nt hothouse. T∼hauseffekt m greenhouse effect. T∼holz nt driftwood. T∼riemen m transmission belt. T∼sand m quicksand. T∼stoff m fuel

Trend m -s,-s trend

trenn|bar a separable. t∼en vt separate/(abmachen) detach (von from); divide, split ⟨Wort⟩; sich t∼en separate; (auseinander gehen) part; sich t∼en von leave; (fortgeben) part with. T∼ung f -,-en separation; (Silben-) division. T∼ungsstrich m hyphen. T∼wand f partition

trepp|ab adv downstairs. t∼auf adv upstairs

Treppe f -,-n stairs pl; (Außen-) steps pl; eine T∼ a flight of stairs/steps. T∼nflur m landing. T∼ngeländer nt banisters pl. T∼nhaus nt stairwell. T∼nstufe f stair, step

Tresor m -s,-e safe

Tresse f -,-n braid

Treteimer m pedal bin

treten† vi (sein/haben) step; (versehentlich) tread; (ausschlagen) kick (nach at); in Verbindung t∼ get in touch □ vt tread; (mit Füßen) kick

treu a faithful, adv -ly; (fest) loyal, adv -ly. T∼e f - faithfulness; loyalty; (eheliche) fidelity. T∼händer m -s,- trustee. t∼herzig a trusting, adv -ly; (arglos) innocent, adv -ly. t∼los a disloyal, adv -ly; (untreu) unfaithful

Tribüne f -,-n platform; (Zuschauer-) stand

Tribut m -[e]s,-e tribute; (Opfer) toll

Trichter m -s,- funnel; (Bomben-) crater

Trick m -s,-s trick. T∼film m cartoon. t∼reich a clever

Trieb m -[e]s,-e drive, urge; (Instinkt) instinct; (Bot) shoot. T∼täter, T∼verbrecher m sex offender. T∼werk nt (Aviat) engine; (Uhr-) mechanism

trief|en† vi (haben) drip; (nass sein) be dripping (von/vor + dat with). t∼nass (t∼naß) a dripping wet

triftig a valid

Trigonometrie f - trigonometry

Trikot¹ /tri'ko:/ m -s (Tex) jersey

Trikot² nt -s,-s (Sport) jersey; (Fußball-) shirt

Trimester nt -s,- term

Trimm-dich nt -s keep-fit

trimmen vt trim, (fam) train; tune ⟨Motor⟩; sich t∼ keep fit

trink|bar a drinkable. t∼en† vt/i (haben) drink. T∼er(in) m -s,- (f -,-nen) alcoholic. T∼geld nt tip. T∼halm m [drinking-] straw. T∼spruch m toast. T∼wasser nt drinking-water

Trio nt -s,-s trio

trippeln vi (sein) trip along

trist a dreary

Tritt m -[e]s,-e step; (Fuß-) kick. T∼brett nt step. T∼leiter f step-ladder

Triumph m -s,-e triumph. t∼ieren vi (haben) rejoice; t∼ieren über (+ acc) triumph over. t∼ierend a triumphant, adv -ly

trocken a dry, adv drily. T∼haube f drier. T∼heit f -,-en dryness; (Dürre) drought. t∼legen vt sep change ⟨Baby⟩; drain ⟨Sumpf⟩. T∼milch f powdered milk

trockn|en vt/i (sein) dry. T∼er m -s,- drier

Troddel f -,-n tassel

Trödel m -s (fam) junk. T∼laden m (fam) junk-shop. T∼markt m (fam) flea market. t∼n vi (haben) dawdle

Trödler m -s,- (fam) slowcoach; (Händler) junk-dealer

Trog m -[e]s,-e trough

Trommel f -,-n drum. T∼fell nt ear-drum. t∼n vi (haben) drum

Trommler m -s,- drummer

Trompete f -,-n trumpet. T∼r m -s,- trumpeter

Tropen pl tropics

Tropf m -[e]s,-e (Med) drip

tröpfeln vt/i (sein/haben) drip; es tröpfelt it's spitting with rain

tropfen vt/i (sein/haben) drip. T∼ m -s,- drop; (fallend) drip. t∼weise adv drop by drop

tropf|nass (tropfnaß) a dripping wet. T∼stein m stalagmite; (hängend) stalactite

Trophäe /tro'fɛ:ə/ f -,-n trophy

tropisch a tropical

Trost m -[e]s consolation, comfort

tröst|en vt console, comfort; sich t∼en console oneself. t∼lich a comforting

trost|los a desolate; (elend) wretched; (öde) dreary. T∼preis m consolation prize. t∼reich a comforting

Trott m -s amble; (fig) routine

Trottel m -s (fam) idiot

trotten vi (sein) traipse; ⟨Tier:⟩ amble

Trottoir /trɔ'toa:ɐ̯/ nt -s,-s pavement, (Amer) sidewalk

trotz *prep* (+ *gen*) despite, in spite of. T∼ *m* -es defiance. t∼dem *adv* nevertheless. t∼en *vi* (*haben*) (+ *dat*) defy. t∼ig *a* defiant, *adv* -ly; ⟨*Kind*⟩ stubborn

trübe *a* dull; ⟨*Licht*⟩ dim; ⟨*Flüssigkeit*⟩ cloudy; (*fig*) gloomy

Trubel *m* -s bustle

trüben *vt* dull; make cloudy ⟨*Flüssigkeit*⟩; (*fig*) spoil; strain ⟨*Verhältnis*⟩. sich t∼ ⟨*Flüssigkeit:*⟩ become cloudy; ⟨*Himmel:*⟩ cloud over; ⟨*Augen:*⟩ dim; ⟨*Verhältnis, Erinnerung:*⟩ deteriorate

Trüb|sal *f* - misery; T∼sal blasen (*fam*) mope. t∼selig *a* miserable; (*trübe*) gloomy, *adv* -ily. T∼sinn *m* melancholy. t∼sinnig *a* melancholy

Trugbild *nt* illusion

trüg|en *vt* deceive □ *vi* (*haben*) be deceptive. t∼erisch *a* false; (*täuschend*) deceptive

Trugschluss (Trugschluß) *m* fallacy

Truhe *f* -,-n chest

Trümmer *pl* rubble *sg*; ⟨T∼teile⟩ wreckage *sg*; (*fig*) ruins. T∼haufen *m* pile of rubble

Trumpf *m* -[e]s,-̈e trump [card]; T∼ sein be trumps. t∼en *vi* (*haben*) play trumps

Trunk *m* -[e]s drink. T∼enbold *m* -[e]s, -e drunkard. T∼enheit *f* - drunkenness; T∼enheit am Steuer drink-driving. T∼sucht *f* alcoholism

Trupp *m* -s,-s group; (*Mil*) squad. T∼e *f* -, -n (*Mil*) unit; (*Theat*) troupe; T∼en troops

Truthahn *m* turkey

Tschech|e *m* -n,-n, T∼in *f* -,-nen Czech. t∼isch *a* Czech. T∼oslowakei (die) - Czechoslovakia

tschüs, tschüss *int* bye, cheerio

Tuba *f* -,-ben (*Mus*) tuba

Tube *f* -,-n tube

Tuberkulose *f* - tuberculosis

Tuch¹ *nt* -[e]s,-̈er cloth; ⟨*Hals-, Kopf-*⟩ scarf; ⟨*Schulter-*⟩ shawl

Tuch² *nt* -[e]s,-e ⟨*Stoff*⟩ cloth

tüchtig *a* competent; ⟨*reichlich, beträchtlich*⟩ good; ⟨*groß*⟩ big □ *adv* competently; ⟨*ausreichend*⟩ well; ⟨*regnen, schneien*⟩ hard. T∼keit *f* - competence

Tück|e *f* -,-n malice; T∼en haben be temperamental; (*gefährlich sein*) be treacherous. t∼isch *a* malicious, *adv* -ly; (*gefährlich*) treacherous

tüfteln *vi* (*haben*) (*fam*) fiddle (an + *dat* with); (*geistig*) puzzle (an + *dat* over)

Tugend *f* -,en virtue. t∼haft *a* virtuous

Tülle *f* -,-n spout

Tulpe *f* -,-n tulip

tummeln (sich) *vr* romp [about]; (*sich beeilen*) hurry [up]

Tümmler *m* -s,- porpoise

Tumor *m* -s,-en /-'mo:rən/ tumour

Tümpel *m* -[e]s,- pond

Tumult *m* -[e]s,-e commotion; ⟨*Aufruhr*⟩ riot

tun† *vt* do; take ⟨*Schritt, Blick*⟩; work ⟨*Wunder*⟩; (*bringen*) put (in + *acc* into); sich tun happen; jdm etwas tun hurt s.o.; viel zu tun haben have a lot to do; das tut man nicht it isn't done; das tut nichts it doesn't matter □ *vi* (*haben*) act (als ob as if); überrascht tun pretend to be surprised; er tut nur so he's just pretending; jdm/etw gut tun do s.o. good; zu tun haben have things/work to do; [es] zu tun haben mit have to deal with; [es] mit dem Herzen zu tun haben have heart trouble. Tun *nt* -s actions *pl*

Tünche *f* -,-n whitewash; (*fig*) veneer. t∼n *vt* whitewash

Tunesien /-jən/ *nt* -s Tunisia

Tunfisch *m* = Thunfisch

Tunke *f* -,-n sauce. t∼n *vt/i* (*haben*) (*fam*) dip (in + *acc* into)

Tunnel *m* -s,- tunnel

tupf|en *vt* dab □ *vi* (*haben*) t∼en an/auf (+ *acc*) touch. T∼en *m* -s,- spot. T∼er *m* -s,- spot; (*Med*) swab

Tür *f* -,-en door

Turban *m* -s,-e turban

Turbine *f* -,-n turbine

turbulen|t *a* turbulent. T∼z *f* -,-en turbulence

Türk|e *m* -n,-n Turk. T∼ei (die) - Turkey. T∼in *f* -,-nen Turk

türkis *inv a* turquoise. T∼ *m* -es,-e turquoise

türkisch *a* Turkish

Turm *m* -[e]s,-̈e tower; ⟨*Schach*⟩ rook, castle

Türm|chen *nt* -s,- turret. t∼en *vt* pile [up]; sich t∼en pile up □ *vi* (*sein*) (*fam*) escape

Turmspitze *f* spire

turn|en *vi* (*haben*) do gymnastics. T∼en *nt* -s gymnastics *sg*; (*Sch*) physical education, (*fam*) gym. T∼er(in) *m* -s,- (*f* -,-nen) gymnast. T∼halle *f* gymnasium

Turnier *nt* -s,-e tournament; ⟨*Reit-*⟩ show

Turnschuhe *mpl* gym shoes; ⟨*Trainingsschuhe*⟩ trainers

Türschwelle *f* doorstep, threshold

Tusch *m* -[e]s,-e fanfare

Tusche *f* -,-n [drawing] ink; ⟨*Wasserfarbe*⟩ watercolour

tuscheln *vt/i* (*haben*) whisper

Tüte *f* -,-n bag; (*Comm*) packet; ⟨*Eis-*⟩ cornet; in die T∼ blasen (*fam*) be breathalysed tu̱ten *vi* (*haben*) hoot; ⟨*Schiff:*⟩ sound its hooter; ⟨*Sirene:*⟩ sound

TÜV *m* - ≈ MOT [test]

Typ *m* -s,-en type; (*fam: Kerl*) bloke. T∼e *f* -,-n type; (*fam: Person*) character

Typhus *m* - typhoid

typisch *a* typical, *adv* -ly (für *of*)

Typographie, Typografie *f* - typography

Typus *m* -, Typen type

Tyrann *m* -en,-en tyrant. T∼ei̱ *f* - tyranny. t∼isch *a* tyrannical. t∼isi̱eren *vt* tyrannize

U

u.a. *abbr* (unter anderem) amongst other things

U-Bahn *f* underground, (*Amer*) subway

ü̱bel *a* bad; (*hässlich*) nasty, *adv* -ily; mir ist/wird ü∼ I feel sick; etw ü∼ nehmen take sth amiss; jdm etw ü∼ nehmen hold sth against s.o. Ü∼ *nt* -s,- evil. Ü∼keit *f* - nausea. ü∼nehmen† *vt sep* (NEW) ü∼ nehmen, *s.* übel. Ü∼täter *m* culprit

ü̱ben *vt/i* (*haben*) practise; sich in etw (*dat*) ü∼ practise sth

ü̱ber *prep* (+ *dat/acc*) over; (*höher als*) above; (*betreffend*) about; (*Buch, Vortrag*) on; (*Scheck, Rechnung*) for; (*quer ü∼*) across; ü∼ Köln fahren go via Cologne; ü∼ Ostern over Easter; die Woche ü∼ during the week; heute ü∼ eine Woche a week today; Fehler ü∼ Fehler mistake after mistake ▫ *adv* ü∼ und ü∼ all over; jdm ü∼ sein be better/(*stärker*) stronger than s.o. ▫ *a* (*fam*) ü∼ sein be left over; etw ü∼ sein be fed up with sth

ü̱berall *adv* everywhere

überanstrengen *vt insep* overtax; strain ⟨*Augen*⟩; sich ü∼ overexert oneself

überarbeit|en *vt insep* revise; sich ü∼en overwork. Ü∼ung *f* - revision; overwork

ü̱beraus *adv* extremely

überbewerten *vt insep* overrate

überbieten† *vt insep* outbid; (*fig*) outdo; (*übertreffen*) surpass

Überblick *m* overall view; (*Abriss*) summary

überblicken *vt insep* overlook; (*abschätzen*) assess

überbringen† *vt insep* deliver

überbrücken *vt insep* (*fig*) bridge

überdauern *vt insep* survive

überdenken† *vt insep* think over

überdi̱es *adv* moreover

überdimensional *a* oversized

Ü̱berdosis *f* overdose

Ü̱berdruss *m* -es (Überdruß *m* -sses) surfeit; bis zum Ü∼ ad nauseam

überdrüssig *a* ü∼ sein/werden be/grow tired (*gen of*)

übereignen *vt insep* transfer

übereilt *a* over-hasty, *adv* -ily

übereinander *adv* one on top of/above the other; ⟨*sprechen*⟩ about each other; die Arme/Beine ü∼ schlagen fold one's arms/cross one's legs. ü∼schlagen† *vt sep* (NEW) ü∼ schlagen, *s.* übereinander

überein|kommen† *vi sep* (*sein*) agree. Ü∼kunft *f* - agreement. ü∼stimmen *vi sep* (*haben*) agree; ⟨*Zahlen:*⟩ tally; ⟨*Ansichten:*⟩ coincide; ⟨*Farben:*⟩ match. Ü∼stimmung *f* agreement

überempfindlich *a* over-sensitive; (*Med*) hypersensitive

überfahren† *vt insep* run over

Ü̱berfahrt *f* crossing

Ü̱berfall *m* attack; (*Bank-*) raid

überfallen† *vt insep* attack; raid ⟨*Bank*⟩; (*bestürmen*) bombard (mit with); (*überkommen*) come over; (*fam: besuchen*) surprise

überfällig *a* overdue

überfliegen† *vt insep* fly over; (*lesen*) skim over

überflügeln *vt insep* outstrip

Ü̱berfluss (Ü̱berfluß) *m* abundance; (*Wohlstand*) affluence

überflüssig *a* superfluous

überfluten *vt insep* flood

überfordern *vt insep* overtax

überführ|en *vt insep* transfer; (*Jur*) convict (*gen of*). Ü∼ung *f* transfer; (*Straße*) flyover; (*Fußgänger-*) foot-bridge

überfüllt *a* overcrowded

Ü̱bergabe *f* (*s.* übergeben) handing over; transfer

Ü̱bergang *m* crossing; (*Wechsel*) transition. Ü∼sstadium *nt* transitional stage

übergeben† *vt insep* hand over; (*übereignen*) transfer; sich ü∼ be sick

übergehen†¹ *vi sep* (*sein*) pass (an + *acc* to); (*überwechseln*) go over (zu to); (*werden zu*) turn (in + *acc* into); zum Angriff ü∼ start the attack

übergehen†² *vt insep* (*fig*) pass over; (*nicht beachten*) ignore; (*auslassen*) leave out

Ü̱bergewicht *nt* excess weight; (*fig*) predominance; Ü∼ haben be overweight

übergießen† *vt insep* mit Wasser ü∼ pour water over

überglücklich *a* overjoyed

über|greifen† *vi sep* (haben) spread (auf + *acc* to). Ü~griff *m* infringement

über|groß *a* outsize; (*übertrieben*) exaggerated. Ü~größe *f* outsize

überhaben† *vt sep* have on; (*fam: satthaben*) be fed up with

überhand *adv* ü~ nehmen increase alarmingly. ü~nehmen† *vi sep* (haben) (NEW) ü~ nehmen, *s.* überhand

überhängen *v sep □ vi†* (haben) overhang □ *vt* (reg) sich (dat) etw ü~ sling over one's shoulder (*Gewehr*); put round one's shoulders (*Jacke*)

überhäufen *vt insep* inundate (mit with)

überhaupt *adv* (*im Allgemeinen*) altogether; (*eigentlich*) anyway; (*überdies*) besides; ü~ nicht/nichts not/nothing at all

überheblich *a* arrogant, *adv* -ly. Ü~keit *f* - arrogance

überholen *vt insep* overtake; (*reparieren*) overhaul. ü~t *a* out-dated. Ü~ung *f* -,-en overhaul. Ü~verbot *nt* 'Ü~verbot' 'no overtaking'

überhören *vt insep* fail to hear; (*nicht beachten*) ignore

überirdisch *a* supernatural

überkochen *vi sep* (sein) boil over

überladen† *vt insep* overload □ *a* overornate

überlassen† *vt insep* jdm etw ü~ leave sth to s.o.; (*geben*) let s.o. have sth; sich seinem Schmerz ü~ abandon oneself to one's grief; sich (dat) selbst ü~ sein be left to one's own devices

überlasten *vt insep* overload; overtax (*Person*)

Überlauf *m* overflow

überlaufen†¹ *vi sep* (sein) overflow; (*Mil, Pol*) defect

überlaufen†² *vt insep* jdn ü~ (*Gefühl:*) come over s.o. □ *a* over-run; (*Kursus*) oversubscribed

Überläufer *m* defector

überleben *vt/i insep* (haben) survive. Ü~de(r) *m/f* survivor

überlegen¹ *vt sep* put over

überlegen² *v insep □ vt* [sich dat] ü~ think over, consider; es sich (dat) anders ü~ change one's mind □ *vi* (haben) think, reflect; ohne zu ü~ without thinking

überlegen³ *a* superior; (*herablassend*) supercilious, *adv* -ly. Ü~heit *f* - superiority

Überlegung *f* -,-en reflection

überliefer|n *vt insep* hand down. Ü~ung *f* tradition

überlisten *vt insep* outwit

überm *prep* = über dem

Über|macht *f* superiority. ü~mächtig *a* superior; (*Gefühl*) overpowering

übermannen *vt insep* overcome

Über|maß *nt* excess. ü~mäßig *a* excessive, *adv* -ly

Übermensch *m* superman. ü~lich *a* superhuman

übermitteln *vt insep* convey; (*senden*) transmit

übermorgen *adv* the day after tomorrow

übermüdet *a* overtired

Über|mut *m* high spirits *pl.* ü~mütig *a* high-spirited □ *adv* in high spirits

übern *prep* = über den

übernächst|e(r,s) *a* next ... but one; ü~es Jahr the year after next

übernacht|en *vi sep* (haben) stay overnight. Ü~ung *f* -,-en overnight stay; Ü~ung und Frühstück bed and breakfast

Übernahme *f* - taking over; (*Comm*) take-over

übernatürlich *a* supernatural

übernehmen† *vt insep* take over; (*annehmen*) take on; sich ü~ overdo things; (*finanziell*) over-reach oneself

überprüf|en *vt insep* check. Ü~ung *f* check

überqueren *vt insep* cross

überragen *vt insep* tower above; (*fig*) surpass. ü~d *a* outstanding

überrasch|en *vt insep* surprise. ü~end *a* surprising, *adv* -ly; (*unerwartet*) unexpected, *adv* -ly. Ü~ung *f* -,-en surprise

überreden *vt insep* persuade

überreichen *vt insep* present

überreizt *a* overwrought

überrennen† *vt insep* overrun

Überreste *mpl* remains

überrrumpeln *vt insep* take by surprise

übers *prep* = über das

Überschall- *pref* supersonic

überschatten *vt insep* overshadow

überschätzen *vt insep* overestimate

Überschlag *m* rough estimate; (*Sport*) somersault

überschlagen†¹ *vt sep* cross (*Beine*)

überschlagen†² *vt insep* estimate roughly; (*auslassen*) skip; sich ü~ somersault; (*Ereignisse:*) happen fast □ *a* tepid

überschnappen *vi sep* (sein) (*fam*) go crazy

überschneiden† (sich) *vr insep* intersect, cross; (*zusammenfallen*) overlap

überschreiben† *vt insep* entitle; (*übertragen*) transfer

überschreiten† *vt insep* cross; (*fig*) exceed

Überschrift f heading; (Zeitungs-) headline

Über|schuss (Überschuß) m surplus. ü~schüssig a surplus

überschütten vt insep ü~ mit cover with; (fig) shower with

überschwänglich a effusive, adv -ly

überschwemm|en vt insep flood; (fig) inundate. Ü~ung f -,-en flood

überschwenglich a (NEW) überschwänglich

Übersee in/nach ü~ overseas; aus/von Ü~ from overseas. Ü~dampfer m ocean liner. ü~isch a overseas

übersehen† vt insep look out over; (abschätzen) assess; (nicht sehen) overlook, miss; (ignorieren) ignore

übersenden† vt insep send

übersetzen¹ vi sep (haben/sein) cross [over]

übersetz|en² vt insep translate. Ü~er(in) m -s,- (f -,-nen) translator. Ü~ung f -,-en translation

Übersicht f overall view; (Abriss) summary; (Tabelle) table. ü~lich a clear, adv -ly

übersied|eln vi sep (sein), übersied|eln vi insep (sein) move (nach to). Ü~lung f move

übersinnlich a supernatural

überspannt a exaggerated; (verschroben) eccentric

überspielen vt insep (fig) cover up; auf Band ü~ tape

überspitzt a exaggerated

überspringen† vt insep jump [over]; (auslassen) skip

überstehen†¹ vi sep (haben) project, jut out

überstehen†² vt insep come through; get over (Krankheit); (überleben) survive

übersteigen† vt insep climb [over]; (fig) exceed

überstimmen vt insep outvote

überstreifen vt sep slip on

Überstunden fpl overtime sg; Ü~ machen work overtime

überstürz|en vt insep rush; sich ü~en (Ereignisse:) happen fast; (Worte:) tumble out. ü~t a hasty, adv -ily

übertölpeln vt insep dupe

übertönen vt insep drown [out]

übertrag|bar a transferable; (Med) infectious. ü~en† vt insep transfer; (übergeben) assign (auf to); (Techn, Med) transmit; (Radio, TV) broadcast; (übersetzen) translate; (anwenden) apply (auf + acc to) □ a transferred, figurative.

Ü~ung f -,-en transfer; transmission; broadcast; translation; application

übertreffen† vt insep surpass; (übersteigen) exceed; sich selbst ü~ excel oneself

übertreib|en† vt insep exaggerate; (zu weit treiben) overdo. Ü~ung f -,-en exaggeration

übertret|en†¹ vi sep (sein) step over the line; (Pol) go over/(Relig) convert (zu to)

übertret|en†² vt insep infringe; break (Gesetz). Ü~ung f -,-en infringement; breach

übertrieben a exaggerated; (übermäßig) excessive, adv -ly

übervölkert a overpopulated

übervorteilen vt insep cheat

überwachen vt insep supervise; (kontrollieren) monitor; (bespitzeln) keep under surveillance

überwachsen a overgrown

überwältigen vt insep overpower; (fig) overwhelm. ü~d a overwhelming

überweis|en† vt insep transfer; refer (Patienten). Ü~ung f transfer; (ärztliche) referral

überwerfen†¹ vt sep put on (Mantel)

überwerfen†² (sich) vr insep fall out (mit with)

überwiegen† v insep □ vi (haben) predominate □ vt outweigh. ü~d a predominant, adv -ly

überwind|en† vt insep overcome; sich ü~en force oneself. Ü~ung f effort

Überwurf m wrap; (Bett-) bedspread

Über|zahl f majority. ü~zählig a spare

überzeug|en vt insep convince; sich [selbst] ü~en satisfy oneself. ü~end a convincing, adv -ly. Ü~ung f -,-en conviction

überziehen†¹ vt sep put on

überziehen†² vt insep cover; overdraw (Konto)

Überzug m cover; (Schicht) coating

üblich a usual; (gebräuchlich) customary

U-Boot nt submarine

übrig a remaining; (andere) other; alles Ü~e (ü~e) [all] the rest; im Ü~en (ü~en) besides; (ansonsten) apart from that; ü~ sein od bleiben be left [over]; etw ü~ haben od behalten have sth left [over]; etw ü~ lassen leave sth left [over]; uns blieb nichts anderes ü~ we had no choice. ü~behalten† vt sep (NEW) ü~ behalten, s. übrig. ü~bleiben† vi sep (sein) (NEW) ü~ bleiben, s. übrig. ü~ens adv by the way. ü~lassen† vt sep (NEW) ü~ lassen, s. übrig

Übung f -,-en exercise; (*Üben*) practice; außer od aus der Ü~ out of practice

UdSSR f - USSR

Ufer nt -s,- shore; (*Fluss-*) bank

Uhr f -,-en clock; (*Armband-*) watch; (*Zähler*) meter; um ein U~ at one o'clock; wie viel U~ ist es? what's the time? U~armband nt watch-strap. U~macher m -s,- watch and clockmaker. U~werk nt clock/watch mechanism. U~zeiger m [clock-/watch-]hand. U~zeigersinn m im/entgegen dem U~zeigersinn clockwise/anticlockwise. U~zeit f time

Uhu m -s,-s eagle owl

UKW abbr (*Ultrakurzwelle*) VHF

Ulk m -s fun; (*Streich*) trick. u~en vi (*haben*) joke. u~ig a funny; (*seltsam*) odd, adv -ly

Ulme f -,-n elm

Ultimatum nt -s,-ten ultimatum

Ultrakurzwelle f very high frequency

Ultraschall m ultrasound

ultraviolett a ultraviolet

um prep (+ acc) [a]round; (*Uhrzeit*) at; (*bitten, kämpfen*) for; (*streiten*) over; (*sich sorgen*) about; (*betrügen*) out of; (*bei Angabe einer Differenz*) by; um [... herum] around, [round] about; Tag um Tag day after day; einen Tag um den andern every other day; um seinetwillen for his sake □ adv (*ungefähr*) around, about; um sein (*fam*) be over; (*Zeit*) be up □ conj um zu to; (*Absicht*) [in order] to; zu müde, um zu ... too tired to ...; um so besser (NEW) umso besser, s. umso

umändern vt sep alter

umarbeiten vt sep alter; (*bearbeiten*) revise

umarm|en vt insep embrace, hug. U~ung f -,-en embrace, hug

Umbau m rebuilding; conversion (zu into). u~en vt sep rebuild; convert (zu into)

umbild|en vt sep change; (*umgestalten*) reorganize; reshuffle (*Kabinett*). U~ung f reorganization; (*Pol*) reshuffle

umbinden† vt sep put on

umblättern v sep □ vt turn [over] □ vi (*haben*) turn the page

umblicken (sich) vr sep look round; (*zurück*) look back

umbringen† vt sep kill; sich u~ kill oneself

Umbruch m (*fig*) radical change

umbuchen v sep □ vt change; (*Comm*) transfer □ vi (*haben*) change one's booking

umdrehen v sep □ vt turn round/(*wenden*) over; turn (*Schlüssel*);

(*umkrempeln*) turn inside out; sich u~ turn round; (*im Liegen*) turn over □ vi (*haben/sein*) turn back

Umdrehung f turn; (*Motor-*) revolution

umeinander adv around each other; sich u~ sorgen worry about each other

umfahren†[^1] vt sep run over

umfahren†[^2] vt insep go round; bypass (*Ort*)

umfallen† vi sep (*sein*) fall over; (*Person:*) fall down

Umfang m girth; (*Geom*) circumference; (*Größe*) size; (*Ausmaß*) extent; (*Mus*) range

umfangen† vt insep embrace; (*fig*) envelop

umfangreich a extensive; (*dick*) big

umfassen vt insep consist of, comprise; (*umgeben*) surround. u~d a comprehensive

Umfrage f survey, poll

umfüllen vt sep transfer

umfunktionieren vt sep convert

Umgang m [social] contact; (*Umgehen*) dealing (mit with); U~ haben mit associate with

umgänglich a sociable

Umgangs|formen fpl manners. U~sprache f colloquial language. u~sprachlich a colloquial, adv -ly

umgeb|en† vt/i insep (*haben*) surround □ a u~en von surrounded by. U~ung f -,-en surroundings pl

umgehen†[^1] vi sep (*sein*) go round; u~ mit treat, handle; (*verkehren*) associate with; in dem Schloss geht ein Gespenst um the castle is haunted

umgehen†[^2] vt insep avoid; (*nicht beachten*) evade; (*Straße:*) bypass

umgehend a immediate, adv -ly

Umgehungsstraße f bypass

umgekehrt a inverse; (*Reihenfolge*) reverse; es war u~ it was the other way round □ adv conversely; und u~ and vice versa

umgraben† vt sep dig [over]

umhaben† vt sep have on

Umhang m cloak

umhauen† vt sep knock down; (*fällen*) chop down

umher adv weit u~ all around. u~gehen† vi sep (*sein*) walk about

umhören (sich) vr sep ask around

Umkehr f - turning back. u~en v sep □ vi (*sein*) turn back □ vt turn round; turn inside out (*Tasche*); (*fig*) reverse. U~ung f - reversal

umkippen *v sep* ⊔ *vt* tip over; (*versehentlich*) knock over ⊡ *vi* (*sein*) fall over; ⟨*Boot:*⟩ capsize; (*fam: ohnmächtig werden*) faint

Umkleide|kabine *f* changing-cubicle. **u~n (sich)** *vr sep* change. **U~raum** *m* changing-room

umknicken *v sep* ⊔ *vt* bend; (*falten*) fold ⊡ *vi* (*sein*) bend; (*mit dem Fuß*) go over on one's ankle

umkommen† *vi sep* (*sein*) perish; **u~ lassen** waste (*Lebensmittel*)

Umkreis *m* surroundings *pl;* 1m **U~** von within a radius of

umkreisen *vt insep* circle; (*Astr*) revolve around; ⟨*Satellit:*⟩ orbit

umkrempeln *vt sep* turn up; (*von innen nach außen*) turn inside out; (*ändern*) change radically

Umlauf *m* circulation; (*Astr*) revolution. **U~bahn** *f* orbit

Umlaut *m* umlaut

umlegen *vt sep* lay *or* put down; flatten ⟨*Getreide*⟩; turn down ⟨*Kragen*⟩; put on ⟨*Schal*⟩; throw ⟨*Hebel*⟩; (*verlegen*) transfer; (*fam: niederschlagen*) knock down; (*töten*) kill

umleit|en *vt sep* divert. **U~ung** *f* diversion

umliegend *a* surrounding

umpflanzen *vt sep* transplant

umrahmen *vt insep* frame

umranden *vt insep* edge

umräumen *vt sep* rearrange

umrechn|en *vt sep* convert. **U~ung** *f* conversion

umreißen†[1] *vt sep* tear down; knock down ⟨*Person*⟩

umreißen†[2] *vt insep* outline

umringen *vt insep* surround

Umriss (Umriß) *m* outline

umrühren *vt/i sep* (*haben*) stir

ums *pron* = um das; **u~ Leben kommen** lose one's life

Umsatz *m* (*Comm*) turnover

umschalten *vt/i sep* (*haben*) switch over; **auf Rot u~** ⟨*Ampel:*⟩ change to red

Umschau *f* **U~** halten look out for. **u~en (sich)** *vr sep* look round/⟨*zurück*⟩ back

Umschlag *m* cover; (*Schutz-*) jacket; (*Brief-*) envelope; (*Med*) compress; (*Hosen-*) turn-up; (*Wechsel*) change. **u~en†** *v sep* ⊔ *vt* turn up; turn over ⟨*Seite*⟩; (*fällen*) chop down ⊡ *vi* (*sein*) topple over; ⟨*Boot:*⟩ capsize; ⟨*Wetter:*⟩ change; ⟨*Wind:*⟩ veer

umschließen† *vt insep* enclose

umschnallen *vt sep* buckle on

umschreiben†[1] *vt sep* rewrite

umschreib|en†[2] *vt insep* define; (*anders ausdrücken*) paraphrase. **U~ung** *f* definition; paraphrase

umschulen *vt sep* retrain; (*Sch*) transfer to another school

Umschweife *pl* **keine U~** machen come straight out with it; **ohne U~** straight out

Umschwung *m* (*fig*) change; (*Pol*) U-turn

umsehen† (sich) *vr sep* look round; (*zurück*) look back; **sich u~ nach** look for

umsein† *vi sep* (*sein*) (NEW) **um sein,** s. **um**

umseitig *a & adv* overleaf

umsetzen *vt sep* move; (*umpflanzen*) transplant; (*Comm*) sell

Umsicht *f* circumspection. **u~ig** *a* circumspect, *adv* -ly

umsied|eln *v sep* ⊡ *vt* resettle ⊡ *vi* (*sein*) move. **U~lung** *f* resettlement

umso *conj* **~ besser/mehr** all the better/more; **je mehr, ~ besser** the more the better

umsonst *adv* in vain; (*grundlos*) without reason; (*gratis*) free

umspringen† *vi sep* (*sein*) change; ⟨*Wind:*⟩ veer; **übel u~ mit** treat badly

Umstand *m* circumstance; (*Tatsache*) fact; (*Aufwand*) fuss; (*Mühe*) trouble; **unter U~en** possibly; **U~e machen** make a fuss; **jdm U~e machen** put s.o. to trouble; **in andern U~en** pregnant

umständlich *a* laborious, *adv* -ly; (*kompliziert*) involved; ⟨*Person*⟩ fussy

Umstands|kleid *nt* maternity dress. **U~wort** *nt* (*pl* -wörter) adverb

umstehen† *vi insep* surround

Umstehende *pl* bystanders

umsteigen† *vi sep* (*sein*) change

umstellen¹ *vt insep* surround

umstell|en² *vt sep* rearrange; transpose ⟨*Wörter*⟩; (*anders einstellen*) reset; (*Techn*) convert; (*ändern*) change; **sich u~en** adjust. **U~ung** *f* rearrangement; transposition; resetting; conversion; change; adjustment

umstimmen *vt sep* **jdn u~** change s.o.'s mind

umstoßen† *vt sep* knock over; (*fig*) overturn; upset ⟨*Plan*⟩

umstritten *a* controversial; (*ungeklärt*) disputed

umstülpen *vt sep* turn upside down; (*von innen nach außen*) turn inside out

Um|sturz *m* coup. **u~stürzen** *v sep* ⊡ *vt* overturn; (*Pol*) overthrow ⊡ *vi* (*sein*) fall over

umtaufen *vt sep* rename

Umtausch m exchange. u∼en vt sep change; exchange (gegen for)

umwälzend a revolutionary

umwandeln vt sep convert; (fig) transform

umwechseln vt sep change

Umweg m detour; auf U∼en (fig) in a roundabout way

Umwelt f environment. u∼freundlich a environmentally friendly. U∼schutz m protection of the environment. U∼schützer m environmentalist

umwenden† vt sep turn over; sich u∼ turn round

umwerfen† v sep knock over; (fig) upset ⟨Plan⟩; ⟨fam⟩ bowl over ⟨Person⟩

umziehen† v sep a vi (sein) move ⊓ vt change; sich u∼ change

umzingeln vt insep surround

Umzug m move; ⟨Prozession⟩ procession

unabänderlich a irrevocable; ⟨Tatsache⟩ unalterable

unabhängig a independent, adv -ly; u∼ davon, ob irrespective of whether. U∼keit f - independence

unabkömmlich pred a busy

unablässig a incessant, adv -ly

unabsehbar a incalculable

unabsichtlich a unintentional, adv -ly

unachtsam a careless, adv -ly. U∼keit f - carelessness

unangebracht a inappropriate

unangemeldet a unexpected, adv -ly

unangemessen a inappropriate, adv -ly

unangenehm a unpleasant, adv -ly; ⟨peinlich⟩ embarrassing

Unannehmlichkeiten fpl trouble sg

unansehnlich a shabby; ⟨Person⟩ plain

unanständig a indecent, adv -ly

unantastbar a inviolable

unappetitlich a unappetizing

Unart f -,-en bad habit. u∼ig a naughty

unauffällig a inconspicuous, adv -ly, unobtrusive, adv -ly

unauffindbar a u∼ sein be nowhere to be found

unaufgefordert adv without being asked

unaufhaltsam a inexorable, adv -bly. u∼hörlich a incessant, adv -ly

unaufmerksam a inattentive

unaufrichtig a insincere

unausbleiblich a inevitable

unausgeglichen a unbalanced; ⟨Person⟩ unstable

unauslöschlich a (fig) indelible, adv -bly. u∼sprechlich a indescribable, adv -bly. u∼stehlich a insufferable

unbarmherzig a merciless, adv -ly

unbeabsichtigt a unintentional, adv -ly

unbedacht a rash, adv -ly

unbedenklich a harmless ⊓ adv without hesitation

unbedeutend a insignificant; ⟨geringfügig⟩ slight, adv -ly

unbedingt a absolute, adv -ly; nicht u∼ not necessarily

unbefangen a natural, adv -ly; ⟨unparteiisch⟩ impartial

unbefriedig|end a unsatisfactory. u∼t a dissatisfied

unbefugt a unauthorized ⊓ adv without authorization

unbegreiflich a incomprehensible

unbegrenzt a unlimited ⊓ adv indefinitely

unbegründet a unfounded

Unbehag|en nt unease; ⟨körperlich⟩ discomfort. u∼lich a uncomfortable, adv -bly

unbeholfen a awkward, adv -ly

unbekannt a unknown; ⟨nicht vertraut⟩ unfamiliar. U∼e(r) m/f stranger

unbekümmert a unconcerned; ⟨unbeschwert⟩ carefree

unbeliebt a unpopular. U∼heit f unpopularity

unbemannt a unmanned

unbemerkt a & adv unnoticed

unbenutzt a unused

unbequem a uncomfortable, adv -bly; ⟨lästig⟩ awkward

unberechenbar a unpredictable

unberechtigt a unjustified; ⟨unbefugt⟩ unauthorized

unberufen int touch wood!

unberührt a untouched; (fig) virgin; ⟨Landschaft⟩ unspoilt

unbescheiden a presumptuous

unbeschrankt a unguarded

unbeschränkt a unlimited ⊓ adv without limit

unbeschreiblich a indescribable, adv -bly

unbeschwert a carefree

unbesiegbar a invincible

unbesiegt a undefeated

unbesonnen a rash, adv -ly

unbespielt a blank

unbeständig a inconsistent; ⟨Wetter⟩ unsettled

unbestechlich a incorruptible

unbestimmt a indefinite; ⟨Alter⟩ indeterminate; ⟨ungewiss⟩ uncertain; ⟨unklar⟩ vague ⊓ adv vaguely

unbestreitbar *a* indisputable, *adv* -bly

unbestritten *a* undisputed □ *adv* indisputably

unbeteiligt *a* indifferent; u~ an (+ *dat*) not involved in

unbetont *a* unstressed

unbewacht *a* unguarded

unbewaffnet *a* unarmed

unbeweglich *a* & *adv* motionless, still

unbewohnt *a* uninhabited

unbewusst (unbewußt) *a* unconscious, *adv* -ly

unbezahlbar *a* priceless

unbezahlt *a* unpaid

unbrauchbar *a* useless

und *conj* and; und so weiter and so on; nach und nach bit by bit

Undank *m* ingratitude. u~bar *a* ungrateful; (*nicht lohnend*) thankless. U~barkeit *f* ingratitude

undefinierbar *a* indefinable

undenk|bar *a* unthinkable. u~lich *a* seit u~lichen Zeiten from time immemorial

undeutlich *a* indistinct, *adv* -ly; (*vage*) vague, *adv* -ly

undicht *a* leaking; u~e Stelle leak

Unding *nt* absurdity

undiplomatisch *a* undiplomatic, *adv* -ally

unduldsam *a* intolerant

undurch|dringlich *a* impenetrable; (*Miene*) inscrutable. u~führbar *a* impracticable

undurch|lässig *a* impermeable. u~sichtig *a* opaque; (*fig*) doubtful

uneben *a* uneven, *adv* -ly. U~heit *f* -,-en unevenness; (*Buckel*) bump

unecht *a* false; u~er Schmuck/Pelz imitation jewellery/fur

unehelich *a* illegitimate

unehr|enhaft *a* dishonourable, *adv* -bly. u~lich *a* dishonest, *adv* -ly. U~lichkeit *f* dishonesty

uneinig *a* (*fig*) divided; [sich (*dat*)] u~ sein disagree. U~keit *f* disagreement; (*Streit*) discord

uneins *a* ~ sein be at odds

unempfindlich *a* insensitive (gegen to); (*widerstandsfähig*) tough, (*Med*) immune

unendlich *a* infinite, *adv* -ly; (*endlos*) endless, *adv* -ly. U~keit *f* - infinity

unentbehrlich *a* indispensable

unentgeltlich *a* free; (*Arbeit*) unpaid □ *adv* free of charge; (*arbeiten*) without pay

unentschieden *a* undecided; (*Sport*) drawn; u~ spielen draw. U~ *nt* -s,- draw

unentschlossen *a* indecisive; (*unentschieden*) undecided. U~heit *f* indecision

unentwegt *a* persistent *adv* -ly; (*unaufhörlich*) incessant, *adv* -ly

unerbittlich *a* implacable, *adv* -bly; (*Schicksal*) inexorable

unerfahren *a* inexperienced. U~heit *f* - inexperience

unerfreulich *a* unpleasant, *adv* -ly

unergründlich *a* unfathomable

unerhört *a* enormous, *adv* -ly; (*empörend*) outrageous, *adv* -ly

unerklärlich *a* inexplicable

unerlässlich (unerläßlich) *a* essential

unerlaubt *a* unauthorized □ *adv* without permission

unermesslich (unermeßlich) *a* immense, *adv* -ly

unermüdlich *a* tireless, *adv* -ly

unersättlich *a* insatiable

unerschöpflich *a* inexhaustible

unerschütterlich *a* unshakeable

unerschwinglich *a* prohibitive

unersetzlich *a* irreplaceable; (*Verlust*) irreparable

unerträglich *a* unbearable, *adv* -bly

unerwartet *a* unexpected, *adv* -ly

unerwünscht *a* unwanted; (*Besuch*) unwelcome

unfähig *a* incompetent; u~, etw zu tun incapable of doing sth; (*nicht in der Lage*) unable to do sth. U~keit *f* incompetence; inability (zu to)

unfair *a* unfair, *adv* -ly

Unfall *m* accident. U~flucht *f* failure to stop after an accident. U~station *f* casualty department

unfassbar (unfaßbar) *a* incomprehensible; (*unglaublich*) unimaginable

unfehlbar *a* infallible. U~keit *f* - infallibility

unfolgsam *a* disobedient

unförmig *a* shapeless

unfreiwillig *a* involuntary, *adv* -ily; (*unbeabsichtigt*) unintentional, *adv* -ly

unfreundlich *a* unfriendly; (*unangenehm*) unpleasant, *adv* -ly. U~keit *f* unfriendliness; unpleasantness

Unfriede[n] *m* discord

unfruchtbar *a* infertile; (*fig*) unproductive. U~keit *f* infertility

Unfug *-s* mischief; (*Unsinn*) nonsense

Ungar|(in) *m* -n,-n (*f* -,-nen) Hungarian. u~isch *a* Hungarian. U~n *nt* -s Hungary

ungastlich *a* inhospitable

ungeachtet *prep* (+ *gen*) in spite of; dessen u~ notwithstanding [this]. ungebärdig *a* unruly. ungebeugt *a* (*Gram*) uninflected. ungebraucht *a* unused. ungebührlich *a* improper, *adv* -ly. ungedeckt *a* uncovered; (*Sport*) unmarked; ⟨*Tisch*⟩ unlaid

Ungeduld *f* impatience. u~ig *a* impatient, *adv* -ly

ungeeignet *a* unsuitable

ungefähr *a* approximate, *adv* -ly, rough, *adv* -ly

ungefährlich *a* harmless

ungehalten *a* angry, *adv* -ily

ungeheuer *a* enormous, *adv* -ly. U~ *nt* -s,- monster

ungeheuerlich *a* outrageous

ungehobelt *a* uncouth

ungehörig *a* improper, *adv* -ly; ⟨*frech*⟩ impertinent, *adv* -ly

ungehorsam *a* disobedient. U~ *m* disobedience

ungeklärt *a* unsolved; ⟨*Frage*⟩ unsettled; ⟨*Ursache*⟩ unknown

ungeladen *a* unloaded; ⟨*Gast*⟩ uninvited

ungelegen *a* inconvenient. U~heiten *fpl* trouble *sg*

ungelernt *a* unskilled. ungemein *a* tremendous, *adv* -ly

ungemütlich *a* uncomfortable, *adv* -bly; ⟨*unangenehm*⟩ unpleasant, *adv* -ly

ungenau *a* inaccurate, *adv* -ly; ⟨*vage*⟩ vague, *adv* -ly. U~igkeit *f* -,-en inaccuracy

ungeniert /'ʊnʒeːniːɐ̯t/ *a* uninhibited □ *adv* openly

ungenießbar *a* inedible; ⟨*Getränk*⟩ undrinkable. ungenügend *a* inadequate, *adv* -ly; (*Sch*) unsatisfactory. ungepflegt *a* neglected; ⟨*Person*⟩ unkempt. ungerade *a* ⟨*Zahl*⟩ odd

ungerecht *a* unjust, *adv* -ly. U~igkeit *f* -,-en injustice

ungern *adv* reluctantly

ungesalzen *a* unsalted

ungeschehen *a* u~ machen undo

Ungeschick|lichkeit *f* clumsiness. u~t *a* clumsy, *adv* -ily

ungeschminkt *a* without make-up: ⟨*Wahrheit*⟩ unvarnished. ungeschrieben *a* unwritten. ungesehen *a & adv* unseen. ungesellig *a* unsociable. ungesetzlich *a* illegal, *adv* -ly. ungestört *a* undisturbed. ungestraft *adv* with impunity. ungestüm *a* impetuous, *adv* -ly. ungesund *a* unhealthy. ungesüßt *a* unsweetened. ungetrübt *a* perfect

Ungetüm *nt* -s,-e monster

ungewiss (ungewiß) *a* uncertain; im Ungewissen (ungewissen) sein/lassen be/leave in the dark. U~heit *f* uncertainty

ungewöhnlich *a* unusual, *adv* -ly. ungewohnt *a* unaccustomed; (*nicht vertraut*) unfamiliar. ungewollt *a* unintentional, *adv* -ly; ⟨*Schwangerschaft*⟩ unwanted

Ungeziefer *nt* -s vermin

ungezogen *a* naughty, *adv* -ly

ungezwungen *a* informal, *adv* -ly; (*natürlich*) natural, *adv* -ly

ungläubig *a* incredulous

unglaublich *a* incredible, *adv* -bly, unbelievable, *adv* -bly

ungleich *a* unequal, *adv* -ly; (*verschieden*) different. U~heit *f* - inequality. u~mäßig *a* uneven, *adv* -ly

Unglück *nt* -s,-e misfortune; (*Pech*) bad luck; (*Missgeschick*) mishap; (*Unfall*) accident; U~ bringen be unlucky. u~lich *a* unhappy, *adv* -ily; (*ungünstig*) unfortunate, *adv* -ly. u~licherweise *adv* unfortunately. u~selig *a* unfortunate. U~sfall *m* accident

ungültig *a* invalid; (*Jur*) void

ungünstig *a* unfavourable, *adv* -bly; (*unpassend*) inconvenient, *adv* -ly

ungut *a* ⟨*Gefühl*⟩ uneasy; nichts für u~! no offence!

unhandlich *a* unwieldy

Unheil *nt* -s disaster; U~ anrichten cause havoc

unheilbar *a* incurable, *adv* -bly

unheimlich *a* eerie; (*gruselig*) creepy; (*fam: groß*) terrific □ *adv* eerily; (*fam: sehr*) terribly

unhöflich *a* rude, *adv* -ly. U~keit *f* rudeness

unhörbar *a* inaudible, *adv* -bly

unhygienisch *a* unhygienic

Uni *f* -,-s (*fam*) university

uni /y'niː/ *inv a* plain

Uniform *f* -,-en uniform

uninteress|ant *a* uninteresting. u~iert *a* uninterested; (*unbeteiligt*) disinterested

Union *f* -,-en union

universal *a* universal

universell *a* universal, *adv* -ly

Universität *f* -,-en university

Universum *nt* -s universe

unkennt|lich *a* unrecognizable. U~nis *f* ignorance

unklar *a* unclear; (*ungewiss*) uncertain; (*vage*) vague, *adv* -ly; im U~en (u~en) sein/lassen be/leave in the dark. U~heit *f* -,-en uncertainty

unklug *a* unwise, *adv* -ly

unkompliziert *a* uncomplicated

Unkosten *pl* expenses

Unkraut *nt* weed; *(coll)* weeds *pl*; U~
jäten weed. U~vertilgungsmittel *nt*
weed-killer

unkultiviert *a* uncultured

unlängst *adv* recently

unlauter *a* dishonest; *(unfair)* unfair

unleserlich *a* illegible, *adv* -bly

unleugbar *a* undeniable, *adv* -bly

unlogisch *a* illogical, *adv* -ly

unlös|bar *a* *(fig)* insoluble. u~lich *a*
(Chem) insoluble

unlustig *a* listless, *adv* -ly

unmäßig *a* excessive, *adv* -ly; *(äußerst)*
extreme, *adv* -ly

Unmenge *f* enormous amount/*(Anzahl)*
number

Unmensch *m* *(fam)* brute. u~lich *a* in-
human; *(entsetzlich)* appalling, *adv* -ly

unmerklich *a* imperceptible, *adv* -bly

unmissverständlich (unmißver-
ständlich) *a* unambiguous, *adv* -ly; *(offen)*
unequivocal, *adv* -ly

unmittelbar *a* immediate, *adv* -ly; *(direkt)* direct, *adv* -ly

unmöbliert *a* unfurnished

unmodern *a* old-fashioned

unmöglich *a* impossible, *adv* -bly. U~
keit *f* - impossibility

Unmoral *f* immorality. u~isch *a* immoral, *adv* -ly

unmündig *a* under-age

Unmut *m* displeasure

unnachahmlich *a* inimitable

unnachgiebig *a* intransigent

unnatürlich *a* unnatural, *adv* -ly

unnormal *a* abnormal, *adv* -ly

unnötig *a* unnecessary, *adv* -ily

unnütz *a* useless □ *adv* needlessly

unord|entlich *a* untidy, *adv* -ily; *(nach-
lässig)* sloppy, *adv* -ily. U~nung *f* dis-
order; *(Durcheinander)* muddle

unorganisiert *a* disorganized

unorthodox *a* unorthodox □ *adv* in an
unorthodox manner

unparteiisch *a* impartial, *adv* -ly

unpassend *a* inappropriate, *adv* -ly; *(Moment)* inopportune

unpässlich (unpäßlich) *a* indisposed

unpersönlich *a* impersonal

unpraktisch *a* impractical

unpünktlich *a* unpunctual □ *adv* late

unrasiert *a* unshaven

Unrast *f* restlessness

unrealistisch *a* unrealistic, *adv* -ally

unrecht *a* wrong, *adv* -ly □ *n* jdm u~ tun
do s.o. an injustice; u~ haben/ge-
ben ⟨NEW⟩ U~ haben/geben, *s.* Unrecht.
U~ *nt* wrong; zu U~ wrongly; U~ haben
be wrong; jdm U~ geben disagree with
s.o. u~mäßig *a* unlawful, *adv* -ly

unregelmäßig *a* irregular, *adv* -ly. U~
keit *f* irregularity

unreif *a* unripe; *(fig)* immature

unrein *a* impure; *(Luft)* polluted; *(Haut)*
bad; ins U~e (u~e) schreiben make a
rough draft of

unrentabel *a* unprofitable, *adv* -bly

unrichtig *a* incorrect

Unruh|e *f* -,-n restlessness; *(Erregung)*
agitation; *(Besorgnis)* anxiety; U~en
(Pol) unrest *sg.* u~ig *a* restless, *adv* -ly;
(Meer) agitated; *(laut)* noisy, *adv* -ily; *(besorgt)* anxious, *adv* -ly

uns *pron* *(acc/dat of* wir) us; *(refl)* ourselves; *(einander)* each other; ein Freund
von uns a friend of ours

unsagbar, unsäglich *a* indescribable,
adv -bly

unsanft *a* rough, *adv* -ly

unsauber *a* dirty; *(nachlässig)* sloppy, *adv*
-ily; *(unlauter)* dishonest, *adv* -ly

unschädlich *a* harmless

unscharf *a* blurred

unschätzbar *a* inestimable

unscheinbar *a* inconspicuous

unschicklich *a* improper, *adv* -ly

unschlagbar *a* unbeatable

unschlüssig *a* undecided

Unschuld *f* - innocence; *(Jungfräulich-
keit)* virginity. u~ig *a* innocent, *adv* -ly

unselbstständig, unselbständig *a* dependent □ *adv* u~ denken not think for
oneself

unser *poss pron* our. u~e(r,s) *poss pron*
ours. u~erseits *adv* for our part.
u~twegen *adv* for our sake; *(wegen uns)*
because of us, on our account. u~twillen
adv um u~twillen for our sake

unsicher *a* unsafe; *(ungewiss)* uncertain;
(nicht zuverlässig) unreliable; *(Schritte,
Hand)* unsteady; *(Person)* insecure □ *adv*
unsteadily. U~heit *f* uncertainty; unreli-
ability; insecurity

unsichtbar *a* invisible

Unsinn *m* nonsense. u~ig *a* nonsensical,
absurd

Unsitt|e *f* bad habit. u~lich *a* indecent,
adv -ly

unsportlich *a* not sporty; *(unfair)* un-
sporting, *adv* -ly

uns|re(r,s) *poss pron* = unsere(r,s). u~
rige *poss pron* der/die/das u~rige ours

unsterblich *a* immortal. U∼keit *f* immortality

unstet *a* restless, *adv* -ly; *(unbeständig)* unstable

Unstimmigkeit *f* -,-en inconsistency; *(Streit)* difference

Unsumme *f* vast sum

unsymmetrisch *a* not symmetrical

unsympathisch *a* unpleasant; er ist mir u∼ I don't like him

untätig *a* idle, *adv* idly. U∼keit *f* - idleness

untauglich *a* unsuitable; *(Mil)* unfit

unteilbar *a* indivisible

unten *adv* at the bottom; *(auf der Unterseite)* underneath; *(eine Treppe tiefer)* downstairs; *(im Text)* below; **hier/da** u∼ down here/there; **nach** u∼ down[wards]; *(die Treppe hinunter)* downstairs; **siehe** u∼ see below

unter *prep* (+ *dat/acc*) under; *(niedriger als)* below; *(inmitten, zwischen)* among; u∼anderem among other things; u∼der Woche during the week; u∼sich by themselves; u∼uns gesagt between ourselves

Unter|arm *m* forearm. U∼bewusstsein (U∼bewußtsein) *nt* subconscious

unterbieten† *vt insep* undercut; beat ⟨Rekord⟩

unterbinden† *vt insep* stop

unterbleiben† *vi insep (sein)* cease; es hat zu u∼ it must stop

unterbrech|en† *vt insep* interrupt; break ⟨Reise⟩. U∼ung *f* -,-en interruption; break

unterbreiten *vt insep* present

unterbringen† *vt sep* put; *(beherbergen)* put up

unterdessen *adv* in the meantime

unterdrück|en *vt insep* suppress; oppress ⟨Volk⟩. U∼ung *f* - suppression; oppression

untere(r,s) *a* lower

untereinander *adv* one below the other; *(miteinander)* among ourselves/yourselves/themselves

unterernähr|t *a* undernourished. U∼ung *f* malnutrition

Unterfangen *nt* -s,- venture

Unterführung *f* underpass; *(Fußgänger-)* subway

Untergang *m (Astr)* setting; *(Naut)* sinking; *(Zugrundegehen)* disappearance; *(der Welt)* end

Untergebene(r) *m/f* subordinate

untergehen† *vi sep (sein) (Astr)* set; *(versinken)* go under; ⟨Schiff:⟩ go down, sink; *(zugrunde gehen)* disappear; ⟨Welt:⟩ come to an end

untergeordnet *a* subordinate

Untergeschoss (Untergeschoß) *nt* basement

untergraben† *vt insep (fig)* undermine

Untergrund *m* foundation; *(Hintergrund)* background; *(Pol)* underground. U∼bahn *f* underground [railway]; *(Amer)* subway

unterhaken *vt sep* jdn u∼ take s.o.'s arm; untergehakt arm in arm

unterhalb *adv & prep* (+ *gen*) below

Unterhalt *m* maintenance

unterhalt|en† *vt insep* maintain; *(ernähren)* support; *(betreiben)* run; *(erheitern)* entertain; sich u∼en talk; *(sich vergnügen)* enjoy oneself. u∼sam *a* entertaining. U∼ung *f* -,-en maintenance; *(Gespräch)* conversation; *(Zeitvertreib)* entertainment

unterhandeln *vi insep (haben)* negotiate

Unter|haus *nt (Pol)* lower house; *(in UK)* House of Commons. U∼hemd *nt* vest. U∼holz *nt* undergrowth. U∼hose *f* underpants *pl.* u∼irdisch *a & adv* underground

unterjochen *vt insep* subjugate

Unterkiefer *m* lower jaw

unter|kommen† *vi sep (sein)* find accommodation; *(eine Stellung finden)* get a job. u∼kriegen *vt sep (fam)* get down

Unterkunft *f* -,-künfte accommodation

Unterlage *f* pad; U∼n papers

Unterlass (Unterlaß) *m* ohne U∼ incessantly

unterlass|en† *vt insep* etw u∼en refrain from [doing] sth; es u∼en, etw zu tun fail or omit to do sth. U∼ung *f* -,-en omission

unterlaufen† *vi insep (sein)* occur; mir ist ein Fehler u∼ I made a mistake

unterlegen[1] *vt sep* put underneath

unterlegen[2] *a* inferior; *(Sport)* losing; zahlenmäßig u∼ out-numbered *(dat* by). U∼e(r) *m/f* loser

Unterleib *m* abdomen

unterliegen† *vi insep (sein)* lose *(dat* to); *(unterworfen sein)* be subject *(dat* to)

Unterlippe *f* lower lip

unterm *prep* = unter dem

Untermiete *f* zur U∼ wohnen be a lodger. U∼r(in) *m(f)* lodger

unterminieren *vt insep* undermine

untern *prep* = unter den

unternehm|en† *vt insep* undertake; take ⟨Schritte⟩; etw/nichts u∼en do sth/nothing. U∼en *nt* -s,- undertaking, enterprise; *(Betrieb)* concern. u∼end *a* enterprising. U∼er *m* -s,- employer; *(Bau-)* contractor; *(Industrieller)* industrialist. U∼ung *f* -,-en undertaking; *(Comm)* venture. u~ungslustig *a* enterprising; (*abenteuerlustig*) adventurous

Unteroffizier *m* non-commissioned officer

unterordnen *vt sep* subordinate; sich u~ accept a subordinate role

Unterredung *f* -,-en talk

Unterricht *m* -[e]s teaching; (*Privat-*) tuition; (*U~sstunden*) lessons *pl*; U~ geben/nehmen give/have lessons

unterrichten *vt/i insep* (*haben*) teach; (*informieren*) inform; sich u~ inform oneself

Unterrock *m* slip

unters *prep* = unter das

untersagen *vt insep* forbid

Untersatz *m* mat; (*mit Füßen*) stand; (*Gläser-*) coaster

unterschätzen *vt insep* underestimate

unterscheid|en† *vt/i insep* (*haben*) distinguish; (*auseinander halten*) tell apart; sich u~en differ. U~ung *f* -,-en distinction

Unterschied *m* -[e]s,-e difference; (*Unterscheidung*) distinction; im U~ zu ihm unlike him. u~lich *a* different; (*wechselnd*) varying; das ist u~lich it varies. u~slos *a* equal, *adv* -ly

unterschlag|en† *vt insep* embezzle; (*verheimlichen*) suppress. U~ung *f* -,-en embezzlement; suppression

Unterschlupf *m* -[e]s shelter; (*Versteck*) hiding-place

unterschreiben† *vt/i insep* (*haben*) sign

Unter|schrift *f* signature; (*Bild-*) caption. U~seeboot *nt* submarine. U~setzer *m* -s,- = Untersatz

untersetzt *a* stocky

Unterstand *m* shelter

unterste(r,s) *a* lowest, bottom

unterstehen†1 *vi sep* (*haben*) shelter

unterstehen†2 *v insep □ vi* (*haben*) be answerable (*dat* to); (*unterliegen*) be subject (*dat* to) □ *vr* sich u~ dare; untersteh dich! don't you dare!

unterstellen1 *vt sep* put underneath; (*abstellen*) store; sich u~ shelter

unterstellen2 *vt insep* place under the control (*of*); (*annehmen*) assume; (*fälschlich zuschreiben*) impute (*dat* to)

unterstreichen† *vt insep* underline

unterstütz|en *vt insep* support; (*helfen*) aid. U~ung *f* -,-en support; (*finanziell*) aid; (*regelmäßiger Betrag*) allowance; (*Arbeitslosen-*) benefit

untersuch|en *vt insep* examine; (*Jur*) investigate; (*prüfen*) test; (*überprüfen*) check; (*durchsuchen*) search. U~ung *f* -,-en examination; investigation; test;

check; search. U~ungshaft *f* detention on remand; in U~ungshaft on remand. U~ungsrichter *m* examining magistrate

Untertan *m* -s & -en, -en subject

Untertasse *f* saucer

untertauchen *v sep □ vt* duck □ *vi* (*sein*) go under; (*fig*) disappear

Unterteil *nt* bottom (part)

unterteilen *vt insep* subdivide; (*aufteilen*) divide

Untertitel *m* subtitle

Unterton *m* undertone

untervermieten *vt/i insep* (*haben*) sublet

unterwandern *vt insep* infiltrate

Unterwäsche *f* underwear

Unterwasser- *pref* underwater

unterwegs *adv* on the way; (*außer Haus*) out; (*verreist*) away

unterweisen† *vt insep* instruct

Unterwelt *f* underworld

unterwerfen† *vt insep* subjugate; sich u~ submit (*dat* to); etw (*dat*) unterworfen sein be subject to sth

unterwürfig *a* obsequious, *adv* -ly

unterzeichnen *vt insep* sign

unterziehen†1 *vt sep* put on underneath; (*Culin*) fold in

unterziehen†2 *vt insep* etw einer Untersuchung/Überprüfung u~ examine/check sth; sich einer Operation/Prüfung u~ have an operation/take a test

Untier *nt* monster

untragbar *a* intolerable

untrennbar *a* inseparable

untreu *a* disloyal; (*in der Ehe*) unfaithful. U~e *f* disloyalty; infidelity

untröstlich *a* inconsolable

untrüglich *a* infallible

Untugend *f* bad habit

unüberlegt *a* rash, *adv* -ly

unüber|sehbar *a* obvious; (*groß*) immense. u~troffen *a* unsurpassed

unum|gänglich *a* absolutely necessary. u~schränkt *a* absolute. u~wunden *adv* frankly

ununterbrochen *a* incessant, *adv* -ly

unveränderlich *a* invariable; (*gleich bleibend*) unchanging

unverändert *a* unchanged

unverantwortlich *a* irresponsible, *adv* bly

unverbesserlich *a* incorrigible

unverbindlich *a* non-committal; (*Comm*) not binding □ *adv* without obligation

unverblümt *a* blunt, *adv* -ly

unverdaulich *a* indigestible

unver|einbar *a* incompatible. **u~gesslich** (u~geßlich) *a* unforgettable. **u~gleichlich** *a* incomparable

unver|hältnismäßig *adv* disproportionately. **u~heiratet** *a* unmarried. **u~hofft** *a* unexpected, *adv* -ly. **u~hohlen** *a* undisguised □ *adv* openly. **u~käuflich** *a* not for sale; ⟨*Muster*⟩ free

unverkennbar *a* unmistakable, *adv* -bly

unverletzt *a* unhurt

unvermeidlich *a* inevitable

unver|mindert *a* & *adv* undiminished. **u~mittelt** *a* abrupt, *adv* -ly. **u~mutet** *a* unexpected, *adv* -ly

Unver|nunft *f* folly. **u~nünftig** *a* foolish, *adv* -ly

unverschämt *a* insolent, *adv* -ly; ⟨*fam: ungeheuer*⟩ outrageous, *adv* -ly. **U~heit** *f* -,-en insolence

unver|sehens *adv* suddenly. **u~sehrt** *a* unhurt; ⟨*unbeschädigt*⟩ intact. **u~söhnlich** *a* irreconcilable; ⟨*Gegner*⟩ implacable

unverständ|lich *a* incomprehensible; ⟨*undeutlich*⟩ indistinct. **U~nis** *nt* lack of understanding

unverträglich *a* incompatible; ⟨*Person*⟩ quarrelsome; ⟨*unbekömmlich*⟩ indigestible

unverwandt *a* fixed, *adv* -ly

unver|wundbar *a* invulnerable. **u~wüstlich** *a* indestructible; ⟨*Person, Humor*⟩ irrepressible; ⟨*Gesundheit*⟩ robust. **u~zeihlich** *a* unforgivable

unverzüglich *a* immediate, *adv* -ly

unvollendet *a* unfinished

unvollkommen *a* imperfect; ⟨*unvollständig*⟩ incomplete. **U~heit** *f* -,-en imperfection

unvollständig *a* incomplete

unvor|bereitet *a* unprepared. **u~eingenommen** *a* unbiased. **u~hergesehen** *a* unforeseen

unvorsichtig *a* careless, *adv* -ly. **U~keit** *f* - carelessness

unvorstellbar *a* unimaginable, *adv* -bly

unvorteilhaft *a* unfavourable; ⟨*nicht hübsch*⟩ unattractive; ⟨*Kleid, Frisur*⟩ unflattering

unwahr *a* untrue. **U~heit** *f* -,-en untruth. **u~scheinlich** *a* unlikely; ⟨*unglaublich*⟩ improbable; ⟨*fam: groß*⟩ incredible, *adv* -bly

unweigerlich *a* inevitable, *adv* -bly

unweit *adv* & *prep* (+ *gen*) not far; **u~ vom Fluss** *od* **des Flusses** not far from the river

unwesentlich *a* unimportant □ *adv* slightly

Unwetter *nt* -s,- storm

unwichtig *a* unimportant

unwider|legbar *a* irrefutable. **u~ruflich** *a* irrevocable, *adv* -bly. **u~stehlich** *a* irresistible

Unwill|e *m* displeasure. **u~ig** *a* angry, *adv* -ily; ⟨*widerwillig*⟩ reluctant, *adv* -ly. **u~kürlich** *a* involuntary, *adv* -ily; ⟨*instinktiv*⟩ instinctive, *adv* -ly

unwirklich *a* unreal

unwirksam *a* ineffective

unwirsch *a* irritable, *adv* -bly

unwirtlich *a* inhospitable

unwirtschaftlich *a* uneconomic, *adv* -ally

unwissen|d *a* ignorant. **U~heit** *f* - ignorance

unwohl *a* unwell; ⟨*unbehaglich*⟩ uneasy. **U~sein** *nt* -s indisposition

unwürdig *a* unworthy ⟨*gen* of⟩; ⟨*würdelos*⟩ undignified

Unzahl *f* vast number. **unzählig** *a* innumerable, countless

unzerbrechlich *a* unbreakable

unzerstörbar *a* indestructible

unzertrennlich *a* inseparable

Unzucht *f* sexual offence; gewerbsmäßige **U~** prostitution

unzüchtig *a* indecent, *adv* -ly; ⟨*Schriften*⟩ obscene

unzufrieden *a* dissatisfied; ⟨*innerlich*⟩ discontented. **U~heit** *f* dissatisfaction; (*Pol*) discontent

unzulänglich *a* inadequate, *adv* -ly

unzulässig *a* inadmissible

unzumutbar *a* unreasonable

unzurechnungsfähig *a* insane. **U~keit** *f* insanity

unzusammenhängend *a* incoherent

unzutreffend *a* inapplicable; ⟨*falsch*⟩ incorrect

unzuverlässig *a* unreliable

unzweckmäßig *a* unsuitable, *adv* -bly

unzweideutig *a* unambiguous

unzweifelhaft *a* undoubted, *adv* -ly

üppig *a* luxuriant, *adv* -ly; ⟨*überreichlich*⟩ lavish, *adv* -ly; ⟨*Busen, Figur*⟩ voluptuous

uralt *a* ancient

Uran *nt* -s uranium

Uraufführung *f* first performance

urbar *a* **u~ machen** cultivate

Ureinwohner *mpl* native inhabitants

Urenkel *m* great-grandson; ⟨*pl*⟩ great-grandchildren

Urgroß|mutter *f* great-grandmother. **U~vater** *m* great-grandfather

Urheber m -s,- originator; (*Verfasser*) author. U~recht nt copyright

Urin m -s,-e urine

Urkunde f -,-n certificate; (*Dokument*) document

Urlaub m -s holiday; (*Mil, Admin*) leave; auf U~ on holiday/leave; U~ haben be on holiday/leave. U~er(in) m -s,- (f -,-nen) holiday-maker. U~sort m holiday resort

Urne f -,-n urn; (*Wahl-*) ballot-box

Ursache f cause; (*Grund*) reason; keine U~! don't mention it!

Ursprung m origin

ursprünglich a original, adv -ly; (*anfänglich*) initial, adv -ly; (*natürlich*) natural

Urteil nt -s,-e judgement; (*Meinung*) opinion; (*U~sspruch*) verdict; (*Strafe*) sentence. u~en vi (haben) judge. U~svermögen nt [power of] judgement

Urwald m primeval forest; (*tropischer*) jungle

urwüchsig a natural; (*derb*) earthy

Urzeit f primeval times pl; seit U~en from time immemorial

USA pl USA sg

usw. abbr (und so weiter) etc.

Utensilien /-jən/ ntpl utensils

utopisch a Utopian

V

vage /'vaːgə/ a vague, adv -ly

Vakuum /'vaːkuʊm/ nt -s vacuum. v~verpackt a vacuum-packed

Vanille /va'nɪljə/ f - vanilla

variabel /va'rjaːbəl/ a variable. v~e f -,-n variant. V~ation /-'tsjoːn/ f -,-en variation. v~ieren vt/i (haben) vary

Vase /'vaːzə/ f -,-n vase

Vater m -s,- father. V~land nt fatherland

väterlich a paternal; (*fürsorglich*) fatherly. v~erseits adv on one's/the father's side

Vater|schaft f - fatherhood; (*Jur*) paternity. V~unser nt -s,- Lord's Prayer

Vati m -s,-s ⟨ⁿⁿⁿ⟩ daddy

v. Chr. abbr (vor Christus) BC

Vegetar|ier(in) /vege'taːrjɐ, -jərɪn/ m(f) -s,- (f -,-nen) vegetarian. v~isch a vegetarian

Vegetation /vegeta'tsjoːn/ f -,-en vegetation

Veilchen nt -s,-n violet

Vene /'veːnə/ f -,-n vein

Venedig /ve'neːdɪç/ nt -s Venice

Ventil /vɛn'tiːl/ nt -s,-e valve. V~ator m -s,-en /-'toːrən/ fan

verabred|en vt arrange; sich [mit jdm] v~en arrange to meet [s.o.]. V~ung f -,-en arrangement; (*Treffen*) appointment

verabreichen vt administer

verabscheuen vt detest, loathe

verabschieden vt say goodbye to; (*aus dem Dienst*) retire; pass (*Gesetz*); sich v~ say goodbye

verachten vt despise. v~swert a contemptible

verächtlich a contemptuous, adv -ly; (*unwürdig*) contemptible

Verachtung f - contempt

verallgemeiner|n vt/i (haben) generalize. V~ung f -,-en generalization

veralte|n vi (sein) become obsolete. v~t a obsolete

Veranda /ve'randa/ f -,-den veranda

veränder|lich a changeable; (*Math*) variable. v~n vt change; sich v~n change; (*beruflich*) change one's job. V~ung f change

verängstigt a frightened, scared

verankern vt anchor

veranlag|t a künstlerisch/musikalisch v~t sein have an artistic/a musical bent; praktisch v~t practically minded. V~ung f -,-en disposition; (*Neigung*) tendency; (*künstlerisch*) bent

veranlass|en vt (reg) arrange for; (*einleiten*) institute; jdn v~en prompt s.o. (zu to). V~ung f - reason; auf meine V~ung at my suggestion; (*Befehl*) on my orders

veranschaulichen vt illustrate

veranschlagen vt (reg) estimate

veranstalt|en vt organize; hold, give (*Party*); make (*Lärm*). V~er m -s,- organizer. V~ung f -,-en event

verantwort|en vt take responsibility for; sich v~en answer (für for). v~lich a responsible; v~lich machen hold responsible. V~ung f - responsibility. v~ungsbewusst (v~ungsbewußt) a responsible, adv -bly. v~ungslos a irresponsible, adv -bly. v~ungsvoll a responsible

verarbeiten vt use; (*Techn*) process; (*verdauen & fig*) digest; v~ zu make into

verärgern vt annoy

verarmt a impoverished

verästeln (sich) vr branch out

verausgaben (sich) vr spend all one's money; (*körperlich*) wear oneself out

veräußern vt sell

Verb /verp/ nt -s,-en verb. v~al /ver'ba:l/ a verbal, adv -ly

Verband m -[e]s,-e association; (Mil) unit; (Med) bandage; (Wund-) dressing. V~szeug nt first-aid kit

verbann|en vt exile; (fig) banish. V~ung f - exile

verbarrikadieren vt barricade

verbeißen† vt suppress; ich konnte mir kaum das Lachen v~ I could hardly keep a straight face

verbergen† vt hide; sich v~ hide

verbesser|n vt improve; (berichtigen) correct. V~ung f -,-en improvement; correction

verbeug|en (sich) vr bow. V~ung f bow

verbeulen vt dent

verbiegen† vt bend; sich v~ bend

verbieten† vt forbid; (Admin) prohibit, ban

verbillig|en vt reduce [in price]. v~t a reduced

verbinden† vt connect (mit to); (zusammenfügen) join; (verknüpfen) combine; (in Verbindung bringen) associate; (Med) bandage; dress (Wunde); sich v~ combine; (sich zusammentun) join together; jdm die Augen v~ blindfold s.o.; jdm verbunden sein (fig) be obliged to s.o.

verbindlich a friendly; (bindend) binding. V~keit f -,-en friendliness; V~keiten obligations; (Comm) liabilities

Verbindung f - connection; (Verknüpfung) combination; (Kontakt) contact; (Vereinigung) association; chemische V~ chemical compound; in V~ stehen/sich in V~ setzen be/get in touch

verbissen a grim, adv -ly; (zäh) dogged, adv -ly

verbitten† vt sich (dat) etw v~ not stand for sth

verbitter|n vt make bitter. v~t a bitter. V~ung f - bitterness

verblassen vi (sein) fade

verbläuen vt (fam) thrash

Verbleib m -s whereabouts pl. v~en† vi (sein) remain

verbleichen† vi (sein) fade

verbleit a (Benzin) leaded

verbleuen vt NEW verbläuen

verblüff|en vt amaze, astound. V~ung f - amazement

verblühen vi (sein) wither, fade

verbluten vi (sein) bleed to death

verborgen¹ a hidden

verborgen² vt lend

Verbot nt -[e]s,-e ban. v~en a forbidden; (Admin) prohibited; 'Rauchen v~en' 'no smoking'

Verbrauch m -[e]s consumption. v~en vt use; consume (Lebensmittel); (erschöpfen) use up, exhaust. V~er m -s,- consumer. v~t a worn; (Luft) stale

verbrechen† vt (fam) perpetrate. V~ nt -s,- crime

Verbrecher m -s,- criminal. v~isch a criminal

verbreit|en vt spread; sich v~en spread. v~ern vt widen; sich v~ern widen. v~et a widespread. V~ung f - spread; (Verbreiten) spreading

verbrenn|en vt/i (sein) burn; cremate (Leiche). V~ung f -,-en burning; cremation; (Wunde) burn

verbringen† vt spend

verbrühen vt scald

verbuchen vt enter; (fig) notch up (Erfolg)

verbünd|en (sich) vr form an alliance. V~ete(r) m/f ally

verbürgen vt guarantee; sich v~ für vouch for

verbüßen vt serve (Strafe)

Verdacht m -[e]s suspicion; in or im V~ haben suspect

verdächtig a suspicious, adv -ly. v~en vt suspect (gen of). V~te(r) m/f suspect

verdamm|en vt condemn; (Relig) damn. V~nis f - damnation. v~t a & adv (sl) damned; v~t! damn!

verdampfen vt/i (sein) evaporate

verdanken vt owe (dat to)

verdau|en vt digest. v~lich a digestible; schwer v~lich indigestible. V~ung f - digestion

Verdeck nt -[e]s,-e hood; (Oberdeck) top deck. v~en vt cover; (verbergen) hide, conceal

verdenken† vt das kann man ihm nicht v~ you can't blame him for it

verderb|en† vi (sein) spoil; (Lebensmittel:) go bad □ vt spoil; (zerstören) ruin; (moralisch) corrupt; ich habe mir den Magen verdorben I have an upset stomach. V~en nt -s ruin. v~lich a perishable; (schädlich) pernicious

verdeutlichen vt make clear

verdichten vt compress; sich v~ (Nebel:) thicken

verdien|en vt/i (haben) earn; (fig) deserve. V~er m -s,- wage-earner

Verdienst¹ m -[e]s earnings pl

Verdienst² nt -[e]s,-e merit

verdient a well-deserved; ⟨Person⟩ of outstanding merit. **v∼ermaßen** adv deservedly

verdoppeln vt double; ⟨fig⟩ redouble; **sich v∼** double

verdorben a spoilt, ruined; ⟨Magen⟩ upset; ⟨moralisch⟩ corrupt; ⟨verkommen⟩ depraved

verdorren vi (sein) wither

verdrängen vt force out; ⟨fig⟩ displace; ⟨psychisch⟩ repress

verdrehen vt twist; roll ⟨Augen⟩; ⟨fig⟩ distort. **v∼t** a ⟨fam⟩ crazy

verdreifachen vt treble, triple

verdreschen† vt ⟨fam⟩ thrash

verdrießlich a morose, adv -ly

verdrücken vt crumple; ⟨fam: essen⟩ polish off; **sich v∼** ⟨fam⟩ slip away

Verdruss m -es (Verdruß m -sses) annoyance

verdunk|eln vt darken; black out ⟨Zimmer⟩; **sich v∼eln** darken. **V∼[e]lung** f - black-out

verdünnen vt dilute; **sich v∼** taper off

verdunst|en vi (sein) evaporate. **V∼ung** f - evaporation

verdursten vi (sein) die of thirst

verdutzt a baffled

veredeln vt refine; ⟨Hort⟩ graft

verehr|en vt revere; ⟨Relig⟩ worship; ⟨bewundern⟩ admire; ⟨schenken⟩ give. **V∼er(in)** m -s,- (f -,-nen) admirer. **V∼ung** f - veneration; worship; admiration

vereidigen vt swear in

Verein m -s,-e society; ⟨Sport-⟩ club

vereinbar a compatible. **v∼en** vt arrange; **nicht zu v∼en** incompatible. **V∼ung** f -,-en agreement

vereinen vt unite; **sich v∼** unite

vereinfachen vt simplify

vereinheitlichen vt standardize

vereinig|en vt unite; merge ⟨Firmen⟩; wieder v∼en reunite; reunify ⟨Land⟩; **sich v∼en** unite; **V∼te Staaten [von Amerika]** United States sg [of America]. **V∼ung** f -,-en union; ⟨Organisation⟩ organization

vereinsamt a lonely

vereinzelt a isolated □ adv occasionally

vereist a frozen; ⟨Straße⟩ icy

vereiteln vt foil, thwart

vereitert a septic

verenden vi (sein) die

verengen vt restrict; **sich v∼** narrow; ⟨Pupille:⟩ contract

vererb|en vt leave (dat to); ⟨Biol & fig⟩ pass on (dat to). **V∼ung** f - heredity

verewigen vt immortalize; **sich v∼** ⟨fam⟩ leave one's mark

verfahren† vi (sein) proceed; **v∼ mit** deal with □ vr **sich v∼** lose one's way □ a muddled. **V∼** nt -s,- procedure; ⟨Techn⟩ process; ⟨Jur⟩ proceedings pl

Verfall m decay; ⟨eines Gebäudes⟩ dilapidation; ⟨körperlich & fig⟩ decline; ⟨Ablauf⟩ expiry. **v∼en†** vi (sein) decay; ⟨Person, Sitten:⟩ decline; ⟨ablaufen⟩ expire; **v∼en in** (+ acc) lapse into; **v∼en auf** (+ acc) hit on ⟨Idee⟩; jdm/etw v∼en sein be under the spell of s.o./sth; be addicted to ⟨Alkohol⟩

verfälschen vt falsify; adulterate ⟨Wein, Lebensmittel⟩

verfänglich a awkward

verfärben (sich) vr change colour; ⟨Stoff:⟩ discolour

verfass|en vt write; ⟨Jur⟩ draw up; ⟨entwerfen⟩ draft. **V∼er** m -s,- author. **V∼ung** f ⟨Pol⟩ constitution; ⟨Zustand⟩ state

verfaulen vi (sein) rot, decay

verfechten† vt advocate

verfehlen vt miss

verfeinde|n (sich) vr become enemies; **v∼t sein** be enemies

verfeinern vt refine; ⟨verbessern⟩ improve

verfilmen vt film

verfilzt a matted

verfliegen† vi (sein) evaporate; ⟨Zeit:⟩ fly

verflixt a ⟨fam⟩ awkward; ⟨verdammt⟩ blessed; **v∼!** damn!

verfluch|en vt curse. **v∼t** a & adv ⟨fam⟩ damned; **v∼t!** damn!

verflüchtigen (sich) vr evaporate

verflüssigen vt liquefy

verfolg|en vt pursue; ⟨folgen⟩ follow; ⟨bedrängen⟩ pester; ⟨Pol⟩ persecute; strafrechtlich v∼en prosecute. **V∼er** m -s,- pursuer. **V∼ung** f - pursuit; persecution

verfrachten vt ship

verfrüht a premature

verfügbar a available

verfüg|en vt order; ⟨Jur⟩ decree □ vi ⟨haben⟩ v∼en über (+ acc) have at one's disposal. **V∼ung** f -,-en order; ⟨Jur⟩ decree; jdm zur V∼ung stehen/stellen be/place at s.o.'s disposal

verführ|en vt seduce; ⟨verlocken⟩ tempt. **V∼er** m seducer. **v∼erisch** a seductive; tempting. **V∼ung** f seduction; temptation

vergammelt a rotten; ⟨Gebäude⟩ decayed; ⟨Person⟩ scruffy

vergangen a past; ⟨letzte⟩ last. **V∼heit** f - past; ⟨Gram⟩ past tense

vergänglich *a* transitory

vergas|en *vt* gas. V~er *m* -s,- carburettor

vergeb|en† *vt* award (an + *dat* to); (*weggeben*) give away; (*verzeihen*) forgive. v~ens *adv* in vain. v~lich *a* futile, vain □ *adv* in vain. V~ung *f* - forgiveness

vergehen† *vi* (*sein*) pass; v~ vor (+ *dat*) nearly die of; sich v~ violate (gegen etw sth); (*sexuell*) sexually assault (an jdm s.o.). V~ *nt* -s,- offence

vergelt|en† *vt* repay. V~ung *f* - retaliation; (*Rache*) revenge. V~ungsmaßnahme *f* reprisal

vergessen† *vt* forget; (*liegen lassen*) leave behind. V~heit *f* - oblivion; in V~heit geraten be forgotten

vergesslich (vergeßlich) *a* forgetful. V~keit *f* - forgetfulness

vergeuden *vt* waste, squander

vergewaltig|en *vt* rape. V~ung *f* -,-en rape

vergewissern (sich) *vr* make sure (*gen* of)

vergießen† *vt* spill; shed ⟨*Tränen, Blut*⟩

vergift|en *vt* poison. V~ung *f* -,-en poisoning

Vergissmeinnicht (Vergißmeinnicht) *nt* -[e]s,-[e] forget-me-not

vergittert *a* barred

verglasen *vt* glaze

Vergleich *m* -[e]s,-e comparison; (*Jur*) settlement. v~bar *a* comparable. v~en† *vt* compare (mit with/to). v~sweise *adv* comparatively

vergnüg|en (sich) *vr* enjoy oneself. V~en *nt* -s,- pleasure; (*Spaß*) fun; viel V~en! have a good time! v~lich *a* enjoyable. v~t *a* cheerful, *adv* -ly; (*zufrieden*) happy, *adv* -ily; (*vergnüglich*) enjoyable. V~ungen *fpl* entertainments

vergolden *vt* gild; (*plattieren*) gold-plate

vergönnen *vt* grant

vergöttern *vt* idolize

vergraben† *vt* bury

vergreifen† (sich) *vr* sich v~an (+ *dat*) assault; (*stehlen*) steal

vergriffen *a* out of print

vergrößer|n *vt* enlarge; ⟨*Linse:*⟩ magnify; (*vermehren*) increase; (*erweitern*) extend; expand ⟨*Geschäft*⟩; sich v~n grow bigger; ⟨*Firma:*⟩ expand; (*zunehmen*) increase. V~ung *f* -,-en magnification; increase; expansion; (*Phot*) enlargement. V~ungsglas *nt* magnifying glass

Vergünstigung *f* -,-en privilege

vergüt|en *vt* pay for; jdm etw v~en reimburse s.o. for sth. V~ung *f* -,-en remuneration; (*Erstattung*) reimbursement

verhaft|en *vt* arrest. V~ung *f* -,-en arrest

verhalten† (sich) *vr* behave; (*handeln*) act; (*beschaffen sein*) be; sich still v~ keep quiet. V~ *nt* -s behaviour, conduct

Verhältnis *nt* -ses,-se relationship; (*Liebes-*) affair; (*Math*) ratio; V~se circumstances; (*Bedingungen*) conditions; über seine V~se leben live beyond one's means. v~mäßig *adv* comparatively, relatively

verhand|eln *vt* discuss; (*Jur*) try □ *vi* (*haben*) negotiate; v~eln gegen (*Jur*) try. V~lung *f* (*Jur*) trial; V~lungen negotiations

verhängen *vt* cover; (*fig*) impose

Verhängnis *nt* -ses fate, doom. v~voll *a* fatal, disastrous

verharmlosen *vt* play down

verharren *vi* (*haben*) remain

verhärten *vt/i* (*sein*) harden; sich v~ harden

verhasst (verhaßt) *a* hated

verhätscheln *vt* spoil, pamper

verhauen† *vt* (*fam*) beat; make a mess of (*Prüfung*)

verheerend *a* devastating; (*fam*) terrible

verhehlen *vt* conceal

verheilen *vi* (*sein*) heal

verheimlichen *vt* keep secret

verheirat|en (sich) *vr* get married (mit to); sich wieder v~en remarry. v~et *a* married

verhelfen† *vi* (*haben*) jdm zu etw v~ help s.o. get sth

verherrlichen *vt* glorify

verhexen *vt* bewitch; es ist wie verhext (*fam*) there is a jinx on it

verhinder|n *vt* prevent; v~t sein be unable to come. V~ung *f* - prevention

verhöhnen *vt* deride

Verhör *nt* -s,-e interrogation; ins V~ nehmen interrogate. v~en *vt* interrogate; sich v~en mishear

verhüllen *vt* cover; (*fig*) disguise. v~d *a* euphemistic, *adv* -ally

verhungern *vi* (*sein*) starve

verhüt|en *vt* prevent. V~ung *f* - prevention. V~ungsmittel *nt* contraceptive

verhutzelt *a* wizened

verirren (sich) *vr* get lost

verjagen *vt* chase away

verjüngen *vt* rejuvenate; sich v~ taper

verkalkt *a* (*fam*) senile

verkalkulieren (sich) *vr* miscalculate

Verkauf *m* sale; zum V~ for sale. v~en *vt* sell; zu v~en for sale

Verkäufer(in) *m(f)* seller; (*im Geschäft*) shop assistant

Verkehr m -s traffic; (Kontakt) contact; (Geschlechts-) intercourse; aus dem V∼ ziehen take out of circulation. v∼en vi (haben) operate; (Bus, Zug·) run; (Umgang haben) associate, mix (mit with); (Gast sein) visit (bei jdm s.o.); frequent (in einem Lokal a restaurant); brieflich v∼en correspond ❑ vt ins Gegenteil v∼en turn round

Verkehrs|ampel f traffic lights pl. V∼büro nt = V∼verein. V∼funk m [radio] traffic information. V∼unfall m road accident. V∼verein m tourist office. V∼zeichen nt traffic sign

verkehrt a wrong, adv -ly; v∼ herum the wrong way round; (links) inside out

verkennen† vt misjudge

verklagen vt sue (auf + acc for)

verkleid|en vt disguise; (Techn) line; sich v∼en disguise oneself; (für Kostümfest) dress up. V∼ung f -,-en disguise; (Kostüm) fancy dress; (Techn) lining

verklein|ern vt reduce [in size]. V∼ung f - reduction. V∼ungsform f diminutive

verklemmt a jammed; (psychisch) inhibited

verkneifen† vt sich (dat) etw v∼ do without sth; (verbeißen) suppress sth

verknittern vt/i (sein) crumple

verknüpfen vt knot together; (verbinden) connect, link; (zugleich tun) combine

verkommen† vi (sein) be neglected; (sittlich) go to the bad; (verfallen) decay; (Haus·) fall into disrepair; (Gegend·) become run-down; (Lebensmittel·) go bad ❑ a neglected; (sittlich) depraved; (Haus) dilapidated; (Gegend) run-down

verkörper|n vt embody, personify. V∼ung f -,-en embodiment, personification

verkraften vt cope with

verkrampft a (fig) tense

verkriechen† (sich) vr hide

verkrümmt a crooked, bent

verkrüppelt a crippled; (Glied) deformed

verkühl|en (sich) vr catch a chill. V∼ung f -,-en chill

verkümmer|n vi (sein) waste/(Pflanze·) wither away. v∼t a stunted

verkünd|en vt announce; pronounce (Urteil). v∼igen vt announce; (predigen) preach

verkürzen vt shorten; (verringern) reduce; (abbrechen) cut short; while away (Zeit)

verladen† vt load

Verlag m -[e]s,-e publishing firm

verlangen vt ask for; (fordern) demand; (berechnen) charge; am Telefon verlangt werden be wanted on the telephone. V∼ nt -s desire; (Bitte) request; auf V∼ on demand

verlänger|n vt extend; lengthen (Kleid); (zeitlich) prolong; renew (Pass, Vertrag); (Culin) thin down. V∼ung f -,-en extension; renewal. V∼ungsschnur f extension cable

verlangsamen vt slow down

Verlass (Verlaß) m auf ihn ist kein V∼ you cannot rely on him

verlassen† vt leave; (im Stich lassen) desert; sich v∼ auf (+ acc) rely or depend on ❑ a deserted. V∼heit f - desolation

verlässlich (verläßlich) a reliable

Verlauf m course; im V∼ (+ gen) in the course of. v∼en† vi (sein) run; (ablaufen) go; (zerlaufen) melt; gut v∼en go [off] well ❑ vr sich v∼en lose one's way; (Menge·) disperse; (Wasser·) drain away

verleben vt spend

verlegen vt move; (verschieben) postpone; (vor-) bring forward; (verlieren) mislay; (versperren) block; (legen) lay (Teppich, Rohre); (veröffentlichen) publish; sich v∼ auf (+ acc) take up (Beruf, Fach); resort to (Taktik, Bitten) ❑ a embarrassed; nie v∼ um never at a loss for. V∼heit f - embarrassment

Verleger m -s,- publisher

verleihen† vt lend; (gegen Gebühr) hire out; (überreichen) award, confer; (fig) give

verleiten vt induce/(verlocken) tempt (zu to)

verlernen vt forget

verlesen†¹ vt read out; ich habe mich v∼ I misread it

verlesen†² vt sort out

verletz|en vt injure; (kränken) hurt; (verstoßen gegen) infringe; violate (Grenze). v∼end a hurtful, wounding. v∼lich a vulnerable. V∼te(r) m/f injured person; (bei Unfall) casualty. V∼ung f -,-en injury; (Verstoß) infringement; violation

verleugnen vt deny; disown (Freund)

verleumd|en vt slander; (schriftlich) libel. v∼erisch a slanderous; libellous. V∼ung f -,-en slander; (schriftlich) libel

verlieben (sich) vr fall in love (in + acc with); verliebt sein be in love (in + acc with)

verlier|en† vt lose; shed (Laub); sich v∼en disappear; (Weg·) peter out ❑ vi (haben) lose (an etw dat sth). V∼er m -s,- loser

verlob|en (sich) vr get engaged (mit to); v∼t sein be engaged. V∼te f fiancée. V∼te(r) m fiancé. V∼ung f -,-en engagement

verlock|en vt tempt; v~end tempting. V~ung f -,-en temptation

verlogen a lying

verloren a lost; v~e Eier poached eggs; v~ gehen get lost. v~gehen† vi sep (sein) (NEW) v~ gehen, s. verloren

verlos|en vt raffle. V~ung f -,-en raffle; (Ziehung) draw

verlottert a run-down; (Person) scruffy; (sittlich) dissolute

Verlust m -[e]s,-e loss

vermachen vt leave, bequeath

Vermächtnis nt -ses,-se legacy

vermähl|en (sich) vr marry. V~ung f -,-en marriage

vermehren vt increase; propagate (Pflanzen); sich v~ increase; (sich fortpflanzen) breed, multiply

vermeiden† vt avoid

vermeintlich a supposed, adv -ly

Vermerk m -[e]s,-e note. v~en vt note [down]; übel v~en take amiss

vermess|en† vt measure; survey (Gelände) □ a presumptuous. V~enheit f - presumption. V~ung f measurement; (Land-) survey

vermiet|en vt let, rent [out]; hire out (Boot, Auto); zu v~en to let; (Boot:) for hire. V~er m landlord. V~erin f landlady

verminder|n vt reduce, lessen. V~ung f - reduction, decrease

vermischen vt mix; sich v~ mix

vermissen vt miss

vermisst (vermißt) a missing. V~e(r) m missing person/(Mil) soldier

vermittel|n vi (haben) mediate □ vt arrange; (beschaffen) find; place (Arbeitskräfte); impart (Wissen); convey (Eindruck). v~s prep (+ gen) by means of

Vermittl|er m -s,- agent; (Schlichter) mediator. V~ung f -,-en arrangement; (Agentur) agency; (Teleph) exchange; (Schlichtung) mediation

vermögen† vt be able (zu to). V~ nt -s,- fortune. v~d a wealthy

vermut|en vt suspect; (glauben) presume. v~lich a probable □ adv presumably. V~ung f -,-en supposition; (Verdacht) suspicion; (Mutmaßung) conjecture

vernachlässig|en vt neglect. V~ung f - neglect

vernehm|en† vt hear; (verhören) question; (Jur) examine. V~ung f -,-en questioning

verneig|en (sich) vr bow. V~ung f -,-en bow

vernein|en vt answer in the negative; (ablehnen) reject. v~end a negative. V~ung f -,-en negative answer; (Gram) negative

vernicht|en vt destroy; (ausrotten) exterminate. v~end a devastating; (Niederlage) crushing. V~ung f - destruction; extermination

Vernunft f - reason; V~ annehmen see reason

vernünftig a reasonable, sensible; (fam: ordentlich) decent □ adv sensibly; (fam) properly

veröffentlich|en vt publish. V~ung f -,-en publication

verordn|en vt prescribe (dat for). V~ung f -,-en prescription; (Verfügung) decree

verpachten vt lease [out]

verpack|en vt pack; (einwickeln) wrap. V~ung f packaging; wrapping

verpassen vt miss; (fam: geben) give

verpfänden vt pawn

verpflanzen vt transplant

verpfleg|en vt feed; sich selbst v~en cater for oneself. V~ung f -board; (Essen) food; Unterkunft und V~ung board and lodging

verpflicht|en vt oblige; (einstellen) engage; (Sport) sign; sich v~en undertake/ (versprechen) promise (zu to); (vertraglich) sign a contract; jdm v~et sein be indebted to s.o. V~ung f -,-en obligation, commitment

verpfuschen vt make a mess of

verpönt a v~ sein be frowned upon

verprügeln vt beat up, thrash

Verputz m -es plaster. v~en vt plaster; (fam: essen) polish off

Verrat m -[e]s betrayal, treachery. v~en† vt betray; give away (Geheimnis); (fam: sagen) tell; sich v~en give oneself away

Verräter m -s,-traitor. v~isch a treacherous; (fig) revealing

verräuchert a smoky

verrech|nen vt settle; clear (Scheck); sich v~nen make a mistake; (fig) miscalculate. V~nungsscheck m crossed cheque

verregnet a spoilt by rain; (Tag) rainy, wet

verreisen vi (sein) go away; verreist sein be away

verreißen† vt (fam) pan, slate

verrenken vt dislocate; sich v~ contort oneself

verricht|en vt perform, do; say (Gebet). V~ung f -,-en task

verriegeln vt bolt

verringer|n vt reduce; sich v~n decrease. V~ung f - reduction; decrease

verrost|en vi (sein) rust. v~et a rusty

verrücken vt move

verrückt *a* crazy, mad; v~ werden/machen go/drive crazy. V~e(r) *m/f* lunatic. V~heit *f* -,-en madness; *(Torheit)* folly

Verruf *m* disrepute. v~en *a* disreputable

verrühren *vt* mix

verrunzelt *a* wrinkled

verrutschen *vt (sein)* slip

Vers /fɛrs/ *m* -es,-e verse

versag|en *vi (haben)* fail □ *vt* jdm/sich etw v~en deny s.o./oneself sth. V~en *nt* -s,- failure. V~er *m* -s,- failure

versalzen† *vt* put too much salt in/on; *(fig)* spoil

versamm|eln *vt* assemble; sich v~eln assemble, meet. V~lung *f* assembly, meeting

Versand *m* -[e]s dispatch. V~haus *nt* mail-order firm

versäum|en *vt* miss; lose *(Zeit)*; *(unterlassen)* neglect; [es] v~en, etw zu tun fail *or* neglect to do sth. V~nis *nt* -ses,-se omission

verschaffen *vt* get; sich *(dat)* v~ obtain; gain *(Respekt)*

verschämt *a* bashful, *adv* -ly

verschandeln *vt* spoil

verschärfen *vt* intensify; tighten *(Kontrolle)*; increase *(Tempo)*; aggravate *(Lage)*; sich v~ intensify; increase; *(Lage)* worsen

verschätzen *(sich) vr* sich v~ in (+ *dat)* misjudge

verschenken *vt* give away

verscheuchen *vt* shoo/*(jagen)* chase away

verschicken *vt* send; *(Comm)* dispatch

verschieb|en *vt* move; *(aufschieben)* put off, postpone; *(sl: handeln mit)* traffic in; sich v~en move, shift; *(verrutschen)* slip; *(zeitlich)* be postponed. V~ung *f* shift; postponement

verschieden *a* different; v~e *(pl)* different; *(mehrere)* various; *(dieses und jenes)* various things; die v~sten Farben a whole variety of colours; das ist v~ it varies □ *adv* differently; v~ groß/lang of different sizes/lengths. V~artig *a* diverse. V~heit *f* - difference; *(Vielfalt)* diversity. v~tlich *adv* several times

verschimmeln *vi (sein)* go mouldy. v~t *a* mouldy

verschlafen† *vi (haben)* oversleep □ *vt* sleep through *(Tag)*; *(versäumen)* miss *(Zug, Termin)*; sich v~ oversleep □ *a* sleepy; noch v~ still half asleep

Verschlag *m* -[e]s,-̈e shed

verschlagen† *vt* lose *(Seite)*; jdm die Sprache/den Atem v~ leave s.o. speechless/take s.o.'s breath away; nach X v~ werden end up in X □ *a* sly, *adv* -ly

verschlechter|n *vt* make worse; sich v~n get worse, deteriorate. V~ung *f* -,-en deterioration

verschleiern *vt* veil; *(fig)* hide

Verschleiß *m* -es wear and tear; *(Verbrauch)* consumption. v~en† *vt/i (sein)* wear out

verschleppen *vt* carry off; *(entführen)* abduct; spread *(Seuche)*; neglect *(Krankheit)*; *(hinausziehen)* delay

verschleudern *vt* sell at a loss; *(verschwenden)* squander

verschließen† *vt* close; *(abschließen)* lock; *(einschließen)* lock up

verschlimmer|n *vt* make worse; aggravate *(Lage)*; sich v~n get worse, deteriorate. V~ung *f* -,-en deterioration

verschlingen† *vt* intertwine; *(fressen)* devour; *(fig)* swallow

verschlissen *a* worn

verschlossen *a* reserved. V~heit *f* - reserve

verschlucken *vt* swallow; sich v~ choke (an + *dat* on)

Verschluss *m* -es,-̈e (Verschluß *m* -sses, -̈sse) fastener, clasp; *(Fenster-, Koffer-)* catch; *(Flaschen-)* top; *(luftdicht)* seal; *(Phot)* shutter; unter V~ under lock and key

verschlüsselt *a* coded

verschmähen *vt* spurn

verschmelzen† *vt/i (sein)* fuse

verschmerzen *vt* get over

verschmutz|en *vt* soil; pollute *(Luft)* □ *vi (sein)* get dirty. V~ung *f* - pollution

verschnaufen *vi/r (haben)* [sich] v~ get one's breath

verschneit *a* snow-covered

verschnörkelt *a* ornate

verschnüren *vt* tie up

verschollen *a* missing

verschonen *vt* spare

verschönern *vt* brighten up; *(verbessern)* improve

verschossen *a* faded

verschrammt *a* scratched

verschränken *vt* cross

verschreiben† *vt* prescribe; sich v~ make a slip of the pen

verschrien *a* notorious

verschroben *a* eccentric

verschrotten *vt* scrap

verschulden *vt* be to blame for; sich v~ get into debt. V~ *nt* -s fault

verschuldet *a* v~ sein be in debt

verschütten *vt* spill; (*begraben*) bury

verschweigen† *vt* conceal, hide

verschwend|en *vt* waste. v~erisch *a* extravagant, *adv* -ly; (*üppig*) lavish, *adv* -ly. V~ung *f* - extravagance; (*Vergeudung*) waste

verschwiegen *a* discreet; (*Ort*) secluded. V~heit *f* - discretion

verschwimmen† *vi* (*sein*) become blurred

verschwinden† *vi* (*sein*) disappear; [mal] v~ (*fam*) spend a penny. V~ *nt* -s disappearance

verschwommen *a* blurred

verschwör|en (*sich*) *vr* conspire. V~ung *f* -,-en conspiracy

versehen† *vt* perform; hold (*Posten*); keep (*Haushalt*); v~ mit provide with; sich v~ make a mistake; ehe man sich's versieht before you know where you are. V~ *nt* -s,- oversight; (*Fehler*) slip; aus V~ by mistake. v~tlich *adv* by mistake

Versehrte(r) *m* disabled person

versenden† *vt* send [out]

versengen *vt* singe; (*stärker*) scorch

versenken *vt* sink; sich v~ in (+ *acc*) immerse oneself in

versessen *a* keen (auf + *acc* on)

versetz|en *vt* move; transfer (*Person*); (*Sch*) move up; (*verpfänden*) pawn; (*verkaufen*) sell; (*vermischen*) blend; (*antworten*) reply; jdn v~en (*fam: warten lassen*) stand s.o. up; jdm einen Stoß/Schreck v~en give s.o. a push/ fright; jdm in Angst/Erstaunen v~en frighten/astonish s.o.; sich in jds Lage v~en put oneself in s.o.'s place. V~ung *f* -,-en move; transfer; (*Sch*) move to a higher class

verseuch|en *vt* contaminate. V~ung *f* - contamination

versicher|n *vt* insure; (*bekräftigen*) affirm; jdm v~n assure s.o (dass that). V~ung *f* -,-en insurance; assurance

versiegeln *vt* seal

versiegen *vi* (*sein*) dry up

versiert /vɛr'ʒiːɐt/ *a* experienced

versilbert *a* silver-plated

versinken† (*sein*) sink; in Gedanken versunken lost in thought

Version /vɛr'ʒioːn/ *f* -,-en version

Versmaß /'fɛrs-/ *nt* metre

versöhn|en *vt* reconcile; sich v~en become reconciled. v~lich *a* conciliatory. V~ung *f* -,-en reconciliation

versorg|en *vt* provide, supply (mit with); provide for (*Familie*); (*betreuen*) look after; keep (*Haushalt*). V~ung *f* - provision, supply; (*Betreuung*) care

verspät|en (sich) *vr* be late. v~et *a* late; (*Zug*) delayed; (*Dank, Glückwunsch*) belated □ *adv* late; belatedly. V~ung *f* - lateness; V~ung haben be late

versperren *vt* block; bar (*Weg*)

verspiel|en *vt* gamble away; sich v~en play a wrong note. v~t *a* playful, *adv* -ly

verspotten *vt* mock, ridicule

versprech|en† *vt* promise; sich v~en make a slip of the tongue; sich (*dat*) viel v~en von have high hopes of; ein viel v~ender Anfang a promising start. V~en *nt* -s,- promise. V~ungen *fpl* promises

verspüren *vt* feel

verstaatlich|en *vt* nationalize. V~ung *f* - nationalization

Verstand *m* -[e]s mind; (*Vernunft*) reason; den V~ verlieren go out of one's mind. v~esmäßig *a* rational, *adv* -ly

verständig *a* sensible, *adv* -bly; (*klug*) intelligent, *adv* -ly. v~en *vt* notify, inform; sich v~en communicate; (*sich verständlich machen*) make oneself understood; (*sich einigen*) reach agreement. V~ung *f* - notification; communication; (*Einigung*) agreement

verständlich *a* comprehensible, *adv* -bly; (*deutlich*) clear, *adv* -ly; (*begreiflich*) understandable; leicht v~ easily understood; sich v~ machen make oneself understood. v~erweise *adv* understandably

Verständnis *nt* -ses understanding. v~los *a* uncomprehending, *adv* -ly. v~voll *a* understanding, *adv* -ly

verstärk|en *vt* strengthen, reinforce; (*steigern*) intensify, increase; amplify (*Ton*); sich v~en intensify. V~er *m* -s,- amplifier. V~ung *f* reinforcement; increase; amplification; (*Truppen*) reinforcements *pl*

verstaubt *a* dusty

verstauchen *vt* sprain

verstauen *vt* stow

Versteck *nt* -[e]s,-e hiding-place; V~ spielen play hide-and-seek. v~en *vt* hide; sich v~en hide. v~t *a* hidden; (*heimlich*) secret; (*verstohlen*) furtive, *adv* -ly

verstehen† *vt* understand; (*können*) know; falsch v~ misunderstand; sich v~ understand one another; (*auskommen*) get on; das versteht sich von selbst that goes without saying

versteif|en *vt* stiffen; sich v~ stiffen; (*fig*) insist (auf + *acc* on)

versteiger|n *vt* auction. V~ung *f* auction

versteinert *a* fossilized

verstell|bar *a* adjustable. **v~en** *vt* adjust; (*versperren*) block; (*verändern*) disguise; sich **v~en** pretend. **V~ung** *f* - pretence

versteuern *vt* pay tax on

verstiegen *a* (*fig*) extravagant

verstimm|t *a* disgruntled; ⟨*Magen*⟩ upset; (*Mus*) out of tune. **V~ung** *f* - ill humour; (*Magen-*) upset

verstockt *a* stubborn, *adv* -ly

verstohlen *a* furtive, *adv* -ly

verstopf|en *vt* plug; (*versperren*) block; **v~t** blocked; ⟨*Person*⟩ constipated. **V~ung** *f* -,-en blockage; (*Med*) constipation

verstorben *a* late, deceased. **V~e(r)** *m*/*f* deceased

verstört *a* bewildered

Verstoß *m* infringement. **v~en†** *vt* disown □ *vi* (*haben*) **v~en gegen** contravene, infringe; offend against ⟨*Anstand*⟩

verstreichen† *vt* spread □ *vi* (*sein*) pass

verstreuen *vt* scatter

verstümmeln *vt* mutilate; garble ⟨*Text*⟩

verstummen *vi* (*sein*) fall silent; ⟨*Gespräch, Lärm*⟩ cease

Versuch *m* -[e]s,-e attempt; (*Experiment*) experiment. **v~en** *vt/i* (*haben*) try; sich **v~en in** (+ *dat*) try one's hand at; **v~t sein** be tempted (zu to). **V~skaninchen** *nt* (*fig*) guinea-pig. **v~sweise** *adv* as an experiment. **V~ung** *f* -,-en temptation

versündigen (sich) *vr* sin (an + *dat* against)

vertagen *vt* adjourn; (*aufschieben*) postpone; sich **v~** adjourn

vertauschen *vt* exchange; (*verwechseln*) mix up

verteidig|en *vt* defend. **V~er** *m* -s,- defender; (*Jur*) defence counsel. **V~ung** *f* -,-en defence

verteil|en *vt* distribute; (*zuteilen*) allocate; (*ausgeben*) hand out; (*verstreichen*) spread; sich **v~en** spread out. **V~ung** *f* - distribution; allocation

vertief|en *vt* deepen; **v~t sein in** (+ *acc*) be engrossed in. **V~ung** *f* -,-en hollow, depression

vertikal /vɛrti'ka:l/ *a* vertical, *adv* -ly

vertilgen *vt* exterminate; kill [off] ⟨*Unkraut*⟩; (*fam: essen*) demolish

vertippen (sich) *vr* make a typing mistake

vertlgnen od ust tr muain

Vertrag *m* -[e]s,-e contract; (*Pol*) treaty

vertragen† *vt* tolerate, stand; take ⟨*Kritik, Spaß*⟩; sich **v~** get on; (*passen*) go (mit with); sich wieder **v~** make it up □ *a* worn

vertraglich *a* contractual

verträglich *a* good-natured; (*bekömmlich*) digestible

vertrauen *vi* (*haben*) trust (jdm/etw s.o./sth; auf + *acc* in). **V~** *nt* -s trust, confidence (zu in); im **V~** in confidence. **V~smann** *m* (*pl* -leute) representative; (*Sprecher*) spokesman. **v~svoll** *a* trusting, *adv* -ly. **v~swürdig** *a* trustworthy

vertraulich *a* confidential, *adv* -ly; (*intim*) familiar, *adv* -ly

vertraut *a* intimate; (*bekannt*) familiar; sich **v~** machen mit familiarize oneself with. **V~heit** *f* - intimacy; familiarity

vertreib|en† *vt* drive away; drive out ⟨*Feind*⟩; (*Comm*) sell; sich (*dat*) die Zeit **v~en** pass the time. **V~ung** *f* -,-en expulsion

vertret|en† *vt* represent; (*einspringen für*) stand in or deputize for; (*verfechten*) support; hold ⟨*Meinung*⟩; sich (*dat*) den Fuß **v~en** twist one's ankle; sich (*dat*) die Beine **v~en** stretch one's legs. **V~er** *m* -s,- representative; deputy; (*Arzt-*) locum; (*Verfechter*) supporter, advocate. **V~ung** *f* -,-en representation; (*Person*) deputy; (*eines Arztes*) locum; (*Handels-*) agency

Vertrieb *m* -[e]s (*Comm*) sale. **V~ene(r)** *m*/*f* displaced person

vertrocknen *vi* (*sein*) dry up

vertrösten *vt* jdn auf später **v~** put s.o. off until later

vertun† *vt* waste; sich **v~** (*fam*) make a mistake

vertuschen *vt* hush up

verübeln *vt* jdm etw **v~** hold sth against s.o.

verüben *vt* commit

verunglimpfen *vt* denigrate

verunglücken *vi* (*sein*) be involved in an accident; (*fam: misslücken*) go wrong; tödlich **v~** be killed in an accident

verunreinigen *vt* pollute; (*verseuchen*) contaminate; (*verschmutzen*) soil

verunstalten *vt* disfigure

veruntreu|en *vt* embezzle. **V~ung** *f* - embezzlement

verursachen *vt* cause

verurteil|en *vt* condemn; (*Jur*) convict (wegen of); sentence (zum Tode to death). **V~ung** *f* - condemnation; (*Jur*) conviction

vervielfachen *vt* multiply

vorvielfältigen *nt* duplicate

vervollkommnen *vt* perfect

vervollständigen *vt* complete

verwachsen *a* deformed

verwählen (sich) *vr* misdial

verwahren *vt* keep; (*verstauen*) put away; sich v~ (*fig*) protest

verwahrlost *a* neglected; (*Haus*) dilapidated; (*sittlich*) depraved

Verwahrung *f* -keeping; in V~ nehmen take into safe keeping

verwaist *a* orphaned

verwalt|en *vt* administer; (*leiten*) manage; govern (*Land*). V~er *m* -s,- administrator; manager. V~ung *f* -,-en administration; management; government

verwand|eln *vt* transform, change (in + *acc* into); sich v~eln change, turn (in + *acc* into). V~lung *f* transformation

verwandt *a* related (mit to). V~e(r) *m/f* relative. V~schaft *f* - relationship; (*Menschen*) relatives *pl*

verwarn|en *vt* warn, caution. V~ung *f* warning, caution

verwaschen *a* washed out, faded

verwechs|eln *vt* mix up, confuse; (*halten für*) mistake (mit for). V~lung *f* -,-en mix-up

verwegen *a* audacious, *adv* -ly

Verwehung *f* -,-en [snow-]drift

verweichlicht *a* (*fig*) soft

verweiger|n *vt/i* (*haben*) refuse (jdm etw s.o. sth); den Gehorsam v~n refuse to obey. V~ung *f* refusal

verweilen *vi* (*haben*) stay

Verweis *m* -es,-e reference (auf + *acc* to); (*Tadel*) reprimand; v~en† *vt* refer (auf/ an + *acc* to); (*tadeln*) reprimand; von der Schule v~en expel

verwelken *vi* (*sein*) wilt

verwend|en† *vt* use; spend (*Zeit, Mühe*). V~ung *f* use

verwerf|en† *vt* reject; sich v~en warp. v~lich *a* reprehensible

verwert|en *vt* utilize, use; (*Comm*) exploit. V~ung *f* - utilization; exploitation

verwesen *vi* (*sein*) decompose

verwick|eln *vt* involve (in + *acc* in); sich v~eln get tangled up; in etw (*acc*) v~elt sein (*fig*) be involved *or* mixed up in sth. v~elt *a* complicated

verwildert *a* wild; (*Garten*) overgrown; (*Aussehen*) unkempt

verwinden† *vt* (*fig*) get over

verwirken *vt* forfeit

verwirklichen *vt* realize; sich v~ be realized

verwirr|en *vt* tangle up; (*fig*) confuse; sich v~en get tangled; (*fig*) become confused. v~t *a* confused. V~ung *f* confusion

verwischen *vt* smudge

verwittert *a* weathered; (*Gesicht*) weather-beaten

verwitwet *a* widowed

verwöhn|en *vt* spoil. v~t *a* spoilt; (*anspruchsvoll*) discriminating

verworren *a* confused

verwund|bar *a* vulnerable. v~en *vt* wound

verwunder|lich *a* surprising. v~n *vt* surprise; sich v~n be surprised. V~ung *f* - surprise

Verwund|ete(r) *m* wounded soldier; die V~eten the wounded *pl*. V~ung *f* -,-en wound

verwünsch|en *vt* curse. v~t *a* confounded

verwüst|en *vt* devastate, ravage. V~ung *f* -,-en devastation

verzagen *vi* (*haben*) lose heart

verzählen (sich) *vr* miscount

verzärteln *vt* mollycoddle

verzaubern *vt* bewitch; (*fig*) enchant; v~ in (+ *acc*) turn into

Verzehr *m* -s consumption. v~en *vt* eat; (*aufbrauchen*) use up; sich v~en (*fig*) pine away

verzeichn|en *vt* list; (*registrieren*) register. V~nis *nt* -ses,-se list; (*Inhalts-*) index

verzeih|en† *vt* forgive; v~en Sie! excuse me! V~ung *f* - forgiveness; um V~ung bitten apologize; V~ung! sorry! (*bei Frage*) excuse me!

verzerren *vt* distort; contort (*Gesicht*); pull (*Muskel*)

Verzicht *m* -[e]s renunciation (auf + *acc* of). v~en *vi* (*haben*) do without; v~en auf (+ *acc*) give up; renounce (*Recht, Erbe*)

verziehen† *vt* pull out of shape; (*verwöhnen*) spoil; sich v~ lose shape; (*Holz:*) warp; (*Gesicht:*) twist; (*verschwinden*) disappear; (*Nebel:*) disperse; (*Gewitter:*) pass; das Gesicht v~ pull a face □ *vi* (*sein*) move [away]

verzier|en *vt* decorate. V~ung *f* -,-en decoration

verzinsen *vt* pay interest on

verzöger|n *vt* delay; (*verlangsamen*) slow down; sich v~n be delayed. V~ung *f* -,-en delay

verzollen *vt* pay duty on; haben Sie etwas zu v~? have you anything to declare?

verzück|t *a* ecstatic, *adv* -ally. V~ung *f* - rapture, ecstasy

Verzug *m* delay; in V~ in arrears

verzweif|eln *vi* (*sein*) despair. v~elt *a* desperate, *adv* -ly; v~elt sein be in despair; (*ratlos*) be desperate. V~lung *f* - despair; (*Ratlosigkeit*) desperation

verzweigen (sich) *vr* branch [out]

verzwickt *a* (*fam*) tricky

Veto /'ve:to/ *nt* -s,-s veto

Vetter *m* -s,-n cousin. V~nwirtschaft *f* nepotism

vgl. *abbr* (vergleiche) cf.

Viadukt /vja'dʊkt/ *nt* -[e]s,-e viaduct

vibrieren /vi'bri:rən/ *vi* (*haben*) vibrate

Video /'vi:deo/ *nt* -s,-s video. V~kassette *f* video cassette. V~recorder /-rəkɔrdɐ/ *m* -s,- video recorder

Vieh *nt* -[e]s livestock; (*Rinder*) cattle *pl*; (*fam: Tier*) creature. v~isch *a* brutal, *adv* -ly

viel *pron* a great deal/(*fam*) lot; (*pl*) many, (*fam*) a lot of; (*substantivisch*) v~[es] much, (*fam*) a lot; nicht/so/wie/zu v~ not/so/how/too much; (*pl*) many; v~e *pl* many; das v~e Geld/ Lesen all that money/reading □ *adv* much, (*fam*) a lot; v~ mehr/weniger much more/less; v~ zu groß/klein/viel much *or* far too big/small/much; so v~ wie möglich as much as possible; so/zu v~ arbeiten work so/too much

viel|deutig *a* ambiguous. v~erlei *inv a* many kinds of □ *pron* many things. v~fach *a* multiple □ *adv* many times; (*fam: oft*) frequently. V~falt *f* -diversity, [great] variety. v~fältig *a* diverse, varied

vielleicht *adv* perhaps, maybe; (*fam: wirklich*) really

vielmals *adv* very much; danke v~! thank you very much!

viel|mehr *adv* rather; (*im Gegenteil*) on the contrary. v~sagend *a* (NEW) v~ sagend, s. sagen

vielseitig *a* varied; (*Person*) versatile □ *adv* v~ begabt versatile. V~keit *f* -versatility

vielversprechend *a* (NEW) viel versprechend, s. versprechen

vier *inv a*, V~ *f* -,-en four; (*Sch*) ≈ fair. V~eck *nt* -[e]s,-e oblong, rectangle; (*Quadrat*) square. v~eckig *a* oblong, rectangular; square. V~fach *a* quadruple. V~linge *mpl* quadruplets

viertel /'fɪrtəl/ *inv a* quarter; eine v~ Million a quarter of a million; um v~ neun at [a] quarter past eight; um drei v~ neun at [a] quarter to nine; eine v~ Stunde = eine Viertelstunde. V~ *nt* -s,- quarter; (*Wein*) quarter litre; V~ vor/ nach sechs [a] quarter to/past six; um V~/drei V~ neun (NEW) v~/drei v~ neun, s. viertel. V~finale *nt* quarter-final. V~jahr *nt* three months *pl*; (*Comm*) quarter. v~jährlich *a* & *adv* quarterly. v~n *vt* quarter. V~note *f* crotchet,

(*Amer*) quarter note. V~stunde *f* quarter of an hour

vier|zehn /'fɪr-/ *inv a* fourteen. v~zehnte(r,s) *a* fourteenth. v~zig *inv a* forty. v~zigste(r,s) *a* fortieth

Villa /'vɪla/ *f* -,-len villa

violett /vio'lɛt/ *a* violet

Vio|line /vjo'li:nə/ *f* -,-n violin. V~linschlüssel *m* treble clef. V~loncello /-lɔn'tʃelo/ *nt* cello

Virtuose /vɪr'tʊo:zə/ *m* -n,-n virtuoso

Virus /'vi:rʊs/ *nt* -,-ren virus

Visier /vi'zi:ɐ/ *nt* -s,-e visor

Vision /vi'zjo:n/ *f* -,-en vision

Visite /vi'zi:tə/ *f* -,-n round; V~ machen do one's round

visuell /vi'zuɛl/ *a* visual, *adv* -ly

Visum /'vi:zʊm/ *nt* -s,-sa visa

vital /vi'ta:l/ *a* vital; (*Person*) energetic. V~ität *f* -vitality

Vitamin /vita'mi:n/ *nt* -s,-e vitamin

Vitrine /vi'tri:nə/ *f* -,-n display cabinet/ (*im Museum*) case

Vizepräsident /'fi:tsə-/ *m* vice president

Vogel *m* -s,- bird; einen V~ haben (*fam*) have a screw loose. V~scheuche *f* -,-n scarecrow

Vokab|eln /vo'ka:bəln/ *fpl* vocabulary *sg*. V~ular *nt* -s,-e vocabulary

Vokal /vo'ka:l/ *m* -s,-e vowel

Volant /vo'lã:/ *m* -s,-s flounce; (*Auto*) steering-wheel

Volk *nt* -[e]s,-er people *sg*; (*Bevölkerung*) people *pl*; (*Bienen-*) colony

Völker|kunde *f* ethnology. V~mord *m* genocide. V~recht *nt* international law

Volks|abstimmung *f* plebiscite. V~fest *nt* public festival. V~hochschule *f* adult education classes *pl*/ (*Gebäude*) centre. V~lied *nt* folk-song. V~tanz *m* folk-dance. v~tümlich *a* popular. V~wirt *m* economist. V~wirtschaft *f* economics *sg*. V~zählung *f* [national] census

voll *a* full (von *od* mit of); (*Haar*) thick; (*Erfolg, Ernst*) complete; (*Wahrheit*) whole; v~ machen fill up; v~ tanken fill up with petrol; die Uhr schlug v~ (*fam*) the clock struck the hour □ *adv* (*ganz*) completely; (*arbeiten*) full-time; (*auszahlen*) in full; v~ und ganz completely

vollauf *adv* fully, completely

Voll|beschäftigung *f* full employment. V~blut *nt* thoroughbred

vollbringen† *vt insep* accomplish; work (*Wunder*)

vollende|n *vt insep* complete. v~t *a* perfect, *adv* -ly; v~te Gegenwart/Vergangenheit perfect/pluperfect

vollends *adv* completely

Vollendung *f* completion; *(Vollkommenheit)* perfection

voller *inv a* full of; v~ Angst/Freude filled with fear/joy; v~ Flecken covered with stains

Völlerei *f* - gluttony

Volleyball /'vɔli-/ *m* volleyball

vollführen *vt insep* perform

vollfüllen *vt sep* fill up

Vollgas *nt* v~ geben put one's foot down; mit V~ flat out

völlig *a* complete, *adv* -ly

volljährig *a* v~ sein *(Jur)* be of age. V~keit *f* - *(Jur)* majority

Vollkaskoversicherung *f* fully comprehensive insurance

vollkommen *a* perfect, *adv* -ly; *(völlig)* complete, *adv* -ly. V~heit *f* - perfection

Voll|kornbrot *nt* wholemeal bread. V~macht *f* -,-en authority; *(Jur)* power of attorney. V~mond *m* full moon. V~pension *f* full board. v~schlank *a* with a fuller figure

vollständig *a* complete, *adv* -ly

vollstrecken *vt insep* execute; carry out *⟨Urteil⟩*

volltanken *vi sep* (haben) (NEW) voll tanken, s. voll

Volltreffer *m* direct hit

vollzählig *a* complete; sind wir v~? are we all here?

vollziehen† *vt insep* carry out; perform *⟨Handlung⟩*; consummate *⟨Ehe⟩*; sich v~ take place

Volt /vɔlt/ *nt* -[s],- volt

Volumen /vo'lu:mən/ *nt* -s,- volume

vom *prep* = von dem; vom Rauchen from smoking

von *prep* (+ *dat*) of; *(über)* about; *(Ausgangspunkt, Ursache)* from; *(beim Passiv)* by; Musik von Mozart music by Mozart; einer von euch one of you; von hier/heute an from here/today; von mir aus I don't mind

voneinander *adv* from each other; *⟨abhängig⟩* on each other

vonseiten *prep* (+ *gen*) on the part of

vonstatten *adv* v~ gehen take place; gut v~ gehen go [off] well

vor *prep* (+ *dat/acc*) in front of; *(zeitlich, Reihenfolge)* before; (+ *dat*) *(bei Uhrzeit)* to; *(warnen, sich fürchten/schämen)* of; *(schützen, davonlaufen)* from; *(Respekt haben)* for; vor Angst/Kälte zittern tremble with fear/cold; vor drei Tagen/

Jahren three days/years ago; vor sich *(acc)* hin murmeln mumble to oneself; vor allen Dingen above all *□ adv* forward; vor und zurück backwards and forwards

Vor|abend *m* eve. V~ahnung *f* premonition

voran *adv* at the front; *(voraus)* ahead; *(vorwärts)* forward. v~gehen† *vi sep* (sein) lead the way; *(Fortschritte machen)* make progress; jdm/etw v~gehen precede s.o./sth. v~kommen† *vi sep* (sein) make progress; *(fig)* get on

Vor|anschlag *m* estimate. V~anzeige *f* advance notice. V~arbeit *f* preliminary work. V~arbeiter *m* foreman

voraus *adv* ahead *(dat* of); *(vorn)* at the front; *(vorwärts)* forward *□ im* Voraus *(voraus)* in advance. v~bezahlen *vt sep* pay in advance. v~gehen† *vi sep* (sein) go on ahead; jdm/etw v~gehen precede s.o./sth. V~sage *f* -,-n prediction. v~sagen *vt sep* predict. v~sehen† *vt sep* foresee

voraussetz|en *vt sep* take for granted; *(erfordern)* require; vorausgesetzt, dass provided that. V~ung *f* -,-en assumption; *(Erfordernis)* prerequisite; unter der V~ung, dass on condition that

Voraussicht *f* foresight; aller V~ nach in all probability. v~lich *a* anticipated, expected *□ adv* probably

Vorbehalt *m* -[e]s,-e reservation. v~en† *vt sep* sich *(dat)* v~en reserve *(Recht)*; jdm v~en sein/bleiben be left to s.o. v~los *a* unreserved, *adv* -ly

vorbei *adv* past (an jdm/etw s.o./sth); *(zu Ende)* over. v~fahren† *vi sep* (sein) drive/go past. v~gehen† *vi sep* (sein) go past; *(verfehlen)* miss; *(vergehen)* pass; *(fam: besuchen)* drop in (bei on). v~kommen† *vi sep* (sein) pass/*(v~können)* get past (an jdm/etw s.o./sth); *(fam: besuchen)* drop in (bei on)

vorbereit|en *vt sep* prepare; prepare for *(Reise)*; sich v~en prepare [oneself] (auf + *acc* for). V~ung *f* -,-en preparation

vorbestellen *vt sep* order/*(im Theater, Hotel)* book in advance

vorbestraft *a* v~ sein have a [criminal] record

vorbeug|en *v sep □ vt* bend forward; sich v~en bend *or* lean forward *□ vi* (haben) prevent (etw *dat* sth); v~end preventive. V~ung *f* - prevention

Vorbild *nt* model. v~lich *a* exemplary, model *□ adv* in an exemplary manner

vorbringen† *vt sep* put forward; offer *⟨Entschuldigung⟩*

vordatieren *vt sep* post-date

Vorder|bein nt foreleg. **v~e(r,s)** a front. **V~grund** m foreground. **V~mann** m (pl **-männer**) person in front; auf V~mann bringen (fam) lick into shape. (aufräumen) tidy up. **V~rad** nt front wheel. **V~seite** f front; (einer Münze) obverse. **v~ste(r,s)** a front, first. **V~teil** nt front

vor|drängeln (sich) vr sep (fam) jump the queue. **v~drängen** (sich) vr sep push forward. **v~dringen†** vi sep (sein) advance

vor|ehelich a pre-marital. **v~eilig** a rash, adv -ly

voreingenommen a biased, prejudiced. **V~heit** f - bias

vorenthalten† vt sep withhold

vorerst adv for the time being

Vorfahr m -en,-en ancestor

vorfahren† vi sep (sein) drive up; (vorwärts-) move forward; (voraus-) drive on ahead

Vorfahrt f right of way; 'V~ beachten' 'give way'. **V~sstraße** f ≈ major road

Vorfall m incident. **v~en†** vi sep (sein) happen

vorfinden† vt sep find

Vorfreude f [happy] anticipation

vorführ|en vt sep present, show; (demonstrieren) demonstrate; (aufführen) perform. **V~ung** f presentation; demonstration; performance

Vor|gabe f (Sport) handicap. **V~gang** m occurrence; (Techn) process. **V~gänger(in)** m -s,- (f -,-nen) predecessor. **V~garten** m front garden

vorgeben† vt sep pretend

vor|gefasst (vor|gefaßt) a preconceived. **v~gefertigt** a prefabricated

vorgehen† vi sep (sein) go forward; (voraus-) go on ahead; (Uhr:) be fast; (wichtig sein) take precedence; (verfahren) act, proceed; (geschehen) happen, go on. **V~** nt -s action

vor|geschichtlich a prehistoric. **V~geschmack** m foretaste. **V~gesetzte(r)** m/f superior. **v~gestern** adv the day before yesterday; **v~gestern Abend/Nacht** the evening/night before last

vorhaben† vt sep propose, intend (zu to); etw v~ have sth planned; nichts v~ have no plans. **V~** nt -s,-plan; (Projekt) project

vorhalt|en v sep □ vt hold up; jdm etw [⎯] reproach s.o. for sth □ vi (haben) last. **V~ungen** fpl jdm Varungen machen reproach s.o. (wegen for)

Vorhand f (Sport) forehand

vorhanden a existing; **v~ sein** exist; (verfügbar sein) be available. **V~sein** nt -s existence

Vorhang m curtain

Vorhängeschloss (**Vorhängeschloß**) nt padlock

vorher adv before[hand]

vorhergehend a previous

vorheriga prior; (vorhergehend) previous

Vorherrsch|aft f supremacy. **v~en** vi sep (haben) predominate. **v~end** a predominant

Vorher|sage f -,-n prediction: (Wetter-) forecast. **v~sagen** vt sep predict; forecast (Wetter). **v~sehen†** vt sep foresee

vorhin adv just now

vorige(r,s) a last, previous

Vor|kämpfer m (fig) champion. **V~kehrungen** fpl precautions. **V~kenntnisse** fpl previous knowledge sg

vorkommen† vi sep (sein) happen; (vorhanden sein) occur; (nach vorn kommen) come forward; (hervorkommen) come out; (zu sehen sein) show; jdm bekannt/verdächtig v~ seem familiar/suspicious to s.o.; sich (dat) dumm/alt v~ feel stupid/old. **V~** nt -s,- occurrence; (Geol) deposit

Vorkriegszeit f pre-war period

vorlad|en† vt sep (Jur) summons. **V~ung** f summons

Vorlage f model; (Muster) pattern; (Gesetzes-) bill

vorlassen† vt sep admit; jdn v~ (fam) let s.o. pass; (den Vortritt lassen) let s.o. go first

Vor|lauf m (Sport) heat. **V~läufer** m forerunner. **v~läufig** a provisional, adv -ly; (zunächst) for the time being. **v~laut** a forward. **V~leben** nt past

vorleg|en vt sep put on (Kette); (unterbreiten) present; (vorzeigen) show; jdm Fleisch v~en serve s.o. with meat. **V~er** m -s,- mat; (Bett-) rug

vorles|en† vt sep read [out]; jdm v~en read to s.o. **V~ung** f (Univ) lecture

vorletzt|e(r,s) a last ... but one; (Silbe) penultimate; **v~es Jahr** the year before last

vorlieb adv **v~ nehmen** make do (mit with). **v~nehmen†** vt sep (NEW) **v~ nehmen, s. vorlieb**

Vorliebe f preference

vorliegen† vt sep (haben) be present/(verfügbar) available; (bestehen) exist, be; es muss ein Irrtum v~ there must be some mistake. **v~d** a present; (Frage) at issue

vorlügen† vt sep lie (dat to)

vorm prep = vor dem

vormachen vt sep put up; put on ⟨Kette⟩; push ⟨Riegel⟩; ⟨zeigen⟩ demonstrate; jdm etwas v∼ ⟨fam: täuschen⟩ kid s.o.

Vormacht f supremacy

vormals adv formerly

Vormarsch m ⟨Mil & fig⟩ advance

vormerken vt sep make a note of; ⟨reservieren⟩ reserve

Vormittag m morning; gestern/heute V∼ yesterday/this morning. v∼ adv gestern/heute v∼ ⟨NEW⟩ gestern/heute V∼, s. Vormittag. v∼s adv in the morning

Vormund m -[e]s,-munde & -münder guardian

vorn adv at the front; nach v∼ to the front; von v∼ from the front/⟨vom Anfang⟩ beginning; wieder von v∼ anfangen start afresh

Vorname m first name

vorne adv = vorn

vornehm a distinguished; ⟨elegant⟩ smart, adv -ly

vornehmen† vt sep carry out; sich ⟨dat⟩ v∼, etw zu tun plan/⟨beschließen⟩ resolve to do sth

vorn|herein adv von v∼herein from the start. v∼über adv forward

Vor|ort m suburb. V∼rang m priority, precedence (vor + dat over). V∼rat m -[e]s,-e supply, stock (an + dat of). v∼rätig a available; v∼rätig haben have in stock. V∼ratskammer f larder. V∼raum m ante-room. V∼recht nt privilege. V∼richtung f device

vorrücken vt/i sep ⟨sein⟩ move forward; ⟨Mil⟩ advance

Vorrunde f qualifying round

vors prep = vor das

vorsagen vt/i sep ⟨haben⟩ recite; jdm [die Antwort] v∼ tell s.o. the answer

Vor|satz m resolution. v∼sätzlich a deliberate, adv -ly; ⟨Jur⟩ premeditated

Vorschau f preview; ⟨Film-⟩ trailer

Vorschein m zum V∼ kommen appear

vorschießen† vt sep advance ⟨Geld⟩

Vorschlag m suggestion, proposal. v∼en† vt sep suggest, propose

vorschnell a rash, adv -ly

vorschreiben† vt sep lay down; dictate ⟨dat⟩ to; vorgeschriebene Dosis prescribed dose

Vorschrift f regulation; ⟨Anweisung⟩ instruction; jdm V∼en machen tell s.o. what to do; Dienst nach V∼ work to rule. v∼smäßig a correct, adv -ly

Vorschule f nursery school

Vorschuss ⟨Vorschuß⟩ m advance

vorschützen vt sep plead [as an excuse]; feign ⟨Krankheit⟩

vorseh|en† v sep ⬜vt intend ⟨für/als for/as⟩; ⟨planen⟩ plan; sich v∼en be careful ⟨vor + dat of⟩ ⬜vi ⟨haben⟩ peep out. V∼ung f · providence

vorsetzen vt sep move forward; jdm etw v∼ serve s.o. sth

Vorsicht f · care; ⟨bei Gefahr⟩ caution: V∼! careful! ⟨auf Schild⟩ 'caution'. v∼ig a careful, adv -ly; cautious, adv -ly. v∼shalber adv to be on the safe side. V∼smaßnahme f precaution

Vorsilbe f prefix

Vorsitz m chairmanship; den V∼ führen be in the chair. v∼en† vi sep ⟨haben⟩ preside ⟨dat over⟩. V∼ende(r) m/f chair[man]

Vorsorge f V∼ treffen take precautions; make provisions ⟨für for⟩. v∼n vi sep ⟨haben⟩ provide ⟨für for⟩. V∼untersuchung f check-up

vorsorglich adv as a precaution

Vorspeise f starter

Vorspiel nt prelude. v∼en v sep ⬜vt perform/ ⟨Mus⟩ play ⟨dat for⟩ ⬜vi ⟨haben⟩ audition

vorsprechen† v sep ⬜vt recite; ⟨zum Nachsagen⟩ say ⟨dat to⟩ ⬜vi ⟨haben⟩ ⟨Theat⟩ audition; bei jdm v∼ call on s.o.

vorspringen† vi sep ⟨sein⟩ jut out; v∼des Kinn prominent chin

Vor|sprung m projection; ⟨Fels-⟩ ledge; ⟨Vorteil⟩ lead ⟨vor + dat over⟩. V∼stadt f suburb. v∼städtisch a suburban. V∼stand m board [of directors]; ⟨Vereins-⟩ committee; ⟨Partei-⟩ executive

vorsteh|en† vi sep ⟨haben⟩ project, protrude; einer Abteilung v∼en be in charge of a department; v∼end protruding; ⟨Augen⟩ bulging. V∼er m -s,- head; ⟨Gemeinde-⟩ chairman

vorstell|bar a imaginable, conceivable. v∼en vt sep put forward ⟨Bein, Uhr⟩; ⟨darstellen⟩ represent; ⟨bekannt machen⟩ introduce; sich v∼en introduce oneself; ⟨als Bewerber⟩ go for an interview; sich ⟨dat⟩ etw v∼en imagine sth. V∼ung f introduction; ⟨bei Bewerbung⟩ interview; ⟨Aufführung⟩ performance; ⟨Idee⟩ idea; ⟨Phantasie⟩ imagination. V∼ungsgespräch nt interview. V∼ungskraft f imagination

Vorstoß m advance

Vorstrafe f previous conviction

Vortag m day before

vortäuschen vt sep feign, fake

Vorteil m advantage. v∼haft a advantageous, adv -ly; ⟨Kleidung, Farbe⟩ flattering

Vortrag m -[e]s,-e talk; ⟨wissenschaftlich⟩ lecture; ⟨Klavier-, Gedicht-⟩ recital. v∼en† vt sep perform; ⟨aufsagen⟩ recite; ⟨singen⟩

sing; (*darlegen*) present (*dat* to); express ⟨*Wunsch*⟩

vortrefflich a excellent, adv -ly

vortreten† vi sep (*sein*) step forward; (*hervor-*) protrude

Vortritt m precedence; jdm den V∼ lassen let s.o. go first

vorüber adv v∼ sein be over; an etw (*dat*) v∼ past sth. v∼gehen† vi sep (*sein*) walk past; (*vergehen*) pass. v∼gehend a temporary, adv -ily

Vor|urteil nt prejudice. V∼verkauf m advance booking

vorverlegen vt sep bring forward

Vor|wahl[nummer] f dialling code. V∼wand m -[e]s,⸚e pretext; (*Ausrede*) excuse

vorwärts adv forward[s]; v∼ kommen make progress; (*fig*) get on or ahead. v∼kommen† vi sep (*sein*) ⟨NEW⟩ v∼ kommen, s. vorwärts

vorweg adv beforehand; (*vorn*) in front; (*voraus*) ahead. v∼nehmen† vt sep anticipate

vorweisen† vt sep show

vorwerfen† vt sep throw (*dat* to); jdm etw v∼ reproach s.o. with sth; (*beschuldigen*) accuse s.o. of sth

vorwiegend adv predominantly

Vorwort nt (*pl* -worte) preface

Vorwurf m reproach; jdm Vorwürfe machen reproach s.o. v∼svoll a reproachful, adv -ly

Vorzeichen nt (*fig*) omen

vorzeigen vt sep show

vorzeitig a premature, adv -ly

vorziehen† vt sep pull forward; draw ⟨*Vorhang*⟩; (*vorverlegen*) bring forward; (*lieber mögen*) prefer; (*bevorzugen*) favour

Vor|zimmer nt ante-room; (*Büro*) outer office. V∼zug m preference; (*gute Eigenschaft*) merit, virtue; (*Vorteil*) advantage

vorzüglich a excellent, adv -ly

vorzugsweise adv preferably

vulgär /vʊlˈgɛːɐ̯/ a vulgar □ adv in a vulgar way

Vulkan /vʊlˈkaːn/ m -s,-e volcano

W

Waage f -,-n scales pl; (*Astr*) Libra. w∼recht a horizontal, adv -ly

Wabe f -,-n honeycomb

wach a awake; (*aufgeweckt*) alert; w∼ werden wake up

Wach|e f -,-n guard; (*Posten*) sentry; (*Dienst*) guard duty; (*Naut*) watch; (*Polizei-*) station; W∼e halten keep watch; W∼e stehen stand guard. w∼en vi (*haben*) be awake; w∼en über (+ *acc*) watch over. W∼hund m guard-dog

Wacholder m -s juniper

Wachposten m sentry

Wachs nt -es wax

wachsam a vigilant, adv -ly. W∼keit f -vigilance

wachsen†¹ vi (*sein*) grow

wachs|en² vt (*reg*) wax. W∼figur f waxwork. W∼tuch nt oil-cloth

Wachstum nt -s growth

Wächter m -s,- guard; (*Park-*) keeper; (*Parkplatz-*) attendant

Wacht|meister m [police] constable. W∼posten m sentry

Wachturm m watch-tower

wackel|ig a wobbly; (*Stuhl*) rickety; (*Person*) shaky. W∼kontakt m loose connection. w∼n vi (*haben*) wobble; (*zittern*) shake □ vi (*sein*) totter

wacklig a = wackelig

Wade f -,-n (*Anat*) calf

Waffe f -,-n weapon; W∼n arms

Waffel f -,-n waffle; (*Eis-*) wafer

Waffen|ruhe f cease-fire. W∼schein m firearms licence. W∼stillstand m armistice

Wagemut m daring. w∼ig a daring, adv -ly

wagen vt risk; es w∼, etw zu tun dare [to] do sth; sich w∼ (*gehen*) venture

Wagen m -s,- cart; (*Eisenbahn-*) carriage, coach; (*Güter-*) wagon; (*Kinder-*) pram; (*Auto*) car. W∼heber m -s,- jack

Waggon /vaˈgõ:/ m -s,-s wagon

waghalsig a daring, adv -ly

Wagnis nt -ses,-se risk

Wagon /vaˈgõ:/ m -s,-s = Waggon

Wahl f -,-en choice; (*Pol, Admin*) election; (*geheime*) ballot; zweite W∼ (*Comm*) seconds pl

wähl|en vt/i (*haben*) choose; (*Pol, Admin*) elect; (*stimmen*) vote; (*Teleph*) dial; jdn wieder w∼en re-elect s.o. W∼er(in) m -s,- (f -,-nen) voter. w∼erisch a choosy, fussy

Wahl|fach nt optional subject. w∼frei a optional. W∼kampf m election campaign. W∼kreis m constituency. W∼lokal nt polling-station. w∼los a indiscriminate, adv -ly. W∼recht nt [right to] vote

Wählscheibe f (*Teleph*) dial

Wahl|spruch m motto. W∼urne f ballot-box

Wahn m -[e]s delusion; (*Manie*) mania

wähnen vt believe

Wahnsinn m madness. w~ig a mad, insane; (*fam: unsinnig*) crazy; (*fam: groß*) terrible; w~ig werden go mad □ adv (*fam*) terribly. W~ige(r) m/f maniac

wahr a true; (*echt*) real; w~ werden come true; du kommst doch, nicht w~? you are coming, aren't you?

wahren vt keep; (*verteidigen*) safeguard; den Schein w~ keep up appearances

währen vi (*haben*) last

während prep (+ gen) during □ conj while; (*wohingegen*) whereas. w~dessen adv in the meantime

wahrhaben vt etw nicht w~ wollen refuse to admit sth

wahrhaftig adv really, truly

Wahrheit f -,-en truth. w~sgemäß a truthful, adv -ly

wahrnehm|bar a perceptible. w~en† vt sep notice; (*nutzen*) take advantage of; exploit (*Vorteil*); look after (*Interessen*). W~ung f -,-en perception

wahrsag|en v sep □ vt predict □ vi (*haben*) jdm w~en tell s.o.'s fortune. W~erin f -,-nen fortune-teller

wahrscheinlich a probable, adv -bly. W~keit f - probability

Währung f -,-en currency

Wahrzeichen nt symbol

Waise f -,-n orphan. W~nhaus nt orphanage. W~nkind nt orphan

Wal m -[e]s,-e whale

Wald m -[e]s,-er wood; (*groß*) forest. w~ig a wooded

Walis|er m -s,- Welshman. w~isch a Welsh

Wall m -[e]s,-e mound; (*Mil*) rampart

Wallfahr|er(in) m(f) pilgrim. W~t f pilgrimage

Walnuss (**Walnuß**) f walnut

Walze f -,-n roller. w~n vt roll

wälzen vt roll; pore over (*Bücher*); mull over (*Probleme*); sich w~ roll [about]; (*schlaflos*) toss and turn

Walzer m -s,- waltz

Wand f -,-e wall; (*Trenn-*) partition; (*Seite*) side; (*Fels-*) face

Wandel m -s change. w~bar a changeable. w~n vi (*sein*) stroll □ vr sich w~n change

Wander|er m -s,-, W~in f -,-nen hiker, rambler. w~n vi (*sein*) hike, ramble; (*ziehen*) travel; (*gemächlich gehen*) wander; (*ziellos*) roam. W~schaft f - travels pl. W~ung f -,-en hike, ramble; (*länger*) walking tour. W~weg m footpath

Wandgemälde nt mural

Wandlung f -,-en change, transformation

Wand|malerei f mural. W~tafel f blackboard. W~teppich m tapestry

Wange f -,-n cheek

wank|elmütig a fickle. w~en vi (*haben*) sway; (*Person;*) stagger; (*fig*) waver □ vi (*sein*) stagger

wann adv when

Wanne f -,-n tub

Wanze f -,-n bug

Wappen nt -s,- coat of arms. W~kunde f heraldry

war, wäre s. sein[1]

Ware f -,-n article; (*Comm*) commodity; (*coll*) merchandise; W~n goods. W~nhaus nt department store. W~nprobe f sample. W~nzeichen nt trademark

warm a (wärmer, wärmst) warm; (*Mahlzeit*) hot; w~ machen heat □ adv warmly; w~ essen have a hot meal

Wärm|e f - warmth; (*Phys*) heat; 10 Grad W~e 10 degrees above zero. w~en vt warm; heat (*Essen, Wasser*). W~flasche f hot-water bottle

warmherzig a warm-hearted

Warn|blinkanlage f hazard [warning] lights pl. w~en vt/i (*haben*) warn (vor + dat of). W~ung f -,-en warning

Warteliste f waiting list

warten vi (*haben*) wait (auf + acc for); auf sich (*acc*) w~ lassen take one's/its time □ vt (*Techn*) service

Wärter(in) m -s,- (f -,-nen) keeper; (*Museums-*) attendant; (*Gefängnis-*) warder, (*Amer*) guard; (*Kranken-*) orderly

Warte|raum, W~saal m waiting-room. W~zimmer nt (*Med*) waiting-room

Wartung f - (*Techn*) service

warum adv why

Warze f -,-n wart

was pron what; was für [ein]? what kind of [a]? was für ein Pech! what bad luck! das gefällt dir, was? you like that, don't you? □ rel pron that; alles, was ich brauche all [that] I need □ indef pron (*fam: etwas*) something; (*fragend, verneint*) anything; was zu essen something to eat; so was Ärgerliches! what a nuisance! □ adv (*fam*) (*warum*) why; (*wie*) how

wasch|bar a washable. W~becken nt wash-basin. W~beutel m sponge-bag

Wäsche f - washing; (*Unter-*) underwear; in der W~ in the wash

waschecht a colour-fast; (*fam*) genuine

Wäsche|klammer f clothes-peg. W~leine f clothes-line

waschen† vt wash; sich w~ have a wash; sich (dat) die Hände w~ wash one's hands; W~ und Legen shampoo and set □ vi (haben) do the washing

Wäscherei f -,-en laundry

Wäsche|schleuder f spin-drier. W~trockner m tumble-drier

Wasch|küche f laundry-room. W~lappen m face-flannel, (Amer) washcloth; (fam: Feigling) sissy. W~maschine f washing machine. W~mittel nt detergent. W~pulver nt washing-powder. W~raum m wash-room. W~salon m launderette. W~zettel m blurb

Wasser nt -s water; (Haar-) lotion; ins W~ fallen (fam) fall through; mir lief das W~ im Mund zusammen my mouth was watering. W~ball m beach-ball; (Spiel) water polo. w~dicht a watertight; (Kleidung) waterproof. W~fall m waterfall. W~farbe f water-colour. W~hahn m tap, (Amer) faucet. W~kasten m cistern. W~kraft f water-power. W~kraftwerk nt hydroelectric power-station. W~leitung f water-main; aus der W~leitung from the tap. W~mann m (Astr) Aquarius

wässern vt soak; (begießen) water □ vi (haben) water

Wasser|scheide f watershed. W~ski nt -s water-skiing. W~stoff m hydrogen. W~straße f waterway. W~waage f spirit-level. W~werfer m -s,- water-cannon. W~zeichen nt watermark

wässrig (wäßrig) a watery

waten vi (sein) wade

watscheln vi (sein) waddle

Watt¹ nt -[e]s mud-flats pl

Watt² nt -s,- (Phys) watt

Watt|e f - cotton wool. w~iert a padded; (gesteppt) quilted

WC /ve'tse:/ nt -s,-s WC

web|en vt/i (haben) weave. W~er m -s,- weaver. W~stuhl m loom

Wechsel m -s,- change; (Tausch) exchange; (Comm) bill of exchange. W~geld nt change. w~haft a changeable. W~jahre npl menopause sg. W~kurs m exchange rate. w~n vt change; (tauschen) exchange □ vi (haben) change; (ab-) alternate; (verschieden sein) vary. w~nd a changing; (verschieden) varying. w~seitig a mutual, adv -ly. W~strom m alternating current. W~stube f bureau de change. w~weise adv alternately. W~wirkung f interaction

weck|en vt wake [up]; (fig) awaken □ vi (haben) (Wecker:) go off. W~er m -s,- alarm [clock]

wedeln vi (haben) wave; mit dem Schwanz w~ wag its tail

weder conj w~ ... noch neither .. nor

Weg m -[e]s,-e way; (Fuß-) path; (Fahr-) track; (Gang) errand; auf dem Weg on the way (nach to); sich auf den Weg machen set off; im Weg sein be in the way; zu W~e bringen = zuwege bringen, s. zuwege

weg adv away, off; (verschwunden) gone; weg sein be away; (gegangen/verschwunden) have gone; (fam: schlafen) be asleep; Hände weg! hands off! w~bleiben† vi sep (sein) stay away. w~bringen† vt sep take away

wegen prep (+ gen) because of; (um ... willen) for the sake of; (bezüglich) about

weg|fahren† vi sep (sein) go away; (abfahren) leave. w~fallen† vi sep (sein) be dropped/(ausgelassen) omitted; (entfallen) no longer apply; (aufhören) cease. w~geben† vt sep give away; send to the laundry (Wäsche). w~gehen† vi sep (sein) leave, go away; (ausgehen) go out; (Fleck:) come out. w~jagen vt sep chase away. w~kommen† vi sep (sein) get away; (verloren gehen) disappear; schlecht w~kommen (fam) get a raw deal. w~lassen† vt sep let go; (auslassen) omit. w~laufen† vi sep (sein) run away. w~machen vt sep remove. w~nehmen† vt sep take away. w~räumen vt sep put away; (entfernen) clear away. w~schicken vt sep send away; (abschicken) send off. w~tun† vt sep put away; (wegwerfen) throw away

Wegweiser m -s,- signpost

weg|werfen† vt sep throw away. w~ziehen† v sep □ vt pull away □ vi (sein) move away

weh a sore; weh tun hurt; (Kopf, Rücken:) ache; jdm weh tun hurt s.o. □ int o weh! oh dear!

wehe int alas; w~ [dir/euch]! (drohend) don't you dare!

wehen vi (haben) blow; (flattern) flutter □ vt blow

Wehen fpl contractions; in den W~ liegen be in labour

weh|leidig a soft; (weinerlich) whining. W~mut f - wistfulness. w~mütig a wistful, adv -ly

Wehr¹ nt -[e]s,-e weir

Wehr² f sich zur W~ setzen resist. W~dienst m military service. W~dienstverweigerer m -s,- conscientious objector

wehren (sich) vr resist; (gegen Anschuldigung) protest; (sich sträuben) refuse

wehr|los *a* defenceless. W~macht *f* armed forces *pl.* W~pflicht *f* conscription

Weib *nt* -[e]s,-er woman; (*Ehe-*) wife. W~chen *nt* -s,- (*Zool*) female. W~erheld *m* womanizer. w~isch *a* effeminate. w~lich *a* feminine; (*Biol*) female. W~lichkeit *f* - femininity

weich *a* soft, *adv* -ly; (*gar*) done; (*Ei*) soft-boiled; (*Mensch*) soft-hearted; w~ werden (*fig*) relent

Weiche *f* -,-n (*Rail*) points *pl*

weichen¹ *vi* (*sein*) (*reg*) soak

weichen¹² *vi* (*sein*) give way (*dat* to); nicht von jds Seite w~ not leave s.o.'s side

Weich|heit *f* - softness. w~herzig *a* soft-hearted. w~lich *a* soft; (*Charakter*) weak. W~spüler *m* -s,- (*Tex*) conditioner. W~tier *nt* mollusc

Weide¹ *f* -,-n (*Bot*) willow

Weide² *f* -,-n pasture. W~n *vt/i* (*haben*) graze; sich w~n an (+ *dat*) enjoy; (*schadenfroh*) gloat over

weiger|n (sich) *vr* refuse. W~ung *f* -,-en refusal

Weihe *f* -,-n consecration; (*Priester-*) ordination. w~n *vt* consecrate; (*zum Priester*) ordain; dedicate (*Kirche*) (*dat* to)

Weiher *m* -s,- pond

Weihnacht|en *nt* -s & *pl* Christmas. w~lich *a* Christmassy. W~sbaum *m* Christmas tree. W~sfest *nt* Christmas. W~slied *nt* Christmas carol. W~smann *m* (*pl* -männer) Father Christmas. W~stag *m* erster/zweiter W~stag Christmas Day/Boxing Day

Weih|rauch *m* incense. W~wasser *nt* holy water

weil *conj* because; (*da*) since

Weile *f* - while

Wein *m* -[e]s,-e wine; (*Bot*) vines *pl*; (*Trauben*) grapes *pl*. W~bau *m* wine-growing. W~beere *f* grape. W~berg *m* vineyard. W~brand *m* -[e]s brandy

wein|en *vt/i* (*haben*) cry, weep. w~erlich *a* tearful, *adv* -ly

Wein|glas *nt* wineglass. W~karte *f* wine-list. W~keller *m* wine-cellar. W~lese *f* grape harvest. W~liste *f* wine-list. W~probe *f* wine-tasting. W~rebe *f*, W~stock *m* vine. W~stube *f* wine-bar. W~traube *f* bunch of grapes; (*W~beere*) grape

weise *a* wise, *adv* -ly

Weise *f* -,-n way; (*Melodie*) tune; auf diese W~ in this way

weisen¹ *vt* show; von sich w~ (*fig*) reject □ *vi* (*haben*) point (auf + *acc* at)

Weisheit *f* -,-en wisdom. W~szahn *m* wisdom tooth

weiß *a*, W~ *nt* -,- white

weissag|en *vt/i insep* (*haben*) prophesy. W~ung *f* -,-en prophecy

Weiß|brot *nt* white bread. W~e(r) *m/f* white man/woman. w~en *vt* whitewash. W~wein *m* white wine

Weisung *f* -,-en instruction; (*Befehl*) order

weit *a* wide; (*ausgedehnt*) extensive; (*lang*) long □ *adv* widely; (*offen, öffnen*) wide; (*lang*) far; von w~em from a distance; bei w~em by far; w~ und breit far and wide; ist es noch w~? is it much further? so w~ wie möglich as far as possible; ich bin so w~ I'm ready; es ist so w~ the time has come; zu w~ gehen (*fig*) go too far; w~ verbreitet widespread; w~blickend (*fig*) far-sighted; w~reichende Folgen far-reaching consequences. w~aus *adv* far. W~blick *m* (*fig*) far-sightedness. w~blickend *a* = w~ blickend, *s.* weit

Weite *f* -,-n expanse; (*Entfernung*) distance; (*Größe*) width. W~n *vt* widen; stretch (*Schuhe*); sich w~n widen; stretch; (*Pupille*) dilate

weiter *a* further □ *adv* further; (*außerdem*) in addition; (*anschließend*) then; etw w~ tun go on doing sth; w~ nichts/niemand nothing/no one else; und so w~ and so on. w~arbeiten *vi sep* (*haben*) go on working

weiter|e(r,s) *a* further; im w~en Sinne in a wider sense; ohne w~es just like that; (*leicht*) easily; bis auf w~es until further notice; (*vorläufig*) for the time being

weiter|erzählen *vt sep* go on with; (*w~sagen*) repeat. w~fahren† *vi sep* (*sein*) go on. w~geben† *vt sep* pass on. w~gehen† *vi sep* (*sein*) go on. w~hin *adv* (*immer noch*) still; (*in Zukunft*) in future; (*außerdem*) furthermore; etw w~hin tun go on doing sth. w~kommen† *vi sep* (*sein*) get on. w~machen *vt sep* (*haben*) carry on. w~sagen *vt sep* pass on; (*verraten*) repeat

weit|gehend *a* extensive □ *adv* to a large extent. w~hin *adv* a long way; (*fig*) widely. w~läufig *a* spacious; (*entfernt*) distant, *adv* -ly; (*ausführlich*) lengthy, *adv* at length. w~reichend *a* = w~ reichend, *s.* weit. w~schweifig *a* long-winded. w~sichtig *a* long-sighted; (*fig*) far-sighted. W~sprung *m* long jump. w~verbreitet *a* = w~ verbreitet, *s.* weit

Weizen *m* -s wheat

welch *inv pron* what; w∼ ein(e) what a. w∼e(r,s) *pron* which; um w∼e Zeit? at what time? □ *rel pron* which; (Person) who □ *indef pron* some; (fragend) any; was für w∼e? what sort of?

welk *a* wilted; (Laub) dead. w∼en *vi* (haben) wilt; (fig) fade

Wellblech *nt* corrugated iron

Well|e *f* -,-n wave; (Techn) shaft. W∼enlänge *f* wavelength. W∼enlinie *f* wavy line. W∼enreiten *nt* surfing. W∼ensittich *m* -s,-e budgerigar. w∼ig *a* wavy

Welt *f* -,-en world; auf der W∼ in the world; auf die *od* zur W∼ kommen be born. W∼all *nt* universe. w∼berühmt *a* world-famous. w∼fremd *a* unworldly. w∼gewandt *a* sophisticated. W∼kugel *f* globe. w∼lich *a* worldly; (nicht geistlich) secular

Weltmeister|(in) *m(f)* world champion. W∼schaft *f* world championship

Weltraum *m* space. W∼fahrer *m* astronaut

Weltrekord *m* world record. w∼weit *a & adv* world-wide

wem *pron* (dat of wer) to whom

wen *pron* (acc of wer) whom

Wende *f* -,-n change. W∼kreis *m* (Geog) tropic

Wendeltreppe *f* spiral staircase

wenden[1] *vt* (reg) turn; sich zum Guten w∼ take a turn for the better □ *vi* (haben) turn [round]

wenden[2] (& reg) *vt* turn; sich w∼ turn; sich an jdn w∼ turn/(schriftlich) write to s.o.

Wend|epunkt *m* (fig) turning-point. w∼ig *a* nimble; (Auto) manœuvrable. W∼ung *f* -,-en turn; (Biegung) bend; (Veränderung) change; eine W∼ung zum Besseren/Schlechteren a turn for the better/worse

wenig *pron* little; (pl) few; so/zu w∼ so/too little/(pl) few; w∼e *pl* few □ *adv* little; (kaum) not much; so/zu w∼ verdienen earn so/too little; so w∼ wie möglich as little as possible. w∼er *pron* less; (pl) fewer; immer w∼er less and less □ *adv & conj* less. w∼ste(r,s) *pron* least; am w∼sten least [of all]. w∼stens *adv* at least

wenn *conj* if; (sobald) when; immer w∼ whenever; w∼ nicht *od* außer w∼ unless; w∼ auch even though

wer *pron* who; (fam: jemand) someone; (fragend) anyone; ist da wer? is anyone there?

Werbe|agentur *f* advertising agency. w∼n† *vt* recruit; attract (Kunden, Besucher) □ *vi* (haben) w∼n für advertise;

canvass for (Partei); w∼n um try to attract (Besucher); court (Frau, Gunst). W∼spot /-sp-/ *m* -s,-s commercial

Werbung *f* advertising

werden† *vi* (sein) become; (müde, alt, länger) get, grow; (blind, wahnsinnig) go; blass w∼ turn pale; krank w∼ fall ill; es wird warm/dunkel it is getting warm/dark; mir wurde schlecht/schwindlig I felt sick/dizzy; er will Lehrer w∼ he wants to be a teacher; was ist aus ihm geworden? what has become of him? □ *v aux* (Zukunft) shall; wir w∼ sehen we shall see; es wird bald regnen it's going to rain soon; würden Sie so nett sein? would you be so kind? □ (Passiv; pp worden) be; geliebt/geboren w∼ be loved/born; es wurde gemunkelt it was rumoured

werfen† *vt* throw; cast (Blick, Schatten); sich w∼ (Holz:) warp □ *vi* (haben) w∼ mit throw

Werft *f* -,-en shipyard

Werk *nt* -[e]s,-e work; (Fabrik) works *sg*, factory; (Trieb-) mechanism. W∼en *nt* -s (Sch) handicraft. W∼statt *f* -,-en workshop; (Auto-) garage; (Künstler-) studio. W∼tag *m* weekday. w∼tags *adv* on weekdays. w∼tätig *a* working. W∼unterricht *m* (Sch) handicraft

Werkzeug *nt* tool; (coll) tools *pl*. W∼maschine *f* machine tool

Wermut *m* -s vermouth

wert *a* viel/50 Mark w∼ worth a lot/50 marks; nichts w∼ sein be worthless; jds/etw (gen) w∼ sein be worthy of s.o./sth. W∼ *m* -[e]s,-e value; (Nenn-) denomination; im W∼ von worth; W∼ legen auf (+ acc) set great store by. w∼en *vt* rate

Wert|gegenstand *m* object of value; W∼gegenstände valuables. w∼los *a* worthless. W∼minderung *f* depreciation. W∼papier *nt* (Comm) security. W∼sachen *fpl* valuables. w∼voll *a* valuable

Wesen *nt* -s,- nature; (Lebe-) being; (Mensch) creature

wesentlich *a* essential; (grundlegend) fundamental; (erheblich) considerable; im W∼en (w∼en) essentially □ *adv* considerably, much

weshalb *adv* why

Wespe *f* -,-n wasp

wessen *pron* (gen of wer) whose

westdeutsch *a* West German

Weste *f* -,-n waistcoat, (Amer) vest

Westen *m* -s west; nach W∼ west

Western *m* -[s],- western

Westfalen *nt* -s Westphalia

Westindien nt West Indies pl

west|lich a western; ⟨Richtung⟩ westerly □ adv & prep (+ gen) w~lich [von] der Stadt [to the] west of the town. w~wärts adv westwards

weswegen adv why

wett a w~ sein be quits

Wett|bewerb m -s,-e competition. W~büro nt betting shop

Wette f -,-n bet; um die W~ laufen race (mit jdm s.o.)

wetteifern vi (haben) compete

wetten vt/i (haben) bet (auf + acc on); mit jdm w~ have a bet with s.o.

Wetter nt -s,- weather; ⟨Un-⟩ storm. W~bericht m weather report. W~hahn m weathercock. W~lage f weather conditions pl. W~vorhersage f weather forecast. W~warte f -,-n meteorological station

Wett|kampf m contest. W~kämpfer(in) m(f) competitor. W~lauf m race. w~machen vt sep make up for. W~rennen nt race. W~streit m contest

wetzen vt sharpen □ vi (sein) ⟨fam⟩ dash

Whisky m -s whisky

wichsen vt polish

wichtig a important; w~ nehmen take seriously. W~keit f - importance. w~tuerisch a self-important

Wicke f -,-n sweet pea

Wickel m -s,- compress

wick|eln vt wind; ⟨ein-⟩ wrap; ⟨bandagieren⟩ bandage; ein Kind frisch w~eln change a baby. W~ler m -s,- curler

Widder m -s,- ram; ⟨Astr⟩ Aries

wider prep (+ acc) against; ⟨entgegen⟩ contrary to; w~ Willen against one's will

widerfahren† vi insep (sein) jdm w~ happen to s.o.

widerhallen vi sep (haben) echo

widerlegen vt insep refute

wider|lich a repulsive; ⟨unangenehm⟩ nasty, adv -ily. w~rechtlich a unlawful, adv -ly. W~rede f contradiction; keine W~rede! don't argue!

widerrufen† vt/i insep (haben) retract; revoke ⟨Befehl⟩

Widersacher m -s,- adversary

widersetzen (sich) vr insep resist (jdm/etw s.o./sth)

wider|sinnig a absurd. w~spenstig a unruly; ⟨störrisch⟩ stubborn

widerspiegeln vt sep reflect; sich w~ be reflected

widersprechen† vi insep (haben) contradict (jdm/etw s.o./sth)

Wider|spruch m contradiction; ⟨Protest⟩ protest. w~sprüchlich a contradictory. w~spruchslos adv without protest

Widerstand m resistance; W~ leisten resist. w~sfähig a resistant; ⟨Bot⟩ hardy

widerstehen† vi insep (haben) resist (jdm/etw s.o./sth); ⟨anwidern⟩ be repugnant (jdm to s.o.)

widerstreben vi insep (haben) es widerstrebt mir I am reluctant (zu to). W~ nt -s reluctance. w~d a reluctant, adv -ly

widerwärtig a disagreeable, unpleasant; ⟨ungünstig⟩ adverse

Widerwill|e m aversion, repugnance. w~ig a reluctant, adv -ly

widm|en vt dedicate (dat to); ⟨verwenden⟩ devote (dat to); sich w~en (+ dat) devote oneself to. W~ung f -,-en dedication

widrig a adverse, unfavourable

wie adv how; wie viel how much/(pl) many; um wie viel Uhr? at what time? wie viele? how many? wie ist Ihr Name? what is your name? wie ist das Wetter? what is the weather like? □ conj as; ⟨gleich wie⟩ like; ⟨sowie⟩ as well as; ⟨als⟩ when, as; genau wie du just like you; so gut/reich wie as good/rich as; nichts wie nothing but; größer wie ich ⟨fam⟩ bigger than me

wieder adv again; er ist w~ da he is back; jdn/etw w~ erkennen recognize s.o./sth; eine Tätigkeit w~aufnehmen resume an activity; etw w~ verwenden/verwerten reuse/recycle sth; etw w~gutmachen make up for ⟨Schaden⟩; redress ⟨Unrecht⟩; ⟨bezahlen⟩ pay for sth

Wiederaufbau m reconstruction. w~en vt sep (NEW) wieder aufbauen, s. aufbauen

wieder|aufnehmen† vt sep (NEW) w~aufnehmen, s. wieder. W~aufrüstung f rearmament

wieder|bekommen† vt sep get back. w~beleben vt sep (NEW) w~ beleben, s. beleben. W~belebung f - resuscitation. w~bringen† vt sep bring back. w~erkennen† vt sep (NEW) w~ erkennen, s. wieder. W~gabe f (s. w~geben) return; portrayal; rendering; reproduction. w~geben† vt sep give back, return; ⟨darstellen⟩ portray; ⟨ausdrücken, übersetzen⟩ render; ⟨zitieren⟩ quote; ⟨Techn⟩ reproduce. W~geburt f reincarnation

wiedergutmach|en vt sep (NEW) w~ gutmachen, s. wieder. W~ung f - reparation; ⟨Entschädigung⟩ compensation

wiederher|stellen vt sep re-establish; restore ⟨Gebäude⟩; restore to health ⟨Kranke⟩; w~gestellt sein be fully recovered. W~stellung f re-establishment; restoration; ⟨Genesung⟩ recovery

wiederholen[1] *vt sep* get back

wiederhol|en[2] *vt insep* repeat; (*Sch*) revise; sich w~en recur; ⟨*Person:*⟩ repeat oneself. w~t *a* repeated, *adv* -ly. W~ung *f* -,-en repetition; (*Sch*) revision

Wieder|hören *nt* auf W~hören! goodbye! W~käuer *m* -s,- ruminant. W~kehr *f* - return; (*W~holung*) recurrence. w~kehren *vi sep* (*sein*) return; (*sich wiederholen*) recur. w~kommen† *vi sep* (*sein*) come back

wiedersehen† *vt sep* (NEW) wieder sehen, *s.* sehen. W~ *nt* -s,- reunion; auf W~! goodbye!

wiederum *adv* again; (*andererseits*) on the other hand

wiedervereinig|en *vt sep* (NEW) wieder vereinigen, *s.* vereinigen. W~ung *f* re-unification

wieder|verheiraten (sich) *vr sep* (NEW) w~ verheiraten (sich), *s.* verheiraten. w~verwenden† *vt sep* (NEW) w~ verwenden, *s.* wieder. w~verwerten *vt sep* (NEW) w~ verwerten, *s.* wieder. w~wählen *vt sep* (NEW) w~ wählen, *s.* wählen

Wiege *f* -,-n cradle

wiegen† *vt/i* (*haben*) weigh

wiegen[2] *vt* (*reg*) rock; sich w~ sway; (*schaukeln*) rock. W~lied *nt* lullaby

wiehern *vi* (*haben*) neigh

Wien *nt* -s Vienna. W~er *a* Viennese; W~er Schnitzel Wiener schnitzel □ *m* -s,- Viennese □ *f* -,- ≈ frankfurter. w~erisch *a* Viennese

Wiese *f* -,-n meadow

Wiesel *nt* -s,- weasel

wieso *adv* why

wieviel *pron* (NEW) wie viel, *s.* wie. w~te(r,s) *a* which; der W~te ist heute? what is the date today?

wieweit *adv* how far

wild *a* wild, *adv* -ly; (*Stamm*) savage; w~er Streik wildcat strike; w~ wachsen grow wild. W~ *nt* -[e]s game; (*Rot-*) deer; (*Culin*) venison. W~dieb *m* poacher. W~e(r) *m|f* savage

Wilder|er *m* -s,- poacher. w~n *vt/i* (*haben*) poach

wildfremd *a* totally strange, w~e Leute total strangers

Wild|heger, W~hüter *m* -s,- gamekeeper. W~leder *nt* suede. w~ledern *a* suede. W~nis *f* - wilderness. W~schwein *nt* wild boar. W~westfilm *m* western

Wille *m* -ns will; letzter W~ will; seinen W~n durchsetzen get one's [own] way; mit W~n intentionally

willen *prep* (+ *gen*) um ... w~ for the sake of ...

Willens|kraft *f* will-power. w~stark *a* strong-willed

willig *a* willing, *adv* -ly

willkommen *a* welcome; w~ heißen welcome. W~ *nt* -s welcome

willkürlich *a* arbitrary, *adv* -ily

wimmeln *vi* (*haben*) swarm

wimmern *vi* (*haben*) whimper

Wimpel *m* -s,- pennant

Wimper *f* -,-n [eye]lash; nicht mit der W~ zucken (*fam*) not bat an eyelid. W~ntusche *f* mascara

Wind *m* -[e]s,-e wind

Winde *f* -,-n (*Techn*) winch

Windel *f* -,-n nappy, (*Amer*) diaper

winden† *vt* wind; make (*Kranz*); in die Höhe w~ winch up; sich w~ wind (um round); (*sich krümmen*) writhe

Wind|hund *m* greyhound. w~ig *a* windy. W~mühle *f* windmill. W~pocken *fpl* chickenpox *sg.* W~schutzscheibe *f* windscreen, (*Amer*) windshield. w~still *a* calm. W~stille *f* calm. W~stoß *m* gust of wind. W~surfen *nt* windsurfing

Windung *f* -,-en bend; (*Spirale*) spiral

Wink *m* -[e]s,-e sign; (*Hinweis*) hint

Winkel *m* -s,- angle; (*Ecke*) corner. W~messer *m* -s,- protractor

winken *vi* (*haben*) wave; jdm w~ wave/(*herbei-*) beckon to s.o.

winseln *vi* (*haben*) whine

Winter *m* -s,- winter. w~lich *a* wintry; (*Winter-*) winter ... W~schlaf *m* hibernation; W~schlaf halten hibernate. W~sport *m* winter sports *pl*

Winzer *m* -s,- winegrower

winzig *a* tiny, minute

Wipfel *m* -s,- [tree-]top

Wippe *f* -,-n see-saw. w~n *vi* (*haben*) bounce; (*auf Wippe*) play on the see-saw

wir *pron* we; wir sind es it's us

Wirbel *m* -s,- eddy; (*Drehung*) whirl; (*Trommel-*) roll; (*Anat*) vertebra; (*Haar-*) crown; (*Aufsehen*) fuss. w~n *vt/i* (*sein/haben*) whirl. W~säule *f* spine. W~sturm *m* cyclone. W~tier *nt* vertebrate. W~wind *m* whirlwind

wird *s.* werden

wirken *vi* (*haben*) have an effect (auf + *acc* on); (*zur Geltung kommen*) be effective; (*tätig sein*) work; (*scheinen*) seem □ *vt* (*Tex*) knit; Wunder w~ work miracles

wirklich *a* real, *adv* -ly. W~keit *f* -,-en reality

wirksam *a* effective, *adv* -ly. W~keit *f* - effectiveness

Wirkung f -,-en effect. w~slos a ineffective, adv -ly. w~svoll a effective, adv -ly

wirr a tangled; (Haar) tousled; (verwirrt, verworren) confused. W~warr m -s tangle; (fig) confusion; (von Stimmen) hubbub

Wirt m -[e]s,-e landlord. W~in f -,-nen landlady

Wirtschaft f -,-en economy; (Gast-) restaurant; (Kneipe) pub. w~en vi (haben) manage one's finances; (sich betätigen) busy oneself; sie kann nicht w~en she's a bad manager. W~erin f -,-nen housekeeper. w~lich a economic, adv -ally; (sparsam) economical, adv -ly. W~sgeld nt housekeeping [money]. W~sprüfer m auditor

Wirtshaus nt inn; (Kneipe) pub

Wisch m -[e]s,-e (fam) piece of paper

wisch|en vt/i (haben) wipe; wash ⟨Fußboden⟩ □vi (sein) slip; ⟨Maus:⟩ scurry. W~lappen m cloth; (Aufwisch-) floorcloth

wispern vt/i (haben) whisper

wissen† vt/i (haben) know; weißt du noch? do you remember? ich wüsste gern… I should like to know…; nichts w~ wollen von not want anything to do with. W~ nt -s knowledge; meines W~s to my knowledge

Wissenschaft f -,-en science. W~ler m -s,- academic; (Natur-) scientist. w~lich a academic, adv -ally; scientific, adv -ally

wissen|swert a worth knowing. w~tlich a deliberate □ adv knowingly

wittern vt scent; (ahnen) sense. W~ung f - scent; (Wetter) weather

Witwe f -,-n widow. W~r m -s,- widower

Witz m -es,-e joke; (Geist) wit. W~bold m -[e]s,-e joker. w~ig a funny; (geistreich) witty

wo adv where; (als) when; (irgendwo) somewhere; wo immer wherever □ conj seeing that; (obwohl) although; (wenn) if

woanders adv somewhere else

wobei adv how; (relativ) during the course of which

Woche f -,-n week. W~nende nt weekend. W~nkarte f weekly ticket. w~nlang adv for weeks. W~ntag m day of the week; (Werktag) weekday. w~tags adv on weekdays

wöchentlich a & adv weekly

Wodka m -s vodka

wodurch adv how; (relativ) through/(Ursache) by which; (Folge) as a result of which

wofür adv what … for; (relativ) for which

Woge f -,-n wave

wogegen adv what … against; (relativ) against which □ conj whereas. **woher** adv where from; (woher weißt du das? how do you know that? **wohin** adv where [to]; wohin gehst du? where are you going? **wohingegen** conj whereas

wohl adv well; (vermutlich) probably; (etwa) about; (zwar) perhaps; w~ kaum hardly; w~ oder übel willy-nilly; sich w~ fühlen feel well/(behaglich) comfortable; jdm w~ tun do s.o. good; der ist w~ verrückt! he must be mad! W~ nt -[e]s welfare, well-being; auf jds W~ trinken drink s.o.'s health; zum W~ (+ gen) for the good of; zum W~! cheers!

wohlauf a w~ sein be well

Wohl|befinden nt well-being. W~behagen nt feeling of well-being. w~behalten a safe, adv -ly. W~ergehen nt -s welfare. w~erzogen a well brought-up

Wohlfahrt f - welfare. W~sstaat m Welfare State

Wohl|gefallen nt -s pleasure. W~geruch m fragrance. w~gesinnt a well disposed (dat towards). w~habend a prosperous, well-to-do. w~ig a comfortable, adv -bly. w~klingend a melodious. w~riechend a fragrant. w~schmeckend a tasty

Wohlstand m prosperity. W~sgesellschaft f affluent society

Wohltat f [act of] kindness; (Annehmlichkeit) treat; (Genuss) bliss

Wohltät|er m benefactor. w~ig a charitable

wohl|tuend a agreeable, adv -bly. w~tun† vi sep (haben) (NEW) w~ tun, s. wohl. w~verdient a well-deserved. w~weislich adv deliberately

Wohlwollen nt -s goodwill; (Gunst) favour. w~d a benevolent, adv -ly

Wohn|anhänger m = Wohnwagen. W~block m block of flats. w~en vi (haben) live; (vorübergehend) stay. W~gegend f residential area. w~haft a resident. W~haus nt [dwelling-]house. W~heim nt hostel; (Alten-) home. w~lich a comfortable, adv -bly. W~mobil nt -s,-e camper. W~ort m place of residence. W~raum m living space; (Zimmer) living-room. W~sitz m place of residence

Wohnung f -,-en flat, (Amer) apartment; (Unterkunft) accommodation. W~snot f housing shortage

Wohn|wagen m caravan, (Amer) trailer. W~zimmer nt living-room

wölb|en vt curve; arch ⟨Rücken⟩. W~ung f -,-en curve; (Archit) vault

Wolf *m* -[e]s,⸗e wolf; (*Fleisch*-) mincer; (*Reiß*-) shredder

Wolke|*f* -,-n cloud. W~enbruch *m* cloudburst. W~enkratzer *m* skyscraper. w~enlos *a* cloudless. w~ig *a* cloudy

Woll|decke *f* blanket. W~e *f* -,-n wool

wollen[1] *vt/i* (*haben*) & *v aux* want; etw tun w~ want to do sth; (*beabsichtigen*) be going to do sth; ich will nach Hause I want to go home; wir wollten gerade gehen we were just going; ich wollte, ich könnte dir helfen I wish I could help you; der Motor will nicht anspringen the engine won't start

woll|en[2] *a* woollen. w~ig *a* woolly. W~sachen *fpl* woollens

wollüstig *a* sensual, *adv* -ly

womit *adv* what ... with; (*relativ*) with which. womöglich *adv* possibly. wonach *adv* what ... after/(*suchen*) for/(*riechen*) of; (*relativ*) after/for/of which

Wonne *f* -,-n bliss; (*Freude*) joy. w~ig *a* sweet

woran *adv* what ... on/(*denken, sterben*) of; (*relativ*) on/of which; woran hast du ihn erkannt? how did you recognize him? worauf *adv* what ... on/(*warten*) for; (*relativ*) on/for which; (*woraufhin*) whereupon. woraufhin *adv* whereupon. woraus *adv* what ... from; (*relativ*) from which. worin *adv* what ... in; (*relativ*) in which

Wort *nt* -[e]s,⸗er & -e word; jdm ins W~ fallen interrupt s.o.; ein paar W~e sagen say a few words. w~brüchig *a* w~brüchig werden break one's word

Wörterbuch *nt* dictionary

Wort|führer *m* spokesman. w~getreu *a* & *adv* word-for-word. w~gewandt *a* eloquent, *adv* -ly. w~karg *a* taciturn. W~laut *m* wording

wörtlich *a* literal, *adv* -ly; (*wortgetreu*) word-for-word

wort|los *a* silent □ *adv* without a word. W~schatz *m* vocabulary. W~spiel *nt* pun, play on words. W~wechsel *m* exchange of words; (*Streit*) argument. w~wörtlich *a* & *adv* = wörtlich

worüber *adv* what ... over/(*lachen, sprechen*) about; (*relativ*) over/about which. worum *adv* what ... round/(*bitten, kämpfen*) for; (*relativ*) round/for which; worum geht es? what is it about? worunter *adv* what ... under/(*wozwischen*) among; (*relativ*) under/among which. wovon *adv* what ... from/(*sprechen*) about; (*relativ*) from/about which. wovor *adv* what ... in front of; (*sichfürchten*) what ... of; (*relativ*) in front of which; of which. wozu *adv* what ...

to/(*brauchen, benutzen*) for; (*relativ*) to/for which; wozu? what for?

Wrack *nt* -s,-s wreck

wringen† *vt* wring

wuchern *vi* (*haben/sein*) grow profusely. W~preis *m* extortionate price. W~ung *f* -,-en growth

Wuchs *m* -es growth; (*Gestalt*) stature

Wucht *f* - force. w~en *vt* heave. w~ig *a* massive

wühlen *vi* (*haben*) rummage; (*in der Erde*) burrow □ *vt* dig

Wulst *m* -[e]s,⸗e bulge; (*Fett*-) roll. w~ig *a* bulging; (*Lippen*) thick

wund *a* sore; w~ reiben chafe; sich w~ liegen get bedsores. W~brand *m* gangrene

Wunde *f* -,-n wound

Wunder *nt* -s,- wonder, marvel; (*übernatürliches*) miracle; kein W~! no wonder! w~bar *a* miraculous; (*herrlich*) wonderful, *adv* -ly, marvellous, *adv* -ly. W~kind *nt* infant prodigy. w~lich *a* odd, *adv* -ly. w~n *vt* surprise; sich w~n be surprised (über + *acc* at). w~schön *a* beautiful, *adv* -ly. w~voll *a* wonderful, *adv* -ly

Wundstarrkrampf *m* tetanus

Wunsch *m* -[e]s,⸗e wish; (*Verlangen*) desire; (*Bitte*) request

wünschen *vt* want; sich (*dat*) etw w~ want sth; (*bitten um*) ask for sth; jdm Glück/gute Nacht w~ wish s.o. luck/good night; ich wünschte, ich könnte ... I wish I could ...; Sie w~? can I help you? zu w~ übrig lassen leave something to be desired. w~swert *a* desirable

Wunsch|konzert *nt* musical request programme. W~traum *m* (*fig*) dream

wurde, würde *s.* werden

Würde *f* -,-n dignity; (*Ehrenrang*) honour. w~los *a* undignified. W~nträger *m* dignitary. w~voll *a* dignified □ *adv* with dignity

würdig *a* dignified; (*wert*) worthy. w~en *vt* recognize; (*schätzen*) appreciate; keines Blickes w~en not deign to look at

Wurf *m* -[e]s,⸗e throw; (*Junge*) litter

Würfel *m* -s,- cube; (*Spiel*-) dice; (*Zucker*-) lump. w~n *vi* (*haben*) throw the dice; w~n um play dice for □ *vt* throw; (*in Würfel schneiden*) dice. W~zucker *m* cube sugar

Wurfgeschoss (Wurfgeschoß) *nt* missile

würgen *vt* choke □ *vi* (*haben*) retch; choke (an + *dat* on)

Wurm *m* -[e]s,⸗er worm; (*Made*) maggot. w~en *vi* (*haben*) jdn w~en (*fam*) rankle [with s.o.]. w~stichig *a* worm-eaten

Wurst *f* -,-̈e sausage; das ist mir W~ (*fam*) I couldn't care less

Würstchen *nt* -s,- small sausage; Frankfurter W~ frankfurter

Würze *f* -,-n spice; (*Aroma*) aroma

Wurzel *f* -,-n root; W~n schlagen take root. w~n *vi* (*haben*) root

würz|en *vt* season. w~ig *a* tasty; (*aromatisch*) aromatic; (*pikant*) spicy

wüst *a* chaotic; (*wirr*) tangled; (*öde*) desolate; (*wild*) wild, *adv* -ly; (*schlimm*) terrible, *adv* -bly

Wüste *f* -,-n desert

Wut *f* - rage, fury. W~anfall *m* fit of rage

wüten *vi* (*haben*) rage. w~d *a* furious, *adv* -ly; w~d machen infuriate

X

x /ɪks/ *inv a* (*Math*) x; (*fam*) umpteen. X-Beine *ntpl* knock-knees. x-beinig, X-beinig *a* knock-kneed. x-beliebig *a* (*fam*) any; eine x-beliebige Zahl any number [you like]. x-mal *adv* (*fam*) umpteen times; zum x-ten Mal for the umpteenth time

Y

Yoga /ˈjoːɡa/ *m & nt* -[s] yoga

Z

Zack|e *f* -,-n point; (*Berg-*) peak; (*Gabel-*) prong. z~ig *a* jagged; (*gezackt*) serrated; (*fam: schneidig*) smart, *adv* -ly

zaghaft *a* timid, *adv* -ly; (*zögernd*) tentative, *adv* -ly

zäh *a* tough; (*hartnäckig*) tenacious, *adv* -ly; (*zähflüssig*) viscous; (*schleppend*) sluggish, *adv* -ly. z~flüssig *a* viscous; (*Verkehr*) slow-moving. Z~igkeit *f* - toughness; tenacity

Zahl *f* -,-en number; (*Ziffer, Betrag*) figure

zahl|bar *a* payable. z~en *vt/i* (*haben*) pay; (*bezahlen*) pay for; bitte z~en! the bill please!

zählen *vi* (*haben*) count; z~ zu (*fig*) be one/(*pl*) some of; z~ auf (+ *acc*) count on □ *vt* count; z~ zu add to; (*fig*) count among; die Stadt zählt 5000 Einwohner the town has 5000 inhabitants

zahlenmäßig *a* numerical, *adv* -ly

Zähler *m* -s,- meter

Zahl|grenze *f* fare-stage. Z~karte *f* paying-in slip. z~los *a* countless. z~reich *a* numerous; (*Anzahl, Gruppe*) large □ *adv* in large numbers. Z~ung *f* -,-en payment; in Z~ung nehmen take in part-exchange

Zählung *f* -,-en count

zahlungsunfähig *a* insolvent

Zahlwort *nt* (*pl* -wörter) numeral

zahm *a* tame

zähmen *vt* tame; (*fig*) restrain

Zahn *m* -[e]s,-̈e tooth; (*am Zahnrad*) cog. Z~arzt *m*, Z~ärztin *f* dentist. Z~belag *m* plaque. Z~bürste *f* toothbrush. z~en *vi* (*haben*) be teething. Z~fleisch *nt* gums *pl*. z~los *a* toothless. Z~pasta *f* -,-en toothpaste. Z~rad *nt* cog-wheel. Z~schmelz *m* enamel. Z~schmerzen *mpl* toothache *sg*. Z~spange *f* brace. Z~stein *m* tartar. Z~stocher *m* -s,- tooth-pick

Zange *f* -,-n pliers *pl*; (*Kneif-*) pincers *pl*; (*Kohlen-, Zucker-*) tongs *pl*; (*Geburts-*) forceps *pl*

Zank *m* -[e]s squabble. z~en *vr* sich z~en squabble □ *vi* (*haben*) scold (mit jdm s.o.)

zänkisch *a* quarrelsome

Zäpfchen *nt* -s,- (*Anat*) uvula; (*Med*) suppository

Zapfen *m* -s,- (*Bot*) cone; (*Stöpsel*) bung; (*Eis-*) icicle. z~ *vt* tap, draw. Z~streich *m* (*Mil*) tattoo

Zapf|hahn *m* tap. Z~säule *f* petrol-pump

zappel|ig *a* fidgety; (*nervös*) jittery. z~n *vi* (*haben*) wriggle; (*Kind:*) fidget

zart *a* delicate, *adv* -ly; (*weich, zärtlich*) tender, *adv* -ly; (*sanft*) gentle, *adv* -ly. Z~gefühl *nt* tact. Z~heit *f* - delicacy; tenderness; gentleness

zärtlich *a* tender, *adv* -ly; (*liebevoll*) loving, *adv* -ly. Z~keit *f* -,-en tenderness; (*Liebkosung*) caress

Zauber *m* -s magic; (*Bann*) spell. Z~er *m* -s,- magician. z~haft *a* enchanting. Z~künstler *m* conjuror. Z~kunststück *nt* = Z~trick. z~n *vi* (*haben*) do magic; (*Zaubertricks ausführen*) do conjuring tricks □ *vt* produce as if by magic. Z~stab *m* magic wand. Z~trick *m* conjuring trick

zaudern *vi* (*haben*) delay; (*zögern*) hesitate

Zaum *m* -[e]s,Zäume bridle; im Z~ halten(*fig*) restrain

Zaun *m* -[e]s,Zäune fence. Z~könig *m* wren

z.B. *abbr* (zum Beispiel) e.g.

Zebra *nt* -s,-s zebra. Z~streifen *m* zebra crossing

Zeche *f* -,-n bill; (*Bergwerk*) pit

zechen *vi* (*haben*) (*fam*) drink

Zeder *f* -,-n cedar

Zeh *m* -[e]s,-en toe. Z~e *f* -,-n toe; (*Knoblauch*-) clove. Z~ennagel *m* toenail

zehn *inv a*, Z~ *f* -,-en ten. z~te(r,s) *a* tenth. Z~tel *nt* -s,-tenth

Zeichen *nt* -s,- sign; (*Signal*) signal. Z~setzung *f* -punctuation. Z~trickfilm *m* cartoon [film]

zeichn|en *vt/i* (*haben*) draw; (*kenn*-) mark; (*unter*-) sign. Z~er *m* -s,-draughtsman. Z~ung *f* -,-en drawing; (*auf Fell*) markings *pl*

Zeige|finger *m* index finger. z~*nvt* show; sich z~n appear; (*sich herausstellen*) become clear; das wird sich z~n we shall see ☐ *vi* (*haben*) point (auf + *acc* to). Z~r *m* -s,-pointer; (*Uhr*-) hand

Zeile *f* -,-n line; (*Reihe*) row

zeit *prep* (+ *gen*) z~ meines/seines Lebens all my/his life

Zeit *f* -,-entime; sich(*dat*) Z~ lassentake one's time; es hat Z~there's no hurry; mit der Z~ in time; in nächster Z~ in the near future; die erste Z~at first; von Z~ zu Z~ from time to time; zur Z~ (*rechtzeitig*) in time; (*derzeit*) NEW zurzeit eine Z~ lang for a time *or* while; [ach] du liebe Z~!(*fam*) good heavens!

Zeit|alter *nt* age, era. Z~arbeit *f* temporary work. Z~bombe *f* time bomb. z~gemäß *a* modern, up-to-date. Z~genosse*m*, Z~genossin *f* contemporary. z~genössisch*a* contemporary. z~ig *a* & *adv* early. Z~lang *f* eine Z~lang NEW eine Z~ lang *s*. Zeit z~lebens*adv* all one's life

zeitlich (*Dauer*) in time; (*Folge*) chronological ☐ *adv* z~ begrenzt for a limited time

zeit|los timeless. Z~lupe *f* slow motion. Z~punkt *m* time. z~raubend *a* time-consuming. Z~raum *m* period. Z~schrift *f* magazine, periodical

Zeitung *f* -,-ennewspaper. Z~spapier *nt* newspaper

Zeit|verschwendung *f* waste of time. Z~vertreib*m* pastime; zum Z~vertreib to pass the time. z~weilig *a* temporary ☐ *adv* temporarily; (*hin und wieder*) at times. z~weise*adv* at times. Z~wort *nt* (*pl* -wörter) verb. Z~zünder*m* time fuse

---

Zelle *f* -,-ncell; (*Telefon*-) box

Zelt *nt* -[e]s,-etent; (*Fest*-) marquee. z~en *vi* (*haben*) camp. Z~en *nt* -s camping. Z~plane *f* tarpaulin. Z~platz *m* campsite

Zement *m* -[e]s cement. z~ieren *vt* cement

zen|sieren *vt* (*Sch*) mark; censor (*Presse, Film*). Z~sur *f* -,-en (*Sch*) mark, (*Amer*) grade; (*Presse*-) censorship

Zentimeter *m* & *nt* centimetre. Z~maß *nt* tape-measure

Zentner *m* -s,- [metric] hundredweight (*50 kg*)

zentral *a* central, *adv* -ly. Z~e *f* -,-ncentral office; (*Partei*-) headquarters *pl*; (*Teleph*) exchange. Z~heizung *f* central heating. z~isieren *vt* centralize

Zentrum *nt* -s,-tren centre

zerbrech|en *vt/i* (*sein*) break; sich(*dat*) den Kopf z~en rack one's brains. z~lich*a* fragile

zerdrücken *vt* crush; mash (*Kartoffeln*)

Zeremonie *f* -,-nceremony

Zeremoniell *nt* -s,-e ceremonial. z~ *a* ceremonial, *adv* -ly

Zerfall *m* disintegration; (*Verfall*) decay. z~en *vi* (*sein*) disintegrate; (*verfallen*) decay; in drei Teile z~enbe divided into three parts

zerfetzen *vt* tear to pieces

zerfließen *vi* (*sein*) melt; (*Tinte*:) run

zergehen *vi* (*sein*) melt; (*sich auflösen*) dissolve

zergliedern *vt* dissect

zerkleinern *vt* chop/(*schneiden*) cut up; (*mahlen*) grind

zerknirscht *a* contrite

zerknüllen *vt* crumple [up]

zerkratzen *vt* scratch

zerlassen *vt* melt

zerlegen *vt* take to pieces, dismantle; (*zerschneiden*) cut up; (*tranchieren*) carve

zerlumpt *a* ragged

zermalmen *vt* crush

zermürb|en *vt* (*fig*) wear down. Z~ungskrieg *m* war of attrition

zerplatzen *vi* (*sein*) burst

zerquetschen *vt* squash, crush; mash (*Kartoffeln*)

Zerrbild *nt* caricature

zerreißen *vt* tear, (*in Stücke*) tear up; break (*Faden, Seil*) ☐ *vi* (*sein*) tear; break

zerren *vt* drag; pull (*Muskel*) ☐ *vi* (*haben*) pull (an + *dat* at)

zerrinnen *vi* (*sein*) melt

zerrissen *a* torn

zerrütten vt ruin, wreck; shatter ⟨Nerven⟩; zerrüttete Ehe broken marriage

zerschlagen† vt smash; smash up ⟨Möbel⟩; sich z∼ ⟨fig⟩ fall through; ⟨Hoffnung:⟩ be dashed □ a ⟨erschöpft⟩ worn out

zerschmettern vt/i ⟨sein⟩ smash

zerschneiden† vt cut; ⟨in Stücke⟩ cut up

zersetzen vt corrode; undermine ⟨Moral⟩; sich z∼ decompose

zersplittern vi ⟨sein⟩ splinter; ⟨Glas:⟩ shatter □ vt shatter

zerspringen† vi ⟨sein⟩ shatter; ⟨bersten⟩ burst

Zerstäuber m -s,- atomizer

zerstör|en vt destroy; ⟨zunichte machen⟩ wreck. Z∼er m -s,- destroyer. Z∼ung f destruction

zerstreu|en vt scatter; disperse ⟨Menge⟩; dispel ⟨Zweifel⟩; sich z∼en disperse; ⟨sich unterhalten⟩ amuse oneself. z∼t a absent-minded, adv -ly. Z∼ung f,-en ⟨Unterhaltung⟩ entertainment

zerstückeln vt cut up into pieces

zerteilen vt divide up

Zertifikat nt -[e]s,-e certificate

zertreten† vt stamp on; ⟨zerdrücken⟩ crush

zertrümmern vt smash [up]; wreck ⟨Gebäude, Stadt⟩

zerzaus|en vt tousle. z∼t a dishevelled; ⟨Haar⟩ tousled

Zettel m -s,- piece of paper; ⟨Notiz⟩ note; ⟨Bekanntmachung⟩ notice; ⟨Reklame-⟩ leaflet

Zeug nt -s ⟨fam⟩ stuff; ⟨Sachen⟩ things pl; ⟨Ausrüstung⟩ gear; dummes Z∼ nonsense; das Z∼ haben zu have the makings of

Zeuge m -n,-n witness. z∼n vi ⟨haben⟩ testify; z∼n von ⟨fig⟩ show □ vt father. Z∼naussage f testimony. Z∼nstand m witness box/⟨Amer⟩ stand

Zeugin f -,-nen witness

Zeugnis nt -ses,-se certificate; ⟨Sch⟩ report; ⟨Referenz⟩ reference; ⟨fig: Beweis⟩ evidence

Zickzack m -[e]s,-e zigzag

Ziege f -,-n goat

Ziegel m -s,- brick; ⟨Dach-⟩ tile. Z∼stein m brick

ziehen† vt pull; ⟨sanfter; zücken; zeichnen⟩ draw; ⟨heraus-⟩ pull out; extract ⟨Zahn⟩; raise ⟨Hut⟩; put on ⟨Bremse⟩; move ⟨Schachfigur⟩; put up ⟨Leine, Zaun⟩; ⟨dehnen⟩ stretch; make ⟨Grimasse, Scheitel⟩; ⟨züchten⟩ breed; grow ⟨Rosen, Gemüse⟩; nach sich z∼ ⟨fig⟩ entail □ vr sich z∼ ⟨sich erstrecken⟩ run; ⟨sich verziehen⟩

warp □ vi ⟨haben⟩ pull (an + dat on/at); ⟨Tee, Ofen:⟩ draw; ⟨Culin⟩ simmer; es zieht there is a draught; solche Filme z∼ nicht mehr films like that are no longer popular □ vi ⟨sein⟩ ⟨um-⟩ move ⟨nach to⟩; ⟨Menge:⟩ march; ⟨Vögel:⟩ migrate; ⟨Wolken, Nebel:⟩ drift. Z∼ nt -s ache

Ziehharmonika f accordion

Ziehung f -,-en draw

Ziel nt -[e]s,-e destination; ⟨Sport⟩ finish; ⟨Z∼scheibe & Mil⟩ target; ⟨Zweck⟩ aim, goal. z∼bewusst ⟨z∼bewußt⟩ a purposeful, adv -ly. z∼en vi ⟨haben⟩ aim ⟨auf + acc at⟩. z∼end a ⟨Gram⟩ transitive. z∼los a aimless, adv -ly. Z∼scheibe f target; ⟨fig⟩ butt. z∼strebig a single-minded, adv -ly

ziemen (sich) vr be seemly

ziemlich a ⟨fam⟩ fair □ adv rather, fairly; ⟨fast⟩ pretty well

Zier|de f -,-n ornament. z∼en vt adorn; sich z∼en make a fuss; ⟨sich bitten lassen⟩ need coaxing

zierlich a dainty, adv -ily; ⟨fein⟩ delicate, adv -ly; ⟨Frau⟩ petite

Ziffer f -,-n figure, digit; ⟨Zahlzeichen⟩ numeral. Z∼blatt nt dial

zig inv a ⟨fam⟩ umpteen

Zigarette f -,-n cigarette

Zigarre f -,-n cigar

Zigeuner(in) m -s,- ⟨f -,-nen⟩ gypsy

Zimmer nt -s,- room. Z∼mädchen nt chambermaid. Z∼mann m ⟨pl -leute⟩ carpenter. z∼n vt make ⟨a fam⟩ do carpentry. Z∼nachweis m accommodation bureau. Z∼pflanze f house plant

zimperlich a squeamish; ⟨wehleidig⟩ soft; ⟨prüde⟩ prudish

Zimt m -[e]s cinnamon

Zink nt -s zinc

Zinke f -,-n prong; ⟨Kamm-⟩ tooth

Zinn m -s tin; ⟨Gefäße⟩ pewter

Zins|en mpl interest sg; Z∼en tragen earn interest. Z∼eszins m -es compound interest. Z∼fuß, Z∼satz m interest rate

Zipfel m -s,- corner; ⟨Spitze⟩ point; ⟨Wurst-⟩ [tail-]end

zirka adv about

Zirkel m -s,- [pair of] compasses pl; ⟨Gruppe⟩ circle

Zirkul|ation /-'tsio:n/ f - circulation. z∼ieren vi ⟨sein⟩ circulate

Zirkus m -,-se circus

zirpen vi ⟨haben⟩ chirp

zischen vi ⟨haben⟩ hiss; ⟨Fett:⟩ sizzle □ vt hiss

Zit|at nt -[e]s,-e quotation. z∼ieren vt/i ⟨haben⟩ quote; ⟨rufen⟩ summon

Zitr|onat nt -[e]s candied lemon-peel.
Z~one f -,-n lemon. Z~onenlimonade f
lemonade

zittern vi (haben) tremble; (vor Kälte)
shiver; (beben) shake

zittrig a shaky, adv -ily

Zitze f -,-n teat

zivil a civilian; ⟨Ehe, Recht, Luftfahrt⟩ civil;
(mäßig) reasonable. Z~ nt -s civilian
clothes pl. Z~courage /-kura:ʒə/ f -
courage of one's convictions. Z~dienst m
community service

Zivili|sation /-'tsjo:n/ f -,-en civilization.
z~sieren vt civilize. z~siert a civilized
□ adv in a civilized manner

Zivilist m -en,-en civilian

zögern vi (haben) hesitate. Z~ nt -s hesitation. z~d a hesitant, adv -ly

Zoll¹ m -[e]s,-̈ inch

Zoll² m -[e]s,-̈e [customs] duty; (Behörde)
customs pl. Z~abfertigung f customs
clearance. Z~beamte(r) m customs officer. z~frei a & adv duty-free. Z~kon-
trolle f customs check

Zone f -,-n zone

Zoo m -s,-s zoo

Zoo|loge /tsoo'lo:gə/ m -n,-n zoologist.
Z~logie f - zoology. z~logisch a zoological

Zopf m -[e]s,-̈e plait

Zorn m -[e]s anger. z~ig a angry, adv -ily

zotig a smutty, dirty

zottig a shaggy

z.T. abbr (zum Teil) partly

zu prep (+ dat) to; (dazu) with; (zeitlich;
preislich) at; (Zweck) for; (über) about; to
... hin towards; zu Hause at home; zu
Fuß/Pferde on foot/horseback; zu
beiden Seiten on both sides; zu Ostern
at Easter; zu diesem Zweck for this purpose; zu meinem Erstaunen/Entsetzen
to my surprise/horror; zu Dutzenden by
the dozen; eine Marke zu 60 Pfennig a
60-pfennig stamp; das Stück zu zwei
Mark at two marks each; wir waren zu
dritt/viert there were three/four of us;
es steht 5 zu 3 the score is 5–3; zu etw
werden turn into sth □ adv (allzu) too;
(Richtung) towards; (geschlossen) closed;
⟨an Schalter, Hahn⟩ off; zu sein be closed;
zu groß/viel/weit too big/much/far;
nach dem Fluss zu towards the river;
Augen zu! shut your eyes! Tür zu! shut
the door! nur zu! go oh! macht zu! (fam)
hurry up! □ conj to; etwas zu essen something to eat; nicht zu glauben unbelievable; zu erörternde Probleme problems
to be discussed

zualler|erst adv first of all. z~letzt adv
last of all

Zubehör nt -s accessories pl

zubereit|en vt sep prepare. Z~ung f -
preparation; (in Rezept) method

zubilligen vt sep grant

zubinden† vt sep tie [up]

zubring|en† vt sep spend. Z~er m -s,- ac-
cess road; (Bus) shuttle

Zucchini /tsu'ki:ni/ pl courgettes

Zucht f -,-en breeding; (Pflanzen-) cultivation; ⟨Art, Rasse⟩ breed; (von Pflanzen)
strain; (Z~farm) farm; (Pferde-) stud;
(Disziplin) discipline

züchten vt breed; cultivate, grow ⟨Rosen,
Gemüse⟩. Z~er m -s,- breeder; grower

Zuchthaus nt prison

züchtigen vt chastise

Züchtung f -,-en breeding; (Pflanzen-)
cultivation; ⟨Art, Rasse⟩ breed; (von
Pflanzen) strain

zucken vi (haben) twitch; (sich z~d bewegen) jerk; ⟨Blitz:⟩ flash; ⟨Flamme:⟩
flicker □ vt die Achseln z~ shrug one's
shoulders

zücken vt draw ⟨Messer⟩

Zucker m -s sugar. Z~dose f sugar basin.
Z~guss (Z~guß) m icing. z~krank a
diabetic. Z~krankheit f diabetes. z~n
vt sugar. Z~rohr nt sugar cane. Z~rübe
f sugar beet. z~süß a sweet; (fig) sugary.
Z~watte f candyfloss. Z~zange f sugar
tongs pl

zuckrig a sugary

zudecken vt sep cover up; (im Bett) tuck
up; cover ⟨Topf⟩

zudem adv moreover

zudrehen vt sep turn off; jdm den Rücken
z~ turn one's back on s.o.

zudringlich a pushing, (fam) pushy

zudrücken vt sep press or push shut; close
⟨Augen⟩

zueinander adv to one another; z~
passen go together; z~ halten (fig) stick
together. z~halten† vi sep (haben) (NEW)
z~ halten, s. zueinander

zuerkennen† vt sep award (dat to)

zuerst adv first; (anfangs) at first; mit dem
Kopf z~ head first

zufahr|en† vi sep (sein) z~en auf (+ acc)
drive towards. Z~t f access; (Einfahrt)
drive

Zufall m chance; (Zusammentreffen) coincidence; durch Z~ by chance/coincid-
ence. z~en† vi sep (sein) close, shut; jdm
n z~en (Aufgabe) fall /(Erbe:) go to s.o.

zufällig a chance, accidental □ adv by
chance; ich war z~ da I happened to be
there

Zuflucht f refuge; (Schutz) shelter.
Z~sort m refuge

zufolge prep (+ dat) according to

zufrieden a contented, adv -ly; (befriedigt) satisfied; sich z~ geben be satisfied; jdn z~ lassen leave s.o. in peace; jdn z~ stellen satisfy s.o.; z~ stellend satisfactory. z~geben† (sich) vr sep (NEW≈) geben (sich), s. zufrieden. Z~heit f - contentment; satisfaction. z~lassen† vt sep (NEW≈) lassen, s. zufrieden. z~stellen vt sep (NEW≈) stellen, s. zufrieden. z~stellend a (NEW≈) z~ stellend, s. zufrieden

zufrieren† vi sep (sein) freeze over

zufügen vt sep inflict (dat on); do (Unrecht) (dat to)

Zufuhr f- supply

zuführen vt sep □ vt supply □ vi (haben) z~ auf (+ acc) lead to

Zug m -[e]s,¨e train; (Kolonne) column; (Um-) procession; (Mil) platoon; (Vogelschar) flock; (Ziehen, Zugkraft) pull; (Wandern, Ziehen) migration; (Schluck, Luft-) draught; (Atem-) breath; (beim Rauchen) puff; (Schach-) move; (beim Schwimmen, Rudern) stroke; (Gesichts-) feature; (Wesens-) trait; etw in vollen Zügen genießen enjoy sth to the full; in einem Zug[e] at one go

Zugabe f (Geschenk) [free] gift; (Mus) encore

Zugang m access

zugänglich a accessible; (Mensch:) approachable; (fig) amenable (dat/für to)

Zugbrücke f drawbridge

zugeben† vt sep add; (gestehen) admit; (erlauben) allow. zugegebenermaßen adv admittedly

zugegen a z~ sein be present

zugehen† vi sep (sein) close; (Tür:) be sent to s.o.; z~ auf (+ acc) go towards; dem Ende z~ draw to a close; (Vorräte:) run low; auf der Party ging es lebhaft zu the party was pretty lively

Zugehörigkeit f- membership

Zügel m -s,- rein

zugelassen a registered

zügel|los a unrestrained, adv -ly; (sittenlos) licentious. z~n vt rein in; (fig) curb

Zuge|ständnis nt concession. z~stehen† vt sep grant

zugetan a fond (dat of)

zugig a draughty

zügig a quick, adv -ly

Zug|kraft f pull; (fig) attraction. z~kräftig a effective; (anreizend) popular; (Titel) catchy

zugleich adv at the same time

Zug|luft f draught. Z~pferd nt draught-horse; (fam) draw

zugreifen† vi sep (haben) grab it/them; (bei Tisch) help oneself; (bei Angebot) jump at it; (helfen) lend a hand

zugrunde adv z~ richten destroy; z~ gehen be destroyed; (Ehe:) founder; (sterben) die; z~ liegen form the basis (dat of)

zugucken vi sep (haben) = zusehen

zugunsten prep (+ gen) in favour of; (Sammlung) in aid of

zugute adv jdm/etw z~ kommen benefit s.o./sth; jdm seine Jugend z~ halten make allowances for s.o.'s youth

Zugvogel m migratory bird

zuhalten† v sep □ vt keep closed; (bedecken) cover; sich (dat) die Nase z~ hold one's nose □ vi (haben) z~ auf (+ acc) head for

Zuhälter m -s,- pimp

zuhause adv = zu Hause, s. Haus. Z~ nt -s,- home

zuhör|en vi sep (haben) listen (dat to). Z~er(in) m(f) listener

zujubeln vi sep (haben) jdm z~ cheer s.o.

zukehren vt sep turn (dat to)

zukleben vt sep seal

zuknallen vt/i sep (sein) slam

zuknöpfen vt sep button up

zukommen† vi sep (sein) z~ auf (+ acc) come towards; (sich nähern) approach; z~ lassen send (jdm s.o.); devote (Pflege) (dat to); jdm z~ be s.o.'s right

Zukunft f - future. zukünftig a future □ adv in future

zulächeln vi sep (haben) smile (dat at)

Zulage f-,-n extra allowance

zulangen vi sep (haben) help oneself; tüchtig z~ tuck in

zulassen† vt sep allow, permit; (teilnehmen lassen) admit; (Admin) license, register; (geschlossen lassen) leave closed; leave unopened (Brief)

zulässig a permissible

Zulassung f -,-en admission; registration; (Lizenz) licence

zulaufen† vi sep (sein) z~en auf (+ acc) run towards; spitz z~en taper to a point

zulegen vt sep add; sich (dat) etw z~ get sth; grow (Bart)

zuleide adv jdm etwas z~ tun hurt s.o.

zuletzt adv last; (schließlich) in the end; nicht z~ not least

zuliebe adv jdm/etw z~ for the sake of s.o./sth

zum prep = zu dem; zum Spaß for fun; etw zum Lesen sth to read

zumachen v sep □ vt close, shut; do up ⟨Jacke⟩; seal ⟨Umschlag⟩; turn off ⟨Hahn⟩; (stilllegen) close down □ vi (haben) close, shut; (stillgelegt werden) close down

zumal adv especially □ conj especially since

zumeist adv for the most part

zumindest adv at least

zumutbar a reasonable

zumute adv mir ist traurig/elend z∼ I feel sad/wretched; mir ist nicht danach z∼ I don't feel like it

zumut|en vt sep jdm etw z∼en ask or expect sth of s.o.; sich (dat) zu viel z∼en overdo things. Z∼ung f· imposition; eine Z∼ung sein be unreasonable

zunächst adv first [of all]; (anfangs) at first; (vorläufig) for the moment □ prep (+ dat) nearest to

Zunahme f·,-n increase

Zuname m surname

zünd|en vt/i (haben) ignite; z∼ende Rede rousing speech. Z∼er m -s,- detonator, fuse. Z∼holz nt match. Z∼kerze f sparking-plug. Z∼schlüssel m ignition key. Z∼schnur f fuse. Z∼ung f·,-en ignition

zunehmen† vt sep (haben) increase (an + dat in); ⟨Mond:⟩ wax; (an Gewicht) put on weight. z∼d a increasing, adv -ly

Zuneigung f· affection

Zunft f·,-̈e guild

zünftig a proper, adv -ly

Zunge f·,-n tongue. Z∼nbrecher m tongue-twister

zunichte a z∼ machen wreck; z∼ werden come to nothing

zunicken vi sep (haben) nod (dat to)

zunutze a sich (dat) etw z∼ machen make use of sth; (ausnutzen) take advantage of sth

zuoberst adv right at the top

zuordnen vt sep assign (dat to)

zupfen vt/i (haben) pluck (an + dat at); pull out ⟨Unkraut⟩

zur prep = zu der; zur Schule/Arbeit to school/work

zurande advz∼ kommen mit (fam) cope with

zurate adv z∼ ziehen consult

zurechnungsfähig a of sound mind

zurecht|finden† (sich) vr sep find one's way. z∼kommen† vi sep (sein) cope (mit with); (rechtzeitig kommen) be in time. z∼legen vt sep put out ready; sich (dat) eine Ausrede z∼legen have an excuse all ready. z∼machen vt sep get ready; sich z∼machen get ready. z∼weisen† vt sep reprimand. Z∼weisung f reprimand

zureden vi sep (haben) jdm z∼ try to persuade s.o.

zurichten vt sep prepare; (beschädigen) damage; (verletzen) injure

zuriegeln vt sep bolt

zurück adv back; Berlin, hin und z∼ return to Berlin. z∼behalten† vt sep keep back; be left with ⟨Narbe⟩. z∼bekommen† vt sep get back; 20 Pfennig z∼bekommen get 20 pfennigs change. z∼bleiben† vi sep (sein) stay behind; (nicht mithalten) lag behind. z∼blicken vi sep (haben) look back. z∼bringen† vt sep bring back; (wieder hinbringen) take back. z∼erobern vt sep recapture; (fig) regain. z∼erstatten vt sep refund. z∼fahren† v sep □ vt drive back □ vi (sein) return, go back; (im Auto) drive back; (zurückweichen) recoil. z∼finden† vi sep (haben) find one's way back. z∼führen v sep □ vt take back; (fig) attribute (auf + acc to) □ vi (haben) lead back. z∼geben† vt sep give back, return. z∼geblieben a retarded. z∼gehen† vi sep (sein) go back, return; (abnehmen) go down; z∼gehen auf (+ acc) (fig) go back to

zurückgezogen a secluded. Z∼heit f· seclusion

zurückhalt|en† vt sep hold back; (abhalten) stop; sich z∼en restrain oneself. z∼end a reserved. Z∼ung f· reserve

zurück|kehren vi sep (sein) return. z∼kommen† vi sep (sein) come back, return; (ankommen) get back; z∼kommen auf (+ acc) (fig) come back to. z∼lassen† vt sep leave behind; (z∼kehren lassen) allow back. z∼legen vt sep put back; (reservieren) keep; (sparen) put by; cover ⟨Strecke⟩. z∼lehnen (sich) vr sep lean back. z∼liegen† vi sep (haben) be in the past; (Sport) be behind; das liegt lange zurück that was long ago. z∼melden (sich) vr sep report back. z∼nehmen† vt sep take back. z∼rufen† vt/i sep (haben) call back. z∼scheuen vi sep (sein) shrink (vor + dat from). z∼schicken vt sep send back. z∼schlagen† v sep □ vi (haben) hit back □ vt hit back; (abwehren) beat back; (umschlagen) turn back. z∼schneiden† vt sep cut back. z∼schrecken† vi sep (sein) shrink back, recoil; (fig) shrink (vor + dat from). z∼setzen v sep □ vt put back; (Auto) reverse, back; (herabsetzen) reduce; (fig) neglect □ vi (haben) reverse, back z∼stellen vt sep put back; (reservieren) keep; (fig) put aside; (aufschieben) postpone. z∼stoßen† v sep □ vt push back □ vi (sein) reverse, back. z∼treten† vi sep (sein) step back; (vom Amt) resign; (verzichten) withdraw. z∼weichen† vi sep (sein) draw back; (z∼schrecken) shrink

back. z~weisen† *vt sep* turn away; (*fig*)
reject. z~werfen† *vt* throw back; (*reflektieren*) reflect. z~zahlen *vt sep* pay back.
z~ziehen† *vt sep* draw back; (*fig*)
withdraw; sich z~ziehen withdraw;
(*vom Beruf*) retire; (*Mil*) retreat

Zuruf *m* shout. z~en† *vt sep* shout (*dat to*)

zurzeit *adv* at present

Zusage *f* -,-n acceptance; (*Versprechen*)
promise. z~n *v sep* □ *vt* promise □ *vi*
(*haben*) accept; jdm z~n appeal to s.o.

zusammen *adv* together; (*insgesamt*) altogether; z~ sein be together. Z~arbeit
f co-operation. z~arbeiten *vi sep* (*haben*)
co-operate. z~bauen *vt sep* assemble.
z~beißen† *vt sep* die Zähne z~beißen
clench/(*fig*) grit one's teeth. z~bleiben†
vi sep (*sein*) stay together. z~brechen†
vi sep (*sein*) collapse. z~bringen† *vt sep*
bring together; (*beschaffen*) raise.
Z~bruch *m* collapse; (*Nerven- & fig*)
breakdown. z~fahren† *vi sep* (*sein*) collide; (z~zucken) start. z~fallen† *vi sep*
(*sein*) collapse; (*zeitlich*) coincide.
z~falten *vt sep* fold up. z~fassen *vt sep*
summarize, sum up. Z~fassung *f* summary. z~fügen *vt sep* fit together.
z~führen *vt sep* bring together. z~gehören *vi sep* (*haben*) belong together;
(z~passen) go together. z~gesetzt *a*
(*Gram*) compound. z~halten† *v sep* □ *vt*
hold together; (*beisammenhalten*) keep together □ *vi* (*haben*) (*fig*) stick together.
Z~hang *m* connection; (*Kontext*) context.
z~hängen† *vi sep* (*haben*) be connected.
z~hanglos *a* incoherent, *adv* -ly.
z~klappen *v sep* □ *vt* fold up □ *vi* (*sein*)
collapse. z~kommen† *vi sep* (*sein*) meet;
(*sich sammeln*) accumulate. Z~kunft *f* -,
-e meeting. z~laufen† *vi sep* (*sein*) gather;
(*Flüssigkeit:*) collect; (*Linien:*) converge.
z~leben *vi sep* (*haben*) live together.
z~legen *v sep* □ *vt* put together;
(z~falten) fold up; (*vereinigen*) amalgamate; pool (*Geld*) □ *vi* (*haben*) club together. z~nehmen† *vt sep* gather up;
summon up (*Mut*); collect (*Gedanken*).
sich z~nehmen pull oneself together.
z~passen *vi sep* (*haben*) go together,
match; (*Personen:*) be well matched.
Z~prall *m* collision. z~prallen *vi sep*
(*sein*) collide. z~rechnen *vt sep* add up.
z~reißen† (sich) *vr sep* (*fam*) pull oneself
together. z~rollen *vt sep* roll up; sich
z~rollen curl up. z~schlagen† *vt sep*
smash up; (*prügeln*) beat up.
z~schließen† (sich) *vr sep* join together;
(*Firmen:*) merge. Z~schluss (Z~schluß)
m union; (*Comm*) merger. z~schreiben†
vt sep write as one word

zusammensein† *vi sep* (*sein*) NEW zusammen sein, *s.* zusammen. Z~ *nt* -s
get-together

zusammensetz|en *vt sep* put together;
(*Techn*) assemble; sich z~en sit [down]
together; (*bestehen*) be made up (*aus*
from). Z~ung *f* -,-en composition;
(*Techn*) assembly; (*Wort*) compound

zusammen|stellen *vt sep* put together;
(*gestalten*) compile. Z~stoß *m* collision;
(*fig*) clash. z~stoßen† *vi sep* (*sein*) collide.
z~treffen† *vi sep* (*sein*) meet; (*zeitlich*)
coincide. Z~treffen *nt* meeting; coincidence. z~zählen *vt sep* add up. z~ziehen†
v sep □ *vt* draw together; (*addieren*) add
up; (*konzentrieren*) mass; sich z~ziehen
contract; (*Gewitter:*) gather □ *vi* (*sein*)
move in together; move in (*mit* with).
z~zucken *vi sep* (*sein*) start; (*vor
Schmerz*) wince

Zusatz *m* addition; (*Jur*) rider;
(*Lebensmittel-*) additive. Z~gerät *nt* attachment. **zusätzlich** *a* additional □ *adv*
in addition

zuschanden *adv* z~ machen ruin,
wreck; z~ werden be wrecked or ruined;
z~ fahren wreck

zuschau|en *vi sep* (*haben*) watch.
Z~er(in) *m* -s,- (*f* -,-nen) spectator; (*TV*)
viewer. Z~erraum *m* auditorium

zuschicken *vt sep* send (*dat to*)

Zuschlag *m* surcharge; (*D-Zug-*) supplement. z~en† *v sep* □ *vt* shut; (*heftig*) slam;
(*bei Auktion*) knock down (*jdm to s.o.*)
□ *vi* (*haben*) hit out; (*Feind:*) strike □ *vi*
(*sein*) slam shut. z~pflichtig *a* (*Zug*) for
which a supplement is payable

zuschließen† *v sep* □ *vt* lock □ *vi* (*haben*)
lock up

zuschneiden† *vt sep* cut out; cut to size
(*Holz*)

zuschreiben† *vt sep* attribute (*dat to*);
jdm die Schuld z~ blame s.o.

Zuschrift *f* letter; (*auf Annonce*) reply

zuschulden *adv* sich (*dat*) etwas z~
kommen lassen do wrong

Zuschuss (**Zuschuß**) *m* contribution;
(*staatlich*) subsidy

zusehen† *vi sep* (*haben*) watch; z~, dass
see [to it] that

zusehends *adv* visibly

zusein† *vi sep* (*sein*) NEW zu sein, *s.* zu sein

zusenden† *vt sep* send (*dat to*)

zusetzen *v sep* □ *vt* add; (*einbüßen*) lose
□ *vi* (*haben*) jdm z~ pester s.o.; (*Hitze:*)
take it out of s.o.

zusicher|n *vt sep* promise. Z~ung *f* promise

Zuspätkommende(r) *m/f* late-comer

zuspielen *vt sep* (*Sport*) pass

zuspitzen (sich) *vr sep* (*fig*) become critical

zusprechen† *v sep* □ *vt* award (jdm s.o.); jdm Trost/Mut z~ comfort/encourage s.o. □ *vi* (*haben*) dem Essen z~ eat heartily

Zustand *m* condition, state

zustande *adv* z~ bringen/kommen bring/come about

zuständig *a* competent; (*verantwortlich*) responsible. Z~keit *f* - competence; responsibility

zustehen† *vi sep* (*haben*) jdm z~ be s.o.'s right; (*Urlaub:*) be due to s.o.; es steht ihm nicht zu he is not entitled to it; (*gebührt*) is not for him (zu to)

zusteigen† *vi sep* (*sein*) get on; noch jemand zugestiegen? tickets please; (*im Bus*) any more fares please?

zustell|en *vt sep* block; (*bringen*) deliver. Z~ung *f* delivery

zusteuern *v sep* □ *vi* (*sein*) head (auf + *acc* for) □ *vt* contribute

zustimm|en *vi sep* (*haben*) agree; (*billigen*) approve (*dat* of). Z~ung *f* consent; approval

zustoßen† *vi sep* (*sein*) happen (*dat* to)

Zustrom *m* influx

zutage *adv* z~ treten *od* kommen/bringen come/bring to light

Zutat *f* (*Culin*) ingredient

zuteil|en *vt sep* allocate; assign (*Aufgabe*). Z~ung *f* allocation

zutiefst *adv* deeply

zutragen† *vt sep* carry/(*fig*) report (*dat* to); sich z~ happen

zutrau|en *vt sep* jdm etw z~ believe s.o. capable of sth. Z~en *nt* -s confidence. z~lich *a* trusting, *adv* -ly; (*Tier*) friendly

zutreffen† *vi sep* (*haben*) be correct; z~ auf (+ *acc*) apply to. z~d *a* applicable (auf + *acc* to); (*richtig*) correct, *adv* -ly

zutrinken† *vi sep* (*haben*) jdm z~ drink to s.o.

Zutritt *m* admittance

zuunterst *adv* right at the bottom

zuverlässig *a* reliable, *adv* -bly. Z~keit *f* - reliability

Zuversicht *f* - confidence. z~lich *a* confident, *adv* -ly

zuviel *pron* & *adv* (NEW)zu viel, *s.* viel

zuvor *adv* before; (*erst*) first

zuvorkommen† *vi sep* (*sein*) (+ *dat*) anticipate; jdm z~ beat s.o. to it. z~d *a* obliging, *adv* -ly

Zuwachs *m* -es increase

zuwege *adv* z~ bringen achieve

zuweilen *adv* now and then

zuweisen† *vt sep* assign; (*zuteilen*) allocate

zuwenden† *vt sep* turn (*dat* to); sich z~en (+ *dat*) turn to; (*fig*) devote oneself to. Z~ung *f* donation; (*Fürsorge*) care

zuwenig *pron* & *adv* (NEW)zu wenig, *s.* wenig

zuwerfen† *vt sep* slam (*Tür*); jdm etw z~ throw s.o. sth; give s.o. (*Blick, Lächeln*)

zuwider *adv* jdm z~ sein be repugnant to s.o. □ *prep* (+ *dat*) contrary to. z~handeln *vi sep* (*haben*) contravene (etw *dat* sth)

zuzahlen *vt sep* pay extra

zuziehen† *v sep* □ *vt* pull tight; draw (*Vorhänge*); (*hinzu-*) call in; sich (*dat*) etw z~ contract (*Krankheit*); sustain (*Verletzung*); incur (*Zorn*) □ *vi* (*sein*) move into the area

zuzüglich *prep* (+ *gen*) plus

Zwang *m* -[e]s,·̈-e compulsion; (*Gewalt*) force; (*Verpflichtung*) obligation

zwängen *vt* squeeze

zwanglos *a* informal, *adv* -ly; (*Benehmen*) free and easy. Z~igkeit *f* - informality

Zwangs|jacke *f* straitjacket. Z~lage *f* predicament. z~läufig *a* inevitable, *adv* -bly

zwanzig *inv a* twenty. z~ste(r,s) *a* twentieth

zwar *adv* admittedly; und z~ to be precise

Zweck *m* -[e]s,-e purpose; (*Sinn*) point; es hat keinen Z~ there is no point. z~dienlich *a* appropriate; (*Information*) relevant. z~los *a* pointless. z~mäßig *a* suitable, *adv* -bly; (*praktisch*) functional, *adv* -ly. z~s *prep* (+ *gen*) for the purpose of

zwei *inv a*, Z~ *f* -,-en two; (*Sch*) ≈ B. Z~bettzimmer *nt* twin-bedded room

zweideutig *a* ambiguous, *adv* -ly; (*schlüpfrig*) suggestive, *adv* -ly. Z~keit *f* -,-en ambiguity

zwei|erlei *inv a* two kinds of □ *pron* two things. z~fach *a* double

Zweifel *m* -s,- doubt. z~haft *a* doubtful; (*fragwürdig*) dubious. z~los *adv* undoubtedly. z~n *vi* (*haben*) doubt (an etw *dat* sth)

Zweig *m* -[e]s,-e branch. Z~geschäft *nt* branch. Z~stelle *f* branch [office]

Zwei|kampf *m* duel. z~mal *adv* twice. z~reihig *a* (*Anzug*) double-breasted. z~sprachig *a* bilingual

zweit *adv* zu z~ in twos; wir waren zu z~ there were two of us. z~beste(r,s) *a* second-best. z~e(r,s) *a* second

zwei|teilig *a* two-piece; (*Film, Programm*) two-part. z~tens *adv* secondly

zweitklassig *a* second-class

Zwerchfell *nt* diaphragm

Zwerg *m* -[e]s,-e dwarf

Zwetsch[g]e *f* -,-n quetsche

Zwickel *m* -s,- gusset

zwicken *vt/i (haben)* pinch

Zwieback *m* -[e]s,-̈e rusk

Zwiebel *f* -,-n onion; *(Blumen-)* bulb

Zwielicht *nt* half-light; *(Dämmerlicht)* twilight. z∼ig *a* shady

Zwie|spalt *m* conflict. z∼spältig *a* conflicting. Z∼tracht *f* - discord

Zwilling *m* -s,-e twin; Z∼e *(Astr)* Gemini

zwingen† *vt* force; sich z∼ force oneself. z∼d *a* compelling

Zwinger *m* -s,- run; *(Zucht-)* kennels *pl*

zwinkern *vi (haben)* blink; *(als Zeichen)* wink

Zwirn *m* -[e]s button thread

zwischen *prep* (+ *dat/acc*) between; *(unter)* among[st]. Z∼bemerkung *f* interjection. Z∼ding *nt (fam)* cross. z∼durch

adv in between; *(in der Z∼zeit)* in the meantime; *(ab und zu)* now and again. Z∼fall *m* incident. Z∼händler *m* middleman. Z∼landung *f* stopover. Z∼raum *m* gap, space. Z∼ruf *m* interjection. Z∼stecker *m* adaptor. Z∼wand *f* partition. Z∼zeit *f* in der Z∼zeit in the meantime

Zwist *m* -[e]s,-e discord; *(Streit)* feud. Z∼igkeiten *fpl* quarrels

zwitschern *vi (haben)* chirp

zwo *inv a* two

zwölf *inv a* twelve. z∼te(r,s) *a* twelfth

zwote(r,s) *a* second

Zyklus *m* -,-klen cycle

Zylind|er *m* -s,- cylinder; *(Hut)* top hat. z∼risch *a* cylindrical

Zyn|iker *m* -s,- cynic. z∼isch *a* cynical, *adv* -ly. Z∼ismus *m* - cynicism

Zypern *nt* -s Cyprus

Zypresse *f* -,-n cypress

Zyste /ˈtsʏstə/ *f* -,-n cyst

1. Join Up the Nouns

These German nouns are all made up of two separate words, but they have split apart. Draw a line between two pieces of paper that make up a noun. Watch out: one of the first words goes with two of the second words!

When you've made all the German words, do the same for the English translations and match them up with the German.

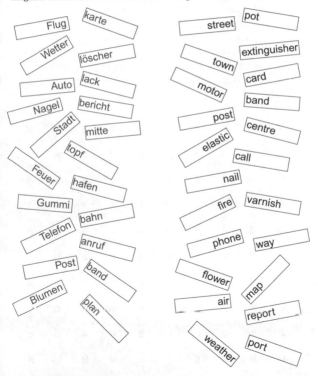

German first words: Flug, Wetter, Auto, Nagel, Stadt, Feuer, Gummi, Telefon, Post, Blumen

German second words: karte, löscher, lack, bericht, mitte, topf, hafen, bahn, anruf, band, plan

English first words: street, town, motor, post, elastic, nail, fire, phone, flower, air, weather

English second words: pot, extinguisher, card, band, centre, call, varnish, way, map, report, port

2. Wordsearch

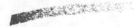

Fifteen German words are hidden among the letters in the grid. Can you find them all? Watch out: six of the words read downwards, while all the others read across.

To help you, here are the English meanings of the German words. You can tick them off as you find the German.

ace	rough
almost	save
also	speak
better	ten
daughter	under
opera	village
powder	wide
quay	

M	W	N	B	U	N	T	E	R	V
Z	E	H	N	C	X	Z	L	K	J
H	I	G	F	P	U	L	V	E	R
D	T	O	C	H	T	E	R	S	A
D	S	P	R	E	C	H	E	N	P
O	B	E	S	S	E	R	A	O	I
R	U	R	K	U	F	A	S	T	A
F	Y	T	A	R	E	W	S	Q	U
Z	X	C	I	V	B	R	A	U	C
N	R	E	T	T	E	N	M	L	H

3. Odd Meaning Out

One word can have several different meanings. In the following exercise, only two of the three English translations given for each German word are correct. Use the dictionary to spot the odd one out, and then look up the right German translation for it:

fordern	demand challenge convince	**Pilz**	mushroom fungus beer
Schnee	snow icing beaten egg-white	**schwer**	swift difficult heavy
patent	obvious resourceful clever	**gerade**	straight grand even
Haken	tick hake hook	**drehen**	turn shoot catch
Brause	bruise fizzy drink shower	**Strom**	power storm stream
neben	next to apart from foggy	**Blase**	blanket blister bladder

4. Troubleshooting

Our computer has developed some annoying little problems. Can you help put them right?

First, when we type any three-letter word beginning with d, the computer shows three d's on the screen! The problem words are all highlighted in our "Recipe of the Week". Can you correct them in the box above each word?

Ddd Rezept ddd Woche

Für ddd Kuchenteig ddd Butter in Stückchen schneiden

und mit ddd Mehl vermischen. Ddd Gemisch mit ddd Honig

und ddd Milch zu einem festen Teig verarbeiten. Ddd

Äpfel waschen, halbieren und in ddd Pfanne mit ddd

Butter, ddd Zimt und ddd Zitronensaft aufkochen lassen.

Ddd Teig in ddd Form geben und mit ddd Obst belegen.

Ddd Kuchen in ddd Backofen schieben und 35 Minuten

backen.

5. Crossword

If you need to, you can use the dictionary to solve this crossword. Just translate the clues into German, and write the translations in capital letters.

Across
- **1** mature (4)
- **3** journeys (6)
- **8** advertisement, small ad (7)
- **9** pale (adjective) (5)
- **10** to hurry (5)
- **11** few (6)
- **13** a (male) industrialist (13)
- **15** to catch (6)
- **17** (male) Russian (5)
- **20** price or prize (5)
- **21** bags or pockets (7)
- **22** saddle (noun) (6)
- **23** stove (4)

Down
- **1** (female) rider (8)
- **2** island (5)
- **4** heiress (5)
- **5** asparagus (7)
- **6** nest (4)
- **7** crane (machine) (4)
- **11** goods, or (they) were (5)
- **12** to appoint (8)
- **14** dialect (7)
- **16** alley (5)
- **17** pink (4)
- **18** sheep (5)
- **19** epic (noun) (4)

6. Curly Words

One word is missing in each of the curly lists. Which day, month, number and capital city are missing?

Can you write out the four lists in the right order?

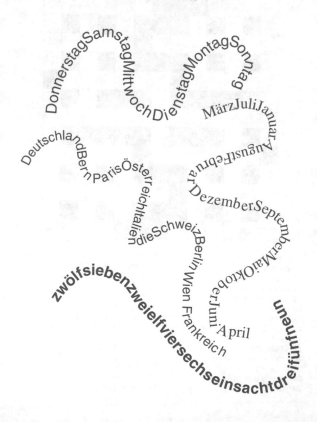

7. True or False?

Can you crack the code to say whether these four statements are
true or false? First use the key to translate the symbols into
German.

Code key

a	♋	A	✌	r	⬛	R	☼
b	♌	B	✊	s	◆	S	♠
c	♍	C	✋	t	◆	T	❋
d	♎	D	✏	u	◆	U	✞
e	♏	E	✐	v	❖	V	✟
f	♐	F	✒	w	✦	W	✦
g	♑	G	✓	x	⊠	X	✺
h	♒	H	✆	y	⊡	Y	✵
i	♓	I	☺	z	⌘	Z	☾
j	♋	J	☺	ä	⑩	Ä	⓪
k	&	K	☺	ö	✑	Ö	⑤
l	●	L	⊗	ü	•	Ü	⑥
m	○	M	✳	ß	▪	🗁	1
n	■	N	☠	,	🖎	🗎	2
o	⬜	O	♉	.	🖎	🗏	3
p	⬜	P	♊	?	✍	🗐	4
q	⬜	Q	✈				

🗁 ✳⬛⬜●✦■ ♓◆◆ ♎♏♏ ♍♋◆⬛◆◆♋♎◆
      ❖⬛■ ✏♏◆◆♍♒●♋■♎🖎

🗎 ☼⬜◆♏■ ◆■♎ ♊◆◆♏⬛♑●⬜♍♍&♏■ ◆♓■♎
      ♑◆■♏♏♍♋◆◆♏■🖎

🗏 ◆♍♒■♏■♏♍&♏■ ◆♓■♎ ♎♓♏
      ◆♍♒■♏♏◗●●◆♓◗●● ✏)♏⬜♏ 🖎

🗐 ✳♋⬜⬜&&⬛ ♓◆◆ ♏♓■
      ⊠◆⬜♓♍♋♑■&♓◆♏■◆♍♒■◆ ☺♋■♎🖎

8. Sporting Links

Can you match each piece of sporting equipment to the right sport?
Can you translate the sports into German?

das Seil	archery
die Zielscheibe	tennis
der Schlittschuh	skittles
der Tennisschläger	surfing
der Kegel	mountaineering
der Ski	football
der Federball	swimming
das Segel	golf
die Kugel	skating
der Fußball	riding
die Flosse	cycling
der Zügel	gymnastics
das Sprungbrett	skiing
das Fahrrad	fencing
der Golfschläger	diving
die Turnschuhe	shot-putting
das Florett	sailing
das Surfbrett	badminton

Answers

1. Join Up the Nouns

Flughafen	airport
Wetterbericht	weather report
Autobahn	motorway
Nagellack	nail varnish
Stadtmitte	*town centre*
Stadtplan	*street map*
Feuerlöscher	fire extinguisher
Gummiband	elastic band
Telefonanruf	phone call
Postkarte	postcard
Blumentopf	flowerpot

2. Wordsearch

Ass	ace	rau	rough
fast	almost	retten	save
auch	also	sprechen	speak
besser	better	zehn	ten
Tochter	daughter	unter	under
Oper	opera	Dorf	village
Pulver	powder	weit	wide
Kai	quay		

3. Odd Meaning Out

convince	überzeugen
icing	Zuckerguss
obvious	offensichtlich
hake	Seehecht
bruise	blauer Fleck
foggy	neblig
beer	Bier
swift	schnell
grand	großartig
catch	fangen
storm	Sturm
blanket	Decke

4. Troubleshooting

Das Rezept *der* Woche

Für *den* Kuchenteig *die* Butter in Stückchen schneiden und mit *dem* Mehl vermischen. *Das* Gemisch mit *dem* Honig und *der* Milch zu einem festen Teig verarbeiten. *Die* Äpfel waschen, halbieren und in *der* Pfanne mit *der* Butter, *dem* Zimt und *dem* Zitronensaft aufkochen lassen. *Den* Teig in *die* Form geben und mit *dem* Obst belegen. *Den* Kuchen in *den* Backofen schieben und 35 Minuten backen.

5. Crossword

The crossword grid contains:

```
R E I F _ _ _ R E I S E N
E _ N _ K _ _ R _ P _ _ E
I N S E R A T _ B L A S S
T _ E _ A _ _ I _ R _ _ T
E I L E N _ W E N I G E _
R _ _ _ A _ _ E _ _ E _ E
I N D U S T R I E L L E R
N _ I _ _ E _ E _ _ _ _ N
_ F A N G E N _ R U S S E
E _ L _ A _ _ O _ C _ _ E
P R E I S _ T A S C H E N
O _ K _ S _ _ A _ A _ _ E
S A T T E L _ _ O F E N _
```

6. Curly Words

Freitag; Sonntag, Montag, Dienstag, Mittwoch, Donnerstag, Freitag,
Samstag;

November; Januar, Februar, März, April, Mai, Juni, Juli, August,
September, Oktober, November, Dezember;

Rom; Deutschland/Berlin, Österreich/Wien, die Schweiz/Bern,
Frankreich/Paris, Italien/Rom

zehn; eins. zwei, drei, vier. fünf, sechs, sieben, acht, neun, zehn, elf, zwölf.

7. True or False?

1) Berlin ist die Hauptstadt von Deutschland.
   True: Berlin is the capital of Germany.
2) Rosen und Osterglocken sind Hundearten.
   False: Roses and daffodils are not kinds of dog.
3) Schnecken sind die schnellsten Tiere.
   False: Snails are not the fastest animals.
4) Marokko ist ein afrikanisches Land.
   True: Morocco is an African country.

8. Sporting Links

das Fahrrad	bicycle	cycling	das Radfahren
der Federball	shuttlecock	badminton	der Federball
das Florett	foil	fencing	das Fechten
die Flosse	flipper	swimming	das Schwimmen
der Fußball	football	football	der Fußball
der Golfschläger	golf-club	golf	das Golf
der Kegel	skittle	skittles	das Kegeln
die Kugel	shot	shot-putting	das Kugelstoßen
der Schlittschuh	ice-skate	skating	das Eislaufen
das Segel	sail	sailing	der Segelsport
das Seil	rope	mountaineering	das Bergsteigen
der Ski	ski	skiing	das Skilaufen
das Sprungbrett	springboard	diving	das Kunstspringen
das Surfbrett	surfboard	surfing	das Surfen
der Tennisschläger	tennis-racket	tennis	das Tennis
die Turnschuhe	gym-shoes	gymnastics	das Turnen
die Zielscheibe	target	archery	das Bogenschießen
der Zügel	rein	riding	das Reiten

A

a /ə, betont eɪ/ (vor einem Vokal an) indef art ein(e); (each) pro; not a kein(e)

aback /ə'bæk/ adv be taken ∼ verblüfft sein

abandon /ə'bændən/ vt verlassen; (give up) aufgeben □ n Hingabe f. ∼ed a verlassen; (behaviour) hemmungslos

abase /ə'beɪs/ vt demütigen

abashed /ə'bæʃt/ a beschämt, verlegen

abate /ə'beɪt/ vi nachlassen

abattoir /'æbətwɑ:(r)/ n Schlachthof m

abb|ey /'æbɪ/ n Abtei f. ∼ot /-ət/ n Abt m

abbreviat|e /ə'bri:vɪeɪt/ vt abkürzen. ∼ion /-'eɪʃn/ n Abkürzung f

abdicat|e /'æbdɪkeɪt/ vi abdanken. ∼ion /-'keɪʃn/ n Abdankung f

abdom|en /'æbdəmən/ n Unterleib m. ∼inal /-'dɒmɪnl/ a Unterleibs-

abduct /əb'dʌkt/ vt entführen. ∼ion /-ʌkʃn/ n Entführung f. ∼or n Entführer m

aberration /æbə'reɪʃn/ n Abweichung f; (mental) Verwirrung f

abet /ə'bet/ vt (pt/pp abetted) aid and ∼ (Jur) Beihilfe leisten (+ dat)

abeyance /ə'beɪəns/ n in ∼ [zeitweilig] außer Kraft; fall into ∼ außer Kraft kommen

abhor /əb'hɔ:(r)/ vt (pt/pp abhorred) verabscheuen. ∼rence /-'hɒrəns/ n Abscheu m. ∼rent /-'hɒrənt/ a abscheulich

abid|e /ə'baɪd/ vt (pt/pp abided) (tolerate) aushalten; ausstehen (person) □ vi ∼e by sich halten an (+ acc). ∼ing a bleibend

ability /ə'bɪlətɪ/ n Fähigkeit f; (talent) Begabung f

abject /'æbdʒekt/ a erbärmlich; (humble) demütig

ablaze /ə'bleɪz/ a in Flammen; be ∼ in Flammen stehen

able /'eɪbl/ a (-r, -st) fähig; be ∼ to do sth etw tun können. ∼-'bodied a körperlich gesund; (Mil) tauglich

ably /'eɪblɪ/ adv gekonnt

abnormal /æb'nɔ:ml/ a anormal; (Med) abnorm. ∼ity /-'mælətɪ/ n Abnormität f. ∼ly adv ungewöhnlich

aboard /ə'bɔ:d/ adv & prep an Bord (+ gen)

abode /ə'bəʊd/ n Wohnsitz m

abol|ish /ə'bɒlɪʃ/ vt abschaffen. ∼ition /æbə'lɪʃn/ n Abschaffung f

abominable /ə'bɒmɪnəbl/ a, -bly adv abscheulich

abominate /ə'bɒmɪneɪt/ vt verabscheuen

aborigines /æbə'rɪdʒəni:z/ npl Ureinwohner pl

abort /ə'bɔ:t/ vt abtreiben. ∼ion /-ɔ:ʃn/ n Abtreibung f; have an ∼ion eine Abtreibung vornehmen lassen. ∼ive /-tɪv/ a (attempt) vergeblich

abound /ə'baʊnd/ vi reichlich vorhanden sein; ∼ in reich sein an (+ dat)

about /ə'baʊt/ adv umher, herum; (approximately) ungefähr; be ∼ (in circulation) umgehen; (in existence) vorhanden sein; be up and ∼ auf den Beinen sein; be ∼ to do sth im Begriff sein, etw zu tun; there are a lot ∼ es gibt viele; there was no one ∼ es war kein Mensch da; run/play ∼ herumlaufen/-spielen □ prep um (+ acc) [. . . herum]; (concerning) über (+ acc); what is it ∼? worum geht es? (book:) wovon handelt es? I know nothing ∼ it ich weiß nichts davon; talk/know ∼ reden/wissen von

about: ∼-'face n, ∼-'turn n Kehrtwendung f

above /ə'bʌv/ adv oben □ prep über (+ dat/acc); ∼ all vor allem

above: ∼-'board a legal. ∼-mentioned a oben erwähnt

abrasion /ə'breɪʒn/ n Schürfwunde f

abrasive /ə'breɪsɪv/ a Scheuer-; (remark) verletzend □ n Scheuermittel nt; (Techn) Schleifmittel nt

abreast /ə'brest/ adv nebeneinander; keep ∼ of Schritt halten mit

abridge /ə'brɪdʒ/ vt kürzen

abroad /ə'brɔ:d/ adv im Ausland; go ∼ ins Ausland fahren

abrupt /ə'brʌpt/ a, -ly adv abrupt; (sudden) plötzlich; (curt) schroff

abscess /'æbsɪs/ n Abszess m

abscond /əb'skɒnd/ vi entfliehen

absence /'æbsəns/ n Abwesenheit f

absent¹ /'æbsənt/ a, -ly adv abwesend; be ∼ fehlen

absent² /æb'sent/ vt ∼ oneself fernbleiben

absentee /æbsən'ti:/ n Abwesende(r) m/f

absent-minded /æbsənt'maɪndɪd/ a, -ly adv geistesabwesend; (forgetful) zerstreut

absolute /'æbsəlu:t/ a, -ly adv absolut

absolution /æbsə'luːʃn/ n Absolution f

absolve /əb'zɒlv/ vt lossprechen

absorb /əb'sɔːb/ vt absorbieren, aufsaugen; ~ed in vertieft in (+ acc). ~ent /-ənt/ a saugfähig

absorption /əb'sɔːpʃn/ n Absorption f

abstain /əb'steɪn/ vi sich enthalten (from gen); ~ from voting sich der Stimme enthalten

abstemious /əb'stiːmɪəs/ a enthaltsam

abstention /əb'stenʃn/ n (Pol) [Stimm]-enthaltung f

abstinence /'æbstɪnəns/ n Enthaltsamkeit f

abstract /'æbstrækt/ a abstrakt □ n (summary) Abriss m

absurd /əb'sɜːd/ a, -ly adv absurd. ~ity n Absurdität f

abundan|ce /ə'bandəns/ n Fülle f (of an + dat). ~t a reichlich

abuse¹ /ə'bjuːz/ vt missbrauchen; (insult) beschimpfen

abus|e² /ə'bjuːs/ n Missbrauch m; (insults) Beschimpfungen pl. ~ive /-ɪv/ a ausfallend

abut /ə'bʌt/ vi (pt/pp abutted) angrenzen (on to an + acc)

abysmal /ə'bɪzml/ a (fam) katastrophal

abyss /ə'bɪs/ n Abgrund m

academic /ækə'demɪk/ a, -ally adv akademisch □ n Akademiker(in) m(f)

academy /ə'kædəmɪ/ n Akademie f

accede /ək'siːd/ vi ~ to zustimmen (+ dat); (throne) besteigen (throne)

accelerat|e /ək'seləreɪt/ vt beschleunigen □ vi die Geschwindigkeit erhöhen. ~ion /-'reɪʃn/ n Beschleunigung f. ~or n (Auto) Gaspedal nt

accent¹ /'æksənt/ n Akzent m

accent² /æk'sent/ vt betonen

accentuate /ək'sentjʊeɪt/ vt betonen

accept /ək'sept/ vt annehmen; (fig) akzeptieren □ vi zusagen. ~able /-əbl/ a annehmbar. ~ance n Annahme f; (of invitation) Zusage f

access /'ækses/ n Zugang m; (road) Zufahrt f. ~ible /ək'sesəbl/ a zugänglich

accession /ək'seʃn/ n (to throne) Thronbesteigung f

accessor|y /ək'sesərɪ/ n (Jur) Mitschuldige(r) m/f; ~ies pl (fashion) Accessoires pl; (Techn) Zubehör nt

accident /'æksɪdənt/ n Unfall m; (chance) Zufall m; by ~ zufällig; (unintentionally) versehentlich. ~al /-'dentl/ a, -ly adv zufällig; (unintentional) versehentlich

acclaim /ə'kleɪm/ n Beifall m □ vt feiern (as als)

acclimate /'æklɪmeɪt/ vt (Amer) = acclimatize

acclimatize /ə'klaɪmətaɪz/ vt become ~d sich akklimatisieren

accolade /'ækəleɪd/ n Auszeichnung f

accommodat|e /ə'kɒmədeɪt/ vt unterbringen; (oblige) entgegenkommen (+ dat). ~ing a entgegenkommend. ~ion /-'deɪʃn/ n (rooms) Unterkunft f

accompan|iment /ə'kʌmpənɪmənt/ n Begleitung f. ~ist n (Mus) Begleiter(in) m(f)

accompany /ə'kʌmpənɪ/ vt (pt/pp -ied) begleiten

accomplice /ə'kʌmplɪs/ n Komplize/-zin m/f

accomplish /ə'kʌmplɪʃ/ vt erfüllen ⟨task⟩; (achieve) erreichen. ~ed a fähig. ~ment n Fertigkeit f; (achievement) Leistung f

accord /ə'kɔːd/ n (treaty) Abkommen nt; of one ~ einmütig; of one's own ~ aus eigenem Antrieb □ vt gewähren. ~ance n in ~ance with entsprechend (+ dat)

according /ə'kɔːdɪŋ/ adv ~ to nach (+ dat). ~ly adv entsprechend

accordion /ə'kɔːdɪən/ n Akkordeon nt

accost /ə'kɒst/ vt ansprechen

account /ə'kaʊnt/ n Konto nt; (bill) Rechnung f; (description) Darstellung f; (report) Bericht m; ~s pl (Comm) Bücher pl; on ~ of wegen (+ gen); on no ~ auf keinen Fall; on this ~ deshalb; on my ~ meinetwegen; of no ~ ohne Bedeutung; take into ~ in Betracht ziehen; berücksichtigen □ vi ~ for Rechenschaft ablegen für; (explain) erklären

accountant /ə'kaʊntənt/ n Buchhalter(in) m(f); (chartered) Wirtschaftsprüfer m; (for tax) Steuerberater m

accoutrements /ə'kuːtrəmənts/ npl Ausrüstung f

accredited /ə'kredɪtɪd/ a akkreditiert

accrue /ə'kruː/ vi sich ansammeln

accumulat|e /ə'kjuːmjʊleɪt/ vt ansammeln, anhäufen □ vi sich ansammeln, sich anhäufen. ~ion /-'leɪʃn/ n Ansammlung f, Anhäufung f. ~or n (Electr) Akkumulator m

accura|cy /'ækjʊrəsɪ/ n Genauigkeit f. ~te /-rət/ a, -ly adv genau

accusation /ækjuː'zeɪʃn/ n Anklage f

accusative /ə'kjuːzətɪv/ a & n ~ [case] (Gram) Akkusativ m

accuse /ə'kjuːz/ vt (Jur) anklagen (of gen); ~ s.o. of doing sth jdn beschuldigen, etw getan zu haben. ~d n the ~d der/die Angeklagte

accustom /ə'kʌstəm/ vt gewöhnen (to an + dat); grow or get ~ed to sich gewöhnen an (+ acc). ~ed a gewohnt

ace /eɪs/ n (Cards, Sport) Ass nt

ache /eɪk/ n Schmerzen pl □ vi weh tun, schmerzen

achieve /ə'tʃiːv/ vt leisten; (gain) erzielen; (reach) erreichen. ~ment n (feat) Leistung f

acid /'æsɪd/ a sauer; (fig) beißend □ n Säure f. ~ity /ə'sɪdətɪ/ n Säure f. ~ 'rain n saurer Regen m

acknowledge /ək'nɒlɪdʒ/ vt anerkennen; (admit) zugeben; erwidern (greeting); ~ receipt of den Empfang bestätigen (+ gen). ~ment n Anerkennung f; (of letter) Empfangsbestätigung f

acne /'æknɪ/ n Akne f

acorn /'eɪkɔːn/ n Eichel f

acoustic /ə'kuːstɪk/ a, -ally adv akustisch. ~s npl Akustik f

acquaint /ə'kweɪnt/ vt ~ s.o. with jdn bekannt machen mit; be ~ed with kennen; vertraut sein mit (fact). ~ance n Bekanntschaft f; (person) Bekannte(r) m/f; make s.o.'s ~ance jdn kennen lernen

acquiesce /ækwɪ'es/ vi einwilligen (to in + acc). ~nce n Einwilligung f

acquire /ə'kwaɪə(r)/ vt erwerben

acquisit|ion /ækwɪ'zɪʃn/ n Erwerb m; (thing) Erwerbung f. ~ive /æ'kwɪzətɪv/ a habgierig

acquit /ə'kwɪt/ vt (pt/pp acquitted) freisprechen; ~ oneself well seiner Aufgabe gerecht werden. ~tal n Freispruch m

acre /'eɪkə(r)/ n ≈ Morgen m

acrid /'ækrɪd/ a scharf

acrimon|ious /ækrɪ'məʊnɪəs/ a bitter. ~y /'ækrɪmənɪ/ n Bitterkeit f

acrobat /'ækrəbæt/ n Akrobat(in) m(f). ~ic /-'bætɪk/ a akrobatisch

across /ə'krɒs/ adv hinüber/herüber; (wide) breit; (not lengthwise) quer; (in crossword) waagerecht; come ~ sth auf etw (acc) stoßen; go ~ hinübergehen; bring ~ herüberbringen □ prep über (+ acc); (crosswise) quer über (+ acc/dat); (on the other side of) auf der anderen Seite (+ gen)

act /ækt/ n Tat f; (action) Handlung f; (law) Gesetz nt; (Theat) Akt m; (item) Nummer f; put on an ~ (fam) sich verstellen □ vi handeln; (behave) sich verhalten; (Theat) spielen; (pretend) sich verstellen; ~ as fungieren als □ vt spielen (role). ~ing a (deputy) stellvertretend □ n (Theat) Schauspielerei f. ~ing profession n Schauspielerberuf m

action /'ækʃn/ n Handlung f; (deed) Tat f; (Mil) Einsatz m; (Jur) Klage f; (effect) Wirkung f; (Techn) Mechanismus m; out of ~ (machine:) außer Betrieb; take ~ handeln; killed in ~ gefallen. ~ 'replay n (TV) Wiederholung f

activate /'æktɪveɪt/ vt betätigen; (Chem, Phys) aktivieren

activ|e /'æktɪv/ a, -ly adv aktiv; on ~e service im Einsatz. ~ity /-'tɪvətɪ/ n Aktivität f

act|or /'æktə(r)/ n Schauspieler m. ~ress n Schauspielerin f

actual /'æktʃʊəl/ a, -ly adv eigentlich; (real) tatsächlich. ~ity /-'ælətɪ/ n Wirklichkeit f

acumen /'ækjʊmən/ n Scharfsinn m

acupuncture /'ækjʊ-/ n Akupunktur f

acute /ə'kjuːt/ a scharf; (angle) spitz; (illness) akut. ~ly adv sehr

ad /æd/ n (fam) = advertisement

AD abbr (Anno Domini) n.Chr.

adamant /'ædəmənt/ a be ~ that darauf bestehen, dass

adapt /ə'dæpt/ vt anpassen; bearbeiten (play) □ vi sich anpassen. ~ability /-ə'bɪlətɪ/ n Anpassungsfähigkeit f. ~able /-əbl/ a anpassungsfähig

adaptation /ædæp'teɪʃn/ n (Theat) Bearbeitung f

adapter, adaptor /ə'dæptə(r)/ n (Techn) Adapter m; (Electr) (two-way) Doppelstecker m

add /æd/ vt hinzufügen; (Math) addieren □ vi zusammenzählen, addieren; ~ to hinzufügen zu; (fig: increase) steigern; (compound) verschlimmern. ~ up vt zusammenzählen (figures) □ vi zusammenzählen, addieren; ~ up to machen; it doesn't ~ up (fig) da stimmt etwas nicht

adder /'ædə(r)/ n Kreuzotter f

addict /'ædɪkt/ n Süchtige(r) m/f

addict|ed /ə'dɪktɪd/ a süchtig; ~ed to drugs drogensüchtig. ~ion /-ɪkʃn/ n Sucht f. ~ive /-ɪv/ a be ~ive zur Süchtigkeit führen

addition /ə'dɪʃn/ n Hinzufügung f; (Math) Addition f; (thing added) Ergänzung f; in ~ zusätzlich. ~al a, -ly adv zusätzlich

additive /'ædɪtɪv/ n Zusatz m

address /ə'dres/ n Adresse f, Anschrift f; (speech) Ansprache f; form of ~ Anrede f □ vt adressieren (to an + acc); (speak to) anreden (person); sprechen vor (+ dat) (meeting). ~ee /ædre'siː/ n Empfänger m

adenoids /'ædənɔɪdz/ npl [Rachen]-polypen pl

adept /'ædept/ a geschickt (at in + dat)

adequate /'ædɪkwət/ a, -ly adv ausreichend

adhere /əd'hɪə(r)/ vi kleben/⟨fig⟩ festhalten (to an + dat). ∼nce n Festhalten nt

adhesive /əd'hi:sɪv/ a klebend □ n Klebstoff m

adjacent /ə'dʒeɪsnt/ a angrenzend

adjective /'ædʒɪktɪv/ n Adjektiv nt

adjoin /ə'dʒɔɪn/ vt angrenzen an (+ acc). ∼ing a angrenzend

adjourn /ə'dʒɜːn/ vt vertagen (until auf + acc) □ vi sich vertagen. ∼ment n Vertagung f

adjudicate /ə'dʒuːdɪkeɪt/ vi entscheiden; ⟨in competition⟩ Preisrichter sein

adjust /ə'dʒʌst/ vt einstellen; ⟨alter⟩ verstellen □ vi sich anpassen (to dat). ∼able /-əbl/ a verstellbar. ∼ment n Einstellung f; Anpassung f

ad lib /æd'lɪb/ adv aus dem Stegreif □ vi (pt/pp ad libbed) ⟨fam⟩ improvisieren

administer /əd'mɪnɪstə(r)/ vt verwalten; verabreichen ⟨medicine⟩

administrat|ion /ədmɪnɪ'streɪʃn/ n Verwaltung f; ⟨Pol⟩ Regierung f. ∼or /əd'mɪnɪstreɪtə(r)/ n Verwaltungsbeamte(r) m /-beamtin f

admirable /'ædmərəbl/ a bewundernswert

admiral /'ædmərəl/ n Admiral m

admiration /ædmə'reɪʃn/ n Bewunderung f

admire /əd'maɪə(r)/ vt bewundern. ∼r n Verehrer(in) m(f)

admissable /əd'mɪsəbl/ a zulässig

admission /əd'mɪʃn/ n Eingeständnis nt; ⟨entry⟩ Eintritt m

admit /əd'mɪt/ vt (pt/pp admitted) ⟨let in⟩ hereinlassen; ⟨acknowledge⟩ zugeben; ∼ to sth etw zugeben. ∼tance n Eintritt m. ∼tedly adv zugegebenermaßen

admoni|sh /əd'mɒnɪʃ/ vt ermahnen. ∼tion /ædmə'nɪʃn/ n Ermahnung f

ado /ə'duː/ n without more ∼ ohne weiteres

adolescen|ce /ædə'lesns/ n Jugend f, Pubertät f. ∼t a Jugend-; ⟨boy, girl⟩ halbwüchsig □ n Jugendliche(r) m/f

adopt /ə'dɒpt/ vt adoptieren; ergreifen ⟨measure⟩; ⟨Pol⟩ annehmen ⟨candidate⟩. ∼ion /-ɒpʃn/ n Adoption. f. ∼ive /-ɪv/ a Adoptiv-

ador|able /ə'dɔːrəbl/ a bezaubernd. ∼ation n Anbetung f

adore /ə'dɔː(r)/ vt ⟨worship⟩ anbeten; ⟨fam: like⟩ lieben

adorn /ə'dɔːn/ vt schmücken. ∼ment n Schmuck m

adrenalin /ə'drenəlɪn/ n Adrenalin nt

Adriatic /eɪdrɪ'ætɪk/ a & n ∼ [Sea] Adria f

adrift /ə'drɪft/ a be ∼ treiben; come ∼ sich losreißen

adroit /ə'drɔɪt/ a, -ly adv gewandt, geschickt

adulation /ædjʊ'leɪʃn/ n Schwärmerei f

adult /'ædʌlt/ n Erwachsene(r) m/f

adulterate /ə'dʌltəreɪt/ vt verfälschen; panschen ⟨wine⟩

adultery /ə'dʌltərɪ/ n Ehebruch m

advance /əd'vɑːns/ n Fortschritt m; ⟨Mil⟩ Vorrücken nt; ⟨payment⟩ Vorschuss m; in ∼ im Voraus □ vi vorankommen; ⟨Mil⟩ vorrücken; ⟨make progress⟩ Fortschritte machen □ vt fördern ⟨cause⟩; vorbringen ⟨idea⟩; vorschießen ⟨money⟩. ∼ booking n Kartenvorverkauf m. ∼d a fortgeschritten; ⟨progressive⟩ fortschrittlich. ∼ment n Förderung f; ⟨promotion⟩ Beförderung f

advantage /əd'vɑːntɪdʒ/ n Vorteil m; take ∼ of ausnutzen. ∼ous /ædvən'teɪdʒəs/ a vorteilhaft

advent /'ædvent/ n Ankunft f; A∼ ⟨season⟩ Advent m

adventur|e /əd'ventʃə(r)/ n Abenteuer nt. ∼er n Abenteurer m. ∼ous /-rəs/ a abenteuerlich; ⟨person⟩ abenteuerlustig

adverb /'ædvɜːb/ n Adverb nt

adversary /'ædvəsərɪ/ n Widersacher m

advers|e /'ædvɜːs/ a ungünstig. ∼ity /əd'vɜːsətɪ/ n Not f

advert /'ædvɜːt/ n ⟨fam⟩ = advertisement

advertise /'ædvətaɪz/ vt Reklame machen für; ⟨by small ad⟩ inserieren □ vi Reklame machen; inserieren; ∼ for per Anzeige suchen

advertisement /əd'vɜːtɪsmənt/ n Anzeige f; ⟨publicity⟩ Reklame f; ⟨small ad⟩ Inserat nt

advertis|er /'ædvətaɪzə(r)/ n Inserent m. ∼ing n Werbung f □ attrib Werbe-

advice /əd'vaɪs/ n Rat m. ∼ note n Benachrichtigung f

advisable /əd'vaɪzəbl/ a ratsam

advis|e /əd'vaɪz/ vt raten (s.o. jdm); ⟨counsel⟩ beraten; ⟨inform⟩ benachrichtigen; ∼e s.o. against sth jdm von etw abraten □ vi raten. ∼er n Berater(in) m(f). ∼ory /-ərɪ/ a beratend

advocate[1] /'ædvəkət/ n ⟨Rechts⟩anwalt m/-anwältin f; ⟨supporter⟩ Befürworter m

advocate[2] /'ædvəkeɪt/ vt befürworten

aerial /'eərɪəl/ a Luft- □ n Antenne f

aerobics /eə'rəʊbɪks/ n Aerobic nt

aero|drome /'eərədrəum/ n Flugplatz m.
~plane n Flugzeug nt

aerosol /'eərəsɒl/ n Spraydose f

aesthetic /iːs'θetik/ a ästhetisch

afar /ə'fɑː(r)/ adv from ~ aus der Ferne

affable /'æfəbl/ a, -bly adv freundlich

affair /ə'feə(r)/ n Angelegenheit f, Sache
f; (scandal) Affäre f; [love-]~ [Liebes]-
verhältnis nt

affect /ə'fekt/ vt sich auswirken auf (+
acc); (concern) betreffen; (move) rühren;
(pretend) vortäuschen. ~ation /æfek-
'teiʃn/ n Affektiertheit f. ~ed a affektiert

affection /ə'fekʃn/ n Liebe f. ~ate /-ət/
a, -ly adv liebevoll

affiliated /ə'filiertid/ a angeschlossen (to
dat)

affinity /ə'finəti/ n Ähnlichkeit f; (attraction) gegenseitige Anziehung f

affirm /ə'fɜːm/ vt behaupten; (Jur) eides-
stattlich erklären

affirmative /ə'fɜːmətiv/ a bejahend □ n
Bejahung f

affix /ə'fiks/ vt anbringen (to dat); (stick)
aufkleben (to auf + acc); setzen (signature) (to unter + acc)

afflict /ə'flikt/ vt be ~ed with behaftet
sein mit. ~ion /-ikʃn/ n Leiden nt

affluen|ce /'æfluəns/ n Reichtum m. ~t a
wohlhabend. ~t society n Wohlstandsge-
sellschaft f

afford /ə'fɔːd/ vt (provide) gewähren; be
able to ~ sth sich (dat) etw leisten
können. ~able /-əbl/ a erschwinglich

affray /ə'frei/ n Schlägerei f

affront /ə'frʌnt/ n Beleidigung f □ vt beleidigen

afield /ə'fiːld/ adv further ~ weiter weg

afloat /ə'fləut/ a be ~ (ship:) flott sein;
keep ~ (person:) sich über Wasser halten

afoot /ə'fut/ a im Gange

aforesaid /ə'fɔːsed/ a (Jur) oben erwähnt

afraid /ə'freid/ a be ~ Angst haben (of
vor + dat); I'm ~ not leider nicht; I'm ~
so [ja] leider; I'm ~ I can't help you ich
kann Ihnen leider nicht helfen

afresh /ə'freʃ/ adv von vorne

Africa /'æfrikə/ n Afrika nt. ~n a afrika-
nisch □ n Afrikaner(in) m(f)

after /'ɑːftə(r)/ adv danach □ prep nach (+
dat); ~ that danach; ~ all schließlich;
the day ~ tomorrow übermorgen; be ~
aus sein auf (+ acc) □ conj nachdem

after: ~-effect n Nachwirkung f. ~math
/-mɑːθ/ n Auswirkungen pl. ~noon n
Nachmittag m; good ~noon! guten Tag!
~-sales service n Kundendienst m.
~shave n Rasierwasser nt. ~thought n

nachträglicher Einfall m. ~wards adv
nachher

again /ə'gen/ adv wieder; (once more) noch
einmal; (besides) außerdem; ~ and ~ immer wieder

against /ə'genst/ prep gegen (+ acc)

age /eidʒ/ n Alter nt; (era) Zeitalter nt; ~s
(fam) ewig; under ~ minderjährig; of ~
volljährig; two years of ~ zwei Jahre alt
□ v (pres p ageing) □ vt älter machen □ vi
altern; (mature) reifen

aged¹ /eidʒd/ a ~ two zwei Jahre alt

aged² /'eidʒid/ a betagt □ n the ~ pl die
Alten

ageless /'eidʒlis/ a ewig jung

agency /'eidʒənsi/ n Agentur f; (office)
Büro nt; have the ~ for die Vertretung
haben für

agenda /ə'dʒendə/ n Tagesordnung f; on
the ~ auf dem Programm

agent /'eidʒənt/ n Agent(in) m(f); (Comm)
Vertreter(in) m(f); (substance) Mittel nt

aggravat|e /'ægrəveit/ vt verschlimmern;
(fam: annoy) ärgern. ~ion /-'veiʃn/ n
(fam) Ärger m

aggregate /'ægrigət/ a gesamt □ n Gesamtzahl f; (sum) Gesamtsumme f

aggress|ion /ə'greʃn/ n Aggression f.
~ive /-siv/ a, -ly adv aggressiv. ~iveness
n Aggressivität f. ~or n Angreifer(in)
m(f)

aggrieved /ə'griːvd/ a verletzt

aggro /'ægrəu/ n (fam) Ärger m

aghast /ə'gɑːst/ a entsetzt

agil|e /'ædʒail/ a flink, behände; (mind)
wendig. ~ity /ə'dʒiləti/ n Flinkheit f, Be-
händigkeit f

agitat|e /'ædʒiteit/ vt bewegen; (shake)
schütteln □ vi (fig) ~ for agitieren für.
~ed a, -ly adv erregt. ~ion /-'teiʃn/ n
Erregung f; (Pol) Agitation f. ~or n Agitator m

agnostic /æg'nɒstik/ n Agnostiker m

ago /ə'gəu/ adv vor (+ dat); a month ~
vor einem Monat; a long time ~ vor
langer Zeit; how long ~ is it? wie lange
ist es her?

agog /ə'gɒg/ a gespannt

agoniz|e /'ægənaiz/ vi [innerlich] ringen.
~ing a qualvoll

agony /'ægəni/ n Qual f; be in ~ furcht-
bare Schmerzen haben

agree /ə'griː/ vt vereinbaren; (admit) zugeben; ~ to do sth sich bereit erklären
etw zu tun □ vi (people, figures:) übereinstimmen; (reach agreement) sich einigen; (get on) gut miteinander auskommen;
(consent) einwilligen (to in + acc); I ~ der
Meinung bin ich auch; ~ with s.o. jdm

zustimmen; ⟨food:⟩ jdm bekommen; ~ with sth (approve of) mit etw einverstanden sein

agreeable /ə'griːəbl/ a angenehm; be ~ einverstanden sein (to mit)

agreed /ə'griːd/ a vereinbart

agreement /ə'griːmənt/ n Übereinstimmung f; ⟨consent⟩ Einwilligung f; ⟨contract⟩ Abkommen nt; reach ~ sich einigen

agricultur|al /ægrɪ'kʌltʃərəl/ a landwirtschaftlich. ~e f /'ægrɪkʌltʃə(r)/ n Landwirtschaft f

aground /ə'graʊnd/ a gestrandet; run ~ ⟨ship:⟩ stranden

ahead /ə'hed/ adv straight ~ geradeaus; be ~ of s.o./sth vor jdm/etw sein; ⟨fig⟩ jdm/etw voraus sein; draw ~ nach vorne ziehen; go on ~ vorgehen; get ~ vorankommen; go ~! ⟨fam⟩ bitte! look/plan ~ vorausblicken/-planen

aid /eɪd/ n Hilfe f; ⟨financial⟩ Unterstützung f; in ~ of zugunsten (+ gen) □ vt helfen (+ dat)

aide /eɪd/ n Berater m

Aids /eɪdz/ n Aids nt

ail|ing /'eɪlɪŋ/ a kränkelnd. ~ment n Leiden nt

aim /eɪm/ n Ziel nt; take ~ zielen □ vt richten (at auf + acc) □ vi zielen (at auf + acc); ~ to do sth beabsichtigen, etw zu tun. ~less a, -ly adv ziellos

air /eə(r)/ n Luft f; ⟨tune⟩ Melodie f; ⟨expression⟩ Miene f; ⟨appearance⟩ Anschein m; be on the ~ ⟨programme:⟩ gesendet werden; ⟨person:⟩ senden, auf Sendung sein; put on ~s vornehm tun; by ~ auf dem Luftweg; ⟨airmail⟩ mit Luftpost □ vt lüften; vorbringen ⟨views⟩

air: ~-bed n Luftmatratze f. ~-conditioned a klimatisiert. ~-conditioning n Klimaanlage f. ~craft n Flugzeug nt. ~fare n Flugpreis m. ~field n Flugplatz m. ~ force n Luftwaffe f. ~ freshener n Raumspray nt. ~gun n Luftgewehr nt. ~ hostess n Stewardess f. ~ letter n Aerogramm nt. ~line n Fluggesellschaft f. ~ lock n Luftblase f. ~mail n Luftpost f. ~man n Flieger m. ~plane n ⟨Amer⟩ Flugzeug nt. ~ pocket n Luftloch nt. ~port n Flughafen m. ~raid n Luftangriff m. ~-raid shelter n Luftschutzbunker m. ~ship n Luftschiff nt. ~ ticket n Flugschein m. ~tight a luftdicht. ~ traffic n Luftverkehr m. ~-traffic controller n Fluglotse m. ~worthy a flugtüchtig

airy /'eərɪ/ a ⟨ier,-iest⟩ luftig; ⟨manner⟩ nonchalant

aisle /aɪl/ n Gang m

ajar /ə'dʒɑː(r)/ a angelehnt

akin /ə'kɪn/ a ~ to verwandt mit; ⟨similar⟩ ähnlich ⟨to dat⟩

alabaster /'æləbɑːstə(r)/ n Alabaster m

alacrity /ə'lækrətɪ/ n Bereitfertigkeit f

alarm /əlɑːm/ n Alarm m; ⟨device⟩ Alarmanlage f; ⟨clock⟩ Wecker m; ⟨fear⟩ Unruhe f □ vt erschrecken; alarmieren. ~ clock n Wecker m

alas /ə'læs/ int ach!

album /'ælbəm/ n Album nt

alcohol /'ælkəhɒl/ n Alkohol m. ~ic /-'hɒlɪk/ a alkoholisch □ n Alkoholiker(in) m(f). ~ism n Alkoholismus m

alcove /'ælkəʊv/ n Nische f

alert /ə'lɜːt/ a aufmerksam □ n Alarm m; on the ~ auf der Hut □ vt alarmieren

algae /'ældʒiː/ npl Algen pl

algebra /'ældʒɪbrə/ n Algebra f

Algeria /æl'dʒɪərɪə/ n Algerien nt

alias /'eɪlɪəs/ n Deckname m □ adv alias

alibi /'ælɪbaɪ/ n Alibi nt

alien /'eɪlɪən/ a fremd □ n Ausländer(in) m(f)

alienat|e /'eɪlɪəneɪt/ vt entfremden. ~ion /-'neɪʃn/ n Entfremdung f

alight[1] /ə'laɪt/ vi aussteigen ⟨from aus⟩; ⟨bird:⟩ sich niederlassen

alight[2] a be ~ brennen; set ~ anzünden

align /ə'laɪn/ vt ausrichten. ~ment n Ausrichtung f; out of ~ment nicht richtig ausgerichtet

alike /ə'laɪk/ a & adv ähnlich; ⟨same⟩ gleich; look ~ sich ⟨dat⟩ ähnlich sehen

alimony /'ælɪmənɪ/ n Unterhalt m

alive /ə'laɪv/ a lebendig; be ~ leben; be ~ with wimmeln von

alkali /'ælkəlaɪ/ n Base f, Alkali nt

all /ɔːl/ a alle pl; ⟨whole⟩ ganz; ~ [the] children alle Kinder; ~ our children alle unsere Kinder; ~ the others alle anderen; ~ day den ganzen Tag; ~ the wine der ganze Wein; for ~ that ⟨nevertheless⟩ trotzdem; in ~ innocence in aller Unschuld □ pron alle pl; ⟨everything⟩ alles; ~ of you/them Sie/sie alle; ~ of the town die ganze Stadt; not at ~ gar nicht; in ~ insgesamt; ~ in ~ alles in allem; most of ~ am meisten; once and for ~ ein für alle Mal □ adv ganz; ~ but fast; ~ at once auf einmal; ~ too soon viel zu früh; ~ the same ⟨nevertheless⟩ trotzdem; ~ the better umso besser; be ~ in ⟨fam⟩ völlig erledigt sein; four ~ ⟨Sport⟩ vier zu vier

allay /ə'leɪ/ vt zerstreuen

allegation /ælɪ'geɪʃn/ n Behauptung f

allege /ə'ledʒ/ vt behaupten. ~d a -ly /-ɪdlɪ/ adv angeblich allegiance /ə'liːdʒəns/ n Treue f

allegor|ical /ælɪ'gɒrɪkl/ a allegorisch. ~y /'ælɪgərɪ/ n Allegorie f

allerg|ic /ə'lɜːdʒɪk/ a allergisch (to gegen). ~y /'ælədʒɪ/ n Allergie f

alleviate /ə'liːvɪeɪt/ vt lindern

alley /'ælɪ/ n Gasse f; (for bowling) Bahn f

alliance /ə'laɪəns/ n Verbindung f; (Pol) Bündnis nt

allied /'ælaɪd/ a alliiert; (fig: related) verwandt (to mit)

alligator /'ælɪgeɪtə(r)/ n Alligator m

allocat|e /'æləkeɪt/ vt zuteilen; (share out) verteilen. ~ion /-'keɪʃn/ n Zuteilung f

allot /ə'lɒt/ vt (pt/pp allotted) zuteilen (s.o. jdm). ~ment n ≈ Schrebergarten m

allow /ə'laʊ/ vt erlauben; (give) geben; (grant) gewähren; (reckon) rechnen; (agree, admit) zugeben; ~ for berücksichtigen; ~ s.o. to do sth jdm erlauben, etw zu tun; be ~ed to do sth etw tun dürfen

allowance /ə'laʊəns/ n [finanzielle] Unterstützung f; ~ for petrol Benzingeld nt; make ~s for berücksichtigen

alloy /'ælɔɪ/ n Legierung f

allude /ə'luːd/ vi anspielen (to auf + acc)

allure /ə'ljʊə(r)/ n Reiz m

allusion /ə'luːʒn/ n Anspielung f

ally[1] /'ælaɪ/ n Verbündete(r) m/f; the Allies pl die Alliierten

ally[2] /ə'laɪ/ vt (pt/pp -ied) verbinden; ~ oneself with sich verbünden mit

almighty /ɔːl'maɪtɪ/ a allmächtig; (fam: big) Riesen-. □ n the A ~ der Allmächtige

almond /'ɑːmənd/ n (Bot) Mandel f

almost /'ɔːlməʊst/ adv fast, beinahe

alms /ɑːmz/ npl (liter) Almosen pl

alone /ə'ləʊn/ a & adv allein; leave me ~ lass mich in Ruhe; leave that ~! lass die Finger davon! let ~ ganz zu schweigen von

along /ə'lɒŋ/ prep entlang (+ acc); ~ the river den Fluss entlang □ adv ~ with zusammen mit; all ~ die ganze Zeit; come ~ komm doch; I'll bring it ~ ich bringe es mit; move ~ weitergehen

along'side adv daneben □ prep neben (+ dat)

aloof /ə'luːf/ a distanziert

aloud /ə'laʊd/ adv laut

alphabet /'ælfəbet/ n Alphabet nt. ~ical /-'betɪkl/ a, -ly adv alphabetisch

alpine /'ælpaɪn/ a alpin; A~ Alpen-

Alps /ælps/ npl Alpen pl

already /ɔːl'redɪ/ adv schon

Alsace /æl'sæs/ n Elsass nt

Alsatian /æl'seɪʃn/ n (dog) [deutscher] Schäferhund m

also /'ɔːlsəʊ/ adv auch

altar /'ɔːltə(r)/ n Altar m

alter /'ɔːltə(r)/ vt ändern □ vi sich verändern. ~ation /-'reɪʃn/ n Änderung f

alternate[1] /'ɔːltəneɪt/ vi [sich] abwechseln □ vt abwechseln

alternate[2] /ɔːl'tɜːnət/ a, -ly adv abwechselnd; (Amer: alternative) andere(r,s); on ~ days jeden zweiten Tag

'alternating current n Wechselstrom m

alternative /ɔːl'tɜːnətɪv/ a andere(r,s) □ n Alternative f. ~ly adv oder aber

although /ɔːl'ðəʊ/ conj obgleich, obwohl

altitude /'æltɪtjuːd/ n Höhe f

altogether /ɔːltə'geðə(r)/ adv insgesamt; (on the whole) alles in allem

altruistic /æltru'ɪstɪk/ a altruistisch

aluminium /æljʊ'mɪnɪəm/ n, (Amer) aluminum /ə'luːmɪnəm/ n Aluminium nt

always /'ɔːlweɪz/ adv immer

am /æm/ see be

a.m. abbr (ante meridiem) vormittags

amalgamate /ə'mælgəmeɪt/ vt vereinigen; (Chem) amalgamieren □ vi sich vereinigen; (Chem) sich amalgamieren

amass /ə'mæs/ vt anhäufen

amateur /'æmətə(r)/ n Amateur m □ attrib Amateur-; (Theat) Laien-. ~ish a laienhaft

amaze /ə'meɪz/ vt erstaunen. ~d a erstaunt. ~ment n Erstaunen nt

amazing /ə'meɪzɪŋ/ a, -ly adv erstaunlich

ambassador /æm'bæsədə(r)/ n Botschafter m

amber /'æmbə(r)/ n Bernstein m □ a (colour) gelb

ambidextrous /æmbɪ'dekstrəs/ a be ~ mit beiden Händen gleich geschickt sein

ambience /'æmbɪəns/ n Atmosphäre f

ambigu|ity /æmbɪ'gjuːətɪ/ n Zweideutigkeit f. ~ous /-'bɪgjʊəs/ a, -ly adv zweideutig

ambiti|on /æm'bɪʃn/ n Ehrgeiz m; (aim) Ambition f. ~ous /-ʃəs/ a ehrgeizig

ambivalent /æm'bɪvələnt/ a zwiespältig; be/feel ~ im Zwiespalt sein

amble /'æmbl/ vi schlendern

ambulance /'æmbjʊləns/ n Krankenwagen m, ~man n Sanitäter m

ambush /'æmbʊʃ/ n Hinterhalt m □ vt aus dem Hinterhalt überfallen

amen /ɑː'men/ int amen

amenable /ə'miːnəbl/ a ~ to zugänglich (+ dat)

amend /ə'mend/ *vt* ändern. ~**ment** *n* Änderung *f*. ~**s** *npl* make ~**s** for sth etw wieder gutmachen

amenities /ə'mi:nətɪz/ *npl* Einrichtungen *pl*

America /ə'merɪkə/ *n* Amerika *nt*. ~**n** *a* amerikanisch □ *n* Amerikaner(in) *m(f)*. ~**nism** *n* Amerikanismus *m*

amiable /'eɪmɪəbl/ *a* nett

amicable /'æmɪkəbl/ *a*, -**bly** *adv* freundschaftlich; ⟨agreement⟩ gütlich

amid(st) /ə'mɪd(st)/ *prep* inmitten (+ *gen*)

amiss /ə'mɪs/ *a* be ~ nicht stimmen □ *adv* not come ~ nicht unangebracht sein; take sth ~ etw übel nehmen

ammonia /ə'məʊnɪə/ *n* Ammoniak *nt*

ammunition /æmjʊ'nɪʃn/ *n* Munition *f*

amnesia /æm'ni:zɪə/ *n* Amnesie *f*

amnesty /'æmnəstɪ/ *n* Amnestie *f*

among[st] /ə'mʌŋ(st)/ *prep* unter (+ *dat/acc*); ~ yourselves untereinander

amoral /eɪ'mɒrəl/ *a* amoralisch

amorous /'æmərəs/ *a* zärtlich

amount /ə'maʊnt/ *n* Menge *f*; ⟨sum of money⟩ Betrag *m*; ⟨total⟩ Gesamtsumme *f* □ *vi* ~ to sich belaufen auf (+ *acc*); ⟨fig⟩ hinauslaufen auf (+ *acc*)

amp /æmp/ *n* Ampere *nt*

amphibi|an /æm'fɪbɪən/ *n* Amphibie *f*. ~**ous** /-rəs/ *a* amphibisch

amphitheatre /'æmfɪ-/ *n* Amphitheater *nt*

ample /'æmpl/ *a* (-r,-st), -**ly** *adv* reichlich; ⟨large⟩ füllig

amplif|ier /'æmplɪfaɪə(r)/ *n* Verstärker *m*. ~**y** /-faɪ/ *vt* (*pt/pp*-ied) weiter ausführen; verstärken ⟨sound⟩

amputat|e /'æmpjʊteɪt/ *vt* amputieren. ~**ion** /-'teɪʃn/ *n* Amputation *f*

amuse /ə'mju:z/ *vt* amüsieren, belustigen; ⟨entertain⟩ unterhalten. ~**ment** *n* Belustigung *f*; Unterhaltung *f*. ~**ment arcade** *n* Spielhalle *f*

amusing /ə'mju:zɪŋ/ *a* amüsant

an /ən, *betont* æn/ *see* a

anaem|ia /ə'ni:mɪə/ *n* Blutarmut *f*, Anämie *f*. ~**ic** *a* blutarm

anaesthesia /ænəs'θi:zɪə/ *n* Betäubung *f*

anaesthetic /ænəs'θetɪk/ *n* Narkosemittel *nt*, Betäubungsmittel *nt*; under [an] ~ in Narkose; give s.o. an ~ jdm eine Narkose geben

anaesthet|ist /ə'ni:sθətɪst/ *n* Narkosearzt *m*. ~**ize** /-taɪz/ *vt* betäuben

analog[ue] /'ænəlɒg/ *a* Analog-

analogy /ə'nælədʒɪ/ *n* Analogie *f*

analyse /'ænəlaɪz/ *vt* analysieren

analysis /ə'næləsɪs/ *n* Analyse *f*

analyst /'ænəlɪst/ *n* Chemiker(in) *m(f)*; ⟨Psych⟩ Analytiker *m*

analytical /ænə'lɪtɪkl/ *a* analytisch

anarch|ist /'ænəkɪst/ *n* Anarchist *m*. ~**y** *n* Anarchie *f*

anathema /ə'næθəmə/ *n* Gräuel *m*

anatom|ical /ænə'tɒmɪkl/ *a*, -**ly** *adv* anatomisch. ~**y** /ə'nætəmɪ/ *n* Anatomie *f*

ancestor /'ænsestə(r)/ *n* Vorfahr *m*. ~**ry** *n* Abstammung *f*

anchor /'æŋkə(r)/ *n* Anker *m* □ *vi* ankern □ *vt* verankern

anchovy /'æntʃəvɪ/ *n* Sardelle *f*

ancient /'eɪnʃənt/ *a* alt

ancillary /æn'sɪlərɪ/ *a* Hilfs-

and /ənd, *betont* ænd/ *conj* und; ~ so on und so weiter; six hundred ~ two sechshundertzwei; more ~ more immer mehr; nice ~ warm schön warm; try ~ come versuche zu kommen

anecdote /'ænɪkdəʊt/ *n* Anekdote *f*

anew /ə'nju:/ *adv* von neuem

angel /'eɪndʒl/ *n* Engel *m*. ~**ic** /æn'dʒelɪk/ *a* engelhaft

anger /'æŋgə(r)/ *n* Zorn *m* □ *vt* zornig machen

angle¹ /'æŋgl/ *n* Winkel *m*; ⟨fig⟩ Standpunkt *m*; at an ~ schräg

angle² *vi* angeln; ~ for ⟨fig⟩ fischen nach. ~**r** *n* Angler *m*

Anglican /'æŋglɪkən/ *a* anglikanisch □ *n* Anglikaner(in) *m(f)*

Anglo-Saxon /æŋgləʊ'sæksn/ *a* angelsächsisch □ *n* Angelsächsisch *nt*

angry /'æŋgrɪ/ *a* (-ier,-iest), -**ily** *adv* zornig; be ~ with böse sein auf (+ *acc*)

anguish /'æŋgwɪʃ/ *n* Qual *f*

angular /'æŋgjʊlə(r)/ *a* eckig; ⟨features⟩ kantig

animal /'ænɪml/ *n* Tier *nt* □ *a* tierisch

animate¹ /'ænɪmət/ *a* lebendig

animat|e² /'ænɪmeɪt/ *vt* beleben. ~**ed** *a* lebhaft. ~**ion** /-'meɪʃn/ *n* Lebhaftigkeit *f*

animosity /ænɪ'mɒsətɪ/ *n* Feindseligkeit *f*

aniseed /'ænɪsi:d/ *n* Anis *m*

ankle /'æŋkl/ *n* [Fuß]knöchel *m*

annex /ə'neks/ *vt* annektieren

annex[e] /'æneks/ *n* Nebengebäude *nt*; ⟨extension⟩ Anbau *m*

annihilat|e /ə'naɪəleɪt/ *vt* vernichten. ~**ion** /-'leɪʃn/ *n* Vernichtung *f*

anniversary /ænɪ'vɜːsərɪ/ *n* Jahrestag *m*

annotate /'ænəteɪt/ *vt* kommentieren

announce /ə'naʊns/ *vt* bekannt geben; ⟨over loudspeaker⟩ durchsagen; ⟨at reception⟩ ankündigen; ⟨Radio, TV⟩ ansagen;

(in newspaper) anzeigen. ∼ment n Bekanntgabe f, Bekanntmachung f; Durchsage f; Ansage f; Anzeige f. ∼r n Ansager(in) m(f)

annoy /ə'nɔɪ/ vt ärgern; (pester) belästigen; get ∼ed sich ärgern. ∼ance n Ärger m. ∼ing a ärgerlich

annual /'ænjʊəl/ a, -ly adv jährlich □ n (Bot) einjährige Pflanze f; (book) Jahresalbum nt

annuity /ə'nju:əti/ n [Leib]rente f

annul /ə'nʌl/ vt (pt/pp annulled) annullieren

anoint /ə'nɔɪnt/ vt salben

anomaly /ə'nɒməli/ n Anomalie f

anonymous /ə'nɒnɪməs/ a, -ly adv anonym

anorak /'ænəræk/ n Anorak m

anorexia /ænə'reksɪə/ n Magersucht f

another /ə'nʌðə(r)/ a & pron ein anderer/ eine andere/ein anderes; (additional) noch ein(e); ∼ [one] noch einer/eine/ eins; ∼ day an einem anderen Tag; in ∼ way auf andere Weise; ∼ time ein andermal; one ∼ einander

answer /'ɑ:nsə(r)/ n Antwort f; (solution) Lösung f □ vt antworten (s.o. jdm); beantworten (question, letter); ∼ the door/ telephone an die Tür/ans Telefon gehen □ vi antworten; (Teleph) sich melden; ∼ back eine freche Antwort geben; ∼ for verantwortlich sein für. ∼able /-əbl/ a verantwortlich. ∼ing machine n (Teleph) Anrufbeantworter m

ant /ænt/ n Ameise f

antagonis|m /æn'tægənɪzm/ n Antagonismus m. ∼tic /-'nɪstɪk/ a feindselig

antagonize /æn'tægənaɪz/ vt gegen sich aufbringen

Antarctic /ænt'ɑ:ktɪk/ n Antarktis f

antelope /'æntɪləʊp/ n Antilope f

antenatal /ænti'neɪtl/ a ∼ care Schwangerschaftsfürsorge f

antenna /æn'tenə/ n Fühler m; (Amer: aerial) Antenne f

ante-room /'ænti-/ n Vorraum m

anthem /'ænθəm/ n Hymne f

anthology /æn'θɒlədʒi/ n Anthologie f

anthropology /ænθrə'pɒlədʒi/ n Anthropologie f

anti-'aircraft /ænti-/ a Flugabwehr-

antibiotic /æntibaɪ'ɒtɪk/ n Antibiotikum nt

'antibody n Antikörper m

anticipat|e /æn'tɪsɪpeɪt/ vt vorhersehen; (forestall) zuvorkommen (+ dat); (expect) erwarten. ∼ion /-'peɪʃn/ n Erwartung f

anti-'climax n Enttäuschung f

anti'clockwise a & adv gegen den Uhrzeigersinn

antics /'æntɪks/ npl Mätzchen pl

anti'cyclone n Hochdruckgebiet nt

antidote /'æntɪdəʊt/ n Gegengift nt

'antifreeze n Frostschutzmittel nt

antipathy /æn'tɪpəθɪ/ n Abneigung f, Antipathie f

antiquarian /ænti'kweərɪən/ a antiquarisch. ∼ bookshop n Antiquariat nt

antiquated /'æntɪkweɪtɪd/ a veraltet

antique /æn'ti:k/ a antik □ n Antiquität f. ∼ dealer n Antiquitätenhändler m

antiquity /æn'tɪkwəti/ n Altertum nt

anti-Semitic /æntɪsɪ'mɪtɪk/ a antisemitisch

anti'septic a antiseptisch □ n Antiseptikum nt

anti'social a asozial; (fam) ungesellig

antithesis /æn'tɪθəsɪs/ n Gegensatz m

antlers /'æntləz/ npl Geweih nt

anus /'eɪnəs/ n After m

anvil /'ænvɪl/ n Amboss m

anxiety /æŋ'zaɪəti/ n Sorge f

anxious /'æŋkʃəs/ a, -ly adv ängstlich; (worried) besorgt; be ∼ to do sth etw gerne machen wollen

any /'enɪ/ a irgendein(e); pl irgendwelche; (every) jede(r,s); pl alle; (after negative) kein(e); pl keine; ∼ colour/number you like eine beliebige Farbe/Zahl; have you ∼ wine/apples? haben Sie Wein/Äpfel? for ∼ reason aus irgendeinem Grund □ pron [irgend]einer/eine/eins; pl [irgend]welche; (some) welche(r,s); pl welche; (all) alle pl; (negative) keiner/keine/ keins; pl keine; I don't want ∼ of it ich will nichts davon; there aren't ∼ es gibt keine; I need wine/apples/money— have we ∼? ich brauche Wein/Äpfel/ Geld—haben wir welchen/welche/ welches? □ adv noch; ∼quicker/slower noch schneller/langsamer; is it ∼ better? geht es etwas besser? would you like ∼ more? möchten Sie noch [etwas]? I can't eat ∼ more ich kann nichts mehr essen; I can't go ∼ further ich kann nicht mehr weiter

'anybody pron [irgend]jemand; (after negative) niemand; ∼ can do that das kann jeder

'anyhow adv jedenfalls; (nevertheless) trotzdem; (badly) irgendwie

'anyone pron = anybody

'anything pron [irgend]etwas; (after negative) nichts; (everything) alles

'anyway adv jedenfalls; (in any case) sowieso

'**anywhere** *adv* irgendwo; (*after negative*) nirgendwo; (*be, live*) überall; I'd go ∼ ich würde überallhin gehen

apart /ə'pɑːt/ *adv* auseinander; live ∼ getrennt leben; ∼ from abgesehen von

apartment /ə'pɑːtmənt/ *n* Zimmer *nt*; (*Amer: flat*) Wohnung *f*

apathy /'æpəθɪ/ *n* Apathie *f*

ape /eɪp/ *n* [Menschen]affe *m* □ *vt* nachäffen

aperitif /ə'perətiːf/ *n* Aperitif *m*

aperture /'æpətʃə(r)/ *n* Öffnung *f*; (*Phot*) Blende *f*

apex /'eɪpeks/ *n* Spitze *f*; (*fig*) Gipfel *m*

apiece /ə'piːs/ *adv* pro Person; (*thing*) pro Stück

apologetic /əpɒlə'dʒetɪk/ *a*, **-ally** *adv* entschuldigend; be ∼ sich entschuldigen

apologize /ə'pɒlədʒaɪz/ *vi* sich entschuldigen (to bei)

apology /ə'pɒlədʒɪ/ *n* Entschuldigung *f*

apostle /ə'pɒsl/ *n* Apostel *m*

apostrophe /ə'pɒstrəfɪ/ *n* Apostroph *m*

appal /ə'pɔːl/ *vt* (*pt/pp* appalled) entsetzen. ∼**ling** *a* entsetzlich

apparatus /æpə'reɪtəs/ *n* Apparatur *f*; (*Sport*) Geräte *pl*; (*single piece*) Gerät *nt*

apparel /ə'pærəl/ *n* Kleidung *f*

apparent /ə'pærənt/ *a* offenbar; (*seeming*) scheinbar. ∼**ly** *adv* offenbar, anscheinend

apparition /æpə'rɪʃn/ *n* Erscheinung *f*

appeal /ə'piːl/ *n* Appell *m*, Aufruf *m*; (*request*) Bitte *f*; (*attraction*) Reiz *m*; (*Jur*) Berufung *f* □ *vi* appellieren (to an + *acc*); (*ask*) bitten (for um); (*be attractive*) zusagen (to *dat*); (*Jur*) Berufung einlegen. ∼**ing** *a* ansprechend

appear /ə'pɪə(r)/ *vi* erscheinen; (*seem*) scheinen; (*Theat*) auftreten. ∼**ance** *n* Erscheinen *nt*; (*look*) Aussehen *nt*; to all ∼**ances** allem Anschein nach

appease /ə'piːz/ *vt* beschwichtigen

append /ə'pend/ *vt* nachtragen; setzen (*signature*) (to unter + *acc*). ∼**age** /-ɪdʒ/ *n* Anhängsel *nt*

appendicitis /əpendɪ'saɪtɪs/ *n* Blinddarmentzündung *f*

appendix /ə'pendɪks/ *n* (*pl* -ices /-ɪsiːz/) (*of book*) Anhang *m* □ (*pl*-es) (*Anat*) Blinddarm *m*

appertain /æpə'teɪn/ *vi* to betreffen

appetite /'æpɪtaɪt/ *n* Appetit *m*

appetizing /'æpɪtaɪzɪŋ/ *a* appetitlich

applau|d /ə'plɔːd/ *vt*/*i* Beifall klatschen (+ *dat*). ∼**se** *n* Beifall *m*

apple /'æpl/ *n* Apfel *m*

appliance /ə'plaɪəns/ *n* Gerät *nt*

applicable /'æplɪkəbl/ *a* anwendbar (to auf + *acc*); (*on form*) not ∼ nicht zutreffend

applicant /'æplɪkənt/ *n* Bewerber(in) *m(f)*

application /æplɪ'keɪʃn/ *n* Anwendung *f*; (*request*) Antrag *m*; (*for job*) Bewerbung *f*; (*diligence*) Fleiß *m*

applied /ə'plaɪd/ *a* angewandt

apply /ə'plaɪ/ *vt* (*pt/pp* -ied) auftragen (*paint*); anwenden (*force, rule*) □ *vi* zutreffen (to auf + *acc*); ∼ for beantragen; sich bewerben um (*job*)

appoint /ə'pɔɪnt/ *vt* ernennen; (*fix*) festlegen; well ∼**ed** gut ausgestattet. ∼**ment** *n* Ernennung *f*; (*meeting*) Verabredung *f*; (*at doctor's, hairdresser's*) Termin *m*; (*job*) Posten *m*; make an ∼**ment** sich anmelden

apposite /'æpəzɪt/ *a* treffend

appraise /ə'preɪz/ *vt* abschätzen

appreciable /ə'priːʃəbl/ *a* merklich; (*considerable*) beträchtlich

appreciat|e /ə'priːʃɪeɪt/ *vt* zu schätzen wissen; (*be grateful for*) dankbar sein für; (*enjoy*) schätzen; (*understand*) verstehen □ *vi* (*increase in value*) im Wert steigen. ∼**ion** /-'eɪʃn/ *n* (*gratitude*) Dankbarkeit *f*; in ∼**ion** als Dank (of für). ∼**ive** /-ətɪv/ *a* dankbar

apprehend /æprɪ'hend/ *vt* festnehmen

apprehens|ion /æprɪ'henʃn/ *n* Festnahme *f*; (*fear*) Angst *f*. ∼**ive** /-sɪv/ *a* ängstlich

apprentice /ə'prentɪs/ *n* Lehrling *m*. ∼**ship** *n* Lehre *f*

approach /ə'prəʊtʃ/ *n* Näherkommen *nt*; (*of time*) Nahen *nt*; (*access*) Zugang *m*; (*road*) Zufahrt *f* □ *vi* sich nähern; (*time*) nahen □ *vt* sich nähern (+ *dat*); (*with request*) herantreten an (+ *acc*); (*set about*) sich heranmachen an (+ *acc*). ∼**able** /-əbl/ *a* zugänglich

approbation /æprə'beɪʃn/ *n* Billigung *f*

appropriate[1] /ə'prəʊprɪət/ *a* angebracht, angemessen

appropriate[2] /ə'prəʊprɪeɪt/ *vt* sich (*dat*) aneignen

approval /ə'pruːvl/ *n* Billigung *f*; on ∼ zur Ansicht

approv|e /ə'pruːv/ *vt* billigen □ *vi* ∼**e** of sth/s.o. mit etw/jdm einverstanden sein. ∼**ing** *a*, **-ly** *adv* anerkennend

approximate[1] /ə'prɒksɪmeɪt/ *vi* ∼ to nahe kommen (+ *dat*)

approximate[2] /ə'prɒksɪmət/ *a* ungefähr. ∼**ly** *adv* ungefähr, etwa

approximation /əprɒksɪ'meɪʃn/ *n* Schätzung *f*

apricot /'eɪprɪkɒt/ n Aprikose f

April /'eɪprəl/ n April m; make an ~ fool of in den April schicken

apron /'eɪprən/ n Schürze f

apropos /'æprəpəʊ/ adv ~ [of] betreffs (+ gen)

apt /æpt/ a, -ly adv passend; ⟨pupil⟩ begabt; be ~ to do sth dazu neigen, etw zu tun

aptitude /'æptɪtjuːd/ n Begabung f

aqualung /'ækwʌlʌŋ/ n Tauchgerät nt

aquarium /ə'kweərɪəm/ n Aquarium nt

Aquarius /ə'kweərɪəs/ n (Astr) Wassermann m

aquatic /ə'kwætɪk/ a Wasser-

Arab /'ærəb/ a arabisch ▢ n Araber(in) m(f). ~ian /ə'reɪbɪən/ a arabisch

Arabic /'ærəbɪk/ a arabisch

arable /'ærəbl/ a ~ land Ackerland nt

arbitrary /'ɑːbɪtrərɪ/ a, -ily adv willkürlich

arbitrat|e /'ɑːbɪtreɪt/ vi schlichten. ~ion /-'treɪʃn/ n Schlichtung f

arc /ɑːk/ n Bogen m

arcade /ɑː'keɪd/ n Laubengang m; ⟨shops⟩ Einkaufspassage f

arch /ɑːtʃ/ n Bogen m; ⟨of foot⟩ Gewölbe nt ▢ vt ~ its back ⟨cat:⟩ einen Buckel machen

archaeological /ɑːkɪə'lɒdʒɪkl/ a archäologisch

archaeolog|ist /ɑːkɪ'ɒlədʒɪst/ n Archäologe m/-login f. ~y n Archäologie f

archaic /ɑː'keɪɪk/ a veraltet

arch'bishop /ɑːtʃ-/ n Erzbischof m

arch-'enemy n Erzfeind m

archer /'ɑːtʃə(r)/ n Bogenschütze m. ~y n Bogenschießen nt

architect /'ɑːkɪtekt/ n Architekt(in) m(f). ~ural /ɑːkɪ'tektʃərəl/ a, -ly adv architektonisch

architecture /'ɑːkɪtektʃə(r)/ n Architektur f

archives /'ɑːkaɪvz/ npl Archiv nt

archway /'ɑːtʃweɪ/ n Torbogen m

Arctic /'ɑːktɪk/ a arktisch ▢ n the ~ die Arktis

ardent /'ɑːdənt/ a, -ly adv leidenschaftlich

ardour /'ɑːdə(r)/ n Leidenschaft f

arduous /'ɑːdjʊəs/ a mühsam

are /ɑː(r)/ see be

area /'eərɪə/ n ⟨surface⟩ Fläche f; ⟨Geom⟩ Flächeninhalt m; ⟨region⟩ Gegend f; ⟨fig⟩ Gebiet nt. ~ code n Vorwahlnummer f

arena /ə'riːnə/ n Arena f

aren't /ɑːnt/ = are not. See be

Argentina /ɑːdʒən'tiːnə/ n Argentinien nt

Argentin|e /'ɑːdʒəntaɪn/, ~ian /-'tɪnɪən/ a argentinisch

argue /'ɑːgjuː/ vi streiten (about über + acc); ⟨two people:⟩ sich streiten, ⟨debate⟩ diskutieren; don't ~! keine Widerrede! ▢ vt ⟨debate⟩ diskutieren; ⟨reason⟩ ~ that argumentieren, dass

argument /'ɑːgjʊmənt/ n Streit m, Auseinandersetzung f; ⟨reasoning⟩ Argument nt; have an ~ sich streiten. ~ative /-'mentətɪv/ a streitlustig

aria /'ɑːrɪə/ n Arie f

arid /'ærɪd/ a dürr

Aries /'eəriːz/ n (Astr) Widder m

arise /ə'raɪz/ vi (pt arose, pp arisen) sich ergeben (from aus)

aristocracy /ærɪ'stɒkrəsɪ/ n Aristokratie f

aristocrat /'ærɪstəkræt/ n Aristokrat(in) m(f). ~ic /-'krætɪk/ a aristokratisch

arithmetic /ə'rɪθmətɪk/ n Rechnen nt

ark /ɑːk/ n Noah's A ~ die Arche Noah

arm /ɑːm/ n Arm m; ⟨of chair⟩ Armlehne f; ~s pl ⟨weapons⟩ Waffen pl; ⟨Heraldry⟩ Wappen nt; up in ~s ⟨fam⟩ empört ▢ vt bewaffnen

armament /'ɑːməmənt/ n Bewaffnung f; ~s pl Waffen pl

'armchair n Sessel m

armed /ɑːmd/ a bewaffnet; ~ forces Streitkräfte pl

armistice /'ɑːmɪstɪs/ n Waffenstillstand m

armour /'ɑːmə(r)/ n Rüstung f. ~ed a Panzer-

'armpit n Achselhöhle f

army /'ɑːmɪ/ n Heer nt; ⟨specific⟩ Armee f; join the ~ zum Militär gehen

aroma /ə'rəʊmə/ n Aroma nt, Duft m. ~tic /ærə'mætɪk/ a aromatisch

arose /ə'rəʊz/ see arise

around /ə'raʊnd/ adv [all] ~ rings herum; he's not ~ er ist nicht da; look/ turn ~ sich umsehen/umdrehen; travel ~ herumreisen ▢ prep um (+ acc) ... herum; ⟨approximately⟩ gegen

arouse /ə'raʊz/ vt aufwecken; ⟨excite⟩ erregen

arrange /ə'reɪndʒ/ vt arrangieren; anordnen ⟨furniture, books⟩; ⟨settle⟩ abmachen; I have ~d to go there ich habe abgemacht, dass ich dahingehe. ~ment n Anordnung f; ⟨agreement⟩ Vereinbarung f; ⟨of flowers⟩ Gesteck nt; make ~ments Vorkehrungen treffen

arrears /ə'rɪəz/ npl Rückstände pl; in ~ im Rückstand

arrest /ə'rest/ n Verhaftung f; under ~ verhaftet ▢ vt verhaften

arrival /əˈraɪvl/ n Ankunft f; new ~s pl Neuankömmlinge pl

arrive /əˈraɪv/ vi ankommen; ~ at (fig) gelangen zu

arrogan|ce /ˈærəgəns/ n Arroganz f. ~t a, -ly adv arrogant

arrow /ˈærəʊ/ n Pfeil m

arse /ɑːs/ n (vulg) Arsch m

arsenic /ˈɑːsənɪk/ n Arsen nt

arson /ˈɑːsn/ n Brandstiftung f. ~ist /-sənɪst/ n Brandstifter m

art /ɑːt/ n Kunst f; work of ~ Kunstwerk nt; ~s and crafts pl Kunstgewerbe nt; A~s pl (Univ) Geisteswissenschaften pl

artery /ˈɑːtəri/ n Schlagader f, Arterie f

artful /ˈɑːtfl/ a gerissen

'art gallery n Kunstgalerie f

arthritis /ɑːˈθraɪtɪs/ n Arthritis f

artichoke /ˈɑːtɪtʃəʊk/ n Artischocke f

article /ˈɑːtɪkl/ n Artikel m; (object) Gegenstand m; ~ of clothing Kleidungsstück nt

articulate¹ /ɑːˈtɪkjʊlət/ a deutlich; be ~ sich gut ausdrücken können

articulate² /ɑːˈtɪkjʊleɪt/ vt aussprechen. ~d lorry n Sattelzug m

artifice /ˈɑːtɪfɪs/ n Arglist f

artificial /ɑːtɪˈfɪʃl/ a, -ly adv künstlich

artillery /ɑːˈtɪləri/ n Artillerie f

artist /ˈɑːtɪst/ n Künstler(in) m(f)

artiste /ɑːˈtiːst/ n (Theat) Artist(in) m(f)

artistic /ɑːˈtɪstɪk/ a, -ally adv künstlerisch

artless /ˈɑːtlɪs/ a unschuldig

as /æz/ conj (because) da; (when) als; (while) während □ prep als; as a child/foreigner als Kind/Ausländer □ adv as well auch; as soon as sobald; as much as so viel wie; as quick as you so schnell wie du; as you know wie Sie wissen; as far as I'm concerned was mich betrifft

asbestos /æzˈbestɒs/ n Asbest m

ascend /əˈsend/ vi [auf]steigen □ vt besteigen (throne)

Ascension /əˈsenʃn/ n (Relig) [Christi] Himmelfahrt f

ascent /əˈsent/ n Aufstieg m

ascertain /æsəˈteɪn/ vt ermitteln

ascribe /əˈskraɪb/ vt zuschreiben (to dat)

ash¹ /æʃ/ n (tree) Esche f

ash² n Asche f

ashamed /əˈʃeɪmd/ a beschämt; be ~ sich schämen (of über + acc)

ashore /əˈʃɔː(r)/ adv an Land

ash: ~tray n Aschenbecher m. A~ ~ 'Wednesday n Aschermittwoch m

Asia /ˈeɪʃə/ n Asien nt. ~n a asiatisch □ n Asiat(in) m(f). ~tic /eɪʃɪˈætɪk/ a asiatisch

aside /əˈsaɪd/ adv beiseite; ~ from (Amer) außer (+ dat)

ask /ɑːsk/ vt/i fragen; stellen (question); (invite) einladen; ~ for bitten um; verlangen (s.o.); ~ after sich erkundigen nach; ~ s.o. in jdn hereinbitten; ~ s.o. to do sth jdn bitten, etw zu tun

askance /əˈskɑːns/ adv look ~ at schief ansehen

askew /əˈskjuː/ a & adv schief

asleep /əˈsliːp/ a be ~ schlafen; fall ~ einschlafen

asparagus /əˈspærəgəs/ n Spargel m

aspect /ˈæspekt/ n Aspekt m

aspersions /əˈspɜːʃnz/ npl cast ~ on schlecht machen

asphalt /ˈæsfælt/ n Asphalt m

asphyxia /æˈsfɪksɪə/ n Erstickung f. ~te /æˈsfɪksɪeɪt/ vt/i ersticken. ~tion /-ˈeɪʃn/ n Erstickung f

aspirations /æspəˈreɪʃnz/ npl Streben nt

aspire /əˈspaɪə(r)/ vi ~ to streben nach

ass /æs/ n Esel m

assail /əˈseɪl/ vt bestürmen. ~ant n Angreifer(in) m(f)

assassin /əˈsæsɪn/ n Mörder(in) m(f). ~ate vt ermorden. ~ation /-ˈneɪʃn/ n [politischer] Mord m

assault /əˈsɔːlt/ n (Mil) Angriff m; (Jur) Körperverletzung f □ vt [tätlich] angreifen

assemble /əˈsembl/ vi sich versammeln □ vt versammeln; (Techn) montieren

assembly /əˈsembli/ n Versammlung f; (Sch) Andacht f; (Techn) Montage f. ~ line n Fließband nt

assent /əˈsent/ n Zustimmung f □ vi zustimmen (to dat)

assert /əˈsɜːt/ vt behaupten; ~ oneself sich durchsetzen. ~ion /-ɜːʃn/ n Behauptung f. ~ive /-tɪv/ a be ~ive sich durchsetzen können

assess /əˈses/ vt bewerten; (fig & for tax purposes) einschätzen: schätzen (value). ~ment n Einschätzung f; (of tax) Steuerbescheid m

asset /ˈæset/ n Vorteil m; ~s pl (money) Vermögen nt; (Comm) Aktiva pl

assiduous /əˈsɪdjʊəs/ a, -ly adv fleißig

assign /əˈsaɪn/ vt zuweisen (to dat). ~ment n (task) Aufgabe f

assimilate /əˈsɪmɪleɪt/ vt aufnehmen; (integrate) assimilieren

assist /əˈsɪst/ vt/i helfen (+ dat). ~ance n Hilfe f. ~ant a Hilfs- □ n Assistent(in) m(f); (in shop) Verkäufer(in) m(f)

associat|e[1] /əˈsəʊʃɪeɪt/ vt verbinden; (Psych) assoziieren □ vi ~ with verkehren mit. ~ion -ˈeɪʃn/ n Verband m. A~ion 'football n Fußball m

associate[2] /əˈsəʊʃɪət/ a assoziiert □ n Kollege m/-gin f

assort|ed /əˈsɔːtɪd/ a gemischt. ~ment n Mischung f

assum|e /əˈsjuːm/ vt annehmen; übernehmen ⟨office⟩; ~ing that angenommen, dass

assumption /əˈsʌmpʃn/ n Annahme f; on the ~ in der Annahme (that dass)

assurance /əˈʃʊərəns/ n Versicherung f; ⟨confidence⟩ Selbstsicherheit f

assure /əˈʃʊə(r)/ vt versichern (s.o. jdm); I ~ you [of that] das versichere ich Ihnen. ~d a sicher

asterisk /ˈæstərɪsk/ n Sternchen nt

astern /əˈstɜːn/ adv achtern

asthma /ˈæsmə/ n Asthma nt. ~tic /-ˈmætɪk/ a asthmatisch

astonish /əˈstɒnɪʃ/ vt erstaunen. ~ing a erstaunlich. ~ment n Erstaunen nt

astound /əˈstaʊnd/ vt in Erstaunen setzen

astray /əˈstreɪ/ adv go ~ verloren gehen; ⟨person:⟩ sich verlaufen; ⟨fig⟩ vom rechten Weg abkommen; lead ~ verleiten

astride /əˈstraɪd/ adv rittlings □ prep rittlings auf (+ dat/acc)

astringent /əˈstrɪndʒənt/ a adstringierend; ⟨fig⟩ beißend

astrolog|er /əˈstrɒlədʒə(r)/ n Astrologe m/-gin f. ~y n Astrologie f

astronaut /ˈæstrənɔːt/ n Astronaut(in) m(f)

astronom|er /əˈstrɒnəmə(r)/ n Astronom m. ~ical /æstrəˈnɒmɪkl/ a astronomisch. ~y n Astronomie f

astute /əˈstjuːt/ a scharfsinnig. ~ness n Scharfsinn m

asylum /əˈsaɪləm/ n Asyl nt; [lunatic] ~ Irrenanstalt f

at /ət, betont æt/ prep an (+ dat/acc); ⟨with town⟩ in; ⟨price⟩ zu; ⟨speed⟩ mit; at the station am Bahnhof; at the beginning/ end am Anfang/Ende; at home zu Hause; at John's bei John; at work/the hairdresser's bei der Arbeit/beim Friseur; at school/the office in der Schule/im Büro; at a party/wedding auf einer Party/Hochzeit; at one o'clock um ein Uhr; at Christmas/Easter zu Weihnachten/Ostern; at the age of im Alter von; not at all gar nicht; at times manchmal; two at a time zwei auf einmal; good/bad at languages gut/schlecht in Sprachen

ate /et/ see eat

atheist /ˈeɪθɪɪst/ n Atheist(in) m(f)

athlet|e /ˈæθliːt/ n Athlet(in) m(f). ~ic /-ˈletɪk/ a sportlich. ~ics /-ˈletɪks/ n Leichtathletik f

Atlantic /ətˈlæntɪk/ a & n the ~ [Ocean] der Atlantik

atlas /ˈætləs/ n Atlas m

atmospher|e /ˈætməsfɪə(r)/ n Atmosphäre f. ~ic /-ˈferɪk/ a atmosphärisch

atom /ˈætəm/ n Atom nt. ~ bomb n Atombombe f

atomic /əˈtɒmɪk/ a Atom-

atone /əˈtəʊn/ vi büßen (for für). ~ment n Buße f

atrocious /əˈtrəʊʃəs/ a abscheulich

atrocity /əˈtrɒsəti/ n Gräueltat f

attach /əˈtætʃ/ vt befestigen (to an + dat); beimessen ⟨importance⟩ (to dat); be ~ed to ⟨fig⟩ hängen an (+ dat)

attaché /əˈtæʃeɪ/ n Attaché m. ~ case n Aktenkoffer m

attachment /əˈtætʃmənt/ n Bindung f; ⟨tool⟩ Zubehörteil nt; ⟨additional⟩ Zusatzgerät nt

attack /əˈtæk/ n Angriff m; ⟨Med⟩ Anfall m □ vt/i angreifen. ~er n Angreifer m

attain /əˈteɪn/ vt erreichen; ⟨get⟩ erlangen. ~able /-əbl/ a erreichbar

attempt /əˈtempt/ n Versuch m □ vt versuchen

attend /əˈtend/ vt anwesend sein bei; ⟨go regularly to⟩ besuchen; ⟨take part in⟩ teilnehmen an (+ dat); ⟨accompany⟩ begleiten; ⟨doctor:⟩ behandeln □ vi anwesend sein; ⟨pay attention⟩ aufpassen; ~ to sich kümmern um; ⟨in shop⟩ bedienen. ~ance n Anwesenheit f; ⟨number⟩ Besucherzahl f. ~ant n Wärter(in) m(f); ⟨in car park⟩ Wächter m

attention /əˈtenʃn/ n Aufmerksamkeit f; ~! ⟨Mil⟩ stillgestanden! pay ~ aufpassen; pay ~ to beachten, achten auf (+ acc); need ~ reparaturbedürftig sein; for the ~ of zu Händen von

attentive /əˈtentɪv/ a, -ly adv aufmerksam

attest /əˈtest/ vt/i ~ [to] bezeugen

attic /ˈætɪk/ n Dachboden m

attire /əˈtaɪə(r)/ n Kleidung f □ vt kleiden

attitude /ˈætɪtjuːd/ n Haltung f

attorney /əˈtɜːnɪ/ n ⟨Amer: lawyer⟩ Rechtsanwalt m; power of ~ Vollmacht f

attract /əˈtrækt/ vt anziehen; erregen ⟨attention⟩; ~ s.o.'s attention jds Aufmerksamkeit auf sich ⟨acc⟩ lenken. ~ion /-ækʃn/ n Anziehungskraft f; ⟨charm⟩ Reiz m; ⟨thing⟩ Attraktion f. ~ive /-tɪv/ a, -ly adv attraktiv

attribute[1] /ˈætrɪbjuːt/ n Attribut nt

attribut|e² /ə'trɪbjuːt/ vt zuschreiben (to dat). ~ive /-ɪv/ a, -ly adv attributiv

attrition /ə'trɪʃn/ n war of ~ Zermürbungskrieg m

aubergine /'əʊbəʒiːn/ n Aubergine f

auburn /'ɔːbən/ a kastanienbraun

auction /'ɔːkʃn/ n Auktion f, Versteigerung f □ vt versteigern. ~eer /-ʃə'nɪə(r)/ n Auktionator m

audaci|ous /ɔː'deɪʃəs/ a, -ly adv verwegen. ~ty /-'dæsəti/ n Verwegenheit f; (impudence) Dreistigkeit f

audible /'ɔːdəbl/ a, -bly adv hörbar

audience /'ɔːdɪəns/ n Publikum nt; (Theat, TV) Zuschauer pl; (Radio) Zuhörer pl; (meeting) Audienz f

audio /'ɔːdɪəʊ/: ~ typist n Phonotypistin f. ~visual a audiovisuell

audit /'ɔːdɪt/ n Bücherrevision f □ vt (Comm) prüfen

audition /ɔː'dɪʃn/ n (Theat) Vorsprechen nt; (Mus) Vorspielen nt; (for singer) Vorsingen nt □ vi vorsprechen; vorspielen; vorsingen

auditor /'ɔːdɪtə(r)/ n Buchprüfer m

auditorium /ɔːdɪ'tɔːrɪəm/ n Zuschauerraum m

augment /ɔːg'ment/ vt vergrößern

augur /'ɔːgə(r)/ vi ~ well/ill etwas/nichts Gutes verheißen

august /ɔː'gʌst/ a hoheitsvoll

August /'ɔːgəst/ n August m

aunt /ɑːnt/ n Tante f

au pair /əʊ'peə(r)/ n ~ [girl] Aupairmädchen nt

aura /'ɔːrə/ n Fluidum nt

auspices /'ɔːspɪsɪz/ npl (protection) Schirmherrschaft f

auspicious /ɔː'spɪʃəs/ a günstig; (occasion) freudig

auster|e /ɒ'stɪə(r)/ a streng; (simple) nüchtern. ~ity /-'sterəti/ n Strenge f; (hardship) Entbehrung f

Australia /ɒ'streɪlɪə/ n Australien nt. ~n a australisch □ n Australier(in) m(f)

Austria /'ɒstrɪə/ n Österreich nt. ~n a österreichisch □ n Österreicher(in) m(f)

authentic /ɔː'θentɪk/ a echt, authentisch. ~ate vt beglaubigen. ~ity /-'tɪsəti/ n Echtheit f

author /'ɔːθə(r)/ n Schriftsteller m, Autor m; (of document) Verfasser m

authoritarian /ɔːθɒrɪ'teərɪən/ a autoritär

authoritative /ɔː'θɒrɪtətɪv/ a maßgebend; be ~ Autorität haben

authority /ɔː'θɒrəti/ n Autorität f; (public) Behörde f; in ~ verantwortlich

authorization /ɔːθəraɪ'zeɪʃn/ n Ermächtigung f

authorize /'ɔːθəraɪz/ vt ermächtigen ⟨s.o.⟩; genehmigen ⟨sth⟩

autobi'ography /ɔːtə-/ n Autobiographie f

autocratic /ɔːtə'krætɪk/ a autokratisch

autograph /'ɔːtə-/ n Autogramm nt

automatic /ɔːtə'mætɪk/ a, -ally adv automatisch □ n (car) Fahrzeug nt mit Automatikgetriebe; (washing machine) Waschautomat m

automation /ɔːtə'meɪʃn/ n Automation f

automobile /'ɔːtəməbiːl/ n Auto nt

autonom|ous /ɔː'tɒnəməs/ a autonom. ~y n Autonomie f

autopsy /'ɔːtɒpsi/ n Autopsie f

autumn /'ɔːtəm/ n Herbst m. ~al /-'tʌmnl/ a herbstlich

auxiliary /ɔːg'zɪlɪərɪ/ a Hilfs- □ n Helfer(in) m(f), Hilfskraft f

avail /ə'veɪl/ n to no ~vergeblich □ vi ~ oneself of Gebrauch machen von

available /ə'veɪləbl/ a verfügbar; (obtainable) erhältlich

avalanche /'ævəlɑːnʃ/ n Lawine f

avaric|e /'ævərɪs/ n Habsucht f. ~ious /-'rɪʃəs/ a habgierig, habsüchtig

avenge /ə'vendʒ/ vt rächen

avenue /'ævənjuː/ n Allee f

average /'ævərɪdʒ/ a Durchschnitts-, durchschnittlich □ n Durchschnitt m; on ~ im Durchschnitt, durchschnittlich □ vt durchschnittlich schaffen □ vi ~ out at im Durchschnitt ergeben

avers|e /ə'vɜːs/ a not be ~e to sth etw (dat) nicht abgeneigt sein. ~ion /-ɜːʃn/ n Abneigung f (to gegen)

avert /ə'vɜːt/ vt abwenden

aviary /'eɪvɪərɪ/ n Vogelhaus nt

aviation /eɪvɪ'eɪʃn/ n Luftfahrt f

avid /'ævɪd/ a gierig (for nach); (keen) eifrig

avocado /ævə'kɑːdəʊ/ n Avocado f

avoid /ə'vɔɪd/ vt vermeiden; ~ s.o. jdm aus dem Weg gehen. ~able /-əbl/ a vermeidbar. ~ance n Vermeidung f

await /ə'weɪt/ vt warten auf (+ acc)

awake /ə'weɪk/ a wach; wide ~ hellwach □ vi (pt awoke, pp awoken) erwachen

awaken /ə'weɪkn/ vt wecken □ vi erwachen. ~ing n Erwachen nt

award /ə'wɔːd/ n Auszeichnung f; (prize) Preis m □ vt zuerkennen (to s.o. dat); verleihen (prize)

aware /ə'weə(r)/ a become ~ gewahr werden (of gen); be ~ that wissen, dass. ~ness n Bewusstsein nt

awash /ə'wɒʃ/ *a* be ~ unter Wasser stehen

away /ə'weɪ/ *adv* weg, fort; (*absent*) abwesend; be ~ nicht da sein; far ~ weit weg; four kilometres ~ vier Kilometer entfernt; play ~ (*Sport*) auswärts spielen; go/stay ~ weggehen/-bleiben. ~ game *n* Auswärtsspiel *nt*

awe /ɔ:/ *n* Ehrfurcht *f*

awful /'ɔ:fl/ *a*, -ly *adv* furchtbar

awhile /ə'waɪl/ *adv* eine Weile

awkward /'ɔ:kwəd/ *a* schwierig; (*clumsy*) ungeschickt; (*embarrassing*) peinlich; (*inconvenient*) ungünstig. ~ly *adv* ungeschickt; (*embarrassedly*) verlegen

awning /'ɔ:nɪŋ/ *n* Markise *f*

awoke(n) /ə'wəʊk(n)/ *see* awake

awry /ə'raɪ/ *adv* schief

axe /æks/ *n* Axt □ *vt* (*pres p* axing) streichen; (*dismiss*) entlassen

axis /'æksɪs/ *n* (*pl* axes /-si:z/) Achse *f*

axle /'æksl/ *n* (*Techn*) Achse *f*

ay[e] /aɪ/ *adv* ja □ *n* Jastimme *f*

B

B /bi:/ *n* (*Mus*) H *nt*

BA *abbr of* Bachelor of Arts

babble /'bæbl/ *vi* plappern; ⟨*stream.*⟩ plätschern

baboon /bə'bu:n/ *n* Pavian *m*

baby /'beɪbɪ/ *n* Baby *nt*; (*Amer, fam*) Schätzchen *nt*

baby: ~ carriage *n* (*Amer*) Kinderwagen *m*. ~ish *a* kindisch. ~minder *n* Tagesmutter *f*. ~sit *vi* babysitten. ~sitter *n* Babysitter *m*

bachelor /'bætʃələ(r)/ *n* Junggeselle *m*; B ~ of Arts/Science Bakkalaureus Artium/Scientium

bacillus /bə'sɪləs/ *n* (*pl* -lli) Bazillus *m*

back /bæk/ *n* Rücken *m*; (*reverse*) Rückseite *f*; (*of chair*) Rückenlehne *f*; (*Sport*) Verteidiger *m*; at/(*Auto*) in the ~ hinten; on the ~ auf der Rückseite; ~ to front verkehrt; at the ~ of beyond am Ende der Welt □ *a* Hinter- □ *adv* zurück; ~ here/ there hier/da hinten; ~ at home zu Hause; go/pay ~ zurückgehen/-zahlen □ *vt* (*support*) unterstützen; (*with money*) finanzieren; (*Auto*) zurücksetzen; (*Betting*) [Geld] setzen auf (+ *acc*); (*cover the back of*) mit einer Verstärkung versehen □ *vi* (*Auto*) zurücksetzen. ~ down *vi* klein beigeben. ~ in *vi* rückwärts hineinfahren. ~ out *vi* rückwärts hinaus-/

herausfahren; (*fig*) aussteigen (of aus). ~ up *vt* unterstützen; (*confirm*) bestätigen □ *vi* (*Auto*) zurücksetzen

back: ~ache *n* Rückenschmerzen *pl*. ~biting *n* gehässiges Gerede *nt*. ~bone *n* Rückgrat *nt*. ~chat *n* Widerrede *f*. ~comb *vt* toupieren. ~date *vt* rückdatieren; ~dated to rückwirkend von. ~'door *n* Hintertür *f*

backer /'bækə(r)/ *n* Geldgeber *m*

back: ~'fire *vi* (*Auto*) fehlzünden; (*fig*) fehlschlagen. ~ground *n* Hintergrund *m*; family ~ground Familienverhältnisse *pl*. ~hand *n* (*Sport*) Rückhand *f*. ~'handed *a* (*compliment*) zweifelhaft. ~'hander *n* (*Sport*) Rückhandschlag *m*; (*fam: bribe*) Schmiergeld *nt*

backing /'bækɪŋ/ *n* (*support*) Unterstützung *f*; (*material*) Verstärkung *f*

back: ~lash *n* (*fig*) Gegenschlag *m*. ~log *n* Rückstand *m* (of an + dat). ~'seat *n* Rücksitz *m*. ~side *n* (*fam*) Hintern *m*. ~stage *adv* hinter der Bühne. ~stroke *n* Rückenschwimmen *nt*. ~-up *n* Unterstützung *f*; (*Amer: traffic jam*) Stau *m*

backward /'bækwəd/ *a* zurückgeblieben; ⟨*country*⟩ rückständig □ *adv* rückwärts. ~s rückwärts; ~s and forwards hin und her

back: ~water *n* (*fig*) unberührtes Fleckchen *nt*. ~ 'yard *n* Hinterhof *m*; not in my ~ yard (*fam*) nicht vor meiner Haustür

bacon /'beɪkn/ *n* [Schinken]speck *m*

bacteria /bæk'tɪərɪə/ *npl* Bakterien *pl*

bad /bæd/ *a* (worse, worst) schlecht; (*serious*) schwer, schlimm; (*naughty*) unartig; ~ language gemeine Ausdrucksweise *f*; feel ~ sich schlecht fühlen; (*feel guilty*) ein schlechtes Gewissen haben; go ~ schlecht werden

bade /bæd/ *see* bid²

badge /bædʒ/ *n* Abzeichen *nt*

badger /'bædʒə(r)/ *n* Dachs *m* □ *vt* plagen

badly /'bædlɪ/ *adv* schlecht; (*seriously*) schwer; ~ off schlecht gestellt; ~ behaved unerzogen; want ~ sich (*dat*) sehnsüchtig wünschen; need ~ dringend brauchen

bad-'mannered *a* mit schlechten Manieren

badminton /'bædmɪntən/ *n* Federball *m*

bad-'tempered *a* schlecht gelaunt

baffle /'bæfl/ *vt* verblüffen

bag /bæg/ *n* Tasche *f*; (*of paper*) Tüte *f*; (*pouch*) Beutel *m*; ~s of (*fam*) jede Menge □ *vt* (*fam: reserve*) in Beschlag nehmen

baggage /'bægɪdʒ/ *n* [Reise]gepäck *nt*

baggy /'bægɪ/ *a* ⟨*clothes*⟩ ausgebeult

'bagpipes *npl* Dudelsack *m*

bail /beɪl/ n Kaution f; on ~ gegen Kaution □ vt ~ s.o. out jdn gegen Kaution freibekommen; (fig) jdm aus der Patsche helfen. ~ out vt (Naut) ausschöpfen □ vi (Aviat) abspringen

bailiff /'beɪlɪf/ n Gerichtsvollzieher m; (of estate) Gutsverwalter m

bait /beɪt/ n Köder m □ vt mit einem Köder versehen; (fig: torment) reizen

bake /beɪk/ vt/i backen

baker /'beɪkə(r)/ n Bäcker m; ~'s [shop] Bäckerei f. ~y n Bäckerei f

baking /'beɪkɪŋ/ n Backen nt. ~-powder n Backpulver nt. ~-tin n Backform f

balance /'bæləns/ n (equilibrium) Gleichgewicht nt, Balance f; (scales) Waage f; (Comm) Saldo m; (outstanding sum) Restbetrag m; [bank] ~ Kontostand m; in the ~ (fig) in der Schwebe □ vt balancieren; (equalize) ausgleichen; (Comm) abschließen (books) □ vi balancieren; (fig & Comm) sich ausgleichen. ~d a ausgewogen. ~ sheet n Bilanz f

balcony /'bælkənɪ/ n Balkon m

bald /bɔːld/ a (-er, -est) kahl; (person) kahlköpfig; go ~ eine Glatze bekommen

balderdash /'bɔːldədæʃ/ n Unsinn m

balding /'bɔːldɪŋ/ a be ~ing eine Glatze bekommen. ~ly adv unverblümt. ~ness n Kahlköpfigkeit f

bale /beɪl/ n Ballen m

baleful /'beɪlfl/ a, -ly adv böse

balk /bɔːlk/ vt vereiteln □ vi ~ at zurückschrecken vor (+ dat)

Balkans /'bɔːlknz/ npl Balkan m

ball[1] /bɔːl/ n Ball m; (Billiards, Croquet) Kugel f; (of yarn) Knäuel m & nt; on the ~ (fam) auf Draht

ball[2] n (dance) Ball m

ballad /'bæləd/ n Ballade f

ballast /'bæləst/ n Ballast m

ball-'bearing n Kugellager nt

ballerina /bælə'riːnə/ n Ballerina f

ballet /'bæleɪ/ n Ballett nt. ~ dancer n Balletttänzer(in) m(f)

ballistic /bə'lɪstɪk/ a ballistisch. ~s n Ballistik f

balloon /bə'luːn/ n Luftballon m; (Aviat) Ballon m

ballot /'bælət/ n [geheime] Wahl f; (on issue) [geheime] Abstimmung f. ~-box n Wahlurne f. ~-paper n Stimmzettel m

ball: ~-point ['pen] n Kugelschreiber m. ~room n Ballsaal m

balm /bɑːm/ n Balsam m

balmy /'bɑːmɪ/ a (-ier, -iest) a sanft; (fam: crazy) verrückt

Baltic /'bɔːltɪk/ a & n the ~ [Sea] die Ostsee

balustrade /bælə'streɪd/ n Balustrade f

bamboo /bæm'buː/ n Bambus m

bamboozle /bæm'buːzl/ vt (fam) übers Ohr hauen

ban /bæn/ n Verbot nt □ vt (pt/pp banned) verbieten

banal /bə'nɑːl/ a banal. ~ity /-'nælətɪ/ n Banalität f

banana /bə'nɑːnə/ n Banane f

band /bænd/ n Band nt; (stripe) Streifen m; (group) Schar f; (Mus) Kapelle f □ vi ~ together sich zusammenschließen

bandage /'bændɪdʒ/ n Verband m; (for support) Bandage f □ vt verbinden; bandagieren (limb)

b. & b. abbr of bed and breakfast

bandit /'bændɪt/ n Bandit m

band: ~stand n Musikpavillon m. ~wagon n jump on•the ~wagon (fig) sich einer erfolgreichen Sache anschließen

bandy[1] /'bændɪ/ vt (pt/pp -ied) wechseln (words)

bandy[2] a (-ier, -iest) be ~ O-Beine haben. ~-legged a O-beinig

bang /bæŋ/ n (noise) Knall m; (blow) Schlag m □ adv go ~ knallen □ int bums! peng! □ vt knallen; (shut noisily) zuknallen; (strike) schlagen auf (+ acc); ~ one's head against (dat) den Kopf stoßen (on an + acc) □ vi schlagen; (door:) zuknallen

banger /'bæŋə(r)/ n (firework) Knallfrosch m; (fam: sausage) Wurst f; old ~ (fam: car) Klapperkiste f

bangle /'bæŋgl/ n Armreifen m

banish /'bænɪʃ/ vt verbannen

banisters /'bænɪstəz/ npl [Treppen]geländer nt

banjo /'bændʒəʊ/ n Banjo nt

bank[1] /bæŋk/ n (of river) Ufer nt; (slope) Hang m □ vi (Aviat) in die Kurve gehen

bank[2] n Bank f □ vt einzahlen; ~ with ein Konto haben bei. ~ on sich verlassen auf (+ acc)

'bank account n Bankkonto nt

banker /'bæŋkə(r)/ n Bankier m

bank: ~ 'holiday n gesetzlicher Feiertag m. ~ing n Bankwesen nt. ~note n Banknote f

bankrupt /'bæŋkrʌpt/ a bankrott; go ~ Bankrott machen □ n Bankrotteur m □ vt Bankrott machen. ~cy n Bankrott m

banner /'bænə(r)/ n Banner nt; (carried by demonstrators) Transparent nt, Spruchband nt

banns /bænz/ npl (Relig) Aufgebot nt

banquet /'bæŋkwɪt/ n Bankett nt

banter /'bæntə(r)/ n Spötterei f

bap /bæp/ n weiches Brötchen nt

baptism /'bæptɪzm/ n Taufe f

Baptist /'bæptɪst/ n Baptist(in) m(f)

baptize /bæp'taɪz/ vt taufen

bar /ˈbɑː(r)/ n Stange f; (of cage) [Gitter]otab m; (of gold) Barren m; (of chocolate) Tafel f; (of soap) Stück nt; (long) Riegel m; (café) Bar f; (counter) Theke f; (Mus) Takt m; (fig: obstacle) Hindernis nt; parallel ~s (Sport) Barren m; be called to the ~ (Jur) als plädierender Anwalt zugelassen werden; behind ~s (fam) hinter Gittern □ vt (pt/pp barred) versperren (way, door); ausschließen (person) □ prep außer; ~ none ohne Ausnahme

barbarian /bɑː'beərɪən/ n Barbar m

barbar|ic /bɑː'bærɪk/ a barbarisch. ~ity n Barbarei f. ~ous /'bɑːbərəs/ a barbarisch

barbecue /'bɑːbɪkjuː/ n Grill m; (party) Grillfest nt □ vt [im Freien] grillen

barbed /'bɑːbd/ a ~ wire Stacheldraht m

barber /'bɑːbə(r)/ n [Herren]friseur m

barbiturate /bɑː'bɪtjʊrət/ n Barbiturat nt

'bar code n Strichkode m

bare /beə/(r)/ a (-r, -st) nackt, bloß; (tree) kahl; (empty) leer; (mere) bloß □ vt entblößen; fletschen (teeth)

bare: ~back adv ohne Sattel. ~faced a schamlos. ~foot adv barfuß. ~'headed a mit unbedecktem Kopf

barely /'beəlɪ/ adv kaum

bargain /'bɑːgɪn/ n (agreement) Geschäft nt; (good buy) Gelegenheitskauf m; into the ~ noch dazu; make a ~ sich einigen □ vi handeln; (haggle) feilschen; ~ for (expect) rechnen mit

barge /bɑːdʒ/ n Lastkahn m; (towed) Schleppkahn m □ vi ~ in (fam) hereinplatzen

baritone /'bærɪtəʊn/ n Bariton m

bark¹ /bɑːk/ n (of tree) Rinde f

bark² n Bellen nt □ vi bellen

barley /'bɑːlɪ/ n Gerste f

bar: ~maid n Schankmädchen nt. ~man n Barmann m

barmy /'bɑːmɪ/ a (fam) verrückt

barn /bɑːn/ n Scheune f

barometer /bə'rɒmɪtə(r)/ n Barometer nt

baron /'bærən/ n Baron m. ~ess n Baronin f

baroque /bə'rɒk/ a barock □ n Barock nt

barracks /'bærəks/ npl Kaserne f

barrage /'bærɑːʒ/ n (in river) Wehr nt; (Mil) Sperrfeuer nt; (fig) Hagel m

barrel /'bærl/ n Fass nt; (of gun) Lauf m; (of cannon) Rohr nt. ~-organ n Drehorgel f

barren /'bærn/ a unfruchtbar; (landscape) öde

barricade /bærɪ'keɪd/ n Barrikade f □ vt verbarrikadieren

barrier /'bærɪə(r)/ n Barriere f; (across road) Schranke f; (Rail) Sperre f; (fig) Hindernis nt

barring /'bɑːrɪŋ/ prep ~ accidents wenn alles gut geht

barrister /'bærɪstə(r)/ n [plädierender] Rechtsanwalt m

barrow /'bærəʊ/ n Karre f, Karren m. ~ boy n Straßenhändler m

barter /'bɑːtə(r)/ vt tauschen (for gegen)

base /beɪs/ n Fuß m; (fig) Basis f; (Mil) Stützpunkt m □ a gemein; (metal) unedel □ vt stützen (on auf + acc); be ~d on basieren auf (+ dat)

base: ~ball n Baseball m. ~less a unbegründet. ~ment n Kellergeschoss nt. ~ment flat n Kellerwohnung f

bash /bæʃ/ n Schlag m; have a ~! (fam) probier es mal! □ vt hauen; (dent) einbeulen; ~ed in verbeult

bashful /'bæʃfl/ a, -ly adv schüchtern

basic /'beɪsɪk/ a Grund-; (fundamental) grundlegend; (essential) wesentlich; (unadorned) einfach; the ~s das Wesentliche. ~ally adv grundsätzlich

basil /'bæzɪl/ n Basilikum nt

basilica /bə'zɪlɪkə/ n Basilika f

basin /'beɪsn/ n Becken nt; (for washing) Waschbecken nt; (for food) Schüssel f

basis /'beɪsɪs/ n (pl -ses /-siːz/) Basis f

bask /bɑːsk/ vi sich sonnen

basket /'bɑːskɪt/ n Korb m. ~ball n Basketball m

Basle /bɑːl/ n Basel nt

bass /beɪs/ a Bass-; ~ voice Bassstimme f □ n Bass m; (person) Bassist m

bassoon /bə'suːn/ n Fagott nt

bastard /'bɑːstəd/ n (sl) Schuft m

baste¹ /beɪst/ vt (sew) heften

baste² vt (Culin) begießen

bastion /'bæstɪən/ n Bastion f

bat¹ /bæt/ n Schläger m; off one's own ~ (fam) auf eigene Faust □ vt (pt/pp batted) schlagen; not ~ an eyelid (fig) nicht mit der Wimper zucken

bat² n (Zool) Fledermaus f

batch /bætʃ/ n (of people) Gruppe f; (of papers) Stoß m; (of goods) Sendung f; (of bread) Schub m

bated /'beɪtɪd/ a with ~ breath mit angehaltenem Atem

bath /bɑːθ/ n (pl ~s /bɑːðz/) Bad nt; (tub) Badewanne f; ~s pl Badeanstalt f; have a ~ baden □ vt/i baden

bathe /beɪð/ n Bad nt □ vt/i baden. ~r n Badende(r) m/f

bathing /'beɪðɪŋ/ n Baden nt. ~cap n Bademütze f. ~costume n Badeanzug m

bath: ~mat n Bademattte f. ~robe n (Amer) Bademantel m. ~room n Badezimmer nt. ~towel n Badetuch nt

baton /'bætn/ n (Mus) Taktstock m; (Mil) Stab m

battalion /bə'tæliən/ n Bataillon nt

batten /'bætn/ n Latte f

batter /'bætə(r)/ n (Culin) flüssiger Teig m □ vt schlagen. ~ed ⟨car⟩ verbeult; ⟨wife⟩ misshandelt

battery /'bætəri/ n Batterie f

battle /'bætl/ n Schlacht f; (fig) Kampf m □ vi (fig) kämpfen (for um)

battle: ~axe n (fam) Drachen m. ~field n Schlachtfeld nt. ~ship n Schlachtschiff nt

batty /'bæti/ a (fam) verrückt

Bavaria /bə'veəriə/ n Bayern nt. ~n a bayrisch □ n Bayer(in) m(f)

bawdy /'bɔːdi/ a (-ier, -iest) derb

bawl /bɔːl/ vt/i brüllen

bay¹ /beɪ/ n (Geog) Bucht f; (Archit) Erker m

bay² n keep at ~ fern halten

bay³ n (horse) Braune(r) m

bay⁴ n (Bot) [echter] Lorbeer m. ~leaf n Lorbeerblatt nt

bayonet /'beɪənet/ n Bajonett nt

bay 'window n Erkerfenster nt

bazaar /bə'zɑː(r)/ n Basar m

BC abbr (before Christ) v. Chr.

be /biː/ vi (pres am, are, is, pl are; pt was, pl were; pp been) sein; (lie) liegen; (stand) stehen; (cost) kosten; he is a teacher er ist Lehrer; be quiet! sei still! I am cold/hot mir ist kalt/heiß; how are you? wie geht es Ihnen? I am well mir geht es gut; there is/are es gibt; what do you want to be? was willst du werden? I have been to Vienna ich bin in Wien gewesen; has the postman been? war der Briefträger schon da? it's hot, isn't it? es ist heiß, nicht [wahr]? you are coming too, aren't you? du kommst mit, nicht [wahr]? it's yours, is it? das gehört also Ihnen? yes he is/I am ja; (negating previous statement) doch; three and three are six drei und drei macht sechs □ v aux ~ reading/going lesen/gehen; I am coming/staying ich komme/bleibe; what is he doing? was macht er? I am being lazy ich faulenze; I was thinking of you ich dachte an dich; you were going to ... du wolltest ...; I am to stay ich soll bleiben; you are not to ... du

darfst nicht ...; you are to do that immediately das musst du sofort machen □ passive werden; be attacked/deceived überfallen/betrogen werden

beach /biːtʃ/ n Strand m. ~wear n Strandkleidung f

beacon /'biːkn/ n Leuchtfeuer nt; (Naut, Aviat) Bake f

bead /biːd/ n Perle f

beak /biːk/ n Schnabel m

beaker /'biːkə(r)/ n Becher m

beam /biːm/ n Balken m; (of light) Strahl m □ vi strahlen. ~ing a [freude]strahlend

bean /biːn/ n Bohne f; spill the ~s (fam) alles ausplaudern

bear¹ /beə(r)/ n Bär m

bear² vt/i (pt bore, pp borne) tragen; (endure) ertragen; gebären ⟨child⟩; ~ right sich rechts halten. ~able /-əbl/ a erträglich

beard /bɪəd/ n Bart m. ~ed a bärtig

bearer /'beərə(r)/ n Träger m; (of news, cheque) Überbringer m; (of passport) Inhaber(in) m(f)

bearing /'beərɪŋ/ n Haltung f; (Techn) Lager nt; have a ~ on von Belang sein für; get one's ~s sich orientieren; lose one's ~s die Orientierung verlieren

beast /biːst/ n Tier nt; (fam: person) Biest nt

beastly /'biːstli/ a (-ier, -iest) (fam) scheußlich; ⟨person⟩ gemein

beat /biːt/ n Schlag m; (of policeman) Runde f; (rhythm) Takt m □ vt/i (pt beat, pp beaten) schlagen; (thrash) verprügeln; klopfen ⟨carpet⟩; (hammer) hämmern (on an + acc); ~ a retreat (Mil) sich zurückziehen; ~ it! (fam) hau ab! it ~s me (fam) das begreife ich nicht. ~ up vt zusammenschlagen

beat|en /'biːtn/ a off the ~en track abseits. ~ing n Prügel pl

beautician /bjuː'tɪʃn/ n Kosmetikerin f

beauti|ful /'bjuːtɪfl/ a, -ly adv schön. ~fy /-faɪ/ vt (pt/pp -ied) verschönern

beauty /'bjuːti/ n Schönheit f. ~ parlour n Kosmetiksalon m. ~ spot n Schönheitsfleck m; (place) landschaftlich besonders reizvolles Fleckchen nt

beaver /'biːvə(r)/ n Biber m

became /bɪ'keɪm/ see become

because /bɪ'kɒz/ conj weil □ adv ~ of wegen (+ gen)

beckon /'bekn/ vt/i ~ [to] herbeiwinken

become /bɪ'kʌm/ vt/i (pt became, pp become) werden. ~ing a ⟨clothes⟩ kleidsam

bed /bed/ n Bett nt; (layer) Schicht f; (of flowers) Beet nt; in ~ im Bett; go to ~ ins od zu Bett gehen; ~ and breakfast

Zimmer mit Frühstück. ∼clothes *npl*, ∼ding *n* Bettzeug *nt*

bedlam /'bedləm/ *n* Chaos *nt*

'**bedpan** *n* Bettpfanne *f*

bedraggled /bɪ'drægld/ *a* nass und verschmutzt

bed: ∼ridden *a* bettlägerig. ∼room *n* Schlafzimmer *nt*

'**bedside** *n* at his ∼ an seinem Bett. ∼ 'lamp *n* Nachttischlampe *f*. ∼ 'rug *n* Bettvorleger *m*. ∼ 'table *n* Nachttisch *m*

bed: ∼'sitter *n*, ∼'sitting-room *n* Wohnschlafzimmer *nt*. ∼spread *n* Tagesdecke *f*. ∼time *n* Schlafenszeit *f*; at ∼time vor dem Schlafengehen

bee /biː/ *n* Biene *f*

beech /biːtʃ/ *n* Buche *f*

beef /biːf/ *n* Rindfleisch *nt*. ∼burger *n* Hamburger *m*

bee: ∼hive *n* Bienenstock *m*. ∼keeper *n* Imker(in) *m(f)*. ∼keeping *n* Bienenzucht *f*. ∼line *n* make a ∼line for *(fam)* zusteuern auf (+ *acc*)

been /biːn/ *see* be

beer /bɪə(r)/ *n* Bier *nt*

beet /biːt/ *n* (*Amer:* beetroot) rote Bete *f*; [sugar] ∼ Zuckerrübe *f*

beetle /'biːtl/ *n* Käfer *m*

'**beetroot** *n* rote Bete *f*

before /bɪ'fɔː(r)/ *prep* vor (+ *dat*/*acc*); the day ∼ yesterday vorgestern; ∼ long bald □ *adv* vorher; (*already*) schon; never ∼ noch nie; ∼ that davor □ *conj* (*time*) ehe, bevor. ∼hand *adv* vorher, im Voraus

befriend /bɪ'frend/ *vt* sich anfreunden mit

beg /beg/ *v* (*pt/pp* begged) □ *vi* betteln □ *vt* (*entreat*) anflehen; (*ask*) bitten (for um)

began /bɪ'gæn/ *see* begin

beggar /'begə(r)/ *n* Bettler(in) *m(f)*; (*fam*) Kerl *m*

begin /bɪ'gɪn/ *vt/i* (*pt* began, *pp* begun, *pres p* beginning) anfangen, beginnen; to ∼ with anfangs. ∼ner *n* Anfänger(in) *m(f)*. ∼ning *n* Anfang *m*, Beginn *m*

begonia /bɪ'gəʊnɪə/ *n* Begonie *f*

begrudge /bɪ'grʌdʒ/ *vt* ∼ s.o. sth jdm etw missgönnen

beguile /bɪ'gaɪl/ *vt* betören

begun /bɪ'gʌn/ *see* begin

behalf /bɪ'hɑːf/ *n* on ∼ of im Namen von; on my ∼ meinetwegen

behave /bɪ'heɪv/ *vi* sich verhalten, ∼ oneself sich benehmen

behaviour /bɪ'heɪvjə(r)/ *n* Verhalten *nt*; good/bad ∼ gutes/schlechtes Benehmen *nt*; ∼ pattern Verhaltensweise *f*

behead /bɪ'hed/ *vt* enthaupten

beheld /bɪ'held/ *see* behold

behind /bɪ'haɪnd/ *prep* hinter (+ *dat*/ *acc*); be ∼ sth hinter etw (*dat*) stecken □ *adv* hinten; (*late*) im Rückstand; a long way ∼ weit zurück; in the car ∼ im Wagen dahinter □ *n* (*fam*) Hintern *m*. ∼hand *adv* im Rückstand

behold /bɪ'həʊld/ *vt* (*pt/pp* beheld) (*liter*) sehen

beholden /bɪ'həʊldn/ *a* verbunden (to *dat*)

beige /beɪʒ/ *a* beige

being /'biːɪŋ/ *n* Dasein *nt*; living ∼ Lebewesen *nt*; come into ∼ entstehen

belated /bɪ'leɪtɪd/ *a*, -ly *adv* verspätet

belch /beltʃ/ *vi* rülpsen □ *vt* ∼ out ausstoßen (*smoke*)

belfry /'belfrɪ/ *n* Glockenstube *f*; (*tower*) Glockenturm *m*

Belgian /'beldʒən/ *a* belgisch □ *n* Belgier(in) *m(f)*

Belgium /'beldʒəm/ *n* Belgien *nt*

belief /bɪ'liːf/ *n* Glaube *m*

believable /bɪ'liːvəbl/ *a* glaubhaft

believe /bɪ'liːv/ *vt/i* glauben (s.o. jdm; in an + *acc*). ∼r *n* (*Relig*) Gläubige(r) *m/f*

belittle /bɪ'lɪtl/ *vt* herabsetzen

bell /bel/ *n* Glocke *f*; (on door) Klingel *f*

belligerent /bɪ'lɪdʒərənt/ *a* Krieg führend; (*aggressive*) streitlustig

bellow /'beləʊ/ *vt/i* brüllen

bellows /'beləʊz/ *npl* Blasebalg *m*

belly /'belɪ/ *n* Bauch *m*

belong /bɪ'lɒŋ/ *vi* gehören (to *dat*); (*be member*) angehören (to *dat*). ∼ings *npl* Sachen *pl*

beloved /bɪ'lʌvɪd/ *a* geliebt □ *n* Geliebte(r) *m/f*

below /bɪ'ləʊ/ *prep* unter (+ *dat*/*acc*) □ *adv* unten; (*Naut*) unter Deck

belt /belt/ *n* Gürtel *m*; (*area*) Zone *f*; (*Techn*) [Treib]riemen *m* □ *vi* (*fam:* rush) rasen □ *vt* (*fam: hit*) hauen

bemused /bɪ'mjuːzd/ *a* verwirrt

bench /bentʃ/ *n* Bank *f*; (*work-*) Werkbank *f*; the B ∼ (*Jur*) ≈ die Richter *pl*

bend /bend/ *n* Biegung *f*; (in road) Kurve *f*; round the ∼ (*fam*) verrückt □ *v* (*pt/pp* bent) □ *vt* biegen; beugen (*arm*, *leg*) □ *vi* sich biegen; (*thing*:) sich bücken; (*road*:) eine Biegung machen. ∼ down *vi* sich bücken. ∼ over *vi* sich vornüberbeugen

beneath /bɪ'niːθ/ *prep* unter (+ *dat*/*acc*); ∼ him (*fig*) unter seiner Würde; ∼ contempt unter aller Würde □ *adv* darunter

benediction /benɪ'dɪkʃn/ *n* (*Relig*) Segen *m*

benefactor /'benɪfæktə(r)/ n Wohltäter(in) m(f)

beneficial /benɪ'fɪʃl/ a nützlich

beneficiary /benɪ'fɪʃərɪ/ n Begünstigte(r) m|f

benefit /'benɪfɪt/ n Vorteil m; (allowance) Unterstützung f; (insurance) Leistung f; sickness ~ Krankengeld nt □ v (pt/pp -fited, pres p -fiting) □ vt nützen (+ dat) □ vi profitieren (from von)

benevolen|ce /bɪ'nevələns/ n Wohlwollen nt. ~t a, -ly adv wohlwollend

benign /bɪ'naɪn/ a, -ly adv gütig; (Med) gutartig

bent /bent/ see bend □ a ⟨person⟩ gebeugt; (distorted) verbogen; ⟨fam: dishonest⟩ korrupt; be ~ on doing sth darauf erpicht sein, etw zu tun □ n Hang m, Neigung f (for zu); artistic ~ künstlerische Ader f

be|queath /bɪ'kwiːð/ vt vermachen (to dat). ~quest /-'kwest/ n Vermächtnis nt

bereave|d /bɪ'riːvd/ n the ~d pl die Hinterbliebenen. ~ment n Trauerfall m; (state) Trauer f

bereft /bɪ'reft/ a ~ of beraubt (+ gen)

beret /'bereɪ/ n Baskenmütze f

Berne /bɜːn/ n Bern nt

berry /'berɪ/ n Beere f

berserk /bə'sɜːk/ a go ~ wild werden

berth /bɜːθ/ n (on ship) [Schlaf]koje f; (ship's anchorage) Liegeplatz m; give a wide ~ to ⟨fam⟩ einen großen Bogen machen um □ vi anlegen

beseech /bɪ'siːtʃ/ vt (pt/pp beseeched or besought) anflehen

beside /bɪ'saɪd/ prep neben (+ dat/acc); ~ oneself außer sich (dat)

besides /bɪ'saɪdz/ prep außer (+ dat) □ adv außerdem

besiege /bɪ'siːdʒ/ vt belagern

besought /bɪ'sɔːt/ see beseech

bespoke /bɪ'spəʊk/ a ⟨suit⟩ maßgeschneidert

best /best/ a & n beste(r,s); the ~ der/die/das Beste; at ~ bestenfalls; all the ~! alles Gute! do one's ~ sein Bestes tun; the ~ part of a year fast ein Jahr; to the ~ of my knowledge so viel ich weiß; make the ~ of it das Beste daraus machen □ adv am besten; as ~ I could so gut ich konnte. ~ 'man n ≈ Trauzeuge m

bestow /bɪ'stəʊ/ vt schenken (on dat)

best'seller n Bestseller m

bet /bet/ n Wette f □ v (pt/pp bet or betted) □ vt ~ s.o. £5 mit jdm um £5 wetten □ vi wetten; ~ on [Geld] setzen auf (+ acc)

betray /bɪ'treɪ/ vt verraten. ~al n Verrat m

better /'betə(r)/ a besser; get ~ sich bessern; (after illness) sich erholen □ adv besser; ~ off besser dran; ~ not lieber nicht; all the ~ umso besser; the sooner the ~ je eher, desto besser; think ~ of sth sich eines Besseren besinnen; you'd ~ stay du bleibst am besten hier □ vt verbessern; (do better than) übertreffen; ~ oneself sich verbessern

'**betting shop** n Wettbüro nt

between /bɪ'twiːn/ prep zwischen (+ dat/acc); ~ you and me unter uns; ~ us (together) zusammen □ adv [in] ~ dazwischen

beverage /'bevərɪdʒ/ n Getränk nt

bevy /'bevɪ/ n Schar f

beware /bɪ'weə(r)/ vi sich in Acht nehmen (of vor + dat); ~ of the dog! Vorsicht, bissiger Hund!

bewilder /bɪ'wɪldə(r)/ vt verwirren. ~ment n Verwirrung f

bewitch /bɪ'wɪtʃ/ vt verzaubern; (fig) bezaubern

beyond /bɪ'jɒnd/ prep über (+ acc) ... hinaus; (further) weiter als; ~ reach außer Reichweite; ~ doubt ohne jeden Zweifel; it's ~ me ⟨fam⟩ das geht über meinen Horizont □ adv darüber hinaus

bias /'baɪəs/ n Voreingenommenheit f; (preference) Vorliebe f; (Jur) Befangenheit f; cut on the ~ schräg geschnitten □ vt (pt/pp biased) (influence) beeinflussen. ~ed a voreingenommen; (Jur) befangen

bib /bɪb/ n Lätzchen nt

Bible /'baɪbl/ n Bibel f

biblical /'bɪblɪkl/ a biblisch

bibliography /bɪblɪ'ɒɡrəfɪ/ n Bibliographie f

bicarbonate /baɪ'kɑːbəneɪt/ n ~ of soda doppeltkohlensaures Natron nt

bicker /'bɪkə(r)/ vi sich zanken

bicycle /'baɪsɪkl/ n Fahrrad nt □ vi mit dem Rad fahren

bid[1] /bɪd/ n Gebot nt; (attempt) Versuch m □ vt/i (pt/pp bid, pres p bidding) bieten (for auf + acc); ⟨Cards⟩ reizen

bid[2] vt (pt bade or bid, pp bidden or bid, pres p bidding) (liter) heißen; ~ s.o. welcome jdn willkommen heißen

bidder /'bɪdə(r)/ n Bieter(in) m(f)

bide /baɪd/ vt ~ one's time den richtigen Moment abwarten

biennial /baɪ'enɪəl/ a zweijährlich; (lasting two years) zweijährig

bier /bɪə(r)/ n [Toten]bahre f

bifocals /baɪ'fəʊklz/ npl [pair of] ~ Bifokalbrille f

big /bɪɡ/ a (bigger, biggest) groß □ adv talk ~ ⟨fam⟩ angeben

bigam|ist /'bɪgəmɪst/ n Bigamist m. ~y n Bigamie f

big-'headed a (fam) eingebildet

bigot /'bɪgət/ n Eiferer m. ~ed a engstirnig

'bigwig n (fam) hohes Tier nt

bike /baɪk/ n (fam) [Fahr]rad nt

bikini /bɪ'kiːnɪ/ n Bikini m

bilberry /'bɪlbərɪ/ n Heidelbeere f

bile /baɪl/ n Galle f

bilingual /baɪ'lɪŋgwəl/ a zweisprachig

bilious /'bɪljəs/ a (Med) ~ attack verdorbener Magen m

bill[1] /bɪl/ n Rechnung f; (poster) Plakat nt; (Pol) Gesetzentwurf m; (Amer: note) Banknote f; ~ of exchange Wechsel m □ vt eine Rechnung schicken (+ dat)

bill[2] (break) Schnabel m

billet /'bɪlɪt/ n (Mil) Quartier nt □ vt (pt/pp billeted) einquartieren (on bei)

billfold n (Amer) Brieftasche f

billiards /'bɪljədz/ n Billard nt

billion /'bɪljən/ n (thousand million) Milliarde f; (million million) Billion f

billy-goat /'bɪlɪ-/ n Ziegenbock m

bin /bɪn/ n Mülleimer m; (for bread) Kasten m

bind /baɪnd/ vt (pt/pp bound) binden (to an + acc); (bandage) verbinden; (Jur) verpflichten; (cover the edge of) einfassen. ~ing a verbindlich □ n Einband m; (braid) Borte f; (on ski) Bindung f

binge /bɪndʒ/ n (fam) go on the ~ eine Sauftour machen

binoculars /bɪ'nɒkjʊləz/ npl [pair of] ~ Fernglas nt

bio|'chemistry /baɪəʊ-/ n Biochemie f. ~degradable /-dɪ'greɪdəbl/ a biologisch abbaubar

biograph|er /baɪ'ɒgrəfə(r)/ n Biograph(in) m(f). ~y n Biographie f

biological /baɪə'lɒdʒɪkl/ a biologisch

biolog|ist /baɪ'ɒlədʒɪst/ n Biologe m. ~y n Biologie f

birch /bɜːtʃ/ n Birke f; (whip) Rute f

bird /bɜːd/ n Vogel m; (fam: girl) Mädchen nt; kill two ~s with one stone zwei Fliegen mit einer Klappe schlagen

Biro (P) /'baɪrəʊ/ n Kugelschreiber m

birth /bɜːθ/ n Geburt f

birth: ~ certificate n Geburtsurkunde f. ~control n Geburtenregelung f. ~day n Geburtstag m. ~mark n Muttermal nt. ~rate n Geburtenziffer f. ~right n Geburtsrecht nt

biscuit /'bɪskɪt/ n Keks m

bisect /baɪ'sekt/ vt halbieren

bishop /'bɪʃəp/ n Bischof m; (Chess) Läufer m

bit[1] /bɪt/ n Stückchen nt; (for horse) Gebiss nt; (Techn) Bohreinsatz m; a ~ ein bisschen; ~ by ~ nach und nach; a ~ of bread ein bisschen Brot; do one's ~ sein Teil tun

bit[2] see bite

bitch /bɪtʃ/ n Hündin f; (sl) Luder nt. ~y a gehässig

bit|e /baɪt/ n Biss m; (mouthful) Bissen m; [insect] ~ Stich m □ vt/i (pt bit, pp bitten) beißen; (insect:) stechen; kauen (one's nails). ~ing a beißend

bitten /'bɪtn/ see bite

bitter /'bɪtə(r)/ a, -ly adv bitter; cry ~ly bitterlich weinen; ~ly cold bitterkalt □ n bitteres Bier nt. ~ness n Bitterkeit f

bitty /'bɪtɪ/ a zusammengestoppelt

bizarre /bɪ'zɑː(r)/ a bizarr

blab /blæb/ vi (pt/pp blabbed) alles ausplaudern

black /blæk/ a (-er, -est) schwarz; be ~ and blue grün und blau sein □ n Schwarz nt; (person) Schwarze(r) m/f □ vt schwärzen; boykottieren (goods). ~ out vt verdunkeln □ vi (lose consciousness) das Bewusstsein verlieren

black: ~berry n Brombeere f. ~bird n Amsel f. ~board n (Sch) [Wand]tafel f. ~'currant n schwarze Johannisbeere f

black: ~ 'eye n blaues Auge nt. B~ 'Forest n Schwarzwald m. ~ 'ice n Glatteis nt. ~leg n Streikbrecher m. ~list vt auf die schwarze Liste setzen. ~mail n Erpressung f □ vt erpressen. ~mailer n Erpresser(in) m(f). ~ 'market n schwarzer Markt m. ~-out n Verdunkelung f; have a ~-out (Med) das Bewusstsein verlieren. ~ 'pudding n Blutwurst f. ~smith n [Huf]schmied m

bladder /'blædə(r)/ n (Anat) Blase f

blade /bleɪd/ n Klinge f; (of grass) Halm m

blame /bleɪm/ n Schuld f □ vt die Schuld geben (+ dat); no one is to ~ keiner ist schuld daran. ~less a schuldlos

blanch /blɑːntʃ/ vi blass werden □ vt (Culin) blanchieren

blancmange /blə'mɒnʒ/ n Pudding m

bland /blænd/ a (-er, -est) mild

blank /blæŋk/ a (-er, -est); (look) ausdruckslos □ n Lücke f; (cartridge) Platzpatrone f. ~ 'cheque n Blankoscheck m

blanket /'blæŋkɪt/ n Decke f; wet ~ (fam) Spielverderber(in) m(f)

blank 'verse n Blankvers m

blare /bleə(r)/ vt/i schmettern

blasé /'blɑːzeɪ/ a blasiert

blaspheme /blæs'fiːm/ vi lästern

blasphem|ous /'blæsfəməs/ a [gottes]lästerlich. ~y n [Gottes]lästerung f

blast /blɑːst/ n (gust) Luftstoß m; (sound) Schmettern nt; (of horn) Tuten nt □ vt sprengen □ int (sl) verdammt. ~ed a (sl) verdammt

blast: ~-furnace n Hochofen m. ~-off n (of missile) Start m

blatant /'bleɪtənt/ a offensichtlich

blaze /bleɪz/ n Feuer nt □ vi brennen

blazer /'bleɪzə(r)/ n Blazer m

bleach /bliːtʃ/ n Bleichmittel n □ vt/i bleichen

bleak /bliːk/ a (-er, -est) öde; (fig) trostlos

bleary-eyed /'blɪərɪ-/ a mit trüben/(on waking up) verschlafenen Augen

bleat /bliːt/ vi blöken; (goat:) meckern

bleed /bliːd/ v (pt/pp bled) □ vi bluten □ vt entlüften (radiator)

bleep /bliːp/ n Piepton m □ vi piepsen □ vt mit dem Piepser rufen. ~er n Piepser m

blemish /'blemɪʃ/ n Makel m

blend /blend/ n Mischung f □ vt mischen □ vi sich vermischen. ~er n (Culin) Mixer m

bless /bles/ vt segnen. ~ed /'blesɪd/ a heilig; (sl) verflixt. ~ing n Segen m

blew /bluː/ see blow²

blight /blaɪt/ n (Bot) Brand m □ vt (spoil) vereiteln

blind /blaɪnd/ a blind; (corner) unübersichtlich; ~ man/woman Blinde(r) m/f □ n [roller] ~ Rouleau nt □ vt blenden

blind: ~ alley n Sackgasse f. ~fold a & adv mit verbundenen Augen □ n Augenbinde f □ vt die Augen verbinden (+ dat). ~ly adv blindlings. ~ness n Blindheit f

blink /blɪŋk/ vi blinzeln; (light:) blinken

blinkers /'blɪŋkəz/ npl Scheuklappen pl

bliss /blɪs/ n Glückseligkeit f. ~ful a glücklich

blister /'blɪstə(r)/ n (Med) Blase f □ vi (paint:) Blasen werfen

blitz /blɪts/ n Luftangriff m; (fam) Großaktion f

blizzard /'blɪzəd/ n Schneesturm m

bloated /'bləʊtɪd/ a aufgedunsen

blob /blɒb/ n Klecks m

bloc /blɒk/ n (Pol) Block m

block /blɒk/ n Block m; (of wood) Klotz m; (of flats) [Wohn]block m □ vt blockieren. ~ up vt zustopfen

blockade /blɒ'keɪd/ n Blockade f □ vt blockieren

blockage /'blɒkɪdʒ/ n Verstopfung f

block: ~head n (fam) Dummkopf m. ~ letters npl Blockschrift f

bloke /bləʊk/ n (fam) Kerl m

blonde /blɒnd/ a blond □ n Blondine f

blood /blʌd/ n Blut nt

blood: ~ count n Blutbild nt. ~-curdling a markerschütternd. ~ donor n Blutspender m. ~ group n Blutgruppe f. ~hound n Bluthund m. ~-poisoning n Blutvergiftung f. ~-pressure n Blutdruck m. ~ relative n Blutsverwandte(r) m/f. ~shed n Blutvergießen nt. ~shot a blutunterlaufen. ~ sports npl Jagdsport m. ~-stained a blutbefleckt. ~stream n Blutbahn f. ~ test n Blutprobe f. ~-thirsty a blutdürstig. ~ transfusion n Blutübertragung f. ~-vessel n Blutgefäß nt

bloody /'blʌdɪ/ a (-ier, -iest) blutig; (sl) verdammt. ~-minded a (sl) stur

bloom /bluːm/ n Blüte f □ vi blühen

bloom|er /'bluːmə(r)/ n (fam) Schnitzer m. ~ing a (fam) verdammt

blossom /'blɒsəm/ n Blüte f □ vi blühen. ~ out vi (fig) aufblühen

blot /blɒt/ n [Tinten]klecks m; (fig) Fleck m □ vt (pt/pp blotted) löschen. ~ out vt (fig) auslöschen

blotch /blɒtʃ/ n Fleck m. ~y a fleckig

blotting-paper n Löschpapier nt

blouse /blaʊz/ n Bluse f

blow¹ /bləʊ/ n Schlag m

blow² /bləʊ/ v (pt blew, pp blown) □ vt blasen; (fam: squander) verpulvern; ~ one's nose sich (dat) die Nase putzen □ vi blasen; (fuse:) durchbrennen. ~ away vt wegblasen □ vi wegfliegen. ~ down vt umwehen □ vi umfallen. ~ out vt (extinguish) ausblasen. ~ over vi umfallen; (fig: die down) vorübergehen. ~ up vt (inflate) aufblasen; (enlarge) vergrößern; (shatter by explosion) sprengen □ vi explodieren

blow: ~-dry vt föhnen. ~fly n Schmeißfliege f. ~lamp n Lötlampe f

blown /bləʊn/ see blow²

blowtorch n (Amer) Lötlampe f

blowy /'bləʊɪ/ a windig

bludgeon /'blʌdʒn/ vt (fig) zwingen

blue /bluː/ a (-r, -st) blau; feel ~ deprimiert sein □ n Blau nt; have the ~s deprimiert sein; out of the ~ aus heiterem Himmel

blue: ~bell n Sternhyazinthe f. ~berry n Heidelbeere f. ~bottle n Schmeißfliege f. ~ film n Pornofilm m. ~print n (fig) Entwurf m

bluff /blʌf/ n Bluff m □ vi bluffen

blunder /'blʌndə(r)/ n Schnitzer m □ vi einen Schnitzer machen

blunt /blʌnt/ a stumpf; ⟨person⟩ geradeheraus. ~ly adv unverblümt, geradeheraus

blur /blɜ:(r)/ n it's all a ~ alles ist verschwommen □ vt (pt/pp **blurred**) verschwommen machen; ~red verschwommen

blurb /blɜ:b/ n Klappentext m

blurt /blɜ:t/ vt ~ out herausplatzen mit

blush /blʌʃ/ n Erröten nt □ vi erröten

bluster /'blʌstə(r)/ n Großtuerei f. ~y a windig

boar /bɔ:(r)/ n Eber m

board /bɔ:d/ n Brett nt; ⟨for notices⟩ schwarzes Brett nt; ⟨committee⟩ Ausschuss m; ⟨of directors⟩ Vorstand m; on ~ an Bord; full ~ Vollpension f; ~ and lodging Unterkunft und Verpflegung pl; go by the ~ ⟨fam⟩ unter den Tisch fallen □ vt einsteigen in (+ acc); ⟨Naut, Aviat⟩ besteigen □ vi an Bord gehen; ~ with in Pension wohnen bei. ~ up vt mit Brettern verschlagen

boarder /'bɔ:də(r)/ n Pensionsgast m; ⟨Sch⟩ Internatsschüler(in) m(f)

board: ~game n Brettspiel nt. ~inghouse n Pension f. ~ing-school n Internat nt

boast /bəʊst/ vt sich rühmen (+ gen) □ vi prahlen (about mit). ~ful a, ~ly adv prahlerisch

boat /bəʊt/ n Boot nt; ⟨ship⟩ Schiff nt. ~er n ⟨hat⟩ flacher Strohhut m

bob /bɒb/ n Bubikopf m □ vi (pt/pp **bobbed**) ⟨curtsy⟩ knicksen; ~ up and down sich auf und ab bewegen

bobbin /'bɒbɪn/ n Spule f

bob-sleigh n Bob m

bode /bəʊd/ vi ~ well/ill etwas/nichts Gutes verheißen

bodice /'bɒdɪs/ n Mieder nt

bodily /'bɒdɪlɪ/ a körperlich □ adv ⟨forcibly⟩ mit Gewalt

body /'bɒdɪ/ n Körper m; ⟨corpse⟩ Leiche f; ⟨corporation⟩ Körperschaft f; the main ~ der Hauptanteil. ~guard n Leibwächter m. ~work n ⟨Auto⟩ Karosserie f

bog /bɒg/ n Sumpf m □ vt (pt/pp **bogged**) get ~ged down stecken bleiben

boggle /'bɒgl/ vi the mind ~s es ist kaum vorstellbar

bogus /'bəʊgəs/ a falsch

boil[1] /bɔɪl/ n Furunkel m

boil[2] n bring/come to the ~ zum Kochen bringen/kommen □ vt/i kochen; ~ed potatoes Salzkartoffeln pl. ~ down vi ⟨fig⟩ hinauslaufen (to auf + acc). ~ over vi überkochen. ~ up vt aufkochen

boiler /'bɔɪlə(r)/ n Heizkessel m. ~ suit n Overall m

boiling point n Siedepunkt m

boisterous /'bɔɪstərəs/ a übermütig

bold /bəʊld/ a (-er, -est), -ly adv kühn; ⟨Typ⟩ fett. ~ness n Kühnheit f

bollard /'bɒlɑ:d/ n Poller m

bolster /'bəʊlstə(r)/ n Nackenrolle f □ vt ~ up Mut machen (+ dat)

bolt /bəʊlt/ n Riegel m; ⟨Techn⟩ Bolzen m; nuts and ~s Schrauben und Muttern pl □ vt schrauben (to an + acc); verriegeln ⟨door⟩; hinunterschlingen ⟨food⟩ □ vi abhauen; ⟨horse⟩ durchgehen □ adv ~ upright kerzengerade

bomb /bɒm/ n Bombe f □ vt bombardieren

bombard /bɒm'bɑ:d/ vt beschießen; ⟨fig⟩ bombardieren

bombastic /bɒm'bæstɪk/ a bombastisch

bomb|er /'bɒmə(r)/ n ⟨Aviat⟩ Bomber m; ⟨person⟩ Bombenleger(in) m(f). ~shell n be a ~shell ⟨fig⟩ wie eine Bombe einschlagen

bond /bɒnd/ n ⟨fig⟩ Band nt; ⟨Comm⟩ Obligation f; be in ~ unter Zollverschluss stehen

bondage /'bɒndɪdʒ/ n ⟨fig⟩ Sklaverei f

bone /bəʊn/ n Knochen m; ⟨of fish⟩ Gräte f □ vt von den Knochen lösen ⟨meat⟩; entgräten ⟨fish⟩. ~-'dry a knochentrocken

bonfire /'bɒn-/ n Gartenfeuer nt; ⟨celebratory⟩ Freudenfeuer nt

bonnet /'bɒnɪt/ n Haube f

bonus /'bəʊnəs/ n Prämie f; ⟨gratuity⟩ Gratifikation f; ⟨fig⟩ Plus nt

bony /'bəʊnɪ/ a (-ier, -iest) knochig; ⟨fish⟩ grätig

boo /bu:/ int buh! □ vt ausbuhen □ vi buhen

boob /bu:b/ n ⟨fam: mistake⟩ Schnitzer m □ vi ⟨fam⟩ einen Schnitzer machen

book /bʊk/ n Buch nt; ⟨of tickets⟩ Heft nt; keep the ~s ⟨Comm⟩ die Bücher führen □ vt/i buchen; ⟨reserve⟩ [vor]bestellen; ⟨for offence⟩ aufschreiben. ~able /-əbl/ a im Vorverkauf erhältlich

book: ~case n Bücherregal nt. ~ends npl Buchstützen pl. ~ing-office in Fahrkartenschalter m. ~keeping n Buchführung f. ~let n Broschüre f. ~maker n Buchmacher m. ~mark n Lesezeichen nt. ~seller n Buchhändler(in) m(f). ~shop n Buchhandlung f. ~stall n Bücherstand m. ~worm n Bücherwurm m

boom /bu:m/ n ⟨Comm⟩ Hochkonjunktur f; ⟨upturn⟩ Aufschwung m □ vi dröhnen; ⟨fig⟩ blühen

boon /bu:n/ n Segen m

boor /bʊə(r)/ n Flegel m. ~ish a flegelhaft

boost /buːst/ n Auftrieb m □ vt Auftrieb geben (+ dat). ~er n (Med) Nachimpfung f

boot /buːt/ n Stiefel m; (Auto) Kofferraum m

booth /buːð/ n Bude f; (cubicle) Kabine f

booty /ˈbuːtɪ/ n Beute f

booze /buːz/ n (fam) Alkohol m □ vi (fam) saufen

border /ˈbɔːdə(r)/ n Rand m; (frontier) Grenze f; (in garden) Rabatte f □ vi ~ on grenzen an (+ acc). ~line n Grenzlinie f. ~line case n Grenzfall m

bore¹ /bɔː(r)/ see bear²

bore² vt/i (Techn) bohren

bor|e³ n (of gun) Kaliber nt; (person) langweiliger Mensch m; (thing) langweilige Sache f □ vt langweilen; be ~ed sich langweilen. ~edom n Langeweile f. ~ing a langweilig

born /bɔːn/ pp be ~ geboren werden □ a geboren

borne /bɔːn/ see bear²

borough /ˈbʌrə/ n Stadtgemeinde f

borrow /ˈbɒrəʊ/ vt [sich (dat)] borgen od leihen (from von)

bosom /ˈbʊzm/ n Busen m

boss /bɒs/ n (fam) Chef m □ vt herumkommandieren. ~y a herrschsüchtig

botanical /bəˈtænɪkl/ a botanisch

botan|ist /ˈbɒtənɪst/ n Botaniker(in) m(f). ~y n Botanik f

botch /bɒtʃ/ vt verpfuschen

both /bəʊθ/ a & pron beide; ~[of] the children beide Kinder; ~ of them beide [von ihnen] □ adv ~ men and women sowohl Männer als auch Frauen

bother /ˈbɒðə(r)/ n Mühe f; (minor trouble) Ärger m □ int (fam) verflixt! □ vt belästigen; (disturb) stören □ vi sich kümmern (about um); don't ~ nicht nötig

bottle /ˈbɒtl/ n Flasche f □ vt auf Flaschen abfüllen; (preserve) einmachen. ~ up vt (fig) in sich (dat) aufstauen

bottle: ~-neck n (fig) Engpass m. ~-opener n Flaschenöffner m

bottom /ˈbɒtəm/ a unterste(r,s) □ n (of container) Boden m; (of river) Grund m; (of page, hill) Fuß m; (buttocks) Hintern m; at the ~ unten; get to the ~ of sth (fig) hinter etw (acc) kommen. ~less a bodenlos

bough /baʊ/ n Ast m

bought /bɔːt/ see buy

boulder /ˈbəʊldə(r)/ n Felsblock m

bounce /baʊns/ vi [auf]springen; (cheque:) (fam) nicht gedeckt sein □ vt aufspringen lassen (ball)

bouncer /ˈbaʊnsə(r)/ n (fam) Rausschmeißer m

bouncing /ˈbaʊnsɪŋ/ a ~ baby strammer Säugling m

bound¹ /baʊnd/ n Sprung m □ vi springen

bound² see bind □ a ~ for ⟨ship⟩ mit Kurs auf (+ acc); be ~ to do sth etw bestimmt machen; (obliged) verpflichtet sein, etw zu machen

boundary /ˈbaʊndərɪ/ n Grenze f

'boundless a grenzenlos

bounds /baʊndz/ npl (fig) Grenzen pl; out of ~ verboten

bouquet /bʊˈkeɪ/ n [Blumen]strauß m; (of wine) Bukett nt

bourgeois /ˈbʊəʒwɑː/ a (pej) spießbürgerlich

bout /baʊt/ n (Med) Anfall m; (Sport) Kampf m

bow¹ /bəʊ/ n (weapon & Mus) Bogen m; (knot) Schleife f

bow² /baʊ/ n Verbeugung f □ vi sich verbeugen □ vt neigen ⟨head⟩

bow³ /baʊ/ n (Naut) Bug m

bowel /ˈbaʊəl/ n Darm m; ~ movement Stuhlgang m. ~s pl Eingeweide pl; (digestion) Verdauung f

bowl¹ /bəʊl/ n Schüssel f; (shallow) Schale f; (of pipe) Kopf m; (of spoon) Schöpfteil m

bowl² n (ball) Kugel f □ vt/i werfen. ~ over vt umwerfen

bow-legged /bəʊˈlegd/ a O-beinig

bowler¹ /ˈbəʊlə(r)/ n (Sport) Werfer m

bowler² n ~ [hat] Melone f

bowling /ˈbəʊlɪŋ/ n Kegeln nt. ~-alley n Kegelbahn f

bowls /bəʊlz/ n Bowlsspiel nt

bow-'tie /bəʊ-/ n Fliege f

box¹ /bɒks/ n Schachtel f; (wooden) Kiste f; (cardboard) Karton m; (Theat) Loge f

box² vt/i (Sport) boxen; ~ s.o.'s ears jdn ohrfeigen

box|er /ˈbɒksə(r)/ n Boxer m. ~ing n Boxen nt. **B~ing Day** n zweiter Weihnachtstag m

box: ~-office n (Theat) Kasse f. ~-room n Abstellraum m

boy /bɔɪ/ n Junge m

boycott /ˈbɔɪkɒt/ n Boykott m □ vt boykottieren

boy: ~friend n Freund m. ~ish a jungenhaft

bra /brɑː/ n BH m

brace /breɪs/ n Strebe f, Stütze f; (dental) Zahnspange f; ~s npl Hosenträger mpl □ vt ~ oneself sich stemmen (against gegen); (fig) sich gefasst machen (for auf + acc)

bracelet /'breɪslɪt/ n Armband nt

bracing /'breɪsɪŋ/ a stärkend

bracken /'brækn/ n Farnkraut nt

bracket /'brækɪt/ n Konsole f; (group) Gruppe f; round/square ~s (Typ) runde/eckige Klammern □ vt einklammern

brag /bræg/ vi (pt/pp bragged) prahlen (about with)

braid /breɪd/ n Borte f

braille /breɪl/ n Blindenschrift f

brain /breɪn/ n Gehirn nt; ~s (fig) Intelligenz f

brain: ~child n geistiges Produkt nt. ~less a dumm. ~wash vt einer Gehirnwäsche unterziehen. ~wave n Geistesblitz m

brainy /'breɪnɪ/ a (-ier, -iest) klug

braise /breɪz/ vt schmoren

brake /breɪk/ n Bremse f □ vt/i bremsen. ~-light n Bremslicht nt

bramble /'bræmbl/ n Brombeerstrauch m

bran /bræn/ n Kleie f

branch /brɑːntʃ/ n Ast m; (fig) Zweig m; (Comm) Zweigstelle f; (shop) Filiale f □ vi sich gabeln. ~ off vi abzweigen. ~ out vi ~ out into sich verlegen auf (+ acc)

brand /brænd/ n Marke f; (on animal) Brandzeichen nt □ vt mit dem Brandeisen zeichnen (animal); (fig) brandmarken

brandish /'brændɪʃ/ vt schwingen

brand-'new a nagelneu

brandy /'brændɪ/ n Weinbrand m

brash /bræʃ/ a nassforsch

brass /brɑːs/ n Messing nt; (Mus) Blech nt; get down to ~ tacks (fam) zur Sache kommen; top ~ (fam) hohe Tiere pl. ~ band n Blaskapelle f

brassiere /'bræzɪə(r)/ n Büstenhalter m

brassy /'brɑːsɪ/ a (-ier, -iest) (fam) ordinär

brat /bræt/ n (pej) Balg nt

bravado /brə'vɑːdəʊ/ n Forschheit f

brave /breɪv/ a (-r, -st), -ly adv tapfer □ vt die Stirn bieten (+ dat). ~ry /-ərɪ/ n Tapferkeit f

bravo /brɑː'vəʊ/ int bravo!

brawl /brɔːl/ n Schlägerei f □ vi sich schlagen

brawn /brɔːn/ n (Culin) Sülze f

brawny /'brɔːnɪ/ a muskulös

bray /breɪ/ vi iahen

brazen /'breɪzn/ a unverschämt

brazier /'breɪzɪə(r)/ n Kohlenbecken nt

Brazil /brə'zɪl/ n Brasilien nt. ~ian a brasilianisch. ~ nut n Paranuss f

breach /briːtʃ/ n Bruch m; (Mil & fig) Bresche f; ~ of contract Vertragsbruch m □ vt durchbrechen; brechen (contract)

bread /bred/ n Brot nt; slice of ~ and butter Butterbrot nt

bread: ~crumbs npl Brotkrümel pl; (Culin) Paniermehl nt. ~line n be on the ~line gerade genug zum Leben haben

breadth /bredθ/ n Breite f

'bread-winner n Brotverdiener m

break /breɪk/ n Bruch m; (interval) Pause f; (interruption) Unterbrechung f; (fam: chance) Chance f □ v (pt broke, pp broken) □ vt brechen; (smash) zerbrechen; (damage) kaputtmachen (fam); (interrupt) unterbrechen; ~ one's arm sich (dat) den Arm brechen □ vi brechen; (day:) anbrechen; (storm:) losbrechen; (thing:) kaputtgehen (fam); (rope, thread:) reißen; (news:) bekannt werden; his voice is ~ing er ist im Stimmbruch. ~ away vi sich losreißen; (fig) sich absetzen (from von). ~ down vi zusammenbrechen; (Techn) eine Panne haben; (negotiations:) scheitern □ vt aufbrechen (smash); aufgliedern (figures). ~ in vi einbrechen. ~ off vt/i abbrechen; lösen (engagement). ~ out vi ausbrechen. ~ up vt zerbrechen □ vi zerbrechen; (crowd:) sich zerstreuen; (marriage, couple:) auseinander gehen; (Sch) Ferien bekommen

break|able /'breɪkəbl/ a zerbrechlich. ~age /-ɪdʒ/ n Bruch m. ~down n (Techn) Panne f; (Med) Zusammenbruch m; (of figures) Aufgliederung f. ~er n (wave) Brecher m

breakfast /'brekfəst/ n Frühstück nt

break: ~through n Durchbruch m. ~water n Buhne f

breast /brest/ n Brust f. ~bone n Brustbein nt. ~-feed vt stillen. ~-stroke n Brustschwimmen nt

breath /breθ/ n Atem m; out of ~ außer Atem; under one's ~ vor sich (acc) hin

breathalyse /'breθəlaɪz/ vt ins Röhrchen blasen lassen. ~r (P) n Röhrchen nt. ~r test n Alcotest (P) m

breathe /briːð/ vt/i atmen. ~ in vt/i einatmen. ~ out vt/i ausatmen

breath|er /'briːðə(r)/ n Atempause f. ~ing n Atmen nt

breath /breθ/: ~less a atemlos. ~-taking a atemberaubend. ~ test n Alcotest (P) m

breeches /'brɪtʃɪz/ npl Kniehose f; (for riding) Reithose f

breed /briːd/ n Rasse f □ v (pt/pp bred) □ vt züchten; (give rise to) erzeugen □ vi sich vermehren. ~er n Züchter m. ~ing n Zucht f; (fig) [gute] Lebensart f

breeze|le /bri:z/ n Lüftchen nt; (Naut) Brise f. ~y a [leicht] windig

brevity /'brevəti/ n Kürze f

brew /bru:/ n Gebräu nt □ vt brauen; kochen ⟨tea⟩ □ vi (fig) sich zusammenbrauen. ~er n Brauer m. ~ery n Brauerei f

bribe /braib/ n (money) Bestechungsgeld nt □ vt bestechen. ~ry /-əri/ n Bestechung f

brick /brik/ n Ziegelstein m, Backstein m □ vt ~ up zumauern

'bricklayer n Maurer m

bridal /'braidl/ a Braut-

bride /braid/ n Braut f. ~groom n Bräutigam m. ~smaid n Brautjungfer f

bridge¹ /bridʒ/ n Brücke f; (of nose) Nasenrücken m; (of spectacles) Steg m □ vt (fig) überbrücken

bridge² n (Cards) Bridge nt

bridle /'braidl/ n Zaum m. ~-path n Reitweg m

brief¹ /bri:f/ a (-er, -est) kurz; be ~ ⟨person⟩ sich kurz fassen

brief² n Instruktionen pl; (Jur: case) Mandat nt □ vt Instruktionen geben (+ dat); (Jur) beauftragen. ~case n Aktentasche f

brief|ing /'bri:fiŋ/ n Informationsgespräch nt. ~ly adv kurz. ~ness n Kürze f

briefs /bri:fs/ npl Slip m

brigad|e /bri'geid/ n Brigade f. ~ier /-ə'diə(r)/ n Brigadegeneral m

bright /brait/ a (-er, -est), -ly adv hell; ⟨day⟩ heiter; ~ red hellrot

bright|en /'braitn/ v ~en [up] □ vt aufheitern □ vi sich aufheitern. ~ness n Helligkeit f

brilliance /'briljəns/ n Glanz m; (of person) Genialität f

brilliant /'briljənt/ a, -ly adv glänzend; ⟨person⟩ genial

brim /brim/ n Rand m; (of hat) Krempe f □ vi (pt/pp brimmed) ~ over überfließen

brine /brain/ n Salzwasser nt; (Culin) [Salz]lake f

bring /briŋ/ vt (pt/pp brought) bringen; ~ them with you bring sie mit; I can't b~ myself to do it ich bringe es nicht fertig. ~ about vt verursachen. ~ along vt mitbringen. ~ back vt zurückbringen. ~ down vt herunterbringen; senken ⟨price⟩. ~ off vt vollbringen. ~ on vt ⟨cause⟩ verursachen. ~ out vt herausbringen. ~ round vt vorbeibringen; ⟨persuade⟩ überreden; wieder zum

Bewusstsein bringen ⟨unconscious person⟩. ~ up vt heraufbringen; (vomit) erbrechen; aufziehen ⟨children⟩; erwähnen ⟨question⟩

brink /briŋk/ n Rand m

brisk /brisk/ a (-er, -est,) -ly adv lebhaft; (quick) schnell

brist|le /'brisl/ n Borste f. ~ly a borstig

Brit|ain /'britn/ n Großbritannien nt. ~ish a britisch; the ~ish die Briten pl. ~on n Brite m/Britin f

Brittany /'britəni/ n die Bretagne

brittle /'britl/ a brüchig, spröde

broach /brəutʃ/ vt anzapfen; anschneiden ⟨subject⟩

broad /brɔ:d/ a (-er, -est) breit; ⟨hint⟩ deutlich; in ~ daylight am helllichten Tag. ~ beans npl dicke Bohnen pl

'broadcast n Sendung f □ vt/i (pt/pp -cast) senden. ~er n Rundfunk- und Fernsehpersönlichkeit f. ~ing n Funk und Fernsehen pl

broaden /'brɔ:dn/ vt verbreitern; (fig) erweitern □ vi sich verbreitern

broadly /'brɔ:dli/ adv breit; ~ speaking allgemein gesagt

broad'minded a tolerant

brocade /brə'keid/ n Brokat m

broccoli /'brɒkəli/ n inv Brokkoli pl

brochure /'brəuʃə(r)/ n Broschüre f

brogue /brəug/ n (shoe) Wanderschuh m; Irish ~ irischer Akzent m

broke /brəuk/ see break □ a (fam) pleite

broken /'brəukn/ see break □ a zerbrochen, (fam) kaputt; ~ English gebrochenes Englisch nt. ~-hearted a untröstlich

broker /'brəukə(r)/ n Makler m

brolly /'brɒli/ n (fam) Schirm m

bronchitis /brɒŋ'kaitis/ n Bronchitis f

bronze /brɒnz/ n Bronze f

brooch /brəutʃ/ n Brosche f

brood /bru:d/ n Brut f □ vi brüten; (fig) grübeln

brook¹ /bruk/ n Bach m

brook² vt dulden

broom /bru:m/ n Besen m; (Bot) Ginster m. ~stick n Besenstiel m

broth /brɒθ/ n Brühe f

brothel /'brɒθl/ n Bordell nt

brother /'brʌðə(r)/ n Bruder m

brother: ~-in-law n (pl -s-in-law) Schwager m. ~ly a brüderlich

brought /brɔ:t/ see bring

brow /brau/ n Augenbraue f; (forehead) Stirn f; (of hill) [Berg]kuppe f

'browbeat vt (pt -beat, pp -beaten) einschüchtern

brown /braʊn/ a (-er, -est) braun; ~
'paper Packpapier nt ▢ n Braun nt ▢ vt
bräunen ▢ vi braun werden
Brownie /'braʊnɪ/ n Wichtel m
browse /braʊz/ vi (read) schmökern; (in
shop) sich umsehen
bruise /bruːz/ n blauer Fleck m ▢ vt beschädigen (fruit); ~ one's arm sich (dat)
den Arm quetschen
brunch /brʌntʃ/ n Brunch m
brunette /bruː'net/ n Brünette f
Brunswick /'brʌnzwɪk/ n Braunschweig nt
brunt /brʌnt/ n the ~ of die volle Wucht
(+ gen)
brush /brʌʃ/ n Bürste f; (with handle)
Handfeger m; (for paint, pastry) Pinsel m;
(bushes) Unterholz nt; (fig: conflict) Zusammenstoß m ▢ vt bürsten putzen (teeth);
~ against streifen [gegen]; ~ aside (fig)
abtun. ~ off vt abbürsten; (reject) zurückweisen. ~ up vt/i (fig) ~ up [on] auffrischen
brusque /brʊsk/ a, -ly adv brüsk
Brussels /'brʌslz/ n Brüssel nt. ~ sprouts
npl Rosenkohl m
brutal /'bruːtl/ a, -ly adv brutal. ~ity
/-'tælətɪ/ n Brutalität f
brute /bruːt/ n Unmensch m. ~ force n
rohe Gewalt f
B.Sc. abbr of Bachelor of Science
bubble /'bʌbl/ n [Luft]blase f ▢ vi sprudeln
buck[1] /bʌk/ n (deer & Gym) Bock m; (rabbit) Rammler m ▢ vi (horse:) bocken. ~
up vi (fam) sich aufheitern; (hurry) sich
beeilen
buck[2] n (Amer, fam) Dollar m
buck[3] n pass the ~ die Verantwortung
abschieben
bucket /'bʌkɪt/ n Eimer m
buckle /'bʌkl/ n Schnalle f ▢ vt zu-
schnallen ▢ vi sich verbiegen
bud /bʌd/ n Knospe f ▢ vi (pt/pp budded)
knospen
Buddhis|m /'bʊdɪzm/ n Buddhismus m.
~t a buddhistisch ▢ n Buddhist(in) m(f)
buddy /'bʌdɪ/ n (fam) Freund m
budge /bʌdʒ/ vt bewegen ▢ vi sich [von
der Stelle] rühren
budgerigar /'bʌdʒərɪgɑː(r)/ n Wellensit-
tich m
budget /'bʌdʒɪt/ n Budget nt; (Pol) Haus-
haltsplan m; (money available) Etat m
▢ vi (pt/pp budgeted) ~ for sth etw einkalkulieren
buff /bʌf/ a (colour) sandfarben ▢ n Sand-
farbe f; (Amer, fam) Fan m ▢ vt polieren

buffalo /'bʌfələʊ/ n (inv or pl -es) Büffel
m
buffer /'bʌfə(r)/ n (Rail) Puffer m; old ~
(fam) alter Knacker m; ~ zone Pufferzone
f
buffet[1] /'bʊfeɪ/ n Büfett nt; (on station)
Imbissstube f
buffet[2] /'bʌfɪt/ vt (pt/pp buffeted) hin und
her werfen
buffoon /bə'fuːn/ n Narr m
bug /bʌg/ n (fam: virus) Bazillus
m; (fam: device) Abhörgerät nt, (fam)
Wanze f ▢ vt (pt/pp bugged) (fam) ver-
wanzen (room); abhören (telephone);
(Amer: annoy) ärgern
buggy /'bʌgɪ/ n [Kinder]sportwagen m
bugle /'bjuːgl/ n Signalhorn nt
build /bɪld/ n (of person) Körperbau m
▢ vt/i (pt/pp built) bauen. ~ on vt anbauen (to an + acc). ~ up vt aufbauen
▢ vi zunehmen; (traffic:) sich stauen
builder /'bɪldə(r)/ n Bauunternehmer m
building /'bɪldɪŋ/ n Gebäude nt. ~ site n
Baustelle f. ~ society n Bausparkasse f
built /bɪlt/ see build. ~-in a eingebaut. ~-
in 'cupboard n Einbauschrank m. ~-
up area n bebautes Gebiet nt; (Auto) geschlossene Ortschaft f
bulb /bʌlb/ n [Blumen]zwiebel f; (Electr)
[Glüh]birne f
bulbous /'bʌlbəs/ a bauchig
Bulgaria /bʌl'geərɪə/ n Bulgarien nt
bulg|e /bʌldʒ/ n Ausbauchung f ▢ vi sich
ausbauchen. ~ing a prall; (eyes) hervor-
quellend; ~ing with prall gefüllt mit
bulk /bʌlk/ n Masse f; (greater part)
Hauptteil m; in ~ en gros; (loose) lose. ~y
a sperrig; (large) massig
bull /bʊl/ n Bulle m, Stier m
'bulldog n Bulldogge f
bulldozer /'bʊldəʊzə(r)/ n Planierraupe
f
bullet /'bʊlɪt/ n Kugel f
bulletin /'bʊlɪtɪn/ n Bulletin nt
'bullet-proof a kugelsicher
'bullfight n Stierkampf m. ~er n Stier-
kämpfer m
'bullfinch n Dompfaff m
bullion /'bʊlɪən/ n gold ~ Barrengold nt
bullock /'bʊlək/ n Ochse m
bull: ~ring n Stierkampfarena f. ~'s-eye
n score a ~'s-eye ins Schwarze treffen
bully /'bʊlɪ/ n Tyrann m ▢ vt tyrannisieren
bum[1] /bʌm/ n (sl) Hintern m
bum[2] n (Amer, fam) Landstreicher m
bumble-bee /'bʌmbl-/ n Hummel f

bump /bʌmp/ n Bums m; (swelling) Beule f; (in road) holperige Stelle f ▫ vt stoßen; ~ into stoßen gegen; (meet) zufällig treffen. ~ off vt (fam) um die Ecke bringen

bumper /'bʌmpə(r)/ a Rekord- ▫ n (Auto) Stoßstange f

bumpkin /'bʌmpkɪn/ n country ~ Tölpel m

bumptious /'bʌmpʃəs/ a aufgeblasen

bumpy /'bʌmpɪ/ a holperig

bun /bʌn/ n Milchbrötchen nt; (hair) [Haar]knoten m

bunch /bʌntʃ/ n (of flowers) Strauß m; (of radishes, keys) Bund m; (of people) Gruppe f; ~ of grapes [ganze] Weintraube f

bundle /'bʌndl/ n Bündel nt ▫ vt ~ [up] bündeln

bung /bʌŋ/ vt (fam) (throw) schmeißen. ~ up vt (fam) verstopfen

bungalow /'bʌŋgələʊ/ n Bungalow m

bungle /'bʌŋgl/ vt verpfuschen

bunion /'bʌnjən/ n (Med) Ballen m

bunk /bʌŋk/ n [Schlaf]koje f. ~-beds npl Etagenbett nt

bunker /'bʌŋkə(r)/ n Bunker m

bunkum /'bʌŋkəm/ n Quatsch m

bunny /'bʌnɪ/ n (fam) Kaninchen nt

buoy /bɔɪ/ n Boje f. ~ up vt (fig) stärken

buoyan|cy /'bɔɪənsɪ/ n Auftrieb m. ~t a be ~t schwimmen; (water:) gut tragen

burden /'bɜːdn/ n Last f ▫ vt belasten. ~some /-səm/ a lästig

bureau /'bjʊərəʊ/ n (pl -x /-əʊz/ or ~s) (desk) Sekretär m; (office) Büro nt

bureaucracy /bjʊə'rɒkrəsɪ/ n Bürokratie f

bureaucrat /'bjʊərəkræt/ n Bürokrat m. ~ic /-'krætɪk/ a bürokratisch

burger /'bɜːgə(r)/ n Hamburger m

burglar /'bɜːglə(r)/ n Einbrecher m. ~ alarm n Alarmanlage f

burglar|ize /'bɜːgləraɪz/ vt (Amer) einbrechen in (+ acc). ~y n Einbruch m

burgle /'bɜːgl/ vt einbrechen in (+ acc); they have been ~d bei ihnen ist eingebrochen worden

Burgundy /'bɜːgəndɪ/ n Burgund nt; b~ (wine) Burgunder m

burial /'berɪəl/ n Begräbnis nt

burlesque /bɜː'lesk/ n Burleske f

burly /'bɜːlɪ/ a (-ier, -iest) stämmig

Burm|a /'bɜːmə/ n Birma nt. ~ese /-'miːz/ a birmanisch

burn /bɜːn/ n Verbrennung f; (on skin) Brandwunde f; (on material) Brandstelle f ▫ v (pt/pp burnt or burned) ▫ vt verbrennen ▫ vi brennen; (food:) anbrennen. ~ down vt/i niederbrennen

burnish /'bɜːnɪʃ/ vt polieren

burnt /bɜːnt/ see burn

burp /bɜːp/ vi (fam) aufstoßen

burrow /'bʌrəʊ/ n Bau m ▫ vi wühlen

bursar /'bɜːsə(r)/ n Rechnungsführer m. ~y n Stipendium nt

burst /bɜːst/ n Bruch m; (surge) Ausbruch m ▫ v (pt/pp burst) ▫ vt platzen machen ▫ vi platzen; (bud:) aufgehen; ~ into tears in Tränen ausbrechen

bury /'berɪ/ vt (pt/pp-ied) begraben; (hide) vergraben

bus /bʌs/ n [Auto]bus m ▫ vt/i (pt/pp bussed) mit dem Bus fahren

bush /bʊʃ/ n Strauch m; (land) Busch m. ~y a (-ier, -iest) buschig

busily /'bɪzɪlɪ/ adv eifrig

business /'bɪznɪs/ n Angelegenheit f; (Comm) Geschäft nt; on ~ geschäftlich; he has no ~ er hat kein Recht (to zu); mind one's own ~ sich um seine eigenen Angelegenheiten kümmern; that's none of your ~ das geht Sie nichts an. ~like a geschäftsmäßig. ~man n Geschäftsmann m

busker /'bʌskə(r)/ n Straßenmusikant m

'bus-stop n Bushaltestelle f

bust[1] /bʌst/ n Büste f. ~ size n Oberweite f

bust[2] a (fam) kaputt; go ~ Pleite gehen ▫ v (pt/pp busted or bust) (fam) ▫ vt kaputtmachen ▫ vt kaputtgehen

bustl|e /'bʌsl/ n Betrieb m, Getriebe nt ▫ vi ~e about geschäftig hin und her laufen. ~ing a belebt

'bust-up n (fam) Streit m, Krach m

busy /'bɪzɪ/ a (-ier, -iest) beschäftigt; (day) voll; (street) belebt; (with traffic) stark befahren; (Amer Teleph) besetzt; be ~ zu tun haben ▫ vt ~ oneself sich beschäftigen (with mit)

'busybody n Wichtigtuer(in) m(f)

but /bʌt, unbetont bət/ conj aber; (after negative) sondern ▫ prep außer (+ dat); ~ for (without) ohne (+ acc); the last ~ one der/die/das vorletzte; the next ~ one der/die/das übernächste ▫ adv nur

butcher /'bʊtʃə(r)/ n Fleischer m, Metzger m; ~'s [shop] Fleischerei f, Metzgerei f ▫ vt [ab]schlachten

butler /'bʌtlə(r)/ n Butler m

butt /bʌt/ n (of gun) [Gewehr]kolben m; (fig: target) Zielscheibe f; (of cigarette) Stummel m; (for water) Regentonne f ▫ vt mit dem Kopf stoßen ▫ vi ~ in unterbrechen

butter /'bʌtə(r)/ n Butter f ◻ vt mit Butter bestreichen. ~ **up** vt (fam) schmeicheln (+ dat)

butter: ~**cup** a Butterblume f. Hahnenfuß m. ~**fly** n Schmetterling m

buttocks /'bʌtəks/ npl Gesäß nt

button /'bʌtn/ n Knopf m ◻ vt ~ [**up**] zuknöpfen ◻ vi geknöpft werden. ~**hole** n Knopfloch nt

buttress /'bʌtrɪs/ n Strebepfeiler m; flying ~ Strebebogen m

buxom /'bʌksəm/ a drall

buy /baɪ/ n Kauf m ◻ vt (pt/pp bought) kaufen. ~**er** n Käufer(in) m(f)

buzz /bʌz/ n Summen nt ◻ vi summen. ~ **off** vi (fam) abhauen

buzzard /'bʌzəd/ n Bussard m

buzzer /'bʌzə(r)/ n Summer m

by /baɪ/ prep (close to) bei (+ dat); (next to) neben (+ dat/acc); (past) an (+ dat) ... vorbei; (to the extent of) um (+ acc); (at the latest) bis; (by means of) durch; by Mozart/Dickens von Mozart/Dickens; ~ oneself allein; ~ **the sea** am Meer; ~ **car/bus** mit dem Auto/Bus; ~ **sea** mit dem Schiff; ~ **day/night** bei Tag/Nacht; ~ **the hour** pro Stunde; ~ **the metre** meterweise; **six metres** ~ **four** sechs mal vier Meter; **win** ~ **a length** mit einer Länge Vorsprung gewinnen; **miss the train** ~ **a minute** den Zug um eine Minute verpassen ◻ adv ~ **and** ~ mit der Zeit; ~ **and large** im Großen und Ganzen; **put** ~ beiseite legen; **go/pass** ~ vorbeigehen

bye /baɪ/ int (fam) tschüs

by: ~-**election** n Nachwahl f. ~**gone** a vergangen. ~-**law** n Verordnung f. ~**pass** n Umgehungsstraße f; (Med) Bypass m ◻ vt umfahren. ~-**product** n Nebenprodukt nt. ~-**road** n Nebenstraße f. ~**stander** n Zuschauer(in) m(f)

Byzantine /bɪˈzæntaɪn/ a byzantinisch

C

cab /kæb/ n Taxi nt; (of lorry, train) Führerhaus nt

cabaret /'kæbəreɪ/ n Kabarett nt

cabbage /'kæbɪdʒ/ n Kohl m

cabin /'kæbɪn/ n Kabine f; (hut) Hütte f

cabinet /'kæbɪnɪt/ n Schrank m; (TV, Radio) Gehäuse nt; **C~** (Pol) Kabinett nt; [**display**] ~ Vitrine f; ~-**maker** n Möbeltischler m

cable /'keɪbl/ n Kabel nt; (rope) Tau nt. ~ 'railway n Seilbahn f. ~ 'television n Kabelfernsehen nt

cache /kæʃ/ n Versteck nt; ~ **of arms** Waffenlager nt

cackle /'kækl/ vi gackern

cactus /'kæktəs/ n (pl -ti /-taɪ/ or -tuses) Kaktus m

caddie /'kædɪ/ n Caddie m

caddy /'kædɪ/ n [tea-]~ Teedose f

cadet /kəˈdet/ n Kadett m

cadge /kædʒ/ vt/i (fam) schnorren

Caesarean /sɪˈzeərɪən/ a & n ~ [**section**] Kaiserschnitt m

café /'kæfeɪ/ n Café nt

cafeteria /kæfəˈtɪərɪə/ n Selbstbedienungsrestaurant nt

caffeine /'kæfiːn/ n Koffein nt

cage /keɪdʒ/ n Käfig m

cagey /'keɪdʒɪ/ a (fam) **be** ~ mit der Sprache nicht herauswollen

cajole /kəˈdʒəʊl/ vt gut zureden (+ dat)

cake /keɪk/ n Kuchen m; (of soap) Stück nt. ~**d** a verkrustet (with mit)

calamity /kəˈlæmətɪ/ n Katastrophe f

calcium /'kælsɪəm/ n Kalzium nt

calculat|e /'kælkjʊleɪt/ vt berechnen; (estimate) kalkulieren. ~**ing** a (fig) berechnend. ~**ion** /-'leɪʃn/ n Rechnung f, Kalkulation f. ~**or** n Rechner m

calendar /'kælɪndə(r)/ n Kalender m

calf¹ /kɑːf/ n (pl calves) Kalb nt

calf² n (pl calves) (Anat) Wade f

calibre /'kælɪbə(r)/ n Kaliber nt

calico /'kælɪkəʊ/ n Kattun m

call /kɔːl/ n Ruf m; (Teleph) Anruf m; (visit) Besuch m; **be on** ~ ⟨doctor:⟩ Bereitschaftsdienst haben ◻ vt rufen; (Teleph) anrufen; (wake) wecken; ausrufen ⟨strike⟩; (name) nennen; **be** ~**ed** heißen ◻ vi rufen; ~ [**in or round**] vorbeikommen. ~ **back** vt zurückrufen ◻ vi noch einmal vorbeikommen. ~ **for** vt rufen nach; (demand) verlangen; (fetch) abholen. ~ **off** vt zurückrufen ⟨dog⟩; (cancel) absagen. ~ **on** vt bitten (for um); (appeal to) appellieren an (+ acc); (visit) besuchen. ~ **out** vt rufen; aufrufen ⟨names⟩ ◻ vi rufen. ~ **up** vt (Mil) einberufen; (Teleph) anrufen

call: ~-**box** n Telefonzelle f. ~**er** n Besucher m; (Teleph) Anrufer m. ~**ing** n Berufung f

callous /'kæləs/ a gefühllos

'call-up n (Mil) Einberufung f

calm /kɑːm/ a (-er, -est), -ly adv ruhig ◻ n Ruhe f ◻ vt ~ [**down**] beruhigen ◻ vi ~ **down** sich beruhigen. ~**ness** n Ruhe f; (of sea) Stille f

calorie /'kælərɪ/ n Kalorie f

calves /kɑːvz/ npl see calf[1] & [2]

camber /'kæmbə(r)/ n Wölbung f

came /keɪm/ see come

camel /'kæml/ n Kamel nt

camera /'kæmərə/ n Kamera f. ~man n Kameramann m

camouflage /'kæməflɑːʒ/ n Tarnung f □ vt tarnen

camp /kæmp/ n Lager nt □ vi campen; (Mil) kampieren

campaign /kæm'peɪn/ n Feldzug m; (Comm, Pol) Kampagne f □ vi kämpfen; (pol) im Wahlkampf arbeiten

camp: ~bed n Feldbett nt. ~er n Camper m; (Auto) Wohnmobil nt. ~ing n Camping nt. ~site n Campingplatz m

campus /'kæmpəs/ n (pl -puses) (Univ) Campus m

can[1] /kæn/ n (for petrol) Kanister m; (tin) Dose f, Büchse f; a ~ of beer eine Dose Bier □ vt in Dosen od Büchsen konservieren

can[2] /kæn, unbetont kən/ v aux (pres can; pt could) können; I cannot/can't go ich kann nicht gehen; he could not go er konnte nicht gehen; if I could go wenn ich gehen könnte

Canad|a /'kænədə/ n Kanada nt. ~ian /kə'neɪdɪən/ a kanadisch □ n Kanadier(in) m(f)

canal /kə'næl/ n Kanal m

Canaries /kə'neərɪz/ npl Kanarische Inseln pl

canary /kə'neərɪ/ n Kanarienvogel m

cancel /'kænsl/ vt/i (pt/pp cancelled) absagen; entwerten ⟨stamp⟩; (annul) rückgängig machen; (Comm) stornieren; abbestellen ⟨newspaper⟩; be ~led ausfallen. ~lation /-ə'leɪʃn/ n Absage f

cancer /'kænsə(r)/ n, & (Astr) C~ Krebs m. ~ous /-rəs/ a krebsig

candelabra /kændə'lɑːbrə/ n Armleuchter m

candid /'kændɪd/ a, -ly adv offen

candidate /'kændɪdət/ n Kandidat(in) m(f)

candied /'kændɪd/ a kandiert

candle /'kændl/ n Kerze f. ~stick n Kerzenständer m, Leuchter m

candour /'kændə(r)/ n Offenheit f

candy /'kændɪ/ n (Amer) Süßigkeiten pl; [piece of] ~ Bonbon m. ~floss /-flɒs/ n Zuckerwatte f

cane /keɪn/ n Rohr nt; (stick) Stock m □ vt mit dem Stock züchtigen

canine /'keɪnaɪn/ a Hunde-. ~ tooth n Eckzahn m

canister /'kænɪstə(r)/ n Blechdose f

cannabis /'kænəbɪs/ n Haschisch nt

canned /kænd/ a Dosen-, Büchsen-; ~ music (fam) Musik f aus der Konserve

cannibal /'kænɪbl/ n Kannibale m. ~ism /-bəlɪzm/ n Kannibalismus m

cannon /'kænən/ n inv Kanone f. ~-ball n Kanonenkugel f

cannot /'kænɒt/ see can[2]

canny /'kænɪ/ a schlau

canoe /kə'nuː/ n Paddelboot nt; (Sport) Kanu nt □ vi paddeln; (Sport) Kanu fahren

canon /'kænən/ n Kanon m; (person) Kanonikus m. ~ize /-aɪz/ vt kanonisieren

'**can-opener** n Dosenöffner m, Büchsenöffner m

canopy /'kænəpɪ/ n Baldachin m

cant /kænt/ n Heuchelei f

can't /kɑːnt/ = cannot. See can[2]

cantankerous /kæn'tæŋkərəs/ a zänkisch

canteen /kæn'tiːn/ n Kantine f; ~ of cutlery Besteckkasten m

canter /'kæntə(r)/ n Kanter m □ vi kantern

canvas /'kænvəs/ n Segeltuch nt; (Art) Leinwand f; (painting) Gemälde nt

canvass /'kænvəs/ vi um Stimmen werben

canyon /'kænjən/ n Cañon m

cap /kæp/ n Kappe f, Mütze f; (nurse's) Haube f; (top, lid) Verschluss m □ vt (pt/pp capped) (fig) übertreffen

capability /keɪpə'bɪlətɪ/ n Fähigkeit f

capable /'keɪpəbl/ a, -bly adv fähig; be ~ of doing sth fähig sein, etw zu tun

capacity /kə'pæsətɪ/ n Fassungsvermögen nt; (ability) Fähigkeit f; in my ~ as in meiner Eigenschaft als

cape[1] /keɪp/ n (cloak) Cape nt

cape[2] n (Geog) Kap nt

caper[1] /'keɪpə(r)/ vi herumspringen

caper[2] n (Culin) Kaper f

capital /'kæpɪtl/ a (letter) groß □ n (town) Hauptstadt f; (money) Kapital nt; (letter) Großbuchstabe m

capital|ism /'kæpɪtəlɪzm/ n Kapitalismus m. ~ist /-ɪst/ a kapitalistisch □ n Kapitalist m. ~ize /-aɪz/ vi ~ize on (fig) Kapital schlagen aus. ~ 'letter n Großbuchstabe m. ~ 'punishment n Todesstrafe f

capitulat|e /kə'pɪtjʊleɪt/ vi kapitulieren. ~ion /-'leɪʃn/ n Kapitulation f

capricious /kə'prɪʃəs/ a launisch

Capricorn /'kæprɪkɔːn/ n (Astr) Steinbock m

capsize /kæp'saɪz/ vi kentern □ vt zum Kentern bringen

capsule /'kæpsjʊl/ n Kapsel f

captain /'kæptɪn/ n Kapitän m; (Mil) Hauptmann m ◻ vt anführen (team)

caption /'kæpʃn/ n Überschrift f; (of illustration) Bildtext m

captivate /'kæptɪveɪt/ vt bezaubern

captiv|e /'kæptɪv/ a hold/take ~e gefangen halten/nehmen □ n Gefangene(r) m/f. ~ity /-'tɪvɪtɪ/ n Gefangenschaft f

capture /'kæptʃə(r)/ n Gefangennahme f □ vt gefangen nehmen; [ein]fangen (animal); (Mil) einnehmen (town)

car /kɑː(r)/ n Auto nt, Wagen m; by ~ mit dem Auto od Wagen

carafe /kə'ræf/ n Karaffe f

caramel /'kærəmel/ n Karamell m

carat /'kærət/ n Karat nt

caravan /'kærəvæn/ n Wohnwagen m; (procession) Karawane f

carbohydrate /kɑːbə'haɪdreɪt/ n Kohlenhydrat nt

carbon /'kɑːbən/ n Kohlenstoff m; (paper) Kohlepapier nt; (copy) Durchschlag m

carbon: ~ **copy** n Durchschlag m. ~ **di-'oxide** n Kohlendioxid nt; (in drink) Kohlensäure f. ~ **paper** n Kohlepapier nt

carburettor /kɑːbjʊ'retə(r)/ n Vergaser m

carcass /'kɑːkəs/ n Kadaver m

card /kɑːd/ n Karte f

'cardboard n Pappe f, Karton m. ~ '**box** n Pappschachtel f; (large) [Papp]karton m

'card-game n Kartenspiel nt

cardiac /'kɑːdiæk/ a Herz-

cardigan /'kɑːdɪgən/ n Strickjacke f

cardinal /'kɑːdɪnl/ a Kardinal-; ~ **number** Kardinalzahl f □ n (Relig) Kardinal m

card 'index n Kartei f

care /keə(r)/ n Sorgfalt f; (caution) Vorsicht f; (protection) Obhut f; (looking after) Pflege f; (worry) Sorge f; ~ **of** (on letter abbr c/o) bei; take ~ vorsichtig sein; take into ~ in Pflege nehmen; take ~ of sich kümmern um □ vi ~ about sich kümmern um; ~ for (like) mögen; (look after) betreuen; I don't ~ das ist mir gleich

career /kə'rɪə(r)/ n Laufbahn f; (profession) Beruf m □ vi rasen

care: ~**free** a sorglos. ~**ful** a, -ly adv sorgfältig; (cautious) vorsichtig. ~**less** a, -ly adv nachlässig. ~**lessness** n Nachlässigkeit f

caress /kə'res/ n Liebkosung f □ vt liebkosen

'caretaker n Hausmeister m

'car ferry n Autofähre f

cargo /'kɑːgəʊ/ n (pl -es) Ladung f

Caribbean /kærɪ'biːən/ n the ~ die Karibik

caricature /'kærɪkətjʊə(r)/ n Karikatur f □ vt karikieren

caring /'keərɪŋ/ a (parent) liebevoll; (profession, attitude) sozial

carnage /'kɑːnɪdʒ/ n Gemetzel nt

carnal /'kɑːnl/ a fleischlich

carnation /kɑː'neɪʃn/ n Nelke f

carnival /'kɑːnɪvl/ n Karneval m

carnivorous /kɑː'nɪvərəs/ a Fleisch fressend

carol /'kærl/ n [Christmas] ~ Weihnachtslied nt

carp¹ /kɑːp/ n inv Karpfen m

carp² vi nörgeln; ~ at herumnörgeln an (+ dat)

'car park n Parkplatz m; (multi-storey) Parkhaus nt; (underground) Tiefgarage f

carpent|er /'kɑːpɪntə(r)/ n Zimmermann m; (joiner) Tischler m. ~**ry** n Tischlerei f

carpet /'kɑːpɪt/ n Teppich m □ vt mit Teppich auslegen

carriage /'kærɪdʒ/ n Kutsche f; (Rail) Wagen m; (of goods) Beförderung f; (cost) Frachtkosten pl; (bearing) Haltung f. ~**way** n Fahrbahn f

carrier /'kærɪə(r)/ n Träger(in) m(f); (Comm) Spediteur m; ~ [**bag**] Tragetasche f

carrot /'kærət/ n Möhre f, Karotte f

carry /'kærɪ/ vt/i (pt/pp -ied) tragen; be carried away (fam) hingerissen sein. ~ **off** vt wegtragen; gewinnen (prize). ~ **on** vi weitermachen; ~ **on at** (fam) herumnörgeln an (+ dat); ~ **on with** (fam) eine Affäre haben mit □ vt führen; (continue) fortführen. ~ **out** vt hinaus-/heraustragen; (perform) ausführen

'carry-cot n Babytragetasche f

cart /kɑːt/ n Karren m; put the ~ before the horse das Pferd beim Schwanz aufzäumen □ vt karren; (fam: carry) schleppen

cartilage /'kɑːtɪlɪdʒ/ n (Anat) Knorpel m

carton /'kɑːtn/ n [Papp]karton m; (for drink) Tüte f; (of cream, yoghurt) Becher m

cartoon /kɑː'tuːn/ n Karikatur f; (joke) Witzzeichnung f; (strip) Comic Strips pl; (film) Zeichentrickfilm m; (Art) Karton m. ~**ist** n Karikaturist m

cartridge /'kɑːtrɪdʒ/ n Patrone f; (for film, typewriter ribbon) Kassette f; (of record player) Tonabnehmer m

carve /kɑːv/ vt schnitzen; (in stone) hauen; (Culin) aufschneiden

carving /'kɑːvɪŋ/ n Schnitzerei f. ~**-knife** n Tranchiermesser nt

'**car wash** n Autowäsche f; (place) Autowaschanlage f

case¹ /keɪs/ n Fall m; in any ~ auf jeden Fall; just in ~ für alle Fälle; in ~ he comes falls er kommt

case² n Kasten m; (crate) Kiste f; (for spectacles) Etui nt; (suitcase) Koffer m; (for display) Vitrine f

cash /kæʃ/ n Bargeld nt; pay [in] ~ [in] bar bezahlen; ~ **on delivery** per Nachnahme □ vt einlösen (cheque). ~ **desk** n Kasse f

cashier /kæ'ʃɪə(r)/ n Kassierer(in) m(f)

'**cash register** n Registrierkasse f

casino /kə'siːnəʊ/ n Kasino nt

cask /kɑːsk/ n Fass nt

casket /'kɑːskɪt/ n Kasten m; (Amer: coffin) Sarg m

casserole /'kæsərəʊl/ n Schmortopf m; (stew) Eintopf m

cassette /kə'set/ n Kassette f. ~ **recorder** n Kassettenrecorder m

cast /kɑːst/ n (throw) Wurf m; (mould) Form f; (model) Abguss m; (Theat) Besetzung f; [**plaster**] ~ (Med) Gipsverband m □ vt (pt/pp cast) (throw) werfen; (shed) abwerfen; abgeben (vote); gießen (metal); (Theat) besetzen (role); ~ **a glance** at einen Blick werfen auf (+ acc). ~ **off** vi (Naut) ablegen □ vt (Knitting) abketten. ~ **on** vt (Knitting) anschlagen

castanets /kæstə'nets/ npl Kastagnetten pl

castaway /'kɑːstəweɪ/ n Schiffbrüchige(r) m/f

caste /kɑːst/ n Kaste f

cast 'iron n Gusseisen nt

cast-'iron a gusseisern

castle /'kɑːsl/ n Schloss nt; (fortified) Burg f; (Chess) Turm m

'**cast-offs** npl abgelegte Kleidung f

castor /'kɑːstə(r)/ n (wheel) [Lauf]rolle f

'**castor sugar** n Streuzucker m

castrat|e /kæ'streɪt/ vt kastrieren. ~**ion** /-eɪʃn/ n Kastration f

casual /'kæʒʊəl/ a, **-ly** adv (chance) zufällig; (offhand) lässig; (informal) zwanglos; (not permanent) Gelegenheits-; ~ **wear** Freizeitbekleidung f

casualty /'kæʒʊəltɪ/ n [Todes]opfer nt; (injured person) Verletzte(r) m/f; ~ [**department**] Unfallstation f

cat /kæt/ n Katze f

catalogue /'kætəlɒg/ n Katalog m □ vt katalogisieren

catalyst /'kætəlɪst/ n (Chem & fig) Katalysator m

catalytic /kætə'lɪtɪk/ a ~ **converter** (Auto) Katalysator m

catapult /'kætəpʌlt/ n Katapult nt □ vt katapultieren

cataract /'kætərækt/ n (Med) grauer Star m

catarrh /kə'tɑː(r)/ n Katarrh m

catastroph|e /kə'tæstrəfi/ n Katastrophe f. ~**ic** /kætə'strɒfɪk/ a katastrophal

catch /kætʃ/ n (of fish) Fang m; (fastener) Verschluss m; (on door) Klinke f; (fam: snag) Haken m (fam) □ v (pt/pp caught) □ vt fangen; (be in time for) erreichen; (travel by) fahren mit; bekommen (illness); ~ **a cold** sich erkälten; ~ **sight of** erblicken; ~ **s.o. stealing** jdn beim Stehlen erwischen; ~ **one's finger in the door** sich (dat) den Finger in der Tür [ein]klemmen □ vi (burn) anbrennen; (get stuck) klemmen. ~ **on** vi (fam) (understand) kapieren; (become popular) sich durchsetzen. ~ **up** vt einholen □ vi aufholen; ~ **up with** einholen (s.o.); nachholen (work)

catching /'kætʃɪŋ/ a ansteckend

catch: ~**-phrase** n, ~**word** n Schlagwort nt

catchy /'kætʃɪ/ a (-ier, -iest) einprägsam

catechism /'kætɪkɪzm/ n Katechismus m

categor|ical /kætɪ'gɒrɪkl/ a, **-ly** adv kategorisch. ~**y** /'kætɪgərɪ/ n Kategorie f

cater /'keɪtə(r)/ vi ~ **for** bekostigen; (firm:) das Essen liefern für (party); (fig) eingestellt sein auf (+ acc). ~**ing** n (trade) Gaststättengewerbe f

caterpillar /'kætəpɪlə(r)/ n Raupe f

cathedral /kə'θiːdrl/ n Dom m, Kathedrale f

Catholic /'kæθəlɪk/ a katholisch □ n Katholik(in) m(f). **c**~**ism** /kə'θɒlɪsɪzm/ n Katholizismus m

catkin /'kætkɪn/ n (Bot) Kätzchen nt

cattle /'kætl/ npl Vieh nt

catty /'kætɪ/ a (-ier, -iest) boshaft

caught /kɔːt/ see catch

cauldron /'kɔːldrən/ n [großer] Kessel m

cauliflower /'kɒlɪ-/ n Blumenkohl m

cause /kɔːz/ n Ursache f; (reason) Grund m; good ~ gute Sache f □ vt verursachen; ~ **s.o. to do sth** jdn veranlassen, etw zu tun

'**causeway** n [Insel]damm m

caustic /'kɔːstɪk/ a ätzend; (fig) beißend

cauterize /'kɔːtəraɪz/ vt kauterisieren

caution /'kɔːʃn/ n Vorsicht f; (warning) Verwarnung f □ vt (Jur) verwarnen

cautious /'kɔːʃəs/ a, **-ly** adv vorsichtig

cavalry /'kævəlrɪ/ n Kavallerie f

cave /keɪv/ n Höhle f □ vi ~ **in** einstürzen

cavern /ˈkævən/ n Höhle f

caviare /ˈkævɪɑː(r)/ n Kaviar m

caving /ˈkeɪvɪŋ/ n Höhlenforschung f

cavity /ˈkævətɪ/ n Hohlraum m; (in tooth) Loch nt

cavort /kəˈvɔːt/ vi tollen

cease /siːs/ v n without ~ unaufhörlich □ vt/i aufhören. ~-fire n Waffenruhe f. ~less a, -ly adv unaufhörlich

cedar /ˈsiːdə(r)/ n Zeder f

cede /siːd/ vt abtreten (to an + acc)

ceiling /ˈsiːlɪŋ/ n [Zimmer]decke f; (fig) oberste Grenze f

celebrat|e /ˈselɪbreɪt/ vt/i feiern. ~ed a berühmt (for wegen). ~ion /-ˈbreɪʃn/ n Feier f

celebrity /sɪˈlebrətɪ/ n Berühmtheit f

celery /ˈselərɪ/ n [Stangen]sellerie m & f

celiba|cy /ˈselɪbəsɪ/ n Zölibat nt. ~te a be ~te im Zölibat leben

cell /sel/ n Zelle f

cellar /ˈselə(r)/ n Keller m

cellist /ˈtʃelɪst/ n Cellist(in) m(f)

cello /ˈtʃeləʊ/ n Cello nt

Celsius /ˈselsɪəs/ a Celsius

Celt /kelt/ n Kelte m/ Keltin f. ~ic a keltisch

cement /sɪˈment/ n Zement m; (adhesive) Kitt m □ vt zementieren; (stick) kitten

cemetery /ˈsemɪtrɪ/ n Friedhof m

censor /ˈsensə(r)/ n Zensor m □ vt zensieren. ~ship n Zensur f

censure /ˈsenʃə(r)/ n Tadel m □ vt tadeln

census /ˈsensəs/ n Volkszählung f

cent /sent/ n (coin) Cent m

centenary /senˈtiːnərɪ/ n, (Amer) centennial /senˈtenɪəl/ n Hundertjahrfeier f

center /ˈsentə(r)/ n (Amer) = centre

centi|grade /ˈsentɪ-/ a Celsius-; 5° ~ 5° Celsius. ~metre n Zentimeter m & nt. ~pede /-piːd/ n Tausendfüßler m

central /ˈsentrəl/ a, -ly adv zentral. ~ heating n Zentralheizung f. ~ize vt zentralisieren. ~ reser'vation n (Auto) Mittelstreifen m

centre /ˈsentə(r)/ n Zentrum nt; (middle) Mitte f □ v (pt/pp centred) □ vt zentrieren; ~ on (fig) sich drehen um. ~'forward n Mittelstürmer m

centrifugal /sentrɪˈfjuːgl/ a ~ force Fliehkraft f

century /ˈsentʃərɪ/ n Jahrhundert nt

ceramic /sɪˈræmɪk/ a Keramik-. ~s n Keramik f

cereal /ˈsɪərɪəl/ n Getreide nt; (breakfast food) Frühstücksflocken pl

cerebral /ˈserɪbrl/ a Gehirn-

ceremon|ial /serɪˈməʊnɪəl/ a, -ly adv zeremoniell, feierlich □ n Zeremoniell nt. ~ious /-ɪəs/ a, -ly adv formell

ceremony /ˈserɪmənɪ/ n Zeremonie f, Feier f; without ~ ohne weitere Umstände

certain /ˈsɜːtn/ a sicher; (not named) gewiss; for ~ mit Bestimmtheit; make ~ (check) sich vergewissern (that dass); (ensure) dafür sorgen (that dass); he is ~ to win er wird ganz bestimmt siegen. ~ly adv bestimmt, sicher; ~ly not! auf keinen Fall! ~ty n Sicherheit f, Gewissheit f; it's a ~ty es ist sicher

certificate /səˈtɪfɪkət/ n Bescheinigung f; (Jur) Urkunde f; (Sch) Zeugnis nt

certify /ˈsɜːtɪfaɪ/ vt (pt/pp -ied) bescheinigen; (declare insane) für geisteskrank erklären

cessation /seˈseɪʃn/ n Ende nt

cesspool /ˈses-/ n Senkgrube f

cf. abbr (compare) vgl.

chafe /tʃeɪf/ vt wund reiben

chaff /tʃɑːf/ n Spreu f

chaffinch /ˈtʃæfɪntʃ/ n Buchfink m

chain /tʃeɪn/ n Kette f □ vt ketten (to an + acc). ~ up vt anketten

chain: ~ re'action n Kettenreaktion f. ~- smoker n Kettenraucher m. ~ store n Kettenladen m

chair /tʃeə(r)/ n Stuhl m; (Univ) Lehrstuhl m; (Adm) Vorsitzende/ m/f □ vt den Vorsitz führen bei. ~-lift n Sessellift m. ~man n Vorsitzende(r) m/f

chalet /ˈʃæleɪ/ n Chalet nt

chalice /ˈtʃælɪs/ n (Relig) Kelch m

chalk /tʃɔːk/ n Kreide f. ~y a kreidig

challeng|e /ˈtʃælɪndʒ/ n Herausforderung f; (Mil) Anruf m □ vt herausfordern; (Mil) anrufen; (fig) anfechten (statement). ~er n Herausforderer m. ~ing a herausfordernd; (demanding) anspruchsvoll

chamber /ˈtʃeɪmbə(r)/ n Kammer f; ~s pl (Jur) [Anwalts]büro nt; C~ of Commerce Handelskammer f

chamber: ~maid n Zimmermädchen nt. ~ music n Kammermusik f. ~pot n Nachttopf m

chamois¹ /ˈʃæmwɑː/ n inv (animal) Gämse f

chamois² /ˈʃæmɪ/ n ~-[leather] Ledertuch nt

champagne /ʃæmˈpeɪn/ n Champagner m

champion /ˈtʃæmpɪən/ n (Sport) Meister(in) m(f); (of cause) Verfechter m □ vt sich einsetzen für. ~ship n (Sport) Meisterschaft f chance /tʃɑːns/ n Zufall m; (prospect) Chancen pl; (likelihood) Aussicht f; (opportinity) Gelegenheit f; by ~ zufällig; take a ~ein Risiko eingehen; give s.o. a ~jdm eine Chance geben □ attrib zufällig □ vt ~ it es riskieren

chancellor /'tʃɑːnsələ(r)/ n Kanzler m; (Univ) Rektor m; C~ of the Exchequer Schatzkanzler m

chancy /'tʃɑːnsɪ/ a riskant

chandelier /ʃændə'lɪə(r)/ n Kronleuchter m

change /tʃeɪndʒ/ n Veränderung f; (alteration) Änderung f; (money) Wechselgeld nt; for a ~ zur Abwechslung □ vt wechseln; (alter) ändern; (exchange) umtauschen (for gegen); (transform) verwandeln; trocken legen (baby); ~ one's clothes sich umziehen; ~ trains umsteigen □ vi sich verändern; (~ clothes) sich umziehen; (~ trains) umsteigen; all ~!alles aussteigen!

changeable /'tʃeɪndʒəbl/ a wechselhaft

'changing-room n Umkleideraum m

channel /'tʃænl/ n Rinne f; (Radio, TV) Kanal m; (fig) Weg m; the [English] C~ der Ärmelkanal; the C~ Islands die Kanalinseln □ vt (pt/pp channelled) leiten; (fig) lenken

chant /tʃɑːnt/ n liturgischer Gesang m □ vt singen; (demonstrators:) skandieren

chao|s /'keɪɒs/ n Chaos nt. ~tic /-'ɒtɪk/ a chaotisch

chap /tʃæp/ n (fam) Kerl m

chapel /'tʃæpl/ n Kapelle f

chaperon /'ʃæpərəʊn/ n Anstandsdame f □ vt begleiten

chaplain /'tʃæplɪn/ n Geistliche(r) m

chapped /tʃæpt/ a (skin) aufgesprungen

chapter /'tʃæptə(r)/ n Kapitel nt

char¹ /tʃɑː(r)/ n (fam) Putzfrau f

char² vt (pt/pp charred) (burn) verkohlen

character /'kærɪktə(r)/ n Charakter m; (in novel, play) Gestalt f; (Typ) Schriftzeichen nt; out of ~ uncharakteristisch; quite a ~ (fam) ein Original

characteristic /kærɪktə'rɪstɪk/ a, -ally adv charakteristisch (of für) □ n Merkmal nt

characterize /'kærɪktəraɪz/ vt charakterisieren

charade /ʃə'rɑːd/ n Scharade f

charcoal /'tʃɑː-/ n Holzkohle f

charge /tʃɑːdʒ/ n (price) Gebühr f; (Electr) Ladung f; (attack) Angriff m; (Jur) Anklage f; free of ~ kostenlos; be in ~ verantwortlich sein (of für); take ~ die Aufsicht übernehmen (of über + acc) □ vt berechnen (fee); (Electr) laden; (attack) angreifen; (Jur) anklagen (with gen); ~ s.o.

for sth jdm etw berechnen □ vi (attack) angreifen

chariot /'tʃærɪət/ n Wagen m

charisma /kə'rɪzmə/ n Charisma nt. ~tic /kærɪz'mætɪk/ a charismatisch

charitable /'tʃærɪtəbl/ a wohltätig; (kind) wohlwollend

charity /'tʃærətɪ/ n Nächstenliebe f; (organization) wohltätige Einrichtung f; for ~ für Wohltätigkeitszwecke; live on ~ von Almosen leben

charlatan /'ʃɑːlətən/ n Scharlatan m

charm /tʃɑːm/ n Reiz m; (of person) Charme f; (object) Amulett nt □ vt bezaubern. ~ing a, -ly adv reizend; (person, smile) charmant

chart /tʃɑːt/ n Karte f; (table) Tabelle f

charter /'tʃɑːtə(r)/ n ~ [flight] Charterflug m □ vt chartern; ~ed accountant Wirtschaftsprüfer(in) m(f)

charwoman /'tʃɑː-/ n Putzfrau f

chase /tʃeɪs/ n Verfolgungsjagd f □ vt jagen, verfolgen. ~ away or off vt wegjagen

chasm /'kæzm/ n Kluft f

chassis /'ʃæsɪ/ n (pl chassis /-sɪz/) Chassis nt

chaste /tʃeɪst/ a keusch

chastise /tʃæ'staɪz/ vt züchtigen

chastity /'tʃæstətɪ/ n Keuschheit f

chat /tʃæt/ n Plauderei f; have a ~ with plaudern mit □ vi (pt/pp chatted) plaudern. ~ show n Talkshow f

chatter /'tʃætə(r)/ n Geschwätz nt □ vi schwatzen; (child:) plappern; (teeth:) klappern. ~box n (fam) Plappermaul nt

chatty /'tʃætɪ/ a (-ier, -iest) geschwätzig

chauffeur /'ʃəʊfə(r)/ n Chauffeur m

chauvin|ism /'ʃəʊvɪnɪzm/ n Chauvinismus m. ~ist n Chauvinist m; male ~ist (fam) Chauvi m

cheap /tʃiːp/ a & adv (-er, -est), -ly adv billig. ~en vt entwürdigen; ~en oneself sich erniedrigen

cheat /tʃiːt/ n Betrüger(in) m(f); (at games) Mogler m □ vt betrügen □ vi (at games) mogeln (fam)

check¹ /tʃek/ a (squared) kariert □ n Karo nt

check² n Überprüfung f; (inspection) Kontrolle f; (Chess) Schach nt; (Amer: bill) Rechnung f; (Amer: cheque) Scheck m; (Amer: tick) Haken m; keep a ~ on kontrollieren □ vt [über]prüfen; (inspect) kontrollieren; (restrain) hemmen; (stop) aufhalten □ vi [go and] ~ nachsehen. ~ in vi sich anmelden; (Aviat) einchecken □ vt abfertigen; einchecken. ~ out vi sich abmelden. ~ up *vi* prüfen, kontrollieren; ~ up on überprüfen

check|ed /tʃekt/ *a* kariert. ~ers *n* (*Amer*) Damespiel *n*

check: ~mate *int* schachmatt! ~out *n* Kasse *f*. ~room *n* (*Amer*) Garderobe *f*. ~up *n* (*Med*) [Kontroll]untersuchung *f*

cheek /tʃiːk/ *n* Backe *f*; (*impudence*) Frechheit *f*. ~y *a*, -ily *adv* frech

cheep /tʃiːp/ *vi* piepen

cheer /tʃɪə(r)/ *n* Beifallsruf *m*; three ~s ein dreifaches Hoch (for auf + *acc*); ~s! prost! (*goodbye*) tschüs! □ *vt* zujubeln (+ *dat*) □ *vi* jubeln. ~ up *vt* aufmuntern; aufheitern □ *vi* munterer werden. ~ful *a*, -ly *adv* fröhlich. ~fulness *n* Fröhlichkeit *f*

cheerio /tʃɪərɪ'əʊ/ *int* (*fam*) tschüs!

'cheerless *a* trostlos

cheese /tʃiːz/ *n* Käse *m*. ~cake *n* Käsekuchen *m*

cheetah /'tʃiːtə/ *n* Gepard *m*

chef /ʃef/ *n* Koch *m*

chemical /'kemɪkl/ *a*, -ly *adv* chemisch □ *n* Chemikalie *f*

chemist /'kemɪst/ *n* (*pharmacist*) Apotheker(in) *m(f)*; (*scientist*) Chemiker(in) *m(f)*; ~'s [shop] Drogerie *f*; (*dispensing*) Apotheke *f*. ~ry *n* Chemie *f*

cheque /tʃek/ *n* Scheck *m*. ~-book *n* Scheckbuch *nt*. ~ card *n* Scheckkarte *f*

cherish /'tʃerɪʃ/ *vt* lieben; (*fig*) hegen

cherry /'tʃerɪ/ *n* Kirsche *f* □ *attrib* Kirschrot

cherub /'tʃerəb/ *n* Engelchen *nt*

chess /tʃes/ *n* Schach *nt*

chess: ~board *n* Schachbrett *nt*. ~-man *n* Schachfigur *f*

chest /tʃest/ *n* Brust *f*; (*box*) Truhe *f*

chestnut /'tʃesnʌt/ *n* Esskastanie *f*, Marone *f*; (*horse-*) [Ross]kastanie *f*

chest of 'drawers *n* Kommode *f*

chew /tʃuː/ *vt* kauen. ~ing-gum *n* Kaugummi *m*

chic /ʃiːk/ *a* schick

chick /tʃɪk/ *n* Küken *nt*

chicken /'tʃɪkɪn/ *n* Huhn *nt* □ *attrib* Hühner- □ *a* (*fam*) feige □ *vi* ~ out (*fam*) kneifen. ~pox *n* Windpocken *pl*

chicory /'tʃɪkərɪ/ *n* Chicorée *m*; (*in coffee*) Zichorie *f*

chief /tʃiːf/ *a* Haupt- □ *n* Chef *m*; (*of tribe*) Häuptling *m*. ~ly *adv* hauptsächlich

chilblain /'tʃɪlbleɪn/ *n* Frostbeule *f*

child /tʃaɪld/ *n* (*pl* ~ren) Kind *nt*

child: ~birth *n* Geburt *f*. ~hood *n* Kindheit *f*. ~ish *a* kindisch. ~less *a* kinderlos. ~like *a* kindlich. ~-minder *n* Tagesmutter *f*

children /'tʃɪldrən/ *npl see* child

Chile /'tʃɪlɪ/ *n* Chile *nt*

chill /tʃɪl/ *n* Kälte *f*; (*illness*) Erkältung *f* □ *vt* kühlen

chilli /'tʃɪlɪ/ *n* (*pl* -es) Chili *m*

chilly /'tʃɪlɪ/ *a* kühl; I felt ~mich fröstelte [es]

chime /tʃaɪm/ *vi* läuten; (*clock:*) schlagen

chimney /'tʃɪmnɪ/ *n* Schornstein *m*. ~pot *n* Schornsteinaufsatz *m*. ~-sweep *n* Schornsteinfeger *m*

chimpanzee /tʃɪmpæn'ziː/ *n* Schimpanse *m*

chin /tʃɪn/ *n* Kinn *nt*

china /'tʃaɪnə/ *n* Porzellan *nt*

Chin|a *n* China *nt*. ~ese /-'niːz/ *a* chinesisch □ *n* (*Lang*) Chinesisch *nt*; the ~ese *pl* die Chinesen. ~ese 'lantern *n* Lampion *m*

chink[1] /tʃɪŋk/ *n* (*slit*) Ritze *f*

chink[2] *n* Geklirr *nt* □ *vi* klirren; (*coins:*) klimpern

chip /tʃɪp/ *n* (*fragment*) Span *m*; (*in china, paintwork*) angeschlagene Stelle *f*; (*Computing, Gambling*) Chip *m*; ~s *pl* (*Culin*) Pommes frites *pl*; (*Amer: crisps*) Chips *pl* □ *vt* (*pt/pp* chipped) (*damage*) anschlagen. ~ped *a* angeschlagen

chiropod|ist /kɪ'rɒpədɪst/ *n* Fußpfleger(in) *m(f)*. ~y *n* Fußpflege *f*

chirp /tʃɜːp/ *vi* zwitschern; (*cricket:*) zirpen. ~y *a* (*fam*) munter

chisel /'tʃɪzl/ *n* Meißel *m* □ *vt/i* (*pt/pp* chiselled) meißeln

chit /tʃɪt/ *n* Zettel *m*

chival|rous /'ʃɪvlrəs/ *a*, -ly *adv* ritterlich. ~ry *n* Ritterlichkeit *f*

chives /tʃaɪvz/ *npl* Schnittlauch *m*

chlorine /'klɔːriːn/ *n* Chlor *nt*

chloroform /'klɒrəfɔːm/ *n* Chloroform *nt*

chocolate /'tʃɒkələt/ *n* Schokolade *f*; (*sweet*) Praline *f*

choice /tʃɔɪs/ *n* Wahl *f*; (*variety*) Auswahl *f* □ *a* auserlesen

choir /'kwaɪə(r)/ *n* Chor *m*. ~boy *n* Chorknabe *m*

choke /tʃəʊk/ *n* (*Auto*) Choke *m* □ *vt* würgen; (*to death*) erwürgen □ *vi* sich verschlucken; ~ on [fast] ersticken an (+ *dat*)

cholera /'kɒlərə/ *n* Cholera *f*

cholesterol /kə'lestərɒl/ *n* Cholesterin *nt*

choose /tʃuːz/ *vt/i* (*pt* chose, *pp* chosen) wählen; (*select*) sich (*dat*) aussuchen; ~ to do/go (*freiwillig*) tun/gehen; as you ~ wie Sie wollen

choos[e]y /'tʃuːzɪ/ *a* (*fam*) wählerisch

chop /tʃɒp/ n (blow) Hieb m; (Culin) Kotelett nt ▢ vt (pt/pp chopped) hacken. ~ down vt abhacken; fällen ⟨tree⟩. ~ off vt abhacken

chop|per /'tʃɒpə(r)/ n Beil nt; (fam) Hubschrauber m. ~py a kabbelig

'chopsticks npl Essstäbchen pl

choral /'kɔːrəl/ a Chor-; ~ society Gesangverein m

chord /kɔːd/ n (Mus) Akkord m

chore /tʃɔː(r)/ n lästige Pflicht f; [household] ~s Hausarbeit f

choreography /kɒrɪ'ɒgrəfɪ/ n Choreographie f

chortle /'tʃɔːtl/ vi [vor Lachen] glucksen

chorus /'kɔːrəs/ n Chor m; (of song) Refrain m

chose, chosen /tʃəʊz, 'tʃəʊzn/ see choose

Christ /kraɪst/ n Christus m

christen /'krɪsn/ vt taufen. ~ing n Taufe f

Christian /'krɪstʃən/ a christlich ▢ n Christ(in) m(f). ~ity /-stɪ'ænətɪ/ n Christentum nt. ~ name n Vorname m

Christmas /'krɪsməs/ n Weihnachten nt. ~ card n Weihnachtskarte f. ~ 'Day n erster Weihnachtstag m. ~ 'Eve n Heiligabend m. ~ tree n Weihnachtsbaum m

chrome /krəʊm/ n, chromium /'krəʊmɪəm/ n Chrom nt

chromosome /'krəʊməsəʊm/ n Chromosom nt

chronic /'krɒnɪk/ a chronisch

chronicle /'krɒnɪkl/ n Chronik f

chronological /krɒnə'lɒdʒɪkl/ a, -ly adv chronologisch

chrysalis /'krɪsəlɪs/ n Puppe f

chrysanthemum /krɪ'sænθəməm/ n Chrysantheme f

chubby /'tʃʌbɪ/ a (-ier, -iest) mollig

chuck /tʃʌk/ vt (fam) schmeißen. ~ out vt (fam) rausschmeißen

chuckle /'tʃʌkl/ vi in sich (acc) hineinlachen

chum /tʃʌm/ n Freund(in) m(f)

chunk /tʃʌŋk/ n Stück nt

church /tʃɜːtʃ/ n Kirche f. ~yard n Friedhof m

churlish /'tʃɜːlɪʃ/ a unhöflich

churn /tʃɜːn/ n Butterfass nt; (for milk) Milchkanne f ▢ vt ~ out am laufenden Band produzieren

chute /ʃuːt/ n Rutsche f; (for rubbish) Müllschlucker m

CID abbr (Criminal Investigation Department) Kripo f

cider /'saɪdə(r)/ n Apfelwein m

cigar /sɪ'gɑː(r)/ n Zigarre f

cigarette /sɪgə'ret/ n Zigarette f

cine-camera /'sɪnɪ-/ n Filmkamera f

cinema /'sɪnɪmə/ n Kino nt

cinnamon /'sɪnəmən/ n Zimt m

cipher /'saɪfə(r)/ n (code) Chiffre f; (numeral) Ziffer f; (fig) Null f

circle /'sɜːkl/ n Kreis m; (Theat) Rang m ▢ vt umkreisen ▢ vi kreisen

circuit /'sɜːkɪt/ n Runde f; (racetrack) Rennbahn f; (Electr) Stromkreis m. ~ous /sə'kjuːɪtəs/ a ~ route Umweg m

circular /'sɜːkjʊlə(r)/ a kreisförmig ▢ n Rundschreiben nt. ~ 'saw n Kreissäge f. ~ 'tour n Rundfahrt f

circulat|e /'sɜːkjʊleɪt/ vt in Umlauf setzen ▢ vi zirkulieren. ~ion /-'leɪʃn/ n Kreislauf m; (of newspaper) Auflage f

circumcis|e /'sɜːkəmsaɪz/ vt beschneiden. ~ion /-'sɪʒn/ n Beschneidung f

circumference /sə'kʌmfərəns/ n Umfang m

circumspect /'sɜːkəmspekt/ a, -ly adv umsichtig

circumstance /'sɜːkəmstəns/ n Umstand m; ~s pl Umstände pl; (financial) Verhältnisse pl

circus /'sɜːkəs/ n Zirkus m

CIS abbr (Commonwealth of Independent States) GUS f

cistern /'sɪstən/ n (tank) Wasserbehälter m; (of WC) Spülkasten m

cite /saɪt/ vt zitieren

citizen /'sɪtɪzn/ n Bürger(in) m(f). ~ship n Staatsangehörigkeit f

citrus /'sɪtrəs/ n ~ [fruit] Zitrusfrucht f

city /'sɪtɪ/ n [Groß]stadt f

civic /'sɪvɪk/ a Bürger-

civil /'ʃɪvl/ a bürgerlich; ⟨aviation, defence⟩ zivil; (polite) höflich. ~ engi'neering n Hoch- und Tiefbau m

civilian /sɪ'vɪljən/ a Zivil-; in ~ clothes in Zivil ▢ n Zivilist m

civility /sɪ'vɪlətɪ/ n Höflichkeit f

civiliz|ation /sɪvəlaɪ'zeɪʃn/ n Zivilisation f. ~e /'sɪvəlaɪz/ vt zivilisieren

civil: ~ 'servant n Beamte(r) m/Beamtin f. C~ 'Service n Staatsdienst m

clad /klæd/ a gekleidet (in in + acc)

claim /kleɪm/ n Anspruch m; (application) Antrag m; (demand) Forderung f; (assertion) Behauptung f ▢ vt beanspruchen; (apply for) beantragen; (demand) fordern; (assert) behaupten; (collect) abholen. ~ant n Antragsteller m

clairvoyant /kleə'vɔɪənt/ n Hellseher(in) m(f)

clam /klæm/ n Klaffmuschel f

clamber /'klæmbə(r)/ vi klettern

clammy /'klæmɪ/ a (-ier, -iest) feucht

clamour /'klæmə(r)/ n Geschrei nt □ vi ~ for schreien nach

clamp /klæmp/ n Klammer f □ vt [ein]spannen □ vi (fam) ~ down durchgreifen; ~ down on vorgehen gegen

clan /klæn/ n Clan m

clandestine /klæn'destɪn/ a geheim

clang /klæŋ/ n Schmettern nt. ~er n (fam) Schnitzer m

clank /klæŋk/ vi klirren

clap /klæp/ n give s.o. a ~ jdm Beifall klatschen; ~ of thunder Donnerschlag m □ vt/i (pt/pp clapped) Beifall klatschen (+ dat); ~ one's hands [in die Hände] klatschen

claret /'klærət/ n roter Bordeaux m

clari|fication /klærɪfɪ'keɪʃn/ n Klärung f. ~fy /'klærɪfaɪ/ vt/i (pt/pp -ied) klären

clarinet /klærɪ'net/ n Klarinette f

clarity /'klærətɪ/ n Klarheit f

clash /klæʃ/ n Geklirr nt; (fig) Konflikt m □ vi klirren; (colours:) sich beißen; (events:) ungünstig zusammenfallen

clasp /klɑːsp/ n Verschluss m □ vt ergreifen; (hold) halten

class /klɑːs/ n Klasse f; travel first/second ~ erster/zweiter Klasse reisen □ vt einordnen

classic /'klæsɪk/ a klassisch □ n Klassiker m; ~s pl (Univ) Altphilologie f. ~al a klassisch

classi|fication /klæsɪfɪ'keɪʃn/ n Klassifikation f. ~fy /'klæsɪfaɪ/ vt (pt/pp -ied) klassifizieren

'classroom n Klassenzimmer nt

classy /'klɑːsɪ/ a (-ier, -iest) (fam) schick

clatter /'klætə(r)/ n Geklapper nt □ vi klappern

clause /klɔːz/ n Klausel f; (Gram) Satzteil m

claustrophobia /klɔːstrə'fəʊbɪə/ n Klaustrophobie f, (fam) Platzangst m

claw /klɔː/ n Kralle f; (of bird of prey & Techn) Klaue f; (of crab, lobster) Schere f □ vt kratzen

clay /kleɪ/ n Lehm m; (pottery) Ton m

clean /kliːn/ a (-er, -est) sauber □ vt sauber machen; putzen (shoes, windows); ~ one's teeth sich (dat) die Zähne putzen; have sth ~ed etw reinigen lassen. ~ up vt sauber machen

cleaner /'kliːnə(r)/ n Putzfrau f; (substance) Reinigungsmittel nt; [dry] ~'s chemische Reinigung f

cleanliness /'klenlɪnɪs/ n Sauberkeit f

cleanse /klenz/ vt reinigen. ~r n Reinigungsmittel nt

clean-shaven a glatt rasiert

cleansing cream /'klenz-/ n Reinigungscreme f

clear /klɪə(r)/ a (-er, -est), -ly adv klar; (obvious) eindeutig; (distinct) deutlich; (conscience) rein; (without obstacles) frei; make sth ~ etw klarmachen (to dat) □ adv stand ~ zurücktreten; keep ~ of aus dem Wege gehen (+ dat) □ vt räumen; abräumen (table); (acquit) freisprechen; (authorize) genehmigen; (jump over) überspringen; ~ one's throat sich räuspern □ vi (fog:) sich auflösen. ~ away vt wegräumen. ~ off vi (fam) abhauen. ~ out vt ausräumen □ vi (fam) abhauen. ~ up vt (tidy) aufräumen; (solve) aufklären □ vi (weather:) sich aufklären

clearance /'klɪərəns/ n Räumung f; (authorization) Genehmigung f; (customs) [Zoll]abfertigung f; (Techn) Spielraum m. ~ sale n Räumungsverkauf m

clear|ing /'klɪərɪŋ/ n Lichtung f. ~way n (Auto) Straße f mit Halteverbot

cleavage /'kliːvɪdʒ/ n Spaltung f; (woman's) Dekolleté nt

clef /klef/ n Notenschlüssel m

cleft /kleft/ n Spalte f

clemen|cy /'klemənsɪ/ n Milde f. ~t a mild

clench /klentʃ/ vt ~ one's fist die Faust ballen; ~ one's teeth die Zähne zusammenbeißen

clergy /'klɜːdʒɪ/ npl Geistlichkeit f. ~man n Geistliche(r) m

cleric /'klerɪk/ n Geistliche(r) m. ~al a Schreib-; (Relig) geistlich

clerk /klɑːk/, Amer: /klɜːk/ n Büroangestellte(r) m/f; (Amer: shop assistant) Verkäufer(in) m(f)

clever /'klevə(r)/ a (-er, -est), -ly adv klug; (skilful) geschickt

cliché /'kliːʃeɪ/ n Klischee nt

click /klɪk/ vi klicken

client /'klaɪənt/ n Kunde m/ Kundin f; (Jur) Klient(in) m(f)

clientele /kliːɒn'tel/ n Kundschaft f

cliff /klɪf/ n Kliff nt

climat|e /'klaɪmət/ n Klima nt. ~ic /-'mætɪk/ a klimatisch

climax /'klaɪmæks/ n Höhepunkt m

climb /klaɪm/ n Aufstieg m □ vt besteigen (mountain); steigen auf (+ acc) (ladder, tree) □ vi klettern; (rise) steigen; (road:) ansteigen. ~ down vi hinunter-/ herunterklettern; (from ladder, tree) heruntersteigen, (fam) nachgeben

climber /'klaɪmə(r)/ n Bergsteiger m; (plant) Kletterpflanze f clinch /klɪntʃ/ vt perfekt machen ⟨deal⟩ □ vi ⟨boxing⟩ clinchen

cling /klɪŋ/ vi ⟨pt/pp clung⟩ sich klammern ⟨to an + acc⟩; ⟨stick⟩ haften ⟨to an + dat⟩.~film n Sichtfolie f mit Hafteffekt

clinic /'klɪnɪk/ n Klinik f.~al a, -ly adv klinisch

clink /klɪŋk/ n Klirren nt; ⟨fam: prison⟩ Knast m □ vi klirren

clip¹ /klɪp/ n Klammer f; ⟨jewellery⟩ Klipp m □ vt ⟨pt/pp clipped⟩ anklammern ⟨to an + acc⟩

clip² n ⟨extract⟩ Ausschnitt m □ vt schneiden; knipsen ⟨ticket⟩. ~board n Klemmbrett nt. ~pers npl Schere f. ~ping n ⟨extract⟩ Ausschnitt m

clique /kliːk/ n Clique f

cloak /kləʊk/ n Umhang m.~room n Garderobe f; ⟨toilet⟩ Toilette f

clobber /'klɒbə(r)/ n ⟨fam⟩ Zeug nt □ vt ⟨fam: hit, defeat⟩ schlagen

clock /klɒk/ n Uhr f; ⟨fam: speedometer⟩ Tacho m □ vi ~ in/out stechen

clock: ~ tower n Uhrenturm m.~wise a & adv im Uhrzeigersinn. ~work n Uhrwerk nt; ⟨of toy⟩ Aufziehmechanismus m; like ~work ⟨fam⟩ wie am Schnürchen

clod /klɒd/ n Klumpen m

clog /klɒg/ n Holzschuh m □ vt/i ⟨pt/pp clogged⟩ ~ [up] verstopfen

cloister /'klɔɪstə(r)/ n Kreuzgang m

close¹ /kləʊs/ a ⟨-r, -st⟩ nah[e] ⟨to dat⟩; ⟨friend⟩ eng; ⟨weather⟩ schwül; have a ~ shave ⟨fam⟩ mit knapper Not davonkommen □ adv nahe; ~ by nicht weit weg □ n ⟨street⟩ Sackgasse f

close² /kləʊz/ n Ende nt; draw to a ~ sich dem Ende nähern □ vt zumachen, schließen; ⟨bring to an end⟩ beenden; sperren ⟨road⟩ □ vi sich schließen; ⟨shop:⟩ schließen, zumachen; ⟨end⟩ enden. ~ down vt schließen; stillegen ⟨factory⟩ □ vi schließen; ⟨factory:⟩ stillgelegt werden

closed 'shop /kləʊzd-/ n ≈ Gewerkschaftszwang m

closely /'kləʊslɪ/ adv eng, nah[e]; ⟨with attention⟩ genau

close season /'kləʊs-/ n Schonzeit f

closet /'klɒzɪt/ n ⟨Amer⟩ Schrank m

close-up /'kləʊs-/ n Nahaufnahme f

closure /'kləʊʒə(r)/ n Schließung f; ⟨of factory⟩ Stillegung f; ⟨of road⟩ Sperrung f

clot /klɒt/ n [Blut]gerinnsel nt; ⟨fam: idiot⟩ Trottel m □ vi ⟨pt/pp clotted⟩ ⟨blood:⟩ gerinnen

cloth /klɒθ/ n Tuch nt

clothe /kləʊð/ vt kleiden

clothes /kləʊðz/ npl Kleider pl. ~brush n Kleiderbürste f. ~line n Wäscheleine f

clothing /'kləʊðɪŋ/ n Kleidung f

cloud /klaʊd/ n Wolke f □ vi ~ over sich bewölken. ~burst n Wolkenbruch m

cloudy /'klaʊdɪ/ a ⟨-ier, -iest⟩ wolkig, bewölkt; ⟨liquid⟩ trübe

clout /klaʊt/ n ⟨fam⟩ Schlag m; ⟨influence⟩ Einfluss m □ vt ⟨fam⟩ hauen

clove /kləʊv/ n [Gewürz]nelke f; ~ of garlic Knoblauchzehe f

clover /'kləʊvə(r)/ n Klee m. ~ leaf n Kleeblatt nt

clown /klaʊn/ n Clown m □ vi ~ [about] herumalbern

club /klʌb/ n Klub m; ⟨weapon⟩ Keule f; ⟨Sport⟩ Schläger m; ~s pl ⟨Cards⟩ Kreuz nt, Treff nt □ v ⟨pt/pp clubbed⟩ □ vt knüppeln □ vi ~ together zusammenlegen

cluck /klʌk/ vi glucken

clue /kluː/ n Anhaltspunkt m; ⟨in crossword⟩ Frage f; I haven't a ~ ⟨fam⟩ ich habe keine Ahnung

clump /klʌmp/ n Gruppe f

clumsiness /'klʌmzɪnɪs/ n Ungeschicklichkeit f

clumsy /'klʌmzɪ/ a ⟨-ier, -iest⟩, -ily adv ungeschickt; ⟨unwieldy⟩ unförmig

clung /klʌŋ/ see cling

cluster /'klʌstə(r)/ n Gruppe f; ⟨of flowers⟩ Büschel nt □ vi sich scharen ⟨round um⟩

clutch /klʌtʃ/ n Griff m; ⟨Auto⟩ Kupplung f; be in s.o.'s ~es ⟨fam⟩ in jds Klauen sein □ vt festhalten; ⟨grab⟩ ergreifen □ vi ~ at greifen nach

clutter /'klʌtə(r)/ n Kram m □ vt ~ [up] vollstopfen

c/o abbr ⟨care of⟩ bei

coach /kəʊtʃ/ n [Reise]bus m; ⟨Rail⟩ Wagen m; ⟨horse-drawn⟩ Kutsche f; ⟨Sport⟩ Trainer m □ vt Nachhilfestunden geben ⟨+ dat⟩; ⟨Sport⟩ trainieren

coagulate /kəʊ'ægjʊleɪt/ vi gerinnen

coal /kəʊl/ n Kohle f

coalition /kəʊə'lɪʃn/ n Koalition f

'coal-mine n Kohlenbergwerk nt

coarse /kɔːs/ a ⟨-r, -st⟩, -ly adv grob

coast /kəʊst/ n Küste f □ vi ⟨freewheel⟩ im Freilauf fahren; ⟨Auto⟩ im Leerlauf fahren. ~al a Küsten-. ~er n ⟨mat⟩ Untersatz m

coast: ~guard n Küstenwache f. ~line n Küste f

coat /kəʊt/ n Mantel m; ⟨of animal⟩ Fell nt; ⟨of paint⟩ Anstrich m; ~ of arms Wappen nt □ vt überziehen; ⟨with paint⟩ streichen. ~-hanger n Kleiderbügel m. ~-hook n Kleiderhaken m

coating /'kəʊtɪŋ/ n Überzug m, Schicht f; (of paint) Anstrich m

coax /kəʊks/ vt gut zureden (+ dat)

cob /kɒb/ n (of corn) [Mais]kolben m

cobble¹ /'kɒbl/ n Kopfstein m; ~s pl Kopfsteinpflaster nt

cobble² vt flicken. ~r m Schuster m

'cobblestones n pl = cobbles

cobweb /'kɒb-/ n Spinnengewebe nt

cocaine /kə'keɪn/ n Kokain nt

cock /kɒk/ n Hahn m; (any male bird) Männchen nt □ vt (animal:) ~ its ears die Ohren spitzen; ~ the gun den Hahn spannen. ~-and-'bull story n (fam) Lügengeschichte f

cockerel /'kɒkərəl/ n [junger] Hahn m

cock-'eyed a (fam) schief; (absurd) verrückt

cockle /'kɒkl/ n Herzmuschel f

cockney /'kɒknɪ/ n (dialect) Cockney nt; (person) Cockney m

cock: ~pit n (Aviat) Cockpit nt. ~roach /-rəʊtʃ/ n Küchenschabe f. ~tail n Cocktail m. ~up n (sl) make a ~up Mist bauen (of bei)

cocky /'kɒkɪ/ a (-ier, -iest) (fam) eingebildet

cocoa /'kəʊkəʊ/ n Kakao m

coconut /'kəʊkənʌt/ n Kokosnuß f

cocoon /kə'kuːn/ n Kokon m

cod /kɒd/ n inv Kabeljau m

COD abbr (cash on delivery) per Nachnahme

coddle /'kɒdl/ vt verhätscheln

code /kəʊd/ n Kode m; (Computing) Code m; (set of rules) Kodex m. ~d a verschlüsselt

coedu'cational /kəʊ-/ a gemischt. ~ school n Koedukationsschule f

coerc|e /kəʊ'ɜːs/ vt zwingen. ~ion /-'ɜːʃn/ n Zwang m

coe'xist vi koexistieren. ~ence n Koexistenz f

coffee /kɒfɪ/ n Kaffee m

coffee: ~-grinder n Kaffeemühle f. ~pot n Kaffeekanne f. ~-table n Couchtisch m

coffin /'kɒfɪn/ n Sarg m

cog /kɒg/ n (Techn) Zahn m

cogent /'kəʊdʒənt/ a überzeugend

cog-wheel n Zahnrad nt

cohabit /kəʊ'hæbɪt/ vi (Jur) zusammenleben

coherent /kəʊ'hɪərənt/ a zusammenhängend; (comprehensible) verständlich

coil /kɔɪl/ n Rolle f; (Electr) Spule f; (one ring) Windung f □ vt ~ [up] zusammenrollen

coin /kɔɪn/ n Münze f □ vt prägen

coincide /kəʊɪn'saɪd/ vi zusammenfallen; (agree) übereinstimmen

coinciden|ce /kəʊ'ɪnsɪdəns/ n Zufall m. ~tal /-'dentl/ a, ~ly adv zufällig

coke /kəʊk/ n Koks m

Coke (P) n (drink) Cola f

colander /'kʌləndə(r)/ n (Culin) Durchschlag m

cold /kəʊld/ a (-er, -est) kalt; I am or feel ~ mir ist kalt □ n Kälte f; (Med) Erkältung f

cold: ~-'blooded a kaltblütig. ~-'hearted a kaltherzig. ~ly adv (fig) kalt, kühl. ~ness n Kälte f

coleslaw /'kəʊlslɔː/ n Krautsalat m

colic /'kɒlɪk/ n Kolik f

collaborat|e /kə'læbəreɪt/ vi zusammenarbeiten (with mit); ~e on sth mitarbeiten bei etw. ~ion /-'reɪʃn/ n Zusammenarbeit f, Mitarbeit f; (with enemy) Kollaboration f. ~or n Mitarbeiter(in) m(f); Kollaborateur m

collaps|e /kə'læps/ n Zusammenbruch m; Einsturz m □ vi zusammenbrechen; (roof, building:) einstürzen. ~ible a zusammenklappbar

collar /'kɒlə(r)/ n Kragen m; (for animal) Halsband nt. ~-bone n Schlüsselbein nt

colleague /'kɒliːg/ n Kollege m/Kollegin f

collect /kə'lekt/ vt sammeln; (fetch) abholen; einsammeln (tickets); einziehen (taxes) □ vi sich [an]sammeln □ adv call ~ (Amer) ein R-Gespräch führen. ~ed /-ɪd/ a gesammelt; (calm) gefasst

collection /kə'lekʃn/ n Sammlung f; (in church) Kollekte f; (of post) Leerung f; (designer's) Kollektion f

collective /kə'lektɪv/ a gemeinsam; (Pol) kollektiv. ~ 'noun n Kollektivum nt

collector /kə'lektə(r)/ n Sammler(in) m(f)

college /'kɒlɪdʒ/ n College nt

collide /kə'laɪd/ vi zusammenstoßen

colliery /'kɒlɪərɪ/ n Kohlengrube f

collision /kə'lɪʒn/ n Zusammenstoß m

colloquial /kə'ləʊkwɪəl/ a, ~ly adv umgangssprachlich. ~ism n umgangssprachlicher Ausdruck m

Cologne /kə'ləʊn/ n Köln nt

colon /'kəʊlən/ n Doppelpunkt m; (Anat) Dickdarm m

colonel /'kɜːnl/ n Oberst m

colonial /kə'ləʊnɪəl/ a Kolonial-

colon|ize /'kɒlənaɪz/ vt kolonisieren. ~y n Kolonie f

colossal /kə'lɒsl/ a riesig

colour /'kʌlə(r)/ n Farbe f; (complexion) Gesichtsfarbe f; (race) Hautfarbe f; ~s pl (*flag*) Fahne *f*; off ~ (*fam*) nicht ganz auf der Höhe □ *vt* färben; ~ [in] ausmalen □ *vi* (*blush*) erröten

colour: ~ **bar** *n* Rassenschranke *f*. ~**blind** *a* farbenblind. ~**ed** *a* farbig □ *n* (*person*) Farbige(r) *m/f*. ~**fast** *a* farbecht. ~ **film** *n* Farbfilm *m*. ~**ful** *a* farbenfroh. ~**less** *a* farblos. ~ **photo[graph]** *n* Farbaufnahme *f*. ~ **television** *n* Farbfernsehen *nt*

colt /kəʊlt/ *n* junger Hengst *m*

column /'kɒləm/ *n* Säule *f*; (*of soldiers, figures*) Kolonne *f*; (*Typ*) Spalte *f*; (*Journ*) Kolumne *f*. ~**ist** /-nɪst/ *n* Kolumnist *m*

coma /'kəʊmə/ *n* Koma *nt*

comb /kəʊm/ *n* Kamm *m* □ *vt* kämmen; (*search*) absuchen; ~ one's hair sich (*dat*) [die Haare] kämmen

combat /'kɒmbæt/ *n* Kampf *m* □ *vt* (*pt/pp* combated) bekämpfen

combination /kɒmbɪ'neɪʃn/ *n* Verbindung *f*; (*for lock*) Kombination *f*

combine[1] /kəm'baɪn/ *vt* verbinden □ *vi* sich verbinden; (*people:*) sich zusammenschließen

combine[2] /'kɒmbaɪn/ *n* (*Comm*) Konzern *m*; ~ [harvester] *n* Mähdrescher *m*

combustion /kəm'bʌstʃn/ *n* Verbrennung *f*

come /kʌm/ *vi* (*pt* came, *pp* come) kommen; (*reach*) reichen (to an + *acc*); that ~s to £10 das macht £10; ~ into money zu Geld kommen; ~ true wahr werden; ~ in two sizes in zwei Größen erhältlich sein; the years to ~ die kommenden Jahre; how ~? (*fam*) wie das? ~ about *vi* geschehen. ~ across *vi* herüberkommen; (*fam*) klar werden □ *vt* stoßen auf (+ *acc*). ~ apart *vi* sich auseinander nehmen lassen; (*accidentally*) auseinander gehen. ~ away *vi* weggehen; ⟨*thing*:⟩ abgehen. ~ back *vi* zurückkommen. ~ by *vi* vorbeikommen □ *vt* (*obtain*) bekommen. ~ in *vi* hereinkommen. ~ off *vi* abgehen; (*take place*) stattfinden; (*succeed*) klappen (*fam*). ~ out *vi* herauskommen; ⟨*book:*⟩ erscheinen; ⟨*stain:*⟩ herausgehen. ~ round *vi* vorbeikommen; (*after fainting*) [wieder] zu sich kommen; (*change one's mind*) sich umstimmen lassen. ~ to *vi* [wieder] zu sich kommen. ~ up *vi* heraufkommen; ⟨*plant:*⟩ aufgehen; (*reach*) reichen (to bis); ~ up with (*dat*) einfallen lassen

'**come-back** *n* Comeback *nt*

comedian /kə'mi:dɪən/ *n* Komiker *m*

'**come-down** *n* Rückschritt *m*

comedy /'kɒmədɪ/ *n* Komödie *f*

comet /'kɒmɪt/ *n* Komet *m*

come-uppance /kʌm'ʌpəns/ *n* get one's ~ (*fam*) sein Fett abkriegen

comfort /'kʌmfət/ *n* Bequemlichkeit *f*; (*consolation*) Trost *m* □ *vt* trösten

comfortable /'kʌmfətəbl/ *a*, **-bly** *adv* bequem

'**comfort station** *n* (*Amer*) öffentliche Toilette *f*

comfy /'kʌmfɪ/ *a* (*fam*) bequem

comic /'kɒmɪk/ *a* komisch □ *n* Komiker *m*; (*periodical*) Comic-Heft *nt*. ~**al** *a*, **-ly** *adv* komisch. ~ **strip** *n* Comic Strips *pl*

coming /'kʌmɪŋ/ *a* kommend □ *n* Kommen *nt*; ~**s and goings** Kommen und Gehen *nt*

comma /'kɒmə/ *n* Komma *nt*

command /kə'mɑ:nd/ *n* Befehl *m*; (*Mil*) Kommando *nt*; (*mastery*) Beherrschung *f* □ *vt* befehlen (+ *dat*); kommandieren (*army*)

commandeer /kɒmən'dɪə(r)/ *vt* beschlagnahmen

command|er /kə'mɑ:ndə(r)/ *n* Befehlshaber *m*; (*of unit*) Kommandeur *m*; (*of ship*) Kommandant *m*. ~**ing** *a* ⟨*view*⟩ beherrschend. ~**ing officer** *n* Befehlshaber *m*. ~**ment** *n* Gebot *nt*

commemorat|e /kə'meməreɪt/ *vt* gedenken (+ *gen*). ~**ion** /-'reɪʃn/ *n* Gedenken *nt*. ~**ive** /-ətɪv/ *a* Gedenk-

commence /kə'mens/ *vt/i* anfangen, beginnen. ~**ment** *n* Anfang *m*, Beginn *m*

commend /kə'mend/ *vt* loben; (*recommend*) empfehlen (to *dat*). ~**able** /-əbl/ *a* lobenswert. ~**ation** /kɒmen'deɪʃn/ *n* Lob *nt*

commensurate /kə'menʃərət/ *a* angemessen; be ~ with entsprechen (+ *dat*)

comment /'kɒment/ *n* Bemerkung *f*; no ~! kein Kommentar! □ *vi* sich äußern (on zu); ~ on (*Journ*) kommentieren

commentary /'kɒməntrɪ/ *n* Kommentar *m*; [running] ~ (*Radio, TV*) Reportage *f*

commentator /'kɒməntɪeɪtə(r)/ *n* Kommentator *m*; (*Sport*) Reporter *m*

commerce /'kɒmɜ:s/ *n* Handel *m*

commercial /kə'mɜ:ʃl/ *a*, **-ly** *adv* kommerziell □ *n* (*Radio, TV*) Werbespot *m*. ~**ize** *vt* kommerzialisieren

commiserate /kə'mɪzəreɪt/ *vi* sein Mitleid ausdrücken (with *dat*)

commission /kə'mɪʃn/ *n* (*order for work*) Auftrag *m*; (*body of people*) Kommission *f*; (*payment*) Provision *f*; (*Mil*) [Offiziers]patent *nt*; out of ~ außer Betrieb □ *vt* beauftragen ⟨*s.o.*⟩; in Auftrag geben⟨*thing*⟩; (*Mil*) zum Offizier ernennen

commissionaire /kəmɪʃə'neə(r)/ *n* Portier *m*

commissioner /kə'mɪʃənə(r)/ *n* Kommissar *m*; ~ **for oaths** Notar *m*

commit /kə'mɪt/ *vt* (*pt/pp* committed) begehen; (*entrust*) anvertrauen (**to** *dat*); (*consign*) einweisen (**to** **in** + *acc*); ~ oneself sich festlegen; (*involve oneself*) sich engagieren; ~ **sth to memory** sich (*dat*) etw einprägen. ~**ment** *n* Verpflichtung *f*; (*involvement*) Engagement *nt*. ~**ted** *a* engagiert

committee /kə'mɪtɪ/ *n* Ausschuss *m*, Komitee *nt*

commodity /kə'mɒdətɪ/ *n* Ware *f*

common /'kɒmən/ *a* (-er, -est) gemeinsam; (*frequent*) häufig; (*ordinary*) gewöhnlich; (*vulgar*) ordinär ☐ *n* Gemeindeland *nt*; **have in** ~ gemeinsam haben; **House of C**~**s** Unterhaus *nt*. ~**er** *n* Bürgerliche(r) *m/f*

common: ~ **'law** *n* Gewohnheitsrecht *nt*. ~**ly** *adv* allgemein. **C**~ **'Market** *n* Gemeinsamer Markt *m*. ~**place** *a* häufig. ~**room** *n* Aufenthaltsraum *m*. ~ **'sense** *n* gesunder Menschenverstand *m*

commotion /kə'məʊʃn/ *n* Tumult *m*

communal /'kɒmjʊnl/ *a* gemeinschaftlich

communicable /kə'mju:nɪkəbl/ *a* (*disease*) übertragbar

communicate /kə'mju:nɪkeɪt/ *vt* mitteilen (**to** *dat*); übertragen (*disease*) ☐ *vi* sich verständigen; (*be in touch*) in Verbindung stehen

communication /kəmju:nɪ'keɪʃn/ *n* Verständigung *f*; (*contact*) Verbindung *f*; (*of disease*) Übertragung *f*; (*message*) Mitteilung *f*; ~**s** *pl* (*technology*) Nachrichtenwesen *nt*. ~ **cord** *n* Notbremse *f*

communicative /kə'mju:nɪkətɪv/ *a* mitteilsam

Communion /kə'mju:nɪən/ *n* **[Holy]** ~ das [heilige] Abendmahl; (*Roman Catholic*) die [heilige] Kommunion

communiqué /kə'mju:nɪkeɪ/ *n* Kommuniqué *nt*

Communis|m /'kɒmjʊnɪzm/ *n* Kommunismus *m*. ~**t** /-ɪst/ *a* kommunistisch ☐ *n* Kommunist(in) *m(f)*

community /kə'mju:nətɪ/ *n* Gemeinschaft *f*; local ~ Gemeinde *f*. ~ **centre** *n* Gemeinschaftszentrum *nt*

commute /kə'mju:t/ *vi* pendeln ☐ *vt* (*Jur*) umwandeln. ~**r** *n* Pendler(in) *m(f)*

compact[1] /kəm'pækt/ *a* kompakt

compact[2] /'kɒmpækt/ *n* Puderdose *f*. ~ **disc** *n* CD *f*

companion /kəm'pænjən/ *n* Begleiter(in) *m(f)*. ~**ship** *n* Gesellschaft *f*

company /'kʌmpənɪ/ *n* Gesellschaft *f*; (*firm*) Firma *f*; (*Mil*) Kompanie *f*; (*fam*: guests) Besuch *m*. ~ **car** *n* Firmenwagen *m*

comparable /'kɒmpərəbl/ *a* vergleichbar

comparative /kəm'pærətɪv/ *a* vergleichend; (*relative*) relativ ☐ *n* (*Gram*) Komparativ *m*. ~**ly** *adv* verhältnismäßig

compare /kəm'peə(r)/ *vt* vergleichen (**with**/**to** mit) ☐ *vi* sich vergleichen lassen

comparison /kəm'pærɪsn/ *n* Vergleich *m*

compartment /kəm'pɑ:tmənt/ *n* Fach *nt*; (*Rail*) Abteil *nt*

compass /'kʌmpəs/ *n* Kompass *m*. ~**es** *npl* **pair of** ~**es** Zirkel *m*

compassion /kəm'pæʃn/ *n* Mitleid *nt*. ~**ate** /-ʃənət/ *a* mitfühlend

compatible /kəm'pætəbl/ *a* vereinbar; (*drugs*) verträglich; (*Techn*) kompatibel; **be** ~ ⟨*people*:⟩ [gut] zueinander passen

compatriot /kəm'pætrɪət/ *n* Landsmann *m* /-männin *f*

compel /kəm'pel/ *vt* (*pt/pp* compelled) zwingen

compensat|e /'kɒmpənseɪt/ *vt* entschädigen ☐ *vi* ~**e for** (*fig*) ausgleichen. ~**ion** /-'seɪʃn/ *n* Entschädigung *f*; (*fig*) Ausgleich *m*

compère /'kɒmpeə(r)/ *n* Conférencier *m*

compete /kəm'pi:t/ *vi* konkurrieren; (*take part*) teilnehmen (**in** **an** + *dat*)

competen|ce /'kɒmpɪtəns/ *n* Tüchtigkeit *f*; (*ability*) Fähigkeit *f*; (*Jur*) Kompetenz *f*. ~**t** *a* tüchtig; fähig; (*Jur*) kompetent

competition /kɒmpə'tɪʃn/ *n* Konkurrenz *f*; (*contest*) Wettbewerb *m*; (*in newspaper*) Preisausschreiben *nt*

competitive /kəm'petətɪv/ *a* (*Comm*) konkurrenzfähig

competitor /kəm'petɪtə(r)/ *n* Teilnehmer *m*; (*Comm*) Konkurrent *m*

compile /kəm'paɪl/ *vt* zusammenstellen; verfassen ⟨*dictionary*⟩

complacen|cy /kəm'pleɪsənsɪ/ *n* Selbstzufriedenheit *f*. ~**t** *a*, ~**ly** *adv* selbstzufrieden

complain /kəm'pleɪn/ *vi* klagen (**about**/ **of** über + *acc*); (*formally*) sich beschweren. ~**t** *n* Klage *f*; (*formal*) Beschwerde *f*; (*Med*) Leiden *nt*

complement[1] /'kɒmplɪmənt/ *n* Ergänzung *f*; **full** ~ volle Anzahl *f*

complement[2] /'kɒmplɪment/ *vt* ergänzen; ~ **each other** sich ergänzen. ~**ary** /-'mentərɪ/ *a* sich ergänzend; **be** ~**ary** sich ergänzen

complete /kəm'pli:t/ *a* vollständig; (*finished*) fertig; (*utter*) völlig ☐ *vt* vervollständigen; (*finish*) abschließen; (*fill in*) ausfüllen. ~**ly** *adv* völlig

completion /kəm'pli:ʃn/ n Vervollständigung f; (end) Abschluss m

complex /'kɒmpleks/ a komplex □ n Komplex m

complexion /kəm'plekʃn/ n Teint m; (colour) Gesichtsfarbe f; (fig) Aspekt m

complexity /kəm'pleksətɪ/ n Komplexität f

compliance /kəm'plaɪəns/ n Einverständnis nt; in ~ with gemäß (+ dat)

complicat|e /'kɒmplɪkeɪt/ vt komplizieren. ~ed a kompliziert. ~ion /-'keɪʃn/ n Komplikation f

complicity /kəm'plɪsətɪ/ n Mittäterschaft f

compliment /'kɒmplɪmənt/ n Kompliment nt; ~s pl Grüße pl □ vt ein Kompliment machen (+ dat). ~ary /-'mentərɪ/ a schmeichelhaft; (given free) Frei-

comply /kəm'plaɪ/ vi (pt/pp -ied) ~ with nachkommen (+ dat)

component /kəm'pəʊnənt/ a & n ~ [part] Bestandteil m, Teil nt

compose /kəm'pəʊz/ vt verfassen; (Mus) komponieren; ~ oneself sich fassen; be ~d of sich zusammensetzen aus. ~d a (calm) gefasst. ~r n Komponist m

composition /kɒmpə'zɪʃn/ n Komposition f; (essay) Aufsatz m

compost /'kɒmpɒst/ n Kompost m

composure /kəm'pəʊʒə(r)/ n Fassung f

compound[1] /kəm'paʊnd/ vt (make worse) verschlimmern

compound[2] /'kɒmpaʊnd/ a zusammengesetzt; (fracture) kompliziert □ n (Chem) Verbindung f; (Gram) Kompositum nt; (enclosure) Einfriedigung f. ~ 'interest n Zinseszins m

comprehen|d /kɒmprɪ'hend/ vt begreifen, verstehen; (include) umfassen. ~sible a, -bly adv verständlich. ~sion /-'henʃn/ n Verständnis nt

comprehensive /kɒmprɪ'hensɪv/ a & n umfassend; ~ [school] Gesamtschule f. ~ insurance n (Auto) Vollkaskoversicherung f

compress[1] /'kɒmpres/ n Kompresse f

compress[2] /kəm'pres/ vt zusammenpressen; ~ed air Druckluft f

comprise /kəm'praɪz/ vt umfassen, bestehen aus

compromise /'kɒmprəmaɪz/ n Kompromiss m □ vt kompromittieren (person) □ vi einen Kompromiss schließen

compuls|ion /kəm'pʌlʃn/ n Zwang m. ~ive -sɪv/ a zwanghaft; ~ive eating Esszwang m. ~ory /-sərɪ/ a obligatorisch; ~ory subject Pflichtfach nt

compunction /kəm'pʌŋkʃn/ n Gewissensbisse pl

comput|er /kəm'pju:tə(r)/ n Computer m. ~erize vt computerisieren (data); auf Computer umstellen (firm). ~ing n Computertechnik f

comrade /'kɒmreɪd/ n Kamerad m; (Pol) Genosse m/Genossin f. ~ship n Kameradschaft f

con[1] /kɒn/ see **pro**

con[2] n (fam) Schwindel m □ vt (pt/pp conned) (fam) beschwindeln

concave /'kɒŋkeɪv/ a konkav

conceal /kən'si:l/ vt verstecken; (keep secret) verheimlichen

concede /kən'si:d/ vt zugeben; (give up) aufgeben

conceit /kən'si:t/ n Einbildung f. ~ed a eingebildet

conceivable /kən'si:vəbl/ a denkbar

conceive /kən'si:v/ vt (Biol) empfangen; (fig) sich (dat) ausdenken □ vi schwanger werden. ~ of (fig) sich (dat) vorstellen

concentrat|e /'kɒnsəntreɪt/ vt konzentrieren □ vi sich konzentrieren. ~ion /-'treɪʃn/ n Konzentration f. ~ion camp n Konzentrationslager nt

concept /'kɒnsept/ n Begriff m. ~ion /kən'sepʃn/ n Empfängnis f; (idea) Vorstellung f

concern /kən'sɜ:n/ n Angelegenheit f; (worry) Sorge f; (Comm) Unternehmen nt □ vt (be about, affect) betreffen; (worry) kümmern; be ~ed about besorgt sein um; ~ oneself with sich beschäftigen mit; as far as I am ~ed was mich angeht od betrifft. ~ing prep bezüglich (+ gen)

concert /'kɒnsət/ n Konzert nt; in ~ im Chor. ~ed /kən'sɜ:tɪd/ a gemeinsam

concertina /kɒnsə'ti:nə/ n Konzertina f

'concertmaster n (Amer) Konzertmeister m

concerto /kən'tʃeətəʊ/ n Konzert nt

concession /kən'seʃn/ n Zugeständnis nt; (Comm) Konzession f; (reduction) Ermäßigung f. ~ary a (reduced) ermäßigt

conciliation /kənsɪlɪ'eɪʃn/ n Schlichtung f

concise /kən'saɪs/ a, -ly adv kurz

conclude /kən'klu:d/ vt/i schließen

conclusion /kən'klu:ʒn/ n Schluss m; in ~ abschließend, zum Schluss

conclusive /kən'klu:sɪv/ a schlüssig

concoct /kən'kɒkt/ vt zusammenstellen; (fig) fabrizieren. ~ion /-ɒkʃn/ n Zusammenstellung f; (drink) Gebräu nt

concourse /'kɒŋkɔ:s/ a Halle f

concrete /'kɒŋkri:t/ a konkret □ n Beton m □ vt betonieren concur /kən'kɜ:(r)/ vi (pt/pp concurred) übereinstimmen

concurrently /kən'kʌrəntlı/ adv gleichzeitig

concussion /kən'kʌʃn/ n Gehirnerschütterung f

condemn /kən'dem/ vt verurteilen; (declare unfit) für untauglich erklären. ~ation /kɒndem'neɪʃn/ n Verurteilung f

condensation /kɒnden'seɪʃn/ n Kondensation f

condense /kən'dens/ vt zusammenfassen; (Phys) kondensieren □ vi sich kondensieren. ~d milk n Kondensmilch f

condescend /kɒndɪ'send/ vi sich herablassen (to zu). ~ing a, -ly adv herablassend

condiment /'kɒndɪmənt/ n Gewürz nt

condition /kən'dɪʃn/ n Bedingung f; (state) Zustand m; ~s pl Verhältnisse pl; on ~ that unter der Bedingung, dass □ vt (Psych) konditionieren. ~al a bedingt; be ~al on abhängen von □ n (Gram) Konditional m. ~er n Haarkur f; (for fabrics) Weichspüler m

condolences /kən'dəʊlənsɪz/ npl Beileid nt

condom /'kɒndəm/ n Kondom nt

condominium /kɒndə'mɪnɪəm/ n (Amer) ≈ Eigentumswohnung f

condone /kən'dəʊn/ vt hinwegsehen über (+ acc)

conducive /kən'dju:sɪv/ a förderlich (to dat)

conduct¹ /'kɒndʌkt/ n Verhalten nt; (Sch) Betragen nt

conduct² /kən'dʌkt/ vt führen; (Phys) leiten; (Mus) dirigieren. ~or n Dirigent m; (of bus) Schaffner m; (Phys) Leiter m. ~ress n Schaffnerin f

cone /kəʊn/ n Kegel m; (Bot) Zapfen m; (for ice-cream) [Eis]tüte f; (Auto) Leitkegel m

confectioner /kən'fekʃənə(r)/ n Konditor m. ~y n Süßwaren pl

confederation /kənfedə'reɪʃn/ n Bund m; (Pol) Konföderation f

confer /kən'fɜ:(r)/ v (pt/pp conferred) □ vt verleihen (on dat) □ vi sich beraten

conference /'kɒnfərəns/ n Konferenz f

confess /kən'fes/ vt/i gestehen; (Relig) beichten. ~ion /-eʃn/ n Geständnis nt; (Relig) Beichte f. ~ional /-əʃənəl/ n Beichtstuhl m. ~or n Beichtvater m

confetti /kən'fetɪ/ n Konfetti nt

confide /kən'faɪd/ vt anvertrauen □ vi ~ in s.o. sich jdm anvertrauen

confidence /'kɒnfɪdəns/ n (trust) Vertrauen nt; (self-assurance) Selbstvertrauen nt; (secret) Geheimnis nt; in ~ im Vertrauen. ~ trick n Schwindel m

confident /'kɒnfɪdənt/ a, -ly adv zuversichtlich; (self-assured) selbstsicher

confidential /kɒnfɪ'denʃl/ a, -ly adv vertraulich

confine /kən'faɪn/ vt beschränken (to auf + acc); be ~d to bed das Bett hüten müssen. ~d a (narrow) eng. ~ment n Haft f

confines /'kɒnfaɪnz/ npl Grenzen pl

confirm /kən'fɜ:m/ vt bestätigen; (Relig) konfirmieren; (Roman Catholic) firmen. ~ation /kɒnfə'meɪʃn/ n Bestätigung f; Konfirmation f; Firmung f. ~ed a ~ed bachelor eingefleischter Junggeselle m

confiscat|e /'kɒnfɪskeɪt/ vt beschlagnahmen. ~ion /-'keɪʃn/ n Beschlagnahme f

conflict¹ /'kɒnflɪkt/ n Konflikt m

conflict² /kən'flɪkt/ vi im Widerspruch stehen (with zu). ~ing a widersprüchlich

conform /kən'fɔ:m/ vi (person.) sich anpassen; (thing.) entsprechen (to dat). ~ist n Konformist m

confounded /kən'faʊndɪd/ a (fam) verflixt

confront /kən'frʌnt/ vt konfrontieren. ~ation /kɒnfrən'teɪʃn/ n Konfrontation f

confus|e /kən'fju:z/ vt verwirren; (mistake for) verwechseln (with mit). ~ing a verwirrend. ~ion /-juːʒn/ n Verwirrung f; (muddle) Durcheinander nt

congeal /kən'dʒi:l/ vi fest werden; (blood.) gerinnen

congenial /kən'dʒi:nɪəl/ a angenehm

congenital /kən'dʒenɪtl/ a angeboren

congest|ed /kən'dʒestɪd/ a verstopft; (with people) überfüllt. ~ion /-estʃn/ n Verstopfung f; Überfüllung f

congratulat|e /kən'grætjʊleɪt/ vt gratulieren (+ dat) (on zu). ~ions /-'leɪʃnz/ npl Glückwünsche pl; ~ions! [ich] gratuliere!

congregat|e /'kɒŋgrɪgeɪt/ vi sich versammeln. ~ion /-'geɪʃn/ n (Relig) Gemeinde f

congress /'kɒŋgres/ n Kongress m. ~man n Kongressabgeordnete(r) m

conical /'kɒnɪkl/ a kegelförmig

conifer /'kɒnɪfə(r)/ n Nadelbaum m

conjecture /kən'dʒektʃə(r)/ n Mutmaßung f □ vt/i mutmaßen

conjugal /'kɒndʒʊgl/ a ehelich

conjugat|e /'kɒndʒʊgeɪt/ vt konjugieren. ~ion /-'geɪʃn/ n Konjugation f

conjunction /kən'dʒʌŋkʃn/ n Konjunktion f; in ~ with zusammen mit

conjunctivitis /kəndʒʌŋktɪˈvaɪtɪs/ n Bindehautentzündung f

conjur|e /ˈkʌndʒə(r)/ vi zaubern □ vt ~e up heraufbeschwören. ~or n Zauberkünstler m

conk /kɒŋk/ vi ~ out (fam) ⟨machine:⟩ kaputtgehen; ⟨person:⟩ zusammenklappen

conker /ˈkɒŋkə/ n (fam) Kastanie f

'con-man n (fam) Schwindler m

connect /kəˈnekt/ vt verbinden (to mit); (Electr) anschließen (to an + acc) □ vi verbunden sein; (train:) Anschluss haben (with an + acc); be ~ed with zu tun haben mit; (be related to) verwandt sein mit

connection /kəˈnekʃn/ n Verbindung f; (Rail, Electr) Anschluss m; in ~ with in Zusammenhang mit. ~s npl Beziehungen pl

conniv|ance /kəˈnaɪvəns/ n stillschweigende Duldung f. ~e vi ~e at stillschweigend dulden

connoisseur /kɒnəˈsɜː(r)/ n Kenner m

connotation /kɒnəˈteɪʃn/ n Assoziation f

conquer /ˈkɒŋkə(r)/ vt erobern; (fig) besiegen. ~or n Eroberer m

conquest /ˈkɒŋkwest/ n Eroberung f

conscience /ˈkɒnʃəns/ n Gewissen nt

conscientious /kɒnʃɪˈenʃəs/ a, -ly adv gewissenhaft. ~ ob'jector n Kriegsdienstverweigerer m

conscious /ˈkɒnʃəs/ a, -ly adv bewusst; [fully] ~ bei [vollem] Bewusstsein; be/ become ~ of sth sich (dat) etw (gen) bewusst sein/werden. ~ness n Bewusstsein nt

conscript¹ /ˈkɒnskrɪpt/ n Einberufene(r) m

conscript² /kənˈskrɪpt/ vt einberufen. ~ion /-ɪpʃn/ n allgemeine Wehrpflicht f

consecrat|e /ˈkɒnsɪkreɪt/ vt weihen; einweihen ⟨church⟩. ~ion /-ˈkreɪʃn/ n Weihe f; Einweihung f

consecutive /kənˈsekjʊtɪv/ a aufeinanderfolgend. -ly adv fortlaufend

consensus /kənˈsensəs/ n Übereinstimmung f

consent /kənˈsent/ n Einwilligung f, Zustimmung f □ vi einwilligen (to in + acc), zustimmen (to dat)

consequen|ce /ˈkɒnsɪkwəns/ n Folge f; (importance) Bedeutung f. ~t a daraus folgend. ~tly adv folglich

conservation /kɒnsəˈveɪʃn/ n Erhaltung f, Bewahrung f. ~ist n Umweltschützer m

conservative /kənˈsɜːvətɪv/ a konservativ; ⟨estimate⟩ vorsichtig. C~ (Pol) a konservativ □ n Konservative(r) m/f

conservatory /kənˈsɜːvətrɪ/ n Wintergarten m

conserve /kənˈsɜːv/ vt erhalten, bewahren; sparen ⟨energy⟩

consider /kənˈsɪdə(r)/ vt erwägen; (think over) sich (dat) überlegen; (take into account) berücksichtigen; ⟨regard as⟩ betrachten als; ~ doing sth erwägen, etw zu tun. ~able /-əbl/ a, -bly adv erheblich

consider|ate /kənˈsɪdərət/ a, -ly adv rücksichtsvoll. ~ation /-ˈreɪʃn/ n Erwägung f; (thoughtfulness) Rücksicht f; (payment) Entgelt nt; take into ~ation berücksichtigen. ~ing prep wenn man bedenkt (that dass); ~ing the circumstances unter den Umständen

consign /kənˈsaɪn/ vt übergeben (to dat). ~ment n Lieferung f

consist /kənˈsɪst/ vi ~ of bestehen aus

consisten|cy /kənˈsɪstənsɪ/ n Konsequenz f; (density) Konsistenz f. ~t a konsequent; (unchanging) gleichbleibend; be ~t with entsprechen (+ dat). ~tly adv konsequent; (constantly) ständig

consolation /kɒnsəˈleɪʃn/ n Trost m. ~ prize n Trostpreis m

console /kənˈsəʊl/ vt trösten

consolidate /kənˈsɒlɪdeɪt/ vt konsolidieren

consonant /ˈkɒnsənənt/ n Konsonant m

consort /ˈkɒnsɔːt/ n Gemahl(in) m(f)

conspicuous /kənˈspɪkjʊəs/ a auffällig

conspiracy /kənˈspɪrəsɪ/ n Verschwörung f

conspire /kənˈspaɪə(r)/ vi sich verschwören

constable /ˈkʌnstəbl/ n Polizist m

constant /ˈkɒnstənt/ a, -ly adv beständig; (continuous) ständig

constellation /kɒnstəˈleɪʃn/ n Sternbild nt

consternation /kɒnstəˈneɪʃn/ n Bestürzung f

constipat|ed /ˈkɒnstɪpeɪtɪd/ a verstopft. ~ion /-ˈpeɪʃn/ n Verstopfung f

constituency /kənˈstɪtjʊənsɪ/ n Wahlkreis m

constituent /kənˈstɪtjʊənt/ n Bestandteil m; (Pol) Wähler(in) m(f)

constitut|e /ˈkɒnstɪtjuːt/ vt bilden. ~ion /-ˈtjuːʃn/ n (Pol) Verfassung f; (of person) Konstitution f. ~ional /-ˈtjuːʃənl/ a Verfassungs- □ n Verdauungsspaziergang m

constrain /kən'streɪn/ vt zwingen. ∼t n Zwang m; (restriction) Beschränkung f; (strained manner) Gezwungenheit f

constrict /kən'strɪkt/ vt einengen

construct /kən'strʌkt/ vt bauen. ∼ion /-ʌkʃn/ n Bau m; (Gram) Konstruktion f; (interpretation) Deutung f; under ∼ion im Bau. ∼ive /-ɪv/ a konstruktiv

construe /kən'stru:/ vt deuten

consul /'kɒnsl/ n Konsul m. ∼ate /'kɒnsjʊlət/ n Konsulat nt

consult /kən'sʌlt/ vt [um Rat] fragen; konsultieren (doctor); nachschlagen in (+ dat) ⟨book⟩. ∼ant n Berater m; (Med) Chefarzt m. ∼ation /kɒnsl'teɪʃn/ n Beratung f; (Med) Konsultation f

consume /kən'sju:m/ vt verzehren; (use) verbrauchen. ∼r n Verbraucher m. ∼r goods npl Konsumgüter pl

consummat|e /'kɒnsəmeɪt/ vt vollziehen. ∼ion /-'meɪʃn/ n Vollzug m

consumption /kən'sʌmpʃn/ n Konsum m; (use) Verbrauch m

contact /'kɒntækt/ n Kontakt m; (person) Kontaktperson f ▯ vt sich in Verbindung setzen mit. ∼ 'lenses npl Kontaktlinsen pl

contagious /kən'teɪdʒəs/ a direkt übertragbar

contain /kən'teɪn/ vt enthalten; (control) beherrschen. ∼er n Behälter m; (Comm) Container m

contaminat|e /kən'tæmɪneɪt/ vt verseuchen. ∼ion /-'neɪʃn/ n Verseuchung f

contemplat|e /'kɒntəmpleɪt/ vt betrachten; (meditate) nachdenken über (+ acc); ∼e doing sth daran denken, etw zu tun. ∼ion /-'pleɪʃn/ n Betrachtung f; Nachdenken nt

contemporary /kən'tempərərɪ/ a zeitgenössisch ▯ n Zeitgenosse m/ -genossin f

contempt /kən'tempt/ n Verachtung f; beneath ∼ verabscheuungswürdig; ∼ of court Missachtung f des Gerichts. ∼ible /-əbl/ a verachtenswert. ∼uous /-tjʊəs/ a, -ly adv verächtlich

contend /kən'tend/ vi kämpfen (with mit) ▯ vt (assert) behaupten. ∼er n Bewerber(in) m(f); (Sport) Wettkämpfer(in) m(f)

content[1] /'kɒntent/ n & contents pl Inhalt m

content[2] /kən'tent/ a zufrieden ▯ n to one's heart's ∼ nach Herzenslust ▯ vt ∼ oneself sich begnügen (with mit). ∼ed a, -ly adv zufrieden

contention /kən'tenʃn/ n (assertion) Behauptung f

contentment /kən'tentmənt/ n Zufriedenheit f

contest[1] /'kɒntest/ n Kampf m; (competition) Wettbewerb m

contest[2] /kən'test/ vt (dispute) bestreiten; (Jur) anfechten; (Pol) kandidieren in (+ dat). ∼ant n Teilnehmer m

context /'kɒntekst/ n Zusammenhang m

continent /'kɒntɪnənt/ n Kontinent m

continental /kɒntɪ'nentl/ a Kontinental-. ∼ breakfast n kleines Frühstück nt. ∼ quilt n Daunendecke f

contingen|cy /kən'tɪndʒənsɪ/ n Eventualität f. ∼t a be ∼t upon abhängen von ▯ n (Mil) Kontingent nt

continual /kən'tɪnjʊəl/ a, -ly adv dauernd

continuation /kəntɪnjʊ'eɪʃn/ n Fortsetzung f

continue /kən'tɪnju:/ vt fortsetzen; ∼ doing or to do sth fortfahren, etw zu tun; to be ∼d Fortsetzung folgt ▯ vi weitergehen; (doing sth) weitermachen; (speaking) fortfahren; ⟨weather:⟩ anhalten

continuity /kɒntɪ'nju:ətɪ/ n Kontinuität f

continuous /kən'tɪnjʊəs/ a, -ly adv anhaltend, ununterbrochen

contort /kən'tɔ:t/ vt verzerren. ∼ion /-ɔ:ʃn/ n Verzerrung f

contour /'kɒntʊə(r)/ n Kontur f; (line) Höhenlinie f

contraband /'kɒntrəbænd/ n Schmuggelware f

contracep|tion /kɒntrə'sepʃn/ n Empfängnisverhütung f. ∼tive /-tɪv/ a empfängnisverhütend ▯ n Empfängnisverhütungsmittel nt

contract[1] /'kɒntrækt/ n Vertrag m

contract[2] /kən'trækt/ vi sich zusammenziehen ▯ vt zusammenziehen; sich (dat) zuziehen (illness). ∼ion /-ækʃn/ n Zusammenziehung f; (abbreviation) Abkürzung f; (in childbirth) Wehe f. ∼or n Unternehmer m

contradict /kɒntrə'dɪkt/ vt widersprechen (+ dat). ∼ion /-ɪkʃn/ n Widerspruch m. ∼ory /-ərɪ/ a widersprüchlich

contra-flow /'kɒntrə-/ n Umleitung f [auf die entgegengesetzte Fahrbahn]

contralto /kən'træltəʊ/ n Alt m; (singer) Altistin f

contraption /kən'træpʃn/ n (fam) Apparat m

contrary[1] /'kɒntrərɪ/ a & adv entgegengesetzt; ∼ to entgegen (+ dat) ▯ n Gegenteil nt; on the ∼ im Gegenteil

contrary[2] /kən'treərɪ/ a widerspenstig

contrast[1] /'kɒntrɑ:st/ n Kontrast m

contrast[2] /kən'trɑ:st/ vt gegenüberstellen (with dat) ▯ vi einen Kontrast bilden (with zu). ~ing a gegensätzlich; ⟨colour⟩ Kontrast-

contraven|e /kɒntrə'viːn/ vt verstoßen gegen. ~tion /-'venʃn/ n Verstoß m (of gegen)

contribut|e /kən'trɪbjuːt/ vt/i beitragen; beisteuern ⟨money⟩; ⟨donate⟩ spenden. ~ion /kɒntrɪ'bjuːʃn/ n Beitrag m; ⟨donation⟩ Spende f. ~or n Beitragende(r) m/f

contrite /kən'traɪt/ a reuig

contrivance /kən'traɪvəns/ n Vorrichtung f

contrive /kən'traɪv/ vt verfertigen; ~ to do sth es fertig bringen, etw zu tun

control /kən'trəʊl/ n Kontrolle f; ⟨mastery⟩ Beherrschung f; ⟨Techn⟩ Regler m; ~s pl ⟨of car, plane⟩ Steuerung f; get out of ~ außer Kontrolle geraten □ vt ⟨pt/pp controlled⟩ kontrollieren; ⟨restrain⟩ unter Kontrolle halten; ~ oneself sich beherrschen

controvers|ial /kɒntrə'vɜːʃl/ a umstritten. ~y /'kɒntrəvɜːsɪ/ n Kontroverse f

conundrum /kə'nʌndrəm/ n Rätsel nt

conurbation /kɒnɜː'beɪʃn/ n Ballungsgebiet nt

convalesce /kɒnvə'les/ vi sich erholen. ~nce n Erholung f

convalescent /kɒnvə'lesnt/ a be ~ noch erholungsbedürftig sein. ~ home n Erholungsheim nt

convector /kən'vektə(r)/ n ~ [heater] Konvektor m

convene /kən'viːn/ vt einberufen □ vi sich versammeln

convenience /kən'viːnɪəns/ n Bequemlichkeit f; [public] ~ öffentliche Toilette f; with all modern ~s mit allem Komfort

convenient /kən'viːnɪənt/ a, -ly adv günstig; be ~ for s.o. jdm gelegen sein od jdm passen; if it is ~ [for you] wenn es Ihnen passt

convent /'kɒnvənt/ n [Nonnen]kloster nt

convention /kən'venʃn/ n ⟨custom⟩ Brauch m, Sitte f; ⟨agreement⟩ Konvention f; ⟨assembly⟩ Tagung f. ~al a, -ly adv konventionell

converge /kən'vɜːdʒ/ vi zusammenlaufen

conversant /kən'vɜːsənt/ a ~ with vertraut mit

conversation /kɒnvə'seɪʃn/ n Gespräch nt; ⟨Sch⟩ Konversation f

converse¹ /kən'vɜːs/ vi sich unterhalten

converse² /'kɒnvɜːs/ n Gegenteil nt. ~ly adv umgekehrt

conversion /kən'vɜːʃn/ n Umbau m; ⟨Relig⟩ Bekehrung f; ⟨calculation⟩ Umrechnung f

convert¹ /'kɒnvɜːt/ n Bekehrte(r) m/f, Konvertit m

convert² /kən'vɜːt/ vt bekehren ⟨person⟩; ⟨change⟩ umwandeln (into in + acc); umbauen ⟨building⟩; ⟨calculate⟩ umrechnen; ⟨Techn⟩ umstellen. ~ible /-ɪbl/ -əbl/ a verwandelbar □ n ⟨Auto⟩ Kabriolett nt

convex /'kɒnveks/ a konvex

convey /kən'veɪ/ vt befördern; vermitteln ⟨idea, message⟩. ~ance n Beförderung f; ⟨vehicle⟩ Beförderungsmittel nt. ~or belt n Förderband nt

convict¹ /'kɒnvɪkt/ n Sträfling m

convict² /kən'vɪkt/ vt verurteilen (of wegen). ~ion /-ɪkʃn/ n Verurteilung f; ⟨belief⟩ Überzeugung f; previous ~ion Vorstrafe f

convinc|e /kən'vɪns/ vt überzeugen. ~ing a, -ly adv überzeugend

convivial /kən'vɪvɪəl/ a gesellig

convoluted /'kɒnvəluːtɪd/ a verschlungen; ⟨fig⟩ verwickelt

convoy /'kɒnvɔɪ/ n Konvoi m

convuls|e /kən'vʌls/ vt be ~edsich krümmen (with vor + dat). ~ion /-ʌlʃn/ n Krampf m

coo /kuː/ vi gurren

cook /kʊk/ n Koch m/ Köchin f □ vt/i kochen; is it ~ed? ist es gar? ~ the books ⟨fam⟩ die Bilanz frisieren. ~book n ⟨Amer⟩ Kochbuch nt

cooker /'kʊkə(r)/ n [Koch]herd m; ⟨apple⟩ Kochapfel m. ~y n Kochen nt. ~y book n Kochbuch nt

cookie /'kʊkɪ/ n ⟨Amer⟩ Keks m

cool /kuːl/ a (-er, -est), -ly adv kühl □ n Kühle f □ vt kühlen □ vi abkühlen. ~box n Kühlbox f. ~ness n Kühle f

coop /kuːp/ n [Hühner]stall m □ vt ~ up einsperren

co-operat|e /kəʊ'ɒpəreɪt/ vi zusammenarbeiten. ~ion /-'reɪʃn/ n Kooperation f

co-operative /kəʊ'ɒpərətɪv/ a hilfsbereit □ n Genossenschaft f

co-opt /kəʊ'ɒpt/ vt hinzuwählen

co-ordinat|e /kəʊ'ɔːdɪneɪt/ vt koordinieren. ~ion /-'neɪʃn/ n Koordination f

cop /kɒp/ n ⟨fam⟩ Polizist m

cope /kəʊp/ vi ⟨fam⟩ zurechtkommen; ~ with fertig werden mit

copious /'kəʊpɪəs/ a reichlich

copper¹ /'kɒpə(r)/ n Kupfer nt; ~s pl Kleingeld nt □ a kupfern

copper² n ⟨fam⟩ Polizist m

copper 'beech n Blutbuche f

coppice /'kɒpɪs/ n, **copse** /kɒps/ n Gehölz nt

copulate /'kɒpjʊleɪt/ vi sich begatten

copy /'kɒpɪ/ n Kopie f; (book) Exemplar nt □ vt (pt/pp -ied) kopieren; (imitate) nachahmen; (Sch) abschreiben

copy: ~right n Copyright nt. ~-writer n Texter m

coral /'kɒrl/ n Koralle f

cord /kɔːd/ n Schnur f; (fabric) Cordsamt m; ~s pl Cordhose f

cordial /'kɔːdɪəl/ a, -ly adv herzlich □ n Fruchtsirup m

cordon /'kɔːdn/ n Kordon m □ vt ~ off absperren

corduroy /'kɔːdərɔɪ/ n Cordsamt m

core /kɔː(r)/ n Kern m; (of apple, pear) Kerngehäuse nt

cork /kɔːk/ n Kork m; (for bottle) Korken m. ~screw n Korkenzieher m

corn¹ /kɔːn/ n Korn nt; (Amer: maize) Mais m

corn² n (Med) Hühnerauge nt

cornea /'kɔːnɪə/ n Hornhaut f

corned beef /kɔːnd'biːf/ n Cornedbeef nt

corner /'kɔːnə(r)/ n Ecke f; (bend) Kurve f; (football) Eckball m □ vt (fig) in die Enge treiben; (Comm) monopolisieren ⟨market⟩. ~stone n Eckstein m

cornet /'kɔːnɪt/ n (Mus) Kornett nt; (for ice-cream) [Eis]tüte f

corn: ~flour n, (Amer) ~starch n Stärkemehl nt

corny /'kɔːnɪ/ a (fam) abgedroschen

coronary /'kɒrənərɪ/ a & n ~ [thrombosis] Koronarthrombose f

coronation /kɒrə'neɪʃn/ n Krönung f

coroner /'kɒrənə(r)/ n Beamte(r) m, der verdächtige Todesfälle untersucht

coronet /'kɒrənət/ n Adelskrone f

corporal¹ /'kɔːpərəl/ n (Mil) Stabsunteroffizier m

corporal² a körperlich; ~ punishment körperliche Züchtigung f

corporate /'kɔːpərət/ a gemeinschaftlich

corporation /kɔːpə'reɪʃn/ n Körperschaft f; (of town) Stadtverwaltung f

corps /kɔː(r)/ n (pl corps /kɔːz/) Korps nt

corpse /kɔːps/ n Leiche f

corpulent /'kɔːpjʊlənt/ a korpulent

corpuscle /'kɔːpʌsl/ n Blutkörperchen nt

correct /kə'rekt/ a, -ly adv richtig; (proper) korrekt □ vt verbessern; (Sch, Typ) korrigieren. ~ion /-ekʃn/ n Verbesserung f; (Typ) Korrektur f

correlation /kɒrə'leɪʃn/ n Wechselbeziehung f

correspond /kɒrɪ'spɒnd/ vi entsprechen (to dat); ⟨two things:⟩ sich entsprechen;

(write) korrespondieren. ~ence n Briefwechsel m; (Comm) Korrespondenz f. ~ent n Korrespondent(in) m(f). ~ing a, -ly adv entsprechend

corridor /'kɒrɪdɔː(r)/ n Gang m; (Pol, Aviat) Korridor m

corroborate /kə'rɒbəreɪt/ vt bestätigen

corro|de /kə'rəʊd/ vt zerfressen □ vi rosten. ~sion /-'rəʊʒn/ n Korrosion f

corrugated /'kɒrəgeɪtɪd/ a gewellt. ~ iron n Wellblech nt

corrupt /kə'rʌpt/ a korrupt □ vt korrumpieren; (spoil) verderben. ~ion /-ʌpʃn/ n Korruption f

corset /'kɔːsɪt/ n & -s pl Korsett nt

Corsica /'kɔːsɪkə/ n Korsika nt

cortège /kɔː'teɪʒ/ n [funeral] ~ Leichenzug m

cosh /kɒʃ/ n Totschläger m

cosmetic /kɒz'metɪk/ a kosmetisch □ n ~s pl Kosmetika pl

cosmic /'kɒzmɪk/ a kosmisch

cosmonaut /'kɒzmənɔːt/ n Kosmonaut(in) m(f)

cosmopolitan /kɒzmə'pɒlɪtən/ a kosmopolitisch

cosmos /'kɒzmɒs/ n Kosmos m

cosset /'kɒsɪt/ vt verhätscheln

cost /kɒst/ n Kosten pl; ~s pl (Jur) Kosten; at all ~s um jeden Preis; I learnt to my ~ es ist mich teuer zu stehen gekommen □ vt (pt/pp cost) kosten; it ~ me £20 es hat mich £20 gekostet □ vt (pt/pp costed) ~ [out] die Kosten kalkulieren für

costly /'kɒstlɪ/ a (-ier, -iest) teuer

cost: ~ of 'living n Lebenshaltungskosten pl. ~ price n Selbstkostenpreis m

costume /'kɒstjuːm/ n Kostüm nt; (national) Tracht f. ~ jewellery n Modeschmuck m

cosy /'kəʊzɪ/ a (-ier, -iest) gemütlich □ n (tea-, egg-) Wärmer m

cot /kɒt/ n Kinderbett nt; (Amer: camp-bed) Feldbett nt

cottage /'kɒtɪdʒ/ n Häuschen nt. ~ 'cheese n Hüttenkäse m

cotton /'kɒtn/ n Baumwolle f; (thread) Nähgarn nt □ a baumwollen □ vi ~ on (fam) kapieren

cotton 'wool n Watte f

couch /kaʊtʃ/ n Liege f

couchette /kuː'ʃet/ n (Rail) Liegeplatz m

cough /kɒf/ n Husten m □ vi husten. ~ up vt/i husten; (fam: pay) blechen

'cough mixture n Hustensaft m

could /kʊd, unbetont kəd/ see can²

council /'kaʊnsl/ n Rat m; (Admin) Stadtverwaltung f; (rural) Gemeindeverwaltung f. ~ house n ≈ Sozialwohnung f

councillor /'kaʊnsələ(r)/ n Stadtverordnete(r) m/f

'council tax n Gemeindesteuer f

counsel /'kaʊnsl/ n Rat m; (Jur) Anwalt m □ vt (pt/pp counselled) beraten. ∼lor n Berater(in) m(f)

count¹ /kaʊnt/ n Graf m

count² n Zählung f; keep ∼ zählen □ vt/i zählen. ∼ on vt rechnen auf (+ acc)

countenance /'kaʊntənəns/ n Gesicht nt □ vt dulden

counter¹ /'kaʊntə(r)/ n (in shop) Ladentisch m; (in bank) Schalter m; (in café) Theke f; (Games) Spielmarke f

counter² adv ∼ to gegen (+ acc) □ a Gegen- □ vt/i kontern

counter'act vt entgegenwirken (+ dat)

'counter-attack n Gegenangriff m

counter-'espionage n Spionageabwehr f

'counterfeit /-fɪt/ a gefälscht □ n Fälschung f □ vt fälschen

'counterfoil n Kontrollabschnitt m

'counterpart n Gegenstück nt

counter-pro'ductive a be ∼ das Gegenteil bewirken

'countersign vt gegenzeichnen

countess /'kaʊntɪs/ n Gräfin f

countless /'kaʊntlɪs/ a unzählig

countrified /'kʌntrɪfaɪd/ a ländlich

country /'kʌntrɪ/ n Land nt; (native land) Heimat f; (countryside) Landschaft f; in the ∼ auf dem Lande. ∼man n (fellow) ∼man Landsmann m. ∼side n Landschaft f

county /'kaʊntɪ/ n Grafschaft f

coup /ku:/ n (Pol) Staatsstreich m

couple /'kʌpl/ n Paar nt; a ∼ of (two) zwei □ vt verbinden; (Rail) koppeln

coupon /'ku:pɒn/ n Kupon m; (voucher) Gutschein m; (entry form) Schein m

courage /'kʌrɪdʒ/ n Mut m. ∼ous /kə-'reɪdʒəs/ a, -ly adv mutig

courgettes /kʊə'ʒets/ npl Zucchini pl

courier /'kʊrɪə(r)/ n Bote m; (diplomatic) Kurier m; (for tourists) Reiseleiter(in) m(f)

course /kɔ:s/ n (Naut, Sch) Kurs m; (Culin) Gang m; (for golf) Platz m; ∼ of treatment (Med) Kur f; of ∼ natürlich, selbstverständlich; in the ∼ of im Lauf[e] (+ gen)

court /kɔ:t/ n Hof m; (Sport) Platz m; (Jur) Gericht nt □ vt werben um; herausfordern ⟨danger⟩

courteous /'kɜ:tɪəs/ a, -ly adv höflich

courtesy /'kɜ:təsɪ/ n Höflichkeit f

court: ∼ 'martial n (pl ∼s martial) Militärgericht nt. ∼ shoes npl Pumps pl. ∼yard n Hof m

cousin /'kʌzn/ n Vetter m, Cousin m; (female) Kusine f

cove /kəʊv/ n kleine Bucht f

cover /'kʌvə(r)/ n Decke f; (of cushion) Bezug m; (of umbrella) Hülle f; (of typewriter) Haube f; (of book; lid) Deckel m; (of magazine) Umschlag m; (protection) Deckung f, Schutz m; take ∼ Deckung nehmen; under separate ∼ mit getrennter Post □ vt bedecken; beziehen ⟨cushion⟩; decken ⟨costs, needs⟩; zurücklegen ⟨distance⟩; (Journ) berichten über (+ acc); (insure) versichern. ∼ up vt zudecken; (fig) vertuschen

coverage /'kʌvərɪdʒ/ n (Journ) Berichterstattung f (of über + acc)

cover: ∼ charge n Gedeck nt. ∼ing n Decke f; (for floor) Belag m. ∼-up n Vertuschung f

covet /'kʌvɪt/ vt begehren

cow /kaʊ/ n Kuh f

coward /'kaʊəd/ n Feigling m. ∼ice /-ɪs/ n Feigheit f. ∼ly a feige

'cowboy n Cowboy m; (fam) unsolider Handwerker m

cower /'kaʊə(r)/ vi sich [ängstlich] ducken

'cowshed n Kuhstall m

cox /kɒks/ n, coxswain /'kɒksn/ n Steuermann m

coy /kɔɪ/ a (-er, -est) gespielt schüchtern

crab /kræb/ n Krabbe f. ∼-apple n Holzapfel m

crack /kræk/ n Riss m; (in china, glass) Sprung m; (noise) Knall m; (fam: joke) Witz m; (fam: attempt) Versuch m □ a (fam) erstklassig □ vt knacken ⟨nut, code⟩; einen Sprung machen in (+ acc) ⟨china, glass⟩; (fam) reißen ⟨joke⟩; (fam) lösen ⟨problem⟩ □ vi ⟨china, glass:⟩ springen; ⟨whip:⟩ knallen. ∼ down (on) (fam) durchgreifen

cracked /krækt/ a gesprungen; ⟨rib⟩ angebrochen; (fam: crazy) verrückt

cracker /'krækə(r)/ n (biscuit) Kräcker m; (firework) Knallkörper m; [Christmas] ∼ Knallbonbon m. ∼s a be ∼s (fam) einen Knacks haben

crackle /'krækl/ vi knistern

cradle /'kreɪdl/ n Wiege f

craft¹ /krɑ:ft/ n inv (boat) [Wasser]-fahrzeug nt

craft² n Handwerk nt; (technique) Fertigkeit f. ∼sman n Handwerker m

crafty /'krɑ:ftɪ/ a (-ier, -iest), -ily adv gerissen

crag /kræg/ n Felszacken m. ∼gy a felsig; ⟨face⟩ kantig

cram /kræm/ v (pt/pp crammed) □ vt hineinstopfen (into in + acc); vollstopfen (with mit) □ vi (for exams) pauken

cramp /kræmp/ n Krampf m. ~ed a eng

crampon /'kræmpən/ n Steigeisen nt

cranberry /'krænbəri/ n (Culin) Preiselbeere f

crane /kreɪn/ n Kran m; (bird) Kranich m □ vt ~ one's neck den Hals recken

crank¹ /kræŋk/ n (fam) Exzentriker m

crank² n (Techn) Kurbel f. ~shaft n Kurbelwelle f

cranky /'kræŋkɪ/ a exzentrisch; (Amer: irritable) reizbar

cranny /'krænɪ/ n Ritze f

crash /kræʃ/ n (noise) Krach m; (Auto) Zusammenstoß m; (Aviat) Absturz m □ vi krachen (into gegen); ⟨cars:⟩ zusammenstoßen; ⟨plane:⟩ abstürzen □ vt einen Unfall haben mit ⟨car⟩

crash: ~ course n Schnellkurs m. ~-helmet n Sturzhelm m. ~-landing n Bruchlandung f

crate /kreɪt/ n Kiste f

crater /'kreɪtə(r)/ n Krater m

cravat /krə'væt/ n Halstuch nt

crav|e /kreɪv/ vi ~e for sich sehnen nach. ~ing n Gelüst nt

crawl /krɔːl/ n (Swimming) Kraul nt; do the ~ kraulen; at a ~ im Kriechtempo □ vi kriechen; ⟨baby:⟩ krabbeln; ~ with wimmeln von. ~er lane n (Auto) Kriechspur f

crayon /'kreɪən/ n Wachsstift m; (pencil) Buntstift m

craze /kreɪz/ n Mode f

crazy /'kreɪzɪ/ a (-ier, -iest) verrückt; be ~ about verrückt sein nach

creak /kriːk/ n Knarren nt □ vi knarren

cream /kriːm/ n Sahne f; (Cosmetic, Med, Culin) Creme f □ a (colour) cremefarben □ vt (Culin) cremig rühren. ~ 'cheese n ≈ Quark m. ~y a sahnig; (smooth) cremig

crease /kriːs/ n Falte f; (unwanted) Knitterfalte f □ vt falten; (accidentally) zerknittern □ vi knittern. ~-resistant a knitterfrei

creat|e /kriː'eɪt/ vt schaffen. ~ion /-'eɪʃn/ n Schöpfung f. ~ive /-tɪv/ a schöpferisch. ~or n Schöpfer m

creature /'kriːtʃə(r)/ n Geschöpf nt

crèche /kreʃ/ n Kinderkrippe f

credentials /krɪ'denʃlz/ npl Beglaubigungsschreiben nt

credibility /kredə'bɪlɪtɪ/ n Glaubwürdigkeit f

credible /'kredəbl/ a glaubwürdig

credit /'kredɪt/ n Kredit m; (honour) Ehre f □ vt glauben; ~ s.o. with sth (Comm)

jdm etw gutschreiben; (fig) jdm etw zuschreiben. ~able /-əbl/ a lobenswert

credit: ~ card n Kreditkarte f. ~or n Gläubiger m

creed /kriːd/ n Glaubensbekenntnis nt

creek /kriːk/ n enge Bucht f; (Amer: stream) Bach m

creep /kriːp/ vi (pt/pp crept) schleichen □ n (fam) fieser Kerl m; it gives me the ~s es ist mir unheimlich. ~er n Kletterpflanze f. ~y a gruselig

cremat|e /krɪ'meɪt/ vt einäschern. ~ion /-'eɪʃn/ n Einäscherung f

crematorium /kremə'tɔːrɪəm/ n Krematorium nt

crêpe /kreɪp/ n Krepp m. ~ paper n Krepppapier nt

crept /krept/ see creep

crescent /'kresənt/ n Halbmond m

cress /kres/ n Kresse f

crest /krest/ n Kamm m; (coat of arms) Wappen nt

Crete /kriːt/ n Kreta nt

crevasse /krɪ'væs/ n [Gletscher]spalte f

crevice /'krevɪs/ n Spalte f

crew /kruː/ n Besatzung f; (gang) Bande f. ~ cut n Bürstenschnitt m

crib¹ /krɪb/ n Krippe f

crib² vt/i (pt/pp cribbed) (fam) abschreiben

crick /krɪk/ n ~ in the neck steifes Genick nt

cricket¹ /'krɪkɪt/ n (insect) Grille f

cricket² n Kricket nt. ~er n Kricketspieler m

crime /kraɪm/ n Verbrechen nt; (rate) Kriminalität f

criminal /'krɪmɪnl/ a kriminell, verbrecherisch; ⟨law, court⟩ Straf- □ n Verbrecher m

crimson /'krɪmzn/ a purpurrot

cringe /krɪndʒ/ vi sich [ängstlich] ducken

crinkle /'krɪŋkl/ vt/i knittern

cripple /'krɪpl/ n Krüppel m □ vt zum Krüppel machen; (fig) lahm legen. ~d a verkrüppelt

crisis /'kraɪsɪs/ n (pl -ses /-siːz/) Krise f

crisp /krɪsp/ a (-er, -est) knusprig. ~bread n Knäckebrot nt. ~s npl Chips pl

criss-cross /'krɪs-/ a schräg gekreuzt

criterion /kraɪ'tɪərɪən/ n (pl -ria /-rɪə/) Kriterium nt

critic /'krɪtɪk/ n Kritiker m. ~al a kritisch. ~ally adv kritisch; ~ally ill schwer krank

criticism /'krɪtɪsɪzm/ n Kritik f

criticize /'krɪtɪsaɪz/ vt kritisieren

croak /krəʊk/ vi krächzen; ⟨frog:⟩ quaken

crochet /'krəʊʃeɪ/ n Häkelarbeit f □ vt/i häkeln. ~-hook n Häkelnadel f

crock /krɒk/ n ⟨fam⟩ old ~ ⟨person⟩ Wrack m; ⟨car⟩ Klapperkiste f

crockery /'krɒkərɪ/ n Geschirr nt

crocodile /'krɒkədaɪl/ n Krokodil nt

crocus /'krəʊkəs/ n ⟨pl -es⟩ Krokus m

crony /'krəʊnɪ/ n Kumpel m

crook /krʊk/ n ⟨stick⟩ Stab m; ⟨fam: criminal⟩ Schwindler m, Gauner m

crooked /'krʊkɪd/ a schief; ⟨bent⟩ krumm; ⟨fam: dishonest⟩ unehrlich

crop /krɒp/ n Feldfrucht f; ⟨harvest⟩ Ernte f; ⟨of bird⟩ Kropf m □ v ⟨pt/pp cropped⟩ □ vt stutzen □ vi ~ up ⟨fam⟩ zur Sprache kommen; ⟨occur⟩ dazwischenkommen

croquet /'krəʊkeɪ/ n Krocket nt

croquette /krəʊ'ket/ n Krokette f

cross /krɒs/ a, -ly adv ⟨annoyed⟩ böse ⟨with auf + acc⟩; talk at ~ purposes aneinander vorbeireden □ n Kreuz nt; ⟨Bot, Zool⟩ Kreuzung f; on the ~ schräg □ vt kreuzen ⟨cheque, animals⟩; überqueren ⟨road⟩; ~ oneself sich bekreuzigen; ~ one's arms die Arme verschränken; ~ one's legs die Beine übereinander schlagen; keep one's fingers ~ed for s.o. jdm die Daumen drücken; it ~ed my mind es fiel mir ein □ vi ⟨go across⟩ hinübergehen/-fahren; ⟨lines:⟩ sich kreuzen. ~ out vt durchstreichen

cross: ~bar n Querlatte f; ⟨on bicycle⟩ Stange f. ~-'country n ⟨Sport⟩ Crosslauf m. ~-ex'amine vt ins Kreuzverhör nehmen. ~-exami'nation n Kreuzverhör nt. ~-'eyed a schielend; be ~-eyed schielen. ~fire n Kreuzfeuer nt. ~ing n Übergang m; ⟨sea journey⟩ Überfahrt f. ~-'reference n Querverweis m. ~roads n [Straßen]kreuzung f. ~-'section n Querschnitt m. ~-'stitch n Kreuzstich m. ~wise adv quer. ~word n ~word [puzzle] Kreuzworträtsel nt

crotchet /'krɒtʃɪt/ n Viertelnote f

crotchety /'krɒtʃɪtɪ/ a griesgrämig

crouch /kraʊtʃ/ vi kauern

crow /krəʊ/ n Krähe f; as the ~ flies Luftlinie □ vi krähen. ~bar n Brechstange f

crowd /kraʊd/ n [Menschen]menge f □ vi sich drängen. ~ed /'kraʊdɪd/ a [gedrängt] voll

crown /kraʊn/ n Krone f □ vt krönen; überkronen ⟨tooth⟩

crucial /'kru:ʃl/ a höchst wichtig; ⟨decisive⟩ entscheidend ⟨to für⟩

crucifix /'kru:sɪfɪks/ n Kruzifix nt

crucif|ixion /kru:sɪ'fɪkʃn/ n Kreuzigung f. ~y /'kru:sɪfaɪ/ vt ⟨pt/pp -ied⟩ kreuzigen

crude /'kru:d/ a (-r, -st) ⟨raw⟩ roh

cruel /'kru:əl/ a (crueller, cruellest), -ly adv grausam ⟨to gegen⟩. ~ty n Grausamkeit f; ~ty to animals Tierquälerei f

cruis|e /kru:z/ n Kreuzfahrt f □ vi kreuzen; ⟨car:⟩ fahren. ~er n ⟨Mil⟩ Kreuzer m; ⟨motor boat⟩ Kajütboot nt. ~ing speed n Reisegeschwindigkeit f

crumb /krʌm/ n Krümel m

crumb|le /'krʌmbl/ vt/i krümeln; ⟨collapse⟩ einstürzen. ~ly a krümelig

crumple /'krʌmpl/ vt zerknittern □ vi knittern

crunch /krʌntʃ/ n ⟨fam⟩ when it comes to the ~ wenn es [wirklich] drauf ankommt □ vt mampfen □ vi knirschen

crusade /kru:'seɪd/ n Kreuzzug m; ⟨fig⟩ Kampagne f. ~r n Kreuzfahrer m; ⟨fig⟩ Kämpfer m

crush /krʌʃ/ n ⟨crowd⟩ Gedränge nt □ vt zerquetschen; zerknittern ⟨clothes⟩; ⟨fig: subdue⟩ niederschlagen

crust /krʌst/ n Kruste f

crutch /krʌtʃ/ n Krücke f

crux /krʌks/ n ⟨fig⟩ springender Punkt m

cry /kraɪ/ n Ruf m; ⟨shout⟩ Schrei m; a far ~ from ⟨fig⟩ weit entfernt von □ vi ⟨pt/pp cried⟩ ⟨weep⟩ weinen; ⟨baby:⟩ schreien; ⟨call⟩ rufen

crypt /krɪpt/ n Krypta f. ~ic a rätselhaft

crystal /'krɪstl/ n Kristall m; ⟨glass⟩ Kristall nt. ~lize vi [sich] kristallisieren

cub /kʌb/ n ⟨Zool⟩ Junge(s) nt; C~ [Scout] Wölfling m

Cuba /'kju:bə/ n Kuba nt

cubby-hole /'kʌbɪ-/ n Fach nt

cub|e /kju:b/ n Würfel m. ~ic a Kubik-

cubicle /'kju:bɪkl/ n Kabine f

cuckoo /'kuku:/ n Kuckuck m. ~ clock n Kuckucksuhr f

cucumber /'kju:kʌmbə(r)/ n Gurke f

cuddl|e /'kʌdl/ vt herzen □ vi ~e up to sich kuscheln an (+ acc). ~y a kuschelig. ~y 'toy n Plüschtier m

cudgel /'kʌdʒl/ n Knüppel m

cue[1] /kju:/ n Stichwort nt

cue[2] n ⟨Billiards⟩ Queue nt

cuff /kʌf/ n Manschette f; ⟨Amer: turn-up⟩ [Hosen]aufschlag m; ⟨blow⟩ Klaps m; off the ~ ⟨fam⟩ aus dem Stegreif □ vt einen Klaps geben (+ dat). ~-link n Manschettenknopf m

cul-de-sac /'kʌldəsæk/ n Sackgasse f

culinary /'kʌlɪnərɪ/ a kulinarisch

cull /kʌl/ vt pflücken (flowers); (kill) ausmerzen

culminat|e /'kʌlmɪneɪt/ vi gipfeln (in in + dat). ~ion /-'neɪʃn/ n Gipfelpunkt m

culottes /kju:'lɒts/ npl Hosenrock m

culprit /'kʌlprɪt/ n Täter m

cult /kʌlt/ n Kult m

cultivate /'kʌltɪveɪt/ vt anbauen (crop); bebauen (land)

cultural /'kʌltʃərəl/ a kulturell

culture /'kʌltʃə(r)/ n Kultur f. ~d a kultiviert

cumbersome /'kʌmbəsəm/ a hinderlich; (unwieldy) unhandlich

cumulative /'kju:mjʊlətɪv/ a kumulativ

cunning /'kʌnɪŋ/ a listig □ n List f

cup /kʌp/ n Tasse f; (prize) Pokal m

cupboard /'kʌbəd/ n Schrank m

Cup 'Final n Pokalendspiel nt

Cupid /'kju:pɪd/ n Amor m

curable /'kjʊərəbl/ a heilbar

curate /'kjʊərət/ n Vikar m; (Roman Catholic) Kaplan m

curator /kjʊə'reɪtə(r)/ n Kustos m

curb /kɜ:b/ vt zügeln

curdle /'kɜ:dl/ vi gerinnen

cure /kjʊə(r)/ n [Heil]mittel nt □ vt heilen; (salt) pökeln; (smoke) räuchern; gerben (skin)

curfew /'kɜ:fju:/ n Ausgangssperre f

curio /'kjʊərɪəʊ/ n Kuriosität f

curiosity /kjʊərɪ'ɒsətɪ/ n Neugier f; (object) Kuriosität f

curious /'kjʊərɪəs/ a, -ly adv neugierig; (strange) merkwürdig, seltsam

curl /kɜ:l/ n Locke f □ vt locken □ vi sich locken. ~ up vi sich zusammenrollen

curler /'kɜ:lə(r)/ n Lockenwickler m

curly /'kɜ:lɪ/ a (-ier, -iest) lockig

currant /'kʌrənt/ n (dried) Korinthe f

currency /'kʌrənsɪ/ n Geläufigkeit f; (money) Währung f; foreign ~ Devisen pl

current /'kʌrənt/ a augenblicklich, gegenwärtig; (in general use) geläufig, gebräuchlich □ n Strömung f; (Electr) Strom m. ~ affairs or events npl Aktuelle(s) nt. ~ly adv zurzeit

curriculum /kə'rɪkjʊləm/ n Lehrplan m. ~ vitae /-'vi:taɪ/ n Lebenslauf m

curry /'kʌrɪ/ n Curry m & nt; (meal) Currygericht nt □ vt (pt/pp -ied) ~ favour sich einschmeicheln (with bei)

curse /kɜ:s/ n Fluch m □ vt verfluchen □ vi fluchen

cursory /'kɜ:sərɪ/ a flüchtig

curt /kɜ:t/ a, -ly adv barsch

curtail /kɜ:'teɪl/ vt abkürzen

curtain /'kɜ:tn/ n Vorhang m

curtsy /'kɜ:tsɪ/ n Knicks m □ vi (pt/pp -ied) knicksen

curve /kɜ:v/ n Kurve f □ vi einen Bogen machen; ~ to the right/left nach rechts/links biegen. ~d a gebogen

cushion /'kʊʃn/ n Kissen nt □ vt dämpfen; (protect) beschützen

cushy /'kʊʃɪ/ a (-ier, -iest) (fam) bequem

custard /'kʌstəd/ n Vanillesoße f

custodian /kʌ'stəʊdɪən/ n Hüter m

custody /'kʌstədɪ/ n Obhut f; (of child) Sorgerecht nt; (imprisonment) Haft f

custom /'kʌstəm/ n Brauch m; (habit) Gewohnheit f; (Comm) Kundschaft f. ~ary a üblich; (habitual) gewohnt. ~er n Kunde m/Kundin f

customs /'kʌstəmz/ npl Zoll m. ~ officer n Zollbeamte(r) m

cut /kʌt/ n Schnitt m; (Med) Schnittwunde f; (reduction) Kürzung f; (in price) Senkung f; ~ [of meat] [Fleisch]stück nt □ vt/i (pt/pp cut, pres p cutting) schneiden; (mow) mähen; abheben (cards); (reduce) kürzen, senken (price); ~ one's finger sich in den Finger schneiden; ~ s.o.'s hair jdm die Haare schneiden; ~ short abkürzen. ~ back vt zurückschneiden; (fig) einschränken, kürzen. ~ down vt fällen; (fig) einschränken. ~ off vt abschneiden; (disconnect) abstellen; be ~ off (Teleph) unterbrochen werden. ~ out vt ausschneiden; (delete) streichen; be ~ out for (fam) geeignet sein zu. ~ up vt zerschneiden; (slice) aufschneiden

'cut-back n Kürzung f, Einschränkung f

cute /kju:t/ a (-r, -st) (fam) niedlich

cut 'glass n Kristall m

cuticle /'kju:tɪkl/ n Nagelhaut f

cutlery /'kʌtlərɪ/ n Besteck nt

cutlet /'kʌtlɪt/ n Kotelett nt

'cut-price a verbilligt

cutting /'kʌtɪŋ/ a (remark) bissig □ n (from newspaper) Ausschnitt m; (of plant) Ableger m

CV abbr of curriculum vitae

cyclamen /'sɪkləmən/ n Alpenveilchen nt

cycl|e /'saɪkl/ n Zyklus m; (bicycle) [Fahr]rad nt □ vi mit dem Rad fahren. ~ing n Radfahren nt. ~ist n Radfahrer(in) m(f)

cyclone /'saɪkləʊn/ n Wirbelsturm m

cylind|er /'sɪlɪndə(r)/ n Zylinder m. ~rical /-'lɪndrɪkl/ a zylindrisch

cymbals /'sɪmblz/ npl (Mus) Becken nt

cynic /'sɪnɪk/ n Zyniker m. ~al a, -ly adv zynisch. ~ism /-sɪzm/ n Zynismus m

cypress /'saɪprəs/ n Zypresse f

Cyprus /'saɪprəs/ n Zypern nt

cyst /sɪst/ n Zyste f. ~**itis** /-'taɪtɪs/ n Blasenentzündung f

Czech /tʃek/ a tschechisch □ n Tscheche m/ Tschechin f

Czechoslovak /tʃekə'sləʊvæk/ a tschechoslowakisch. ~**ia** /-'vækɪə/ n die Tschechoslowakei. ~**ian** /-'vækɪən/ a tschechoslowakisch

D

dab /dæb/ n Tupfer m; (of butter) Klecks m; a ~ of ein bisschen □ vt (pt/pp dabbed) abtupfen; betupfen (with mit)

dabble /'dæbl/ vi ~ in sth (fig) sich nebenbei mit etw befassen

dachshund /'dækshʊnd/ n Dackel m

dad[dy] /'dæd[i]/ n (fam) Vati m

daddy-'long-legs n [Kohl]schnake f; (Amer: spider) Weberknecht m

daffodil /'dæfədɪl/ n Osterglocke f, gelbe Narzisse f

daft /dɑːft/ a (-er, -est) dumm

dagger /'dægə(r)/ n Dolch m; (Typ) Kreuz nt; be at ~s drawn (fam) auf Kriegsfuß stehen

dahlia /'deɪlɪə/ n Dahlie f

daily /'deɪli/ a & adv täglich □ n (newspaper) Tageszeitung f; (fam: cleaner) Putzfrau f

dainty /'deɪnti/ a (-ier, -iest) zierlich

dairy /'deəri/ n Molkerei f; (shop) Milchgeschäft nt. ~ **cow** n Milchkuh f. ~ **products** n Milchprodukte pl

dais /'deɪɪs/ n Podium nt

daisy /'deɪzi/ n Gänseblümchen nt

dale /deɪl/ n (liter) Tal nt

dally /'dæli/ vi (pt/pp -ied) trödeln

dam /dæm/ n [Stau]damm m □ vt (pt/pp dammed) eindämmen

damage /'dæmɪdʒ/ n Schaden m (to an + dat); ~**s** pl (Jur) Schadenersatz m □ vt beschädigen; (fig) beeinträchtigen. ~**ing** a schädlich

damask /'dæməsk/ n Damast m

dame /deɪm/ n (liter) Dame f; (Amer sl) Weib nt

damn /dæm/ a, int & adv (fam) verdammt □ n I don't care or give a ~ (fam) ich schere mich einen Dreck darum □ vt verdammen. ~**ation** /-'neɪʃn/ n Verdammnis f □ int (fam) verdammt!

damp /dæmp/ a (-er, -est) feucht □ n Feuchtigkeit f □ vt = dampen

damp|en vt anfeuchten; (fig) dämpfen. ~**ness** n Feuchtigkeit f

dance /dɑːns/ n Tanz m; (function) Tanzveranstaltung f □ vt/i tanzen. ~-**hall** n Tanzlokal nt. ~ **music** n Tanzmusik f

dancer /'dɑːnsə(r)/ n Tänzer(in) m(f)

dandelion /'dændɪlaɪən/ n Löwenzahn m

dandruff /'dændrʌf/ n Schuppen pl

Dane /deɪn/ n Däne m/Dänin f; Great ~ [deutsche] Dogge f

danger /'deɪndʒə(r)/ n Gefahr f; in/out of ~ in/außer Gefahr. ~**ous** /-rəs/ a, -**ly** adv gefährlich; ~**ously ill** schwer erkrankt

dangle /'dæŋgl/ vi baumeln □ vt baumeln lassen

Danish /'deɪnɪʃ/ a dänisch. ~ 'pastry n Hefeteilchen nt, Plunderstück nt

dank /dæŋk/ a (-er, -est) nasskalt

Danube /'dænjuːb/ n Donau f

dare /deə(r)/ n Mutprobe f □ vt/i (challenge) herausfordern (to zu); ~ [to] do sth [es] wagen, etw zu tun; I ~ say! das mag wohl sein! ~**devil** n Draufgänger m

daring /'deərɪŋ/ a verwegen □ n Verwegenheit f

dark /dɑːk/ a (-er, -est) dunkel; ~ **blue**/ **brown** dunkelblau/ -braun; ~ **horse** (fig) stilles Wasser nt; **keep sth** ~ (fig) etw geheim halten □ n Dunkelheit f; **after** ~ nach Einbruch der Dunkelheit; **in the** ~ im Dunkeln; **keep in the** ~ (fig) im Dunkeln lassen

dark|en /'dɑːkn/ vt verdunkeln □ vi dunkler werden. ~**ness** n Dunkelheit f

'dark-room n Dunkelkammer f

darling /'dɑːlɪŋ/ a allerliebst □ n Liebling m

darn /dɑːn/ vt stopfen. ~**ing-needle** n Stopfnadel f

dart /dɑːt/ n Pfeil m; (Sewing) Abnäher m; ~**s** sg (game) [Wurf]pfeil m □ vi flitzen

dash /dæʃ/ n (Typ) Gedankenstrich m; (in Morse) Strich m; a ~ of milk ein Schuss Milch; **make a** ~ losstürzen (for auf + acc) □ vi rennen □ vt schleudern. ~ **off** vi losstürzen □ vt (write quickly) hinwerfen

'dashboard n Armaturenbrett nt

dashing /'dæʃɪŋ/ a schneidig

data /'deɪtə/ npl & sg Daten pl. ~ **processing** n Datenverarbeitung f

date¹ /deɪt/ n (fruit) Dattel f

date² n Datum nt; (fam) Verabredung f; to ~ bis heute; out of ~ überholt; (expired) ungültig; be up to ~ auf dem Laufenden sein □ vt/i datieren; (Amer, fam: go out with) ausgehen mit; ~ back to zurückgehen auf (+ acc)

dated /'deɪtɪd/ a altmodisch

'date-line n Datumsgrenze f

dative /'deɪtɪv/ a & n (Gram) ~ [case] Dativ m

daub /dɔːb/ vt beschmieren (with mit); schmieren (paint)

daughter /'dɔːtə(r)/ n Tochter f. ~-in-law n (pl ~s-in-law) Schwiegertochter f

daunt /dɔːnt/ vt entmutigen; nothing ~ed unverzagt. ~less a furchtlos

dawdle /'dɔːdl/ vi trödeln

dawn /dɔːn/ n Morgendämmerung f; at ~ bei Tagesanbruch □ vi anbrechen; it ~ed on me (fig) es ging mir auf

day /deɪ/ n Tag m; ~ by ~ Tag für Tag; ~ after ~ Tag um Tag; these ~s heutzutage; in those ~s zu der Zeit; it's had its ~ (fam) es hat ausgedient

day: ~break n at ~break bei Tagesanbruch m. ~dream n Tagtraum m □ vi [mit offenen Augen] träumen. ~light n Tageslicht nt. ~ re'turn (ticket) Tagesrückfahrkarte f. ~time n in the ~time am Tage

daze /deɪz/ n in a ~ wie benommen. ~d a benommen

dazzle /'dæzl/ vt blenden

deacon /'diːkn/ n Diakon m

dead /ded/ a tot; (flower) verwelkt; (numb) taub; ~ body Leiche f; be ~ on time auf die Minute pünktlich kommen; ~ centre genau in der Mitte □ adv ~ tired todmüde; ~ slow sehr langsam; stop ~ stehen bleiben □ n the ~ pl die Toten; in the ~ of night mitten in der Nacht

deaden /'dedn/ vt dämpfen (sound); betäuben (pain)

dead: ~'end n Sackgasse f. ~'heat n totes Rennen nt. ~line n [letzter] Termin m. ~lock n reach ~lock (fig) sich festfahren

deadly /'dedlɪ/ a (-ier, -iest) tödlich; (fam: dreary) sterbenslangweilig; ~ sins pl Todsünden pl

deaf /def/ a (-er, -est) taub; ~ and dumb taubstumm. ~-aid n Hörgerät nt

deaf|en /'defn/ vt betäuben; (permanently) taub machen. ~ening a ohrenbetäubend. ~ness n Taubheit f

deal /diːl/ n (transaction) Geschäft nt; whose ~? (Cards) wer gibt? a good or great ~ eine Menge; get a raw ~ (fam) schlecht wegkommen □ v (pt/pp dealt

/delt/) □ vt (Cards) geben; ~ out austeilen; ~ s.o. a blow jdm einen Schlag versetzen □ vi ~ in handeln mit; ~ with zu tun haben mit; (handle) sich befassen mit; (cope with) fertig werden mit; (be about) handeln von; that's been dealt with das ist schon erledigt

deal|er /'diːlə(r)/ n Händler m; (Cards) Kartengeber m. ~ings npl have ~ings with zu tun haben mit

dean /diːn/ n Dekan m

dear /dɪə(r)/ a (-er, -est) lieb; (expensive) teuer; (in letter) liebe(r,s) (formal) sehr geehrte(r,s) □ n Liebe(r) m/f □ int oh ~! oje! ~ly adv (love) sehr; (pay) teuer

dearth /dɜːθ/ n Mangel m (of an + dat)

death /deθ/ n Tod m; three ~s drei Todesfälle. ~ certificate n Sterbeurkunde f. ~ duty n Erbschaftssteuer f

deathly a ~ silence Totenstille f □ adv ~ pale totenblass

death: ~ penalty n Todesstrafe f. ~'s head n Totenkopf m. ~-trap n Todesfalle f

debar /dɪ'bɑː(r)/ vt (pt/pp debarred) ausschließen

debase /dɪ'beɪs/ vt erniedrigen

debatable /dɪ'beɪtəbl/ a strittig

debate /dɪ'beɪt/ n Debatte f □ vt/i debattieren

debauchery /dɪ'bɔːtʃərɪ/ n Ausschweifung f

debility /dɪ'bɪlətɪ/ n Entkräftung f

debit /'debɪt/ n Schuldbetrag m; ~ [side] Soll nt □ vt (pt/pp debited) (Comm) belasten; abbuchen (sum)

debris /'debriː/ n Trümmer pl

debt /det/ n Schuld f; in ~ verschuldet. ~or n Schuldner m

début /'deɪbuː/ n Debüt nt

decade /'dekeɪd/ n Jahrzehnt nt

decaden|ce /'dekədəns/ n Dekadenz f. ~t a dekadent

decaffeinated /dɪ'kæfɪneɪtɪd/ a koffeinfrei

decant /dɪ'kænt/ vt umfüllen. ~er n Karaffe f

decapitate /dɪ'kæpɪteɪt/ vt köpfen

decay /dɪ'keɪ/ n Verfall m; (rot) Verwesung f; (of tooth) Zahnfäule f □ vi verfallen; (rot) verwesen; (tooth:) schlecht werden

decease /dɪ'siːs/ n Ableben nt. ~d a verstorben □ n the ~d der/die Verstorbene

deceit /dɪ'siːt/ n Täuschung f. ~ful a, ~ly adv unaufrichtig

deceive /dɪ'siːv/ vt täuschen; (be unfaithful to) betrügen

December /dɪ'sembə(r)/ n Dezember m

decency /'di:sənsɪ/ n Anstand m

decent /'di:sənt/ a, **-ly** adv anständig

decentralize /di:'sentrəlaɪz/ vt dezentralisieren

decept|ion /dɪ'sepʃn/ n Täuschung f; (fraud) Betrug m. ∼**ive** /-tɪv/ a, **-ly** adv täuschend

decibel /'desɪbel/ n Dezibel nt

decide /dɪ'saɪd/ vt entscheiden ▫ vi sich entscheiden (on für)

decided /dɪ'saɪdɪd/ a, **-ly** adv entschieden

deciduous /dɪ'sɪdjʊəs/ a ∼ tree Laubbaum m

decimal /'desɪml/ a Dezimal-. ▫ n Dezimalzahl f. ∼ point n Komma nt. ∼ system n Dezimalsystem nt

decimate /'desɪmeɪt/ vt dezimieren

decipher /dɪ'saɪfə(r)/ vt entziffern

decision /dɪ'sɪʒn/ n Entscheidung f; (firmness) Entschlossenheit f

decisive /dɪ'saɪsɪv/ a ausschlaggebend; (firm) entschlossen

deck¹ /dek/ vt schmücken

deck² n (Naut) Deck nt; on ∼ an Deck; top ∼ (of bus) Oberdeck nt; ∼ of cards (Amer) [Karten]spiel nt. ∼**-chair** n Liegestuhl m

declaration /deklə'reɪʃn/ n Erklärung f

declare /dɪ'kleə(r)/ vt erklären; angeben (goods); anything to ∼? etwas zu verzollen?

declension /dɪ'klenʃn/ n Deklination f

decline /dɪ'klaɪn/ n Rückgang m; (in health) Verfall m ▫ vt ablehnen; (Gram) deklinieren ▫ vi ablehnen; (fall) sinken; (decrease) nachlassen

decode /dɪ'kəʊd/ vt entschlüsseln

decompos|e /di:kəm'pəʊz/ vi sich zersetzen

décor /'deɪkɔ:(r)/ n Ausstattung f

decorat|e /'dekəreɪt/ vt (adorn) schmücken; verzieren (cake); (paint) streichen; (wallpaper) tapezieren; (award medal to) einen Orden verleihen (+ dat). ∼**ion** /-'reɪʃn/ n Verzierung f; (medal) Orden m; ∼**ions** pl Schmuck m. ∼**ive** /-rətɪv/ a dekorativ. ∼**or** n painter and ∼**or** Maler und Tapezierer m

decorous /'dekərəs/ a, **-ly** adv schamhaft

decorum /dɪ'kɔ:rəm/ n Anstand m

decoy¹ /'di:kɔɪ/ n Lockvogel m

decoy² /dɪ'kɔɪ/ vt locken

decrease¹ /'di:kri:s/ n Verringerung f; (in number) Rückgang m; be on the ∼ zurückgehen

decrease² /dɪ'kri:s/ vt verringern; herabsetzen (price) ▫ vi sich verringern; (price:) sinken

decree /dɪ'kri:/ n Erlass m ▫ vt (pt/pp decreed) verordnen

decrepit /dɪ'krepɪt/ a altersschwach

dedicat|e /'dedɪkeɪt/ vt widmen; (Relig) weihen. ∼**ed** a hingebungsvoll; (person) aufopfernd. ∼**ion** /-'keɪʃn/ n Hingabe f; (in book) Widmung f

deduce /dɪ'dju:s/ vt folgern (from aus)

deduct /dɪ'dʌkt/ vt abziehen

deduction /dɪ'dʌkʃn/ n Abzug m; (conclusion) Folgerung f

deed /di:d/ n Tat f; (Jur) Urkunde f

deem /di:m/ vt halten für

deep /di:p/ a (-er, -est), **-ly** adv tief; go off the ∼ end (fam) auf die Palme gehen ▫ adv tief

deepen /'di:pn/ vt vertiefen ▫ vi tiefer werden; (fig) sich vertiefen

deep-'freeze n Gefriertruhe f; (upright) Gefrierschrank m

deer /dɪə(r)/ n inv Hirsch m; (roe) Reh nt

deface /dɪ'feɪs/ vt beschädigen

defamat|ion /defə'meɪʃn/ n Verleumdung f. ∼**ory** /dɪ'fæmətərɪ/ a verleumderisch

default /dɪ'fɔ:lt/ n (Jur) Nichtzahlung f; (failure to appear) Nichterscheinen nt; win by ∼ (Sport) kampflos gewinnen ▫ vi nicht zahlen; nicht erscheinen

defeat /dɪ'fi:t/ n Niederlage f; (defeating) Besiegung f; (rejection) Ablehnung f ▫ vt besiegen; ablehnen; (frustrate) vereiteln

defect¹ /dɪ'fekt/ vi (Pol) überlaufen

defect² /'di:fekt/ n Fehler m; (Techn) Defekt m. ∼**ive** /dɪ'fektɪv/ a fehlerhaft; (Techn) defekt

defence /dɪ'fens/ n Verteidigung f. ∼**less** a wehrlos

defend /dɪ'fend/ vt verteidigen; (justify) rechtfertigen. ∼**ant** n (Jur) Beklagte(r) m/f; (in criminal court) Angeklagte(r) m/f

defensive /dɪ'fensɪv/ a defensiv ▫ n Defensive f

defer /dɪ'fɜ:(r)/ vt (pt/pp deferred) (postpone) aufschieben; ∼ to s.o. sich jdm fügen

deferen|ce /'defərəns/ n Ehrerbietung f. ∼**tial** /-'renʃl/ a, **-ly** adv ehrerbietig

defian|ce /dɪ'faɪəns/ n Trotz m; in ∼ce of zum Trotz (+ dat). ∼**t** a, **-ly** adv aufsässig

deficien|cy /dɪ'fɪʃənsɪ/ n Mangel m. ∼**t** a mangelhaft; he is ∼**t** in ... ihm mangelt es an ... (dat)

deficit /'defɪsɪt/ n Defizit nt

defile /dɪ'faɪl/ vt (fig) schänden

define /dɪ'faɪn/ vt bestimmen; definieren (word)

definite /'defɪnɪt/ a, **-ly** adv bestimmt; (certain) sicher

definition /defɪ'nɪʃn/ n Definition f; (Phot, TV) Schärfe f

definitive /dɪ'fɪnətɪv/ a endgültig; (authoritative) maßgeblich

deflat|e /dɪ'fleɪt/ vt die Luft auslassen aus. ∼ion /-eɪʃn/ n (Comm) Deflation f

deflect /dɪ'flekt/ vt ablenken

deform|ed /dɪ'fɔːmd/ a missgebildet. ∼ity n Missbildung f

defraud /dɪ'frɔːd/ vt betrügen (of um)

defray /dɪ'freɪ/ vt bestreiten

defrost /diː'frɒst/ vt entfrosten; abtauen (fridge); auftauen (food)

deft /deft/ a (-er, -est), -ly adv geschickt. ∼ness n Geschicklichkeit f

defunct /dɪ'fʌŋkt/ a aufgelöst; (law) außer Kraft gesetzt

defuse /diː'fjuːz/ vt entschärfen

defy /dɪ'faɪ/ vt (pt/pp -ied) trotzen (+ dat); widerstehen (+ dat) (attempt)

degenerate¹ /dɪ'dʒenəreɪt/ vi degenerieren; ∼ into (fig) ausarten in (+ acc)

degenerate² /dɪ'dʒenərət/ a degeneriert

degrading /dɪ'greɪdɪŋ/ a entwürdigend

degree /dɪ'griː/ n Grad m; (Univ) akademischer Grad m; 20 ∼s 20 Grad

dehydrate /diː'haɪdreɪt/ vt Wasser entziehen (+ dat). ∼d /-ɪd/ a ausgetrocknet

de-ice /diː'aɪs/ vt enteisen

deign /deɪn/ vi ∼ to do sth sich herablassen, etw zu tun

deity /'diːɪtɪ/ n Gottheit f

dejected /dɪ'dʒektɪd/ a, -ly adv niedergeschlagen

delay /dɪ'leɪ/ n Verzögerung f; (of train, aircraft) Verspätung f; without ∼ unverzüglich □ vt aufhalten; (postpone) aufschieben; be ∼ed (person:) aufgehalten werden; (train, aircraft:) Verspätung haben □ vi zögern

delegate¹ /'delɪgət/ n Delegierte(r) m/f

delegate² /'delɪgeɪt/ vt delegieren. ∼ion /-'geɪʃn/ n Delegation f

delet|e /dɪ'liːt/ vt streichen. ∼ion /-iːʃn/ n Streichung f

deliberate¹ /dɪ'lɪbərət/ a, -ly adv absichtlich; (slow) bedächtig

deliberat|e² /dɪ'lɪbəreɪt/ vt/i überlegen. ∼ion /-'reɪʃn/ n Überlegung f; with ∼ion mit Bedacht

delicacy /'delɪkəsɪ/ n Feinheit f; Zartheit f; (food) Delikatesse f

delicate /'delɪkət/ a fein; (fabric, health) zart; (situation) heikel; (mechanism) empfindlich

delicatessen /delɪkə'tesn/ n Delikatessengeschäft nt

delicious /dɪ'lɪʃəs/ a köstlich

delight /dɪ'laɪt/ n Freude f □ vt entzücken □ vi ∼ in sich erfreuen an (+ dat). ∼ed a hocherfreut; be ∼ed sich sehr freuen. ∼ful a reizend

delinquen|cy /dɪ'lɪŋkwənsɪ/ n Kriminalität f. ∼t a straffällig □ n Straffällige(r) m/f

deli|rious /dɪ'lɪrɪəs/ a be ∼rious im Delirium sein. ∼rium /-rɪəm/ n Delirium nt

deliver /dɪ'lɪvə(r)/ vt liefern; zustellen (post, newspaper); halten (speech); überbringen (message); versetzen (blow); (set free) befreien; ∼ a baby ein Kind zur Welt bringen. ∼ance n Erlösung f. ∼y n Lieferung f; (of post) Zustellung f; (Med) Entbindung f; cash on ∼y per Nachnahme

delta /'deltə/ n Delta nt

delude /dɪ'luːd/ vt täuschen; ∼ oneself sich (dat) Illusionen machen

deluge /'deljuːdʒ/ n Flut f; (heavy rain) schwerer Guss m □ vt überschwemmen

delusion /dɪ'luːʒn/ n Täuschung f

de luxe /də'lʌks/ a Luxus-

delve /delv/ vi hineingreifen (into in + acc); (fig) eingehen (into auf + acc)

demand /dɪ'mɑːnd/ n Forderung f; (Comm) Nachfrage f; in ∼ gefragt; on ∼ auf Verlangen □ vt verlangen, fordern (of/ from von). ∼ing a anspruchsvoll

demarcation /diːmɑː'keɪʃn/ n Abgrenzung f

demean /dɪ'miːn/ vt ∼ oneself sich erniedrigen

demeanour /dɪ'miːnə(r)/ n Verhalten nt

demented /dɪ'mentɪd/ a verrückt

demise /dɪ'maɪz/ n Tod m

demister /diː'mɪstə(r)/ n (Auto) Defroster m

demo /'deməʊ/ n (pl ∼s) (fam) Demonstration f

demobilize /diː'məʊbɪlaɪz/ vt (Mil) entlassen

democracy /dɪ'mɒkrəsɪ/ n Demokratie f

democrat /'deməkræt/ n Demokrat m. ∼ic /-'krætɪk/ a, -ally adv demokratisch

demo|lish /dɪ'mɒlɪʃ/ vt abbrechen; (destroy) zerstören. ∼lition /demə'lɪʃn/ n Abbruch m

demon /'diːmən/ n Dämon m

demonstrat|e /'demənstreɪt/ vt beweisen; vorführen (appliance) □ vi (Pol) demonstrieren. ∼ion /-'streɪʃn/ n Vorführung f; (Pol) Demonstration f

demonstrative /dɪ'mɒnstrətɪv/ a (Gram) demonstrativ; be ∼ seine Gefühle zeigen

demonstrator /'demənstreɪtə(r)/ n Vorführer m; (Pol) Demonstrant m

demoralize /dɪ'mɒrəlaɪz/ *vt* demoralisieren

demote /dɪ'məʊt/ *vt* degradieren

demure /dɪ'mjʊə(r)/ *a*, **-ly** *adv* sittsam

den /den/ *n* Höhle *f*; (*room*) Bude *f*

denial /dɪ'naɪəl/ *n* Leugnen *nt*; official ~ Dementi *nt*

denigrate /'denɪgreɪt/ *vt* herabsetzen

denim /'denɪm/ *n* Jeansstoff *m*; ~s *pl* Jeans *pl*

Denmark /'denmɑːk/ *n* Dänemark *nt*

denomination /dɪnɒmɪ'neɪʃn/ *n* (*Relig*) Konfession *f*; (*money*) Nennwert *m*

denote /dɪ'nəʊt/ *vt* bezeichnen

denounce /dɪ'naʊns/ *vt* denunzieren; (*condemn*) verurteilen

dens|e /dens/ *a* (-r, -st), **-ly** *adv* dicht; (*fam: stupid*) blöd[e]. ~ity *n* Dichte *f*

dent /dent/ *n* Delle *f*, Beule *f* □ *vt* einbeulen; ~ed /-ɪd/ verbeult

dental /'dentl/ *a* Zahn-; (*treatment*) zahnärztlich. ~ floss /flɒs/ *n* Zahnseide *f*. ~ surgeon *n* Zahnarzt *m*

dentist /'dentɪst/ *n* Zahnarzt *m*/-ärztin *f*. ~ry *n* Zahnmedizin *f*

denture /'dentʃə(r)/ *n* Zahnprothese *f*; ~s *pl* künstliches Gebiss *nt*

denude /dɪ'njuːd/ *vt* entblößen

denunciation /dɪnʌnsɪ'eɪʃn/ *n* Denunziation *f*; (*condemnation*) Verurteilung *f*

deny /dɪ'naɪ/ *vt* (*pt/pp* -ied) leugnen; (*officially*) dementieren; ~ s.o. sth jdm etw verweigern

deodorant /diː'əʊdərənt/ *n* Deodorant *nt*

depart /dɪ'pɑːt/ *vi* abfahren; (*Aviat*) abfliegen; (*go away*) weggehen/-fahren; (*deviate*) abweichen (from von)

department /dɪ'pɑːtmənt/ *n* Abteilung *f*; (*Pol*) Ministerium *nt*. ~ store *n* Kaufhaus *nt*

departure /dɪ'pɑːtʃə(r)/ *n* Abfahrt *f*; (*Aviat*) Abflug *m*; (*from rule*) Abweichung *f*; new ~ Neuerung *f*

depend /dɪ'pend/ *vi* abhängen (on von); (*rely*) sich verlassen (on auf + *acc*); it all ~s das kommt darauf an. ~able /-əbl/ *a* zuverlässig. ~ant *n* Abhängige(r) *m*/*f*. ~ence *n* Abhängigkeit *f*. ~ent *a* abhängig (on von)

depict /dɪ'pɪkt/ *vt* darstellen

depilatory /dɪ'pɪlətərɪ/ *n* Enthaarungsmittel *nt*

deplete /dɪ'pliːt/ *vt* verringern

deplor|able /dɪ'plɔːrəbl/ *a* bedauerlich. ~e *vt* bedauern

deploy /dɪ'plɔɪ/ *vt* (*Mil*) einsetzen □ *vi* sich aufstellen

depopulate /diː'pɒpjʊleɪt/ *vt* entvölkern

deport /dɪ'pɔːt/ *vt* deportieren, ausweisen. ~ation /diːpɔː'teɪʃn/ *n* Ausweisung *f*

deportment /dɪ'pɔːtmənt/ *n* Haltung *f*

depose /dɪ'pəʊz/ *vt* absetzen

deposit /dɪ'pɒzɪt/ *n* Anzahlung *f*; (*against damage*) Kaution *f*; (*on bottle*) Pfand *nt*; (*sediment*) Bodensatz *m*; (*Geol*) Ablagerung *f* □ *vt* (*pt/pp* deposited) legen; (*for safety*) deponieren; (*Geol*) ablagern. ~ account *n* Sparkonto *nt*

depot /'depəʊ/ *n* Depot *nt*; (*Amer: railway station*) Bahnhof *m*

deprav|e /dɪ'preɪv/ *vt* verderben. ~ed *a* verkommen. ~ity /-'prævəti/ *n* Verderbtheit *f*

deprecate /'deprəkeɪt/ *vt* missbilligen

depreciat|e /dɪ'priːʃɪeɪt/ *vi* an Wert verlieren. ~ion /-'eɪʃn/ *n* Wertminderung *f*; (*Comm*) Abschreibung *f*

depress /dɪ'pres/ *vt* deprimieren; (*press down*) herunterdrücken. ~ed *a* deprimiert; ~ed area Notstandsgebiet *nt*. ~ing *a* deprimierend. ~ion /-eʃn/ *n* Vertiefung *f*; (*Med*) Depression *f*; (*Meteorol*) Tief *nt*

deprivation /deprɪ'veɪʃn/ *n* Entbehrung *f*

deprive /dɪ'praɪv/ *vt* entziehen; ~ s.o. of sth jdm etw entziehen. ~d *a* benachteiligt

depth /depθ/ *n* Tiefe *f*; in ~ gründlich; in the ~s of winter im tiefsten Winter

deputation /depjʊ'teɪʃn/ *n* Abordnung *f*

deputize /'depjʊtaɪz/ *vi* ~ for vertreten

deputy /'depjʊti/ *n* Stellvertreter *m* □ *attrib* stellvertretend

derail /dɪ'reɪl/ *vt* be ~ed entgleisen. ~ment *n* Entgleisung *f*

deranged /dɪ'reɪndʒd/ *a* geistesgestört

derelict /'derəlɪkt/ *a* verfallen; (*abandoned*) verlassen

deri|de /dɪ'raɪd/ *vt* verhöhnen. ~sion /-'rɪʒn/ *n* Hohn *m*

derisive /dɪ'raɪsɪv/ *a*, **-ly** *adv* höhnisch

derisory /dɪ'raɪsərɪ/ *a* höhnisch; (*offer*) lächerlich

derivation /derɪ'veɪʃn/ *n* Ableitung *f*

derivative /dɪ'rɪvətɪv/ *a* abgeleitet □ *n* Ableitung *f*

derive /dɪ'raɪv/ *vt/i* (*obtain*) gewinnen (from aus); be ~d from (*word:*) hergeleitet sein aus

dermatologist /dɜːmə'tɒlədʒɪst/ *n* Hautarzt *m* /-ärztin *f*

derogatory /dɪ'rɒgətrɪ/ *a* abfällig

derrick /'derɪk/ *n* Bohrturm *m*

derv /dɜːv/ *n* Diesel[kraftstoff] *m*

descend /dɪ'send/ *vt/i* hinunter-/heruntergehen; ⟨*vehicle, lift:*⟩ hinunter-/herunterfahren; be ~ed from abstammen von. ~ant *n* Nachkomme *m*

descent /dɪ'sent/ *n* Abstieg *m*; ⟨*lineage*⟩ Abstammung *f*

describe /dɪ'skraɪb/ *vt* beschreiben

descrip|tion /dɪ'skrɪpʃn/ *n* Beschreibung *f*; ⟨*sort*⟩ Art *f*. ~tive /-tɪv/ *a* beschⸯⸯⸯend; ⟨*vivid*⟩ anschaulich

desecrat|e /'desɪkreɪt/ ⸯⸯ entweihen. ~ion /-'kreɪʃn/ ⸯⸯ Entweihung *f*

desert[1] /'dezⸯⸯⸯ/ *n* Wüste *f* □ *a* Wüsten-; ~ isⸯⸯ verlassene Insel *f*

desert[2] /dɪ'zɜːt/ *vt* verlassen □ *vt* desertieren. ~ed *a* verlassen. ~er *n* ⟨*Mil*⟩ Deserteur *m*. ~ion /-ɜːʃn/ *n* Fahnenflucht *f*

deserts /dɪ'zɜːts/ *npl* get one's ~ seinen verdienten Lohn bekommen

deserv|e /dɪ'zɜːv/ *vt* verdienen. ~edly /-ɪdlɪ/ *adv* verdientermaßen. ~ing *a* verdienstvoll; ~ing cause guter Zweck *m*

design /dɪ'zaɪn/ *n* Entwurf *m*; ⟨*pattern*⟩ Muster *nt*; ⟨*construction*⟩ Konstruktion *f*; ⟨*aim*⟩ Absicht *f* □ *vt* entwerfen; ⟨*construct*⟩ konstruieren; be ~ed for bestimmt sein für

designat|e /'dezɪgneɪt/ *vt* bezeichnen; ⟨*appoint*⟩ ernennen. ~ion /-'neɪʃn/ *n* Bezeichnung *f*

designer /dɪ'zaɪnə(r)/ *n* Designer *m*; ⟨*Techn*⟩ Konstrukteur *m*; ⟨*Theat*⟩ Bühnenbildner *m*

desirable /dɪ'zaɪrəbl/ *a* wünschenswert; ⟨*sexually*⟩ begehrenswert

desire /dɪ'zaɪə(r)/ *n* Wunsch *m*; ⟨*longing*⟩ Verlangen *nt* (for nach); ⟨*sexual*⟩ Begierde *f* □ *vt* [sich ⟨*dat*⟩] wünschen; ⟨*sexually*⟩ begehren

desk /desk/ *n* Schreibtisch *m*; ⟨*Sch*⟩ Pult *nt*; ⟨*Comm*⟩ Kasse *f*; ⟨*in hotel*⟩ Rezeption *f*

desolat|e /'desələt/ *a* trostlos. ~ion /-'leɪʃn/ *n* Trostlosigkeit *f*

despair /dɪ'speə(r)/ *n* Verzweiflung *f*; in ~ verzweifelt □ *vi* verzweifeln

desperat|e /'despərət/ *a*, -ly *adv* verzweifelt; ⟨*urgent*⟩ dringend; be ~e ⟨*criminal:*⟩ zum Äußersten entschlossen sein; be ~e for dringend brauchen. ~ion /-'reɪʃn/ *n* Verzweiflung *f*; in ~ion aus Verzweiflung

despicable /dɪ'spɪkəbl/ *a* verachtenswert

despise /dɪ'spaɪz/ *vt* verachten

despite /dɪ'spaɪt/ *prep* trotz (+ *gen*)

despondent /dɪ'spɒndənt/ *a* niedergeschlagen

despot /'despɒt/ *n* Despot *m*

dessert /dɪ'zɜːt/ *n* Dessert *nt*, Nachtisch *m*. ~ spoon *n* Dessertlöffel *m*

destination /destɪ'neɪʃn/ *n* [Reise]ziel *nt*; ⟨*of goods*⟩ Bestimmungsort *m*

destine /'destɪn/ *vt* bestimmⸯⸯ ⸯⸯ

destiny /'destɪnɪ/ *n* ⟨*ⸯⸯ*⟩ ⸯⸯ Schicksal *nt*

destitute /'destⸯⸯ tⸯ/ *a* völlig mittellos

destroy /dɪ'strɔɪ/ *vt* zerstören; ⟨*totally*⟩ ⸯⸯ nichten. ~er *n* ⟨*Naut*⟩ Zerstörer *m*

destruc|tion /dɪ'strʌkʃn/ *n* Zerstörung *f*; Vernichtung *f*. ~tive /-tɪv/ *a* zerstörerisch; ⟨*fig*⟩ destruktiv

detach /dɪ'tætʃ/ *vt* abnehmen; ⟨*tear off*⟩ abtrennen. ~able /-əbl/ *a* abnehmbar. ~ed *a* ⟨*fig*⟩ distanziert; ~ed house Einzelhaus *nt*

detachment /dɪ'tætʃmənt/ *n* Distanz *f*; ⟨*objectivity*⟩ Abstand *m*; ⟨*Mil*⟩ Sonderkommando *nt*

detail /'diːteɪl/ *n* Einzelheit *f*, Detail *nt*; in ~ ausführlich □ *vt* einzeln aufführen; ⟨*Mil*⟩ abkommandieren. ~ed *a* ausführlich

detain /dɪ'teɪn/ *vt* aufhalten; ⟨*police:*⟩ in Haft behalten; ⟨*take into custody*⟩ in Haft nehmen. ~ee /diːteɪ'niː/ *n* Häftling *m*

detect /dɪ'tekt/ *vt* entdecken; ⟨*perceive*⟩ wahrnehmen. ~ion /-ekʃn/ *n* Entdeckung *f*

detective /dɪ'tektɪv/ *n* Detektiv *m*. ~ story *n* Detektivroman *m*

detector /dɪ'tektə(r)/ *n* Suchgerät *nt*; ⟨*for metal*⟩ Metalldetektor *m*

detention /dɪ'tenʃn/ *n* Haft *f*; ⟨*Sch*⟩ Nachsitzen *nt*

deter /dɪ'tɜː(r)/ *vt* ⟨*pt/pp* deterred⟩ abschrecken; ⟨*prevent*⟩ abhalten

detergent /dɪ'tɜːdʒənt/ *n* Waschmittel *nt*

deteriorat|e /dɪ'tɪərɪəreɪt/ *vi* sich verschlechtern. ~ion /-'reɪʃn/ *n* Verschlechterung *f*

determination /dɪtɜːmɪ'neɪʃn/ *n* Entschlossenheit *f*

determine /dɪ'tɜːmɪn/ *vt* bestimmen; ~ to ⟨*resolve*⟩ sich entschließen zu. ~d *a* entschlossen

deterrent /dɪ'terənt/ *n* Abschreckungsmittel *nt*

detest /dɪ'test/ *vt* verabscheuen. ~able /-əbl/ *a* abscheulich

detonat|e /'detəneɪt/ *vt* zünden □ *vi* explodieren. ~or *n* Zünder *m*

detour /'diːtʊə(r)/ *n* Umweg *m*; ⟨*for traffic*⟩ Umleitung *f*

detract /dɪ'trækt/ *vi* ~ from beeinträchtigen

detriment /'detrɪmənt/ *n* to the ~ zum Schaden (of *gen*). ~al /-'mentl/ *a* schädlich (to *dat*)

deuce /djuːs/ *n* ⟨*Tennis*⟩ Einstand *m*

devaluation /diːvæljuˈeɪʃn/ n Abwertung f

de'value vt abwerten ⟨currency⟩

devastat|e /ˈdevəsteɪt/ vt verwüsten. ~ed /-ɪd/ a ⟨fam⟩ erschüttert. ~ing a verheerend. ~ion /-ˈsteɪʃn/ n Verwüstung f

develop /dɪˈveləp/ vt entwickeln; bekommen ⟨illness⟩; erschließen ⟨area⟩ □ vi sich entwickeln (into zu). ~er n [property] ~er Bodenspekulant m

de'veloping country n Entwicklungsland nt

development /dɪˈveləpmənt/ n Entwicklung f

deviant /ˈdiːvɪənt/ a abweichend

deviat|e /ˈdiːvɪeɪt/ vi abweichen. ~ion /-ˈeɪʃn/ n Abweichung f

device /dɪˈvaɪs/ n Gerät nt; ⟨fig⟩ Mittel nt; leave s.o. to his own ~s jdn sich ⟨dat⟩ selbst überlassen

devil /ˈdevl/ n Teufel m. ~ish a teuflisch

devious /ˈdiːvɪəs/ a verschlagen; ~ route Umweg m

devise /dɪˈvaɪz/ vt sich ⟨dat⟩ ausdenken

devoid /dɪˈvɔɪd/ a ~ of ohne

devolution /diːvəˈluːʃn/ n Dezentralisierung f; ⟨of power⟩ Übertragung f

devot|e /dɪˈvəʊt/ vt widmen (to dat). ~ed a, -ly adv ergeben; ⟨care⟩ liebevoll; be ~ed to s.o. sehr an jdm hängen. ~ee /devəˈtiː/ n Anhänger(in) m(f)

devotion /dɪˈvəʊʃn/ n Hingabe f; ~s pl ⟨Relig⟩ Andacht f

devour /dɪˈvaʊə(r)/ vt verschlingen

devout /dɪˈvaʊt/ a fromm

dew /djuː/ n Tau m

dexterity /dekˈsterətɪ/ n Geschicklichkeit f

diabet|es /daɪəˈbiːtiːz/ n Zuckerkrankheit f. ~ic /-ˈbetɪk/ a zuckerkrank □ n Zuckerkranke(r) m/f, Diabetiker(in) m(f)

diabolical /daɪəˈbɒlɪkl/ a teuflisch

diagnose /daɪəgˈnəʊz/ vt diagnostizieren

diagnosis /daɪəgˈnəʊsɪs/ n (pl -oses /-siːz/) Diagnose f

diagonal /daɪˈægənl/ a, -ly adv diagonal □ n Diagonale f

diagram /ˈdaɪəgræm/ n Diagramm nt

dial /ˈdaɪəl/ n ⟨of clock⟩ Zifferblatt nt; ⟨Techn⟩ Skala f; ⟨Teleph⟩ Wählscheibe f □ vt/i ⟨pt/pp dialled⟩ ⟨Teleph⟩ wählen; ~ direct durchwählen

dialect /ˈdaɪəlekt/ n Dialekt m

dialling: ~ code n Vorwahlnummer f. ~ tone n Amtszeichen nt

dialogue /ˈdaɪəlɒg/ n Dialog m

'dial tone n ⟨Amer, Teleph⟩ Amtszeichen nt

diameter /daɪˈæmɪtə(r)/ n Durchmesser m

diametrically /daɪəˈmetrɪkəlɪ/ adv ~ opposed genau entgegengesetzt (to dat)

diamond /ˈdaɪəmənd/ n Diamant m; ⟨cut⟩ Brillant m; ⟨shape⟩ Raute f; ~s pl ⟨Cards⟩ Karo nt

diaper /ˈdaɪəpə(r)/ n ⟨Amer⟩ Windel f

diaphragm /ˈdaɪəfræm/ n ⟨Anat⟩ Zwerchfell nt; ⟨Phot⟩ Blende f

diarrhoea /daɪəˈrɪə/ n Durchfall m

diary /ˈdaɪərɪ/ n Tagebuch nt; ⟨for appointments⟩ [Termin]kalender m

dice /daɪs/ n inv Würfel m □ vt ⟨Culin⟩ in Würfel schneiden

dicey /ˈdaɪsɪ/ a ⟨fam⟩ riskant

dictat|e /dɪkˈteɪt/ vt/i diktieren. ~ion /-eɪʃn/ n Diktat nt

dictator /dɪkˈteɪtə(r)/ n Diktator m. ~ial /-təˈtɔːrɪəl/ a diktatorisch. ~ship n Diktatur f

diction /ˈdɪkʃn/ n Aussprache f

dictionary /ˈdɪkʃənrɪ/ n Wörterbuch nt

did /dɪd/ see do

didactic /dɪˈdæktɪk/ a didaktisch

diddle /ˈdɪdl/ vt ⟨fam⟩ übers Ohr hauen

didn't /ˈdɪdnt/ = did not

die¹ /daɪ/ n ⟨Techn⟩ Prägestempel m; ⟨metal mould⟩ Gussform f

die² vi ⟨pres p dying⟩ sterben ⟨of an + dat⟩; ⟨plant, animal:⟩ eingehen; ⟨flower:⟩ verwelken; be dying to do sth ⟨fam⟩ darauf brennen, etw zu tun; be dying for sth ⟨fam⟩ sich nach etw sehnen. ~ down vi nachlassen; ⟨fire:⟩ herunterbrennen. ~ out vi aussterben

diesel /ˈdiːzl/ n Diesel m. ~ engine n Dieselmotor m

diet /ˈdaɪət/ n Kost f; ⟨restricted⟩ Diät f; ⟨for slimming⟩ Schlankheitskur f; be on a ~ Diät leben; eine Schlankheitskur machen □ vi Diät leben; eine Schlankheitskur machen

dietician /daɪəˈtɪʃn/ n Diätassistent(in) m(f)

differ /ˈdɪfə(r)/ vi sich unterscheiden; ⟨disagree⟩ verschiedener Meinung sein

differen|ce /ˈdɪfrəns/ n Unterschied m; ⟨disagreement⟩ Meinungsverschiedenheit f. ~t a andere(r,s); ⟨various⟩ verschiedene; be ~t anders sein (from als)

differential /dɪfəˈrenʃl/ a Differential- □ n Unterschied m; ⟨Techn⟩ Differenzial nt

differentiate /dɪfəˈrenʃɪeɪt/ vt/i unterscheiden (between zwischen + dat)

differently /ˈdɪfrəntlɪ/ adv anders

difficult /ˈdɪfɪkəlt/ a schwierig, schwer. ~y n Schwierigkeit f

diffiden|ce /'dɪfɪdəns/ n Zaghaftigkeit f. ~t a zaghaft

diffuse[1] /dɪ'fjuːs/ a ausgebreitet; (wordy) langatmig

diffuse[2] /dɪ'fjuːz/ vt (Phys) streuen

dig /dɪg/ n (poke) Stoß m; (remark) spitze Bemerkung f; (Archaeol) Ausgrabung f; ~s pl (fam) möbliertes Zimmer nt □ vt/i (pt/pp dug, pres p digging) graben; umgraben (garden); ~ s.o. in the ribs jdm einen Rippenstoß geben. ~ out vt ausgraben. ~ up vt ausgraben; umgraben (garden); aufreißen (street)

digest[1] /'daɪdʒest/ n Kurzfassung f

digest[2] /dɪ'dʒest/ vt verdauen. ~ible a verdaulich. ~ion /-ɪən/ /-estʃn/ n Verdauung f

digger /'dɪgə(r)/ n (Techn) Bagger m

digit /'dɪdʒɪt/ n Ziffer f; (finger) Finger m; (toe) Zehe f

digital /'dɪdʒɪtl/ a Digital-; ~ clock Digitaluhr f

dignified /'dɪgnɪfaɪd/ a würdevoll

dignitary /'dɪgnɪtərɪ/ n Würdenträger m

dignity /'dɪgnɪtɪ/ n Würde f

digress /daɪ'gres/ vi abschweifen. ~ion /-eʃn/ n Abschweifung f

dike /daɪk/ n Deich m; (ditch) Graben m

dilapidated /dɪ'læpɪdeɪtɪd/ a baufällig

dilate /daɪ'leɪt/ vt erweitern □ vi sich erweitern

dilatory /'dɪlətərɪ/ a langsam

dilemma /dɪ'lemə/ n Dilemma f

dilettante /dɪlɪ'tæntɪ/ n Dilettant(in) m(f)

diligen|ce /'dɪlɪdʒəns/ n Fleiß m. ~t a, -ly adv fleißig

dill /dɪl/ n Dill m

dilly-dally /'dɪlɪdælɪ/ vi (pt/pp -ied) (fam) trödeln

dilute /daɪ'luːt/ vt verdünnen

dim /dɪm/ a (dimmer, dimmest), -ly adv (weak) schwach; (dark) trüb[e]; (indistinct) undeutlich; (fam: stupid) dumm, (fam) doof □ v (pt/pp dimmed) □ vt dämpfen □ vi schwächer werden

dime /daɪm/ n (Amer) Zehncentstück nt

dimension /daɪ'menʃn/ n Dimension f; ~s pl Maße pl

diminish /dɪ'mɪnɪʃ/ vt verringern □ vi sich verringern

diminutive /dɪ'mɪnjʊtɪv/ a winzig □ n Verkleinerungsform f

dimple /'dɪmpl/ n Grübchen nt

din /dɪn/ n Krach m, Getöse nt

dine /daɪn/ vi speisen. ~r n Speisende(r) m/f; (Amer: restaurant) Esslokal nt

dinghy /'dɪŋgɪ/ n Dinghi nt; (inflatable) Schlauchboot nt

dingy /'dɪndʒɪ/ a (-ier, -iest) trübe

dining /'daɪnɪŋ/: ~-car n Speisewagen m. ~-room n Esszimmer nt. ~-table n Esstisch m

dinner /'dɪnə(r)/ n Abendessen nt; (at midday) Mittagessen nt; (formal) Essen nt. ~-jacket n Smoking m

dinosaur /'daɪnəsɔː(r)/ n Dinosaurier m

dint /dɪnt/ n by ~ of durch (+ acc)

diocese /'daɪəsɪs/ n Diözese f

dip /dɪp/ n (in ground) Senke f; (Culin) Dip m; go for a ~ kurz schwimmen gehen □ v (pt/pp dipped) vt [ein]tauchen; ~ one's headlights (Auto) [die Scheinwerfer] abblenden □ vi sich senken

diphtheria /dɪf'θɪərɪə/ n Diphtherie f

diphthong /'dɪfθɒŋ/ n Diphthong m

diploma /dɪ'pləʊmə/ n Diplom nt

diplomacy /dɪ'pləʊməsɪ/ n Diplomatie f

diplomat /'dɪpləmæt/ n Diplomat m. ~ic /-'mætɪk/ a, -ally adv diplomatisch

'dip-stick n (Auto) Ölmessstab m

dire /daɪə(r)/ a (-r, -st) bitter; (situation, consequences) furchtbar

direct /dɪ'rekt/ a & adv direkt □ vt (aim) richten (at auf / (fig) an + acc); (control) leiten; (order) anweisen; ~ s.o. (show the way) jdm den Weg sagen; ~ a film/play bei einem Film/Theaterstück Regie führen. ~ 'current n Gleichstrom m

direction /dɪ'rekʃn/ n Richtung f; (control) Leitung f; (of play, film) Regie f; ~s pl Anweisungen pl; ~s for use Gebrauchsanweisung f

directly /dɪ'rektlɪ/ adv direkt; (at once) sofort □ conj (fam) sobald

director /dɪ'rektə(r)/ n (Comm) Direktor m; (of play, film) Regisseur m

directory /dɪ'rektərɪ/ n Verzeichnis nt; (Teleph) Telefonbuch nt

dirt /dɜːt/ n Schmutz m; (soil) Erde f; ~ cheap (fam) spottbillig

dirty /'dɜːtɪ/ a (-ier, -iest) schmutzig □ vt schmutzig machen

dis|a'bility /dɪs-/ n Behinderung f. ~abled /dɪ'seɪbld/ a [körper]behindert

disad'van|tage n Nachteil m; at a ~tage im Nachteil. ~taged a benachteiligt. ~tageous a nachteilig

disaf'fected a unzufrieden; (disloyal) illoyal

disa'gree vi nicht übereinstimmen (with mit); I ~ ich bin anderer Meinung; we ~ wir sind verschiedener Meinung; oysters ~ with me Austern bekommen mir nicht

disa'greeable a unangenehm

disa'greement n Meinungsverschiedenheit f

disap'pear vi verschwinden. ~ance n Verschwinden nt

disap'point *vt* enttäuschen. ∼ment *n* Enttäuschung *f*

disap'proval *n* Missbilligung *f*

disap'prove *vi* dagegen sein; ∼ of missbilligen

dis'arm *vt* entwaffnen ◻ *vi* (*Mil*) abrüsten. ∼ament *n* Abrüstung *f*. ∼ing *a* entwaffnend

disar'ray *n* Unordnung *f*

disast|er /dɪ'zɑːstə(r)/ *n* Katastrophe *f*; (*accident*) Unglück *nt*. ∼rous /-rəs/ *a* katastrophal

dis'band *vt* auflösen ◻ *vi* sich auflösen

disbe'lief *n* Ungläubigkeit *f*; in ∼ ungläubig

disc /dɪsk/ *n* Scheibe *f*; (*record*) [Schall]platte *f*; (*CD*) CD *f*

discard /dɪ'skɑːd/ *vt* ablegen; (*throw away*) wegwerfen

discern /dɪ'sɜːn/ *vt* wahrnehmen. ∼ible *a* wahrnehmbar. ∼ing *a* anspruchsvoll

'discharge[1] *n* Ausstoßen *nt*; (*Naut, Electr*) Entladung *f*; (*dismissal*) Entlassung *f*; (*Jur*) Freispruch *m*; (*Med*) Ausfluss *m*

dis'charge[2] *vt* ausstoßen; (*Naut, Electr*) entladen; (*dismiss*) entlassen; (*Jur*) freisprechen (*accused*); ∼ a duty sich einer Pflicht entledigen

disciple /dɪ'saɪpl/ *n* Jünger *m*; (*fig*) Schüler *m*

disciplinary /'dɪsɪplɪnərɪ/ *a* disziplinarisch

discipline /'dɪsɪplɪn/ *n* Disziplin *f* ◻ *vt* Disziplin beibringen (+ *dat*); (*punish*) bestrafen

'disc jockey *n* Diskjockey *m*

dis'claim *vt* abstreiten. ∼er *n* Verzichterklärung *f*

dis'clos|e *vt* enthüllen. ∼ure *n* Enthüllung *f*

disco /'dɪskəʊ/ *n* (*fam*) Disko *f*

dis'colour *vt* verfärben ◻ *vi* sich verfärben

dis'comfort *n* Beschwerden *pl*; (*fig*) Unbehagen *nt*

disconcert /dɪskən'sɜːt/ *vt* aus der Fassung bringen

discon'nect *vt* trennen; (*Electr*) ausschalten; (*cut supply*) abstellen

disconsolate /dɪs'kɒnsələt/ *a* untröstlich

discon'tent *n* Unzufriedenheit *f*. ∼ed *a* unzufrieden

discon'tinue *vt* einstellen; (*Comm*) nicht mehr herstellen

'discord *n* Zwietracht *f*; (*Mus & fig*) Missklang *m*. ∼ant /dɪ'skɔːdənt/ *a* ∼ant note Missklang *m*

discothèque /'dɪskətek/ *n* Diskothek *f*

'discount[1] *n* Rabatt *m*

dis'count[2] *vt* außer Acht lassen

dis'courage *vt* entmutigen; (*dissuade*) abraten (+ *dat*)

'discourse *n* Rede *f*

dis'courteous *a*, -ly *adv* unhöflich

discover /dɪ'skʌvə(r)/ *vt* entdecken. ∼y *n* Entdeckung *f*

dis'credit *n* Misskredit *m* ◻ *vt* in Misskredit bringen

discreet /dɪ'skriːt/ *a*, -ly *adv* diskret

discrepancy /dɪ'skrepənsɪ/ *n* Diskrepanz *f*

discretion /dɪ'skreʃn/ *n* Diskretion *f*; (*judgement*) Ermessen *nt*

discriminat|e /dɪ'skrɪmɪneɪt/ *vi* unterscheiden (between zwischen + *dat*); ∼e against diskriminieren. ∼ing *a* anspruchsvoll. ∼ion /-'neɪʃn/ *n* Diskriminierung *f*; (*quality*) Urteilskraft *f*

discus /'dɪskəs/ *n* Diskus *m*

discuss /dɪ'skʌs/ *vt* besprechen; (*examine critically*) diskutieren. ∼ion /-ʌʃn/ *n* Besprechung *f*; Diskussion *f*

disdain /dɪs'deɪn/ *n* Verachtung *f* ◻ *vt* verachten. ∼ful *a* verächtlich

disease /dɪ'ziːz/ *n* Krankheit *f*. ∼d *a* krank

disem'bark *vi* an Land gehen

disen'chant *vt* ernüchtern. ∼ment *n* Ernüchterung *f*

disen'gage *vt* losmachen; ∼ the clutch (*Auto*) auskuppeln

disen'tangle *vt* entwirren

dis'favour *n* Ungnade *f*; (*disapproval*) Missfallen *nt*

dis'figure *vt* entstellen

dis'gorge *vt* ausspeien

dis'grace *n* Schande *f*; in ∼ in Ungnade ◻ *vt* Schande machen (+ *dat*). ∼ful *a* schändlich

disgruntled /dɪs'grʌntld/ *a* verstimmt

disguise /dɪs'ɡaɪz/ *n* Verkleidung *f*; in ∼ verkleidet ◻ *vt* verkleiden; verstellen (*voice*); (*conceal*) verhehlen

disgust /dɪs'ɡʌst/ *n* Ekel *m*; in ∼ empört ◻ *vt* anekeln; (*appal*) empören. ∼ing *a* eklig; (*appalling*) abscheulich

dish /dɪʃ/ *n* Schüssel *f*; (*shallow*) Schale *f*; (*small*) Schälchen *nt*; (*food*) Gericht *nt*. ∼ out *vt* austeilen. ∼ up *vt* auftragen

'dishcloth *n* Spültuch *m*

dis'hearten *vt* entmutigen. ∼ing *a* entmutigend

dishevelled /dɪ'ʃevld/ *a* zerzaust

dis'honest *a* -ly *adv* unehrlich. ∼y *n* Unehrlichkeit *f* dis'honour *n* Schande *f* ◻ *vt* entehren; nicht honorieren ⟨*cheque*⟩. ∼able *a*, -bly *adv* unehrenhaft

'dishwasher *n* Geschirrspülmaschine *f*

disil'lusion *vt* ernüchtern. ∼ment *n* Ernüchterung *f*

disin'fect *vt* desinfizieren. ∼ant *n* Desinfektionsmittel *nt*

disin'herit *vt* enterben

dis'integrate *vi* zerfallen

dis'interested *a* unvoreingenommen; ⟨*uninterested*⟩ uninteressiert

dis'jointed *a* unzusammenhängend

disk /dɪsk/ *n* = disc

dis'like *n* Abneigung *f* ◻ *vt* nicht mögen

dislocate /'dɪsləkeɪt/ *vt* ausrenken; ∼ one's shoulder sich ⟨*dat*⟩ den Arm ausrenken kugeln

dis'lodge *vt* entfernen

dis'loyal *a*, -ly *adv* illoyal. ∼ty *n* Illoyalität *f*

dismal /'dɪzməl/ *a* trüb[e]; ⟨*person*⟩ trübselig; ⟨*fam: poor*⟩ kläglich

dismantle /dɪs'mæntl/ *vt* auseinander nehmen; ⟨*take down*⟩ abbauen

dis'may *n* Bestürzung *f*. ∼ed *a* bestürzt

dis'miss *vt* entlassen; ⟨*reject*⟩ zurückweisen. ∼al *n* Entlassung *f*; Zurückweisung *f*

dis'mount *vi* absteigen

diso'bedi|ence *n* Ungehorsam *m*. ∼t *a* ungehorsam

diso'bey *vt/i* nicht gehorchen (+ *dat*); nicht befolgen ⟨*rule*⟩

dis'order *n* Unordnung *f*; ⟨*Med*⟩ Störung *f*. ∼ly *a* unordentlich; ∼ly conduct ungebührliches Benehmen *nt*

dis'organized *a* unorganisiert

dis'orientate *vt* verwirren; be ∼d die Orientierung verloren haben

dis'own *vt* verleugnen

disparaging /dɪ'spærɪdʒɪŋ/ *a*, -ly *adv* abschätzig

disparity /dɪ'spærətɪ/ *n* Ungleichheit *f*

dispassionate /dɪ'spæʃənət/ *a*, -ly *adv* gelassen; ⟨*impartial*⟩ unparteiisch

dispatch /dɪ'spætʃ/ *n* ⟨*Comm*⟩ Versand *m*; ⟨*Mil*⟩ Nachricht *f*; ⟨*report*⟩ Bericht *m*; with ∼ prompt ◻ *vt* [ab]senden; ⟨*deal with*⟩ erledigen; ⟨*kill*⟩ töten. ∼-rider *n* Meldefahrer *m*

dispel /dɪ'spel/ *vt* (*pt/pp* dispelled) vertreiben

dispensable /dɪ'spensəbl/ *a* entbehrlich

dispensary /dɪ'spensərɪ/ *n* Apotheke *f*

dispense /dɪ'spens/ *vt* austeilen; ∼ with verzichten auf (+ *acc*). ∼r *n* Apotheker(in) *m(f)*; ⟨*device*⟩ Automat *m*

dispers|al /dɪ'spɜːsl/ *n* Zerstreuung *f*. ∼e /dɪ'spɜːs/ *vt* zerstreuen ◻ *vi* sich zerstreuen

dispirited /dɪ'spɪrɪtɪd/ *a* entmutigt

dis'place *vt* verschieben; ∼d person Vertriebene(r) *m|f*

display /dɪ'spleɪ/ *n* Ausstellung *f*; ⟨*Comm*⟩ Auslage *f*; ⟨*performance*⟩ Vorführung *f* ◻ *vt* zeigen; ausstellen ⟨*goods*⟩

dis'please *vt* missfallen (+ *dat*)

dis'pleasure *n* Missfallen *nt*

disposable /dɪ'spəʊzəbl/ *a* Wegwerf-; ⟨*income*⟩ verfügbar

disposal /dɪ'spəʊzl/ *n* Beseitigung *f*; be at s.o.'s ∼ jdm zur Verfügung stehen

dispose /dɪ'spəʊz/ *vt*; ∼ of beseitigen; ⟨*deal with*⟩ erledigen; be well ∼d wohlgesinnt sein (to *dat*)

disposition /dɪspə'zɪʃn/ *n* Veranlagung *f*; ⟨*nature*⟩ Wesensart *f*

disproportionate /dɪsprə'pɔːʃənət/ *a*, -ly *adv* unverhältnismäßig

dis'prove *vt* widerlegen

dispute /dɪ'spjuːt/ *n* Disput *m*; ⟨*quarrel*⟩ Streit *m* ◻ *vt* bestreiten

disquali'fication *n* Disqualifikation *f*

dis'qualify *vt* disqualifizieren; ∼ s.o. from driving jdm den Führerschein entziehen

disquieting /dɪs'kwaɪətɪŋ/ *a* beunruhigend

disre'gard *n* Nichtbeachtung *f* ◻ *vt* nicht beachten, ignorieren

disre'pair *n* fall into ∼ verfallen

disre'putable *a* verrufen

disre'pute *n* Verruf *m*

disre'spect *n* Respektlosigkeit *f*. ∼ful *a*, -ly *adv* respektlos

disrupt /dɪs'rʌpt/ *vt* stören. ∼ion /-ʌpʃn/ *n* Störung *f*. ∼ive /-ɪv/ *a* störend

dissatis'faction *n* Unzufriedenheit *f*

dis'satisfied *a* unzufrieden

dissect /dɪ'sekt/ *vt* zergliedern; ⟨*Med*⟩ sezieren. ∼ion /-ekʃn/ *n* Zergliederung *f*; ⟨*Med*⟩ Sektion *f*

disseminat|e /dɪ'semɪneɪt/ *vt* verbreiten. ∼ion /-'neɪʃn/ *n* Verbreitung *f*

dissent /dɪ'sent/ *n* Nichtübereinstimmung *f* ◻ *vi* nicht übereinstimmen

dissertation /dɪsə'teɪʃn/ *n* Dissertation *f*

dis'service *n* schlechter Dienst *m*

dissident /'dɪsɪdənt/ *n* Dissident *m*

dis'similar *a* unähnlich (to *dat*)

dissociate /dɪ'səʊʃɪeɪt/ *vt* trennen; ∼ oneself sich distanzieren (from von)

dissolute /'dɪsəluːt/ *a* zügellos; ⟨*life*⟩ ausschweifend

dissolution /dɪsə'lu:ʃn/ n Auflösung f

dissolve /dɪ'zɒlv/ vt auflösen □ vi sich auflösen

dissuade /dɪ'sweɪd/ vt abbringen (from von)

distance /'dɪstəns/ n Entfernung f; long/ short ~ lange/kurze Strecke f; in the/ from a ~ in/aus der Ferne

distant /'dɪstənt/ a fern; (aloof) kühl; (relative) entfernt

dis'taste n Abneigung f. ~ful a unangenehm

distend /dɪ'stend/ vi sich [auf]blähen

distil /dɪ'stɪl/ vt (pt/pp distilled) brennen; (Chem) destillieren. ~lation /-'leɪʃn/ n Destillation f. ~lery /-ərɪ/ n Brennerei f

distinct /dɪ'stɪŋkt/ a deutlich; (different) verschieden. ~ion /-ɪŋkʃn/ n Unterschied m; (Sch) Auszeichnung f. ~ive /-tɪv/ a kennzeichnend; (unmistakable) unverwechselbar. ~ly adv deutlich

distinguish /dɪ'stɪŋgwɪʃ/ vt/i unterscheiden; (make out) erkennen; ~ oneself sich auszeichnen. ~ed a angesehen; (appearance) distinguiert

distort /dɪ'stɔ:t/ vt verzerren; (fig) verdrehen. ~ion /-ɔ:ʃn/ n Verzerrung f; (fig) Verdrehung f

distract /dɪ'strækt/ vt ablenken. ~ed /-ɪd/ a [völlig] aufgelöst. ~ion /-ækʃn/ n Ablenkung f; (despair) Verzweiflung f

distraught /dɪ'strɔ:t/ a [völlig] aufgelöst

distress /dɪ'stres/ n Kummer m; (pain) Schmerz m; (poverty, danger) Not f □ vt Kummer/Schmerz bereiten (+ dat); (sadden) bekümmern; (shock) erschüttern. ~ing a schmerzlich; (shocking) erschütternd. ~ signal n Notsignal nt

distribut|e /dɪ'strɪbju:t/ vt verteilen; (Comm) vertreiben. ~ion /-'bju:ʃn/ n Verteilung f; Vertrieb m. ~or n Verteiler m

district /'dɪstrɪkt/ n Gegend f; (Admin) Bezirk m. ~ nurse n Gemeindeschwester f

dis'trust n Misstrauen nt □ vt misstrauen (+ dat). ~ful a misstrauisch

disturb /dɪ'stɜ:b/ vt stören; (perturb) beunruhigen; (touch) anrühren. ~ance n Unruhe f; (interruption) Störung f. ~ed a beunruhigt; [mentally] ~ed geistig gestört. ~ing a beunruhigend

dis'used a stillgelegt; (empty) leer

ditch /dɪtʃ/ n Graben m □ vt (fam: abandon) fallen lassen (plan); wegschmeißen (thing)

dither /'dɪðə(r)/ vi zaudern

ditto /'dɪtəʊ/ n dito; (fam) ebenfalls

divan /dɪ'væn/ n Polsterbett nt

dive /daɪv/ n [Kopf]sprung m; (Aviat) Sturzflug m; (fam: place) Spelunke f □ vi einen Kopfsprung machen; (when in water) tauchen; (Aviat) einen Sturzflug machen; (fam: rush) stürzen

diver /'daɪvə(r)/ n Taucher m; (Sport) [Kunst]springer m

diver|ge /daɪ'vɜ:dʒ/ vi auseinander gehen. ~gent /-ənt/ a abweichend

diverse /daɪ'vɜ:s/ a verschieden

diversify /daɪ'vɜ:sɪfaɪ/ vt/i (pt/pp -ied) variieren; (Comm) diversifizieren

diversion /daɪ'vɜ:ʃn/ n Umleitung f; (distraction) Ablenkung f

diversity /daɪ'vɜ:sətɪ/ n Vielfalt f

divert /daɪ'vɜ:t/ vt umleiten; ablenken (attention); (entertain) unterhalten

divest /daɪ'vest/ vt sich entledigen (of + gen); (fig) entkleiden

divide /dɪ'vaɪd/ vt teilen; (separate) trennen; (Math) dividieren (by durch) □ vi sich teilen

dividend /'dɪvɪdend/ n Dividende f

divine /dɪ'vaɪn/ a göttlich

diving /'daɪvɪŋ/ n (Sport) Kunstspringen nt. ~-board n Sprungbrett nt. ~-suit n Taucheranzug m

divinity /dɪ'vɪnətɪ/ n Göttlichkeit f; (subject) Theologie f

divisible /dɪ'vɪzɪbl/ a teilbar (by durch)

division /dɪ'vɪʒn/ n Teilung f; (separation) Trennung f; (Math, Mil) Division f; (Parl) Hammelsprung m; (line) Trennlinie f; (group) Abteilung f

divorce /dɪ'vɔ:s/ n Scheidung f □ vt sich scheiden lassen von. ~d a geschieden; get ~d sich scheiden lassen

divorcee /dɪvɔ:'si:/ n Geschiedene(r) m/f

divulge /daɪ'vʌldʒ/ vt preisgeben

DIY abbr of do-it-yourself

dizziness /'dɪzɪnɪs/ n Schwindel m

dizzy /'dɪzɪ/ a (-ier, -iest) schwindlig; I feel ~ mir ist schwindlig

do /du:/ n (pl dos or do's) (fam) Veranstaltung f □ v (3 sg pres tense does; pt did; pp done) □ vt/i tun, machen; (be suitable) passen; (be enough) reichen, genügen; (cook) kochen; (clean) putzen; (Sch: study) durchnehmen; (fam: cheat) beschwindeln (out of um); do without auskommen ohne; do away with abschaffen; be done (Culin) gar sein; well done gut gemacht! (Culin) gut durchgebraten; done in (fam) kaputt, fertig; done for (fam) verloren, erledigt; do the flowers die Blumen arrangieren; do the potatoes die Kartoffeln schälen; do the washing up abwaschen, spülen; do one's hair sich frisieren; do well/badly gut/schlecht abschneiden;

how is he doing? wie geht es ihm? this won't do das geht nicht; are you doing anything today? haben Sie heute etwas vor? I could do with a spanner ich könnte einen Schraubenschlüssel gebrauchen □ *vaux* do you speak German? sprechen Sie Deutsch? yes, I do ja; (*emphatic*) doch; no, I don't nein; I don't smoke ich rauche nicht; don't you/ doesn't he? nicht [wahr]? so do I ich auch; do come in kommen Sie doch herein; how do you do? guten Tag. do in *vt* (*fam*) um die Ecke bringen. do up *vt* (*fasten*) zumachen; (*renovate*) renovieren; (*wrap*) einpacken

docile /'dəʊsaɪl/ *a* fügsam

dock[1] /dɒk/ *n* (*Jur*) Anklagebank *f*

dock[2] *n* Dock *nt* □ *vi* anlegen, docken □ *vt* docken. ~er *n* Hafenarbeiter *m*. ~yard *n* Werft *f*

doctor /'dɒktə(r)/ *n* Arzt *m*/ Ärztin *f*; (*Univ*) Doktor *m* □ *vt* kastrieren; (*spay*) sterilisieren. ~ate /-ət/ *n* Doktorwürde *f*

doctrine /'dɒktrɪn/ *n* Lehre *f*, Doktrin *f*

document /'dɒkjʊmənt/ *n* Dokument *nt*. ~ary /-'mentərɪ/ *a* Dokumentar- □ *n* Dokumentarbericht *m*; (*film*) Dokumentarfilm *m*

doddery /'dɒdərɪ/ *a* (*fam*) tatterig

dodge /dɒdʒ/ *n* (*fam*) Trick *m*, Kniff *m* □ *vt/i* ausweichen (+ *dat*); ~ out of the way zur Seite springen

dodgems /'dɒdʒəmz/ *npl* Autoskooter *pl*

dodgy /'dɒdʒɪ/ *a* (-ier, -iest) (*fam*) (*awkward*) knifflig; (*dubious*) zweifelhaft

doe /dəʊ/ *n* Ricke *f*; (*rabbit*) [Kaninchen]weibchen *nt*

does /dʌz/ *see* do

doesn't /'dʌznt/ = does not

dog /dɒg/ *n* Hund *m* □ *vt* (*pt/pp* dogged) verfolgen

dog: ~-biscuit *n* Hundekuchen *m*. ~-collar *n* Hundehalsband *nt*; (*Relig., fam*) Kragen *m* eines Geistlichen. ~-eared *a* be ~-eared Eselsohren haben

dogged /'dɒgɪd/ *a*, -ly *adv* beharrlich

dogma /'dɒgmə/ *n* Dogma *nt*. ~tic /-'mætɪk/ *a* dogmatisch

'dogsbody *n* (*fam*) Mädchen *nt* für alles

doily /'dɔɪlɪ/ *n* Deckchen *nt*

do-it-yourself /du:ɪtjə'self/ *n* Heimwerken *nt*. ~ shop *n* Heimwerkerladen *m*

doldrums /'dɒldrəmz/ *npl* be in the ~ niedergeschlagen sein; (*business:*) daniederliegen

dole /dəʊl/ *n* Stempelgeld *nt*; be on the ~ arbeitslos sein □ *vt* ~ out austeilen

doleful /'dəʊlfl/ *a*, -ly *adv* traurig

doll /dɒl/ *n* Puppe *f* □ *vt* (*fam*) ~ oneself up sich herausputzen

dollar /'dɒlə(r)/ *n* Dollar *m*

dollop /'dɒləp/ *n* (*fam*) Klecks *m*

dolphin /'dɒlfɪn/ *n* Delphin *m*

domain /də'meɪn/ *n* Gebiet *nt*

dome /dəʊm/ *n* Kuppel *f*

domestic /də'mestɪk/ *a* häuslich; (*Pol*) Innen-; (*Comm*) Binnen-. ~ animal *n* Haustier *nt*

domesticated /də'mestɪkeɪtɪd/ *a* häuslich; ⟨*animal*⟩ zahm

domestic: ~ flight *n* Inlandflug *m*. ~ 'servant *n* Hausangestellte(r) *m/f*

dominant /'dɒmɪnənt/ *a* vorherrschend

dominat|e /'dɒmɪneɪt/ *vt* beherrschen □ *vi* dominieren; ~ over beherrschen. ~ion /-'neɪʃn/ *n* Vorherrschaft *f*

domineer /dɒmɪ'nɪə(r)/ *vi* ~ over tyrannisieren. ~ing *a* herrschsüchtig

dominion /də'mɪnjən/ *n* Herrschaft *f*

domino /'dɒmɪnəʊ/ *n* (*pl*-es) Dominostein *m*; ~es *sg* (*game*) Domino *nt*

don[1] /dɒn/ *vt* (*pt/pp* donned) (*liter*) anziehen

don[2] *n* [Universitäts]dozent *m*

donat|e /dəʊ'neɪt/ *vt* spenden. ~ion /-eɪʃn/ *n* Spende *f*

done /dʌn/ *see* do

donkey /'dɒŋkɪ/ *n* Esel *m*; ~'s years (*fam*) eine Ewigkeit. ~-work *n* Routinearbeit *f*

donor /'dəʊnə(r)/ *n* Spender(in) *m(f)*

don't /dəʊnt/ = do not

doodle /'du:dl/ *vi* kritzeln

doom /du:m/ *n* Schicksal *nt*; (*ruin*) Verhängnis *nt* □ *vt* be ~ed to failure zum Scheitern verurteilt sein

door /dɔ:(r)/ *n* Tür *f*; out of ~s im Freien

door: ~man *n* Portier *m*. ~mat *n* [Fuß]abtreter *m*. ~step *n* Türschwelle *f*; on the ~step vor der Tür. ~way *n* Türöffnung *f*

dope /dəʊp/ *n* (*fam*) Drogen *pl*; (*fam: information*) Informationen *pl*; (*fam: idiot*) Trottel *m* □ *vt* betäuben; (*Sport*) dopen

dopey /'dəʊpɪ/ *a* (*fam*) benommen; (*stupid*) blöd[e]

dormant /'dɔ:mənt/ *a* ruhend

dormer /'dɔ:mə(r)/ *n* ~ [window] Mansardenfenster *nt*

dormitory /'dɔ:mɪtərɪ/ *n* Schlafsaal *m*

dormouse /'dɔ:-/ *n* Haselmaus *f*

dosage /'dəʊsɪdʒ/ *n* Dosierung *f*

dose /dəʊs/ *n* Dosis *f*

doss /dɒs/ *vi* (*sl*) pennen. ~er *n* Penner *m*. ~house *n* Penne *f*

dot /dɒt/ *n* Punkt *m*; on the ~ pünktlich

dote /dəʊt/ vi ~ on vernarrt sein in (+ acc)

dotted /'dɒtɪd/ a ~ line punktierte Linie f; be ~ with bestreut sein mit

dotty /'dɒtɪ/ a (-ier, -iest) (fam) verdreht

double /'dʌbl/ a & adv doppelt; ⟨bed, chin⟩ Doppel-; ⟨flower⟩ gefüllt □ n das Doppelte; ⟨person⟩ Doppelgänger m; ~s pl (Tennis) Doppel nt; at the ~ im Laufschritt □ vt verdoppeln; ⟨fold⟩ falten □ vi sich verdoppeln. ~ back vi zurückgehen. ~ up vi sich krümmen (with vor + dat)

double: ~-bass n Kontrabass m. ~-breasted a zweireihig. ~-'cross vt ein Doppelspiel treiben mit. ~-'decker n Doppeldecker m. ~ 'Dutch n (fam) Kauderwelsch nt. ~ 'glazing n Doppelverglasung f. ~ 'room n Doppelzimmer nt

doubly /'dʌblɪ/ adv doppelt

doubt /daʊt/ n Zweifel m □ vt bezweifeln. ~ful a, -ly adv zweifelhaft; ⟨disbelieving⟩ skeptisch. ~less adv zweifellos

dough /dəʊ/ n [fester] Teig m; ⟨fam: money⟩ Pinke f. ~nut n Berliner [Pfannkuchen] m, Krapfen m

douse /daʊs/ vt übergießen; ausgießen ⟨flames⟩

dove /dʌv/ n Taube f. ~tail n (Techn) Schwalbenschwanz m

dowdy /'daʊdɪ/ a (-ier, -iest) unschick

down[1] /daʊn/ n ⟨feathers⟩ Daunen pl

down[2] adv unten; ⟨with movement⟩ nach unten; go ~ hinuntergehen; come ~ herunterkommen; ~ there da unten; £50 ~ £50 Anzahlung; ~! (to dog) Platz! ~ with ...! nieder mit ...! □ prep ~ the road/stairs die Straße/Treppe hinunter; ~ the river den Fluss abwärts; be ~ the pub (fam) in der Kneipe sein □ vt ⟨fam⟩ ⟨drink⟩ runterkippen; ~ tools die Arbeit niederlegen

down: ~-and-'out n Penner m. ~cast a niedergeschlagen. ~fall n Sturz m; ⟨ruin⟩ Ruin m. ~'grade vt niedriger einstufen. ~-'hearted a entmutigt. ~'hill adv bergab. ~ payment n Anzahlung f. ~pour n Platzregen m. ~right a & adv ausgesprochen. ~'stairs adv unten; ⟨go⟩ nach unten □ a /'--/ im Erdgeschoss. ~'stream adv stromabwärts. ~-to-'earth a sachlich. ~town adv (Amer) im Stadtzentrum. ~trodden a unterdrückt. ~ward a nach unten; ⟨slope⟩ abfallend □ adv ~[s] abwärts, nach unten

downy /'daʊnɪ/ a (-ier, -iest) flaumig

dowry /'daʊrɪ/ n Mitgift f

doze /dəʊz/ n Nickerchen n □ vi dösen. ~ off vi einnicken

dozen /'dʌzn/ n Dutzend nt

Dr abbr of doctor

draft[1] /drɑːft/ n Entwurf m; (Comm) Tratte f; (Amer Mil) Einberufung f □ vt entwerfen; (Amer Mil) einberufen

draft[2] n (Amer) = draught

drag /dræg/ n (fam) Klotz m am Bein; in ~ ⟨fam⟩ ⟨man⟩ als Frau gekleidet □ vt ⟨pt/pp dragged⟩ schleppen; absuchen ⟨river⟩. ~ on vi sich in die Länge ziehen

dragon /'drægən/ n Drache m. ~-fly n Libelle f

'drag show n Transvestitenshow f

drain /dreɪn/ n Abfluss m; ⟨underground⟩ Kanal m; the ~s die Kanalisation □ vt entwässern ⟨land⟩; ablassen ⟨liquid⟩; das Wasser ablassen aus ⟨tank⟩; abgießen ⟨vegetables⟩; austrinken ⟨glass⟩ □ vi ~ [away] ablaufen; leave sth to ~ etw abtropfen lassen

drain|age /'dreɪnɪdʒ/ n Kanalisation f; ⟨of land⟩ Dränage f. ~ing board n Abtropfbrett nt. ~-pipe n Abflussrohr nt

drake /dreɪk/ n Enterich m

drama /'drɑːmə/ n Drama nt; ⟨quality⟩ Dramatik f

dramatic /drə'mætɪk/ a, -ally adv dramatisch

dramat|ist /'dræmətɪst/ n Dramatiker m. ~ize vt für die Bühne bearbeiten; (fig) dramatisieren

drank /dræŋk/ see drink

drape /dreɪp/ n (Amer) Vorhang m □ vt drapieren

drastic /'dræstɪk/ a, -ally adv drastisch

draught /drɑːft/ n [Luft]zug m; ~s sg ⟨game⟩ Damespiel nt; there is a ~ es zieht

draught: ~ beer n Bier nt vom Fass. ~sman n technischer Zeichner m

draughty /'drɑːftɪ/ a zugig; it's ~ es zieht

draw /drɔː/ n Attraktion f; (Sport) Unentschieden nt; ⟨in lottery⟩ Ziehung f □ v ⟨pt drew, pp drawn⟩ □ vt ziehen; ⟨attract⟩ anziehen; zeichnen ⟨picture⟩; abheben ⟨money⟩; holen ⟨water⟩; ~ the curtains die Vorhänge zuziehen/⟨back⟩ aufziehen; ~ lots losen (for um) □ vi ⟨tea:⟩ ziehen; (Sport) unentschieden spielen. ~ back vt zurückziehen □ vi ⟨recoil⟩ zurückweichen. ~ in vt/i einziehen □ vi einfahren; ⟨days:⟩ kürzer werden. ~ out vt herausziehen; abheben ⟨money⟩ □ vi ausfahren; ⟨days:⟩ länger werden. ~ up vt aufsetzen ⟨document⟩; heranrücken ⟨chair⟩; ~ oneself up sich aufrichten □ vi [an]halten

draw: ~back n Nachteil m. ~bridge n Zugbrücke f

drawer /drɔː(r)/ n Schublade f

drawing /'drɔːɪŋ/ n Zeichnung f

drawing: ~-board *n* Reißbrett *nt.* ~-pin *n* Reißzwecke *f.* ~-room *n* Wohnzimmer *nt*

drawl /drɔːl/ *n* schleppende Aussprache *f*

drawn /drɔːn/ *see* draw

dread /dred/ *n* Furcht *f* (of vor + *dat*) □ *vt* fürchten. ~-ful *a*, ~-fully *adv* fürchterlich

dream /driːm/ *n* Traum *m* □ *attrib* Traum- □ *vt/i* (*pt/pp* dreamt /dremt/ *or* dreamed) träumen (about/of von)

dreary /'drɪərɪ/ *a* (-ier, -iest) trüb[e]; (*boring*) langweilig

dredge /dredʒ/ *vt/i* baggern. ~r *n* [Nass]bagger *m*

dregs /dregz/ *npl* Bodensatz *m*

drench /drentʃ/ *vt* durchnässen

dress /dres/ *n* Kleid *nt*; (*clothing*) Kleidung *f* □ *vt* anziehen; (*decorate*) schmücken; (*Culin*) anmachen; (*Med*) verbinden; ~ oneself, get ~ed sich anziehen □ *vi* sich anziehen. ~ up *vi* sich schön anziehen; (*in disguise*) sich verkleiden (as als)

dress: ~ circle *n* (*Theat*) erster Rang *m.* ~er *n* (*furniture*) Anrichte *f*; (*Amer: dressing-table*) Frisiertisch *m*

dressing *n* (*Culin*) Soße *f*; (*Med*) Verband *m*

dressing: ~ 'down *n* Standpauke *f.* ~-gown *n* Morgenmantel *m.* ~-room *n* Ankleidezimmer *nt*; (*Theat*) [Künstler]garderobe *f.* ~-table *n* Frisiertisch *m*

dress: ~maker *n* Schneiderin *f.* ~making *n* Damenschneiderei *f.* ~ rehearsal *n* Generalprobe *f*

dressy /'dresɪ/ *a* (-ier, -iest) schick

drew /druː/ *see* draw

dribble /'drɪbl/ *vi* sabbern; (*Sport*) dribbeln

dried /draɪd/ *a* getrocknet; ~ fruit Dörrobst *nt*

drier /'draɪə(r)/ *n* Trockner *m*

drift /drɪft/ *n* Abtrift *f*; (*of snow*) Schneewehe *f*; (*meaning*) Sinn *m* □ *vi* treiben; (*off course*) abtreiben; (*snow:*) Wehen bilden; (*fig*) (*person:*) sich treiben lassen; ~ apart (*persons:*) sich auseinander leben. ~wood *n* Treibholz *nt*

drill /drɪl/ *n* Bohrer *m*; (*Mil*) Drill *m* □ *vt/i* bohren (for nach); (*Mil*) drillen

drily /'draɪlɪ/ *adv* trocken

drink /drɪŋk/ *n* Getränk *nt*; (*alcoholic*) Drink *m*; (*alcohol*) Alkohol *m*; have a ~ etwas trinken □ *vt/i* (*pt* drank, *pp* drunk) trinken. ~ up *vt/i* austrinken

drink|able /'drɪŋkəbl/ *a* trinkbar. ~er *n* Trinker *m*

'drinking-water *n* Trinkwasser *nt*

drip /drɪp/ *n* Tropfen *nt*; (*drop*) Tropfen *m*; (*Med*) Tropf *m*; (*fam: person*) Niete *f* □ *vi*

(*pt/pp* dripped) tropfen. ~-'dry *a* bügelfrei. ~ping *n* Schmalz *nt*

drive /draɪv/ *n* [Auto]fahrt *f*; (*entrance*) Einfahrt *f*; (*energy*) Elan *m*, (*Psych*) Trieb *m*; (*Pol*) Aktion *f*; (*Sport*) Treibschlag *m*; (*Techn*) Antrieb *m* □ *v* (*pt* drove, *pp* driven) □ *vt* treiben; fahren (*car*); (*Sport: hit*) schlagen; (*Techn*) antreiben; ~ s.o. mad (*fam*) jdn verrückt machen; what are you driving at? (*fam*) worauf willst du hinaus? □ *vi* fahren. ~ away *vt* vertreiben □ *vi* abfahren. ~ in *vi* hinein-/hereinfahren. ~ off *vt* vertreiben □ *vi* abfahren. ~ on *vi* weiterfahren. ~ up *vi* vorfahren

'drive-in *a* ~ cinema Autokino *nt*

drivel /'drɪvl/ *n* (*fam*) Quatsch *m*

driven /'drɪvn/ *see* drive

driver /'draɪvə(r)/ *n* Fahrer(in) *m(f)*; (*of train*) Lokführer *m*

driving /'draɪvɪŋ/ *a* (*rain*) peitschend; (*force*) treibend

driving: ~ lesson *n* Fahrstunde *f.* ~ licence *n* Führerschein *m.* ~ school *n* Fahrschule *f.* ~ test *n* Fahrprüfung *f*; take one's ~ test den Führerschein machen

drizzle /'drɪzl/ *n* Nieselregen *m* □ *vi* nieseln

drone /drəʊn/ *n* Drohne *f*; (*sound*) Brummen *nt*

droop /druːp/ *vi* herabhängen; (*flowers:*) die Köpfe hängen lassen

drop /drɒp/ *n* Tropfen *m*; (*fall*) Fall *m*; (*in price, temperature*) Rückgang *m* □ *v* (*pt/pp* dropped) □ *vt* fallen lassen; abwerfen (*bomb*); (*omit*) auslassen; (*give up*) aufgeben □ *vi* fallen; (*fall lower*) sinken; (*wind:*) nachlassen. ~ in *vi* vorbeikommen. ~ off *vt* absetzen (*person*) □ *vi* abfallen; (*fall asleep*) einschlafen. ~ out *vi* herausfallen; (*give up*) aufgeben

'drop-out *n* Aussteiger *m*

droppings /'drɒpɪŋz/ *npl* Kot *m*

drought /draʊt/ *n* Dürre *f*

drove /drəʊv/ *see* drive

droves /drəʊvz/ *npl* in ~ in Scharen

drown /draʊn/ *vi* ertrinken □ *vt* ertränken; übertönen (*noise*); be ~ed ertrinken

drowsy /'draʊzɪ/ *a* schläfrig

drudgery /'drʌdʒərɪ/ *n* Plackerei *f*

drug /drʌg/ *n* Droge *f* □ *vt* (*pt/pp* drugged) betäuben

drug: ~ addict *n* Drogenabhängige(r) *m/f.* ~gist *n* (*Amer*) Apotheker *m.* ~store *n* (*Amer*) Drogerie *f*, (*dispensing*) Apotheke *f*

drum /drʌm/ *n* Trommel *f*; (*for oil*) Tonne *f* □ *v* (*pt/pp* drummed) □ *vi* trommeln

□ *vt* ∼sth into s.o. (*fam*) jdm etw einbläuen. ∼mer *n* Trommler *m*; (*in popgroup*) Schlagzeuger *m*. ∼stick *n* Trommelschlägel *m*; (*Culin*) Keule *f*

drunk /drʌŋk/ *see* drink □ *a* betrunken; get ∼ sich betrinken □ *n* Betrunkene(r) *m*

drunk|ard /'drʌŋkəd/ *n* Trinker *m*. ∼en *a* betrunken; ∼en driving Trunkenheit *f* am Steuer

dry /draɪ/ *a* (drier, driest) trocken □ *vt/i* trocknen; ∼ one's eyes sich *dat* die Tränen abwischen. ∼ up *vi* austrocknen; (*fig*) versiegen □ *vt* austrocknen; abtrocknen ⟨*dishes*⟩

dry: ∼'clean *vt* chemisch reinigen. ∼-'cleaner's *n* (*shop*) chemische Reinigung *f*. ∼ness *n* Trockenheit *f*

dual /'djuːəl/ *a* doppelt

dual: ∼ 'carriageway *n* ≈ Schnellstraße *f*. ∼-'purpose *a* zweifach verwendbar

dub /dʌb/ *vt* (*pt/pp* dubbed) synchronisieren ⟨*film*⟩; kopieren ⟨*tape*⟩; (*name*) nennen

dubious /'djuːbɪəs/ *a* zweifelhaft; be ∼ about sich *dat* nicht sicher sein über (+ *acc*)

duchess /'dʌtʃɪs/ *n* Herzogin *f*

duck /dʌk/ *n* Ente *f* □ *vt* (*in water*) untertauchen; ∼ one's head den Kopf einziehen □ *vi* sich ducken. ∼ling *n* Entchen *nt*; (*Culin*) Ente *f*

duct /dʌkt/ *n* Rohr *nt*; (*Anat*) Gang *m*

dud /dʌd/ *a* (*fam*) nutzlos; ⟨*coin*⟩ falsch; ⟨*cheque*⟩ ungedeckt; (*forged*) gefälscht □ *n* (*fam*) ⟨*banknote*⟩ Blüte *f*; (*Mil: shell*) Blindgänger *m*

due /djuː/ *a* angemessen; be ∼ fällig sein; ⟨*baby:*⟩ erwartet werden; ⟨*train:*⟩ planmäßig ankommen; ∼ to (*owing to*) wegen (+ *gen*); be ∼ to zurückzuführen sein auf (+ *acc*); in ∼ course im Laufe der Zeit; ⟨*write*⟩ zu gegebener Zeit □ *adv* ∼ west genau westlich

duel /'djuːəl/ *n* Duell *nt*

dues /djuːz/ *npl* Gebühren *pl*

duet /djuː'et/ *n* Duo *nt*; (*vocal*) Duett *nt*

dug /dʌg/ *see* dig

duke /djuːk/ *n* Herzog *m*

dull /dʌl/ *a* (-er, -est) (*overcast, not bright*) trüb[e]; (*not shiny*) matt; ⟨*sound*⟩ dumpf; (*boring*) langweilig; (*stupid*) schwerfällig □ *vt* betäuben; abstumpfen ⟨*mind*⟩

duly /'djuːlɪ/ *adv* ordnungsgemäß

dumb /dʌm/ *a* (-er, -est) stumm; (*fam: stupid*) dumm. ∼founded *a* sprachlos

dummy /'dʌmɪ/ *n* (*tailor's*) [Schneider]-puppe *f*; (*for baby*) Schnuller *m*; (*Comm*) Attrappe *f*

dump /dʌmp/ *n* Abfallhaufen *m*; (*for refuse*) Müllhalde *f*, Deponie *f*; (*fam: town*) Kaff *nt*; be down in the ∼s (*fam*) deprimiert sein □ *vt* abladen; (*fam: put down*) hinwerfen (on auf + *acc*)

dumpling /'dʌmplɪŋ/ *n* Kloß *m*, Knödel *m*

dunce /dʌns/ *n* Dummkopf *m*

dune /djuːn/ *n* Düne *f*

dung /dʌŋ/ *n* Mist *m*

dungarees /dʌŋgə'riːz/ *npl* Latzhose *f*

dungeon /'dʌndʒən/ *n* Verlies *nt*

dunk /dʌŋk/ *vt* eintunken

duo /'djuːəʊ/ *n* Paar *nt*; (*Mus*) Duo *nt*

dupe /djuːp/ *n* Betrogene(r) *m/f* □ *vt* betrügen

duplicate[1] /'djuːplɪkət/ *a* Zweit- □ *n* Doppel *nt*; (*document*) Duplikat *nt*; in ∼ in doppelter Ausfertigung

duplicat|e[2] /'djuːplɪkeɪt/ *vt* kopieren; (*do twice*) zweimal machen. ∼or *n* Vervielfältigungsapparat *m*

durable /'djʊərəbl/ *a* haltbar

duration /djʊə'reɪʃn/ *n* Dauer *f*

duress /djʊə'res/ *n* Zwang *m*

during /'djʊərɪŋ/ *prep* während (+ *gen*)

dusk /dʌsk/ *n* [Abend]dämmerung *f*

dust /dʌst/ *n* Staub *m* □ *vt* abstauben; (*sprinkle*) bestäuben (with mit) □ *vi* Staub wischen

dust: ∼bin *n* Mülltonne *f*. ∼cart *n* Müllwagen *m*. ∼er *n* Staubtuch *nt*. ∼jacket *n* Schutzumschlag *m*. ∼man *n* Müllmann *m*. ∼pan *n* Kehrschaufel *f*

dusty /'dʌstɪ/ *a* (-ier, -iest) staubig

Dutch /dʌtʃ/ *a* holländisch; go ∼ (*fam*) getrennte Kasse machen □ *n* (*Lang*) Holländisch *nt*; the ∼ *pl* die Holländer. ∼man *n* Holländer *m*

dutiable /'djuːtɪəbl/ *a* zollpflichtig

dutiful /'djuːtɪfl/ *a*, -ly *adv* pflichtbewusst; (*obedient*) gehorsam

duty /'djuːtɪ/ *n* Pflicht *f*; (*task*) Aufgabe *f*; (*tax*) Zoll *m*; be on ∼ Dienst haben. ∼free *a* zollfrei

duvet /'duːveɪ/ *n* Steppdecke *f*

dwarf /dwɔːf/ *n* (*pl* -s *or* dwarves) Zwerg *m*

dwell /dwel/ *vi* (*pt/pp* dwelt) (*liter*) wohnen; ∼ on (*fig*) verweilen bei. ∼ing *n* Wohnung *f*

dwindle /'dwɪndl/ *vi* abnehmen, schwinden

dye /daɪ/ *n* Farbstoff *m* □ *vt* (*pres p* dyeing) färben

dying /'daɪɪŋ/ *see* die[2]

dynamic /daɪ'næmɪk/ *a* dynamisch. ∼s *n* Dynamik *f*

dynamite /'daɪnəmaɪt/ n Dynamit nt

dynamo /'daɪnəməʊ/ n Dynamo m

dynasty /'dɪnəstɪ/ n Dynastie f

dysentery /'dɪsəntrɪ/ n Ruhr f

dyslex|ia /dɪs'leksɪə/ n Legasthenie f. ~ic a legasthenisch; be ~ic Legastheniker sein

E

each /iːtʃ/ a & pron jede(r,s); (per) je; ~ other einander; £1 ~ £1 pro Person/ (for thing) pro Stück

eager /'iːgə(r)/ a, -ly adv eifrig; be ~ to do sth etw gerne machen wollen. ~ness n Eifer m

eagle /'iːgl/ n Adler m

ear[1] /ɪə(r)/ n (of corn) Ähre f

ear[2] n Ohr nt. ~ache n Ohrenschmerzen pl. ~drum n Trommelfell nt

earl /ɜːl/ n Graf m

early /'ɜːlɪ/ a & adv (-ier, -iest) früh; (reply) baldig; be ~ früh dran sein; ~ in the morning früh am Morgen

'earmark vt ~ for bestimmen für

earn /ɜːn/ vt verdienen

earnest /'ɜːnɪst/ a, -ly adv ernsthaft □ n in ~ im Ernst

earnings /'ɜːnɪŋz/ npl Verdienst m

ear: ~phones npl Kopfhörer pl. ~-ring n Ohrring m; (clip-on) Ohrklips m. ~shot n within/out of ~shot in/außer Hörweite

earth /ɜːθ/ n Erde f; (of fox) Bau m; where/ what on ~? wo/was in aller Welt? □ vt (Electr) erden

earthenware /'ɜːθn-/ n Tonwaren pl

earthly /'ɜːθlɪ/ a irdisch; be no ~ use (fam) völlig nutzlos sein

'earthquake n Erdbeben nt

earthy /'ɜːθɪ/ a erdig; (coarse) derb

earwig /'ɪəwɪg/ n Ohrwurm m

ease /iːz/ n Leichtigkeit f; at ~! (Mil) rührt euch! be or feel ill at ~ ein ungutes Gefühl haben □ vt erleichtern; lindern (pain) □ vi (pain:) nachlassen; (situation:) sich entspannen

easel /'iːzl/ n Staffelei f

easily /'iːzɪlɪ/ adv leicht, mit Leichtigkeit

east /iːst/ n Osten m; to the ~ of östlich von □ a Ost-, ost- □ adv nach Osten

Easter /'iːstə(r)/ n Ostern nt □ attrib Oster-. ~ egg n Osterei nt

east|erly /'iːstəlɪ/ a östlich. ~ern a östlich. ~ward[s] /-wəd[z]/ adv nach Osten

easy /'iːzɪ/ a (-ier, -iest) leicht; take it ~ (fam) sich schonen; take it ~! beruhige dich! go ~ with (fam) sparsam umgehen mit

easy: ~ chair n Sessel m. ~'going a gelassen; too ~going lässig

eat /iːt/ vt/i (pt ate, pp eaten) essen; (animal:) fressen. ~ up vt aufessen

eat|able /'iːtəbl/ a genießbar. ~er n (apple) Essapfel m

eau-de-Cologne /əʊdəkə'ləʊn/ n Kölnischwasser nt

eaves /iːvz/ npl Dachüberhang m. ~drop vi (pt/pp -dropped) [heimlich] lauschen; ~drop on belauschen

ebb /eb/ n (tide) Ebbe f; at a low ~ (fig) auf einem Tiefstand □ vi zurückgehen; (fig) verebben

ebony /'ebənɪ/ n Ebenholz nt

ebullient /ɪ'bʌlɪənt/ a überschwänglich

EC abbr (European Community) EG f

eccentric /ɪk'sentrɪk/ a exzentrisch □ n Exzentriker m

ecclesiastical /ɪkliːzɪ'æstɪkl/ a kirchlich

echo /'ekəʊ/ n (pl -es) Echo nt, Widerhall m □ v (pt/pp echoed, pres p echoing) □ vt zurückwerfen; (imitate) nachsagen □ vi widerhallen (with von)

eclipse /ɪ'klɪps/ n (Astr) Finsternis f □ vt (fig) in den Schatten stellen

ecolog|ical /iːkə'lɒdʒɪkl/ a ökologisch. ~y /iː'kɒlədʒɪ/ n Ökologie f

economic /iːkə'nɒmɪk/ a wirtschaftlich. ~al a sparsam. ~ally adv wirtschaftlich; (thriftily) sparsam. ~s n Volkswirtschaft f

economist /ɪ'kɒnəmɪst/ n Volkswirt m; (Univ) Wirtschaftswissenschaftler m

economize /ɪ'kɒnəmaɪz/ vi sparen (on an + dat)

economy /ɪ'kɒnəmɪ/ n Wirtschaft f; (thrift) Sparsamkeit f

ecstasy /'ekstəsɪ/ n Ekstase f

ecstatic /ɪk'stætɪk/ a, -ally adv ekstatisch

ecu /'eɪkjuː/ n Ecu m

ecumenical /iːkjʊ'menɪkl/ a ökumenisch

eczema /'eksɪmə/ n Ekzem nt

eddy /'edɪ/ n Wirbel m

edge /edʒ/ n Rand m; (of table, lawn) Kante f; (of knife) Schneide f; on ~ (fam) nervös; have the ~ on (fam) etwas besser sein als □ vt einfassen. ~ forward vi sich nach vorn schieben

edging /'edʒɪŋ/ n Einfassung f

edgy /'edʒɪ/ a (fam) nervös

edible /'edɪbl/ a essbar

edict /'iːdɪkt/ n Erlass m

edifice /'edɪfɪs/ n [großes] Gebäude nt

edify /'edɪfaɪ/ vt (pt/pp -ied) erbauen. ~ing a erbaulich

edit /'edɪt/ vt (pt/pp edited) redigieren; herausgeben ⟨anthology, dictionary⟩; schneiden ⟨film, tape⟩

edition /ɪ'dɪʃn/ n Ausgabe f; (impression) Auflage f

editor /'edɪtə(r)/ n Redakteur m; (of anthology, dictionary) Herausgeber m; (of newspaper) Chefredakteur m; (of film) Cutter(in) m(f)

editorial /edɪ'tɔːrɪəl/ a redaktionell, Redaktions- □ n (Journ) Leitartikel m

educate /'edjʊkeɪt/ vt erziehen; be ~d at X auf die X-Schule gehen. ~d a gebildet

education /edjʊ'keɪʃn/ n Erziehung f; (culture) Bildung f. ~al a pädagogisch; ⟨visit⟩ kulturell

eel /iːl/ n Aal m

eerie /'ɪərɪ/ a (-ier, -iest) unheimlich

effect /ɪ'fekt/ n Wirkung f, Effekt m; in ~ in Wirklichkeit; take ~ in Kraft treten □ vt bewirken

effective /ɪ'fektɪv/ a, -ly adv wirksam, effektiv; (striking) wirkungsvoll, effektvoll; (actual) tatsächlich. ~ness n Wirksamkeit f

effeminate /ɪ'femɪnət/ a unmännlich

effervescent /efə'vesnt/ a sprudelnd

efficiency /ɪ'fɪʃənsɪ/ n Tüchtigkeit f; (of machine, organization) Leistungsfähigkeit f

efficient /ɪ'fɪʃənt/ a tüchtig; ⟨machine, organization⟩ leistungsfähig; ⟨method⟩ rationell. ~ly adv gut; ⟨function⟩ rationell

effigy /'efɪdʒɪ/ n Bildnis nt

effort /'efət/ n Anstrengung f; make an ~ sich (dat) Mühe geben. ~less a, -ly adv mühelos

effrontery /ɪ'frʌntərɪ/ n Unverschämtheit f

effusive /ɪ'fjuːsɪv/ a, -ly adv überschwänglich

e.g. abbr (exempli gratia) z.B.

egalitarian /ɪɡælɪ'teərɪən/ a egalitär

egg¹ /eɡ/ vt ~ on (fam) anstacheln

egg² n Ei nt. ~cup n Eierbecher m. ~shell n Eierschale f. ~timer n Eieruhr f

ego /'iːɡəʊ/ n Ich nt. ~centric /-'sentrɪk/ a egozentrisch. ~ism n Egoismus m. ~ist n Egoist m. ~tism n Ichbezogenheit f. ~tist n ichbezogener Mensch m

Egypt /'iːdʒɪpt/ n Ägypten nt. ~ian /ɪ'dʒɪpʃn/ a ägyptisch □ n Ägypter(in) m(f)

eiderdown /'aɪdə-/ n (quilt) Daunendecke f

eigh|t /eɪt/ a acht □ n Acht f; (boat) Achter m. ~'teen a achtzehn. ~'teenth a achtzehnte(r,s)

eighth /eɪtθ/ a achte(r,s) □ n Achtel nt

eightieth /'eɪtɪɪθ/ a achtzigste(r,s)

eighty /'eɪtɪ/ a achtzig

either /'aɪðə(r)/ a & pron ~ [of them] einer von [den] beiden; (both) beide; on ~ side auf beiden Seiten □ adv I don't ~ ich auch nicht □ conj ~ ... or entweder ... oder

eject /ɪ'dʒekt/ vt hinauswerfen

eke /iːk/ vt ~ out strecken; (increase) ergänzen; ~ out a living sich kümmerlich durchschlagen

elaborate¹ /ɪ'læbərət/ a, -ly adv kunstvoll; (fig) kompliziert

elaborate² /ɪ'læbəreɪt/ vi ausführlicher sein; ~ on näher ausführen

elapse /ɪ'læps/ vi vergehen

elastic /ɪ'læstɪk/ a elastisch □ n Gummiband nt. ~ 'band n Gummiband nt

elasticity /ɪlæs'tɪsətɪ/ n Elastizität f

elated /ɪ'leɪtɪd/ a überglücklich

elbow /'elbəʊ/ n Ellbogen m

elder¹ /'eldə(r)/ n Holunder m

eld|er² a ältere(r,s) □ n the ~er der/die Ältere. ~erly a alt. ~est a älteste(r,s) □ n the ~est der/die Älteste

elect /ɪ'lekt/ a the president ~ der designierte Präsident □ vt wählen; ~ to do sich dafür entscheiden, etw zu tun. ~ion /-ekʃn/ n Wahl f

elector /ɪ'lektə(r)/ n Wähler(in) m(f). ~al a Wahl-; ~al roll Wählerverzeichnis nt. ~ate /-rət/ n Wählerschaft f

electric /ɪ'lektrɪk/ a, -ally adv elektrisch

electrical /ɪ'lektrɪkl/ a elektrisch; ~ engineering Elektrotechnik f

electric: ~ 'blanket n Heizdecke f. ~ 'fire n elektrischer Heizofen m

electrician /ɪlek'trɪʃn/ n Elektriker m

electricity /ɪlek'trɪsətɪ/ n Elektrizität f; (supply) Strom m

electrify /ɪ'lektrɪfaɪ/ vt (pt/pp -ied) elektrifizieren. ~ing a (fig) elektrisierend

electrocute /ɪ'lektrəkjuːt/ vt durch einen elektrischen Schlag töten; (execute) auf dem elektrischen Stuhl hinrichten

electrode /ɪ'lektrəʊd/ n Elektrode f

electron /ɪ'lektrɒn/ n Elektron nt

electronic /ɪlek'trɒnɪk/ a elektronisch. ~s n Elektronik f

elegance /'elɪɡəns/ n Eleganz f

elegant /'elɪɡənt/ a, -ly adv elegant

elegy /'elɪdʒɪ/ n Elegie f

element /'elɪmənt/ n Element nt. ∼ary /-'mentəri/ a elementar

elephant /'elɪfənt/ n Elefant m

elevat|e /'elɪveɪt/ vt heben; (fig) erheben. ∼ion /-'veɪʃn/ n Erhebung f

elevator /'elɪveɪtə(r)/ n (Amer) Aufzug m, Fahrstuhl m

eleven /ɪ'levn/ a elf □ n Elf f. ∼th a elfte(r,s); at the ∼th hour (fam) in letzter Minute

elf /elf/ n (pl elves) Elfe f

elicit /ɪ'lɪsɪt/ vt herausbekommen

eligible /'elɪdʒəbl/ a berechtigt; ∼ young man gute Partie f

eliminate /ɪ'lɪmɪneɪt/ vt ausschalten; (excrete) ausscheiden

élite /eɪ'li:t/ n Elite f

ellip|se /ɪ'lɪps/ n Ellipse f. ∼tical a elliptisch

elm /elm/ n Ulme f

elocution /elə'kju:ʃn/ n Sprecherziehung f

elongate /'i:lɒŋgeɪt/ vt verlängern

elope /ɪ'əʊp/ vi durchbrennen (fam)

eloquen|ce /'eləkwəns/ n Beredsamkeit f. ∼t a, ∼ly adv beredt

else /els/ adv sonst; who ∼? wer sonst? nothing ∼ sonst nichts; or ∼ oder; (otherwise) sonst; someone/somewhere ∼ jemand/irgendwo anders; anyone ∼ jeder andere; (as question) sonst noch jemand? anything ∼ alles andere; (as question) sonst noch etwas? ∼where adv woanders

elucidate /ɪ'lu:sɪdeɪt/ vt erläutern

elude /ɪ'lu:d/ vt entkommen (+ dat); (avoid) ausweichen (+ dat)

elusive /ɪ'lu:sɪv/ a be ∼ schwer zu fassen sein

emaciated /ɪ'meɪsɪeɪtɪd/ a abgezehrt

emanate /'eməneɪt/ vi ausgehen (from von)

emancipat|ed /ɪ'mænsɪpeɪtɪd/ a emanzipiert. ∼ion /-'peɪʃn/ n Emanzipation f; (of slaves) Freilassung f

embalm /ɪm'ba:m/ vt einbalsamieren

embankment /ɪm'bæŋkmənt/ n Böschung f; (of railway) Bahndamm m

embargo /em'ba:gəʊ/ n (pl -es) Embargo nt

embark /ɪm'ba:k/ vi sich einschiffen; ∼ on anfangen mit. ∼ation /emba:'keɪʃn/ n Einschiffung f

embarrass /ɪm'bærəs/ vt in Verlegenheit bringen. ∼ed a verlegen. ∼ing a peinlich. ∼ment n Verlegenheit f

embassy /'embəsi/ n Botschaft f

embedded /ɪm'bedɪd/ a be deeply ∼ in tief stecken in (+ dat)

embellish /ɪm'belɪʃ/ vt verzieren; (fig) ausschmücken

embers /'embəz/ npl Glut f

embezzle /ɪm'bezl/ vt unterschlagen. ∼ment n Unterschlagung f

embitter /ɪm'bɪtə(r)/ vt verbittern

emblem /'embləm/ n Emblem nt

embodiment /ɪm'bɒdɪmənt/ n Verkörperung f

embody /ɪm'bɒdɪ/ vt (pt/pp -ied) verkörpern; (include) enthalten

emboss /ɪm'bɒs/ vt prägen

embrace /ɪm'breɪs/ n Umarmung f □ vt umarmen; (fig) umfassen □ vi sich umarmen

embroider /ɪm'brɔɪdə(r)/ vt besticken; sticken (design); (fig) ausschmücken □ vi sticken. ∼y n Stickerei f

embroil /ɪm'brɔɪl/ vt become ∼ed in sth in etw (acc) verwickelt werden

embryo /'embrɪəʊ/ n Embryo m

emerald /'emərəld/ n Smaragd m

emer|ge /ɪ'mɜ:dʒ/ vi auftauchen (from aus); (become known) sich herausstellen; (come into being) entstehen. ∼gence /-əns/ n Auftauchen nt; Entstehung f

emergency /ɪ'mɜ:dʒənsɪ/ n Notfall m; in an ∼ im Notfall. ∼ exit n Notausgang m

emery-paper /'emərɪ-/ n Schmirgelpapier nt

emigrant /'emɪgrənt/ n Auswanderer m

emigrat|e /'emɪgreɪt/ vi auswandern. ∼ion /-'greɪʃn/ n Auswanderung f

eminent /'emɪnənt/ a, -ly adv eminent

emission /ɪ'mɪʃn/ n Ausstrahlung f; (of pollutant) Emission f

emit /ɪ'mɪt/ vt (pt/pp emitted) ausstrahlen ⟨light, heat⟩; ausstoßen ⟨smoke, fumes, cry⟩

emotion /ɪ'məʊʃn/ n Gefühl nt. ∼al a emotional; become ∼al sich erregen

emotive /ɪ'məʊtɪv/ a emotional

empath|ize /'empəθaɪz/ vi ∼ize with s.o. sich in jdn einfühlen. ∼y n Einfühlungsvermögen nt

emperor /'empərə(r)/ n Kaiser m

emphasis /'emfəsɪs/ n Betonung f

emphasize /'emfəsaɪz/ vt betonen

emphatic /ɪm'fætɪk/ a, -ally adv nachdrücklich

empire /'empaɪə(r)/ n Reich nt

empirical /em'pɪrɪkl/ a empirisch

employ /ɪm'plɔɪ/ vt beschäftigen; (appoint) einstellen; (fig) anwenden. ∼ee /emplɔɪ'i:/ n Beschäftigte(r) m/f; (in contrast to employer) Arbeitnehmer m. ∼er n Arbeitgeber m. ∼ment n Beschäftigung f; (*work*) Arbeit f. **~ment agency** n Stellenvermittlung f

empower /ɪmˈpaʊə(r)/ vt ermächtigen

empress /ˈemprɪs/ n Kaiserin f

empties /ˈemptɪz/ npl leere Flaschen pl

emptiness /ˈemptɪnɪs/ n Leere f

empty /ˈemptɪ/ a leer □ vt leeren; ausleeren ⟨*container*⟩ □ vi sich leeren

emulate /ˈemjʊleɪt/ vt nacheifern (+ *dat*)

emulsion /ɪˈmʌlʃn/ n Emulsion f

enable /ɪˈneɪbl/ vt ~ s.o. to es jdm möglich machen, zu

enact /ɪˈnækt/ vt (*Theat*) aufführen

enamel /ɪˈnæml/ n Email nt; (*on teeth*) Zahnschmelz m; (*paint*) Lack m □ vt (pt/pp enamelled) emaillieren

enamoured /ɪˈnæməd/ a be ~ of sehr angetan sein von

enchant /ɪnˈtʃɑːnt/ vt bezaubern. **~ing** a bezaubernd. **~ment** n Zauber m

encircle /ɪnˈsɜːkl/ vt einkreisen

enclave /ˈenkleɪv/ n Enklave f

enclos|e /ɪnˈkləʊz/ vt einschließen; (*in letter*) beilegen (with *dat*). **~ure** /-ʒə/ n (*at zoo*) Gehege nt; (*in letter*) Anlage f

encompass /ɪnˈkʌmpəs/ vt umfassen

encore /ˈɒŋkɔː(r)/ n Zugabe f □ int bravo!

encounter /ɪnˈkaʊntə(r)/ n Begegnung f; (*battle*) Zusammenstoß m □ vt begegnen (+ *dat*); (*fig*) stoßen auf (+ *acc*)

encourag|e /ɪnˈkʌrɪdʒ/ vt ermutigen; (*promote*) fördern. **~ement** n Ermutigung f. **~ing** a ermutigend

encroach /ɪnˈkrəʊtʃ/ vi ~ on eindringen in (+ *acc*) ⟨*land*⟩; beanspruchen ⟨*time*⟩

encumb|er /ɪnˈkʌmbə(r)/ vt belasten (with mit). **~rance** /-rəns/ n Belastung f

encyclopaed|ia /ɪnsaɪklə'piːdɪə/ n Enzyklopädie f, Lexikon nt. **~ic** a enzyklopädisch

end /end/ n Ende nt; (*purpose*) Zweck m; in the ~ schließlich; at the ~ of May Ende Mai; on ~ hochkant; for days on ~ tagelang; make ~s meet ⟨*fam*⟩ [gerade] auskommen; no ~ of ⟨*fam*⟩ unheimlich viel(e) □ vt beenden □ vi enden; ~ up in ⟨*fam: arrive at*⟩ landen in (+ *dat*)

endanger /ɪnˈdeɪndʒə(r)/ vt gefährden

endear|ing /ɪnˈdɪərɪŋ/ a liebenswert. **~ment** n term of ~ment Kosewort nt

endeavour /ɪnˈdevə(r)/ n Bemühung f □ vi sich bemühen (to zu)

ending /ˈendɪŋ/ n Schluss m, Ende nt; (*Gram*) Endung f

endive /ˈendaɪv/ n Endivie f

endless /ˈendlɪs/ a, -ly adv endlos

endorse /enˈdɔːs/ vt (*Comm*) indossieren; (*confirm*) bestätigen. **~ment** n (*Comm*) Indossament nt; (*fig*) Bestätigung f; (*on driving licence*) Strafvermerk m

endow /ɪnˈdaʊ/ vt stiften; be **~ed** with (*fig*) haben. **~ment** n Stiftung f

endur|able /ɪnˈdjʊərəbl/ a erträglich. **~ance** /-rəns/ n Durchhaltevermögen nt; beyond **~ance** unerträglich

endur|e /ɪnˈdjʊə(r)/ vt ertragen □ vi [lange] bestehen. **~ing** a dauernd

enemy /ˈenəmɪ/ n Feind m □ attrib feindlich

energetic /enəˈdʒetɪk/ a tatkräftig; be ~ voller Energie sein

energy /ˈenədʒɪ/ n Energie f

enforce /ɪnˈfɔːs/ vt durchsetzen. **~d** a unfreiwillig

engage /ɪnˈgeɪdʒ/ vt einstellen ⟨*staff*⟩; (*Theat*) engagieren; (*Auto*) einlegen ⟨*gear*⟩ □ vi sich beteiligen (in an + *dat*); (*Techn*) ineinander greifen. **~d** a besetzt; ⟨*person*⟩ beschäftigt; (*to be married*) verlobt; get **~d** sich verloben (to mit). **~ment** n Verlobung f; (*appointment*) Verabredung f; (*Mil*) Gefecht nt

engaging /ɪnˈgeɪdʒɪŋ/ a einnehmend

engender /ɪnˈdʒendə(r)/ vt (*fig*) erzeugen

engine /ˈendʒɪn/ n Motor m; (*Naut*) Maschine f; (*Rail*) Lokomotive f; (*of jet-plane*) Triebwerk nt. **~-driver** n Lokomotivführer m

engineer /endʒɪˈnɪə(r)/ n Ingenieur m; (*service, installation*) Techniker m; (*Naut*) Maschinist m; (*Amer*) Lokomotivführer m □ vt (*fig*) organisieren. **~ing** n [mechanical] **~ing** Maschinenbau m

England /ˈɪŋglənd/ n England nt

English /ˈɪŋglɪʃ/ a englisch; the ~ Channel der Ärmelkanal □ n (*Lang*) Englisch nt; in ~ auf Englisch; into ~ ins Englische; the ~ pl die Engländer. **~man** n Engländer m. **~woman** n Engländerin f

engrav|e /ɪnˈgreɪv/ vt eingravieren. **~ing** n Stich m

engross /ɪnˈgrəʊs/ vt be **~ed** in vertieft sein in (+ *acc*)

engulf /ɪnˈgʌlf/ vt verschlingen

enhance /ɪnˈhɑːns/ vt verschönern; (*fig*) steigern

enigma /ɪˈnɪgmə/ n Rätsel nt. **~tic** /enɪgˈmætɪk/ a rätselhaft

enjoy /ɪnˈdʒɔɪ/ vt genießen; ~ oneself sich amüsieren; ~ cooking/painting gern kochen/malen; I **~ed** it es hat mir gut gefallen ⟨*food:*⟩ geschmeckt. **~able** /-əbl/ a angenehm, nett. **~ment** n Vergnügen nt

enlarge /ɪnˈlɑːdʒ/ *vt* vergrößern □ *vi* ~ upon sich näher auslassen über (+ *acc*). ~ment *n* Vergrößerung *f*

enlighten /ɪnˈlaɪtn/ *vt* aufklären. ~ment *n* Aufklärung *f*

enlist /ɪnˈlɪst/ *vt* (*Mil*) einziehen; ~ s.o.'s help jdn zur Hilfe heranziehen □ *vi* (*Mil*) sich melden

enliven /ɪnˈlaɪvn/ *vt* beleben

enmity /ˈenmətɪ/ *n* Feindschaft *f*

enormity /ɪˈnɔːmətɪ/ *n* Ungeheuerlichkeit *f*

enormous /ɪˈnɔːməs/ *a*, -ly *adv* riesig

enough /ɪˈnʌf/ *a*, *adv* & *n* genug; be ~ reichen; funnily ~ komischerweise; I've had ~! (*fam*) jetzt reicht's mir aber!

enquir|e /ɪnˈkwaɪə(r)/ *vi* sich erkundigen (about nach) □ *vt* sich erkundigen nach. ~y *n* Erkundigung *f*; (*investigation*) Untersuchung *f*

enrage /ɪnˈreɪdʒ/ *vt* wütend machen

enrich /ɪnˈrɪtʃ/ *vt* bereichern; (*improve*) anreichern

enrol /ɪnˈrəʊl/ *v* (*pt/pp* -rolled) □ *vt* einschreiben □ *vi* sich einschreiben. ~ment *n* Einschreibung *f*

ensemble /ɒnˈsɒmbl/ *n* (*clothing & Mus*) Ensemble *nt*

ensign /ˈensaɪn/ *n* Flagge *f*

enslave /ɪnˈsleɪv/ *vt* versklaven

ensue /ɪnˈsjuː/ *vi* folgen; (*result*) sich ergeben (from aus)

ensure /ɪnˈʃʊə(r)/ *vt* sicherstellen; ~ that dafür sorgen, dass

entail /ɪnˈteɪl/ *vt* erforderlich machen; what does it ~? was ist damit verbunden?

entangle /ɪnˈtæŋgl/ *vt* get ~d sich verfangen (in in + *dat*); (*fig*) sich verstricken (in in + *acc*)

enter /ˈentə(r)/ *vt* eintreten (*vehicle:*) einfahren in (+ *acc*); einreisen in (+ *acc*) (*country*); (*register*) eintragen; sich anmelden zu (*competition*) □ *vi* eintreten; (*vehicle:*) einfahren; (*Theat*) auftreten; (*register as competitor*) sich anmelden; (*take part*) sich beteiligen (in an + *dat*)

enterpris|e /ˈentəpraɪz/ *n* Unternehmen *nt*; (*quality*) Unternehmungsgeist *m*. ~ing *a* unternehmend

entertain /entəˈteɪn/ *vt* unterhalten; (*invite*) einladen; (*to meal*) bewirten (*guest*); (*fig*) in Erwägung ziehen □ *vi* unterhalten; (*have guests*) Gäste haben. ~er *n* Unterhalter *m*. ~ment *n* Unterhaltung *f*

enthral /ɪnˈθrɔːl/ *vt* (*pt/pp* enthralled) be ~led gefesselt sein (by von)

enthuse /ɪnˈθjuːz/ *vi* ~ over schwärmen von

enthusias|m /ɪnˈθjuːzɪæzm/ *n* Begeisterung *f*. ~t *n* Enthusiast *m*. ~tic /-ˈæstɪk/ *a*, -ally *adv* begeistert

entice /ɪnˈtaɪs/ *vt* locken. ~ment *n* Anreiz *m*

entire /ɪnˈtaɪə(r)/ *a* ganz. ~ly *adv* ganz, völlig. ~ty /-rətɪ/ *n* in its ~ty in seiner Gesamtheit

entitle /ɪnˈtaɪtl/ *vt* berechtigen; ~d ... mit dem Titel ...; be ~d to sth das Recht auf etw (*acc*) haben. ~ment *n* Berechtigung *f*; (*claim*) Anspruch *m* (to auf + *acc*)

entity /ˈentɪtɪ/ *n* Wesen *nt*

entomology /entəˈmɒlədʒɪ/ *n* Entomologie *f*

entourage /ˈɒntʊrɑːʒ/ *n* Gefolge *nt*

entrails /ˈentreɪlz/ *npl* Eingeweide *pl*

entrance[1] /ɪnˈtrɑːns/ *vt* bezaubern

entrance[2] /ˈentrəns/ *n* Eintritt *m*; (*Theat*) Auftritt *m*; (*way in*) Eingang *m*; (*for vehicle*) Einfahrt *f*. ~ examination *n* Aufnahmeprüfung *f*. ~ fee *n* Eintrittsgebühr *f*

entrant /ˈentrənt/ *n* Teilnehmer(in) *m(f)*

entreat /ɪnˈtriːt/ *vt* anflehen (for um)

entrench /ɪnˈtrentʃ/ *vt* be ~ed in verwurzelt sein in (+ *dat*)

entrust /ɪnˈtrʌst/ *vt* ~ s.o. with sth, ~ sth to s.o. jdm etw anvertrauen

entry /ˈentrɪ/ *n* Eintritt *m*; (*into country*) Einreise *f*; (*on list*) Eintrag *m*; no ~ Zutritt/ (*Auto*) Einfahrt verboten. ~ form *n* Anmeldeformular *nt*. ~ visa *n* Einreisevisum *nt*

enumerate /ɪˈnjuːməreɪt/ *vt* aufzählen

enunciate /ɪˈnʌnsɪeɪt/ *vt* (*deutlich*) aussprechen; (*state*) vorbringen

envelop /ɪnˈveləp/ *vt* (*pt/pp* enveloped) einhüllen

envelope /ˈenvələʊp/ *n* [Brief]umschlag *m*

enviable /ˈenvɪəbl/ *a* beneidenswert

envious /ˈenvɪəs/ *a*, -ly *adv* neidisch (of auf + *acc*)

environment /ɪnˈvaɪərənmənt/ *n* Umwelt *f*

environmental /ɪnvaɪərənˈmentl/ *a* Umwelt-. ~ist *n* Umweltschützer *m*. ~ly *adv* ~ly friendly umweltfreundlich

envisage /ɪnˈvɪzɪdʒ/ *vt* sich (*dat*) vorstellen

envoy /ˈenvɔɪ/ *n* Gesandte(r) *m*

envy /ˈenvɪ/ *n* Neid *m* □ *vt* (*pt/pp* -ied) ~ s.o. sth jdm um etw beneiden

enzyme /ˈenzaɪm/ *n* Enzym *nt*

epic /ˈepɪk/ *a* episch □ *n* Epos *nt*

epidemic /epɪˈdemɪk/ *n* Epidemie *f*

epilep|sy /'epɪlepsɪ/ n Epilepsie f. ~tic /-'leptɪk/ a epileptisch □ n Epileptiker(in) m(f)

epilogue /'epɪlɒg/ n Epilog m

episode /'epɪsəʊd/ n Episode f; (instalment) Folge f

epistle /ɪ'pɪsl/ n (liter) Brief m

epitaph /'epɪtɑ:f/ n Epitaph nt

epithet /'epɪθet/ n Beiname m

epitom|e /ɪ'pɪtəmɪ/ n Inbegriff m. ~ize vt verkörpern

epoch /'i:pɒk/ n Epoche f. ~-making a epochemachend

equal /'i:kwl/ a gleich (to dat); be ~ to a task einer Aufgabe gewachsen sein □ n Gleichgestellte(r) m/f □ vt (pt/pp equalled) gleichen (+ dat); (fig) gleichkommen (+ dat). ~ity /ɪ'kwɒlətɪ/ n Gleichheit f

equalize /'i:kwəlaɪz/ vt/i ausgleichen. ~r n (Sport) Ausgleich[streffer] m

equally /'i:kwəlɪ/ adv gleich; (divide) gleichmäßig; (just as) genauso

equanimity /ekwə'nɪmətɪ/ n Gleichmut m

equat|e /ɪ'kweɪt/ vt gleichsetzen (with mit). ~ion /-eɪʒn/ n (Math) Gleichung f

equator /ɪ'kweɪtə(r)/ n Äquator m. ~ial /ekwə'tɔ:rɪəl/ a Äquator-

equestrian /ɪ'kwestrɪən/ a Reit-

equilibrium /i:kwɪ'lɪbrɪəm/ n Gleichgewicht nt

equinox /'i:kwɪnɒks/ n Tagundnachtgleiche f

equip /ɪ'kwɪp/ vt (pt/pp equipped) ausrüsten; (furnish) ausstatten. ~ment n Ausrüstung f; Ausstattung f

equitable /'ekwɪtəbl/ a gerecht

equity /'ekwətɪ/ n Gerechtigkeit f

equivalent /ɪ'kwɪvələnt/ a gleichwertig; (corresponding) entsprechend □ n Äquivalent nt; (value) Gegenwert m; (counterpart) Gegenstück nt

equivocal /ɪ'kwɪvəkl/ a zweideutig

era /'ɪərə/ n Ära f, Zeitalter nt

eradicate /ɪ'rædɪkeɪt/ vt ausrotten

erase /ɪ'reɪz/ vt ausradieren; (from tape) löschen; (fig) auslöschen. ~r n Radiergummi m

erect /ɪ'rekt/ a aufrecht □ vt errichten. ~ion /-ekʃn/ n Errichtung f; (building) Bau m; (Biol) Erektion f

ermine /'ɜ:mɪn/ n Hermelin m

ero|de /ɪ'rəʊd/ vt (water:) auswaschen; (acid:) angreifen. ~sion /-əʊʒn/ n Erosion f

erotic /ɪ'rɒtɪk/ a erotisch. ~ism /-tɪsɪzm/ n Erotik f

err /ɜ:(r)/ vi sich irren; (sin) sündigen

errand /'erənd/ n Botengang m

erratic /ɪ'rætɪk/ a unregelmäßig; (person) unberechenbar

erroneous /ɪ'rəʊnɪəs/ a falsch; (belief, assumption) irrig. ~ly adv fälschlich; irrigerweise

error /'erə(r)/ n Irrtum m; (mistake) Fehler m; in ~ irrtümlicherweise

erudit|e /'erʊdaɪt/ a gelehrt. ~ion /-'dɪʃn/ n Gelehrsamkeit f

erupt /ɪ'rʌpt/ vi ausbrechen. ~ion /-ʌpʃn/ n Ausbruch m

escalat|e /'eskəleɪt/ vt/i eskalieren. ~ion /-'leɪʃn/ n Eskalation f. ~or n Rolltreppe f

escapade /'eskəpeɪd/ n Eskapade f

escape /ɪ'skeɪp/ n Flucht f; (from prison) Ausbruch m; have a narrow ~ gerade noch davonkommen □ vi flüchten; (prisoner:) ausbrechen; entkommen (from aus; from s.o. jdm); (gas:) entweichen □ vt ~ notice unbemerkt bleiben; the name ~s me der Name entfällt mir

escapism /ɪ'skeɪpɪzm/ n Flucht f vor der Wirklichkeit, Eskapismus m

escort¹ /'eskɔ:t/ n (of person) Begleiter m; (Mil) Eskorte f; under ~ unter Bewachung

escort² /ɪ'skɔ:t/ vt begleiten; (Mil) eskortieren

Eskimo /'eskɪməʊ/ n Eskimo m

esoteric /esə'terɪk/ a esoterisch

especial /ɪ'speʃl/ a besondere(r,s). ~ly adv besonders

espionage /'espɪənɑ:ʒ/ n Spionage f

essay /'eseɪ/ n Aufsatz m

essence /'esns/ n Wesen nt; (Chem, Culin) Essenz f; in ~ im Wesentlichen

essential /ɪ'senʃl/ a wesentlich; (indispensable) unentbehrlich □ n the ~s das Wesentliche; (items) das Nötigste. ~ly adv im Wesentlichen

establish /ɪ'stæblɪʃ/ vt gründen; (form) bilden; (prove) beweisen. ~ment n (firm) Unternehmen nt

estate /ɪ'steɪt/ n Gut nt; (possessions) Besitz m; (after death) Nachlass m; (housing) [Wohn]siedlung f. ~ agent n Immobilienmakler m. ~ car n Kombi[wagen] m

esteem /ɪ'sti:m/ n Achtung f □ vt hochschätzen

estimate¹ /'estɪmət/ n Schätzung f; (Comm) [Kosten]voranschlag m; at a rough ~ grob geschätzt

estimat|e² /'estɪmeɪt/ vt schätzen. ~ion /-'meɪʃn/ n Einschätzung f; (esteem) Achtung f; in my ~ion meiner Meinung nach estuary /'estjʊərɪ/ n Mündung f

etc. /et'setərə/ abbr (et cetera) und so weiter, usw.

etching /'etʃɪŋ/ n Radierung f

eternal /ɪ'tɜːnl/ a, -ly adv ewig

eternity /ɪ'tɜːnətɪ/ n Ewigkeit f

ether /'iːθə(r)/ n Äther m

ethic /'eθɪk/ n Ethik f. ~al a ethisch; (morally correct) moralisch einwandfrei. ~s n Ethik f

Ethiopia /iːθɪ'əʊpɪə/ n Äthiopien nt

ethnic /'eθnɪk/ a ethnisch

etiquette /'etɪket/ n Etikette f

etymology /etɪ'mɒlədʒɪ/ n Etymologie f

eucalyptus /juːkə'lɪptəs/ n Eukalyptus m

eulogy /'juːlədʒɪ/ n Lobrede f

euphemis|m /'juːfəmɪzm/ n Euphemismus m. ~tic /-'mɪstɪk/ a, -ally adv verhüllend

euphoria /juː'fɔːrɪə/ n Euphorie f

Euro /'jʊərəʊ/ n Euro m. ~cheque n Euroscheck m. ~ passport n Europaß m

Europe /'jʊərəp/ n Europa nt

European /jʊərə'piːən/ a europäisch; ~ Community Europäische Gemeinschaft f □ n Europäer(in) m(f)

evacuat|e /ɪ'vækjʊeɪt/ vt evakuieren; räumen ⟨building, area⟩. ~ion /-'eɪʃn/ n Evakuierung f; Räumung f

evade /ɪ'veɪd/ vt sich entziehen (+ dat); hinterziehen ⟨taxes⟩; ~ the issue ausweichen

evaluate /ɪ'væljʊeɪt/ vt einschätzen

evange|lical /iːvæn'dʒelɪkl/ a evangelisch. ~list /ɪ'vændʒəlɪst/ n Evangelist m

evaporat|e /ɪ'væpəreɪt/ vi verdunsten; ~ed milk Kondensmilch f, Dosenmilch f. ~ion /-'reɪʃn/ n Verdampfung f

evasion /ɪ'veɪʒn/ n Ausweichen nt; ~ of taxes Steuerhinterziehung f

evasive /ɪ'veɪsɪv/ a, -ly adv ausweichend; be ~ ausweichen

eve /iːv/ n (liter) Vorabend m

even /'iːvn/ a (level) eben; (same, equal) gleich; (regular) gleichmäßig; ⟨number⟩ gerade; get ~ with (fam) es jdm heimzahlen □ adv sogar, selbst; ~ so trotzdem; not ~ nicht einmal □ vt ~ the score ausgleichen. ~ up vt ausgleichen □ vi sich ausgleichen

evening /'iːvnɪŋ/ n Abend m; this ~ heute Abend; in the ~ abends, am Abend. ~ class n Abendkurs m

evenly /'iːvnlɪ/ adv gleichmäßig

event /ɪ'vent/ n Ereignis nt; (function) Veranstaltung f; (Sport) Wettbewerb m; in

the ~ of im Falle (+ gen); in the ~ wie es sich ergab. ~ful a ereignisreich

eventual /ɪ'ventjʊəl/ a his ~ success der Erfolg, der ihm schließlich zuteil wurde. ~ity /-'ælətɪ/ n Eventualität f, Fall m. ~ly adv schließlich

ever /'evə(r)/ adv je[mals]; not ~ nie; for ~ für immer; hardly ~ fast nie; ~ since seitdem; ~ so (fam) sehr, furchtbar (fam)

'evergreen n immergrüner Strauch m/ (tree) Baum m

ever'lasting a ewig

every /'evrɪ/ a jede(r,s); ~ one jede(r,s) Einzelne; ~ other day jeden zweiten Tag

every|~body pron jeder[mann]; alle pl. ~day a alltäglich. ~ one pron jeder [-mann]; alle pl. ~thing pron alles. ~where adv überall

evict /ɪ'vɪkt/ vt [aus der Wohnung] hinausweisen. ~ion /-ɪkʃn/ n Ausweisung f

eviden|ce /'evɪdəns/ n Beweise pl; (Jur) Beweismaterial nt; (testimony) Aussage f; give ~ce aussagen. ~t a, -ly adv offensichtlich

evil /'iːvl/ a böse □ n Böse nt

evocative /ɪ'vɒkətɪv/ a be ~ of heraufbeschwören

evoke /ɪ'vəʊk/ vt heraufbeschwören

evolution /iːvə'luːʃn/ n Evolution f

evolve /ɪ'vɒlv/ vt entwickeln □ vi sich entwickeln

ewe /juː/ n [Mutter]schaf nt

exacerbate /ek'sæsəbeɪt/ vt verschlimmern; verschärfen ⟨situation⟩

exact /ɪg'zækt/ a, -ly adv genau; not ~ly nicht gerade □ vt erzwingen. ~ing a anspruchsvoll. ~itude /-ɪtjuːd/ n, ~ness n Genauigkeit f

exaggerat|e /ɪg'zædʒəreɪt/ vt/i übertreiben. ~ion /-'reɪʃn/ n Übertreibung f

exalt /ɪg'zɔːlt/ vt erheben; (praise) preisen

exam /ɪg'zæm/ n (fam) Prüfung f

examination /ɪgzæmɪ'neɪʃn/ n Untersuchung f; (Sch) Prüfung f

examine /ɪg'zæmɪn/ vt untersuchen; (Sch) prüfen; (Jur) verhören. ~r n (Sch) Prüfer m

example /ɪg'zɑːmpl/ n Beispiel nt (of für); for ~ zum Beispiel; make an ~ of ein Exempel statuieren an (+ dat)

exasperat|e /ɪg'zæspəreɪt/ vt zur Verzweiflung treiben. ~ion /-'reɪʃn/ n Verzweiflung f

excavat|e /'ekskəveɪt/ vt ausschachten; (Archaeol) ausgraben. ~ion /-'veɪʃn/ n Ausgrabung f

exceed /ɪk'siːd/ vt übersteigen. ~ingly adv äußerst

excel /ɪk'sel/ v (pt/pp **excelled**) vi sich auszeichnen □ vt ~ oneself sich selbst übertreffen

excellen|ce /'eksələns/ n Vorzüglichkeit f. **E** ~**cy** n (title) Exzellenz f. ~**t** a, -ly adv ausgezeichnet, vorzüglich

except /ɪk'sept/ prep außer (+ dat); ~ **for** abgesehen von □ vt ausnehmen. ~**ing** prep außer (+ dat)

exception /ɪk'sepʃn/ n Ausnahme f; take ~ **to** Anstoß nehmen an (+ dat). ~**al** a, -ly adv außergewöhnlich

excerpt /'eksɜ:pt/ n Auszug m

excess /ɪk'ses/ n Übermaß nt (of an + dat); (surplus) Überschuss m; ~**es** pl Exzesse pl; **in** ~ **of** über (+ dat)

excess 'fare /ekses–/ n Nachlösegebühr f

excessive /ɪk'sesɪv/ a, -ly adv übermäßig

exchange /ɪks'tʃeɪndʒ/ n Austausch m; (Teleph) Fernsprechamt nt; (Comm) [Geld]wechsel m; (stock) ~ Börse f; in ~ **dafür** □ vt austauschen (for gegen); tauschen ⟨places, greetings, money⟩. ~ **rate** n Wechselkurs m

exchequer /ɪks'tʃekə(r)/ n (Pol) Staatskasse f

excise[1] /'eksaɪz/ n ~ **duty** Verbrauchssteuer f

excise[2] /ek'saɪz/ vt herausschneiden

excitable /ɪk'saɪtəbl/ a [leicht] erregbar

excit|e /ɪk'saɪt/ vt aufregen; (cause) erregen. ~**ed** a, -ly adv aufgeregt; **get** ~**ed** sich aufregen. ~**ement** n Aufregung f; Erregung f. ~**ing** a aufregend; ⟨story⟩ spannend

exclaim /ɪk'skleɪm/ vt/i ausrufen

exclamation /eksklə'meɪʃn/ n Ausruf m. ~ **mark** n, (Amer) ~ **point** n Ausrufezeichen nt

exclu|de /ɪk'sklu:d/ vt ausschließen. ~**ding** prep ausschließlich (+ gen). ~**sion** /-ʒn/ n Ausschluss m

exclusive /ɪk'sklu:sɪv/ a, -ly adv ausschließlich; (select) exklusiv; ~ **of** ausschließlich (+ gen)

excommunicate /ekskə'mju:nɪkeɪt/ vt exkommunizieren

excrement /'ekskrɪmənt/ n Kot m

excrete /ɪk'skri:t/ vt ausscheiden

excruciating /ɪk'skru:ʃɪeɪtɪŋ/ a grässlich

excursion /ɪk'skɜ:ʃn/ n Ausflug m

excusable /ɪk'skju:zəbl/ a entschuldbar

excuse[1] /ɪk'skju:s/ n Entschuldigung f; (pretext) Ausrede f

excuse[2] /ɪk'skju:z/ vt entschuldigen; ~ **from** freistellen von; ~ **me!** Entschuldigung!

ex-di'rectory a **be** ~ nicht im Telefonbuch stehen

execute /'eksɪkju:t/ vt ausführen; (put to death) hinrichten

execution /eksɪ'kju:ʃn/ n (see execute) Ausführung f; Hinrichtung f. ~**er** n Scharfrichter m

executive /ɪg'zekjʊtɪv/ a leitend □ n leitende(r) Angestellte(r) m/f; (Pol) Exekutive f

executor /ɪg'zekjʊtə(r)/ n (Jur) Testamentsvollstrecker m

exemplary /ɪg'zemplərɪ/ a beispielhaft; (as a warning) exemplarisch

exemplify /ɪg'zemplɪfaɪ/ vt (pt/pp -ied) veranschaulichen

exempt /ɪg'zempt/ a befreit □ vt befreien (from von). ~**ion** /-empʃn/ n Befreiung f

exercise /'eksəsaɪz/ n Übung f; physical ~ körperliche Bewegung f; **take** ~ sich bewegen □ vt (use) ausüben; bewegen ⟨horse⟩; spazieren führen ⟨dog⟩ □ vi sich bewegen. ~ **book** n [Schul]heft nt

exert /ɪg'zɜ:t/ vt ausüben; ~ **oneself** sich anstrengen. ~**ion** /-ɜ:ʃn/ n Anstrengung f

exhale /eks'heɪl/ vt/i ausatmen

exhaust /ɪg'zɔ:st/ n (Auto) Auspuff m; (pipe) Auspuffrohr nt; (fumes) Abgase pl □ vt erschöpfen. ~**ed** a erschöpft. ~**ing** a anstrengend. ~**ion** /-ɔ:stʃn/ n Erschöpfung f. ~**ive** /-ɪv/ a (fig) erschöpfend

exhibit /ɪg'zɪbɪt/ n Ausstellungsstück nt; (Jur) Beweisstück nt □ vt ausstellen; (fig) zeigen

exhibition /eksɪ'bɪʃn/ n Ausstellung f; (Univ) Stipendium nt. ~**ist** n Exhibitionist(in) m(f)

exhibitor /ɪg'zɪbɪtə(r)/ n Aussteller m

exhilarat|ed /ɪg'zɪləreɪtɪd/ a beschwingt. ~**ing** a berauschend. ~**ion** /-'reɪʃn/ n Hochgefühl nt

exhort /ɪg'zɔ:t/ vt ermahnen

exhume /ɪg'zju:m/ vt exhumieren

exile /'eksaɪl/ n Exil nt; (person) im Exil Lebende(r) m/f □ vt ins Exil schicken

exist /ɪg'zɪst/ vi bestehen, existieren. ~**ence** /-əns/ n Existenz f; **be in** ~**ence** existieren

exit /'eksɪt/ n Ausgang m; (Auto) Ausfahrt f; (Theat) Abgang m □ vi (Theat) abgehen. ~ **visa** n Ausreisevisum nt

exonerate /ɪg'zɒnəreɪt/ vt entlasten

exorbitant /ɪg'zɔ:bɪtənt/ a übermäßig hoch

exorcize /'eksɔ:saɪz/ vt austreiben

exotic /ɪg'zɒtɪk/ a exotisch

expand /ɪk'spænd/ vt ausdehnen; (explain better) weiter ausführen □ vi sich ausdehnen; (Comm) expandieren; ~ **on** (fig) weiter ausführen

expans|e /ɪk'spæns/ n Weite f. ~ion /-ænʃn/ n Ausdehnung f; (Techn, Pol, Comm) Expansion f. ~ive /-ɪv/ a mitteilsam

expatriate /eks'pætrɪət/ n be an ~ im Ausland leben

expect /ɪk'spekt/ vt erwarten; (suppose) annehmen; I ~ so wahrscheinlich; we ~ to arrive on Monday wir rechnen damit, dass wir am Montag ankommen

expectan|cy /ɪk'spektənsɪ/ n Erwartung f. ~t a, -ly adv erwartungsvoll; ~t mother werdende Mutter f

expectation /ekspek'teɪʃn/ n Erwartung f; ~ of life Lebenserwartung f

expedient /ɪk'spiːdɪənt/ a zweckdienlich

expedite /'ekspɪdaɪt/ vt beschleunigen

expedition /ekspɪ'dɪʃn/ n Expedition f. ~ary a (Mil) Expeditions-

expel /ɪk'spel/ vt (pt/pp expelled) ausweisen (from aus); (from school) von der Schule verweisen

expend /ɪk'spend/ vt aufwenden. ~able /-əbl/ a entbehrlich

expenditure /ɪk'spendɪtʃə(r)/ n Ausgaben pl

expense /ɪk'spens/ n Kosten pl; business ~s pl Spesen pl; at my ~ auf meine Kosten; at the ~ of (fig) auf Kosten (+ gen)

expensive /ɪk'spensɪv/ a, -ly adv teuer

experience /ɪk'spɪərɪəns/ n Erfahrung f; (event) Erlebnis nt □ vt erleben. ~d a erfahren

experiment /ɪk'sperɪmənt/ n Versuch m, Experiment nt □ /-ment/ vi experimentieren. ~al /-'mentl/ a experimentell

expert /'ekspɜːt/ a, -ly adv fachmännisch □ n Fachmann m, Experte m

expertise /ekspɜː'tiːz/ n Sachkenntnis f; (skill) Geschick nt

expire /ɪk'spaɪə(r)/ vi ablaufen

expiry /ɪk'spaɪərɪ/ n Ablauf m. ~ date n Verfallsdatum nt

explain /ɪk'spleɪn/ vt erklären

explana|tion /eksplə'neɪʃn/ n Erklärung f. ~tory /ɪk'splænətərɪ/ a erklärend

expletive /ɪk'spliːtɪv/ n Kraftausdruck m

explicit /ɪk'splɪsɪt/ a, -ly adv deutlich

explode /ɪk'spləʊd/ vi explodieren □ vt zur Explosion bringen

exploit[1] /'eksplɔɪt/ n [Helden]tat f

exploit[2] /ɪk'splɔɪt/ vt ausbeuten. ~ation /eksplɔɪ'teɪʃn/ n Ausbeutung f

explora|tion /eksplə'reɪʃn/ n Erforschung f. ~tory /ɪk'splɒrətərɪ/ a Probe-

explore /ɪk'splɔː(r)/ vt erforschen. ~r n Forschungsreisende(r) m

explos|ion /ɪk'spləʊʒn/ n Explosion f. ~ive /-sɪv/ a explosiv □ n Sprengstoff m

exponent /ɪk'spəʊnənt/ n Vertreter m

export[1] /'ekspɔːt/ n Export m, Ausfuhr f

export[2] /ɪk'spɔːt/ vt exportieren, ausführen. ~er n Exporteur m

expos|e /ɪk'spəʊz/ vt freilegen; (to danger) aussetzen (to dat); (reveal) aufdecken; (Phot) belichten. ~ure /-ʒə(r)/ n Aussetzung f; (Med) Unterkühlung f; (Phot) Belichtung f; 24 ~ures 24 Aufnahmen

expound /ɪk'spaʊnd/ vt erläutern

express /ɪk'spres/ a ausdrücklich; (purpose) fest □ adv (send) per Eilpost □ n (train) Schnellzug m □ vt ausdrücken; ~ oneself sich ausdrücken. ~ion /-ʃn/ n Ausdruck m. ~ive /-ɪv/ a ausdrucksvoll. ~ly adv ausdrücklich

expulsion /ɪk'spʌlʃn/ n Ausweisung f; (Sch) Verweisung f von der Schule

expurgate /'ekspəgeɪt/ vt zensieren

exquisite /ek'skwɪzɪt/ a erlesen

ex-'serviceman n Veteran m

extempore /ɪk'stempərɪ/ adv (speak) aus dem Stegreif

extend /ɪk'stend/ vt verlängern; (stretch out) ausstrecken; (enlarge) vergrößern □ vi sich ausdehnen; (table:) sich ausziehen lassen

extension /ɪk'stenʃn/ n Verlängerung f; (to house) Anbau m; (Teleph) Nebenanschluss m; ~ 7 Apparat 7

extensive /ɪk'stensɪv/ a weit; (fig) umfassend. ~ly adv viel

extent /ɪk'stent/ n Ausdehnung f; (scope) Ausmaß nt, Umfang m; to a certain ~ in gewissem Maße

extenuating /ɪk'stenjʊeɪtɪŋ/ a mildernd

exterior /ɪk'stɪərɪə(r)/ a äußere(r,s) □ n the ~ das Äußere

exterminat|e /ɪk'stɜːmɪneɪt/ vt ausrotten. ~ion /-'neɪʃn/ n Ausrottung f

external /ɪk'stɜːnl/ a äußere(r,s); for ~ use only (Med) nur äußerlich. ~ly adv äußerlich

extinct /ɪk'stɪŋkt/ a ausgestorben; (volcano) erloschen. ~ion /-ɪŋkʃn/ n Aussterben nt

extinguish /ɪk'stɪŋgwɪʃ/ vt löschen. ~er n Feuerlöscher m

extol /ɪk'stəʊl/ vt (pt/pp extolled) preisen

extort /ɪk'stɔːt/ vt erpressen. ~ion /-ɔːʃn/ n Erpressung f

extortionate /ɪk'stɔːʃənət/ a übermäßig hoch

extra /'ekstrə/ a zusätzlich □ adv extra; (especially) besonders; ~ strong extrastark □ n (Theat) Statist(in) m/f; ~s pl Nebenkosten pl; (Auto) Extras pl

extract¹ /'ekstrækt/ n Auszug m; (Culin) Extrakt m

extract² /ık'strækt/ vt herausziehen; ziehen ⟨tooth⟩; (fig) erzwingen. ~or [fan] n Entlüfter m

extradit|e /'ekstrədaıt/ vt ausliefern. ~ion /-'dıʃn/ n (Jur) Auslieferung f

extra'marital a außerehelich

extraordinary /ık'strɔ:dınərı/ a, -ily adv außerordentlich; ⟨strange⟩ seltsam

extravagan|ce /ık'strævəgəns/ n Verschwendung f; an ~ce ein Luxus m. ~t a verschwenderisch; ⟨exaggerated⟩ extravagant

extrem|e /ık'stri:m/ a äußerste⟨r,s⟩; (fig) extrem ▫ n Extrem nt; in the ~e im höchsten Grade. ~ely adv äußerst. ~ist n Extremist m

extremit|y /ık'stremətı/ n ⟨distress⟩ Not f; the ~ies pl die Extremitäten pl

extricate /'ekstrıkeıt/ vt befreien

extrovert /'ekstrəvз:t/ n extravertierter Mensch m

exuberant /ıg'zju:bərənt/ a überglücklich

exude /ıg'zju:d/ vt absondern; (fig) ausstrahlen

exult /ıg'zʌlt/ vi frohlocken

eye /aı/ n Auge nt; ⟨of needle⟩ Öhr nt; ⟨for hook⟩ Öse f; keep an ~ on aufpassen auf (+ acc); see ~ to ~ einer Meinung sein ▫ vt ⟨pt/pp eyed, pres p ey[e]ing⟩ ansehen

eye: ~ball n Augapfel m. ~brow n Augenbraue f. ~lash n Wimper f. ~let /-lıt/ n Öse f. ~lid n Augenlid nt. ~-shadow n Lidschatten m. ~sight n Sehkraft f. ~sore n (fam) Schandfleck m. ~-tooth n Eckzahn m. ~witness n Augenzeuge m

F

fable /'feıbl/ n Fabel f

fabric /'fæbrık/ n Stoff m; (fig) Gefüge nt

fabrication /fæbrı'keıʃn/ n Erfindung f

fabulous /'fæbjuləs/ a (fam) phantastisch

façade /fə'sa:d/ n Fassade f

face /feıs/ n Gesicht nt; ⟨grimace⟩ Grimasse f; ⟨surface⟩ Fläche f; ⟨of clock⟩ Zifferblatt nt; pull ~s Gesichter schneiden; in the ~ of angesichts (+ gen); on the ~ of it allem Anschein nach ▫ vt/i gegenüberstehen (+ dat); ~ north ⟨house:⟩ nach Norden liegen; ~ me! sieh mich an! ~ the fact that sich damit abfinden, dass; ~ up to s.o. jdm die Stirn bieten

face: ~-flannel n Waschlappen m. ~less a anonym. ~-lift n Gesichtsstraffung f

facet /'fæsıt/ n Facette f; (fig) Aspekt m

facetious /fə'si:ʃəs/ a, -ly adv spöttisch

'face value n Nennwert m

facial /'feıʃl/ a Gesichts-

facile /'fæsaıl/ a oberflächlich

facilitate /fə'sılıteıt/ vt erleichtern

facilit|y /fə'sılətı/ n Leichtigkeit f; ⟨skill⟩ Gewandtheit f; ~ies pl Einrichtungen pl

facing /'feısıŋ/ n Besatz m

facsimile /fæk'sıməlı/ n Faksimile nt

fact /fækt/ n Tatsache f; in ~ tatsächlich; ⟨actually⟩ eigentlich

faction /'fækʃn/ n Gruppe f

factor /'fæktə(r)/ n Faktor m

factory /'fæktərı/ n Fabrik f

factual /'fæktʃuəl/ a, -ly adv sachlich

faculty /'fækəltı/ n Fähigkeit f; (Univ) Fakultät f

fad /fæd/ n Fimmel m

fade /feıd/ vi verblassen; ⟨material:⟩ verbleichen; ⟨sound:⟩ abklingen; ⟨flower:⟩ verwelken. ~ in/out vt (Radio, TV) ein-/ausblenden

fag /fæg/ n ⟨chore⟩ Plage f; ⟨fam: cigarette⟩ Zigarette f; ⟨Amer sl⟩ Homosexuelle⟨r⟩ m

fagged /fægd/ a ~ out (fam) völlig erledigt

Fahrenheit /'færənhaıt/ a Fahrenheit

fail /feıl/ n without ~ unbedingt ▫ vi ⟨attempt:⟩ scheitern; ⟨grow weak⟩ nachlassen; ⟨break down⟩ versagen; (in exam) durchfallen; ~ to do sth etw nicht tun; he ~ed to break the record es gelang ihm nicht, den Rekord zu brechen ▫ vt nicht bestehen ⟨exam⟩; durchfallen lassen ⟨candidate⟩; ⟨disappoint⟩ enttäuschen; words ~ me ich weiß nicht, was ich sagen soll

failing /'feılıŋ/ n Fehler m ▫ prep ~ that andernfalls

failure /'feıljə(r)/ n Misserfolg m; ⟨breakdown⟩ Versagen nt; ⟨person⟩ Versager m

faint /feınt/ a (-er, -est), -ly adv schwach; I feel ~ mir ist schwach ▫ n Ohnmacht f ▫ vi ohnmächtig werden

faint: ~-hearted a zaghaft. ~ness n Schwäche f

fair¹ /feə(r)/ n Jahrmarkt m; (Comm) Messe f

fair² (-er, -est) ⟨hair⟩ blond; ⟨skin⟩ hell; ⟨weather⟩ heiter; ⟨just⟩ gerecht, fair; ⟨quite good⟩ ziemlich gut; (Sch) genügend; a ~ amount ziemlich viel ▫ adv play ~ fair sein. ~ly adv gerecht; ⟨rather⟩ ziemlich. ~ness n Blondheit f; Helle f; Gerechtigkeit f; (Sport) Fairness f

fairy /'feərɪ/ *n* Elfe *f*; good/wicked ~ gute/böse Fee *f*. ~ story, ~tale *n* Märchen *nt*

faith /feɪθ/ *n* Glaube *m*; (*trust*) Vertrauen *nt* (ln zu); in good ~ in gutem Glauben

faithful /'feɪθfl/ *a*, -ly *adv* treu; (*exact*) genau; Yours ~ly Hochachtungsvoll. ~ness *n* Treue *f*; Genauigkeit *f*

'**faith-healer** *n* Gesundbeter(in) *m(f)*

fake /feɪk/ *a* Fälschung *f*; (*person*) Schwindler *m* □ *vt* fälschen; (*pretend*) vortäuschen

falcon /'fɔːlkən/ *n* Falke *m*

fall /fɔːl/ *n* Fall *m*; (*heavy*) Sturz *m*; (*in prices*) Fallen *nt*; (*Amer: autumn*) Herbst *m*; have a ~ fallen □ *vi* (*pt* fell, *pp* fallen) fallen; (*heavily*) stürzen; ⟨*night:*⟩ anbrechen; ~ in love sich verlieben; ~ back on zurückgreifen auf (+ *acc*); ~ for s.o. (*fam*) sich in jdn verlieben; ~ for sth (*fam*) auf etw (*acc*) hereinfallen. ~ about *vi* (*with laughter*) sich [vor Lachen] kringeln. ~ down *vi* umfallen; ⟨*thing:*⟩ herunterfallen; (*building:*) einstürzen. ~ in *vi* hineinfallen; (*collapse*) einfallen; (*Mil*) antreten; ~ in with sich anschließen (+ *dat*). ~ off *vi* herunterfallen; (*diminish*) abnehmen. ~ out *vi* herausfallen; ⟨*hair:*⟩ ausfallen; (*quarrel*) sich überwerfen. ~ over *vi* hinfallen. ~ through *vi* durchfallen; ⟨*plan:*⟩ ins Wasser fallen

fallacy /'fæləsɪ/ *n* Irrtum *m*

fallible /'fæləbl/ *a* fehlbar

'**fall-out** *n* [radioaktiver] Niederschlag *m*

fallow /'fæləʊ/ *a* lie ~ brachliegen

false /fɔːls/ *a* falsch; (*artificial*) künstlich; ~ start (*Sport*) Fehlstart *m*. ~hood *n* Unwahrheit *f*. ~ly *adv* falsch. ~ness *n* Falschheit *f*

false 'teeth *npl* [künstliches] Gebiss *nt*

falsify /'fɔːlsɪfaɪ/ *vt* (*pt/pp* -ied) fälschen; (*misrepresent*) verfälschen

falter /'fɔːltə(r)/ *vi* zögern; (*stumble*) straucheln

fame /feɪm/ *n* Ruhm *m*. ~d *a* berühmt

familiar /fə'mɪljə(r)/ *a* vertraut; (*known*) bekannt; too ~ familiär. ~ity /-lɪ'ærɪtɪ/ *n* Vertrautheit *f*. ~ize *vt* vertraut machen (with mit)

family /'fæməlɪ/ *n* Familie *f*

family: ~ al'lowance *n* Kindergeld *nt*. ~ 'doctor *n* Hausarzt *m*. ~ 'life *n* Familienleben *nt*. ~ 'planning *n* Familienplanung *f*. ~ 'tree *n* Stammbaum *m*

famine /'fæmɪn/ *n* Hungersnot *f*

famished /'fæmɪʃt/ *a* sehr hungrig

famous /'feɪməs/ *a* berühmt

fan¹ /fæn/ *n* Fächer *m*; (*Techn*) Ventilator *m* □ *v* (*pt/pp* fanned) □ *vt* fächeln; ~ oneself sich fächeln □ *vi* ~ out sich fächerförmig ausbreiten

fan² *n* (*admirer*) Fan *m*

fanatic /fə'nætɪk/ *n* Fanatiker *m*. ~al *a*, -ly *adv* fanatisch. ~ism /-sɪzm/ *n* Fanatismus *m*

'**fan belt** *n* Keilriemen *m*

fanciful /'fænsɪfl/ *a* phantastisch; (*imaginative*) phantasiereich

fancy /'fænsɪ/ *n* Phantasie *f*; have a ~ to Lust haben, zu; I have taken a real ~ to him er hat es mir angetan □ *a* ausgefallen; ~ cakes and biscuits Feingebäck *nt* □ *vt* (*believe*) meinen; (*imagine*) sich (*dat*) einbilden; (*fam: want*) Lust haben auf (+ *acc*); ~ that! stell dir vor! (*really*) tatsächlich! ~ 'dress *n* Kostüm *nt*

fanfare /'fænfeə(r)/ *n* Fanfare *f*

fang /fæŋ/ *n* Fangzahn *m*; (*of snake*) Giftzahn *m*

fan: ~ heater *n* Heizlüfter *m*. ~light *n* Oberlicht *nt*

fantasize /'fæntəsaɪz/ *vi* phantasieren. ~tic /-'tæstɪk/ *a* phantastisch. ~y *n* Phantasie *f*; (*Mus*) Fantasie *f*

far /fɑː(r)/ *adv* weit; (*much*) viel; by ~ bei weitem; ~ away weit weg; as ~ as I know soviel ich weiß; as ~ as the church bis zur Kirche □ *a* at the ~ end am anderen Ende; the F~ East der Ferne Osten

farc|e /fɑːs/ *n* Farce *f*. ~ical *a* lächerlich

fare /feə(r)/ *n* Fahrpreis *m*; (*money*) Fahrgeld *nt*; (*food*) Kost *f*; air ~ Flugpreis *m*. ~-dodger /-dɒdʒə(r)/ *n* Schwarzfahrer *m*

farewell /feə'wel/ *int* (*liter*) lebe wohl! ~ *n* Lebewohl *nt*; ~ dinner *n* Abschiedsessen *nt*

far-'fetched *a* weit hergeholt; be ~ an den Haaren herbeigezogen sein

farm /fɑːm/ *n* Bauernhof *m* □ *vi* Landwirtschaft betreiben □ *vt* bewirtschaften ⟨*land*⟩. ~er *n* Landwirt *m*

farm: ~house *n* Bauernhaus *nt*. ~ing *n* Landwirtschaft *f*. ~yard *n* Hof *m*

far: ~-'reaching *a* weit reichend. ~-'sighted *a* (*fig*) umsichtig; (*Amer: longsighted*) weitsichtig

fart /fɑːt/ *n* (*vulg*) Furz *m* □ *vi* (*vulg*) furzen

farther /'fɑːðə(r)/ *adv* weiter; ~ off weiter entfernt □ *a* at the ~ end am anderen Ende

fascinat|e /'fæsɪneɪt/ *vt* faszinieren. ~ing *a* faszinierend. ~ion /-'neɪʃn/ *n* Faszination *f*

fascis|m /'fæʃɪzm/ *n* Faschismus *m*. ~t *n* Faschist *m* □ *a* faschistisch

fashion /'fæʃn/ n Mode f; (manner) Art f □ vt machen; (mould) formen. ~able /-əbl/ a, -bly adv modisch; be ~able Mode sein

fast[1] /fɑ:st/ a & adv (-er, -est) schnell; (firm) fest; (colour) waschecht; be ~ (clock:) vorgehen; be ~ asleep fest schlafen

fast[2] n Fasten nt □ vi fasten

'fastback n (Auto) Fließheck nt

fasten /'fɑ:sn/ vt zumachen; (fix) befestigen (to an + dat); (seat belt) anschnallen. ~er n, ~ing n Verschluss m

fastidious /fə'stɪdɪəs/ a wählerisch; (particular) penibel

fat /fæt/ a (fatter, fattest) dick; (meat) fett □ n Fett nt

fatal /'feɪtl/ a tödlich; (error) verhängnisvoll. ~ism /-təlɪzm/ n Fatalismus m. ~ist /-təlɪst/ n Fatalist m. ~ity /fə'tælətɪ/ n Todesopfer nt. ~ly /-təlɪ/ adv tödlich

fate /feɪt/ n Schicksal nt. ~ful a verhängnisvoll

'fat-head n (fam) Dummkopf m

father /'fɑ:ðə(r)/ n Vater m; F ~ Christmas der Weihnachtsmann □ vt zeugen

father: ~hood n Vaterschaft f. ~-in-law n (pl ~s-in-law) Schwiegervater m. ~ly a väterlich

fathom /'fæðəm/ n (Naut) Faden m □ vt verstehen; ~ out ergründen

fatigue /fə'ti:g/ n Ermüdung f □ vt ermüden

fatten /'fætn/ vt mästen (animal). ~ing a cream is ~ing Sahne macht dick

fatty /'fætɪ/ a fett; (foods) fetthaltig

fatuous /'fætjʊəs/ a, -ly adv albern

faucet /'fɔ:sɪt/ n (Amer) Wasserhahn m

fault /fɔ:lt/ n Fehler m; (Techn) Defekt m; (Geol) Verwerfung f; at ~ im Unrecht; find ~ with etwas auszusetzen haben an (+ dat); it's your ~ du bist schuld □ vt etwas auszusetzen haben an (+ dat). ~less a, -ly adv fehlerfrei

faulty /'fɔ:ltɪ/ a fehlerhaft

fauna /'fɔ:nə/ n Fauna f

favour /'feɪvə(r)/ n Gunst f; I am in ~ ich bin dafür; do s.o. a ~ jdm einen Gefallen tun □ vt begünstigen; (prefer) bevorzugen. ~able /-əbl/ a, -bly adv günstig; (reply) positiv

favourit|e /'feɪvərɪt/ a Lieblings- □ n Liebling m; (Sport) Favorit(in) m(f). ~ism n Bevorzugung f

fawn[1] /fɔ:n/ a rehbraun □ n Hirschkalb nt

fawn[2] vi sich einschmeicheln (on bei)

fax /fæks/ n Fax nt □ vt faxen (s.o. jdm). ~ machine n Faxgerät nt

fear /fɪə(r)/ n Furcht f, Angst f (of vor + dat); no ~! (fam) keine Angst! □ vt/i fürchten

fear|ful /'fɪəfl/ a besorgt; (awful) furchtbar. ~less a, -ly adv furchtlos. ~some /-səm/ a Furcht erregend

feas|ibility /fi:zə'bɪlətɪ/ n Durchführbarkeit f. ~ible a durchführbar; (possible) möglich

feast /fi:st/ n Festmahl nt; (Relig) Fest nt □ vi ~ [on] schmausen

feat /fi:t/ n Leistung f

feather /'feðə(r)/ n Feder f

feature /'fi:tʃə(r)/ n Gesichtszug m; (quality) Merkmal nt; (Journ) Feature nt □ vt darstellen; (film:) in der Hauptrolle zeigen. ~ film n Hauptfilm m

February /'februərɪ/ n Februar m

feckless /'feklɪs/ a verantwortungslos

fed /fed/ see feed □ a be ~ up (fam) die Nase voll haben (with von)

federal /'fedərəl/ a Bundes-

federation /fedə'reɪʃn/ n Föderation f

fee /fi:/ n Gebühr f; (professional) Honorar nt

feeble /'fi:bl/ a (-r, -st), -bly adv schwach

feed /fi:d/ n Futter nt; (for baby) Essen nt □ v (pt/pp fed) □ vt füttern; (support) ernähren; (into machine) eingeben; speisen (computer) □ vi sich ernähren (on von)

'feedback n Feedback nt

feel /fi:l/ v (pt/pp felt) □ vt fühlen; (experience) empfinden; (think) meinen □ vi sich fühlen; ~ soft/hard sich weich/hart anfühlen; I ~ hot/ill mir ist heiß/schlecht; I don't ~ like it ich habe keine Lust dazu. ~er n Fühler m. ~ing n Gefühl nt; no hard ~ings nichts für ungut

feet /fi:t/ see foot

feign /feɪn/ vt vortäuschen

feint /feɪnt/ n Finte f

feline /'fi:laɪn/ a Katzen-; (catlike) katzenartig

fell[1] /fel/ vt fällen

fell[2] see fall

fellow /'feləʊ/ n (of society) Mitglied nt; (fam: man) Kerl m

fellow: ~'countryman n Landsmann m. ~ men pl Mitmenschen pl. ~ship n Kameradschaft f; (group) Gesellschaft f

felony /'felənɪ/ n Verbrechen nt

felt[1] /felt/ see feel

felt[2] n Filz m. ~[-tipped] 'pen n Filzstift m

female /'fi:meɪl/ a weiblich □ nt Weibchen nt; (pej: woman) Weib nt

femin|ine /'feminɪn/ a weiblich □ n (Gram) Femininum nt. ~inity /-'nɪnəti/ n Weiblichkeit f. ~ist a feministisch □ n Feminist(in) m(f)

fenc|e /fens/ n Zaun m; (fam: person) Hehler m □ vi (Sport) fechten □ vt ~e in einzäunen. ~er n Fechter m. ~ing n Zaun m; (Sport) Fechten nt

fend /fend/ vi ~ for oneself sich allein durchschlagen. ~ off vt abwehren

fender /'fendə(r)/ n Kaminvorsetzer m; (Naut) Fender m; (Amer: wing) Kotflügel m

fennel /'fenl/ n Fenchel m

ferment[1] /'fɜ:ment/ n Erregung f

ferment[2] /fə'ment/ vi gären □ vt gären lassen. ~ation /fɜ:men'teɪʃn/ n Gärung f

fern /fɜ:n/ n Farn m

feroc|ious /fə'rəʊʃəs/ a wild. ~ity /-'rɒsəti/ n Wildheit f

ferret /'ferit/ n Frettchen nt

ferry /'feri/ n Fähre f □ vt ~ [across] übersetzen

fertil|e /'fɜ:taɪl/ a fruchtbar. ~ity /fɜ:-'tɪləti/ n Fruchtbarkeit f

fertilize /'fɜ:təlaɪz/ vt befruchten; düngen (land). ~r n Dünger m

fervent /'fɜ:vənt/ a leidenschaftlich

fervour /'fɜ:və(r)/ n Leidenschaft f

fester /'festə(r)/ vi eitern

festival /'festɪvl/ n Fest nt; (Mus, Theat) Festspiele pl

festiv|e /'festɪv/ a festlich; ~e season Festzeit. f. ~ities /fe'stɪvəti/ npl Feierlichkeiten f

festoon /fe'stu:n/ vt behängen (with mit)

fetch /fetʃ/ vt holen; (collect) abholen; (be sold for) einbringen

fetching /'fetʃɪŋ/ a anziehend

fête /feɪt/ n Fest nt □ vt feiern

fetish /'fetɪʃ/ n Fetisch m

fetter /'fetə(r)/ vt fesseln

fettle /'fetl/ n in fine ~ in bester Form

feud /fju:d/ n Fehde f

feudal /'fju:dl/ a Feudal-

fever /'fi:və(r)/ n Fieber nt. ~ish a fiebrig; (fig) fieberhaft

few /fju:/ a (-er, -est) wenige; every ~ days alle paar Tage □ n a ~ ein paar; quite a ~ ziemlich viele

fiancé /fɪ'ɒnseɪ/ n Verlobte(r) m. fiancée n Verlobte f

fiasco /fɪ'æskəʊ/ n Fiasko nt

fib /fɪb/ n kleine Lüge; tell a ~ schwindeln

fibre /'faɪbə(r)/ n Faser f

fickle /'fɪkl/ a unbeständig

fiction /'fɪkʃn/ n Erfindung f; [works of] ~ Erzählungsliteratur f. ~al a erfunden

fictitious /fɪk'tɪʃəs/ a [frei] erfunden

fiddle /'fɪdl/ n (fam) Geige f; (cheating) Schwindel m □ vi herumspielen (with mit) □ vt (fam) frisieren (accounts); (arrange) arrangieren

fiddly /'fɪdli/ a knifflig

fidelity /fɪ'deləti/ n Treue f

fidget /'fɪdʒɪt/ vi zappeln. ~y a zappelig

field /fi:ld/ n Feld nt; (meadow) Wiese f; (subject) Gebiet nt

field: ~events npl Sprung- und Wurfdisziplinen pl. ~glasses npl Feldstecher m. F~ 'Marshal n Feldmarschall m. ~work n Feldforschung f

fiend /fi:nd/ n Teufel m. ~ish a teuflisch

fierce /fɪəs/ a (-r, -st). wild; (fig) heftig. ~ness n Wildheit f; (fig) Heftigkeit f

fiery /'faɪəri/ a (-ier, -iest) feurig

fifteen /fɪf'ti:n/ a fünfzehn □ n Fünfzehn f. ~th a fünfzehnte(r,s)

fifth /fɪfθ/ a fünfte(r,s)

fiftieth /'fɪftɪɪθ/ a fünfzigste(r,s)

fifty /'fɪfti/ a fünfzig

fig /fɪg/ n Feige f

fight /faɪt/ n Kampf m; (brawl) Schlägerei f; (between children, dogs) Rauferei f □ v (pt/pp fought) □ vt kämpfen gegen; (fig) bekämpfen □ vi kämpfen; (brawl) sich schlagen; (children, dogs.) sich raufen. ~er n Kämpfer m; (Aviat) Jagdflugzeug nt. ~ing n Kampf m

figment /'fɪgmənt/ n ~ of the imagination Hirngespinst nt

figurative /'fɪgjərətɪv/ a, -ly adv bildlich, übertragen

figure /'fɪgə(r)/ n (digit) Ziffer f; (number) Zahl f; (sum) Summe f; (carving, sculpture, woman's) Figur f; (form) Gestalt f; (illustration) Abbildung f. ~ of speech Redefigur f; good at ~s gut im Rechnen □ vi (appear) erscheinen □ vt (Amer: think) glauben. ~ out vt ausrechnen

figure: ~head n Galionsfigur f; (fig) Repräsentationsfigur f. ~ skating n Eiskunstlauf m

filament /'fɪləmənt/ n Faden m; (Electr) Glühfaden m

filch /fɪltʃ/ vt (fam) klauen

file[1] /faɪl/ n Akte f; (for documents) [Akten]ordner m □ vt ablegen (documents); (Jur) einreichen

file[2] n (line) Reihe f; in single ~ im Gänsemarsch

file[3] n (Techn) Feile f □ vt feilen

filigree /'fɪligri:/ n Filigran nt

filings /'faɪlɪŋz/ npl Feilspäne pl

fill /fɪl/ n eat one's ~ sich satt essen □ vt füllen; plombieren ⟨tooth⟩ □ vi sich füllen. ~ in vt auffüllen; ausfüllen ⟨form⟩. ~ out vt ausfüllen ⟨form⟩. ~ up vi sich füllen □ vt vollfüllen; ⟨Auto⟩ volltanken; ausfüllen ⟨form⟩

fillet /ˈfɪlɪt/ n Filet nt □ vt (pt/pp filleted) entgräten

filling /ˈfɪlɪŋ/ n Füllung f; ⟨of tooth⟩ Plombe f. ~ station f Tankstelle f

filly /ˈfɪlɪ/ n junge Stute f

film /fɪlm/ n Film m; ⟨Culin⟩ [cling] ~ Klarsichtfolie f □ vt/i filmen; verfilmen ⟨book⟩. ~ star n Filmstar m

filter /ˈfɪltə(r)/ n Filter m □ vt vi filtern. ~ through vi durchsickern. ~ tip n Filter m; ⟨cigarette⟩ Filterzigarette f

filth /fɪlθ/ n Dreck m. ~y a (-ier, -iest) dreckig

fin /fɪn/ n Flosse f

final /ˈfaɪnl/ a letzte(r,s); ⟨conclusive⟩ endgültig; ~ result Endresultat nt □ n ⟨Sport⟩ Finale nt, Endspiel nt; ~s pl ⟨Univ⟩ Abschlussprüfung f

finale /fɪˈnɑːlɪ/ n Finale nt

finalist /ˈfaɪnlɪst/ n Finalist(in) m(f). ~ity /-ˈnælətɪ/ n Endgültigkeit f

finalize /ˈfaɪnlaɪz/ vt endgültig festlegen. ~ly adv schließlich

finance /faɪˈnæns/ n Finanz f □ vt finanzieren

financial /faɪˈnænʃl/ a, -ly adv finanziell

finch /fɪntʃ/ n Fink m

find /faɪnd/ n Fund m □ vt (pt/pp found) finden; ⟨establish⟩ feststellen; go and ~ holen; try to ~ suchen; ~ guilty ⟨Jur⟩ schuldig sprechen. ~ out vt herausfinden; ⟨learn⟩ erfahren □ vi ⟨enquire⟩ sich erkundigen

findings /ˈfaɪndɪŋz/ npl Ergebnisse pl

fine¹ /faɪn/ n Geldstrafe f □ vt zu einer Geldstrafe verurteilen

fine² a (-r, -st,) -ly adv fein; ⟨weather⟩ schön; he's ~ es geht ihm gut □ adv gut; cut it ~ ⟨fam⟩ sich ⟨dat⟩ wenig Zeit lassen. ~ arts npl schöne Künste pl

finery /ˈfaɪnərɪ/ n Putz m, Staat m

finesse /fɪˈnes/ n Gewandtheit f

finger /ˈfɪŋgə(r)/ n Finger m □ vt anfassen

finger: ~-mark n Fingerabdruck m. ~-nail n Fingernagel m. ~print n Fingerabdruck m. ~tip n Fingerspitze f; have sth at one's ~tips etw im kleinen Finger haben

finicky /ˈfɪnɪkɪ/ a knifflig; ⟨choosy⟩ wählerisch

finish /ˈfɪnɪʃ/ n Schluss m; ⟨Sport⟩ Finish nt; ⟨line⟩ Ziel nt; ⟨of product⟩ Ausführung f □ vt beenden; ⟨use up⟩ aufbrauchen; ~

one's drink austrinken; ~ reading zu Ende lesen □ vi fertig werden; ⟨performance:⟩ zu Ende sein; ⟨runner:⟩ durchs Ziel gehen

finite /ˈfaɪnaɪt/ a begrenzt

Finland /ˈfɪnlənd/ n Finnland nt

Finn /fɪn/ n Finne m/ Finnin f. ~ish a finnisch

fiord /fjɔːd/ n Fjord m

fir /fɜː(r)/ n Tanne f

fire /ˈfaɪə(r)/ n Feuer nt; ⟨forest, house⟩ Brand m; be on ~ brennen; catch ~ Feuer fangen; set ~ to anzünden; ⟨arsonist:⟩ in Brand stecken; under ~ unter Beschuss □ vt brennen ⟨pottery⟩; abfeuern ⟨shot⟩; schießen mit ⟨gun⟩; ⟨fam: dismiss⟩ feuern □ vi schießen (at auf + acc); ⟨engine:⟩ anspringen

fire: ~ alarm n Feueralarm m; ⟨apparatus⟩ Feuermelder m. ~arm n Schusswaffe f. ~ brigade n Feuerwehr f. ~-engine n Löschfahrzeug nt. ~-escape n Feuertreppe f. ~ extinguisher n Feuerlöscher m. ~man n Feuerwehrmann m. ~place n Kamin m. ~side n by or at the ~side am Kamin. ~ station n Feuerwache f. ~wood n Brennholz nt. ~work n Feuerwerkskörper m; ~works pl ⟨display⟩ Feuerwerk nt

'firing squad n Erschießungskommando nt

firm¹ /fɜːm/ n Firma f

firm² a (-er, -est), -ly adv fest; ⟨resolute⟩ entschlossen; ⟨strict⟩ streng

first /fɜːst/ a & n erste(r,s); at ~ zuerst; who's ~? wer ist der Erste? at ~ sight auf den ersten Blick; for the ~ time zum ersten Mal; from the ~ von Anfang an □ adv zuerst; ⟨firstly⟩ erstens

first: ~ 'aid n erste Hilfe. ~-'aid kit n Verbandkasten m. ~-class a erstklassig; ⟨Rail⟩ erster Klasse □ /-'-/ adv ⟨travel⟩ erster Klasse. ~ e'dition n Erstausgabe f. ~ 'floor n erster Stock; ⟨Amer: ground floor⟩ Erdgeschoss nt. ~ly adv erstens. ~ name n Vorname m. ~-rate a erstklassig

fish /fɪʃ/ n Fisch m □ vt/i fischen; ⟨with rod⟩ angeln. ~ out vt herausfischen

fish: ~bone n Gräte f. ~erman n Fischer m. ~-farm n Fischzucht f. ~ 'finger n Fischstäbchen n

fishing /ˈfɪʃɪŋ/ n Fischerei f. ~ boat n Fischerboot nt. ~-rod n Angel[rute] f

fish: ~monger /-mʌŋgə(r)/ n Fischhändler m. ~-slice n Fischheber m. ~y a Fisch-; ⟨fam: suspicious⟩ verdächtig

fission /ˈfɪʃn/ n ⟨Phys⟩ Spaltung f

fist /fɪst/ n Faust f

fit¹ /fɪt/ n ⟨attack⟩ Anfall m

fit² *a* (fitter, fittest) ⟨*suitable*⟩ geeignet; ⟨*healthy*⟩ gesund; ⟨*Sport*⟩ fit; ~ to eat essbar; keep ~ sich fit halten; see ~ es für angebracht halten (to zu)

fit³ *n* ⟨*of clothes*⟩ Sitz *m*; be a good ~ gut passen □ *v* ⟨*pt/pp* fitted⟩ □ *vi* ⟨*be the right size*⟩ passen □ *vt* anbringen (to an + *dat*); ⟨*install*⟩ einbauen; ⟨*clothes:*⟩ passen (+ *dat*); ~ with versehen mit. ~ in *vi* hineinpassen; ⟨*adapt*⟩ sich einfügen (with in + *acc*) □ *vt* ⟨*accommodate*⟩ unterbringen

fit|ful /'fɪtfl/ *a*, -ly *adv* ⟨*sleep*⟩ unruhig. ~ment *n* Einrichtungsgegenstand *m*; ⟨*attachment*⟩ Zusatzgerät *nt*. ~ness *n* Eignung *f*; [physical] ~ness Gesundheit *f*; ⟨*Sport*⟩ Fitness *f*. ~ted *a* eingebaut; ⟨*garment*⟩ tailliert

fitted: ~ 'carpet *n* Teppichboden *m*. ~ 'cupboard *n* Einbauschrank *m*. ~ 'kitchen *n* Einbauküche *f*. ~ 'sheet *n* Spannlaken *nt*

fitter /'fɪtə(r)/ *n* Monteur *m*

fitting /'fɪtɪŋ/ *a* passend □ *n* ⟨*of clothes*⟩ Anprobe *f*; ⟨*of shoes*⟩ Weite *f*; ⟨*Techn*⟩ Zubehörteil *nt*; ~s *pl* Zubehör *nt*. ~ room *n* Anprobekabine *f*

five /faɪv/ *a* fünf □ *n* Fünf *f*. ~r *n* Fünfpfundschein *m*

fix /fɪks/ *n* ⟨*sl: drugs*⟩ Fix *m*; be in a ~ ⟨*fam*⟩ in der Klemme sitzen □ *vt* befestigen (to an + *dat*); ⟨*arrange*⟩ festlegen; ⟨*repair*⟩ reparieren; ⟨*Phot*⟩ fixieren; ~ a meal ⟨*Amer*⟩ Essen machen

fixation /fɪk'seɪʃn/ *n* Fixierung *f*

fixed /'fɪkst/ *a* fest

fixture /'fɪkstʃə(r)/ *n* ⟨*Sport*⟩ Veranstaltung *f*; ~s and fittings zu einer Wohnung gehörende Einrichtungen *pl*

fizz /fɪz/ *vi* sprudeln

fizzle /'fɪzl/ *vi* ~ out verpuffen

fizzy /'fɪzɪ/ *a* sprudelnd. ~ drink *n* Brause[limonade] *f*

flabbergasted /'flæbəgɑːstɪd/ *a* be ~ platt sein ⟨*fam*⟩

flabby /'flæbɪ/ *a* schlaff

flag¹ /flæg/ *n* Fahne *f*; ⟨*Naut*⟩ Flagge *f* □ *vt* ⟨*pt/pp* flagged⟩ ~ down anhalten ⟨*taxi*⟩

flag² *vi* ⟨*pt/pp* flagged⟩ ermüden

flagon /'flægən/ *n* Krug *m*

'flag-pole *n* Fahnenstange *f*

flagrant /'fleɪgrənt/ *a* flagrant

'flagstone *n* [Pflaster]platte *f*

flair /fleə(r)/ *n* Begabung *f*

flake /fleɪk/ *n* Flocke *f* □ *vi* ~ [off] abblättern

flaky /'fleɪkɪ/ *a* blättrig. ~ pastry *n* Blätterteig *m*

flamboyant /flæm'bɔɪənt/ *a* extravagant

flame /fleɪm/ *n* Flamme *f*

flammable /'flæməbl/ *a* feuergefährlich

flan /flæn/ *n* [fruit] ~ Obsttorte *f*

flank /flæŋk/ *n* Flanke *f* □ *vt* flankieren

flannel /'flænl/ *n* Flanell *m*; ⟨*for washing*⟩ Waschlappen *m*

flannelette /flænə'let/ *n* ⟨*Tex*⟩ Biber *m*

flap /flæp/ *n* Klappe *f*; in a ~ ⟨*fam*⟩ aufgeregt □ *v* ⟨*pt/pp* flapped⟩ *vi* flattern; ⟨*fam*⟩ sich aufregen □ *vt* ~ its wings mit den Flügeln schlagen

flare /fleə(r)/ *n* Leuchtsignal *nt* □ *vi* ~ up auflodern; ⟨*fam: get angry*⟩ aufbrausen. ~d *a* ⟨*garment*⟩ ausgestellt

flash /flæʃ/ *n* Blitz *m*; in a ~ ⟨*fam*⟩ im Nu □ *vi* blitzen; ⟨*repeatedly*⟩ blinken; ~ past vorbeirasen □ *vt* aufleuchten lassen; ~ one's headlights die Lichthupe betätigen

flash: ~back *n* Rückblende *f*. ~bulb *n* ⟨*Phot*⟩ Blitzbirne *f*. ~er *n* ⟨*Auto*⟩ Blinker *m*. ~light *n* ⟨*Phot*⟩ Blitzlicht *nt*; ⟨*Amer: torch*⟩ Taschenlampe *f*. ~y *a* auffällig

flask /flɑːsk/ *n* Flasche *f*; ⟨*Chem*⟩ Kolben *m*; ⟨*vacuum* ~⟩ Thermosflasche (P) *f*

flat /flæt/ *a* ⟨*flatter, flattest*⟩ flach; ⟨*surface*⟩ eben; ⟨*refusal*⟩ glatt; ⟨*beer*⟩ schal; ⟨*battery*⟩ verbraucht; ⟨*Auto*⟩ leer; ⟨*tyre*⟩ platt; ⟨*Mus*⟩ A ~ As *nt*; B ~ B *nt* □ *n* Wohnung *f*; ⟨*Mus*⟩ Erniedrigungszeichen *nt*; ⟨*fam: puncture*⟩ Reifenpanne *f*

flat: ~ 'feet *npl* Plattfüße *pl*. ~fish *n* Plattfisch *m*. ~ly *adv* ⟨*refuse*⟩ glatt. ~ rate *n* Einheitspreis *m*

flatten /'flætn/ *vt* platt drücken

flatter /'flætə(r)/ *vt* schmeicheln (+ *dat*). ~y *n* Schmeichelei *f*

flat 'tyre *n* Reifenpanne *f*

flatulence /'flætjʊləns/ *n* Blähungen *pl*

flaunt /flɔːnt/ *vt* prunken mit

flautist /'flɔːtɪst/ *n* Flötist(in) *m(f)*

flavour /'fleɪvə(r)/ *n* Geschmack *m* □ *vt* abschmecken. ~ing *n* Aroma *nt*

flaw /flɔː/ *n* Fehler *m*. ~less *a* tadellos; ⟨*complexion*⟩ makellos

flax /flæks/ *n* Flachs *m*. ~en *a* flachsblond

flea /fliː/ *n* Floh *m*. ~ market *n* Flohmarkt *m*

fleck /flek/ *n* Tupfen *m*

fled /fled/ *see* flee

flee /fliː/ *v* ⟨*pt/pp* fled⟩ □ *vi* fliehen (from vor + *dat*) □ *vt* flüchten aus

fleec|e /fliːs/ *n* Vlies *nt* □ *vt* ⟨*fam*⟩ schröpfen. ~y *a* flauschig

fleet /fliːt/ *n* Flotte *f*; ⟨*of cars*⟩ Wagenpark *m*

fleeting /'fliːtɪŋ/ *a* flüchtig

Flemish /'flemɪʃ/ *a* flämisch

flesh /fleʃ/ *n* Fleisch *nt*; in the ~ ⟨*fam*⟩ in Person. ~y *a* fleischig

flew /fluː/ *see* fly²

flex¹ /fleks/ *vt* anspannen ⟨muscle⟩

flex² *n* (*Electr*) Schnur *f*

flexib|ility /fleksə'bɪlətɪ/ *n* Biegsamkeit *f*; (*fig*) Flexibilität *f*. ~le *a* biegsam; (*fig*) flexibel

'flexitime /'fleksɪ-/ *n* Gleitzeit *f*

flick /flɪk/ *vt* schnippen. ~ through *vi* schnell durchblättern

flicker /'flɪkə(r)/ *vi* flackern

flier /'flaɪə(r)/ *n* = flyer

flight¹ /flaɪt/ *n* (*fleeing*) Flucht *f*; take ~ die Flucht ergreifen

flight² *n* (*flying*) Flug *m*; ~ of stairs Treppe *f*

flight: ~ path *n* Flugschneise *f*. ~ recorder *n* Flugschreiber *m*

flighty /'flaɪtɪ/ *a* (-ier, -iest) flatterhaft

flimsy /'flɪmzɪ/ *a* (-ier, -iest) dünn; ⟨excuse⟩ fadenscheinig

flinch /flɪntʃ/ *vi* zurückzucken

fling /flɪŋ/ *n* have a ~ (*fam*) sich austoben □ *vt* (*pt/pp* flung) schleudern

flint /flɪnt/ *n* Feuerstein *m*

flip /flɪp/ *vt/i* schnippen; ~ through durchblättern

flippant /'flɪpənt/ *a*, -ly *adv* leichtfertig

flipper /'flɪpə(r)/ *n* Flosse *f*

flirt /flɜːt/ *n* kokette Frau *f* □ *vi* flirten

flirtat|ion /flɜː'teɪʃn/ *n* Flirt *m*. ~ious /-ʃəs/ *a* kokett

flit /flɪt/ *vi* (*pt/pp* flitted) flattern

float /fləʊt/ *n* Schwimmer *m*; (*in procession*) Festwagen *m*; (*money*) Wechselgeld *nt* □ *vi* ⟨thing:⟩ schwimmen; ⟨person:⟩ sich treiben lassen; (*in air*) schweben; (*Comm*) floaten

flock /flɒk/ *n* Herde *f*; (*of birds*) Schwarm *m* □ *vi* strömen

flog /flɒg/ *vt* (*pt/pp* flogged) auspeitschen; (*fam: sell*) verkloppen

flood /flʌd/ *n* Überschwemmung *f*; (*fig*) Flut *f*; be in ~ ⟨river:⟩ Hochwasser führen □ *vt* überschwemmen □ *vi* ⟨river:⟩ über die Ufer treten

'floodlight *n* Flutlicht *nt* □ *vt* (*pt/pp* floodlit) anstrahlen

floor /flɔː(r)/ *n* Fußboden *m*; (*storey*) Stock *m* □ *vt* (*baffle*) verblüffen

floor: ~ board *n* Dielenbrett *nt*. ~ cloth *n* Scheuertuch *nt*. ~ polish *n* Bohnerwachs *nt*. ~ show *n* Kabarettvorstellung *f*

flop /flɒp/ *n* (*fam*) (*failure*) Reinfall *m*; (*Theat*) Durchfall *m* □ *vi* (*pt/pp* flopped) (*fam*) (*fail*) durchfallen; ~ down sich plumpsen lassen

floppy /'flɒpɪ/ *a* schlapp. ~ 'disc *n* Diskette *f*

flora /'flɔːrə/ *n* Flora *f*

floral /'flɔːrl/ *a* Blumen-

florid /'flɒrɪd/ *a* ⟨complexion⟩ gerötet; ⟨style⟩ blumig

florist /'flɒrɪst/ *n* Blumenhändler(in) *m(f)*

flounce /flaʊns/ *n* Volant *m* □ *vi* ~ out hinausstolzieren

flounder¹ /'flaʊndə(r)/ *vi* zappeln

flounder² *n* (*fish*) Flunder *f*

flour /'flaʊə(r)/ *n* Mehl *nt*

flourish /'flʌrɪʃ/ *n* große Geste *f*; (*scroll*) Schnörkel *m* □ *vi* gedeihen; (*fig*) blühen □ *vt* schwenken

floury /'flaʊərɪ/ *a* mehlig

flout /flaʊt/ *vt* missachten

flow /fləʊ/ *n* Fluss *m*; (*of traffic, blood*) Strom *m* □ *vi* fließen

flower /'flaʊə(r)/ *n* Blume *f* □ *vi* blühen

flower: ~ bed *n* Blumenbeet *nt*. ~ ed *a* geblümt. ~ pot *n* Blumentopf *m*. ~ y *a* blumig

flown /fləʊn/ *see* fly²

flu /fluː/ *n* (*fam*) Grippe *f*

fluctuat|e /'flʌktjʊeɪt/ *vi* schwanken. ~ ion /-'eɪʃn/ *n* Schwankung *f*

fluent /'fluːənt/ *a*, -ly *adv* fließend

fluff /flʌf/ *n* Fusseln *pl*; (*down*) Flaum *m*. ~ y *a* (-ier, -iest) flauschig

fluid /'fluːɪd/ *a* flüssig; (*fig*) veränderlich □ *n* Flüssigkeit *f*

fluke /fluːk/ *n* [glücklicher] Zufall *m*

flung /flʌŋ/ *see* fling

flunk /flʌŋk/ *vt/i* (*Amer, fam*) durchfallen (in + *dat*)

fluorescent /flʊə'resnt/ *a* fluoreszierend; ~ lighting Neonbeleuchtung *f*

fluoride /'flʊəraɪd/ *n* Fluor *nt*

flurry /'flʌrɪ/ *n* (*snow*) Gestöber *nt*; (*fig*) Aufregung *f*

flush /flʌʃ/ *n* (*blush*) Erröten *nt* □ *vi* rot werden □ *vt* spülen □ *a* in einer Ebene (with mit); (*fam: affluent*) gut bei Kasse

flustered /'flʌstəd/ *a* nervös

flute /fluːt/ *n* Flöte *f*

flutter /'flʌtə(r)/ *n* Flattern *nt* □ *vi* flattern

flux /flʌks/ *n* in a state of ~ im Fluss

fly¹ /flaɪ/ *n* (*pl* flies) Fliege *f*

fly² *v* (*pt* flew, *pp* flown) □ *vi* fliegen; ⟨flag:⟩ wehen; (*rush*) sausen □ *vt* fliegen; führen ⟨flag⟩

fly³ *n* & flies *pl* (*on trousers*) Hosenschlitz *m*

flyer /'flaɪə(r)/ *n* Flieger(in) *m(f)*; (*Amer: leaflet*) Flugblatt *nt*

flying: ~ 'buttress *n* Strebebogen *m*. ~ 'saucer *n* fliegende Untertasse *f*. ~ 'visit *n* Stippvisite *f*

fly: ~leaf n Vorsatzblatt nt. ~over n Überführung f

foal /'fəʊl/ n Fohlen nt

foam /fəʊm/ n Schaum m; (synthetic) Schaumstoff m □ vi schäumen. ~'rubber n Schaumgummi m

fob /fɒb/ vt (pt/pp fobbed) ~ sth off etw andrehen (on s.o. jdm); ~ s.o. off ab-speisen (with mit)

focal /'fəʊkl/ n Brenn-

focus /'fəʊkəs/ n Brennpunkt m; in ~ scharf eingestellt □ v (pt/pp focused or focussed) □ vt einstellen (on auf + acc); (fig) konzentrieren (on auf + acc) □ vi (fig) sich konzentrieren (on auf + acc)

fodder /'fɒdə(r)/ n Futter nt

foe /fəʊ/ n Feind m

foetus /'fiːtəs/ n (pl -tuses) Fötus m

fog /fɒg/ n Nebel m

foggy /'fɒgɪ/ a (foggier, foggiest) neblig

'fog-horn n Nebelhorn nt

fogy /'fəʊgɪ/ n old ~ alter Knacker m

foible /'fɔɪbl/ n Eigenart f

foil[1] /fɔɪl/ n Folie f; (Culin) Alufolie f

foil[2] vt (thwart) vereiteln

foil[3] n (Fencing) Florett nt

foist /fɔɪst/ vt andrehen (on s.o. jdm)

fold[1] /fəʊld/ n (for sheep) Pferch m

fold[2] n Falte f; (in paper) Kniff m □ vt falten; ~ one's arms die Arme verschränken □ vi sich falten lassen; (fail) ein-gehen. ~ up vt zusammenfalten; zusammenklappen ⟨chair⟩ □ vi sich zu-sammenfalten/-klappen lassen; (fam) ⟨business:⟩ eingehen

fold|er /'fəʊldə(r)/ n Mappe f. ~ing a Klapp-

foliage /'fəʊlɪɪdʒ/ n Blätter pl; (of tree) Laub nt

folk /fəʊk/ npl Leute pl

folk: ~dance n Volkstanz m. ~lore n Folk-klore f. ~song n Volkslied nt

follow /'fɒləʊ/ vt/i folgen (+ dat); (pursue) verfolgen; (in vehicle) nachfahren (+ dat); ~ suit (fig) dasselbe tun. ~ up vt nach-gehen (+ dat)

follow|er /'fɒləʊə(r)/ n Anhänger(in) m(f). ~ing a folgend □ n Folgende(s) nt; (supporters) Anhängerschaft f □ prep im Anschluss an (+ acc)

folly /'fɒlɪ/ n Torheit f

fond /fɒnd/ a (-er, -est), -ly adv liebevoll; be ~ of gern haben; gern essen ⟨food⟩

fondle /'fɒndl/ vt liebkosen

fondness /'fɒndnɪs/ n Liebe f (for zu)

font /fɒnt/ n Taufstein m

food /fuːd/ n Essen nt; (for animals) Futter nt; (groceries) Lebensmittel pl

food: ~ mixer n Küchenmaschine f. ~ poisoning n Lebensmittelvergiftung f. ~ processor n Küchenmaschine f. ~ value n Nährwert m

fool[1] /fuːl/ n (Culin) Fruchtcreme f

fool[2] n Narr m; you are a ~ du bist dumm; make a ~ of oneself sich lächerlich machen □ vt hereinlegen □ vi ~ around herumalbern

'fool|hardy a tollkühn. ~ish a, -ly adv dumm. ~ishness n Dummheit f. ~proof a narrensicher

foot /fʊt/ n (pl feet) Fuß m; (measure) Fuß m (30,48 cm); (of bed) Fußende nt; on ~ zu Fuß; on one's feet auf den Beinen; put one's ~ in it (fam) ins Fettnäpfchen tre-ten

foot: ~-and-'mouth disease n Maul- und Klauenseuche f. ~ball n Fußball m. ~baller n Fußballspieler m. ~ball pools npl Fußballtoto nt. ~brake n Fußbremse f. ~bridge n Fußgängerbrücke f. ~hills npl Vorgebirge nt. ~hold n Halt m. ~ing n Halt m; (fig) Basis f. ~lights npl Ram-penlicht nt. ~man n Lakai m. ~note n Fußnote f. ~path n Fußweg m. ~print n Fußabdruck m. ~step n Schritt m; follow in s.o.'s ~steps (fig) in jds Fußstapfen treten. ~stool n Fußbank f. ~wear n Schuhwerk nt

for /fə(r), betont fɔː(r)/ prep für (+ acc); ⟨send, long⟩ nach; ⟨ask, fight⟩ um; what ~? wozu? ~ supper zum Abendessen; ~ nothing umsonst; ~ all that trotz allem; ~ this reason aus diesem Grund; ~ a month einen Monat; I have lived here ~ ten years ich wohne seit zehn Jahren hier □ conj denn

forage /'fɒrɪdʒ/ n Futter nt □ vi ~ for suchen nach

forbade /fə'bæd/ see forbid

forbear|ance /fɔː'beərəns/ n Nachsicht f. ~ing a nachsichtig

forbid /fə'bɪd/ vt (pt forbade, pp for-bidden) verbieten (s.o. jdm). ~ding a be-drohlich; (stern) streng

force /fɔːs/ n Kraft f; (of blow) Wucht f; (violence) Gewalt f; in ~ gültig; (in large numbers) in großer Zahl; come into ~ in Kraft treten; the ~s pl die Streitkräfte pl □ vt zwingen; (break open) aufbrechen; ~ sth on s.o. jdm etw aufdrängen

forced /fɔːst/ a erzwungen; ~ landing Notlandung f

force: ~'feed vt (pt/pp -fed) zwangser-nähren. ~ful a, -ly adv energisch

forceps /'fɔːseps/ n inv Zange f

forcibl|e /'fɔːsəbl/ *a* gewaltsam. ~y *adv* mit Gewalt

ford /fɔːd/ *n* Furt *f* □ *vt* durchwaten; (*in vehicle*) durchfahren

fore /fɔː(r)/ *a* vordere(r,s) □ *n* to the ~ im Vordergrund

fore: ~**arm** *n* Unterarm *m*. ~**boding** /-'bəʊdɪŋ/ *n* Vorahnung *f*. ~**cast** *n* Voraussage *f*; (*for weather*) Vorhersage *f* □ *vt* (*pt/pp* ~cast) voraussagen, vorhersagen. ~**court** *n* Vorhof *m*. ~**fathers** *npl* Vorfahren *pl*. ~**finger** *n* Zeigefinger *m*. ~**front** *n* be in the ~front führend sein. ~**gone** *a* be a ~gone conclusion von vornherein feststehen. ~**ground** *n* Vordergrund *m*. ~**head** /'fɒrɪd/ *n* Stirn *f*. ~**hand** *n* Vorhand *f*

foreign /'fɒrən/ *a* ausländisch; (*country*) fremd; he is ~ er ist Ausländer. ~ **currency** *n* Devisen *pl*. ~**er** *n* Ausländer(in) *m(f)*. ~ **language** *n* Fremdsprache *f*

Foreign: ~ Office *n* ≈ Außenministerium *nt*. ~ 'Secretary *n* ≈ Außenminister *m*

fore: ~**leg** *n* Vorderbein *nt*. ~**man** *n* Vorarbeiter *m*. ~**most** *a* führend □ *adv* first and ~most zuallerest. ~**name** *n* Vorname *m*

forensic /fə'rensɪk/ *a* ~ medicine Gerichtsmedizin *f*

'forerunner *n* Vorläufer *m*

fore'see *vt* (*pt* -saw, *pp* -seen) voraussehen, vorhersehen. ~**able** /-əbl/ *a* in the ~able future in absehbarer Zeit

'foresight *n* Weitblick *m*

forest /'fɒrɪst/ *n* Wald *m*. ~**er** *n* Förster *m*

fore'stall *vt* zuvorkommen (+ *dat*)

forestry /'fɒrɪstrɪ/ *n* Forstwirtschaft *f*

'foretaste *n* Vorgeschmack *m*

fore'tell *vt* (*pt/pp* -told) vorhersagen

forever /fə'revə(r)/ *adv* für immer

fore'warn *vt* vorher warnen

foreword /'fɔːwɜːd/ *n* Vorwort *nt*

forfeit /'fɔːfɪt/ *n* (*in game*) Pfand *nt* □ *vt* verwirken

forgave /fə'geɪv/ *see* forgive

forge¹ /fɔːdʒ/ *vi* ~ ahead (*fig*) Fortschritte machen

forge² *n* Schmiede *f* □ *vt* schmieden; (*counterfeit*) fälschen. ~**r** *n* Fälscher *m*. ~**ry** *n* Fälschung *f*

forget /fə'get/ *vt/i* (*pt* -got, *pp* -gotten) vergessen; verlernen (*language, skill*). ~**ful** *a* vergesslich. ~**fulness** *n* Vergesslichkeit *f*. ~**me-not** *n* Vergissmeinnicht *nt*

forgive /fə'gɪv/ *vt* (*pt* -gave, *pp* -given) ~ s.o. for sth jdm etw vergeben *od* verzeihen. ~**ness** *n* Vergebung *f*, Verzeihung *f*

forgo /fɔː'gəʊ/ *vt* (*pt* -went, *pp* -gone) verzichten auf (+ *acc*)

forgot(ten) /fə'gɒt(n)/ *see* forget

fork /fɔːk/ *n* Gabel *f*; (*in road*) Gabelung *f* □ *vi* (*road:*) sich gabeln; ~ right rechts abzweigen. ~ out *vt* (*fam*) blechen

fork-lift 'truck *n* Gabelstapler *m*

forlorn /fə'lɔːn/ *a* verlassen; (*hope*) schwach

form /fɔːm/ *n* Form *f*; (*document*) Formular *nt*; (*bench*) Bank *f*; (*Sch*) Klasse *f* □ *vt* formen (into zu); (*create*) bilden □ *vi* sich bilden; (*idea:*) Gestalt annehmen

formal /'fɔːml/ *a*, -ly *adv* formell, förmlich. ~**ity** /-'mælətɪ/ *n* Förmlichkeit *f*; (*requirement*) Formalität *f*

format /'fɔːmæt/ *n* Format *nt*

formation /fɔː'meɪʃn/ *n* Formation *f*

formative /'fɔːmətɪv/ *a* ~ years Entwicklungsjahre *pl*

former /'fɔːmə(r)/ *a* ehemalig; the ~ der/die/das Erstere. ~**ly** *adv* früher

formidable /'fɔːmɪdəbl/ *a* gewaltig

formula /'fɔːmjʊlə/ *n* (*pl* -ae /-liː/ *or* -s) Formel *f*

formulate /'fɔːmjʊleɪt/ *vt* formulieren

forsake /fə'seɪk/ *vt* (*pt* -sook /-sʊk/, *pp* -saken) verlassen

fort /fɔːt/ *n* (*Mil*) Fort *nt*

forte /'fɔːteɪ/ *n* Stärke *f*

forth /fɔːθ/ *adv* back and ~ hin und her; and so ~ und so weiter

forth: ~'coming *a* bevorstehend; (*fam: communicative*) mitteilsam. ~right *a* direkt. ~'with *adv* umgehend

fortieth /'fɔːtɪɪθ/ *a* vierzigste(r,s)

fortification /fɔːtɪfɪ'keɪʃn/ *n* Befestigung *f*

fortify /'fɔːtɪfaɪ/ *vt* (*pt/pp* -ied) befestigen; (*fig*) stärken

fortitude /'fɔːtɪtjuːd/ *n* Standhaftigkeit *f*

fortnight /'fɔːt-/ *n* vierzehn Tage *pl*. ~**ly** *a* vierzehntäglich □ *adv* alle vierzehn Tage

fortress /'fɔːtrɪs/ *n* Festung *f*

fortuitous /fɔː'tjuːɪtəs/ *a*, -ly *adv* zufällig

fortunate /'fɔːtʃʊnət/ *a* glücklich; be ~ Glück haben. ~**ly** *adv* glücklicherweise

fortune /'fɔːtʃuːn/ *n* Glück *nt*; (*money*) Vermögen *nt*. ~**teller** *n* Wahrsagerin *f*

forty /'fɔːtɪ/ *a* vierzig; have ~ winks (*fam*) ein Nickerchen machen □ *n* Vierzig *f*

forum /'fɔːrəm/ *n* Forum *nt*

forward /'fɔːwəd/ *adv* vorwärts; (*to the front*) nach vorn □ *a* Vorwärts-; (*presumptuous*) anmaßend □ *n* (*Sport*) Stürmer *m* □ *vt* nachsenden (*letter*). ~**s** *adv* vorwärts

fossil /'fɒsl/ n Fossil nt. ∼ized a versteinert

foster /'fɒstə(r)/ vt fördern; in Pflege nehmen ⟨child⟩. ∼-child n Pflegekind nt. ∼-mother n Pflegemutter f

fought /fɔːt/ see fight

foul /faʊl/ a (-er, -est) widerlich; ⟨language⟩ unflätig; ∼ play ⟨Jur⟩ Mord m □ n ⟨Sport⟩ Foul nt □ vt verschmutzen; ⟨obstruct⟩ blockieren; ⟨Sport⟩ foulen. ∼-smelling a übel riechend

found¹ /faʊnd/ see find

found² vt gründen

foundation /faʊn'deɪʃn/ n ⟨basis⟩ Grundlage f; ⟨charitable⟩ Stiftung f; ∼s pl Fundament nt. ∼-stone n Grundstein m

founder¹ /'faʊndə(r)/ n Gründer(in) m(f)

founder² vi ⟨ship⟩ sinken; ⟨fig⟩ scheitern

foundry /'faʊndrɪ/ n Gießerei f

fountain /'faʊntɪn/ n Brunnen m. ∼-pen n Füllfederhalter m

four /fɔː(r)/ a vier □ n Vier f

four: ∼-'poster n Himmelbett nt. ∼some /'fɔːsəm/ n in a ∼some zu viert. ∼'teen a vierzehn □ n Vierzehn f. ∼'teenth a vierzehnte(r,s)

fourth /fɔːθ/ a vierte(r,s)

fowl /faʊl/ n Geflügel nt

fox /fɒks/ n Fuchs m □ vt ⟨puzzle⟩ verblüffen

foyer /'fɔɪeɪ/ n Foyer nt; ⟨in hotel⟩ Empfangshalle f

fraction /'frækʃn/ n Bruchteil m; ⟨Math⟩ Bruch m

fracture /'fræktʃə(r)/ n Bruch m □ vt/i brechen

fragile /'frædʒaɪl/ a zerbrechlich

fragment /'frægmənt/ n Bruchstück nt, Fragment nt. ∼ary a bruchstückhaft

fragrance /'freɪgrəns/ n Duft m. ∼t a duftend

frail /freɪl/ a (-er, -est) gebrechlich

frame /freɪm/ n Rahmen m; ⟨of spectacles⟩ Gestell nt; ⟨Anat⟩ Körperbau m; ∼ of mind Gemütsverfassung f □ vt einrahmen; ⟨fig⟩ formulieren; ⟨sl⟩ ein Verbrechen anhängen (+ dat). ∼work n Gerüst nt; ⟨fig⟩ Gerippe nt

franc /fræŋk/ n ⟨French, Belgian⟩ Franc m; ⟨Swiss⟩ Franken m

France /frɑːns/ n Frankreich nt

franchise /'fræntʃaɪz/ n ⟨Pol⟩ Wahlrecht nt; ⟨Comm⟩ Franchise nt

frank¹ /fræŋk/ vt frankieren

frank² a, -ly adv offen

frankfurter /'fræŋkfɜːtə(r)/ n Frankfurter f

frantic /'fræntɪk/ a, -ally adv verzweifelt; be ∼ außer sich ⟨dat⟩ sein (with vor)

fraternal /frə'tɜːnl/ a brüderlich

fraud /frɔːd/ n Betrug m; ⟨person⟩ Betrüger(in) m(f). ∼ulent /-jʊlənt/ a betrügerisch

fraught /frɔːt/ a ∼ with danger gefahrvoll

fray¹ /freɪ/ n Kampf m

fray² vi ausfransen

freak /friːk/ n Missbildung f; ⟨person⟩ Missgeburt f; ⟨phenomenon⟩ Ausnahmeerscheinung f □ a anormal. ∼ish a anormal

freckle /'frekl/ n Sommersprosse f. ∼d a sommersprossig

free /friː/ a (freer, freest) frei; ⟨ticket, copy, time⟩ Frei-; ⟨lavish⟩ freigebig; ∼ [of charge] kostenlos; set ∼ freilassen; ⟨rescue⟩ befreien; you are ∼ to … es steht Ihnen frei, zu … □ vt ⟨pt/pp freed⟩ freilassen; ⟨rescue⟩ befreien; ⟨disentangle⟩ freibekommen

free: ∼dom n Freiheit f. ∼hand adv aus freier Hand. ∼hold n [freier] Grundbesitz m. ∼'kick n Freistoß m. ∼lance a & adv freiberuflich. ∼ly adv frei; ⟨voluntarily⟩ freiwillig; ⟨generously⟩ großzügig. F∼mason n Freimaurer m. F∼masonry n Freimaurerei f. ∼-range a ∼-range eggs Landeier pl. ∼ 'sample n Gratisprobe f. ∼-style n Freistil m. ∼way n ⟨Amer⟩ Autobahn f. ∼'wheel vi im Freilauf fahren

freeze /friːz/ vt ⟨pt froze, pp frozen⟩ einfrieren; stoppen ⟨wages⟩ □ vi gefrieren; it's ∼ing es friert

freezer /'friːzə(r)/ n Gefriertruhe f; ⟨upright⟩ Gefrierschrank m. ∼ing a eiskalt □ n below ∼ing unter Null

freight /freɪt/ n Fracht f. ∼er n Frachter m. ∼ train n ⟨Amer⟩ Güterzug m

French /frentʃ/ a französisch □ n ⟨Lang⟩ Französisch nt; the ∼ pl die Franzosen

French: ∼ 'beans npl grüne Bohnen pl. ∼ 'bread n Stangenbrot nt. ∼ 'fries npl Pommes frites pl. ∼man n Franzose m. ∼ 'window n Terrassentür f. ∼woman n Französin f

frenzied /'frenzɪd/ a rasend

frenzy /'frenzɪ/ n Raserei f

frequency /'friːkwənsɪ/ n Häufigkeit f; ⟨Phys⟩ Frequenz f

frequent¹ /'friːkwənt/ a, -ly adv häufig

frequent² /frɪ'kwent/ vt regelmäßig besuchen

fresco /'freskəʊ/ n Fresko nt

fresh /freʃ/ a (-er, -est), -ly adv frisch; ⟨new⟩ neu; ⟨Amer: cheeky⟩ frech

freshen /'freʃn/ vi ⟨wind:⟩ auffrischen. ~ up vt auffrischen ▫ vi sich frisch machen

freshness /'freʃnɪs/ n Frische f

'freshwater a Süßwasser-

fret /fret/ vi (pt/pp fretted) sich grämen. ~ful a weinerlich

'fretsaw n Laubsäge f

friar /'fraɪə(r)/ n Mönch m

friction /'frɪkʃn/ n Reibung f; (fig) Reibereien pl

Friday /'fraɪdeɪ/ n Freitag m

fridge /frɪdʒ/ n Kühlschrank m

fried /fraɪd/ see fry² ▫ a gebraten; ~ egg Spiegelei nt

friend /frend/ n Freund(in) m(f). ~liness n Freundlichkeit f. ~ly a (-ier, -iest) freundlich; ~ly with befreundet mit. ~ship n Freundschaft f

frieze /fri:z/ n Fries m

fright /fraɪt/ n Schreck m

frighten /'fraɪtn/ vt Angst machen (+ dat); (startle) erschrecken; be ~ed Angst haben (of vor + dat). ~ing a Angst erregend

frightful /'fraɪtfl/ a, -ly adv schrecklich

frigid /'frɪdʒɪd/ a frostig; (Psych) frigide. ~ity /-'dʒɪdəti/ n Frostigkeit f; Frigidität f

frill /frɪl/ n Rüsche f; (paper) Manschette f. ~y a rüschenbesetzt

fringe /frɪndʒ/ n Fransen pl; (of hair) Pony m; (fig: edge) Rand m. ~ benefits npl zusätzliche Leistungen pl

frisk /frɪsk/ vi herumspringen ▫ vt (search) durchsuchen, (fam) filzen

frisky /'frɪskɪ/ a (-ier, -iest) lebhaft

fritter /'frɪtə(r)/ vt ~ [away] verplempern (fam)

frivolity /frɪ'vɒlətɪ/ n Frivolität f. ~ous /'frɪvələs/ a, -ly adv frivol, leichtfertig

frizzy /'frɪzɪ/ a kraus

fro /frəʊ/ adv to and ~ hin und her

frock /frɒk/ n Kleid nt

frog /frɒg/ n Frosch m. ~man n Froschmann m. ~spawn n Froschlaich m

frolic /'frɒlɪk/ vi (pt/pp frolicked) herumtollen

from /frɒm/ prep von (+ dat); (out of) aus (+ dat); (according to) nach (+ dat); ~ Monday ab Montag; ~ that day seit dem Tag

front /frʌnt/ n Vorderseite f; (fig) Fassade f; (of garment) Vorderteil nt; (sea-) Strandpromenade f; (Mil, Pol, Meteorol) Front f; in ~ of vor; in or at the ~ vorne; to the

~ nach vorne ▫ a vordere(r,s); ⟨page, row⟩ erste(r,s); ⟨tooth, wheel⟩ Vorder-

frontal /'frʌntl/ a Frontal-

front: ~ 'door n Haustür f. ~ 'garden n Vorgarten m

frontier /'frʌntɪə(r)/ n Grenze f

front-wheel 'drive n Vorderradantrieb m

frost /frɒst/ n Frost m; (hoar-) Raureif m; ten degrees of ~ zehn Grad Kälte. ~bite n Erfrierung f. ~bitten a erfroren

frost|ed /'frɒstɪd/ a ~ed glass Mattglas nt. ~ing n (Amer Culin) Zuckerguss m. ~y a, -ily adv frostig

froth /frɒθ/ n Schaum m ▫ vi schäumen. ~y a schaumig

frown /fraʊn/ n Stirnrunzeln nt ▫ vi die Stirn runzeln; ~ on missbilligen

froze /frəʊz/ see freeze

frozen /'frəʊzn/ see freeze ▫ a gefroren; (Culin) tiefgekühlt; I'm ~ (fam) mir ist eiskalt. ~ food n Tiefkühlkost f

frugal /'fru:gl/ a, -ly adv sparsam; ⟨meal⟩ frugal

fruit /fru:t/ n Frucht f; (collectively) Obst nt. ~ cake n englischer [Tee]kuchen m

fruit|erer /'fru:tərə(r)/ n Obsthändler m. ~ful a fruchtbar

fruition /fru:'ɪʃn/ n come to ~ sich verwirklichen

fruit: ~ juice n Obstsaft m. ~less a, -ly adv fruchtlos. ~ machine n Spielautomat m. ~ 'salad n Obstsalat m

fruity /'fru:tɪ/ a fruchtig

frumpy /'frʌmpɪ/ a unmodisch

frustrat|e /frʌ'streɪt/ vt vereiteln; (psych) frustrieren. ~ing a frustrierend. ~ion /-eɪʃn/ n Frustration f

fry¹ /fraɪ/ n inv small ~ (fig) kleine Fische pl

fry² vt/i (pt/pp fried) [in der Pfanne] braten. ~ing-pan n Bratpfanne f

fuck /fʌk/ vt/i (vulg) ficken. ~ing a (vulg) Scheiß-

fuddy-duddy /'fʌdɪdʌdɪ/ n (fam) verknöcherter Kerl m

fudge /fʌdʒ/ n weiche Karamellen pl

fuel /'fju:əl/ n Brennstoff m; (for car) Kraftstoff m; (for aircraft) Treibstoff m

fugitive /'fju:dʒətɪv/ n Flüchtling m

fugue /fju:g/ n (Mus) Fuge f

fulfil /fʊl'fɪl/ vt (pt/pp -filled) erfüllen. ~ment n Erfüllung f

full /fʊl/ a & adv (-er, -est) voll; (detailed) ausführlich; ⟨skirt⟩ weit; ~ of voll von (+ dat), voller (+ gen); at ~ speed in voller Fahrt ▫ n in ~ vollständig

full: ~ 'moon n Vollmond m. ~-scale a
⟨model⟩ in Originalgröße; ⟨rescue, alert⟩
groß angelegt. ~ 'stop n Punkt m. ~-
time a ganztägig ▫ adv ganztags

fully /'fʊlɪ/ adv völlig; (in detail) ausführlich

fulsome /'fʊlsəm/ a übertrieben

fumble /'fʌmbl/ vi herumfummeln (with
an + dat)

fume /fju:m/ vi vor Wut schäumen

fumes /fju:mz/ npl Dämpfe pl; (from car)
Abgase pl

fumigate /'fju:mɪgeɪt/ vt ausräuchern

fun /fʌn/ n Spaß m; for ~ aus od zum Spaß;
make ~ of sich lustig machen über (+
acc); have ~! viel Spaß!

function /'fʌŋkʃn/ n Funktion f; (event)
Veranstaltung f ▫ vi funktionieren;
(serve) dienen (as als). ~al a zweckmäßig

fund /fʌnd/ n Fonds m; (fig) Vorrat m; ~s
pl Geldmittel pl ▫ vt finanzieren

fundamental /fʌndə'mentl/ a grundlegend; (essential) wesentlich

funeral /'fju:nərl/ n Beerdigung f; (cremation) Feuerbestattung f

funeral: ~ directors pl, (Amer) ~ home
n Bestattungsinstitut nt. ~ march n
Trauermarsch m. ~ parlour n (Amer) Bestattungsinstitut nt. ~ service n Trauer-
gottesdienst m

'funfair n Jahrmarkt m, Kirmes f

fungus /'fʌŋgəs/ n (pl -gi /-gaɪ/) Pilz m

funicular /fju:'nɪkjʊlə(r)/ n Seilbahn f

funnel /'fʌnl/ n Trichter m; (on ship, train)
Schornstein m

funnily /'fʌnɪlɪ/ adv komisch; ~ enough
komischerweise

funny /'fʌnɪ/ a (-ier, -iest) komisch. ~-
bone n (fam) Musikantenknochen m

fur /fɜ:(r)/ n Fell nt; (for clothing) Pelz m;
(in kettle) Kesselstein m. ~ 'coat n Pelz-
mantel m

furious /'fjʊərɪəs/ a, -ly adv wütend (with
auf + acc)

furnace /'fɜ:nɪs/ n (Techn) Ofen m

furnish /'fɜ:nɪʃ/ vt einrichten; (supply) liefern. ~ed a ~ed room möbliertes
Zimmer m. ~ings npl Einrichtungsge-
genstände pl

furniture /'fɜ:nɪtʃə(r)/ n Möbel pl

furred /fɜ:d/ a ⟨tongue⟩ belegt

furrow /'fʌrəʊ/ n Furche f

furry /'fɜ:rɪ/ a ⟨animal⟩ Pelz-; ⟨toy⟩ Plüsch-

further /'fɜ:ðə(r)/ a weitere(r,s); at the ~
end am anderen Ende; until ~ notice bis
auf weiteres ▫ adv weiter; ▫ vt weiter
entfernt ▫ vi fördern

further: ~ edu'cation n Weiterbildung f.
~'more adv überdies

furthest /'fɜ:ðɪst/ a am weitesten entfernt
▫ adv am weitesten

furtive /'fɜ:tɪv/ a, -ly adv verstohlen

fury /'fjʊərɪ/ n Wut f

fuse¹ /fju:z/ n (of bomb) Zünder m; (cord)
Zündschnur f

fuse² n (Electr) Sicherung f ▫ vt/i ver-
schmelzen; the lights have ~d die
Sicherung [für das Licht] ist durchge-
brannt. ~-box n Sicherungskasten m

fuselage /'fju:zəlɑːʒ/ n (Aviat) Rumpf m

fusion /'fju:ʒn/ n Verschmelzung f, Fusion f

fuss /fʌs/ n Getue nt; make a ~ of verwöhnen; (caress) liebkosen ▫ vi Umstände
machen

fussy /'fʌsɪ/ a (-ier, -iest) wählerisch; (particular) penibel

fusty /'fʌstɪ/ a moderig

futile /'fju:taɪl/ a zwecklos. ~ity /-'tɪlətɪ/
n Zwecklosigkeit f

future /'fju:tʃə(r)/ a zukünftig ▫ n Zukunft
f; (Gram) [erstes] Futur nt; ~ perfect
zweites Futur nt; in ~ in Zukunft

futuristic /fju:tʃə'rɪstɪk/ a futuristisch

fuzz /fʌz/ n the ~ (sl) die Bullen pl

fuzzy /'fʌzɪ/ a (-ier, -iest) ⟨hair⟩ kraus;
(blurred) verschwommen

G

gab /gæb/ n (fam) have the gift of the ~
gut reden können

gabble /'gæbl/ vi schnell reden

gable /'geɪbl/ n Giebel m

gad /gæd/ vi (pt/pp gadded) ~ about
dauernd ausgehen

gadget /'gædʒɪt/ n [kleines] Gerät nt

Gaelic /'geɪlɪk/ n Gälisch nt

gaffe /gæf/ n Fauxpas m

gag /gæg/ n Knebel m; (joke) Witz m;
(Theat) Gag m ▫ vt (pt/pp gagged) kneb-
eln

gaiety /'geɪətɪ/ n Fröhlichkeit f

gaily /'geɪlɪ/ adv fröhlich

gain /geɪn/ n Gewinn m, (increase) Zunahme f ▫ vt gewinnen; (obtain) erlangen; ~ weight zunehmen ▫ vi ⟨clock:⟩
vorgehen. ~ful a ~ful employment
Erwerbstätigkeit f

gait /geɪt/ n Gang m

gala /'gɑːlə/ n Fest nt; swimming ~ Schwimmfest nt □ attrib Gala-

galaxy /'gæləksɪ/ n Galaxie f; the G~ die Milchstraße

gale /geɪl/ n Sturm m

gall /gɔːl/ n Galle f; (impudence) Frechheit f

gallant /'gælənt/ a, -ly adv tapfer; (chivalrous) galant. ~ry n Tapferkeit f

'gall-bladder n Gallenblase f

gallery /'gælərɪ/ n Galerie f

galley /'gælɪ/ n (ship's kitchen) Kombüse f; ~ [proof] [Druck]fahne f

gallivant /'gælɪvænt/ vi (fam) ausgehen

gallon /'gælən/ n Gallone f (= 4,5 l; Amer = 3,785 l)

gallop /'gæləp/ n Galopp m □ vi galoppieren

gallows /'gæləʊz/ n Galgen m

'gallstone n Gallenstein m

galore /gə'lɔː(r)/ adv in Hülle und Fülle

galvanize /'gælvənaɪz/ vt galvanisieren

gambit /'gæmbɪt/ n Eröffnungsmanöver nt

gamble /'gæmbl/ n (risk) Risiko nt □ vi [um Geld] spielen; ~ on (rely) sich verlassen auf (+ acc). ~r n Spieler(in) m(f)

game /geɪm/ n Spiel nt; (animals, birds) Wild nt; ~s (Sch) Sport m □ a (brave) tapfer; (willing) bereit (for zu). ~keeper n Wildhüter m

gammon /'gæmən/ n [geräucherter] Schinken m

gamut /'gæmət/ n Skala f

gander /'gændə(r)/ n Gänserich m

gang /gæŋ/ n Bande f; (of workmen) Kolonne f □ vi ~ up sich zusammenrotten (on gegen)

gangling /'gæŋglɪŋ/ a schlaksig

gangrene /'gæŋgriːn/ n Wundbrand m

gangster /'gæŋstə(r)/ n Gangster m

gangway /'gæŋweɪ/ n Gang m; (Naut, Aviat) Gangway f

gaol /dʒeɪl/ n Gefängnis nt □ vt ins Gefängnis sperren. ~er n Gefängniswärter m

gap /gæp/ n Lücke f; (interval) Pause f; (difference) Unterschied m

gape /geɪp/ vi gaffen; ~e at anstarren. ~ing a klaffend

garage /'gærɑːʒ/ n Garage f; (for repairs) Werkstatt f; (for petrol) Tankstelle f

garb /gɑːb/ n Kleidung f

garbage /'gɑːbɪdʒ/ n Müll m. ~ can n (Amer) Mülleimer m

garbled /'gɑːbld/ a verworren

garden /'gɑːdn/ n Garten m; [public] ~s pl [öffentliche] Anlagen pl □ vi im Garten arbeiten. ~er n Gärtner(in) m(f). ~ing n Gartenarbeit f

gargle /'gɑːgl/ n (liquid) Gurgelwasser nt □ vi gurgeln

gargoyle /'gɑːgɔɪl/ n Wasserspeier m

garish /'geərɪʃ/ a grell

garland /'gɑːlənd/ n Girlande f

garlic /'gɑːlɪk/ n Knoblauch m

garment /'gɑːmənt/ n Kleidungsstück nt

garnet /'gɑːnɪt/ n Granat m

garnish /'gɑːnɪʃ/ n Garnierung f □ vt garnieren

garret /'gærɪt/ n Dachstube f

garrison /'gærɪsn/ n Garnison f

garrulous /'gærʊləs/ a geschwätzig

garter /'gɑːtə(r)/ n Strumpfband nt; (Amer: suspender) Strumpfhalter m

gas /gæs/ n Gas nt; (Amer fam: petrol) Benzin nt □ v (pt/pp gassed) □ vt vergasen □ vi (fam) schwatzen. ~ cooker n Gasherd m. ~ 'fire n Gasofen m

gash /gæʃ/ n Schnitt m; (wound) klaffende Wunde f □ vt ~ one's arm sich (dat) den Arm aufschlitzen

gasket /'gæskɪt/ n (Techn) Dichtung f

gas: ~ mask n Gasmaske f. ~-meter n Gaszähler m

gasoline /'gæsəliːn/ n (Amer) Benzin nt

gasp /gɑːsp/ vi keuchen; (in surprise) hörbar die Luft einziehen

'gas station n (Amer) Tankstelle f

gastric /'gæstrɪk/ a Magen-. ~ 'flu n Darmgrippe f. ~ 'ulcer n Magengeschwür nt

gastronomy /gæ'strɒnəmɪ/ n Gastronomie f

gate /geɪt/ n Tor nt; (to field) Gatter nt; (barrier) Schranke f; (at airport) Flugsteig m

gâteau /'gætəʊ/ n Torte f

gate: ~crasher n ungeladener Gast m. ~way n Tor nt

gather /'gæðə(r)/ vt sammeln; (pick) pflücken; (conclude) folgern (from aus); (Sewing) kräuseln; ~ speed schneller werden □ vi sich versammeln; ⟨storm:⟩ sich zusammenziehen. ~ing n family ~ing Familientreffen nt

gaudy /'gɔːdɪ/ a (-ier, -iest) knallig

gauge /geɪdʒ/ n Stärke f; (Rail) Spurweite f; (device) Messinstrument nt □ vt messen; (estimate) schätzen

gaunt /gɔːnt/ a hager

gauntlet /'gɔːntlɪt/ n run the ~ Spießruten laufen

gauze /gɔːz/ n Gaze f

gave /geɪv/ see give

gawky /'gɔːkɪ/ a (-ier, -iest) schlaksig

gawp /gɔːp/ vi (fam) glotzen; ~ at
anglotzen

gay /geɪ/ a (er, -est) fröhlich; (fam) homosexuell, (fam) schwul

gaze /geɪz/ n [langer] Blick m □ vi sehen;
~ at ansehen

gazelle /gə'zel/ n Gazelle f

GB abbr of Great Britain

gear /gɪə(r)/ n Ausrüstung f; (Techn) Getriebe nt; (Auto) Gang m; in ~ mit einge-
legtem Gang; change ~ schalten □ vt
anpassen (to dat)

gear: ~box n (Auto) Getriebe nt. ~lever
n, (Amer) ~-shift n Schalthebel m

geese /giːs/ see goose

geezer /'giːzə(r)/ n (sl) Typ m

gel /dʒel/ n Gel nt

gelatine /'dʒelətɪn/ n Gelatine f

gelignite /'dʒelɪgnaɪt/ n Gelatinedynamit
nt

gem /dʒem/ n Juwel nt

Gemini /'dʒemɪnaɪ/ n (Astr) Zwillinge pl

gender /'dʒendə(r)/ n (Gram) Geschlecht
nt

gene /dʒiːn/ n Gen nt

genealogy /dʒiːnɪ'ælədʒɪ/ n Genealogie f

general /'dʒenrəl/ a allgemein □ n
General m; in ~ im Allgemeinen. ~ e'lec-
tion n allgemeine Wahlen pl

generaliz|ation /dʒenrəlaɪ'zeɪʃn/ n Ver-
allgemeinerung f. ~e /'dʒenrəlaɪz/ vt/i
verallgemeinern

generally /'dʒenrəlɪ/ adv im Allgemeinen

general prac'titioner n praktischer
Arzt m

generate /'dʒenəreɪt/ vt erzeugen

generation /dʒenə'reɪʃn/ n Generation f

generator /'dʒenəreɪtə(r)/ n Generator m

generic /dʒɪ'nerɪk/ a ~ term Oberbegriff
m

generosity /dʒenə'rɒsɪtɪ/ n Großzügig-
keit f

generous /'dʒenərəs/ a, -ly adv großzügig

genetic /dʒɪ'netɪk/ a genetisch. ~ engineering n Gentechnologie f. ~s n Genetik
f

Geneva /dʒɪ'niːvə/ n Genf nt

genial /'dʒiːnɪəl/ a, -ly adv freundlich

genitals /'dʒenɪtlz/ pl [äußere] Ge-
schlechtsteile pl

genitive /'dʒenɪtɪv/ a & n ~ [case] Genitiv m

genius /'dʒiːnɪəs/ n (pl -uses) Genie nt;
(quality) Genialität f

genocide /'dʒenəsaɪd/ n Völkermord m

genre /'ʒãrə/ n Gattung f, Genre nt

gent /dʒent/ n (fam) Herr m; the ~s sg die
Herrentoilette f

genteel /dʒen'tiːl/ a vornehm

gentle /'dʒentl/ a (-r, -st) sanft

gentleman /'dʒentlmən/ n Herr m; (well-
mannered) Gentleman m

gent|leness /'dʒentlnɪs/ n Sanftheit f.
~ly adv sanft

genuine /'dʒenjuɪn/ a echt; (sincere) aufrichtig. ~ly adv (honestly) ehrlich

genus /'dʒiːnəs/ n (Biol) Gattung f

geograph|ical /dʒɪə'græfɪkl/ a, -ly adv
geographisch. ~y /dʒɪ'ɒgrəfɪ/ n Geo-
graphie f, Erdkunde f

geological /dʒɪə'lɒdʒɪkl/ a, -ly adv geolo-
gisch

geolog|ist /dʒɪ'ɒlədʒɪst/ n Geologe m
/-gɪn f. ~y n Geologie f

geometr|ic(al) /dʒɪə'metrɪk(l)/ a geome-
trisch. ~y /dʒɪ'ɒmətrɪ/ n Geometrie f

geranium /dʒə'reɪnɪəm/ n Geranie f

geriatric /dʒerɪ'ætrɪk/ a geriatrisch □ n
geriatrischer Patient m. ~s n Geriatrie f

germ /dʒɜːm/ n Keim m; ~s pl (fam) Ba-
zillen pl

German /'dʒɜːmən/ a deutsch □ n (person) Deutsche(r) m/f; (Lang) Deutsch nt;
in ~ auf Deutsch; into ~ ins Deutsche

Germanic /dʒə'mænɪk/ a germanisch

German: ~ 'measles n Röteln pl. ~
'shepherd [dog] n [deutscher] Schäferhund m

Germany /'dʒɜːmənɪ/ n Deutschland nt

germinate /'dʒɜːmɪneɪt/ vi keimen

gesticulate /dʒe'stɪkjʊleɪt/ vi gestiku-
lieren

gesture /'dʒestʃə(r)/ n Geste f

get /get/ v (pt/pp got, pp Amer also gotten,
pres p getting) □ vt bekommen, (fam)
kriegen; (procure) besorgen; (buy) kaufen;
(fetch) holen; (take) bringen; (on telephone) erreichen; (fam: understand) kapieren; machen ⟨meal⟩; ~ s.o. to do sth
jdn dazu bringen, etw zu tun □ vi (become)
werden; ~ to kommen zu/nach ⟨town⟩;
(reach) erreichen; ~ dressed sich anziehen; ~ married heiraten. ~ at herankommen an (+ acc); what are you
~ting at? worauf willst du hinaus? ~
away vi (leave) wegkommen; (escape)
entkommen. ~ back vi zurückkommen
□ vt (recover) zurückbekommen; one's
own back sich revanchieren. ~ by vi vorbeikommen; (manage) sein Auskommen
haben. ~ down vi heruntersteigen; ~
down to sich [heran]machen an (+ acc)
□ vt (depress) deprimieren. ~ in vi einsteigen □ vt (fetch) hereinholen. ~ off vi

(*dismount*) absteigen; (*from bus*) aussteigen; (*leave*) wegkommen; (*Jur*) freigesprochen werden □ *vt* (*remove*) abbekommen. ~ on *vi* (*mount*) aufsteigen; (*to bus*) einsteigen; (*be on good terms*) gut auskommen (with mit); (*make progress*) Fortschritte machen; how are you ~ting on? wie geht's? ~ out *vi* herauskommen; (*of car*) aussteigen; ~ out of (*avoid doing*) sich drücken um □ *vt* herausholen; herausbekommen (*cork, stain*). ~ over *vi* hinübersteigen □ *vt* (*fig*) hinwegkommen über (+ *acc*). ~ round *vi* herumkommen; I never ~ round to it ich komme nie dazu □ *vt* herumkriegen; (*avoid*) umgehen. ~ through *vi* durchkommen. ~ up *vi* aufstehen

get: ~away *n* Flucht *f*. ~up *n* Aufmachung *f*

geyser /'giːzə(r)/ *n* Durchlauferhitzer *m*; (*Geol*) Geysir *m*

ghastly /'gɑːstlɪ/ *a* (-ier, -iest) grässlich; (*pale*) blass

gherkin /'gɜːkɪn/ *n* Essiggurke *f*

ghetto /'getəʊ/ *n* Getto *nt*

ghost /gəʊst/ *n* Geist *m*, Gespenst *nt*. ~ly *a* geisterhaft

ghoulish /'guːlɪʃ/ *a* makaber

giant /'dʒaɪənt/ *n* Riese *m* □ *a* riesig

gibberish /'dʒɪbərɪʃ/ *n* Kauderwelsch *nt*

gibe /dʒaɪb/ *n* spöttische Bemerkung *f* □ *vi* spotten (at über + *acc*)

giblets /'dʒɪblɪts/ *npl* Geflügelklein *nt*

giddiness /'gɪdɪnɪs/ *n* Schwindel *m*

giddy /'gɪdɪ/ *a* (-ier, -iest) schwindlig; I feel ~ mir ist schwindlig

gift /gɪft/ *n* Geschenk *nt*; (*to charity*) Gabe *f*; (*talent*) Begabung *f*. ~ed /-ɪd/ *a* begabt. ~wrap *vt* als Geschenk einpacken

gig /gɪg/ *n* (*fam, Mus*) Gig *m*

gigantic /dʒaɪ'gæntɪk/ *a* riesig, riesengroß

giggle /'gɪgl/ *n* Kichern *nt* □ *vi* kichern

gild /gɪld/ *vt* vergolden

gills /gɪlz/ *npl* Kiemen *pl*

gilt /gɪlt/ *a* vergoldet □ *n* Vergoldung *f*. ~edged *a* (*Comm*) mündelsicher

gimmick /'gɪmɪk/ *n* Trick *m*

gin /dʒɪn/ *n* Gin *m*

ginger /'dʒɪndʒə(r)/ *a* rotblond; (*cat*) rot □ *n* Ingwer *m*. ~bread *n* Pfefferkuchen *m*

gingerly /'dʒɪndʒəlɪ/ *adv* vorsichtig

gipsy /'dʒɪpsɪ/ *n* = gypsy

giraffe /dʒɪ'rɑːf/ *n* Giraffe *f*

girder /'gɜːdə(r)/ *n* (*Techn*) Träger *m*

girdle /'gɜːdl/ *n* Bindegürtel *m*; (*corset*) Hüfthalter *m*

girl /gɜːl/ *n* Mädchen *nt*; (*young woman*) junge Frau *f*. ~friend *n* Freundin *f*. ~ish *a*, -ly *adv* mädchenhaft

giro /'dʒaɪərəʊ/ *n* Giro *nt*; (*cheque*) Postscheck *m*

girth /gɜːθ/ *n* Umfang *m*; (*for horse*) Bauchgurt *m*

gist /dʒɪst/ *n* the ~ das Wesentliche

give /gɪv/ *n* Elastizität *f* □ *v* (*pt* gave, *pp* given) □ *vt* geben; (*as present*) schenken (to *dat*); (*donate*) spenden; (*lecture*) halten; (*one's name*) angeben □ *vi* geben; (*yield*) nachgeben. ~ away *vt* verschenken; (*betray*) verraten; (*distribute*) verteilen; ~ away the bride ≈ Brautführer sein. ~ back *vt* zurückgeben. ~ in *vt* einreichen □ *vi* (*yield*) nachgeben. ~ off *vt* abgeben. ~ up *vt/i* aufgeben; ~ oneself up sich stellen. ~ way *vi* nachgeben; (*Auto*) die Vorfahrt beachten

given /'gɪvn/ *see* give □ *a* ~ name Vorname *m*

glacier /'glæsɪə(r)/ *n* Gletscher *m*

glad /glæd/ *a* froh (of über + *acc*). ~den /'glædn/ *vt* erfreuen

glade /gleɪd/ *n* Lichtung *f*

gladly /'glædlɪ/ *adv* gern[e]

glamorous /'glæmərəs/ *a* glanzvoll; (*film star*) glamourös

glamour /'glæmə(r)/ *n* [betörender] Glanz *m*

glance /glɑːns/ *n* [flüchtiger] Blick *m* □ *vi* ~ at einen Blick werfen auf (+ *acc*). ~ up *vi* aufblicken

gland /glænd/ *n* Drüse *f*

glandular /'glændjʊlə(r)/ *a* Drüsen-

glare /gleə(r)/ *n* grelles Licht *nt*; ärgerlicher Blick *m* □ *vi* ~ at böse ansehen

glaring /'gleərɪŋ/ *a* grell; (*mistake*) krass

glass /glɑːs/ *n* Glas *nt*; (*mirror*) Spiegel *m*; ~es *pl* (*spectacles*) Brille *f*. ~y *a* glasig

glaze /gleɪz/ *n* Glasur *f* □ *vt* verglasen; (*Culin, Pottery*) glasieren

glazier /'gleɪzɪə(r)/ *n* Glaser *m*

gleam /gliːm/ *n* Schein *m* □ *vi* glänzen

glean /gliːn/ *vi* Ähren lesen □ *vt* (*learn*) erfahren

glee /gliː/ *n* Frohlocken *nt*. ~ful *a*, -ly *adv* frohlockend

glen /glen/ *n* [enges] Tal *nt*

glib /glɪb/ *a*, -ly *adv* (*pej*) gewandt

glid|e /glaɪd/ *vi* gleiten; (*through the air*) schweben. ~er *n* Segelflugzeug *nt*. ~ing *n* Segelfliegen *nt*

glimmer /'glɪmə(r)/ *n* Glimmen *nt* □ *vi* glimmen

glimpse /glɪmps/ *n* catch a ~ of flüchtig sehen □ *vt* flüchtig sehen

glint /glɪnt/ n Blitzen nt ▯ vi blitzen

glisten /'glɪsn/ vi glitzern

glitter /'glɪtə(r)/ vi glitzern

gloat /gləʊt/ vi schadenfroh sein; ~ over sich weiden an (+ dat)

global /'gləʊbl/ a, -ly adv global

globe /gləʊb/ n Kugel f; (map) Globus m

gloom /gluːm/ n Düsterkeit f; (fig) Pessimismus m

gloomy /'gluːmɪ/ a (-ier, -iest), -ily adv düster; (fig) perssimistisch

glorif|y /'glɔːrɪfaɪ/ vt (pt/pp -ied) verherrlichen; **a** ~**ied** waitress eine bessere Kellnerin f

glorious /'glɔːrɪəs/ a herrlich; ⟨deed, hero⟩ glorreich

glory /'glɔːrɪ/ n Ruhm m; (splendour) Pracht f ▯ vi ~ in genießen

gloss /glɒs/ n Glanz m ▯ a Glanz- ▯ vi ~ over beschönigen

glossary /'glɒsərɪ/ n Glossar nt

glossy /'glɒsɪ/ a (-ier, -iest) glänzend

glove /glʌv/ n Handschuh m. ~ compartment n (Auto) Handschuhfach nt

glow /gləʊ/ n Glut f; (of candle) Schein m ▯ vi glühen; ⟨candle:⟩ scheinen. ~**ing** a glühend; ⟨account⟩ begeistert

glow-worm n Glühwürmchen nt

glucose /'gluːkəʊs/ n Traubenzucker m, Glukose f

glue /gluː/ n Klebstoff m ▯ vt (pres p gluing) kleben (to an + acc)

glum /glʌm/ a (glummer, glummest), -ly adv niedergeschlagen

glut /glʌt/ n Überfluss m (of an + dat); ~ of fruit Obstschwemme f

glutton /'glʌtən/ n Vielfraß m. ~**ous** /-əs/ a gefräßig. ~**y** n Gefräßigkeit f

gnarled /nɑːld/ a knorrig; ⟨hands⟩ knotig

gnash /næʃ/ vt ~ one's teeth mit den Zähnen knirschen

gnat /næt/ n Mücke f

gnaw /nɔː/ vt/i nagen (at an + dat)

gnome /nəʊm/ n Gnom m

go /gəʊ/ n (pl goes) Energie f; (attempt) Versuch m; on the go auf Trab; at one go auf einmal; it's your go du bist dran; **make a go** of it Erfolg haben ▯ vi (pt went, pp gone) gehen; (in vehicle) fahren; (leave) weggehen; (on journey) abfahren; ⟨time:⟩ vergehen; (vanish) verschwinden; (fail) versagen; (become) werden; (belong) kommen; **go swimming/shopping** schwimmen/einkaufen gehen; **where are you going?** wo gehst du hin? it's all gone es ist nichts mehr übrig; **I am not going** to ich werde es nicht tun; 'to go' (Amer) 'zum Mitnehmen'. **go away** vi weggehen/ -fahren. **go back** vi zurückgehen/-fahren.

go by vi vorbeigehen/-fahren; ⟨time:⟩ vergehen. **go down** vi hinuntergehen/ -fahren; ⟨sun, ship:⟩ untergehen; ⟨prices:⟩ fallen; ⟨temperature, swelling:⟩ zurückgehen. **go for** vt holen; ⟨fam: attack⟩ losgehen auf (+ acc). **go in** vi hineingehen /-fahren; **go in for** teilnehmen an (+ dat) ⟨competition⟩; ⟨take up⟩ sich verlegen auf (+ acc). **go off** vi weggehen/-fahren; ⟨alarm:⟩ klingeln; ⟨gun, bomb:⟩ losgehen; ⟨go bad⟩ schlecht werden; **go off well** gut verlaufen. **go on** vi weitergehen/-fahren; ⟨continue⟩ weitermachen; ⟨talking⟩ fortfahren; ⟨happen⟩ vorgehen; **go on at** ⟨fam⟩ herumnörgeln an (+ dat). **go out** vi ausgehen; ⟨leave⟩ hinausgehen/-fahren. **go over** vi hinübergehen/-fahren ▯ vt ⟨check⟩ durchgehen. **go round** vi herumgehen/-fahren; ⟨visit⟩ vorbeigehen; ⟨turn⟩ sich drehen; ⟨be enough⟩ reichen. **go through** vi durchgehen/-fahren ▯ vt ⟨suffer⟩ durchmachen; ⟨check⟩ durchgehen. **go under** vi untergehen; ⟨fail⟩ scheitern. **go up** vi hinaufgehen/-fahren; ⟨lift:⟩ hochfahren; ⟨prices:⟩ steigen. **go without** vt verzichten auf (+ acc) ▯ vi darauf verzichten

goad /gəʊd/ vt anstacheln (into zu); (taunt) reizen

go-ahead a fortschrittlich; (enterprising) unternehmend ▯ n (fig) grünes Licht nt

goal /gəʊl/ n Ziel nt; (sport) Tor nt. ~**keeper** n Torwart m. ~**-post** n Torpfosten m

goat /gəʊt/ n Ziege f

gobble /'gɒbl/ vt hinunterschlingen

go-between n Vermittler(in) m(f)

goblet /'gɒblɪt/ n Pokal m; (glass) Kelchglas nt

goblin /'gɒblɪn/ n Kobold m

God, god /gɒd/ n Gott m

god: ~**child** n Patenkind nt. ~**daughter** n Patentochter f. ~**dess** n Göttin f. ~**father** n Pate m. **G**~**forsaken** a gottverlassen. ~**mother** n Patin f. ~**parents** npl Paten pl. ~**send** n Segen m. ~**son** n Patensohn m

goggle /'gɒgl/ vi (fam) ~ at anglotzen. ~**s** npl Schutzbrille f

going /'gəʊɪŋ/ a ⟨price, rate⟩ gängig; ⟨concern⟩ gut gehend ▯ n it is hard ~ es ist schwierig; **while the** ~ **is good** solange es noch geht. ~**s-'on** npl [seltsame] Vorgänge pl

gold /gəʊld/ n Gold nt ▯ a golden

golden /'gəʊldn/ a golden. ~ **handshake** n hohe Abfindungssumme f. ~ **'wedding** n goldene Hochzeit f

gold: ~**fish** n inv Goldfisch m. ~**mine** n Goldgrube f. ~**plated** a vergoldet. ~**smith** n Goldschmied m

golf /gɒlf/ n Golf nt

golf: ~-club n Golfklub m; (implement) Golfschläger m. ~-course n Golfplatz m. ~er m Golfspieler(in) m(f)

gondo|la /'gɒndələ/ n Gondel f. ~lier /-'lɪə(r)/ n Gondoliere m

gone /gɒn/ see go

gong /gɒŋ/ n Gong m

good /gʊd/ a (better, best) gut; (well-behaved) brav, artig; ~ at gut in (+ dat); a ~ deal ziemlich viel; as ~ as so gut wie; (almost) fast; ~ morning/evening guten Morgen/Abend; ~ afternoon guten Tag; ~ night gute Nacht □ n the ~ das Gute; for ~ für immer; do ~ Gutes tun; do s.o. ~ jdm gut tun; it's no ~ es ist nutzlos; (hopeless) da ist nichts zu machen; be up to no ~ nichts Gutes im Schilde führen

goodbye /gʊd'baɪ/ int auf Wiedersehen; (Teleph, Radio) auf Wiederhören

good: ~-for-nothing a nichtsnutzig □ n Taugenichts m. G~ 'Friday n Karfreitag m. ~-'looking a gut aussehend. ~-'natured a gutmütig

goodness /'gʊdnɪs/ n Güte f; my ~! du meine Güte! thank ~! Gott sei Dank!

goods /gʊdz/ npl Waren pl. ~ train n Güterzug m

good'will n Wohlwollen nt; (Comm) Goodwill m

goody /'gʊdɪ/ n (fam) Gute(r) m/f. ~-goody n Musterkind nt

gooey /'guːɪ/ a (fam) klebrig

goof /guːf/ vi (fam) einen Schnitzer machen

goose /guːs/ n (pl geese) Gans f

gooseberry /'gʊzbərɪ/ n Stachelbeere f

goose /guːs/: ~-flesh n, ~-pimples npl Gänsehaut f

gore1 /gɔː(r)/ n Blut nt

gore2 vt mit den Hörnern aufspießen

gorge /gɔːdʒ/ n (Geog) Schlucht f □ vt ~ oneself sich vollessen

gorgeous /'gɔːdʒəs/ a prachtvoll; (fam) herrlich

gorilla /gə'rɪlə/ n Gorilla m

gormless /'gɔːmlɪs/ a (fam) doof

gorse /gɔːs/ n inv Stechginster m

gory /'gɔːrɪ/ a (-ier, -iest) blutig; (story) blutrünstig

gosh /gɒʃ/ int (fam) Mensch!

go-'slow n Bummelstreik m

gospel /'gɒspl/ n Evangelium nt

gossip /'gɒsɪp/ n Klatsch m; (person) Klatschbase f □ vi klatschen. ~y a geschwätzig

got /gɒt/ see get; have ~ haben; have ~ to müssen; have ~ to do sth etw tun müssen

Gothic /'gɒθɪk/ a gotisch

gotten /'gɒtn/ see get

gouge /gaʊdʒ/ vt ~ out aushöhlen

goulash /'guːlæʃ/ n Gulasch nt

gourmet /'gʊəmeɪ/ n Feinschmecker m

gout /gaʊt/ n Gicht f

govern /'gʌvn/ vt/i regieren; (determine) bestimmen. ~ess n Gouvernante f

government /'gʌvnmənt/ n Regierung f. ~al /-'mentl/ a Regierungs-

governor /'gʌvənə(r)/ n Gouverneur m; (on board) Vorstandsmitglied nt; (of prison) Direktor m; (fam: boss) Chef m

gown /gaʊn/ n [elegantes] Kleid nt; (Univ, Jur) Talar m

GP abbr of general practitioner

grab /græb/ vt (pt/pp grabbed) ergreifen; ~ [hold of] packen

grace /greɪs/ n Anmut f; (before meal) Tischgebet nt; (Relig) Gnade f; with good ~ mit Anstand; say ~ [vor dem Essen] beten; three days' ~ drei Tage Frist. ~ful a, ~ly adv anmutig

gracious /'greɪʃəs/ a gnädig; (elegant) vornehm

grade /greɪd/ n Stufe f; (Comm) Güteklasse f; (Sch) Note f; (Amer, Sch: class) Klasse f; (Amer) = gradient □ vt einstufen; (Comm) sortieren. ~ crossing n (Amer) Bahnübergang m

gradient /'greɪdɪənt/ n Steigung f; (downward) Gefälle nt

gradual /'grædjʊəl/ a, ~ly adv allmählich

graduate1 /'grædjʊət/ n Akademiker(in) m(f)

graduate2 /'grædjʊeɪt/ vi (Univ) sein Examen machen. ~d a abgestuft; (container) mit Maßeinteilung

graffiti /grə'fiːtiː/ npl Graffiti pl

graft /grɑːft/ n (Bot) Pfropfreis nt; (Med) Transplantat nt; (fam: hard work) Plackerei f □ vt (Bot) aufpfropfen; (Med) übertragen

grain /greɪn/ n (sand, salt, rice) Korn nt; (cereals) Getreide nt; (in wood) Maserung f; against the ~ (fig) gegen den Strich

gram /græm/ n Gramm nt

grammar /'græmə(r)/ n Grammatik f. ~ school n ≈ Gymnasium nt

grammatical /grə'mætɪkl/ a, ~ly adv grammatisch

granary /'grænərɪ/ n Getreidespeicher m

grand /grænd/ a (-er, -est) großartig

grandad /'grændæd/ n (fam) Opa m

'grandchild n Enkelkind nt

'granddaughter n Enkelin f

grandeur /'grændʒə(r)/ n Pracht f

'**grandfather** n Großvater m. ~ **clock** n Standuhr f

grandiose /'grændɪəʊs/ a grandios

grand: ~**mother** n Großmutter f. ~**parents** npl Großeltern pl. ~ **pi'ano** n Flügel m. ~**son** n Enkel m. ~**stand** n Tribüne f

granite /'grænɪt/ n Granit m

granny /'grænɪ/ n (fam) Oma f

grant /grɑːnt/ n Subvention f; (Univ) Studienbeihilfe f □ vt gewähren; (admit) zugeben; **take sth for** ~**ed** etw als selbstverständlich hinnehmen

granular /'grænjʊlə(r)/ a körnig

granulated /'grænjʊleɪtɪd/ a ~ **sugar** Kristallzucker m

granule /'grænjuːl/ n Körnchen nt

grape /greɪp/ n [Wein]traube f; **bunch of** ~**s** [ganze] Weintraube f

grapefruit /'greɪp-/ n invar Grapefruit f, Pampelmuse f

graph /grɑːf/ n Kurvendiagramm nt

graphic /'græfɪk/ a, -ally adv grafisch; (vivid) anschaulich. ~**s** n (design) grafische Gestaltung f

'**graph paper** n Millimeterpapier nt

grapple /'græpl/ vi ringen

grasp /grɑːsp/ n Griff m □ vt ergreifen; (understand) begreifen. ~**ing** a habgierig

grass /grɑːs/ n Gras nt; (lawn) Rasen m; **at the** ~ **roots** an der Basis. ~**hopper** n Heuschrecke f. ~**land** n Weideland nt

grassy /'grɑːsɪ/ a grasig

grate[1] /greɪt/ n Feuerrost m; (hearth) Kamin m

grate[2] vt (Culin) reiben; (grind); ~ **one's teeth** mit den Zähnen knirschen

grateful /'greɪtfl/ a, -ly adv dankbar (to dat)

grater /'greɪtə(r)/ n (Culin) Reibe f

gratify /'grætɪfaɪ/ vt (pt/pp -ied) befriedigen. ~**ing** a erfreulich

grating /'greɪtɪŋ/ n Gitter nt

gratis /'grɑːtɪs/ adv gratis

gratitude /'grætɪtjuːd/ n Dankbarkeit f

gratuitous /grə'tjuːɪtəs/ a (uncalled for) überflüssig

gratuity /grə'tjuːɪtɪ/ n (tip) Trinkgeld nt

grave[1] /greɪv/ a (-r, -st), -ly adv ernst; ~**ly ill** schwer krank

grave[2] n Grab nt. ~-**digger** n Totengräber m

gravel /'grævl/ n Kies m

grave: ~**stone** n Grabstein m. ~**yard** n Friedhof m

gravitate /'grævɪteɪt/ vi gravitieren

gravity /'grævɪtɪ/ n Ernst m; (force) Schwerkraft f

gravy /'greɪvɪ/ n [Braten]soße f

gray /greɪ/ a (Amer) = grey

graze[1] /greɪz/ vi (animal:) weiden

graze[2] n Schürfwunde f □ vt (car) streifen; (knee) aufschürfen

grease /griːs/ n Fett nt; (lubricant) Schmierfett nt □ vt einfetten; (lubricate) schmieren. ~-**proof** '**paper** n Pergamentpapier nt

greasy /'griːsɪ/ a (-ier, -iest) fettig

great /greɪt/ a (-er, -est) groß; (fam: marvellous) großartig

great: ~-'**aunt** n Großtante f. G~ '**Britain** n Großbritannien n. ~'**grandchildren** npl Urenkel pl. ~-'**grandfather** n Urgroßvater m. ~-'**grandmother** n Urgroßmutter f

great|ly /'greɪtlɪ/ adv sehr. ~**ness** n Größe f

great-'uncle n Großonkel m

Greece /griːs/ n Griechenland nt

greed /griːd/ n [Hab]gier f

greedy /'griːdɪ/ a (-ier, -iest), -ily adv gierig; **don't be** ~ sei nicht so unbescheiden

Greek /griːk/ a griechisch □ n Grieche m/Griechin f; (Lang) Griechisch nt

green /griːn/ a (-er, -est) grün; (fig) unerfahren □ n Grün nt; (grass) Wiese f; ~**s** pl Kohl m; **the G**~**s** pl (Pol) die Grünen pl

greenery /'griːnərɪ/ n Grün nt

'**greenfly** n Blattlaus f

greengage /'griːngeɪdʒ/ n Reneklode f

green: ~**grocer** n Obst- und Gemüsehändler m. ~**house** n Gewächshaus nt. ~**house effect** n Treibhauseffekt m

Greenland /'griːnlənd/ n Grönland nt

greet /griːt/ vt grüßen; (welcome) begrüßen. ~**ing** n Gruß m; (welcome) Begrüßung f. ~**ings card** n Glückwunschkarte f

gregarious /grɪ'geərɪəs/ a gesellig

grenade /grɪ'neɪd/ n Granate f

grew /gruː/ see **grow**

grey /greɪ/ a (-er, -est) grau □ n Grau nt □ vi grau werden. ~**hound** n Windhund m

grid /grɪd/ n Gitter nt; (on map) Gitternetz nt; (Electr) Überlandleitungsnetz nt

grief /griːf/ n Trauer f; **come to** ~ scheitern

grievance /'griːvəns/ n Beschwerde f

grieve /griːv/ vt betrüben □ vi trauern (for um)

grievous /'griːvəs/ a, -ly adv schwer

grill /grɪl/ n Gitter nt; (Culin) Grill m; **mixed** ~ Gemischtes nt vom Grill □ vt/i grillen; (interrogate) [streng] verhören

grille /grɪl/ n Gitter nt

grim /grɪm/ a (grimmer, grimmest), -ly adv ernst; (determination) verbissen

grimace /grɪˈmeɪs/ n Grimasse f □ vi Grimassen schneiden

grime /graɪm/ n Schmutz m

grimy /ˈgraɪmɪ/ a (-ier, -iest) schmutzig

grin /grɪn/ n Grinsen nt □ vi (pt/pp grinned) grinsen

grind /graɪnd/ n (fam: hard work) Plackerei f □ vt (pt/pp ground) mahlen; (smooth, sharpen) schleifen; (Amer: mince) durchdrehen; ~ one's teeth mit den Zähnen knirschen

grip /grɪp/ n Griff m; (bag) Reisetasche f □ vt (pt/pp gripped) ergreifen; (hold) festhalten; fesseln (interest)

gripe /graɪp/ vi (sl: grumble) meckern

gripping /ˈgrɪpɪŋ/ a fesselnd

grisly /ˈgrɪzlɪ/ a (-ier, -iest) grausig

gristle /ˈgrɪsl/ n Knorpel m

grit /grɪt/ n [grober] Sand m; (for roads) Streugut nt; (courage) Mut m □ vt (pt/pp gritted) streuen (road); ~ one's teeth die Zähne zusammenbeißen

grizzle /ˈgrɪzl/ vi quengeln

groan /grəʊn/ n Stöhnen nt □ vi stöhnen

grocer /ˈgrəʊsə(r)/ n Lebensmittelhändler m; ~'s [shop] Lebensmittelgeschäft nt. ~ies npl Lebensmittel pl

groggy /ˈgrɒgɪ/ a schwach; (unsteady) wackelig [auf den Beinen]

groin /grɔɪn/ n (Anat) Leiste f

groom /gru:m/ n Bräutigam m; (for horse) Pferdepfleger(in) m(f) □ vt striegeln (horse)

groove /gru:v/ n Rille f

grope /grəʊp/ vi tasten (for nach)

gross /grəʊs/ a (-er, -est) fett; (coarse) derb; (glaring) grob; (Comm) brutto; (salary, weight) Brutto- □ n inv Gros nt. ~ly adv (very) sehr

grotesque /grəʊˈtesk/ a, -ly adv grotesk

grotto /ˈgrɒtəʊ/ n (pl -es) Grotte f

grotty /ˈgrɒtɪ/ a (fam) mies

ground¹ /graʊnd/ see grind

ground² n /graʊnd/ n Boden m; (terrain) Gelände nt; (reason) Grund m; (Amer, Electr) Erde f; ~s pl (park) Anlagen pl; (of coffee) Satz m □ vi (ship:) auflaufen □ vt aus dem Verkehr ziehen (aircraft); (Amer, Electr) erden

ground: ~ floor n Erdgeschoss nt. ~ing n Grundlage f. ~less a grundlos. ~ 'meat n (Amer) Hackfleisch nt. ~sheet n Bodenplane f. ~work n Vorarbeiten pl

group /gru:p/ n Gruppe f □ vt gruppieren □ vi sich gruppieren

grouse¹ /graʊs/ n inv schottisches Moorschneehuhn nt

grouse² vi (fam) meckern

grovel /ˈgrɒvl/ vi (pt/pp grovelled) kriechen. ~ling a kriecherisch

grow /grəʊ/ v (pt grew, pp grown) □ vi wachsen; (become) werden; (increase) zunehmen □ vt anbauen; ~ one's hair sich (dat) die Haare wachsen lassen. ~ up vi aufwachsen; (town:) entstehen

growl /graʊl/ n Knurren nt □ vi knurren

grown /grəʊn/ see grow. ~-up a erwachsen □ n Erwachsene(r) m/f

growth /grəʊθ/ n Wachstum nt; (increase) Zunahme f; (Med) Gewächs nt

grub /grʌb/ n (larva) Made f; (fam: food) Essen nt

grubby /ˈgrʌbɪ/ a (-ier, -iest) schmuddelig

grudge /grʌdʒ/ n Groll m; bear s.o. a ~e einen Groll gegen jdn hegen □ vt ~e s.o. sth jdm etw missgönnen. ~ing a, -ly adv widerwillig

gruelling /ˈgru:əlɪŋ/ a strapaziös

gruesome /ˈgru:səm/ a grausig

gruff /grʌf/ a, -ly adv barsch

grumble /ˈgrʌmbl/ vi schimpfen (at mit)

grumpy /ˈgrʌmpɪ/ a (-ier, -iest) griesgrämig

grunt /grʌnt/ n Grunzen nt □ vi grunzen

guarant|ee /gærənˈti:/ n Garantie f; (document) Garantieschein m □ vt garantieren; garantieren für (quality, success); be ~eed (product:) Garantie haben. ~or n Bürge m

guard /gɑ:d/ n Wache f; (security) Wächter m; (on train) ≈ Zugführer m; (Techn) Schutz m; be on ~ Wache stehen; on one's ~ auf der Hut sein □ vt bewachen; (protect) schützen □ vi ~ against sich hüten vor (+ dat). ~dog n Wachhund m

guarded /ˈgɑ:dɪd/ a vorsichtig

guardian /ˈgɑ:dɪən/ n Vormund m

guerrilla /gəˈrɪlə/ n Guerillakämpfer m. ~ warfare n Partisanenkrieg m

guess /ges/ n Vermutung f □ vt erraten □ vi raten; (Amer: believe) glauben. ~work n Vermutung f

guest /gest/ n Gast m. ~-house n Pension f

guffaw /gʌˈfɔ:/ n derbes Lachen nt □ vi derb lachen

guidance /ˈgaɪdəns/ n Führung f, Leitung f; (advice) Beratung f

guide /gaɪd/ n Führer(in) m(f); (book) Führer m; [Girl] G~ Pfadfinderin f □ vt führen, leiten. ~book n Führer m

guided /ˈgaɪdɪd/ a ~ missile Fernlenkgeschoss nt; ~ tour Führung f

guide: ~-dog n Blindenhund m. ~-lines npl Richtlinien pl

guild /gɪld/ n Gilde f, Zunft f

guile /gaɪl/ n Arglist f

guillotine /'gɪləti:n/ n Guillotine f; (for paper) Papierschneidemaschine f

guilt /gɪlt/ n Schuld f. **~ily** adv schuldbewusst

guilty /'gɪlti/ a (-ier, -iest) a schuldig (of gen); (look) schuldbewusst; (conscience) schlecht

guinea-pig /'gɪnɪ-/ n Meerschweinchen nt; (person) Versuchskaninchen nt

guise /gaɪz/ n in the ~ of in Gestalt (+ gen)

guitar /gɪ'tɑ:(r)/ n Gitarre f. **~ist** n Gitarrist(in) m(f)

gulf /gʌlf/ n (Geog) Golf m; (fig) Kluft f

gull /gʌl/ n Möwe f

gullet /'gʌlɪt/ n Speiseröhre f; (throat) Kehle f

gullible /'gʌlɪbl/ a leichtgläubig

gully /'gʌlɪ/ n Schlucht f; (drain) Rinne f

gulp /gʌlp/ n Schluck m ◻ vi schlucken ◻ vt ~ **down** hinunterschlucken

gum[1] /gʌm/ n & -s pl (Anat) Zahnfleisch nt

gum[2] n Gummi[harz] nt; (glue) Klebstoff m; (chewing-gum) Kaugummi m ◻ vt (pt/pp gummed) kleben (to an + acc). **~boot** n Gummistiefel m

gummed /gʌmd/ see**gum**[2] ◻ a ⟨label⟩ gummiert

gumption /'gʌmpʃn/ n (fam) Grips m

gun /gʌn/ n Schusswaffe f; (pistol) Pistole f; (rifle) Gewehr nt; (cannon) Geschütz nt ◻ vt (pt/pp gunned) ~ **down** niederschießen

gun: **~fire** n Geschützfeuer nt. **~man** n bewaffneter Bandit m

gunner /'gʌnə(r)/ n Artillerist m

gun: **~powder** n Schießpulver nt. **~shot** n Schuss m

gurgle /'gɜ:gl/ vi gluckern; (of baby) glucksen

gush /gʌʃ/ vi strömen; (enthuse) schwärmen (over von). **~ out** vi herausströmen

gusset /'gʌsɪt/ n Zwickel m

gust /gʌst/ n (of wind) Windstoß m; (Naut) Bö f

gusto /'gʌstəʊ/ n with ~ mit Schwung

gusty /'gʌstɪ/ a böig

gut /gʌt/ n Darm m; **~s** pl Eingeweide pl; (fam: courage) Schneid m ◻ vt (pt/pp gutted) (Culin) ausnehmen; **~ted by fire** ausgebrannt

gutter /'gʌtə(r)/ n Rinnstein m; (fig) [Gosse] f; (on roof) Dachrinne f

guttural /'gʌtərl/ a guttural

guy /gaɪ/ n (fam) Kerl m

guzzle /'gʌzl/ vt/i schlingen; (drink) schlürfen

gym /dʒɪm/ n (fam) Turnhalle f; (gymnastics) Turnen nt

gymnasium /dʒɪm'neɪzɪəm/ n Turnhalle f

gymnast /'dʒɪmnæst/ n Turner(in) m(f). **~ics** /-'næstɪks/ n Turnen nt

gym: **~ shoes** pl Turnschuhe pl. **~slip** n (Sch) Trägerkleid nt

gynaecolog|ist /gaɪnɪ'kɒlədʒɪst/ n Frauenarzt m /-ärztin f. **~y** n Gynäkologie f

gypsy /'dʒɪpsɪ/ n Zigeuner(in) m(f)

gyrate /dʒaɪə'reɪt/ vi sich drehen

H

haberdashery /'hæbədæʃərɪ/ n Kurzwaren pl; (Amer) Herrenmoden pl

habit /'hæbɪt/ n Gewohnheit f; (Relig: costume) Ordenstracht f; **be in the ~** die Angewohnheit haben (of zu)

habitable /'hæbɪtəbl/ a bewohnbar

habitat /'hæbɪtæt/ n Habitat nt

habitation /hæbɪ'teɪʃn/ n **unfit for human ~** für Wohnzwecke ungeeignet

habitual /hə'bɪtjʊəl/ a gewohnt; (inveterate) gewohnheitsmäßig. **~ly** adv gewohnheitsmäßig; (constantly) ständig

hack[1] /hæk/ n (writer) Schreiberling m; (hired horse) Mietpferd nt

hack[2] vt hacken; **~ to pieces** zerhacken

hackneyed /'hæknɪd/ a abgedroschen

'**hacksaw** n Metallsäge f

had /hæd/ see have

haddock /'hædək/ n inv Schellfisch m

haemorrhage /'hemərɪdʒ/ n Blutung f

haemorrhoids /'hemərɔɪdz/ npl Hämorrhoiden pl

hag /hæg/ n old ~ alte Hexe f

haggard /'hægəd/ a abgehärmt

haggle /'hægl/ vi feilschen (over um)

hail[1] /heɪl/ vt begrüßen; herbeirufen ⟨taxi⟩ ◻ vi ~ **from** kommen aus

hail[2] n Hagel m ◻ vi hageln. **~stone** n Hagelkorn nt

hair /heə(r)/ n Haar nt; **wash one's ~** sich (dat) die Haare waschen

hair: **~brush** n Haarbürste f. **~cut** n Haarschnitt m; **have a ~cut** sich (dat) die Haare schneiden lassen. **~do** n (fam) Frisur f. **~dresser** n Friseur m /Friseuse f. **~-drier** n Haartrockner m; (hand-held)

Föhn *m.* ∼-grip *n* [Haar]klemme *f.* ∼pin *n* Haarnadel *f.* ∼pin 'bend *n* Haarnadel-kurve *f.* ∼-raising *a* haarsträubend. ∼-style *n* Frisur *f*

hairy /'heərɪ/ *a* (-ier, -iest) behaart; (*excessively*) haarig; (*fam: frightening*) brenzlig

hake /heɪk/ *n inv* Seehecht *m*

hale /heɪl/ *a* ∼ and hearty gesund und munter

half /ha:f/ *n* (*pl* halves) Hälfte *f*; cut in ∼ halbieren; one and a ∼ eineinhalb, anderthalb; a dozen ein halbes Dutzend; ∼ an hour eine halbe Stunde □ *a & adv* halb; ∼ past two halb drei; [at] ∼ price zum halben Preis

half: ∼-board *n* Halbpension *f.* ∼-caste *n* Mischling *m.* ∼-'hearted *a* lustlos. ∼'hourly *a & adv* halbstündlich. ∼-'mast *n* at ∼-mast auf halbmast. ∼-measure *n* Halbheit *f.* ∼-'term *n* schulfreie Tage nach dem halben Trimester. ∼-'timbered *a* Fachwerk-. ∼-'time *n* (*Sport*) Halbzeit *f.* ∼-'way *a* the ∼-way mark/stage die Hälfte □ *adv* auf halbem Weg; get ∼-way den halben Weg zurücklegen; (*fig*) bis zur Hälfte kommen. ∼-wit *n* Idiot *m*

halibut /'hælɪbət/ *n inv* Heilbutt *m*

hall /hɔ:l/ *n* Halle *f*; (*room*) Saal *m*; (*Sch*) Aula *f*; (*entrance*) Flur *m*; (*mansion*) Gutshaus *nt*; ∼ of residence (*Univ*) Studentenheim *nt*

'**hallmark** *n* [Feingehalts]stempel *m*; (*fig*) Kennzeichen *nt* (of für) □ *vt* stempeln

hallo /hə'ləʊ/ *int* [guten] Tag! (*fam*) hallo!

Hallowe'en /hæləʊ'i:n/ *n* der Tag vor Allerheiligen

hallucination /həluːsɪ'neɪʃn/ *n* Halluzination *f*

halo /'heɪləʊ/ *n* (*pl* -es) Heiligenschein *m*; (*Astr*) Hof *m*

halt /hɔ:lt/ *n* Halt *m*; come to a ∼ stehen bleiben; (*traffic:*) zum Stillstand kommen □ *vi* Halt machen; ∼! halt! ∼ing *a, adv* -ly zögernd

halve /ha:v/ *vt* halbieren; (*reduce*) um die Hälfte reduzieren

ham /hæm/ *n* Schinken *m*

hamburger /'hæmbɜ:gə(r)/ *n* Hamburger *m*

hamlet /'hæmlɪt/ *n* Weiler *m*

hammer /'hæmə(r)/ *n* Hammer *m* □ *vt/i* hämmern (at an + *acc*)

hammock /'hæmək/ *n* Hängematte *f*

hamper[1] /'hæmpə(r)/ *n* Picknickkorb *m*; [gift] ∼ Geschenkkorb *m*

hamper[2] *vt* behindern

hamster /'hæmstə(r)/ *n* Hamster *m*

hand /hænd/ *n* Hand *f*; (*of clock*) Zeiger *m*; (*writing*) Handschrift *f*; (*worker*) Arbeiter(in) *m(f)*; (*Cards*) Blatt *nt*; all ∼s (*Naut*) alle Mann; at ∼ in der Nähe; on the one/ other ∼ einer-/andererseits; out of ∼ außer Kontrolle; (*summarily*) kurzerhand; in ∼ unter Kontrolle; (*available*) verfügbar; give s.o. a ∼ jdm behilflich sein □ *vt* reichen (to *dat*). ∼ in *vt* abgeben. ∼ out *vt* austeilen. ∼ over *vt* überreichen

hand: ∼bag *n* Handtasche *f.* ∼book *n* Handbuch *nt.* ∼brake *n* Handbremse *f.* ∼cuffs *npl* Handschellen *pl.* ∼ful *n* Handvoll *f*; be [quite] a ∼ful (*fam*) nicht leicht zu haben sein

handicap /'hændɪkæp/ *n* Behinderung *f*; (*Sport & fig*) Handikap *nt.* ∼ped *a* mentally/physically ∼ped geistig/körperlich behindert

handi|craft /'hændɪkrɑːft/ *n* Basteln *nt*; (*Sch*) Werken *nt.* ∼work *n* Werk *nt*

handkerchief /'hæŋkətʃɪf/ *n* (*pl* ∼s & -chieves) Taschentuch *nt*

handle /'hændl/ *n* Griff *m*; (*of door*) Klinke *f*; (*of cup*) Henkel *m*; (*of broom*) Stiel *m*; fly off the ∼ (*fam*) aus der Haut fahren □ *vt* handhaben; (*treat*) umgehen mit; (*touch*) anfassen. ∼bars *npl* Lenkstange *f*

hand: ∼-luggage *n* Handgepäck *nt.* ∼made *a* handgemacht. ∼out *n* Prospekt *m*; (*money*) Unterstützung *f.* ∼rail *n* Handlauf *m.* ∼shake *n* Händedruck *m*

handsome /'hænsəm/ *a* gut aussehend; (*generous*) großzügig; (*large*) beträchtlich

hand: ∼stand *n* Handstand *m.* ∼writing *n* Handschrift *f.* ∼'written *a* handgeschrieben

handy /'hændɪ/ *a* (-ier, -iest) handlich; (*person*) geschickt; have/keep ∼ griffbereit haben/halten. ∼man *n* [home] ∼man Heimwerker *m*

hang /hæŋ/ *vt/i* (*pt/pp* hung) hängen; ∼ wallpaper tapezieren □ *vt* (*pt/pp* hanged) hängen (*criminal*); ∼ oneself sich erhängen □ *n* get the ∼ of it (*fam*) den Dreh herauskriegen. ∼ about *vi* sich herumdrücken. ∼ on *vi* sich festhalten (to an + *dat*); (*fam: wait*) warten. ∼ out *vi* heraushängen; (*fam: live*) wohnen □ *vt* draußen aufhängen (*washing*). ∼ up *vt/i* aufhängen

hangar /'hæŋə(r)/ *n* Flugzeughalle *f*

hanger /'hæŋə(r)/ *n* [Kleider]bügel *m*

hang: ∼-glider *n* Drachenflieger *m.* ∼-gliding *n* Drachenfliegen *nt.* ∼man *n* Henker *m.* ∼over *n* (*fam*) Kater *m* (*fam*). ∼-up *n* (*fam*) Komplex *m*

hanker /'hæŋkə(r)/ *vi* ∼ after sth sich (*dat*) etw wünschen hanky /'hæŋkɪ/ n (fam) Taschentuch nt

hanky-panky /hæŋkɪ'pæŋkɪ/ n (fam) Mauscheleien pl

haphazard /hæp'hæzəd/ a, ~ly adv planlos

happen /'hæpn/ vi geschehen, passieren; as it ~s zufälligerweise; I ~ed to be there ich war zufällig da; what has ~ed to him? was ist mit ihm los? (become of) was ist aus ihm geworden? ~ing n Ereignis nt

happi|ly /'hæpɪlɪ/ adv glücklich; (fortunately) glücklicherweise. ~ness n Glück nt

happy /'hæpɪ/ a (-ier, -iest) glücklich. ~-go-'lucky a sorglos

harass /'hærəs/ vt schikanieren. ~ed a abgehetzt. ~ment n Schikane f; (sexual) Belästigung f

harbour /'hɑːbə(r)/ n Hafen m □ vt Unterschlupf gewähren (+ dat); hegen (grudge)

hard /hɑːd/ a (-er, -est) hart; (difficult) schwer; ~ of hearing schwerhörig □ adv hart; (work) schwer; (pull) kräftig; (rain, snow) stark; think ~! denk mal nach! be ~ up (fam) knapp bei Kasse sein; be ~ done by (fam) ungerecht behandelt werden

hard: ~back n gebundene Ausgabe f. ~board n Hartfaserplatte f. ~-boiled a hart gekocht

harden /'hɑːdn/ vi hart werden

hard-'hearted a hartherzig

hard|ly /'hɑːdlɪ/ adv kaum; ~ly ever kaum [jemals]. ~ness n Härte f. ~ship n Not f

hard: ~ 'shoulder n (Auto) Randstreifen m. ~ware n Haushaltswaren pl; (Computing) Hardware f. ~-'wearing a strapazierfähig. ~-'working a fleißig

hardy /'hɑːdɪ/ a (-ier, -iest) abgehärtet; (plant) winterhart

hare /heə(r)/ n Hase m. ~ 'lip n Hasenscharte f

hark /hɑːk/ vi ~! hört! ~ back vi ~ back to (fig) zurückkommen auf (+ acc)

harm /hɑːm/ n Schaden m; out of ~'s way in Sicherheit; it won't do any ~ es kann nichts schaden □ vt ~ s.o. jdm etwas antun. ~ful a schädlich. ~less a harmlos

harmonica /hɑː'mɒnɪkə/ n Mundharmonika f

harmonious /hɑː'məʊnɪəs/ a, ~ly adv harmonisch

harmon|ize /'hɑːmənaɪz/ vi (fig) harmonieren. ~y n Harmonie f

harness /'hɑːnɪs/ n Geschirr nt; (of parachute) Gurtwerk nt □ vt anschirren (horse); (use) nutzbar machen

harp /hɑːp/ n Harfe f □ vi ~ on [about] (fam) herumreiten auf (+ dat). ~ist n Harfenist(in) m(f)

harpoon /hɑː'puːn/ n Harpune f

harpsichord /'hɑːpsɪkɔːd/ n Cembalo nt

harrow /'hærəʊ/ n Egge f. ~ing a grauenhaft

harsh /hɑːʃ/ a (-er, -est), -ly adv hart; (voice) rau; (light) grell. ~ness n Härte f; Rauheit f

harvest /'hɑːvɪst/ n Ernte f □ vt ernten

has /hæz/ see have

hash /hæʃ/ n (Culin) Haschee nt; make a ~ of (fam) verpfuschen

hashish /'hæʃɪʃ/ n Haschisch nt

hassle /'hæsl/ n (fam) Ärger m □ vt schikanieren

hassock /'hæsək/ n Kniekissen nt

haste /heɪst/ n Eile f; make ~ sich beeilen

hasten /'heɪsn/ vi sich beeilen (to zu); (go quickly) eilen □ vt beschleunigen

hasty /'heɪstɪ/ a (-ier, -iest), -ily adv hastig; (decision) voreilig

hat /hæt/ n Hut m; (knitted) Mütze f

hatch¹ /hætʃ/ n (for food) Durchreiche f; (Naut) Luke f

hatch² vi ~ [out] ausschlüpfen □ vt ausbrüten

'hatchback n (Auto) Modell nt mit Hecktür

hatchet /'hætʃɪt/ n Beil nt

hate /heɪt/ n Hass m □ vt hassen. ~ful a abscheulich

hatred /'heɪtrɪd/ n Hass m

haughty /'hɔːtɪ/ a (-ier, -iest), -ily adv hochmütig

haul /hɔːl/ n (fish) Fang m; (loot) Beute f □ vt/i ziehen (on an + dat). ~age /-ɪdʒ/ n Transport m. ~ier /-ɪə(r)/ n Spediteur m

haunt /hɔːnt/ n Lieblingsaufenthalt m □ vt umgehen in (+ dat); this house is ~ed in diesem Haus spukt es

have /hæv/ vt (3 sg pres tense has; pt/pp had) haben; bekommen (baby); holen (doctor); ~ a meal/drink etwas essen/trinken; ~ lunch zu Mittag essen; ~ a walk spazieren gehen; ~ a dream träumen; ~ a rest sich ausruhen; ~ a swim schwimmen; ~ sth done etw machen lassen; ~ sth made sich (dat) etw machen lassen; ~ to do sth etw tun müssen; ~ it out with zur Rede stellen; so I ~! tatsächlich! he has [got] two houses er hat zwei Häuser; you have got the money, haven't you? du hast das Geld, nicht [wahr]? □ v aux haben; (with verbs of motion & some others) sein; I ~ seen him ich habe ihn gesehen; he has never been there er ist nie da gewesen. ~ on *vt (be wearing)* anhaben; *(dupe)* anführen

haven /'heɪvn/ n *(fig)* Zuflucht f

haversack /'hævə-/ n Rucksack m

havoc /'hævək/ n Verwüstung f; play ~ with *(fig)* völlig durcheinander bringen

haw /hɔ:/ *see* hum

hawk[1] /hɔ:k/ n Falke m

hawk[2] *vt* hausieren mit. ~er n Hausierer m

hawthorn /'hɔ:-/ n Hagedorn m

hay /heɪ/ n Heu nt. ~ fever n Heuschnupfen m. ~stack n Heuschober m

haywire a *(fam)* go ~ verrückt spielen; *(plans:)* über den Haufen geworfen werden

hazard /'hæzəd/ n Gefahr f; *(risk)* Risiko nt ▫ *vt* riskieren. ~ous /-əs/ a gefährlich; *(risky)* riskant. ~ [warning] lights npl *(Auto)* Warnblinkanlage f

haze /heɪz/ n Dunst m

hazel /'heɪzl/ n Haselbusch m. ~-nut n Haselnuss f

hazy /'heɪzɪ/ a (-ier, -iest) dunstig; *(fig)* unklar

he /hi:/ pron er

head /hed/ n Kopf m; *(chief)* Oberhaupt nt; *(of firm)* Chef(in) m(f); *(of school)* Schulleiter(in) m(f); *(on beer)* Schaumkrone f; *(of bed)* Kopfende nt; 20 ~ of cattle 20 Stück Vieh; ~ first kopfüber ▫ *vt* anführen; *(Sport)* köpfen *(ball)* ▫ *vi* ~ for zusteuern auf (+ acc). ~ache n Kopfschmerzen pl. ~dress n Kopfschmuck m

head|er /'hedə(r)/ n Kopfball m; *(dive)* Kopfsprung m. ~ing n Überschrift f

head: ~lamp n *(Auto)* Scheinwerfer m. ~land n Landspitze f. ~light n *(Auto)* Scheinwerfer m. ~line n Schlagzeile f. ~long adv kopfüber. ~'master n Schulleiter m. ~'mistress n Schulleiterin f. ~-on a & adv frontal. ~phones npl Kopfhörer m. ~quarters npl Hauptquartier nt; *(Pol)* Zentrale f. ~rest n Kopfstütze f. ~room n lichte Höhe f. ~scarf n Kopftuch nt. ~strong a eigenwillig. ~'waiter n Oberkellner m. ~way n make ~way Fortschritte machen. ~wind n Gegenwind m. ~word n Stichwort nt

heady /'hedɪ/ a berauschend

heal /hi:l/ *vt/i* heilen

health /helθ/ n Gesundheit f

health: ~ farm n Schönheitsfarm f. ~ foods npl Reformkost f. ~-food shop n Reformhaus m. ~ insurance n Krankenversicherung f

healthy /'helθɪ/ a (-ier, -iest), -ily adv gesund

heap /hi:p/ n Haufen m; ~s *(fam)* jede Menge ▫ *vt* ~ [up] häufen; ~ed teaspoon gehäufter Teelöffel

hear /hɪə(r)/ *vt/i (pt/pp* heard) hören; ~, ~! hört, hört! he would not ~ of it er ließ es nicht zu

hearing /'hɪərɪŋ/ n Gehör nt; *(Jur)* Verhandlung f. ~-aid n Hörgerät nt

'hearsay n from ~ vom Hörensagen

hearse /hɜ:s/ n Leichenwagen m

heart /hɑ:t/ n Herz nt; *(courage)* Mut m; ~s pl *(Cards)* Herz nt; by ~ auswendig

heart: ~ache n Kummer m. ~attack n Herzanfall m. ~beat n Herzschlag m. ~break n Leid nt. ~breaking a herzzerreißend. ~broken a untröstlich. ~burn n Sodbrennen nt. ~en *vt* ermutigen. ~felt a herzlich[st]

hearth /hɑ:θ/ n Herd m; *(fireplace)* Kamin m. ~rug n Kaminvorleger m

heart|ily /'hɑ:tɪlɪ/ adv herzlich; *(eat)* viel. ~less a, -ly adv herzlos. ~y a herzlich; *(meal)* groß; *(person)* burschikos

heat /hi:t/ n Hitze f; *(Sport)* Vorlauf m ▫ *vt* heiß machen; heizen *(room)*. ~ed a geheizt; *(swimming pool)* beheizt; *(discussion)* hitzig. ~er n Heizgerät nt; *(Auto)* Heizanlage f

heath /hi:θ/ n Heide f

heathen /'hi:ðn/ a heidnisch ▫ n Heide m/Heidin f

heather /'heðə(r)/ n Heidekraut nt

heating /'hi:tɪŋ/ n Heizung f

heat: ~-stroke n Hitzschlag m. ~wave n Hitzewelle f

heave /hi:v/ *vt/i* ziehen; *(lift)* heben; *(fam: throw)* schmeißen; ~ a sigh einen Seufzer ausstoßen

heaven /'hevn/ n Himmel m. ~ly a himmlisch

heavy /'hevɪ/ a (-ier, -iest), -ily adv schwer; *(traffic, rain)* stark; *(sleep)* tief. ~weight n Schwergewicht nt

Hebrew /'hi:bru:/ a hebräisch

heckle /'hekl/ *vt* [durch Zwischenrufe] unterbrechen. ~r n Zwischenrufer m

hectic /'hektɪk/ a hektisch

hedge /hedʒ/ n Hecke f ▫ *vi (fig)* ausweichen. ~hog n Igel m

heed /hi:d/ n pay ~ to Beachtung schenken (+ dat) ▫ *vt* beachten. ~less a ungeachtet *(of any)*

heel[1] /hi:l/ n Ferse f; *(of shoe)* Absatz m; down at ~ heruntergekommen; take to one's ~s *(fam)* Fersengeld geben

heel[2] *vi* ~ over *(Naut)* sich auf die Seite legen

hefty /'heftɪ/ a (-ier, -iest) kräftig; *(heavy)* schwer

heifer /'hefə(r)/ n Färse f

height /haɪt/ n Höhe f; (of person) Größe f. ~en vt (fig) steigern

heir /eə(r)/ n Erbe m. ~ess n Erbin f. ~loom n Erbstück nt

held /held/ see hold²

helicopter /'helɪkɒptə(r)/ n Hubschrauber m

hell /hel/ n Hölle f; go to ~! (sl) geh zum Teufel! □ int verdammt!

hello /hə'ləʊ/ int [guten] Tag! (fam) hallo!

helm /helm/ n [Steuer]ruder nt; at the ~ (fig) am Ruder

helmet /'helmɪt/ n Helm m

help /help/ n Hilfe f; (employees) Hilfskräfte pl; that's no ~ das nützt nichts □ vt/i helfen (s.o. jdm); ~ oneself to sth sich (dat) etw nehmen; ~ yourself (at table) greif zu; I could not ~ laughing ich musste lachen; it cannot be ~ed es lässt sich nicht ändern; I can't ~ it ich kann nichts dafür

help|er /'helpə(r)/ n Helfer(in) m(f). ~ful a, -ly adv hilfsbereit; (advice) nützlich. ~ing n Portion f. ~less a, -ly adv hilflos

helter-skelter /heltə'skeltə(r)/ adv holterdiepolter □ n Rutschbahn f

hem /hem/ n Saum m □ vt (pt/pp hemmed) säumen; ~ in umzingeln

hemisphere /'hemɪ-/ n Hemisphäre f

'hem-line n Rocklänge f

hemp /hemp/ n Hanf m

hen /hen/ n Henne f; (any female bird) Weibchen nt

hence /hens/ adv daher; five years ~ in fünf Jahren. ~'forth adv von nun an

henchman /'hentʃmən/ n (pej) Gefolgsmann m

'henpecked a ~ husband Pantoffelheld m

her /hɜ:(r)/ a ihr □ pron (acc) sie; (dat) ihr; I know ~ ich kenne sie; give ~ the money gib ihr das Geld

herald /'herəld/ vt verkünden. ~ry n Wappenkunde f

herb /hɜ:b/ n Kraut nt

herbaceous /hɜ:'beɪʃəs/ a krautartig; ~ border Staudenrabatte f

herd /hɜ:d/ n Herde f □ vt (tend) hüten; (drive) treiben. ~ together vi sich zusammendrängen □ vt zusammentreiben

here /hɪə(r)/ adv hier; (to this place) hierher; in ~ hier drinnen; come/bring ~ herkommen/herbringen. ~'after adv im Folgenden. ~'by adv hiermit

hereditary /hə'redɪtəri/ a erblich. ~y n Vererbung f

heresy /'herəsi/ n Ketzerei f. ~tic n Ketzer(in) m(f)

here'with adv (Comm) beiliegend

heritage /'herɪtɪdʒ/ n Erbe nt

hermetic /hɜ:'metɪk/ a, -ally adv hermetisch

hermit /'hɜ:mɪt/ n Einsiedler m

hernia /'hɜ:nɪə/ n Bruch m, Hernie f

hero /'hɪərəʊ/ n (pl -es) Held m

heroic /hɪ'rəʊɪk/ a, -ally adv heldenhaft

heroin /'herəʊɪn/ n Heroin nt

hero|ine /'herəʊɪn/ n Heldin f. ~ism n Heldentum nt

heron /'hern/ n Reiher m

herring /'herɪŋ/ n Hering m; red ~ (fam) falsche Spur f. ~bone n (pattern) Fischgrätenmuster nt

hers /hɜ:z/ poss pron ihre(r), ihrs; a friend of ~ ein Freund von ihr; that is ~ das gehört ihr

her'self pron selbst; (refl) sich; by ~ allein

hesitant /'hezɪtənt/ a, -ly adv zögernd

hesitat|e /'hezɪteɪt/ vi zögern. ~ion /-'teɪʃn/ n Zögern nt; without ~ion ohne zu zögern

het /het/ a ~ up (fam) aufgeregt

hetero'sexual /hetərəʊ-/ a heterosexuell

hew /hju:/ vt (pt hewed, pp hewed or hewn) hauen

hexagonal /hek'sægənl/ a sechseckig

heyday /'heɪ-/ n Glanzzeit f

hi /haɪ/ int he! (hallo) Tag!

hiatus /haɪ'eɪtəs/ n (pl -tuses) Lücke f

hibernat|e /'haɪbəneɪt/ vi Winterschlaf halten. ~ion /-'neɪʃn/ n Winterschlaf m

hiccup /'hɪkʌp/ n Hick m; (fam: hitch) Panne f; have the ~s den Schluckauf haben □ vi hick machen

hid /hɪd/, **hidden** see hide²

hide¹ /haɪd/ n (Comm) Haut f; (leather) Leder nt

hide² vt (pt hid, pp hidden) □ vt verstecken; (keep secret) verheimlichen □ vt sich verstecken. ~-and-seek n play ~-and-seek Versteck spielen

hideous /'hɪdɪəs/ a, -ly adv hässlich; (horrible) grässlich

'hide-out n Versteck nt

hiding¹ /'haɪdɪŋ/ n (fam) give s.o. a ~ jdn verdreschen

hiding² n go into ~ untertauchen

hierarchy /'haɪərɑ:kɪ/ n Hierarchie f

hieroglyphics /haɪərə'glɪfɪks/ npl Hieroglyphen pl

higgledy-piggledy /hɪgldɪ'pɪgldɪ/ adv kunterbunt durcheinander

high /haɪ/ a (-er, -est) hoch; attrib hohe(r,s); (meat) angegangen; (wind) stark;

(*on drugs*) high; it's ~ time es ist höchste Zeit □ *adv* hoch; ~ and low überall □ *n* Hoch *nt*; (*temperature*) Höchsttemperatur *f*

high: ~**brow** *a* intellektuell. ~ **chair** *n* Kinderhochstuhl *m*. ~'-**handed** *a* selbstherrlich. ~-'**heeled** *a* hochhackig. ~ **jump** *n* Hochsprung *m*

'**highlight** *n* (*fig*) Höhepunkt *m*; ~**s** *pl* (*in hair*) helle Strähnen *pl* □ *vt* (*emphasize*) hervorheben

highly /'haɪlɪ/ *adv* hoch; **speak** ~ **of** loben; **think** ~ **of** sehr schätzen. ~-'**strung** *a* nervös

Highness /'haɪnɪs/ *n* Hoheit *f*

high: ~-**rise** *a* ~-**rise flats** *pl* Wohnturm *m*. ~ **season** *n* Hochsaison *f*. ~ **street** *n* Hauptstraße *f*. ~ '**tide** *n* Hochwasser *nt*. ~**way** *n* public ~**way** öffentliche Straße

hijack /'haɪdʒæk/ *vt* entführen. ~**er** *n* Entführer *m*

hike /haɪk/ *n* Wanderung *f* □ *vi* wandern. ~**r** *n* Wanderer *m*

hilarious /hɪ'leərɪəs/ *a* sehr komisch

hill /hɪl/ *n* Berg *m*; (*mound*) Hügel *m*; (*slope*) Hang *m*

hill: ~-**billy** *n* (*Amer*) Hinterwäldler *m*. ~**side** *n* Hang *m*. ~**y** *a* hügelig

hilt /hɪlt/ *n* Griff *m*; **to the** ~ (*fam*) voll und ganz

him /hɪm/ *pron* (*acc*) ihn; (*dat*) ihm; **I know** ~ ich kenne ihn; **give** ~ **the money** gib ihm das Geld. ~'**self** *pron* selbst; (*refl*) sich; **by** ~**self** allein

hind /haɪnd/ *a* Hinter-

hind|er /'hɪndə(r)/ *vt* hindern. ~**rance** /-rəns/ *n* Hindernis *nt*

hindsight /'haɪnd-/ *n* **with** ~ rückblickend

Hindu /'hɪndu:/ *n* Hindu *m* □ *a* Hindu-. ~**ism** *n* Hinduismus *m*

hinge /hɪndʒ/ *n* Scharnier *nt*; (*on door*) Angel *f* □ *vi* ~ **on** (*fig*) ankommen auf (+ *acc*)

hint /hɪnt/ *n* Wink *m*, Andeutung *f*; (*advice*) Hinweis *m*; (*trace*) Spur *f* □ *vi* ~ **at** anspielen auf (+ *acc*)

hip /hɪp/ *n* Hüfte *f*

hippie /'hɪpɪ/ *n* Hippie *m*

hip 'pocket *n* Gesäßtasche *f*

hippopotamus /hɪpə'pɒtəməs/ *n* (*pl* -**muses** *or* -**mi** /-maɪ/) Nilpferd *nt*

hire /'haɪə(r)/ *vt* mieten (*car*); leihen (*suit*); einstellen (*person*); ~ [**out**] vermieten; verleihen □ *n* Mieten *nt*; Leihen *nt*. ~-**car** *n* Leihwagen *m*

his /hɪz/ *a* sein □ *poss pron* seine(r), seins; **a friend of** ~ ein Freund von ihm; **that is** ~ das gehört ihm

hiss /hɪs/ *n* Zischen *nt* □ *vt/i* zischen

historian /hɪ'stɔːrɪən/ *n* Historiker(in) *m(f)*

historic /hɪ'stɒrɪk/ *a* historisch. ~**al** *a*, -**ly** *adv* geschichtlich, historisch

history /'hɪstərɪ/ *n* Geschichte *f*

hit /hɪt/ *n* (*blow*) Schlag *m*; (*fam: success*) Erfolg *m*; **direct** ~ Volltreffer *m* □ *vt/i* (*pt/pp* **hit**, *pres p* **hitting**) schlagen; (*knock against, collide with, affect*) treffen; ~ **the target** das Ziel treffen; ~ **on** (*fig*) kommen auf (+ *acc*); ~ **it off** gut auskommen (**with** mit); ~ **one's head on sth** sich (*dat*) den Kopf an etw (*dat*) stoßen

hitch /hɪtʃ/ *n* Problem *nt*; **technical** ~ Panne *f* □ *vt* festmachen (**to** an + *dat*); ~ **up** hochziehen; ~ **a lift** per Anhalter fahren, (*fam*) trampen. ~**hike** *vi* per Anhalter fahren, (*fam*) trampen. ~**hiker** *n* Anhalter(in) *m(f)*

hither /'hɪðə(r)/ *adv* hierher; ~ **and thither** hin und her. ~'**to** *adv* bisher

hive /haɪv/ *n* Bienenstock *m*. ~ **off** *vt* (*Comm*) abspalten

hoard /hɔːd/ *n* Hort *m* □ *vt* horten, hamstern

hoarding /'hɔːdɪŋ/ *n* Bauzaun *m*; (*with advertisements*) Reklamewand *f*

hoar-frost /'hɔː-/ *n* Raureif *m*

hoarse /hɔːs/ *a* (-r, -st), -**ly** *adv* heiser. ~**ness** *n* Heiserkeit *f*

hoax /həʊks/ *n* übler Scherz *m*; (*false alarm*) blinder Alarm *m*

hob /hɒb/ *n* Kochmulde *f*

hobble /'hɒbl/ *vi* humpeln

hobby /'hɒbɪ/ *n* Hobby *nt*. ~-**horse** *n* (*fig*) Lieblingsthema *nt*

hobnailed /'hɒb-/ *a* ~ **boots** *pl* genagelte Schuhe *pl*

hock /hɒk/ *n* [weißer] Rheinwein *m*

hockey /'hɒkɪ/ *n* Hockey *nt*

hoe /həʊ/ *n* Hacke *f* □ *vt* (*pres p* **hoeing**) hacken

hog /hɒg/ *n* [Mast]schwein *nt* □ *vt* (*pt/pp* **hogged**) (*fam*) mit Beschlag belegen

hoist /hɔɪst/ *n* Lastenaufzug *m* □ *vt* hochziehen; hissen (*flag*)

hold[1] /həʊld/ *n* (*Naut*) Laderaum *m*

hold[2] *n* Halt *m*; (*Sport*) Griff *m*; (*fig: influence*) Einfluss *m*; **get** ~ **of** fassen; (*fam: contact*) erreichen □ *v* (*pt/pp* **held**) □ *vt* halten; (*container:*) fassen; (*believe*) meinen; (*possess*) haben; **anhalten** (*breath*); ~ **one's tongue** den Mund halten □ *vi* (*rope:*) halten; (*weather:*) sich halten; **not** ~ **with** (*fam*) nicht einverstanden sein mit. ~ **back** *vt* zurückhalten □ *vi* zögern. ~ **on** *vi* (*wait*) warten; (*on telephone*) am Apparat bleiben; ~ **on to**

(*keep*) behalten; (*cling to*) sich festhalten an (+ *dat.*). ~ out *vt* hinhalten □ *vi* (*resist*) aushalten. ~ up *vt* hochhalten; (*delay*) aufhalten; (*rob*) überfallen

'hold|all *n* Reisetasche *f*. ~er *n* Inhaber(in) *m(f)*; (*container*) Halter *m*. ~-up *n* Verzögerung *f*; (*attack*) Überfall *m*

hole /həʊl/ *n* Loch *nt*

holiday /'hɒlədeɪ/ *n* Urlaub *m*; (*Sch*) Ferien *pl*; (*public*) Feiertag *m*; (*day off*) freier Tag *m*; go on ~ in Urlaub fahren. ~-maker *n* Urlauber(in) *m(f)*

holiness /'həʊlɪnɪs/ *n* Heiligkeit *f*

Holland /'hɒlənd/ *n* Holland *nt*

hollow /'hɒləʊ/ *a* hohl; (*promise*) leer □ *n* Vertiefung *f*; (*in ground*) Mulde *f*. ~ out *vt* aushöhlen

holly /'hɒlɪ/ *n* Stechpalme *f*

'hollyhock *n* Stockrose *f*

hologram /'hɒləɡræm/ *n* Hologramm *nt*

holster /'həʊlstə(r)/ *n* Pistolentasche *f*

holy /'həʊlɪ/ *a* (-ier, -est) heilig. H~ Ghost *or* Spirit *n* Heiliger Geist *m*. ~ water *n* Weihwasser *nt*. H~ Week *n* Karwoche *f*

homage /'hɒmɪdʒ/ *n* Huldigung *f*; pay ~ to huldigen (+ *dat*)

home /həʊm/ *n* Zuhause *nt*; (*house*) Haus *nt*; (*institution*) Heim *nt*; (*native land*) Heimat *f* □ *adv* at ~ zu Hause; come/go ~ nach Hause kommen/gehen

home: ~ ad'dress *n* Heimatanschrift *f*. ~ com'puter *n* Heimcomputer *m*. ~ game *n* Heimspiel *nt*. ~ help *n* Haushaltshilfe *f*. ~land *n* Heimatland *nt*. ~less *a* obdachlos

homely /'həʊmlɪ/ *a* (-ier, -iest) *a* gemütlich; (*Amer: ugly*) unscheinbar

home: ~-'made *a* selbst gemacht. H~ Office *n* Innenministerium *nt*. H~ 'Secretary Innenminister *m*. ~sick *a* be ~ sick Heimweh haben (for nach). ~ sickness *n* Heimweh *nt*. ~ 'town *n* Heimatstadt *f*. ~work *n* (*Sch*) Hausaufgaben *pl*

homicide /'hɒmɪsaɪd/ *n* Totschlag *m*; (*murder*) Mord *m*

homoeopath|ic /həʊmɪə'pæθɪk/ *a* homöopathisch. ~y /-'ɒpəθɪ/ *n* Homöopathie *f*

homogeneous /hɒmə'dʒiːnɪəs/ *a* homogen

homo'sexual *a* homosexuell □ *n* Homosexuelle(r) *m/f*

honest /'ɒnɪst/ *a*, -ly *adv* ehrlich. ~y *n* Ehrlichkeit *f*

honey /'hʌnɪ/ *n* Honig *m*; (*fam: darling*) Schatz *m*

honey: ~comb *n* Honigwabe *f*. ~moon *n* Flitterwochen *pl*; (*journey*) Hochzeitsreise *f*. ~suckle *n* Geißblatt *nt*

honk /hɒŋk/ *vi* hupen

honorary /'ɒnərərɪ/ *a* ehrenamtlich; (*member, doctorate*) Ehren-

honour /'ɒnə(r)/ *n* Ehre *f* □ *vt* ehren; honorieron (*cheque*). ~able / əbl/ *a*, bly *adv* ehrenhaft

hood /hʊd/ *n* Kapuze *f*; (*of pram*) [Klapp]verdeck *nt*; (*Amer, Auto*) Kühlerhaube *f*

hoodlum /'huːdləm/ *n* Rowdy *m*

'hoodwink /'hʊd-/ *vt* (*fam*) reinlegen

hoof /huːf/ *n* (*pl* ~s *or* hooves) Huf *m*

hook /hʊk/ *n* Haken *m*; by ~ or by crook mit allen Mitteln □ *vt* festhaken (to an + *acc*)

hook|ed /hʊkt/ *a* ~ed nose Hakennase *f*; ~ed on (*fam*) abhängig von; (*keen on*) besessen von. ~er *n* (*Amer, sl*) Nutte *f*

hookey /'hʊkɪ/ *n* play ~ (*Amer, fam*) schwänzen

hooligan /'huːlɪɡən/ *n* Rowdy *m*. ~ism *n* Rowdytum *nt*

hoop /huːp/ *n* Reifen *m*

hooray /hʊ'reɪ/ *int* & *n* = hurrah

hoot /huːt/ *n* Ruf *m*; ~s of laughter schallendes Gelächter *nt* □ *vi* (*owl:*) rufen; (*car:*) hupen; (*jeer*) johlen. ~er *n* (*of factory*) Sirene *f*; (*Auto*) Hupe *f*

hoover /'huːvə(r)/ *n* H~ (P) Staubsauger *m* □ *vt/i* [staub]saugen

hop¹ /hɒp/ *n*, & ~s *pl* Hopfen *m*

hop² *n* Hüpfer *m*; catch s.o. on the ~ (*fam*) jdm ungelegen kommen □ *vi* (*pt/pp* hopped) hüpfen; ~ it! (*fam*) hau ab! ~ in *vi* (*fam*) einsteigen. ~ out *vi* (*fam*) aussteigen

hope /həʊp/ *n* Hoffnung *f*; (*prospect*) Aussicht *f* (of auf + *acc*) □ *vt/i* hoffen (for auf + *acc*); I ~ so hoffentlich

hope|ful /'həʊpfl/ *a* hoffnungsvoll; be ~ful that hoffen, dass. ~fully *adv* hoffnungsvoll; (*it is hoped*) hoffentlich. ~less *a*, -ly *adv* hoffnungslos; (*useless*) nutzlos; (*incompetent*) untauglich

horde /hɔːd/ *n* Horde *f*

horizon /hə'raɪzn/ *n* Horizont *m*; on the ~ am Horizont

horizontal /hɒrɪ'zɒntl/ *a*, -ly *adv* horizontal. ~'bar *n* Reck *nt*

horn /hɔːn/ *n* Horn *nt*; (*Auto*) Hupe *f*

hornet /'hɔːnɪt/ *n* Hornisse *f*

horny /'hɔːnɪ/ *a* schwielig

horoscope /'hɒrəskəʊp/ *n* Horoskop *nt*

horrible /'hɒrɪbl/ *a*, -bly *adv* schrecklich

horrid /'hɒrɪd/ *a* grässlich

horrific /hə'rɪfɪk/ *a* entsetzlich

horrify /'hɒrɪfaɪ/ *vt* (*pt/pp* -ied) entsetzen

horror /'hɒrə(r)/ n Entsetzen nt. ~ film n Horrorfilm m

hors-d'œuvre /ɔː'dɜːvr/ n Vorspeise f

horse /hɔːs/ n Pferd nt

horse: ~back n on ~back zu Pferde. ~ 'chestnut n [Ross]kastanie f. ~man n Reiter m. ~play n Toben nt. ~power n Pferdestärke f. ~racing n Pferderennen nt. ~radish n Meerrettich m. ~shoe n Hufeisen nt

horti'cultural /hɔːtɪ-/ a Garten- 'horticulture n Gartenbau m

hose /həʊz/ n (pipe) Schlauch m ▢ vt ~ down abspritzen

hosiery /'həʊʒərɪ/ n Strumpfwaren pl

hospice /'hɒspɪs/ n Heim nt; (for the terminally ill) Sterbeklinik f

hospitable /hə'spɪtəbl/ a, -bly adv gastfreundlich

hospital /'hɒspɪtl/ n Krankenhaus nt

hospitality /hɒspɪ'tælətɪ/ n Gastfreundschaft f

host¹ /həʊst/ n a ~ of eine Menge von

host² n Gastgeber m

host³ n (Relig) Hostie f

hostage /'hɒstɪdʒ/ n Geisel f

hostel /'hɒstl/ n [Wohn]heim nt

hostess /'həʊstɪs/ n Gastgeberin f

hostile /'hɒstaɪl/ a feindlich; (unfriendly) feindselig

hostility /hɒ'stɪlətɪ/ n Feindschaft f; ~ies pl Feindseligkeiten pl

hot /hɒt/ a (hotter, hottest) heiß; ⟨meal⟩ warm; (spicy) scharf; I am or feel ~ mir ist heiß

'hotbed n (fig) Brutstätte f

hotchpotch /'hɒtʃpɒtʃ/ n Mischmasch m

hotel /həʊ'tel/ n Hotel nt. ~ier /-ɪə(r)/ n Hotelier m

hot: ~head n Hitzkopf m. ~-'headed a hitzköpfig. ~house n Treibhaus nt. ~ly adv (fig) heiß, heftig. ~plate n Tellerwärmer m; (of cooker) Kochplatte f. ~ tap n Warmwasserhahn m. ~-tempered a jähzornig. ~'water bottle n Wärmflasche f

hound /haʊnd/ n Jagdhund m ▢ vt (fig) verfolgen

hour /'aʊə(r)/ n Stunde f. ~ly a & adv stündlich; ~ly pay or rate Stundenlohn m

house¹ /haʊs/ n Haus nt; at my ~ bei mir

house² /haʊz/ vt unterbringen

house /haʊs/: ~boat n Hausboot nt. ~breaking n Einbruch m. ~hold n Haushalt m. ~holder n Hausinhaber(in) m(f). ~keeper n Haushälterin f. ~keeping n Hauswirtschaft f; (money) Haushaltsgeld

nt. ~plant n Zimmerpflanze f. ~trained a stubenrein. ~warming n have a ~warming party Einstand feiern. ~wife n Hausfrau f. ~work n Hausarbeit f

housing /'haʊzɪŋ/ n Wohnungen pl; (Techn) Gehäuse nt. ~ estate n Wohnsiedlung f

hovel /'hɒvl/ n elende Hütte f

hover /'hɒvə(r)/ vi schweben; (be undecided) schwanken; (linger) herumstehen. ~craft n Luftkissenfahrzeug nt

how /haʊ/ adv wie; ~ do you do? guten Tag! ~ many wie viele; ~ much wie viel; and ~! und ob!

how'ever adv (in question) wie; (nevertheless) jedoch, aber; ~ small wie klein es auch sein mag

howl /haʊl/ n Heulen nt ▢ vi heulen; ⟨baby:⟩ brüllen. ~er n (fam) Schnitzer m

hub /hʌb/ n Nabe f; (fig) Mittelpunkt m

hubbub /'hʌbʌb/ n Stimmengewirr nt

'hub-cap n Radkappe f

huddle /'hʌdl/ vi ~ together sich zusammendrängen

hue¹ /hjuː/ n Farbe f

hue² n ~ and cry Aufruhr m

huff /hʌf/ n in a ~ beleidigt

hug /hʌg/ n Umarmung f ▢ vt (pt/pp hugged) umarmen

huge /hjuːdʒ/ a, -ly adv riesig

hulking /'hʌlkɪŋ/ a (fam) ungeschlacht

hull /hʌl/ n (Naut) Rumpf m

hullo /hə'ləʊ/ int = hallo

hum /hʌm/ n Summen nt; Brummen nt ▢ vt/i (pt/pp hummed) summen; ⟨motor:⟩ brummen; ~ and haw nicht mit der Sprache herauswollen

human /'hjuːmən/ a menschlich ▢ n Mensch m. ~ 'being n Mensch m

humane /hjuː'meɪn/ a, -ly adv human

humanitarian /hjuːmænɪ'teərɪən/ a humanitär

humanit|y /hjuː'mænətɪ/ n Menschheit f; ~ies pl (Univ) Geisteswissenschaften pl

humble /'hʌmbl/ a (-r, -st), -bly adv demütig ▢ vt demütigen

'humdrum a eintönig

humid /'hjuːmɪd/ a feucht. ~ity /-'mɪdətɪ/ n Feuchtigkeit f

humiliat|e /hjuː'mɪlɪeɪt/ vt demütigen. ~ion /-'eɪʃn/ n Demütigung f

humility /hjuː'mɪlətɪ/ n Demut f

'humming-bird n Kolibri m

humorous /'hjuːmərəs/ a, -ly adv humorvoll; ⟨story⟩ humoristisch

humour /'hju:mə(r)/ n Humor m; (mood) Laune f; **have a sense of ~** Humor haben □ vt ~ s.o jdm seinen Willen lassen

hump /hʌmp/ n Buckel m; (of camel) Höcker m □ vt schleppen

hunch /hʌntʃ/ n (idea) Ahnung f

'hunch|back n Bucklige(r) m/f. **~ed** a **~ed up** gebeugt

hundred /'hʌndrəd/ a **one/a ~** [ein]hundert □ n Hundert nt; (written figure) Hundert f. **~th** a hundertste(r,s) □ n Hundertstel nt. **~weight** n ≈ Zentner m

hung /hʌŋ/ see **hang**

Hungarian /hʌŋ'geəriən/ a ungarisch □ n Ungar(in) m(f)

Hungary /'hʌŋgəri/ n Ungar nt

hunger /'hʌŋgə(r)/ n Hunger m. **~-strike** n Hungerstreik m

hungry /'hʌŋgri/ a (-ier, -iest), -ily adv hungrig; **be ~** Hunger haben

hunk /hʌŋk/ n [großes] Stück nt

hunt /hʌnt/ n Jagd f; (for criminal) Fahndung f □ vt/i jagen; fahnden nach (criminal); **~ for** suchen. **~er** n Jäger m; (horse) Jagdpferd nt. **~ing** n Jagd f

hurdle /'hɜ:dl/ n (Sport & fig) Hürde f. **~r** n Hürdenläufer(in) m(f)

hurl /hɜ:l/ vt schleudern

hurrah /hʊ'rɑ:/, **hurray** /hʊ'reɪ/ int hurra! □ n Hurra nt

hurricane /'hʌrɪkən/ n Orkan m

hurried /'hʌrɪd/ a, -ly adv eilig; (superficial) flüchtig

hurry /'hʌrɪ/ n Eile f; **be in a ~** es eilig haben □ vi (pt/pp -ied) sich beeilen; (go quickly) eilen. **~ up** vi sich beeilen □ vt antreiben

hurt /hɜ:t/ n Schmerz m □ vt/i (pt/pp hurt) weh tun (+ dat); (injure) verletzen; (offend) kränken. **~ful** a verletzend

hurtle /'hɜ:tl/ vi **~ along** rasen

husband /'hʌzbənd/ n [Ehe]mann m

hush /hʌʃ/ n Stille f □ vt **~ up** vertuschen. **~ed** a gedämpft. **~·'hush** a (fam) streng geheim

husk /hʌsk/ n Spelze f

husky /'hʌski/ a (-ier, -iest) heiser; (burly) stämmig

hustle /'hʌsl/ vt drängen □ n Gedränge nt; **~ and bustle** geschäftiges Treiben n

hut /hʌt/ n Hütte f

hutch /hʌtʃ/ n [Kaninchen]stall m

hybrid /'haɪbrɪd/ a hybrid □ n Hybride f

hydrangea /haɪ'dreɪndʒə/ n Hortensie f

hydrant /'haɪdrənt/ n [fire] Hydrant m

hydraulic /haɪ'drɔ:lɪk/ a, -ally adv hydraulisch

hydrochloric /haɪdrə'klɔ:rɪk/ a **~ acid** Salzsäure f

hydroe'lectric /haɪdrəʊ-/ a hydroelektrisch. **~ power station** n Wasserkraftwerk nt

hydrofoil /'haɪdrə-/ n Tragflügelboot nt

hydrogen /'haɪdrədʒən/ n Wasserstoff m

hyena /haɪ'i:nə/ n Hyäne f

hygien|e /'haɪdʒi:n/ n Hygiene f. **~ic** /haɪ'dʒi:nɪk/ a, -ally adv hygienisch

hymn /hɪm/ n Kirchenlied nt. **~-book** n Gesangbuch nt

hyphen /'haɪfn/ n Bindestrich m. **~ate** vt mit Bindestrich schreiben

hypno|sis /hɪp'nəʊsɪs/ n Hypnose f. **~tic** /-'nɒtɪk/ a hypnotisch

hypno|tism /'hɪpnətɪzm/ n Hypnotik f. **~tist** /-tɪst/ n Hypnotiseur m. **~tize** vt hypnotisieren

hypochondriac /haɪpə'kɒndriæk/ a hypochondrisch □ n Hypochonder m

hypocrisy /hɪ'pɒkrəsɪ/ n Heuchelei f

hypocrit|e /'hɪpəkrɪt/ n Heuchler(in) m(f). **~ical** /-'krɪtɪkl/ a, -ly adv heuchlerisch

hypodermic /haɪpə'dɜ:mɪk/ a & n **~ [syringe]** Injektionsspritze f

hypothe|sis /haɪ'pɒθəsɪs/ n Hypothese f. **~tical** /-ə'θetɪkl/ a, -ly adv hypothetisch

hyster|ia /hɪ'stɪəriə/ n Hysterie f. **~ical** /-'sterɪkl/ a, -ly adv hysterisch. **~ics** /hɪ'sterɪks/ npl hysterischer Anfall m

I

I /aɪ/ pron ich

ice /aɪs/ n Eis nt □ vt mit Zuckerguss überziehen (cake)

ice: ~ age n Eiszeit f. **~-axe** n Eispickel m. **~berg** /-bɜːg/ n Eisberg m. **~-box** n (Amer) Kühlschrank m. **~-'cream** n [Speise]eis nt. **~-'cream parlour** n Eisdiele f. **~-cube** n Eiswürfel m

Iceland /'aɪslənd/ n Island nt

ice: ~ 'lolly n Eis nt am Stiel. **~ rink** n Eisbahn f

icicle /'aɪsɪkl/ n Eiszapfen m

icing /'aɪsɪŋ/ n Zuckerguss m. **~ sugar** n Puderzucker m

icon /'aɪkɒn/ n Ikone f

icy /'aɪsɪ/ a (-ier, -iest), -ily adv eisig; (road) vereist

idea /aɪ'dɪə/ n Idee f; (conception) Vorstellung f; **I have no ~!** ich habe keine Ahnung!

ideal /aɪˈdɪəl/ a ideal ▫ n Ideal nt. ~ism n Idealismus m. ~ist n Idealist(in) m(f). ~istic /-ˈlɪstɪk/ a idealistisch. ~ize vt idealisieren. ~ly adv ideal; (in ideal circumstances) idealerweise

identical /aɪˈdentɪkl/ a identisch; (twins) eineiig

identi|fication /aɪdentɪfɪˈkeɪʃn/ n Identifizierung f; (proof of identity) Ausweispapiere pl. ~fy /aɪˈdentɪfaɪ/ vt (pt/pp -ied) identifizieren

identity /aɪˈdentɪtɪ/ n Identität f. ~ card n [Personal]ausweis m

ideolog|ical /aɪdɪəˈlɒdʒɪkl/ a ideologisch. ~y /aɪdɪˈɒlədʒɪ/ n Ideologie f

idiom /ˈɪdɪəm/ n [feste] Redewendung f. ~atic /-ˈmætɪk/ a, -ally adv idiomatisch

idiosyncrasy /ɪdɪəˈsɪŋkrəsɪ/ n Eigenart f

idiot /ˈɪdɪət/ n Idiot m. ~ic /-ˈɒtɪk/ a idiotisch

idle /ˈaɪdl/ a (-r, -st), -ly adv untätig; (lazy) faul; (empty) leer; (machine) nicht in Betrieb ▫ vi faulenzen; (engine:) leer laufen. ~ness n Untätigkeit f; Faulheit f

idol /ˈaɪdl/ n Idol nt. ~ize /ˈaɪdəlaɪz/ vt vergöttern

idyllic /ɪˈdɪlɪk/ a idyllisch

i.e. abbr (id est) d.h.

if /ɪf/ conj wenn; (whether) ob; as if als ob

ignite /ɪgˈnaɪt/ vt entzünden ▫ vi sich entzünden

ignition /ɪgˈnɪʃn/ n (Auto) Zündung f. ~ key n Zündschlüssel m

ignoramus /ɪgnəˈreɪməs/ n Ignorant m

ignoran|ce /ˈɪgnərəns/ n Unwissenheit f. ~t a unwissend; (rude) ungehobelt

ignore /ɪgˈnɔ:(r)/ vt ignorieren

ilk /ɪlk/ n (fam) of that ~ von der Sorte

ill /ɪl/ a krank; (bad) schlecht; feel ~ at ease sich unbehaglich fühlen ▫ adv schlecht ▫ n Schlechte(s) nt; (evil) Übel nt. ~-advised a unklug. ~bred a schlecht erzogen

illegal /ɪˈli:gl/ a, -ly adv illegal

illegible /ɪˈledʒəbl/ a, -bly adv unleserlich

illegitima|cy /ɪlɪˈdʒɪtɪməsɪ/ n Unehelichkeit f. ~te /-mət/ a unehelich; (claim) unberechtigt

illicit /ɪˈlɪsɪt/ a, -ly adv illegal

illitera|cy /ɪˈlɪtərəsɪ/ n Analphabetentum nt. ~te /-rət/ a be ~te nicht lesen und schreiben können ▫ n Analphabet(in) m(f)

illness /ˈɪlnɪs/ n Krankheit f

illogical /ɪˈlɒdʒɪkl/ a, -ly adv unlogisch

ill-treat /ɪlˈtri:t/ vt misshandeln. ~ment n Misshandlung f

illuminat|e /ɪˈlu:mɪneɪt/ vt beleuchten. ~ing a aufschlussreich. ~ion /-ˈneɪʃn/ n Beleuchtung f

illusion /ɪˈlu:ʒn/ n Illusion f; be under the ~ that sich (dat) einbilden, dass

illusory /ɪˈlu:sərɪ/ a illusorisch

illustrat|e /ˈɪləstreɪt/ vt illustrieren. ~ion /-ˈstreɪʃn/ n Illustration f

illustrious /ɪˈlʌstrɪəs/ a berühmt

image /ˈɪmɪdʒ/ n Bild nt; (statue) Standbild nt; (figure) Figur f; (exact likeness) Ebenbild nt; [public] ~ Image nt

imagin|able /ɪˈmædʒɪnəbl/ a vorstellbar. ~ary /-ərɪ/ a eingebildet

imaginat|ion /ɪmædʒɪˈneɪʃn/ n Phantasie f; (fancy) Einbildung f. ~ive /ɪˈmædʒɪnətɪv/ a, -ly adv phantasievoll; (full of ideas) einfallsreich

imagine /ɪˈmædʒɪn/ vt sich (dat) vorstellen; (wrongly) sich (dat) einbilden

im'balance n Unausgeglichenheit f

imbecile /ˈɪmbəsi:l/ n Schwachsinnige(r) m|f; (pej) Idiot m

imbibe /ɪmˈbaɪb/ vt trinken; (fig) aufnehmen

imbue /ɪmˈbju:/ vt be ~d with erfüllt sein von

imitat|e /ˈɪmɪteɪt/ vt nachahmen, imitieren. ~ion /-ˈteɪʃn/ n Nachahmung f, Imitation f

immaculate /ɪˈmækjʊlət/ a, -ly adv tadellos; (Relig) unbefleckt

imma'terial a (unimportant) unwichtig, unwesentlich

imma'ture a unreif

immediate /ɪˈmi:dɪət/ a sofortig; (nearest) nächste(r,s). ~ly adv sofort; ~ly next to unmittelbar neben ▫ conj sobald

immemorial /ɪməˈmɔ:rɪəl/ a from time ~ seit Urzeiten

immense /ɪˈmens/ a, -ly adv riesig; (fam) enorm; (extreme) äußerst

immers|e /ɪˈmɜ:s/ vt untertauchen; be ~ed in (fig) vertieft sein in (+ acc). ~ion /-ɜ:ʃn/ n Untertauchen nt. ~ion heater n Heißwasserbereiter m

immigrant /ˈɪmɪgrənt/ n Einwanderer m

immigrat|e /ˈɪmɪgreɪt/ vi einwandern. ~ion /-ˈgreɪʃn/ n Einwanderung f

imminent /ˈɪmɪnənt/ a be ~ unmittelbar bevorstehen

immobil|e /ɪˈməʊbaɪl/ a unbeweglich. ~ize /-bəlaɪz/ vt (fig) lähmen; (Med) ruhig stellen

immoderate /ɪˈmɒdərət/ a übermäßig

immodest /ɪˈmɒdɪst/ a unbescheiden

immoral /ɪˈmɒrəl/ a, -ly adv unmoralisch. ~ity /ɪməˈrælətɪ/ n Unmoral f

immortal /ɪˈmɔːtl/ a unsterblich. ~ity /-ˈtælətɪ/ n Unsterblichkeit f. ~ize vt verewigen

immovable /ɪˈmuːvəbl/ a unbeweglich; (fig) fest

immune /ɪˈmjuːn/ a immun (to/from gegen). ~ system n Abwehrsystem nt

immunity /ɪˈmjuːnɪtɪ/ n Immunität f

immunize /ˈɪmjʊnaɪz/ vt immunisieren

imp /ɪmp/ n Kobold m

impact /ˈɪmpækt/ n Aufprall m; (collision) Zusammenprall m; (of bomb) Einschlag m; (fig) Auswirkung f

impair /ɪmˈpeə(r)/ vt beeinträchtigen

impale /ɪmˈpeɪl/ vt aufspießen

impart /ɪmˈpɑːt/ vt übermitteln (to dat); vermitteln ⟨knowledge⟩

im'parti|al a unparteiisch. ~'ality n Unparteilichkeit f

im'passable a unpassierbar

impasse /æmˈpɑːs/ n (fig) Sackgasse f

impassioned /ɪmˈpæʃnd/ a leidenschaftlich

im'passive a, -ly adv unbeweglich

im'patien|ce n Ungeduld f. ~t a, -ly adv ungeduldig

impeach /ɪmˈpiːtʃ/ vt anklagen

impeccable /ɪmˈpekəbl/ a, -bly adv tadellos

impede /ɪmˈpiːd/ vt behindern

impediment /ɪmˈpedɪmənt/ n Hindernis nt; (in speech) Sprachfehler m

impel /ɪmˈpel/ vt (pt/pp impelled) treiben; feel ~led sich genötigt fühlen (to zu)

impending /ɪmˈpendɪŋ/ a bevorstehend

impenetrable /ɪmˈpenɪtrəbl/ a undurchdringlich

imperative /ɪmˈperətɪv/ a be ~ dringend notwendig sein □ n (Gram) Imperativ m, Befehlsform f

imper'ceptible a nicht wahrnehmbar

im'perfect a unvollkommen; (faulty) fehlerhaft □ n (Gram) Imperfekt nt. ~ion /-ˈfekʃn/ n Unvollkommenheit f; (fault) Fehler m

imperial /ɪmˈpɪərɪəl/ a kaiserlich. ~ism n Imperialismus m

imperil /ɪmˈperəl/ vt (pt/pp imperilled) gefährden

imperious /ɪmˈpɪərɪəs/ a, -ly adv herrisch

im'personal a unpersönlich

impersonat|e /ɪmˈpɜːsəneɪt/ vt sich ausgeben als; (Theat) nachahmen, imitieren. ~or n Imitator m

impertinen|ce /ɪmˈpɜːtɪnəns/ n Frechheit f. ~t a frech

imperturbable /ɪmpəˈtɜːbəbl/ a unerschütterlich

impervious /ɪmˈpɜːvɪəs/ a ~ to (fig) unempfänglich für

impetuous /ɪmˈpetjʊəs/ a, -ly adv ungestüm

impetus /ˈɪmpɪtəs/ n Schwung m

impish /ˈɪmpɪʃ/ a schelmisch

implacable /ɪmˈplækəbl/ a unerbittlich

im'plant[1] vt einpflanzen

'implant[2] n Implantat nt

implement[1] /ˈɪmplɪmənt/ n Gerät nt

implement[2] /ˈɪmplɪment/ vt ausführen

implicat|e /ˈɪmplɪkeɪt/ vt verwickeln. ~ion /-ˈkeɪʃn/ n Verwicklung f; ~ions pl Auswirkungen pl; by ~ion implizit

implicit /ɪmˈplɪsɪt/ a, -ly adv unausgesprochen; (absolute) unbedingt

implore /ɪmˈplɔː(r)/ vt anflehen

imply /ɪmˈplaɪ/ vt (pt/pp -ied) andeuten; what are you ~ing? was wollen Sie damit sagen?

impo'lite a, -ly adv unhöflich

import[1] /ˈɪmpɔːt/ n Import m, Einfuhr f; (importance) Wichtigkeit f; (meaning) Bedeutung f

import[2] /ɪmˈpɔːt/ vt importieren, einführen

importan|ce /ɪmˈpɔːtns/ n Wichtigkeit f. ~t a wichtig

importer /ɪmˈpɔːtə(r)/ n Importeur m

impos|e /ɪmˈpəʊz/ vt auferlegen (on dat) □ vi sich aufdrängen (on dat). ~ing a eindrucksvoll. ~ition /ɪmpəˈzɪʃn/ n be an ~ition eine Zumutung sein

impossi'bility n Unmöglichkeit f

im'possible a, -bly adv unmöglich

impostor /ɪmˈpɒstə(r)/ n Betrüger(in) m(f)

impoten|ce /ˈɪmpətəns/ n Machtlosigkeit f; (Med) Impotenz f. ~t a machtlos; (Med) impotent

impound /ɪmˈpaʊnd/ vt beschlagnahmen

impoverished /ɪmˈpɒvərɪʃt/ a verarmt

im'practicable a undurchführbar

im'practical a unpraktisch

impre'cise a ungenau

impregnable /ɪmˈpregnəbl/ a uneinnehmbar

impregnate /ˈɪmpregneɪt/ vt tränken; (Biol) befruchten

im'press vt beeindrucken; ~ sth [up]on s.o. jdm etw einprägen

impression /ɪmˈpreʃn/ n Eindruck m; (imitation) Nachahmung f; (imprint) Abdruck m; (edition) Auflage f. ~ism n Impressionismus m

impressive /ɪmˈpresɪv/ a eindrucksvoll

'imprint¹ n Abdruck m

im'print² vt prägen; (fig) einprägen (on dat)

im'prison vt gefangen halten; (put in prison) ins Gefängnis sperren

im'probable a unwahrscheinlich

impromptu /ɪm'prɒmptju:/ a improvisiert □ adv aus dem Stegreif

im'proper a, -ly adv inkorrekt; (indecent) unanständig

impro'priety n Unkorrektheit f

improve /ɪm'pru:v/ vt verbessern; verschönern ⟨appearance⟩ □ vi sich bessern; ∼ [up]on übertreffen. ∼ment /-mənt/ n Verbesserung f; (in health) Besserung f

improvise /'ɪmprəvaɪz/ vt/i improvisieren

im'prudent a unklug

impuden|ce /'ɪmpjʊdəns/ n Frechheit f. ∼t a, -ly adv frech

impuls|e /'ɪmpʌls/ n Impuls m; on [an] ∼e impulsiv. ∼ive /-'pʌlsɪv/ a, -ly adv impulsiv

impunity /ɪm'pju:nətɪ/ n with ∼ ungestraft

im'pur|e a unrein. ∼ity n Unreinheit f; ∼ities pl Verunreinigungen pl

impute /ɪm'pju:t/ vt zuschreiben (to dat)

in /ɪn/ prep in (+ dat/(into) + acc); sit in the garden im Garten sitzen; go in the garden in den Garten gehen; in May im Mai; in the summer/winter im Sommer/ Winter; in 1992 [im Jahre] 1992; in this heat bei dieser Hitze; in the rain/sun im Regen/in der Sonne; in the evening am Abend; in the sky am Himmel; in the world auf der Welt; in the street auf der Straße; deaf in one ear auf einem Ohr taub; in the army beim Militär; in English/German auf Englisch/Deutsch; in ink/pencil mit Tinte/Bleistift; in a soft/loud voice mit leiser/lauter Stimme; in doing this, he ... indem er das tut/tat, ... er □ adv (at home) zu Hause; (indoors) drinnen; he's not in yet er ist noch nicht da; all in alles inbegriffen; (fam: exhausted) kaputt; day in, day out tagaus, tagein; keep in with s.o. sich mit jdm gut stellen; have it in for s.o. (fam) es auf jdn abgesehen haben; let oneself in for sth sich auf etw (acc) einlassen; send/go in hineinschicken/-gehen; come/bring in hereinkommen/-bringen □ a (fam: in fashion) in □ n the ins and outs alle Einzelheiten pl

ina'bility n Unfähigkeit f

inac'cessible a unzugänglich

in'accura|cy n Ungenauigkeit f. ∼te a, -ly adv ungenau

in'ac|tive a untätig. ∼'tivity n Untätigkeit f

in'adequate a, -ly adv unzulänglich; feel ∼ sich der Situation nicht gewachsen fühlen

inad'missable a unzulässig

inadvertently /ɪnəd'vɜ:təntlɪ/ adv versehentlich

inad'visable a nicht ratsam

inane /ɪ'neɪn/ a, -ly adv albern

in'animate a unbelebt

in'applicable a nicht zutreffend

inap'propriate a unangebracht

inar'ticulate a undeutlich; be ∼ sich nicht gut ausdrücken können

inat'tentive a unaufmerksam

in'audible a, -bly adv unhörbar

inaugural /ɪ'nɔ:gjʊrl/ a Antritts-

inaugurat|e /ɪ'nɔ:gjʊreɪt/ vt [feierlich] in sein Amt einführen. ∼ion /-'reɪʃn/ n Amtseinführung f

inau'spicious a ungünstig

inborn /'ɪnbɔ:n/ a angeboren

inbred /ɪn'bred/ a angeboren

incalculable /ɪn'kælkjʊləbl/ a nicht berechenbar; (fig) unabsehbar

in'capable a unfähig; be ∼ of doing sth nicht fähig sein, etw zu tun

incapacitate /ɪnkə'pæsɪteɪt/ vt unfähig machen

incarcerate /ɪn'kɑ:səreɪt/ vt einkerkern

incarnat|e /ɪn'kɑ:nət/ a the devil ∼e der leibhaftige Satan. ∼ion /-'neɪʃn/ n Inkarnation f

incendiary /ɪn'sendɪərɪ/ a & n ∼ [bomb] Brandbombe f

incense¹ /'ɪnsens/ n Weihrauch m

incense² /ɪn'sens/ vt wütend machen

incentive /ɪn'sentɪv/ n Anreiz m

inception /ɪn'sepʃn/ n Beginn m

incessant /ɪn'sesnt/ a, -ly adv unaufhörlich

incest /'ɪnsest/ n Inzest m, Blutschande f

inch /ɪntʃ/ n Zoll m □ vi ∼ forward sich ganz langsam vorwärts schieben

inciden|ce /'ɪnsɪdəns/ n Vorkommen nt. ∼t n Zwischenfall m

incidental /ɪnsɪ'dentl/ a nebensächlich; ⟨remark⟩ beiläufig; ⟨expenses⟩ Neben-. ∼ly adv übrigens

incinerat|e /ɪn'sɪnəreɪt/ vt verbrennen. ∼or n Verbrennungsofen m

incipient /ɪn'sɪpɪənt/ a angehend

incision /ɪn'sɪʒn/ n Einschnitt m

incisive /ɪn'saɪsɪv/ a scharfsinnig

incisor /ɪn'saɪzə(r)/ n Schneidezahn m

incite /ɪnˈsaɪt/ vt aufhetzen. ~ment n Aufhetzung f

inci'vility n Unhöflichkeit f

in'clement a rau

inclination /ˌɪnklɪˈneɪʃn/ n Neigung f

incline¹ /ɪnˈklaɪn/ vt neigen; be ~d to do sth dazu neigen, etw zu tun ☐ vi sich neigen

incline² /ˈɪnklaɪn/ n Neigung f

inclu|de /ɪnˈkluːd/ vt einschließen; (contain) enthalten; (incorporate) aufnehmen (in in + acc). ~ding prep einschließlich (+ gen). ~sion /-ˈuːʒn/ n Aufnahme f

inclusive /ɪnˈkluːsɪv/ a Inklusiv-; ~ of einschließlich (+ gen) ☐ adv inklusive

incognito /ɪnkɒgˈniːtəʊ/ adv inkognito

inco'herent a, -ly adv zusammenhanglos; (incomprehensible) unverständlich

income /ˈɪnkʌm/ n Einkommen nt. ~ tax n Einkommensteuer f

'incoming a ankommend; (mail, call) eingehend. ~ tide n steigende Flut f

in'comparable a unvergleichlich

incom'patible a unvereinbar; be ~ ⟨people:⟩ nicht zueinander passen

in'competen|ce n Unfähigkeit f. ~t a unfähig

incom'plete a unvollständig

incompre'hensible a unverständlich

incon'ceivable a undenkbar

incon'clusive a nicht schlüssig

incongruous /ɪnˈkɒŋgrʊəs/ a unpassend

inconsequential /ɪnkɒnsɪˈkwenʃl/ a unbedeutend

incon'siderate a rücksichtslos

incon'sisten|t a, -ly adv widersprüchlich; (illogical) inkonsequent; be ~ nicht übereinstimmen

inconsolable /ɪnkənˈsəʊləbl/ a untröstlich

incon'spicuous a unauffällig

incon'tinen|ce n /ɪnˈkɒntɪnəns/ n Inkontinenz f. ~t a inkontinent

incon'venien|ce n Unannehmlichkeit f; (drawback) Nachteil m; put s.o. to ~ce jdm Umstände machen. ~t a, -ly adv ungünstig; be ~t for s.o. jdm nicht passen

incorporate /ɪnˈkɔːpəreɪt/ vt aufnehmen; (contain) enthalten

incor'rect a, -ly adv inkorrekt

incorrigible /ɪnˈkɒrɪdʒəbl/ a unverbesserlich

incorruptible /ɪnkəˈrʌptəbl/ a unbestechlich

increase¹ /ˈɪnkriːs/ n Zunahme f; (rise) Erhöhung f; be on the ~ zunehmen

increas|e² /ɪnˈkriːs/ vt vergrößern; (raise) erhöhen ☐ vi zunehmen; (rise) sich erhöhen. ~ing a, -ly adv zunehmend

in'credible a, -bly adv unglaublich

incredulous /ɪnˈkredjʊləs/ a ungläubig

increment /ˈɪnkrɪmənt/ n Gehaltszulage f

incriminate /ɪnˈkrɪmɪneɪt/ vt (Jur) belasten

incubat|e /ˈɪŋkjʊbeɪt/ vt ausbrüten. ~ion /-ˈbeɪʃn/ n Ausbrüten nt. ~ion period n (Med) Inkubationszeit f. ~or n (for baby) Brutkasten m

inculcate /ˈɪnkʌlkeɪt/ vt einprägen (in dat)

incumbent /ɪnˈkʌmbənt/ a be ~ on s.o. jds Pflicht sein

incur /ɪnˈkɜː(r)/ vt (pt/pp incurred) sich (dat) zuziehen; machen ⟨debts⟩

in'curable a, -bly adv unheilbar

incursion /ɪnˈkɜːʃn/ n Einfall m

indebted /ɪnˈdetɪd/ a verpflichtet (to dat)

in'decent a, -ly adv unanständig

inde'cision n Unentschlossenheit f

inde'cisive a ergebnislos; ⟨person⟩ unentschlossen

indeed /ɪnˈdiːd/ adv in der Tat, tatsächlich; yes ~! allerdings! ~ I am/do oh doch! very much ~ sehr; thank you very much ~ vielen herzlichen Dank

indefatigable /ɪndɪˈfætɪgəbl/ a unermüdlich

in'definite a unbestimmt. ~ly adv unbegrenzt; (postpone) auf unbestimmte Zeit

indelible /ɪnˈdelɪbl/ a, -bly adv nicht zu entfernen; (fig) unauslöschlich

indemni|fy /ɪnˈdemnɪfaɪ/ vt (pt/pp -ied) versichern; (compensate) entschädigen. ~ty n Versicherung f; Entschädigung f

indent /ɪnˈdent/ vt (Typ) einrücken. ~ation /-ˈteɪʃn/ n Einrückung f; (notch) Kerbe f

inde'penden|ce n Unabhängigkeit f; (self-reliance) Selbstständigkeit f. ~t a, -ly adv unabhängig; selbstständig

indescribable /ɪndɪˈskraɪbəbl/ a, -bly adv unbeschreiblich

indestructible /ɪndɪˈstrʌktəbl/ a unzerstörbar

indeterminate /ɪndɪˈtɜːmɪnət/ a unbestimmt

index /ˈɪndeks/ n Register nt

index: ~ card n Karteikarte f. ~ finger n Zeigefinger m. ~-linked a ⟨pension⟩ dynamisch

India /ˈɪndɪə/ n Indien nt. ~n a indisch; (American) indianisch ☐ n Inder(in) m(f); (American) Indianer(in) m(f)

Indian: ~ 'ink *n* Tusche *f*. ~ 'summer *n* Nachsommer *m*

indicat|e /'ɪndɪkeɪt/ *vt* zeigen; (*point at*) zeigen auf (+ *acc*); (*hint*) andeuten; (*register*) anzeigen □ *vi* (*Auto*) blinken. ~ion /-'keɪʃn/ *n* Anzeichen *nt*

indicative /ɪn'dɪkətɪv/ *a* be ~ of schließen lassen auf (+ *acc*) □ *n* (*Gram*) Indikativ *m*

indicator /'ɪndɪkeɪtə(r)/ *n* (*Auto*) Blinker *m*

indict /ɪn'daɪt/ *vt* anklagen. ~ment *n* Anklage *f*

in'differen|ce *n* Gleichgültigkeit *f*. ~t *a*, -ly *adv* gleichgültig; (*not good*) mittelmäßig

indigenous /ɪn'dɪdʒɪnəs/ *a* einheimisch

indi'gest|ible *a* unverdaulich; (*difficult to digest*) schwer verdaulich; ~ion *n* Magenverstimmung *f*

indigna|nt /ɪn'dɪgnənt/ *a*, -ly *adv* entrüstet, empört. ~tion /-'neɪʃn/ *n* Entrüstung *f*, Empörung *f*

in'dignity *n* Demütigung *f*

indi'rect *a*, -ly *adv* indirekt

indi'screet *a* indiskret

indis'cretion *n* Indiskretion *f*

indiscriminate /ɪndɪ'skrɪmɪnət/ *a*, -ly *adv* wahllos

indi'spensable *a* unentbehrlich

indisposed /ɪndɪ'spəʊzd/ *a* indisponiert

indisputable /ɪndɪ'spju:təbl/ *a*, -bly *adv* unbestreitbar

indi'stinct *a*, -ly *adv* undeutlich

indistinguishable /ɪndɪ'stɪŋgwɪʃəbl/ *a* be ~ nicht zu unterscheiden sein; (*not visible*) nicht erkennbar sein

individual /ɪndɪ'vɪdjʊəl/ *a*, -ly *adv* individuell; (*single*) einzeln □ *n* Individuum *nt*. ~ity /-'ælətɪ/ *n* Individualität *f*

indi'visible *a* unteilbar

indoctrinate /ɪn'dɒktrɪneɪt/ *vt* indoktrinieren

indolen|ce /'ɪndələns/ *n* Faulheit *f*. ~t *a* faul

indomitable /ɪn'dɒmɪtəbl/ *a* unbeugsam

indoor /'ɪndɔ:(r)/ *a* Innen-; (*clothes*) Haus-; (*plant*) Zimmer-; (*Sport*) Hallen-. ~s /-'dɔ:z/ *adv* im Haus, drinnen; go ~s ins Haus gehen

induce /ɪn'dju:s/ *vt* dazu bewegen (to zu); (*produce*) herbeiführen. ~ment *n* (*incentive*) Anreiz *m*

indulge /ɪn'dʌldʒ/ *vt* frönen (+ *dat*); verwöhnen (*child*) □ *vi* ~ in frönen (+ *dat*). ~nce /-əns/ *n* Nachgiebigkeit *f*; (*leniency*) Nachsicht *f*. ~nt *a* [zu] nachgiebig; nachsichtig

industrial /ɪn'dʌstrɪəl/ *a* Industrie-; take ~ action streiken. ~ist *n* Industrielle(r) *m*. ~ized *a* industrialisiert

industr|ious /ɪn'dʌstrɪəs/ *a*, -ly *adv* fleißig. ~y /'ɪndəstrɪ/ *n* Industrie *f*; (*zeal*) Fleiß *m*

inebriated /ɪ'ni:brɪeɪtɪd/ *a* betrunken

in'edible *a* nicht essbar

inef'fective *a*, -ly *adv* unwirksam; (*person*) untauglich

ineffectual /ɪnɪ'fektʃʊəl/ *a* unwirksam; (*person*) untauglich

inef'ficient *a* unfähig; (*organization*) nicht leistungsfähig; (*method*) nicht rationell

in'eligible *a* nicht berechtigt

inept /ɪ'nept/ *a* ungeschickt

ine'quality *n* Ungleichheit *f*

inert /ɪ'nɜ:t/ *a* unbeweglich; (*Phys*) träge. ~ia /ɪ'nɜ:ʃə/ *n* Trägheit *f*

inescapable /ɪnɪ'skeɪpəbl/ *a* unvermeidlich

inestimable /ɪn'estɪməbl/ *a* unschätzbar

inevitab|le /ɪn'evɪtəbl/ *a* unvermeidlich. ~ly *adv* zwangsläufig

ine'xact *a* ungenau

inex'cusable *a* unverzeihlich

inexhaustible /ɪnɪg'zɔ:stəbl/ *a* unerschöpflich

inexorable /ɪn'eksərəbl/ *a* unerbittlich

inex'pensive *a*, -ly *adv* preiswert

inex'perience *n* Unerfahrenheit *f*. ~d *a* unerfahren

inexplicable /ɪnɪk'splɪkəbl/ *a* unerklärlich

in'fallible *a* unfehlbar

infam|ous /'ɪnfəməs/ *a* niederträchtig; (*notorious*) berüchtigt. ~y *n* Niederträchtigkeit *f*

infan|cy /'ɪnfənsɪ/ *n* frühe Kindheit *f*; (*fig*) Anfangsstadium *nt*. ~t *n* Kleinkind *nt*. ~tile *a* kindisch

infantry /'ɪnfəntrɪ/ *n* Infanterie *f*

infatuated /ɪn'fætʃʊeɪtɪd/ *a* vernarrt (with in + *acc*)

infect /ɪn'fekt/ *vt* anstecken, infizieren; become ~ed (*wound*) sich infizieren. ~ion /-'fekʃn/ *n* Infektion *f*. ~ious /-'fekʃəs/ *a* ansteckend

infer /ɪn'fɜ:(r)/ *vt* (*pt/pp* inferred) folgern (from aus); (*imply*) andeuten. ~ence /'ɪnfərəns/ *n* Folgerung *f*

inferior /ɪn'fɪərɪə(r)/ *a* minderwertig; (*in rank*) untergeordnet □ *n* Untergebene(r) *m/f*

inferiority /ɪnfɪərɪ'ɒrətɪ/ *n* Minderwertigkeit *f*. ~ complex *n* Minderwertigkeitskomplex *m*

infern|al /ɪnˈfɜːnl/ a höllisch. ∼o n flammendes Inferno nt

in'fer|tile a unfruchtbar. ∼'tility n Unfruchtbarkeit f

infest /ɪnˈfest/ vt be ∼ed with befallen sein von; ⟨place⟩ verseucht sein mit

infi'delity n Untreue f

infighting /ˈɪnfaɪtɪŋ/ n (fig) interne Machtkämpfe pl

infiltrate /ˈɪnfɪltreɪt/ vt infiltrieren; (Pol) unterwandern

infinite /ˈɪnfɪnət/ a, -ly adv unendlich

infinitesimal /ɪnfɪnɪˈtesɪml/ a unendlich klein

infinitive /ɪnˈfɪnətɪv/ n (Gram) Infinitiv m

infinity /ɪnˈfɪnətɪ/ n Unendlichkeit f

infirm /ɪnˈfɜːm/ a gebrechlich. ∼ary n Krankenhaus nt. ∼ity n Gebrechlichkeit f

inflame /ɪnˈfleɪm/ vt entzünden; become ∼d sich entzünden. ∼d a entzündet

in'flammable a feuergefährlich

inflammation /ɪnfləˈmeɪʃn/ n Entzündung f

inflammatory /ɪnˈflæmətrɪ/ a aufrührerisch

inflatable /ɪnˈfleɪtəbl/ a aufblasbar

inflat|e /ɪnˈfleɪt/ vt aufblasen; (with pump) aufpumpen. ∼ion /-eɪʃn/ n Inflation f. ∼ionary /-eɪʃənrɪ/ a inflationär

in'flexible a starr; ⟨person⟩ unbeugsam

inflexion /ɪnˈflekʃn/ n Tonfall m; (Gram) Flexion f

inflict /ɪnˈflɪkt/ vt zufügen (on dat); versetzen ⟨blow⟩ (on dat)

influen|ce /ˈɪnfluəns/ n Einfluss m ◻ vt beeinflussen. ∼tial /-ˈenʃl/ a einflussreich

influenza /ɪnfluˈenzə/ n Grippe f

influx /ˈɪnflʌks/ n Zustrom m

inform /ɪnˈfɔːm/ vt benachrichtigen; (officially) informieren; ∼ s.o. of sth jdm etw mitteilen; keep s.o. ∼ed jdn auf dem Laufenden halten ◻ vi ∼ against denunzieren

in'for|mal a, -ly adv zwanglos; (unofficial) inoffiziell. ∼'mality n Zwanglosigkeit f

informant /ɪnˈfɔːmənt/ n Gewährsmann m

informat|ion /ɪnfəˈmeɪʃn/ n Auskunft f; a piece of ∼ion eine Auskunft. ∼ive /ɪnˈfɔːmətɪv/ a aufschlussreich; (instructive) lehrreich

informer /ɪnˈfɔːmə(r)/ n Spitzel m; (Pol) Denunziant m

infra-red /ɪnfrə-/ a infrarot

in'frequent a, -ly adv selten

infringe /ɪnˈfrɪndʒ/ vt/i ∼ [on] verstoßen gegen. ∼ment n Verstoß m

infuriat|e /ɪnˈfjʊərɪeɪt/ vt wütend machen. ∼ing a ärgerlich; he is ∼ing er kann einen zur Raserei bringen

infusion /ɪnˈfjuːʒn/ n Aufguss m

ingenious /ɪnˈdʒiːnɪəs/ a erfinderisch; ⟨thing⟩ raffiniert

ingenuity /ɪndʒɪˈnjuːətɪ/ n Geschicklichkeit f

ingenuous /ɪnˈdʒenjʊəs/ a unschuldig

ingot /ˈɪŋgət/ n Barren m

ingrained /ɪnˈgreɪnd/ a eingefleischt; be ∼ ⟨dirt:⟩ tief sitzen

ingratiate /ɪnˈgreɪʃɪeɪt/ vt ∼ oneself sich einschmeicheln (with bei)

in'gratitude n Undankbarkeit f

ingredient /ɪnˈgriːdɪənt/ n (Culin) Zutat f

ingrowing /ˈɪngrəʊɪŋ/ a ⟨nail⟩ eingewachsen

inhabit /ɪnˈhæbɪt/ vt bewohnen. ∼ant n Einwohner(in) m(f)

inhale /ɪnˈheɪl/ vt/i einatmen; (Med & when smoking) inhalieren

inherent /ɪnˈhɪərənt/ a natürlich

inherit /ɪnˈherɪt/ vt erben. ∼ance /-əns/ n Erbschaft f, Erbe nt

inhibit /ɪnˈhɪbɪt/ vt hemmen. ∼ed a gehemmt. ∼ion /-ˈbɪʃn/ n Hemmung f

inho'spitable a ungastlich

in'human a unmenschlich

inimitable /ɪˈnɪmɪtəbl/ a unnachahmlich

iniquitous /ɪˈnɪkwɪtəs/ a schändlich; (unjust) ungerecht

initial /ɪˈnɪʃl/ n anfänglich, Anfangs- ◻ n Anfangsbuchstabe m; my ∼s meine Initialen ◻ vt (pt/pp initialled) abzeichnen; (Pol) paraphieren. ∼ly adv anfangs, am Anfang

initiat|e /ɪˈnɪʃɪeɪt/ vt einführen. ∼ion /-ˈeɪʃn/ n Einführung f

initiative /ɪˈnɪʃətɪv/ n Initiative f

inject /ɪnˈdʒekt/ vt einspritzen, injizieren. ∼ion /-ekʃn/ n Spritze f, Injektion f

injunction /ɪnˈdʒʌŋkʃn/ n gerichtliche Verfügung f

injur|e /ˈɪndʒə(r)/ vt verletzen. ∼y n Verletzung f

in'justice n Ungerechtigkeit f; do s.o. an ∼ jdm unrecht tun

ink /ɪŋk/ n Tinte f

inkling /ˈɪŋklɪŋ/ n Ahnung f

inlaid /ɪnˈleɪd/ a eingelegt

inland /ˈɪnlənd/ a Binnen- ◻ adv landeinwärts. I ∼ Revenue n ≈ Finanzamt nt

in-laws /ˈɪnlɔːz/ npl (fam) Schwiegereltern pl

inlay /'ınleı/ n Einlegearbeit f

inlet /'ınlet/ n schmale Bucht f; (Techn) Zuleitung f

inmate /'ınmeıt/ n Insasse m

inn /ın/ n Gasthaus nt

innards /'ınədz/ npl (fam) Eingeweide pl

innate /ı'neıt/ a angeboren

inner /'ınə(r)/ a innere(r,s). ~most a innerste(r,s)

'innkeeper n Gastwirt m

innocen|ce /'ınəsəns/ n Unschuld f. ~t a unschuldig. ~tly adv in aller Unschuld

innocuous /ı'nɒkjʊəs/ a harmlos

innovat|e /'ınəveıt/ vi neu einführen. ~ion /-'veıʃn/ n Neuerung f. ~or n Neuerer m

innuendo /ınju:'endəʊ/ n (pl -es) [versteckte] Anspielung f

innumerable /ı'nju:mərəbl/ a unzählig

inoculat|e /ı'nɒkjʊleıt/ vt impfen. ~ion /-'leıʃn/ n Impfung f

inof'fensive a harmlos

in'operable a nicht operierbar

in'opportune a unpassend

inordinate /ı'nɔ:dınət/ a, -ly adv übermäßig

inor'ganic a anorganisch

'in-patient n [stationär behandelter] Krankenhauspatient m

input /'ınpʊt/ n Input m & nt

inquest /'ınkwest/ n gerichtliche Untersuchung f

inquir|e /ın'kwaıə(r)/ vi sich erkundigen (about nach); ~e into untersuchen □ vt sich erkundigen nach. ~y n Erkundigung f; (investigation) Untersuchung f

inquisitive /ın'kwızətıv/ a, -ly adv neugierig

inroad /'ınrəʊd/ n Einfall m; make ~s into sth etw angreifen

in'sane a geisteskrank; (fig) wahnsinnig

in'sanitary a unhygienisch

in'sanity n Geisteskrankheit f

insatiable /ın'seıʃəbl/ a unersättlich

inscri|be /ın'skraıb/ vt eingravieren. ~ption /-'skrıpʃn/ n Inschrift f

inscrutable /ın'skru:təbl/ a unergründlich; (expression) undurchdringlich

insect /'ınsekt/ n Insekt nt. ~icide /-'sektı-saıd/ n Insektenvertilgungsmittel nt

inse'cur|e a nicht sicher; (fig) unsicher. ~ity n Unsicherheit f

insemination /ınsemı'neıʃn/ n Besamung f; (Med) Befruchtung f

in'sensible a (unconscious) bewusstlos

in'sensitive a gefühllos; ~ to unempfindlich gegen

in'separable a untrennbar; (people) unzertrennlich

insert¹ /'ınsɜ:t/ n Einsatz m

insert² /ın'sɜ:t/ vt einfügen, einsetzen; einstecken (key); einwerfen (coin). ~ion /-ɔ:ʃn/ n (insert) Einsatz m; (in text) Einfügung f

inside /ın'saıd/ n Innenseite f; (of house) Innere(s) nt □ attrib Innen- □ adv innen; (indoors) drinnen; go ~ hineingehen; come ~ hereinkommen; ~ out links [herum]; know sth ~ out etw in- und auswendig kennen □ prep ~ [of] in (+ dat) (into) + acc)

insidious /ın'sıdıəs/ a, -ly adv heimtückisch

insight /'ınsaıt/ n Einblick m (into in + acc); (understanding) Einsicht f

insignia /ın'sıgnıə/ npl Insignien pl

insig'nificant a unbedeutend

insin'cere a unaufrichtig

insinuat|e /ın'sınjʊeıt/ vt andeuten. ~ion /-'eıʃn/ n Andeutung f

insipid /ın'sıpıd/ a fade

insist /ın'sıst/ vi darauf bestehen; ~ on bestehen auf (+ dat) □ vt ~ that darauf bestehen, dass. ~ence n Bestehen nt. ~ent a, -ly adv beharrlich; be ~ent darauf bestehen

'insole n Einlegesohle f

insolen|ce /'ınsələns/ n Unverschämtheit f. ~t a, -ly adv unverschämt

in'soluble a unlöslich; (fig) unlösbar

in'solvent a zahlungsunfähig

insomnia /ın'sɒmnıə/ n Schlaflosigkeit f

inspect /ın'spekt/ vt inspizieren; (test) prüfen; kontrollieren (ticket). ~ion /-ekʃn/ n Inspektion f. ~or n Inspektor m; (of tickets) Kontrolleur m

inspiration /ınspə'reıʃn/ n Inspiration f

inspire /ın'spaıə(r)/ vt inspirieren; ~ sth in s.o. jdm etw einflößen

insta'bility n Unbeständigkeit f; (of person) Labilität f

install /ın'stɔ:l/ vt installieren; [in ein Amt] einführen (person). ~ation /-stə-'leıʃn/ n Installation f; Amtseinführung f

instalment /ın'stɔ:lmənt/ n (Comm) Rate f; (of serial) Fortsetzung f; (Radio, TV) Folge f

instance /'ınstəns/ n Fall m; (example) Beispiel nt; in the first ~ zunächst; for ~ zum Beispiel

instant /'ınstənt/ a sofortig; (Culin) Instant- □ n Augenblick m, Moment m. ~aneous /-'teınıəs/ a unverzüglich, unmittelbar; death was ~aneous der Tod trat sofort ein

instant 'coffee n Pulverkaffee m

instantly /'ɪnstəntlɪ/ adv sofort

instead /ɪn'sted/ adv statt dessen; ∼ of statt (+ gen), anstelle von; ∼ of me an meiner Stelle; ∼ of going anstatt zu gehen

'instep n Spann m, Rist m

instigat|e /'ɪnstɪgeɪt/ vt anstiften; einleiten ⟨proceedings⟩. ∼ion /-'geɪʃn/ n Anstiftung f; at his ∼ion auf seine Veranlassung. ∼or n Anstifter(in) m(f)

instil /ɪn'stɪl/ vt (pt/pp instilled) einprägen (into s.o. jdm)

instinct /'ɪnstɪŋkt/ n Instinkt m. ∼ive /ɪn'stɪŋktɪv/ a, -ly adv instinktiv

institut|e /'ɪnstɪtjuːt/ n Institut nt □ vt einführen: einleiten ⟨search⟩. ∼ion /-'tjuːʃn/ n Institution f; ⟨home⟩ Anstalt f

instruct /ɪn'strʌkt/ vt unterrichten; ⟨order⟩ anweisen. ∼ion /-ʌkʃn/ n Unterricht m; Anweisung f; ∼ions pl for use Gebrauchsanweisung f. ∼ive /-ɪv/ a lehrreich. ∼or n Lehrer(in) m(f); ⟨Mil⟩ Ausbilder m

instrument /'ɪnstrəmənt/ n Instrument nt. ∼al /-'mentl/ a Instrumental-; be ∼al in eine entscheidende Rolle spielen bei

insu'bordi|nate a ungehorsam. ∼nation /-'neɪʃn/ n Ungehorsam m; ⟨Mil⟩ Insubordination f

in'sufferable a unerträglich

insuf'ficient a, -ly adv nicht genügend

insular /'ɪnsjʊlə(r)/ a ⟨fig⟩ engstirnig

insulat|e /'ɪnsjʊleɪt/ vt isolieren. ∼ing tape n Isolierband nt. ∼ion /-'leɪʃn/ n Isolierung f

insulin /'ɪnsjʊlɪn/ n Insulin nt

insult¹ /'ɪnsʌlt/ n Beleidigung f

insult² /ɪn'sʌlt/ vt beleidigen

insuperable /ɪn'suːpərəbl/ a unüberwindlich

insur|ance /ɪn'ʃʊərəns/ n Versicherung f. ∼e vt versichern

insurrection /ɪnsə'rekʃn/ n Aufstand m

intact /ɪn'tækt/ a unbeschädigt; ⟨complete⟩ vollständig

'intake n Aufnahme f

in'tangible a nicht greifbar

integral /'ɪntɪgrl/ a wesentlich

integrat|e /'ɪntɪgreɪt/ vt integrieren □ vi sich integrieren. ∼ion /-'greɪʃn/ n Integration f

integrity /ɪn'tegrətɪ/ n Integrität f

intellect /'ɪntəlekt/ n Intellekt m. ∼ual /-'lektjʊəl/ a intellektuell

intelligen|ce /ɪn'telɪdʒəns/ n Intelligenz f; ⟨Mil⟩ Nachrichtendienst m; ⟨information⟩ Meldungen pl. ∼t a, -ly adv intelligent

intelligentsia /ɪntelɪ'dʒentsɪə/ n Intelligenz f

intelligible /ɪn'telɪdʒəbl/ a verständlich

intend /ɪn'tend/ vt beabsichtigen; be ∼ed for bestimmt sein für

intense /ɪn'tens/ a intensiv; ⟨pain⟩ stark. ∼ly adv äußerst; ⟨study⟩ intensiv

intensi|fication /ɪntensɪfɪ'keɪʃn/ n Intensivierung f. ∼fy /-'tensɪfaɪ/ v (pt/pp -ied) □ vt intensivieren □ vi zunehmen

intensity /ɪn'tensətɪ/ n Intensität f

intensive /ɪn'tensɪv/ a, -ly adv intensiv; be in ∼ care auf der Intensivstation sein

intent /ɪn'tent/ a, -ly adv aufmerksam; ∼ on ⟨absorbed in⟩ vertieft in (+ acc); be ∼ on doing sth fest entschlossen sein, etw zu tun □ n Absicht f; to all ∼s and purposes im Grunde

intention /ɪn'tenʃn/ n Absicht f. ∼al a, -ly adv absichtlich

inter /ɪn'tɜː(r)/ vt (pt/pp interred) bestatten

inter'action n Wechselwirkung f

intercede /ɪntə'siːd/ vi Fürsprache einlegen (on behalf of für)

intercept /ɪntə'sept/ vt abfangen

'interchange¹ n Austausch m; ⟨Auto⟩ Autobahnkreuz nt

inter'change² vt austauschen. ∼able a austauschbar

intercom /'ɪntəkɒm/ n [Gegen]sprechanlage f

'intercourse n Verkehr m; ⟨sexual⟩ Geschlechtsverkehr m

interest /'ɪntrəst/ n Interesse nt; ⟨Comm⟩ Zinsen pl; have an ∼ ⟨Comm⟩ beteiligt sein (in an + dat) □ vt interessieren; be ∼ed sich interessieren (in für). ∼ing a interessant. ∼ rate n Zinssatz m

interfere /ɪntə'fɪə(r)/ vi sich einmischen. ∼nce /-əns/ n Einmischung f; ⟨Radio, TV⟩ Störung f

interim /'ɪntərɪm/ a Zwischen-; ⟨temporary⟩ vorläufig □ n in the ∼ in der Zwischenzeit

interior /ɪn'tɪərɪə(r)/ a innere(r,s), Innen- □ n Innere(s) nt

interject /ɪntə'dʒekt/ vt einwerfen. ∼ion /-ekʃn/ n Interjektion f; ⟨remark⟩ Einwurf m

inter'lock vi ineinander greifen

interloper /'ɪntələʊpə(r)/ n Eindringling m

interlude /'ɪntəluːd/ n Pause f; ⟨performance⟩ Zwischenspiel n

inter'marry vi untereinander heiraten; ⟨different groups:⟩ Mischehen schließen

intermediary /ɪntə'miːdɪərɪ/ n Vermittler(in) m(f)

intermediate /ɪntəˈmiːdɪət/ a Zwischen-

interminable /ɪnˈtɜːmɪnəbl/ a endlos [lang]

intermission /ɪntəˈmɪʃn/ n Pause f

intermittent /ɪntəˈmɪtənt/ a in Abständen auftretend

intern /ɪnˈtɜːn/ vt internieren

internal /ɪnˈtɜːnl/ a innere(r,s); ⟨matter, dispute⟩ intern. ~ly adv innerlich; ⟨deal with⟩ intern

inter'national a, -ly adv international □ n Länderspiel nt; ⟨player⟩ Nationalspieler(in) m(f)

internist /ɪnˈtɜːnɪst/ n (Amer) Internist m

internment /ɪnˈtɜːnmənt/ n Internierung f

'interplay n Wechselspiel nt

interpolate /ɪnˈtɜːpəleɪt/ vt einwerfen

interpret /ɪnˈtɜːprɪt/ vt interpretieren; auslegen ⟨text⟩; deuten ⟨dream⟩; ⟨translate⟩ dolmetschen □ vi dolmetschen. ~ation /-ˈteɪʃn/ n Interpretation f. ~er n Dolmetscher(in) m(f)

interre'lated a verwandt; ⟨facts⟩ zusammenhängend

interrogate /ɪnˈterəgeɪt/ vt verhören. ~ion /-ˈgeɪʃn/ n Verhör nt

interrogative /ɪntəˈrɒgətɪv/ a & n ~ [pronoun] Interrogativpronomen nt

interrupt /ɪntəˈrʌpt/ vt/i unterbrechen; don't ~! red nicht dazwischen! ~ion /-ˈʌpʃn/ n Unterbrechung f

intersect /ɪntəˈsekt/ vi sich kreuzen; (Geom) sich schneiden. ~ion /-ekʃn/ n Kreuzung f

interspersed /ɪntəˈspɜːst/ a ~ with durchsetzt mit

inter'twine vi sich ineinander schlingen

interval /ˈɪntəvl/ n Abstand m; (Theat) Pause f; (Mus) Intervall nt; at hourly ~s alle Stunde; bright ~s pl Aufheiterungen pl

intervene /ɪntəˈviːn/ vi eingreifen; ⟨occur⟩ dazwischenkommen. ~tion /-ˈvenʃn/ n Eingreifen nt; (Mil, Pol) Intervention f

interview /ˈɪntəvjuː/ n (Journ) Interview nt; (for job) Vorstellungsgespräch nt; go for an ~ sich vorstellen □ vt interviewen; ein Vorstellungsgespräch führen mit. ~er n Interviewer(in) m(f)

intestine /ɪnˈtestɪn/ n Darm m

intimacy /ˈɪntɪməsɪ/ n Vertrautheit f; (sexual) Intimität f

intimate¹ /ˈɪntɪmət/ a, -ly adv vertraut; ⟨friend⟩ eng; (sexually) intim

intimate² /ˈɪntɪmeɪt/ vt zu verstehen geben; (imply) andeuten

intimidate /ɪnˈtɪmɪdeɪt/ vt einschüchtern. ~ion /-ˈdeɪʃn/ n Einschüchterung f

into /ˈɪntə, vor einem Vokal ˈɪntʊ/ prep in (+ acc); go ~ the house ins Haus [hinein]gehen; be ~ (fam) sich auskennen mit; 7 ~ 21 21 [geteilt] durch 7

in'tolerable a unerträglich

in'toleran|ce n Intoleranz f. ~t a intolerant

intonation /ɪntəˈneɪʃn/ n Tonfall m

intoxicat|ed /ɪnˈtɒksɪkeɪtɪd/ a betrunken; (fig) berauscht. ~ion /-ˈkeɪʃn/ n Rausch m

intractable /ɪnˈtræktəbl/ a widerspenstig; ⟨problem⟩ hartnäckig

intransigent /ɪnˈtrænsɪdʒənt/ a unnachgiebig

in'transitive a, -ly adv intransitiv

intravenous /ɪntrəˈviːnəs/ a, -ly adv intravenös

intrepid /ɪnˈtrepɪd/ a kühn, unerschrocken

intricate /ˈɪntrɪkət/ a kompliziert

intrigue /ɪnˈtriːg/ n Intrige f □ vt faszinieren □ vi intrigieren. ~ing a faszinierend

intrinsic /ɪnˈtrɪnsɪk/ a ~ value Eigenwert m

introduce /ɪntrəˈdjuːs/ vt vorstellen; (bring in, insert) einführen

introduct|ion /ɪntrəˈdʌkʃn/ n Einführung f; (to person) Vorstellung f; (to book) Einleitung f. ~ory /-tərɪ/ a einleitend

introspective /ɪntrəˈspektɪv/ a in sich (acc) gerichtet

introvert /ˈɪntrəvɜːt/ n introvertierter Mensch m

intru|de /ɪnˈtruːd/ vi stören. ~der n Eindringling m. ~sion /-uːʒn/ n Störung f

intuit|ion /ɪntjuːˈɪʃn/ n Intuition f. ~ive /-ˈtjuːɪtɪv/ a, -ly adv intuitiv

inundate /ˈɪnəndeɪt/ vt überschwemmen

invade /ɪnˈveɪd/ vt einfallen in (+ acc). ~r n Angreifer m

invalid¹ /ˈɪnvəlɪd/ n Kranke(r) m/f

invalid² /ɪnˈvælɪd/ a ungültig. ~ate vt ungültig machen

in'valuable a unschätzbar; ⟨person⟩ unersetzlich

in'variab|le a unveränderlich. ~ly adv immer

invasion /ɪnˈveɪʒn/ n Invasion f

invective /ɪnˈvektɪv/ n Beschimpfungen pl

invent /ɪnˈvent/ vt erfinden. ~ion /-enʃn/ n Erfindung f. ~ive /-tɪv/ a erfinderisch. ~or n Erfinder m

inventory /'ınvəntrı/ n Bestandsliste f; make an ~ ein Inventar aufstellen

inverse /ın'vɜ:s/ a, -ly adv umgekehrt □ n Gegenteil nt

invert /ın'vɜ:t/ vt umkehren. ~ed commas npl Anführungszeichen pl

invest /ın'vest/ vt investieren, anlegen; ~ in (fam: buy) sich (dat) zulegen

investigat|e /ın'vestıgeıt/ vt untersuchen. ~ion /-'geıʃn/ n Untersuchung f

invest|ment /ın'vestmənt/ n Anlage f; be a good ~ment (fig) sich bezahlt machen. ~or n Kapitalanleger m

inveterate /ın'vetərət/ a Gewohnheits-; ⟨liar⟩ unverbesserlich

invidious /ın'vıdıəs/ a unerfreulich; (unfair) ungerecht

invigilate /ın'vıdʒıleıt/ vi (Sch) Aufsicht führen

invigorate /ın'vıgəreıt/ vt beleben

invincible /ın'vınsəbl/ a unbesiegbar

inviolable /ın'vaıələbl/ a unantastbar

in'visible a unsichtbar. ~ mending n Kunststopfen nt

invitation /ınvı'teıʃn/ n Einladung f

invit|e /ın'vaıt/ vt einladen. ~ing a einladend

invoice /'ınvɔıs/ n Rechnung f □ vt ~ s.o. jdm eine Rechnung schicken

invoke /ın'vəʊk/ vt anrufen

in'voluntary a, -ily adv unwillkürlich

involve /ın'vɒlv/ vt beteiligen; (affect) betreffen; (implicate) verwickeln; (entail) mit sich bringen; (mean) bedeuten; be ~d in beteiligt sein an (+ dat); (implicated) verwickelt sein in (+ acc); get ~d with s.o. sich mit jdm einlassen. ~d a kompliziert

in'vulnerable a unverwundbar; ⟨position⟩ unangreifbar

inward /'ınwəd/ a innere(r,s). ~ly adv innerlich. ~s adv nach innen

iodine /'aıədi:n/ n Jod nt

iota /aı'əʊtə/ n Jota nt, (fam) Funke m

IOU abbr (I owe you) Schuldschein m

Iran /ı'rɑ:n/ n der Iran

Iraq /ı'rɑ:k/ n der Irak

irascible /ı'ræsəbl/ a aufbrausend

irate /aı'reıt/ a wütend

Ireland /'aıələnd/ n Irland nt

iris /'aıərıs/ n (Anat) Regenbogenhaut f, Iris f; (Bot) Schwertlilie f

Irish /'aıərıʃ/ a irisch □ n the ~ pl die Iren. ~man n Ire m. ~woman n Irin f

irk /ɜ:k/ vt ärgern. ~some /-səm/ a lästig

iron /'aıən/ a Eisen-; (fig) eisern □ n Eisen nt; (appliance) Bügeleisen nt □ vt/i bügeln. ~ out vt ausbügeln

ironic[al] /aı'rɒnık[l]/ a ironisch

ironing /'aıənıŋ/ n Bügeln nt; (articles) Bügelwäsche f; do the ~ bügeln. ~board n Bügelbrett nt

ironmonger /-mʌŋgə(r)/ n ~'s [shop] Haushaltswarengeschäft nt

irony /'aıərənı/ n Ironie f

irradiate /ı'reıdıeıt/ vt bestrahlen

irrational /ı'ræʃənl/ a irrational

irreconcilable /ı'rekənsaıləbl/ a unversöhnlich

irrefutable /ırı'fju:təbl/ a unwiderlegbar

irregular /ı'regjʊlə(r)/ a, -ly adv unregelmäßig; (against rules) regelwidrig. ~ity /-'lærətı/ n Unregelmäßigkeit f; Regelwidrigkeit f

irrelevant /ı'reləvənt/ a irrelevant

irreparable /ı'repərəbl/ a unersetzlich; be ~ nicht wieder gutzumachen sein

irreplaceable /ırı'pleısəbl/ a unersetzlich

irrepressible /ırı'presəbl/ a unverwüstlich; be ~ ⟨person:⟩ nicht unterzukriegen sein

irresistible /ırı'zıstəbl/ a unwiderstehlich

irresolute /ı'rezəlu:t/ a unentschlossen

irrespective /ırı'spektıv/ a ~ of ungeachtet (+ gen)

irresponsible /ırı'spɒnsəbl/ a, -bly adv unverantwortlich; ⟨person⟩ verantwortungslos

irreverent /ı'revərənt/ a, -ly adv respektlos

irreversible /ırı'vɜ:səbl/ a unwiderruflich; (Med) irreversibel

irrevocable /ı'revəkəbl/ a, -bly adv unwiderruflich

irrigat|e /'ırıgeıt/ vt bewässern. ~ion /-'geıʃn/ n Bewässerung f

irritability /ırıtə'bılətı/ n Gereiztheit f

irritable /'ırıtəbl/ a reizbar

irritant /'ırıtənt/ n Reizstoff m

irritat|e /'ırıteıt/ vt irritieren; (Med) reizen. ~ion /-'teıʃn/ n Ärger m; (Med) Reizung f

is /ız/ see be

Islam /'ızlɑ:m/ n der Islam. ~ic /ı'læmık/ a islamisch

island /'aılənd/ n Insel f. ~er n Inselbewohner(in) m(f)

isle /aıl/ n Insel f

isolat|e /'aısəleıt/ vt isolieren. ~d a (remote) abgelegen; (single) einzeln. ~ion /-'leıʃn/ n Isoliertheit f; (Med) Isolierung f

Israel /'ızreıl/ n Israel nt. ~i /ız'reılı/ a israelisch □ n Israeli m/f issue /'ıʃu:/ n Frage f; (outcome) Ergebnis nt; (of magazine, stamps) Ausgabe f; (offspring) Nachkommen pl; what is at ∼? worum geht es? take ∼ with s.o. jdm widersprechen ◻ vt ausgeben; ausstellen (passport); erteilen (order); herausgeben (book); be ∼d with sth etw erhalten ◻ vi ∼ from herausströmen aus

isthmus /'ısməs/ n (pl -muses) Landenge f

it /ıt/ pron es; (m) er; (f) sie; (as direct object) es; (m) ihn; (f) sie; (as indirect object) ihm; (f) ihr; it is raining es regnet; it's me ich bin's; who is it? wer ist da? of/from it davon; with it damit; out of it daraus

Italian /ı'tæljən/ a italienisch ◻ n Italiener(in) m(f); (Lang) Italienisch nt

italic /ı'tælık/ a kursiv. ∼s npl Kursivschrift f; in ∼s kursiv

Italy /'ıtəlı/ n Italien nt

itch /ıtʃ/ n Juckreiz m; I have an ∼ es juckt mich ◻ vi jucken; I'm ∼ing (fam) es juckt mich (to zu). ∼y a be ∼y jucken

item /'aıtəm/ n Gegenstand m; (Comm) Artikel m; (on agenda) Punkt m; (on invoice) Posten m; (act) Nummer f; ∼ [of news] Nachricht f. ∼ize vt einzeln aufführen; spezifizieren (bill)

itinerant /aı'tınərənt/ a Wander-

itinerary /aı'tınərərı/ n [Reise]route f

its /ıts/ poss pron sein; (f) ihr

it's = it is, it has

itself /ıt'self/ pron selbst; (refl) sich; by ∼ von selbst; (alone) allein

ivory /'aıvərı/ n Elfenbein nt ◻ attrib Elfenbein-

ivy /'aıvı/ n Efeu m

J

jab /dʒæb/ n Stoß m; (fam: injection) Spritze f ◻ vt (pt/pp jabbed) stoßen

jabber /'dʒæbə(r)/ vi plappern

jack /dʒæk/ n (Auto) Wagenheber m; (Cards) Bube m ◻ vt ∼ up (Auto) aufbocken

jackdaw /'dʒækdɔ:/ n Dohle f

jacket /'dʒækıt/ n Jacke f; (of book) Schutzumschlag m. ∼ potato n in der Schale gebackene Kartoffel f

'jackpot n hit the ∼ das große Los ziehen

jade /dʒeıd/ n Jade m

jaded /'dʒeıdıd/ a abgespannt

jagged /'dʒægıd/ a zackig

jail /dʒeıl/ = gaol

jalopy /dʒə'lɒpı/ n (fam) Klapperkiste f

jam¹ /dʒæm/ n Marmelade f

jam² n Gedränge nt; (Auto) Stau m; (fam: difficulty) Klemme f ◻ v (pt/pp jammed) ◻ vt klemmen (in in + acc); stören (broadcast) ◻ vi klemmen

Jamaica /dʒə'meıkə/ n Jamaika f

jangle /'dʒæŋgl/ vi klimpern ◻ vt klimpern mit

janitor /'dʒænıtə(r)/ n Hausmeister m

January /'dʒænjʊərı/ n Januar m

Japan /dʒə'pæn/ n Japan nt. ∼ese /dʒæpə'ni:z/ a japanisch ◻ n Japaner(in) m(f); (Lang) Japanisch nt

jar¹ /dʒɑ:(r)/ n Glas nt; (earthenware) Topf m

jar² v (pt/pp jarred) vi stören ◻ vt erschüttern

jargon /'dʒɑ:gən/ n Jargon m

jaundice /'dʒɔ:ndıs/ n Gelbsucht f. ∼d a (fig) zynisch

jaunt /dʒɔ:nt/ n Ausflug m

jaunty /'dʒɔ:ntı/ a (-ier, -iest) -ily adv keck

javelin /'dʒævlın/ n Speer m

jaw /dʒɔ:/ n Kiefer m; ∼s pl Rachen m ◻ vi (fam) quatschen

jay /dʒeı/ n Eichelhäher m. ∼-walker n achtloser Fußgänger m

jazz /dʒæz/ n Jazz m. ∼y a knallig

jealous /'dʒeləs/ a, -ly adv eifersüchtig (of auf + acc). ∼y n Eifersucht f

jeans /dʒi:nz/ npl Jeans pl

jeer /dʒıə(r)/ n Johlen nt ◻ vi johlen; ∼ at verhöhnen

jell /dʒel/ vi gelieren

jelly /'dʒelı/ n Gelee nt; (dessert) Götterspeise f. ∼fish n Qualle f

jemmy /'dʒemı/ n Brecheisen nt

jeopar|dize /'dʒepədaız/ vt gefährden. ∼dy /-dı/ n in ∼dy gefährdet

jerk /dʒɜ:k/ n Ruck m ◻ vt stoßen; (pull) reißen ◻ vi rucken; (limb, muscle:) zucken. ∼ily adv ruckweise. ∼y a ruckartig

jersey /'dʒɜ:zı/ n Pullover m; (Sport) Trikot nt; (fabric) Jersey m

jest /dʒest/ n Scherz m; in ∼ im Spaß ◻ vi scherzen

jet¹ /dʒet/ n (Miner) Jett m

jet² n (of water) [Wasser]strahl m; (nozzle) Düse f; (plane) Düsenflugzeug nt

jet: ∼-'black a pechschwarz. ∼lag n Jetlag nt. ∼-pro'pelled a mit Düsenantrieb

jettison /'dʒetısn/ vt über Bord werfen

jetty /'dʒetı/ n Landesteg m; (breakwater) Buhne f

Jew /dʒu:/ n Jude m /Jüdin f

jewel /'dʒuːəl/ n Edelstein m; (fig) Juwel nt. ∼ler n Juwelier m; ∼ler's [shop] Juweliergeschäft nt. ∼lery n Schmuck m

Jew|ess /'dʒuːɪs/ n Jüdin f. ∼ish a jüdisch

jib /dʒɪb/ vi (pt/pp jibbed) (fig) sich sträuben (at gegen)

jiffy /'dʒɪfɪ/ n (fam) in a ∼ in einem Augenblick

jigsaw /'dʒɪgsɔː/ n ∼ [puzzle] Puzzlespiel nt

jilt /dʒɪlt/ vt sitzen lassen

jingle /'dʒɪŋgl/ n (rhyme) Verschen nt □ vi klimpern □ vt klimpern mit

jinx /dʒɪŋks/ n (fam) it's got a ∼ on it es ist verhext

jitter|s /'dʒɪtəz/ npl (fam) have the ∼s nervös sein. ∼y a (fam) nervös

job /dʒɒb/ n Aufgabe f; (post) Stelle f, (fam) Job m; be a ∼ (fam) nicht leicht sein; it's a good ∼ that es ist [nur] gut, dass. ∼centre n Arbeitsvermittlungsstelle f. ∼less a arbeitslos

jockey /'dʒɒkɪ/ n Jockei m

jocular /'dʒɒkjʊlə(r)/ a, -ly adv spaßhaft

jog /dʒɒg/ n Stoß m; at a ∼ im Dauerlauf □ v (pt/pp jogged) □ vt anstoßen; ∼ s.o.'s memory jds Gedächtnis nachhelfen □ vi (Sport) joggen. ∼ging n Jogging nt

john /dʒɒn/ n (Amer, fam) Klo nt

join /dʒɔɪn/ n Nahtstelle f □ vt verbinden (to mit); sich anschließen (+ dat) ⟨person⟩; (become member of) beitreten (+ dat); eintreten in (+ acc) ⟨firm⟩ □ vi ⟨roads:⟩ sich treffen. ∼ in vi mitmachen. ∼ up vi (Mil) Soldat werden □ vt zusammenfügen

joiner /'dʒɔɪnə(r)/ n Tischler m

joint /dʒɔɪnt/ a, -ly adv gemeinsam □ n Gelenk nt; (in wood, brickwork) Fuge f; (Culin) Braten m; (fam: bar) Lokal nt

joist /dʒɔɪst/ n Dielenbalken m

jok|e /dʒəʊk/ n Scherz m; (funny story) Witz m; (trick) Streich m □ vi scherzen. ∼er n Witzbold m; (Cards) Joker m. ∼ing n ∼ing apart Spaß beiseite. ∼ingly adv im Spaß

jollity /'dʒɒlətɪ/ n Lustigkeit f

jolly /'dʒɒlɪ/ a (-ier, -iest) lustig □ adv (fam) sehr

jolt /dʒəʊlt/ n Ruck m □ vt einen Ruck versetzen (+ dat) □ vi holpern

Jordan /'dʒɔːdn/ n Jordanien nt

jostle /'dʒɒsl/ vt anrempeln □ vi drängeln

jot /dʒɒt/ n Jota nt □ vt (pt/pp jotted) ∼ [down] sich (dat) notieren. ∼ter n Notizblock m

journal /'dʒɜːnl/ n Zeitschrift f; (diary) Tagebuch nt. ∼ese /-ə'liːz/ n Zeitungsjargon m. ∼ism n Journalismus m. ∼ist n Journalist(in) m(f)

journey /'dʒɜːnɪ/ n Reise f

jovial /'dʒəʊvɪəl/ a lustig

joy /dʒɔɪ/ n Freude f. ∼ful a, -ly adv freudig, froh. ∼ride n (fam) Spritztour f [im gestohlenen Auto]

jubil|ant /'dʒuːbɪlənt/ a überglücklich. ∼ation /-'leɪʃn/ n Jubel m

jubilee /'dʒuːbɪliː/ n Jubiläum nt

Judaism /'dʒuːdeɪɪzm/ n Judentum nt

judder /'dʒʌdə(r)/ vi rucken

judge /dʒʌdʒ/ n Richter m; (of competition) Preisrichter m □ vt beurteilen; (estimate) [ein]schätzen □ vi urteilen (by nach). ∼ment n Beurteilung f; (Jur) Urteil nt; (fig) Urteilsvermögen nt

judic|ial /dʒuː'dɪʃl/ a gerichtlich. ∼iary /-ʃərɪ/ n Richterstand m. ∼ious /-ʃəs/ a klug

judo /'dʒuːdəʊ/ n Judo nt

jug /dʒʌg/ n Kanne f; (small) Kännchen nt; (for water, wine) Krug m

juggernaut /'dʒʌgənɔːt/ n (fam) Riesenlaster m

juggle /'dʒʌgl/ vi jonglieren. ∼r n Jongleur m

juice /dʒuːs/ n Saft m. ∼ extractor n Entsafter m

juicy /'dʒuːsɪ/ a (-ier, -iest) saftig; (fam) ⟨story⟩ pikant

juke-box /'dʒuːk-/ n Musikbox f

July /dʒʊ'laɪ/ n Juli m

jumble /'dʒʌmbl/ n Durcheinander nt □ vt ∼ [up] durcheinander bringen. ∼ sale n [Wohltätigkeits]basar m

jumbo /'dʒʌmbəʊ/ n ∼ [jet] Jumbo[jet] m

jump /dʒʌmp/ n Sprung m; (in prices) Anstieg m; (in horse racing) Hindernis nt □ vi springen; (start) zusammenzucken; make s.o. ∼ jdn erschrecken; ∼ at (fig) sofort zugreifen bei ⟨offer⟩; ∼ to conclusions voreilige Schlüsse ziehen □ vt überspringen; ∼ the gun (fig) vorschnell handeln. ∼ up vi aufspringen

jumper /'dʒʌmpə(r)/ n Pullover m, Pulli m

jumpy /'dʒʌmpɪ/ a nervös

junction /'dʒʌŋkʃn/ n Kreuzung f; (Rail) Knotenpunkt m

juncture /'dʒʌŋktʃə(r)/ n at this ∼ zu diesem Zeitpunkt

June /dʒuːn/ n Juni m

jungle /'dʒʌŋgl/ n Dschungel m

junior /'dʒuːnɪə(r)/ a jünger; (in rank) untergeordnet; (Sport) Junioren- □ n Junior m. ∼ school n Grundschule f

juniper /'dʒuːnɪpə(r)/ n Wacholder m

junk /dʒʌŋk/ n Gerümpel nt, Trödel m

junkie /'dʒʌŋkɪ/ n (sl) Fixer m

'**junk-shop** n Trödelladen m

juris|diction /dʒʊərɪs'dɪkʃn/ n Ge-
richtsbarkeit f. ~'prudence n Rechts-
wissenschaft f

juror /'dʒʊərə(r)/ n Geschworene(r) m/f

jury /'dʒʊərɪ/ n the ~ die Geschworenen
pl; (for competition) die Jury

just /dʒʌst/ a gerecht □ adv gerade; (only)
nur; (simply) einfach; (exactly) genau; ~
as tall ebenso groß; ~ listen! hör doch
mal! I'm ~ going ich gehe schon; ~ put
it down stell es nur hin

justice /'dʒʌstɪs/ n Gerechtigkeit f; do ~
to gerecht werden (+ dat); J~ of the
Peace ≈ Friedensrichter m

justifiab|le /'dʒʌstɪfaɪəbl/ a berechtigt.
~ly adv berechtigterweise

justi|fication /dʒʌstɪfɪ'keɪʃn/ n Rechtfer-
tigung f. ~fy /'dʒʌstɪfaɪ/ vt (pt/pp -ied)
rechtfertigen

justly /'dʒʌstlɪ/ adv zu Recht

jut /dʒʌt/ vi(pt/pp jutted) ~ out vorstehen

juvenile /'dʒuːvənaɪl/ a jugendlich;
(childish) kindisch □ n Jugendliche(r)
m/f. ~ delinquency n Jugendkriminali-
tät f

juxtapose /dʒʌkstə'pəʊz/ vt nebeneinander stellen

K

kangaroo /kæŋgə'ruː/ n Känguru nt

karate /kə'rɑːtɪ/ n Karate nt

kebab /kɪ'bæb/ n (Culin) Spießchen nt

keel /kiːl/ n Kiel m □ vi ~ over umkippen;
(Naut) kentern

keen /kiːn/ a (-er, -est) (sharp) scharf; (intense) groß; (eager) eifrig, begeistert; ~ on
(fam) erpicht auf (+ acc); ~ on s.o. von
jdm sehr angetan; be ~ to do sth etw
gerne machen wollen. ~ly adv tief. ~ness
n Eifer m, Begeisterung f

keep /kiːp/ n (maintenance) Unterhalt m;
(of castle) Bergfried m; for ~s für immer
□ v (pt/pp kept) □ vt behalten; (store) aufbewahren; (not throw away) aufheben;
(support) unterhalten; (detain) aufhalten;
freihalten (seat); halten (promise, animals); führen, haben (shop); einhalten
(law, rules); ~ sth hot etw warm halten;
~ s.o. from doing sth jdn davon abhalten, etw zu tun; ~ s.o. waiting jdn
warten lassen; ~ sth to oneself etw nicht
weitersagen; where do you ~ the sugar?
wo hast du den Zucker? □ vi (remain)
bleiben; (food:) sich halten; ~ left/right

sich links/rechts halten; ~ doing sth etw
dauernd machen; ~ on doing sth etw
weitermachen; ~ in with sich gut stellen
mit. ~ up vi Schritt halten □ vt (continue)
weitermachen

keep|er /'kiːpə(r)/ n Wärter(in) m(f). ~ing
n Obhut f; be in ~ing with passen zu.
~sake n Andenken nt

keg /keg/ n kleines Fass nt

kennel /'kenl/ n Hundehütte f; ~s pl
(boarding) Hundepension f; (for breeding)
Zwinger m

Kenya /'kenjə/ n Kenia nt

kept /kept/ see keep

kerb /kɜːb/ n Bordstein m

kernel /'kɜːnl/ n Kern m

kerosene /'kerəsiːn/ n (Amer) Petroleum
nt

ketchup /'ketʃʌp/ n Ketschup m

kettle /'ketl/ n [Wasser]kessel m; put the
~ on Wasser aufsetzen; a pretty ~ of fish
(fam) eine schöne Bescherung f

key /kiː/ n Schlüssel m; (Mus) Tonart f;
(of piano, typewriter) Taste f □ vt ~ in
eintasten

key: ~board n Tastatur f; (Mus) Klaviatur
f. ~boarder n Taster(in) m(f). ~hole n
Schlüsselloch nt. ~-ring n Schlüsselring
m

khaki /'kɑːkɪ/ a khakifarben □ n Khaki nt

kick /kɪk/ n [Fuß]tritt m; for ~s (fam)
zum Spaß □ vt treten; ~ the bucket (fam)
abkratzen □ vi (animal) ausschlagen. ~-
off n (Sport) Anstoß m

kid /kɪd/ n Kitz nt; (fam: child) Kind nt □ vt
(pt/pp kidded) (fam) ~ s.o. jdm etwas
vormachen. ~ gloves npl Glacéhand-
schuhe pl

kidnap /'kɪdnæp/ vt (pt/pp -napped)
entführen. ~per n Entführer m. ~ping n
Entführung f

kidney /'kɪdnɪ/ n Niere f. ~ machine n
künstliche Niere f

kill /kɪl/ vt töten; (fam) totschlagen (time);
~ two birds with one stone zwei Fliegen
mit einer Klappe schlagen. ~er n Mör-
der(in) m(f). ~ing n Tötung f; (murder)
Mord m

'**killjoy** n Spielverderber m

kiln /kɪln/ n Brennofen m

kilo /'kiːləʊ/ n Kilo nt

kilo /'kɪlə/: ~gram n Kilogramm nt.
~hertz /-hɜːts/ n Kilohertz nt. ~metre n
Kilometer m. ~watt n Kilowatt nt

kilt /kɪlt/ n Schottenrock m

kin /kɪn/ n Verwandtschaft f; next of ~
nächster Verwandter m/nächste Verwandte f

kind[1] /kaɪnd/ n Art f; (brand, type) Sorte f; what ~ of car? was für ein Auto? ~ of (fam) irgendwie

kind[2] a (-er, -est) nett; ~ to animals gut zu Tieren; ~ regards herzliche Grüße

kindergarten /ˈkɪndəgɑːtn/ n Vorschule f

kindle /ˈkɪndl/ vt anzünden

kind|ly /ˈkaɪndlɪ/ a (-ier, -iest) nett □ adv netterweise; (if you please) gefälligst. ~ness n Güte f; (favour) Gefallen m

kindred /ˈkɪndrɪd/ a ~ spirit Gleichgesinnte(r) m/f

kinetic /kɪˈnetɪk/ a kinetisch

king /kɪŋ/ n König m; (Draughts) Dame f. ~dom n Königreich nt; (fig & Relig) Reich nt

king: ~fisher n Eisvogel m. ~-sized a extragroß

kink /kɪŋk/ n Knick m. ~y a (fam) pervers

kiosk /ˈkiːɒsk/ n Kiosk m

kip /kɪp/ n have a ~ (fam) pennen □ vi (pt/pp kipped) (fam) pennen

kipper /ˈkɪpə(r)/ n Räucherhering m

kiss /kɪs/ n Kuss m □ vt/i küssen

kit /kɪt/ n Ausrüstung f; (tools) Werkzeug nt; (construction ~) Bausatz m □ vt (pt/pp kitted) ~ out ausrüsten. ~bag n See sack m

kitchen /ˈkɪtʃɪn/ n Küche f □ attrib Küchen-. ~ette /kɪtʃɪˈnet/ n Kochnische f

kitchen: ~ 'garden n Gemüsegarten m. ~ 'sink n Spülbecken nt

kite /kaɪt/ n Drachen m

kith /kɪθ/ n with ~ and kin mit der ganzen Verwandtschaft

kitten /ˈkɪtn/ n Kätzchen nt

kitty /ˈkɪtɪ/ n (money) [gemeinsame] Kasse f

kleptomaniac /kleptəˈmeɪnɪæk/ n Kleptomane m/ -manin f

knack /næk/ n Trick m, Dreh m

knapsack /ˈnæp-/ n Tornister m

knead /niːd/ vt kneten

knee /niː/ n Knie nt. ~cap n Kniescheibe f

kneel /niːl/ vi (pt/pp knelt) knien; ~ [down] sich [nieder]knien

knelt /nelt/ see kneel

knew /njuː/ see know

knickers /ˈnɪkəz/ npl Schlüpfer m

knick-knacks /ˈnɪknæks/ npl Nippsachen pl

knife /naɪf/ n (pl knives) Messer nt □ vt einen Messerstich versetzen (+ dat); (to death) erstechen

knight /naɪt/ n Ritter m; (Chess) Springer m □ vt adeln

knit /nɪt/ vt/i (pt/pp knitted) stricken; ~ one, purl one eine rechts eine links; ~ one's brow die Stirn runzeln. ~ting n Stricken nt; (work) Strickzeug nt. ~ting-needle n Stricknadel f. ~wear n Strickwaren pl

knives /naɪvz/ npl see knife

knob /nɒb/ n Knopf m; (on door) Knauf m; (small lump) Beule f; (small piece) Stückchen m. ~bly a knorrig; (bony) knochig

knock /nɒk/ n Klopfen nt; (blow) Schlag m; there was a ~ at the door es klopfte □ vt anstoßen; (at door) klopfen an (+ acc); (fam: criticize) heruntermachen; ~ a hole in sth ein Loch in etw (acc) schlagen; ~ one's head (dat) den Kopf stoßen (on an + dat) □ vi klopfen. ~ about vt schlagen □ vi (fam) herumkommen. ~ down vt herunterwerfen; (with fist) niederschlagen; (in car) anfahren; (demolish) abreißen; (fam: reduce) herabsetzen. ~ off vt herunterwerfen; (fam: steal) klauen; (fam: complete quickly) hinhauen □ vi (fam: cease work) Feierabend machen. ~ out vt ausschlagen; (make unconscious) bewusstlos schlagen; (Boxing) k.o. schlagen. ~ over vt umwerfen; (in car) anfahren

knock: ~down a ~-down prices Schleuderpreise pl. ~er n Türklopfer m. ~-kneed /-ˈniːd/ a X-beinig. ~-out n (Boxing) K.o. m

knot /nɒt/ n Knoten m □ vt (pt/pp knotted) knoten

knotty /ˈnɒtɪ/ a (-ier, -iest) verwickelt

know /nəʊ/ vt/i (pt knew, pp known) wissen; kennen (person); können (language); get to ~ kennen lernen □ n in the ~ (fam) im Bild

know: ~all n (fam) Alleswisser m. ~how n (fam) [Sach]kenntnis f. ~ing a wissend. ~ingly adv wissend; (intentionally) wissentlich

knowledge /ˈnɒlɪdʒ/ n Kenntnis f (of von/gen); (general) Wissen nt; (specialized) Kenntnisse pl. ~able /-əbl/ a be ~able viel wissen

known /nəʊn/ see know □ a bekannt

knuckle /ˈnʌkl/ n [Finger]knöchel m; (Culin) Hachse f □ vi ~ under sich fügen; ~ down sich dahinter klemmen

kosher /ˈkəʊʃə(r)/ a koscher

kowtow /kaʊˈtaʊ/ vi Kotau machen (to vor + dat)

kudos /ˈkjuːdɒs/ n (fam) Prestige nt

L

lab /læb/ n (fam) Labor nt
label /'leɪbl/ n Etikett nt ▢ vt (pt/pp labelled) etikettieren
laboratory /ləˈbɒrətrɪ/ n Labor nt
laborious /ləˈbɔːrɪəs/ a, -ly adv mühsam
labour /'leɪbə(r)/ n Arbeit f; (workers) Arbeitskräfte pl; (Med) Wehen pl; L~ (Pol) die Labourpartei ▢ attrib Labour- ▢ vi arbeiten ▢ vt (fig) sich lange auslassen über (+ acc). ~er n Arbeiter m
'labour-saving a arbeitssparend
laburnum /ləˈbɜːnəm/ n Goldregen m
labyrinth /'læbərɪnθ/ n Labyrinth nt
lace /leɪs/ n Spitze f; (of shoe) Schnürsenkel m ▢ vt schnüren; ~d with rum mit einem Schuss Rum
lacerate /'læsəreɪt/ vt zerreißen
lack /læk/ n Mangel m (of an + dat) ▢ vt I ~ the time mir fehlt die Zeit ▢ vi be ~ing fehlen
lackadaisical /lækəˈdeɪzɪkl/ a lustlos
laconic /ləˈkɒnɪk/ a, -ally adv lakonisch
lacquer /'lækə(r)/ n Lack m; (for hair) [Haar]spray m
lad /læd/ n Junge m
ladder /'lædə(r)/ n Leiter f; (in fabric) Laufmasche f
laden /'leɪdn/ a beladen
ladle /'leɪdl/ n [Schöpf]kelle f ▢ vt schöpfen
lady /'leɪdɪ/ n Dame f; (title) Lady f
lady: ~bird n, (Amer) ~bug n Marienkäfer m. ~like a damenhaft
lag¹ /læg/ vi (pt/pp lagged) ~ behind zurückbleiben; (fig) nachhinken
lag² vt (pt/pp lagged) umwickeln (pipes)
lager /'lɑːgə(r)/ n Lagerbier nt
lagoon /ləˈguːn/ n Lagune f
laid /leɪd/ see lay³
lain /leɪn/ see lie²
lair /leə(r)/ n Lager nt
laity /'leɪətɪ/ n Laienstand m
lake /leɪk/ n See m
lamb /læm/ n Lamm nt
lame /leɪm/ a (-r, -st) lahm
lament /ləˈment/ n Klage f; (song) Klagelied nt ▢ vt beklagen ▢ vi klagen. ~able /'læməntəbl/ a beklagenswert
laminated /'læmɪneɪtɪd/ a laminiert

lamp /læmp/ n Lampe f; (in street) Laterne f. ~post n Laternenpfahl m. ~shade n Lampenschirm m
lance /lɑːns/ n Lanze f ▢ vt (Med) aufschneiden. ~'corporal n Gefreite(r) m
land /lænd/ n Land nt; plot of ~ Grundstück nt ▢ vt/i landen; ~ s.o. with sth (fam) jdm etw aufhalsen
landing /'lændɪŋ/ n Landung f; (top of stairs) Treppenflur m. ~-stage n Landesteg m
land: ~lady n Wirtin f. ~-locked a ~-locked country Binnenstaat m. ~lord n Wirt m; (of land) Grundbesitzer m; (of building) Hausbesitzer m. ~mark n Erkennungszeichen nt; (fig) Meilenstein m. ~owner n Grundbesitzer m. ~scape /-skeɪp/ n Landschaft f. ~slide n Erdrutsch m
lane /leɪn/ n kleine Landstraße f; (Auto) Spur f; (Sport) Bahn f; 'get in ~' (Auto) 'bitte einordnen'
language /'læŋgwɪdʒ/ n Sprache f; (speech, style) Ausdrucksweise f. ~ laboratory n Sprachlabor nt
languid /'læŋgwɪd/ a, -ly adv träge
languish /'læŋgwɪʃ/ vi schmachten
lank /læŋk/ a (hair) strähnig
lanky /'læŋkɪ/ a (-ier, -iest) schlaksig
lantern /'læntən/ n Laterne f
lap¹ /læp/ n Schoß m
lap² n (Sport) Runde f; (of journey) Etappe f ▢ vi (pt/pp lapped) plätschern (against gegen)
lap³ vt (pt/pp lapped) ~ up aufschlecken
lapel /ləˈpel/ n Revers nt
lapse /læps/ n Fehler m; (moral) Fehltritt m; (of time) Zeitspanne f ▢ vi (expire) erlöschen; ~ into verfallen in (+ acc)
larceny /'lɑːsənɪ/ n Diebstahl m
lard /lɑːd/ n [Schweine]schmalz nt
larder /'lɑːdə(r)/ n Speisekammer f
large /lɑːdʒ/ a (-r, -st) & adv groß; by and ~ im Großen und Ganzen; at ~ auf freiem Fuß; (in general) im Allgemeinen. ~ly adv großenteils
lark¹ /lɑːk/ n (bird) Lerche f
lark² n (joke) Jux m ▢ vi ~ about herumalbern
larva /'lɑːvə/ n (pl -vae /-viː/) Larve f
laryngitis /lærɪnˈdʒaɪtɪs/ n Kehlkopfentzündung f
larynx /'lærɪŋks/ n Kehlkopf m
lascivious /ləˈsɪvɪəs/ a lüstern
laser /'leɪzə(r)/ n Laser m
lash /læʃ/ n Peitschenhieb m; (eyelash) Wimper f ▢ vt peitschen; (tie) festbinden (to an + acc). ~ out vi um sich schlagen; (spend) viel Geld ausgeben (on für)

lashings /'læʃɪŋz/ npl ~ of (fam) eine Riesenmenge von

lass /læs/ n Mädchen nt

lasso /lə'suː/ n Lasso nt

last¹ /lɑːst/ n (for shoe) Leisten m

last² a & n letzte(r,s); ~ night heute od gestern Nacht; (evening) gestern Abend; at ~ endlich; the ~ time das letzte Mal; for the ~ time zum letzten Mal; the ~ but one der/die/das vorletzte; that's the ~ straw (fam) das schlägt dem Fass den Boden aus □ adv zuletzt; (last time) das letzte Mal; do sth ~ etw zuletzt od als Letztes machen; he/she went ~ er/sie ging als Letzter/Letzte □ vi dauern; ⟨weather:⟩ sich halten; ⟨relationship:⟩ halten. ~ing a dauerhaft. ~ly adv schließlich, zum Schluss

latch /lætʃ/ n [einfache] Klinke f; on the ~ nicht verschlossen

late /leɪt/ a & adv (-r, -st) spät; (delayed) verspätet; (deceased) verstorben; the ~st news die neuesten Nachrichten; stay up ~ bis spät aufbleiben; of ~ in letzter Zeit; arrive ~ zu spät ankommen; I am ~ ich komme zu spät od habe mich verspätet; the train is ~ der Zug hat Verspätung. ~comer n Zuspätkommende(r) m/f. ~ly adv in letzter Zeit. ~ness n Zuspätkommen nt; (delay) Verspätung f

latent /'leɪtnt/ a latent

later /'leɪtə(r)/ a & adv später; ~ on nachher

lateral /'lætərəl/ a seitlich

lathe /leɪð/ n Drehbank f

lather /'lɑːðə(r)/ n [Seifen]schaum m □ vt einseifen □ vi schäumen

Latin /'lætɪn/ a lateinisch □ n Latein nt. ~ A'merica n Lateinamerika nt

latitude /'lætɪtjuːd/ n (Geog) Breite f; (fig) Freiheit f

latter /'lætə(r)/ a & n the ~ der/die/das Letztere. ~ly adv in letzter Zeit

lattice /'lætɪs/ n Gitter nt

Latvia /'lætvɪə/ n Lettland nt

laudable /'lɔːdəbl/ a lobenswert

laugh /lɑːf/ n Lachen nt; with a ~ lachend □ vi lachen (at/about über + acc); ~ at s.o. (mock) jdn auslachen. ~able /-əbl/ a lachhaft, lächerlich. ~ing-stock n Gegenstand m des Spottes

laughter /'lɑːftə(r)/ n Gelächter nt

launch¹ /lɔːntʃ/ n (boat) Barkasse f

launch² n Stapellauf m; (of rocket) Abschuss m; (of product) Lancierung f □ vt vom Stapel lassen ⟨ship⟩; zu Wasser lassen ⟨lifeboat⟩; abschießen ⟨rocket⟩; starten ⟨attack⟩; (Comm) lancieren ⟨product⟩

launder /'lɔːndə(r)/ vt waschen. ~ette /-'dret/ n Münzwäscherei f

laundry /'lɔːndrɪ/ n Wäscherei f; (clothes) Wäsche f

laurel /'lɒrl/ n Lorbeer m

lava /'lɑːvə/ n Lava f

lavatory /'lævətrɪ/ n Toilette f

lavender /'lævəndə(r)/ n Lavendel m

lavish /'lævɪʃ/ a, -ly adv großzügig; (wasteful) verschwenderisch; on a ~ scale mit viel Aufwand □ vt ~ sth on s.o. jdn mit etw überschütten

law /lɔː/ n Gesetz nt; (system) Recht nt; study ~ Jura studieren; ~ and order Recht und Ordnung

law: ~-abiding a gesetzestreu. ~court n Gerichtshof m. ~ful a rechtmäßig. ~less a gesetzlos

lawn /lɔːn/ n Rasen m. ~-mower n Rasenmäher m

'law suit n Prozess m

lawyer /'lɔːjə(r)/ n Rechtsanwalt m /-anwältin f

lax /læks/ a lax, locker

laxative /'læksətɪv/ n Abführmittel nt

laxity /'læksətɪ/ n Laxheit f

lay¹ /leɪ/ a Laien-

lay² see lie²

lay³ vt (pt/pp laid) legen; decken ⟨table⟩; ~ a trap eine Falle stellen. ~ down vt hinlegen; festlegen ⟨rules, conditions⟩. ~ off vt entlassen ⟨workers⟩ □ vi (fam: stop) aufhören. ~ out vt hinlegen; aufbahren ⟨corpse⟩; anlegen ⟨garden⟩; (Typ) gestalten

lay: ~about n Faulenzer m. ~-by n Parkbucht f; (on motorway) Rastplatz m

layer /'leɪə(r)/ n Schicht f

layette /leɪ'et/ n Babyausstattung f

lay: ~man n Laie m. ~out n Anordnung f; (design) Gestaltung f; (Typ) Layout nt. ~ 'preacher n Laienprediger m

laze /leɪz/ vi ~ [about] faulenzen

laziness /'leɪzɪnɪs/ n Faulheit f

lazy /'leɪzɪ/ a (-ier, -iest) faul. ~-bones n Faulenzer m

lb /paʊnd/ abbr (pound) Pfd.

lead¹ /led/ n Blei nt; (of pencil) [Blei]stift]mine f

lead² /liːd/ n Führung f; (leash) Leine f; (flex) Schnur f; (clue) Hinweis m, Spur f; (Theat) Hauptrolle f; (distance ahead) Vorsprung m; be in the ~ in Führung liegen □ vt/i (pt/pp led) führen; leiten ⟨team⟩; (induce) bringen; (at cards) ausspielen; ~ the way vorangehen; ~ up to sth (fig) etw (dat) vorangehen. ~ away vt wegführen

leaded /'ledɪd/ a verbleit

leader /'li:də(r)/ n Führer m; (of expedition, group) Leiter(in) m(f); (of orchestra) Konzertmeister m; (in newspaper) Leitartikel m. ∼ship n Führung f; Leitung f

leading /'li:dɪŋ/ a führend; ∼ lady Hauptdarstellerin f; ∼ question Suggestivfrage f

leaf /li:f/ n (pl leaves) Blatt nt; (of table) Ausziehplatte f □ vi ∼ through sth etw durchblättern. ∼let n Merkblatt nt; (advertising) Reklameblatt nt; (political) Flugblatt nt

league /li:g/ n Liga f; be in ∼ with unter einer Decke stecken mit

leak /li:k/ n (hole) undichte Stelle f; (Naut) Leck nt; (of gas) Gasausfluss m □ vi undicht sein; (ship:) leck sein, lecken; (liquid:) auslaufen; (gas:) ausströmen □ vt auslaufen lassen; ∼ sth to s.o. (fig) jdm etw zuspielen. ∼y a undicht; (Naut) leck

lean[1] /li:n/ a (-er, -est) mager

lean[2] v (pt/pp leaned or leant /lent/) □ vt lehnen (against/on an + acc) □ vi (person) sich lehnen (against/on an + acc); (not be straight) sich neigen; be ∼ing against lehnen an (+ dat); ∼ on s.o. (depend) bei jdm festen Halt finden. ∼ back vi sich zurücklehnen. ∼ forward vi sich vorbeugen. ∼ out vi sich hinauslehnen. ∼ over vi sich vorbeugen

leaning /'li:nɪŋ/ a schief □ n Neigung f

leap /li:p/ n Sprung m □ vi (pt/pp leapt /lept/ or leaped) springen; he leapt at it (fam) er griff sofort zu. ∼-frog n Bockspringen nt. ∼ year n Schaltjahr nt

learn /lɜ:n/ vt/i (pt/pp learnt or learned) lernen; (hear) erfahren; ∼ to swim schwimmen lernen

learn|ed /'lɜ:nɪd/ a gelehrt. ∼er n Anfänger m; ∼er [driver] Fahrschüler(in) m(f). ∼ing n Gelehrsamkeit f

lease /li:s/ n Pacht f; (contract) Mietvertrag m; (Comm) Pachtvertrag m □ vt pachten; ∼ [out] verpachten

leash /li:ʃ/ n Leine f

least /li:st/ a geringste(r,s); have ∼ time am wenigsten Zeit haben □ n the ∼ das wenigste; at ∼ wenigstens, mindestens; not in the ∼ nicht im Geringsten □ adv am wenigsten

leather /'leðə(r)/ n Leder nt. ∼y a ledern; (tough) zäh

leave /li:v/ n Erlaubnis f; (holiday) Urlaub m; on ∼ auf Urlaub; take one's ∼ sich verabschieden □ v (pt/pp left) □ vt lassen; (go out of, abandon) verlassen; (forget) liegen lassen; (bequeath) vermachen (to dat); ∼ it to me! überlassen Sie es mir! there is nothing left es ist nichts mehr übrig □ vi [weg]gehen/-fahren; (train,

bus:) abfahren. ∼ behind vt zurücklassen; (forget) liegen lassen. ∼ out vt liegen lassen; (leave outside) draußen lassen; (omit) auslassen

leaves /li:vz/ see **leaf**

Lebanon /'lebənən/ n Libanon m

lecherous /'letʃərəs/ a lüstern

lectern /'lektən/ n [Lese]pult nt

lecture /'lektʃə(r)/ n Vortrag m; (Univ) Vorlesung f; (reproof) Strafpredigt f □ vi einen Vortrag/eine Vorlesung halten (on über + acc) □ vt ∼ s.o. jdm eine Strafpredigt halten. ∼r n Vortragende(r) m/f; (Univ) Dozent(in) m(f)

led /led/ see **lead**[2]

ledge /ledʒ/ n Leiste f; (shelf, of window) Sims m; (in rock) Vorsprung m

ledger /'ledʒə(r)/ n Hauptbuch nt

lee /li:/ n (Naut) Lee f

leech /li:tʃ/ n Blutegel m

leek /li:k/ n Stange f Porree; ∼s pl Porree m

leer /lɪə(r)/ n anzügliches Grinsen nt □ vi anzüglich grinsen

lee|ward /'li:wəd/ adv nach Lee. ∼way n (fig) Spielraum m

left[1] /left/ see **leave**

left[2] a linke(r,s) □ adv links; (go) nach links □ n linke Seite f; on the ∼ links; from/to the ∼ von/nach links; the ∼ (Pol) die Linke

left: ∼-'handed a linkshändig. ∼-'luggage [office] n Gepäckaufbewahrung f. ∼overs npl Reste pl. ∼-'wing a (Pol) linke(r,s)

leg /leg/ n Bein nt; (Culin) Keule f; (of journey) Etappe f

legacy /'legəsɪ/ n Vermächtnis nt, Erbschaft f

legal /'li:gl/ a, -ly adv gesetzlich; (matters) rechtlich; (department, position) Rechts-; be ∼ [gesetzlich] erlaubt sein; take ∼ action gerichtlich vorgehen

legality /lɪ'gælətɪ/ n Legalität f

legalize /'li:gəlaɪz/ vt legalisieren

legend /'ledʒənd/ n Legende f. ∼ary a legendär

legible /'ledʒəbl/ a, -bly adv leserlich

legion /'li:dʒn/ n Legion f

legislat|e /'ledʒɪsleɪt/ vi Gesetze erlassen. ∼ion /-'leɪʃn/ n Gesetzgebung f; (laws) Gesetze pl

legislat|ive /'ledʒɪslətɪv/ a gesetzgebend. ∼ure /-leɪtʃə(r)/ n Legislative f

legitimate /lɪ'dʒɪtɪmət/ a rechtmäßig; (justifiable) berechtigt; (child) ehelich

leisure /'leʒə(r)/ n Freizeit f; at your ∼ wenn Sie Zeit haben. ∼ly a gemächlich

lemon /'lemən/ n Zitrone f. ~ade /-'neɪd/ n Zitronenlimonade f

lend /lend/ vt (pt/pp lent) leihen; ~ s.o. sth jdm etw leihen; ~ a hand (fam) helfen. ~ing library n Leihbücherei f

length /leŋθ/ n Länge f; (piece) Stück nt; (of wallpaper) Bahn f; (of time) Dauer f; at ~ ausführlich; (at last) endlich

length|en /'leŋθən/ vt länger machen □ vi länger werden. ~ways adv der Länge nach, längs

lengthy /'leŋθɪ/ a (-ier, -iest) langwierig

lenien|ce /'li:nɪəns/ n Nachsicht f. ~t a, -ly adv nachsichtig

lens /lenz/ n Linse f; (Phot) Objektiv nt; (of spectacles) Glas nt

lent /lent/ see lend

Lent n Fastenzeit f

lentil /'lentl/ n (Bot) Linse f

Leo /'li:əʊ/ n (Astr) Löwe m

leopard /'lepəd/ n Leopard m

leotard /'li:ətɑ:d/ n Trikot nt

leper /'lepə(r)/ n Leprakranke(r) m/f; (Bible & fig) Aussätzige(r) m/f

leprosy /'leprəsɪ/ n Lepra f

lesbian /'lezbɪən/ a lesbisch □ n Lesbierin f

lesion /'li:ʒn/ n Verletzung f

less /les/ a, adv, n & prep weniger; ~ and ~ immer weniger; not any the ~ um nichts weniger

lessen /'lesn/ vt verringern □ vi nachlassen; (value:) abnehmen

lesser /'lesə(r)/ a geringere(r,s)

lesson /'lesn/ n Stunde f; (in text-book) Lektion f; (Relig) Lesung f; teach s.o. a ~ (fig) jdm eine Lehre erteilen

lest /lest/ conj (liter) damit ... nicht

let /let/ vt (pt/pp let, pres p letting) lassen; (rent) vermieten; ~ alone (not to mention) geschweige denn; 'to ~' 'zu vermieten'; ~ us go when we ~ me know sagen Sie mir Bescheid; ~ him do it lass ihn das machen; just ~ him! soll er doch! ~ s.o. sleep/win jdn schlafen/gewinnen lassen; ~ oneself in for sth (fam) sich (dat) etw einbrocken. ~ down vt hinunter-/herunterlassen; (lengthen) länger machen; ~ s.o. down (fam) jdn im Stich lassen; (disappoint) jdn enttäuschen. ~ in vt hereinlassen. ~ off vt abfeuern (gun); hochgehen lassen (firework, bomb); (emit) ausstoßen; (excuse from) befreien von; (not punish) frei ausgehen lassen. ~ out vt hinauslassen/herauslassen; (make larger) auslassen. ~ through vt durchlassen. ~ up vi (fam) nachlassen

'let-down n Enttäuschung f, (fam) Reinfall m

lethal /'li:θl/ a tödlich

letharg|ic /lɪ'θɑ:dʒɪk/ a lethargisch. ~y /'leθədʒɪ/ n Lethargie f

letter /'letə(r)/ n Brief m; (of alphabet) Buchstabe m; by ~ brieflich. ~box n Briefkasten m. ~head n Briefkopf m. ~ing n Beschriftung f

lettuce /'letɪs/ n [Kopf]salat m

'let-up n (fam) Nachlassen nt

leukaemia /lu:'ki:mɪə/ n Leukämie f

level /'levl/ a eben; (horizontal) waagerecht; (in height) auf gleicher Höhe; (spoonful) gestrichen; draw ~ with gleichziehen mit; one's ~ best sein Möglichstes □ n Höhe f; (fig) Ebene f, Niveau nt; (stage) Stufe f; on the ~ (fam) ehrlich □ vt (pt/pp levelled) einebnen; (aim) richten (at auf + acc)

level-: ~'crossing n Bahnübergang m. ~'headed a vernünftig

lever /'li:və(r)/ n Hebel m □ vt ~ up mit einem Hebel anheben. ~age /-rɪdʒ/ n Hebelkraft f

levity /'levətɪ/ n Heiterkeit f; (frivolity) Leichtfertigkeit f

levy /'levɪ/ vt (pt/pp levied) erheben (tax)

lewd /lju:d/ a (-er, -est) anstößig

liabilit|y /laɪə'bɪlətɪ/ n Haftung f; ~ies pl Verbindlichkeiten pl

liable /'laɪəbl/ a haftbar; be ~ to do sth leicht etw tun können

liaise /lɪ'eɪz/ vi (fam) Verbindungsperson sein

liaison /lɪ'eɪzɒn/ n Verbindung f; (affair) Verhältnis nt

liar /'laɪə(r)/ n Lügner(in) m(f)

libel /'laɪbl/ n Verleumdung f □ vt (pt/pp libelled) verleumden. ~lous a verleumderisch

liberal /'lɪbərl/ a, -ly adv tolerant; (generous) großzügig. L~ a (Pol) liberal □ n Liberale(r) m/f

liberat|e /'lɪbəreɪt/ vt befreien. ~ed a (woman) emanzipiert. ~ion /-'reɪʃn/ n Befreiung f. ~or n Befreier m

liberty /'lɪbətɪ/ n Freiheit f; take the ~ of doing sth sich (dat) erlauben, etw zu tun; take liberties sich (dat) Freiheiten erlauben

Libra /'li:brə/ n (Astr) Waage f

librarian /laɪ'breərɪən/ n Bibliothekar(in) m(f)

library /'laɪbrərɪ/ n Bibliothek f

Libya /'lɪbɪə/ n Libyen nt

lice /laɪs/ see louse

licence /'laɪsns/ n Genehmigung f; (Comm) Lizenz f; (for TV) Fernsehgebühr f; (for driving) Führerschein m; (for

alcohol) Schankkonzession *f*; *(freedom)* Freiheit *f*

license /'laɪsn/ *vt* eine Genehmigung/(*Comm*) Lizenz erteilen (+ *dat*); be ~d *(car:)* zugelassen sein; *(restaurant:)* Schankkonzession haben. ~-**plate** *n* Nummernschild *nt*

licentious /laɪ'senʃəs/ *a* lasterhaft

lichen /'laɪkən/ *n (Bot)* Flechte *f*

lick /lɪk/ *n* Lecken *nt*; a ~ of paint ein bisschen Farbe □ *vt* lecken; *(fam: defeat)* schlagen

lid /lɪd/ *n* Deckel *m*; *(of eye)* Lid *nt*

lie¹ /laɪ/ *n* Lüge *f*; tell a ~ lügen □ *vi (pt/pp* lied, *pres p* lying) lügen; ~ to belügen

lie² *vi (pt* lay, *pp* lain, *pres p* lying) liegen; here ~s ... hier ruht ... ~ **down** □ *vi* sich hinlegen

Liège /lɪ'eɪʒ/ *n* Lüttich *nt*

'**lie-in** *n* have a ~ [sich] ausschlafen

lieu /lju:/ *n* in ~ of statt (+ *gen*)

lieutenant /lef'tenənt/ *n* Oberleutnant *m*

life /laɪf/ *n (pl* lives) Leben *nt*; *(biography)* Biographie *f*; lose one's ~ ums Leben kommen

life: ~**belt** *n* Rettungsring *m*. ~**boat** *n* Rettungsboot *nt*. ~**buoy** *n* Rettungsring *m*. ~**guard** *n* Lebensretter *m*. ~**jacket** *n* Schwimmweste *f*. ~**less** *a* leblos. ~**like** *a* naturgetreu. ~**line** *n* Rettungsleine *f*. ~**long** *a* lebenslang. ~ **preserver** *n (Amer)* Rettungsring *m*. ~-**size(d)** *a* ... in Lebensgröße. ~**time** *n* Leben *nt*; in s.o.'s ~**time** zu jds Lebzeiten; the chance of a ~**time** eine einmalige Gelegenheit

lift /lɪft/ *n* Aufzug *m*, Lift *m*; give s.o. a ~ jdn mitnehmen; get a ~ mitgenommen werden □ *vt* heben; aufheben *(restrictions)* □ *vi (fog:)* sich lichten. ~ **up** *vt* hochheben

'**lift-off** *n* Abheben *nt*

ligament /'lɪgəmənt/ *n (Anat)* Band *nt*

light¹ /laɪt/ *a* (-er, -est) *(not dark)* hell; ~ blue hellblau □ *n* Licht *nt*; *(lamp)* Lampe *f*; in the ~ of *(fig)* angesichts (+ *gen*); have you [got] a ~? haben Sie Feuer? □ *vt (pt/pp* lit *or* lighted) anzünden *(fire, cigarette)*; anmachen *(lamp)*; *(illuminate)* beleuchten. ~ **up** *vi (face:)* sich erhellen

light² *a* (-er, -est) *(not heavy)* leicht; ~ sentence milde Strafe *f* □ *adv* travel ~ mit wenig Gepäck reisen

'**light-bulb** *n* Glühbirne *f*

lighten¹ /'laɪtn/ *vt* heller machen □ *vi* heller werden

lighten² *vt* leichter machen *(load)*

lighter /'laɪtə(r)/ *n* Feuerzeug *nt*

light: ~-'**headed** *a* benommen. ~-'**hearted** *a* unbekümmert. ~**house** *n* Leuchtturm *m*. ~**ing** *n* Beleuchtung *f*.

~**ly** *adv* leicht; *(casually)* leichthin; get off ~**ly** glimpflich davonkommen

lightning /'laɪtnɪŋ/ *n* Blitz *m*. ~-**conductor** *n* Blitzableiter *m*

'**lightweight** *a* leicht □ *n (Boxing)* Leichtgewicht *nt*

like¹ /laɪk/ *a* ähnlich; *(same)* gleich □ *prep* wie; *(similar to)* ähnlich (+ *dat*); ~ this so; a man ~ that so ein Mann; what's he ~? wie ist er denn? □ *conj (fam: as)* wie; *(Amer: as if)* als ob

like² *vt* mögen; I should/would ~ ich möchte; I ~ the car das Auto gefällt mir; I ~ chocolate ich esse gern Schokolade; ~ **dancing/singing** gern tanzen/singen; I ~ that! *(fam)* das ist doch die Höhe! □ *n* ~s and dislikes *pl* Vorlieben und Abneigungen *pl*

like|able /'laɪkəbl/ *a* sympathisch. ~**lihood** /-lɪhʊd/ *n* Wahrscheinlichkeit *f*. ~**ly** *a* (-ier, -iest) & *adv* wahrscheinlich; not ~**ly!** *(fam)* auf gar keinen Fall!

'**like-minded** *a* gleich gesinnt

liken /'laɪkən/ *vt* vergleichen (to mit)

like|ness /'laɪknɪs/ *n* Ähnlichkeit *f*. ~**wise** *adv* ebenso

liking /'laɪkɪŋ/ *n* Vorliebe *f*; is it to your ~? gefällt es Ihnen?

lilac /'laɪlək/ *n* Flieder *m* □ *a* fliederfarben

lily /'lɪlɪ/ *n*. Lilie *f*. ~ of the valley *n* Maiglöckchen *nt*

limb /lɪm/ *n* Glied *nt*

limber /'lɪmbə(r)/ *vi* ~ up Lockerungsübungen machen

lime¹ /laɪm/ *n (fruit)* Limone *f*; *(tree)* Linde *f*

lime² *n* Kalk *m*. ~**light** *n* be in the ~**light** im Rampenlicht stehen. ~**stone** *n* Kalkstein *m*

limit /'lɪmɪt/ *n* Grenze *f*; *(limitation)* Beschränkung *f*; that's the ~! *(fam)* das ist doch die Höhe! □ *vt* beschränken (to auf + *acc*). ~**ation** /-'teɪʃn/ *n* Beschränkung *f*; ~**ed** *a* beschränkt; ~**ed company** Gesellschaft *f* mit beschränkter Haftung

limousine /'lɪməzi:n/ *n* Limousine *f*

limp¹ /lɪmp/ *n* Hinken *nt*; have a ~ hinken □ *vi* hinken

limp² *a* (-er -est), -**ly** *adv* schlaff

limpet /'lɪmpɪt/ *n* like a ~ *(fig)* wie eine Klette

limpid /'lɪmpɪd/ *a* klar

linctus /'lɪŋktəs/ *n* [cough] ~ Hustensirup *m*

line¹ /laɪn/ *n* Linie *f*; *(length of rope, cord)* Leine *f*; *(Teleph)* Leitung *f*; *(of writing)* Zeile *f*; *(row)* Reihe *f*; *(wrinkle)* Falte *f*; *(of business)* Branche *f*; *(Amer: queue)* Schlange *f*; in ~ with gemäß (+ *dat*) □ *vt* säumen ⟨street⟩. ~ up vi sich aufstellen □ vt aufstellen

line² vt füttern ⟨garment⟩; (Techn) auskleiden

lineage /'lɪniɪdʒ/ n Herkunft f

linear /'lɪnɪə(r)/ a linear

lined¹ /laɪnd/ a ⟨paper⟩ liniert; ⟨wrinkled⟩ faltig

lined² a ⟨garment⟩ gefüttert

linen /'lɪnɪn/ n Leinen nt; ⟨articles⟩ Wäsche f

liner /'laɪnə(r)/ n Passagierschiff nt

'linesman n (Sport) Linienrichter m

linger /'lɪŋgə(r)/ vi [zurück]bleiben

lingerie /'læʒərɪ/ n Damenunterwäsche f

linguist /'lɪŋgwɪst/ n Sprachkundige(r) m/f

linguistic /lɪŋ'gwɪstɪk/ a, -ally adv sprachlich. ~s n Linguistik f

lining /'laɪnɪŋ/ n ⟨of garment⟩ Futter nt; (Techn) Auskleidung f

link /lɪŋk/ n ⟨of chain⟩ Glied nt ⟨fig⟩ Verbindung f □ vt verbinden; ~ arms sich unterhaken

links /lɪŋks/ n or npl Golfplatz m

lino /'laɪnəʊ/ n, linoleum /lɪ'nəʊlɪəm/ n Linoleum nt

lint /lɪnt/ n Verbandstoff m

lion /'laɪən/ n Löwe m; ~'s share ⟨fig⟩ Löwenanteil m. ~ess n Löwin f

lip /lɪp/ n Lippe f; ⟨edge⟩ Rand m; ⟨of jug⟩ Schnabel m

lip: ~-reading n Lippenlesen nt. ~-service n pay ~-service ein Lippenbekenntnis ablegen (to zu). ~stick n Lippenstift m

liquefy /'lɪkwɪfaɪ/ vt ⟨pt/pp -ied⟩ verflüssigen □ vi sich verflüssigen

liqueur /lɪ'kjʊə(r)/ n Likör m

liquid /'lɪkwɪd/ n Flüssigkeit f □ a flüssig

liquidat|e /'lɪkwɪdeɪt/ vt liquidieren. ~ion /-'deɪʃn/ n Liquidation f

liquidize /'lɪkwɪdaɪz/ vt [im Mixer] pürieren. ~r n (Culin) Mixer m

liquor /'lɪkə(r)/ n Alkohol m; ⟨juice⟩ Flüssigkeit f

liquorice /'lɪkərɪs/ n Lakritze f

'liquor store n (Amer) Spirituosengeschäft nt

lisp /lɪsp/ n Lispeln nt □ vt/i lispeln

list¹ /lɪst/ n Liste f □ vt aufführen

list² vi ⟨ship⟩ Schlagseite haben

listen /'lɪsn/ vi zuhören (to dat); ~ to the radio Radio hören. ~er n Zuhörer(in) m(f); (Radio) Hörer(in) m(f)

listless /'lɪstlɪs/ a, -ly adv lustlos

lit /lɪt/ see light¹

litany /'lɪtənɪ/ n Litanei f

literacy /'lɪtərəsɪ/ n Lese- und Schreibfertigkeit f

literal /'lɪtərl/ a wörtlich. ~ly adv buchstäblich

literary /'lɪtərərɪ/ a literarisch

literate /'lɪtərət/ a be ~ lesen und schreiben können

literature /'lɪtrətʃə(r)/ n Literatur f; (fam) Informationsmaterial nt

lithe /laɪð/ a geschmeidig

Lithuania /lɪθjʊ'eɪnɪə/ n Litauen nt

litigation /lɪtɪ'geɪʃn/ n Rechtsstreit m

litre /'liːtə(r)/ n Liter m & nt

litter /'lɪtə(r)/ n Abfall m; (Zool) Wurf m □ vt be ~ed with übersät sein mit. ~-bin n Abfalleimer m

little /'lɪtl/ a klein; ⟨not much⟩ wenig □ adv & n wenig; a ~ ein bisschen/wenig; ~ by ~ nach und nach

liturgy /'lɪtədʒɪ/ n Liturgie f

live¹ /laɪv/ a lebendig; ⟨ammunition⟩ scharf; ~ broadcast Live-Sendung f; be ~ (Electr) unter Strom stehen □ adv (Radio, TV) live

live² /lɪv/ vi leben; ⟨reside⟩ wohnen; ~ up to get married werden (+ dat). ~ on vt leben von; ⟨eat⟩ sich ernähren von □ vi weiterleben

liveli|hood /'laɪvlɪhʊd/ n Lebensunterhalt m. ~ness n Lebendigkeit f

lively /'laɪvlɪ/ a (-ier, -iest) lebhaft, lebendig

liven /'laɪvn/ v ~ up vt beleben □ vi lebhaft werden

liver /'lɪvə(r)/ n Leber f

lives /laɪvz/ see life

livestock /'laɪv-/ n Vieh nt

livid /'lɪvɪd/ a (fam) wütend

living /'lɪvɪŋ/ a lebend □ n earn one's ~ seinen Lebensunterhalt verdienen; the ~ pl die Lebenden. ~-room n Wohnzimmer nt

lizard /'lɪzəd/ n Eidechse f

load /ləʊd/ n Last f; ⟨quantity⟩ Ladung f; (Electr) Belastung f; ~s of (fam) jede Menge □ vt laden ⟨goods, gun⟩; beladen ⟨vehicle⟩; ~ a camera einen Film in eine Kamera einlegen. ~ed a beladen; (fam: rich) steinreich; ~ed question Fangfrage f

loaf¹ /ləʊf/ n (pl loaves) Brot nt

loaf² vi faulenzen

loan /ləʊn/ n Leihgabe f; ⟨money⟩ Darlehen nt; on ~ geliehen □ vt leihen (to dat)

loath /ləʊθ/ a be ~ to do sth etw ungern tun

loath|e /ləʊð/ vt verabscheuen. ~**ing** n Abscheu m. ~**some** a abscheulich

loaves /ləʊvz/ see loaf¹

lobby /'lɒbɪ/ n Foyer nt; (ante-room) Vorraum m; (Pol) Lobby f

lobe /ləʊb/ n (of ear) Ohrläppchen nt

lobster /'lɒbstə(r)/ n Hummer m

local /'ləʊkl/ a hiesig; ⟨time, traffic⟩ Orts-; under ~ anaesthetic unter örtlicher Betäubung; I'm not ~ ich bin nicht von hier □ n Hiesige(r) m/f; (fam: public house) Stammkneipe f. ~ au'thority n Kommunalbehörde f. ~ **call** n (Teleph) Ortsgespräch nt

locality /ləʊ'kælətɪ/ n Gegend f

localized /'ləʊkəlaɪzd/ a lokalisiert

locally /'ləʊkəlɪ/ adv am Ort

locat|e /ləʊ'keɪt/ vt ausfindig machen; be ~**ed** sich befinden. ~**ion** /-'keɪʃn/ n Lage f; filmed on ~**ion** als Außenaufnahme gedreht

lock¹ /lɒk/ n (hair) Strähne f

lock² n (on door) Schloss nt; (on canal) Schleuse f □ vt abschließen □ vi sich abschließen lassen. ~ **in** vt einschließen. ~ **out** vt ausschließen. ~ **up** vt abschließen; einsperren ⟨person⟩ □ vi zuschließen

locker /'lɒkə(r)/ n Schließfach nt; (Mil) Spind m; (in hospital) kleiner Schrank m

locket /'lɒkɪt/ n Medaillon nt

lock: ~**out** n Aussperrung f. ~**smith** n Schlosser m

locomotion /ləʊkə'məʊʃn/ n Fortbewegung f

locomotive /ləʊkə'məʊtɪv/ n Lokomotive f

locum /'ləʊkəm/ n Vertreter(in) m(f)

locust /'ləʊkəst/ n Heuschrecke f

lodge /lɒdʒ/ n (porter's) Pförtnerhaus nt; (masonic) Loge f □ vt ⟨submit⟩ einreichen; ⟨deposit⟩ deponieren □ vi zur Untermiete wohnen (with bei); ⟨become fixed⟩ stecken bleiben. ~**r** n Untermieter(in) m(f)

lodging /'lɒdʒɪŋ/ n Unterkunft f; ~**s** npl möbliertes Zimmer nt

loft /lɒft/ n Dachboden m

lofty /'lɒftɪ/ a (-ier, -iest) hoch; (haughty) hochmütig

log /lɒg/ n Baumstamm m; (for fire) [Holz]scheit nt; sleep like a ~ (fam) wie ein Murmeltier schlafen

logarithm /'lɒgərɪðm/ n Logarithmus m

'log-book n (Naut) Logbuch nt

loggerheads /'lɒgə-/ npl be at ~ (fam) sich in den Haaren liegen

logic /'lɒdʒɪk/ n Logik f. ~**al** a, ~**ly** adv logisch

logistics /lə'dʒɪstɪks/ npl Logistik f

logo /'ləʊgəʊ/ n Symbol nt, Logo nt

loin /lɔɪn/ n (Culin) Lende f

loiter /'lɔɪtə(r)/ vi herumlungern

loll /lɒl/ vi sich lümmeln

loll|ipop /'lɒlɪpɒp/ n Lutscher m. ~**y** n Lutscher m; (fam: money) Moneten pl

London /'lʌndən/ n London nt □ attrib Londoner. ~**er** n Londoner(in) m(f)

lone /ləʊn/ a einzeln. ~**liness** n Einsamkeit f

lonely /'ləʊnlɪ/ a (-ier, -iest) einsam

lone|r /'ləʊnə(r)/ n Einzelgänger m. ~**some** a einsam

long¹ /lɒŋ/ a (-er /'lɒŋgə(r)/, -est /'lɒŋgɪst/) lang; (journey) weit; a ~ **time** lange; a ~ **way** weit; in the ~ **run** auf lange Sicht; (in the end) letzten Endes □ adv lange; all day ~ den ganzen Tag; not ~ ago vor kurzem; before ~ bald; no ~**er** nicht mehr; as or so ~ as solange; so ~! (fam) tschüs! will you be ~? dauert es noch lange [bei dir]? it won't take ~ es dauert nicht lange

long² vi ~ **for** sich sehnen nach

long-'distance a Fern-; (Sport) Langstrecken-

longevity /lɒn'dʒevətɪ/ n Langlebigkeit f

'longhand n Langschrift f

longing /'lɒŋɪŋ/ a, ~**ly** adv sehnsüchtig □ n Sehnsucht f

longitude /'lɒŋgɪtjuːd/ n (Geog) Länge f

long: ~ **jump** n Weitsprung m. ~**life** 'milk n H-Milch f. ~**lived** /-lɪvd/ a langlebig. ~**range** a (Mil, Aviat) Langstrecken-; (forecast) langfristig. ~**sighted** a weitsichtig. ~**sleeved** a langärmelig. ~**suffering** a langmütig. ~**term** a langfristig. ~ **wave** n Langwelle f. ~**winded** /-'wɪndɪd/ a langatmig

loo /luː/ n (fam) Klo nt

look /lʊk/ n Blick m; (appearance) Aussehen nt; [good] ~**s** pl [gutes] Aussehen nt; have a ~ **at** sich (dat) ansehen; go and have a ~ sich mal nach □ vi sehen; (search) nachsehen; (seem) aussehen; don't ~ sieh nicht hin; ~ **here!** hören Sie mal! ~ **at** ansehen; ~ **for** suchen; ~ **forward to** sich freuen auf (+ acc); ~ **in** on vorbeischauen bei; ~ **into** (examine) nachgehen (+ dat); ~ **like** aussehen wie; ~ **on to** ⟨room:⟩ gehen auf (+ acc). ~ **after** vt betreuen; ~ **down** vi hinuntersehen; ~ **down** on s.o. (fig) auf jdn herabsehen. ~ **out** vi hinaus-/heraussehen; (take care) aufpassen; ~ **out for** Ausschau halten nach; ~ **out!** Vorsicht! ~ **round** vi sich umsehen. ~ **up** vi aufblicken; ~ **up to** s.o. (fig) zu jdm aufsehen □ vt nachschlagen ⟨word⟩

'**look-out** n Wache f; (*prospect*) Aussicht f; be on the ∼ for Ausschau halten nach

loom¹ /luːm/ n Webstuhl m

loom² vi auftauchen; (*fig*) sich abzeichnen

loony /'luːnɪ/ a (*fam*) verrückt

loop /luːp/ n Schlinge f; (*in road*) Schleife f; (*on garment*) Aufhänger m □ vt schlingen. ∼hole n Hintertürchen nt; (*in the law*) Lücke f

loose /luːs/ a (-r, -st), -ly adv lose; (*not tight enough*) locker; (*inexact*) frei; be at a ∼ end nichts zu tun haben; set ∼ freilassen; run ∼ frei herumlaufen. ∼ 'change n Kleingeld nt. ∼'chippings npl Rollsplit m

loosen /'luːsn/ vt lockern □ vi sich lockern

loot /luːt/ n Beute f □ vt/i plündern. ∼er n Plünderer m

lop /lɒp/ vt (*pt/pp* lopped) stutzen. ∼ off vt abhacken

lop'**sided** a schief

loquacious /lə'kweɪʃəs/ a redselig

lord /lɔːd/ n Herr m; (*title*) Lord m; House of L∼s ≈ Oberhaus nt; the L∼'s Prayer das Vaterunser; good L∼! du liebe Zeit!

lore /lɔː(r)/ n Überlieferung f

lorry /'lɒrɪ/ n Last[kraft]wagen m

lose /luːz/ v (*pt/pp* lost) □ vt verlieren; (*miss*) verpassen □ vi verlieren; (*clock:*) nachgehen; get lost verloren gehen; (*person:*) sich verlaufen. ∼r n Verlierer m

loss /lɒs/ n Verlust m; be at a ∼ nicht mehr weiter wissen; be at a ∼ for words nicht wissen, was man sagen soll

lost /lɒst/ see lose. ∼ 'property office n Fundbüro nt

lot¹ /lɒt/ Los nt; (*at auction*) Posten m; draw ∼s losen (for um)

lot² n the ∼ alle; (*everything*) alles; a ∼ [of] viel; (*many*) viele; ∼s of (*fam*) eine Menge; it has changed a ∼ es hat sich sehr verändert

lotion /'ləʊʃn/ n Lotion f

lottery /'lɒtərɪ/ n Lotterie f. ∼ ticket n Los nt

loud /laʊd/ a (-er, -est), -ly adv laut; (*colours*) grell □ adv [out] ∼ laut. ∼ 'hailer n Megaphon nt. ∼'speaker n Lautsprecher m

lounge /laʊndʒ/ n Wohnzimmer nt; (*in hotel*) Aufenthaltsraum m. □ vi sich lümmeln. ∼ suit n Straßenanzug m

louse /laʊs/ n (*pl* lice) Laus f

lousy /'laʊzɪ/ a (-ier, -iest) (*fam*) lausig ▮▮.▮▮.▮ .▮ ▮▮▮.▮▮▮ ▮ ▮▮▮▮▮▮ ▮ ▮▮▮▮▮▮ ▮▮ ▮▮ ▮▮ flegelhaft

lovable /'lʌvəbl/ a liebenswert

love /lʌv/ n Liebe f; (*Tennis*) null; in ∼ verliebt □ vt lieben; ∼ doing sth etw sehr gerne machen; I ∼ chocolate ich esse sehr gerne Schokolade. ∼-affair n Liebesverhältnis nt. ∼ letter n Liebesbrief m

lovely /'lʌvlɪ/ a (-ier, -iest) schön; we had a ∼ time es war sehr schön

lover /'lʌvə(r)/ n Liebhaber m

love: ∼ song n Liebeslied nt. ∼ story n Liebesgeschichte f

loving /'lʌvɪŋ/ a, -ly adv liebevoll

low /ləʊ/ a (-er, -est) niedrig; (*cloud, note*) tief; (*voice*) leise; (*depressed*) niedergeschlagen □ adv niedrig; (*fly, sing*) tief; (*speak*) leise; feel ∼ deprimiert sein □ n (*Meteorol*) Tief nt; (*fig*) Tiefstand m

low: ∼brow a geistig anspruchslos. ∼-cut a (*dress*) tief ausgeschnitten

lower /'ləʊə(r)/ a & adv see low □ vt niedriger machen; (*let down*) herunterlassen; (*reduce*) senken; ∼ oneself sich herabwürdigen

low: ∼-'fat a fettarm. ∼-'grade a minderwertig. ∼lands /-ləndz/ npl Tiefland nt. ∼ 'tide n Ebbe f

loyal /'lɔɪəl/ a, -ly adv treu. ∼ty n Treue f

lozenge /'lɒzɪndʒ/ n Pastille f

Ltd abbr (Limited) GmbH

lubricant /'luːbrɪkənt/ n Schmiermittel nt

lubricat|e /'luːbrɪkeɪt/ vt schmieren. ∼ion /-'keɪʃn/ n Schmierung f

lucid /'luːsɪd/ a klar. ∼ity /-'sɪdətɪ/ n Klarheit f

luck /lʌk/ n Glück nt; bad ∼ Pech nt; good ∼! viel Glück! ∼ily adv glücklicherweise, zum Glück

lucky /'lʌkɪ/ a (-ier, -iest) glücklich; (*day, number*) Glücks-; be ∼ Glück haben; (*thing:*) Glück bringen. ∼ 'charm n Amulett nt

lucrative /'luːkrətɪv/ a einträglich

ludicrous /'luːdɪkrəs/ a lächerlich

lug /lʌg/ vt (*pt/pp* lugged) (*fam*) schleppen

luggage /'lʌgɪdʒ/ n Gepäck nt

luggage: ∼-rack n Gepäckablage f. ∼ trolley n Kofferkuli m. ∼-van n Gepäckwagen m

lugubrious /luː'guːbrɪəs/ a traurig

lukewarm /'luːk-/ a lauwarm

lull /lʌl/ n Pause f □ vt ∼ to sleep einschläfern

lullaby /'lʌləbaɪ/ n Wiegenlied nt

lumbago /lʌm'beɪgəʊ/ n Hexenschuss m

lumber /'lʌmbə(r)/ n Gerümpel nt; (*Amer:*) ▮▮▮▮▮▮. jdm etw aufhalsen. ∼jack n (*Amer*) Holzfäller m

luminous /'luːmɪnəs/ a leuchtend; be ∼ leuchten

lump¹ /lʌmp/ n Klumpen m; (of sugar) Stück nt; (swelling) Beule f; (in breast) Knoten m; (tumour) Geschwulst f; a ~ in one's throat (fam) ein Kloß im Hals ▫ vt ~ together zusammentun

lump² vt ~ it (fam) sich damit abfinden

lump: ~ sugar n Würfelzucker m. ~ 'sum n Pauschalsumme f

lumpy /'lʌmpɪ/ a (-ier, -iest) klumpig

lunacy /'luːnəsɪ/ n Wahnsinn m

lunar /'luːnə(r)/ a Mond-

lunatic /'luːnətɪk/ n Wahnsinnige(r) m/f

lunch /lʌntʃ/ n Mittagessen nt ▫ vi zu Mittag essen

luncheon /'lʌntʃn/ n Mittagessen nt. ~ meat n Frühstücksfleisch nt. ~ voucher n Essensbon m

lunch: ~-hour n Mittagspause f. ~-time n Mittagszeit f

lung /lʌŋ/ n Lungenflügel m; ~s pl Lunge f. ~ cancer n Lungenkrebs m

lunge /lʌndʒ/ vi sich stürzen (at auf + acc)

lurch¹ /lɜːtʃ/ n leave in the ~ (fam) im Stich lassen

lurch² vi schleudern; ⟨person:⟩ torkeln

lure /ljʊə(r)/ n Lockung f; (bait) Köder m ▫ vt locken

lurid /'lʊərɪd/ a grell; (sensational) reißerisch

lurk /lɜːk/ vi lauern

luscious /'lʌʃəs/ a lecker, köstlich

lush /lʌʃ/ a üppig

lust /lʌst/ n Begierde f ▫ vi ~ after gieren nach. ~ful a lüstern

lustre /'lʌstə(r)/ n Glanz m

lusty /'lʌstɪ/ a (-ier, -iest) kräftig

lute /luːt/ n Laute f

luxuriant /lʌg'ʒʊərɪənt/ a üppig

luxurious /lʌg'ʒʊərɪəs/ a, -ly adv luxuriös

luxury /'lʌkʃərɪ/ n Luxus m ▫ attrib Luxus-

lying /'laɪɪŋ/ see lie¹, lie²

lymph gland /'lɪmf-/ n Lymphdrüse f

lynch /lɪntʃ/ vt lynchen

lynx /lɪŋks/ n Luchs m

lyric /'lɪrɪk/ a lyrisch. ~al a lyrisch; (fam: enthusiastic) schwärmerisch. ~ poetry n Lyrik f. ~s npl [Lied]text m

M

mac /mæk/ n (fam) Regenmantel m

macabre /mə'kɑːbr/ a makaber

macaroni /mækə'rəʊnɪ/ n Makkaroni pl

macaroon /mækə'ruːn/ n Makrone f

mace¹ /meɪs/ n Amtsstab m

mace² n (spice) Muskatblüte f

machinations /mækɪ'neɪʃnz/ pl Machenschaften pl

machine /mə'ʃiːn/ n Maschine f ▫ vt (sew) mit der Maschine nähen; (Techn) maschinell bearbeiten. ~-gun n Maschinengewehr nt

machinery /mə'ʃiːnərɪ/ n Maschinerie f

machine tool n Werkzeugmaschine f

machinist /mə'ʃiːnɪst/ n Maschinist m; (on sewing machine) Maschinennäherin f

mackerel /'mækrl/ n inv Makrele f

mackintosh /'mækɪntoʃ/ n Regenmantel m

mad /mæd/ a (madder, maddest) verrückt; (dog) tollwütig; (fam: angry) böse (at auf + acc)

madam /'mædəm/ n gnädige Frau f

madden /'mædn/ vt (make angry) wütend machen

made /meɪd/ see make; ~ to measure maßgeschneidert

Madeira cake /mə'dɪərə-/ n Sandkuchen m

mad|ly /'mædlɪ/ adv (fam) wahnsinnig. ~man n Irre(r) m. ~ness n Wahnsinn m

madonna /mə'dɒnə/ n Madonna f

magazine /mægə'ziːn/ n Zeitschrift f; (Mil, Phot) Magazin nt

maggot /'mægət/ n Made f. ~y a madig

Magi /'meɪdʒaɪ/ npl the ~ die Heiligen Drei Könige

magic /'mædʒɪk/ n Zauber m; (tricks) Zauberkunst f ▫ a magisch; ⟨word, wand, flute⟩ Zauber-. ~al a zauberhaft

magician /mə'dʒɪʃn/ n Zauberer m; (entertainer) Zauberkünstler m

magistrate /'mædʒɪstreɪt/ n ≈ Friedensrichter m

magnanim|ity /mægnə'nɪmətɪ/ n Großmut f. ~ous /-'nænɪməs/ a großmütig

magnesia /mæg'niːʃə/ n Magnesia f

magnet /'mægnɪt/ n Magnet m. ~ic /-'netɪk/ a magnetisch. ~ism n Magnetismus m. ~ize vt magnetisieren

magnification /mægnɪfɪ'keɪʃn/ n Vergrößerung f

magnificen|ce /mæg'nıfısəns/ n Großartigkeit f. ~t a, -ly adv großartig

magnify /'mægnıfaı/ vt (pt/pp -ied) vergrößern; (exaggerate) übertreiben. ~ing glass n Vergrößerungsglas nt

magnitude /'mægnıtjuːd/ n Größe f; (importance) Bedeutung f

magpie /'mægpaı/ n Elster f

mahogany /mə'hogənı/ n Mahagoni nt

maid /meıd/ n Dienstmädchen nt; (liter: girl) Maid f; old ~ (pej) alte Jungfer f

maiden /'meıdn/ n (liter) Maid f □ a (speech, voyage) Jungfern-. ~ 'aunt n unverheiratete Tante f. ~ name n Mädchenname m

mail¹ /meıl/ n Kettenpanzer m

mail² n Post f □ vt mit der Post schicken; (send off) abschicken

mail: ~-bag n Postsack m. ~box n (Amer) Briefkasten m. ~ing list n Postversandliste f. ~man n (Amer) Briefträger m. ~-order firm n Versandhaus nt

maim /meım/ vt verstümmeln

main¹ /meın/ n (water, gas, electricity) Hauptleitung f

main² a Haupt- □ n in the ~ im Großen und Ganzen

main: ~land /-lənd/ n Festland nt. ~ly adv hauptsächlich. ~stay n (fig) Stütze f. ~ street n Hauptstraße f

maintain /meın'teın/ vt aufrechterhalten; (keep in repair) instand halten; (support) unterhalten; (claim) behaupten

maintenance /'meıntənəns/ n Aufrechterhaltung f; (care) Instandhaltung f; (allowance) Unterhalt m

maisonette /meızə'net/ n Wohnung f [auf zwei Etagen]

maize /meız/ n Mais m

majestic /mə'dʒestık/ a, -ally adv majestätisch

majesty /'mædʒəstı/ n Majestät f

major /'meıdʒə(r)/ a größer □ n (Mil) Major m; (Mus) Dur nt □ vi (Amer) ~ in als Hauptfach studieren

Majorca /mə'jɔːkə/ n Mallorca nt

majority /mə'dʒorətı/ n Mehrheit f; in the ~ in der Mehrzahl

major road n Hauptverkehrsstraße f

make /meık/ n (brand) Marke f □ v (pt/pp made) □ vt machen; (force) zwingen; (earn) verdienen; halten (speech); treffen (decision); erreichen (destination) □ vi ~ as if to Miene machen zu. ~ do vi zurechtkommen (with mit). ~ for vt zusteuern auf (+ acc). ~ off vi sich davonmachen (with mit). ~ out vt (distinguish) ausmachen; (write out) ausstellen; (assert) behaupten. ~ over vt überschreiben (to auf

+ acc). ~ up vt (constitute) bilden; (invent) erfinden; (apply cosmetics to) schminken; ~ up one's mind sich entschließen □ vi sich versöhnen; ~ up for sth etw wieder gutmachen; ~ up for lost time verlorene Zeit aufholen

'make-believe n Phantasie f

maker /'meıkə(r)/ n Hersteller m

make: ~shift a behelfsmäßig □ n Notbehelf m. ~-up n Make-up nt

making /'meıkıŋ/ n have the ~s of das Zeug haben zu

maladjusted /mælə'dʒʌstıd/ a verhaltensgestört

malaise /mə'leız/ n (fig) Unbehagen nt

male /meıl/ a männlich □ n Mann m; (animal) Männchen nt. ~ nurse n Krankenpfleger m. ~ voice 'choir n Männerchor m

malevolen|ce /mə'levələns/ n Bosheit f. ~t a boshaft

malfunction /mæl'fʌŋkʃn/ n technische Störung f; (Med) Funktionsstörung f □ vi nicht richtig funktionieren

malice /'mælıs/ n Bosheit f; bear s.o. ~ einen Groll gegen jdn hegen

malicious /mə'lıʃəs/ a, -ly adv böswillig

malign /mə'laın/ vt verleumden

malignan|cy /mə'lıgnənsı/ n Bösartigkeit f. ~t a bösartig

malinger /mə'lıŋgə(r)/ vi simulieren, sich krank stellen. ~er n Simulant m

malleable /'mælıəbl/ a formbar

mallet /'mælıt/ n Holzhammer m

malnu'trition /mæl-/ n Unterernährung f

malpractice n Berufsvergehen nt

malt /mɔːlt/ n Malz nt

mal'treat /mæl-/ vt misshandeln. ~ment n Misshandlung f

mammal /'mæml/ n Säugetier nt

mammoth /'mæməθ/ a riesig □ n Mammut nt

man /mæn/ n (pl men) Mann m; (mankind) der Mensch; (chess) Figur f; (draughts) Stein m □ vt (pt/pp manned) bemannen (ship); bedienen (pump); besetzen (counter)

manacle /'mænəkl/ vt fesseln (to an + acc); ~ d in Handschellen

manage /'mænıdʒ/ vt leiten; verwalten (estate); (cope with) fertig werden mit; ~ to do sth es schaffen, etw zu tun □ vi zurechtkommen; ~ on auskommen mit. ~able /-əbl/ a (tool) handlich; (person) fügsam. ~ment /-mənt/ n the ~ment die Geschäftsleitung f

manager /'mænıdʒə(r)/ n Geschäftsführer m; (of bank) Direktor m; (of estate)

Verwalter *m*; (*Sport*) [Chef]trainer *m*. ~ess *n* Geschäftsführerin *f*. ~ial /-'dʒɪə-rɪəl/ *a* ~ial staff Führungskräfte *pl*

managing /'mænɪdʒɪŋ/ *a* ~ director Generaldirektor *m*

mandarin /'mændərɪn/ *n* ~ [orange] Mandarine *f*

mandat|e /'mændeɪt/ *n* Mandat *nt*. ~ory /-dətrɪ/ *a* obligatorisch

mane /meɪn/ *n* Mähne *f*

manful /'mænfl/ *a*, -ly *adv* mannhaft

manger /'meɪndʒə(r)/ *n* Krippe *f*

mangle¹ /'mæŋgl/ *n* Wringmaschine *f*; (*for smoothing*) Mangel *f*

mangle² *vt* (*damage*) verstümmeln

mango /'mæŋgəʊ/ *n* (*pl* -es) Mango *f*

mangy /'meɪndʒɪ/ *a* (*dog*) räudig

man: ~'handle *vt* grob behandeln (*person*). ~hole *n* Kanalschacht *m*. ~hole cover *n* Kanaldeckel *m*. ~hood *n* Mannesalter *nt*; (*quality*) Männlichkeit *f*. ~-hour *n* Arbeitsstunde *f*. ~-hunt *n* Fahndung *f*

man|ia /'meɪnɪə/ *n* Manie *f*. ~iac /-ɪæk/ *n* Wahnsinnige(r) *m/f*

manicur|e /'mænɪkjʊə/ *n* Maniküre *f* □ *vt* maniküren. ~ist *n* Maniküre *f*

manifest /'mænɪfest/ *a*, -ly *adv* offensichtlich □ *vt* ~ itself sich manifestieren

manifesto /mænɪ'festəʊ/ *n* Manifest *nt*

manifold /'mænɪfəʊld/ *a* mannigfaltig

manipulat|e /mə'nɪpjʊleɪt/ *vt* handhaben; (*pej*) manipulieren. ~ion /-'leɪʃn/ *n* Manipulation *f*

man'kind *n* die Menschheit

manly /'mænlɪ/ *a* männlich

'man-made *a* künstlich. ~ fibre *n* Kunstfaser *f*

manner /'mænə(r)/ *n* Weise *f*; (*kind, behaviour*) Art *f*; in this ~ auf diese Weise; [good/bad] ~s [gute/schlechte] Manieren *pl*. ~ism *n* Angewohnheit *f*

mannish /'mænɪʃ/ *a* männlich

manœuvrable /mə'nu:vrəbl/ *a* manövrierfähig

manœuvre /mə'nu:və(r)/ *n* Manöver *nt* □ *vt/i* manövrieren

manor /'mænə(r)/ *n* Gutshof *m*; (*house*) Gutshaus *nt*

man: ~power *n* Arbeitskräfte *pl*. ~servant *n* (*pl* menservants) Diener *m*

mansion /'mænʃn/ *n* Villa *f*

'manslaughter *n* Totschlag *m*

mantelpiece /'mæntl-/ *n* Kaminsims *m* & *nt*

manual /'mænjʊəl/ *a* Hand- □ *n* Handbuch *nt*

manufacture /mænjʊ'fæktʃə(r)/ *vt* herstellen □ *n* Herstellung *f*. ~r *n* Hersteller *m*

manure /mə'njʊə(r)/ *n* Mist *m*

manuscript /'mænjʊskrɪpt/ *n* Manuskript *nt*

many /'menɪ/ *a* viele; ~ a time oft □ *n* a good/great ~ sehr viele

map /mæp/ *n* Landkarte *f*; (*of town*) Stadtplan *m* □ *vt* (*pt/pp* mapped) ~ out (*fig*) ausarbeiten

maple /'meɪpl/ *n* Ahorn *m*

mar /mɑ:(r)/ *vt* (*pt/pp* marred) verderben

marathon /'mærəθən/ *n* Marathon *m*

marauding /mə'rɔ:dɪŋ/ *a* plündernd

marble /'mɑ:bl/ *n* Marmor *m*; (*for game*) Murmel *f*

March /mɑ:tʃ/ *n* März *m*

march *n* Marsch *m* □ *vi* marschieren □ *vt* marschieren lassen; ~ s.o. off jdn abführen

mare /'meə(r)/ *n* Stute *f*

margarine /mɑ:dʒə'ri:n/ *n* Margarine *f*

margin /'mɑ:dʒɪn/ *n* Rand *m*; (*leeway*) Spielraum *m*; (*Comm*) Spanne *f*. ~al *a*, -ly *adv* geringfügig

marigold /'mærɪgəʊld/ *n* Ringelblume *f*

marijuana /mærɪ'hwɑ:nə/ *n* Marihuana *nt*

marina /mə'ri:nə/ *n* Jachthafen *m*

marinade /mærɪ'neɪd/ *n* Marinade *f* □ *vt* marinieren

marine /mə'ri:n/ *a* Meeres- □ *n* Marine *f*; (*sailor*) Marineinfanterist *m*

marionette /mærɪə'net/ *n* Marionette *f*

marital /'mærɪtl/ *a* ehelich. ~ status *n* Familienstand *m*

maritime /'mærɪtaɪm/ *a* See-

marjoram /'mɑ:dʒərəm/ *n* Majoran *m*

mark¹ /mɑ:k/ *n* (*currency*) Mark *f*

mark² *n* Fleck *m*; (*sign*) Zeichen *nt*; (*trace*) Spur *f*; (*target*) Ziel *nt*; (*Sch*) Note *f* □ *vt* markieren; (*spoil*) beschädigen; (*characterize*) kennzeichnen; (*Sch*) korrigieren; (*Sport*) decken; ~ time (*Mil*) auf der Stelle treten; (*fig*) abwarten; ~ my words das [eine] will ich dir sagen. ~ out *vt* markieren

marked /mɑ:kt/ *a*, ~ly /-kɪdlɪ/ *adv* deutlich; (*pronounced*) ausgeprägt

marker /'mɑ:kə(r)/ *n* Marke *f*; (*of exam*) Korrektor(in) *m(f)*

market /'mɑ:kɪt/ *n* Markt *m* □ *vt* vertreiben; (*launch*) auf den Markt bringen. ~ing *n* Marketing *nt*. ~ re'search *n* Marktforschung *f*

marking /'mɑ:kɪŋ/ *n* Markierung *f*; (*on animal*) Zeichnung *f*

marksman /'mɑːksmən/ n Scharfschütze m

marmalade /'mɑːməleɪd/ n Orangenmarmelade f

marmot /'mɑːmət/ n Murmeltier nt

maroon /mə'ruːn/ a dunkelrot

marooned /mə'ruːnd/ a (fig) von der Außenwelt abgeschnitten

marquee /mɑː'kiː/ n Festzelt nt; (Amer: awning) Markise f

marquetry /'mɑːkɪtrɪ/ n Einlegearbeit f

marquis /'mɑːkwɪs/ n Marquis m

marriage /'mærɪdʒ/ n Ehe f; (wedding) Hochzeit f. ~able /-əbl/ a heiratsfähig

married /'mærɪd/ see marry □ a verheiratet. ~ life n Eheleben nt

marrow /'mærəʊ/ n (Anat) Mark nt; (vegetable) Kürbis m

marr|y /'mærɪ/ vt/i (pt/pp married) heiraten; (unite) trauen; get ~ied heiraten

marsh /mɑːʃ/ n Sumpf m

marshal /'mɑːʃl/ n Marschall m; (steward) Ordner m □ vt (pt/pp marshalled) (Mil) formieren; (fig) ordnen

marshy /'mɑːʃɪ/ a sumpfig

marsupial /mɑː'suːpɪəl/ n Beuteltier nt

martial /'mɑːʃl/ a kriegerisch. ~ 'law n Kriegsrecht nt

martyr /'mɑːtə(r)/ n Märtyrer(in) m(f) □ vt zum Märtyrer machen. ~dom /-dəm/ n Martyrium nt

marvel /'mɑːvl/ n Wunder nt □ vi (pt/pp marvelled) staunen (at über + acc). ~lous /-vələs/ a, -ly adv wunderbar

Marxis|m /'mɑːksɪzm/ n Marxismus m. ~t a marxistisch □ n Marxist(in) m(f)

marzipan /'mɑːzɪpæn/ n Marzipan nt

mascara /mæ'skɑːrə/ n Wimperntusche f

mascot /'mæskət/ n Maskottchen nt

masculin|e /'mæskjʊlɪn/ a männlich □ n (Gram) Maskulinum nt. ~ity /-'lɪnətɪ/ n Männlichkeit f

mash /mæʃ/ n (fam, Culin) Kartoffelpüree nt □ vt stampfen. ~ed potatoes npl Kartoffelpüree nt

mask /mɑːsk/ n Maske f □ vt maskieren

masochis|m /'mæsəkɪzm/ n Masochismus m. ~t /-ɪst/ n Masochist m

mason /'meɪsn/ n Steinmetz m

Mason n Freimaurer m. ~ic /mə'sɒnɪk/ a freimaurerisch

masonry /'meɪsnrɪ/ n Mauerwerk nt

masquerade /mæskə'reɪd/ n (fig) Maskerade f □ vi ~ as (pose) sich ausgeben als

mass¹ /mæs/ n (Relig) Messe f

mass² n Masse f □ vi sich sammeln; (Mil) sich massieren

massacre /'mæsəkə(r)/ n Massaker nt □ vt niedermetzeln

massage /'mæsɑːʒ/ n Massage f □ vt massieren

masseu|r /mæ'sɜː(r)/ n Masseur m. ~se /-'sɜːz/ n Masseuse f

massive /'mæsɪv/ a massiv; (huge) riesig

mass: ~ 'media npl Massenmedien pl. ~-pro'duce vt in Massenproduktion herstellen. ~pro'duction n Massenproduktion f

mast /mɑːst/ n Mast m

master /'mɑːstə(r)/ n Herr m; (teacher) Lehrer m; (craftsman, artist) Meister m; (of ship) Kapitän m □ vt meistern; beherrschen (language)

master: ~-key n Hauptschlüssel m. ~ly a meisterhaft. ~-mind n führender Kopf m □ vt der führende Kopf sein von. ~piece n Meisterwerk nt. ~y n (of subject) Beherrschung f

masturbat|e /'mæstəbeɪt/ vi masturbieren. ~ion /-'beɪʃn/ n Masturbation f

mat /mæt/ n Matte f; (on table) Untersatz m

match¹ /mætʃ/ n Wettkampf m; (in ball games) Spiel nt; (Tennis) Match nt; (marriage) Heirat f; be a good ~ (colours:) gut zusammenpassen; be no ~ for s.o. jdm nicht gewachsen sein □ vt (equal) gleichkommen (+ dat); (be like) passen zu; (find sth similar) etwas Passendes finden zu □ vi zusammenpassen

match² n Streichholz nt. ~box n Streichholzschachtel f

matching /'mætʃɪŋ/ a [zusammen]passend

mate¹ /meɪt/ n Kumpel m; (assistant) Gehilfe m; (Naut) Maat m; (Zool) Männchen nt; (female) Weibchen nt □ vi sich paaren □ vt paaren

mate² n (Chess) Matt nt

material /mə'tɪərɪəl/ n Material nt; (fabric) Stoff m; raw ~s Rohstoffe pl □ a materiell

material|ism /mə'tɪərɪəlɪzm/ n Materialismus m. ~istic /-'lɪstɪk/ a materialistisch. ~ize /-laɪz/ vi sich verwirklichen

maternal /mə'tɜːnl/ a mütterlich

maternity /mə'tɜːnətɪ/ n Mutterschaft f. ~ clothes npl Umstandskleidung f. ~ ward n Entbindungsstation f

matey /'meɪtɪ/ a (fam) freundlich

mathematic|al /mæθə'mætɪkl/ a, -ly adv mathematisch. ~ian /-mə'tɪʃn/ n Mathematiker(in) m(f)

mathematics /mæθə'mætɪks/ n Mathematik f

maths /mæθs/ n (fam) Mathe f

matinée /'mætɪneɪ/ n (Theat) Nachmittagsvorstellung f

matriculat|e /məˈtrɪkjʊleɪt/ vi sich immatrikulieren. ~ion /-'leɪʃn/ n Immatrikulation f

matrimon|ial /mætrɪˈməʊnɪəl/ a Ehe-. ~y /'mætrɪmənɪ/ n Ehe f

matrix /'meɪtrɪks/ n (pl matrices /-si:z/) n (Techn: mould) Matrize f

matron /'meɪtrən/ n (of hospital) Oberin f; (of school) Hausmutter f. ~ly a matronenhaft

matt /mæt/ a matt

matted /'mætɪd/ a verfilzt

matter /'mætə(r)/ n (affair) Sache f; (pus) Eiter m; (Phys: substance) Materie f; money ~s Geldangelegenheiten pl; as a ~ of fact eigentlich; what is the ~? was ist los? □ vi wichtig sein; ~ to s.o. jdm etwas ausmachen; it doesn't ~ es macht nichts. ~-of-fact a sachlich

matting /'mætɪŋ/ n Matten pl

mattress /'mætrɪs/ n Matratze f

matur|e /məˈtjʊə(r)/ a reif; (Comm) fällig □ vi reifen; (person:) reifer werden; (Comm) fällig werden □ vt reifen lassen. ~ity n Reifer f; (Comm) Fälligkeit f

maul /mɔ:l/ vt übel zurichten

Maundy /'mɔ:ndɪ/ n ~ Thursday Gründonnerstag m

mauve /məʊv/ a lila

mawkish /'mɔ:kɪʃ/ a rührselig

maxim /'mæksɪm/ n Maxime f

maximum /'mæksɪməm/ a maximal □ n (pl -ima) Maximum nt. ~ speed n Höchstgeschwindigkeit f

may /meɪ/ v aux (nur Präsens) (be allowed to) dürfen; (be possible) können; may I come in? darf ich reinkommen? may he succeed möge es ihm gelingen; I may as well stay am besten bleibe ich hier; it may be true es könnte wahr sein

May n Mai m

maybe /'meɪbɪ/ adv vielleicht

'May Day n der Erste Mai

mayonnaise /meɪəˈneɪz/ n Mayonnaise f

mayor /'meə(r)/ n Bürgermeister m. ~ess n Bürgermeisterin f; (wife of mayor) Frau Bürgermeister f

maze /meɪz/ n Irrgarten m; (fig) Labyrinth nt

me /mi:/ pron (acc) mich; (dat) mir; he knows ~ er kennt mich; give ~ the money gib mir das Geld; it's ~ (fam) ich bin es

meadow /'medəʊ/ n Wiese f

meagre /'mi:gə(r)/ a dürftig

meal¹ /mi:l/ n Mahlzeit f; (food) Essen nt

meal² n (grain) Schrot m

mealy-mouthed /mi:lɪ'maʊðd/ a heuchlerisch

mean¹ /mi:n/ a (-er, -est) geizig; (unkind) gemein; (poor) schäbig

mean² a mittlere(r,s) □ n (average) Durchschnitt m; the golden ~ die goldene Mitte

mean³ vt (pt/pp meant) heißen; (signify) bedeuten; (intend) beabsichtigen; I ~ it das ist mein Ernst; ~ well es gut meinen; be meant for (present:) bestimmt sein für; (remark:) gerichtet sein an (+ acc)

meander /mɪˈændə(r)/ vi sich schlängeln; (person:) schlendern

meaning /'mi:nɪŋ/ n Bedeutung f. ~ful a bedeutungsvoll. ~less a bedeutungslos

means /mi:nz/ n Möglichkeit f, Mittel nt; ~ of transport Verkehrsmittel nt; by ~ of durch; by all ~! aber natürlich! by no ~ keineswegs □ npl (resources) [Geld]mittel pl. ~s test n Bedürftigkeitsnachweis m

meant /ment/ see mean³

'meantime n in the ~ in der Zwischenzeit □ adv inzwischen

'meanwhile adv inzwischen

measles /'mi:zlz/ n Masern pl

measly /'mi:zlɪ/ a (fam) mickerig

measurable /'meʒərəbl/ a messbar

measure /'meʒə(r)/ n Maß nt; (action) Maßnahme f □ vt/i messen; ~ up to (fig) herankommen an (+ acc). ~d a gemessen. ~ment /-mənt/ n Maß nt

meat /mi:t/ n Fleisch nt. ~ ball n (Culin) Klops m. ~ loaf n falscher Hase m

mechan|ic /mɪˈkænɪk/ n Mechaniker m. ~ical a, -ly adv mechanisch. ~ical engineering Maschinenbau m. ~ics n Mechanik f □ n pl Mechanismus m

mechan|ism /'mekənɪzm/ n Mechanismus m. ~ize vt mechanisieren

medal /'medl/ n Orden m; (Sport) Medaille f

medallion /mɪˈdælɪən/ n Medaillon nt

medallist /'medəlɪst/ n Medaillengewinner(in) m(f)

meddle /'medl/ vi sich einmischen (in in + acc); (tinker) herumhantieren (with an + acc)

media /'mi:dɪə/ see medium □ n pl the ~ die Medien pl

median /'mi:dɪən/ a ~ strip (Amer) Mittelstreifen m

mediat|e /'mi:dɪeɪt/ vi vermitteln. ~or n Vermittler(in) m(f)

medical /'medɪkl/ a medizinisch; (treatment) ärztlich □ n ärztliche Untersuchung f. ~ insurance n Krankenversicherung f. ~ student n Medizinstudent m

medicat|ed /'medɪkeɪtɪd/ a medizinisch. ∼ion /-'keɪʃn/ n (drugs) Medikamente pl

medicinal /mɪ'dɪsɪnl/ a medizinisch; ⟨plant⟩ heilkräftig

medicine /'medsən/ n Medizin f; (preparation) Medikament nt

medieval /medɪ'iːvl/ a mittelalterlich

mediocr|e /miːdɪ'əʊkə(r)/ a mittelmäßig. ∼ity /-'ɒkrətɪ/ n Mittelmäßigkeit f

meditat|e /'medɪteɪt/ vi nachdenken (on über + acc); ⟨Relig⟩ meditieren. ∼ion /-'teɪʃn/ n Meditation f

Mediterranean /medɪtə'reɪnɪən/ n Mittelmeer nt □ a Mittelmeer-

medium /'miːdɪəm/ a mittlere(r,s); ⟨steak⟩ medium; of ∼ size von mittlerer Größe □ n (pl media) Medium nt; (means) Mittel nt □ (pl -s) (person) Medium nt

medium: ∼-sized a mittelgroß. ∼ wave n Mittelwelle f

medley /'medlɪ/ n Gemisch nt; (Mus) Potpourri nt

meek /miːk/ a (-er, -est), -ly adv sanftmütig; (unprotesting) widerspruchslos

meet /miːt/ v (pt/pp met) □ vt treffen; (by chance) begegnen (+ dat); (at station) abholen; (make the acquaintance of) kennenlernen; stoßen auf (+ acc) ⟨problem⟩; bezahlen ⟨bill⟩; erfüllen ⟨requirements⟩ □ vi sich treffen; (for the first time) sich kennenlernen; ∼ with stoßen auf (+ acc) ⟨problem⟩; sich treffen mit ⟨person⟩ □ n Jagdtreffen f

meeting /'miːtɪŋ/ n Treffen nt; (by chance) Begegnung f; (discussion) Besprechung f; (of committee) Sitzung f; (large) Versammlung f

megalomania /megələ'meɪnɪə/ n Größenwahnsinn m

megaphone /'megəfəʊn/ n Megaphon nt

melancholy /'melənkəlɪ/ a melancholisch □ n Melancholie f

mellow /'meləʊ/ a(-er, -est) ⟨fruit⟩ ausgereift; ⟨sound, person⟩ sanft □ vi reifer werden

melodic /mɪ'lɒdɪk/ a melodisch

melodious /mɪ'ləʊdɪəs/ a melodiös

melodrama /'melə-/ n Melodrama nt. ∼tic /-drə'mætɪk/ a, -ally adv melodramatisch

melody /'melədɪ/ n Melodie f

melon /'melən/ n Melone f

melt /melt/ vt/i schmelzen; damm vt einschmelzen. ∼ing-pot n (fig) Schmelztiegel m

member /'membə(r)/ n Mitglied nt; (of family) Angehörige(r) m/f; M∼ of Parliament Abgeordnete(r) m/f. ∼ship n

Mitgliedschaft f; (members) Mitgliederzahl f

membrane /'membreɪn/ n Membran f

memento /mɪ'mentəʊ/ n Andenken nt

memo /'meməʊ/ n Mitteilung f

memoirs /'memwɑːz/ n pl Memoiren pl

memorable /'memərəbl/ a denkwürdig

memorandum /memə'rændəm/ n Mitteilung f

memorial /mɪ'mɔːrɪəl/ n Denkmal nt. ∼ service n Gedenkfeier f

memorize /'meməraɪz/ vt sich (dat) einprägen

memory /'memərɪ/ n Gedächtnis nt; (thing remembered) Erinnerung f; (of computer) Speicher m; from ∼ auswendig; in ∼ of zur Erinnerung an (+ acc)

men /men/ see man

menac|e /'menɪs/ n Drohung f; (nuisance) Plage f □ vt bedrohen. ∼ing a, ∼ly adv drohend

mend /mend/ vt reparieren; (patch) flicken; ausbessern ⟨clothes⟩ □ n on the ∼ auf dem Weg der Besserung

'menfolk n pl Männer pl

menial /'miːnɪəl/ a niedrig

meningitis /menɪn'dʒaɪtɪs/ n Hirnhautentzündung f, Meningitis f

menopause /'menə-/ n Wechseljahre pl

menstruat|e /'menstrʊeɪt/ vi menstruieren. ∼ion /-'eɪʃn/ n Menstruation f

mental /'mentl/ a, -ly adv geistig; (fam: mad) verrückt. ∼ a'rithmetic n Kopfrechnen nt. ∼ 'illness n Geisteskrankheit f

mentality /men'tælətɪ/ n Mentalität f

mention /'menʃn/ n Erwähnung f □ vt erwähnen; don't ∼ it keine Ursache; bitte

menu /'menjuː/ n Speisekarte f

mercantile /'mɜːkəntaɪl/ a Handels-

mercenary /'mɜːsɪnərɪ/ a geldgierig □ n Söldner m

merchandise /'mɜːtʃəndaɪz/ n Ware f

merchant /'mɜːtʃənt/ n Kaufmann m; (dealer) Händler m. ∼ 'navy n Handelsmarine f

merci|ful /'mɜːsɪfl/ a barmherzig. ∼fully adv (fam) glücklicherweise. ∼less a, -ly adv erbarmungslos

mercury /'mɜːkjʊrɪ/ n Quecksilber nt

mercy /'mɜːsɪ/ n Barmherzigkeit f, Gnade f; be at s.o.'s ∼ jdm ausgeliefert sein

mere /mɪə(r)/ a, -ly adv bloß

merest /'mɪərɪst/ a kleinste(r,s)

merge /mɜːdʒ/ vi zusammenlaufen; (Comm) fusionieren □ vt (Comm) zusammenschließen

merger /'mɜːdʒə(r)/ n Fusion f

meridian /mə'rɪdɪən/ n Meridian m

meringue /mə'ræŋ/ n Baiser nt

merit /'merɪt/ n Verdienst nt; (advantage) Vorzug m; (worth) Wert m ▫ vt verdienen

mermaid /'mɜːmeɪd/ n Meerjungfrau f

merri|ly /'merɪlɪ/ adv fröhlich. ∼ment /-mənt/ n Fröhlichkeit f; (laughter) Gelächter nt

merry /'merɪ/ a (-ier, -iest) fröhlich. ∼ Christmas! fröhliche Weihnachten!

merry: ∼-go-round n Karussell nt. ∼-making n Feiern nt

mesh /meʃ/ n Masche f; (size) Maschenweite f; (fig: network) Netz nt

mesmerize /'mezməraɪz/ vt hypnotisieren. ∼d a (fig) [wie] gebannt

mess /mes/ n Durcheinander nt; (trouble) Schwierigkeiten pl; (something spilt) Bescherung f (fam); (Mil) Messe f; make a ∼ of (botch) verpfuschen ▫ vt ∼ up in Unordnung bringen; (botch) verpfuschen ▫ vi ∼ about herumalbern; (tinker) herumspielen (with mit)

message /'mesɪdʒ/ n Nachricht f; give s.o. a ∼ jdm etwas ausrichten

messenger /'mesɪndʒə(r)/ n Bote m

Messiah /mɪ'saɪə/ n Messias m

Messrs /'mesəz/ n pl see Mr; (on letter) ∼ Smith Firma Smith

messy /'mesɪ/ a (-ier, -iest) schmutzig; (untidy) unordentlich

met /met/ see meet

metabolism /mɪ'tæbəlɪzm/ n Stoffwechsel m

metal /'metl/ n Metall nt ▫ a Metall-. ∼lic /mɪ'tælɪk/ a metallisch. ∼lurgy /mɪ'tælədʒɪ/ n Metallurgie f

metamorphosis /metə'mɔːfəsɪs/ n (pl -phoses /-siːz/) Metamorphose f

metaphor /'metəfə(r)/ n Metapher f. ∼ical /-'fɒrɪkl/ a, -ly adv metaphorisch

meteor /'miːtɪə(r)/ n Meteor m. ∼ic /-'ɒrɪk/ a kometenhaft

meteorological /miːtɪərə'lɒdʒɪkl/ a Wetter-

meteorolog|ist /miːtɪə'rɒlədʒɪst/ n Meteorologe m/ -gin f. ∼y n Meteorologie f

meter¹ /'miːtə(r)/ n Zähler m

meter² n (Amer) = metre

method /'meθəd/ n Methode f; (Culin) Zubereitung f

methodical /mɪ'θɒdɪkl/ a, -ly adv systematisch, methodisch

Methodist /'meθədɪst/ n Methodist(in) m(f)

meths /meθs/ n (fam) Brennspiritus m

methylated /'meθɪleɪtɪd/ a ∼ spirit[s] Brennspiritus m

meticulous /mɪ'tɪkjʊləs/ a, -ly adv sehr genau

metre /'miːtə(r)/ n Meter m & n; (rhythm) Versmaß nt

metric /'metrɪk/ a metrisch

metropolis /mɪ'trɒpəlɪs/ n Metropole f

metropolitan /metrə'pɒlɪtən/ a hauptstädtisch; (international) weltstädtisch

mettle /'metl/ n Mut m

mew /mjuː/ n Miau nt ▫ vi miauen

Mexican /'meksɪkən/ a mexikanisch ▫ n Mexikaner(in) m(f). 'Mexico n Mexiko nt

miaow /mɪ'aʊ/ n Miau nt ▫ vi miauen

mice /maɪs/ see mouse

microbe /'maɪkrəʊb/ n Mikrobe f

micro /'maɪkrəʊ/: ∼chip n Mikrochip nt. ∼computer n Mikrocomputer m. ∼film n Mikrofilm m. ∼phone n Mikrofon m. ∼processor n Mikroprozessor m. ∼scope /-skəʊp/ n Mikroskop nt. ∼scopic /-'skɒpɪk/ a mikroskopisch. ∼wave n Mikrowelle f. ∼wave [oven] n Mikrowellenherd m

mid /mɪd/ a ∼ May Mitte Mai; in ∼ air in der Luft

midday /mɪd'deɪ/ n Mittag m

middle /'mɪdl/ a mittlere(r,s); the M∼ Ages das Mittelalter; the ∼ class[es] der Mittelstand; the M∼ East der Nahe Osten ▫ n Mitte f; in the ∼ of the night mitten in der Nacht

middle: ∼-aged a mittleren Alters. ∼-class a bürgerlich. ∼man n (Comm) Zwischenhändler m

middling /'mɪdlɪŋ/ a mittelmäßig

midge /mɪdʒ/ n [kleine] Mücke f

midget /'mɪdʒɪt/ n Liliputaner(in) m(f)

Midlands /'mɪdləndz/ npl the ∼ Mittelengland n

'midnight n Mitternacht f

midriff /'mɪdrɪf/ n (fam) Taille f

midst /mɪdst/ n in the ∼ of mitten in (+ dat); in our ∼ unter uns

mid: ∼summer n Hochsommer m; (solstice) Sommersonnenwende f. ∼way adv auf halbem Wege. ∼wife n Hebamme f. ∼wifery /-wɪfrɪ/ n Geburtshilfe f. ∼'winter n Mitte f des Winters

might¹ /maɪt/ v aux I ∼ vielleicht; it ∼ be true es könnte wahr sein; I ∼ as well stay am besten bleibe ich hier; he asked if he ∼ go er fragte, ob er gehen dürfte; you ∼ have drowned du hättest ertrinken können

might² n Macht f

mighty /'maɪtɪ/ a (-ier, -iest) mächtig

migraine /'miːgreɪn/ n Migräne f

migrant /'maɪgrənt/ a Wander- ▫ n (bird) Zugvogel m

migrat|e /maɪˈgreɪt/ vi abwandern; (birds:) ziehen. ∼ion /-ˈgreɪʃn/ n Wanderung f; (of birds) Zug m

mike /maɪk/ n (fam) Mikrofon nt

mild /maɪld/ a (-er, -est) mild

mildew /ˈmɪldju:/ n Schimmel m; (Bot) Mehltau m

mild|ly /ˈmaɪldlɪ/ adv leicht; to put it ∼ly gelinde gesagt. ∼ness n Milde f

mile /maɪl/ n Meile f (= 1,6 km); ∼s too big (fam) viel zu groß

mile|age /-ɪdʒ/ n Meilenzahl f; (of car) Meilenstand m. ∼stone n Meilenstein m

militant /ˈmɪlɪtənt/ a militant

military /ˈmɪlɪtrɪ/ a militärisch. ∼ service n Wehrdienst m

militate /ˈmɪlɪteɪt/ vi ∼ against sprechen gegen

militia /mɪˈlɪʃə/ n Miliz f

milk /mɪlk/ n Milch f □ vt melken

milk: ∼man n Milchmann m. ∼ shake n Milchmixgetränk nt. ∼ tooth n Milchzahn m ·

milky /ˈmɪlkɪ/ a (-ier, -iest) milchig. M∼ Way n (Astr) Milchstraße f

mill /mɪl/ n Mühle f; (factory) Fabrik f □ vt/i mahlen; (Techn) fräsen. ∼ about, ∼ around vi umherlaufen

millenium /mɪˈlenɪəm/ n Jahrtausend nt

miller /ˈmɪlə(r)/ n Müller m

millet /ˈmɪlɪt/ n Hirse f

milli|gram /ˈmɪlɪ-/ n Milligramm nt. ∼metre n Millimeter m & nt

milliner /ˈmɪlɪnə(r)/ n Modistin f; (man) Hutmacher m. ∼y n Damenhüte pl

million /ˈmɪljən/ n Million f; a ∼ pounds eine Million Pfund. ∼aire /-ˈneə(r)/ n Millionär(in) m(f)

'**millstone** n Mühlstein m

mime /maɪm/ n Pantomime f □ vt pantomimisch darstellen

mimic /ˈmɪmɪk/ n Imitator m □ vt (pt/pp mimicked) nachahmen. ∼ry n Nachahmung f

mimosa /mɪˈməʊzə/ n Mimose f

mince /mɪns/ n Hackfleisch nt □ vt (Culin) durchdrehen; not ∼ one's words kein Blatt vor den Mund nehmen

mince: ∼meat n Masse f aus Korinthen, Zitronat usw; make ∼ meat of (fig) vernichtend schlagen. ∼'pie n mit 'mincemeat' gefülltes Pastetchen m

mincer /ˈmɪnsə(r)/ n Fleischwolf m

mind /maɪnd/ n Geist m; (sanity) Verstand m; to my ∼ meiner Meinung nach; give s.o. a piece of one's ∼ jdm gehörig die Meinung sagen; make up one's ∼ sich entschließen; be out of one's ∼ nicht bei Verstand sein; have sth in ∼ etw im Sinn haben; bear sth in ∼ an etw (acc) denken; have a good ∼ to große Lust haben, zu; I have changed my ∼ ich habe es mir anders überlegt □ vt aufpassen auf (+ acc); I don't ∼ the noise der Lärm stört mich nicht; ∼ the step! Achtung Stufe! □ vi (care) sich kümmern (about um); I don't ∼ mir macht es nichts aus; never ∼! macht nichts! do you ∼ if? haben Sie etwas dagegen, wenn? ∼ out vi aufpassen

mind|ful a ∼ful of eingedenk (+ gen). ∼less a geistlos

mine¹ /maɪn/ poss pron meine(r), meins; a friend of ∼ ein Freund von mir; that is ∼ das gehört mir

mine² n Bergwerk nt; (explosive) Mine f □ vt abbauen; (Mil) verminen. ∼ detector n Minensuchgerät nt. ∼field n Minenfeld nt

miner /ˈmaɪnə(r)/ n Bergarbeiter m

mineral /ˈmɪnərl/ n Mineral nt. ∼ogy /-ˈrælədʒɪ/ n Mineralogie f. ∼ water n Mineralwasser nt

minesweeper /ˈmaɪn-/ n Minenräumboot nt

mingle /ˈmɪŋgl/ vi ∼ with sich mischen unter (+ acc)

miniature /ˈmɪnɪtʃə(r)/ a Klein- □ n Miniatur f

mini|bus /ˈmɪnɪ-/ n Kleinbus m. ∼cab n Taxi nt

minim /ˈmɪnɪm/ n (Mus) halbe Note f

minim|al /ˈmɪnɪməl/ a minimal. ∼ize vt auf ein Minimum reduzieren. ∼um n (pl -ima) Minimum nt □ a Mindest-

mining /ˈmaɪnɪŋ/ n Bergbau m

miniskirt /ˈmɪnɪ-/ n Minirock m

minist|er /ˈmɪnɪstə(r)/ n Minister m; (Relig) Pastor m. ∼erial /-ˈstɪərɪəl/ a ministeriell

ministry /ˈmɪnɪstrɪ/ n (Pol) Ministerium nt; the ∼ (Relig) das geistliche Amt

mink /mɪŋk/ n Nerz m

minor /ˈmaɪnə(r)/ a kleiner; (less important) unbedeutend □ n Minderjährige(r) m/f; (Mus) Moll m

minority /maɪˈnɒrətɪ/ n Minderheit f; (age) Minderjährigkeit f

minor road n Nebenstraße f

mint¹ /mɪnt/ n Münzstätte f □ a (stamp) postfrisch; in ∼ condition wie neu □ vt prägen

mint² n (herb) Minze f; (sweet) Pfefferminzbonbon m & nt

minuet /mɪnjʊˈet/ n Menuett nt

minus /ˈmaɪnəs/ prep minus, weniger; (fam: without) ohne □ n ∼ [sign] Minuszeichen nt

minute¹ /'mɪnɪt/ n Minute f; in a ~ (shortly) gleich; ~s pl (of meeting) Protokoll nt

minute² /maɪ'njuːt/ a winzig; (precise) genau

mirac|le /'mɪrəkl/ n Wunder nt. ~ulous /-'rækjʊləs/ a wunderbar

mirage /'mɪrɑːʒ/ n Fata Morgana f

mire /'maɪə(r)/ n Morast m

mirror /'mɪrə(r)/ n Spiegel m □ vt widerspiegeln

mirth /mɜːθ/ n Heiterkeit f

misad'venture /mɪs-/ n Missgeschick nt

misanthropist /mɪ'zænθrəpɪst/ n Menschenfeind m

misappre'hension n Missverständnis nt; be under a ~ sich irren

misbe'have vi sich schlecht benehmen. ~iour n schlechtes Benehmen nt

mis'calcu|late vt falsch berechnen □ vi sich verrechnen. ~lation n Fehlkalkulation f

'**miscarriage** n Fehlgeburt f; ~ of justice Justizirrtum m. mis'carry vi eine Fehlgeburt haben

miscellaneous /mɪsə'leɪnɪəs/ a vermischt

mischief /'mɪstʃɪf/ n Unfug m; (harm) Schaden m

mischievous /'mɪstʃɪvəs/ a, -ly adv schelmisch; (malicious) boshaft

miscon'ception n falsche Vorstellung f

mis'conduct n unkorrektes Verhalten nt; (adultery) Ehebruch m

miscon'strue vt missdeuten

mis'deed n Missetat f

misde'meanour n Missetat f

miser /'maɪzə(r)/ n Geizhals m

miserable /'mɪzrəbl/ a, -bly adv unglücklich; (wretched) elend

miserly /'maɪzəlɪ/ adv geizig

misery /'mɪzərɪ/ n Elend nt; (fam: person) Miesepeter m

mis'fire vi fehlzünden; (go wrong) fehlschlagen

'**misfit** n Außenseiter(in) m(f)

mis'fortune n Unglück nt

mis'givings npl Bedenken pl

mis'guided a töricht

mishap /'mɪshæp/ n Missgeschick nt

misin'form vt falsch unterrichten

misin'terpret vt missdeuten

mis'judge vt falsch beurteilen; (estimate wrongly) falsch einschätzen

mis'lay vt (pt/pp -laid) verlegen

mis'lead vt (pt/pp -led) irreführen. ~ing a irreführend

mis'manage vt schlecht verwalten. ~ment n Misswirtschaft f

misnomer /mɪs'nəʊmə(r)/ n Fehlbezeichnung f

'**misprint** n Druckfehler m

mis'quote vt falsch zitieren

misrepre'sent vt falsch darstellen

miss /mɪs/ n Fehltreffer m □ vt verpassen; (fail to hit or find) verfehlen; (fail to attend) versäumen; (fail to notice) übersehen; (feel the loss of) vermissen □ vi (fail to hit) nicht treffen. ~ out vt auslassen

Miss n (pl -es) Fräulein nt

misshapen /mɪs'ʃeɪpn/ a missgestaltet

missile /'mɪsaɪl/ n [Wurf]geschoss nt; (Mil) Rakete f

missing /'mɪsɪŋ/ a fehlend (lost) verschwunden; (Mil) vermisst; be ~ fehlen

mission /'mɪʃn/ n Auftrag m; (Mil) Einsatz m; (Relig) Mission f

missionary /'mɪʃənrɪ/ n Missionar(in) m(f)

mis'spell vt (pt/pp -spelt or -spelled) falsch schreiben

mist /mɪst/ n Dunst m; (fog) Nebel m; (on window) Beschlag m □ vi ~ up beschlagen

mistake /mɪ'steɪk/ n Fehler m; by ~ aus Versehen □ vt (pt mistook, pp mistaken) missverstehen; ~ for verwechseln mit

mistaken /mɪ'steɪkən/ a falsch; be ~ sich irren; ~ identity Verwechslung f. ~ly adv irrtümlicherweise

mistletoe /'mɪsltəʊ/ n Mistel f

mistress /'mɪstrɪs/ n Herrin f; (teacher) Lehrerin f; (lover) Geliebte f

mis'trust n Misstrauen nt □ vt misstrauen (+ dat)

misty /'mɪstɪ/ a (-ier, -iest) dunstig; (foggy) neblig; (fig) unklar

misunder'stand vt (pt/pp -stood) missverstehen. ~ing n Missverständnis nt

misuse¹ /mɪs'juːz/ vt missbrauchen

misuse² /mɪs'juːs/ n Missbrauch m

mite /maɪt/ n (Zool) Milbe f; little ~ (child) kleines Ding nt

mitigat|e /'mɪtɪgeɪt/ vt mildern. ~ing a mildernd

mitten /'mɪtn/ n Fausthandschuh m

mix /mɪks/ n Mischung f □ vt mischen □ vi sich mischen; ~ with (associate with) verkehren mit. ~ up vt mischen; (muddle) durcheinander bringen; (mistake for) verwechseln (mit)

mixed /mɪkst/ a gemischt; be ~ up durcheinander sein

mixer /'mɪksə(r)/ n Mischmaschine f; (Culin) Küchenmaschine f mixture /'mɪkstʃə(r)/ n Mischung f; (medicine) Mixtur f; (Culin) Teig m

'mix up n Durcheinander nt; (confusion) Verwirrung f; (mistake) Verwechslung f

moan /məʊn/ n Stöhnen nt ▢ vi stöhnen; (complain) jammern

moat /məʊt/ n Burggraben m

mob /mɒb/ n Horde f; (rabble) Pöbel m; (fam: gang) Bande f ▢ vt (pt/pp mobbed) herfallen über (+ acc); belagern ⟨celebrity⟩

mobile /'məʊbaɪl/ a beweglich ▢ n Mobile nt; (telephone) Handy nt. ~ 'home n Wohnwagen m. ~ 'phone n Mobiltelefon nt, Handy nt

mobility /məˈbɪlətɪ/ n Beweglichkeit f

mobi|lization /məʊbɪlaɪ'zeɪʃn/ n Mobilisierung f. ~lize /'məʊbɪlaɪz/ vt mobilisieren

mocha /'mɒkə/ n Mokka m

mock /mɒk/ a Schein- ▢ vt verspotten. ~ery n Spott m

'mock-up n Modell nt

modal /'məʊdl/ a ~ auxiliary Modalverb nt

mode /məʊd/ n [Art und] Weise f; (fashion) Mode f

model /'mɒdl/ n Modell nt; (example) Vorbild nt; [fashion] ~ Mannequin nt ▢ a Modell-; (exemplary) Muster- ▢ v (pt/pp modelled) ▢ vt formen, modellieren; vorführen ⟨clothes⟩ ▢ vi Mannequin sein; (for artist) Modell stehen

moderate¹ /'mɒdəreɪt/ vt mäßigen ▢ vi sich mäßigen

moderate² /'mɒdərət/ a mäßig; ⟨opinion⟩ gemäßigt ▢ n (Pol) Gemäßigte(r) m/f. ~ly adv mäßig; (fairly) einigermaßen

moderation /mɒdəˈreɪʃn/ n Mäßigung f; in ~ mit Maß[en]

modern /'mɒdn/ a modern. ~ize vt modernisieren. ~ 'languages npl neuere Sprachen pl

modest /'mɒdɪst/ a bescheiden; (decorous) schamhaft. ~y n Bescheidenheit f

modicum /'mɒdɪkəm/ n a ~ of ein bisschen

modifi|cation /mɒdɪfɪ'keɪʃn/ n Abänderung f. ~y /'mɒdɪfaɪ/ vt (pt/pp -fied) abändern

modulate /'mɒdjʊleɪt/ vt/i modulieren

moist /mɔɪst/ a (-er, -est) feucht

moisten /'mɔɪsn/ vt befeuchten

moistur|e /'mɔɪstʃə(r)/ n Feuchtigkeit f. ~izer n Feuchtigkeitscreme f

molar /'məʊlə(r)/ n Backenzahn m

molasses /məˈlæsɪz/ n (Amer) Sirup m

mole¹ /məʊl/ n Leberfleck m

mole² n (Zool) Maulwurf m

mole³ n (breakwater) Mole f

molecule /'mɒlɪkjuːl/ n Molekül nt

'molehill n Maulwurfshaufen m

molest /məˈlest/ vt belästigen

mollify /'mɒlɪfaɪ/ vt (pt/pp -ied) besänftigen

mollusc /'mɒləsk/ n Weichtier nt

mollycoddle /'mɒlɪkɒdl/ vt verzärteln

molten /'məʊltən/ a geschmolzen

mom /mɒm/ n (Amer fam) Mutti f

moment /'məʊmənt/ n Moment m, Augenblick m; at the ~ im Augenblick, augenblicklich. ~ary a vorübergehend

momentous /məˈmentəs/ a bedeutsam

momentum /məˈmentəm/ n Schwung m

monarch /'mɒnək/ n Monarch(in) m(f). ~y n Monarchie f

monast|ery /'mɒnəstrɪ/ n Kloster nt. ~ic /mə'næstɪk/ a Kloster-

Monday /'mʌndeɪ/ n Montag m

money /'mʌnɪ/ n Geld nt

money: ~box n Sparbüchse f. ~-lender n Geldverleiher m. ~ order n Zahlungsanweisung f

mongrel /'mʌŋgrəl/ n Promenadenmischung f

monitor /'mɒnɪtə(r)/ n (Techn) Monitor m ▢ vt überwachen ⟨progress⟩; abhören ⟨broadcast⟩

monk /mʌŋk/ n Mönch m

monkey /'mʌŋkɪ/ n Affe m. ~-nut n Erdnuss f. ~-wrench n (Techn) Engländer m

mono /'mɒnəʊ/ n Mono nt

monocle /'mɒnəkl/ n Monokel nt

monogram /'mɒnəgræm/ n Monogramm nt

monologue /'mɒnəlɒg/ n Monolog m

monopol|ize /məˈnɒpəlaɪz/ vt monopolisieren. ~y n Monopol nt

monosyll|abic /mɒnəsɪ'læbɪk/ a einsilbig. ~able /'mɒnəsɪləbl/ n einsilbiges Wort nt

monotone /'mɒnətəʊn/ n in a ~ mit monotoner Stimme

monoton|ous /məˈnɒtənəs/ a, -ly adv eintönig, monoton; (tedious) langweilig. ~y n Eintönigkeit f, Monotonie f

monsoon /mɒn'suːn/ n Monsun m

monster /'mɒnstə(r)/ n Ungeheuer nt; (cruel person) Unmensch m

monstrosity /mɒn'strɒsətɪ/ n Monstrosität f

monstrous /'mɒnstrəs/ a ungeheuer, (outrageous) ungeheuerlich

montage /mɒn'tɑːʒ/ n Montage f

month /mʌnθ/ n Monat m. ~ly a & adv monatlich ▢ n (periodical) Monatszeitschrift f

monument /'mɒnjʊmənt/ n Denkmal nt.
~al /-'mentl/ a (fig) monumental

moo /muː/ n Muh nt □ vi (pt/pp mooed)
muhen

mooch /muːtʃ/ vi ~ about (fam)
herumschleichen

mood /muːd/ n Laune f; be in a good/bad
~ gute/schlechte Laune haben

moody /'muːdɪ/ a (-ier, -iest) launisch

moon /muːn/ n Mond m; over the ~ (fam)
überglücklich

moon: ~light n Mondschein m. ~light-
ing n (fam) ≈ Schwarzarbeit f. ~lit a
mondhell

moor¹ /mʊə(r)/ n Moor nt

moor² vt (Naut) festmachen □ vi anlegen.
~ings npl (chains) Verankerung f; (place)
Anlegestelle f

moose /muːs/ n Elch m

moot /muːt/ a it's a ~ point darüber lässt
sich streiten □ vt aufwerfen (question)

mop /mɒp/ n Mopp m; ~ of hair Wuschelk-
opf m □ vt (pt/pp mopped) wischen. ~ up
vt aufwischen

mope /məʊp/ vi Trübsal blasen

moped /'məʊped/ n Moped nt

moral /'mɒrl/ a, -ly adv moralisch,
sittlich; (virtuous) tugendhaft □ n Moral
f; ~s pl Moral f

morale /mə'rɑːl/ n Moral f

morality /mə'rælətɪ/ n Sittlichkeit f

moralize /'mɒrəlaɪz/ vi moralisieren

morbid /'mɔːbɪd/ a krankhaft; (gloomy)
trübe

more /mɔː(r)/ a, adv & n mehr; (in addition) noch; a few ~ noch ein paar; any ~
noch etwas; once ~ noch einmal; ~ or
less mehr oder weniger; some ~ tea?
noch etwas Tee? ~ interesting inte-
ressanter; ~ [and ~] quickly [immer]
schneller; no ~, thank you, nichts mehr,
danke; no ~ bread kein Brot mehr; no ~
apples keine Äpfel mehr

moreover /mɔː'rəʊvə(r)/ adv außerdem

morgue /mɔːg/ n Leichenschauhaus nt

moribund /'mɒrɪbʌnd/ a sterbend

morning /'mɔːnɪŋ/ n Morgen m; in the ~
morgens, am Morgen; (tomorrow) morgen
früh

Morocco /mə'rɒkəʊ/ n Marokko nt

moron /'mɔːrɒn/ n (fam) Idiot m

morose /mə'rəʊs/ a, -ly adv mürrisch

morphine /'mɔːfiːn/ n Morphium nt

Morse /mɔːs/ n ~ [code] Morsealphabet
nt

morsel /'mɔːsl/ n (food) Happen m

mortal /'mɔːtl/ a sterblich; (fatal) tödlich
□ n Sterbliche(r) m/f. ~ity /mɔː'tælətɪ/ n
Sterblichkeit f. ~ly adv tödlich

mortar /'mɔːtə(r)/ n Mörtel m

mortgage /'mɔːgɪdʒ/ n Hypothek f □ vt
hypothekarisch belasten

mortify /'mɔːtɪfaɪ/ vt (pt/pp -ied) demütigen

mortuary /'mɔːtjʊərɪ/ n Leichenhalle f;
(public) Leichenschauhaus nt; (Amer: undertaker's) Bestattungsinstitut nt

mosaic /məʊ'zeɪɪk/ n Mosaik nt

Moscow /'mɒskəʊ/ n Moskau nt

Moselle /məʊ'zel/ n Mosel f; (wine) Mo-
selwein m

mosque /mɒsk/ n Moschee f

mosquito /mɒs'kiːtəʊ/ n (pl -es)
[Stech]mücke f, Schnake f; (tropical)
Moskito m

moss /mɒs/ n Moos nt. ~y a moosig

most /məʊst/ a der/die/das meiste;
(majority) die meisten; for the ~ part
zum größten Teil □ adv am meisten; (very)
höchst; the ~ interesting day der inte-
ressanteste Tag; ~ unlikely höchst unwahrscheinlich □ n das meiste; ~ of them
die meisten [von ihnen]; at [the] ~ höchstens; ~ of the time die meiste Zeit. ~ly
adv meist

MOT n ≈ TÜV m

motel /məʊ'tel/ n Motel nt

moth /mɒθ/ n Nachtfalter m; [clothes-]~
Motte f

moth: ~ball n Mottenkugel f. ~-eaten a
mottenzerfressen

mother /'mʌðə(r)/ n Mutter f; M~'s Day
Muttertag m □ vt bemuttern

mother: ~hood n Mutterschaft f. ~-in-
law n (pl ~s-in-law) Schwiegermutter f.
~land n Mutterland nt. ~ly a mütterlich.
~-of-pearl n Perlmutter f. ~-to-be n werdende Mutter f. ~ tongue n Muttersprache f

mothproof /'mɒθ-/ a mottenfest

motif /məʊ'tiːf/ n Motiv nt

motion /'məʊʃn/ n Bewegung f; (proposal) Antrag m □ vt/i ~ [to] s.o. jdm ein
Zeichen geben (to zu). ~less a, -ly adv
bewegungslos

motivate /'məʊtɪveɪt/ vt motivieren.
~ion /-'veɪʃn/ n Motivation f

motive /'məʊtɪv/ n Motiv nt

motley /'mɒtlɪ/ a bunt

motor /'məʊtə(r)/ n Motor m; (car) Auto
nt □ a Motor-; (Anat) motorisch □ vi [mit
dem Auto] fahren

Motorail /'məʊtəreɪl/ n Autozug m

motor: ~ bike n (fam) Motorrad nt. ~
boat n Motorboot nt. ~cade /-keɪd/ n
(Amer) Autokolonne f. ~ car n Auto nt,

Wagen m. ~ cycle n Motorrad nt. ~cyclist n Motorradfahrer m. ~ing n Autofahren nt. ~ist n Autofahrer(in) m(f). ~ize vt motorisieren. ~ vehicle n Kraftfahrzeug nt. ~way n Autobahn f

mottled /'mɒtld/ a gesprenkelt

motto /'mɒtəʊ/ n (pl -es) Motto nt

mould¹ /məʊld/ n (fungus) Schimmel m

mould² n Form f □ vt formen (into zu). ~ing n (Archit) Fries m

mouldy /'məʊldɪ/ a schimmelig; (fam: worthless) schäbig

moult /məʊlt/ vi (bird:) sich mausern; (animal:) sich haaren

mound /maʊnd/ n Hügel m; (of stones) Haufen m

mount¹ /maʊnt/ n Berg m

mount² n (animal) Reittier nt; (of jewel) Fassung f; (of photo, picture) Passepartout nt □ vt (get on) steigen auf (+ acc); (on pedestal) montieren auf (+ acc); besteigen (horse); fassen (jewel); aufziehen (photo, picture) □ vi aufsteigen; (increase) steigen. ~ up vi sich häufen; (add up) sich anhäufen; (increase) steigen

mountain /'maʊntɪn/ n Berg m

mountaineer /maʊntɪ'nɪə(r)/ n Bergsteiger(in) m(f). ~ing n Bergsteigen nt

mountainous /'maʊntɪnəs/ a bergig, gebirgig

mourn /mɔːn/ vt betrauern □ vi trauern (for um). ~er n Trauernde(r) m/f. ~ful a, -ly adv trauervoll. ~ing n Trauer f

mouse /maʊs/ n (pl mice) Maus f. ~trap n Mausefalle f

mousse /muːs/ n Schaum m; (Culin) Mousse f

moustache /mə'stɑːʃ/ n Schnurrbart m

mousy /'maʊsɪ/ a graubraun; (person) farblos

mouth¹ /maʊð/ vt ~ sth etw lautlos mit den Lippen sagen

mouth² /maʊθ/ n Mund m; (of animal) Maul nt; (of river) Mündung f

mouth: ~ful n Mundvoll m; (bite) Bissen m. ~organ n Mundharmonika f. ~piece n Mundstück nt; (fig: person) Sprachrohr nt. ~wash n Mundwasser nt

movable /'muːvəbl/ a beweglich

move /muːv/ n Bewegung f; (fig) Schritt m; (moving house) Umzug m; (in board-game) Zug m; on the ~ unterwegs; get a ~ on (fam) sich beeilen □ vt bewegen; (emotionally) rühren; (move along) rücken; (in board-game) ziehen; (take away) wegnehmen; wegfahren (car); (rearrange) umstellen; (transfer) versetzen (person); verlegen (office); (propose) beantragen; ~ house umziehen □ vi sich bewegen; (move house) umziehen; don't ~! stillhalten! (stop) stillstehen! ~ along vt/i weiterrücken. ~ away vt/i wegrücken; (move house) wegziehen. ~ forward vt/i vorrücken; (vehicle) vorwärts fahren. ~ in vi einziehen. ~ off vi (vehicle:) losfahren. ~ out vi ausziehen. ~ over vt/i [zur Seite] rücken. ~ up vi aufrücken

movement /'muːvmənt/ n Bewegung f; (Mus) Satz m; (of clock) Uhrwerk nt

movie /'muːvɪ/ n (Amer) Film m; go to the ~s ins Kino gehen

moving /'muːvɪŋ/ a beweglich; (touching) rührend

mow /məʊ/ vt (pt mowed, pp mown or mowed) mähen. ~ down vt (destroy) niedermähen

mower /'məʊə(r)/ n Rasenmäher m

MP abbr see Member of Parliament

Mr /'mɪstə(r)/ n (pl Messrs) Herr m

Mrs /'mɪsɪz/ n Frau f

Ms /mɪz/ n Frau f

much /mʌtʃ/ a, adv & n viel; as ~ as so viel wie; very ~ loved/interested sehr geliebt/interessiert

muck /mʌk/ n Mist m; (fam: filth) Dreck m. ~ about vi herumalbern; (tinker) herumspielen (with mit). ~ in vi (fam) mitmachen. ~ out vi ausmisten. ~ up vi (fam) vermasseln; (make dirty) schmutzig machen

mucky /'mʌkɪ/ a (-ier, -iest) dreckig

mucus /'mjuːkəs/ n Schleim m

mud /mʌd/ n Schlamm m

muddle /'mʌdl/ n Durcheinander nt; (confusion) Verwirrung f □ vt ~ [up] durcheinander bringen

muddy /'mʌdɪ/ a (-ier, -iest) schlammig; (shoes) schmutzig

mudguard n Kotflügel m; (on bicycle) Schutzblech nt

muesli /'muːzlɪ/ n Müsli nt

muff /mʌf/ n Muff m

muffle /'mʌfl/ vt dämpfen (sound); ~ [up] (for warmth) einhüllen (in in + acc)

muffler /'mʌflə(r)/ n Schal m; (Amer, Auto) Auspufftopf m

mufti /'mʌftɪ/ n in ~ in Zivil

mug¹ /mʌg/ n Becher m; (for beer) Bierkrug m; (fam: face) Visage f; (fam: simpleton) Trottel m

mug² vt (pt/pp mugged) überfallen. ~ger n Straßenräuber m. ~ging n Straßenraub m

muggy /'mʌgɪ/ a (-ier, -iest) schwül

mule¹ /mjuːl/ n Maultier nt

mule² n (slipper) Pantoffel m

mull /mʌl/ vt ~ over nachdenken über (+ acc)

mulled /mʌld/ a ~ wine Glühwein m

multi /'mʌltɪ/: ~coloured *a* vielfarbig, bunt. ~lingual /-'lɪŋgwəl/ *a* mehrsprachig. ~national *a* multinational

multiple /'mʌltɪpl/ *a* vielfach; (*with pl*) mehrere □ *n* Vielfache(s) *nt*

multiplication /mʌltɪplɪ'keɪʃn/ *n* Multiplikation *f*

multiply /'mʌltɪplaɪ/ *v* (*pt/pp* -ied) □ *vt* multiplizieren (by mit) □ *vi* sich vermehren

multi-storey *a* ~ car park Parkhaus *nt*

mum¹ /mʌm/ *a* keep ~ (*fam*) den Mund halten

mum² *n* (*fam*) Mutti *f*

mumble /'mʌmbl/ *vt/i* murmeln

mummy¹ /'mʌmɪ/ *n* (*fam*) Mutti *f*

mummy² *n* (*Archaeol*) Mumie *f*

mumps /mʌmps/ *n* Mumps *m*

munch /mʌntʃ/ *vt/i* mampfen

mundane /mʌn'deɪn/ *a* banal; (*worldly*) weltlich

municipal /mju:'nɪsɪpl/ *a* städtisch

munitions /mju:'nɪʃnz/ *npl* Kriegsmaterial *nt*

mural /'mjʊərəl/ *n* Wandgemälde *nt*

murder /'mɜ:də(r)/ *n* Mord *m* □ *vt* ermorden; (*fam: ruin*) verhunzen. ~er *n* Mörder *m*. ~ess *n* Mörderin *f*. ~ous /-rəs/ *a* mörderisch

murky /'mɜ:kɪ/ *a* (-ier, -iest) düster

murmur /'mɜ:mə(r)/ *n* Murmeln *nt* □ *vt/i* murmeln

muscle /'mʌsl/ *n* Muskel *m*

muscular /'mʌskjʊlə(r)/ *a* Muskel-; (*strong*) muskulös

muse /mju:z/ *vi* nachsinnen (on über + *acc*)

museum /mju:'zɪəm/ *n* Museum *nt*

mush /mʌʃ/ *n* Brei *m*

mushroom /'mʌʃrʊm/ *n* [essbarer] Pilz *m, esp* Champignon *m* □ *vi* (*fig*) wie Pilze aus dem Boden schießen

mushy /'mʌʃɪ/ *a* breiig

music /'mju:zɪk/ *n* Musik *f*; (*written*) Noten *pl*; set to ~ vertonen

musical /'mju:zɪkl/ *a* musikalisch □ *n* Musical *nt*. ~ box *n* Spieldose *f*. ~ instrument *n* Musikinstrument *nt*

'music-hall *n* Varieté *nt*

musician /mju:'zɪʃn/ *n* Musiker(in) *m(f)*

'music-stand *n* Notenständer *m*

Muslim /'mʊzlɪm/ *a* mohammedanisch □ *n* Mohammedaner(in) *m(f)*

muslin /'mʌzlɪn/ *n* Musselin *m*

mussel /'mʌsl/ *n* [Mies]muschel *f*

must /mʌst/ *v aux* (*nur Präsens*) müssen; (*with negative*) dürfen □ *n* a ~ (*fam*) ein Muss *nt*

mustard /'mʌstəd/ *n* Senf *m*

muster /'mʌstə(r)/ *vt* versammeln; aufbringen ⟨strength⟩ □ *vi* sich versammeln

musty /'mʌstɪ/ *a* (-ier, -iest) muffig

mutation /mju:'teɪʃn/ *n* Veränderung *f*; (*Biol*) Mutation *f*

mute /mju:t/ *a* stumm

muted /'mju:tɪd/ *a* gedämpft

mutilat|e /'mju:tɪleɪt/ *vt* verstümmeln. ~ion /-'leɪʃn/ *n* Verstümmelung *f*

mutin|ous /'mju:tɪnəs/ *a* meuterisch. ~y *n* Meuterei *f* □ *vi* (*pt/pp* -ied) meutern

mutter /'mʌtə(r)/ *n* Murmeln *nt* □ *vt/i* murmeln

mutton /'mʌtn/ *n* Hammelfleisch *nt*

mutual /'mju:tjʊəl/ *a* gegenseitig; (*fam: common*) gemeinsam. ~ly *adv* gegenseitig

muzzle /'mʌzl/ *n* (*of animal*) Schnauze *f*; (*of firearm*) Mündung *f*; (*for dog*) Maulkorb *m* □ *vt* einen Maulkorb anlegen (+ *dat*)

my /maɪ/ *a* mein

myopic /maɪ'ɒpɪk/ *a* kurzsichtig

myself /maɪ'self/ *pron* selbst; (*refl*) mich; by ~ allein; I thought to ~ ich habe mir gedacht

mysterious /mɪ'stɪərɪəs/ *a*, ~ly *adv* geheimnisvoll; (*puzzling*) mysteriös, rätselhaft

mystery /'mɪstərɪ/ *n* Geheimnis *nt*; (*puzzle*) Rätsel *nt*; ~ [story] Krimi *m*

mysti|c[al] /'mɪstɪk[l]/ *a* mystisch. ~cism /-sɪzm/ *n* Mystik *f*

mystification /mɪstɪfɪ'keɪʃn/ *n* Verwunderung *f*

mystified /'mɪstɪfaɪd/ *a* be ~ vor einem Rätsel stehen

mystique /mɪ'sti:k/ *n* geheimnisvoller Zauber *m*

myth /mɪθ/ *n* Mythos *m*; (*fam: untruth*) Märchen *nt*. ~ical *a* mythisch; (*fig*) erfunden

mythology /mɪ'θɒlədʒɪ/ *n* Mythologie *f*

N

nab /næb/ *vt* (*pt/pp* nabbed) (*fam*) erwischen

nag¹ /næg/ *n* (*horse*) Gaul *m*

nag² *vt/i* (*pp/pp* nagged) herumnörgeln (s.o. an jdm). ~ging (*pain*) nagend □ *n* Nörgelei *f* nail /neɪl/ n (Anat, Techn) Nagel m; on the ~ (fam) sofort □ vt nageln (to an + acc). ~ down vt festnageln; (close) zunageln

nail: ~-brush n Nagelbürste f. ~-file n Nagelfeile f. ~ polish n Nagellack m. ~ scissors npl Nagelschere f. ~ varnish n Nagellack m

naïve /naɪˈiːv/ a, -ly adv naiv. ~ty /-ətɪ/ n Naivität f

naked /ˈneɪkɪd/ a nackt; (flame) offen; with the ~ eye mit bloßem Auge. ~ness n Nacktheit f

name /neɪm/ n Name m; (reputation) Ruf m; by ~ dem Namen nach; by the ~ of namens; call s.o. ~s (fam) jdn beschimpfen □ vt nennen; (give a name to) einen Namen geben (+ dat); (announce publicly) den Namen bekannt geben von. ~less a namenlos. ~ly adv nämlich

name: ~-plate n Namensschild nt. ~sake n Namensvetter m/Namensschwester f

nanny /ˈnænɪ/ n Kindermädchen nt. ~goat n Ziege f

nap /næp/ n Nickerchen nt; have a ~ ein Nickerchen machen □ vi catch s.o. ~ping jdn überrumpeln

nape /neɪp/ n ~ [of the neck] Nacken m

napkin /ˈnæpkɪn/ n Serviette f; (for baby) Windel f

nappy /ˈnæpɪ/ n Windel f

narcotic /nɑːˈkɒtɪk/ a betäubend □ n Narkotikum nt; (drug) Rauschgift nt

narrat|e /nəˈreɪt/ vt erzählen. ~ion /-eɪʃn/ n Erzählung f

narrative /ˈnærətɪv/ a erzählend □ n Erzählung f

narrator /nəˈreɪtə(r)/ n Erzähler(in) m(f)

narrow /ˈnærəʊ/ a (-er, -est) schmal; (restricted) eng; (margin, majority) knapp; (fig) beschränkt; have a ~ escape, adv ~ly escape mit knapper Not davonkommen □ vi sich verengen. ~-minded a engstirnig

nasal /ˈneɪzl/ a nasal; (Med & Anat) Nasen-

nastily /ˈnɑːstɪlɪ/ adv boshaft

nasturtium /nəˈstɜːʃəm/ n Kapuzinerkresse f

nasty /ˈnɑːstɪ/ a (-ier, -iest) übel; (unpleasant) unangenehm; (unkind) boshaft; (serious) schlimm; turn ~ gemein werden

nation /ˈneɪʃn/ n Nation f; (people) Volk nt

national /ˈnæʃənl/ a national; (newspaper) überregional; (campaign) landesweit □ n Staatsbürger(in) m(f)

national: ~ 'anthem n Nationalhymne f. N~ 'Health Service n staatlicher Gesundheitsdienst m. N~ In'surance n Sozialversicherung f

nationalism /ˈnæʃənəlɪzm/ n Nationalismus m

nationality /næʃəˈnælətɪ/ n Staatsangehörigkeit f

national|ization /næʃənəlaɪˈzeɪʃn/ n Verstaatlichung f. ~ize /ˈnæʃənəlaɪz/ vt verstaatlichen. ~ly /ˈnæʃənəlɪ/ adv landesweit

'nation-wide a landesweit

native /ˈneɪtɪv/ a einheimisch; (innate) angeboren □ n Eingeborene(r) m/f; (local inhabitant) Einheimische(r) m/f; a ~ of Vienna ein gebürtiger Wiener

native: ~ 'land n Heimatland nt. ~ 'language n Muttersprache f

Nativity /nəˈtɪvətɪ/ n the ~ Christi Geburt f. ~ play n Krippenspiel nt

natter /ˈnætə(r)/ n have a ~ (fam) einen Schwatz halten □ vi (fam) schwatzen

natural /ˈnætʃrəl/ a, -ly adv natürlich; ~[coloured] naturfarben

natural: ~ 'gas n Erdgas nt. ~ 'history n Naturkunde f

naturalist /ˈnætʃrəlɪst/ n Naturforscher m

natural|ization /nætʃrəlaɪˈzeɪʃn/ n Einbürgerung f. ~ize /ˈnætʃrəlaɪz/ vt einbürgern

nature /ˈneɪtʃə(r)/ n Natur f; (kind) Art f; by ~ von Natur aus. ~ reserve n Naturschutzgebiet nt

naturism /ˈneɪtʃərɪzm/ n Freikörperkultur f

naught /nɔːt/ n = nought

naughty /ˈnɔːtɪ/ a (-ier, -iest), -ily adv unartig; (slightly indecent) gewagt

nausea /ˈnɔːzɪə/ n Übelkeit f

nause|ate /ˈnɔːzɪeɪt/ vt anekeln. ~ating a ekelhaft. ~ous /-ɪəs/ a I feel ~ous mir ist übel

nautical /ˈnɔːtɪkl/ a nautisch. ~ mile n Seemeile f

naval /ˈneɪvl/ a Marine-

nave /neɪv/ n Kirchenschiff nt

navel /ˈneɪvl/ n Nabel m

navigable /ˈnævɪgəbl/ a schiffbar

navigat|e /ˈnævɪgeɪt/ vi navigieren □ vt befahren (river). ~ion /-ˈgeɪʃn/ n Navigation f. ~or n Navigator m

navvy /ˈnævɪ/ n Straßenarbeiter m

navy /ˈneɪvɪ/ n [Kriegs]marine f □ a ~ [blue] marineblau

near /nɪə(r)/ a (-er, -est) nah[e]; the ~est bank die nächste Bank □ adv nahe; ~ by nicht weit weg; ~ at hand in der Nähe; draw ~ sich nähern □ prep nahe an (+ dat/acc); in der Nähe von; ~ to tears den Tränen nahe; go ~ [to] sth nahe an etw (acc) herangehen □ vt sich nähern (+ dat)

near: ∼by a nahe gelegen, nahe liegend
□ adv /-'-/ nicht weit weg. ∼ly adv fast,
beinahe; not ∼ly bei weitem nicht.
∼ness n Nähe f. ∼ side n Beifahrerseite
f. ∼sighted a (Amer) kurzsichtig

neat /ni:t/ a (-er, -est), -ly adv adrett; (tidy)
ordentlich; (clever) geschickt; (undiluted)
pur. ∼ness n Ordentlichkeit f

necessarily /'nesəsərəlɪ/ adv notwendi-
gerweise; not ∼ nicht unbedingt

necessary /'nesəsərɪ/ a nötig, notwendig

necessit|ate /nɪ'sesɪteɪt/ vt notwendig
machen. ∼y n Notwendigkeit f; she
works from ∼y sie arbeitet, weil sie es
nötig hat

neck /nek/ n Hals m; ∼ and ∼ Kopf an
Kopf

necklace /'neklɪs/ n Halskette f

neck: ∼line n Halsausschnitt m. ∼tie n
Schlips m

nectar /'nektə(r)/ n Nektar m

née /neɪ/ a ∼ Brett geborene Brett

need /ni:d/ n Bedürfnis nt; (misfortune)
Not f; be in ∼ Not leiden; be in ∼ of
brauchen; in case of ∼ notfalls; if ∼ be
wenn nötig; there is a ∼ for es besteht
ein Bedarf an (+ dat); there is no ∼ for
that das ist nicht nötig; there is no ∼ for
you to go du brauchst nicht zu gehen □ vt
brauchen; you ∼ not go du brauchst
nicht zu gehen; ∼ I come? muss ich kommen? I ∼ to know ich muss es wissen; it
∼s to be done es muss gemacht werden

needle /'ni:dl/ n Nadel f □ vt (annoy) ärgern

needless /'ni:dlɪs/ a, -ly adv unnötig; ∼
to say selbstverständlich, natürlich

'needlework n Nadelarbeit f

needy /'ni:dɪ/ a (-ier, -iest) bedürftig

negation /nɪ'geɪʃn/ n Verneinung f

negative /'negətɪv/ a negativ □ n Verneinung f; (photo) Negativ nt

neglect /nɪ'glekt/ n Vernachlässigung f;
state of ∼ verwahrloster Zustand m □ vt
vernachlässigen; (omit) versäumen (to
zu). ∼ed a verwahrlost. ∼ful a nachlässig; be ∼ful of vernachlässigen

negligen|ce /'neglɪdʒəns/ n Nachlässig-
keit f; (Jur) Fahrlässigkeit f. ∼t a, -ly adv
nachlässig; (Jur) fahrlässig

negligible /'neglɪdʒəbl/ a unbedeutend

negotiable /nɪ'gəʊʃəbl/ a (road) befahrbar; (Comm) unverbindlich; not ∼
nicht übertragbar

negotiat|e /nɪ'gəʊʃɪeɪt/ vt aushandeln;
(Auto) nehmen (bend) □ vi verhandeln.
∼ion /-'eɪʃn/ n Verhandlung f. ∼or n Un-
terhändler(in) m(f)

Negro /'ni:grəʊ/ a Neger- □ n (pl -es) Neger
m

neigh /neɪ/ vi wiehern

neighbour /'neɪbə(r)/ n Nachbar(in)
m(f). ∼hood n Nachbarschaft f; in the
∼hood of in der Nähe von; (fig) um ...
herum. ∼ing a Nachbar-. ∼ly a
[gut]nachbarlich

neither /'naɪðə(r)/ a & pron keine(r, s)
[von beiden] □ adv ∼ ... nor weder ...
noch □ conj auch nicht

neon /'ni:ɒn/ n Neon nt. ∼ light n
Neonlicht nt

nephew /'nevju:/ n Neffe m

nepotism /'nepətɪzm/ n Vetternwirt-
schaft f

nerve /nɜ:v/ n Nerv m; (fam: courage) Mut
m; (fam: impudence) Frechheit f; lose
one's ∼ den Mut verlieren. ∼-racking a
nervenaufreibend

nervous /'nɜ:vəs/ a, -ly adv (afraid)
ängstlich; (highly strung) nervös; (Anat,
Med) Nerven-; be ∼ Angst haben. ∼
'breakdown n Nervenzusammen-
bruch m. ∼ness n Ängstlichkeit f; (Med)
Nervosität f

nervy /'nɜ:vɪ/ a (-ier, -iest) nervös; (Amer:
impudent) frech

nest /nest/ n Nest nt □ vi nisten. ∼-egg n
Notgroschen m

nestle /'nesl/ vi sich schmiegen (against
an + acc)

net¹ /net/ n Netz nt; (curtain) Store m □ vt
(pt/pp netted) (catch) [mit dem Netz] fangen

net² /net/ a netto; (salary, weight) Netto- □ vt
(pt/pp netted) netto einnehmen; (yield)
einbringen

'netball n ≈ Korbball m

Netherlands /'neðələndz/ npl the ∼ die
Niederlande pl

netting /'netɪŋ/ n [wire] ∼ Maschendraht
m

nettle /'netl/ n Nessel f

'network n Netz nt

neuralgia /njʊə'rældʒə/ n Neuralgie f

neurolog|ist /njʊə'rɒlədʒɪst/ n Neuro-
loge m/ -gin f. ∼y n Neurologie f

neur|osis /njʊə'rəʊsɪs/ n (pl -oses /-si:z/)
Neurose f. ∼otic /-'rɒtɪk/ a neurotisch

neuter /'nju:tə(r)/ a (Gram) sächlich □ n
(Gram) Neutrum nt □ vt kastrieren; (spay)
sterilisieren

neutral /'nju:trl/ a neutral □ n in ∼ (Auto)
im Leerlauf. ∼ity /-'trælətɪ/ n Neutralität
f. ∼ize vt neutralisieren

never /'nevə(r)/ adv nie, niemals; (fam:
not) nicht; ∼ mind macht nichts; well I
∼! ja so was! ∼-ending a endlos

nevertheless /nevəðə'les/ adv dennoch, trotzdem

new /nju:/ a (-er, -est) neu

new: ∼born a neugeboren. ∼comer n Neuankömmling m. ∼fangled /-'fæŋgld/ a (pej) neumodisch. ∼-laid a frisch gelegt

'**newly** adv frisch. ∼-weds npl Jungverheiratete pl

new: ∼ 'moon n Neumond m. ∼ness n Neuheit f

news /nju:z/ n Nachricht f; (Radio, TV) Nachrichten pl; piece of ∼ Neuigkeit f

news: ∼agent n Zeitungshändler m. ∼bulletin n Nachrichtensendung f. ∼caster n Nachrichtensprecher(in) m(f). ∼flash n Kurzmeldung f. ∼letter n Mitteilungsblatt nt. ∼paper n Zeitung f; (material) Zeitungspapier nt. ∼reader n Nachrichtensprecher(in) m(f)

newt /nju:t/ n Molch m

New: ∼ Year's 'Day n Neujahr nt. ∼ Year's 'Eve n Silvester nt. ∼ Zealand /'zi:lənd/ n Neuseeland nt

next /nekst/ a & n nächste(r, s); who's ∼? wer kommt als Nächster dran? the ∼ best das nächstbeste; ∼ door nebenan; my ∼ of kin mein nächster Verwandter; ∼ to nothing fast gar nichts; the week after ∼ übernächste Woche □ adv als Nächstes; ∼ to neben

NHS abbr see National Health Service

nib /nɪb/ n Feder f

nibble /'nɪbl/ vt/i knabbern (at an + dat)

nice /naɪs/ a (-r, -st) nett; (day, weather) schön; (food) gut; (distinction) fein. ∼ly adv nett; (well) gut. ∼ties /'naɪsətɪz/ npl Feinheiten pl

niche /niːʃ/ n Nische f; (fig) Platz m

nick /nɪk/ n Kerbe f; (fam: prison) Knast m; (fam: police station) Revier nt; in the ∼ of time (fam) gerade noch rechtzeitig; in good ∼ (fam) in gutem Zustand □ vt einkerben; (steal) klauen; (fam: arrest) schnappen

nickel /'nɪkl/ n Nickel nt; (Amer) Fünfcentstück nt

'**nickname** n Spitzname m

nicotine /'nɪkəti:n/ n Nikotin nt

niece /niːs/ n Nichte f

Nigeria /naɪ'dʒɪərɪə/ n Nigeria nt. ∼n a nigerianisch □ n Nigerianer(in) m(f)

niggardly /'nɪgədlɪ/ a knauserig

niggling /'nɪglɪŋ/ a gering; (petty) kleinlich; (pain) quälend

night /naɪt/ n Nacht f; (evening) Abend m; at ∼ nachts; Monday ∼ Montag Nacht/ Abend

night: ∼cap n Schlafmütze f; (drink) Schlaftrunk m. ∼club n Nachtklub m. ∼dress n Nachthemd nt. ∼fall n at ∼fall bei Einbruch der Dunkelheit. ∼ gown n, (fam) ∼ie /'naɪtɪ/ n Nachthemd nt

nightingale /'naɪtɪŋgeɪl/ n Nachtigall f

night: ∼life n Nachtleben nt. ∼ly a nächtlich □ adv jede Nacht. ∼mare n Alptraum m. ∼shade n (Bot) deadly ∼shade Tollkirsche f. ∼-time n at ∼-time bei Nacht. ∼-'watchman n Nachtwächter m

nil /nɪl/ n null

nimble /'nɪmbl/ a (-r, -st), -bly adv flink

nine /naɪn/ a neun □ n Neun f. ∼teen a neunzehn. ∼teenth a neunzehnte(r, s)

ninetieth /'naɪntɪɪθ/ a neunzigste(r, s)

ninety /'naɪntɪ/ a neunzig

ninth /naɪnθ/ a neunte(r, s)

nip /nɪp/ n Kniff m; (bite) Biss m □ vt kneifen; (bite) beißen; ∼ in the bud (fig) im Keim ersticken □ vi (fam: run) laufen

nipple /'nɪpl/ n Brustwarze f; (Amer: on bottle) Sauger m

nippy /'nɪpɪ/ a (-ier, -iest) (fam) (cold) frisch; (quick) flink

nitrate /'naɪtreɪt/ n Nitrat nt

nitrogen /'naɪtrədʒən/ n Stickstoff m

nitwit /'nɪtwɪt/ n (fam) Dummkopf m

no /nəʊ/ adv nein □ n (pl noes) Nein nt □ a kein(e); (pl) keine; in no time [sehr] schnell; no parking/smoking Parken/ Rauchen verboten; no one = nobody

nobility /nəʊ'bɪlətɪ/ n Adel m

noble /'nəʊbl/ a (-r, -st) edel; (aristocratic) adlig. ∼man n Adlige(r) m

nobody /'nəʊbədɪ/ pron niemand, keiner; he knows ∼ er kennt niemanden od keinen □ n a ∼ ein Niemand m

nocturnal /nɒk'tɜːnl/ a nächtlich; (animal, bird) Nacht-

nod /nɒd/ n Nicken nt □ v (pt/pp nodded) □ vi nicken □ vt ∼ one's head mit dem Kopf nicken. ∼ off vi einnicken

nodule /'nɒdjuːl/ n Knötchen nt

noise /nɔɪz/ n Geräusch nt; (loud) Lärm m. ∼less a, -ly adv geräuschlos

noisy /'nɔɪzɪ/ a (-ier, -iest), -ily adv laut; (eater) geräuschvoll

nomad /'nəʊmæd/ n Nomade m. ∼ic /-'mædɪk/ a nomadisch; (life, tribe) Nomaden-

nominal /'nɒmɪnl/ a, -ly adv nominell

nominat|e /'nɒmɪneɪt/ vt nominieren, aufstellen; (appoint) ernennen. ∼ion /-'neɪʃn/ n Nominierung f; Ernennung f

nominative /'nɒmɪnətɪv/ a & n (Gram) ∼ [case] Nominativ m

nonchalant /'nɒnʃələnt/ a, -ly adv nonchalant; (gesture) lässig

non-com'missioned /nɒn-/ a ~ officer Unteroffizier m

non-com'mittal a unverbindlich; be ~ sich nicht festlegen

nondescript /'nɒndɪskrɪpt/ a unbestimmbar; (*person*) unscheinbar

none /nʌn/ pron keine(r)/keins; ~ of us keiner von uns; ~ of it/this nichts davon □ adv ~ too nicht gerade; ~ too soon [um] keine Minute zu früh; ~ the wiser um nichts klüger; ~ the less dennoch

nonentity /nɒ'nentətɪ/ n Null f

non-ex'istent a nicht vorhanden; be ~ nicht vorhanden sein

non-'fiction n Sachliteratur f

non-'iron a bügelfrei

nonplussed /nɒn'plʌst/ a verblüfft

nonsens|e /'nɒnsəns/ n Unsinn m. ~ical /-'sensɪkl/ a unsinnig

non-'smoker n Nichtraucher m; (*compartment*) Nichtraucherabteil nt

non-'stop adv ununterbrochen; (*fly*) nonstop; ~ 'flight Nonstopflug m

non-'swimmer n Nichtschwimmer m

non-'violent a gewaltlos

noodles /'nuːdlz/ npl Bandnudeln pl

nook /nʊk/ n Eckchen nt, Winkel m

noon /nuːn/ n Mittag m; at ~ um 12 Uhr mittags

noose /nuːs/ n Schlinge f

nor /nɔː(r)/ adv noch □ conj auch nicht

Nordic /'nɔːdɪk/ a nordisch

norm /nɔːm/ n Norm f

normal /'nɔːml/ a normal. ~ity /-'mælətɪ/ n Normalität f. ~ly adv normal; (*usually*) normalerweise

north /nɔːθ/ n Norden m; to the ~ of nördlich von □ a Nord-, nord- □ adv nach Norden

north: N~ America n Nordamerika nt. ~-east a Nordost- □ n Nordosten m

norther|ly /'nɔːðəlɪ/ a nördlich. ~n a nördlich. N~n Ireland n Nordirland nt

north: N~ 'Pole n Nordpol m. N~ 'Sea n Nordsee f. ~ward[s] /-wəd[z]/ adv nach Norden. ~-west a Nordwest- □ n Nordwesten m

Nor|way /'nɔːweɪ/ n Norwegen nt. ~wegian /-'wiːdʒn/ a norwegisch □ n Norweger(in) m(f)

nose /nəʊz/ n Nase f □ vi ~ about herumschnüffeln

nose: ~bleed n Nasenbluten nt. ~dive n (*Aviat*) Sturzflug m

nostalg|ia /nɒ'stældʒɪə/ n Nostalgie f. ~ic a nostalgisch

nostril /'nɒstrəl/ n Nasenloch nt; (*of horse*) Nüster f

nosy /'nəʊzɪ/ a (-ier, -iest) (*fam*) neugierig

not /nɒt/ adv nicht; ~ a kein(e); if ~ wenn nicht; ~ at all gar nicht; ~ a bit kein bisschen; ~ even nicht mal; ~ yet noch nicht; he is ~ a German er ist kein Deutscher

notab|le /'nəʊtəbl/ a bedeutend; (*remarkable*) bemerkenswert. ~ly adv insbesondere

notary /'nəʊtərɪ/ n ~ 'public ≈ Notar m

notation /nəʊ'teɪʃn/ n Notation f; (*Mus*) Notenschrift f

notch /nɒtʃ/ n Kerbe f. ~ up vt (*score*) erzielen

note /nəʊt/ n (*written comment*) Notiz f, Anmerkung f; (*short letter*) Briefchen nt, Zettel m; (*bank* ~) Banknote f, Schein m; (*Mus*) Note f; (*sound*) Ton m; (*on piano*) Taste f; eighth/quarter ~ (*Amer*) Achtel-/Viertelnote f; half/whole ~ (*Amer*) halbe/ganze Note f; of ~ von Bedeutung; make a ~ of notieren □ vt beachten; (*notice*) bemerken (that dass). ~ down vt notieren

'notebook n Notizbuch nt

noted /'nəʊtɪd/ a bekannt (for für)

note: ~paper n Briefpapier nt. ~worthy a beachtenswert

nothing /'nʌθɪŋ/ n, pron & adv nichts; for ~ umsonst; ~ but nichts als; ~ much nicht viel; ~ interesting nichts Interessantes; it's ~ to do with you das geht dich nichts an

notice /'nəʊtɪs/ n (*on board*) Anschlag m, Bekanntmachung f; (*announcement*) Anzeige f; (*review*) Kritik f; (*termination of lease, employment*) Kündigung f; [advance] ~ Bescheid m; give [in one's] ~ kündigen; give s.o. ~ jdm kündigen; take no ~ of keine Notiz nehmen von; take no ~! ignoriere es! □ vt bemerken. ~able /-əbl/ a, -bly adv merklich. ~-board n Anschlagbrett nt

noti|fication /nəʊtɪfɪ'keɪʃn/ n Benachrichtigung f. ~fy /'nəʊtɪfaɪ/ vt (pt/pp -ied) benachrichtigen

notion /'nəʊʃn/ n Idee f; ~s pl (*Amer: haberdashery*) Kurzwaren pl

notorious /nəʊ'tɔːrɪəs/ a berüchtigt

notwith'standing prep trotz (+ gen) □ adv trotzdem, dennoch

nought /nɔːt/ n Null f

noun /naʊn/ n Substantiv nt

nourish /'nʌrɪʃ/ vt nähren. ~ing a nahrhaft. ~ment n Nahrung f

novel /'nɒvl/ a neu[artig] □ n Roman m. ~ist n Romanschriftsteller(in) m(f). ~ty n Neuheit f; ~ties pl kleine Geschenkartikel pl

November /nəʊ'vembə(r)/ n November m

novice /'nɒvɪs/ n Neuling m; (Relig) Novize m/Novizin f

now /naʊ/ adv & conj jetzt; ~ [that] jetzt; wo; just ~ gerade, eben; right ~ sofort; ~ and again hin und wieder; now, now! na, na!

'nowadays adv heutzutage

nowhere /'nəʊ-/ adv nirgendwo, nirgends

noxious /'nɒkʃəs/ a schädlich

nozzle /'nɒzl/ n Düse f

nuance /'njuːɑ̃s/ n Nuance f

nuclear /'njuːklɪə(r)/ a Kern-. ~ deterrent n nukleares Abschreckungsmittel nt

nucleus /'njuːklɪəs/ n (pl -lei /-lɪaɪ/) Kern m

nude /njuːd/ a nackt □ n (Art) Akt m; in the ~ nackt

nudge /nʌdʒ/ n Stups m □ vt stupsen

nud|ist /'njuːdɪst/ n Nudist m. ~ity n Nacktheit f

nugget /'nʌgɪt/ n [Gold]klumpen m

nuisance /'njuːsns/ n Ärgernis nt; (pest) Plage f; be a ~ ärgerlich sein; ⟨person:⟩ lästig sein; what a ~! wie ärgerlich!

null /nʌl/ a ~ and void null und nichtig. ~ify /'nʌlɪfaɪ/ vt (pt/pp -ied) für nichtig erklären

numb /nʌm/ a gefühllos, taub; ~ with cold taub vor Kälte □ vt betäuben

number /'nʌmbə(r)/ n Nummer f; (amount) Anzahl f; (Math) Zahl f □ vt nummerieren; (include) zählen (among zu). ~-plate n Nummernschild nt

numeral /'njuːmərl/ n Ziffer f

numerate /'njuːmərət/ a be ~ rechnen können

numerical /njuː'merɪkl/ a, -ly adv numerisch; in ~ order zahlenmäßig geordnet

numerous /'njuːmərəs/ a zahlreich

nun /nʌn/ n Nonne f

nuptial /'nʌpʃl/ a Hochzeits-. ~s npl (Amer) Hochzeit f

nurse /nɜːs/ n [Kranken]schwester f; (male) Krankenpfleger m; children's ~ Kindermädchen nt □ vt pflegen. ~maid n Kindermädchen nt

nursery /'nɜːsərɪ/ n Kinderzimmer nt; (Hort) Gärtnerei f; [day] ~ Kindertagesstätte f. ~ rhyme n Kinderreim m. ~ school n Kindergarten m

nursing /'nɜːsɪŋ/ n Krankenpflege f, ~ home n Pflegeheim nt

nurture /'nɜːtʃə(r)/ vt nähren; (fig) hegen

nut /nʌt/ n Nuss f; (Techn) [Schrauben]mutter f; (fam: head) Birne f (fam); be ~s (fam) spinnen (fam). ~crackers npl Nussknacker m. ~meg n Muskat m

nutrient /'njuːtrɪənt/ n Nährstoff m

nutrit|ion /njuː'trɪʃn/ n Ernährung f. ~ious /-ʃəs/ a nahrhaft

'nutshell n Nussschale f; in a ~ (fig) kurz gesagt

nuzzle /'nʌzl/ vt beschnüffeln

nylon /'naɪlɒn/ n Nylon nt; ~s pl Nylonstrümpfe pl

nymph /nɪmf/ n Nymphe f

O

O /əʊ/ n (Teleph) null

oaf /əʊf/ n (pl oafs) Trottel m

oak /əʊk/ n Eiche f □ attrib Eichen-

OAP abbr (old-age pensioner) Rentner(in) m(f)

oar /ɔː(r)/ n Ruder nt. ~sman n Ruderer m

oasis /əʊ'eɪsɪs/ n (pl oases /-siːz/) Oase f

oath /əʊθ/ n Eid m; (swear-word) Fluch m

oatmeal /'əʊt-/ n Hafermehl nt

oats /əʊts/ npl Hafer m; (Culin) [rolled] ~ Haferflocken pl

obedien|ce /ə'biːdɪəns/ n Gehorsam m. ~t a, -ly adv gehorsam

obes|e /əʊ'biːs/ a fettleibig. ~ity n Fettleibigkeit f

obey /ə'beɪ/ vt/i gehorchen (+ dat); befolgen ⟨instructions, rules⟩

obituary /ə'bɪtjʊərɪ/ n Nachruf m; (notice) Todesanzeige f

object¹ /'ɒbdʒɪkt/ n Gegenstand m; (aim) Zweck m; (intention) Absicht f; (Gram) Objekt nt; money is no ~ Geld spielt keine Rolle

object² /əb'dʒekt/ vi Einspruch erheben (to gegen); (be against) etwas dagegen haben

objection /əb'dʒekʃn/ n Einwand m; have no ~ nichts dagegen haben. ~able /-əbl/ a anstößig; ⟨person⟩ unangenehm

objectiv|e /əb'dʒektɪv/ a, -ly adv objektiv □ n Ziel nt. ~ity n /-'tɪvətɪ/ n Objektivität f

objector /əb'dʒektə(r)/ n Gegner m

obligation /ɒblɪ'geɪʃn/ n Pflicht f; be under an ~ verpflichtet sein; without ~ unverbindlich

obligatory /ə'blɪgətrɪ/ a obligatorisch; be ~ Vorschrift sein

oblig|e /ə'blaɪdʒ/ vt verpflichten; (compel) zwingen; (do a small service) einen Gefallen tun (+ dat); much ~ed! vielen Dank! ~ing a entgegenkommend

oblique /ə'bliːk/ a schräg; ⟨angle⟩ schief; ⟨fig⟩ indirekt. ~ **stroke** n Schrägstrich m

obliterate /ə'blɪtəreɪt/ vt auslöschen

oblivion /ə'blɪvɪən/ n Vergessenheit f

oblivious /ə'blɪvɪəs/ a be ~ sich ⟨dat⟩ nicht bewusst sein (of or to gen)

oblong /'ɒblɒŋ/ a rechteckig ◻ n Rechteck nt

obnoxious /əb'nɒkʃəs/ a widerlich

oboe /'əʊbəʊ/ n Oboe f

obscen|e /əb'siːn/ a obszön; ⟨atrocious⟩ abscheulich. ~ity /-'senətɪ/ n Obszönität f; Abscheulichkeit f

obscur|e /əb'skjʊə(r)/ a dunkel; ⟨unknown⟩ unbekannt ◻ vt verdecken; ⟨confuse⟩ verwischen. ~ity n Dunkelheit f; Unbekanntheit f

obsequious /əb'siːkwɪəs/ a unterwürfig

observa|nce /əb'zɜːvns/ n ⟨of custom⟩ Einhaltung f. ~nt a aufmerksam. ~tion /ɒbzə'veɪʃn/ n Beobachtung f; ⟨remark⟩ Bemerkung f

observatory /əb'zɜːvətrɪ/ n Sternwarte f; ⟨weather⟩ Wetterwarte f

observe /əb'zɜːv/ vt beobachten; ⟨say, notice⟩ bemerken; ⟨keep, celebrate⟩ feiern; ⟨obey⟩ einhalten. ~r n Beobachter m

obsess /əb'ses/ vt be ~ed by besessen sein von. ~ion /-eʃn/ n Besessenheit f; ⟨persistent idea⟩ fixe Idee f. ~ive /-ɪv/ a, -ly adv zwanghaft

obsolete /'ɒbsəliːt/ a veraltet

obstacle /'ɒbstəkl/ n Hindernis nt

obstetrician /ɒbstə'trɪʃn/ n Geburtshelfer m. **obstetrics** /-'stetrɪks/ n Geburtshilfe f

obstina|cy /'ɒbstɪnəsɪ/ n Starrsinn m. ~te /-nət/ a, -ly adv starrsinnig; ⟨refusal⟩ hartnäckig

obstreperous /əb'strepərəs/ a widerspenstig

obstruct /əb'strʌkt/ vt blockieren; ⟨hinder⟩ behindern. ~ion /-ʌkʃn/ n Blockierung f; Behinderung f; ⟨obstacle⟩ Hindernis nt. ~ive /-ɪv/ a be ~ive Schwierigkeiten bereiten

obtain /əb'teɪn/ vt erhalten, bekommen ◻ vi gelten. ~able /-əbl/ a erhältlich

obtrusive /əb'truːsɪv/ a aufdringlich; ⟨thing⟩ auffällig

obtuse /əb'tjuːs/ a ⟨Geom⟩ stumpf; ⟨stupid⟩ begriffsstutzig

obviate /'ɒbvɪeɪt/ vt beseitigen

obvious /'ɒbvɪəs/ a, -ly adv offensichtlich, offenbar

occasion /ə'keɪʒn/ n Gelegenheit f; ⟨time⟩ Mal nt; ⟨event⟩ Ereignis nt; ⟨cause⟩ Anlass m, Grund m; on ~ gelegentlich, hin und wieder; on the ~ of anlässlich (+ gen) ◻ vt veranlassen

occasional /ə'keɪʒənl/ a gelegentlich; he has the ~ glass of wine er trinkt gelegentlich ein Glas Wein. ~ly adv gelegentlich, hin und wieder

occult /ɒ'kʌlt/ a okkult

occupant /'ɒkjʊpənt/ n Bewohner(in) m(f); ⟨of vehicle⟩ Insasse m

occupation /ɒkjʊ'peɪʃn/ n Beschäftigung f; ⟨job⟩ Beruf m; ⟨Mil⟩ Besetzung f; ⟨period⟩ Besatzung f. ~al a Berufs-. ~al **therapy** n Beschäftigungstherapie f

occupier /'ɒkjʊpaɪə(r)/ n Bewohner(in) m(f)

occupy /'ɒkjʊpaɪ/ vt (pt/pp **occupied**) besetzen ⟨seat, Mil country⟩; einnehmen ⟨space⟩; in Anspruch nehmen ⟨time⟩; ⟨live in⟩ bewohnen ⟨fig⟩ bekleiden ⟨office⟩; ⟨keep busy⟩ beschäftigen; ~ **oneself** sich beschäftigen

occur /ə'kɜː(r)/ vi (pt/pp **occurred**) geschehen; ⟨exist⟩ vorkommen, auftreten; it ~red to me that es fiel mir ein, dass. ~rence /ə'kʌrəns/ n Auftreten nt; ⟨event⟩ Ereignis nt

ocean /'əʊʃn/ n Ozean m

o'clock /ə'klɒk/ adv [at] 7 ~ [um] 7 Uhr

octagonal /ɒk'tægənl/ a achteckig

octave /'ɒktɪv/ n ⟨Mus⟩ Oktave f

October /ɒk'təʊbə(r)/ n Oktober m

octopus /'ɒktəpəs/ n (pl **-puses**) Tintenfisch m

odd /ɒd/ a (-ier, -est) seltsam, merkwürdig; ⟨number⟩ ungerade; ⟨not of set⟩ einzeln; **forty** ~ über vierzig; ~ **jobs** Gelegenheitsarbeiten pl; the ~ **one out** die Ausnahme; at ~ **moments** zwischendurch; **have the** ~ **glass of wine** gelegentlich ein Glas Wein trinken

odd|ity /'ɒdɪtɪ/ n Kuriosität f. ~ly adv merkwürdig; ~ly **enough** merkwürdigerweise. ~ment n ⟨of fabric⟩ Rest m

odds /ɒdz/ npl ⟨chances⟩ Chancen pl; at ~ uneinig; ~ **and ends** Kleinkram m; it **makes no** ~ es spielt keine Rolle

ode /əʊd/ n Ode f

odious /'əʊdɪəs/ a widerlich, abscheulich

odour /'əʊdə(r)/ n Geruch m. ~less a geruchlos

oesophagus /iː'sɒfəgəs/ n Speiseröhre f

of /ɒv, unbetont əv/ prep von (+ dat); ⟨made of⟩ aus (+ dat); **the two of us** wir zwei; a **child of three** ein dreijähriges Kind; **the fourth of January** der vierte Januar; a **pound of butter** ein Pfund Butter; a **cup of tea/coffee** eine Tasse Tee/Kaffee; a **bottle of wine** eine Flasche Wein; **half of it** die Hälfte davon; **the whole of the room** das ganze Zimmer

off /ɒf/ *prep* von (+ *dat*); £10 ~ the price £10 Nachlass; ~ the coast vor der Küste; get ~ the ladder/bus von der Leiter/aus dem Bus steigen; take/leave the lid ~ the saucepan den Topf abdecken/nicht zudecken □ *adv* weg; ⟨button, lid, handle⟩ ab; ⟨light⟩ aus; ⟨brake⟩ los; ⟨machine⟩ abgeschaltet; ⟨tap⟩ zu; ⟨on appliance⟩ 'off' 'aus'; 2 kilometres ~ 2 Kilometer entfernt; a long way ~ weit weg; ⟨time⟩ noch lange hin; ~ and on hin und wieder; with his hat/coat ~ ohne Hut/Mantel; with the light/lid ~ ohne Licht/Deckel; 20% ~ 20% Nachlass; be ~ ⟨leave⟩ [weg]gehen; ⟨Sport⟩ starten; ⟨food:⟩ schlecht/⟨all gone⟩ alle sein; be better/worse ~ besser/schlechter dran sein; be well ~ gut dran sein; ⟨financially⟩ wohlhabend sein; have a day ~ einen freien Tag haben; go/drive ~ weggehen/-fahren; turn/take sth ~ etw abdrehen/-nehmen

offal /ˈɒfl/ *n* ⟨Culin⟩ Innereien *pl*

offence /əˈfens/ *n* ⟨illegal act⟩ Vergehen *nt*; give/take ~ Anstoß erregen/nehmen (at an + *dat*)

offend /əˈfend/ *vt* beleidigen. ~er *n* ⟨Jur⟩ Straftäter *m*

offensive /əˈfensɪv/ *a* anstößig; ⟨Mil, Sport⟩ offensiv □ *n* Offensive *f*

offer /ˈɒfə(r)/ *n* Angebot *nt*; on special ~ im Sonderangebot □ *vt* anbieten (to *dat*); leisten ⟨resistance⟩; ~ s.o. sth jdm etw anbieten; ~ to do sth sich anbieten, etw zu tun. ~ing *n* Gabe *f*

off'hand *a* brüsk; ⟨casual⟩ lässig □ *adv* so ohne weiteres

office /ˈɒfɪs/ *n* Büro *nt*; ⟨post⟩ Amt *nt*; in ~ im Amt; ~ hours *pl* Dienststunden *pl*

officer /ˈɒfɪsə(r)/ *n* Offizier *m*; ⟨official⟩ Beamte(r) *m*/Beamtin *f*; ⟨police⟩ Polizeibeamte(r) *m*/-beamtin *f*

official /əˈfɪʃl/ *a* offiziell, amtlich □ *n* Beamte(r) *m*/Beamtin *f*; ⟨Sport⟩ Funktionär *m*. ~ly *adv* offiziell

officiate /əˈfɪʃɪeɪt/ *vi* amtieren

officious /əˈfɪʃəs/ *a*, -ly *adv* übereifrig

'offing *n* in the ~ in Aussicht

'off-licence *n* Wein- und Spirituosenhandlung *f*

off'load *vt* ausladen

off-putting *a* ⟨fam⟩ abstoßend

off'set *vt* ⟨pt/pp -set, pres p -setting⟩ ausgleichen

'offshoot *n* Schössling *m*; ⟨fig⟩ Zweig *m*

'offshore *a* offshore-. ~ rig *n* Bohrinsel *f*

off'side *a* ⟨Sport⟩ abseits

'offspring *n* Nachwuchs *m*

off'stage *adv* hinter den Kulissen

off-'white *a* fast weiß

often /ˈɒfn/ *adv* oft; every so ~ von Zeit zu Zeit

ogle /ˈəʊgl/ *vt* beäugeln

ogre /ˈəʊgə(r)/ *n* Menschenfresser *m*

oh /əʊ/ *int* oh! ach! oh dear! o weh!

oil /ɔɪl/ *n* Öl *nt*; ⟨petroleum⟩ Erdöl *nt* □ *vt* ölen

oil: ~cloth *n* Wachstuch *nt*. ~field *n* Ölfeld *nt*. ~-painting *n* Ölgemälde *nt*. ~ refinery *n* [Erd]ölraffinerie *f*. ~skins *npl* Ölzeug *nt*. ~-slick *n* Ölteppich *m*. ~-tanker *n* Öltanker *m*. ~ well *n* Ölquelle *f*

oily /ˈɔɪlɪ/ *a* (-ier, -iest) ölig

ointment /ˈɔɪntmənt/ *n* Salbe *f*

OK /əʊˈkeɪ/ *a* & *int* ⟨fam⟩ in Ordnung; okay □ *adv* ⟨well⟩ gut □ *vt* ⟨auch okay⟩ ⟨pt/pp okayed⟩ genehmigen

old /əʊld/ *a* (-er, -est) alt; ⟨former⟩ ehemalig

old: ~ 'age *n* Alter *nt*. ~-age 'pensioner *n* Rentner(in) *m(f)*. ~ boy *n* ehemaliger Schüler. ~-'fashioned *a* altmodisch. ~ girl *n* ehemalige Schülerin *f*. ~ 'maid *n* alte Jungfer *f*

olive /ˈɒlɪv/ *n* Olive *f*; ⟨colour⟩ Oliv *nt* □ *a* olivgrün. ~ branch *n* Ölzweig *m*; ⟨fig⟩ Friedensangebot *nt*. ~ 'oil *n* Olivenöl *nt*

Olympic /əˈlɪmpɪk/ *a* olympisch □ *n* the ~s die Olympischen Spiele *pl*

omelette /ˈɒmlɪt/ *n* Omelett *nt*

omen /ˈəʊmən/ *n* Omen *nt*

ominous /ˈɒmɪnəs/ *a* bedrohlich

omission /əˈmɪʃn/ *n* Auslassung *f*; ⟨failure to do⟩ Unterlassung *f*

omit /əˈmɪt/ *vt* ⟨pt/pp omitted⟩ auslassen; ~ to do sth es unterlassen, etw zu tun

omnipotent /ɒmˈnɪpətənt/ *a* allmächtig

on /ɒn/ *prep* auf (+ *dat*/⟨on to⟩ + *acc*); ⟨on vertical surface⟩ an (+ *dat*/⟨on to⟩ + *acc*); ⟨about⟩ über (+ *acc*); on Monday [am] Montag; on Mondays montags; on the first of May am ersten Mai; on arriving als ich ankam; on one's finger am Finger; on the right/left rechts/links; on the Rhine/Thames am Rhein/an der Themse; on the radio/television im Radio/Fernsehen; on the bus/train im Bus/Zug; go on the bus/train mit dem Bus/Zug fahren; get on the bus/train in den Bus/Zug einsteigen; on me ⟨with me⟩ bei mir; it's on me ⟨fam⟩ das spendiere ich □ *adv* ⟨further on⟩ weiter; ⟨switched on⟩ an; ⟨brake⟩ angezogen; ⟨machine⟩ angeschaltet; ⟨on appliance⟩ 'on' 'ein'; with/without his hat/coat on mit/ohne Hut/Mantel; with/without the lid on mit/ohne Deckel; be on ⟨film:⟩ laufen; ⟨event:⟩ stattfinden; be on at ⟨fam⟩ bedrängen (zu to); it's not on ⟨fam⟩ das geht nicht; on and on immer weiter; on and off hin und wieder; **and so on** und so weiter; **later on** später; **drive on** weiterfahren; **stick/sew on** ankleben/-nähen; **from then on** von da an

once /wʌns/ adv einmal; (formerly) früher; **at ~** sofort; (at the same time) gleichzeitig; **~ and for all** ein für alle Mal ◻ conj wenn; (with past tense) als. **~-over** n (fam) give s.o./sth the **~-over** sich (dat) jdn/etw kurz ansehen

'oncoming a ~ traffic Gegenverkehr m

one /wʌn/ a ein(e); (only) einzig; **not ~** kein(e); **~ day/evening** eines Tages/Abends ◻ n Eins f ◻ pron eine(r)/eins; (impersonal) man; **which ~** welche(r,s); **~ another** einander; **~ by ~** einzeln; **~ never knows** man kann nie wissen

one: **~-eyed** a einäugig. **~-parent 'family** n Einelternfamilie f. **~'self** pron selbst; (refl) sich; **by ~self** allein. **~-sided** a einseitig. **~-way** a (street) Einbahn-; (ticket) einfach

onion /'ʌnjən/ n Zwiebel f

'onlooker n Zuschauer(in) m(f)

only /'əʊnlɪ/ a einzige(r,s); **an ~ child** ein Einzelkind nt ◻ adv & conj nur; **~ just** gerade erst; (barely) gerade noch

'onset n Beginn m; (of winter) Einsetzen nt

onslaught /'ɒnslɔːt/ n heftiger Angriff m

onus /'əʊnəs/ n **the ~ is on me** es liegt an mir (to zu)

onward[s] /'ɒnwəd[z]/ adv vorwärts; **from then ~** von der Zeit an

ooze /uːz/ vi sickern

opal /'əʊpl/ n Opal m

opaque /əʊ'peɪk/ a undurchsichtig

open /'əʊpən/ a, -ly adv offen; be **~** (shop:) geöffnet sein; **in the ~ air** im Freien ◻ n **in the ~** im Freien ◻ vt öffnen, aufmachen; (start, set up) eröffnen ◻ vi sich öffnen; (flower:) aufgehen; (shop:) öffnen, aufmachen; (be started) eröffnet werden. **~ up** vt öffnen, aufmachen; (fig) eröffnen ◻ vi sich öffnen; (fig) sich eröffnen

open: **~-air** 'swimming pool n Freibad nt. **~ day** n Tag m der offenen Tür

opener /'əʊpənə(r)/ n Öffner m

opening /'əʊpənɪŋ/ n Öffnung f; (beginning) Eröffnung f; (job) Einstiegsmöglichkeit f. **~ hours** npl Öffnungszeiten pl

open: **~-'minded** a aufgeschlossen. **~ plan** a **~-plan office** Großraumbüro nt. **~ 'sandwich** n belegtes Brot nt

opera /'ɒpərə/ n Oper f

operable /'ɒpərəbl/ a operierbar

opera: **~-glasses** npl Opernglas nt. **~ house** n Opernhaus nt. **~-singer** n Opernsänger(in) m(f)

operate /'ɒpəreɪt/ vt bedienen (machine, lift); betätigen (lever, brake); (fig: run) betreiben ◻ vi (Techn) funktionieren; (be in action) in Betrieb sein; (Mil & fig) operieren; **~ [on]** (Med) operieren

operatic /ɒpə'rætɪk/ a Opern-

operation /ɒpə'reɪʃn/ n (see operate) Bedienung f; Betätigung f; Operation f; **in ~** (Techn) in Betrieb; **come into ~** (fig) in Kraft treten; **have an ~** (Med) operiert werden. **~al** a **be ~al** in Betrieb sein; (law:) in Kraft sein

operative /'ɒpərətɪv/ a wirksam

operator /'ɒpəreɪtə(r)/ n (user) Bedienungsperson f; (Teleph) Vermittlung f

operetta /ɒpə'retə/ n Operette f

opinion /ə'pɪnjən/ n Meinung f; **in my ~** meiner Meinung nach. **~ated** a rechthaberisch

opium /'əʊpɪəm/ n Opium nt

opponent /ə'pəʊnənt/ n Gegner(in) m(f)

opportune /'ɒpətjuːn/ a günstig. **~ist** /-'tjuːnɪst/ a opportunistisch ◻ n Opportunist m

opportunity /ɒpə'tjuːnətɪ/ n Gelegenheit f

oppose /ə'pəʊz/ vt Widerstand leisten (+ dat); (argue against) sprechen gegen; be **~ed to sth** gegen etw sein; **as ~ed to** im Gegensatz zu. **~ing** a gegnerisch; (opposite) entgegengesetzt

opposite /'ɒpəzɪt/ a entgegengesetzt; (house, side) gegenüberliegend; **~ number** (fig) Gegenstück nt; **the ~ sex** das andere Geschlecht ◻ n Gegenteil nt ◻ adv gegenüber ◻ prep gegenüber (+ dat)

opposition /ɒpə'zɪʃn/ n Widerstand m; (Pol) Opposition f

oppress /ə'pres/ vt unterdrücken. **~ion** /-eʃn/ n Unterdrückung f. **~ive** /-ɪv/ a tyrannisch; (heat) drückend. **~or** n Unterdrücker m

opt /ɒpt/ vi **~ for** sich entscheiden für; **~ out** ausscheiden (of aus)

optical /'ɒptɪkl/ a optisch; **~ illusion** optische Täuschung f

optician /ɒp'tɪʃn/ n Optiker m

optics /'ɒptɪks/ n Optik f

optimis|m /'ɒptɪmɪzm/ n Optimismus m. **~t** /-mɪst/ n Optimist m. **~tic** /-'mɪstɪk/ a, -ally adv optimistisch

optimum /'ɒptɪməm/ a optimal ◻ n (pl -ima) Optimum nt

option /'ɒpʃn/ n Wahl f; (Comm) Option f. **~al** a auf Wunsch erhältlich; (subject) wahlfrei; **~al extras** pl Extras pl

opulence /'ɒpjʊləns/ n Prunk m; (wealth) Reichtum m. **~nt** a prunkvoll; (wealthy) sehr reich

or /ɔ:(r)/ *conj* oder; (*after negative*) noch; or [else] sonst; in a year or two in ein bis zwei Jahren

oracle /'ɒrəkl/ *n* Orakel *nt*

oral /'ɔ:rl/ *a*, **-ly** *adv* mündlich; (*Med*) oral □ *n* (*fam*) Mündliche(s) *nt*

orange /'ɒrɪndʒ/ *n* Apfelsine *f*, Orange *f*; (*colour*) Orange *nt* □ *a* orangefarben. ∼ade /-'dʒeɪd/ *n* Orangeade *f*

oration /ə'reɪʃn/ *n* Rede *f*

orator /'ɒrətə(r)/ *n* Redner *m*

oratorio /ɒrə'tɔ:rɪəʊ/ *n* Oratorium *nt*

oratory /'ɒrətərɪ/ *n* Redekunst *f*

orbit /'ɔ:bɪt/ *n* Umlaufbahn *f* □ *vt* umkreisen. ∼al *a* ∼al road Ringstraße *f*

orchard /'ɔ:tʃəd/ *n* Obstgarten *m*

orchestra /'ɔ:kɪstrə/ *n* Orchester *nt*. ∼tral /-'kestrəl/ *a* Orchester-. ∼trate *vt* orchestrieren

orchid /'ɔ:kɪd/ *n* Orchidee *f*

ordain /ɔ:'deɪn/ *vt* bestimmen; (*Relig*) ordinieren

ordeal /ɔ:'di:l/ *n* (*fig*) Qual *f*

order /'ɔ:də(r)/ *n* Ordnung *f*; (*sequence*) Reihenfolge *f*; (*condition*) Zustand *m*; (*command*) Befehl *m*; (*in restaurant*) Bestellung *f*; (*Comm*) Auftrag *m*; (*Relig, medal*) Orden *m*; out of ∼ ⟨*machine*⟩ außer Betrieb; in ∼ that damit; in ∼ to help um zu helfen; take holy ∼s Geistlicher werden □ *vt* (*put in* ∼) ordnen; (*command*) befehlen (+ *dat*); (*Comm, in restaurant*) bestellen; (*prescribe*) verordnen

orderly /'ɔ:dəlɪ/ *a* ordentlich; (*not unruly*) friedlich □ *n* (*Mil, Med*) Sanitäter *m*

ordinary /'ɔ:dɪnərɪ/ *a* gewöhnlich, normal; ⟨*meeting*⟩ ordentlich

ordination /ɔ:dɪ'neɪʃn/ *n* (*Relig*) Ordination *f*

ore /ɔ:(r)/ *n* Erz *nt*

organ /'ɔ:gən/ *n* (*Biol & fig*) Organ *nt*; (*Mus*) Orgel *f*

organic /ɔ:'gænɪk/ *a*, **-ally** *adv* organisch; (*without chemicals*) biodynamisch; ⟨*crop*⟩ biologisch angebaut; ⟨*food*⟩ Bio-; ∼ally grown biologisch angebaut. ∼ farm *n* Biohof *m*. ∼ farming *n* biologischer Anbau *m*

organism /'ɔ:gənɪzm/ *n* Organismus *m*

organist /'ɔ:gənɪst/ *n* Organist *m*

organization /ɔ:gənaɪ'zeɪʃn/ *n* Organisation *f*

organize /'ɔ:gənaɪz/ *vt* organisieren; veranstalten ⟨*event*⟩. ∼r *n* Organisator *m*; Veranstalter *m*

orgasm /'ɔ:gæzm/ *n* Orgasmus *m*

orgy /'ɔ:dʒɪ/ *n* Orgie *f*

Orient /'ɔ:rɪənt/ *n* Orient *m*. o∼al /-'entl/ *a* orientalisch; ∼al carpet Orientteppich *m* □ *n* Orientale *m*/Orientalin *f*

orient|ate /'ɔ:rɪənteɪt/ *vt* ∼ate oneself sich orientieren. ∼ation /-'teɪʃn/ *n* Orientierung *f*

orifice /'ɒrɪfɪs/ *n* Öffnung *f*

origin /'ɒrɪdʒɪn/ *n* Ursprung *m*; (*of person, goods*) Herkunft *f*

original /ə'rɪdʒənl/ *a* ursprünglich; (*not copied*) original; (*new*) originell □ *n* Original *nt*. ∼ity /-'nælətɪ/ *n* Originalität *f*. ∼ly *adv* ursprünglich

originat|e /ə'rɪdʒɪneɪt/ *vi* entstehen □ *vt* hervorbringen. ∼or *n* Urheber *m*

ornament /'ɔ:nəmənt/ *n* Ziergegenstand *m*; (*decoration*) Verzierung *f*. ∼al /-'mentl/ *a* dekorativ. ∼ation /-'teɪʃn/ *n* Verzierung *f*

ornate /ɔ:'neɪt/ *a* reich verziert

ornithology /ɔ:nɪ'θɒlədʒɪ/ *n* Vogelkunde *f*

orphan /'ɔ:fn/ *n* Waisenkind *nt*, Waise *f* □ *vt* zur Waise machen; ∼ed verwaist. ∼age /-ɪdʒ/ *n* Waisenhaus *nt*

orthodox /'ɔ:θədɒks/ *a* orthodox

orthography /ɔ:'θɒgrəfɪ/ *n* Rechtschreibung *f*

orthopaedic /ɔ:θə'pi:dɪk/ *a* orthopädisch

oscillate /'ɒsɪleɪt/ *vi* schwingen

ostensible /ɒ'stensəbl/ *a*, **-bly** *adv* angeblich

ostentat|tion /ɒsten'teɪʃn/ *n* Protzerei *f* (*fam*). ∼ious /-ʃəs/ *a* protzig (*fam*)

osteopath /'ɒstɪəpæθ/ *n* Osteopath *m*

ostracize /'ɒstrəsaɪz/ *vt* ächten

ostrich /'ɒstrɪtʃ/ *n* Strauß *m*

other /'ʌðə(r)/ *a, pron & n* andere(r,s); the ∼ [one] der/die/das andere; the ∼ two die zwei anderen; two ∼s zwei andere; (*more*) noch zwei; no ∼s sonst keine; any ∼ questions? sonst noch Fragen? every ∼ day jeden zweiten Tag; the ∼ day neulich; the ∼ evening neulich abends; someone/something ∼ irgendjemand/-etwas □ *adv* anders; ∼ than him außer ihm; somehow/somewhere or ∼ irgendwie/irgendwo

'otherwise *adv* sonst; (*differently*) anders

otter /'ɒtə(r)/ *n* Otter *m*

ouch /aʊtʃ/ *int* autsch

ought /ɔ:t/ *v aux* I/we ∼ to stay ich sollte/ wir sollten eigentlich bleiben; he ∼ not to have done it er hätte es nicht machen sollen; that ∼ to be enough das sollte eigentlich genügen

ounce /aʊns/ *n* Unze *f* (*28, 35 g*)

our /'aʊə(r)/ *a* unser

ours /ˈauəz/ *poss pron* unsere(r,s); a friend of ∼ ein Freund von uns; that is ∼ das gehört uns

ourselves /auəˈselvz/ *pron* selbst; (*refl*) uns; by ∼ allein

oust /aust/ *vt* entfernen

out /aut/ *adv* (*not at home*) weg; (*outside*) draußen; (*not alight*) aus; (*unconscious*) bewusstlos; be ∼ (*sun:*) scheinen; (*flower*) blühen; (*workers*) streiken; (*calculation:*) nicht stimmen; (*Sport*) aus sein; (*fig: not feasible*) nicht infrage kommen; ∼ and about unterwegs; have it ∼ with s.o. (*fam*) jdn zur Rede stellen; get ∼! (*fam*) raus! ∼ with it! (*fam*) heraus damit! go/ send ∼ hinausgehen/-schicken; come/ bring ∼ herauskommen/-bringen □ *prep* ∼ of aus (+ *dat*); go ∼ of the door zur Tür hinausgehen; be ∼ of bed/ the room nicht im Bett/im Zimmer sein; ∼ of breath/danger außer Atem/Gefahr; ∼ of work arbeitslos; nine ∼ of ten neun von zehn; be ∼ of sugar/bread keinen Zucker/kein Brot mehr haben □ *prep* aus (+ *dat*); go ∼ the door zur Tür hinausgehen

out'bid *vt* (*pt/pp* -bid, *pres p* -bidding) überbieten

'outboard *a* ∼ motor Außenbordmotor *m*

'outbreak *n* Ausbruch *m*

'outbuilding *n* Nebengebäude *nt*

'outburst *n* Ausbruch *m*

'outcast *n* Ausgestoßene(r) *m/f*

'outcome *n* Ergebnis *nt*

'outcry *n* Aufschrei *m* [der Entrüstung]

out'dated *a* überholt

out'do *vt* (*pt* -did, *pp* -done) übertreffen, übertrumpfen

'outdoor *a* ⟨*life, sports*⟩ im Freien; ∼ shoes *pl* Straßenschuhe *pl*; ∼ swimming pool Freibad *nt*

out'doors *adv* draußen; go ∼ nach draußen gehen

'outer *a* äußere(r,s)

'outfit *n* Ausstattung *f*; (*clothes*) Ensemble *nt*; (*fam: organization*) Betrieb *m*; (*fam*) Laden *m*. ∼ter *n* men's ∼ter's Herrenbekleidungsgeschäft *nt*

'outgoing *a* ausscheidend; ⟨*mail*⟩ ausgehend; (*sociable*) kontaktfreudig. ∼s *npl* Ausgaben *pl*

out'grow *vi* (*pt* -grew, *pp* -grown) herauswachsen aus

'outhouse *n* Nebengebäude *nt*

outing /ˈautɪŋ/ *n* Ausflug *m*

outlandish /aut'lændɪʃ/ *a* ungewöhnlich

'outlaw *n* Geächtete(r) *m/f* □ *vt* ächten

'outlay *n* Auslagen *pl*

'outlet *n* Abzug *m*; (*for water*) Abfluss *m*; (*fig*) Ventil *nt*; (*Comm*) Absatzmöglichkeit *f*

'outline *n* Umriss *m*; (*summary*) kurze Darstellung *f* □ *vt* umreißen

out'live *vt* überleben

'outlook *n* Aussicht *f*; (*future prospect*) Aussichten *pl*; (*attitude*) Einstellung *f*

'outlying *a* entlegen; ∼ areas *pl* Außengebiete *pl*

out'moded *a* überholt

out'number *vt* zahlenmäßig überlegen sein (+ *dat*)

'out-patient *n* ambulanter Patient *m*; ∼s' department Ambulanz *f*

'outpost *n* Vorposten *m*

'output *n* Leistung *f*; Produktion *f*

'outrage *n* Gräueltat *f*; (*fig*) Skandal *m*; (*indignation*) Empörung *f* □ *vt* empören. ∼ous /-ˈreɪdʒəs/ *a* empörend

out'right¹ *a* völlig, total; ⟨*refusal*⟩ glatt

out'right² *adv* ganz; (*at once*) sofort; (*frankly*) offen

'outset *n* Anfang *m*; from the ∼ von Anfang an

'outside¹ *a* äußere(r,s); ∼ wall Außenwand *f* □ *n* Außenseite *f*; from the ∼ von außen; at the ∼ höchstens

out'side² *adv* außen; (*out of doors*) draußen; go ∼ nach draußen gehen □ *prep* außerhalb (+ *gen*); (*in front of*) vor (+ *dat/acc*)

out'sider *n* Außenseiter *m*

'outsize *a* übergroß

'outskirts *npl* Rand *m*

out'spoken *a* offen; be ∼ kein Blatt vor den Mund nehmen

out'standing *a* hervorragend; (*conspicuous*) bemerkenswert; (*not settled*) unerledigt; (*Comm*) ausstehend

out'stretched *a* ausgestreckt

out'strip *vt* (*pt/pp* -stripped) davonlaufen (+ *dat*); (*fig*) übertreffen

out'vote *vt* überstimmen

'outward /-wəd/ *a* äußerlich; ∼ journey Hinreise *f* □ *adv* nach außen; be ∼ bound ⟨*ship:*⟩ auslaufen. ∼ly *adv* nach außen hin, äußerlich. ∼s *adv* nach außen

out'weigh *vt* überwiegen

out'wit *vt* (*pt/pp* -witted) überlisten

oval /ˈəuvl/ *a* oval □ *n* Oval *nt*

ovary /ˈəuvərɪ/ *n* (*Anat*) Eierstock *m*

ovation /əuˈveɪʃn/ *n* Ovation *f*

oven /ˈʌvn/ *n* Backofen *m*. ∼-ready *a* bratfertig

over /ˈəuvə(r)/ *prep* über (+ *acc/dat*); ∼ dinner beim Essen; ∼ the weekend übers Wochenende; ~ the phone am Telefon; ~ the page auf der nächsten Seite; all ~ Germany in ganz Deutschland; ⟨travel⟩ durch ganz Deutschland; all ~ the place (fam) überall ▢ adv ⟨remaining⟩ übrig; ⟨ended⟩ zu Ende; ~ again noch einmal; ~ and ~ immer wieder; ~ here/there hier/da drüben; all ~ ⟨everywhere⟩ überall; it's all ~ es ist vorbei; I ache all ~ mir tut alles weh; go/drive ~ hinübergehen/ -fahren; come/bring ~ herüberkommen/-bringen; turn ~ herumdrehen

overall¹ /'əʊvərɔːl/ n Kittel m; ~s pl Overall m

overall² /əʊvər'ɔːl/ a gesamt; ⟨general⟩ allgemein ▢ adv insgesamt

over'awe vt ⟨fig⟩ überwältigen

over'balance vi das Gleichgewicht verlieren

over'bearing a herrisch

'overboard adv ⟨Naut⟩ über Bord

'overcast a bedeckt

over'charge vt ~ s.o. jdm zu viel berechnen ▢ vi zu viel verlangen

'overcoat n Mantel m

over'come vt ⟨pt -came, pp -come⟩ überwinden; be ~ by überwältigt werden von

over'crowded a überfüllt

over'do vt ⟨pt -did, pp -done⟩ übertreiben; ⟨cook too long⟩ zu lange kochen; ~ it ⟨fam: do too much⟩ sich übernehmen

'overdose n Überdosis f

'overdraft n [Konto]überziehung f; have an ~ sein Konto überzogen haben

over'draw vt ⟨pt -drew, pp -drawn⟩ ⟨Comm⟩ überziehen

over'due a überfällig

over'estimate vt überschätzen

'overflow¹ n Überschuss m; ⟨outlet⟩ Überlauf m

over'flow² vi überlaufen

over'grown a ⟨garden⟩ überwachsen

'overhang¹ n Überhang m

over'hang² vt/i ⟨pt/pp -hung⟩ überhängen (über + acc)

'overhaul¹ n Überholung f

over'haul² vt ⟨Techn⟩ überholen

over'head¹ adv oben

'overhead² a Ober-; ⟨ceiling⟩ Decken-. ~s npl allgemeine Unkosten pl

over'hear vt ⟨pt/pp -heard⟩ mit anhören ⟨conversation⟩; I overheard him saying it ich hörte zufällig, wie er das sagte

over'heat vi zu heiß werden ▢ vt zu stark erhitzen

over'joyed a überglücklich

'overland a & adv /--'-/ auf dem Landweg; ~ route Landroute f

over'lap v ⟨pt/pp -lapped⟩ ▢ vi sich überschneiden ▢ vt überlappen

over'leaf adv umseitig

over'load vt überladen; ⟨Electr⟩ überlasten

'overlook¹ n ⟨Amer⟩ Aussichtspunkt m

over'look² vt überblicken; ⟨fail to see, ignore⟩ übersehen

overly /'əʊvəli/ adv übermäßig

over'night¹ adv über Nacht; stay ~ übernachten

'overnight² a Nacht-; ~ stay Übernachtung f

'overpass n Überführung f

over'pay vt ⟨pt/pp -paid⟩ überbezahlen

over'populated a überbevölkert

over'power vt überwältigen. ~ing a überwältigend

over'priced a zu teuer

overpro'duce vt überproduzieren

over'rate vt überschätzen. ~d a überbewertet

over'reach vt ~ oneself sich übernehmen

overre'act vi überreagieren. ~ion n Überreaktion f

over'rid|e vt ⟨pt -rode, pp -ridden⟩ sich hinwegsetzen über (+ acc). ~ing a Haupt-

over'rule vt ablehnen; we were ~d wir wurden überstimmt

over'run vt ⟨pt -ran, pp -run, pres p -running⟩ überrennen; überschreiten ⟨time⟩; be ~ with überlaufen sein von

over'seas¹ adv in Übersee; go ~ nach Übersee gehen

'overseas² a Übersee-

over'see vt ⟨pt -saw, pp -seen⟩ beaufsichtigen

'overseer /-sɪə(r)/ n Aufseher m

over'shadow vt überschatten

over'shoot vt ⟨pt/pp -shot⟩ hinausschießen über (+ acc)

'oversight n Versehen nt

over'sleep vi ⟨pt/pp -slept⟩ [sich] verschlafen

over'step vt ⟨pt/pp -stepped⟩ überschreiten

over'strain vt überanstrengen

overt /əʊ'vɜːt/ a offen

over'tak|e vt/i ⟨pt -took, pp -taken⟩ überholen. ~ing n Überholen nt; no ~ing Überholverbot nt

over'tax vt zu hoch besteuern; ⟨fig⟩ überfordern

'overthrow¹ n ⟨Pol⟩ Sturz m

over'throw² vt ⟨pt -threw, pp -thrown⟩ ⟨Pol⟩ stürzen

'overtime n Überstunden pl □ adv work ~ Überstunden machen

over'tired a übermüdet

'overtone n (fig) Unterton m

overture /'əuvətjuə(r)/ n (Mus) Ouvertüre f; ~s pl (fig) Annäherungsversuche pl

over'turn vt umstoßen □ vi umkippen

over'weight a übergewichtig; be ~ Übergewicht haben

overwhelm /-'welm/ vt überwältigen. ~ing a überwältigend

over'work n Überarbeitung f □ vt überfordern □ vi sich überarbeiten

over'wrought a überreizt

ovulation /ɒvju'leiʃn/ n Eisprung m

ow|e /əu/ vt schulden (fig) verdanken ([to] s.o. jdm); ~e s.o. sth jdm etw schuldig sein; be ~ing (money:) ausstehen. ~ing to prep wegen (+ gen)

owl /aul/ n Eule f

own¹ /əun/ a & pron eigen; it's my ~ es gehört mir; a car of my ~ mein eigenes Auto; on one's ~ allein; hold one's ~ sich behaupten; get one's ~ back (fam) sich revanchieren

own² vt besitzen; (confess) zugeben; I don't ~ it es gehört mir nicht. ~ up vi es zugeben

owner /'əunə(r)/ n Eigentümer(in) m(f), Besitzer(in) m(f); (of shop) Inhaber(in) m(f). ~ship n Besitz m

ox /ɒks/ n (pl oxen) Ochse m

oxide /'ɒksaɪd/ n Oxid nt

oxygen /'ɒksɪdʒən/ n Sauerstoff m

oyster /'ɔɪstə(r)/ n Auster f

ozone /'əuzəun/ n Ozon nt. ~-'friendly a ≈ ohne FCKW. ~ layer n Ozonschicht f

P

pace /peis/ n Schritt m; (speed) Tempo nt; keep ~ with Schritt halten mit □ vi ~ up and down auf und ab gehen. ~-maker n (Sport & Med) Schrittmacher m

Pacific /pə'sɪfɪk/ a & n the ~ [Ocean] der Pazifik

pacifier /'pæsɪfaɪə(r)/ n (Amer) Schnuller m

pacifist /'pæsɪfɪst/ n Pazifist m

pacify /'pæsɪfaɪ/ vt (pt/pp -ied) beruhigen

pack /pæk/ n Packung f; (Mil) Tornister m; (of cards) [Karten]spiel nt; (gang) Bande f; (of hounds) Meute f; (of wolves) Rudel nt; a ~ of lies ein Haufen Lügen □ vt/i packen;

einpacken (article); be ~ed (crowded) [gedrängt] voll sein; send s.o. ~ing (fam) jdn wegschicken. ~ up vt einpacken □ vi (fam) (machine:) kaputtgehen; (person:) einpacken (fam)

package /'pækɪdʒ/ n Paket nt □ vt verpacken. ~ holiday n Pauschalreise f

packed 'lunch n Lunchpaket nt

packet /'pækɪt/ n Päckchen nt; cost a ~ (fam) einen Haufen Geld kosten

packing /'pækɪŋ/ n Verpackung f

pact /pækt/ n Pakt m

pad¹ /pæd/ n Polster nt; (for writing) [Schreib]block m; (fam: home) Wohnung f □ vt (pt/pp padded) polstern

pad² vi (pt/pp padded) tappen

padding /'pædɪŋ/ n Polsterung f; (in written work) Füllwerk nt

paddle¹ /'pædl/ n Paddel nt □ vt (row) paddeln

paddle² vi waten

paddock /'pædək/ n Koppel f

padlock /'pædlɒk/ n Vorhängeschloss nt □ vt mit einem Vorhängeschloss verschließen

paediatrician /piːdɪə'trɪʃn/ n Kinderarzt m -ärztin f

pagan /'peɪgən/ a heidnisch □ n Heide m/Heidin f

page¹ /peɪdʒ/ n Seite f

page² n (boy) Page m □ vt ausrufen (person)

pageant /'pædʒənt/ n Festzug m. ~ry n Prunk m

paid /peɪd/ see pay □ a bezahlt; put ~ to (fam) zunichte machen

pail /peɪl/ n Eimer m

pain /peɪn/ n Schmerz m; be in ~ Schmerzen haben; take ~s sich (dat) Mühe geben; ~ in the neck (fam) Nervensäge f □ vt (fig) schmerzen

pain|~ful a schmerzhaft; (fig) schmerzlich. ~-killer n schmerzstillendes Mittel nt. ~less a, -ly adv schmerzlos

painstaking /'peɪnzteɪkɪŋ/ a sorgfältig

paint /peɪnt/ n Farbe f □ vt/i streichen; (artist:) malen. ~brush n Pinsel m. ~er n Maler m; (decorator) Anstreicher m. ~ing n Malerei f; (picture) Gemälde nt

pair /peə(r)/ n Paar nt; ~ of trousers Hose f; ~ of scissors Schere f □ vt paaren □ vi ~ off Paare bilden

pajamas /pə'dʒɑːməz/ n pl (Amer) Schlafanzug m

Pakistan /pɑːkɪ'stɑːn/ n Pakistan nt. ~i a pakistanisch □ n Pakistaner(in) m(f)

pal /pæl/ n Freund(in) m(f)

palace /'pælɪs/ n Palast m

palatable /'pælətəbl/ a schmackhaft

palate /'pælət/ n Gaumen m

palatial /pə'leɪʃl/ a palastartig

palaver /pə'lɑːvə(t)/ n (fam: fuss) Theater nt (fam)

pale[1] /peɪl/ n (stake) Pfahl m; beyond the ~ (fam) unmöglich

pale[2] a (-r, -st) blass □ vi blass werden. ~ness n Blässe f

Palestin|e /'pælɪstaɪn/ n Palästina nt. ~ian /pælə'stɪnɪən/ a palästinensisch □ n Palästinenser(in) m(f)

palette /'pælɪt/ n Palette f

pall /pɔːl/ n Sargtuch nt; (fig) Decke f □ vi an Reiz verlieren

pallid /'pælɪd/ a bleich. ~or n Blässe f

palm /pɑːm/ n Handfläche f; (tree, symbol) Palme f □ vt ~ sth off on s.o. jdm etw andrehen. P~ 'Sunday n Palmsonntag m

palpable /'pælpəbl/ a tastbar; (perceptible) spürbar

palpitat|e /'pælpɪteɪt/ vi klopfen. ~ions /-'teɪʃnz/ npl Herzklopfen nt

paltry /'pɔːltrɪ/ a (-ier, -iest) armselig

pamper /'pæmpə(r)/ vt verwöhnen

pamphlet /'pæmflɪt/ n Broschüre f

pan /pæn/ n Pfanne f; (saucepan) Topf m; (of scales) Schale f □ vt (pt/pp panned) (fam) verreißen

panacea /pænə'siːə/ n Allheilmittel nt

panache /pə'næʃ/ n Schwung m

'pancake n Pfannkuchen m

pancreas /'pæŋkrɪəs/ n Bauchspeicheldrüse f

panda /'pændə/ n Panda m. ~ car n Streifenwagen m

pandemonium /pændɪ'məʊnɪəm/ n Höllenlärm m

pander /'pændə(r)/ vi ~ to s.o. jdm zu sehr nachgeben

pane /peɪn/ n [Glas]scheibe f

panel /'pænl/ n Tafel f, Platte f; ~ of experts Expertenrunde f; ~ of judges Jury f. ~ling n Täfelung f

pang /pæŋ/ n ~s of hunger Hungergefühl nt; ~s of conscience Gewissensbisse pl

panic /'pænɪk/ n Panik f □ vi (pt/pp panicked) in Panik geraten. ~-stricken a von Panik ergriffen

panoram|a /pænə'rɑːmə/ n Panorama f. ~ic /-'ræmɪk/ a Panorama-

pansy /'pænzɪ/ n Stiefmütterchen nt

pant /pænt/ vi keuchen; (dog:) hecheln

pantechnicon /pæn'teknɪkən/ n Möbelwagen m

panther /'pænθə(r)/ n Panther m

panties /'pæntɪz/ npl [Damen]slip m

pantomime /'pæntəmaɪm/ n [zu Weihnachten aufgeführte] Märchenvorstellung f

pantry /'pæntrɪ/ n Speisekammer f

pants /pænts/ npl Unterhose f, (woman's) Schlüpfer m; (trousers) Hose f

'pantyhose n (Amer) Strumpfhose f

papal /'peɪpl/ a päpstlich

paper /'peɪpə(r)/ n Papier nt; (wall~) Tapete f; (newspaper) Zeitung f; (exam ~) Testbogen m; (exam) Klausur f; (treatise) Referat nt; ~s pl (documents) Unterlagen pl; (for identification) [Ausweis]papiere pl; on ~ schriftlich □ vt tapezieren

paper: ~back n Taschenbuch nt. ~-clip n Büroklammer f. ~-knife n Brieföffner m. ~weight n Briefbeschwerer m. ~work n Schreibarbeit f

par /pɑː(r)/ n (Golf) Par nt; on a ~ gleichwertig (with dat); feel below ~ sich nicht ganz auf der Höhe fühlen

parable /'pærəbl/ n Gleichnis nt

parachut|e /'pærəʃuːt/ n Fallschirm m □ vi [mit dem Fallschirm] abspringen. ~ist n Fallschirmspringer m

parade /pə'reɪd/ n Parade f; (procession) Festzug m □ vi marschieren □ vt (show off) zur Schau stellen

paradise /'pærədaɪs/ n Paradies nt

paradox /'pærədɒks/ n Paradox nt. ~ical a /-'dɒksɪkl/ paradox

paraffin /'pærəfɪn/ n Paraffin nt

paragon /'pærəgən/ n ~ of virtue Ausbund m der Tugend

paragraph /'pærəgrɑːf/ n Absatz m

parallel /'pærəlel/ a & adv parallel □ n (Geog) Breitenkreis m; (fig) Parallele f

paralyse /'pærəlaɪz/ vt lähmen; (fig) lahm legen

paralysis /pə'rælɪsɪs/ n (pl -ses /-siːz/) Lähmung f

paramount /'pærəmaʊnt/ a überragend; be ~ vorgehen

paranoid /'pærənɔɪd/ a [krankhaft] misstrauisch

parapet /'pærəpɪt/ n Brüstung f

paraphernalia /pærəfə'neɪlɪə/ n Kram m

paraphrase /'pærəfreɪz/ n Umschreibung f □ vt umschreiben

paraplegic /pærə'pliːdʒɪk/ a querschnittsgelähmt □ n Querschnittsgelähmte(r) m/f

parasite /'pærəsaɪt/ n Parasit m, Schmarotzer m

parasol /'pærəsɒl/ n Sonnenschirm m

paratrooper /'pærətruːpə(r)/ n Fallschirmjäger m

parcel /'pɑ:sl/ n Paket nt

parch /pɑ:tʃ/ vt austrocknen; be ~ed (person.) furchtbaren Durst haben

parchment /'pɑ:tʃmənt/ n Pergament nt

pardon /'pɑ:dn/ n Verzeihung f; (Jur) Begnadigung f; ~? (fam) bitte? I beg your ~ wie bitte? (sorry) Verzeihung! □ vt verzeihen; (Jur) begnadigen

pare /peə(r)/ vt (peel) schälen

parent /'peərənt/ n Elternteil m; ~s pl Eltern pl. ~al /pə'rentl/ a elterlich

parenthesis /pə'renθəsɪs/ n (pl -ses /-si:z/) Klammer f

parish /'pærɪʃ/ n Gemeinde f. ~ioner /pə'rɪʃənə(r)/ n Gemeindemitglied nt

parity /'pærətɪ/ n Gleichheit f

park /pɑ:k/ n Park m □ vt/i parken

parking /'pɑ:kɪŋ/ n Parken nt; 'no ~' 'Parken verboten'. ~-lot n (Amer) Parkplatz m. ~-meter n Parkuhr f. ~ space n Parkplatz m

parliament /'pɑ:ləmənt/ n Parlament nt. ~ary /pɑ:lə'mentərɪ/ a parlamentarisch

parlour /'pɑ:lə(r)/ n Wohnzimmer nt

parochial /pə'rəʊkɪəl/ a Gemeinde-; (fig) beschränkt

parody /'pærədɪ/ n Parodie f □ vt (pt/pp -ied) parodieren

parole /pə'rəʊl/ n on ~ auf Bewährung

paroxysm /'pærəksɪzm/ n Anfall m

parquet /'pɑ:keɪ/ n ~ floor Parkett nt

parrot /'pærət/ n Papagei m

parry /'pærɪ/ vt (pt/pp -ied) abwehren (blow); (Fencing) parieren

parsimonious /pɑ:sɪ'məʊnɪəs/ a geizig

parsley /'pɑ:slɪ/ n Petersilie f

parsnip /'pɑ:snɪp/ n Pastinake f

parson /'pɑ:sn/ n Pfarrer m

part /pɑ:t/ n Teil m; (Techn) Teil nt; (area) Gegend f; (Theat) Rolle f; (Mus) Part m; spare ~ Ersatzteil m; for my ~ meinerseits; on the ~ of vonseiten (+ gen); take s.o.'s ~ für jdn Partei ergreifen; take ~ in teilnehmen an (+ dat) □ adv teils □ vt trennen; scheiteln (hair) □ vi (people:) sich trennen; ~ with sich trennen von

partake /pɑ:'teɪk/ vt (pt -took, pp -taken) teilnehmen; ~ of (eat) zu sich nehmen

part-ex'change n take in ~ in Zahlung nehmen

partial /'pɑ:ʃl/ a Teil-; be ~ to mögen. ~ity /pɑ:ʃɪ'ælətɪ/ n Voreingenommenheit f; (liking) Vorliebe f. -ly adv teilweise

particip|ant /pɑ:'tɪsɪpənt/ n Teilnehmer(in) m(f). ~ate /-peɪt/ vi teilnehmen (in an + dat). ~ation /-'peɪʃn/ n Teilnahme f

participle /'pɑ:tɪsɪpl/ n Partizip nt; present/past ~ erstes/zweites Partizip

particle /'pɑ:tɪkl/ n Körnchen nt; (Phys) Partikel nt; (Gram) Partikel f

particular /pə'tɪkjʊlə(r)/ a besondere(r,s); (precise) genau; (fastidious) penibel; in ~ besonders. ~ly adv besonders. ~s npl nähere Angaben pl

parting /'pɑ:tɪŋ/ n Abschied m; (in hair) Scheitel m □ attrib Abschieds-

partition /pɑ:'tɪʃn/ n Trennwand f; (Pol) Teilung f □ vt teilen. ~ off vt abtrennen

partly /'pɑ:tlɪ/ adv teilweise

partner /'pɑ:tnə(r)/ n Partner(in) m(f); (Comm) Teilhaber m. ~ship n Partnerschaft f; (Comm) Teilhaberschaft f

partridge /'pɑ:trɪdʒ/ n Rebhuhn n

part-'time a & adv Teilzeit-; be or work ~ Teilzeitarbeit machen

party /'pɑ:tɪ/ n Party f, Fest nt; (group) Gruppe f; (Pol, Jur) Partei f; be ~ to sich beteiligen an (+ dat)

'party line¹ n (Teleph) Gemeinschaftsanschluss m

party 'line² n (Pol) Parteilinie f

pass /pɑ:s/ n Ausweis m; (Geog, Sport) Pass m; (Sch) ≈ ausreichend; get a ~ bestehen □ vt vorbeigehen/-fahren an (+ dat); (overtake) überholen; (hand) reichen; (Sport) abgeben, abspielen; (approve) annehmen; (exceed) übersteigen; bestehen (exam); machen (remark); fällen (judgement); (Jur) verhängen (sentence); ~ water Wasser lassen; ~ the time sich (dat) die Zeit vertreiben; ~ sth off as sth etw als etw ausgeben; ~ one's hand over sth mit der Hand über etw (acc) fahren □ vi vorbeigehen/-fahren; (get by) vorbeikommen; (overtake) überholen; (time:) vergehen; (in exam) bestehen; let sth ~ (fig) etw übergehen; [I] ~! [ich] passe! ~ away vi sterben. ~ down vt herunterreichen; (fig) weitergeben. ~ out vi ohnmächtig werden. ~ round vt herumreichen. ~ up vt heraufreichen; (fam: miss) vorübergehen lassen

passable /'pɑ:səbl/ a (road) befahrbar; (satisfactory) passabel

passage /'pæsɪdʒ/ n Durchgang m; (corridor) Gang m; (voyage) Überfahrt f; (in book) Passage f

passenger /'pæsɪndʒə(r)/ n Fahrgast m; (Naut, Aviat) Passagier m; (in car) Mitfahrer m. ~ seat n Beifahrersitz m

passer-by /pɑ:sə'baɪ/ n (pl -s-by) Passant(in) m(f)

'passing place n Ausweichstelle f

passion /'pæʃn/ n Leidenschaft f. ~ate /-ət/ a, -ly adv leidenschaftlich

passive /'pæsɪv/ a passiv □ n Passiv nt

Passover /'pɑːsəʊvə(r)/ n Passah nt

pass: ∼port n [Reise]pass m. ∼word n Kennwort nt; (Mil) Losung f

past /pɑːst/ a vergangene(r,ŝ); (former) ehemalig; in the ∼ few days in den letzten paar Tagen; that's all ∼ das ist jetzt vorbei n Vergangenheit f ◻ prep an (+ dat) ... vorbei; (after) nach; at ten ∼ two um zehn nach zwei ◻ adv vorbei; go/come ∼ vorbeigehen/-kommen

pasta /'pæstə/ n Nudeln pl

paste /peɪst/ n Brei m; (dough) Teig m; (fish-, meat-) Paste f; (adhesive) Kleister m; (jewellery) Strass m ◻ vt kleistern

pastel /'pæstl/ n Pastellfarbe f; (crayon) Pastellstift m; (drawing) Pastell nt ◻ attrib Pastell-

pasteurize /'pɑːstʃəraɪz/ vt pasteurisieren

pastille /'pæstɪl/ n Pastille f

pastime /'pɑːstaɪm/ n Zeitvertreib m

pastoral /'pɑːstərl/ a ländlich; (care) seelsorgerisch

pastr|y /'peɪstrɪ/ n Teig m; cakes and ∼ies Kuchen und Gebäck

pasture /'pɑːstʃə(r)/ n Weide f

pasty¹ /'pæstɪ/ n Pastete f

pasty² /'peɪstɪ/ a blass, (fam) käsig

pat /pæt/ n Klaps m; (of butter) Stückchen nt ◻ adv have sth off ∼ etw aus dem Effeff können ◻ vt (pt/pp patted) tätscheln; ∼ s.o. on the back jdm auf die Schulter klopfen

patch /pætʃ/ n Flicken m; (spot) Fleck m; not a ∼ on (fam) gar nicht zu vergleichen mit ◻ vt flicken. ∼ up vt [zusammen]flicken; beilegen (quarrel)

patchy /'pætʃɪ/ a ungleichmäßig

pâté /'pæteɪ/ n Pastete f

patent /'peɪtnt/ a, -ly adv offensichtlich ◻ n Patent nt ◻ vt patentieren. ∼ leather n Lackleder nt

patern|al /pə'tɜːnl/ a väterlich. ∼ity n Vaterschaft f

path /pɑːθ/ n (pl ∼s /pɑːðz/) [Fuß]weg m, Pfad m; (orbit, track) Bahn f; (fig) Weg m

pathetic /pə'θetɪk/ a mitleiderregend; (attempt) erbärmlich

patholog|ical /pæθə'lɒdʒɪkl/ a pathologisch. ∼ist /pə'θɒlədʒɪst/ n Pathologe m

pathos /'peɪθɒs/ n Rührseligkeit f

patience /'peɪʃns/ n Geduld f; (game) Patience f

patient /'peɪʃnt/ a, -ly adv geduldig ◻ n Patient(in) m(f)

patio /'pætɪəʊ/ n Terrasse f

patriot /'pætrɪət/ n Patriot(in) m(f). ∼ic /-'ɒtɪk/ a patriotisch. ∼ism n Patriotismus m

Patrol /pə'trəʊl/ n Patrouille f ◻ vt/i patrouillieren [in (+ dat)]; (police:) auf Streife gehen/fahren [in (+ dat)]. ∼ car n Streifenwagen m

patron /'peɪtrən/ n Gönner m; (of charity) Schirmherr m; (of the arts) Mäzen m; (customer) Kunde m/Kundin f; (Theat) Besucher m. ∼age /'pætrənɪdʒ/ n Schirmherrschaft f

patroniz|e /'pætrənaɪz/ vt (fig) herablassend behandeln. ∼ing a, -ly adv gönnerhaft

patter¹ /'pætə(r)/ n Getrippel nt; (of rain) Plätschern nt ◻ vi trippeln; plätschern

patter² n (speech) Gerede nt

pattern /'pætn/ n Muster nt

paunch /pɔːntʃ/ n [Schmer]bauch m

pauper /'pɔːpə(r)/ n Arme(r) m/f

pause /pɔːz/ n Pause f ◻ vi innehalten

pave /peɪv/ vt pflastern; ∼ the way den Weg bereiten (for dat). ∼ment n Bürgersteig m

pavilion /pə'vɪljən/ n Pavillon m; (Sport) Klubhaus nt

paw /pɔː/ n Pfote f; (of large animal) Pranke f, Tatze f

pawn¹ /pɔːn/ n (Chess) Bauer m; (fig) Schachfigur f

pawn² vt verpfänden ◻ n in ∼ verpfändet. ∼ broker n Pfandleiher m. ∼shop n Pfandhaus nt

pay /peɪ/ n Lohn m; (salary) Gehalt nt; be in the ∼ of bezahlt werden von ◻ v (pt/pp paid) ◻ vt bezahlen; zahlen (money); ∼ s.o. a visit jdm einen Besuch abstatten; ∼ s.o. a compliment jdm ein Kompliment machen ◻ vi zahlen; (be profitable) sich bezahlt machen; (fig) sich lohnen; ∼ for sth etw bezahlen. ∼ back vt zurückzahlen. ∼ in vt einzahlen. ∼ off vt abzahlen (debt) ◻ vi (fig) sich auszahlen. ∼ up vi zahlen

payable /'peɪəbl/ a zahlbar; make ∼ to ausstellen auf (+ acc)

payee /peɪ'iː/ n [Zahlungs]empfänger m

payment /'peɪmənt/ n Bezahlung f; (amount) Zahlung f

pay: ∼ packet n Lohntüte f. ∼phone n Münzfernsprecher m

pea /piː/ n Erbse f

peace /piːs/ n Frieden m; for my ∼ of mind zu meiner eigenen Beruhigung

peace|able /'piːsəbl/ a friedlich. ∼ful a, -ly adv friedlich. ∼maker n Friedensstifter m

peach /piːtʃ/ n Pfirsich m

peacock /'piːkɒk/ n Pfau m

peak /piːk/ n Gipfel m; (fig) Höhepunkt m. ∼ed 'cap n Schirmmütze f. ∼ hours npl

Hauptbelastungszeit *f*; (*for traffic*) Hauptverkehrszeit *f*

peaky /'pi:kɪ/ *a* kränklich

peal /pi:l/ *n* (*of bells*) Glockengeläut *nt*; ~s of laughter schallendes Gelächter *nt*

'peanut *n* Erdnuss *f*; for ~s (*fam*) für einen Apfel und ein Ei

pear /peə(r)/ *n* Birne *f*

pearl /pɜ:l/ *n* Perle *f*

peasant /'peznt/ *n* Bauer *m*

peat /pi:t/ *n* Torf *m*

pebble /'pebl/ *n* Kieselstein *m*

peck /pek/ *n* Schnabelhieb *m*; (*kiss*) flüchtiger Kuss *m* ▢ *vt/i* picken/(*nip*) hacken (at nach). ~ing order *n* Hackordnung *f*

peckish /'pekɪʃ/ *a* be ~ (*fam*) Hunger haben

peculiar /pɪ'kju:lɪə(r)/ *a* eigenartig, seltsam; ~ to eigentümlich (+ *dat*). ~ity /-'ærətɪ/ *n* Eigenart *f*

pedal /'pedl/ *n* Pedal *nt* ▢ *vt* fahren (*bicycle*) ▢ *vi* treten. ~ bin *n* Treteimer *m*

pedantic /pɪ'dæntɪk/ *a*, -ally *adv* pedantisch

peddle /'pedl/ *vt* handeln mit

pedestal /'pedɪstl/ *n* Sockel *m*

pedestrian /pɪ'destrɪən/ *n* Fußgänger(in) *m(f)* ▢ *a* (*fig*) prosaisch. ~ 'crossing *n* Fußgängerüberweg *m*. ~ 'precinct *n* Fußgängerzone *f*

pedicure /'pedɪkjʊə(r)/ *n* Pediküre *f*

pedigree /'pedɪgri:/ *n* Stammbaum *m* ▢ *attrib* (*animal*) Rasse-

pedlar /'pedlə(r)/ *n* Hausierer *m*

pee /pi:/ *vi* (*pt/pp* peed) (*fam*) pinkeln

peek /pi:k/ *vi* (*fam*) gucken

peel /pi:l/ *n* Schale *f* ▢ *vt* schälen; ▢ *vi* ⟨*skin:*⟩ sich schälen; ⟨*paint:*⟩ abblättern. ~ings *npl* Schalen *pl*

peep /pi:p/ *n* kurzer Blick *m* ▢ *vi* gucken. ~-hole *n* Guckloch *nt*. P~ing 'Tom *n* (*fam*) Spanner *m*

peer¹ /pɪə(r)/ *vi* ~ at forschend ansehen

peer² *n* Peer *m*; his ~s *pl* seinesgleichen

peev|ed /pi:vd/ *a* (*fam*) ärgerlich. ~ish *a* reizbar

peg /peg/ *n* (*hook*) Haken *m*; (*for tent*) Pflock *m*, Hering *m*; (*for clothes*) [Wäsche]klammer *f*; off the ~ (*fam*) von der Stange ▢ *vt* (*pt/pp* pegged) anpflocken; anklammern ⟨*washing*⟩

pejorative /pɪ'dʒɒrətɪv/ *a*, -ly *adv* abwertend

pelican /'pelɪkən/ *n* Pelikan *m*

pellet /'pelɪt/ *n* Kügelchen *nt*

pelt¹ /pelt/ *n* (*skin*) Pelz *m*, Fell *nt*

pelt² *vt* bewerfen ▢ *vi* (*fam: run fast*) rasen; ~ [down] ⟨*rain:*⟩ [hernieder]prasseln

pelvis /'pelvɪs/ *n* (*Anat*) Becken *nt*

pen¹ /pen/ *n* (*for animals*) Hürde *f*

pen² *n* Federhalter *m*; (*ball-point*) Kugelschreiber *m*

penal /'pi:nl/ *a* Straf-. ~ize *vt* bestrafen; (*fig*) benachteiligen

penalty /'penltɪ/ *n* Strafe *f*; (*fine*) Geldstrafe *f*; (*Sport*) Strafstoß *m*; (*Football*) Elfmeter *m*

penance /'penəns/ *n* Buße *f*

pence /pens/ *see* penny

pencil /'pensl/ *n* Bleistift *m* ▢ *vt* (*pt/pp* pencilled) mit Bleistift schreiben. ~-sharpener *n* Bleistiftspitzer *m*

pendant /'pendənt/ *n* Anhänger *m*

pending /'pendɪŋ/ *a* unerledigt ▢ *prep* bis zu

pendulum /'pendjʊləm/ *n* Pendel *nt*

penetrat|e /'penɪtreɪt/ *vt* durchdringen; ~e [into] eindringen in (+ *acc*). ~ing *a* durchdringend. ~ion /-'treɪʃn/ *n* Durchdringen *nt*

'penfriend *n* Brieffreund(in) *m(f)*

penguin /'pengwɪn/ *n* Pinguin *m*

penicillin /penɪ'sɪlɪn/ *n* Penizillin *nt*

peninsula /pə'nɪnsʊlə/ *n* Halbinsel *f*

penis /'pi:nɪs/ *n* Penis *m*

peniten|ce /'penɪtəns/ *n* Reue *f*. ~t *a* reuig ▢ *n* Büßer *m*

penitentiary /penɪ'tenʃərɪ/ *n* (*Amer*) Gefängnis *nt*

pen: ~knife *n* Taschenmesser *nt*. ~name *n* Pseudonym *nt*

pennant /'penənt/ *n* Wimpel *m*

penniless /'penɪlɪs/ *a* mittellos

penny /'penɪ/ *n* (*pl* pence; *single coins* pennies) Penny *m*; (*Amer*) Centstück *nt*; spend a ~ (*fam*) mal verschwinden; the ~'s dropped (*fam*) der Groschen ist gefallen

pension /'penʃn/ *n* Rente *f*; (*of civil servant*) Pension *f*. ~er *n* Rentner(in) *m(f)*; Pensionär(in) *m(f)*

pensive /'pensɪv/ *a* nachdenklich

Pentecost /'pentɪkɒst/ *n* Pfingsten *nt*

pent-up /'pentʌp/ *a* angestaut

penultimate /pe'nʌltɪmət/ *a* vorletzte(r,s)

penury /'penjʊrɪ/ *n* Armut *f*

peony /'pɪənɪ/ *n* Pfingstrose *f*

people /'pi:pl/ *npl* Leute *pl*, Menschen *pl*; (*citizens*) Bevölkerung *f*; the ~ das Volk; English ~ die Engländer; ~ say man sagt; for four ~ für vier Personen ▢ *vt* bevölkern

pep /pep/ *n* (*fam*) Schwung *m*

pepper /'pepə(r)/ n Pfeffer m; (vegetable) Paprika m; a ~ (fruit) eine Paprika[schote] ❑ vt (Culin) pfeffern

pepper: ~corn n Pfefferkorn nt. ~mint n Pfefferminz nt; (Bot) Pfefferminze f. ~pot n Pfefferstreuer m

per /pɜ:(r)/ prep pro; ~ cent Prozent nt

perceive /pə'si:v/ vt wahrnehmen

percentage /pə'sentɪdʒ/ n Prozentsatz m; (part) Teil m

perceptible /pə'septəbl/ a wahrnehmbar

percept|ion /pə'sepʃn/ n Wahrnehmung f. ~ive /-tɪv/ a feinsinnig

perch¹ /pɜ:tʃ/ n Stange f ❑ vi (bird:) sich niederlassen

perch² n inv (fish) Barsch m

percolat|e /'pɜ:kəleɪt/ vi durchsickern. ~or n Kaffeemaschine f

percussion /pə'kʌʃn/ n Schlagzeug nt. ~ instrument n Schlaginstrument nt

peremptory /pə'remptərɪ/ a herrisch

perennial /pə'renɪəl/ a (problem) immer wiederkehrend ❑ n (Bot) mehrjährige Pflanze f

perfect¹ /'pɜ:fɪkt/ a perfekt, vollkommen; (fam: utter) völlig ❑ n (Gram) Perfekt nt

perfect² /pə'fekt/ vt vervollkommnen. ~ion /-ekʃn/ n Vollkommenheit f; to ~ion perfekt

perfectly /'pɜ:fɪktlɪ/ adv perfekt; (completely) vollkommen, völlig

perforate /'pɜ:fəreɪt/ vt perforieren; (make a hole in) durchlöchern. ~d a perforiert

perform /pə'fɔ:m/ vt ausführen; erfüllen (duty); (Theat) aufführen (play); spielen (role) ❑ vi (Theat) auftreten; (Techn) laufen. ~ance n Aufführung f; (at theatre, cinema) Vorstellung f; (Techn) Leistung f. ~er n Künstler(in) m(f)

perfume /'pɜ:fju:m/ n Parfüm nt; (smell) Duft m

perfunctory /pə'fʌŋktərɪ/ a flüchtig

perhaps /pə'hæps/ adv vielleicht

peril /'perəl/ n Gefahr f. ~ous /-əs/ a gefährlich

perimeter /pə'rɪmɪtə(r)/ n [äußere] Grenze f; (Geom) Umfang m

period /'pɪərɪəd/ n Periode f; (Sch) Stunde f, (full stop) Punkt m ❑ attrib (costume) zeitgenössisch; (furniture) antik. ~ic /-'ɒdɪk/, ~ally adv periodisch. ~ical /-'ɒdɪkl/ n Zeitschrift f

peripher|al /pə'rɪfərl/ a nebensächlich. ~y n Peripherie f

periscope /'perɪskəʊp/ n Periskop nt

perish /'perɪʃ/ vi (rubber:) verrotten; (food:) verderben; (die) ums Leben kommen. ~able /-əbl/ a leicht verderblich. ~ing a (fam; cold) eiskalt

perjur|e /'pɜ:dʒə(r)/ vt ~e oneself einen Meineid leisten. ~y n Meineid m

perk¹ /pɜ:k/ n (fam) [Sonder]vergünstigung f

perk² vi ~ up munter werden

perky /'pɜ:kɪ/ a munter

perm /pɜ:m/ n Dauerwelle f ❑ vt ~ s.o.'s hair jdm eine Dauerwelle machen

permanent /'pɜ:mənənt/ a ständig; (job, address) fest. ~ly adv ständig; (work, live) dauernd, permanent; (employed) fest

permeable /'pɜ:mɪəbl/ a durchlässig

permeate /'pɜ:mɪeɪt/ vt durchdringen

permissible /pə'mɪsəbl/ a erlaubt

permission /pə'mɪʃn/ n Erlaubnis f

permissive /pə'mɪsɪv/ a (society) permissiv

permit¹ /pə'mɪt/ vt (pt/pp -mitted) erlauben (s.o. jdm); ~ me! gestatten Sie!

permit² /'pɜ:mɪt/ n Genehmigung f

pernicious /pə'nɪʃəs/ a schädlich; (Med) perniziös

perpendicular /pɜ:pən'dɪkjʊlə(r)/ a senkrecht ❑ n Senkrechte f

perpetrat|e /'pɜ:pɪtreɪt/ vt begehen. ~or n Täter m

perpetual /pə'petjʊəl/ a, -ly adv ständig, dauernd

perpetuate /pə'petjʊeɪt/ vt bewahren; verewigen (error)

perplex /pə'pleks/ vt verblüffen. ~ed a verblüfft. ~ity n Verblüffung f

persecut|e /'pɜ:sɪkju:t/ vt verfolgen. ~ion /-'kju:ʃn/ n Verfolgung f

perseverance /pɜ:sɪ'vɪərəns/ n Ausdauer f

persever|e /pɜ:sɪ'vɪə(r)/ vi beharrlich weitermachen. ~ing a ausdauernd

Persia /'pɜ:ʃə/ n Persien nt

Persian /'pɜ:ʃn/ a persisch; (cat, carpet) Perser-

persist /pə'sɪst/ vi beharrlich weitermachen; (continue) anhalten; (view:) weiter bestehen; ~ in doing sth dabei bleiben, etw zu tun. ~ence n Beharrlichkeit f. ~ent a, -ly adv beharrlich; (continuous) anhaltend

person /'pɜ:sn/ n Person f; in ~ persönlich

personal /'pɜ:sənl/ a, -ly adv persönlich. ~ 'hygiene n Körperpflege f

personality /pɜ:sə'nælətɪ/ n Persönlichkeit f

personify /pə'sɒnɪfaɪ/ vt (pt/pp -ied) personifizieren, verkörpern

personnel /pɜːsə'nel/ n Personal nt

perspective /pə'spektɪv/ n Perspektive f

perspicacious /pɜːspɪ'keɪʃəs/ a scharfsichtig

perspi|ration /pə:spɪ'reɪʃn/ n Schweiß m. ~ire /-'spaɪə(r)/ vi schwitzen

persua|de /pə'sweɪd/ vt überreden; (convince) überzeugen. ~sion /-eɪʒn/ n Überredung f; (powers of ~sion) Überredungskunst f; (belief) Glaubensrichtung f

persuasive /pə'sweɪsɪv/ a, -ly adv beredsam; (convincing) überzeugend

pert /pɜːt/ a, -ly adv kess

pertain /pə'teɪn/ vi ~ to betreffen; (belong) gehören zu

pertinent /'pɜːtɪnənt/ a relevant (to für)

perturb /pə'tɜːb/ vt beunruhigen

peruse /pə'ruːz/ vt lesen

perva|de /pə'veɪd/ vt durchdringen. ~sive /-sɪv/ a durchdringend

pervers|e /pə'vɜːs/ a eigensinnig. ~ion /-ɜːʃn/ n Perversion f

pervert[1] /pə'vɜːt/ vt verdrehen; verführen (person)

pervert[2] /'pɜːvɜːt/ n Perverse(r) m

perverted /pə'vɜːtɪd/ a abartig

pessimis|m /'pesɪmɪzm/ n Pessimismus m. ~t /-mɪst/ n Pessimist m. ~tic /-'mɪstɪk/ a, -ally adv pessimistisch

pest /pest/ n Schädling m; (fam: person) Nervensäge f

pester /'pestə(r)/ vt belästigen; ~ s.o. for sth jdm wegen etw in den Ohren liegen

pesticide /'pestɪsaɪd/ n Schädlingsbekämpfungsmittel nt

pet /pet/ n Haustier nt; (favourite) Liebling m □ vt (pt/pp petted) liebkosen

petal /'petl/ n Blütenblatt nt

peter /'piːtə(r)/ vi ~ out allmählich aufhören; (stream:) versickern

petite /pə'tiːt/ a klein und zierlich

petition /pə'tɪʃn/ n Bittschrift f □ vt eine Bittschrift richten an (+ acc)

pet 'name n Kosename m

petrify /'petrɪfaɪ/ vt/i (pt/pp -ied) versteinern; ~ied (frightened) vor Angst wie versteinert

petrol /'petrl/ n Benzin nt

petroleum /pɪ'trəʊlɪəm/ n Petroleum nt

petrol: ~-pump n Zapfsäule f. ~ station n Tankstelle f. ~ tank n Benzintank m

'pet shop n Tierhandlung f

petticoat /'petɪkəʊt/ n Unterrock m

petty /'petɪ/ a (-ier, -iest) kleinlich. ~ 'cash n Portokasse f

petulant /'petjʊlənt/ a gekränkt

pew /pjuː/ n [Kirchen]bank f

pewter /'pjuːtə(r)/ n Zinn nt

phantom /'fæntəm/ n Gespenst nt

pharmaceutical /fɑːmə'sjuːtɪkl/ a pharmazeutisch

pharmac|ist /'fɑːməsɪst/ n Apotheker(in) m(f). ~y n Pharmazie f; (shop) Apotheke f

phase /feɪz/ n Phase f □ vt ~ in/out allmählich einführen/abbauen

Ph.D. (abbr of Doctor of Philosophy) Dr. phil.

pheasant /'feznt/ n Fasan m

phenomen|al /fɪ'nɒmɪnl/ a phänomenal. ~on n (pl -na) Phänomen nt

phial /'faɪəl/ n Fläschchen nt

philanderer /fɪ'lændərə(r)/ n Verführer m

philanthrop|ic /fɪlən'θrɒpɪk/ a menschenfreundlich. ~ist /fɪ'lænθrəpɪst/ n Philanthrop m

philately /fɪ'lætəlɪ/ n Philatelie f, Briefmarkenkunde f

philharmonic /fɪlə'mɒnɪk/ n (orchestra) Philharmoniker pl

Philippines /'fɪlɪpiːnz/ npl Philippinen pl

philistine /'fɪlɪstaɪn/ n Banause m

philosoph|er /fɪ'lɒsəfə(r)/ n Philosoph m. ~ical /fɪlə'sɒfɪkl/ a, -ly adv philosophisch. ~y n Philosophie f

phlegm /flem/ n (Med) Schleim m

phlegmatic /fleg'mætɪk/ a phlegmatisch

phobia /'fəʊbɪə/ n Phobie f

phone /fəʊn/ n Telefon nt; be on the ~ Telefon haben; (be phoning) telefonieren □ vt anrufen □ vi telefonieren. ~ back vt/i zurückrufen. ~ book n Telefonbuch nt. ~ box n Telefonzelle f. ~ card n Telefonkarte f. ~-in n (Radio) Hörersendung f. ~ number n Telefonnummer f

phonetic /fə'netɪk/ a phonetisch. ~s n Phonetik f

phoney /'fəʊnɪ/ a (-ier, -iest) falsch; (forged) gefälscht

phosphorus /'fɒsfərəs/ n Phosphor m

photo /'fəʊtəʊ/ n Foto nt, Aufnahme f. ~copier n Fotokopiergerät nt. ~copy n Fotokopie f □ vt fotokopieren

photogenic /fəʊtəʊ'dʒenɪk/ a fotogen

photograph /'fəʊtəɡrɑːf/ n Fotografie f, Aufnahme f □ vt fotografieren

photograph|er /fə'tɒɡrəfə(r)/ n Fotograf(in) m(f). ~ic /-ə'ɡræfɪk/ a, -ally adv fotografisch. ~y n Fotografie f

phrase /freɪz/ n Redensart f □ vt formulieren. ~-book n Sprachführer m

physical /'fızıkl/ a, -ly adv körperlich; ⟨geography, law⟩ physikalisch. ∼ edu'cation n Turnen nt

physician /fı'zıʃn/ n Arzt m/ Ärztin f

physic|ist /'fızısıst/ n Physiker(in) m(f). ∼s n Physik f

physiology /fızı'ɒlədʒı/ n Physiologie f

physio'therap|ist /fızıəʊ-/ n Physiotherapeut(in) m(f). ∼y n Physiotherapie f

physique /fı'zi:k/ n Körperbau m

pianist /'pıənıst/ n Klavierspieler(in) m(f); ⟨professional⟩ Pianist(in) m(f)

piano /pı'ænəʊ/ n Klavier nt

pick¹ /pık/ n Spitzhacke f

pick² n Auslese f; take one's ∼ sich ⟨dat⟩ aussuchen □ vt/i ⟨pluck⟩ pflücken; ⟨select⟩ wählen, sich ⟨dat⟩ aussuchen; ∼ and choose wählerisch sein; ∼ one's nose in der Nase bohren; ∼ a quarrel einen Streit anfangen; ∼ a hole in sth ein Loch in etw ⟨acc⟩ machen; ∼ holes in ⟨fam⟩ kritisieren; ∼ at one's food im Essen herumstochern. ∼ on vt wählen; ⟨fam: find fault with⟩ herumhacken auf (+ dat). ∼ up vt in die Hand nehmen; ⟨off the ground⟩ aufheben; hochnehmen ⟨baby⟩; lernen; ⟨acquire⟩ erwerben; ⟨buy⟩ kaufen; ⟨Teleph⟩ abnehmen ⟨receiver⟩; auffangen ⟨signal⟩; ⟨collect⟩ abholen; aufnehmen ⟨passengers⟩; ⟨police:⟩ aufgreifen ⟨criminal⟩; sich holen ⟨illness⟩; ⟨fam⟩ aufgabeln ⟨girl⟩; ∼ oneself up aufstehen □ vi ⟨improve⟩ sich bessern

'**pickaxe** n Spitzhacke f

picket /'pıkıt/ n Streikposten m □ vt Streikposten aufstellen vor (+ dat). ∼ line n Streikpostenkette f

pickle /'pıkl/ n ⟨Amer: gherkin⟩ Essiggurke f; ∼s pl [Mixed] Pickles pl □ vt einlegen

pick: ∼pocket n Taschendieb m. ∼up n ⟨truck⟩ Lieferwagen m; ⟨on record-player⟩ Tonabnehmer m

picnic /'pıknık/ n Picknick nt □ vi ⟨pt/pp -nicked⟩ picknicken

pictorial /pık'tɔːrıəl/ a bildlich

picture /'pıktʃə(r)/ n Bild nt; ⟨film⟩ Film m; as pretty as a ∼ bildhübsch; put s.o. in the ∼ ⟨fig⟩ jdn ins Bild setzen □ vt ⟨imagine⟩ sich ⟨dat⟩ vorstellen

picturesque /pıktʃə'resk/ a malerisch

pie /paı/ n Pastete f; ⟨fruit ∼⟩ Kuchen m

piece /niːs/ n Stück nt; ⟨of set⟩ Teil nt; ⟨in game⟩ Stein m; ⟨Journ⟩ Artikel m; a ∼ of bread/paper ein Stück Brot/Papier; a ∼ of news/advice eine Nachricht/ein Rat; take to ∼s auseinander nehmen □ vt ∼ together zusammensetzen; ⟨fig⟩

zusammenstückeln. ∼meal adv stückweise. ∼-work n Akkordarbeit f

pier /pıə(r)/ n Pier m; ⟨pillar⟩ Pfeiler m

pierc|e /pıəs/ vt durchstechen; ∼e a hole in sth ein Loch in etw ⟨acc⟩ stechen. ∼ing a durchdringend

piety /'paıətı/ n Frömmigkeit f

piffle /'pıfl/ n ⟨fam⟩ Quatsch m

pig /pıg/ n Schwein nt

pigeon /'pıdʒın/ n Taube f. ∼-hole n Fach nt

piggy /'pıgı/ n ⟨fam⟩ Schweinchen nt. ∼back n give s.o. a ∼back jdn huckepack tragen. ∼ bank n Sparschwein nt

pig'headed a ⟨fam⟩ starrköpfig

pigment /'pıgmənt/ n Pigment nt. ∼ation /-men'teıʃn/ n Pigmentierung f

pig: ∼skin n Schweinsleder nt. ∼sty n Schweinestall m. ∼tail n ⟨fam⟩ Zopf m

pike /paık/ n inv ⟨fish⟩ Hecht m

pilchard /'pıltʃəd/ n Sardine f

pile¹ /paıl/ n ⟨of fabric⟩ Flor m

pile² n Haufen m □ vt ∼ sth on to sth etw auf etw ⟨acc⟩ häufen. ∼ up vt aufhäufen □ vi sich häufen

piles /paılz/ npl Hämorrhoiden pl

'**pile-up** n Massenkarambolage f

pilfer /'pılfə(r)/ vt/i stehlen

pilgrim /'pılgrım/ n Pilger(in) m(f). ∼age /-ıdʒ/ n Pilgerfahrt f, Wallfahrt f

pill /pıl/ n Pille f

pillage /'pılıdʒ/ vt plündern

pillar /'pılə(r)/ n Säule f. ∼-box n Briefkasten m

pillion /'pıljən/ n Sozius[sitz] m

pillory /'pılərı/ n Pranger m □ vt ⟨pt/pp -ied⟩ anprangern

pillow /'pıləʊ/ n Kopfkissen nt. ∼case n Kopfkissenbezug m

pilot /'paılət/ n Pilot m; ⟨Naut⟩ Lotse m □ vt fliegen ⟨plane⟩; lotsen ⟨ship⟩. ∼-light n Zündflamme f

pimp /pımp/ n Zuhälter m

pimple /'pımpl/ n Pickel m

pin /pın/ n Stecknadel f; ⟨Techn⟩ Bolzen m, Stift m; ⟨Med⟩ Nagel m; I have ∼s and needles in my leg ⟨fam⟩ mein Bein ist eingeschlafen □ vt ⟨pt/pp pinned⟩ anstecken (to/on an + acc); ⟨sewing⟩ stecken; ⟨hold down⟩ festhalten; ∼ sth on s.o. ⟨fam⟩ jdm etw anhängen. ∼ up vt hochstecken; ⟨on wall⟩ anheften, anschlagen

pinafore /'pınəfɔː(r)/ n Schürze f. ∼ dress n Kleiderrock m

pincers /'pınsəz/ npl Kneifzange f; ⟨Zool⟩ Scheren pl

pinch /pıntʃ/ n Kniff m; ⟨of salt⟩ Prise f; at a ∼ ⟨fam⟩ zur Not □ vt kneifen, zwicken;

(fam: steal) klauen; ~ one's finger sich *(dat)* den Finger klemmen □ *vi (shoe:)* drücken

'**pincushion** *n* Nadelkissen *nt*

pine¹ /paɪn/ *n (tree)* Kiefer *f*

pine² *vi* ~ for sich sehnen nach; ~ away sich verzehren

pineapple /'paɪn-/ *n* Ananas *f*

ping /pɪŋ/ *n* Klingeln *nt*

'**ping-pong** *n* Tischtennis *nt*

pink /pɪŋk/ *a* rosa

pinnacle /'pɪnəkl/ *n* Gipfel *m; (on roof)* Turmspitze *f*

pin: ~point *vt* genau festlegen. ~stripe *n* Nadelstreifen *m*

pint /paɪnt/ *n* Pint *nt (0,571, Amer: 0,47 l)*

'**pin-up** *n* Pin-up-Girl *nt*

pioneer /paɪə'nɪə(r)/ *n* Pionier *m* □ *vt* bahnbrechende Arbeit leisten für

pious /'paɪəs/ *a, -ly adv* fromm

pip¹ /pɪp/ *n (seed)* Kern *m*

pip² *n (sound)* Tonsignal *nt*

pipe /paɪp/ *n* Pfeife *f; (for water, gas)* Rohr *nt* □ *vt* in Rohren leiten; *(Culin)* spritzen. ~ down *vi (fam)* den Mund halten

pipe: ~dream *n* Luftschloss *nt.* ~line *n* Pipeline *f;* in the ~line *(fam)* in Vorbereitung

piper /'paɪpə(r)/ *n* Pfeifer *m*

piping /'paɪpɪŋ/ *a* ~ hot kochend heiß

piquant /'pi:kənt/ *a* pikant

pique /pi:k/ *n* in a fit of ~ beleidigt

pirate /'paɪərət/ *n* Pirat *m*

Pisces /'paɪsi:z/ *n (Astr)* Fische *pl*

piss /pɪs/ *vi (sl)* pissen

pistol /'pɪstl/ *n* Pistole *f*

piston /'pɪstən/ *n (Techn)* Kolben *m*

pit /pɪt/ *n* Grube *f; (for orchestra)* Orchestergraben *m* □ *vt (pt/pp* pitted) *(fig)* messen *(against* mit)

pitch¹ /pɪtʃ/ *n (steepness)* Schräge *f; (of voice)* Stimmlage *f; (of sound)* [Ton]höhe *f; (Sport)* Feld *nt; (of street-trader)* Standplatz *m; (fig: degree)* Grad *m* □ *vt* werfen; aufschlagen *(tent)* □ *vi* fallen

pitch² *n (tar)* Pech *nt.* ~-'black *a* pechschwarz. ~-'dark *a* stockdunkel

pitcher /'pɪtʃə(r)/ *n* Krug *m*

'**pitchfork** *n* Heugabel *f*

piteous /'pɪtɪəs/ *a* erbärmlich

'**pitfall** *n (fig)* Falle *f*

pith /pɪθ/ *n (Bot)* Mark *nt; (of orange)* weiße Haut *f; (fig)* Wesentliche(s) *nt*

pithy /'pɪθɪ/ *a (-ier, -iest) (fig)* prägnant

piti|ful /'pɪtɪfl/ *a* bedauernswert. ~less *a* mitleidslos

pittance /'pɪtns/ *n* Hungerlohn *m*

pity /'pɪtɪ/ *n* Mitleid *nt,* Erbarmen *nt;* [what a] ~! [wie] schade! take ~ on sich erbarmen über *(+ acc)* □ *vt* bemitleiden

pivot /'pɪvət/ *n* Drehzapfen *m; (fig)* Angelpunkt *m* □ *vi* sich drehen *(on* um)

pixie /'pɪksɪ/ *n* Kobold *m*

pizza /'pi:tsə/ *n* Pizza *f*

placard /'plæka:d/ *n* Plakat *nt*

placate /plə'keɪt/ *vt* beschwichtigen

place /pleɪs/ *n* Platz *m; (spot)* Stelle *f; (town, village)* Ort *m; (fam: house)* Haus *nt;* out of ~ fehl am Platze; take ~ stattfinden; all over the ~ überall □ *vt* setzen; *(upright)* stellen; *(flat)* legen; *(remember)* unterbringen *(fam);* ~ an order eine Bestellung aufgeben; be ~d *(in race)* sich platzieren. ~mat *n* Set *nt*

placid /'plæsɪd/ *a* gelassen

plagiar|ism /'pleɪdʒərɪzm/ *n* Plagiat *nt.* ~ize *vt* plagiieren

plague /pleɪg/ *n* Pest *f* □ *vt* plagen

plaice /pleɪs/ *n inv* Scholle *f*

plain /pleɪn/ *a (-er, -est)* klar; *(simple)* einfach; *(not pretty)* nicht hübsch; *(not patterned)* einfarbig; *(chocolate)* zartbitter; in ~ clothes in Zivil □ *adv (simply)* einfach □ *n* Ebene *f; (Knitting)* rechte Masche *f.* ~ly *adv* klar, deutlich; *(simply)* einfach; *(obviously)* offensichtlich

plaintiff /'pleɪntɪf/ *n (Jur)* Kläger(in) *m(f)*

plaintive /'pleɪntɪv/ *a, -ly adv* klagend

plait /plæt/ *n* Zopf *m* □ *vt* flechten

plan /plæn/ *n* Plan *m* □ *vt (pt/pp* planned) planen; *(intend)* vorhaben

plane¹ /pleɪn/ *n (tree)* Platane *f*

plane² *n* Flugzeug *nt; (Geom & fig)* Ebene *f*

plane³ *n (Techn)* Hobel *m* □ *vt* hobeln

planet /'plænɪt/ *n* Planet *m*

plank /plæŋk/ *n* Brett *nt; (thick)* Planke *f*

planning /'plænɪŋ/ *n* Planung *f.* ~ permission *n* Baugenehmigung *f*

plant /plɑ:nt/ *n* Pflanze *f; (Techn)* Anlage *f; (factory)* Werk *nt* □ *vt* pflanzen; *(place in position)* setzen; ~ oneself in front of s.o. sich vor jdn hinstellen. ~ation /plæn'teɪʃn/ *n* Plantage *f*

plaque /plɑ:k/ *n* [Gedenk]tafel *f; (on teeth)* Zahnbelag *m*

plasma /'plæzmə/ *n* Plasma *nt*

plaster /'plɑ:stə(r)/ *n* Verputz *m; (sticking* ~) Pflaster *nt;* ~ [of Paris] Gips *m* □ *vt* verputzen *(wall); (cover)* bedecken mit. ~ed *a (sl)* besoffen. ~er *n* Gipser *m*

plastic /'plæstɪk/ *n* Kunststoff *m,* Plastik *nt* □ *a* Kunststoff-, Plastik-; *(malleable)* formbar, plastisch

Plasticine (P) /'plæstɪsi:n/ *n* Knetmasse *f*

plastic 'surgery *n* plastische Chirurgie *f*

plate /pleıt/ *n* Teller *m*; *(flat sheet)* Platte *f*; *(with name, number)* Schild *nt*; *(gold and silverware)* vergoldete/versilberte Ware *f*; *(in book)* Tafel *f* □ *vt (with gold)* vergolden; *(with silver)* versilbern

plateau /'plætəʊ/ *n (pl ∼x /-əʊz/)* Hochebene *f*

platform /'plætfɔ:m/ *n* Plattform *f*; *(stage)* Podium *nt*; *(Rail)* Bahnsteig *m*; ∼ 5 Gleis 5

platinum /'plætınəm/ *n* Platin *nt*

platitude /'plætıtjuːd/ *n* Plattitüde *f*

platonic /plə'tɒnık/ *a* platonisch

platoon /plə'tuːn/ *n (Mil)* Zug *m*

platter /'plætə(r)/ *n* Platte *f*

plausible /'plɔːzəbl/ *a* plausibel

play /pleı/ *n* Spiel *nt*; *(Theater)*stück *nt*; *(Radio)* Hörspiel *nt*; *(TV)* Fernsehspiel *nt*; ∼ on words Wortspiel *nt* □ *vt/i* spielen; ausspielen *(card)*; ∼ safe sichergehen. ∼ down *vt* herunterspielen. ∼ up *vi (fam)* Mätzchen machen

play: ∼boy *n* Playboy *m*. ∼er *n* Spieler(in) *m(f)*. ∼ful *a*, -ly *adv* verspielt. ∼ground *n* Spielplatz *m*; *(Sch)* Schulhof *m*. ∼group *n* Kindergarten *m*

playing: ∼-card *n* Spielkarte *f*. ∼-field *n* Sportplatz *m*

play: ∼mate *n* Spielkamerad *m*. ∼-pen *n* Laufstall *m*, Laufgitter *nt*. ∼thing *n* Spielzeug *nt*. ∼wright /-raıt/ *n* Dramatiker *m*

plc *abbr* (public limited company) ≈ GmbH

plea /pliː/ *n* Bitte *f*; make a ∼ for bitten um

plead /pliːd/ *vt* vorschützen; *(Jur)* vertreten *(case)* □ *vi* flehen (for um); ∼ guilty sich schuldig bekennen; ∼ with s.o. jdn anflehen

pleasant /'plezənt/ *a* angenehm; *(person)* nett. ∼ly *adv* angenehm; *(say, smile)* freundlich

please /pliːz/ *adv* bitte □ *vt* gefallen (+ *dat*); ∼ e s.o. jdm eine Freude machen; ∼ e oneself tun, was man will. ∼ed *a* erfreut; be ∼ed with/about sth sich über etw *(acc)* freuen. ∼ing *a* erfreulich

pleasurable /'pleʒərəbl/ *a* angenehm

pleasure /'pleʒə(r)/ *n* Vergnügen *nt*; *(joy)* Freude *f*; with ∼ gern[e]

pleat /pliːt/ *n* Falte *f* □ *vt* fälteln. ∼ed 'skirt *n* Faltenrock *m*

plebiscite /'plebısıt/ *n* Volksabstimmung *f*

pledge /pledʒ/ *n* Pfand *nt*; *(promise)* Versprechen *nt* □ *vt* verpfänden; versprechen

plentiful /'plentıfl/ *a* reichlich; be ∼ reichlich vorhanden sein

plenty /'plentı/ *n* eine Menge; *(enough)* reichlich; ∼ of money/people viel Geld/viele Leute

pleurisy /'plʊərəsı/ *n* Rippenfellentzündung *f*

pliable /'plaıəbl/ *a* biegsam

pliers /'plaıəz/ *npl* [Flach]zange *f*

plight /plaıt/ *n* [Not]lage *f*

plimsolls /'plımsɒlz/ *npl* Turnschuhe *pl*

plinth /plınθ/ *n* Sockel *m*

plod /plɒd/ *vi (pt/pp* plodded) trotten; *(work hard)* sich abmühen

plonk /plɒŋk/ *n (fam)* billiger Wein *m*

plot /plɒt/ *n* Komplott *nt*; *(of novel)* Handlung *f*; ∼ of land Stück *nt* Land □ *vt* einzeichnen □ *vi* ein Komplott schmieden

plough /plaʊ/ *n* Pflug *m* □ *vt/i* pflügen. ∼ back *vt (Comm)* wieder investieren

ploy /plɔı/ *n (fam)* Trick *m*

pluck /plʌk/ *n* Mut *m* □ *vt* zupfen; rupfen *(bird)*; pflücken *(flower)*; ∼ up courage Mut fassen

plucky /'plʌkı/ *a (-ier, -iest)* tapfer, mutig

plug /plʌg/ *n* Stöpsel *m*; *(wood)* Zapfen *m*; *(cotton wool)* Bausch *m*; *(Electr)* Stecker *m*; *(Auto)* Zündkerze *f*; *(fam: advertisement)* Schleichwerbung *f* □ *vt* zustopfen; *(fam: advertise)* Schleichwerbung machen für. ∼ in *vt (Electr)* einstecken

plum /plʌm/ *n* Pflaume *f*

plumage /'pluːmıdʒ/ *n* Gefieder *nt*

plumb /plʌm/ *n* Lot *nt* □ *adv* lotrecht □ *vt* loten. ∼ in *vt* installieren

plumb|er /'plʌmə(r)/ *n* Klempner *m*. ∼ing *n* Wasserleitungen *pl*

'plumb-line *n* [Blei]lot *nt*

plume /pluːm/ *n* Feder *f*

plummet /'plʌmıt/ *vi* herunterstürzen

plump /plʌmp/ *a (-er, -est)* mollig, rundlich □ *vt* ∼ for wählen

plunder /'plʌndə(r)/ *n* Beute *f* □ *vt* plündern

plunge /plʌndʒ/ *n* Sprung *m*; take the ∼ *(fam)* den Schritt wagen □ *vt/i* tauchen

plu'perfect /pluː-/ *n* Plusquamperfekt *nt*

plural /'plʊərl/ *a* pluralisch □ *n* Mehrzahl *f*, Plural *m*

plus /plʌs/ *prep* plus (+ *dat*) □ *a* Plus- □ *n* Pluszeichen *nt*; *(advantage)* Plus *nt*

plush[y] /'plʌʃ[ı]/ *a* luxuriös

ply /plaı/ *vt (pt/pp* plied) ausüben *(trade)*; ∼ s.o. with drink jdm ein Glas nach dem anderen eingießen. ∼wood *n* Sperrholz *nt*

p.m. *adv (abbr of* post meridiem) nachmittags

pneumatic /nju:'mætɪk/ a pneumatisch. ~ 'drill n Presslufthammer m

pneumonia /nju:'məʊnɪə/ n Lungenentzündung f

poach /pəʊtʃ/ vt (Culin) pochieren; (steal) wildern. ~er n Wilddieb m

pocket /'pɒkɪt/ n Tasche f; ~ of resistance Widerstandsnest nt; be out of ~ [an einem Geschäft] verlieren □ vt einstecken. ~book n Notizbuch nt; (wallet) Brieftasche f. ~-money n Taschengeld nt

pock-marked /'pɒk-/ a pockennarbig

pod /pɒd/ n Hülse f

podgy /'pɒdʒɪ/ a (-ier, -iest) dick

poem /'pəʊɪm/ n Gedicht nt

poet /'pəʊɪt/ n Dichter(in) m(f). ~ic /-'etɪk/ a dichterisch

poetry /'pəʊɪtrɪ/ n Dichtung f

poignant /'pɔɪnjənt/ a ergreifend

point /pɔɪnt/ n Punkt m; (sharp end) Spitze f; (meaning) Sinn m; (purpose) Zweck m; (Electr) Steckdose f; ~s pl (Rail) Weiche f; ~ of view Standpunkt m; good/bad ~s gute/schlechte Seiten; what is the ~? wozu? the ~ is es geht darum; I don't see the ~ das sehe ich nicht ein; up to a ~ bis zu einem gewissen Grade; be on the ~ of doing sth im Begriff sein, etw zu tun □ vt richten (at auf + acc); ausfugen ⟨brickwork⟩ □ vi deuten (at/to auf + acc); (with finger) mit dem Finger zeigen. ~ out vt zeigen auf (+ acc); ~ sth out to s.o. jdn auf etw (acc) hinweisen

point-'blank a aus nächster Entfernung; (fig) rundweg

point|ed /'pɔɪntɪd/ a spitz; (question) gezielt. ~er n (hint) Hinweis m. ~less a zwecklos, sinnlos

poise /pɔɪz/ n Haltung f. ~d a (confident) selbstsicher; ~d to bereit zu

poison /'pɔɪzn/ n Gift nt □ vt vergiften. ~ous a giftig

poke /pəʊk/ n Stoß m □ vt stoßen; schüren ⟨fire⟩; (put) stecken; ~ fun at sich lustig machen über (+ acc)

poker¹ /'pəʊkə(r)/ n Schüreisen nt

poker² n (Cards) Poker m

poky /'pəʊkɪ/ a (-ier, -iest) eng

Poland /'pəʊlənd/ n Polen nt

polar /'pəʊlə(r)/ a Polar-. ~ 'bear n Eisbär m. ~ize vt polarisieren

Pole /pəʊl/ n Pole m/Polin f

pole¹ n Stange f

pole² n (Geog, Electr) Pol m

'polecat n Iltis m

'pole-star n Polarstern m

'pole-vault n Stabhochsprung m

police /pə'li:s/ npl Polizei f □ vt polizeilich kontrollieren

police: ~man n Polizist m. ~ state n Polizeistaat m. ~ station n Polizeiwache f. ~woman n Polizistin f

policy¹ /'pɒlɪsɪ/ n Politik f

policy² n (insurance) Police f

polio /'pəʊlɪəʊ/ n Kinderlähmung f

Polish /'pəʊlɪʃ/ a polnisch

polish /'pɒlɪʃ/ n (shine) Glanz m; (for shoes) [Schuh]creme f; (for floor) Bohnerwachs m; (for furniture) Politur f; (for silver) Putzmittel nt; (for nails) Lack m; (fig) Schliff m □ vt polieren; bohnern ⟨floor⟩. ~ off vt (fam) verputzen ⟨food⟩; erledigen ⟨task⟩

polisher /'pɒlɪʃə(r)/ n (machine) Poliermaschine f; (for floor) Bohnermaschine f

polite /pə'laɪt/ a, -ly adv höflich. ~ness n Höflichkeit f

politic /'pɒlɪtɪk/ a ratsam

politic|al /pə'lɪtɪkl/ a, -ly adv politisch. ~ian /pɒlɪ'tɪʃn/ n Politiker(in) m(f)

politics /'pɒlɪtɪks/ n Politik f

polka /'pɒlkə/ n Polka f

poll /pəʊl/ n Abstimmung f; (election) Wahl f; [opinion] ~ [Meinungs]umfrage f; go to the ~s wählen □ vt erhalten ⟨votes⟩

pollen /'pɒlən/ n Blütenstaub m, Pollen m

polling /'pəʊlɪŋ/: ~booth n Wahlkabine f. ~station n Wahllokal nt

'poll tax n Kopfsteuer f

pollutant /pə'lu:tənt/ n Schadstoff m

pollut|e /pə'lu:t/ vt verschmutzen. ~ion /-'u:ʃn/ n Verschmutzung f

polo /'pəʊləʊ/ n Polo nt. ~-neck n Rollkragen m. ~ shirt n Polohemd nt

polyester /pɒlɪ'estə(r)/ n Polyester m

polystyrene /pɒlɪ'staɪri:n/ n Polystyrol nt; (for packing) Styropor (P) nt

polytechnic /pɒlɪ'teknɪk/ n ≈ technische Hochschule f

polythene /'pɒlɪθi:n/ n Polyäthylen nt. ~ bag n Plastiktüte f

polyun'saturated a mehrfach ungesättigt

pomegranate /'pɒmɪɡrænɪt/ n Granatapfel m

pomp /pɒmp/ n Pomp m

pompon /'pɒmpɒn/ n Pompon m

pompous /'pɒmpəs/ a, -ly adv großspurig

pond /pɒnd/ n Teich m

ponder /'pɒndə(r)/ vi nachdenken

ponderous /'pɒndərəs/ a schwerfällig

pong /pɒŋ/ n (fam) Mief m

pony /'pəʊnɪ/ n Pony nt. ~-tail n Pferdeschwanz m. ~-trekking n Ponyreiten nt

poodle /'pu:dl/ n Pudel m

pool¹ /puːl/ n [Schwimm]becken nt; (pond) Teich m; (of blood) Lache f

pool² n (common fund) [gemeinsame] Kasse f; ~s pl [Fußball]toto nt □ vt zusammenlegen

poor /puə(r)/ a (-er, -est) arm; (not good) schlecht; in ~ health nicht gesund □ npl the ~ die Armen. ~ly a be ~ly krank sein □ adv ärmlich; (badly) schlecht

pop¹ /pɒp/ n Knall m; (drink) Brause f □ v (pt/pp popped) □ vt (fam: put) stecken (in in + acc) □ vi knallen; (burst) platzen. ~ in vi (fam) reinschauen. ~ out vi (fam) kurz rausgehen

pop² n (fam) Popmusik f, Pop m □ attrib Pop-

'popcorn n Puffmais m

pope /pəʊp/ n Papst m

poplar /'pɒplə(r)/ n Pappel f

poppy /'pɒpɪ/ n Mohn m

popular /'pɒpjʊlə(r)/ a beliebt, populär; (belief) volkstümlich. ~ity /-'lærətɪ/ n Beliebtheit f, Popularität f

populat|e /'pɒpjʊleɪt/ vt bevölkern. ~ion /-'leɪʃn/ n Bevölkerung f

porcelain /'pɔːsəlɪn/ n Porzellan nt

porch /pɔːtʃ/ n Vorbau m; (Amer) Veranda f

porcupine /'pɔːkjʊpaɪn/ n Stachelschwein nt

pore¹ /pɔː(r)/ n Pore f

pore² vi ~ over studieren

pork /pɔːk/ n Schweinefleisch nt

porn /pɔːn/ n (fam) Porno m

pornograph|ic /pɔːnə'græfɪk/ a pornographisch. ~y /-'nɒgrəfɪ/ n Pornographie f

porous /'pɔːrəs/ a porös

porpoise /'pɔːpəs/ n Tümmler m

porridge /'pɒrɪdʒ/ n Haferbrei m

port¹ /pɔːt/ n Hafen m; (town) Hafenstadt f

port² n (Naut) Backbord nt

port³ n (wine) Portwein m

portable /'pɔːtəbl/ a tragbar

porter /'pɔːtə(r)/ n Portier m; (for luggage) Gepäckträger m

portfolio /pɔːt'fəʊlɪəʊ/ n Mappe f; (Comm) Portefeuille nt

porthole n Bullauge nt

portion /'pɔːʃn/ n Portion f; (part, share) Teil m

portly /'pɔːtlɪ/ a (-ier, -iest) beleibt

portrait /'pɔːtrɪt/ n Porträt nt

portray /pɔː'treɪ/ vt darstellen. ~al n Darstellung f

Portug|al /'pɔːtjʊgl/ n Portugal nt. ~uese /-'giːz/ a portugiesisch □ n Portugiese m /-giesin f

pose /pəʊz/ n Pose f □ vt aufwerfen (problem); stellen (question) □ vi posieren; (for painter) Modell stehen; ~ as sich ausgeben als

posh /pɒʃ/ a (fam) feudal

position /pə'zɪʃn/ n Platz m; (posture) Haltung f; (job) Stelle f; (situation) Lage f, Situation f; (status) Stellung f □ vt platzieren; ~ oneself sich stellen

positive /'pɒzətɪv/ a, -ly adv positiv; (definite) eindeutig; (real) ausgesprochen □ n Positiv nt

possess /pə'zes/ vt besitzen. ~ion /pə'zeʃn/ n Besitz m; ~ions pl Sachen pl

possess|ive /pə'zesɪv/ a Possessiv-; be ~ive zu sehr an jdm hängen. ~or n Besitzer m

possibility /pɒsə'bɪlətɪ/ n Möglichkeit f

possib|le /'pɒsəbl/ a möglich. ~ly adv möglicherweise; not ~ly unmöglich

post¹ /pəʊst/ n (pole) Pfosten m □ vt anschlagen (notice)

post² n (place of duty) Posten m; (job) Stelle f □ vt postieren; (transfer) versetzen

post³ n (mail) Post f; by ~ mit der Post □ vt aufgeben (letter); (send by ~) mit der Post schicken; keep s.o. ~ed jdn auf dem Laufenden halten

postage /'pəʊstɪdʒ/ n Porto nt. ~ stamp n Briefmarke f

postal /'pəʊstl/ a Post-. ~ order n ≈ Geldanweisung f

post: ~-box n Briefkasten m. ~card n Postkarte f; (picture) Ansichtskarte f. ~code n Postleitzahl f. ~-'date vt vordatieren

poster /'pəʊstə(r)/ n Plakat nt

posterior /pɒ'stɪərɪə(r)/ a hintere(r,s) □ n (fam) Hintern m

posterity /pɒ'sterətɪ/ n Nachwelt f

posthumous /'pɒstjʊməs/ a, -ly adv postum

post: ~man n Briefträger m. ~mark n Poststempel m

post-mortem /-'mɔːtəm/ n Obduktion f

'post office n Post f

postpone /pəʊst'pəʊn/ vt aufschieben; ~ until verschieben auf (+ acc). ~ment n Verschiebung f

postscript /'pəʊstskrɪpt/ n Nachschrift f

posture /'pɒstʃə(r)/ n Haltung f

post-'war a Nachkriegs-

posy /'pəʊzɪ/ n Sträußchen nt

pot /pɒt/ n Topf m; (for tea, coffee) Kanne f; ~s of money (fam) eine Menge Geld; go to ~ (fam) herunterkommen potassium /pə'tæsɪəm/ n Kalium nt

potato /pə'teɪtəʊ/ n (pl -es) Kartoffel f

poten|cy /'pəʊtənsɪ/ n Stärke f. ~t a stark

potential /pə'tenʃl/ a, -ly adv potenziell
□ n Potenzial nt

pot: ~-hole n Höhle f; (in road) Schlagloch
nt. ~-holer n Höhlenforscher m. ~-shot
n take a ~-shot at schießen auf (+ acc)

potted /'pɒtɪd/ a eingemacht; (shortened)
gekürzt. ~-plant n Topfpflanze f

potter¹ /'pɒtə(r)/ vi ~ [about] herum-
werkeln

potter² n Töpfer(in) m(f). ~y n Töpferei
f; (articles) Töpferwaren pl

potty /'pɒtɪ/ a (-ier, -iest) (fam) verrückt
□ n Töpfchen nt

pouch /paʊtʃ/ n Beutel m

pouffe /puːf/ n Sitzkissen nt

poultry /'pəʊltrɪ/ n Geflügel nt

pounce /paʊns/ vi zuschlagen; ~ on sich
stürzen auf (+ acc)

pound¹ /paʊnd/ n (money & 0,454 kg)
Pfund nt

pound² vt hämmern □ vi (heart:) hämmern; (run heavily) stampfen

pour /pɔː(r)/ vt gießen; einschenken
(drink) □ vi strömen; (with rain) gießen.
~ out vi ausströmen □ vt ausschütten;
einschenken (drink)

pout /paʊt/ vi einen Schmollmund machen

poverty /'pɒvətɪ/ n Armut f

powder /'paʊdə(r)/ n Pulver nt; (cosmetic)
Puder m □ vt pudern. ~y a pulverig

power /'paʊə(r)/ n Macht f; (strength)
Kraft f; (Electr) Strom m; (nuclear) Energie f; (Math) Potenz f. ~ cut n Strom-
sperre f. ~ed a betrieben (by mit); ~ed
by electricity mit Elektroantrieb. ~ful a
mächtig; (strong) stark. ~less a machtlos.
~-station n Kraftwerk nt

practicable /'præktɪkəbl/ a durchführbar, praktikabel

practical /'præktɪkl/ a, -ly adv praktisch.
~-joke n Streich m

practice /'præktɪs/ n Praxis f; (custom)
Brauch m; (habit) Gewohnheit f; (exercise) Übung f; (Sport) Training nt; in ~
(in reality) in der Praxis; out of ~ außer
Übung; put into ~ ausführen

practise /'præktɪs/ vt üben; (carry out)
praktizieren; ausüben (profession) □ vi
üben; (doctor:) praktizieren. ~d a geübt

pragmatic /præg'mætɪk/ a, ~ally adv
pragmatisch

praise /preɪz/ n Lob nt □ vt loben. ~wor-
thy a lobenswert

pram /præm/ n Kinderwagen m

prance /prɑːns/ vi herumhüpfen; (horse:)
tänzeln

prank /præŋk/ n Streich m

prattle /'prætl/ vi plappern

prawn /prɔːn/ n Garnele f, Krabbe f. ~
'cocktail n Krabbencocktail m

pray /preɪ/ vi beten. ~er /preə(r)/ n Gebet
nt; ~ers pl (service) Andacht f

preach /priːtʃ/ vt/i predigen. ~er n Predi-
ger m

preamble /priː'æmbl/ n Einleitung f

pre-ar'range /priː-/ vt im Voraus arrangieren

precarious /prɪ'keərɪəs/ a, -ly adv unsicher

precaution /prɪ'kɔːʃn/ n Vorsichtsmaßn-
ahme f; as a ~ zur Vorsicht. ~ary a Vors-
ichts-

precede /prɪ'siːd/ vt vorangehen (+ dat)

preceden|ce /'presɪdəns/ n Vorrang m. ~t
n Präzedenzfall m

preceding /prɪ'siːdɪŋ/ a vorhergehend

precinct /'priːsɪŋkt/ n Bereich m; (traffic-
free) Fußgängerzone f; (Amer: district) Bezirk m

precious /'preʃəs/ a kostbar; (style) pre-
ziös □ adv (fam) ~ little recht wenig

precipice /'presɪpɪs/ n Steilabfall m

precipitate¹ /prɪ'sɪpɪtət/ a voreilig

precipitate² /prɪ'sɪpɪteɪt/ vt schleudern;
(fig: accelerate) beschleunigen. ~ion
/-'teɪʃn/ n (Meteorol) Niederschlag m

précis /'preɪsiː/ n (pl précis /-siːz/) Zusammenfassung f

precis|e /prɪ'saɪs/ a, -ly adv genau. ~ion
/-'sɪʒn/ n Genauigkeit f

preclude /prɪ'kluːd/ vt ausschließen

precocious /prɪ'kəʊʃəs/ a frühreif

pre|con'ceived /priː-/ a vorgefasst.
~con'ception n vorgefasste Meinung f

precursor /priː'kɜːsə(r)/ n Vorläufer m

predator /'predətə(r)/ n Raubtier nt

predecessor /'priːdɪsesə(r)/ n Vorgän-
ger(in) m(f)

predicament /prɪ'dɪkəmənt/ n Zwangs-
lage f

predicat|e /'predɪkət/ n (Gram) Prädikat
nt. ~ive /prɪ'dɪkətɪv/ a, -ly adv prädikativ

predict /prɪ'dɪkt/ vt voraussagen. ~able
/-əbl/ a voraussehbar; (person) berechenbar. ~ion /-'dɪkʃn/ n Voraussage f

pre'domin|ant /prɪ-/ a vorherrschend.
~antly adv hauptsächlich, überwiegend.
~ate vi vorherrschen

pre-'eminent /priː-/ a hervorragend

pre-empt /priː'empt/ vt zuvorkommen (+
dat)

preen /priːn/ vt putzen; ~ oneself (fig)
selbstgefällig tun

pre|fab /'pri:fæb/ n (fam) [einfaches] Fertighaus nt. ~'fabricated a vorgefertigt

preface /'prefɪs/ n Vorwort nt

prefect /'pri:fekt/ n Präfekt m

prefer /prɪ'fɜ:(r)/ vt (pt/pp preferred) vorziehen; I ~ to walk ich gehe lieber zu Fuß; I ~ wine ich trinke lieber Wein

prefera|ble /'prefərəbl/ a be ~ble vorzuziehen sein (to dat). ~bly adv vorzugsweise

preferen|ce /'prefərəns/ n Vorzug m. ~tial /-'renʃl/ a bevorzugt

prefix /'pri:fɪks/ n Vorsilbe f

pregnan|cy /'pregnənsɪ/ n Schwangerschaft f. ~t a schwanger; ⟨animal⟩ trächtig

prehi'storic /pri:-/ a prähistorisch

prejudice /'predʒʊdɪs/ n Vorurteil nt; ⟨bias⟩ Voreingenommenheit f □ vt einnehmen (against gegen). ~d a voreingenommen

preliminary /prɪ'lɪmɪnərɪ/ a Vor-

prelude /'prelju:d/ n Vorspiel nt

pre-'marital a vorehelich

premature /'premətjʊə(r)/ a vorzeitig; ⟨birth⟩ Früh-. ~ly adv zu früh

pre'meditated /pri:-/ a vorsätzlich

premier /'premɪə(r)/ a führend □ n (Pol) Premier[minister] m

première /'premɪeə(r)/ n Premiere f

premises /'premɪsɪz/ npl Räumlichkeiten pl; on the ~ im Haus

premiss /'premɪs/ n Prämisse f

premium /'pri:mɪəm/ n Prämie f; be at a ~ hoch im Kurs stehen

premonition /premə'nɪʃn/ n Vorahnung f

preoccupied /prɪ'ɒkjʊpaɪd/ a [in Gedanken] beschäftigt

prep /prep/ n (Sch) Hausaufgaben pl

pre-'packed /pri:-/ a abgepackt

preparation /prepə'reɪʃn/ n Vorbereitung f; ⟨substance⟩ Präparat nt

preparatory /prɪ'pærətrɪ/ a Vor- □ adv ~ to vor (+ dat)

prepare /prɪ'peə(r)/ vt vorbereiten; anrichten ⟨meal⟩ □ vi sich vorbereiten (for auf + acc); ~d to bereit zu

pre'pay /pri:-/ vt (pt/pp -paid) im Voraus bezahlen

preposition /prepə'zɪʃn/ n Präposition f

prepossessing /pri:pə'zesɪŋ/ a ansprechend

preposterous /prɪ'pɒstərəs/ a absurd

prerequisite /pri:'rekwɪzɪt/ n Voraussetzung f

prerogative /prɪ'rɒgətɪv/ n Vorrecht nt

Presbyterian /prezbɪ'tɪərɪən/ a presbyterianisch □ n Presbyterianer(in) m(f)

prescribe /prɪ'skraɪb/ vt vorschreiben; (Med) verschreiben

prescription /prɪ'skrɪpʃn/ n (Med) Rezept nt

presence /'prezns/ n Anwesenheit f, Gegenwart f; ~ of mind Geistesgegenwart f

present[1] /'preznt/ a gegenwärtig; be ~ anwesend sein; (occur) vorkommen □ n Gegenwart f; (Gram) Präsens nt; at ~ zurzeit; for the ~ vorläufig

present[2] n (gift) Geschenk nt

present[3] /prɪ'zent/ vt überreichen; (show) zeigen; vorlegen ⟨cheque⟩; (introduce) vorstellen; ~ s.o. with sth jdm etw überreichen. ~able /-əbl/ a be ~able sich zeigen lassen können

presentation /prezn'teɪʃn/ n Überreichung f. ~ ceremony n Verleihungszeremonie f

presently /'prezntlɪ/ adv nachher; (Amer: now) zurzeit

preservation /prezə'veɪʃn/ n Erhaltung f

preservative /prɪ'zɜ:vətɪv/ n Konservierungsmittel nt

preserve /prɪ'zɜ:v/ vt erhalten; (Culin) konservieren; ⟨bottle⟩ einmachen □ n (Hunting & fig) Revier nt; ⟨jam⟩ Konfitüre f

preside /prɪ'zaɪd/ vi den Vorsitz haben (over bei)

presidency /'prezɪdənsɪ/ n Präsidentschaft f

president /'prezɪdənt/ n Präsident m; (Amer: chairman) Vorsitzende(r) m/f. ~ial /-'denʃl/ a Präsidenten-; ⟨election⟩ Präsidentschafts-

press /pres/ n Presse f □ vt/i drücken; drücken auf (+ acc) ⟨button⟩; pressen ⟨flower⟩; (iron) bügeln; (urge) bedrängen; ~ for drängen auf (+ acc); be ~ed for time in Zeitdruck sein. ~ on vi weitergehen/-fahren; (fig) weitermachen

press: ~ cutting n Zeitungsausschnitt m. ~ing a dringend. ~-stud n Druckknopf m. ~-up n Liegestütz m

pressure /'preʃə(r)/ n Druck m □ vt = pressurize. ~-cooker n Schnellkochtopf m. ~ group n Interessengruppe f

pressurize /'preʃəraɪz/ vt Druck ausüben auf (+ acc). ~d a Druck-

prestige /pre'sti:ʒ/ n Prestige nt. ~ious /-'stɪdʒəs/ a Prestige-

presumably /prɪ'zju:məblɪ/ adv vermutlich

presume /prɪˈzjuːm/ *vt* vermuten; ~ to do sth sich (*dat*) anmaßen, etw zu tun ▯ *vi* ~ on ausnutzen

presumpt|ion /prɪˈzʌmpʃn/ *n* Vermutung *f*; (*boldness*) Anmaßung *f*. ~uous /-ˈzʌmptjʊəs/ *a*, -ly *adv* anmaßend

presup'pose /priː-/ *vt* voraussetzen

pretence /prɪˈtens/ *n* Verstellung *f*; (*pretext*) Vorwand *m*; it's all ~ das ist alles gespielt

pretend /prɪˈtend/ *vt* (*claim*) vorgeben; ~ that so tun, als ob; ~ to be sich ausgeben als

pretentious /prɪˈtenʃəs/ *a* protzig

pretext /ˈpriːtekst/ *n* Vorwand *m*

pretty /ˈprɪtɪ/ *a* (-ier, -iest), ~ily *adv* hübsch ▯ *adv* (*fam: fairly*) ziemlich

pretzel /ˈpretsl/ *n* Brezel *f*

prevail /prɪˈveɪl/ *vi* siegen; (*custom*:) vorherrschen; ~ on s.o. to do sth jdn dazu bringen, etw zu tun

prevalen|ce /ˈprevələns/ *n* Häufigkeit *f*. ~t *a* vorherrschend

prevent /prɪˈvent/ *vt* verhindern, verhüten; ~ s.o. [from] doing sth jdn daran hindern, etw zu tun. ~able /-əbl/ *a* vermeidbar. ~ion /-enʃn/ *n* Verhinderung *f*, Verhütung *f*. ~ive /-ɪv/ *a* vorbeugend

preview /ˈpriːvjuː/ *n* Voraufführung *f*

previous /ˈpriːvɪəs/ *a* vorhergehend; ~ to vor (+ *dat*). ~ly *adv* vorher, früher

pre-'war /priː-/ *a* Vorkriegs-

prey /preɪ/ *n* Beute *f*; bird of ~ Raubvogel *m* ▯ *vi* ~ on Jagd machen auf (+ *acc*); ~ on s.o.'s mind jdm schwer auf der Seele liegen

price /praɪs/ *n* Preis *m* ▯ *vt* (*Comm*) auszeichnen. ~less *a* unschätzbar; (*fig*) unbezahlbar

prick /prɪk/ *n* Stich *m* ▯ *vt/i* stechen; ~ up one's ears die Ohren spitzen

prickl|e /ˈprɪkl/ *n* Stachel *m*; (*thorn*) Dorn *m*. ~y *a* stachelig; (*sensation*) stechend

pride /praɪd/ *n* Stolz *m*; (*arrogance*) Hochmut *m*; (*of lions*) Rudel *nt* ▯ *vt* ~ oneself on stolz sein auf (+ *acc*)

priest /priːst/ *n* Priester *m*

prig /prɪg/ *n* Tugendbold *m*

prim /prɪm/ *a* (primmer, primmest) prüde

primarily /ˈpraɪmərɪlɪ/ *adv* hauptsächlich, in erster Linie

primary /ˈpraɪmərɪ/ *a* Haupt-. ~ school *n* Grundschule *f*

prime[1] /praɪm/ *a* Haupt-; (*first-rate*) erstklassig ▯ *n* be in one's ~ in den besten Jahren sein

prime[2] *vt* scharf machen (*bomb*); grundieren (*surface*); (*fig*) instruieren

Prime Minister /praɪˈmɪnɪstə(r)/ *n* Premierminister(in) *m(f)*

primeval /praɪˈmiːvl/ *a* Ur-

primitive /ˈprɪmɪtɪv/ *a* primitiv

primrose /ˈprɪmrəʊz/ *n* gelbe Schlüsselblume *f*

prince /prɪns/ *n* Prinz *m*

princess /prɪnˈses/ *n* Prinzessin *f*

principal /ˈprɪnsəpl/ *a* Haupt- ▯ *n* (*Sch*) Rektor(in) *m(f)*

principality /prɪnsɪˈpælətɪ/ *n* Fürstentum *nt*

principally /ˈprɪnsəplɪ/ *adv* hauptsächlich

principle /ˈprɪnsəpl/ *n* Prinzip *nt*, Grundsatz *m*; in/on ~ im/aus Prinzip

print /prɪnt/ *n* Druck *m*; (*Phot*) Abzug *m*; in ~ gedruckt; (*available*) erhältlich; out of ~ vergriffen ▯ *vt* drucken; (*write in capitals*) in Druckschrift schreiben; (*Computing*) ausdrucken; (*Phot*) abziehen. ~ed matter *n* Drucksache *f*

print|er /ˈprɪntə(r)/ *n* Drucker *m*. ~ing *n* Druck *m*

'printout *n* (*Computing*) Ausdruck *m*

prior /ˈpraɪə(r)/ *a* frühere(r,s); ~ to vor (+ *dat*)

priority /praɪˈɒrɪtɪ/ *n* Priorität *f*, Vorrang *m*; (*matter*) vordringliche Sache *f*

prise /praɪz/ *vt* ~ open/up aufstemmen/hochstemmen

prism /ˈprɪzm/ *n* Prisma *nt*

prison /ˈprɪzn/ *n* Gefängnis *nt*. ~er *n* Gefangene(r) *m/f*

pristine /ˈprɪstiːn/ *a* tadellos

privacy /ˈprɪvəsɪ/ *n* Privatsphäre *f*; have no ~ nie für sich sein

private /ˈpraɪvət/ *a*, -ly *adv* privat; (*confidential*) vertraulich; (*car, secretary, school*) Privat- ▯ *n* (*Mil*) [einfacher] Soldat *m*; in ~ privat; (*confidentially*) vertraulich

privation /praɪˈveɪʃn/ *n* Entbehrung *f*

privatize /ˈpraɪvətaɪz/ *vt* privatisieren

privilege /ˈprɪvɪlɪdʒ/ *n* Privileg *nt*. ~d *a* privilegiert

privy /ˈprɪvɪ/ *a* be ~ to wissen

prize /praɪz/ *n* Preis *m* ▯ *vt* schätzen. ~-giving *n* Preisverleihung *f*. ~-winner *n* Preisgewinner(in) *m(f)*

pro /prəʊ/ *n* (*fam*) Profi *m*; the ~s and cons das Für und Wider

probability /prɒbəˈbɪlətɪ/ *n* Wahrscheinlichkeit *f*

probable /ˈprɒbəbl/ *a*, -bly *adv* wahrscheinlich

probation /prəˈbeɪʃn/ *n* (*Jur*) Bewährung *f*. ~ary *a* Probe-; ~ary period Probezeit *f*

probe /prəʊb/ n Sonde f; (fig: investigation) Untersuchung f □ vt/i ~ [into] untersuchen

problem /'prɒbləm/ n Problem nt; (Math) Textaufgabe f. ~atic /-'mætɪk/ a problematisch

procedure /prə'si:dʒə(r)/ n Verfahren nt

proceed /prə'si:d/ vi gehen; (in vehicle) fahren; (continue) weitergehen/-fahren; (speaking) fortfahren; (act) verfahren □ vt ~ to do sth anfangen, etw zu tun

proceedings /prə'si:dɪŋz/ npl Verfahren nt; (Jur) Prozess m

proceeds /'prəʊsi:dz/ npl Erlös m

process /'prəʊses/ n Prozess m; (procedure) Verfahren nt; in the ~ dabei □ vt verarbeiten; (Admin) bearbeiten; (Phot) entwickeln

procession /prə'seʃn/ n Umzug m, Prozession f

proclaim /prə'kleɪm/ vt ausrufen

proclamation /prɒklə'meɪʃn/ n Proklamation f

procure /prə'kjʊə(r)/ vt beschaffen

prod /prɒd/ n Stoß m □ vt stoßen; (fig) einen Stoß geben (+ dat)

prodigal /'prɒdɪgl/ a verschwenderisch

prodigious /prə'dɪdʒəs/ a gewaltig

prodigy /'prɒdɪdʒɪ/ n [infant] ~ Wunderkind nt

produce[1] /'prɒdju:s/ n landwirtschaftliche Erzeugnisse pl

produce[2] /prə'dju:s/ vt erzeugen, produzieren; (manufacture) herstellen; (bring out) hervorholen; (cause) hervorrufen; inszenieren. (play); (Radio, TV) redigieren. ~r n Erzeuger m, Produzent m; Hersteller m; (Theat) Regisseur m; (Radio, TV) Redakteur(in) m(f)

product /'prɒdʌkt/ n Erzeugnis nt, Produkt nt. ~ion /prə'dʌkʃn/ n Produktion f; (Theat) Inszenierung f

productive /prə'dʌktɪv/ a produktiv; (land, talks) fruchtbar. ~ity /-'tɪvətɪ/ n Produktivität f

profane /prə'feɪn/ a weltlich; (blasphemous) [gottes]lästerlich. ~ity /-'fænətɪ/ n (oath) Fluch m

profess /prə'fes/ vt behaupten; bekennen (faith)

profession /prə'feʃn/ n Beruf m. ~al a, -ly adv beruflich; (not amateur) Berufs-; (expert) fachmännisch; (Sport) professionell □ n Fachmann m; (Sport) Profi m

professor /prə'fesə(r)/ n Professor m

proficien|cy /prə'fɪʃnsɪ/ n Können nt. ~t a be ~t in beherrschen

profile /'prəʊfaɪl/ n Profil nt; (character study) Porträt nt

profit /'prɒfɪt/ n Gewinn m, Profit m □ vi ~ from profitieren von. ~able /-əbl/ a, -bly adv gewinnbringend; (fig) nutzbringend

profound /prə'faʊnd/ a, -ly adv tief

profus|e /prə'fju:s/ a, -ly adv üppig; (fig) überschwenglich. ~ion /-ju:ʒn/ n in ~ion in großer Fülle

progeny /'prɒdʒənɪ/ n Nachkommenschaft f

program /'prəʊgræm/ n Programm nt; □ vt (pt/pp programmed) programmieren

programme /'prəʊgræm/ n Programm nt; (Radio, TV) Sendung f. ~r n (Computing) Programmierer(in) m(f)

progress[1] /'prəʊgres/ n Vorankommen nt; (fig) Fortschritt m; in ~ im Gange; make ~ (fig) Fortschritte machen

progress[2] /prə'gres/ vi vorankommen; (fig) fortschreiten. ~ion /-eʃn/ n Folge f; (development) Entwicklung f

progressive /prə'gresɪv/ a fortschrittlich; (disease) fortschreitend. ~ly adv zunehmend

prohibit /prə'hɪbɪt/ vt verbieten (s.o. jdm). ~ive /-ɪv/ a unerschwinglich

project[1] /'prɒdʒekt/ n Projekt nt; (Sch) Arbeit f

project[2] /prə'dʒekt/ vt projizieren (film); (plan) planen □ vi (jut out) vorstehen

projectile /prə'dʒektaɪl/ n Geschoss nt

projector /prə'dʒektə(r)/ n Projektor m

proletariat /prəʊlɪ'teərɪət/ n Proletariat nt

prolific /prə'lɪfɪk/ a fruchtbar; (fig) produktiv

prologue /'prəʊlɒg/ n Prolog m

prolong /prə'lɒŋ/ vt verlängern

promenade /prɒmə'nɑ:d/ n Promenade f □ vi spazieren gehen

prominent /'prɒmɪnənt/ a vorstehend; (important) prominent; (conspicuous) auffällig; (place) gut sichtbar

promiscu|ity /prɒmɪ'skju:ətɪ/ n Promiskuität f. ~ous /prə'mɪskjʊəs/ a be ~ous häufig den Partner wechseln

promis|e /'prɒmɪs/ n Versprechen nt □ vt/i versprechen (s.o. jdm); the P~ed Land das Gelobte Land. ~ing a viel versprechend

promot|e /prə'məʊt/ vt befördern (to); (advance) fördern; (publicize) Reklame machen für; be ~ed (Sport) aufsteigen. ~ion /-əʊʃn/ n Beförderung f; (Sport) Aufstieg m; (Comm) Reklame f

prompt /prɒmpt/ a prompt, unverzüglich; (punctual) pünktlich □ adv pünktlich ɒr/i veranlassen (to zu); (*Theat*) soufflieren (+ *dat*). ~er *n* Souffleur *m*/Souffleuse *f*. ~ly *adv* prompt

prone /prəʊn/ *a* be *or* lie ~ auf dem Bauch liegen; be ~ to neigen zu; be ~ to do sth dazu neigen, etw zu tun

prong /prɒŋ/ *n* Zinke *f*

pronoun /'prəʊnaʊn/ *n* Fürwort *nt*, Pronomen *nt*

pronounce /prə'naʊns/ *vt* aussprechen; (*declare*) erklären. ~d *a* ausgeprägt; (*noticeable*) deutlich. ~ment *n* Erklärung *f*

pronunciation /prənʌnsɪ'eɪʃn/ *n* Aussprache *f*

proof /pru:f/ *n* Beweis *m*; (*Typ*) Korrekturbogen *m* □ *a* ~ against water/theft wasserfest/diebessicher. ~-reader *n* Korrektor *m*

prop[1] /prɒp/ *n* Stütze *f* □ *vt* (*pt/pp* propped) ~ open offen halten; ~ against (*lean*) lehnen an (+ *acc*). ~ up *vt* stützen

prop[2] *n* (*Theat, fam*) Requisit *nt*

propaganda /prɒpə'gændə/ *n* Propaganda *f*

propagate /'prɒpəgeɪt/ *vt* vermehren; (*fig*) verbreiten, propagieren

propel /prə'pel/ *vt* (*pt/pp* propelled) [an]treiben. ~ler *n* Propeller *m*. ~ling 'pencil *n* Drehbleistift *m*

propensity /prə'pensətɪ/ *n* Neigung *f* (for zu)

proper /'prɒpə(r)/ *a*, -ly *adv* richtig; (*decent*) anständig. ~ 'name, ~ 'noun *n* Eigenname *m*

property /'prɒpətɪ/ *n* Eigentum *nt*; (*quality*) Eigenschaft *f*; (*Theat*) Requisit *nt*; (*land*) [Grund]besitz *m*; (*house*) Haus *nt*. ~ market *n* Immobilienmarkt *m*

prophecy /'prɒfəsɪ/ *n* Prophezeiung *f*

prophesy /'prɒfɪsaɪ/ *vt* (*pt/pp* -ied) prophezeien

prophet /'prɒfɪt/ *n* Prophet *m*. ~ic /prə'fetɪk/ *a* prophetisch

proportion /prə'pɔ:ʃn/ *n* Verhältnis *nt*; (*share*) Teil *m*; ~s *pl* Proportionen; (*dimensions*) Maße. ~al *a*, -ly *adv* proportional

proposal /prə'pəʊzl/ *n* Vorschlag *m*; (*of marriage*) [Heirats]antrag *m*

propose /prə'pəʊz/ *vt* vorschlagen; (*intend*) vorhaben; einbringen (*motion*); ausbringen (*toast*) □ *vi* einen Heiratsantrag machen

proposition /prɒpə'zɪʃn/ *n* Vorschlag *m*

propound /prə'paʊnd/ *vt* darlegen

proprietor /prə'praɪətə(r)/ *n* Inhaber(in) *m*(*f*)

propriety /prə'praɪətɪ/ *n* Korrektheit *f*; (*decorum*) Anstand *m*

propulsion /prə'pʌlʃn/ *n* Antrieb *m*

prosaic /prə'zeɪɪk/ *a* prosaisch

prose /prəʊz/ *n* Prosa *f*

prosecut|**e** /'prɒsɪkju:t/ *vt* strafrechtlich verfolgen. ~**ion** /-'kju:ʃn/ *n* strafrechtliche Verfolgung *f*; the ~**ion** die Anklage. ~or *n* [Public] P~or Staatsanwalt *m*

prospect[1] /'prɒspekt/ *n* Aussicht *f*

prospect[2] /prə'spekt/ *vi* suchen (for nach)

prospect|**ive** /prə'spektɪv/ *a* (*future*) zukünftig. ~or *n* Prospektor *m*

prospectus /prə'spektəs/ *n* Prospekt *m*

prosper /'prɒspə(r)/ *vi* gedeihen, florieren; (*person*) Erfolg haben. ~**ity** /-'sperətɪ/ *n* Wohlstand *m*

prosperous /'prɒspərəs/ *a* wohlhabend

prostitut|**e** /'prɒstɪtju:t/ *n* Prostituierte *f*. ~**ion** /-'tju:ʃn/ *n* Prostitution *f*

prostrate /'prɒstreɪt/ *a* ausgestreckt; ~ with grief (*fig*) vor Kummer gebrochen

protagonist /prəʊ'tægənɪst/ *n* Kämpfer *m*; (*fig*) Protagonist *m*

protect /prə'tekt/ *vt* schützen (from vor + *dat*); beschützen (*person*). ~**ion** /-ekʃn/ *n* Schutz *m*. ~**ive** /-ɪv/ *a* Schutz-; (*fig*) beschützend. ~or *n* Beschützer *m*

protégé /'prɒtɪʒeɪ/ *n* Schützling *m*, Protegé *m*

protein /'prəʊti:n/ *n* Eiweiß *nt*

protest[1] /'prəʊtest/ *n* Protest *m*

protest[2] /prə'test/ *vi* protestieren

Protestant /'prɒtɪstənt/ *a* protestantisch, evangelisch □ *n* Protestant(in) *m*(*f*), Evangelische(r) *m/f*

protester /prə'testə(r)/ *n* Protestierende(r) *m/f*

protocol /'prəʊtəkɒl/ *n* Protokoll *nt*

prototype /'prəʊtə-/ *n* Prototyp *m*

protract /prə'trækt/ *vt* verlängern. ~or *n* Winkelmesser *m*

protrude /prə'tru:d/ *vi* [her]vorstehen

proud /praʊd/ *a*, -ly *adv* stolz (of auf + *acc*)

prove /pru:v/ *vt* beweisen □ *vi* ~ to be sich erweisen als

proverb /'prɒvɜ:b/ *n* Sprichwort *nt*. ~**ial** /prə'vɜ:bɪəl/ *a* sprichwörtlich

provide /prə'vaɪd/ *vt* zur Verfügung stellen; spenden (*shade*); ~ s.o. with sth jdn mit etw versorgen *od* versehen □ *vi* ~ for sorgen für

provided /prə'vaɪdɪd/ *conj* ~ [that] vorausgesetzt [dass]

providen|**ce** /'prɒvɪdəns/ *n* Vorsehung *f*. ~**tial** /-'denʃl/ *a* be ~**tial** ein Glück sein

providing /prə'vaɪdɪŋ/ *conj* = provided

provin|**ce** /'prɒvɪns/ *n* Provinz *f*; (*fig*) Bereich *m*. ~**ial** /prə'vɪnʃl/ *a* provinziell

provision /prəˈvɪʒn/ n Versorgung f (of mit); ~s pl Lebensmittel pl. ~al a, -ly adv vorläufig

proviso /prəˈvaɪzəʊ/ n Vorbehalt m

provocat|ion /prɒvəˈkeɪʃn/ n Provokation f. ~ive /prəˈvɒkətɪv/ a, -ly adv provozierend; (sexually) aufreizend

provoke /prəˈvəʊk/ vt provozieren; (cause) hervorrufen

prow /praʊ/ n Bug m

prowess /ˈpraʊɪs/ n Kraft f

prowl /praʊl/ vi herumschleichen ▢ n be on the ~ herumschleichen

proximity /prɒkˈsɪmətɪ/ n Nähe f

proxy /ˈprɒksɪ/ n Stellvertreter(in) m(f); (power) Vollmacht f

prude /pruːd/ n be a ~ prüde sein

pruden|ce /ˈpruːdns/ n Umsicht f. ~t a, -ly adv umsichtig; (wise) klug

prudish /ˈpruːdɪʃ/ a prüde

prune[1] /pruːn/ n Backpflaume f

prune[2] vt beschneiden

pry /praɪ/ vi (pt/pp pried) neugierig sein

psalm /sɑːm/ n Psalm m

pseudonym /ˈsjuːdənɪm/ n Pseudonym nt

psychiatric /saɪkɪˈætrɪk/ a psychiatrisch

psychiatr|ist /saɪˈkaɪətrɪst/ n Psychiater(in) m(f). ~y n Psychiatrie f

psychic /ˈsaɪkɪk/ a übersinnlich; I'm not ~ ich kann nicht hellsehen

psycho|ˈanalyse /saɪkəʊ-/ vt psychoanalysieren. ~aˈnalysis n Psychoanalyse f. ~aˈnalyst Psychoanalytiker(in) m(f)

psychological /saɪkəˈlɒdʒɪkl/ a, -ly adv psychologisch; (illness) psychisch

psycholog|ist /saɪˈkɒlədʒɪst/ n Psychologe m/ -login f. ~y n Psychologie f

psychopath /ˈsaɪkəpæθ/ n Psychopath(in) m(f)

P.T.O. abbr (please turn over) b.w.

pub /pʌb/ n (fam) Kneipe f

puberty /ˈpjuːbətɪ/ n Pubertät f

public /ˈpʌblɪk/ a, -ly adv öffentlich; make ~ publik machen ▢ n the ~ die Öffentlichkeit; in ~ in aller Öffentlichkeit

publican /ˈpʌblɪkən/ n [Gast]wirt m

publication /pʌblɪˈkeɪʃn/ n Veröffentlichung f

public: ~ conˈvenience n öffentliche Toilette f. ~ ˈholiday n gesetzlicher Feiertag m. ~ ˈhouse n [Gast]wirtschaft f

publicity /pʌbˈlɪsətɪ/ n Publicity f; (advertising) Reklame f

publicize /ˈpʌblɪsaɪz/ vt Reklame machen für

public: ~ ˈlibrary n öffentliche Bücherei f. ~ ˈschool n Privatschule f; (Amer)

staatliche Schule f. ~-ˈspirited a be ~-spirited Gemeinsinn haben. ~ ˈtransport n öffentliche Verkehrsmittel pl

publish /ˈpʌblɪʃ/ vt veröffentlichen. ~er n Verleger(in) m(f); (firm) Verlag m. ~ing n Verlagswesen nt

pucker /ˈpʌkə(r)/ vt kräuseln

pudding /ˈpʊdɪŋ/ n Pudding m; (course) Nachtisch m

puddle /ˈpʌdl/ n Pfütze f

puerile /ˈpjʊəraɪl/ a kindisch

puff /pʌf/ n (of wind) Hauch m; (of smoke) Wölkchen nt; (for powder) Quaste f ▢ vt blasen, pusten; ~ out ausstoßen ▢ vi keuchen; ~ at paffen an (+ dat) (pipe). ~ed a (out of breath) aus der Puste. ~ pastry n Blätterteig m

puffy /ˈpʌfɪ/ a geschwollen

pugnacious /pʌgˈneɪʃəs/ a, -ly adv aggressiv

pull /pʊl/ n Zug m; (jerk) Ruck m; (fam: influence) Einfluss m ▢ vt ziehen; ziehen an (+ dat) (rope); ~ a muscle sich (dat) einen Muskel zerren; ~ oneself together sich zusammennehmen; ~ one's weight tüchtig mitarbeiten; ~ s.o.'s leg (fam) jdn auf den Arm nehmen. ~ down vt herunterziehen; (demolish) abreißen. ~ in vt hereinziehen ▢ vi (Auto) einscheren. ~ off vt abziehen; (fam) schaffen. ~ out vt herausziehen ▢ vi (Auto) ausscheren. ~ through vt durchziehen ▢ vi (recover) durchkommen. ~ up vt heraufziehen; ausziehen (plant); (reprimand) zurechtweisen ▢ vi (Auto) anhalten

pulley /ˈpʊlɪ/ n (Techn) Rolle f

pullover /ˈpʊləʊvə(r)/ n Pullover m

pulp /pʌlp/ n Brei m; (of fruit) [Frucht]-fleisch nt

pulpit /ˈpʊlpɪt/ n Kanzel f

pulsate /pʌlˈseɪt/ vi pulsieren

pulse /pʌls/ n Puls m

pulses /ˈpʌlsɪz/ npl Hülsenfrüchte pl

pulverize /ˈpʌlvəraɪz/ vt pulverisieren

pumice /ˈpʌmɪs/ n Bimsstein m

pummel /ˈpʌml/ vt (pt/pp pummelled) mit den Fäusten bearbeiten

pump /pʌmp/ n Pumpe f ▢ vt pumpen; (fam) aushorchen. ~ up vt hochpumpen; (inflate) aufpumpen

pumpkin /ˈpʌmpkɪn/ n Kürbis m

pun /pʌn/ n Wortspiel nt

punch[1] /pʌntʃ/ n Faustschlag m; (device) Locher m ▢ vt boxen; lochen (ticket); stanzen (hole)

punch[2] n (drink) Bowle f

punch: ~ line n Pointe f. ~-up n Schlägerei f

punctual /'pʌŋktjʊəl/ a, -ly adv pünktlich. ~ity /-'ælətı/ n Pünktlichkeit f

punctuat|e /'pʌŋktjʊeɪt/ vt mit Satzzeichen versehen. ~ion /-'eɪʃn/ n Interpunktion f. ~ion mark n Satzzeichen nt

puncture /'pʌŋktʃə(r)/ n Loch nt; (tyre) Reifenpanne f □ vt durchstechen

pundit /'pʌndɪt/ n Experte m

pungent /'pʌndʒənt/ a scharf

punish /'pʌnɪʃ/ vt bestrafen. ~able /-əbl/ a strafbar. ~ment n Strafe f

punitive /'pju:nɪtɪv/ a Straf-

punnet /'pʌnɪt/ n Körbchen nt

punt /pʌnt/ n (boat) Stechkahn m

punter /'pʌntə(r)/ n (gambler) Wetter m; (client) Kunde m

puny /'pju:nɪ/ a (-ier, -iest) mickerig

pup /pʌp/ n = puppy

pupil /'pju:pl/ n Schüler(in) m(f); (of eye) Pupille f

puppet /'pʌpɪt/ n Puppe f; (fig) Marionette f

puppy /'pʌpɪ/ n junger Hund m

purchase /'pɜ:tʃəs/ n Kauf m; (leverage) Hebelkraft f □ vt kaufen. ~r n Käufer m

pure /pjʊə/ a (-r, -st,) -ly adv rein

purée /'pjʊəreɪ/ n Püree nt, Brei m

purgatory /'pɜ:gətrɪ/ n (Relig) Fegefeuer nt; (fig) Hölle f

purge /pɜ:dʒ/ n (Pol) Säuberungsaktion f □ vt reinigen; (Pol) säubern

puri|fication /pjʊərɪfɪ'keɪʃn/ n Reinigung f. ~fy /'pjʊərɪfaɪ/ vt (pt/pp -ied) reinigen

puritanical /pjʊərɪ'tænɪkl/ a puritanisch

purity /'pjʊərɪtɪ/ n Reinheit f

purl /pɜ:l/ n (Knitting) linke Masche f □ vt/i links stricken

purple /'pɜ:pl/ a (dunkel)lila

purport /pə'pɔ:t/ vt vorgeben

purpose /'pɜ:pəs/ n Zweck m; (intention) Absicht f; (determination) Entschlossenheit f; on ~ absichtlich; to no ~ unnützerweise. ~ful a, -ly adv entschlossen. ~ly adv absichtlich

purr /pɜ:(r)/ vi schnurren

purse /pɜ:s/ n Portemonnaie nt; (Amer: handbag) Handtasche f □ vt schürzen (lips)

pursue /pə'sju:/ vt verfolgen; (fig) nachgehen (+ dat). ~r /-ə(r)/ n Verfolger m

pursuit /pə'sju:t/ n Verfolgung f; Jagd f; (pastime) Beschäftigung f; in ~ hinterher

pus /pʌs/ n Eiter m

push /pʊʃ/ n Stoß m, (fam) Schubs m; get the ~ (fam) hinausfliegen □ vt/i schieben; (press) drücken; (roughly) stoßen; be

~ed for time (fam) unter Zeitdruck stehen. ~ off vt hinunterstoßen □ vi (fam: leave) abhauen. ~ on vi (continue) weitergehen/-fahren; (with activity) weitermachen. ~ up vt hochschieben; hochtreiben (price)

push: ~-button n Druckknopf m. ~-chair n [Kinder]sportwagen m. ~-over n (fam) Kinderspiel nt. ~-up n (Amer) Liegestütz m

pushy /'pʊʃɪ/ a (fam) aufdringlich

puss /pʊs/ n, **pussy** /'pʊsɪ/ n Mieze f

put /pʊt/ vt (pt/pp put, pres p putting) tun; (place) setzen; (upright) stellen; (flat) legen; (express) ausdrücken; (say) sagen; (estimate) schätzen (at auf + acc); ~ aside or by beiseite legen; ~ one's foot down (fam) energisch werden; (Auto) Gas geben □ vi ~ to sea auslaufen □ a stay ~ dableiben. ~ away vt wegräumen. ~ back vt wieder hinsetzen/-stellen/-legen; zurückstellen (clock). ~ down vt hinsetzen/-stellen/-legen; (suppress) niederschlagen; (kill) töten; (write) niederschreiben; (attribute) zuschreiben (to dat). ~ forward vt vorbringen, vorstellen (clock). ~ in vt hineinsetzen/-stellen/-legen; (insert) einstecken; (submit) einreichen □ vi ~ in for beantragen. ~ off vt ausmachen (light); (postpone) verschieben; ~ s.o. off jdn abbestellen; (disconcert) jdn aus der Fassung bringen; ~ s.o. off sth jdm etw verleiden (clothes, brake); sich (dat) aufsetzen (hat); (Culin) aufsetzen; anmachen (light); aufführen (play); annehmen (accent); ~ on weight zunehmen. ~ out vt hinaussetzen/-stellen/-legen; ausmachen (fire, light); ausstrecken (hand); (disconcert) aus der Fassung bringen; ~ s.o./oneself out jdm/sich Umstände machen. ~ through vt durchstecken; (Teleph) verbinden (to mit). ~ up vt errichten (building); aufschlagen (tent); aufspannen (umbrella); anschlagen (notice); erhöhen (price); unterbringen (guest); ~ s.o. up to sth jdn zu etw anstiften □ vi (at hotel) absteigen in (+ dat); ~ up with sth sich (dat) etw bieten lassen

putrefy /'pju:trɪfaɪ/ vi (pt/pp -ied) verwesen

putrid /'pju:trɪd/ a faulig

putty /'pʌtɪ/ n Kitt m

put-up /'pʊtʌp/ a a ~ job ein abgekartetes Spiel nt

puzzl|e /'pʌzl/ n Rätsel nt; (jigsaw) Puzzlespiel nt □ vt it ~es me es ist mir rätselhaft □ vi ~ over sich (dat) den Kopf zerbrechen über (+ acc). ~ing a rätselhaft

pyjamas /pə'dʒɑ:məz/ npl Schlafanzug m

pylon /'paɪlən/ n Mast m
pyramid /'pɪrəmɪd/ n Pyramide f
python /'paɪθn/ n Pythonschlange f

Q

quack[1] /kwæk/ n Quaken nt □ vi quaken
quack[2] n (doctor) Quacksalber m
quad /kwɒd/ n (fam: court) Hof m; ~s pl = quadruplets
quadrangle /'kwɒdræŋgl/ n Viereck nt; (court) Hof m
quadruped /'kwɒdruped/ n Vierfüßer m
quadruple /'kwɒdrʊpl/ a vierfach □ vt vervierfachen □ vi sich vervierfachen. ~ts /-plɪts/ npl Vierlinge pl
quagmire /'kwɒgmaɪə(r)/ n Sumpf m
quaint /kweɪnt/ a (-er, -est) malerisch; (odd) putzig
quake /kweɪk/ n (fam) Erdbeben nt □ vi beben; (with fear) zittern
Quaker /'kweɪkə(r)/ n Quäker(in) m(f)
qualification /kwɒlɪfɪ'keɪʃn/ n Qualifikation f; (reservation) Einschränkung f. ~ied /-faɪd/ a qualifiziert; (trained) ausgebildet; (limited) bedingt
qualify /'kwɒlɪfaɪ/ v (pt/pp -ied) □ vt qualifizieren; (entitle) berechtigen; (limit) einschränken □ vi sich qualifizieren
quality /'kwɒlətɪ/ n Qualität f; (characteristic) Eigenschaft f
qualm /kwɑːm/ n Bedenken pl
quandary /'kwɒndərɪ/ n Dilemma nt
quantity /'kwɒntətɪ/ n Quantität f, Menge f; in ~ in großen Mengen
quarantine /'kwɒrəntiːn/ n Quarantäne f
quarrel /'kwɒrl/ n Streit m □ vi (pt/pp quarrelled) sich streiten. ~some a streitsüchtig
quarry[1] /'kwɒrɪ/ n (prey) Beute f
quarry[2] n Steinbruch m
quart /kwɔːt/ n Quart nt
quarter /'kwɔːtə(r)/ n Viertel nt; (of year) Vierteljahr nt; (Amer) 25-Cent-Stück nt; ~s pl Quartier nt; at [a] ~ to six um Viertel vor sechs; from all ~s aus allen Richtungen. □ vt vierteln; (Mil) einquartieren (on bei). ~-final n Viertelfinale nt
quarterly /'kwɔːtəlɪ/ a & adv vierteljährlich
quartet /kwɔː'tet/ n Quartett nt
quartz /kwɔːts/ n Quarz m. ~ watch n Quarzuhr f

quash /kwɒʃ/ vt aufheben; niederschlagen ⟨rebellion⟩
quaver /'kweɪvə(r)/ n (Mus) Achtelnote f □ vi zittern
quay /kiː/ n Kai m
queasy /'kwiːzɪ/ a I feel ~ mir ist übel
queen /kwiːn/ n Königin f; (Cards, Chess) Dame f
queer /kwɪə(r)/ a (-er, -est) eigenartig; (dubious) zweifelhaft; (fam: homosexual) schwul □ n (fam) Schwule(r) m
quell /kwel/ vt unterdrücken
quench /kwentʃ/ vt löschen
query /'kwɪərɪ/ n Frage f; (question mark) Fragezeichen nt □ vt (pt/pp -ied) infrage stellen; reklamieren ⟨bill⟩
quest /kwest/ n Suche f (for nach)
question /'kwestʃn/ n Frage f; (for discussion) Thema nt; out of the ~ ausgeschlossen; without ~ ohne Frage; the person in ~ die fragliche Person □ vt infrage stellen; ~ s.o. jdn ausfragen; (police:) jdn verhören. ~able /-əbl/ a zweifelhaft. ~ mark n Fragezeichen nt
questionnaire /kwestʃə'neə(r)/ n Fragebogen m
queue /kjuː/ n Schlange f □ vi ~ [up] Schlange stehen, sich anstellen (for nach)
quibble /'kwɪbl/ vi Haarspalterei treiben
quick /kwɪk/ a (-er, -est), -ly adv schnell; be ~! mach schnell! have a ~ meal schnell etwas essen □ adv schnell □ n cut to the ~ (fig) ins Mark getroffen. ~en vt beschleunigen □ vi sich beschleunigen
quick: ~sand n Treibsand m. ~-tempered a aufbrausend
quid /kwɪd/ n inv (fam) Pfund nt
quiet /'kwaɪət/ a (-er, -est), -ly adv still; (calm) ruhig; (soft) leise; keep ~ about (fam) nichts sagen von □ n Stille f; Ruhe f; on the ~ heimlich
quieten /'kwaɪətn/ vt beruhigen □ vi ~en down ruhig werden. ~ness n (see quiet) Stille f; Ruhe f
quill /kwɪl/ n Feder f; (spine) Stachel m
quilt /kwɪlt/ n Steppdecke f. ~ed a Steppquince /kwɪns/ n Quitte f
quins /kwɪnz/ npl (fam) = quintuplets
quintet /kwɪn'tet/ n Quintett nt
quintuplets /'kwɪntjʊplɪts/ npl Fünflinge pl
quip /kwɪp/ n Scherz m □ vi (pt/pp quipped) scherzen
quirk /kwɜːk/ n Eigenart f
quit /kwɪt/ v (pt/pp quitted or quit) □ vt verlassen; (give up) aufgeben; ~ doing sth aufhören, etw zu tun □ vi gehen; give

s.o. notice to ~ jdm die Wohnung kündigen

quite /kwaɪt/ *adv* ganz; (*really*) wirklich; ~ [so]! genau! ~ a few ziemlich viele

quits /kwɪts/ *a* quitt

quiver /'kwɪvə(r)/ *vi* zittern

quiz /kwɪz/ *n* Quiz *nt* □ *vt* (*pt/pp* quizzed) ausfragen. ~zical *a*, -ly *adv* fragend

quorum /'kwɔːrəm/ *n* have a ~ beschlussfähig sein

quota /'kwəʊtə/ *n* Anteil *m*; (*Comm*) Kontingent *nt*

quotation /kwəʊ'teɪʃn/ *n* Zitat *nt*; (*price*) Kostenvoranschlag *m*; (*of shares*) Notierung *f*. ~ marks *npl* Anführungszeichen *pl*

quote /kwəʊt/ *n* (*fam*) = quotation; in ~s in Anführungszeichen □ *vt/i* zitieren

R

rabbi /'ræbaɪ/ *n* Rabbiner *m*; (*title*) Rabbi *m*

rabbit /'ræbɪt/ *n* Kaninchen *nt*

rabble /'ræbl/ *n* the ~ der Pöbel

rabid /'ræbɪd/ *a* fanatisch; ⟨*animal*⟩ tollwütig

rabies /'reɪbiːz/ *n* Tollwut *f*

race[1] /reɪs/ *n* Rasse *f*

race[2] *n* Rennen *nt*; (*fig*) Wettlauf *m* □ *vi* [am Rennen] teilnehmen; ⟨*athlete, horse:*⟩ laufen; (*fam: rush*) rasen □ *vt* um die Wette laufen mit; an einem Rennen teilnehmen lassen ⟨*horse*⟩

race: ~course *n* Rennbahn *f*. ~horse *n* Rennpferd *nt*. ~-track *n* Rennbahn *f*

racial /'reɪʃl/ *a*, -ly *adv* rassisch; ⟨*discrimination, minority*⟩ Rassen-

racing /'reɪsɪŋ/ *n* Rennsport *m*; (*horse-*) Pferderennen *nt*. ~ car *n* Rennwagen *m*. ~ driver *n* Rennfahrer *m*

racis|m /'reɪsɪzm/ *n* Rassismus *m*. ~t /-ɪst/ *a* rassistisch □ *n* Rassist *m*

rack[1] /ræk/ *n* Ständer *m*; (*for plates*) Gestell *nt* □ *vt* ~ one's brains sich (*dat*) den Kopf zerbrechen

rack[2] *n* go to ~ and ruin verfallen; (*fig*) herunterkommen

racket[1] /'rækɪt/ *n* (*Sport*) Schläger *m*

racket[2] *n* (*din*) Krach *m*; (*swindle*) Schwindelgeschäft *nt*

racy /'reɪsɪ/ *a* (-ier, -iest) schwungvoll; (*risqué*) gewagt

radar /'reɪdɑː(r)/ *n* Radar *m*

radian|ce /'reɪdɪəns/ *n* Strahlen *nt*. ~t *a*, -ly *adv* strahlend

radiat|e /'reɪdɪeɪt/ *vt* ausstrahlen □ *vi* ⟨*heat:*⟩ ausgestrahlt werden; ⟨*roads:*⟩ strahlenförmig ausgehen. ~ion /-'eɪʃn/ *n* Strahlung *f*

radiator /'reɪdɪeɪtə(r)/ *n* Heizkörper *m*; (*Auto*) Kühler *m*

radical /'rædɪkl/ *a*, -ly *adv* radikal □ *n* Radikale(r) *m/f*

radio /'reɪdɪəʊ/ *n* Radio *nt*; by ~ über Funk □ *vt* funken ⟨*message*⟩

radio|'active *a* radioaktiv. ~ac'tivity *n* Radioaktivität *f*

radiography /reɪdɪ'ɒgrəfɪ/ *n* Röntgenographie *f*

'radio ham *n* Hobbyfunker *m*

radio'therapy *n* Strahlenbehandlung *f*

radish /'rædɪʃ/ *n* Radieschen *nt*

radius /'reɪdɪəs/ *n* (*pl* -dii /-dɪaɪ/) Radius *m*, Halbmesser *m*

raffle /'ræfl/ *n* Tombola *f* □ *vt* verlosen

raft /rɑːft/ *n* Floß *nt*

rafter /'rɑːftə(r)/ *n* Dachsparren *m*

rag[1] /ræg/ *n* Lumpen *m*; (*pej: newspaper*) Käseblatt *nt*; in ~s in Lumpen

rag[2] *vt* (*pt/pp* ragged) (*fam*) aufziehen

rage /reɪdʒ/ *n* Wut *f*; all the ~ (*fam*) der letzte Schrei □ *vi* rasen; ⟨*storm:*⟩ toben

ragged /'rægɪd/ *a* zerlumpt; ⟨*edge*⟩ ausgefranst

raid /reɪd/ *n* Überfall *m*; (*Mil*) Angriff *m*; (*police*) Razzia *f* □ *vt* überfallen; (*Mil*) angreifen; (*police*) eine Razzia durchführen in (+ *dat*); (*break in*) eindringen in (+ *acc*). ~er *n* Eindringling *m*; (*of bank*) Bankräuber *m*

rail /reɪl/ *n* Schiene *f*; (*pole*) Stange *f*; (*hand-*) Handlauf *m*; (*Naut*) Reling *f*; by ~ mit der Bahn

railings /'reɪlɪŋz/ *npl* Geländer *nt*

'railroad *n* (*Amer*) = railway

'railway *n* [Eisen]bahn *f*. ~man *n* Eisenbahner *m*. ~ station *n* Bahnhof *m*

rain /reɪn/ *n* Regen *m* □ *vi* regnen

rain: ~bow *n* Regenbogen *m*. ~check *n* (*Amer*) take a ~check on aufschieben. ~coat *n* Regenmantel *m*. ~fall *n* Niederschlag *m*

rainy /'reɪnɪ/ *a* (-ier, -iest) regnerisch

raise /reɪz/ *n* (*Amer*) Lohnerhöhung *f* □ *vt* erheben; (*upright*) aufrichten; (*make higher*) erhöhen; (*lift*) [hoch]heben; lüften ⟨*hat*⟩; aufziehen ⟨*children, animals*⟩; aufwerfen ⟨*question*⟩; aufbringen ⟨*money*⟩

raisin /'reɪzn/ *n* Rosine *f*

rake /reɪk/ *n* Harke *f*, Rechen *m* □ *vt* harken, rechen. ~ up *vt* zusammenharken; (*fam*) wieder aufführen

'**rake-off** n (fam) Prozente pl

rally /'rælɪ/ n Versammlung f; (Auto) Rallye f; (Tennis) Ballwechsel m □ vt sammeln □ vi sich sammeln; (recover strength) sich erholen

ram /ræm/ n Schafbock m; (Astr) Widder m □ vt (pt/pp rammed) rammen

ramble /'ræmbl/ n Wanderung f □ vi wandern; (in speech) irrereden. ~er n Wanderer m; (rose) Kletterrose f. ~ing a weitschweifig; (club) Wander-

ramp /ræmp/ n Rampe f; (Aviat) Gangway f

rampage¹ /'ræmpeɪdʒ/ n be/go on the ~ randalieren

rampage² /ræm'peɪdʒ/ vi randalieren

rampant /'ræmpənt/ a weit verbreitet; (in heraldry) aufgerichtet

rampart /'ræmpɑːt/ n Wall m

ramshackle /'ræmʃækl/ a baufällig

ran /ræn/ see run

ranch /rɑːntʃ/ n Ranch f

rancid /'rænsɪd/ a ranzig

rancour /'ræŋkə(r)/ n Groll m

random /'rændəm/ a willkürlich; a ~ sample eine Stichprobe □ n at ~ aufs Geratewohl; (choose) willkürlich

randy /'rændɪ/ a (-ier, -iest) (fam) geil

rang /ræŋ/ see ring²

range /reɪndʒ/ n Serie f, Reihe f; (Comm) Auswahl f, Angebot nt (of an + dat); (of mountains) Kette f; (Mus) Umfang m; (distance) Reichweite f; (for shooting) Schießplatz m; (stove) Kohlenherd m; at a ~ of auf eine Entfernung von □ vi reichen; ~ from ... to gehen von ... bis. ~r n Aufseher m

rank¹ /ræŋk/ n (row) Reihe f; (Mil) Rang m; (social position) Stand m; the ~ and file die breite Masse; the ~s pl die gemeinen Soldaten □ vt/i einstufen; ~ among zählen zu

rank² a (bad) übel; (plants) üppig; (fig) krass

ransack /'rænsæk/ vt durchwühlen; (pillage) plündern

ransom /'rænsəm/ n Lösegeld nt; hold s.o. to ~ Lösegeld für jdn fordern

rant /rænt/ vi rasen

rap /ræp/ n Klopfen nt; (blow) Schlag m □ v (pt/pp rapped) □ vt klopfen auf (+ acc) □ vi ~ at/on klopfen an/auf (+ acc)

rape¹ /reɪp/ n (Bot) Raps m

rape² n Vergewaltigung f □ vt vergewaltigen

rapid /'ræpɪd/ a, -ly adv schnell. ~ity /rə'pɪdətɪ/ n Schnelligkeit f

rapids /'ræpɪdz/ npl Stromschnellen pl

rapist /'reɪpɪst/ n Vergewaltiger m

rapport /ræ'pɔː(r)/ n (innerer) Kontakt m

rapt /ræpt/ a, -ly adv gespannt; (look) andächtig; ~ in versunken in (+ acc)

rapture /'ræptʃə(r)/ n Entzücken nt. ~ous /-rəs/ a, -ly adv begeistert

rare¹ /reə(r)/ a (-r, -st), -ly adv selten

rare² a (Culin) englisch gebraten

rarefied /'reərɪfaɪd/ a dünn

rarity /'reərətɪ/ n Seltenheit f

rascal /'rɑːskl/ n Schlingel m

rash¹ /ræʃ/ n (Med) Ausschlag m

rash² a (-er, -est), -ly adv voreilig

rasher /'ræʃə(r)/ n Speckscheibe f

rasp /rɑːsp/ n Raspel f

raspberry /'rɑːzbərɪ/ n Himbeere f

rat /ræt/ n Ratte f; (fam: person) Schuft m; smell a ~ (fam) Lunte riechen

rate /reɪt/ n Rate f; (speed) Tempo nt; (of payment) Satz m; (of exchange) Kurs m; ~s pl (taxes) ≈ Grundsteuer f; at any ~ auf jeden Fall; at this ~ auf diese Weise □ vt einschätzen; ~ among zählen zu □ vi ~ as gelten als

rather /'rɑːðə(r)/ adv lieber; (fairly) ziemlich; ~! und ob!

ratification /rætɪfɪ'keɪʃn/ n Ratifizierung f. ~fy /'rætɪfaɪ/ vt (pt/pp -ied) ratifizieren

rating /'reɪtɪŋ/ n Einschätzung f; (class) Klasse f; (sailor) [einfacher] Matrose m; ~s pl (Radio, TV) ≈ Einschaltquote f

ratio /'reɪʃɪəʊ/ n Verhältnis nt

ration /'ræʃn/ n Ration f □ vt rationieren

rational /'ræʃənl/ a, -ly adv rational. ~ize vt/i rationalisieren

'**rat race** n (fam) Konkurrenzkampf m

rattle /'rætl/ n Rasseln nt; (of china, glass) Klirren nt; (of windows) Klappern nt; (toy) Klapper f □ vi rasseln; klirren; klappern □ vt rasseln mit; (shake) schütteln. ~ off vt herunterrasseln

'**rattlesnake** n Klapperschlange f

raucous /'rɔːkəs/ a rauh

ravage /'rævɪdʒ/ vt verwüsten, verheeren

rave /reɪv/ vi toben; ~ about schwärmen von

raven /'reɪvn/ n Rabe m

ravenous /'rævənəs/ a heißhungrig

ravine /rə'viːn/ n Schlucht f

raving /'reɪvɪŋ/ a ~ mad (fam) total verrückt

ravishing /'rævɪʃɪŋ/ a hinreißend

raw /rɔː/ a (-er, -est) roh; (not processed) Roh-; (skin) wund; (weather) nasskalt; (inexperienced) unerfahren; get a ~ deal (fam) schlecht wegkommen. ~ ma'terials npl Rohstoffe pl

ray /reɪ/ *n* Strahl *m*; ~ of hope Hoffnungsschimmer *m*

raze /reɪz/ *vt* ~ to the ground dem Erdboden gleichmachen

razor /'reɪzə(r)/ *n* Rasierapparat *m*. ~ blade *n* Rasierklinge *f*

re /riː/ *prep* betreffs (+ *gen*)

reach /riːtʃ/ *n* Reichweite *f*; (*of river*) Strecke *f*; within/out of ~ in/außer Reichweite; within easy ~ leicht erreichbar ◻ *vt* erreichen; (*arrive at*) ankommen in (+ *dat*); (~ *as far as*) reichen bis zu; kommen zu ⟨*decision, conclusion*⟩; (*pass*) reichen ◻ *vi* reichen (to bis zu); ~ for greifen nach; I can't ~ ich komme nicht daran

re'act /rɪ-/ *vi* reagieren (to auf + *acc*)

re'action /rɪ-/ *n* Reaktion *f*. ~ary *a* reaktionär

reactor /rɪ'æktə(r)/ *n* Reaktor *m*

read /riːd/ *vt/i* (*pt/pp* read /red/) lesen; (*aloud*) vorlesen (to *dat*); (*Univ*) studieren; ablesen ⟨*meter*⟩. ~ out *vt* vorlesen

readable /'riːdəbl/ *a* lesbar

reader /'riːdə(r)/ *n* Leser(in) *m(f)*; (*book*) Lesebuch *nt*

readi|ly /'redɪlɪ/ *adv* bereitwillig; (*easily*) leicht. ~ness *n* Bereitschaft *f*; in ~ness bereit

reading /'riːdɪŋ/ *n* Lesen *nt*; (*Pol, Relig*) Lesung *f*

rea'djust /riː-/ *vt* neu einstellen ◻ *vi* sich umstellen (to auf + *acc*)

ready /'redɪ/ *a* (-ier, -iest) fertig; (*willing*) bereit; (*quick*) schnell; get ~ sich fertig machen; (*prepare to*) sich bereitmachen

ready: ~-'made *a* fertig. ~ 'money *n* Bargeld *nt*. ~-to-'wear *a* Konfektions-

real /rɪəl/ *a* wirklich; (*genuine*) echt; (*actual*) eigentlich ◻ *adv* (*Amer, fam*) echt. ~ estate *n* Immobilien *pl*

realis|m /'rɪəlɪzm/ *n* Realismus *m*. ~t /-lɪst/ *n* Realist *m*. ~tic /-'lɪstɪk/ *a*, -ally *adv* realistisch

reality /rɪ'ælətɪ/ *n* Wirklichkeit *f*, Realität *f*

realization /rɪəlaɪ'zeɪʃn/ *n* Erkenntnis *f*

realize /'rɪəlaɪz/ *vt* einsehen; (*become aware*) gewahr werden; verwirklichen ⟨*hopes, plans*⟩; (*Comm*) realisieren; einbringen ⟨*price*⟩; I didn't ~ das wusste ich nicht

really /'rɪəlɪ/ *adv* wirklich; (*actually*) eigentlich

realm /relm/ *n* Reich *nt*

realtor /'riːəltə(r)/ *n* (*Amer*) Immobilienmakler *m*

reap /riːp/ *vt* ernten

reap'pear /riː-/ *vi* wiederkommen

rear¹ /rɪə(r)/ *a* Hinter-; (*Auto*) Heck- ◻ *n* the ~ der hintere Teil; from the ~ von hinten

rear² *vt* aufziehen ◻ *vi* ~ [up] ⟨*horse:*⟩ sich aufbäumen

'rear-light *n* Rücklicht *nt*

re'arm /riː-/ *vi* wieder aufrüsten

rear'range /riː-/ *vt* umstellen

rear-view 'mirror *n* (*Auto*) Rückspiegel *m*

reason /'riːzn/ *n* Grund *m*; (*good sense*) Vernunft *f*; (*ability to think*) Verstand *m*; within ~ in vernünftigen Grenzen ◻ *vi* argumentieren; ~ with vernünftig reden mit. ~able /-əbl/ *a* vernünftig; (*not expensive*) preiswert. ~ably /-əblɪ/ *adv* (*fairly*) ziemlich

reas'sur|ance /riː-/ *n* Beruhigung *f*; Versicherung *f*. ~e *vt* beruhigen; ~ s.o. of sth jdm etw ⟨*gen*⟩ versichern

rebate /'riːbeɪt/ *n* Rückzahlung *f*; (*discount*) Nachlass *m*

rebel¹ /'rebl/ *n* Rebell *m*

rebel² /rɪ'bel/ *vi* (*pt/pp* rebelled) rebellieren. ~lion /-lɪən/ *n* Rebellion *f*. ~lious /-lɪəs/ *a* rebellisch

re'bound¹ /rɪ-/ *vi* abprallen

'rebound² /riː-/ *n* Rückprall *m*

rebuff /rɪ'bʌf/ *n* Abweisung *f* ◻ *vt* abweisen; eine Abfuhr erteilen (s.o. jdm)

re'build /riː-/ *vt* (*pt/pp* -built) wieder aufbauen

rebuke /rɪ'bjuːk/ *n* Tadel *m* ◻ *vt* tadeln

rebuttal /rɪ'bʌtl/ *n* Widerlegung *f*

re'call /rɪ-/ *n* Erinnerung *f*; beyond ~ unwiderruflich ◻ *vt* zurückrufen; abberufen ⟨*diplomat*⟩; vorzeitig einberufen ⟨*parliament*⟩; (*remember*) sich erinnern an (+ *acc*)

recant /rɪ'kænt/ *vi* widerrufen

recap /'riːkæp/ *vt/i* (*fam*) = recapitulate

recapitulate /riːkə'pɪtjʊleɪt/ *vt/i* zusammenfassen; rekapitulieren

re'capture /riː-/ *vt* wieder gefangen nehmen ⟨*person*⟩; wieder einfangen ⟨*animal*⟩

reced|e /rɪ'siːd/ *vi* zurückgehen. ~ing *a* ⟨*forehead, chin*⟩ fliehend; ~ing hair Stirnglatze *f*

receipt /rɪ'siːt/ *n* Quittung *f*; (*receiving*) Empfang *m*; ~s *pl* (*Comm*) Einnahmen *pl*

receive /rɪ'siːv/ *vt* erhalten, bekommen; empfangen ⟨*guests*⟩. ~r *n* (*Teleph*) Hörer *m*; (*Radio, TV*) Empfänger *m*; (*of stolen goods*) Hehler *m*

recent /'riːsnt/ *a* kürzlich erfolgte(r,s). ~ly *adv* in letzter Zeit; (*the other day*) kürzlich, vor kurzem

receptacle /rɪ'septəkl/ *n* Behälter *m*

reception /rɪ'sepʃn/ n Empfang m; ~ [desk] (in hotel) Rezeption f. ~ist n Empfangsdame f

receptive /rɪ'septɪv/ a aufnahmefähig; ~ to empfänglich für

recess /rɪ'ses/ n Nische f; (holiday) Ferien pl; (Amer, Sch) Pause f

recession /rɪ'seʃn/ n Rezession f

re'charge /riː-/ vt [wieder] aufladen

recipe /'resəpɪ/ n Rezept nt

recipient /rɪ'sɪpɪənt/ n Empfänger m

recipro|cal /rɪ'sɪprəkl/ a gegenseitig. ~cate /-keɪt/ vt erwidern

recital /rɪ'saɪtl/ n (of poetry, songs) Vortrag m; (on piano) Konzert nt

recite /rɪ'saɪt/ vt aufsagen; (before audience) vortragen; (list) aufzählen

reckless /'reklɪs/ a, -ly adv leichtsinnig; (careless) rücksichtslos. ~ness n Leichtsinn m; Rücksichtslosigkeit f

reckon /'rekən/ vt rechnen; (consider) glauben □ vi ~ on/with rechnen mit

re'claim /rɪ-/ vt zurückfordern; zurückgewinnen (land)

reclin|e /rɪ'klaɪn/ vi liegen. ~ing seat n Liegesitz m

recluse /rɪ'kluːs/ n Einsiedler(in) m(f)

recognition /rekəg'nɪʃn/ n Erkennen nt; (acknowledgement) Anerkennung f; in ~ als Anerkennung (of gen); be beyond ~ nicht wieder zu erkennen sein

recognize /'rekəgnaɪz/ vt erkennen; (know again) wieder erkennen; (acknowledge) anerkennen

re'coil /rɪ-/ vi zurückschnellen; (in fear) zurückschrecken

recollect /rekə'lekt/ vt sich erinnern an (+ acc). ~ion /-ekʃn/ n Erinnerung f

recommend /rekə'mend/ vt empfehlen. ~ation /-'deɪʃn/ n Empfehlung f

recompense /'rekəmpens/ n Entschädigung f □ vt entschädigen

recon|cile /'rekənsaɪl/ vt versöhnen; ~cile oneself to sich abfinden mit. ~ciliation /-sɪlɪ'eɪʃn/ n Versöhnung f

recon'dition /riː-/ vt generalüberholen. ~ed engine n Austauschmotor m

reconnaissance /rɪ'kɒnɪsns/ n (Mil) Aufklärung f

reconnoitre /rekə'nɔɪtə(r)/ vi (pres p -tring) auf Erkundung ausgehen

recon'sider /riː-/ vt sich [dat] noch einmal überlegen

recon'struct /riː-/ vt wieder aufbauen; rekonstruieren (crime). ~ion n Wiederaufbau m; Rekonstruktion f

record¹ /rɪ'kɔːd/ vt aufzeichnen; (register) registrieren; (on tape) aufnehmen

record² /'rekɔːd/ n Aufzeichnung f; (Jur) Protokoll nt; (Mus) [Schall]platte f; (Sport) Rekord m; ~s pl Unterlagen pl; keep a ~ of sich (dat) notieren; off the ~ inoffiziell; have a [criminal] ~ vorbestraft sein

recorder /rɪ'kɔːdə(r)/ n (Mus) Blockflöte f

recording /rɪ'kɔːdɪŋ/ n Aufzeichnung f, Aufnahme f

'record-player n Plattenspieler m

recount /rɪ'kaʊnt/ vt erzählen

re-'count¹ /riː-/ vt nachzählen

're-count² /riː-/ n (Pol) Nachzählung f

recoup /rɪ'kuːp/ vt wieder einbringen; ausgleichen (losses)

recourse /rɪ'kɔːs/ n have ~ to Zuflucht nehmen zu

re-'cover /riː-/ vt neu beziehen

recover /rɪ'kʌvə(r)/ vt zurückbekommen; bergen (wreck) □ vi sich erholen. ~y n Wiedererlangung f; Bergung f; (of health) Erholung f

recreation /rekrɪ'eɪʃn/ n Erholung f; (hobby) Hobby nt. ~al a Freizeit-; be ~al erholsam sein

recrimination /rɪkrɪmɪ'neɪʃn/ n Gegenbeschuldigung f

recruit /rɪ'kruːt/ n (Mil) Rekrut m; new ~ (member) neues Mitglied nt; (worker) neuer Mitarbeiter m □ vt rekrutieren; anwerben (staff). ~ment n Rekrutierung f; Anwerbung f

rectang|le /'rektæŋgl/ n Rechteck nt. ~ular /-'tæŋgjʊlə(r)/ a rechteckig

rectify /'rektɪfaɪ/ vt (pt/pp -ied) berichtigen

rector /'rektə(r)/ n Pfarrer m; (Univ) Rektor m. ~y n Pfarrhaus nt

recuperat|e /rɪ'kjuːpəreɪt/ vi sich erholen. ~ion /-'reɪʃn/ n Erholung f

recur /rɪ'kɜː(r)/ vi (pt/pp recurred) sich wiederholen; (illness:) wiederkehren

recurren|ce /rɪ'kʌrəns/ n Wiederkehr f. ~t a wiederkehrend

recycle /riː'saɪkl/ vt wieder verwerten. ~d paper n Umweltschutzpapier nt

red /red/ a (redder, reddest) rot □ n Rot nt. ~'currant n rote Johannisbeere f

redd|en /'redn/ vt röten □ vi rot werden. ~ish a rötlich

re'decorate /riː-/ vt renovieren; (paint) neu streichen; (wallpaper) neu tapezieren

redeem /rɪ'diːm/ vt einlösen; (Relig) erlösen

redemption /rɪ'dempʃn/ n Erlösung f

rede'ploy /riː-/ vt an anderer Stelle einsetzen

red: ~-haired *a* rothaarig. ~-'handed *a*
catch s.o. ~-handed jdn auf frischer Tat
ertappen. ~ 'herring *n* falsche Spur *f.* ~-
hot *a* glühend heiß. R~ 'Indian *n* Indi-
aner(in) *m(f)*

redi'rect /riː-/ *vt* nachsenden ‹*letter*›; umleiten ‹*traffic*›

red: ~ 'light *n* ‹*Auto*› rote Ampel *f.* ~ness
n Röte *f*

re'do /riː-/ *vt* (*pt* -did, *pp* -done) noch einmal machen

re'double /riː-/ *vt* verdoppeln

redress /rɪ'dres/ *n* Entschädigung *f* □ *vt*
wieder gutmachen; wiederherstellen
‹*balance*›

red 'tape *n* (*fam*) Bürokratie *f*

reduc|e /rɪ'djuːs/ *vt* verringern, vermin-
dern; (*in size*) verkleinern; ermäßigen
‹*costs*›; herabsetzen ‹*price, goods*›; ‹*Culin*›
einkochen lassen. ~tion /-'dʌkʃn/ *n* Verringerung *f*; (*in price*) Ermäßigung *f*; (*in
size*) Verkleinerung *f*

redundan|cy /rɪ'dʌndənsɪ/ *n* Beschäfti-
gungslosigkeit *f*; (*payment*) Abfindung *f*.
~t *a* überflüssig; make ~t entlassen; be
made ~t beschäftigungslos werden

reed /riːd/ *n* [Schilf]rohr *nt*; ~s *pl* Schilf
nt

reef /riːf/ *n* Riff *nt*

reek /riːk/ *vi* riechen (of nach)

reel /riːl/ *n* Rolle *f*, Spule *f* □ *vi* ‹*stagger*›
taumeln □ *vt* ~ off ‹*fig*› herunterrasseln

refectory /rɪ'fektərɪ/ *n* Refektorium *nt*;
‹*Univ*› Mensa *f*

refer /rɪ'fɜː(r)/ *v* (*pt/pp* referred) □ *vt*
verweisen (to an + *acc*); übergeben, wei-
terleiten ‹*matter*› (to an + *acc*) □ *vi* ~ to
sich beziehen auf (+ *acc*); (*mention*)
erwähnen; (*concern*) betreffen; (*consult*)
sich wenden an (+ *acc*); nachschlagen in
(+ *dat*) ‹*book*›; are you ~ring to me?
meinen Sie mich?

referee /refə'riː/ *n* Schiedsrichter *m*; ‹*Boxing*› Ringrichter *m*; (*for job*) Referenz *f*
□ *vt/i* (*pt/pp* refereed) Schiedsrichter/
Ringrichter sein (bei)

reference /'refərəns/ *n* Erwähnung *f*; (*in
book*) Verweis *m*; (*for job*) Referenz *f*;
(*Comm*) 'your ~' 'Ihr Zeichen'; with ~
to in Bezug auf (+ *acc*); (*in letter*) unter
Bezugnahme auf (+ *acc*); make [a] ~ to
erwähnen. ~ book *n* Nachschlagewerk
nt. ~ number *n* Aktenzeichen *nt*

referendum /refə'rendəm/ *n* Volksabstimmung *f*

re'fill¹ /riː-/ *vt* nachfüllen

'refill² /riː-/ *n* (*for pen*) Ersatzmine *f*

refine /rɪ'faɪn/ *vt* raffinieren. ~d *a* fein,
vornehm. ~ment *n* Vornehmheit *f*;

(*Techn*) Verfeinerung *f*. ~ry /-ərɪ/ *n* Raf-
finerie *f*

reflect /rɪ'flekt/ *vt* reflektieren; ‹*mirror:*›
[wider]spiegeln; be ~ed in sich spiegeln
in (+ *dat*) □ *vi* nachdenken (on über +
acc); ~ badly upon s.o. ‹*fig*› jdn in ein
schlechtes Licht stellen. ~ion /-ekʃn/ *n*
Reflexion *f*; (*image*) Spiegelbild *nt*; on
~ion nach nochmaliger Überlegung.
~ive /-ɪv/ *a*, -ly *adv* nachdenklich. ~or
n Rückstrahler *m*

reflex /'riːfleks/ *n* Reflex *m* □ *attrib* Reflex-

reflexive /rɪ'fleksɪv/ *a* reflexiv

reform /rɪ'fɔːm/ *n* Reform *f* □ *vt* re-
formieren □ *vi* sich bessern. R~ation
/refə'meɪʃn/ *n* ‹*Relig*› Reformation *f*. ~er
n Reformer *m*; ‹*Relig*› Reformator *m*

refract /rɪ'frækt/ *vt* ‹*Phys*› brechen

refrain¹ /rɪ'freɪn/ *n* Refrain *m*

refrain² *vi* ~ from doing sth etw nicht
tun

refresh /rɪ'freʃ/ *vt* erfrischen. ~ing *a* er-
frischend. ~ments *npl* Erfrischungen *pl*

refrigerat|e /rɪ'frɪdʒəreɪt/ *vt* kühlen. ~or
n Kühlschrank *m*

re'fuel /riː-/ *vt/i* (*pt/pp* -fuelled) auf-
tanken

refuge /'refjuːdʒ/ *n* Zuflucht *f*; take ~ in
Zuflucht nehmen in (+ *dat*)

refugee /refjʊ'dʒiː/ *n* Flüchtling *m*

'refund¹ /riː-/ get a ~ sein Geld zurückbekommen

re'fund² /rɪ-/ *vt* zurückerstatten

refurbish /riː'fɜːbɪʃ/ *vt* renovieren

refusal /rɪ'fjuːzl/ *n* (*see* refuse¹) Ablehnung *f*; Weigerung *f*

refuse¹ /rɪ'fjuːz/ *vt* ablehnen; (*not grant*)
verweigern; ~ to do sth sich weigern, etw
zu tun □ *vi* ablehnen; sich weigern

refuse² /'refjuːs/ *n* Müll *m*, Abfall *m*. ~
collection *n* Müllabfuhr *f*

refute /rɪ'fjuːt/ *vt* widerlegen

re'gain /rɪ-/ *vt* wiedergewinnen

regal /'riːgl/ *a*, -ly *adv* königlich

regalia /rɪ'geɪlɪə/ *npl* Insignien *pl*

regard /rɪ'gɑːd/ *n* ‹*heed*› Rücksicht *f*; ‹*respect*› Achtung *f*; ~s *pl* Grüße *pl*; with
~ to in Bezug auf (+ *acc*) □ *vt* ansehen,
betrachten (as als); as ~s in Bezug auf (+
acc). ~ing *prep* bezüglich (+ *gen*). ~less
adv ohne Rücksicht (of auf + *acc*)

regatta /rɪ'gætə/ *n* Regatta *f*

regenerate /rɪ'dʒenəreɪt/ *vt* regenerieren
□ *vi* sich regenerieren

regime /reɪ'ʒiːm/ *n* Regime *nt*

regiment /'redʒɪmənt/ *n* Regiment *nt*.
~al /-'mentl/ *a* Regiments-. ~ation
/-'teɪʃn/ *n* Reglementierung *f*

region /'riːdʒən/ n Region f; in the ~ of (fig) ungefähr. ~al a, -ly adv regional

register /'redʒɪstə(r)/ n Register nt; (Sch) Anwesenheitsliste f □ vt registrieren; (report) anmelden; einschreiben (letter); aufgeben (luggage) □ vi (report) sich anmelden; it didn't ~ (fig) ich habe es nicht registriert

registrar /redʒɪ'strɑː(r)/ n Standesbeamte(r) m

registration /redʒɪ'streɪʃn/ n Registrierung f; Anmeldung f. ~ number n Autonummer f

registry office /'redʒɪstrɪ-/ n Standesamt nt

regret /rɪ'gret/ n Bedauern nt □ vt (pt/pp regretted) bedauern. ~fully adv mit Bedauern

regrettab|le /rɪ'gretəbl/ a bedauerlich. ~ly adv bedauerlicherweise

regular /'regjʊlə(r)/ a, -ly adv regelmäßig; (usual) üblich; (Mil) Berufs- □ n Berufssoldat m; (in pub) Stammgast m; (in shop) Stammkunde m. ~ity /-'lærəti/ n Regelmäßigkeit f

regulat|e /'regjʊleɪt/ vt regulieren. ~ion /-'leɪʃn/ n (rule) Vorschrift f

rehabilitat|e /riːhə'bɪlɪteɪt/ vt rehabilitieren. ~ion /-'teɪʃn/ n Rehabilitation f

rehears|al /rɪ'hɜːsl/ n (Theat) Probe f. ~e vt/i proben

reign /reɪn/ n Herrschaft f □ vi herrschen, regieren

reimburse /riːɪm'bɜːs/ vt ~ s.o. for sth jdm etw zurückerstatten

rein /reɪn/ n Zügel m

reincarnation /riːɪnkɑː'neɪʃn/ f Reinkarnation f, Wiedergeburt f

reindeer /'reɪndɪə(r)/ n inv Rentier nt

reinforce /riːɪn'fɔːs/ vt verstärken. ~d 'concrete n Stahlbeton m. ~ment n Verstärkung f; send ~ments Verstärkung schicken

reinstate /riːɪn'steɪt/ vt wieder einstellen; (to office) wieder einsetzen

reiterate /riː'ɪtəreɪt/ vt wiederholen

reject /rɪ'dʒekt/ vt ablehnen. ~ion /-ekʃn/ n Ablehnung f

rejects /'riːdʒekts/ npl (Comm) Ausschussware f

rejoic|e /rɪ'dʒɔɪs/ vi (liter) sich freuen. ~ing n Freude f

re'join /riː-/ vt sich wieder anschließen (+ dat); wieder beitreten (+ dat) (club, party); (answer) erwidern

rejuvenate /rɪ'dʒuːvəneɪt/ vt verjüngen

relapse /rɪ'læps/ n Rückfall m □ vi einen Rückfall erleiden

relate /rɪ'leɪt/ vt (tell) erzählen; (connect) verbinden □ vi zusammenhängen (to mit). ~d a verwandt (to mit)

relation /rɪ'leɪʃn/ n Beziehung f; (person) Verwandte(r) m/f. ~ship n Beziehung f, (link) Verbindung f; (blood tie) Verwandtschaft f; (affair) Verhältnis nt

relative /'relətɪv/ n Verwandte(r) m/f □ a relativ; (Gram) Relativ-. ~ly adv relativ, verhälnismäßig

relax /rɪ'læks/ vt lockern, entspannen □ vi sich lockern, sich entspannen. ~ation /-'seɪʃn/ n Entspannung f. ~ing a entspannend

relay[1] /riː'leɪ/ vt (pt/pp -layed) weitergeben; (Radio, TV) übertragen

relay[2] /'riːleɪ/ n (Electr) Relais nt; work in ~s sich bei der Arbeit ablösen. ~ [race] n Staffel f

release /rɪ'liːs/ n Freilassung f, Entlassung f; (Techn) Auslöser m □ vt freilassen; (let go of) loslassen; (Techn) auslösen; veröffentlichen ⟨information⟩

relegate /'relɪgeɪt/ vt verbannen; be ~d (Sport) absteigen

relent /rɪ'lent/ vi nachgeben. ~less a, -ly adv erbarmungslos; (unceasing) unaufhörlich

relevan|ce /'reləvəns/ n Relevanz f. ~t a relevant (to für)

reliab|ility /rɪlaɪə'bɪlɪti/ n Zuverlässigkeit f. ~le /-'laɪəbl/ a, -ly adv zuverlässig

relian|ce /rɪ'laɪəns/ n Abhängigkeit f (on von). ~t a angewiesen (on auf + acc)

relic /'relɪk/ n Überbleibsel nt; (Relig) Reliquie f

relief /rɪ'liːf/ n Erleichterung f; (assistance) Hilfe f; (distraction) Abwechslung f; (replacement) Ablösung f; (Art) Relief nt; in ~ im Relief. ~ map n Reliefkarte f. ~ train n Entlastungszug m

relieve /rɪ'liːv/ vt erleichtern; (take over from) ablösen; ~ of entlasten von

religion /rɪ'lɪdʒən/ n Religion f

religious /rɪ'lɪdʒəs/ a religiös. ~ly adv (conscientiously) gewissenhaft

relinquish /rɪ'lɪŋkwɪʃ/ vt loslassen; (give up) aufgeben

relish /'relɪʃ/ n Genuss m; (Culin) Würze f □ vt genießen

relo'cate /riː-/ vt verlegen

reluctan|ce /rɪ'lʌktəns/ n Widerstreben nt. ~t a widerstrebend; be ~t zögern (to ...); ~tly adv ungern, widerstrebend

rely /rɪ'laɪ/ vi (pt/pp -ied) ~ on sich verlassen auf (+ acc); (be dependent on) angewiesen sein auf (+ acc)

remain /rɪ'meɪn/ vi bleiben; (be left) übrig bleiben. ~der n Rest m. ~ing a restlich.

~ *npl* Reste *pl*; [mortal] ~s [sterbliche] Überreste *pl*

remand /rɪˈmɑːnd/ *n* on ~ in Untersuchungshaft ☐ *vt* ~ in custody in Untersuchungshaft schicken

remark /rɪˈmɑːk/ *n* Bemerkung *f* ☐ *vt* bemerken. ~able /-əbl/ *a*, -bly *adv* bemerkenswert

re'marry /riː-/ *vi* wieder heiraten

remedial /rɪˈmiːdɪəl/ *a* Hilfs-; (*Med*) Heil-

remedy /ˈremədɪ/ *n* [Heil]mittel *nt* (for gegen); (*fig*) Abhilfe *f* ☐ *vt* (*pt/pp* -ied) abhelfen (+ *dat*); beheben (*fault*)

remember /rɪˈmembə(r)/ *vt* sich erinnern an (+ *acc*); ~er to do sth daran denken, etw zu tun; ~er me to him grüßen Sie ihn von mir ☐ *vi* sich erinnern. ~rance *n* Erinnerung *f*

remind /rɪˈmaɪnd/ *vt* erinnern (of an + *acc*). ~er *n* Andenken *nt*; (*letter, warning*) Mahnung *f*

reminisce /remɪˈnɪs/ *vi* sich seinen Erinnerungen hingeben. ~nces /-ənsɪs/ *npl* Erinnerungen *pl*. ~nt *a* be ~nt of erinnern an (+ *acc*)

remiss /rɪˈmɪs/ *a* nachlässig

remission /rɪˈmɪʃn/ *n* Nachlass *m*; (*of sentence*) [Straf]erlass *m*; (*Med*) Remission *f*

remit /rɪˈmɪt/ *vt* (*pt/pp* remitted) überweisen (*money*). ~tance *n* Überweisung *f*

remnant /ˈremnənt/ *n* Rest *m*

remonstrate /ˈremənstreɪt/ *vi* protestieren; ~ with s.o. jdm Vorhaltungen machen

remorse /rɪˈmɔːs/ *n* Reue *f*. ~ful *a*, -ly *adv* reumütig. ~less *a*, -ly *adv* unerbittlich

remote /rɪˈməʊt/ *a* fern; (*isolated*) abgelegen; (*slight*) gering. ~ con'trol *n* Fernsteuerung *f*; (*for TV*) Fernbedienung *f*. ~con'trolled *a* ferngesteuert; fernbedient

remotely /rɪˈməʊtlɪ/ *adv* entfernt; not ~ nicht im Entferntesten

re'movable /rɪ-/ *a* abnehmbar

removal /rɪˈmuːvl/ *n* Entfernung *f*; (*from house*) Umzug *m*. ~ van *n* Möbelwagen *m*

remove /rɪˈmuːv/ *vt* entfernen; (*take off*) abnehmen; (*take out*) herausnehmen

remunerate /rɪˈmjuːnəreɪt/ *vt* bezahlen. ~ion /-ˈreɪʃn/ *n* Bezahlung *f*. ~ive /-ətɪv/ *a* einträglich

render /ˈrendə(r)/ *vt* machen; erweisen (*service*); (*translate*) wiedergeben; (*Mus*) vortragen

renegade /ˈrenɪgeɪd/ *n* Abtrünnige(r) *m/f*

renew /rɪˈnjuː/ *vt* erneuern; verlängern (*contract*). ~al *n* Erneuerung *f*; Verlängerung *f*

renounce /rɪˈnaʊns/ *vt* verzichten auf (+ *acc*); (*Relig*) abschwören (+ *dat*)

renovate /ˈrenəveɪt/ *vt* renovieren. ~ion /-ˈveɪʃn/ *n* Renovierung *f*

renown /rɪˈnaʊn/ *n* Ruf *m*. ~ed *a* berühmt

rent /rent/ *n* Miete *f* ☐ *vt* mieten; (*hire*) leihen; ~ [out] vermieten; verleihen. ~al *n* Mietgebühr *f*; Leihgebühr *f*

renunciation /rɪnʌnsɪˈeɪʃn/ *n* Verzicht *m*

re'open /riː-/ *vt/i* wieder aufmachen

re'organize /riː-/ *vt* reorganisieren

rep /rep/ *n* (*fam*) Vertreter *m*

repair /rɪˈpeə(r)/ *n* Reparatur *f*; in good/bad ~ in gutem/schlechtem Zustand ☐ *vt* reparieren

repartee /repɑːˈtiː/ *n* piece of ~ schlagfertige Antwort *f*

repatriate /riːˈpætrɪeɪt/ *vt* repatriieren. ~ion /-ˈeɪʃn/ *n* Repatriierung *f*

re'pay /riː-/ *vt* (*pt/pp* -paid) zurückzahlen; ~ s.o. for sth jdm etw zurückzahlen. ~ment *n* Rückzahlung *f*

repeal /rɪˈpiːl/ *n* Aufhebung *f* ☐ *vt* aufheben

repeat /rɪˈpiːt/ *n* Wiederholung *f* ☐ *vt/i* wiederholen; ~ after me sprechen Sie mir nach. ~ed *a*, -ly *adv* wiederholt

repel /rɪˈpel/ *vt* (*pt/pp* repelled) abwehren; (*fig*) abstoßen. ~lent *a* abstoßend

repent /rɪˈpent/ *vi* Reue zeigen. ~ance *n* Reue *f*. ~ant *a* reuig

repercussions /riːpəˈkʌʃnz/ *npl* Auswirkungen *pl*

repertoire /ˈrepətwɑː(r)/ *n* Repertoire *nt*

repertory /ˈrepətrɪ/ *n* Repertoire *nt*

repetition /repɪˈtɪʃn/ *n* Wiederholung *f*. ~ive /rɪˈpetɪtɪv/ *a* eintönig

re'place /rɪ-/ *vt* zurücktun; (*take the place of*) ersetzen; (*exchange*) austauschen, auswechseln. ~ment *n* Ersatz *m*. ~ment part *n* Ersatzteil *nt*

'replay /riː-/ *n* (*Sport*) Wiederholungsspiel *nt*; (*action*) ~ Wiederholung *f*

replenish /rɪˈplenɪʃ/ *vt* auffüllen (*stocks*); (*refill*) nachfüllen

replete /rɪˈpliːt/ *a* gesättigt

replica /ˈreplɪkə/ *n* Nachbildung *f*

reply /rɪˈplaɪ/ *n* Antwort *f* (to auf + *acc*) ☐ *vt/i* (*pt/pp* replied) antworten

report /rɪˈpɔːt/ *n* Bericht *m*; (*Sch*) Zeugnis *nt*; (*rumour*) Gerücht *nt*; (*of gun*) Knall *m* ☐ *vt* berichten; (*notify*) melden; ~ s.o. to the police jdn anzeigen ☐ *vi* berichten (on über + *acc*); (*present oneself*) sich melden (to bei). ~er *n* Reporter(in) *m(f)*

repose /rɪˈpəʊz/ *n* Ruhe *f*

repos'sess /riː-/ *vt* wieder in Besitz nehmen

reprehensible /reprɪ'hensəbl/ a tadelnswert

represent /reprɪ'zent/ vt darstellen; (act for) vertreten, repräsentieren. ~ation /-'teɪʃn/ n Darstellung f; make ~ations to vorstellig werden bei

representative /reprɪ'zentətɪv/ a repräsentativ (of für) □ n Bevollmächtigte(r) m(f); (Comm) Vertreter(in) m(f); (Amer, Pol) Abgeordnete(r) m/f

repress /rɪ'pres/ vt unterdrücken. ~ion /-eʃn/ n Unterdrückung f. ~ive /-ɪv/ a repressiv

reprieve /rɪ'priːv/ n Begnadigung f; (postponement) Strafaufschub m; (fig) Gnadenfrist f □ vt begnadigen

reprimand /'reprɪmɑːnd/ n Tadel m □ vt tadeln

reprint¹ /riː-/ n Nachdruck m

re'print² /riː-/ vt neu auflegen

reprisal /rɪ'praɪzl/ n Vergeltungsmaßnahme f

reproach /rɪ'prəʊtʃ/ n Vorwurf m □ vt Vorwürfe pl machen (+ dat). ~ful a, -ly adv vorwurfsvoll

repro'duc|e /riː-/ vt wiedergeben, reproduzieren □ vi sich fortpflanzen. ~tion /-'dʌkʃn/ n Reproduktion f; (Biol) Fortpflanzung f. ~tion furniture n Stilmöbel pl. ~tive /-'dʌktɪv/ a Fortpflanzungs-

reprove /rɪ'pruːv/ vt tadeln

reptile /'reptaɪl/ n Reptil nt

republic /rɪ'pʌblɪk/ n Republik f. ~an a republikanisch □ n Republikaner(in) m(f)

repudiate /rɪ'pjuːdɪeɪt/ vt zurückweisen

repugnan|ce /rɪ'pʌgnəns/ n Widerwille m. ~t a widerlich

repuls|e /rɪ'pʌls/ vt abwehren; (fig) abweisen. ~ion /-ʌlʃn/ n Widerwille m. ~ive /-ɪv/ a abstoßend, widerlich

reputable /'repjʊtəbl/ a ⟨firm⟩ von gutem Ruf; (respectable) anständig

reputation /repjʊ'teɪʃn/ n Ruf m

repute /rɪ'pjuːt/ n Ruf m. ~d /-ɪd/ a, -ly adv angeblich

request /rɪ'kwest/ n Bitte f □ vt bitten. ~ stop n Bedarfshaltestelle f

require /rɪ'kwaɪə(r)/ vt (need) brauchen; (demand) erfordern; be ~d to do sth etw tun müssen. ~ment n Bedürfnis nt; (condition) Erfordernis nt

requisite /'rekwɪzɪt/ a erforderlich □ n toilet/travel ~s pl Toiletten-/Reiseartikel pl

requisition /rekwɪ'zɪʃn/ n ~ [order] Anforderung f □ vt anfordern

re'sale /riː-/ n Weiterverkauf m

rescind /rɪ'sɪnd/ vt aufheben

rescue /'reskjuː/ n Rettung f □ vt retten. ~r n Retter m

research /rɪ'sɜːtʃ/ n Forschung f □ vt erforschen; (Journ) recherchieren □ vi ~ into erforschen. ~er n Forscher m; (Journ) Rechercheur m

resem|blance /rɪ'zembləns/ n Ähnlichkeit f. ~ble /-bl/ vt ähneln (+ dat)

resent /rɪ'zent/ vt übel nehmen; einen Groll hegen gegen ⟨person⟩. ~ful a, -ly adv verbittert. ~ment n Groll m

reservation /rezə'veɪʃn/ n Reservierung f; (doubt) Vorbehalt m; (enclosure) Reservat nt

reserve /rɪ'zɜːv/ n Reserve f; (for animals) Reservat nt; (Sport) Reservespieler(in) m(f) □ vt reservieren; ⟨client:⟩ reservieren lassen; (keep) aufheben; sich (dat) vorbehalten ⟨right⟩. ~d a reserviert

reservoir /'rezəvwɑː(r)/ n Reservoir nt

re'shape /riː-/ vt umformen

re'shuffle /riː-/ n (Pol) Umbildung f □ vt (Pol) umbilden

reside /rɪ'zaɪd/ vi wohnen

residence /'rezɪdəns/ n Wohnsitz m; (official) Residenz f; (stay) Aufenthalt m. ~ permit n Aufenthaltsgenehmigung f

resident /'rezɪdənt/ a ansässig (in in + dat); ⟨housekeeper, nurse⟩ im Haus wohnend □ n Bewohner(in) m(f); (of street) Anwohner m. ~ial /-'denʃl/ a Wohn-

residue /'rezɪdjuː/ n Rest m; (Chem) Rückstand m

resign /rɪ'zaɪn/ vt ~ oneself to sich abfinden mit □ vi kündigen; (from public office) zurücktreten. ~ation /rezɪg'neɪʃn/ n Resignation f; (from job) Kündigung f; Rücktritt m. ~ed a, -ly adv resigniert

resilient /rɪ'zɪlɪənt/ a federnd; (fig) widerstandsfähig

resin /'rezɪn/ n Harz nt

resist /rɪ'zɪst/ vt/i sich widersetzen (+ dat); (fig) widerstehen (+ dat). ~ance n Widerstand m. ~ant a widerstandsfähig

resolut|e /'rezəluːt/ a, -ly adv entschlossen. ~ion /-'luːʃn/ n Entschlossenheit f; (intention) Vorsatz m; (Pol) Resolution f

resolve /rɪ'zɒlv/ n Entschlossenheit f; (decision) Beschluss m □ vt beschließen; (solve) lösen. ~d a entschlossen (to zu)

resonan|ce /'rezənəns/ n Resonanz f. ~t a klangvoll

resort /rɪ'zɔːt/ n (place) Urlaubsort m; as a last ~ wenn alles andere fehlschlägt □ vi ~ to (fig) greifen zu

resound /rɪ'zaʊnd/ vi widerhallen. ~ing a widerhallend; (loud) laut; (notable) groß

resource /rɪˈsɔːs/ n ~s pl Ressourcen pl. ~ful a findig. ~fulness n Findigkeit f

respect /rɪˈspekt/ n Respekt m, Achtung f (for vor + dat); (aspect) Hinsicht f; with ~ to in Bezug auf (+ acc) □ vt respektieren, achten

respectability /rɪspektəˈbɪlətɪ/ n (see respectable) Ehrbarkeit f; Anständigkeit f

respect|able /rɪˈspektəbl/ a, -bly adv ehrbar; (decent) anständig; (considerable) ansehnlich. ~ful a, -ly adv respektvoll

respective /rɪˈspektɪv/ a jeweilig. ~ly adv beziehungsweise

respiration /respəˈreɪʃn/ n Atmung f

respite /ˈrespaɪt/ n [Ruhe]pause f; (delay) Aufschub m

resplendent /rɪˈsplendənt/ a glänzend

respond /rɪˈspɒnd/ vi antworten; (react) reagieren (to auf + acc); (patient:) ansprechen (to auf + acc)

response /rɪˈspɒns/ n Antwort f; Reaktion f

responsibility /rɪspɒnsɪˈbɪlətɪ/ n Verantwortung f; (duty) Verpflichtung f

responsi|ble /rɪˈspɒnsəbl/ a verantwortlich; (trustworthy) verantwortungsvoll. ~ly adv verantwortungsbewusst

responsive /rɪˈspɒnsɪv/ a be ~ reagieren

rest¹ /rest/ n Ruhe f; (holiday) Erholung f; (interval & Mus) Pause f; have a ~ eine Pause machen; (rest) sich ausruhen □ vt ausruhen; (lean) lehnen (on an/auf + acc) □ vi ruhen; (have a rest) sich ausruhen

rest² n the ~ der Rest; (people) die Übrigen pl □ vi it ~s with you es ist an Ihnen (to zu)

restaurant /ˈrestərɒnt/ n Restaurant nt, Gaststätte f. ~ car n Speisewagen m

restful /ˈrestfl/ a erholsam

restitution /restɪˈtjuːʃn/ n Entschädigung f; (return) Rückgabe f

restive /ˈrestɪv/ a unruhig

restless /ˈrestlɪs/ a, -ly adv unruhig

restoration /restəˈreɪʃn/ n (of building) Restaurierung f

restore /rɪˈstɔː(r)/ vt wiederherstellen; restaurieren (building); (give back) zurückgeben

restrain /rɪˈstreɪn/ vt zurückhalten; ~ oneself sich beherrschen. ~ed a zurückhaltend. ~t n Zurückhaltung f

restrict /rɪˈstrɪkt/ vt einschränken; ~ to beschränken auf (+ acc). ~ion /-ɪkʃn/ n Einschränkung f; Beschränkung f. ~ive /-ɪv/ a einschränkend

ˈrest room n (Amer) Toilette f

result /rɪˈzʌlt/ n Ergebnis nt, Resultat nt; (consequence) Folge f; as a ~ als Folge (of gen) □ vi sich ergeben (from aus); ~ in enden in (+ dat); (lead to) führen zu

resume /rɪˈzjuːm/ vt wieder aufnehmen; wieder einnehmen (seat) □ vi wieder beginnen

résumé /ˈrezjʊmeɪ/ n Zusammenfassung f

resumption /rɪˈzʌmpʃn/ n Wiederaufnahme f

resurgence /rɪˈsɜːdʒəns/ n Wiederaufleben nt

resurrect /rezəˈrekt/ vt (fig) wieder beleben. ~ion /-ekʃn/ n the R~ion (Relig) die Auferstehung

resuscitat|e /rɪˈsʌsɪteɪt/ vt wieder beleben. ~ion /-ˈteɪʃn/ n Wiederbelebung f

retail /ˈriːteɪl/ n Einzelhandel m □ a Einzelhandels- □ adv im Einzelhandel □ vt im Einzelhandel verkaufen □ vi ~ at im Einzelhandel kosten. ~er n Einzelhändler m. ~ price n Ladenpreis m

retain /rɪˈteɪn/ vt behalten

retaliat|e /rɪˈtælɪeɪt/ vi zurückschlagen. ~ion /-ˈeɪʃn/ n Vergeltung f; in ~ion als Vergeltung

retarded /rɪˈtɑːdɪd/ a zurückgeblieben

retentive /rɪˈtentɪv/ a (memory) gut

reticen|ce /ˈretɪsns/ n Zurückhaltung f. ~t a zurückhaltend

retina /ˈretɪnə/ n Netzhaut f

retinue /ˈretɪnjuː/ n Gefolge nt

retire /rɪˈtaɪə(r)/ vi in den Ruhestand treten; (withdraw) sich zurückziehen. ~d a im Ruhestand. ~ment n Ruhestand m; since my ~ment seit ich nicht mehr arbeite

retiring /rɪˈtaɪərɪŋ/ a zurückhaltend

retort /rɪˈtɔːt/ n scharfe Erwiderung f; (Chem) Retorte f □ vt scharf erwidern

re'touch /riː-/ vt (Phot) retuschieren

re'trace /rɪ-/ vt zurückverfolgen; ~ one's steps denselben Weg zurückgehen

retract /rɪˈtrækt/ vt einziehen; zurücknehmen (remark) □ vi widerrufen

re'train /riː-/ vt umschulen □ vi umgeschult werden

retreat /rɪˈtriːt/ n Rückzug m; (place) Zufluchtsort m □ vi sich zurückziehen

re'trial /riː-/ n Wiederaufnahmeverfahren nt

retribution /retrɪˈbjuːʃn/ n Vergeltung f

retrieve /rɪˈtriːv/ vt zurückholen; (from wreckage) bergen; (Computing) wieder auffinden; (dog:) apportieren

retrograde /ˈretrəgreɪd/ a rückschrittlich

retrospect /ˈretrəspekt/ n in ~ rückblickend. ~ive /-ɪv/ a, -ly adv rückwirkend; (looking back) rückblickend

return /rɪ'tɜːn/ n Rückkehr f; (giving back) Rückgabe f; (Comm) Ertrag m, (ticket) Rückfahrkarte f; (Aviat) Rückflugschein m; by ~ [of post] postwendend; in ~ dafür; in ~ for für; many happy ~s! herzlichen Glückwunsch zum Geburtstag! □ vt zurückgehen/-fahren; (come back) zurückkommen □ vt zurückgeben; (put back) zurückstellen/-legen; (send back) zurückschicken; (elect) wählen

return: ~ flight n Rückflug m. ~ match n Rückspiel nt. ~ ticket n Rückfahrkarte f; (Aviat) Rückflugschein m

reunion /riː'juːnɪən/ n Wiedervereinigung f; (social gathering) Treffen nt

reunite /riːjuː'naɪt/ vt wieder vereinigen □ vi sich wieder vereinigen

re'us|able /riː-/ a wieder verwendbar. ~e vt wieder verwenden

rev /rev/ n (Auto, fam) Umdrehung f □ vt/i ~ [up] den Motor auf Touren bringen

reveal /rɪ'viːl/ vt zum Vorschein bringen; (fig) enthüllen. ~ing a (fig) aufschlussreich

revel /'revl/ vi (pt/pp revelled) ~ in sth etw genießen

revelation /revə'leɪʃn/ n Offenbarung f, Enthüllung f

revelry /'revlrɪ/ n Lustbarkeit f

revenge /rɪ'vendʒ/ n Rache f; (fig & Sport) Revanche f □ vt rächen

revenue /'revənjuː/ n [Staats]einnahmen pl

reverberate /rɪ'vɜːbəreɪt/ vi nachhallen

revere /rɪ'vɪə(r)/ vt verehren. ~nce /'revərəns/ n Ehrfurcht f

Reverend /'revərənd/ a the ~ X Pfarrer X; (Catholic) Hochwürden X

reverent /'revərənt/ a, -ly adv ehrfürchtig

reverie /'revərɪ/ n Träumerei f

revers /rɪ'vɪə/ n (pl revers /-z/) Revers nt

reversal /rɪ'vɜːsl/ n Umkehrung f

reverse /rɪ'vɜːs/ a umgekehrt □ n Gegenteil nt; (back) Rückseite f; (Auto) Rückwärtsgang m □ vt umkehren; (Auto) zurücksetzen; ~ the charges (Teleph) ein R-Gespräch führen □ vi zurücksetzen

revert /rɪ'vɜːt/ vi ~ to zurückfallen an (+ dat), [...] [...]kommen auf (+ acc) (topic)

review /rɪ'vjuː/ n Rückblick [...] (of auf + acc); (re-examination) Überprüfung f, (Mil) Truppenschau f; (of book, play) Kritik f, Rezension f □ vt zurückblicken auf (+ acc); überprüfen (situation); (Mil) besichtigen; kritisieren, rezensieren (book, play). ~er n Kritiker m, Rezensent f

revile /rɪ'vaɪl/ vt verunglimpfen

revis|e /rɪ'vaɪz/ vt revidieren; (for exam) wiederholen. ~ion /-'vɪʒn/ n Revision f; Wiederholung f

revival /rɪ'vaɪvl/ n Wiederbelebung f

revive /rɪ'vaɪv/ vt wieder beleben; (fig) wieder aufleben lassen □ vi wieder aufleben

revoke /rɪ'vəʊk/ vt aufheben; widerrufen (command, decision)

revolt /rɪ'vəʊlt/ n Aufstand m □ vi rebellieren □ vt anwidern. ~ing a widerlich, eklig

revolution /revə'luːʃn/ n Revolution f; (Auto) Umdrehung f. ~ary /-ərɪ/ a revolutionär. ~ize vt revolutionieren

revolve /rɪ'vɒlv/ vi sich drehen; ~ around kreisen um

revolv|er /rɪ'vɒlvə(r)/ n Revolver m. ~ing a Dreh-

revue /rɪ'vjuː/ n Revue f; (satirical) Kabarett nt

revulsion /rɪ'vʌlʃn/ n Abscheu m

reward /rɪ'wɔːd/ n Belohnung f □ vt belohnen. ~ing a lohnend

re'write /riː-/ vt (pt rewrote, pp rewritten) noch einmal [neu] schreiben; (alter) umschreiben

rhapsody /'ræpsədɪ/ n Rhapsodie f

rhetoric /'retərɪk/ n Rhetorik f. ~al /rɪ'tɒrɪkl/ a rhetorisch

rheuma|tic /ruː'mætɪk/ a rheumatisch. ~tism /'ruːmətɪzm/ n Rheumatismus m, Rheuma nt

Rhine /raɪn/ n Rhein m

rhinoceros /raɪ'nɒsərəs/ n Nashorn nt, Rhinozeros nt

rhubarb /'ruːbaːb/ n Rhabarber m

rhyme /raɪm/ n Reim m □ vt reimen □ vi sich reimen

rhythm /'rɪðm/ n Rhythmus m. ~ic[al] a, -ally adv rhythmisch

rib /rɪb/ n Rippe f □ vt (pt/pp ribbed) (fam) aufziehen (fam)

ribald /'rɪbld/ a derb

ribbon /'rɪbən/ n Band nt; (for typewriter) Farbband nt; in ~s in Fetzen

rice /raɪs/ n Reis m

rich /rɪtʃ/ a (-er, -est), -ly adv reich; (food) gehaltvoll; (heavy) schwer □ n the ~ pl die Reichen; ~es pl Reichtum m

rickets /'rɪkɪts/ n Rachitis f

rickety /'rɪkətɪ/ a wackelig

ricochet /'rɪkəʃeɪ/ vi abprallen

rid /rɪd/ vt (pt/pp rid, pres p ridding) befreien (of von); get ~ of [...] [...]den

riddance /'rɪdns/ n good ~! auf Nimmerwiedersehen!

ridden /'rɪdn/ see ride

riddle /'rɪdl/ n Rätsel nt

riddled /'rɪdld/ *a* ~ with durchlöchert mit

ride /raɪd/ *n* Ritt *m*; (*in vehicle*) Fahrt *f*; take s.o. for a ~ (*fam*) jdn reinlegen □ *v* (*pt* rode, *pp* ridden) □ *vt* reiten ⟨*horse*⟩; fahren mit ⟨*bicycle*⟩ □ *vi* reiten; (*in vehicle*) fahren. ~r *n* Reiter(in) *m(f)*; (*on bicycle*) Fahrer(in) *m(f)*; (*in document*) Zusatzklausel *f*

ridge /rɪdʒ/ *n* Erhebung *f*; (*on roof*) First *m*; (*of mountain*) Grat *m*, Kamm *m*; (*of high pressure*) Hochdruckkeil *m*

ridicule /'rɪdɪkjuːl/ *n* Spott *m* □ *vt* verspotten, spotten über (+ *acc*)

ridiculous /rɪ'dɪkjʊləs/ *a*, -ly *adv* lächerlich

riding /'raɪdɪŋ/ *n* Reiten *nt* □ *attrib* Reit-

rife /raɪf/ *a* be ~ weit verbreitet sein

riff-raff /'rɪfræf/ *n* Gesindel *nt*

rifle /'raɪfl/ *n* Gewehr *nt* □ *vt* plündern; ~ through durchwühlen

rift /rɪft/ *n* Spalt *m*; (*fig*) Riss *m*

rig¹ /rɪg/ *n* Ölbohrturm *m*; (*at sea*) Bohrinsel *f* □ *vt* (*pt/pp* rigged) ~ out ausrüsten; ~ up aufbauen

rig² *vt* (*pt/pp* rigged) manipulieren

right /raɪt/ *a* richtig; (*not left*) rechte(r,s); be ~ ⟨*person:*⟩ Recht haben; ⟨*clock:*⟩ richtig gehen; put ~ wieder in Ordnung bringen; (*fig*) richtig stellen; that's ~! das stimmt! □ *adv* richtig; (*directly*) direkt; (*completely*) ganz; (*not left*) rechts; ⟨*go*⟩ nach rechts; ~ away sofort □ *n* Recht *nt*; (*not left*) rechte Seite *f*; on the ~ rechts; from/to the ~ von/nach rechts; be in the ~ Recht haben; by ~s eigentlich; the R~ (*Pol*) die Rechte. ~ angle *n* rechter Winkel *m*

righteous /'raɪtʃəs/ *a* rechtschaffen

rightful /'raɪtfl/ *a*, -ly *adv* rechtmäßig

right: ~-'handed *a* rechtshändig. ~-hand 'man *n* (*fig*) rechte Hand *f*

rightly /'raɪtlɪ/ *adv* mit Recht

right: ~ of way *n* Durchgangsrecht *nt*; (*path*) öffentlicher Fußweg *m*; (*Auto*) Vorfahrt *f*. ~-'wing *a* (*Pol*) rechte(r,s)

rigid /'rɪdʒɪd/ *a* starr; (*strict*) streng. ~ity /-'dʒɪdətɪ/ *n* Starrheit *f*; Strenge *f*

rigmarole /'rɪgmərəʊl/ *n* Geschwätz *nt*; (*procedure*) Prozedur *f*

rigorous /'rɪgərəs/ *a*, -ly *adv* streng

rigour /'rɪgə(r)/ *n* Strenge *f*

rile /raɪl/ *vt* (*fam*) ärgern

rim /rɪm/ *n* Rand *m*; (*of wheel*) Felge *f*

rind /raɪnd/ *n* (*on fruit*) Schale *f*; (*on cheese*) Rinde *f*; (*on bacon*) Schwarte *f*

ring¹ /rɪŋ/ *n* Ring *m*; (*for circus*) Manege *f*; stand in a ~ im Kreis stehen □ *vt* umringen; ~ in red rot einkreisen

ring² /rɪŋ/ *n* Klingeln *nt*; give s.o. a ~ (*Teleph*) jdn anrufen □ *v* (*pt* rang, *pp* rung) □ *vt* läuten; ~ [up] (*Teleph*) anrufen □ *vi* läuten, klingeln. ~ back *vt/i* (*Teleph*) zurückrufen. ~ off *vi* (*Teleph*) auflegen

ring: ~leader *n* Rädelsführer *m*. ~ road *n* Umgehungsstraße *f*

rink /rɪŋk/ *n* Eisbahn *f*

rinse /rɪns/ *n* Spülung *f*; (*hair colour*) Tönung *f* □ *vt* spülen; tönen ⟨*hair*⟩. ~ off *vt* abspülen

riot /'raɪət/ *n* Aufruhr *m*; ~s *pl* Unruhen *pl*; ~ of colours bunte Farbenpracht *f*; run ~ randalieren □ *vi* randalieren. ~er *n* Randalierer *m*. ~ous /-əs/ *a* aufrührerisch; (*boisterous*) wild

rip /rɪp/ *n* Riss *m* □ *vt/i* (*pt/pp* ripped) zerreißen; ~ open aufreißen. ~ off *vt* (*fam*) neppen

ripe /raɪp/ *a* (-r, -st) reif

ripen /'raɪpn/ *vi* reifen □ *vt* reifen lassen

ripeness /'raɪpnɪs/ *n* Reife *f*

'rip-off *n* (*fam*) Nepp *m*

ripple /'rɪpl/ *n* kleine Welle *f* □ *vt* kräuseln □ *vi* sich kräuseln

rise /raɪz/ *n* Anstieg *m*; (*fig*) Aufstieg *m*; (*increase*) Zunahme *f*; (*in wages*) Lohnerhöhung *f*; (*in salary*) Gehaltserhöhung *f*; give ~ to Anlass geben zu □ *vi* (*pt* rose, *pp* risen) steigen; ⟨*ground:*⟩ ansteigen; ⟨*sun, dough:*⟩ aufgehen; ⟨*river:*⟩ entspringen; (*get up*) aufstehen; (*fig*) aufsteigen (to zu); ⟨*rebel*⟩ sich erheben; ⟨*court:*⟩ sich vertagen. ~r *n* early ~r Frühaufsteher *m*

rising /'raɪzɪŋ/ *a* steigend; ⟨*sun*⟩ aufgehend; the ~ generation die heranwachsende Generation □ *n* (*revolt*) Aufstand *m*

risk /rɪsk/ *n* Risiko *nt*; at one's own ~ auf eigene Gefahr □ *vt* riskieren

risky /'rɪskɪ/ *a* (-ier, -iest) riskant

risqué /'rɪskeɪ/ *a* gewagt

rissole /'rɪsəʊl/ *n* Frikadelle *f*

rite /raɪt/ *n* Ritus *m*; last ~s Letzte Ölung *f*

ritual /'rɪtjʊəl/ *a* rituell □ *n* Ritual *nt*

rival /'raɪvl/ *a* rivalisierend □ *n* Rivale *m*/Rivalin *f*; ~s *pl* (*Comm*) Konkurrenten *pl* □ *vt* (*pt/pp* rivalled) gleichkommen (+ *dat*); (*compete with*) rivalisieren mit. ~ry *n* Rivalität *f*; (*Comm*) Konkurrenzkampf *m*

river /'rɪvə(r)/ *n* Fluss *m*. ~-bed *n* Flussbett *nt*

rivet /'rɪvɪt/ *n* Niete *f* □ *vt* [ver]nieten; ~ed by (*fig*) gefesselt von

road /rəʊd/ *n* Straße *f*; (*fig*) Weg *m*

road: ∼-block n Straßensperre f. ∼-hog n (fam) Straßenschreck m. ∼-map n Straßenkarte f. ∼ safety n Verkehrssicherheit f. ∼ sense n Verkehrssinn m. ∼side n Straßenrand m. ∼way n Fahrbahn f. ∼-works npl Straßenarbeiten pl. ∼worthy a verkehrssicher

roam /rəʊm/ vi wandern

roar /rɔː(r)/ n Gebrüll nt; ∼s of laughter schallendes Gelächter nt □ vi brüllen; (with laughter) schallend lachen. ∼ing a (fire) prasselnd; do a ∼ing trade (fam) ein Bombengeschäft machen

roast /rəʊst/ a gebraten, Brat-; ∼ beef/pork Rinder-/Schweinebraten m □ n Braten m □ vt/i braten; rösten (coffee, chestnuts)

rob /rɒb/ vt (pt/pp robbed) berauben (of gen); ausrauben (bank). ∼ber n Räuber m. ∼bery n Raub m

robe /rəʊb/ n Robe f; (Amer: bathrobe) Bademantel m

robin /'rɒbɪn/ n Rotkehlchen nt

robot /'rəʊbɒt/ n Roboter m

robust /rəʊ'bʌst/ a robust

rock¹ /rɒk/ n Fels m; stick of ∼ Zuckerstange f; on the ∼s (ship) aufgelaufen; (marriage) kaputt; (drink) mit Eis

rock² vt/i schaukeln

rock³ n (Mus) Rock m

rock-'bottom n Tiefpunkt m

rockery /'rɒkərɪ/ n Steingarten m

rocket /'rɒkɪt/ n Rakete f □ vi in die Höhe schießen

rocking: ∼-chair n Schaukelstuhl m. ∼-horse n Schaukelpferd nt

rocky /'rɒkɪ/ a (-ier, -iest) felsig; (unsteady) wackelig

rod /rɒd/ n Stab m; (stick) Rute f; (for fishing) Angel[rute] f

rode /rəʊd/ see ride

rodent /'rəʊdnt/ n Nagetier nt

roe¹ /rəʊ/ n Rogen m; (soft) Milch f

roe² n (pl roe or roes) ∼-[deer] Reh nt

rogue /rəʊg/ n Gauner m

role /rəʊl/ n Rolle f

roll /rəʊl/ n Rolle f; (bread) Brötchen nt; (list) Liste f; (of drum) Wirbel m □ vi rollen; be ∼ing in money (fam) Geld wie Heu haben □ vt rollen; walzen (lawn); ausrollen (pastry). ∼ over vi sich auf die andere Seite rollen. ∼ up vt aufrollen; hochkrempeln (sleeves) □ vi (fam) auftauchen

'roll-call n Namensaufruf m; (Mil) Appell m

roller /'rəʊlə(r)/ n Rolle f; (lawn, road) Walze f; (hair) Lockenwickler m. ∼ blind

n Rollo nt. ∼-coaster n Berg-und-Tal-Bahn f. ∼-skate n Rollschuh m

'rolling-pin n Teigrolle f

Roman /'rəʊmən/ a römisch □ n Römer(in) m(f)

romance /rə'mæns/ n Romantik f; (love-affair) Romanze f; (book) Liebesgeschichte f

Romania /rəʊ'meɪnɪə/ n Rumänien nt. ∼n a rumänisch □ n Rumäne m/-nin f

romantic /rəʊ'mæntɪk/ a, -ally adv romantisch. ∼ism /-tɪsɪzm/ n Romantik f

Rome /rəʊm/ n Rom nt

romp /rɒmp/ n Tollen nt □ vi [herum]tollen. ∼ers npl Strampelhöschen nt

roof /ruːf/ n Dach nt; (of mouth) Gaumen m □ vt ∼ over überdachen. ∼-rack n Dachgepäckträger m. ∼-top n Dach nt

rook /rʊk/ n Saatkrähe f; (Chess) Turm m □ vt (fam: swindle) schröpfen

room /ruːm/ n Zimmer nt; (for functions) Saal m; (space) Platz m. ∼y a geräumig

roost /ruːst/ n Hühnerstange f □ vi schlafen

root¹ /ruːt/ n Wurzel f; take ∼ anwachsen □ vi Wurzeln schlagen. ∼ out vt (fig) ausrotten

root² vi ∼ about wühlen; ∼ for s.o. (Amer, fam) für jdn sein

rope /rəʊp/ n Seil nt; know the ∼s (fam) sich auskennen. ∼ in vt (fam) einspannen

rope-'ladder n Strickleiter f

rosary /'rəʊzərɪ/ n Rosenkranz m

rose¹ /rəʊz/ n Rose f; (of watering-can) Brause f

rose² see rise

rosemary /'rəʊzmərɪ/ n Rosmarin m

rosette /rəʊ'zet/ n Rosette f

roster /'rɒstə(r)/ n Dienstplan m

rostrum /'rɒstrəm/ n Podest nt, Podium nt

rosy /'rəʊzɪ/ a (-ier, -iest) rosig

rot /rɒt/ n Fäulnis f; (fam: nonsense) Quatsch m □ vi (pt/pp rotted) [ver]faulen

rota /'rəʊtə/ n Dienstplan m

rotary /'rəʊtərɪ/ a Dreh-; (Techn) Rotations-

rotat|e /rəʊ'teɪt/ vt drehen; im Wechsel anbauen (crops) □ vi sich drehen; (Techn) rotieren. ∼ion /-eɪʃn/ n Drehung f; (of crops) Fruchtfolge f; in ∼ion im Wechsel

rote /rəʊt/ n by ∼ auswendig

rotten /'rɒtn/ a faul; (fam) mies; (person) fies

rotund /rəʊ'tʌnd/ a rundlich

rough /rʌf/ a (-er, -est) rau; (uneven) uneben; (coarse, not gentle) grob; (brutal) roh; (turbulent) stürmisch; (approximate) ungefähr □ *adv* sleep ~ im Freien übernachten; play ~ holzen □ *n* do sth in ~ etw ins Unreine schreiben □ *vt* ~ it primitiv leben. ~ out *vt* im Groben entwerfen

roughage /'rʌfɪdʒ/ *n* Ballaststoffe *pl*

rough 'draft *n* grober Entwurf *m*

rough|ly /'rʌflɪ/ *adv* (*see* rough) rau; grob; roh; ungefähr. ~ness *n* Rauheit *f*

'rough paper *n* Konzeptpapier *nt*

round /raʊnd/ *a* (-er, -est) rund □ *n* Runde *f*; (*slice*) Scheibe *f*; do one's ~ seine Runde machen □ *prep* um (+ *acc*); ~ the clock rund um die Uhr □ *adv* ~ herum; ~ and ~ im Kreis; ask s.o. ~ jdn einladen; turn/look ~ sich umdrehen/umsehen □ *vt* biegen um (*corner*) □ *vi* ~ on s.o. jdn anfahren. ~ off *vt* abrunden. ~ up *vt* aufrunden; zusammentreiben ⟨*animals*⟩; festnehmen ⟨*criminals*⟩

roundabout /'raʊndəbaʊt/ *a* ~ route Umweg *m* □ *n* Karussell *nt*; (*for traffic*) Kreisverkehr *m*

round: ~'shouldered *a* mit einem runden Rücken. ~ 'trip *n* Rundreise *f*

rouse| /raʊz/ *vt* wecken; (*fig*) erregen. ~ing *a* mitreißend

route /ruːt/ *n* Route *f*; (*of bus*) Linie *f*

routine /ruːˈtiːn/ *a*, -ly *adv* routinemäßig □ *n* Routine *f*; (*Theat*) Nummer *f*

roux /ruː/ *n* Mehlschwitze *f*

rove /rəʊv/ *vi* wandern

row¹ /rəʊ/ *n* (*line*) Reihe *f*; in a ~ (*one after the other*) nacheinander

row² *vt/i* rudern

row³ /raʊ/ *n* (*fam*) Krach *m* □ *vi* (*fam*) sich streiten

rowan /'rəʊən/ *n* Eberesche *f*

rowdy /'raʊdɪ/ *a* (-ier, -iest) laut

rowing boat /'rəʊɪŋ-/ *n* Ruderboot *nt*

royal /rɔɪəl/ *a*, -ly *adv* königlich

royal|ty /'rɔɪəltɪ/ *n* Königtum *nt*; (*persons*) Mitglieder *pl* der königlichen Familie; -ies *pl* (*payments*) Tantiemen *pl*

rub /rʌb/ *n* give sth a ~ etw reiben/(*polish*) polieren □ *vt* (*pt/pp* rubbed) reiben; (*polish*) polieren; don't ~ it in (*fam*) reib es mir nicht unter die Nase. ~ off *vt* abreiben; ~ off against □ *vi* abgeben; ~ off on abfärben auf (+ *acc*). ~ out *vt* ausradieren

rubber /'rʌbə(r)/ *n* Gummi *m*; (*eraser*) Radiergummi *m*. ~ band *n* Gummiband *nt*. ~y *a* gummiartig

rubbish /'rʌbɪʃ/ *n* Abfall *m*, Müll *m*; (*fam: nonsense*) Quatsch *m*; (*fam: junk*) Plunder *m*, Kram *m* □ *vt* (*fam*) schlecht machen. ~ bin *n* Mülleimer *m*, Abfalleimer *m*. ~

dump *n* Abfallhaufen *m*; (*official*) Müllhalde *f*

rubble /'rʌbl/ *n* Trümmer *pl*, Schutt *m*

ruby /'ruːbɪ/ *n* Rubin *m*

rucksack /'rʌksæk/ *n* Rucksack *m*

rudder /'rʌdə(r)/ *n* [Steuer]ruder *nt*

ruddy /'rʌdɪ/ *a* (-ier, -iest) rötlich; (*sl*) verdammt

rude /ruːd/ *a* (-r, -st), -ly *adv* unhöflich; (*improper*) unanständig. ~ness *n* Unhöflichkeit *f*

rudiment /'ruːdɪmənt/ *n* ~s *pl* Anfangsgründe *pl*. ~ary /-'mentərɪ/ *a* elementar; (*Biol*) rudimentär

rueful /'ruːfl/ *a*, -ly *adv* reumütig

ruffian /'rʌfɪən/ *n* Rüpel *m*

ruffle /'rʌfl/ *n* Rüsche *f* □ *vt* zerzausen

rug /rʌg/ *n* Vorleger *m*, [kleiner] Teppich *m*; (*blanket*) Decke *f*

rugged /'rʌgɪd/ *a* (*coastline*) zerklüftet

ruin /'ruːɪn/ *n* Ruine *f*; (*fig*) Ruin *m* □ *vt* ruinieren. ~ous /-əs/ *a* ruinös

rule /ruːl/ *n* Regel *f*; (*control*) Herrschaft *f*; (*government*) Regierung *f*; (*for measuring*) Lineal *nt*; as a ~ in der Regel □ *vt* regieren, herrschen über (+ *acc*); (*fig*) beherrschen; (*decide*) entscheiden; ziehen ⟨*line*⟩ □ *vi* regieren, herrschen. ~ out *vt* ausschließen

ruled /ruːld/ *a* (*paper*) liniert

ruler /'ruːlə(r)/ *n* Herrscher(in) *m(f)*; (*measure*) Lineal *nt*

ruling /'ruːlɪŋ/ *a* herrschend; (*factor*) entscheidend; (*Pol*) regierend □ *n* Entscheidung *f*

rum /rʌm/ *n* Rum *m*

rumble /'rʌmbl/ *n* Grollen *nt* □ *vi* grollen; (*stomach:*) knurren

ruminant /'ruːmɪnənt/ *n* Wiederkäuer *m*

rummage /'rʌmɪdʒ/ *vi* wühlen; ~ through durchwühlen

rummy /'rʌmɪ/ *n* Rommé *nt*

rumour /'ruːmə(r)/ *n* Gerücht *nt* □ *vt* it is ~ed that es geht das Gerücht, dass

rump /rʌmp/ *n* Hinterteil *nt*. ~ steak *n* Rumpsteak *nt*

rumpus /'rʌmpəs/ *n* (*fam*) Spektakel *m*

run /rʌn/ *n* Lauf *m*; (*journey*) Fahrt *f*; (*series*) Serie *f*, Reihe *f*; (*for measuring*) Lineal *nt*; (*Skiing*) Abfahrt *f*; (*enclosure*) Auslauf *m*; (*Amer: ladder*) Laufmasche *f*; at a ~ im Laufschritt; ~ of bad luck Pechsträhne *f*; be on the ~ flüchtig sein; have the ~ of sth etw zu seiner freien Verfügung haben; in the long ~ auf lange Sicht □ *v* (*pt* ran, *pp* run, *pres p* running) □ *vi* laufen; (*flow*) fließen; (*eyes:*) tränen; (*bus:*) verkehren, fahren; (*butter, ink:*) zerfließen; (*colours:*) [ab]färben; (*in election*)

kandidieren; ~ across s.o./sth auf jdn/
etw stoßen ◻ vt laufen lassen; einlaufen
lassen ⟨bath⟩; ⟨manage⟩ führen, leiten;
⟨drive⟩ fahren; eingehen ⟨risk⟩; ⟨Journ⟩
bringen ⟨article⟩; ~ one's hand over sth
mit der Hand über etw ⟨acc⟩ fahren. ~
away vi weglaufen. ~ down vi hinunter-/
herunterlaufen; ⟨clockwork:⟩ ablaufen;
⟨stocks:⟩ sich verringern ◻ vt ⟨run over⟩
überfahren; ⟨reduce⟩ verringern; ⟨fam:
criticize⟩ heruntermachen. ~ in vi hinein-/
hereinlaufen. ~ off vi weglaufen ◻ vt abziehen ⟨copies⟩. ~ out vi hinaus-/heraus-
laufen; ⟨supplies, money:⟩ ausgehen; I've
~ out of sugar Ich habe keinen Zucker
mehr. ~ over vi hinüber-/herüberlaufen;
⟨overflow⟩ überlaufen ◻ vt überfahren. ~
through vi durchlaufen. ~ up vi hinauf-/
herauflaufen; ⟨towards⟩ hinlaufen ◻ vt
machen ⟨debts⟩ auflaufen lassen ⟨bill⟩;
⟨sew⟩ schnell nähen

'runaway n Ausreißer m

run-'down a ⟨area⟩ verkommen

rung¹ /rʌŋ/ n ⟨of ladder⟩ Sprosse f

rung² see ring²

runner /'rʌnə(r)/ n Läufer m; ⟨Bot⟩ Ausläufer m; ⟨on sledge⟩ Kufe f. ~ bean n
Stangenbohne f. ~·up n Zweite(r) m/f

running /'rʌnɪŋ/ a laufend; ⟨water⟩
fließend; four times ~ viermal nacheinander ◻ n Laufen nt; ⟨management⟩
Führung f, Leitung f; be/not be in the
~ eine/keine Chance haben. ~ 'commentary n fortlaufender Kommentar m

runny /'rʌnɪ/ a flüssig

run: ~-of-the-'mill a gewöhnlich. ~-up n
⟨Sport⟩ Anlauf m; ⟨to election⟩ Zeit f vor
der Wahl. ~way n Start- und Landebahn
f, Piste f

rupture /'rʌptʃə(r)/ n Bruch m ◻ vt/i
brechen; ~ oneself sich ⟨dat⟩ einen
Bruch heben

rural /'rʊərəl/ a ländlich

ruse /ru:z/ n List f

rush¹ /rʌʃ/ n ⟨Bot⟩ Binse f

rush² n Hetze f; in a ~ in Eile ◻ vi sich
hetzen; ⟨run⟩ rasen; ⟨water:⟩ rauschen ◻ vt
hetzen, drängen; ~ s.o. to hospital jdn
schnellstens ins Krankenhaus bringen.
~-hour n Hauptverkehrszeit f, Stoßzeit
f

rusk /rʌsk/ n Zwieback m

Russia /'rʌʃə/ n Russland nt. ~n a rus-
sisch ◻ n Russe m/Russin f; ⟨Lang⟩ Rus-
sisch nt

rust /rʌst/ n Rost m ◻ vi rosten

rustic /'rʌstɪk/ a bäuerlich; ⟨furniture⟩
rustikal

rustle /'rʌsl/ vi rascheln ◻ vt rascheln mit;
⟨Amer⟩ stehlen ⟨cattle⟩. ~ up vt ⟨fam⟩ improvisieren

'rustproof a rostfrei

rusty /'rʌstɪ/ a (-ier, -iest) rostig

rut /rʌt/ n Furche f; be in a ~ ⟨fam⟩ aus
dem alten Trott nicht herauskommen

ruthless /'ru:θlɪs/ a, -ly adv rücksichtslos.
~ness n Rücksichtslosigkeit f

rye /raɪ/ n Roggen m

S

sabbath /'sæbəθ/ n Sabbat m

sabbatical /sə'bætɪkl/ n ⟨Univ⟩ For-
schungsurlaub m

sabot|age /'sæbətɑ:ʒ/ n Sabotage f ◻ vt
sabotieren. ~eur /-'tɜ:(r)/ n Saboteur m

sachet /'sæʃeɪ/ n Beutel m; ⟨scented⟩
Kissen nt

sack¹ /sæk/ vt ⟨plunder⟩ plündern

sack² n Sack m; get the ~ ⟨fam⟩ rausge-
schmissen werden ◻ vt ⟨fam⟩ rausschmeißen. ~ing n Sackleinen nt; ⟨fam:
dismissal⟩ Rausschmiss m

sacrament /'sækrəmənt/ n Sakrament nt

sacred /'seɪkrɪd/ a heilig

sacrifice /'sækrɪfaɪs/ n Opfer nt ◻ vt op-
fern

sacrilege /'sækrɪlɪdʒ/ n Sakrileg nt

sad /sæd/ a (sadder, saddest) traurig;
⟨loss, death⟩ schmerzlich. ~den vt traurig
machen

saddle /'sædl/ n Sattel m ◻ vt satteln; ~
s.o. with sth ⟨fam⟩ jdm etw aufhalsen

sadis|m /'seɪdɪzm/ n Sadismus m. ~t
/-dɪst/ n Sadist m. ~tic /sə'dɪstɪk/ a,
-ally adv sadistisch

sad|ly /'sædlɪ/ adv traurig; ⟨unfortunately⟩
leider. ~ness n Traurigkeit f

safe /seɪf/ a (-r, -st) sicher; ⟨journey⟩ gut;
⟨not dangerous⟩ ungefährlich; ~ and
sound gesund und wohlbehalten ◻ n Safe
m. ~guard n Schutz m ◻ vt schützen. ~ly
adv sicher; ⟨arrive⟩ gut

safety /'seɪftɪ/ n Sicherheit f. ~-belt n
Sicherheitsgurt m. ~-pin n Sicherheits-
nadel f. ~-valve n [Sicherheits]ventil nt

sag /sæg/ vi ⟨pt/pp sagged⟩ durchhängen

saga /'sɑ:gə/ n Saga f; ⟨fig⟩ Geschichte f

sage¹ /seɪdʒ/ n ⟨herb⟩ Salbei m

sage² a weise ◻ n Weise m

Sagittarius /sædʒɪ'teərɪəs/ n ⟨Astr⟩
Schütze m

said /sed/ *see* say

sail /seɪl/ *n* Segel *nt*; (*trip*) Segelfahrt *f* □ *vi* segeln; (*on liner*) fahren; (*leave*) abfahren (for nach) □ *vt* segeln mit

'sailboard *n* Surfbrett *nt*. ~ing *n* Windsurfen *nt*

sailing /'seɪlɪŋ/ *n* Segelsport *m*. ~-boat *n* Segelboot *nt*. ~-ship *n* Segelschiff *nt*

sailor /'seɪlə(r)/ *n* Seemann *m*; (*in navy*) Matrose *m*

saint /seɪnt/ *n* Heilige(r) *m*/*f*. ~ly *a* heilig

sake /seɪk/ *n* for the ~ of … um … (*gen*) willen; for my/your ~ um meinet-/deinetwillen

salad /'sæləd/ *n* Salat *m*. ~ cream *n* ≈ Mayonnaise *f*. ~-dressing *n* Salatsoße *f*

salary /'sælərɪ/ *n* Gehalt *nt*

sale /seɪl/ *n* Verkauf *m*; (*event*) Basar *m*; (*at reduced prices*) Schlussverkauf *m*; for ~ zu verkaufen

sales|man *n* Verkäufer *m*. ~woman *n* Verkäuferin *f*

salient /'seɪlɪənt/ *a* wichtigste(r,s)

saliva /sə'laɪvə/ *n* Speichel *m*

sallow /'sæləʊ/ *a* (-er, -est) bleich

salmon /'sæmən/ *n* Lachs *m*. ~-pink *a* lachsrosa

saloon /sə'luːn/ *n* Salon *m*; (*Auto*) Limousine *f*; (*Amer: bar*) Wirtschaft *f*

salt /sɔːlt/ *n* Salz *nt* □ *a* salzig; (*water, meat*) Salz- □ *vt* salzen; (*cure*) pökeln; streuen (*road*). ~-cellar *n* Salzfass *nt*. ~ 'water *n* Salzwasser *nt*. ~y *a* salzig

salutary /'sæljʊtərɪ/ *a* heilsam

salute /sə'luːt/ *n* (*Mil*) Gruß *m* □ *vt*/*i* (*Mil*) grüßen

salvage /'sælvɪdʒ/ *n* (*Naut*) Bergung *f* □ *vt* bergen

salvation /sæl'veɪʃn/ *n* Rettung *f*; (*Relig*) Heil *nt*. S~ 'Army *n* Heilsarmee *f*

salvo /'sælvəʊ/ *n* Salve *f*

same /seɪm/ *a & pron* the ~ der/die/das gleiche; (*pl*) die gleichen; (*identical*) der-/die-/dasselbe; (*pl*) dieselben □ *adv* the ~ gleich; all the ~ trotzdem; the ~ to you gleichfalls

sample /'sɑːmpl/ *n* Probe *f*; (*Comm*) Muster *nt* □ *vt* probieren, kosten

sanatorium /sænə'tɔːrɪəm/ *n* Sanatorium *nt*

sanctify /'sæŋktɪfaɪ/ *vt* (*pt/pp* -fied) heiligen

sanctimonious /sæŋktɪ'məʊnɪəs/ *a*, -ly *adv* frömmlerisch

sanction /'sæŋkʃn/ *n* Sanktion *f* □ *vt* sanktionieren

sanctity /'sæŋktətɪ/ *n* Heiligkeit *f*

sanctuary /'sæŋktjʊərɪ/ *n* (*Relig*) Heiligtum *nt*; (*refuge*) Zuflucht *f*; (*for wildlife*) Tierschutzgebiet *nt*

sand /sænd/ *n* Sand *m* □ *vt* ~ [down] [ab]schmirgeln

sandal /'sændl/ *n* Sandale *f*

sand: ~bank *n* Sandbank *f*. ~paper *n* Sandpapier *nt* □ *vt* [ab]schmirgeln. ~-pit *n* Sandkasten *m*

sandwich /'sænwɪdʒ/ *n* ≈ belegtes Brot *nt*; Sandwich *m* □ *vt* ~ed between eingeklemmt zwischen

sandy /'sændɪ/ *a* (-ier, -iest) sandig; (*beach, soil*) Sand-; (*hair*) rotblond

sane /seɪn/ *a* (-r, -st) geistig normal; (*sensible*) vernünftig

sang /sæŋ/ *see* sing

sanitary /'sænɪtərɪ/ *a* hygienisch; (*system*) sanitär. ~ napkin *n* (*Amer*), ~ towel *n* [Damen]binde *f*

sanitation /sænɪ'teɪʃn/ *n* Kanalisation und Abfallbeseitigung *pl*

sanity /'sænətɪ/ *n* [gesunder] Verstand *m*

sank /sæŋk/ *see* sink

sap /sæp/ *n* (*Bot*) Saft *m* □ *vt* (*pt/pp* sapped) schwächen

sapphire /'sæfaɪə(r)/ *n* Saphir *m*

sarcas|m /'sɑːkæzm/ *n* Sarkasmus *m*. ~tic /-'kæstɪk/ *a*, -ally *adv* sarkastisch

sardine /sɑː'diːn/ *n* Sardine *f*

Sardinia /sɑː'dɪnɪə/ *n* Sardinien *nt*

sardonic /sɑː'dɒnɪk/ *a*, -ally *adv* höhnisch; (*smile*) sardonisch

sash /sæʃ/ *n* Schärpe *f*

sat /sæt/ *see* sit

satanic /sə'tænɪk/ *a* satanisch

satchel /'sætʃl/ *n* Ranzen *m*

satellite /'sætəlaɪt/ *n* Satellit *m*. ~ dish *n* Satellitenschüssel *f*. ~ television *n* Satellitenfernsehen *nt*

satin /'sætɪn/ *n* Satin *m*

satire /'sætaɪə(r)/ *n* Satire *f*

satirical /sə'tɪrɪkl/ *a*, -ly *adv* satirisch

satir|ist /'sætərɪst/ *n* Satiriker(in) *m*(*f*). ~ize *vt* satirisch darstellen; (*book:*) eine Satire sein auf (+ *acc*)

satisfaction /sætɪs'fækʃn/ *n* Befriedigung *f*; to my ~ zu meiner Zufriedenheit

satisfactory /sætɪs'fæktərɪ/ *a*, -ily *adv* zufrieden stellend

satisf|y /'sætɪsfaɪ/ *vt* (*pt/pp* -fied) befriedigen; zufrieden stellen (*customer*); (*convince*) überzeugen; be ~ied zufrieden sein. ~ying *a* befriedigend; (*meal*) sättigend

saturat|e /'sætʃəreɪt/ *vt* durchtränken; (*Chem & fig*) sättigen. ~ed *a* durchnässt; (*fat*) gesättigt

Saturday /'sætədeɪ/ n Samstag m, Sonnabend m

sauce /sɔːs/ n Soße f; (cheek) Frechheit f. ~pan n Kochtopf m

saucer /'sɔːsə(r)/ n Untertasse f

saucy /'sɔːʃɪ/ a (-ier, -iest) frech

Saudi Arabia /saʊdɪə'reɪbɪə/ n Saudi-Arabien n

sauna /'sɔːnə/ n Sauna f

saunter /'sɔːntə(r)/ vi schlendern

sausage /'sɒsɪdʒ/ n Wurst f

savage /'sævɪdʒ/ a wild; (fierce) scharf; (brutal) brutal □ n Wilde(r) m/f □ vt anfallen. ~ry n Brutalität f

save /seɪv/ n (Sport) Abwehr f □ vt retten (from vor + dat); (keep) aufheben; (not waste) sparen; (collect) sammeln; (avoid) ersparen; (Sport) abwehren (shot); verhindern (goal) □ vi ~ [up] sparen □ prep außer (+ dat), mit Ausnahme (+ gen)

saver /'seɪvə(r)/ n Sparer m

saving /'seɪvɪŋ/ n (see save) Rettung f; Sparen nt; Ersparnis f; ~s pl (money) Ersparnisse pl. ~s account n Sparkonto nt. ~s bank n Sparkasse f

saviour /'seɪvjə(r)/ n Retter m

savour /'seɪvə(r)/ n Geschmack m □ vt auskosten. ~y a herzhaft, würzig; (fig) angenehm

saw[1] /sɔː/ see see[1]

saw[2] n Säge f □ vt/i (pt sawed, pp sawn or sawed) sägen. ~dust n Sägemehl nt

saxophone /'sæksəfəʊn/ n Saxophon nt

say /seɪ/ n Mitspracherecht nt; have one's ~ seine Meinung sagen □ vt/i (pt/pp said) sagen; sprechen (prayer); that is to ~ das heißt; that goes without ~ing das versteht sich von selbst; when all is said and done letzten Endes; I ~! (attracting attention) hallo! ~ing n Redensart f

scab /skæb/ n Schorf m; (pej) Streikbrecher m

scaffold /'skæfəld/ n Schafott nt. ~ing n Gerüst nt

scald /skɔːld/ vt verbrühen

scale[1] /skeɪl/ n (of fish) Schuppe f

scale[2] n Skala f; (Mus) Tonleiter f; (ratio) Maßstab m; on a grand ~ in großem Stil □ vt (climb) erklettern. ~ down vt verkleinern

scales /skeɪlz/ npl (for weighing) Waage f

scalp /skælp/ n Kopfhaut f □ vt skalpieren

scalpel /'skælpl/ n Skalpell nt

scam /skæm/ n (fam) Schwindel m

scamper /'skæmpə(r)/ vi huschen

scan /skæn/ n (Med) Szintigramm nt □ v (pt/pp scanned) □ vt absuchen; (quickly) flüchtig ansehen; (Med) szintigraphisch

untersuchen □ vi (poetry:) das richtige Versmaß haben

scandal /'skændl/ n Skandal m; (gossip) Skandalgeschichten pl. ~ize /-dəlaɪz/ vt schockieren. ~ous /-əs/ a skandalös

Scandinavia /skændɪ'neɪvɪə/ n Skandinavien nt. ~n a skandinavisch □ n Skandinavier(in) m(f)

scant /skænt/ a wenig

scanty /'skæntɪ/ a (-ier, -iest), -ily adv spärlich; (clothing) knapp

scapegoat /'skeɪp-/ n Sündenbock m

scar /skɑː(r)/ n Narbe f □ vt (pt/pp scarred) eine Narbe hinterlassen auf (+ dat)

scarce /skeəs/ a (-r, -st) knapp; make oneself ~e (fam) sich aus dem Staub machen. ~ely adv kaum. ~ity n Knappheit f

scare /skeə(r)/ n Schreck m; (panic) [allgemeine] Panik f; (bomb ~) Bombendrohung f □ vt Angst machen (+ dat); be ~d Angst haben (of vor + dat)

'scarecrow n Vogelscheuche f

scarf /skɑːf/ n (pl scarves) Schal m; (square) Tuch nt

scarlet /'skɑːlət/ a scharlachrot. ~ 'fever n Scharlach m

scary /'skeərɪ/ a unheimlich

scathing /'skeɪðɪŋ/ a bissig

scatter /'skætə(r)/ vt verstreuen; (disperse) zerstreuen □ vi sich zerstreuen. ~brained a (fam) schusselig. ~ed a verstreut; (showers) vereinzelt

scatty /'skætɪ/ a (-ier, -iest) (fam) verrückt

scavenge /'skævɪndʒ/ vi [im Abfall] Nahrung suchen; (animal:) Aas fressen. ~r n Aasfresser m

scenario /sɪ'nɑːrɪəʊ/ n Szenario nt

scene /siːn/ n Szene f; (sight) Anblick m; (place of event) Schauplatz m; behind the ~s hinter den Kulissen; ~ of the crime Tatort m

scenery /'siːnərɪ/ n Landschaft f; (Theat) Szenerie f

scenic /'siːnɪk/ a landschaftlich schön; (Theat) Bühnen-

scent /sent/ n Duft m; (trail) Fährte f; (perfume) Parfüm nt. ~ed a parfümiert

sceptic|al /'skeptɪkl/ a, -ly adv skeptisch. ~ism /-tɪsɪzm/ n Skepsis f

schedule /'ʃedjuːl/ n Programm nt; (of work) Zeitplan m; (timetable) Fahrplan m; behind ~ im Rückstand; according to ~ planmäßig □ vt planen. ~d flight n Linienflug m

scheme /skiːm/ n Programm nt; (plan) Plan m; (plot) Komplott n □ vi Ränke schmieden schizophren|ia /skɪtsə'friːnɪə/ n Schizophrenie f. ~ic /-'frenɪk/ a schizophren

scholar /'skɒlə(r)/ n Gelehrte(r) m/f. ~ly a gelehrt. ~ship n Gelehrtheit f; (grant) Stipendium nt

school /skuːl/ n Schule f; (Univ) Fakultät f □ vt schulen; dressieren (animal)

school: ~boy n Schüler m. ~girl n Schülerin f. ~ing n Schulbildung f. ~master n Lehrer m. ~mistress n Lehrerin f. ~teacher n Lehrer(in) m(f)

sciatica /saɪ'ætɪkə/ n Ischias m

scien|ce /'saɪəns/ n Wissenschaft f. ~tific /-'tɪfɪk/ a wissenschaftlich. ~tist n Wissenschaftler m

scintillating /'sɪntɪleɪtɪŋ/ a sprühend

scissors /'sɪzəz/ npl Schere f; a pair of ~ eine Schere

scoff¹ /skɒf/ vi ~ at spotten über (+ acc)

scoff² vt (fam) verschlingen

scold /skəʊld/ vt ausschimpfen

scoop /skuːp/ n Schaufel f; (Culin) Portionierer m; (Journ) Exklusivmeldung f □ vt ~ out aushöhlen; (remove) auslöffeln; ~ up schaufeln; schöpfen (liquid)

scoot /skuːt/ vi (fam) rasen. ~er n Roller m

scope /skəʊp/ n Bereich m; (opportunity) Möglichkeiten pl

scorch /skɔːtʃ/ vt versengen. ~ing a glühend heiß

score /skɔː(r)/ n [Spiel]stand m; (individual) Punktzahl f; (Mus) Partitur f; (Cinema) Filmmusik f; a ~ [of] (twenty) zwanzig; keep [the] ~ zählen; (written) aufschreiben; on that ~ was das betrifft □ vt erzielen; schießen (goal); (cut) einritzen □ vi Punkte erzielen; (Sport) ein Tor schießen; (keep score) Punkte zählen. ~r n Punktezähler m; (of goals) Torschütze m

scorn /skɔːn/ n Verachtung f □ vt verachten. ~ful a, -ly adv verächtlich

Scorpio /'skɔːpɪəʊ/ n (Astr) Skorpion m

Scorpion /'skɔːpɪən/ n Skorpion m

Scot /skɒt/ n Schotte m/Schottin f

Scotch /skɒtʃ/ a schottisch □ n (whisky) Scotch m

scotch vt unterbinden

scot-'free a get off ~ straffrei ausgehen

Scot|land /'skɒtlənd/ n Schottland nt. ~s, ~tish a schottisch

scoundrel /'skaʊndrl/ n Schurke m

scour¹ /'skaʊə(r)/ vt (search) absuchen

scour² vt (clean) scheuern

scourge /skɜːdʒ/ n Geißel f

scout /skaʊt/ n (Mil) Kundschafter m □ vi ~ for Ausschau halten nach

Scout n [Boy] ~ Pfadfinder m

scowl /skaʊl/ n böser Gesichtsausdruck m □ vi ein böses Gesicht machen

scraggy /'skrægɪ/ a (-ier, -iest) (pej) dürr, hager

scram /skræm/ vi (fam) abhauen

scramble /'skræmbl/ n Gerangel nt □ vi klettern; ~ for sich drängen nach □ vt (Teleph) verschlüsseln. ~d 'egg[s] n[pl] Rührei nt

scrap¹ /skræp/ n (fam: fight) Rauferei f □ vi sich raufen

scrap² /skræp/ n Stückchen nt; (metal) Schrott m; ~s pl Reste; not a ~ kein bisschen □ vt (pt/pp scrapped) aufgeben

'scrap-book n Sammelalbum nt

scrape /skreɪp/ vt schaben; (clean) abkratzen; (damage) [ver]schrammen. ~ through vi gerade noch durchkommen. ~ together vt zusammenkriegen

scraper /'skreɪpə(r)/ n Kratzer m

'scrap iron n Alteisen nt

scrappy /'skræpɪ/ a lückenhaft

'scrap-yard n Schrottplatz m

scratch /skrætʃ/ n Kratzer m; start from ~ von vorne anfangen; not be up to ~ zu wünschen übrig lassen □ vt/i kratzen; (damage) zerkratzen

scrawl /skrɔːl/ n Gekrakel nt □ vt/i krakeln

scrawny /'skrɔːnɪ/ a (-ier, -iest) (pej) dürr, hager

scream /skriːm/ n Schrei m □ vt/i schreien

screech /skriːtʃ/ n Kreischen nt □ vt/i kreischen

screen /skriːn/ n Schirm m; (Cinema) Leinwand f; (TV) Bildschirm m □ vt schützen; (conceal) verdecken; vorführen (film); (examine) überprüfen; (Med) untersuchen. ~ing n (Med) Reihenuntersuchung f. ~play n Drehbuch nt

screw /skruː/ n Schraube f □ vt schrauben. ~ up vt festschrauben; (crumple) zusammenknüllen; zusammenkneifen (eyes); (sl: bungle) vermasseln; ~ up one's courage seinen Mut zusammennehmen

'screwdriver n Schraubenzieher m

screwy /'skruːɪ/ a (-ier, -iest) (fam) verrückt

scribble /'skrɪbl/ n Gekritzel nt □ vt/i kritzeln

script /skrɪpt/ n Schrift f; (of speech, play) Text m; (Radio, TV) Skript nt; (of film) Drehbuch nt

Scripture /'skrɪptʃə(r)/ n (Sch) Religion f; the ~s pl die Heilige Schrift f

scroll /skrəʊl/ n Schriftrolle f; (decoration) Volute f

scrounge /skraʊndʒ/ vt/i schnorren. ~r n Schnorrer m

scrub[1] /skrʌb/ n (land) Buschland nt, Gestrüpp nt

scrub[2] vt/i (pt/pp scrubbed) schrubben; (fam: cancel) absagen; fallen lassen (plan)

scruff /skrʌf/ n by the ~ of the neck beim Genick

scruffy /'skrʌfɪ/ a (-ier, -iest) vergammelt

scrum /skrʌm/ n Gedränge nt

scruple /'skru:pl/ n Skrupel m

scrupulous /'skru:pjʊləs/ a, -ly adv gewissenhaft

scrutin|ize /'skru:tɪnaɪz/ vt [genau] ansehen. ~y n (look) prüfender Blick m

scuff /skʌf/ vt abstoßen

scuffle /'skʌfl/ n Handgemenge nt

scullery /'skʌlərɪ/ n Spülküche f

sculpt|or /'skʌlptə(r)/ n Bildhauer(in) m(f). ~ure /-tʃə(r)/ n Bildhauerei f; (piece of work) Skulptur f, Plastik f

scum /skʌm/ n Schmutzschicht f; (people) Abschaum m

scurrilous /'skʌrɪləs/ a niederträchtig

scurry /'skʌrɪ/ vi (pt/pp -ied) huschen

scuttle[1] /'skʌtl/ n Kohleneimer m

scuttle[2] vt versenken ⟨ship⟩

scuttle[3] vi schnell krabbeln

scythe /saɪð/ n Sense f

sea /si:/ n Meer nt, See f; at ~ auf See; by ~ mit dem Schiff. ~board n Küste f. ~food n Meeresfrüchte pl. ~gull n Möwe f

seal[1] /si:l/ n (Zool) Seehund m

seal[2] n Siegel nt; (Techn) Dichtung f ⟐ vt versiegeln; (Techn) abdichten; (fig) besiegeln. ~ off vt abriegeln

'sea-level n Meeresspiegel m

seam /si:m/ n Naht f; (of coal) Flöz nt

'seaman n Seemann m; (sailor) Matrose m

seamless /'si:mlɪs/ a nahtlos

seance /'seɪɑ:ns/ n spiritistische Sitzung f

sea: ~plane n Wasserflugzeug nt. ~port n Seehafen m

search /sɜ:tʃ/ n Suche f; (official) Durchsuchung f ⟐ vt durchsuchen; absuchen ⟨area⟩ ⟐ vi suchen (for nach). ~ing a prüfend, forschend

search: ~light n [Such]scheinwerfer m. ~party n Suchmannschaft f

sea: ~ sick a seekrank. ~ness n at/to the ~side am/ans Meer

season /'si:zn/ n Jahreszeit f; (social, tourist, sporting) Saison f ⟐ vt (flavour) würzen. ~able /-əbl/ a der Jahreszeit gemäß. ~al a Saison-. ~ing n Gewürze pl

'season ticket n Dauerkarte f

seat /si:t/ n Sitz m; (place) Sitzplatz m; (bottom) Hintern m; take a ~ Platz nehmen ⟐ vt setzen; (have seats for) Sitzplätze bieten (+ dat); remain ~ed sitzen bleiben. ~-belt n Sicherheitsgurt m; fasten one's ~-belt sich anschnallen

sea: ~weed n [See]tang m. ~worthy a seetüchtig

secateurs /sekə'tɜ:z/ npl Gartenschere f

seclu|de /sɪ'klu:d/ vt absondern. ~ded a abgelegen. ~sion /-ʒn/ n Zurückgezogenheit f

second[1] /sɪ'kɒnd/ vt (transfer) [vorübergehend] versetzen

second[2] /'sekənd/ a zweite(r,s); on ~ thoughts nach weiterer Überlegung ⟐ n Sekunde f; (Sport) Sekundant m; ~s pl (goods) Waren zweiter Wahl; the ~ der/die/das Zweite ⟐ adv (in race) an zweiter Stelle ⟐ vt unterstützen ⟨proposal⟩

secondary /'sekəndrɪ/ a zweitrangig; (Phys) Sekundär-. ~ school n höhere Schule f

second: ~-best a zweitbeste(r,s). ~ 'class adv (travel, send) zweiter Klasse. ~-class a zweitklassig

'second hand n (on clock) Sekundenzeiger m

second-'hand a gebraucht ⟐ adv aus zweiter Hand

secondly /'sekəndlɪ/ adv zweitens

second-'rate a zweitklassig

secrecy /'si:krəsɪ/ n Heimlichkeit f

secret /'si:krɪt/ a geheim; ⟨agent, police⟩ Geheim-; ⟨drinker, lover⟩ heimlich ⟐ n Geheimnis nt; in ~ heimlich

secretarial /sekrə'teərɪəl/ a Sekretärinnen-; ⟨work, staff⟩ Sekretariats-

secretary /'sekrətərɪ/ n Sekretär(in) m(f)

secret|e /sɪ'kri:t/ vt absondern. ~ion /-i:ʃn/ n Absonderung f

secretive /'si:krətɪv/ a geheimtuerisch. ~ness n Heimlichtuerei f

secretly /'si:krɪtlɪ/ adv heimlich

sect /sekt/ n Sekte f

section /'sekʃn/ n Teil m; (of text) Abschnitt m; (of firm) Abteilung f; (of organization) Sektion f

sector /'sektə(r)/ n Sektor m

secular /'sekjʊlə(r)/ a weltlich

secure /sɪ'kjʊə(r)/ a, -ly adv sicher; (firm) fest; (emotionally) geborgen ⟐ vt sichern; (fasten) festmachen; (obtain) sich (dat) sichern

securit|y /sɪ'kjʊərətɪ/ n Sicherheit f; (*emotional*) Geborgenheit f; ~ies pl Wertpapiere pl; (*Fin*) Effekten pl

sedan /sɪ'dæn/ n (*Amer*) Limousine f

sedate¹ /sɪ'deɪt/ a, -ly adv gesetzt

sedate² vt sedieren

sedation /sɪ'deɪʃn/ n Sedierung f; be under ~ sediert sein

sedative /'sedətɪv/ a beruhigend □ n Beruhigungsmittel nt

sedentary /'sedəntərɪ/ a sitzend

sediment /'sedɪmənt/ n [Boden]satz m

seduce /sɪ'dju:s/ vt verführen

seduct|ion /sɪ'dʌkʃn/ n Verführung f. ~ive /-tɪv/ a, -ly adv verführerisch

see¹ /si:/ v (pt saw, pp seen) □ vt sehen; (*understand*) einsehen; (*imagine*) sich (dat) vorstellen; (*escort*) begleiten; go and ~ nachsehen; (*visit*) besuchen; ~ you later! bis nachher! ~ing that da □ vi sehen; (*check*) nachsehen; ~ about sich kümmern um. ~ off vt verabschieden; (*chase away*) vertreiben. ~ through vi durchsehen □ vt (*fig*) ~ through s.o. jdn durchschauen

see² n (*Relig*) Bistum nt

seed /si:d/ n Samen m; (*of grape*) Kern m; (*fig*) Saat f; (*Tennis*) gesetzter Spieler m; go to ~ Samen bilden; (*fig*) herunterkommen. ~ed a (*Tennis*) gesetzt. ~ling n Sämling m

seedy /'si:dɪ/ a (-ier, -iest) schäbig; (*area*) heruntergekommen

seek /si:k/ vt (pt/pp sought) suchen

seem /si:m/ vi scheinen. ~ingly adv scheinbar

seemly /'si:mlɪ/ a schicklich

seen /si:n/ see see¹

seep /si:p/ vi sickern

see-saw /'si:sɔ:/ n Wippe f

seethe /si:ð/ vi ~ with anger vor Wut schäumen

'see-through a durchsichtig

segment /'segmənt/ n Teil m; (*of worm*) Segment nt; (*of orange*) Spalte f

segregat|e /'segrɪgeɪt/ vt trennen. ~ion /-'geɪʃn/ n Trennung f

seize /si:z/ vt ergreifen; (*Jur*) beschlagnahmen; ~ s.o. by the arm jdn am Arm packen. ~ up vi (*Techn*) sich festfressen

seizure /'si:ʒə(r)/ n (*Jur*) Beschlagnahme f; (*Med*) Anfall m

seldom /'seldəm/ adv selten

select /sɪ'lekt/ a ausgewählt; (*exclusive*) exklusiv □ vt auswählen; aufstellen; (*team*). ~ion /-ekʃn/ n Auswahl f. ~ive /-ɪv/ a, -ly adv selektiv; (*choosy*) wählerisch

self /self/ n (pl selves) Ich nt

self: ~-ad'dressed a adressiert. ~-ad'hesive a selbstklebend. ~-as'surance n Selbstsicherheit f. ~-as'sured a selbstsicher. ~-'catering n Selbstversorgung f. ~-'centred a egozentrisch. ~-'confidence n Selbstbewusstsein nt, Selbstvertrauen nt. ~-'confident a selbstbewusst. ~-'conscious a befangen. ~-con'tained a ⟨flat⟩ abgeschlossen. ~-con-'trol n Selbstbeherrschung f. ~-de'fence n Selbstverteidigung f; (*Jur*) Notwehr f. ~-de'nial n Selbstverleugnung f. ~-determi'nation n Selbstbestimmung f. ~-em'ployed selbstständig. ~-e'steem n Selbstachtung f. ~-'evident a offensichtlich. ~-'governing a selbst verwaltet. ~-'help n Selbsthilfe f. ~-in'dulgent a maßlos. ~-'interest n Eigennutz m

self|ish /'selfɪʃ/ a, -ly adv egoistisch, selbstsüchtig. ~less a, -ly adv selbstlos

self: ~-'pity n Selbstmitleid nt. ~-'portrait n Selbstporträt nt. ~-pos'sessed a selbstbeherrscht. ~-preser'vation n Selbsterhaltung f. ~-re'spect n Selbstachtung f. ~-'righteous a selbstgerecht. ~-'sacrifice n Selbstaufopferung f. ~-'satisfied a selbstgefällig. ~-'service n Selbstbedienung f □ attrib Selbstbedienungs-. ~-suf'ficient a selbstständig. ~-'willed a eigenwillig

sell /sel/ v (pt/pp sold) □ vt verkaufen; be sold out ausverkauft sein □ vi sich verkaufen. ~ off vt verkaufen

seller /'selə(r)/ n Verkäufer m

Sellotape (P) /'seləʊ-/ n ≈ Tesafilm (P) m

'sell-out n be a ~ ausverkauft sein; (*fam: betrayal*) Verrat sein

selves /selvz/ see self

semblance /'sembləns/ n Anschein m

semen /'si:mən/ n (*Anat*) Samen m

semester /sɪ'mestə(r)/ n (*Amer*) Semester nt

semi|breve /'semɪbri:v/ n (*Mus*) ganze Note f. ~circle n Halbkreis m. ~'circular a halbkreisförmig. ~'colon n Semikolon nt. ~-de'tached a & n ~-detached [house] Doppelhaushälfte f. ~-'final n Halbfinale nt

seminar /'semɪnɑ:(r)/ n Seminar nt. ~y /-nərɪ/ n Priesterseminar nt

'semitone n (*Mus*) Halbton m

semolina /semə'li:nə/ n Grieß m

senat|e /'senət/ n Senat m. ~or n Senator m

send /send/ vt/i (pt/pp sent) schicken; ~ one's regards grüßen lassen; ~ for kommen lassen ⟨person⟩; sich (dat) schicken lassen ⟨thing⟩. ~er n Absender m. ~-off n Verabschiedung f

senil|e /'si:naɪl/ a senil. ~**ity** /sɪ'nɪlətɪ/ n Senilität f

senior /'si:nɪə(r)/ a älter; (in rank) höher □ n Ältere(r) m/f; (in rank) Vorgesetzte(r) m/f. ~ **citizen** n Senior(in) m(f)

seniority /si:nɪ'ɒrətɪ/ n höheres Alter nt; (in rank) höherer Rang m

sensation /sen'seɪʃn/ n Sensation f; (feeling) Gefühl nt. ~**al** a, -ly adv sensationell

sense /sens/ n Sinn m; (feeling) Gefühl n; (common ~) Verstand m; in a ~ in gewisser Hinsicht; make ~ Sinn ergeben □ vt spüren. ~**less** a, -ly adv sinnlos; (unconscious) bewusstlos

sensible /'sensəbl/ a, -**bly** adv vernünftig; (suitable) zweckmäßig

sensitiv|e /'sensətɪv/ a, -ly adv empfindlich; (understanding) einfühlsam. ~**ity** /-'tɪvətɪ/ n Empfindlichkeit f

sensory /'sensərɪ/ a Sinnes-

sensual /'sensjʊəl/ a sinnlich. -**ity** /-'æləti/ n Sinnlichkeit f

sensuous /'sensjʊəs/ a sinnlich

sent /sent/ see send

sentence /'sentəns/ n Satz m; (Jur) Urteil nt; (punishment) Strafe f □ vt verurteilen

sentiment /'sentɪmənt/ n Gefühl nt; (opinion) Meinung f; (sentimentality) Sentimentalität f. ~**al** a /-'mentl/ a sentimental. ~**ality** /-'tæləti/ n Sentimentalität f

sentry /'sentrɪ/ n Wache f

separable /'sepərəbl/ a trennbar

separate[1] /'sepərət/ a, -ly adv getrennt, separat

separat|e[2] /'sepəreɪt/ vt trennen □ vi sich trennen. ~**ion** /-'reɪʃn/ n Trennung f

September /sep'tembə(r)/ n September m

septic /'septɪk/ a vereitert; go ~ vereitern

sequel /'si:kwl/ n Folge f; (fig) Nachspiel nt

sequence /'si:kwəns/ n Reihenfolge f

sequin /'si:kwɪn/ n Paillette f

serenade /serə'neɪd/ n Ständchen nt □ vt ~ s.o. jdm ein Ständchen bringen

seren|e /sɪ'ri:n/ a, -ly adv gelassen. ~**ity** /-'renətɪ/ n Gelassenheit f

sergeant /'sɑ:dʒənt/ n (Mil) Feldwebel m; (in police) Polizeimeister m

serial /'sɪərɪəl/ n Fortsetzungsgeschichte f; (Radio, TV) Serie f. ~**ize** vt in Fortsetzungen veröffentlichen/(Radio, TV) senden

series /'sɪəri:z/ n inv Serie f

serious /'sɪərɪəs/ a, -ly adv ernst; (illness, error) schwer. ~**ness** n Ernst m

sermon /'sɜ:mən/ n Predigt f

serpent /'sɜ:pənt/ n Schlange f

serrated /se'reɪtɪd/ a gezackt

serum /'sɪərəm/ n Serum nt

servant /'sɜ:vənt/ n Diener(in) m(f)

serve /sɜ:v/ n (Tennis) Aufschlag m □ vt dienen (+ dat); bedienen (customer, guest); servieren (food); (Jur) zustellen (on s.o. jdm); verbüßen (sentence); ~ its purpose seinen Zweck erfüllen; it ~s you right! das geschieht dir recht! ~s two für zwei Personen □ vi dienen; (Tennis) aufschlagen

service /'sɜ:vɪs/ n Dienst m; (Relig) Gottesdienst m; (in shop, restaurant) Bedienung f; (transport) Verbindung f; (maintenance) Wartung f; (set of crockery) Service nt; (Tennis) Aufschlag m; ~s pl Dienstleistungen pl; (on motorway) Tankstelle und Raststätte f; in the ~s beim Militär; be of ~ nützlich sein; out of/in ~ (machine:) außer/ in Betrieb □ vt (Techn) warten. ~**able** /-əbl/ a nützlich; (durable) haltbar

service: ~ **area** n Tankstelle und Raststätte f. ~ **charge** n Bedienungszuschlag m. ~**man** n Soldat m. ~ **station** n Tankstelle f

serviette /sɜ:vɪ'et/ n Serviette f

servile /'sɜ:vaɪl/ a unterwürfig

session /'seʃn/ n Sitzung f; (Univ) Studienjahr nt

set /set/ n Satz m; (of crockery) Service nt; (of cutlery) Garnitur f; (TV, Radio) Apparat m; (Math) Menge f; (Theat) Bühnenbild nt; (Cinema) Szenenaufbau m; (of people) Kreis m; shampoo and ~ Waschen und Legen □ a (ready) fertig, bereit; (rigid) fest; (book) vorgeschrieben; be ~ on doing sth entschlossen sein, etw zu tun; be ~ in one's ways in seinen Gewohnheiten festgefahren sein □ v (pt/pp set, pres p setting) □ vt setzen; (adjust) einstellen; stellen (task, alarm clock); festsetzen, festlegen (date, limit); aufgeben (homework); zusammenstellen (questions); [ein]fassen (gem); einrichten (bone); legen (hair); decken (table) □ vi (sun:) untergehen; (become hard) fest werden; ~ about sth sich an etw (acc) machen; ~ about doing sth sich daranmachen, etw zu tun. ~ **back** vt zurücksetzen; (hold up) aufhalten; (fam: cost) kosten. ~ **off** vi losgehen; (in vehicle) losfahren □ vt auslösen (alarm); explodieren lassen (bomb). ~ **out** vi losgehen; (in vehicle) losfahren; ~ **out to** do sth sich vornehmen, etw zu tun □ vt auslegen; (state) darlegen. ~ **up** vt aufbauen; (fig) gründen

set 'meal n Menü nt

settee /se'ti:/ n Sofa nt, Couch f

setting /'setɪŋ/ n Rahmen m; (surroundings) Umgebung f; (of sun) Untergang m; (of jewel) Fassung f

settle /'setl/ vt (decide) entscheiden; (agree) regeln; (fix) festsetzen; (calm) beruhigen; (pay) bezahlen □ vi sich niederlassen; ⟨snow, dust:⟩ liegen bleiben; (subside) sich senken; ⟨sediment:⟩ sich absetzen. ~ down vi sich beruhigen; (permanently) sesshaft werden. ~ up vi abrechnen

settlement /'setlmənt/ n (see settle) Entscheidung f; Regelung f; Bezahlung f; (Jur) Vergleich m; (colony) Siedlung f

settler /'setlə(r)/ n Siedler m

'set-to n (fam) Streit m

'set-up n System nt

seven /'sevn/ a sieben. ~teen a siebzehn. ~teenth a siebzehnte(r,s)

seventh /'sevnθ/ a siebte(r,s)

seventieth /'sevntiθ/ a siebzigste(r,s)

seventy /'sevntɪ/ a siebzig

sever /'sevə(r)/ vt durchtrennen; abbrechen (relations)

several /'sevrl/ a & pron mehrere, einige

sever|e /sɪ'vɪə(r)/ a (-r, -st,) -ly adv streng; (pain) stark; (illness) schwer. ~ity /-'verətɪ/ n Strenge f; Schwere f

sew /səʊ/ vt/i (pt sewed, pp sewn or sewed) nähen. ~ up vt zunähen

sewage /'suːɪdʒ/ n Abwasser nt

sewer /'suːə(r)/ n Abwasserkanal m

sewing /'səʊɪŋ/ n Nähen nt; (work) Näharbeit f. ~ machine n Nähmaschine f

sewn /səʊn/ see sew

sex /seks/ n Geschlecht nt; (sexuality, intercourse) Sex m. ~ist a sexistisch. ~ offender n Triebverbrecher m

sexual /'seksjʊəl/ a, -ly adv sexuell. ~ 'intercourse n Geschlechtsverkehr m

sexuality /seksjʊ'ælətɪ/ n Sexualität f

sexy /'seksɪ/ a (-ier, -iest) sexy

shabby /'ʃæbɪ/ a (-ier, -iest), -ily adv schäbig

shack /ʃæk/ n Hütte f

shackles /'ʃæklz/ npl Fesseln pl

shade /ʃeɪd/ n Schatten m; (of colour) [Farb]ton m; (for lamp) [Lampen]schirm m; (Amer: window-blind) Jalousie f □ vt beschatten; (draw lines on) schattieren

shadow /'ʃædəʊ/ n Schatten m □ vt (follow) beschatten. ~y a schattenhaft

shady /'ʃeɪdɪ/ a (-ier, -iest) schattig; (fam: disreputable) zwielichtig

shaft /ʃɑːft/ n Schaft m; (Techn) Welle f; (of light) Strahl m; (of lift) Schacht m; ~s pl (of cart) Gabeldeichsel f

shaggy /'ʃægɪ/ a (-ier, -iest) zottig

shake /ʃeɪk/ n Schütteln nt □ v (pt shook, pp shaken) □ vt schütteln; (cause to tremble, shock) erschüttern; ~ hands with s.o. jdm die Hand geben □ vi wackeln; (tremble) zittern. ~ off vt abschütteln

shaky /'ʃeɪkɪ/ a (-ier, -iest) wackelig; ⟨hand, voice⟩ zittrig

shall /ʃæl/ v aux I ~ go ich werde gehen; we ~ see wir werden sehen; what ~ I do? was soll ich machen? I ~ come too, ~ I? ich komme mit, ja? thou shalt not kill (liter) du sollst nicht töten

shallow /'ʃæləʊ/ a (-er, -est) seicht; (dish) flach; (fig) oberflächlich

sham /ʃæm/ a unecht □ n Heuchelei f; (person) Heuchler(in) m(f) □ vt (pt/pp shammed) vortäuschen

shambles /'ʃæmblz/ n Durcheinander nt

shame /ʃeɪm/ n Scham f; (disgrace) Schande f; be a ~ schade sein; what a ~! wie schade! ~-faced a betreten

shame|ful /'ʃeɪmfl/ a, -ly adv schändlich. ~less a, -ly adv schamlos

shampoo /ʃæm'puː/ n Shampoo nt □ vt schamponieren

shandy /'ʃændɪ/ n Radler m

shan't /ʃɑːnt/ = shall not

shape /ʃeɪp/ n Form f; (figure) Gestalt f; take ~ Gestalt annehmen □ vt formen (into zu) □ vi ~ up sich entwickeln. ~less a formlos; (clothing) unförmig

shapely /'ʃeɪplɪ/ a (-ier, -iest) wohlgeformt

share /ʃeə(r)/ n [An]teil m; (Comm) Aktie f □ vt/i teilen. ~holder n Aktionär(in) m(f)

shark /ʃɑːk/ n Hai[fisch] m

sharp /ʃɑːp/ a (-er, -est), -ly adv scharf; (pointed) spitz; (severe) heftig; (sudden) steil; (alert) clever; (unscrupulous) gerissen □ adv scharf; (Mus) zu hoch; at six o'clock ~ Punkt sechs Uhr; look ~! beeil dich! □ n (Mus) Kreuz nt. ~en vt schärfen; [an]spitzen (pencil)

shatter /'ʃætə(r)/ vt zertrümmern; (fig) zerstören; be ~ed (person:) erschüttert sein; (fam: exhausted) kaputt sein □ vi zersplittern

shave /ʃeɪv/ n Rasur f; have a ~ sich rasieren □ vt rasieren □ vi sich rasieren. ~r n Rasierapparat m

shaving /'ʃeɪvɪŋ/ n Rasieren nt. ~-brush n Rasierpinsel m

shawl /ʃɔːl/ n Schultertuch nt

she /ʃiː/ pron sie

sheaf /ʃiːf/ n (pl sheaves) Garbe f; (of papers) Bündel nt shear /ʃɪə(r)/ vt (pt sheared, pp shorn or sheared) scheren

shears /ʃɪəz/ npl [große] Schere f

sheath /ʃiːθ/ n (pl ~s /ʃiːðz/) Scheide f

sheaves /ʃiːvz/ see sheaf

shed¹ /ʃed/ n Schuppen m; (for cattle) Stall m

shed² vt (pt/pp shed, pres p shedding) verlieren; vergießen ⟨blood, tears⟩; ~ light on Licht bringen in (+ acc)

sheen /ʃiːn/ n Glanz m

sheep /ʃiːp/ n inv Schaf nt. ~-dog n Hütehund m

sheepish /ˈʃiːpɪʃ/ a, -ly adv verlegen

'sheepskin n Schaffell nt

sheer /ʃɪə(r)/ a rein; (steep) steil; (transparent) hauchdünn □ adv steil

sheet /ʃiːt/ n Laken nt, Betttuch nt; (of paper) Blatt nt; (of glass, metal) Platte f

sheikh /ʃeɪk/ n Scheich m

shelf /ʃelf/ n (pl shelves) Brett nt, Bord nt; (set of shelves) Regal nt

shell /ʃel/ n Schale f; (of snail) Haus nt; (of tortoise) Panzer m; (on beach) Muschel f; (of unfinished building) Rohbau m; (Mil) Granate f □ vt pellen; enthülsen ⟨peas⟩; (Mil) [mit Granaten] beschießen. ~ out vi (fam) blechen

'shellfish n inv Schalentiere pl; (Culin) Meeresfrüchte pl

shelter /ˈʃeltə(r)/ n Schutz m; (air-raid ~) Luftschutzraum m □ vt schützen (from vor + dat) □ vi sich unterstellen. ~ed a geschützt; ⟨life⟩ behütet

shelve /ʃelv/ vt auf Eis legen; (abandon) aufgeben □ vi ⟨slope:⟩ abfallen

shelves /ʃelvz/ see shelf

shelving /ˈʃelvɪŋ/ n (shelves) Regale pl

shepherd /ˈʃepəd/ n Schäfer m; (Relig) Hirte m □ vt führen. ~ess n Schäferin f. ~'s pie n Auflauf m aus mit Kartoffelbrei bedecktem Hackfleisch

sherry /ˈʃerɪ/ n Sherry m

shield /ʃiːld/ n Schild m; (for eyes) Schirm m; (Techn & fig) Schutz m □ vt schützen (from vor + dat)

shift /ʃɪft/ n Verschiebung f; (at work) Schicht f; make ~ sich ⟨dat⟩ behelfen (with mit) □ vt rücken; (take away) wegnehmen; (rearrange) umstellen; schieben ⟨blame⟩ (on to auf + acc) □ vi sich verschieben; (fam: move quickly) rasen

'shift work n Schichtarbeit f

shifty /ˈʃɪftɪ/ a (-ier, -iest) (pej) verschlagen

shilly-shally /ˈʃɪlɪʃælɪ/ vi fackeln (fam)

shimmer /ˈʃɪmə(r)/ n Schimmer m □ vi schimmern

shin /ʃɪn/ n Schienbein nt

shine /ʃaɪn/ n Glanz m □ vi (pt/pp shone) □ vi leuchten; (reflect light) glänzen; ⟨sun:⟩ scheinen □ vt ~ a light on beleuchten

shingle /ˈʃɪŋgl/ n (pebbles) Kiesel pl

shingles /ˈʃɪŋglz/ n (Med) Gürtelrose f

shiny /ˈʃaɪnɪ/ a (-ier, -iest) glänzend

ship /ʃɪp/ n Schiff nt □ vt (pt/pp shipped) verschiffen

ship: ~building n Schiffbau m. ~ment n Sendung f. ~per n Spediteur m. ~ping n (traffic) Schifffahrt f. ~shape a & adv in Ordnung. ~wreck n Schiffbruch m. ~wrecked a schiffbrüchig. ~yard n Werft f

shirk /ʃɜːk/ vt sich drücken vor (+ dat). ~er n Drückeberger m

shirt /ʃɜːt/ n [Ober]hemd nt; (for woman) Hemdbluse f

shit /ʃɪt/ n (vulg) Scheiße f □ vi (pt/pp shit) (vulg) scheißen

shiver /ˈʃɪvə(r)/ n Schauder m □ vi zittern

shoal /ʃəʊl/ n (of fish) Schwarm m

shock /ʃɒk/ n Schock m; (Electr) Schlag m; (impact) Erschütterung f □ vt einen Schock versetzen (+ dat); (scandalize) schockieren. ~ing a schockierend; (fam: dreadful) fürchterlich

shod /ʃɒd/ see shoe

shoddy /ˈʃɒdɪ/ a (-ier, -iest) minderwertig

shoe /ʃuː/ n Schuh m; (of horse) Hufeisen nt □ vt (pt/pp shod, pres p shoeing) beschlagen ⟨horse⟩

shoe: ~horn n Schuhanzieher m. ~-lace n Schnürsenkel m. ~maker n Schuhmacher m. ~-string n on a ~string (fam) mit ganz wenig Geld

shone /ʃɒn/ see shine

shoo /ʃuː/ vt scheuchen □ int sch!

shook /ʃʊk/ see shake

shoot /ʃuːt/ n (Bot) Trieb m; (hunt) Jagd f □ v (pt/pp shot) □ vt schießen; (kill) erschießen; drehen ⟨film⟩ □ vi schießen. ~ down vt abschießen. ~ out vi (rush) herausschießen. ~ up vi (grow) in die Höhe schießen ⟨prices:⟩ schnellen

'shooting-range n Schießstand m

shop /ʃɒp/ n Laden m, Geschäft nt; (workshop) Werkstatt f; talk ~ (fam) fachsimpeln □ vi (pt/pp shopped, pres p shopping) einkaufen; go ~ping einkaufen gehen

shop: ~ assistant n Verkäufer(in) m(f). ~keeper n Ladenbesitzer(in) m(f). ~lifter n Ladendieb m. ~lifting n Ladendiebstahl m

shopping /ˈʃɒpɪŋ/ n Einkaufen nt; (articles) Einkäufe pl; do the ~ einkaufen. ~ bag n Einkaufstasche f ~ centre n

Einkaufszentrum *nt*. ~ trolley *n* Einkaufswagen *m*

shop: ~ 'steward *n* [gewerkschaftlicher] Vertrauensmann *m*. ~'window *n* Schaufenster *nt*

shore /ʃɔ:(r)/ *n* Strand *m*; (*of lake*) Ufer *nt*

shorn /ʃɔ:n/ *see* shear

short /ʃɔ:t/ *a* (-er, -est) kurz; (*person*) klein; (*curt*) schroff; a ~ time ago vor kurzem; be ~ of . . . zu wenig . . . haben; be in ~ supply knapp sein □ *adv* kurz; (*abruptly*) plötzlich; (*curtly*) kurz angebunden; in ~ kurzum; ~ of (*except*) außer; go ~ Mangel leiden; stop ~ of doing sth davor zurückschrecken, etw zu tun

shortage /ʃɔ:tɪdʒ/ *n* Mangel *m* (of an + *dat*); (*scarcity*) Knappheit *f*

short: ~bread *n* ≈ Mürbekekse *pl*. ~'circuit *n* Kurzschluss *m*. ~coming *n* Fehler *m*. ~ 'cut *n* Abkürzung *f*

shorten /ʃɔ:tn/ *vt* [ab]kürzen; kürzer machen (*garment*)

short: ~hand *n* Kurzschrift *f*, Stenographie *f*. ~'handed *a* be ~-handed zu wenig Personal haben. ~hand 'typist *n* Stenotypistin *f*. ~ list *n* engere Auswahl *f*. ~lived /-lɪvd/ *a* kurzlebig

shortly /ʃɔ:tlɪ/ *adv* in Kürze; ~ly before/after kurz vorher/danach. ~ness *n* Kürze *f*; (*of person*) Kleinheit *f*

shorts /ʃɔ:ts/ *npl* kurze Hose *f*, Shorts *pl*

short: ~-'sighted *a* kurzsichtig. ~sleeved *a* kurzärmelig. ~-'staffed *a* be ~-staffed zu wenig Personal haben. ~'story *n* Kurzgeschichte *f*. ~-'tempered *a* aufbrausend. ~-term *a* kurzfristig. ~wave *n* Kurzwelle *f*

shot /ʃɒt/ *see* shoot □ *n* Schuss *m*; (*pellets*) Schrot *m*; (*person*) Schütze *m*; (*Phot*) Aufnahme *f*; (*injection*) Spritze *f*; (*fam: attempt*) Versuch *m*; like a ~ (*fam*) sofort. ~gun *n* Schrotflinte *f*. ~-putting *n* (*Sport*) Kugelstoßen *nt*

should /ʃʊd/ *v aux* you ~ go du solltest gehen; I ~ have seen him ich hätte ihn sehen sollen; I ~ like to ich möchte; this ~ be enough das müsste eigentlich reichen; if he ~ be there falls er da sein sollte

shoulder /ʃəʊldə(r)/ *n* Schulter *f* □ *vt* schultern; (*fig*) auf sich (*acc*) nehmen. ~blade *n* Schulterblatt *nt*. ~-strap *n* Trägriemen *m*; (*on garment*) Träger *m*

shout /ʃaʊt/ *n* Schrei *m* □ *vt/i* schreien. ~ down *vt* niederschreien

shouting /ʃaʊtɪŋ/ *n* Geschrei *nt*

shove /ʃʌv/ *n* Stoß *m*; (*fam*) Schubs *m* □ *vt* stoßen; (*fam*) schubsen; (*fam: put*) tun □ *vi* drängeln. ~ off *vi* (*fam*) abhauen

shovel /ʃʌvl/ *n* Schaufel *f* □ *vt* (*pt/pp* shovelled) schaufeln

show /ʃəʊ/ *n* (*display*) Pracht *f*; (*exhibition*) Ausstellung *f*, Schau *f*; (*performance*) Vorstellung *f*; (*Theat, TV*) Show *f*; on ~ ausgestellt □ *v* (*pt* showed, *pp* shown) □ *vt* zeigen; (*put on display*) ausstellen; vorführen (*film*) □ *vi* sichtbar sein; (*film:*) gezeigt werden. ~ in *vt* hereinführen. ~ off *vi* (*fam*) angeben □ *vt* vorführen; (*flaunt*) angeben mit. ~ up *vi* [deutlich] zu sehen sein; (*fam: arrive*) auftauchen □ *vt* deutlich zeigen; (*fam: embarrass*) blamieren

'show-down *n* Entscheidungskampf *m*

shower /ʃaʊə(r)/ *n* Dusche *f*; (*of rain*) Schauer *m*; have a ~ duschen □ *vt* ~ with überschütten mit □ *vi* duschen. ~proof *a* regendicht. ~y *a* regnerisch

'show-jumping *n* Springreiten *nt*

shown /ʃəʊn/ *see* show

show: ~-off *n* Angeber(in) *m(f)*. ~-piece *n* Paradestück *nt*. ~-room *n* Ausstellungsraum *m*

showy /ʃəʊɪ/ *a* protzig

shrank /ʃræŋk/ *see* shrink

shred /ʃred/ *n* Fetzen *m*; (*fig*) Spur *f* □ *vt* (*pt/pp* shredded) zerkleinern; (*Culin*) schnitzeln. ~der *n* Reißwolf *m*; (*Culin*) Schnitzelwerk *nt*

shrewd /ʃru:d/ *a* (-er, -est), -ly *adv* klug. ~ness *n* Klugheit *f*

shriek /ʃri:k/ *n* Schrei *m* □ *vt/i* schreien

shrift /ʃrɪft/ *n* give s.o. short ~ jdn kurz abfertigen

shrill /ʃrɪl/ *a*, -y *adv* schrill

shrimp /ʃrɪmp/ *n* Garnele *f*, Krabbe *f*

shrine /ʃraɪn/ *n* Heiligtum *nt*

shrink /ʃrɪŋk/ *vi* (*pt* shrank, *pp* shrunk) schrumpfen; (*garment:*) einlaufen; (*draw back*) zurückschrecken (from vor + *dat*)

shrivel /ʃrɪvl/ *vi* (*pt/pp* shrivelled) verschrumpeln

shroud /ʃraʊd/ *n* Leichentuch *nt*; (*fig*) Schleier *m*

Shrove /ʃrəʊv/ *n* ~ 'Tuesday Fastnachtsdienstag *m*

shrub /ʃrʌb/ *n* Strauch *m*

shrug /ʃrʌg/ *n* Achselzucken *nt* □ *vt/i* (*pt/pp* shrugged) ~ [one's shoulders] die Achseln zucken

shrunk /ʃrʌŋk/ *see* shrink. ~en *a* geschrumpft

shudder /ʃʌdə(r)/ *n* Schauder *m* □ *vi* schaudern; (*tremble*) zittern

shuffle /ʃʌfl/ *vi* schlurfen □ *vt* mischen (*cards*)

shun /ʃʌn/ *vt* (*pt/pp* shunned) meiden

shunt /ʃʌnt/ *vt* rangieren

shush /ʃʊʃ/ *int* sch!

shut /ʃʌt/ v (pt/pp shut, pres p shutting)
□ vt zumachen, schließen; ~ one's finger
in the door sich (dat) den Finger in der
Tür einklemmen □ vi sich schließen;
⟨shop:⟩ schließen, zumachen. ~ down vt
schließen; stilllegen ⟨factory⟩ □ vi schließen; ⟨factory:⟩ stillgelegt werden. ~ up
vt abschließen; ⟨lock in⟩ einsperren □ vi
(fam) den Mund halten

'shut-down n Stilllegung f

shutter /'ʃʌtə(r)/ n [Fenster]laden m;
(Phot) Verschluss m

shuttle /'ʃʌtl/ n (Tex) Schiffchen nt □ vi
pendeln

shuttle: ~cock n Federball m. ~ service
n Pendelverkehr m

shy /ʃaɪ/ a (-er, -est), -ly adv schüchtern;
(timid) scheu □ vi (pt/pp shied) ⟨horse:⟩
scheuen. ~ness n Schüchternheit f

Siamese /saɪə'miːz/ a siamesisch

siblings /'sɪblɪŋz/ npl Geschwister pl

Sicily /'sɪsɪlɪ/ n Sizilien nt

sick /sɪk/ a krank; ⟨humour⟩ makaber; be
~ ⟨vomit⟩ sich übergeben; be ~ of sth
(fam) etw satt haben; I feel ~ mir ist
schlecht

sicken /'sɪkn/ vt anwidern □ vi be ~ing
for something krank werden

sickle /'sɪkl/ n Sichel f

sick|ly /'sɪklɪ/ a (-ier, -iest) kränklich.
~ness n Krankheit f; (vomiting) Erbrechen nt

'sick-room n Krankenzimmer nt

side /saɪd/ n Seite f; on the ~ (as sideline)
nebenbei; ~ by ~ nebeneinander; (fig)
Seite an Seite; take ~s Partei ergreifen
(with für); to be on the safe ~ vorsichts-
halber □ attrib Seiten- □ vi ~ with Partei
ergreifen für

side: ~board n Anrichte f. ~burns npl
Koteletten pl. ~effect n Nebenwirkung
f. ~lights npl Standlicht nt. ~line n Ne-
benbeschäftigung f. ~show n Nebenat-
traktion f. ~step vt ausweichen (+ dat).
~track vt ablenken. ~walk n (Amer)
Bürgersteig m. ~ways adv seitwärts

siding /'saɪdɪŋ/ n Abstellgleis nt

sidle /'saɪdl/ vi sich heranschleichen (up
to an + acc)

siege /siːdʒ/ n Belagerung f; (by police) Um-
stellung f

sieve /sɪv/ n Sieb nt □ vt sieben

sift /sɪft/ vt sieben; (fig) durchsehen

sigh /saɪ/ n Seufzer m □ vi seufzen

sight /saɪt/ n Sicht f; (faculty) Sehver-
mögen nt; (spectacle) Anblick m; (on gun)
Visier nt; ~s pl Sehenswürdigkeiten pl;
at first ~ auf den ersten Blick; within/
out of ~ in/außer Sicht; lose ~ of aus

dem Auge verlieren; know by ~ vom
Sehen kennen; have bad ~ schlechte
Augen haben □ vt sichten

'sightseeing n go ~ die Sehenswürdigkeiten besichtigen

sign /saɪn/ n Zeichen nt; (notice) Schild nt
□ vt/i unterschreiben; ⟨author, artist:⟩
signieren. ~ on vi (as unemployed) sich
arbeitslos melden; (Mil) sich verpflichten

signal /'sɪgnl/ n Signal nt □ vt/i (pt/pp sig-
nalled) signalisieren; ~ to s.o. jdm ein
Signal geben (to zu). ~-box n Stellwerk
nt

signature /'sɪgnətʃə(r)/ n Unterschrift f;
(of artist) Signatur f. ~ tune n Kennmelo-
die f

signet-ring /'sɪgnɪt-/ n Siegelring m

significan|ce /sɪg'nɪfɪkəns/ n Bedeutung
f. ~t a, -ly adv bedeutungsvoll; (important) bedeutend

signify /'sɪgnɪfaɪ/ vt (pt/pp -ied) bedeuten

signpost /'saɪn-/ n Wegweiser m

silence /'saɪləns/ n Stille f; (of person)
Schweigen nt □ vt zum Schweigen
bringen. ~r n (on gun) Schalldämpfer m;
(Auto) Auspufftopf m

silent /'saɪlənt/ a, -ly adv still; (without
speaking) schweigend; remain ~
schweigen. ~ film n Stummfilm m

silhouette /sɪlu:'et/ n Silhouette f; (picture) Schattenriss m □ vt be ~d sich als
Silhouette abheben

silicon /'sɪlɪkən/ n Silizium nt

silk /sɪlk/ n Seide f □ attrib Seiden-.
~worm n Seidenraupe f

silky /'sɪlkɪ/ a (-ier, -iest) seidig

sill /sɪl/ n Sims m & nt

silly /'sɪlɪ/ a (-ier, -iest) dumm, albern

silo /'saɪləʊ/ n Silo m

silt /sɪlt/ n Schlick m

silver /'sɪlvə(r)/ a silbern; ⟨coin, paper⟩
Silber- □ n Silber nt

silver: ~-plated a versilbert. ~ware n
Silber nt. ~ 'wedding n Silberhochzeit f

similar /'sɪmɪlə(r)/ a, -ly adv ähnlich.
~ity /-'lærətɪ/ n Ähnlichkeit f

simile /'sɪmɪlɪ/ n Vergleich m

simmer /'sɪmə(r)/ vi leise kochen, ziehen
□ vt ziehen lassen

simple /'sɪmpl/ a (-r, -st) einfach; ⟨person⟩
einfältig. ~-'minded a einfältig. ~ton
/'sɪmpltən/ n Einfaltspinsel m

simplicity /sɪm'plɪsətɪ/ n Einfachheit f

simpli|fication /sɪmplɪfɪ'keɪʃn/ n Ver-
einfachung f. ~fy /'sɪmplɪfaɪ/ vt (pt/
pp -ied) vereinfachen

simply /'sɪmplɪ/ adv einfach

simulat|e /'sɪmjʊleɪt/ *vt* vortäuschen; *(Techn)* simulieren. ∼ion /-'leɪʃn/ *n* Vortäuschung *f*; Simulation *f*

simultaneous /sɪml'teɪnɪəs/ *a*, **-ly** *adv* gleichzeitig; *(interpreting)* Simultan-

sin /sɪn/ *n* Sünde *f* □ *vi (pt/pp* sinned) sündigen

since /sɪns/ *prep* seit (+ *dat*) □ *adv* seitdem □ *conj* seit; *(because)* da

sincere /sɪn'sɪə(r)/ *a* aufrichtig; *(heartfelt)* herzlich. ∼ly *adv* aufrichtig; Yours ∼ly Mit freundlichen Grüßen

sincerity /sɪn'serətɪ/ *n* Aufrichtigkeit *f*

sinew /'sɪnju:/ *n* Sehne *f*

sinful /'sɪnfl/ *a* sündhaft

sing /sɪŋ/ *vt/i (pt* sang, *pp* sung) singen

singe /sɪndʒ/ *vt (pres p* singeing) versengen

singer /'sɪŋə(r)/ *n* Sänger(in) *m(f)*

single /'sɪŋgl/ *a* einzeln; *(one only)* einzig; *(unmarried)* ledig; *(ticket)* einfach; *(room, bed)* Einzel- □ *n (ticket)* einfache Fahrkarte *f*; *(record)* Single *f*; ∼s *pl (Tennis)* Einzel *nt* □ *vt* ∼ out auswählen

single: ∼-**breasted** *a* einreihig. ∼-**handed** *a & adv* allein. ∼-**minded** *a* zielstrebig. ∼ '**parent** *n* Alleinerziehende(r) *m/f*

singlet /'sɪŋglɪt/ *n* Unterhemd *nt*

singly /'sɪŋglɪ/ *adv* einzeln

singular /'sɪŋgjʊlə(r)/ *a* eigenartig; *(Gram)* im Singular □ *n* Singular *m*. ∼ly *adv* außerordentlich

sinister /'sɪnɪstə(r)/ *a* finster

sink /sɪŋk/ *n* Spülbecken *nt* □ *v (pt* sank, *pp* sunk) □ *vi* sinken □ *vt* versenken *⟨ship⟩*; senken *⟨shaft⟩*. ∼ **in** *vi* einsinken; *⟨fam: be understood⟩* kapiert werden

'**sink unit** *n* Spüle *f*

sinner /'sɪnə(r)/ *n* Sünder(in) *m(f)*

sinus /'saɪnəs/ *n* Nebenhöhle *f*

sip /sɪp/ *n* Schlückchen *nt* □ *vt (pt/pp* sipped) in kleinen Schlucken trinken

siphon /'saɪfn/ *n (bottle)* Siphon *m*. ∼ **off** *vt* mit einem Saugheber ablassen

sir /sɜ:(r)/ *n* mein Herr; S∼ *(title)* Sir; Dear S∼s Sehr geehrte Herren

siren /'saɪrən/ *n* Sirene *f*

sissy /'sɪsɪ/ *n* Waschlappen *m*

sister /'sɪstə(r)/ *n* Schwester *f*; *(nurse)* Oberschwester *f*. ∼-**in-law** *n (pl* ∼s-in-law) Schwägerin *f*. ∼ly *a* schwesterlich

sit /sɪt/ *v (pt/pp* sat, *pres p* sitting) □ *vi* sitzen; *(sit down)* sich setzen; *⟨committee:⟩* tagen □ *vt* setzen; machen *⟨exam⟩*. ∼ **back** *vi* sich zurücklehnen. ∼ **down** *vi* sich setzen. ∼ **up** *vi* [aufrecht] sitzen; *(rise)* sich aufsetzen; *(not slouch)* gerade sitzen; *(stay up)* aufbleiben

'**site** /saɪt/ *n* Gelände *nt*; *(for camping)* Platz *m*; *(Archaeol)* Stätte *f* □ *vt* legen

sitting /'sɪtɪŋ/ *n* Sitzung *f*; *(for meals)* Schub *m*

situat|e /'sɪtjʊeɪt/ *vt* legen; be ∼ed liegen. ∼ion /-'eɪʃn/ *n* Lage *f*; *(circumstances)* Situation *f*; *(job)* Stelle *f*

six /sɪks/ *a* sechs. ∼teen *a* sechzehn. ∼teenth *a* sechzehnte(r,s)

sixth /sɪksθ/ *a* sechste(r,s)

sixtieth /'sɪkstɪɪθ/ *a* sechzigste(r,s)

sixty /'sɪkstɪ/ *a* sechzig

size /saɪz/ *n* Größe *f* □ *vt* ∼ **up** *(fam)* taxieren

sizeable /'saɪzəbl/ *a* ziemlich groß

sizzle /'sɪzl/ *vi* brutzeln

skate[1] /skeɪt/ *n inv (fish)* Rochen *m*

skate[2] *n* Schlittschuh *m*; *(roller-)* Rollschuh *m* □ *vi* Schlittschuh/Rollschuh laufen. ∼r *n* Eisläufer(in) *m(f)*; Rollschuhläufer(in) *m(f)*

skating /'skeɪtɪŋ/ *n* Eislaufen *nt*. ∼-**rink** *n* Eisbahn *f*

skeleton /'skelɪtn/ *n* Skelett *nt*. ∼ '**key** *n* Dietrich *m*. ∼ '**staff** *n* Minimalbesetzung *f*

sketch /sketʃ/ *n* Skizze *f*; *(Theat)* Sketch *m* □ *vt* skizzieren

sketchy /'sketʃɪ/ *a* (-ier, -iest), **-ily** *adv* skizzenhaft

skew /skju:/ *n* on the ∼ schräg

skewer /'skjʊə(r)/ *n* [Brat]spieß *m*

ski /ski:/ *n* Ski *m* □ *vi (pt/pp* skied, *pres p* skiing) Ski fahren *or* laufen

skid /skɪd/ *n* Schleudern *nt* □ *vi (pt/pp* skidded) schleudern

skier /'ski:ə(r)/ *n* Skiläufer(in) *m(f)*

skiing /'ski:ɪŋ/ *n* Skilaufen *nt*

skilful /'skɪlfl/ *a*, **-ly** *adv* geschickt

skill /skɪl/ *n* Geschick *nt*. ∼ed *a* geschickt; *(trained)* ausgebildet

skim /skɪm/ *vt (pt/pp* skimmed) entrahmen *⟨milk⟩*. ∼ **off** *vt* abschöpfen. ∼ **through** *vt* überfliegen

skimp /skɪmp/ *vt* sparen an (+ *dat*)

skimpy /'skɪmpɪ/ *a* (-ier, -iest) knapp

skin /skɪn/ *n* Haut *f*; *(on fruit)* Schale *f* □ *vt (pt/pp* skinned) häuten; schälen *⟨fruit⟩*

skin: ∼-**deep** *a* oberflächlich. ∼-**diving** *n* Sporttauchen *nt*

skinflint /'skɪnflɪnt/ *n* Geizhals *m*

skinny /'skɪnɪ/ *a* (-ier, -iest) dünn

skip[1] /skɪp/ *n* Container *m*

skip[2] *n* Hüpfer *m* □ *v (pt/pp* skipped) *vi* hüpfen; *(with rope)* seilspringen □ *vt* überspringen

skipper /'skɪpə(r)/ *n* Kapitän *m*

'**skipping-rope** *n* Sprungseil *nt*

skirmish /'skɜ:mɪʃ/ n Gefecht nt

skirt /skɜ:t/ n Rock m ▪ vt herumgehen um

skit /skɪt/ n parodistischer Sketch m

skittle /'skɪtl/ n Kegel m

skive /skaɪv/ vi (fam) blaumachen

skulk /skʌlk/ vi lauern

skull /skʌl/ n Schädel m

skunk /skʌŋk/ n Stinktier nt

sky /skaɪ/ n Himmel m. ∼light n Dachluke f. ∼scraper n Wolkenkratzer m

slab /slæb/ n Platte f; (slice) Scheibe f; (of chocolate) Tafel f

slack /slæk/ a (-er, -est) schlaff, locker; (person) nachlässig; (Comm) flau ▪ vi bummeln

slacken /'slækn/ vi sich lockern; (diminish) nachlassen; (speed:) sich verringern ▪ vt lockern; (diminish) verringern

slacks /slæks/ npl Hose f

slag /slæg/ n Schlacke f

slain /sleɪn/ see slay

slake /sleɪk/ vt löschen

slam /slæm/ v (pt/pp slammed) ▪ vt zuschlagen; (put) knallen (fam); (fam: criticize) verreißen ▪ vi zuschlagen

slander /'slɑ:ndə(r)/ n Verleumdung f ▪ vt verleumden. ∼ous /-rəs/ a verleumderisch

slang /slæŋ/ n Slang m. ∼y a salopp

slant /slɑ:nt/ n Schräge f; on the ∼ schräg ▪ vt abschrägen; (fig) färben (report) ▪ vi sich neigen

slap /slæp/ n Schlag m ▪ vt (pt/pp slapped) schlagen; (put) knallen (fam) ▪ adv direkt

slap: ∼dash a (fam) schludrig. ∼-up a (fam) toll

slash /slæʃ/ n Schlitz m ▪ vt aufschlitzen; [drastisch] reduzieren (prices)

slat /slæt/ n Latte f

slate /sleɪt/ n Schiefer m ▪ vt (fam) heruntermachen; verreißen (performance)

slaughter /'slɔ:tə(r)/ n Schlachten nt; (massacre) Gemetzel nt ▪ vt schlachten; abschlachten. ∼house n Schlachthaus nt

Slav /slɑ:v/ a slawisch ▪ n Slawe m/ Slawin f

slave /sleɪv/ n Sklave m/ Sklavin f ▪ vi ∼ [away] schuften. ∼-driver n Leuteschinder m

slav|ery /'sleɪvərɪ/ n Sklaverei f. ∼ish a, -ly adv sklavisch

Slavonic /slə'vɒnɪk/ a slawisch

slay /sleɪ/ vt (pt slew, pp slain) ermorden

sleazy /'sli:zɪ/ a (-ier, -iest) schäbig

sledge /sledʒ/ n Schlitten m. ∼-hammer n Vorschlaghammer m

sleek /sli:k/ a (-er, -est) seidig; (well-fed) wohlgenährt

sleep /sli:p/ n Schlaf m; go to ∼ einschlafen; put to ∼ einschläfern ▪ v (pt/pp slept) ▪ vi schlafen ▪ vt (accommodate) Unterkunft bieten für. ∼er n Schläfer(in) m(f); (Rail) Schlafwagen m; (on track) Schwelle f

sleeping: ∼-bag n Schlafsack m. ∼-car n Schlafwagen m. ∼-pill n Schlaftablette f

sleep: ∼less a schlaflos. ∼-walking n Schlafwandeln nt

sleepy /'sli:pɪ/ a (-ier, -iest), -ily adv schläfrig

sleet /sli:t/ n Schneeregen m ▪ vi it is ∼ing es gibt Schneeregen

sleeve /sli:v/ n Ärmel m; (for record) Hülle f. ∼less a ärmellos

sleigh /sleɪ/ n [Pferde]schlitten m

sleight /slaɪt/ n ∼ of hand Taschenspielerei f

slender /'slendə(r)/ a schlank; (fig) gering

slept /slept/ see sleep

sleuth /slu:θ/ n Detektiv m

slew¹ /slu:/ vi schwenken

slew² see slay

slice /slaɪs/ n Scheibe f ▪ vt in Scheiben schneiden; ∼d bread Schnittbrot nt

slick /slɪk/ a clever ▪ n (of oil) Ölteppich m

slid|e /slaɪd/ n Rutschbahn f; (for hair) Spange f; (Phot) Dia nt ▪ v (pt/pp slid) ▪ vi rutschen ▪ vt schieben. ∼ing a gleitend; (door, seat) Schiebe-

slight /slaɪt/ a (-er, -est), -ly adv leicht; (importance) gering; (acquaintance) flüchtig; (slender) schlank; not in the ∼est nicht im Geringsten; ∼ly better ein bisschen besser ▪ vt kränken, beleidigen ▪ n Beleidigung f

slim /slɪm/ a (slimmer, slimmest) schlank; (volume) schmal; (fig) gering ▪ vi eine Schlankheitskur machen

slim|e /slaɪm/ n Schleim m. ∼y a schleimig

sling /slɪŋ/ n (Med) Schlinge f ▪ vt (pt/pp slung) (fam) schmeißen

slip /slɪp/ n (mistake) Fehler m, (fam) Patzer m; (petticoat) Unterrock m; (for pillow) Bezug m; (paper) Zettel m; give s.o. the ∼ (fam) jdm entwischen; ∼ of the tongue Versprecher m ▪ v (pt/pp slipped) ▪ vi rutschen; (fall) ausrutschen; (go quickly) schlüpfen; (decline) nachlassen ▪ vt schieben; ∼ s.o.'s mind jdm entfallen. ∼ away vi sich fortschleichen; (time:) verfliegen. ∼ up vi (fam) einen Schnitzer machen slipped 'disc n (Med) Bandscheiben-vorfall m

slipper /'slɪpə(r)/ n Hausschuh m

slippery /'slɪpərɪ/ a glitschig; ⟨surface⟩ glatt

slipshod /'slɪpʃɒd/ a schludrig

'slip-up n (fam) Schnitzer m

slit /slɪt/ n Schlitz m □ vt (pt/pp slit) aufschlitzen

slither /'slɪðə(r)/ vi rutschen

sliver /'slɪvə(r)/ n Splitter m

slobber /'slɒbə(r)/ vi sabbern

slog /slɒg/ n [hard] ~ Schinderei f □ v (pt/pp slogged) □ vi schuften □ vt schlagen

slogan /'sləʊgən/ n Schlagwort nt; ⟨advertising⟩ Werbespruch m

slop /slɒp/ v (pt/pp slopped) □ vt verschütten □ vi ~ over überschwappen. ~s npl Schmutzwasser nt

slop|e /sləʊp/ n Hang m; ⟨inclination⟩ Neigung f □ vi sich neigen. ~ing a schräg

sloppy /'slɒpɪ/ a (-ier, -iest) schludrig; ⟨sentimental⟩ sentimental

slosh /slɒʃ/ vi (fam) platschen; ⟨water:⟩ schwappen □ vt (fam: hit) schlagen

slot /slɒt/ n Schlitz m; (TV) Sendezeit f □ v (pt/pp slotted) □ vt einfügen □ vi sich einfügen (in in + acc)

sloth /sləʊθ/ n Trägheit f

'slot-machine n Münzautomat m; ⟨for gambling⟩ Spielautomat m

slouch /slaʊtʃ/ vi sich schlecht halten

slovenly /'slʌvnlɪ/ a schlampig

slow /sləʊ/ a (-er, -est), -ly adv langsam; be ~ ⟨clock:⟩ nachgehen; in ~ motion in Zeitlupe □ adv langsam □ vt verlangsamen □ vi ~ down, ~ up langsamer werden

slow: ~coach n (fam) Trödler m. ~ness n Langsamkeit f

sludge /slʌdʒ/ n Schlamm m

slug /slʌg/ n Nacktschnecke f

sluggish /'slʌgɪʃ/ a, -ly adv träge

sluice /sluːs/ n Schleuse f

slum /slʌm/ n ⟨house⟩ Elendsquartier nt; ~s pl Elendsviertel nt

slumber /'slʌmbə(r)/ n Schlummer m □ vi schlummern

slump /slʌmp/ n Sturz m □ vi fallen; ⟨crumple⟩ zusammensacken; ⟨prices:⟩ stürzen; ⟨sales:⟩ zurückgehen

slung /slʌŋ/ see sling

slur /slɜː(r)/ n ⟨discredit⟩ Schande f □ vt (pt/pp slurred) undeutlich sprechen

slurp /slɜːp/ vt/i schlürfen

slush /slʌʃ/ n [Schnee]matsch m; ⟨fig⟩ Kitsch m. ~ fund n Fonds m für Bestechungsgelder

slushy /'slʌʃɪ/ a matschig; ⟨sentimental⟩ kitschig

slut /slʌt/ n Schlampe f (fam)

sly /slaɪ/ a (-er, -est), -ly adv verschlagen □ n on the ~ heimlich

smack¹ /smæk/ n Schlag m, Klaps m □ vt schlagen; ~ one's lips mit den Lippen schmatzen □ adv (fam) direkt

smack² vi ~ of ⟨fig⟩ riechen nach

small /smɔːl/ a (-er, -est) klein; in the ~ hours in den frühen Morgenstunden □ adv chop up ~ klein hacken □ n ~ of the back Kreuz nt

small: ~ ads npl Kleinanzeigen pl. ~ 'change n Kleingeld nt. ~holding n landwirtschaftlicher Kleinbetrieb m. ~pox n Pocken pl. ~ talk n leichte Konversation f

smarmy /'smɑːmɪ/ a (-ier, -iest) (fam) ölig

smart /smɑːt/ a (-er, -est), -ly adv schick; ⟨clever⟩ schlau, clever; ⟨brisk⟩ flott; ⟨Amer fam: cheeky⟩ frech □ vi brennen

smarten /'smɑːtn/ vt ~ oneself up mehr auf sein Äußeres achten

smash /smæʃ/ n Krach m; ⟨collision⟩ Zusammenstoß m; ⟨Tennis⟩ Schmetterball m □ vt zerschlagen; ⟨strike⟩ schlagen; ⟨Tennis⟩ schmettern □ vi zerschmettern; ⟨crash⟩ krachen (into gegen). ~ing a (fam) toll

smattering /'smætərɪŋ/ n a ~ of German ein paar Brocken Deutsch

smear /smɪə(r)/ n verschmierter Fleck m; (Med) Abstrich m; ⟨fig⟩ Verleumdung f □ vt schmieren; ⟨coat⟩ beschmieren (with mit); ⟨fig⟩ verleumden □ vi schmieren

smell /smel/ n Geruch m; ⟨sense⟩ Geruchssinn m □ v (pt/pp smelt or smelled) □ vt riechen; ⟨sniff⟩ riechen an (+ dat) □ vi riechen (of nach)

smelly /'smelɪ/ a (-ier, -iest) übel riechend

smelt¹ /smelt/ see smell

smelt² vt schmelzen

smile /smaɪl/ n Lächeln nt □ vi lächeln; ~ at anlächeln

smirk /smɜːk/ vi feixen

smith /smɪθ/ n Schmied m

smithereens /smɪðə'riːnz/ npl smash to ~ in tausend Stücke springs

smitten /'smɪtn/ a ~ with sehr angetan von

smock /smɒk/ n Kittel m

smog /smɒg/ n Smog m

smoke /sməʊk/ n Rauch m □ vt/i rauchen; ⟨Culin⟩ räuchern. ~less a rauchfrei; ⟨fuel⟩ rauchlos smoker /'sməʊkə(r)/ n Raucher m; (Rail) Raucherabteil nt

'smoke-screen n [künstliche] Nebelwand f

smoking /'sməʊkɪŋ/ n Rauchen nt; 'no ~' 'Rauchen verboten'

smoky /'sməʊkɪ/ a (-ier, -iest) verraucht; ⟨taste⟩ rauchig

smooth /smuːð/ a (-er, -est), -ly adv glatt ▫ vt glätten. ~ out vt glatt streichen

smother /'smʌðə(r)/ vt ersticken; (cover) bedecken; (suppress) unterdrücken

smoulder /'sməʊldə(r)/ vi schwelen

smudge /smʌdʒ/ n Fleck m ▫ vt verwischen ▫ vi schmieren

smug /smʌg/ a (smugger, smuggest), -ly adv selbstgefällig

smuggl|e /'smʌgl/ vt schmuggeln. ~er n Schmuggler m. ~ing n Schmuggel m

smut /smʌt/ n Rußflocke f; (mark) Rußfleck m; (fig) Schmutz m

smutty /'smʌtɪ/ a (-ier, -iest) schmutzig

snack /snæk/ n Imbiss m. ~-bar n Imbissstube f

snag /snæg/ n Schwierigkeit f, (fam) Haken m

snail /sneɪl/ n Schnecke f; at a ~'s pace im Schneckentempo

snake /sneɪk/ n Schlange f

snap /snæp/ n Knacken nt; (photo) Schnappschuss m ▫ attrib (decision) plötzlich ▫ v (pt/pp snapped) ▫ vi [entzwei]brechen; ~ at (bite) schnappen nach; (speak sharply) [scharf] anfahren ▫ vt zerbrechen; (say) fauchen; (Phot) knipsen. ~ up vt wegschnappen

snappy /'snæpɪ/ a (-ier, -iest) bissig; (smart) flott; make it ~! ein bisschen schnell!

'snapshot n Schnappschuss m

snare /sneə(r)/ n Schlinge f

snarl /snɑːl/ vi [mit gefletschten Zähnen] knurren

snatch /snætʃ/ n (fragment) Fetzen pl; (theft) Raub m; make a ~ at greifen nach ▫ vt schnappen; (steal) klauen; entführen ⟨child⟩; ~ sth from s.o. jdm etw entreißen

sneak /sniːk/ n (fam) Petze f ▫ vi schleichen; (fam: tell tales) petzen ▫ vt (take) mitgehen lassen ▫ vi ~ in/out sich hinein-/hinausschleichen

sneakers /'sniːkəz/ npl (Amer) Turnschuhe pl

sneaking /'sniːkɪŋ/ a heimlich; (suspicion) leise

sneaky /'sniːkɪ/ a hinterhältig

sneer /snɪə(r)/ vi höhnisch lächeln; (mock) spotten

sneeze /sniːz/ n Niesen nt ▫ vi niesen

snide /snaɪd/ a (fam) abfällig

sniff /snɪf/ vi schnüffeln ▫ vt schnüffeln an (+ dat); schnüffeln (glue)

snigger /'snɪgə(r)/ vi [boshaft] kichern

snip /snɪp/ n Schnitt m; (fam: bargain) günstiger Kauf m ▫ vt/i ~ [at] schnippeln an (+ dat)

snipe /snaɪp/ vi ~ at aus dem Hinterhalt schießen auf (+ acc); (fig) anschießen. ~r n Heckenschütze m

snippet /'snɪpɪt/ n Schnipsel m; (of information) Bruchstück nt

snivel /'snɪvl/ vi (pt/pp snivelled) flennen

snob /snɒb/ n Snob m. ~bery n Snobismus m. ~bish a snobistisch

snoop /snuːp/ vi (fam) schnüffeln

snooty /'snuːtɪ/ a (fam) hochnäsig

snooze /snuːz/ n Nickerchen nt ▫ vi dösen

snore /snɔː(r)/ vi schnarchen

snorkel /'snɔːkl/ n Schnorchel m

snort /snɔːt/ vi schnauben

snout /snaʊt/ n Schnauze f

snow /snəʊ/ n Schnee m ▫ vi schneien; ~ed under with (fig) überhäuft mit

snow: ~ball n Schneeball m ▫ vi lawinenartig anwachsen. ~drift n Schneewehe f. ~drop n Schneeglöckchen nt. ~fall n Schneefall m. ~flake n Schneeflocke f. ~ flurry n Schneegestöber nt. ~man n Schneemann m. ~plough n Schneepflug m. ~storm n Schneesturm m

snub /snʌb/ n Abfuhr f ▫ vt (pt/pp snubbed) brüskieren

'snub-nosed a stupsnasig

snuff¹ /snʌf/ n Schnupftabak m

snuff² vt ~ [out] löschen

snuffle /'snʌfl/ vi schnüffeln

snug /snʌg/ a (snugger, snuggest) behaglich, gemütlich

snuggle /'snʌgl/ vi sich kuscheln (up to an + acc)

so /səʊ/ adv so; not so fast nicht so schnell; so am I ich auch; so does he er auch; so I see das sehe ich; that is so das stimmt; so much the better umso besser; so it is tatsächlich; if so wenn ja; so as to um zu; so long! (fam) tschüs! ▫ pron I hope so hoffentlich; I think so ich glaube schon; I told you so ich hab's dir gleich gesagt; because I say so weil ich es sage; I'm afraid so leider ja; so saying/doing, he/she . . . indem er/sie das sagte/tat, . . .; an hour or so eine Stunde oder so; very much so durchaus ▫ conj (therefore) also; so that damit; so there! fertig! so what! na und! so you see wie du siehst; so where have you been? wo warst du denn?

soak /səʊk/ vt nass machen; (steep) einweichen; (fam: fleece) schröpfen □ vi weichen; (liquid:) sickern. ~ up vt aufsaugen

soaking /ˈsəʊkɪŋ/ a & adv ~ [wet] patschnass (fam)

soap /səʊp/ n Seife f. ~ opera n Seifenoper f. ~ powder n Seifenpulver nt

soapy /ˈsəʊpɪ/ a (-ier, -iest) seifig

soar /sɔː(r)/ vi aufsteigen; (prices:) in die Höhe schnellen

sob /sɒb/ n Schluchzer m □ vi (pt/pp sobbed) schluchzen

sober /ˈsəʊbə(r)/ a, -ly adv nüchtern; (serious) ernst; (colour) gedeckt. ~ up vi nüchtern werden

'so-called a sogenannt

soccer /ˈsɒkə(r)/ n (fam) Fußball m

sociable /ˈsəʊʃəbl/ a gesellig

social /ˈsəʊʃl/ a gesellschaftlich; (Admin, Pol, Zool) sozial

socialis|m /ˈsəʊʃəlɪzm/ n Sozialismus m. ~t /-ɪst/ a sozialistisch □ n Sozialist m

socialize /ˈsəʊʃəlaɪz/ vi [gesellschaftlich] verkehren

socially /ˈsəʊʃəlɪ/ adv gesellschaftlich; know ~ privat kennen

social: ~ se'curity n Sozialhilfe f. ~ work n Sozialarbeit f. ~ worker n Sozialarbeiter(in) m(f)

society /səˈsaɪətɪ/ n Gesellschaft f; (club) Verein m

sociolog|ist /səʊsɪˈɒlədʒɪst/ n Soziologe m. ~y n Soziologie f

sock¹ /sɒk/ n Socke f; (knee-length) Kniestrumpf m

sock² n (fam) Schlag m □ vt (fam) hauen

socket /ˈsɒkɪt/ n (of eye) Augenhöhle f; (of joint) Gelenkpfanne f; (wall plug) Steckdose f; (for bulb) Fassung f

soda /ˈsəʊdə/ n Soda nt; (Amer) Limonade f. ~ water n Sodawasser nt

sodden /ˈsɒdn/ a durchnässt

sodium /ˈsəʊdɪəm/ n Natrium nt

sofa /ˈsəʊfə/ n Sofa nt. ~ bed n Schlafcouch f

soft /sɒft/ a (-er, -est), -ly adv weich; (quiet) leise; (gentle) sanft; (fam: silly) dumm; have a ~ spot for s.o. jdn mögen. ~ drink n alkoholfreies Getränk nt

soften /ˈsɒfn/ vt weich machen; (fig) mildern □ vi weich werden

soft: ~ toy n Stofftier nt. ~ware n Software f

soggy /ˈsɒgɪ/ a (-ier, -iest) aufgeweicht

soil¹ /sɔɪl/ n Erde f, Boden m

soil² vt verschmutzen

solace /ˈsɒləs/ n Trost m

solar /ˈsəʊlə(r)/ a Sonnen-

sold /səʊld/ see sell

solder /ˈsəʊldə(r)/ n Lötmetall nt □ vt löten

soldier /ˈsəʊldʒə(r)/ n Soldat m □ vi ~ on [unbeirrt] weitermachen

sole¹ /səʊl/ n Sohle f

sole² n (fish) Seezunge f

sole³ a einzig. ~ly adv einzig und allein

solemn /ˈsɒləm/ a, -ly adv feierlich; (serious) ernst. ~ity /səˈlemnətɪ/ n Feierlichkeit f; Ernst m

solicit /səˈlɪsɪt/ vt bitten um □ vi (prostitute:) sich an Männer heranmachen

solicitor /səˈlɪsɪtə(r)/ n Rechtsanwalt m /-anwältin f

solicitous /səˈlɪsɪtəs/ a besorgt

solid /ˈsɒlɪd/ a fest; (sturdy) stabil; (not hollow, of same substance) massiv; (unanimous) einstimmig; (complete) ganz □ n (Geom) Körper m; ~s pl (food) feste Nahrung f

solidarity /sɒlɪˈdærətɪ/ n Solidarität f

solidify /səˈlɪdɪfaɪ/ vi (pt/pp -ied) fest werden

soliloquy /səˈlɪləkwɪ/ n Selbstgespräch nt

solitary /ˈsɒlɪtərɪ/ a einsam; (sole) einzig. ~ con'finement n Einzelhaft f

solitude /ˈsɒlɪtjuːd/ n Einsamkeit f

solo /ˈsəʊləʊ/ n Solo nt □ a Solo-; (flight) Allein- □ adv solo. ~ist n Solist(in) m(f)

solstice /ˈsɒlstɪs/ n Sonnenwende f

soluble /ˈsɒljʊbl/ a löslich; (solvable) lösbar

solution /səˈluːʃn/ n Lösung f

solvable /ˈsɒlvəbl/ a lösbar

solve /sɒlv/ vt lösen

solvent /ˈsɒlvənt/ a zahlungsfähig; (Chem) lösend □ n Lösungsmittel nt

sombre /ˈsɒmbə(r)/ a dunkel; (mood) düster

some /sʌm/ a & pron etwas; (a little) ein bisschen; (with pl noun) einige; (a few) ein paar; (certain) manche(r,s); (one or the other) [irgend]ein; ~ day eines Tages; I want ~ ich möchte etwas/ (pl) welche; will you have ~ wine? möchten Sie Wein? I need ~ money/books ich brauche Geld/Bücher; do ~ shopping einkaufen

some: ~body /-bədɪ/ pron & n jemand; (emphatic) irgendjemand. ~how adv irgendwie. ~one pron & n = somebody

somersault /ˈsʌməsɔːlt/ n Purzelbaum m (fam); (Sport) Salto m; turn a ~ einen Purzelbaum schlagen/einen Salto springen

'something pron & adv etwas; (emphatic) irgendetwas; ~ different etwas anderes;

~ like so etwas wie; see ~ of s.o. jdn mal sehen

some: ~time *adv* irgendwann □ *a* ehemalig. ~times *adv* manchmal. ~what *adv* ziemlich. ~where *adv* irgendwo; (*go*) irgendwohin

son /sʌn/ *n* Sohn *m*

sonata /sə'nɑːtə/ *n* Sonate *f*

song /sɒŋ/ *n* Lied *nt*. ~bird *n* Singvogel *m*

sonic /'sɒnɪk/ *a* Schall-. ~ 'boom *n* Überschallknall *m*

'son-in-law *n* (*pl* ~s-in-law) Schwiegersohn *m*

soon /suːn/ *adv* (-er, -est) bald; (*quickly*) schnell; too ~ zu früh; as ~ as sobald; as ~ as possible so bald wie möglich; ~er or later früher oder später; no ~er had I arrived than ... kaum war ich angekommen, da ...; I would ~er stay ich würde lieber bleiben

soot /sʊt/ *n* Ruß *m*

soothe /suːð/ *vt* beruhigen; lindern (*pain*). ~ing *a*, -ly *adv* beruhigend; lindernd

sooty /'sʊtɪ/ *a* rußig

sop /sɒp/ *n* Beschwichtigungsmittel *nt*

sophisticated /sə'fɪstɪkeɪtɪd/ *a* weltgewandt; (*complex*) hoch entwickelt

soporific /sɒpə'rɪfɪk/ *a* einschläfernd

sopping /'sɒpɪŋ/ *a* & *adv* ~ [wet] durchnässt

soppy /'sɒpɪ/ *a* (-ier, -iest) (*fam*) rührselig

soprano /sə'prɑːnəʊ/ *n* Sopran *m*; (*woman*) Sopranistin *f*

sordid /'sɔːdɪd/ *a* schmutzig

sore /sɔː(r)/ *a* (-r, -st) wund; (*painful*) schmerzhaft; have a ~ throat Halsschmerzen haben □ *n* wunde Stelle *f*. ~ly *adv* sehr

sorrow /'sɒrəʊ/ *n* Kummer *m*, Leid *nt*. ~ful *a* traurig

sorry /'sɒrɪ/ *a* (-ier, -iest) (*sad*) traurig; (*wretched*) erbärmlich; I am ~ es tut mir Leid; she is *or* feels ~ for him er tut ihr Leid; I am ~ to say leider; ~! Entschuldigung!

sort /sɔːt/ *n* Art *f*; (*brand*) Sorte *f*; he's a good ~ (*fam*) er ist in Ordnung; be out of ~s (*fam*) nicht auf der Höhe sein □ *vt* sortieren. ~ out *vt* sortieren; (*fig*) klären

sought /sɔːt/ *see* seek

soul /səʊl/ *n* Seele *f*. ~ful *a* gefühlvoll

sound¹ /saʊnd/ *a* (-er, -est) gesund; (*sensible*) vernünftig; (*secure*) solide; (*thorough*) gründlich □ *adv* be ~ asleep fest schlafen

sound² *vt* (*Naut*) loten. ~ out *vt* (*fig*) aushorchen

sound³ *n* (*strait*) Meerenge *f*

sound⁴ *n* Laut *m*; (*noise*) Geräusch *nt*; (*Phys*) Schall *m*; (*Radio, TV*) Ton *m*; (*of bells, music*) Klang *m*; I don't like the ~ of it (*fam*) das hört sich nicht gut an □ *vi* [er]tönen; (*seem*) sich anhören □ *vt* (*pronounce*) aussprechen; schlagen (*alarm*); (*Med*) abhorchen (*chest*). ~ barrier *n* Schallmauer *f*. ~less *a*, -ly *adv* lautlos

soundly /'saʊndlɪ/ *adv* solide; (*sleep*) fest; (*defeat*) vernichtend

'soundproof *a* schalldicht

soup /suːp/ *n* Suppe *f*. ~ed-up *a* (*fam*) (*engine*) frisiert

soup: ~-plate *n* Suppenteller *m*. ~-spoon *n* Suppenlöffel *m*

sour /'saʊə(r)/ *a* (-er, -est) sauer; (*bad-tempered*) griesgrämig, verdrießlich

source /sɔːs/ *n* Quelle *f*

south /saʊθ/ *n* Süden *m*; to the ~ of südlich von □ *a* Süd-, süd- □ *adv* nach Süden

south: S~ 'Africa *n* Südafrika *nt*. S~ A'merica *n* Südamerika *nt*. ~-'east *n* Südosten *m*

southerly /'sʌðəlɪ/ *a* südlich

southern /'sʌðən/ *a* südlich

South 'Pole *n* Südpol *m*

'southward[s] /-wəd[z]/ *adv* nach Süden

souvenir /suːvə'nɪə(r)/ *n* Andenken *nt*, Souvenir *nt*

sovereign /'sɒvrɪn/ *a* souverän □ *n* Souverän *m*. ~ty *n* Souveränität *f*

Soviet /'səʊvɪət/ *a* sowjetisch; ~ Union Sowjetunion *f*

sow¹ /saʊ/ *n* Sau *f*

sow² /səʊ/ *vt* (*pt* sowed, *pp* sown *or* sowed) säen

soya /'sɔɪə/ *n* ~ bean Sojabohne *f*

spa /spɑː/ *n* Heilbad *nt*

space /speɪs/ *n* Raum *m*; (*gap*) Platz *m*; (*Astr*) Weltraum *m*; leave/clear a ~ Platz lassen/schaffen □ *vt* ~ [out] [in Abständen] verteilen

space: ~craft *n* Raumfahrzeug *nt*. ~ship *n* Raumschiff *nt*

spacious /'speɪʃəs/ *a* geräumig

spade /speɪd/ *n* Spaten *m*; (*for child*) Schaufel *f*; ~s *pl* (*Cards*) Pik *nt*; call a ~ a ~ das Kind beim rechten Namen nennen. ~work *n* Vorarbeit *f*

Spain /speɪn/ *n* Spanien *nt*

span¹ /spæn/ *n* Spanne *f*; (*of arch*) Spannweite *f* □ *vt* (*pt/pp* spanned) überspannen; umspannen (*time*)

span² *see* spick

Spaniard /'spænjəd/ *n* Spanier(in) *m*(*f*). ~ish *a* spanisch □ *n* (*Lang*) Spanisch *nt*; the ~ish *pl* die Spanier

spank /spæŋk/ *vt* verhauen

spanner /'spænə(r)/ n Schraubenschlüssel m

spar /spɑː(r)/ vi (pt/pp sparred) (Sport) sparren; (argue) sich zanken

spare /speə(r)/ a (surplus) übrig; (additional) zusätzlich; (seat, time) frei; (room) Gäste-; (bed, cup) Extra- □ n (part) Ersatzteil nt □ vt ersparen; (not hurt) verschonen; (do without) entbehren; (afford to give) erübrigen; to ~ (surplus) übrig. ~ 'wheel n Reserverad nt

sparing /'speərɪŋ/ a, -ly adv sparsam

spark /spɑːk/ n Funke m □ vt ~ off zünden; (fig) auslösen. ~ing-plug n (Auto) Zündkerze f

sparkl|e /'spɑːkl/ n Funkeln nt □ vi funkeln. ~ing a funkelnd; (wine) Schaum-

sparrow /'spærəʊ/ n Spatz m

sparse /spɑːs/ a spärlich. ~ly adv spärlich; (populated) dünn

Spartan /'spɑːtn/ a spartanisch

spasm /'spæzm/ n Anfall m; (cramp) Krampf m. ~odic /-'mɒdɪk/ a, -ally adv sporadisch; (Med) krampfartig

spastic /'spæstɪk/ a spastisch [gelähmt] □ n Spastiker(in) m(f)

spat /spæt/ see spit²

spate /speɪt/ n Flut f; (series) Serie f; be in full ~ Hochwasser führen

spatial /'speɪʃl/ a räumlich

spatter /'spætə(r)/ vt spritzen; ~ with bespritzen mit

spatula /'spætjʊlə/ n Spachtel m; (Med) Spatel m

spawn /spɔːn/ n Laich m □ vi laichen □ vt (fig) hervorbringen

spay /speɪ/ vt sterilisieren

speak /spiːk/ v (pt spoke, pp spoken) □ vi sprechen (to mit) ~ing! (Teleph) am Apparat! □ vt sprechen; sagen (truth). ~ up vi lauter sprechen; ~ up for oneself seine Meinung äußern

speaker /spiːkə(r)/ n Sprecher(in) m(f); (in public) Redner(in) m(f); (loudspeaker) Lautsprecher m

spear /spɪə(r)/ n Speer m □ vt aufspießen. ~head vt (fig) anführen

spec /spek/ n on ~ (fam) auf gut Glück

special /'speʃl/ a besondere(r,s), speziell. ~ist n Spezialist m; (Med) Facharzt m /-ärztin f. ~ity /-ʃi'ælətɪ/ n Spezialität f

special|ize /'speʃəlaɪz/ vi sich spezialisieren (in auf + acc). ~ly adv speziell; (particularly) besonders

species /'spiːʃiːz/ n Art f

specific /spə'sɪfɪk/ a bestimmt; (precise) genau; (Phys) spezifisch. ~ally adv ausdrücklich

specification /spesɪfɪ'keɪʃn/ n & ~s pl genaue Angaben pl

specify /'spesɪfaɪ/ vt (pt/pp -ied) [genau] angeben

specimen /'spesɪmən/ n Exemplar nt; (sample) Probe f; (of urine) Urinprobe f

speck /spek/ n Fleck m; (particle) Teilchen nt

speckled /'spekld/ a gesprenkelt

specs /speks/ npl (fam) Brille f

spectacle /'spektəkl/ n (show) Schauspiel nt; (sight) Anblick m. ~s npl Brille f

spectacular /spek'tækjʊlə(r)/ a spektakulär

spectator /spek'teɪtə(r)/ n Zuschauer(in) m(f)

spectre /'spektə(r)/ n Gespenst nt; (fig) Schreckgespenst nt

spectrum /'spektrəm/ n (pl -tra) Spektrum nt

speculat|e /'spekjʊleɪt/ vi spekulieren. ~ion /-'leɪʃn/ n Spekulation f. ~or n Spekulant m

sped /sped/ see speed

speech /spiːtʃ/ n Sprache f; (address) Rede f. ~less a sprachlos

speed /spiːd/ n Geschwindigkeit f; (rapidity) Schnelligkeit f; (gear) Gang m; at ~ mit hoher Geschwindigkeit □ vi (pt/pp sped) schnell fahren □ (pt/pp speeded) (go too fast) zu schnell fahren. ~ up (pt/pp speeded up) □ vt beschleunigen □ vi schneller werden; (vehicle:) schneller fahren

speed: ~boat n Rennboot nt. ~ing n Geschwindigkeitsüberschreitung f. ~ limit n Geschwindigkeitsbeschränkung f

speedometer /spiː'dɒmɪtə(r)/ n Tachometer m

speedy /'spiːdɪ/ a (-ier, -iest), -ily adv schnell

spell¹ /spel/ n Weile f; (of weather) Periode f

spell² v (pt/pp spelled or spelt) □ vt schreiben; (aloud) buchstabieren; (fig: mean) bedeuten □ vi richtig schreiben; (aloud) buchstabieren. ~ out vt buchstabieren; (fig) genau erklären

spell³ n Zauber m; (words) Zauberspruch m. ~bound a wie verzaubert

spelling /'spelɪŋ/ n Schreibweise f; (orthography) Rechtschreibung f

spelt /spelt/ see spell²

spend /spend/ vt/i (pt/pp spent) ausgeben; verbringen (time)

spent /spent/ see spend

sperm /spɜːm/ n Samen m

spew /spjuː/ vt speien

spher|e /ˈsfɪə(r)/ n Kugel f; (fig) Sphäre f.
~ical /ˈsferɪkl/ a kugelförmig

spice /spaɪs/ n Gewürz nt; (fig) Würze f

spick /spɪk/ a ~ and span blitzsauber

spicy /ˈspaɪsɪ/ a würzig, pikant

spider /ˈspaɪdə(r)/ n Spinne f

spik|e /spaɪk/ n Spitze f; (Bot, Zool) Stachel
m; (on shoe) Spike m. ~y a stachelig

spill /spɪl/ v (pt/pp spilt or spilled) □ vt
verschütten; vergießen ⟨blood⟩ □ vi überlaufen

spin /spɪn/ v (pt/pp spun, pres p spinning)
□ vt drehen; spinnen ⟨wool⟩; schleudern
⟨washing⟩ □ vi sich drehen. ~ out vt in
die Länge ziehen

spinach /ˈspɪnɪdʒ/ n Spinat m

spinal /ˈspaɪnl/ a Rückgrat-. ~ cord n Rü-
ckenmark nt

spindl|e /ˈspɪndl/ n Spindel f. ~y a spin-
deldürr

spin-ˈdrier n Wäscheschleuder f

spine /spaɪn/ n Rückgrat nt; (of book)
[Buch]rücken m; (Bot, Zool) Stachel m.
~less a (fig) rückgratlos

spinning /ˈspɪnɪŋ/ n Spinnen nt. ~-wheel
n Spinnrad nt

'spin-off n Nebenprodukt nt

spinster /ˈspɪnstə(r)/ n ledige Frau f

spiral /ˈspaɪrl/ a spiralig □ n Spirale f □ vi
(pt/pp spiralled) sich hochwinden;
⟨smoke:⟩ in einer Spirale aufsteigen. ~
ˈstaircase n Wendeltreppe f

spire /ˈspaɪə(r)/ n Turmspitze f

spirit /ˈspɪrɪt/ n Geist m; (courage) Mut m;
~s pl (alcohol) Spirituosen pl; in high
~s in gehobener Stimmung; in low ~s
niedergedrückt. ~ away vt verschwinden
lassen

spirited /ˈspɪrɪtɪd/ a lebhaft; (courageous)
beherzt

spirit: ~-level n Wasserwaage f. ~ stove
n Spirituskocher m

spiritual /ˈspɪrɪtjʊəl/ a geistig; (Relig)
geistlich. ~ism /-ɪzm/ n Spiritismus m.
~ist /-ɪst/ a spiritistisch □ n Spiritist m

spit¹ /spɪt/ n (for roasting) [Brat]spieß m

spit² /spɪt/ n Spucke f □ vt/i (pt/pp spat, pres
p spitting) spucken; ⟨cat:⟩ fauchen; ⟨fat:⟩
spritzen; it's ~ting with rain es tröpfelt;
be the ~ting image of s.o. jdm wie aus
dem Gesicht geschnitten sein

spite /spaɪt/ n Boshaftigkeit f; in ~ of twto
(+ gen) □ vt ärgern. ~ful a, -ly adv gehässig

spittle /ˈspɪtl/ n Spucke f

splash /splæʃ/ n Platschen nt; (fam: drop)
Schuss m; ~ of colour Farbfleck m □ vt

spritzen; ~ s.o. with sth jdn mit etw bespritzen □ vi spritzen. ~ about vi plan-
schen

spleen /spliːn/ n Milz f

splendid /ˈsplendɪd/ a herrlich, großartig

splendour /ˈsplendə(r)/ n Pracht f

splint /splɪnt/ n (Med) Schiene f

splinter /ˈsplɪntə(r)/ n Splitter m □ vi zersplittern

split /splɪt/ n Spaltung f; (Pol) Bruch m;
(tear) Riss m □ v (pt/pp split, pres p split-
ting) □ vt spalten; (share) teilen; (tear) zerreißen; ~ one's sides sich kaputtlachen
□ vi sich spalten; (tear) zerreißen; ~ on
s.o. (fam) jdn verpfeifen. ~ up vt aufteilen
□ vi ⟨couple:⟩ sich trennen

splutter /ˈsplʌtə(r)/ vi prusten

spoil /spɔɪl/ n ~s pl Beute f □ v (pt/pp
spoilt or spoiled) □ vt verderben; verwöhnen ⟨person⟩ □ vi verderben. ~sport
n Spielverderber m

spoke¹ /spəʊk/ n Speiche f

spoke², spoken /ˈspəʊkn/ see speak

'spokesman n Sprecher m

sponge /spʌndʒ/ n Schwamm m □ vt abwaschen □ vi ~ on schmarotzen bei. ~-
bag n Waschbeutel m. ~-cake n Biskuit-
kuchen m

spong|er /ˈspʌndʒə(r)/ n Schmarotzer m.
~y a schwammig

sponsor /ˈspɒnsə(r)/ n Sponsor m; (god-
parent) Pate m/Patin f; (for membership)
Bürge m □ vt sponsern; bürgen für

spontaneous /spɒnˈteɪnɪəs/ a, -ly adv
spontan

spoof /spuːf/ n (fam) Parodie f

spooky /ˈspuːkɪ/ a (-ier, -iest) (fam) ge-
spenstisch

spool /spuːl/ n Spule f

spoon /spuːn/ n Löffel m □ vt löffeln. ~-
feed vt (pt/pp -fed) (fig) alles vorkauen
(+ dat). ~ful n Löffel m

sporadic /spəˈrædɪk/ a, -ally adv sporadisch

sport /spɔːt/ n Sport m; (amusement) Spaß
m □ vt [stolz] tragen. ~ing a sportlich; a
~ing chance eine faire Chance

sports: ~car n Sportwagen m. ~ coat n,
~ jacket n Sakko m. ~man n Sportler m.
~woman n Sportlerin f

sporty /ˈspɔːtɪ/ a (-ier, -iest) sportlich

spot /spɒt/ n Fleck m; (place) Stelle f; (dot)
Punkt m; (drop) Tropfen m; (pimple) Pickel m; ~s pl (rash) Ausschlag m; a ~
of (fam) ein bisschen; on the ~ auf der
Stelle; be in a tight ~ (fam) in der
Klemme sitzen □ vt (pt/pp spotted) entdecken

spot: ~ 'check n Stichprobe f. ~less a makellos; (fam: very clean) blitzsauber. ~light n Scheinwerfer m; (fig) Rampenlicht nt

spotted /'spɒtɪd/ a gepunktet

spotty /'spɒtɪ/ a (-ier, -iest) fleckig; (pimply) pickelig

spouse /spauz/ n Gatte m/Gattin f

spout /spaut/ n Schnabel m, Tülle f □ vi schießen (from aus)

sprain /spreɪn/ n Verstauchung f □ vt verstauchen

sprang /spræŋ/ see spring²

sprat /spræt/ n Sprotte f

sprawl /sprɔːl/ vi sich ausstrecken; (fall) der Länge nach hinfallen

spray¹ /spreɪ/ n (of flowers) Strauß m

spray² n Sprühnebel m; (from sea) Gischt m; (device) Spritze f; (container) Sprühdose f; (preparation) Spray m □ vt spritzen; (with aerosol) sprühen

spread /spred/ n Verbreitung f; (paste) Aufstrich m; (fam: feast) Festessen nt □ v (pt/pp spread) □ vt ausbreiten; streichen (butter, jam); bestreichen (bread, surface); streuen (sand, manure); verbreiten (news, disease); verteilen (payments) □ vi sich ausbreiten. ~ out vt ausbreiten; (space out) verteilen □ vi sich verteilen

spree /spriː/ n (fam) go on a shopping ~ groß einkaufen gehen

sprig /sprɪg/ n Zweig m

sprightly /'spraɪtlɪ/ a (-ier, -iest) rüstig

spring¹ /sprɪŋ/ n Frühling m □ attrib Frühlings-

spring² n (jump) Sprung m; (water) Quelle f; (device) Feder f; (elasticity) Elastizität f □ v (pt sprang, pp sprung) □ vi springen; (arise) entspringen (from dat) □ vt ~ sth on s.o. jdn mit etw überfallen

spring: ~board n Sprungbrett nt. ~-'cleaning n Frühjahrsputz m. ~time n Frühling m

sprinkl|e /'sprɪŋkl/ vt sprengen; (scatter) streuen; bestreuen (surface). ~er n Sprinkler m; (Hort) Sprenger m. ~ing n dünne Schicht f

sprint /sprɪnt/ n Sprint m □ vi rennen; (Sport) sprinten. ~er n Kurzstreckenläufer(in) m(f)

sprout /spraut/ n Trieb m; [Brussels] ~s pl Rosenkohl m □ vi sprießen

spruce /spruːs/ a gepflegt □ n Fichte f

sprung /sprʌŋ/ see spring² □ a gefedert

spry /spraɪ/ a (-er, -est) rüstig

spud /spʌd/ n (fam) Kartoffel f

spun /spʌn/ see spin

spur /spɜː(r)/ n Sporn m; (stimulus) Ansporn m; (road) Nebenstraße f; on the ~ of the moment ganz spontan □ vt (pt/pp spurred) ~ [on] (fig) anspornen

spurious /'spjʊərɪəs/ a, -ly adv falsch

spurn /spɜːn/ vt verschmähen

spurt /spɜːt/ n Strahl m; (Sport) Spurt m; put on a ~ spurten □ vi spritzen

spy /spaɪ/ n Spion(in) m(f) □ vi spionieren; ~ on s.o. jdm nachspionieren □ vt (fam: see) sehen. ~ out vt auskundschaften

spying /'spaɪɪŋ/ n Spionage f

squabble /'skwɒbl/ n Zank m □ vi sich zanken

squad /skwɒd/ n Gruppe f; (Sport) Mannschaft f

squadron /'skwɒdrən/ n (Mil) Geschwader nt

squalid /'skwɒlɪd/ a, -ly adv schmutzig

squall /skwɔːl/ n Bö f □ vi brüllen

squalor /'skwɒlə(r)/ n Schmutz m

squander /'skwɒndə(r)/ vt vergeuden

square /skweə(r)/ a quadratisch; (metre, mile) Quadrat-; (meal) anständig; all ~ (fam) quitt □ n Quadrat nt; (area) Platz m; (on chessboard) Feld nt □ vt (settle) klären; (Math) quadrieren □ vi (agree) übereinstimmen

squash /skwɒʃ/ n Gedränge nt; (drink) Fruchtsaftgetränk nt; (Sport) Squash nt □ vt zerquetschen; (suppress) niederschlagen. ~y a weich

squat /skwɒt/ a gedrungen □ n (fam) besetztes Haus nt □ vi (pt/pp squatted) hocken; ~ in a house ein Haus besetzen. ~ter n Hausbesetzer m

squawk /skwɔːk/ vi krächzen

squeak /skwiːk/ n Quieken nt; (of hinge, brakes) Quietschen nt □ vi quieken; quietschen

squeal /skwiːl/ n Schrei m; (screech) Kreischen nt □ vi schreien; kreischen

squeamish /'skwiːmɪʃ/ a empfindlich

squeeze /skwiːz/ n Druck m; (crush) Gedränge nt □ vt drücken; (to get juice) ausdrücken; (force) zwängen; (fam: extort) herauspressen (from aus) □ vi ~ in/out sich hinein-/hinauszwängen

squelch /skweltʃ/ vi quatschen

squid /skwɪd/ n Tintenfisch m

squiggle /'skwɪgl/ n Schnörkel m

squint /skwɪnt/ n Schielen nt □ vi schielen

squire /'skwaɪə(r)/ n Gutsherr m

squirm /skwɜːm/ vi sich winden

squirrel /'skwɪrl/ n Eichhörnchen nt

squirt /skwɜːt/ n Spritzer m □ vt/i spritzen

St abbr (Saint) St.; (Street) Str.

stab /stæb/ n Stich m; (fam: attempt) Versuch m □ vt (pt/pp stabbed) stechen; (to death) erstechen stability /stə'bɪlətɪ/ n Stabilität f

stabilize /'steɪbɪlaɪz/ vt stabilisieren □ vi sich stabilisieren

stable¹ /'steɪbl/ a (-r, -st) stabil

stable² n Stall m; (establishment) Reitstall m

stack /stæk/ n Stapel m; (of chimney) Schornstein m; (fam: large quantity) Haufen m □ vt stapeln

stadium /'steɪdɪəm/ n Stadion nt

staff /stɑːf/ n (stick & Mil) Stab m □ (& pl) (employees) Personal nt; (Sch) Lehrkräfte pl □ vt mit Personal besetzen. ~room n (Sch) Lehrerzimmer nt

stag /stæg/ n Hirsch m

stage /steɪdʒ/ n Bühne f; (in journey) Etappe f; (in process) Stadium nt; by or in ~s in Etappen □ vt aufführen; (arrange) veranstalten

stage: ~ door n Bühneneingang m. ~ fright n Lampenfieber nt

stagger /'stægə(r)/ vi taumeln □ vt staffeln (holidays); versetzt anordnen (seats); I was ~ed es hat mir die Sprache verschlagen. ~ing a unglaublich

stagnant /'stægnənt/ a stehend; (fig) stagnierend

stagnat|e /'stægneɪt/ vi (fig) stagnieren. ~ion /-'neɪʃn/ n Stagnation f

staid /steɪd/ a gesetzt

stain /steɪn/ n Fleck m; (for wood) Beize f □ vt färben; beizen (wood); (fig) beflecken; ~ed glass farbiges Glas nt. ~less a fleckenlos; (steel) rostfrei. ~ remover n Fleckentferner m

stair /steə(r)/ n Stufe f; ~s pl Treppe f. ~case n Treppe f

stake /steɪk/ n Pfahl m; (wager) Einsatz m; (Comm) Anteil m; be at ~ auf dem Spiel stehen □ vt [an einem Pfahl] anbinden; (wager) setzen; ~ a claim to sth Anspruch auf etw (acc) erheben

stale /steɪl/ a (-r, -st) alt; (air) verbraucht. ~mate n Patt nt

stalk¹ /stɔːk/ n Stiel m, Stängel m

stalk² vt pirschen auf (+ acc) □ vi stolzieren

stall /stɔːl/ n Stand m; ~s pl (Theat) Parkett nt □ vi (engine:) stehen bleiben; (fig) ausweichen □ vt abwürgen (engine)

stallion /'stæljən/ n Hengst m

stalwart /'stɔːlwət/ a treu □ n treuer Anhänger m

stamina /'stæmɪnə/ n Ausdauer f

stammer /'stæmə(r)/ n Stottern nt □ vt/i stottern

stamp /stæmp/ n Stempel m; (postage ~) [Brief]marke f □ vt stempeln; (impress) prägen; (put postage on) frankieren; ~

one's feet mit den Füßen stampfen □ vi stampfen. ~ out vt [aus]stanzen; (fig) ausmerzen

stampede /stæm'piːd/ n wilde Flucht f; (fam) Ansturm m □ vi in Panik fliehen

stance /stɑːns/ n Haltung f

stand /stænd/ n Stand m; (rack) Ständer m; (pedestal) Sockel m; (Sport) Tribüne f; (fig) Einstellung f □ v (pt/pp stood) □ vi stehen; (rise) aufstehen; (be candidate) kandidieren; (stay valid) gültig bleiben; ~ still stillstehen; ~ firm (fig) festbleiben; ~ together zusammenhalten; ~ to lose/ gain gewinnen/verlieren können; ~ to reason logisch sein; ~ in for vertreten; ~ for (mean) bedeuten; I won't ~ for that das lasse ich mir nicht bieten □ vt stellen; (withstand) standhalten (+ dat); (endure) ertragen, vertragen (climate); (put up with) aushalten; haben (chance); ~ one's ground nicht nachgeben; ~ the test of time sich bewähren; ~ s.o. a beer jdm ein Bier spendieren; I can't ~ her (fam) ich kann sie nicht ausstehen. ~ by vi daneben stehen; (be ready) sich bereithalten □ vt by s.o. (fig) zu jdm stehen. ~ down vi (retire) zurücktreten. ~ out vi hervorstehen; (fig) herausragen. ~ up vi aufstehen; ~ up for eintreten für; ~ up to sich wehren gegen

standard /'stændəd/ a Normal-; be ~ practice allgemein üblich sein □ n Maßstab m; (Techn) Norm f; (level) Niveau nt; (flag) Standarte f; ~s pl (morals) Prinzipien pl; ~ of living Lebensstandard m. ~ize vt standardisieren; (Techn) normen

'standard lamp n Stehlampe f

'stand-in n Ersatz m

standing /'stændɪŋ/ a (erect) stehend; (permanent) ständig □ n Rang m; (duration) Dauer f. ~ 'order n Dauerauftrag m. ~room n Stehplätze pl

stand: ~-offish /stænd'ɒfɪʃ/ a distanziert. ~point n Standpunkt m. ~still n Stillstand m; come to a ~still zum Stillstand kommen

stank /stæŋk/ see stink

staple¹ /'steɪpl/ a Grund- □ n (product) Haupterzeugnis nt

staple² n Heftklammer f □ vt heften. ~r n Heftmaschine f

star /stɑː(r)/ n Stern m; (asterisk) Sternchen nt; (Theat, Sport) Star m □ vi (pt/pp starred) die Hauptrolle spielen

starboard /'stɑːbəd/ n Steuerbord nt

starch /stɑːtʃ/ n Stärke f □ vt stärken. ~y a stärkehaltig; (fig) steif

stare /steə(r)/ n Starren nt □ vi starren; ~ at anstarren

'starfish n Seestern m

stark /stɑːk/ a (-er, -est) scharf; ⟨contrast⟩ krass □ adv ~ naked splitternackt

starling /'stɑːlɪŋ/ n Star m

'starlit a sternhell

starry /'stɑːrɪ/ a sternklar

start /stɑːt/ n Anfang m, Beginn m; ⟨departure⟩ Aufbruch m; ⟨Sport⟩ Start m; from the ~ von Anfang an; for a ~ erstens □ vi anfangen, beginnen; ⟨set out⟩ aufbrechen; ⟨engine:⟩ anspringen; ⟨Auto, Sport⟩ starten; ⟨jump⟩ aufschrecken; to ~ with zuerst □ vt anfangen, beginnen; ⟨cause⟩ verursachen; ⟨found⟩ gründen; starten ⟨car, race⟩; in Umlauf setzen ⟨rumour⟩. ~er n ⟨Culin⟩ Vorspeise f; ⟨Auto, Sport⟩ Starter m. ~ing-point n Ausgangspunkt m

startle /'stɑːtl/ vt erschrecken

starvation /stɑːˈveɪʃn/ n Verhungern nt

starve /stɑːv/ vi hungern; ⟨to death⟩ verhungern □ vt verhungern lassen

stash /stæʃ/ vt ⟨fam⟩ ~ [away] beiseite schaffen

state /steɪt/ n Zustand m; ⟨grand style⟩ Prunk m; ⟨Pol⟩ Staat m; ~ of play Spielstand m; be in a ~ ⟨person:⟩ aufgeregt sein; lie in ~ feierlich aufgebahrt sein □ attrib Staats-, staatlich □ vt erklären; ⟨specify⟩ angeben. ~-aided a staatlich gefördert. ~less a staatenlos

stately /'steɪtlɪ/ a (-ier, -iest) stattlich. ~ 'home n Schloss nt

statement /'steɪtmənt/ n Erklärung f; ⟨Jur⟩ Aussage f; ⟨Banking⟩ Auszug m

'statesman n Staatsmann m

static /'stætɪk/ a statisch; remain ~ unverändert bleiben

station /'steɪʃn/ n Bahnhof m; ⟨police⟩ Wache f; ⟨radio⟩ Sender m; ⟨space, weather⟩ Station f; ⟨Mil⟩ Posten m; ⟨status⟩ Rang m □ vt stationieren; ⟨post⟩ postieren. ~ary /-ərɪ/ a stehend; be ~ary stehen

stationer /'steɪʃənə(r)/ n ~'s [shop] Schreibwarengeschäft nt. ~y n Briefpapier nt; ⟨writing-materials⟩ Schreibwaren pl

'station-wagon n ⟨Amer⟩ Kombi[wagen] n

statistic /stəˈtɪstɪk/ n statistische Tatsache f. ~al a, -ly adv statistisch. ~s n & pl Statistik f

statue /'stætjuː/ n Statue f

stature /'stætʃə(r)/ n Statur f; ⟨fig⟩ Format nt

status /'steɪtəs/ n Status m, Rang m. ~ symbol n Statussymbol m

statut|e /'stætjuːt/ n Statut nt. ~ory a gesetzlich

staunch /stɔːntʃ/ a (-er, -est), -ly adv treu

stave /steɪv/ vt ~ off abwenden

stay /steɪ/ n Aufenthalt m □ vi bleiben; ⟨reside⟩ wohnen; ~ the night übernachten; ~ put dableiben □ vt ~ the course durchhalten. ~ away vi wegbleiben. ~ behind vi zurückbleiben. ~ in vi zu Hause bleiben; ⟨Sch⟩ nachsitzen. ~ up vi oben bleiben; ⟨upright⟩ stehen bleiben; ⟨on wall⟩ hängen bleiben; ⟨person:⟩ aufbleiben

stead /sted/ n in his ~ an seiner Stelle; stand s.o. in good ~ jdm zustatten kommen. ~fast a, -ly adv standhaft

steadily /'stedɪlɪ/ adv fest; ⟨continually⟩ stetig

steady /'stedɪ/ a (-ier, -iest) fest; ⟨not wobbly⟩ stabil; ⟨hand⟩ ruhig; ⟨regular⟩ regelmäßig; ⟨dependable⟩ zuverlässig

steak /steɪk/ n Steak nt

steal /stiːl/ vt/i ⟨pt stole, pp stolen⟩ stehlen ⟨from dat⟩. ~ in/out vi sich hinein-/hinausstehlen

stealth /stelθ/ n Heimlichkeit f; by ~ heimlich. ~y a heimlich

steam /stiːm/ n Dampf m; under one's own ~ ⟨fam⟩ aus eigener Kraft □ vt ⟨Culin⟩ dämpfen, dünsten □ vi dampfen. ~ up vi beschlagen

'steam-engine n Dampfmaschine f; ⟨Rail⟩ Dampflokomotive f

steamer /'stiːmə(r)/ n Dampfer m

'steamroller n Dampfwalze f

steamy /'stiːmɪ/ a dampfig

steel /stiːl/ n Stahl m □ vt ~ oneself allen Mut zusammennehmen

steep¹ /stiːp/ vt ⟨soak⟩ einweichen

steep² a, -ly adv steil; ⟨fam: exorbitant⟩ gesalzen

steeple /'stiːpl/ n Kirchturm m. ~chase n Hindernisrennen nt

steer /stɪə(r)/ vt/i steuern; ~ clear of s.o./sth jdm/ etw aus dem Weg gehen. ~ing n ⟨Auto⟩ Steuerung f. ~ing-wheel n Lenkrad nt

stem¹ /stem/ n Stiel m; ⟨of word⟩ Stamm m □ vi ⟨pt/pp stemmed⟩ ~ from zurückzuführen sein auf (+ acc)

stem² vt ⟨pt/pp stemmed⟩ eindämmen; stillen ⟨bleeding⟩

stench /stentʃ/ n Gestank m

stencil /'stensl/ n Schablone f; ⟨for typing⟩ Matrize f

step /step/ n Schritt m; ⟨stair⟩ Stufe f; ~s pl ⟨ladder⟩ Trittleiter f; in ~ im Schritt; ~ by ~ Schritt für Schritt; take ~s ⟨fig⟩ Schritte unternehmen □ vi ⟨pt/pp stepped⟩ treten; ~ in ⟨fig⟩ eingreifen; ~ into s.o.'s shoes an jds Stelle treten; ~ out of line aus der Reihe tanzen. ~ up *vi* hinaufsteigen □ *vt* (*increase*) erhöhen, steigern; verstärken (*efforts*)

step: ∼**brother** *n* Stiefbruder *m*. ∼**child** *n* Stiefkind *nt*. ∼**daughter** *n* Stieftochter *f*. ∼**father** *n* Stiefvater *m*. ∼ **ladder** *n* Trittleiter *f*. ∼**mother** *n* Stiefmutter *f*

'**stepping-stone** *n* Trittstein *m*; (*fig*) Sprungbrett *nt*

step: ∼**sister** *n* Stiefschwester *f*. ∼**son** *n* Stiefsohn *m*

stereo /'steriəʊ/ *n* Stereo *nt*; (*equipment*) Stereoanlage *f*; **in** ∼ **stereo**. ∼**phonic** /-'fɒnɪk/ *a* stereophon

stereotype /'steriətaɪp/ *n* stereotype Figur *f*. ∼**d** *a* stereotyp

steril|e /'steraɪl/ *a* steril. ∼**ity** /stə'rɪlətɪ/ *n* Sterilität *f*

steriliz|ation /sterəlaɪ'zeɪʃn/ *n* Sterilisation *f*. ∼**e** *vt* sterilisieren

sterling /'stɜːlɪŋ/ *a* Sterling-; (*fig*) gediegen □ *n* Sterling *m*

stern[1] /stɜːn/ *a* (-er, -est), -ly *adv* streng

stern[2] *n* (*of boat*) Heck *nt*

stew /stjuː/ *n* Eintopf *m*; **in a** ∼ (*fam*) aufgeregt □ *vt/i* schmoren; ∼**ed fruit** Kompott *nt*

steward /'stjuːəd/ *n* Ordner *m*; (*on ship, aircraft*) Steward *m*. ∼**ess** *n* Stewardess *f*

stick[1] /stɪk/ *n* Stock *m*; (*of chalk*) Stück *nt*; (*of rhubarb*) Stange *f*; (*Sport*) Schläger *m*

stick[2] *v* (*pt/pp* stuck) □ *vt* stecken; (*stab*) stechen; (*glue*) kleben; (*fam: put*) tun; (*fam: endure*) aushalten □ *vi* stecken; (*adhere*) kleben, haften (**to** an + *dat*); (*jam*) klemmen; ∼ **to sth** (*fig*) bei etw bleiben; ∼ **at it** (*fam*) dranbleiben; ∼ **at nothing** (*fam*) vor nichts zurückschrecken; ∼ **up for** (*fam*) eintreten für; **be stuck** nicht weiterkönnen; (*vehicle:*) festsitzen, festgefahren sein; (*drawer:*) klemmen; **be stuck with sth** (*fam*) etw am Hals haben. ∼ **out** *vi* abstehen; (*project*) vorstehen □ *vt* (*fam*) hinausstrecken; herausstrecken (*tongue*)

sticker /'stɪkə(r)/ *n* Aufkleber *m*

'**sticking plaster** *n* Heftpflaster *nt*

stickler /'stɪklə(r)/ *n* **be a** ∼ **for** es sehr genau nehmen mit

sticky /'stɪkɪ/ *a* (-ier, -iest) klebrig; (*adhesive*) Klebe-

stiff /stɪf/ *a* (-er, -est), -ly *adv* steif; (*brush*) hart; (*dough*) fest; (*difficult*) schwierig; (*penalty*) schwer; **be bored** ∼ (*fam*) sich zu Tode langweilen. ∼**en** *vt* steif machen □ *vi* steif werden. ∼**ness** *n* Steifheit *f*

stifle /'staɪfl/ *vt* ersticken; (*fig*) unterdrücken. ∼**ing** *a* **be** ∼**ing** zum Ersticken sein

stigma /'stɪgmə/ *n* Stigma *nt*

stile /staɪl/ *n* Zauntritt *m*

stiletto /stɪ'letəʊ/ *n* Stilett *nt*; (*heel*) Bleistiftabsatz *m*

still[1] /stɪl/ *n* Destillierapparat *m*

still[2] *a* still; (*drink*) ohne Kohlensäure; **keep** ∼ stillhalten; **stand** ∼ stillstehen □ *n* Stille *f* □ *adv* noch; (*emphatic*) immer noch; (*nevertheless*) trotzdem; ∼ **not** immer noch nicht

'**stillborn** *a* tot geboren

still 'life *n* Stillleben *nt*

stilted /'stɪltɪd/ *a* gestelzt, geschraubt

stilts /stɪlts/ *npl* Stelzen *pl*

stimulant /'stɪmjʊlənt/ *n* Anregungsmittel *nt*

stimulat|e /'stɪmjʊleɪt/ *vt* anregen. ∼**ion** /-'leɪʃn/ *n* Anregung *f*

stimulus /'stɪmjʊləs/ *n* (*pl* -**li** /-laɪ/) Reiz *m*

sting /stɪŋ/ *n* Stich *m*; (*from nettle, jellyfish*) Brennen *nt*; (*organ*) Stachel *m* □ *v* (*pt/pp* stung) □ *vt* stechen; (*insect:*) stechen. ∼**ing nettle** *n* Brennnessel *f*

stingy /'stɪndʒɪ/ *a* (-ier, -iest) geizig, (*fam*) knauserig

stink /stɪŋk/ *n* Gestank *m* □ *vi* (*pt* stank, *pp* stunk) stinken (**of** nach)

stint /stɪnt/ *n* Pensum *nt* □ *vi* ∼ **on** sparen an (+ *dat*)

stipulat|e /'stɪpjʊleɪt/ *vt* vorschreiben. ∼**ion** /-'leɪʃn/ *n* Bedingung *f*

stir /stɜː(r)/ *n* (*commotion*) Aufregung *f* □ *v* (*pt/pp* stirred) *vt* rühren □ *vi* sich rühren

stirrup /'stɪrəp/ *n* Steigbügel *m*

stitch /stɪtʃ/ *n* Stich *m*; (*Knitting*) Masche *f*; (*pain*) Seitenstechen *nt*; **be in** ∼**es** (*fam*) sich kaputtlachen □ *vt* nähen

stoat /stəʊt/ *n* Hermelin *nt*

stock /stɒk/ *n* Vorrat *m* (**of** an + *dat*); (*in shop*) [Waren]bestand *m*; (*livestock*) Vieh *nt*; (*lineage*) Abstammung *f*; (*Finance*) Wertpapiere *pl*; (*Culin*) Brühe *f*; (*plant*) Levkoje *f*; **in**/**out of** ∼ vorrätig/nicht vorrätig; **take** ∼ (*fig*) Bilanz ziehen □ *a* Standard- □ *vt* (*shop:*) führen; auffüllen (*shelves*). ∼ **up** *vi* sich eindecken (**with** mit)

stock: ∼**broker** *n* Börsenmakler *m*. ∼ **cube** *n* Brühwürfel *m*. **S∼ Exchange** *n* Börse *f*

stocking /'stɒkɪŋ/ *n* Strumpf *m*

stockist /'stɒkɪst/ *n* Händler *m*

stock: ∼**market** *n* Börse *f*. ∼**pile** *vt* horten; anhäufen (*weapons*). ∼-'**still** *a* bewegungslos. **∼taking** *n* (*Comm*) Inventur *f*

stocky /'stɒkɪ/ *a* (-ier, -iest) untersetzt

stodgy /'stɒdʒɪ/ *a* pappig [und schwer verdaulich]

stoical /'stəʊɪkl/ a, -ly adv stoisch

stoke /stəʊk/ vt heizen

stole[1] /stəʊl/ n Stola f

stole[2], **stolen** /'stəʊlən/ see steal

stolid /'stɒlɪd/ a, -ly adv stur

stomach /'stʌmək/ n Magen m ם vt vertragen. ~ache n Magenschmerzen pl

stone /stəʊn/ n Stein m; (weight) 6,35kg ם a steinern; ⟨wall, Age⟩ Stein- ם vt mit Steinen bewerfen; entsteinen ⟨fruit⟩. ~-cold a eiskalt. ~-'deaf n (fam) stocktaub

stony /'stəʊnɪ/ a steinig

stood /stʊd/ see stand

stool /stuːl/ n Hocker m

stoop /stuːp/ n walk with a ~ gebeugt gehen ם vi sich bücken; (fig) sich erniedrigen

stop /stɒp/ n Halt m; (break) Pause f; (for bus) Haltestelle f; (for train) Station f; (Gram) Punkt m; (on organ) Register nt; come to a ~ stehen bleiben; put a ~ to sth etw unterbinden ם v (pt/pp stopped) ם vt anhalten, stoppen; (switch off) abstellen; (plug, block) zustopfen; (prevent) verhindern; ~ s.o. doing sth jdn daran hindern, etw zu tun; ~ doing sth aufhören, etw zu tun; ~ that! hör auf damit! lass das sein! ם vi anhalten; (cease) aufhören; ⟨clock:⟩ stehen bleiben; (fam: stay) bleiben (with bei) ם int halt! stopp!

stop: ~gap n Notlösung f. ~over n Zwischenaufenthalt m; (Aviat) Zwischenlandung f

stoppage /'stɒpɪdʒ/ n Unterbrechung f; (strike) Streik m; (deduction) Abzug m

stopper /'stɒpə(r)/ n Stöpsel m

stop: ~-press n letzte Meldungen pl. ~watch n Stoppuhr f

storage /'stɔːrɪdʒ/ n Aufbewahrung f; (in warehouse) Lagerung f; (Computing) Speicherung f

store /stɔː(r)/ n (stock) Vorrat m; (shop) Laden m; (department ~) Kaufhaus nt; (depot) Lager nt; in ~ auf Lager m; put in ~ lagern; set great ~ by großen Wert legen auf (+ acc); be in ~ for s.o. (fig) jdm bevorstehen ם vt aufbewahren; (in warehouse) lagern; (Computing) speichern. ~room n Lagerraum m

storey /'stɔːrɪ/ n Stockwerk nt

stork /stɔːk/ n Storch m

storm /stɔːm/ n Sturm m; (with thunder) Gewitter nt ם vt/i stürmen. ~y a stürmisch

story /'stɔːrɪ/ n Geschichte f; (in newspaper) Artikel m; (fam: lie) Märchen nt

stout /staʊt/ a (-er, -est) beleibt; (strong) fest

stove /stəʊv/ n Ofen m; (for cooking) Herd m

stow /stəʊ/ vt verstauen. ~away n blinder Passagier m

straddle /'strædl/ vt rittlings sitzen auf (+ dat); (standing) mit gespreizten Beinen stehen über (dat)

straggl|e /'strægl/ vi hinterherhinken. ~er n Nachzügler m. ~y a strähnig

straight /streɪt/ a (-er, -est) gerade; (direct) direkt; (clear) klar; (hair) glatt; (drink) pur; be ~ (tidy) in Ordnung sein ם adv gerade; (directly) direkt, geradewegs; (clearly) klar; ~ away sofort; ~ on or ahead geradeaus; ~ out (fig) geradeheraus; go ~ (fam) ein ehrliches Leben führen; put sth ~ etw in Ordnung bringen; sit/stand up ~ gerade sitzen/ stehen

straighten /'streɪtn/ vt gerade machen; (put straight) gerade richten ם vi gerade werden; ~ [up] ⟨person:⟩ sich aufrichten. ~ out vt gerade biegen

straight'forward a offen; (simple) einfach

strain[1] /'streɪn/ n Rasse f; (Bot) Sorte f; (of virus) Art f

strain[2] n Belastung f; ~s pl (of music) Klänge pl ם vt belasten; (overexert) überanstrengen; (injure) zerren ⟨muscle⟩; (Culin) durchseihen; abgießen ⟨vegetables⟩ ם vi sich anstrengen. ~ed a ⟨relations⟩ gespannt. ~er n Sieb nt

strait /streɪt/ n Meerenge f; in dire ~s in großen Nöten. ~-jacket n Zwangsjacke f. ~-'laced a puritanisch

strand[1] /strænd/ n (of thread) Faden m; (of beads) Kette f; (of hair) Strähne f

strand[2] vt be ~ed festsitzen

strange /streɪndʒ/ a (-r, -st) fremd; (odd) seltsam, merkwürdig. ~r n Fremde(r) m/f

strangely /'streɪndʒlɪ/ adv seltsam, merkwürdig; ~ enough seltsamerweise

strangle /'stræŋgl/ vt erwürgen; (fig) unterdrücken

strangulation /stræŋgjʊ'leɪʃn/ n Erwürgen nt

strap /stræp/ n Riemen m; (for safety) Gurt m; (to grasp in vehicle) Halteriemen m; (of watch) Armband nt; (shoulder-) Träger m ם vt (pt/pp strapped) schnallen; ~ in or down festschnallen

strapping /'stræpɪŋ/ a stramm

strata /'strɑːtə/ npl see stratum

stratagem /'strætədʒəm/ n Kriegslist f

strategic /strə'tiːdʒɪk/ a, -ally adv strategisch

strategy /'strætədʒɪ/ n Strategie f

stratum /'strɑːtəm/ n (pl strata) Schicht f

straw /strɔː/ n Stroh nt; (single piece, drinking) Strohhalm m; that's the last ~ jetzt reicht's aber

strawberry /'strɔːbəri/ n Erdbeere f

stray /streɪ/ a streunend ⃟ n streunendes Tier nt ⃟ vi sich verirren; (deviate) abweichen

streak /striːk/ n Streifen m; (in hair) Strähne f; (fig: trait) Zug m ⃟ vi flitzen. ~y a streifig; (bacon) durchwachsen

stream /striːm/ n Bach m; (flow) Strom m; (current) Strömung f; (Sch) Parallelzug m ⃟ vi strömen; ~ in/out hinaus-/herausströmen

streamer /'striːmə(r)/ n Luftschlange f; (flag) Wimpel m

'streamline vt (fig) rationalisieren. ~d a stromlinienförmig

street /striːt/ n Straße f. ~car n (Amer) Straßenbahn f. ~lamp n Straßenlaterne f

strength /streŋθ/ n Stärke f; (power) Kraft f; on the ~ of auf Grund (+ gen). ~en vt stärken; (reinforce) verstärken

strenuous /'strenjʊəs/ a anstrengend

stress /stres/ n (emphasis) Betonung f; (strain) Belastung f; (mental) Stress m ⃟ vt betonen; (put a strain on) belasten. ~ful a stressig (fam)

stretch /stretʃ/ n (of road) Strecke f; (elasticity) Elastizität f; at a ~ ohne Unterbrechung; a long ~ eine lange Zeit; have a ~ sich strecken ⃟ vt strecken; (widen) dehnen; (spread) ausbreiten; fordern (person); ~ one's legs sich (dat) die Beine vertreten ⃟ vi sich erstrecken; (become wider) sich dehnen; (person:) sich strecken. ~er n Tragbahre f

strew /struː/ vt (pp strewn or strewed) streuen

stricken /'strɪkn/ a betroffen; ~ with heimgesucht von

strict /strɪkt/ a (-er, -est), -ly adv streng; ~ly speaking streng genommen

stride /straɪd/ n [großer] Schritt m; make great ~s (fig) große Fortschritte machen; take sth in one's ~ mit etw gut fertig werden ⃟ vi (pt strode, pp stridden) [mit großen Schritten] gehen

strident /'straɪdnt/ a, -ly adv schrill; (colour) grell

strife /straɪf/ n Streit m

strike /straɪk/ n Streik m; (Mil) Angriff m; be on ~ streiken ⃟ v (pt/pp struck) ⃟ vt schlagen; (knock against, collide with) treffen; prägen (coin); anzünden (match); stoßen auf (+ acc) (oil, gold); abbrechen (camp); (delete) streichen; (impress)

beeindrucken; (occur to) einfallen (+ dat); (Mil) angreifen; ~ s.o. a blow jdm einen Schlag versetzen ⃟ vi treffen; (lightning:) einschlagen; (clock:) schlagen; (attack) ⃟ vi schlagen; (workers:) streiken; ~ lucky Glück haben. ~breaker n Streikbrecher m

striker /'straɪkə(r)/ n Streikende(r) m/f

striking /'straɪkɪŋ/ a auffallend

string /strɪŋ/ n Schnur f; (thin) Bindfaden m; (of musical instrument, racket) Saite f; (of bow) Sehne f; (of pearls) Kette f; the ~s (Mus) die Streicher pl; pull ~s (fam) seine Beziehungen spielen lassen, Fäden ziehen ⃟ vt (pt/pp strung) (thread) aufziehen (beads). ~ed a (Mus) Saiten-; (played with bow) Streich-

stringent /'strɪndʒnt/ a streng

strip /strɪp/ n Streifen m ⃟ v (pt/pp stripped) ⃟ vt ablösen; ausziehen (clothes); abziehen (bed); abbeizen (wood, furniture); auseinander nehmen (machine); (deprive) berauben (of gen); ~ sth off sth etw von etw entfernen ⃟ vi (undress) sich ausziehen. ~ club n Stripteaselokal nt

stripe /straɪp/ n Streifen m. ~d a gestreift

'striplight n Neonröhre f

stripper /'strɪpə(r)/ n Stripperin f; (male) Stripper m

strip-'tease n Striptease m

strive /straɪv/ vi (pt strove, pp striven) sich bemühen (to zu); ~ for streben nach

strode /strəʊd/ see stride

stroke[1] /strəʊk/ n Schlag m; (of pen) Strich m; (Swimming) Zug m; (style) Stil m; (Med) Schlaganfall m; ~ of luck Glücksfall m; put s.o. off his ~ jdn aus dem Konzept bringen

stroke[2] ⃟ vt streicheln

stroll /strəʊl/ n Spaziergang m, (fam) Bummel m ⃟ vi spazieren, (fam) bummeln. ~er n (Amer: push-chair) [Kinder]-sportwagen m

strong /strɒŋ/ a (-er /-ɡə(r)/, -est /-ɡɪst/), -ly adv stark; (powerful, healthy) kräftig; (severe) streng; (sturdy) stabil; (convincing) gut

strong: ~box n Geldkassette f. ~hold n Festung f; (fig) Hochburg f. ~-'minded a willensstark. ~room n Tresorraum m

stroppy /'strɒpi/ a widerspenstig

strove /strəʊv/ see strive

struck /strʌk/ see strike

structural /'strʌktʃərl/ a, -ly adv baulich

structure /'strʌktʃə(r)/ n Struktur f; (building) Bau m

struggle /'strʌgl/ n Kampf m; with a ~ mit Mühe ⃟ vt kämpfen; ~ for breath nach Atem ringen; ~ to do sth sich abmühen, etw zu tun; ~ to one's feet mühsam aufstehen

strum /strʌm/ v (pt/pp strummed) □ vt klimpern auf (+ dat) □ vi klimpern

strung /strʌŋ/ see string

strut[1] /strʌt/ n Strebe f

strut[2] vi (pt/pp strutted) stolzieren

stub /stʌb/ n Stummel m; (counterfoil) Abschnitt m □ vt (pt/pp stubbed) ~ one's toe sich (dat) den Zeh stoßen (on an + dat). ~ out vt ausdrücken ⟨cigarette⟩

stubb|le /'stʌbl/ n Stoppeln pl. ~ly a stoppelig

stubborn /'stʌbən/ a, -ly adv starrsinnig; ⟨refusal⟩ hartnäckig

stubby /'stʌbɪ/ a, (-ier, -iest) kurz und dick

stucco /'stʌkəʊ/ n Stuck m

stuck /stʌk/ see stick[2]. ~-'up a (fam) hochnäsig

stud[1] /stʌd/ n Nagel m; (on clothes) Niete f; (for collar) Kragenknopf m; (for ear) Ohrstecker m

stud[2] n (of horses) Gestüt nt

student /'stju:dnt/ n Student(in) m(f); (Sch) Schüler(in) m(f). ~ nurse n Lernschwester f

studied /'stʌdɪd/ a gewollt

studio /'stju:dɪəʊ/ n Studio nt; (for artist) Atelier nt

studious /'stju:dɪəs/ a lerneifrig; ⟨earnest⟩ ernsthaft

stud|y /'stʌdɪ/ n Studie f; (room) Studierzimmer nt; (investigation) Untersuchung f; ~ies pl Studium nt □ v (pt/pp studied) □ vt studieren; (examine) untersuchen □ vi lernen; (at university) studieren

stuff /stʌf/ n Stoff m; (fam: things) Zeug nt □ vt vollstopfen; (with padding, Culin) füllen; ausstopfen ⟨animal⟩; ~ sth into sth etw in etw (acc) [hinein]stopfen. ~ing n Füllung f

stuffy /'stʌfɪ/ a (-ier, -iest) stickig; (oldfashioned) spießig

stumb|le /'stʌmbl/ vi stolpern; ~e across zufällig stoßen auf (+ acc). ~ing-block n Hindernis nt

stump /stʌmp/ n Stumpf m □ ~ up vt/i (fam) blechen. ~ed a (fam) überfragt

stun /stʌn/ vt (pt/pp stunned) betäuben; ~ned by ⟨fig⟩ wie betäubt von

stung /stʌŋ/ see sting

stunk /stʌŋk/ see stink

stunning /'stʌnɪŋ/ a (fam) toll

stunt[1] /stʌnt/ n (fam) Kunststück m

stunt[2] vt hemmen. ~ed a verkümmert

stupendous /stju:'pendəs/ a, -ly adv enorm

stupid /'stju:pɪd/ a dumm. ~ity /-'pɪdətɪ/ n Dummheit f. ~ly adv dumm; ~ly [enough] dummerweise

stupour /'stju:pə(r)/ n Benommenheit f

sturdy /'stɜ:dɪ/ a (-ier, -iest) stämmig; ⟨furniture⟩ stabil; ⟨shoes⟩ fest

stutter /'stʌtə(r)/ n Stottern nt □ vt/i stottern

sty[1] /staɪ/ n (pl sties) Schweinestall m

sty[2], stye n (pl styes) (Med) Gerstenkorn nt

style /staɪl/ n Stil m; (fashion) Mode f; (sort) Art f; (hair~) Frisur f; in ~ in großem Stil

stylish /'staɪlɪʃ/ a, -ly adv stilvoll

stylist /'staɪlɪst/ n Friseur m/ Friseuse f. ~ic /-'lɪstɪk/ a, -ally adv stilistisch

stylized /'staɪlaɪzd/ a stilisiert

stylus /'staɪləs/ n (on record-player) Nadel f

suave /swɑ:v/ a (pej) gewandt

sub'conscious /sʌb-/ a, -ly adv unterbewusst □ n Unterbewusstsein nt

subcon'tract vt [vertraglich] weitervergeben (to an + acc)

'**subdivi|de** vt unterteilen. ~sion n Unterteilung f

subdue /səb'dju:/ vt unterwerfen; (make quieter) beruhigen. ~d a gedämpft; ⟨person⟩ still

subject[1] /'sʌbdʒɪkt/ a be ~ to sth etw (dat) unterworfen sein □ n Staatsbürger(in) m(f); (of ruler) Untertan m; (theme) Thema nt; (of investigation) Gegenstand m; (Sch) Fach nt; (Gram) Subjekt nt

subject[2] /səb'dʒekt/ vt unterwerfen (to dat); (expose) aussetzen (to dat)

subjective /səb'dʒektɪv/ a, -ly adv subjektiv

subjugate /'sʌbdʒʊgeɪt/ vt unterjochen

subjunctive /səb'dʒʌŋktɪv/ n Konjunktiv m

sub'let vt (pt/pp -let) untervermieten

sublime /sə'blaɪm/ a, -ly adv erhaben

subliminal /sʌ'blɪmɪnl/ a unterschwellig

sub-ma'chine-gun n Maschinenpistole f

subma'rine n Unterseeboot nt

submerge /səb'mɜ:dʒ/ vt untertauchen; be ~d unter Wasser stehen □ vi untertauchen

submiss|ion /səb'mɪʃn/ n Unterwerfung f. ~ive /-sɪv/ a gehorsam; (pej) unterwürfig

submit /səb'mɪt/ v (pt/pp -mitted, pres p -mitting) □ vt vorlegen (to dat); (hand in) einreichen □ vi sich unterwerfen (to dat)

subordinate[1] /sə'bɔ:dɪnət/ a untergeordnet □ n Untergebene(r) m/f

subordinate² /sə'bɔ:dɪneɪt/ *vt* unterordnen (*to dat*)

subscribe /səb'skraɪb/ *vi* spenden; ~ to abonnieren ⟨*newspaper*⟩; (*fig*) sich anschließen (+ *dat*). ~r *n* Spender *m*; Abonnent *m*

subscription /səb'skrɪpʃn/ *n* (*to club*) [Mitglieds]beitrag *m*; (*to newspaper*) Abonnement *nt*; by ~ mit Spenden; (*buy*) im Abonnement

subsequent /'sʌbsɪkwənt/ *a*, -ly *adv* folgend; (*later*) später

subservient /səb'sɜ:vɪənt/ *a*, -ly *adv* untergeordnet; (*servile*) unterwürfig

subside /səb'saɪd/ *vi* sinken; ⟨*ground:*⟩ sich senken; ⟨*storm:*⟩ nachlassen

subsidiary /səb'sɪdɪərɪ/ *a* untergeordnet □ *n* Tochtergesellschaft *f*

subsid|ize /'sʌbsɪdaɪz/ *vt* subventionieren. ~y *n* Subvention *f*

subsist /səb'sɪst/ *vi* leben (on von). ~ence *n* Existenz *f*

substance /'sʌbstəns/ *n* Substanz *f*

sub'standard *a* unzulänglich; ⟨*goods*⟩ minderwertig

substantial /səb'stænʃl/ *a* solide; ⟨*meal*⟩ reichhaltig; (*considerable*) beträchtlich. ~ly *adv* solide; (*essentially*) im Wesentlichen

substantiate /səb'stænʃɪeɪt/ *vt* erhärten

substitut|e /'sʌbstɪtju:t/ *n* Ersatz *m*; (*Sport*) Ersatzspieler(in) *m(f)* □ *vt* ~e A for B B durch A ersetzen □ *vi* ~e for s.o. jdn vertreten. ~ion /-'tju:ʃn/ *n* Ersetzung *f*

subterfuge /'sʌbtəfju:dʒ/ *n* List *f*

subterranean /sʌbtə'reɪnɪən/ *a* unterirdisch

'subtitle *n* Untertitel *m*

subtle /'sʌtl/ *a* (-r, -st), -tly *adv* fein; (*fig*) subtil

subtract /səb'trækt/ *vt* abziehen, subtrahieren. ~ion /-ækʃn/ *n* Subtraktion *f*

suburb /'sʌbɜ:b/ *n* Vorort *m*; in the ~s am Stadtrand. ~an /sə'bɜ:bən/ *a* Vorort-; (*pej*) spießig. ~ia /sə'bɜ:bɪə/ *n* die Vororte *pl*

subversive /səb'vɜ:sɪv/ *a* subversiv

'subway *n* Unterführung *f*; (*Amer: railway*) U-Bahn *f*

succeed /sək'si:d/ *vi* Erfolg haben; ⟨*plan:*⟩ gelingen; (*follow*) nachfolgen (+ *dat*); I ~ed es ist mir gelungen; he ~ed in escaping es gelang ihm zu entkommen □ *vt* folgen (+ *dat*). ~ing *a* folgend

success /sək'ses/ *n* Erfolg *m*. ~ful *a*, -ly *adv* erfolgreich

succession /sək'seʃn/ *n* Folge *f*; (*series*) Serie *f*; (*to title, office*) Nachfolge *f*; (*to throne*) Thronfolge *f*; in ~ hintereinander

successive /sək'sesɪv/ *a* aufeinander folgend. ~ly *adv* hintereinander

successor /sək'sesə(r)/ *n* Nachfolger(in) *m(f)*

succinct /sək'sɪŋkt/ *a*, -ly *adv* prägnant

succulent /'sʌkjʊlənt/ *a* saftig

succumb /sə'kʌm/ *vi* erliegen (to *dat*)

such /sʌtʃ/ *a* solche(r,s); ~ a book ein solches *od* solch ein Buch; ~ a thing so etwas; ~ a long time so lange; there is no ~ thing das gibt es gar nicht; there is no ~ person eine solche Person gibt es nicht □ *pron* as ~ als solche(r,s); (*strictly speaking*) an sich; ~ as wie [zum Beispiel]; and ~ und dergleichen. ~like *pron* (*fam*) dergleichen

suck /sʌk/ *vt/i* saugen; lutschen ⟨*sweet*⟩. ~ up *vt* aufsaugen □ *vi* ~ up to s.o. (*fam*) sich bei jdm einschmeicheln

sucker /'sʌkə(r)/ *n* (*Bot*) Ausläufer *m*; (*fam: person*) Dummer(r) *m/f*

suckle /'sʌkl/ *vt* säugen

suction /'sʌkʃn/ *n* Saugwirkung *f*

sudden /'sʌdn/ *a*, -ly *adv* plötzlich; (*abrupt*) jäh □ *n* all of a ~ auf einmal

sue /su:/ *vt* (*pres p* suing) verklagen (for auf + *acc*) □ *vi* klagen

suede /sweɪd/ *n* Wildleder *nt*

suet /'su:ɪt/ *n* [Nieren]talg *m*

suffer /'sʌfə(r)/ *vi* leiden (from an + *dat*) □ *vt* erleiden; (*tolerate*) dulden. ~ance /-əns/ *n* on ~ance bloß geduldet. ~ing *n* Leiden *nt*

suffice /sə'faɪs/ *vi* genügen

sufficient /sə'fɪʃnt/ *a*, -ly *adv* genug, genügend; be ~ genügen

suffix /'sʌfɪks/ *n* Nachsilbe *f*

suffocat|e /'sʌfəkeɪt/ *vt/i* ersticken. ~ion /-'keɪʃn/ *n* Ersticken *nt*

sugar /'ʃʊgə(r)/ *n* Zucker *m* □ *vt* zuckern; (*fig*) versüßen. ~ basin, ~-bowl *n* Zuckerschale *f*. ~y *a* süß; (*fig*) süßlich

suggest /sə'dʒest/ *vt* vorschlagen; (*indicate, insinuate*) andeuten. ~ion /-estʃn/ *n* Vorschlag *m*; Andeutung *f*; (*trace*) Spur *f*. ~ive *a*, -ly *adv* anzüglich; be ~ive of schließen lassen auf (+ *acc*)

suicidal /su:ɪ'saɪdl/ *a* selbstmörderisch

suicide /'su:ɪsaɪd/ *n* Selbstmord *m*

suit /su:t/ *n* Anzug *m*; (*woman's*) Kostüm *nt*; (*Cards*) Farbe *f*; (*Jur*) Prozess *m*; follow ~ (*fig*) das Gleiche tun □ *vt* (*adapt*) anpassen (to *dat*); (*be convenient for*) passen (+ *dat*); (*go with*) passen zu; (*clothing:*) stehen (s.o. *jdm*); be ~ed for geeignet sein für; ~ yourself! wie du willst!

suit|able /'su:təbl/ *a* geeignet; (*convenient*) passend; (*appropriate*) angemessen;

(*for weather, activity*) zweckmäßig. ∼ably *adv* angemessen; zweckmäßig

'suitcase *n* Koffer *m*

suite /swiːt/ *n* Suite *f*; (*of furniture*) Garnitur *f*

sulk /sʌlk/ *vi* schmollen. ∼y *a* schmollend

sullen /'sʌlən/ *a*, -ly *adv* mürrisch

sulphur /'sʌlfə(r)/ *n* Schwefel *f*. ∼ic /-'fjʊərɪk/ *a* ∼ic acid Schwefelsäure *f*

sultana /sʌl'tɑːnə/ *n* Sultanine *f*

sultry /'sʌltrɪ/ *a* (-ier, -iest) (*weather*) schwül

sum /sʌm/ *n* Summe *f*; (*Sch*) Rechenaufgabe *f* ◻ *vt/i* (*pt/pp* summed) ∼ up zusammenfassen; (*assess*) einschätzen

summar|ize /'sʌməraɪz/ *vt* zusammenfassen. ∼y *n* Zusammenfassung *f* ◻ *a*, -ily *adv* summarisch; (*dismissal*) fristlos

summer /'sʌmə(r)/ *n* Sommer *m*. ∼house *n* [Garten]laube *f*. ∼time *n* Sommer *m*

summery /'sʌmərɪ/ *a* sommerlich

summit /'sʌmɪt/ *n* Gipfel *m*. ∼ conference *n* Gipfelkonferenz *f*

summon /'sʌmən/ *vt* rufen; holen (*help*); (*Jur*) vorladen. ∼ up *vt* aufbringen

summons /'sʌmənz/ *n* (*Jur*) Vorladung *f* ◻ *vt* vorladen

sump /sʌmp/ *n* (*Auto*) Ölwanne *f*

sumptuous /'sʌmptjʊəs/ *a*, -ly *adv* prunkvoll; (*meal*) üppig

sun /sʌn/ *n* Sonne *f* ◻ *vt* (*pt/pp* sunned) ∼ oneself sich sonnen

sun: ∼bathe *vi* sich sonnen. ∼bed *n* Sonnenbank *f*. ∼burn *n* Sonnenbrand *m*

sundae /'sʌndeɪ/ *n* Eisbecher *m*

Sunday /'sʌndeɪ/ *n* Sonntag *m*

'sundial *n* Sonnenuhr *f*

sundry /'sʌndrɪ/ *a* verschiedene *pl*; all and ∼ alle *pl*

'sunflower *n* Sonnenblume *f*

sung /sʌŋ/ *see* sing

'sun-glasses *npl* Sonnenbrille *f*

sunk /sʌŋk/ *see* sink

sunken /'sʌŋkn/ *a* gesunken; (*eyes*) eingefallen

sunny /'sʌnɪ/ *a* (-ier, -iest) sonnig

sun: ∼rise *n* Sonnenaufgang *m*. ∼roof *n* (*Auto*) Schiebedach *nt*. ∼set *n* Sonnenuntergang *m*. ∼shade *n* Sonnenschirm *m*. ∼shine *n* Sonnenschein *m*. ∼stroke *n* Sonnenstich *m*. ∼tan *n* [Sonnen]bräune *f*. ∼tanned *a* braun [gebrannt]. ∼tan oil *n* Sonnenöl *nt*

super /'suːpə(r)/ *a* (*fam*) prima, toll

superb /sʊ'pɜːb/ *a* erstklassig

supercilious /suːpə'sɪlɪəs/ *a* überlegen

superficial /suːpə'fɪʃl/ *a*, -ly *adv* oberflächlich

superfluous /sʊ'pɜːflʊəs/ *a* überflüssig

super'human *a* übermenschlich

superintendent /suːpərɪn'tendənt/ *n* (*of police*) Kommissar *m*

superior /suː'pɪərɪə(r)/ *a* überlegen; (*in rank*) höher ◻ *n* Vorgesetzte(r) *m/f*. ∼ity /-'ɒrətɪ/ *n* Überlegenheit *f*

superlative /suː'pɜːlətɪv/ *a* unübertrefflich ◻ *n* Superlativ *m*

'superman *n* Übermensch *m*

'supermarket *n* Supermarkt *m*

super'natural *a* übernatürlich

'superpower *n* Supermacht *f*

supersede /suːpə'siːd/ *vt* ersetzen

super'sonic *a* Überschall-

superstiti|on /suːpə'stɪʃn/ *n* Aberglaube *m*. ∼ous /-'stɪʃəs/ *a*, -ly *adv* abergläubisch

supervis|e /'suːpəvaɪz/ *vt* beaufsichtigen; überwachen (*work*). ∼ion /-'vɪʒn/ *n* Aufsicht *f*; Überwachung *f*. ∼or *n* Aufseher(in) *m(f)*

supper /'sʌpə(r)/ *n* Abendessen *nt*

supple /'sʌpl/ *a* geschmeidig

supplement /'sʌplɪmənt/ *n* Ergänzung *f*; (*addition*) Zusatz *m*; (*to fare*) Zuschlag *m*; (*book*) Ergänzungsband *m*; (*to newspaper*) Beilage *f* ◻ *vt* ergänzen. ∼ary /-'mentərɪ/ *a* zusätzlich

supplier /sə'plaɪə(r)/ *n* Lieferant *m*

supply /sə'plaɪ/ *n* Vorrat *m*; supplies *pl* (*Mil*) Nachschub *m* ◻ *vt* (*pt/pp* -ied) liefern; ∼ s.o. with sth jdn mit etw versorgen

support /sə'pɔːt/ *n* Stütze *f*; (*fig*) Unterstützung *f* ◻ *vt* stützen; (*bear weight of*) tragen; (*keep*) ernähren; (*give money to*) unterstützen; (*speak in favour of*) befürworten; (*Sport*) Fan sein von. ∼er *n* Anhänger(in) *m(f)*; (*Sport*) Fan *m*. ∼ive /-ɪv/ *a* be ∼ive [to s.o.] [jdm] eine große Stütze sein

suppose /sə'pəʊz/ *vt* annehmen; (*presume*) vermuten; (*imagine*) sich (*dat*) vorstellen; be ∼d to do sth etw tun sollen; not be ∼d to (*fam*) nicht dürfen; I ∼ so vermutlich. ∼dly /-ɪdlɪ/ *adv* angeblich

supposition /sʌpə'zɪʃn/ *n* Vermutung *f*

suppository /sʌ'pɒzɪtrɪ/ *n* Zäpfchen *nt*

suppress /sə'pres/ *vt* unterdrücken. ∼ion /-eʃn/ *n* Unterdrückung *f*

supremacy /suː'preməsɪ/ *n* Vorherrschaft *f*

supreme /suːˈpriːm/ a höchste(r,s); ⟨court⟩ oberste(r,s)

surcharge /ˈsɜːtʃɑːdʒ/ n Zuschlag m

sure /ʃʊə(r)/ a (-r, -st) sicher; make ~ sich vergewissern (of gen); (check) nachprüfen; be ~ to do it sieh zu, dass du es tust □ adv (Amer, fam) klar; ~ enough tatsächlich. ~ly adv sicher; (for emphasis) doch; (Amer: gladly) gern

surety /ˈʃʊərətɪ/ n Bürgschaft f; stand ~ for bürgen für

surf /ˈsɜːf/ n Brandung f

surface /ˈsɜːfɪs/ n Oberfläche f □ vi (emerge) auftauchen. ~ mail n by ~ mail auf dem Land-/Seeweg

'surfboard n Surfbrett nt

surfeit /ˈsɜːfɪt/ n Übermaß nt;

surfing /ˈsɜːfɪŋ/ n Surfen nt

surge /sɜːdʒ/ n (of sea) Branden nt; (fig) Welle f □ vi branden; ~ forward nach vorn drängen

surgeon /ˈsɜːdʒən/ n Chirurg(in) m(f)

surgery /ˈsɜːdʒərɪ/ n Chirurgie f; (place) Praxis f; (room) Sprechzimmer nt; (hours) Sprechstunde f; have ~ operiert werden

surgical /ˈsɜːdʒɪkl/ a, -ly adv chirurgisch

surly /ˈsɜːlɪ/ a (-ier, -iest) mürrisch

surmise /səˈmaɪz/ vt mutmaßen

surmount /səˈmaʊnt/ vt überwinden

surname /ˈsɜːneɪm/ n Nachname m

surpass /səˈpɑːs/ vt übertreffen

surplus /ˈsɜːpləs/ a überschüssig; be ~ to requirements nicht benötigt werden □ n Überschuss m (of an + dat)

surprise /səˈpraɪz/ n Überraschung f □ vt überraschen; be ~ed sich wundern (at über + acc). ~ing a, -ly adv überraschend

surrender /səˈrendə(r)/ n Kapitulation f □ vi sich ergeben; (Mil) kapitulieren □ vt aufgeben

surreptitious /sʌrəpˈtɪʃəs/ a, -ly adv heimlich, verstohlen

surrogate /ˈsʌrəgət/ n Ersatz m. ~ 'mother n Leihmutter f

surround /səˈraʊnd/ vt umgeben; (encircle) umzingeln; ~ed by umgeben von. ~ing a umliegend. ~ings npl Umgebung f

surveillance /səˈveɪləns/ n Überwachung f; be under ~ überwacht werden

survey¹ /ˈsɜːveɪ/ n Überblick m; (poll) Umfrage f; (investigation) Untersuchung f; (of land) Vermessung f; (of house) Gutachten nt

survey² /səˈveɪ/ vt betrachten; vermessen ⟨land⟩; begutachten ⟨building⟩. ~or n Landvermesser m; Gutachter m

survival /səˈvaɪvl/ n Überleben nt; (of tradition) Fortbestand m

survive /səˈvaɪv/ vt überleben □ vi überleben; (tradition:) erhalten bleiben. ~or n Überlebende(r) m/f; be a ~or (fam) nicht unterzukriegen sein

susceptible /səˈseptəbl/ a empfänglich; (Med) anfällig (to für)

suspect¹ /səˈspekt/ vt verdächtigen; (assume) vermuten; he ~s nothing er ahnt nichts

suspect² /ˈsʌspekt/ a verdächtig □ n Verdächtige(r) m/f

suspend /səˈspend/ vt aufhängen; (stop) [vorläufig] einstellen; (from duty) vorläufig beurlauben. ~er n Strumpfband-gürtel m. ~ders npl Strumpfbänder pl; (Amer: braces) Hosenträger pl

suspense /səˈspens/ n Spannung f

suspension /səˈspenʃn/ n (Auto) Federung f. ~ bridge n Hängebrücke f

suspicion /səˈspɪʃn/ n Verdacht m; (mistrust) Misstrauen nt; (trace) Spur f. ~ous /-ɪʃəs/ a, -ly adv misstrauisch; (arousing suspicion) verdächtig

sustain /səˈsteɪn/ vt tragen; (fig) aufrechterhalten; erhalten ⟨life⟩; erleiden ⟨injury⟩

sustenance /ˈsʌstɪnəns/ n Nahrung f

swab /swɒb/ n (Med) Tupfer m; (specimen) Abstrich m

swagger /ˈswægə(r)/ vi stolzieren

swallow¹ /ˈswɒləʊ/ vt/i schlucken. ~ up vt verschlucken; verschlingen ⟨resources⟩

swallow² n (bird) Schwalbe f

swam /swæm/ see swim

swamp /swɒmp/ n Sumpf m □ vt überschwemmen. ~y a sumpfig

swan /swɒn/ n Schwan m

swank /swæŋk/ vi (fam) angeben

swap /swɒp/ n (fam) Tausch m □ vt/i (pt/pp swapped) (fam) tauschen (for gegen)

swarm /swɔːm/ n Schwarm m □ vi schwärmen; be ~ing with wimmeln von

swarthy /ˈswɔːðɪ/ a (-ier, -iest) dunkel

swastika /ˈswɒstɪkə/ n Hakenkreuz nt

swat /swɒt/ vt (pt/pp swatted) totschlagen

sway /sweɪ/ n (fig) Herrschaft f □ vi schwanken; (gently) sich wiegen □ vt wiegen; (influence) beeinflussen

swear /sweə(r)/ v (pt swore, pp sworn) □ vt schwören □ vi schwören (by auf + acc); (curse) fluchen. ~-word n Kraftausdruck m

sweat /swet/ n Schweiß m □ vi schwitzen

sweater /ˈswetə(r)/ n Pullover m

sweaty /ˈswetɪ/ a verschwitzt

swede /swiːd/ n Kohlrübe f

Swede n Schwede m /-din f. ~en n Schweden nt. ~ish a schwedisch sweep /swiːp/ n Schornsteinfeger m; (curve) Bogen m; (movement) ausholende Bewegung f; make a clean ~ (fig) gründlich aufräumen □ v (pt/pp swept) □ vt fegen, kehren □ vi (go swiftly) rauschen; ⟨wind:⟩ fegen. ~ up vt zusammenfegen/-kehren

sweeping /'swiːpɪŋ/ a ausholend; ⟨statement⟩ pauschal; ⟨changes⟩ weit reichend

sweet /swiːt/ a (-er, -est) süß; have a ~ tooth gern Süßes mögen □ n Bonbon m & nt; (dessert) Nachtisch m. ~ corn n [Zucker]mais m

sweeten /'swiːtn/ vt süßen. ~er n Süßstoff m; ⟨fam: bribe⟩ Schmiergeld nt

sweet: ~heart n Schatz m. ~shop n Süßwarenladen m. ~ness n Süße f. ~ 'pea n Wicke f

swell /swel/ n Dünung f □ v (pt swelled, pp swollen or swelled) □ vi [an]schwellen; ⟨sails:⟩ sich blähen; ⟨wood:⟩ aufquellen □ vt anschwellen lassen; ⟨increase⟩ vergrößern. ~ing n Schwellung f

swelter /'sweltə(r)/ vi schwitzen

swept /swept/ see sweep

swerve /swɜːv/ vi einen Bogen machen

swift /swɪft/ a (-er, -est), -ly adv schnell

swig /swɪg/ n ⟨fam⟩ Schluck m, Zug m □ vt (pt/pp swigged) ⟨fam⟩ [herunter]kippen

swill /swɪl/ n ⟨for pigs⟩ Schweinefutter nt □ vt ~ [out] [aus]spülen

swim /swɪm/ n have a ~ schwimmen □ vi (pt swam, pp swum) schwimmen; my head is ~ming mir dreht sich der Kopf. ~mer n Schwimmer(in) m(f)

swimming /'swɪmɪŋ/ n Schwimmen nt. ~-baths npl Schwimmbad nt. ~-pool n Schwimmbecken nt; (private) Swimmingpool m

'swim-suit n Badeanzug m

swindle /'swɪndl/ n Schwindel m, Betrug m □ vt betrügen. ~r n Schwindler m

swine /swaɪn/ n Schwein nt

swing /swɪŋ/ n Schwung m; (shift) Schwenk m; (seat) Schaukel f; in full ~ in vollem Gange □ v (pt/pp swung) □ vi schwingen; (on swing) schaukeln; (sway) schwanken; (dangle) baumeln; (turn) schwenken □ vt schwingen; (influence) beeinflussen. ~'door n Schwingtür f

swingeing /'swɪndʒɪŋ/ a hart; (fig) drastisch

swipe /swaɪp/ n ⟨fam⟩ Schlag m □ vt ⟨fam⟩ knallen; (steal) klauen

swirl /swɜːl/ n Wirbel m □ vt/i wirbeln

swish /swɪʃ/ a ⟨fam⟩ schick □ vi zischen

Swiss /swɪs/ a Schweizer, schweizerisch □ n Schweizer(in) m(f); the ~ pl die Schweizer. ~ 'roll n Biskuitrolle f

switch /swɪtʃ/ n Schalter m; (change) Wechsel m; (Amer, Rail) Weiche f □ vt wechseln; (exchange) tauschen □ vi wechseln; ~ to umstellen auf (+ acc). ~ off vt ausschalten; abschalten ⟨engine⟩. ~ on vt einschalten, anschalten

switch: ~back n Achterbahn f. ~board n [Telefon]zentrale f

Switzerland /'swɪtsələnd/ n die Schweiz

swivel /'swɪvl/ v (pt/pp swivelled) □ vt drehen □ vi sich drehen

swollen /'swəʊlən/ see swell □ a geschwollen. ~-'headed a eingebildet

swoop /swuːp/ n Sturzflug m; (by police) Razzia f □ vi ~ down herabstoßen

sword /sɔːd/ n Schwert nt

swore /swɔː(r)/ see swear

sworn /swɔːn/ see swear

swot /swɒt/ n ⟨fam⟩ Streber m □ vt (pt/pp swotted) ⟨fam⟩ büffeln

swum /swʌm/ see swim

swung /swʌŋ/ see swing

syllable /'sɪləbl/ n Silbe f

syllabus /'sɪləbəs/ n Lehrplan m; (for exam) Studienplan m

symbol /'sɪmbəl/ n Symbol nt (of für). ~ic /-'bɒlɪk/ a, -ally adv symbolisch ~ism /-ɪzm/ n Symbolik f. ~ize vt symbolisieren

symmetr|ical /sɪ'metrɪkl/ a, -ly adv symmetrisch. ~y /'sɪmətrɪ/ n Symmetrie f

sympathetic /sɪmpə'θetɪk/ a, -ally adv mitfühlend; (likeable) sympathisch

sympathize /'sɪmpəθaɪz/ vi mitfühlen. ~r n (Pol) Sympathisant m

sympathy /'sɪmpəθɪ/ n Mitgefühl nt; (condolences) Beileid nt

symphony /'sɪmfənɪ/ n Sinfonie f

symptom /'sɪmptəm/ n Symptom nt. ~atic /-'mætɪk/ a symptomatisch (of für)

synagogue /'sɪnəgɒg/ n Synagoge f

synchronize /'sɪŋkrənaɪz/ vt synchronisieren

syndicate /'sɪndɪkət/ n Syndikat nt

syndrome /'sɪndrəʊm/ n Syndrom nt

synonym /'sɪnənɪm/ n Synonym nt. ~ous /-'nɒnɪməs/ a, -ly adv synonym

synopsis /sɪ'nɒpsɪs/ n (pl -opses /-siːz/) Zusammenfassung f; (of opera, ballet) Inhaltsangabe f

syntax /'sɪntæks/ n Syntax f

synthesis /'sɪnθəsɪs/ n (pl -ses /-siːz/) Synthese f

synthetic /sɪn'θetɪk/ a synthetisch □ n Kunststoff m

Syria /'sɪrɪə/ n Syrien nt

syringe /sɪ'rɪndʒ/ n Spritze f □ vt spritzen; ausspritzen ⟨ears⟩

syrup /'sɪrəp/ n Sirup m

system /'sɪstəm/ n System nt. ~atic /-'mætɪk/ a, -ally adv systematisch

T

tab /tæb/ n (projecting) Zunge f; (with name) Namensschild nt; (loop) Aufhänger m; keep ~s on (fam) [genau] beobachten; pick up the ~ (fam) bezahlen

tabby /'tæbɪ/ n getigerte Katze f

table /'teɪbl/ n Tisch m; (list) Tabelle f; at [the] ~ bei Tisch □ vt einbringen. ~cloth n Tischdecke f, Tischtuch nt. ~spoon n Servierlöffel m

tablet /'tæblɪt/ n Tablette f; (of soap) Stück nt; (slab) Tafel f

'table tennis n Tischtennis nt

tabloid /'tæblɔɪd/ n kleinformatige Zeitung f; (pej) Boulevardzeitung f

taboo /tə'buː/ a tabu □ n Tabu nt

tacit /'tæsɪt/ a, -ly adv stillschweigend

taciturn /'tæsɪtɜːn/ a wortkarg

tack /tæk/ n (nail) Stift m; (stitch) Heftstich m; (Naut & fig) Kurs m □ vt festnageln; (sew) heften □ vi (Naut) kreuzen

tackle /'tækl/ n Ausrüstung f □ vt angehen

tacky /'tækɪ/ a klebrig

tact /tækt/ n Takt m, Taktgefühl nt. ~ful a, -ly adv taktvoll

tactic|al /'tæktɪkl/ a, -ly adv taktisch. ~s npl Taktik f

tactless /'tæktlɪs/ a, -ly adv taktlos. ~ness n Taktlosigkeit f

tadpole /'tædpəʊl/ n Kaulquappe f

tag[1] /tæg/ n (label) Schild nt □ vi (pt/pp tagged) ~ along mitkommen

tag[2] n (game) Fangen nt

tail /teɪl/ n Schwanz m; ~s pl (tailcoat) Frack m; heads or ~s? Kopf oder Zahl? □ vt (fam: follow) beschatten □ vi ~ off zurückgehen

tail: ~back n Rückstau m. ~coat n Frack m. ~end n Ende nt. ~ light n Rücklicht nt

tailor /'teɪlə(r)/ n Schneider m. ~-made a maßgeschneidert

'tail wind n Rückenwind m

taint /teɪnt/ vt verderben

take /teɪk/ v (pt took, pp taken) □ vt nehmen; (with one) mitnehmen; (to a place) bringen; (steal) stehlen; (win) gewinnen; (capture) einnehmen; (require) brauchen; (last) dauern; (teach) geben;

machen ⟨exam, subject holiday, photograph⟩; messen ⟨pulse, temperature⟩; ~ s.o. home jdn nach Hause bringen; ~ sth to the cleaner's etw in die Reinigung bringen; ~ s.o. prisoner jdn gefangen nehmen; be ~n ill krank werden; ~ sth calmly etw gelassen aufnehmen □ vi ⟨plant:⟩ angehen; (in game) gewinnen. ~ after vt nachschlagen; (in looks) jdm ähnlich sehen; ~ to (like) mögen; (as a habit) sich ⟨dat⟩ angewöhnen. ~ away vt wegbringen; (remove) wegnehmen; (subtract) abziehen; 'to ~ away' 'zum Mitnehmen'. ~ back vt zurücknehmen; (return) zurückbringen. ~ down vt herunternehmen; (remove) abnehmen; (write down) aufschreiben. ~ in vt hineinbringen; (bring indoors) hereinholen; (to one's home) aufnehmen; (understand) begreifen; (deceive) hereinlegen; (make smaller) enger machen. ~ off vt abnehmen; ablegen ⟨coat⟩; sich ⟨dat⟩ ausziehen ⟨clothes⟩; (deduct) abziehen; (mimic) nachmachen; ~ time off sich ⟨dat⟩ freinehmen; ~ oneself off [fort]gehen □ vi (Aviat) starten. ~ on vt annehmen; (undertake) übernehmen; (engage) einstellen; (as opponent) antreten gegen. ~ out vt hinausbringen; (for pleasure) ausgehen mit; ausführen ⟨dog⟩; (remove) herausnehmen; (withdraw) abheben ⟨money⟩; (from library) ausleihen; ~ out a subscription to sth etw abonnieren; ~ it out on s.o. (fam) seinen Ärger an jdm auslassen. ~ over vt hinüberbringen; übernehmen ⟨firm, control⟩ □ vi ~ over from s.o. jdn ablösen. ~ up vt hinaufbringen; annehmen ⟨offer⟩; ergreifen ⟨profession⟩; sich ⟨dat⟩ zulegen ⟨hobby⟩; in Anspruch nehmen ⟨time⟩; einnehmen ⟨space⟩; aufreißen ⟨floorboards⟩; ~ sth up with s.o. mit jdm über etw (acc) sprechen □ vi ~ up with s.o. sich mit jdm einlassen

take: ~-away n Essen nt zum Mitnehmen; (restaurant) Restaurant nt mit Straßenverkauf. ~-off n (Aviat) Start m, Abflug m. ~-over n Übernahme f

takings /'teɪkɪŋz/ npl Einnahmen pl

talcum /'tælkəm/ n ~ [powder] Körperpuder m

tale /teɪl/ n Geschichte f

talent /'tælənt/ n Talent nt. ~ed a talentiert

talk /tɔːk/ n Gespräch nt; (lecture) Vortrag m; make small ~ Konversation machen □ vi reden, sprechen (to/with mit) □ vt reden; ~ s.o. into sth jdn zu etw überreden. ~ over vt besprechen

talkative /'tɔːkətɪv/ a gesprächig

'talking-to n Standpauke f

tall /tɔːl/ a (-er, -est) groß; ⟨building, tree⟩ hoch; that's a ∼ order das ist ziemlich viel verlangt. ∼boy n hohe Kommode f. ∼ 'story n übertriebene Geschichte f

tally /'tælɪ/ n keep a ∼ of Buch führen über (+ acc) □ vi übereinstimmen

talon /'tælən/ n Klaue f

tambourine /tæmbə'riːn/ n Tamburin n

tame /teɪm/ a (-r, -st), -ly adv zahm; (dull) lahm (fam) □ vt zähmen. ∼r n Dompteur m

tamper /'tæmpə(r)/ vi ∼ with sich (dat) zu schaffen machen an (+ dat)

tampon /'tæmpɒn/ n Tampon m

tan /tæn/ a gelbbraun □ n Gelbbraun nt; (from sun) Bräune f □ v (pt/pp tanned) □ vt gerben ⟨hide⟩ □ vi braun werden

tang /tæŋ/ n herber Geschmack m; (smell) herber Geruch m

tangent /'tændʒənt/ n Tangente f; go off at a ∼ (fam) vom Thema abschweifen

tangible /'tændʒɪbl/ a greifbar

tangle /'tæŋgl/ n Gewirr nt; (in hair) Verfilzung f □ vt ∼ [up] verheddern □ vi sich verheddern

tango /'tæŋgəʊ/ n Tango m

tank /tæŋk/ n Tank m; (Mil) Panzer m

tankard /'tæŋkəd/ n Krug m

tanker /'tæŋkə(r)/ n Tanker m; (lorry) Tank[last]wagen m

tantaliz|e /'tæntəlaɪz/ vt quälen. ∼ing a verlockend

tantamount /'tæntəmaʊnt/ a be ∼ to gleichbedeutend sein mit

tantrum /'tæntrəm/ n Wutanfall m

tap /tæp/ n Hahn m; (knock) Klopfen nt; on ∼ zur Verfügung □ v (pt/pp tapped) □ vt klopfen an (+ acc); anzapfen ⟨barrel, tree⟩; erschließen ⟨resources⟩; abhören ⟨telephone⟩ □ vi klopfen. ∼-dance n Stepptanz m □ vi Stepp tanzen, steppen

tape /teɪp/ n Band nt; (adhesive) Klebstreifen m; (for recording) Tonband nt □ vt mit Klebstreifen zukleben; (record) auf Band aufnehmen

'tape-measure n Bandmaß nt

taper /'teɪpə(r)/ n dünne Wachskerze f □ vi sich verjüngen

'tape recorder n Tonbandgerät nt

tapestry /'tæpɪstrɪ/ n Gobelinstickerei f

tapeworm n Bandwurm m

'tap water n Leitungswasser nt

tar /tɑː(r)/ n Teer m □ vt (pt/pp tarred) teeren

tardy /'tɑːdɪ/ a (-ier, -iest) langsam; (late) spät

target /'tɑːgɪt/ n Ziel nt; (board) [Ziel]scheibe f

tariff /'tærɪf/ n Tarif m; (duty) Zoll m

tarnish /'tɑːnɪʃ/ vi anlaufen

tarpaulin /tɑː'pɔːlɪn/ n Plane f

tarragon /'tærəgən/ n Estragon m

tart¹ /tɑːt/ a (-er, -est) sauer; (fig) scharf

tart² n ≈ Obstkuchen m; (individual) Törtchen nt; (sl: prostitute) Nutte f □ vt ∼ oneself up (fam) sich auftakeln

tartan /'tɑːtn/ n Schottenmuster nt; (cloth) Schottenstoff m □ attrib schottisch kariert

tartar /'tɑːtə(r)/ n (on teeth) Zahnstein m

tartar 'sauce /tɑːtə-/ n ≈ Remouladensoße f

task /tɑːsk/ n Aufgabe f; take s.o. to ∼ jdm Vorhaltungen machen. ∼ force n Sonderkommando nt

tassel /'tæsl/ n Quaste f

taste /teɪst/ n Geschmack m; (sample) Kostprobe f □ vt kosten, probieren; schmecken ⟨flavour⟩ □ vi schmecken (of nach). ∼ful a, -ly adv (fig) geschmackvoll. ∼less a, -ly adv geschmacklos

tasty /'teɪstɪ/ a (-ier, -iest) lecker, schmackhaft

tat /tæt/ see tit²

tatter|ed /'tætəd/ a zerlumpt; ⟨pages⟩ zerfleddert. ∼s npl in ∼s in Fetzen

tattoo¹ /tə'tuː/ n Tätowierung f □ vt tätowieren

tattoo² n (Mil) Zapfenstreich m

tatty /'tætɪ/ a (-ier, -iest) schäbig; ⟨book⟩ zerfleddert

taught /tɔːt/ see teach

taunt /tɔːnt/ n höhnische Bemerkung f □ vt verhöhnen

Taurus /'tɔːrəs/ n (Astr) Stier m

taut /tɔːt/ a straff

tavern /'tævən/ n (liter) Schenke f

tawdry /'tɔːdrɪ/ a (-ier, -iest) billig und geschmacklos

tawny /'tɔːnɪ/ a gelbbraun

tax /tæks/ n Steuer f □ vt besteuern; (fig) strapazieren; ∼ with beschuldigen (+ gen). ∼able /-əbl/ a steuerpflichtig. ∼ation /-'seɪʃn/ n Besteuerung f. ∼-free a steuerfrei

taxi /'tæksɪ/ n Taxi nt □ vi (pt/pp taxied, pres p taxiing) ⟨aircraft:⟩ rollen. ∼ driver n Taxifahrer m. ∼ rank n Taxistand m

'taxpayer n Steuerzahler m

tea /tiː/ n Tee m. ∼ bag n Teebeutel m. ∼ break n Teepause f

teach /tiːtʃ/ vt/i (pt/pp taught) unterrichten; ∼ s.o. sth jdm etw beibringen. ∼er n Lehrer(in) m(f)

tea: ∼-cloth n (for drying) Geschirrtuch nt. ∼cup n Teetasse f

teak /ti:k/ n Teakholz nt

team /ti:m/ n Mannschaft f; (fig) Team nt; (of animals) Gespann nt □ vi ~ up sich zusammentun

'team-work n Teamarbeit f

'teapot n Teekanne f

tear¹ /teə(r)/ n Riss m □ v (pt tore, pp torn) □ vt reißen; (damage) zerreißen; ~ open aufreißen; ~ oneself away sich losreißen □ vi [zer]reißen; (run) rasen. ~ up vt zerreißen

tear² /tɪə(r)/ n Träne f. ~ful a weinend. ~fully adv unter Tränen. ~gas n Tränengas nt

tease /ti:z/ vt necken

tea: ~-set n Teeservice nt. ~shop n Café nt. ~spoon n Teelöffel m. ~strainer n Teesieb nt

teat /ti:t/ n Zitze f; (on bottle) Sauger m

'tea-towel n Geschirrtuch nt

technical /'teknɪkl/ a technisch; (specialized) fachlich. ~ity /-'kælətɪ/ n technisches Detail nt; (Jur) Formfehler m. ~ly adv technisch; (strictly) streng genommen. ~ term n Fachausdruck m

technician /tek'nɪʃn/ n Techniker m

technique /tek'ni:k/ n Technik f

technological /teknə'lɒdʒɪkl/ a, -ly adv technologisch

technology /tek'nɒlədʒɪ/ n Technologie f

teddy /'tedɪ/ n ~ [bear] Teddybär m

tedious /'ti:dɪəs/ a langweilig

tedium /'ti:dɪəm/ n Langeweile f

teem /ti:m/ vi (rain) in Strömen gießen; be ~ing with (full of) wimmeln von

teenage /'ti:neɪdʒ/ a Teenager-; ~ boy/girl Junge m/Mädchen nt im Teenageralter. ~r n Teenager m

teens /ti:nz/ npl the ~ die Teenagerjahre pl

teeny /'ti:nɪ/ a (-ier, -iest) winzig

teeter /'ti:tə(r)/ vi schwanken

teeth /ti:θ/ see tooth

teeth|e /ti:ð/ vi zahnen. ~ing troubles npl (fig) Anfangsschwierigkeiten pl

teetotal /ti:'təʊtl/ a abstinent. ~ler n Abstinenzler m

telecommunications /telɪkəmju:nɪ-'keɪʃnz/ npl Fernmeldewesen nt

telegram /'telɪgræm/ n Telegramm nt

telegraph /'telɪgrɑ:f/ n Telegraf m. ~ic /-'græfɪk/ a telegrafisch. ~ pole n Telegrafenmast m

telepathy /tɪ'lepəθɪ/ n Telepathie f; by ~ telepathisch

telephone /'telɪfəʊn/ n Telefon nt; be on the ~ Telefon haben; (be telephoning) telefonieren □ vt anrufen □ vi telefonieren

telephone: ~ book n Telefonbuch nt. ~ booth n, ~ box n Telefonzelle f. ~ directory n Telefonbuch nt. ~ number n Telefonnummer f

telephonist /tɪ'lefənɪst/ n Telefonist(in) m(f)

tele'photo /telɪ-/ a ~ lens Teleobjektiv nt

teleprinter /'telɪ-/ n Fernschreiber m

telescop|e /'telɪskəʊp/ n Teleskop nt, Fernrohr nt. ~ic /-'skɒpɪk/ a teleskopisch; (collapsible) ausziehbar

televise /'telɪvaɪz/ vt im Fernsehen übertragen

television /'telɪvɪʒn/ n Fernsehen nt; watch ~ fernsehen. ~ set n Fernsehapparat m, Fernseher m

telex /'teleks/ n Telex nt □ vt telexen

tell /tel/ vt/i (pt/pp told) sagen (s.o. jdm); (relate) erzählen; (know) wissen; (distinguish) erkennen; ~ the time die Uhr lesen; time will ~ das wird man sehen; his age is beginning to ~ sein Alter macht sich bemerkbar; don't ~ me sag es mir nicht; you musn't ~ du darfst nichts sagen. ~ off vt ausschimpfen

teller /'telə(r)/ n (cashier) Kassierer(in) m(f)

telly /'telɪ/ n (fam) = television

temerity /tɪ'merətɪ/ n Kühnheit f

temp /temp/ n (fam) Aushilfssekretärin f

temper /'tempə(r)/ n (disposition) Naturell nt; (mood) Laune f; (anger) Wut f; lose one's ~ wütend werden □ vt (fig) mäßigen

temperament /'tempərəmənt/ n Temperament nt. ~al /-'mentl/ a temperamentvoll; (moody) launisch

temperance /'tempərəns/ n Mäßigung f; (abstinence) Abstinenz f

temperate /'tempərət/ a gemäßigt

temperature /'temprətʃə(r)/ n Temperatur f; have or run a ~ Fieber haben

tempest /'tempɪst/ n Sturm m. ~uous /-'pestjʊəs/ a stürmisch

template /'templɪt/ n Schablone f

temple¹ /'templ/ n Tempel m

temple² n (Anat) Schläfe f

tempo /'tempəʊ/ n Tempo nt

temporary /'tempərɪ/ a, -ily adv vorübergehend; (measure, building) provisorisch

tempt /tempt/ vt verleiten; (Relig) versuchen; herausfordern (fate); (entice) [ver]locken; be ~ed versucht sein (to zu), I am ~ed by it es lockt mich. ~ation /-'teɪʃn/ n Versuchung f. ~ing a verlockend

ten /ten/ a zehn

tenable /'tenəbl/ a (fig) haltbar

tenaci|ous /tɪ'neɪʃəs/ a, -ly adv hartnäckig. ~ty /-'næsətɪ/ n Hartnäckigkeit f

tenant /'tenənt/ n Mieter(in) m(f); (Comm) Pächter(in) m(f)

tend¹ /tend/ vt (look after) sich kümmern um

tend² vi ~ to do sth dazu neigen, etw zu tun

tendency /'tendənsɪ/ n Tendenz f; (inclination) Neigung f

tender¹ /'tendə(r)/ n □ (Comm) Angebot nt; legal ~ gesetzliches Zahlungsmittel nt □ vt anbieten; einreichen (resignation)

tender² a zart; (loving) zärtlich; (painful) empfindlich. ~ly adv zärtlich. ~ness n Zartheit f; Zärtlichkeit f

tendon /'tendən/ n Sehne f

tenement /'tenəmənt/ n Mietshaus nt

tenet /'tenɪt/ n Grundsatz m

tenner /'tenə(r)/ n (fam) Zehnpfundschein m

tennis /'tenɪs/ n Tennis nt. ~-court n Tennisplatz m

tenor /'tenə(r)/ n Tenor m

tense¹ /tens/ n (Gram) Zeit f

tense² a (-r, -st) gespannt □ vt anspannen (muscle)

tension /'tenʃn/ n Spannung f

tent /tent/ n Zelt nt

tentacle /'tentəkl/ n Fangarm m

tentative /'tentətɪv/ a, -ly adv vorläufig; (hesitant) zaghaft

tenterhooks /'tentəhʊks/ npl be on ~ wie auf glühenden Kohlen sitzen

tenth /tenθ/ a zehnte(r,s) □ n Zehntel nt

tenuous /'tenjʊəs/ a (fig) schwach

tepid /'tepɪd/ a lauwarm

term /tɜːm/ n Zeitraum m; (Sch) ≈ Halbjahr nt; (Univ) ≈ Semester nt; (expression) Ausdruck m; ~s pl (conditions) Bedingungen pl; ~ of office Amtszeit f; in the short/long ~ kurz-/langfristig; be on good/bad ~s gut/nicht gut miteinander auskommen; come to ~s with sich abfinden mit

terminal /'tɜːmɪnl/ a End-; (Med) unheilbar □ n (Aviat) Terminal m; (of bus) Endstation f; (on battery) Pol m; (Computing) Terminal nt

terminat|e /'tɜːmɪneɪt/ vt beenden; lösen (contract); unterbrechen (pregnancy) □ vi enden. ~ion /-'neɪʃn/ n Beendigung f, (Med) Schwangerschaftsabbruch m

terminology /tɜːmɪ'nɒlədʒɪ/ n Terminologie f

terminus /'tɜːmɪnəs/ n (pl -ni /-naɪ/) Endstation f

terrace /'terəs/ n Terrasse f; (houses) Häuserreihe f; the ~s (Sport) die [Steh]ränge pl. ~d house n Reihenhaus nt

terrain /te'reɪn/ n Gelände nt

terrible /'terəbl/ a, -bly adv schrecklich

terrier /'terɪə(r)/ n Terrier m

terrific /tə'rɪfɪk/ a (fam) (excellent) sagenhaft; (huge) riesig

terri|fy /'terɪfaɪ/ vt (pt/pp -ied) Angst machen (+ dat); be ~fied Angst haben. ~fying a Furcht erregend

territorial /terɪ'tɔːrɪəl/ a Territorial-

territory /'terɪtərɪ/ n Gebiet nt

terror /'terə(r)/ n [panische] Angst f; (Pol) Terror m. ~ism /-ɪzm/ n Terrorismus m. ~ist /-ɪst/ n Terrorist m. ~ize vt terrorisieren

terse /tɜːs/ a, -ly adv kurz, knapp

test /test/ n Test m; (Sch) Klassenarbeit f; put to the ~ auf die Probe stellen □ vt prüfen; (examine) untersuchen (for auf + acc)

testament /'testəmənt/ n Testament nt; Old/New T~ Altes/Neues Testament nt

testicle /'testɪkl/ n Hoden m

testify /'testɪfaɪ/ v (pt/pp -ied) □ vt beweisen; ~ that bezeugen, dass □ vi aussagen; ~ to bezeugen

testimonial /testɪ'məʊnɪəl/ n Zeugnis nt

testimony /'testɪmənɪ/ n Aussage f

'test-tube n Reagenzglas nt. ~ 'baby n (fam) Retortenbaby nt

testy /'testɪ/ a gereizt

tetanus /'tetənəs/ n Tetanus m

tetchy /'tetʃɪ/ a gereizt

tether /'teðə(r)/ n be at the end of one's ~ am Ende seiner Kraft sein □ vt anbinden

text /tekst/ n Text m. ~book n Lehrbuch nt

textile /'tekstaɪl/ a Textil- □ n ~s pl Textilien pl

texture /'tekstʃə(r)/ n Beschaffenheit f; (Tex) Struktur f

Thai /taɪ/ a thailändisch. ~land n Thailand nt

Thames /temz/ n Themse f

than /ðən, betont ðæn/ conj als; older ~ me älter als ich

thank /θæŋk/ vt danken (+ dat); ~ you [very much] danke [schön]. ~ful a, -ly adv dankbar. ~less a undankbar

thanks /θæŋks/ npl Dank m; ~! (fam) danke! ~ to dank (+ dat or gen)

that /ðæt/ a & pron (pl those) der/die/das; (pl) die; ~ one der/die/das da; I'll take ~ ich nehme den/die/das; I don't like those die mag ich nicht; ~ is das heißt; is ~ you? bist du es? who is ~? wer ist da? with/after ∼ damit/danach; like ∼ so; a man like ∼ so ein Mann; ∼ is why deshalb; ∼'s it! genau! all ∼ I know alles was ich weiß; the day ∼ I saw him an dem Tag, als ich ihn sah ◻ adv so; ∼ good/ hot so gut/heiß ◻ conj dass

thatch /θætʃ/ n Strohdach nt. ∼ed a strohgedeckt

thaw /θɔ:/ n Tauwetter nt ◻ vt/i auftauen; it's ∼ing es taut

the /ðə, vor einem Vokal ði:/ def art der/ die/das; (pl) die; play ∼ piano/violin Klavier/Geige spielen ◻ adv ∼ more ∼ better je mehr, desto besser; all ∼ better umso besser

theatre /ˈθɪətə(r)/ n Theater nt; (Med) Operationssaal m

theatrical /θɪˈætrɪkl/ a Theater-; (showy) theatralisch

theft /θeft/ n Diebstahl m

their /ðeə(r)/ a ihr

theirs /ðeəz/ poss pron ihre(r), ihrs; a friend of ∼ ein Freund von ihnen; those are ∼ die gehören ihnen

them /ðem/ pron (acc) sie; (dat) ihnen; I know ∼ ich kenne sie; give ∼ the money gib ihnen das Geld

theme /θi:m/ n Thema nt

them'selves pron selbst; (refl) sich; by ∼ allein

then /ðen/ adv dann; (at that time in past) damals; by ∼ bis dahin; since ∼ seitdem; before ∼ vorher; from ∼ on von da an; now and ∼ dann und wann; there and ∼ auf der Stelle ◻ a damalig

theolo̱gian /θɪəˈləʊdʒɪən/ n Theologe m. ∼y /-ˈɒlədʒɪ/ n Theologie f

theorem /ˈθɪərəm/ n Lehrsatz m

theoretical /θɪəˈretɪkl/ a, -ly adv theoretisch

theory /ˈθɪərɪ/ n Theorie f; in ∼ theoretisch

therapeutic /θerəˈpju:tɪk/ a therapeutisch

therap|ist /ˈθerəpɪst/ n Therapeut(in) m(f). ∼y n Therapie f

there /ðeə(r)/ adv da; (with movement) dahin, dorthin; down/up ∼ da unten/oben; ∼ is/are da ist/sind; (in existence) es gibt; ∼ he/she is da ist er/sie; send/take ∼ hinschicken/-bringen ◻ int there, there! nun, nun!

there: ∼abouts adv da [in der Nähe]; or ∼abouts (roughly) ungefähr. ∼'after adv danach. ∼by adv dadurch. ∼fore /-fɔ:(r)/ adv deshalb, also

thermal /ˈθɜ:ml/ a Thermal-; ∼ 'underwear n Thermowäsche f

thermometer /θəˈmɒmɪtə(r)/ n Thermometer nt

Thermos (P) /ˈθɜ:məs/ n ∼ [flask] Thermosflasche (P) f

thermostat /ˈθɜ:məstæt/ n Thermostat m

these /ði:z/ see this

thesis /ˈθi:sɪs/ n (pl -ses /-si:z/) Dissertation f; (proposition) These f

they /ðeɪ/ pron sie; ∼ say (generalizing) man sagt

thick /θɪk/ a (-er, -est), -ly adv dick; (dense) dicht; (liquid) dickflüssig; (fam: stupid) dumm ◻ adv dick ∼ n in the ∼ of mitten in (+ dat). ∼en vt dicker machen; eindicken (sauce) ◻ vi dicker werden; (fog:) dichter werden; (plot:) kompliziert werden. ∼ness n Dicke f; Dichte f; Dickflüssigkeit f

thick: ∼set a untersetzt. ∼-'skinned a (fam) dickfellig

thief /θi:f/ n (pl thieves) Dieb(in) m(f)

thieving /ˈθi:vɪŋ/ a diebisch ◻ n Stehlen nt

thigh /θaɪ/ n Oberschenkel m

thimble /ˈθɪmbl/ n Fingerhut m

thin /θɪn/ a (thinner, thinnest), -ly adv dünn ◻ adv dünn ∼ v (pt/pp thinned) ◻ vt verdünnen (liquid) ◻ vi sich lichten. ∼ out vt ausdünnen

thing /θɪŋ/ n Ding nt; (subject, affair) Sache f; ∼s pl (belongings) Sachen pl; for one ∼ erstens; the right ∼ das Richtige; just the ∼! genau das Richtige; how are ∼s? wie geht's? the latest ∼ (fam) der letzte Schrei; the best ∼ would be am besten wäre es

think /θɪŋk/ vt/i (pt/pp thought) denken (about/of an + acc); (believe) meinen; (consider) nachdenken; (regard as) halten für; I ∼ so ich glaube schon; what do you ∼? was meinen Sie? what do you ∼ of it? was halten Sie davon? ∼ better of it es sich (dat) anders überlegen. ∼ over vt sich (dat) überlegen. ∼ up vt sich (dat) ausdenken

third /θɜ:d/ a dritte(r,s) ◻ n Drittel nt. ∼ly adv drittens. ∼-rate a drittrangig

thirst /θɜ:st/ n Durst m. ∼y a, -ily adv durstig; be ∼y Durst haben

thirteen /θɜ:ˈti:n/ a dreizehn. ∼th a dreizehnte(r,s)

thirtieth /ˈθɜ:tɪɪθ/ a dreißigste(r,s)

thirty /ˈθɜ:tɪ/ a dreißig

this /ðɪs/ a (pl these) diese(r,s); (pl) diese; ∼ one diese(r,s) da; I'll take ∼ ich nehme diesen/diese/ dieses; ∼ evening/morning heute Abend/Morgen; these days heutzutage ◻ pron (pl these) das, dies[es]; (pl) die, diese; ∼ and that dies und das; ∼ or that dieses oder das da; like ∼ so;

~ is Peter das ist Peter; (*Teleph*) hier [spricht] Peter; who is ~? wer ist das? (*Amer, Teleph*) wer ist am Apparat?

thistle /'θɪsl/ n Distel f

thorn /θɔːn/ n Dorn m. ~y a dornig

thorough /'θʌrə/ a gründlich

thorough: ~bred n reinrassiges Tier nt; (*horse*) Rassepferd nt. ~fare n Durchfahrtsstraße f; 'no ~fare' 'keine Durchfahrt'

thorough|ly /'θʌrəlɪ/ adv gründlich; (*completely*) völlig; (*extremely*) äußerst. ~ness n Gründlichkeit f

those /ðəʊz/ see that

though /ðəʊ/ conj obgleich, obwohl; as ~ als ob a adv (*fam*) doch

thought /θɔːt/ see think □ n Gedanke m; (*thinking*) Denken nt. ~ful a, -ly adv nachdenklich; (*considerate*) rücksichtsvoll. ~less a, -ly adv gedankenlos

thousand /'θaʊznd/ a one/a ~ [ein]tausend □ n Tausend nt; ~s of Tausende von. ~th a tausendste(r,s) □ n Tausendstel n

thrash /θræʃ/ vt verprügeln; (*defeat*) [vernichtend] schlagen. ~ about vi sich herumwälzen; (*fish:*) zappeln. ~ out vt ausdiskutieren

thread /θred/ n Faden m; (*of screw*) Gewinde nt □ vt einfädeln; auffädeln (*beads*); ~ one's way through sich schlängeln durch. ~bare a fadenscheinig

threat /θret/ n Drohung f; (*danger*) Bedrohung f

threaten /'θretn/ vt drohen (+ dat); (*with weapon*) bedrohen; ~ to do sth drohen, etw zu tun; ~ s.o. with sth jdm etw androhen □ vi drohen. ~ing a, -ly adv drohend; (*ominous*) bedrohlich

three /θriː/ a drei. ~fold a & adv dreifach. ~some /-səm/ n Trio nt

thresh /θreʃ/ vt dreschen

threshold /'θreʃəʊld/ n Schwelle f

threw /θruː/ see throw

thrift /θrɪft/ n Sparsamkeit f. ~y a sparsam

thrill /θrɪl/ n Erregung f; (*fam*) Nervenkitzel m □ vt (*excite*) erregen; be ~ed with sich sehr freuen über (+ acc). ~er n Thriller m. ~ing a aufregend

thrive /θraɪv/ vi (*pt* thrived *or* throve, *pp* thrived *or* thriven /'θrɪvn/) gedeihen (on bei); (*business:*) florieren

throat /θrəʊt/ n Hals m; sore ~ Halsschmerzen pl; cut s.o.'s ~ jdm die Kehle durchschneiden

throb /θrɒb/ n Pochen nt □ vi (*pt/pp* throbbed) pochen; (*vibrate*) vibrieren

throes /θrəʊz/ npl in the ~ of (*fig*) mitten in (+ dat)

thrombosis /θrɒm'bəʊsɪs/ n Thrombose f

throne /θrəʊn/ n Thron m

throng /θrɒŋ/ n Menge f

throttle /'θrɒtl/ vt erdrosseln

through /θruː/ prep durch (+ acc); (*during*) während (+ gen); (*Amer: up to & including*) bis einschließlich □ adv durch; all ~ die ganze Zeit; ~ and ~ durch und durch; wet ~ durch und durch nass; read sth ~ etw durchlesen; let/walk ~ durchlassen/-gehen a (*train*) durchgehend; be ~ (*finished*) fertig sein; (*Teleph*) durch sein

throughout /θruː'aʊt/ prep ~ the country im ganzen Land; ~ the night die Nacht durch □ adv ganz; (*time*) die ganze Zeit

throve /θrəʊv/ see thrive

throw /θrəʊ/ n Wurf m □ vt (*pt* threw, *pp* thrown) werfen; schütten (*liquid*); betätigen (*switch*); abwerfen (*rider*); (*fam: disconcert*) aus der Fassung bringen; (*fam*) geben (*party*); ~ sth to s.o. jdm etw zuwerfen; ~ sth at s.o. etw nach jdm werfen; (*pelt with*) jdn mit etw bewerfen. ~ away vt wegwerfen. ~ out vt hinauswerfen; (~ away) wegwerfen; verwerfen (*plan*). ~ up vt hochwerfen □ vi (*fam*) sich übergeben

'throw-away a Wegwerf-

thrush /θrʌʃ/ n Drossel f

thrust /θrʌst/ n Stoß m; (*Phys*) Schub m □ vt (*pt/pp* thrust) stoßen; (*insert*) stecken; ~ [up]on aufbürden (s.o. jdm)

thud /θʌd/ n dumpfer Schlag m

thug /θʌg/ n Schläger m

thumb /θʌm/ n Daumen m; rule of ~ Faustregel f; under s.o.'s ~ unter jds Fuchtel □ vt ~ a lift (*fam*) per Anhalter fahren. ~-index n Daumenregister nt. ~tack n (*Amer*) Reißzwecke f

thump /θʌmp/ n Schlag m; (*noise*) dumpfer Schlag m □ vt schlagen □ vi hämmern (on an/auf + acc); (*heart:*) pochen

thunder /'θʌndə(r)/ n Donner m □ vi donnern. ~clap n Donnerschlag m. ~storm n Gewitter nt. ~y a gewittrig

Thursday /'θɜːzdeɪ/ n Donnerstag m

thus /ðʌs/ adv so

thwart /θwɔːt/ vt vereiteln; ~ s.o. jdm einen Strich durch die Rechnung machen

thyme /taɪm/ n Thymian m

thyroid /'θaɪrɔɪd/ n Schilddrüse f

tiara /tɪ'ɑːrə/ n Diadem nt

tick[1] /tɪk/ n on ~ (*fam*) auf Pump

tick[2] n (*sound*) Ticken nt; (*mark*) Häkchen nt; (*fam: instant*) Sekunde f □ vi ticken

□ *vt* abhaken. ~ off *vt* abhaken; (*fam*) rüffeln. ~ over *vi* ⟨*engine*:⟩ im Leerlauf laufen

ticket /'tıkıt/ *n* Karte *f*; ⟨*for bus, train*⟩ Fahrschein *m*; (*Aviat*) Flugschein *m*; ⟨*for lottery*⟩ Los *nt*; ⟨*for article deposited*⟩ Schein *m*; ⟨*label*⟩ Schild *nt*; ⟨*for library*⟩ Lesekarte *f*; ⟨*fine*⟩ Strafzettel *m*. ~-collector *n* Fahrkartenkontrolleur *m*. ~-office *n* Fahrkartenschalter *m*; ⟨*for entry*⟩ Kasse *f*

tick|le /'tıkl/ *n* Kitzeln *nt* □ *vt/i* kitzeln. ~lish /'tıklıʃ/ *a* kitzlig

tidal /'taıdl/ *a* ⟨*river, harbour*⟩ Tide-. ~ wave *n* Flutwelle *f*

tiddly-winks /'tıdlıwıŋks/ *n* Flohspiel *nt*

tide /taıd/ *n* Gezeiten *pl*; ⟨*of events*⟩ Strom *m*; the ~ is in/out es ist Flut/Ebbe □ *vt* ~ s.o. over jdm über die Runden helfen

tidiness /'taıdınıs/ *n* Ordentlichkeit *f*

tidy /'taıdı/ *a* (-ier, -iest), -ily *adv* ordentlich *v vt* ~ [up] aufräumen; ~ oneself up sich zurechtmachen

tie /taı/ *n* Krawatte *f*; Schlips *m*; ⟨*cord*⟩ Schnur *f*; ⟨*fig: bond*⟩ Band *nt*, ⟨*restriction*⟩ Bindung *f*; (*Sport*) Unentschieden *nt*; ⟨*in competition*⟩ Punktgleichheit *f* □ *v* ⟨*pres p* tying⟩ □ *vt* binden; machen ⟨*knot*⟩ □ *vi* (*Sport*) unentschieden spielen; ⟨*have equal scores, votes*⟩ punktgleich sein; ~ in with passen zu. ~ up *vt* festbinden; verschnüren ⟨*parcel*⟩; fesseln ⟨*person*⟩; be ~d up ⟨*busy*⟩ beschäftigt sein

tier /tıə(r)/ *n* Stufe *f*; ⟨*of cake*⟩ Etage *f*; ⟨*in stadium*⟩ Rang *m*

tiff /tıf/ *n* Streit *m*, (*fam*) Krach *m*

tiger /'taıgə(r)/ *n* Tiger *m*

tight /taıt/ *a* (-er, -est), -ly *adv* fest; ⟨*taut*⟩ straff; ⟨*clothes*⟩ eng; ⟨*control*⟩ streng; ⟨*fam: drunk*⟩ blau; in a ~ corner (*fam*) in der Klemme □ *adv* fest

tighten /'taıtn/ *vt* fester ziehen; straffen ⟨*rope*⟩; anziehen ⟨*screw*⟩; verschärfen ⟨*control*⟩ □ *vi* sich spannen

tight: ~-'fisted *a* knauserig. ~rope *n* Hochseil *nt*

tights /taıts/ *npl* Strumpfhose *f*

tile /taıl/ *n* Fliese *f*; ⟨*on wall*⟩ Kachel *f*; ⟨*on roof*⟩ [Dach]ziegel *m* □ *vt* mit Fliesen auslegen; kacheln ⟨*wall*⟩; decken ⟨*roof*⟩

till[1] /tıl/ *prep & conj* = until

till[2] *n* Kasse *f*

tiller /'tılə(r)/ *n* Ruderpinne *f*

tilt /tılt/ *n* Neigung *f*; at full ~ mit voller Wucht □ *vt* kippen; [zur Seite] neigen ⟨*head*⟩ □ *vi* sich neigen

timber /'tımbə(r)/ *n* [Nutz]holz *nt*

time /taım/ *n* Zeit *f*; ⟨*occasion*⟩ Mal *nt*; ⟨*rhythm*⟩ Takt *m*; ~s (*Math*) mal; at any

~ jederzeit; this ~ dieses Mal, diesmal; at ~s manchmal; ~ and again immer wieder; two at a ~ zwei auf einmal; on ~ pünktlich; in ~ rechtzeitig; ⟨*eventually*⟩ mit der Zeit; in no ~ im Handumdrehen; in a year's ~ in einem Jahr; behind ~ verspätet; behind the ~s rückständig; for the ~ being vorläufig; what is the ~? wie spät ist es? wie viel Uhr ist es? by the ~ we arrive bis wir ankommen; did you have a nice ~? hat es dir gut gefallen? have a good ~! viel Vergnügen! □ *vt* stoppen ⟨*race*⟩; be well ~d gut abgepaßt sein

time: ~ bomb *n* Zeitbombe *f*. ~-lag *n* Zeitdifferenz *f*. ~less *a* zeitlos. ~ly *a* rechtzeitig. ~-switch *n* Zeitschalter *m*. ~-table *n* Fahrplan *m*; (*Sch*) Stundenplan *m*

timid /'tımıd/ *a*, -ly *adv* scheu; ⟨*hesitant*⟩ zaghaft

timing /'taımıŋ/ *n* Wahl *f* des richtigen Zeitpunkts; (*Sport, Techn*) Timing *nt*

tin /tın/ *n* Zinn *nt*; ⟨*container*⟩ Dose *f* □ *vt* ⟨*pt/pp* tinned⟩ in Dosen *od* Büchsen konservieren. ~ foil *n* Stanniol *nt*; (*Culin*) Alufolie *f*

tinge /tındʒ/ *n* Hauch *m* □ *vt* ~d with mit einer Spur von

tingle /'tıŋgl/ *vi* kribbeln

tinker /'tıŋkə(r)/ *vi* herumbasteln (with an + *dat*)

tinkle /'tıŋkl/ *n* Klingeln *nt* □ *vi* klingeln

tinned /tınd/ *a* Dosen-, Büchsen-

'tin opener *n* Dosen-/Büchsenöffner *m*

'tinpot *a* (*pej*) ⟨*firm*⟩ schäbig

tinsel /'tınsl/ *n* Lametta *nt*

tint /tınt/ *n* Farbton *m* □ *vt* tönen

tiny /'taını/ *a* (-ier, -iest) winzig

tip[1] /tıp/ *n* Spitze *f*

tip[2] *n* ⟨*money*⟩ Trinkgeld *nt*; ⟨*advice*⟩ Rat *m*, (*fam*) Tipp *m*; ⟨*for rubbish*⟩ Mülldeponie *f* □ *v* ⟨*pt/pp* tipped⟩ □ *vt* kippen; ⟨*reward*⟩ Trinkgeld geben (s.o. jdm) □ *vi* kippen. ~ off *vt* ~ s.o. off jdm einen Hinweis geben. ~ out *vt* auskippen. ~ over *vt/i* umkippen

'tip-off *n* Hinweis *m*

tipped /tıpt/ *a* Filter-

tipsy /'tıpsı/ *a* (*fam*) beschwipst

tiptoe /'tıptəʊ/ *n* on ~ auf Zehenspitzen

tiptop /tıp'tɒp/ *a* (*fam*) erstklassig

tire /'taıə(r)/ *vt/i* ermüden. ~d *a* müde; be ~d of sth etw satt haben; ~d out [völlig] erschöpft. ~less *a*, -ly *adv* unermüdlich. ~some /-səm/ *a* lästig

tiring /'taıərıŋ/ *a* ermüdend

tissue /ˈtɪʃuː/ n Gewebe nt; (handkerchief) Papiertaschentuch nt. ~-paper n Seidenpapier nt

tit¹ /tɪt/ n (bird) Meise f

tit² n ~ for tat wie du mir, so ich dir

'titbit n Leckerbissen m

titillate /ˈtɪtɪleɪt/ vt erregen

title /ˈtaɪtl/ n Titel m. ~-role n Titelrolle f

tittle-tattle /ˈtɪtlˌtætl/ n Klatsch m

titular /ˈtɪtjʊlə(r)/ a nominell

to /tuː, unbetont tə/ prep zu (+ dat); (with place, direction) nach; (to cinema, theatre) in (+ acc); (to wedding, party) auf (+ acc); ⟨address, send, fasten⟩ an (+ acc); (per) pro; (up to, until) bis; to the station zum Bahnhof; to Germany/Switzerland nach Deutschland/ in die Schweiz; to the toilet/one's room auf die Toilette/sein Zimmer; to the office/an exhibition ins Büro/ in eine Ausstellung; to university auf die Universität; twenty/quarter to eight zwanzig/Viertel vor acht; 5 to 6 pounds 5 bis 6 Pfund; to the end bis zum Schluss; to this day bis heute; to the best of my knowledge nach meinem besten Wissen; give/say sth to s.o. jdm etw geben/sagen; go/come to s.o. zu jdm gehen/kommen; I've never been to Berlin ich war noch nie in Berlin; there's nothing to it es ist nichts dabei □ verbal construction to go gehen; to stay bleiben; learn to swim schwimmen lernen; want to/have to go gehen wollen/müssen; be easy/difficult to forget leicht/schwer zu vergessen sein; too ill/tired to go zu krank/müde, um zu gehen; he did it to annoy me er tat es, um mich zu ärgern; you have to du musst; I don't want to ich will nicht; I'd love to gern; I forgot to ich habe es vergessen; he wants to be a teacher er will Lehrer werden; live to be 90 90 werden; he was the last to arrive er kam als Letzter; to be honest ehrlich gesagt □ adv pull to anlehnen; to and fro hin und her

toad /təʊd/ n Kröte f. ~stool n Giftpilz m

toast /təʊst/ n Toast m □ vt toasten (bread); (drink a ~ to) trinken auf (+ acc). ~er n Toaster m

tobacco /təˈbækəʊ/ n Tabak m. ~nist's [shop] n Tabakladen m

toboggan /təˈbɒgən/ n Schlitten m □ vi Schlitten fahren

today /təˈdeɪ/ n & adv heute; ~ week heute in einer Woche; ~'s paper die heutige Zeitung

toddler /ˈtɒdlə(r)/ n Kleinkind nt

to-do /təˈduː/ n (fam) Getue nt, Theater nt

toe /təʊ/ n Zeh m; (of footwear) Spitze f □ vt ~ the line spuren. ~nail n Zehennagel m

toffee /ˈtɒfɪ/ n Karamellbonbon m & nt

together /təˈgeðə(r)/ adv zusammen; (at the same time) gleichzeitig

toil /tɔɪl/ n [harte] Arbeit f □ vi schwer arbeiten

toilet /ˈtɔɪlɪt/ n Toilette f. ~ bag n Kulturbeutel m. ~ paper n Toilettenpapier nt

toiletries /ˈtɔɪlɪtrɪz/ npl Toilettenartikel pl

toilet: ~ roll n Rolle f Toilettenpapier. ~ water n Toilettenwasser nt

token /ˈtəʊkən/ n Zeichen nt; (counter) Marke f; (voucher) Gutschein m □ attrib symbolisch

told /təʊld/ see tell □ a all ~ insgesamt

tolerable /ˈtɒlərəbl/ a, -bly adv erträglich; (not bad) leidlich

toleran|ce /ˈtɒlərəns/ n Toleranz f. ~t a, -ly adv tolerant

tolerate /ˈtɒləreɪt/ vt dulden, tolerieren; (bear) ertragen

toll¹ /təʊl/ n Gebühr f; (for road) Maut f (Aust); death ~ Zahl f der Todesopfer; take a heavy ~ einen hohen Tribut fordern

toll² vi läuten

tom /tɒm/ n (cat) Kater m

tomato /təˈmɑːtəʊ/ n (pl -es) Tomate f. ~ purée n Tomatenmark nt

tomb /tuːm/ n Grabmal nt

tomboy /ˈtɒm-/ n Wildfang m

'tombstone n Grabstein m

'tom-cat n Kater m

tome /təʊm/ n dicker Band m

tomfoolery /tɒmˈfuːlərɪ/ n Blödsinn m

tomorrow /təˈmɒrəʊ/ n & adv morgen; ~ morning morgen früh; the day after ~ übermorgen; see you ~! bis morgen!

ton /tʌn/ n Tonne f. ~s of (fam) jede Menge

tone /təʊn/ n Ton m; (colour) Farbton m □ vt ~ down dämpfen; (fig) mäßigen. ~ up vt kräftigen; straffen ⟨muscles⟩

tongs /tɒŋz/ npl Zange f

tongue /tʌŋ/ n Zunge f; ~ in cheek (fam) nicht ernst. ~-twister n Zungenbrecher m

tonic /ˈtɒnɪk/ n Tonikum nt; (for hair) Haarwasser nt; (fig) Wohltat f; ~ [water] n Tonic nt

tonight /təˈnaɪt/ n & adv heute Nacht; (evening) heute Abend

tonne /tʌn/ n Tonne f

tonsil /ˈtɒnsl/ n (Anat) Mandel f. ~litis /-səˈlaɪtɪs/ n Mandelentzündung f

too /tu:/ *adv* zu; (*also*) auch; ~ much/little
zu viel/zu wenig

took /tʊk/ *see* take

tool /tu:l/ *n* Werkzeug *nt*; (*for gardening*)
Gerät *nt*

toot /tu:t/ *n* Hupsignal *nt* □ *vi* tuten; (*Auto*)
hupen

tooth /tu:θ/ *n* (*pl* teeth) Zahn *m*

tooth: ~ache *n* Zahnschmerzen *pl.*
~brush *n* Zahnbürste *f.* ~less *a* zahnlos.
~paste *n* Zahnpasta *f.* ~pick *n* Zahn-
stocher *m*

top¹ /tɒp/ *n* (*toy*) Kreisel *m*

top² *n* oberer Teil *m*; (*apex*) Spitze *f*; (*summit*) Gipfel *m*; (*Sch*) Erste(r) *m/f*; (*top part
or half*) Oberteil *nt*; (*head*) Kopfende *nt*;
(*of road*) oberes Ende *nt*; (*upper surface*)
Oberfläche *f*; (*lid*) Deckel *m*; (*of bottle*)
Verschluss *m*; (*garment*) Top *nt*; at the/on
~ oben; on ~ of oben auf (+ *dat/acc*); on
~ of that (*besides*) obendrein; from ~ to
bottom von oben bis unten □ *a* oberste(r,s); (*highest*) höchste(r,s); (*best*) bes-
te(r,s) □ *vt* (*pt/pp* topped) an erster Stelle
stehen auf (+ *dat*) ⟨*list*⟩; (*exceed*) übersteigen; (*remove the* ~ *of*) die Spitze abschneiden von. ~ up *vt* nachfüllen, auffüllen

top: ~ 'hat *n* Zylinder[hut] *m*. ~-heavy *a*
kopflastig

topic /'tɒpɪk/ *n* Thema *nt*. ~al *a* aktuell

top: ~less *a* & *adv* oben ohne. ~most *a*
oberste(r,s)

topple /'tɒpl/ *vt/i* umstürzen. ~ off *vi*
stürzen

top-'secret *a* streng geheim

topsy-turvy /tɒpsɪ'tɜ:vɪ/ *adv* völlig
durcheinander

torch /tɔ:tʃ/ *n* Taschenlampe *f*; (*flaming*)
Fackel *f*

tore /tɔ:(r)/ *see* tear¹

torment¹ /'tɔ:ment/ *n* Qual *f*

torment² /tɔ:'ment/ *vt* quälen

torn /tɔ:n/ *see* tear¹ □ *a* zerrissen

tornado /tɔ:'neɪdəʊ/ *n* (*pl* -es) Wirbelsturm *m*

torpedo /tɔ:'pi:dəʊ/ *n* (*pl* -es) Torpedo *m*
□ *vt* torpedieren

torrent /'tɒrənt/ *n* reißender Strom *m*.
~ial /tə'renʃl/ *a* (*rain*) wolkenbruchartig

torso /'tɔ:səʊ/ *n* Rumpf *m*; (*Art*) Torso *m*

tortoise /'tɔ:təs/ *n* Schildkröte *f*. ~shell
n Schildpatt *nt*

tortuous /'tɔ:tjʊəs/ *a* verschlungen; (*fig*)
umständlich

torture /'tɔ:tʃə(r)/ *n* Folter *f*; (*fig*) Qual *f*
□ *vt* foltern; (*fig*) quälen

toss /tɒs/ *vt* werfen; (*into the air*)
hochwerfen; (*shake*) schütteln; (*unseat*)

abwerfen; mischen ⟨*salad*⟩; wenden ⟨*pancake*⟩; ~ a coin mit einer Münze losen □ *vi*
~ and turn (*in bed*) sich [schlaflos] im
Bett wälzen. ~ up *vi* [mit einer Münze]
losen

tot¹ /tɒt/ *n* kleines Kind *nt*; (*fam: of liquor*)
Gläschen *nt*

tot² *vt* (*pt/pp* totted) ~ up (*fam*) zusammenzählen

total /'təʊtl/ *a* gesamt; (*complete*) völlig,
total □ *n* Gesamtzahl *f*; (*sum*) Gesamtsumme *f* □ *vt* (*pt/pp* totalled) zusammenzählen; (*amount to*) sich belaufen auf
(+ *acc*)

totalitarian /təʊtælɪ'teərɪən/ *a* totalitär

totally /'təʊtəlɪ/ *adv* völling, total

totter /'tɒtə(r)/ *vi* taumeln; (*rock*)
schwanken. ~y *a* wackelig

touch /tʌtʃ/ *n* Berührung *f*; (*sense*) Tast-
sinn *m*; (*Mus*) Anschlag *m*; (*contact*) Kontakt *m*; (*trace*) Spur *f*; (*fig*) Anflug *m*;
get/be in ~ sich in Verbindung setzen/in
Verbindung stehen (with mit) □ *vt* berühren; (*get hold of*) anfassen; (*lightly*)
tippen auf/an (+ *acc*); (*brush against*)
streifen [gegen]; (*reach*) erreichen; (*equal*)
herankommen an (+ *acc*); (*fig: move*)
rühren; anrühren ⟨*food, subject*⟩; don't ~
that! fass das nicht an! □ *vi* sich berühren;
~ on (*fig*) berühren. ~ down *vi* (*Aviat*)
landen. ~ up *vt* ausbessern

touching /'tʌtʃɪŋ/ *a* rührend. ~y *a*
empfindlich; (*subject*) heikel

tough /tʌf/ *a* (-er, -est) zäh; (*severe, harsh*)
hart; (*difficult*) schwierig; (*durable*) strapazierfähig

toughen /'tʌfn/ *vt* härten; ~ up abhärten

tour /tʊə(r)/ *n* Reise *f*, Tour *f*; (*of building,
town*) Besichtigung *f*; (*Theat, Sport*)
Tournee *f*; (*of duty*) Dienstzeit *f* □ *vt*
fahren durch; besichtigen ⟨*building*⟩ □ *vi*
herumreisen

tourism /'tʊərɪzm/ *n* Tourismus *m*,
Fremdenverkehr *m*. ~t /-rɪst/ *n* Tou-
rist(in) *m(f)* □ *attrib* Touristen-. ~t office
n Fremdenverkehrsbüro *nt*

tournament /'tʊənəmənt/ *n* Turnier *nt*

'tour operator *n* Reiseveranstalter *m*

tousle /'taʊzl/ *vt* zerzausen

tout /taʊt/ *n* Anreißer *m*; (*ticket* ~) Kar-
tenschwarzhändler *m* □ *vi* ~ for cus-
tomers Kunden werben

tow /təʊ/ *n* give s.o./a car a ~ jdn/ein
Auto abschleppen; 'on ~' 'wird ge-
schleppt'; in ~ (*fam*) im Schlepptau □ *vt*
schleppen; ziehen ⟨*trailer*⟩. ~ away *vt* abschleppen

toward[s] /tə'wɔ:d(z)/ *prep* zu (+ *dat*);
(*with direction*) nach; (*with time*) gegen (+
acc); (*with respect to*) gegenüber (+ *dat*)

towel /ˈtauəl/ n Handtuch nt. ∼ling n (Tex) Frottee nt

tower /ˈtauə(r)/ n Turm m ◻ vi ∼ above überragen. ∼ block n Hochhaus nt. ∼ing a hoch aufragend

town /taun/ n Stadt f. ∼ 'hall n Rathaus nt

tow: ∼-path n Treidelpfad m. ∼rope n Abschleppseil nt

toxic /ˈtɒksɪk/ a giftig. ∼'waste n Giftmüll m

toxin /ˈtɒksɪn/ n Gift nt

toy /tɔɪ/ n Spielzeug nt ◻ vi ∼ with spielen mit; stochern in (+ dat) ⟨food⟩. ∼shop n Spielwarengeschäft nt

trac|e /treɪs/ n Spur f ◻ vt folgen (+ dat); ⟨find⟩ finden; ⟨draw⟩ zeichnen; ⟨with tracing-paper⟩ durchpausen. ∼ing-paper n Pauspapier nt

track /træk/ n Spur f; ⟨path⟩ [unbefestigter] Weg m; ⟨Sport⟩ Bahn f; ⟨Rail⟩ Gleis nt; keep ∼ of im Auge behalten ◻ vt verfolgen. ∼ down vt aufspüren; ⟨find⟩ finden

'tracksuit n Trainingsanzug m

tract¹ /trækt/ n ⟨land⟩ Gebiet nt

tract² n ⟨pamphlet⟩ ⟨Flug⟩schrift f

tractor /ˈtræktə(r)/ n Traktor m

trade /treɪd/ n Handel m; ⟨line of business⟩ Gewerbe nt; ⟨business⟩ Geschäft nt; ⟨craft⟩ Handwerk nt; by ∼ von Beruf ◻ vt tauschen; ∼ in ⟨give in part exchange⟩ in Zahlung geben ◻ vi handeln (in mit)

'trade mark n Warenzeichen nt

trader /ˈtreɪdə(r)/ n Händler m

trade: ∼ 'union n Gewerkschaft f. ∼ 'unionist n Gewerkschaftler(in) m(f)

trading /ˈtreɪdɪŋ/ n Handel m. ∼ estate n Gewerbegebiet nt. ∼ stamp n Rabattmarke f

tradition /trəˈdɪʃn/ n Tradition f. ∼al a, -ly adv traditionell

traffic /ˈtræfɪk/ n Verkehr m; ⟨trading⟩ Handel m ◻ vi handeln (in mit)

traffic: ∼ circle n ⟨Amer⟩ Kreisverkehr m. ∼ jam n [Verkehrs]stau m. ∼ lights npl [Verkehrs]ampel f. ∼ warden n ≈ Hilfspolizist m; ⟨woman⟩ Politesse f

tragedy /ˈtrædʒədɪ/ n Tragödie f

tragic /ˈtrædʒɪk/ a, -ally adv tragisch

trail /treɪl/ n Spur f; ⟨path⟩ Weg m, Pfad m ◻ vi schleifen; ⟨plant:⟩ sich ranken; ∼ [behind] zurückbleiben; ⟨Sport⟩ zurückliegen ◻ vt verfolgen, folgen (+ dat); ⟨drag⟩ schleifen

trailer /ˈtreɪlə(r)/ n ⟨Auto⟩ Anhänger m; ⟨Amer: caravan⟩ Wohnwagen m; ⟨film⟩ Vorschau f

train /treɪn/ n Zug m; ⟨of dress⟩ Schleppe f; ∼ of thought Gedankengang m ◻ vt ausbilden; ⟨Sport⟩ trainieren; ⟨aim⟩ richten auf (+ acc); erziehen ⟨child⟩; abrichten/⟨to do tricks⟩ dressieren ⟨animal⟩; ziehen ⟨plant⟩ ◻ vi eine Ausbildung machen; ⟨Sport⟩ trainieren. ∼ed a ausgebildet

trainee /treɪˈniː/ n Auszubildende(r) m/f; ⟨Techn⟩ Praktikant(in) m(f)

train|er /ˈtreɪnə(r)/ n ⟨Sport⟩ Trainer m; ⟨in circus⟩ Dompteur m; ∼ers pl Trainingsschuhe pl. ∼ing n Ausbildung f; ⟨Sport⟩ Training nt; ⟨of animals⟩ Dressur f

traipse /treɪps/ vi ⟨fam⟩ latschen

trait /treɪt/ n Eigenschaft f

traitor /ˈtreɪtə(r)/ n Verräter m

tram /træm/ n Straßenbahn f. ∼-lines npl Straßenbahnschienen pl

tramp /træmp/ n Landstreicher m; ⟨hike⟩ Wanderung f ◻ vi stapfen; ⟨walk⟩ marschieren

trample /ˈtræmpl/ vt/i trampeln (on auf + acc)

trampoline /ˈtræmpəlɪn/ n Trampolin nt

trance /trɑːns/ n Trance f

tranquil /ˈtræŋkwɪl/ a ruhig. ∼lity /-ˈkwɪlətɪ/ n Ruhe f

tranquillizer /ˈtræŋkwɪlaɪzə(r)/ n Beruhigungsmittel nt

transact /trænˈzækt/ vt abschließen. ∼ion /-ækʃn/ n Transaktion f

transcend /trænˈsend/ vt übersteigen

transcript /ˈtrænskrɪpt/ n Abschrift f; ⟨of official proceedings⟩ Protokoll nt. ∼ion /-ˈskrɪpʃn/ n Abschrift f

transept /ˈtrænsept/ n Querschiff nt

transfer¹ /ˈtrænsfɜː(r)/ n ⟨see transfer²⟩ Übertragung f; Verlegung f; Versetzung f; Überweisung f; ⟨Sport⟩ Transfer m; ⟨design⟩ Abziehbild nt

transfer² /trænsˈfɜː(r)/ v ⟨pt/pp transferred⟩ ◻ vt übertragen; verlegen ⟨firm, prisoners⟩; versetzen ⟨employee⟩; überweisen ⟨money⟩; ⟨Sport⟩ transferieren ◻ vi [über]wechseln; ⟨when travelling⟩ umsteigen. ∼able /-ˈəbl/ a übertragbar

transform /trænsˈfɔːm/ vt verwandeln. ∼ation /-fəˈmeɪʃn/ n Verwandlung f. ∼er n Transformator m

transfusion /trænsˈfjuːʒn/ n Transfusion f

transient /ˈtrænzɪənt/ a kurzlebig; ⟨life⟩ kurz

transistor /trænˈzɪstə(r)/ n Transistor m

transit /ˈtrænsɪt/ n Transit m; ⟨of goods⟩ Transport m; in ∼ ⟨goods⟩ auf dem Transport

transition /træn'sɪʒn/ n Übergang m. ~al a Übergangs-

transitive /'trænsɪtɪv/ a, -ly adv transitiv

transitory /'trænsɪtərɪ/ a vergänglich; ⟨life⟩ kurz

translat|e /træns'leɪt/ vt übersetzen. ~ion /-'leɪʃn/ n Übersetzung f. ~or n Übersetzer(in) m(f)

translucent /trænz'luːsnt/ a durchscheinend

transmission /trænz'mɪʃn/ n Übertragung f

transmit /trænz'mɪt/ vt (pt/pp transmitted) übertragen. ~ter n Sender m

transparen|cy /træns'pærənsɪ/ n (Phot) Dia nt. ~t a durchsichtig

transpire /træn'spaɪə(r)/ vi sich herausstellen; ⟨fam: happen⟩ passieren

transplant[1] /'trænsplɑːnt/ n Verpflanzung f, Transplantation f

transplant[2] /træns'plɑːnt/ vt umpflanzen; (Med) verpflanzen

transport[1] /'trænspɔːt/ n Transport m

transport[2] /træn'spɔːt/ vt transportieren. ~ation /-'teɪʃn/ n Transport m

transpose /træns'pəʊz/ vt umstellen

transvestite /træns'vestaɪt/ n Transvestit m

trap /træp/ n Falle f; ⟨fam: mouth⟩ Klappe f; pony and ~ Einspänner m ▫ vt (pt/pp trapped) [mit einer Falle] fangen; ⟨jam⟩ einklemmen; be ~ped festsitzen; ⟨shut in⟩ eingeschlossen sein; ⟨cut off⟩ abgeschnitten sein. ~door n Falltür f

trapeze /trə'piːz/ n Trapez nt

trash /træʃ/ n Schund m; ⟨rubbish⟩ Abfall m; ⟨nonsense⟩ Quatsch m. ~can n (Amer) Mülleimer m. ~y a Schund-

trauma /'trɔːmə/ n Trauma nt. ~tic /-'mætɪk/ a traumatisch

travel /'trævl/ n Reisen nt ▫ v (pt/pp travelled) ▫ vi reisen; ⟨go in vehicle⟩ fahren; ⟨light, sound⟩ sich fortpflanzen; (Techn) sich bewegen ▫ vt bereisen; fahren ⟨distance⟩. ~ agency n Reisebüro nt. ~ agent n Reisebürokaufmann m

traveller /'trævələ(r)/ n Reisende(r) m/f; (Comm) Vertreter m; ~s pl ⟨gypsies⟩ fahrendes Volk. ~'s cheque n Reisescheck m

trawler /'trɔːlə(r)/ n Fischdampfer m

tray /treɪ/ n Tablett nt; ⟨for oven⟩ [Back]blech nt; ⟨for documents⟩ Ablagekorb m

treacher|ous /'tretʃərəs/ a treulos; ⟨dangerous⟩ tückisch. ~y n Verrat m

treacle /'triːkl/ n Sirup m

tread /tred/ n Schritt m; ⟨step⟩ Stufe f; ⟨of tyre⟩ Profil nt ▫ v (pt trod, pp trodden)

▫ vi ⟨walk⟩ gehen; ~ on/in treten auf/ in (+ acc) ▫ vt treten

treason /'triːzn/ n Verrat m

treasure /'treʒə(r)/ n Schatz m ▫ vt in Ehren halten. ~r n Kassenwart m

treasury /'treʒərɪ/ n Schatzkammer f; the T~ das Finanzministerium

treat /triːt/ n [besonderes] Vergnügen nt; give s.o. a ~ jdm etwas Besonderes bieten ▫ vt behandeln; ~ s.o. to sth jdm etw spendieren

treatise /'triːtɪz/ n Abhandlung f

treatment /'triːtmənt/ n Behandlung f

treaty /'triːtɪ/ n Vertrag m

treble /'trebl/ a dreifach; ~ the amount dreimal so viel ▫ n (Mus) Diskant m; ⟨voice⟩ Sopran m ▫ vt verdreifachen ▫ vi sich verdreifachen. ~ clef n Violinschlüssel m

tree /triː/ n Baum m

trek /trek/ n Marsch m ▫ vi (pt/pp trekked) latschen

trellis /'trelɪs/ n Gitter nt

tremble /'trembl/ vi zittern

tremendous /trɪ'mendəs/ a, -ly adv gewaltig; ⟨fam: excellent⟩ großartig

tremor /'tremə(r)/ n Zittern nt; [earth] ~ Beben nt

trench /trentʃ/ n Graben m; (Mil) Schützengraben m

trend /trend/ n Tendenz f; ⟨fashion⟩ Trend m. ~y a (-ier, -iest) ⟨fam⟩ modisch

trepidation /trepɪ'deɪʃn/ n Beklommenheit f

trespass /'trespəs/ vi ~ on unerlaubt betreten. ~er n Unbefugte(r) m/f

trial /'traɪəl/ n (Jur) [Gerichts]verfahren nt, Prozess m; ⟨test⟩ Probe f; ⟨ordeal⟩ Prüfung f; be on ~ auf Probe sein; (Jur) angeklagt sein ⟨for wegen⟩; by ~ and error durch Probieren

triang|le /'traɪæŋgl/ n Dreieck nt; (Mus) Triangel m. ~ular /-'æŋgjʊlə(r)/ a dreieckig

tribe /traɪb/ n Stamm m

tribulation /trɪbjʊ'leɪʃn/ n Kummer m

tribunal /traɪ'bjuːnl/ n Schiedsgericht nt

tributary /'trɪbjʊtərɪ/ n Nebenfluss m

tribute /'trɪbjuːt/ n Tribut m; pay ~ Tribut zollen (to dat)

trice /traɪs/ n in a ~ im Nu

trick /trɪk/ n Trick m; ⟨joke⟩ Streich m; ⟨Cards⟩ Stich m; ⟨feat of skill⟩ Kunststück nt; that should do the ~ damit dürfte es klappen ▫ vt täuschen, ⟨fam⟩ hereinlegen

trickle /'trɪkl/ vi rinnen

trick|ster /'trɪkstə(r)/ n Schwindler m. **~y** a (-ier, -iest) a schwierig

tricycle /'traɪsɪkl/ n Dreirad nt

tried /traɪd/ see try

trifl|e /'traɪfl/ n Kleinigkeit f; (Culin) Trifle nt. **~ing** a unbedeutend

trigger /'trɪgə(r)/ n Abzug m; (fig) Auslöser m □ vt **~** [off] auslösen

trigonometry /trɪgə'nɒmɪtrɪ/ n Trigonometrie f

trim /trɪm/ a (trimmer, trimmest) gepflegt □ n (cut) Nachschneiden nt; (decoration) Verzierung f; (condition) Zustand m □ vt schneiden; (decorate) besetzen; (Naut) trimmen. **~ming** n Besatz m; **~mings** pl (accessories) Zubehör nt; (decorations) Verzierungen pl; with all the **~mings** mit allem Drum und Dran

Trinity /'trɪnətɪ/ n the [Holy] **~** die [Heilige] Dreieinigkeit f

trinket /'trɪŋkɪt/ n Schmuckgegenstand m

trio /'triːəʊ/ n Trio nt

trip /trɪp/ n Reise f; (excursion) Ausflug m □ v (pt/pp tripped) □ vt **~** s.o. up jdm ein Bein stellen □ vi stolpern (on/over über + acc)

tripe /traɪp/ n Kaldaunen pl; (nonsense) Quatsch m

triple /'trɪpl/ a dreifach □ vt verdreifachen □ vi sich verdreifachen

triplets /'trɪplɪts/ npl Drillinge pl

triplicate /'trɪplɪkət/ n in **~** in dreifacher Ausfertigung

tripod /'traɪpɒd/ n Stativ nt

tripper /'trɪpə(r)/ n Ausflügler m

trite /traɪt/ a banal

triumph /'traɪʌmf/ n Triumph m □ vi triumphieren (over über + acc). **~ant** /-'ʌmfnt/ a, **-ly** adv triumphierend

trivial /'trɪvɪəl/ a belanglos. **~ity** /-'ælɪtɪ/ n Belanglosigkeit f

trod, trodden /trɒd, 'trɒdn/ see tread

trolley /'trɒlɪ/ n (for serving food) Servierwagen m; (for shopping) Einkaufswagen m; (for luggage) Kofferkuli m; (Amer: tram) Straßenbahn f. **~ bus** n O-Bus m

trombone /trɒm'bəʊn/ n Posaune f

troop /truːp/ n Schar f; **~s** pl Truppen pl □ vi **~** in/out hinein-/hinausströmen

trophy /'trəʊfɪ/ n Trophäe f; (in competition) ≈ Pokal m

tropic /'trɒpɪk/ n Wendekreis m; **~s** pl Tropen pl. **~al** a tropisch; (fruit) Südfrucht

trot /trɒt/ n Trab m □ vi (pt/pp trotted) traben

trouble /'trʌbl/ n Ärger m; (difficulties) Schwierigkeiten pl; (inconvenience) Mühe f; (conflict) Unruhe f; (Med) Beschwerden pl; (Techn) Probleme pl; get into **~** Ärger bekommen; take **~** sich (dat) Mühe geben □ vt (disturb) stören; (worry) beunruhigen □ vi sich bemühen. **~-maker** n Unruhestifter m. **~some** /-səm/ a schwierig; (flies, cough) lästig

trough /trɒf/ n Trog m

trounce /traʊns/ vt vernichtend schlagen; (thrash) verprügeln

troupe /truːp/ n Truppe f

trousers /'traʊzəz/ npl Hose f

trousseau /'truːsəʊ/ n Aussteuer f

trout /traʊt/ n inv Forelle f

trowel /'traʊəl/ n Kelle f; (for gardening) Pflanzkelle f

truant /'truːənt/ n play **~** die Schule schwänzen

truce /truːs/ n Waffenstillstand m

truck /trʌk/ n Last[kraft]wagen m; (Rail) Güterwagen m

truculent /'trʌkjʊlənt/ a aufsässig

trudge /trʌdʒ/ n [mühseliger] Marsch m □ vi latschen

true /truː/ a (-r, -st) wahr; (loyal) treu; (genuine) echt; come **~** in Erfüllung gehen; is that **~**? stimmt das?

truism /'truːɪzm/ n Binsenwahrheit f

truly /'truːlɪ/ adv wirklich; (faithfully) treu; Yours **~** Hochachtungsvoll

trump /trʌmp/ n (Cards) Trumpf m □ vt übertrumpfen. **~ up** vt (fam) erfinden

trumpet /'trʌmpɪt/ n Trompete f. **~er** n Trompeter m

truncheon /'trʌntʃn/ n Schlagstock m

trundle /'trʌndl/ vt/i rollen

trunk /trʌŋk/ n (Baum]stamm m; (body) Rumpf m; (of elephant) Rüssel m; (for travelling) [Überseekoffer m; (for storage) Truhe f; (Amer: of car) Kofferraum m; **~s** pl Badehose f

truss /trʌs/ n (Med) Bruchband nt

trust /trʌst/ n Vertrauen nt; (group of companies) Trust m; (organization) Treuhandgesellschaft f; (charitable) Stiftung f □ vt trauen (+ dat), vertrauen (+ dat); (hope) hoffen □ vi vertrauen (in/to auf + acc)

trustee /trʌs'tiː/ n Treuhänder m

trust|ful /'trʌstfl/ a, **-ly** adv vertrauensvoll. **~ing** a vertrauensvoll. **~worthy** a vertrauenswürdig

truth /truːθ/ n (pl -s /truːðz/) Wahrheit f. **~ful** a, **-ly** adv ehrlich

try /traɪ/ n Versuch m □ v (pt/pp tried) □ vt versuchen; (sample, taste) probieren; (be a strain on) anstrengen; (Jur) vor Gericht stellen; verhandeln (case) □ vi versuchen; (make an effort) sich bemühen. **~ on** vt anprobieren; aufprobieren (hat). **~ out** vt ausprobieren

trying /'traɪɪŋ/ a schwierig

T-shirt /'tiː-/ n T-Shirt nt

tub /tʌb/ n Kübel m; (carton) Becher m; (bath) Wanne f

tuba /'tjuːbə/ a (Mus) Tuba f

tubby /'tʌbɪ/ a (-ier, -iest) rundlich

tube /tjuːb/ n Röhre f; (pipe) Rohr nt; (flexible) Schlauch m; (of toothpaste) Tube f; (Rail, fam) U-Bahn f

tuber /'tjuːbə(r)/ n Knolle f

tuberculosis /tjuːbɜːkjuˈləʊsɪs/ n Tuberkulose f

tubing /'tjuːbɪŋ/ n Schlauch m

tubular /'tjuːbjʊlə(r)/ a röhrenförmig

tuck /tʌk/ n Saum m; (decorative) Biese f □ vt (put) stecken. ~ in vt hineinstecken; ~ s.o. in jdn zudecken □ vi (fam: eat) zulangen. ~ up vt hochkrempeln ⟨sleeves⟩; (in bed) zudecken

Tuesday /'tjuːzdeɪ/ n Dienstag m

tuft /tʌft/ n Büschel nt

tug /tʌg/ n Ruck m; (Naut) Schleppdampfer m □ v (pt/pp tugged) □ vt ziehen □ vi zerren (at an + dat). ~ of war n Tauziehen nt

tuition /tjuːˈɪʃn/ n Unterricht m

tulip /'tjuːlɪp/ n Tulpe f

tumble /'tʌmbl/ n Sturz m □ vi fallen; ~ to sth (fam) etw kapieren. ~down a verfallen. ~-drier n Wäschetrockner m

tumbler /'tʌmblə(r)/ n Glas nt

tummy /'tʌmɪ/ n (fam) Magen m; (abdomen) Bauch m

tumour /'tjuːmə(r)/ n Geschwulst f, Tumor m

tumult /'tjuːmʌlt/ n Tumult m. ~uous /-'mʌltjʊəs/ a stürmisch

tuna /'tjuːnə/ n Thunfisch m

tune /tjuːn/ n Melodie f; out of ~ ⟨instrument⟩ verstimmt; to the ~ of (fam) in Höhe von □ vt stimmen; (Techn) einstellen. ~ in vt einstellen □ vi ~ in to a station einen Sender einstellen. ~ up vi (Mus) stimmen

tuneful /'tjuːnfl/ a melodisch

tunic /'tjuːnɪk/ n (Mil) Uniformjacke f; (Sch) Trägerkleid nt

Tunisia /tjuːˈnɪzɪə/ n Tunesien nt

tunnel /'tʌnl/ n Tunnel m □ vi (pt/pp tunnelled) einen Tunnel graben

turban /'tɜːbən/ n Turban m

turbine /'tɜːbaɪn/ n Turbine f

tur**b**o**t** /ˈtɜːbət/ n **S**te**inbutt** m

turbulen|ce /'tɜːbjʊləns/ n Turbulenz f. ~t a stürmisch

tureen /tjʊəˈriːn/ n Terrine f

turf /tɜːf/ n Rasen m; (segment) Rasenstück nt. ~ out vt (fam) rausschmeißen

'turf accountant n Buchmacher m

Turk /tɜːk/ n Türke m/Türkin f

turkey /'tɜːkɪ/ n Pute f, Truthahn m

Turk|ey n die Türkei. ~ish a türkisch

turmoil /'tɜːmɔɪl/ n Aufruhr m; (confusion) Durcheinander nt

turn /tɜːn/ n (rotation) Drehung f; (in road) Kurve f; (change of direction) Wende f; (short walk) Runde f; (Theat) Nummer f; (fam: attack) Anfall m; do s.o. a good ~ jdm einen guten Dienst erweisen; take ~s sich abwechseln; in ~ der Reihe nach; out of ~ außer der Reihe; it's your ~ du bist an der Reihe □ vt drehen; (~ over) wenden; (reverse) umdrehen; (Techn) drechseln ⟨wood⟩; ~ the page umblättern; ~ the corner um die Ecke biegen □ vi sich drehen; (~ round) sich umdrehen; ⟨car:⟩ wenden; ⟨leaves:⟩ sich färben; ⟨weather:⟩ umschlagen; (become) werden; ~ right/left nach rechts/links abbiegen; ~ to s.o. sich an jdn wenden; have ~ed against s.o. gegen jdn sein. ~ away vt abweisen □ vi sich abwenden. ~ down vt herunterschlagen ⟨collar⟩; herunterdrehen ⟨heat, gas⟩; leiser stellen ⟨sound⟩; (reject) ablehnen; abweisen ⟨person⟩. ~ in vt einschlagen ⟨edges⟩ □ vi ⟨car:⟩ einbiegen; (fam: go to bed) ins Bett gehen. ~ off vt zudrehen ⟨tap⟩; ausschalten ⟨light, radio⟩; abstellen ⟨water, gas, engine, machine⟩ □ vi abbiegen. ~ on vt aufdrehen ⟨tap⟩; einschalten ⟨light, radio⟩; anstellen ⟨water, gas, engine, machine⟩. ~ out vt (expel) vertreiben, (fam) hinauswerfen; ausschalten ⟨light⟩; abdrehen ⟨gas⟩; (produce) produzieren; (empty) ausleeren; [gründlich] aufräumen ⟨room, cupboard⟩ □ vi (go out) hinausgehen; (transpire) sich herausstellen; ~ out well/badly gut/schlecht gehen. ~ over vt umdrehen □ vi sich umdrehen. ~ up vt hochschlagen ⟨collar⟩; aufdrehen ⟨heat, gas⟩; lauter stellen ⟨sound, radio⟩ □ vi auftauchen

turning /'tɜːnɪŋ/ n Abzweigung f. ~point n Wendepunkt m

turnip /'tɜːnɪp/ n weiße Rübe f

turn: ~out n (of people) Teilnahme f, Beteiligung f; (of goods) Produktion f. ~over n (Comm) Umsatz m; (of staff) Personalwechsel m. ~pike n (Amer) gebührenpflichtige Autobahn f. ~stile n Drehkreuz nt. ~table n Drehscheibe f; (on record-player) Plattenteller m. ~up n [Hosen]aufschlag m

tur**pentine** /ˈtɜːpəntaɪn/ n **T**erpentin nt

turquoise /'tɜːkwɔɪz/ a türkis[farben] □ n (gem) Türkis m

turret /'tʌrɪt/ n Türmchen nt

turtle /'tɜːtl/ n Seeschildkröte f

tusk /tʌsk/ n Stoßzahn m

tussle /'tʌsl/ n Balgerei f; (fig) Streit m □ vi sich balgen

tutor /'tju:tə(r)/ n [Privat]lehrer m

tuxedo /tʌk'si:dəʊ/ n (Amer) Smoking m

TV /ti:'vi:/ abbr of television

twaddle /'twɒdl/ n Geschwätz nt

twang /twæŋ/ n (in voice) Näseln n □ vt zupfen

tweed /twi:d/ n Tweed m

tweezers /'twi:zəz/ npl Pinzette f

twelfth /twelfθ/ a zwölfter(r,s)

twelve /twelv/ a zwölf

twentieth /'twentɪθ/ a zwanzigste(r,s)

twenty /'twentɪ/ a zwanzig

twerp /twɜ:p/ n (fam) Trottel m

twice /twaɪs/ adv zweimal

twiddle /'twɪdl/ vt drehen an (+ dat)

twig¹ /twɪg/ n Zweig m

twig² vt/i (pt/pp twigged) (fam) kapieren

twilight /'twaɪ-/ n Dämmerlicht nt

twin /twɪn/ n Zwilling m □ attrib Zwillings-. ∼ beds npl zwei Einzelbetten pl

twine /twaɪn/ n Bindfaden m □ vi sich winden; (plant:) sich ranken

twinge /twɪndʒ/ n Stechen nt; ∼ of conscience Gewissensbisse pl

twinkle /'twɪŋkl/ n Funkeln nt □ vi funkeln

twin 'town n Partnerstadt f

twirl /twɜ:l/ vt/i herumwirbeln

twist /twɪst/ n Drehung f; (curve) Kurve f; (unexpected occurrence) überraschende Wendung ○ vt drehen; (distort) verdrehen; (fam: swindle) beschummeln; ∼ one's ankle sich (dat) den Knöchel verrenken □ vi sich drehen; (road:) sich winden. ∼er n (fam) Schwindler m

twit /twɪt/ n (fam) Trottel m

twitch /twɪtʃ/ n Zucken nt □ vi zucken

twitter /'twɪtə(r)/ n Zwitschern nt □ vi zwitschern

two /tu:/ a zwei

two: ∼-faced a falsch. ∼-piece a zweiteilig. ∼some /-səm/ n Paar nt. ∼-way a ∼-way traffic Gegenverkehr m

tycoon /taɪ'ku:n/ n Magnat m

tying /'taɪɪŋ/ see tie

type /taɪp/ n Art f, Sorte f; (person) Typ m; (printing) Type f □ vt mit der Maschine schreiben, (fam) tippen; ∼d letter maschinegeschriebener Brief □ vi Maschine schreiben, (fam) tippen. ∼writer n Schreibmaschine f. ∼written a maschinegeschrieben

typhoid /'taɪfɔɪd/ n Typhus m

typical /'tɪpɪkl/ a, -ly adv typisch (of für)

typify /'tɪpɪfaɪ/ vt (pt/pp -ied) typisch sein für

typing /'taɪpɪŋ/ n Maschineschreiben nt. ∼ paper n Schreibmaschinenpapier nt

typist /'taɪpɪst/ n Schreibkraft f

typography /taɪ'pɒgrəfɪ/ n Typographie f

tyrannical /tɪ'rænɪkl/ a tyrannisch

tyranny /'tɪrənɪ/ n Tyrannei f

tyrant /'taɪrənt/ n Tyrann m

tyre /'taɪə(r)/ n Reifen m

U

ubiquitous /ju:'bɪkwɪtəs/ a allgegenwärtig; be ∼ überall zu finden sein

udder /'ʌdə(r)/ n Euter nt

ugl|iness /'ʌglɪnɪs/ n Hässlichkeit f. ∼y a (-ier, -iest) hässlich; (nasty) übel

UK abbr see United Kingdom

ulcer /'ʌlsə(r)/ n Geschwür nt

ulterior /ʌl'tɪərɪə(r)/ a ∼ motive Hintergedanke m

ultimate /'ʌltɪmət/ a letzte(r,s); (final) endgültig; (fundamental) grundlegend, eigentlich. ∼ly adv schließlich

ultimatum /ʌltɪ'meɪtəm/ n Ultimatum nt

ultrasound /'ʌltrə-/ n (Med) Ultraschall m

ultra'violet a ultraviolett

umbilical /ʌm'bɪlɪkl/ a ∼ cord Nabelschnur f

umbrella /ʌm'brelə/ n [Regen]schirm m

umpire /'ʌmpaɪə(r)/ n Schiedsrichter m □ vt/i Schiedsrichter sein (bei)

umpteen /ʌmp'ti:n/ a (fam) zig. ∼th a (fam) zigste(r,s); for the ∼th time zum zigsten Mal

un'able /ʌn-/ a be ∼ to do sth etw nicht tun können

una'bridged a ungekürzt

unac'companied a ohne Begleitung; (luggage) unbegleitet

unac'countable a unerklärlich. ∼y adv unerklärlicherweise

unac'customed a ungewohnt; be ∼ to sth etw nicht gewohnt sein

una'dulterated a unverfälscht, rein; (utter) völlig

un'aided a ohne fremde Hilfe

unalloyed /ʌnə'lɔɪd/ a (fig) ungetrübt

unanimity /ju:nə'nɪmətɪ/ n Einstimmigkeit f

unanimous /ju:'nænɪməs/ a, -ly adv einmütig; (vote, decision) einstimmig un'armed *a* unbewaffnet; ~ combat Kampf *m* ohne Waffen

unas'suming *a* bescheiden

unat'tached *a* nicht befestigt; ⟨person⟩ ungebunden

unat'tended *a* unbeaufsichtigt

un'authorized *a* unbefugt

una'voidable *a* unvermeidlich

una'ware *a* be ~ of sth sich ⟨dat⟩ etw ⟨gen⟩ nicht bewusst sein. ~s /-eəz/ *adv* catch so. ~s jdn überraschen

un'balanced *a* unausgewogen; ⟨mentally⟩ unausgeglichen

un'bearable *a*, -bly *adv* unerträglich

unbeat|able /ʌnˈbiːtəbl/ *a* unschlagbar. ~en *a* ungeschlagen; ⟨record⟩ ungebrochen

unbeknown /ʌnbɪˈnəʊn/ *a* ⟨fam⟩ ~ to me ohne mein Wissen

unbe'lievable *a* unglaublich

un'bend *vi* ⟨pt/pp -bent⟩ ⟨relax⟩ aus sich herausgehen

un'biased *a* unvoreingenommen

un'block *vt* frei machen

un'bolt *vt* aufriegeln

un'breakable *a* unzerbrechlich

unbridled /ʌnˈbraɪdld/ *a* ungezügelt

un'burden *vt* ~ oneself ⟨fig⟩ sich aussprechen

un'button *vt* aufknöpfen

uncalled-for /ʌnˈkɔːldfɔː(r)/ *a* unangebracht

un'canny *a* unheimlich

un'ceasing *a* unaufhörlich

uncere'monious *a*, -ly *adv* formlos; ⟨abrupt⟩ brüsk

un'certain *a* ⟨doubtful⟩ ungewiss; ⟨origins⟩ unbestimmt; be ~ nicht sicher sein; in no ~ terms ganz eindeutig. ~ty *n* Ungewissheit *f*

un'changed *a* unverändert

un'charitable *a* lieblos

uncle /ˈʌŋkl/ *n* Onkel *m*

un'comfortable *a*, -bly *adv* unbequem; feel ~ ⟨fig⟩ sich nicht wohl fühlen

un'common *a* ungewöhnlich

un'compromising *a* kompromisslos

uncon'ditional *a*, ~ly *adv* bedingungslos

un'conscious *a* bewusstlos; ⟨unintended⟩ unbewusst; be ~ of sth sich ⟨dat⟩ etw ⟨gen⟩ nicht bewusst sein. ~ly *adv* unbewusst

uncon'ventional *a* unkonventionell

unco'operative *a* nicht hilfsbereit

un'cork *vt* entkorken

uncouth /ʌnˈkuːθ/ *a* ungehobelt

un'cover *vt* aufdecken

unctuous /ˈʌŋktjʊəs/ *a*, -ly *adv* salbungsvoll

unde'cided *a* unentschlossen; ⟨not settled⟩ nicht entschieden

undeniable /ʌndɪˈnaɪəbl/ *a*, -bly *adv* unbestreitbar

under /ˈʌndə(r)/ *prep* unter (+ *dat/acc*); ~ it darunter; ~ there da drunter; ~ repair in Reparatur; ~ construction im Bau; ~ age minderjährig; ~ way unterwegs; ⟨fig⟩ im Gange □ *adv* darunter

'undercarriage *n* ⟨Aviat⟩ Fahrwerk *nt*, Fahrgestell *nt*

'underclothes *npl* Unterwäsche *f*

'undercover *a* geheim

'undercurrent *n* Unterströmung *f*; ⟨fig⟩ Unterton *m*

under'cut *vt* ⟨pt/pp -cut⟩ ⟨Comm⟩ unterbieten

'underdog *n* Unterlegene(r) *m*

under'done *a* nicht gar; ⟨rare⟩ nicht durchgebraten

under'estimate *vt* unterschätzen

under'fed *a* unterernährt

under'foot *adv* am Boden; trample ~ zertrampeln

under'go *vt* ⟨pt -went, pp -gone⟩ durchmachen; sich unterziehen (+ *dat*) ⟨operation, treatment⟩; ~ repairs repariert werden

under'graduate *n* Student(in) *m(f)*

under'ground¹ *adv* unter der Erde; ⟨mining⟩ unter Tage

'underground² *a* unterirdisch; ⟨secret⟩ Untergrund- □ *n* ⟨railway⟩ U-Bahn *f*. ~ car park *n* Tiefgarage *f*

'undergrowth *n* Unterholz *nt*

'underhand *a* hinterhältig

'underlay *n* Unterlage *f*

under'lie *vt* ⟨pt -lay, pp -lain, pres p -lying⟩ ⟨fig⟩ zugrunde liegen (+ *dat*)

under'line *vt* unterstreichen

underling /ˈʌndəlɪŋ/ *n* ⟨pej⟩ Untergebene(r) *m/f*

under'lying *a* ⟨fig⟩ eigentlich

under'mine *vt* ⟨fig⟩ unterminieren, untergraben

underneath /ʌndəˈniːθ/ *prep* unter (+ *dat/acc*); ~ it darunter □ *adv* darunter

'underpants *npl* Unterhose *f*

'underpass *n* Unterführung *f*

under'privileged *a* unterprivilegiert

under'rate *vt* unterschätzen

'underseal *n* ⟨Auto⟩ Unterbodenschutz *m*

'undershirt *n* ⟨Amer⟩ Unterhemd *nt*

understaffed /-ˈstɑːft/ *a* unterbesetzt

under'stand vt/i (pt/pp -stood) verstehen; I ~ that ... (have heard) ich habe gehört, dass ... ~able /-əbl/ a verständlich. ~ably /-əblı/ adv verständlicherweise

under'standing a verständnisvoll □ n Verständnis nt; (agreement) Vereinbarung f; reach an ~ sich verständigen; on the ~ that unter der Voraussetzung, dass

'understatement n Untertreibung f

'understudy n (Theat) Ersatzspieler(in) m(f)

under'take vt (pt -took, pp -taken) unternehmen; ~ to do sth sich verpflichten, etw zu tun

'undertaker n Leichenbestatter m; [firm of] ~s Bestattungsinstitut n

under'taking n Unternehmen nt; (promise) Versprechen nt

'undertone n (fig) Unterton m; in an ~ mit gedämpfter Stimme

under'value vt unterbewerten

'underwater¹ a Unterwasser-

under'water² adv unter Wasser

'underwear n Unterwäsche f

under'weight a untergewichtig; be ~ Untergewicht haben

'underworld n Unterwelt f

'underwriter n Versicherer m

unde'sirable a unerwünscht

undies /'ʌndız/ npl (fam) [Damen]unterwäsche f

un'dignified a würdelos

un'do vt (pt -did, pp -done) aufmachen; (fig) ungeschehen machen; (ruin) zunichte machen

un'done a offen; (not accomplished) unerledigt

un'doubted a unzweifelhaft. ~ly adv zweifellos

un'dress vt ausziehen; get ~ed sich ausziehen □ vi sich ausziehen

un'due a übermäßig

undulating /'ʌndjʊleıtıŋ/ a Wellen-; (country) wellig

un'duly adv übermäßig

un'dying a ewig

un'earth vt ausgraben; (fig) zutage bringen. ~ly a unheimlich; at an ~ly hour (fam) in aller Herrgottsfrühe

un'eas|e n Unbehagen nt. ~y a unbehaglich; I feel ~y mir ist unbehaglich zumute

un'eatable a ungenießbar

uneco'nomic a, -ally adv unwirtschaftlich

uneco'nomical a verschwenderisch

unem'ployed a arbeitslos □ npl the ~ die Arbeitslosen

unem'ployment n Arbeitslosigkeit f. ~ benefit n Arbeitslosenunterstützung f

un'ending a endlos

un'equal a unterschiedlich; (struggle) ungleich; be ~ to a task einer Aufgabe nicht gewachsen sein. ~ly adv ungleichmäßig

unequivocal /ʌnɪ'kwıvəkl/ a, -ly adv eindeutig

unerring /ʌn'ɜːrıŋ/ a unfehlbar

un'ethical a unmoralisch; be ~ gegen das Berufsethos verstoßen

un'even a uneben; (unequal) ungleich; (not regular) ungleichmäßig; (number) ungerade. ~ly adv ungleichmäßig

unex'pected a, -ly adv unerwartet

un'failing a nie versagend

un'fair a, -ly adv ungerecht, unfair. ~ness n Ungerechtigkeit f

un'faithful a untreu

unfa'miliar a ungewohnt; (unknown) unbekannt

un'fasten vt aufmachen; (detach) losmachen

un'favourable a ungünstig

un'feeling a gefühllos

un'finished a unvollendet; (business) unerledigt

un'fit a ungeeignet; (incompetent) unfähig; (Sport) nicht fit; ~ for work arbeitsunfähig

unflinching /ʌn'flıntʃıŋ/ a unerschrocken

un'fold vt auseinander falten, entfalten; (spread out) ausbreiten □ vi sich entfalten

unfore'seen a unvorhergesehen

unforgettable /ʌnfə'getəbl/ a unvergesslich

unforgivable /ʌnfə'gıvəbl/ a unverzeihlich

un'fortunate a unglücklich; (unfavourable) ungünstig; (regrettable) bedauerlich; be ~ (person:) Pech haben. ~ly adv leider

un'founded a unbegründet

unfurl /ʌn'fɜːl/ vt entrollen □ vi sich entrollen

un'furnished a unmöbliert

ungainly /ʌn'geınlı/ a unbeholfen

ungodly /ʌn'gɒdlı/ a gottlos; at an ~ hour (fam) in aller Herrgottsfrühe

un'grateful a, -ly adv undankbar

un'happi|ly adv unglücklich; (unfortunately) leider. ~ness n Kummer m

un'happy a unglücklich; (not content) unzufrieden

un'harmed a unverletzt

un'healthy a ungesund

un'hook *vt* vom Haken nehmen; aufhaken ⟨*dress*⟩

un'hurt *a* unverletzt

unhy'gienic *a* unhygienisch

unicorn /'juːnɪkɔːn/ *n* Einhorn *nt*

unification /juːnɪfɪ'keɪʃn/ *n* Einigung *f*

uniform /'juːnɪfɔːm/ *a*, -ly *adv* einheitlich ▫ *n* Uniform *f*

unify /'juːnɪfaɪ/ *vt* (*pt/pp* -ied) einigen

uni'lateral /juːnɪ-/ *a*, -ly *adv* einseitig

uni'maginable *a* unvorstellbar

unim'portant *a* unwichtig

unin'habited *a* unbewohnt

unin'tentional *a*, -ly *adv* unabsichtlich

union /'juːnɪən/ *n* Vereinigung *f*; (*Pol*) Union *f*; (*trade* ∼) Gewerkschaft *f*. ∼ist *n* (*Pol*) Unionist *m*

unique /juː'niːk/ *a* einzigartig. ∼ly *adv* einmalig

unison /'juːnɪsn/ *n* in ∼ einstimmig

unit /'juːnɪt/ *n* Einheit *f*; (*Math*) Einer *m*; (*of furniture*) Teil *nt*, Element *nt*

unite /juː'naɪt/ *vt* vereinigen ▫ *vi* sich vereinigen

united /juː'naɪtɪd/ *a* einig. U∼ 'Kingdom *n* Vereinigtes Königreich *nt*. U∼ 'Nations *n* Vereinte Nationen *pl*. U∼ States [of America] *n* Vereinigte Staaten *pl* [von Amerika]

unity /'juːnətɪ/ *n* Einheit *f*; (*harmony*) Einigkeit *f*

universal /juːnɪ'vɜːsl/ *a*, -ly *adv* allgemein

universe /'juːnɪvɜːs/ *n* [Welt]all *nt*, Universum *nt*

university /juːnɪ'vɜːsətɪ/ *n* Universität *f* ▫ *attrib* Universitäts-

un'just *a*, -ly *adv* ungerecht

unkempt /ʌn'kempt/ *a* ungepflegt

un'kind *a*, -ly *adv* unfreundlich; (*harsh*) hässlich. ∼ness *n* Unfreundlichkeit *f*; Hässlichkeit *f*

un'known *a* unbekannt

un'lawful *a*, -ly *adv* gesetzwidrig

unleaded /ʌn'ledɪd/ *a* bleifrei

un'leash *vt* (*fig*) entfesseln

unless /ən'les/ *conj* wenn . . . nicht; ∼ I am mistaken wenn ich mich nicht irre

un'like *a* nicht ähnlich, unähnlich; (*not the same*) ungleich ▫ *prep* im Gegensatz zu (+ *dat*)

un'likely *a* unwahrscheinlich

un'limited *a* unbegrenzt

un'load *vt* entladen; ausladen ⟨*luggage*⟩

un'lock *vt* aufschließen

un'lucky *a* unglücklich; ⟨*day, number*⟩ Unglücks-; be ∼ Pech haben; ⟨*thing:*⟩ Unglück bringen

un'manned *a* unbemannt

un'married *a* unverheiratet. ∼ 'mother *n* ledige Mutter *f*

un'mask *vt* (*fig*) entlarven

unmistakable /ʌnmɪ'steɪkəbl/ *a*, -bly *adv* unverkennbar

un'mitigated *a* vollkommen

un'natural *a*, -ly *adv* unnatürlich; (*not normal*) nicht normal

un'necessary *a*, -ily *adv* unnötig

un'noticed *a* unbemerkt

unob'tainable *a* nicht erhältlich

unob'trusive *a*, -ly *adv* unaufdringlich; ⟨*thing*⟩ unauffällig

unof'ficial *a*, -ly *adv* inoffiziell

un'pack *vt/i* auspacken

un'paid *a* unbezahlt

un'palatable *a* ungenießbar

un'paralleled *a* beispiellos

un'pick *vt* auftrennen

un'pleasant *a*, -ly *adv* unangenehm. ∼ness *n* (*bad feeling*) Ärger *m*

un'plug *vt* (*pt/pp* -plugged) den Stecker herausziehen von

un'popular *a* unbeliebt

un'precedented *a* beispiellos

unpre'dictable *a* unberechenbar

unpre'meditated *a* nicht vorsätzlich

unpre'pared *a* nicht vorbereitet

unprepos'sessing *a* wenig attraktiv

unpre'tentious *a* bescheiden

un'principled *a* skrupellos

unpro'fessional *a* be ∼ gegen das Berufsethos verstoßen; (*Sport*) unsportlich sein

un'profitable *a* unrentabel

un'qualified *a* unqualifiziert; (*fig: absolute*) uneingeschränkt

un'questionable *a* unbezweifelbar; ⟨*right*⟩ unbestreitbar

unravel /ʌn'rævl/ *vt* (*pt/pp* -ravelled) entwirren; (*Knitting*) aufziehen

un'real *a* unwirklich

un'reasonable *a* unvernünftig; be ∼ zu viel verlangen

unre'lated *a* unzusammenhängend; be ∼ nicht verwandt sein; ⟨*events:*⟩ nicht miteinander zusammenhängen

unre'liable *a* unzuverlässig

unrequited /ʌnrɪ'kwaɪtɪd/ *a* unerwidert

unreservedly /ʌnrɪ'zɜːvɪdlɪ/ *adv* uneingeschränkt; ⟨*frankly*⟩ offen

un'rest *n* Unruhen *pl*

un'rivalled *a* unübertroffen

un'roll *vt* aufrollen ▫ *vi* sich aufrollen

unruly /ʌn'ruːlɪ/ *a* ungebärdig

un'safe *a* nicht sicher

un'said *a* ungesagt

un'salted *a* ungesalzen

unsatis'factory *a* unbefriedigend

un'savoury *a* unangenehm; ⟨*fig*⟩ unerfreulich

unscathed /ʌnˈskeɪðd/ *a* unversehrt

un'screw *vt* abschrauben

un'scrupulous *a* skrupellos

un'seemly *a* unschicklich

un'selfish *a* selbstlos

un'settled *a* ungeklärt; ⟨*weather*⟩ unbeständig; ⟨*bill*⟩ unbezahlt

unshakeable /ʌnˈʃeɪkəbl/ *a* unerschütterlich

unshaven /ʌnˈʃeɪvn/ *a* unrasiert

un'sightly /ʌnˈsaɪtlɪ/ *a* unansehnlich

un'skilled *a* ungelernt; ⟨*work*⟩ unqualifiziert

un'sociable *a* ungesellig

unso'phisticated *a* einfach

un'sound *a* krank, nicht gesund; ⟨*building*⟩ nicht sicher; ⟨*advice*⟩ unzuverlässig; ⟨*reasoning*⟩ nicht stichhaltig; of ∼ mind unzurechnungsfähig

unspeakable /ʌnˈspiːkəbl/ *a* unbeschreiblich

un'stable *a* nicht stabil; ⟨*mentally*⟩ labil

un'steady *a*, -ily *adv* unsicher; ⟨*wobbly*⟩ wackelig

un'stuck *a* come ∼ sich lösen; ⟨*fam: fail*⟩ scheitern

unsuc'cessful *a*, -ly *adv* erfolglos; be ∼ keinen Erfolg haben

un'suitable *a* ungeeignet; ⟨*inappropriate*⟩ unpassend; ⟨*for weather, activity*⟩ unzweckmäßig

unsu'specting *a* ahnungslos

un'sweetened *a* ungesüßt

unthinkable /ʌnˈθɪŋkəbl/ *a* unvorstellbar

un'tidiness *n* Unordentlichkeit *f*

un'tidy *a*, -ily *adv* unordentlich

un'tie *vt* aufbinden; losbinden ⟨*person, boat, horse*⟩

until /ʌnˈtɪl/ *prep* bis (+ *acc*); not ∼ erst; ∼ the evening bis zum Abend; ∼ his arrival bis zu seiner Ankunft ◻ *conj* bis; not ∼ erst wenn; ⟨*in past*⟩ erst als

untimely /ʌnˈtaɪmlɪ/ *a* ungelegen; ⟨*premature*⟩ vorzeitig

un'tiring *a* unermüdlich

un'told *a* unermesslich

unto'ward *a* ungünstig; ⟨*unseemly*⟩ ungehörig; if nothing ∼ happens wenn nichts dazwischenkommt

un'true *a* unwahr; that's ∼ das ist nicht wahr

unused[1] /ʌnˈjuːzd/ *a* unbenutzt; ⟨*not utilized*⟩ ungenutzt

unused[2] /ʌnˈjuːst/ *a* be ∼ to sth etw nicht gewohnt sein

un'usual *a*, -ly *adv* ungewöhnlich

un'veil *vt* enthüllen

un'versed *a* nicht bewandert (in in + *dat*)

un'wanted *a* unerwünscht

un'warranted *a* ungerechtfertigt

un'welcome *a* unwillkommen

un'well *a* be *or* feel ∼ sich nicht wohl fühlen

unwieldy /ʌnˈwiːldɪ/ *a* sperrig

un'willing *a*, -ly *adv* widerwillig; be ∼ to do sth etw nicht tun wollen

un'wind *v* ⟨*pt/pp* unwound⟩ ◻ *vt* abwickeln ◻ *vi* sich abwickeln; ⟨*fam: relax*⟩ sich entspannen

un'wise *a*, -ly *adv* unklug

un'witting *a*, -ly *adv* unwissentlich

un'worthy *a* unwürdig

un'wrap *vt* ⟨*pt/pp* -wrapped⟩ auswickeln; auspacken ⟨*present*⟩

un'written *a* ungeschrieben

up /ʌp/ *adv* oben; ⟨*with movement*⟩ nach oben; ⟨*not in bed*⟩ auf; ⟨*collar*⟩ hochgeklappt; ⟨*road*⟩ aufgerissen; ⟨*price*⟩ gestiegen; ⟨*curtains*⟩ aufgehängt; ⟨*shelves*⟩ angebracht; ⟨*notice*⟩ angeschlagen; ⟨*tent*⟩ aufgebaut; ⟨*building*⟩ gebaut; be up for sale zu verkaufen sein; up there dort oben; up to ⟨*as far as*⟩ bis; time's up die Zeit ist um; what's up? ⟨*fam*⟩ was ist los? what's he up to? ⟨*fam*⟩ was hat er vor? I don't feel up to it ich fühle mich dem nicht gewachsen; be one up on s.o. ⟨*fam*⟩ jdm etwas voraushaben; go up hinaufgehen; come up heraufkommen ◻ *prep* be up on sth [oben] auf etw ⟨*dat*⟩ sein; up the mountain oben am Berg; ⟨*movement*⟩ den Berg hinauf; be up the tree oben im Baum sein; up the road die Straße entlang; up the river stromaufwärts; go up the stairs die Treppe hinaufgehen; be up the pub ⟨*fam*⟩ in der Kneipe sein

'upbringing *n* Erziehung *f*

up'date *vt* auf den neuesten Stand bringen

up'grade *vt* aufstufen

upheaval /ʌpˈhiːvl/ *n* Unruhe *f*; ⟨*Pol*⟩ Umbruch *m*

up'hill *a* ⟨*fig*⟩ mühsam ◻ *adv* bergauf

up'hold *vt* ⟨*pt/pp* upheld⟩ unterstützen; bestätigen ⟨*verdict*⟩

upholster /ʌpˈhəʊlstə(r)/ *vt* polstern. ∼er *n* Polsterer *m*. ∼y *n* Polsterung *f*

'upkeep *n* Unterhalt *m*

up-'market *a* anspruchsvoll

upon /əˈpɒn/ *prep* auf (+ *dat/acc*)

upper /'ʌpə(r)/ a obere(r,s); ⟨deck, jaw, lip⟩ Ober-; have the ∼ hand die Oberhand haben. □ n ⟨of shoe⟩ Obermaterial nt

upper: ∼ circle n zweiter Rang m. ∼ class n Oberschicht f. ∼most a oberste(r,s)

'upright a aufrecht □ n Pfosten m

'uprising n Aufstand m

'uproar n Aufruhr m

up'root vt entwurzeln

up'set¹ vt (pt/pp upset, pres p upsetting) umstoßen; (spill) verschütten; durcheinander bringen ⟨plan⟩; (distress) erschüttern; ⟨food:⟩ nicht bekommen (+ dat); get ∼ about sth sich über etw (acc) ∼ aufregen; be very ∼ sehr bestürzt sein

'upset² n Aufregung f; have a stomach ∼ einen verdorbenen Magen haben

'upshot n Ergebnis nt

upside 'down adv verkehrt herum; turn ∼ umdrehen

up'stairs¹ adv oben; ⟨go⟩ nach oben

'upstairs² a im Obergeschoss

'upstart n Emporkömmling m

up'stream adv stromaufwärts

'upsurge n Zunahme f

'uptake n slow on the ∼ schwer von Begriff; be quick on the ∼ schnell begreifen

up'tight a nervös

'upturn n Aufschwung m

upward /'ʌpwəd/ a nach oben; ⟨movement⟩ Aufwärts-; ∼ slope Steigung f □ adv ∼[s] aufwärts, nach oben

uranium /jʊ'reɪnɪəm/ n Uran nt

urban /'ɜ:bən/ a städtisch

urbane /ɜ:'beɪn/ a weltmännisch

urge /ɜ:dʒ/ n Trieb m, Drang m □ vt drängen; ∼ on antreiben

urgen|cy /'ɜ:dʒənsɪ/ n Dringlichkeit f. ∼t a, -ly adv dringend

urinate /'jʊərɪneɪt/ vi urinieren

urine /'jʊərɪn/ n Urin m, Harn m

urn /ɜ:n/ n Urne f; ⟨for tea⟩ Teemaschine f

us /ʌs/ pron uns; it's us wir sind es

US[A] abbr USA pl

usable /'ju:zəbl/ a brauchbar

usage /'ju:zɪdʒ/ n Brauch m; ⟨of word⟩ [Sprach]gebrauch m

use¹ /ju:s/ n (see use²) Benutzung f; Verwendung f; Gebrauch m; be of ∼ nützlich sein; be of no ∼ nichts nützen; make ∼ of Gebrauch machen von; (exploit) ausnutzen; it is no ∼ es hat keinen Zweck; what's the ∼? wozu?

use² /ju:z/ vt benutzen ⟨implement, room, lift⟩; verwenden ⟨ingredient, method, book, money⟩; gebrauchen ⟨words, force, brains⟩; ∼ [up] aufbrauchen

used¹ /ju:zd/ a benutzt; ⟨car⟩ Gebraucht-

used² /ju:st/ pt be ∼ to sth an etw (acc) gewöhnt sein; get ∼ to sich gewöhnen an (+ acc); he ∼ to say er hat immer gesagt; he ∼ to live here er hat früher hier gewohnt

useful /'ju:sfl/ a nützlich. ∼ness n Nützlichkeit f

useless /'ju:slɪs/ a nutzlos; (not usable) unbrauchbar; (pointless) zwecklos

user /'ju:zə(r)/ n Benutzer(in) m(f). ∼-'friendly a benutzerfreundlich

usher /'ʌʃə(r)/ n Platzanweiser m; (in court) Gerichtsdiener m □ vt ∼ in hineinführen

usherette /ʌʃə'ret/ n Platzanweiserin f

USSR abbr UdSSR f

usual /'ju:ʒʊəl/ a üblich. ∼ly adv gewöhnlich

usurp /ju:'zɜ:p/ vt sich (dat) widerrechtlich aneignen

utensil /ju:'tensl/ n Gerät nt

uterus /'ju:tərəs/ n Gebärmutter f

utilitarian /ju:tɪlɪ'teərɪən/ a zweckmäßig

utility /ju:'tɪlətɪ/ a Gebrauchs- □ n Nutzen m. ∼ room n ≈ Waschküche f

utiliz|ation /ju:tɪlaɪ'zeɪʃn/ n Nutzung f. ∼e /'ju:tɪlaɪz/ vt nutzen

utmost /'ʌtməʊst/ a äußerste(r,s), größte(r,s) □ n do one's ∼ sein Möglichstes tun

utter¹ /'ʌtə(r)/ a, -ly adv völlig

utter² vt von sich geben ⟨sigh, sound⟩; sagen ⟨word⟩. ∼ance /-əns/ n Äußerung f

U-turn /'ju:-/ n ⟨fig⟩ Kehrtwendung f; 'no ∼s' ⟨Auto⟩ 'Wenden verboten'

V

vacan|cy /'veɪkənsɪ/ n ⟨job⟩ freie Stelle f; ⟨room⟩ freies Zimmer nt; 'no ∼cies' 'belegt'. ∼t a frei; ⟨look⟩ [gedanken]leer

vacate /və'keɪt/ vt räumen

vacation /və'keɪʃn/ n (Univ & Amer) Ferien pl

vaccinat|e /'væksɪneɪt/ vt impfen. ∼ion /-'neɪʃn/ n Impfung f

vaccine /'væksi:n/ n Impfstoff m

vacuum /'vækjʊəm/ n Vakuum nt, luftleerer Raum m □ vt saugen. ∼ cleaner n Staubsauger m. ∼ flask n Thermosflasche (P) f. ∼-packed a vakuumverpackt

vagaries /'veɪgərɪz/ npl Launen pl

vagina /vəˈdʒaɪnə/ n (Anat) Scheide f

vagrant /ˈveɪɡrənt/ n Landstreicher m

vague /veɪɡ/ a (-r,-st), -ly adv vage; ⟨outline⟩ verschwommen

vain /veɪn/ a (-er,-est) eitel; ⟨hope, attempt⟩ vergeblich; in ~ vergeblich. ~ly adv vergeblich

vale /veɪl/ n (liter) Tal nt

valet /ˈvæleɪ/ n Kammerdiener m

valiant /ˈvæliənt/ a, -ly adv tapfer

valid /ˈvælɪd/ a gültig; ⟨claim⟩ berechtigt; ⟨argument⟩ stichhaltig; ⟨reason⟩ triftig. ~ate vt ⟨confirm⟩ bestätigen. ~ity /vəˈlɪdətɪ/ n Gültigkeit f

valley /ˈvælɪ/ n Tal nt

valour /ˈvælə(r)/ n Tapferkeit f

valuable /ˈvæljʊəbl/ a wertvoll. ~s npl Wertsachen pl

valuation /væljʊˈeɪʃn/ n Schätzung f

value /ˈvæljuː/ n Wert m; ⟨usefulness⟩ Nutzen m □ vt schätzen. ~ 'added tax n Mehrwertsteuer f

valve /vælv/ n Ventil nt; (Anat) Klappe f; (Electr) Röhre f

vampire /ˈvæmpaɪə(r)/ n Vampir m

van /væn/ n Lieferwagen m

vandal /ˈvændl/ n Rowdy n. ~ism /-ɪzm/ n mutwillige Zerstörung f. ~ize vt demolieren

vanilla /vəˈnɪlə/ n Vanille f

vanish /ˈvænɪʃ/ vi verschwinden

vanity /ˈvænətɪ/ n Eitelkeit f. ~ bag n Kosmetiktäschchen nt

vantage-point /ˈvɑːntɪdʒ-/ n Aussichtspunkt m

vapour /ˈveɪpə(r)/ n Dampf m

variable /ˈveərɪəbl/ a unbeständig; (Math) variabel; ⟨adjustable⟩ regulierbar

variance /ˈveərɪəns/ n be at ~ nicht übereinstimmen

variant /ˈveərɪənt/ n Variante f

variation /veərɪˈeɪʃn/ n Variation f; ⟨difference⟩ Unterschied m

varicose /ˈværɪkəʊs/ a ~ veins Krampfadern pl

varied /ˈveərɪd/ a vielseitig; ⟨diet:⟩ abwechslungsreich

variety /vəˈraɪətɪ/ n Abwechslung f; ⟨quantity⟩ Vielfalt f; (Comm) Auswahl f; ⟨type⟩ Art f; (Bot) Abart f; (Theat) Varieté nt

various /ˈveərɪəs/ a verschieden. ~ly adv unterschiedlich

varnish /ˈvɑːnɪʃ/ n Lack m □ vt lackieren

vary /ˈveərɪ/ v (pt/pp -ied) □ vi sich ändern; ⟨be different⟩ verschieden sein □ vt [ver]ändern; ⟨add variety to⟩

abwechslungsreicher gestalten. ~ing a wechselnd; ⟨different⟩ unterschiedlich

vase /vɑːz/ n Vase f

vast /vɑːst/ a riesig; ⟨expanse⟩ weit. ~ly adv gewaltig

vat /væt/ n Bottich m

VAT /viːeɪˈtiː, væt/ abbr (value added tax) Mehrwertsteuer f, MwSt.

vault[1] /vɔːlt/ n ⟨roof⟩ Gewölbe nt; ⟨in bank⟩ Tresor m; ⟨tomb⟩ Gruft f

vault[2] n Sprung m □ vt/i ~ [over] springen über (+ acc)

VDU abbr (visual display unit) Bildschirmgerät nt

veal /viːl/ n Kalbfleisch nt □ attrib Kalbs-

veer /vɪə(r)/ vi sich drehen; (Naut) abdrehen; (Auto) ausscheren

vegetable /ˈvedʒtəbl/ n Gemüse nt; ~s pl Gemüse nt □ attrib Gemüse-; ⟨oil, fat⟩ Pflanzen-

vegetarian /vedʒɪˈteərɪən/ a vegetarisch □ n Vegetarier(in) m(f)

vegetat|e /ˈvedʒɪteɪt/ vi dahinvegetieren. ~ion /-ˈteɪʃn/ n Vegetation f

vehemen|ce /ˈviːəməns/ n Heftigkeit f. ~t a, -ly adv heftig

vehicle /ˈviːɪkl/ n Fahrzeug nt; ⟨fig: medium⟩ Mittel nt

veil /veɪl/ n Schleier m □ vt verschleiern

vein /veɪn/ n Ader f; ⟨mood⟩ Stimmung f; ⟨manner⟩ Art f; ~s and arteries Venen und Arterien. ~ed a geädert

Velcro (P) /ˈvelkrəʊ/ n ~ fastening Klettverschluss m

velocity /vɪˈlɒsətɪ/ n Geschwindigkeit f

velvet /ˈvelvɪt/ n Samt m. ~y a samtig

vending-machine /ˈvendɪŋ-/ n [Verkaufs]automat m

vendor /ˈvendə(r)/ n Verkäufer(in) m(f)

veneer /vəˈnɪə(r)/ n Furnier nt; ⟨fig⟩ Tünche f. ~ed a furniert

venerable /ˈvenərəbl/ a ehrwürdig

venereal /vɪˈnɪərɪəl/ a ~ disease Geschlechtskrankheit f

Venetian /vəˈniːʃn/ a venezianisch. v~ blind n Jalousie f

vengeance /ˈvendʒəns/ n Rache f; with a ~ ⟨fam⟩ gewaltig

Venice /ˈvenɪs/ n Venedig nt

venison /ˈvenɪsn/ n (Culin) Wild nt

venom /ˈvenəm/ n Gift nt; ⟨fig⟩ Hass m. ~ous /-əs/ a giftig

vent[1] /vent/ n Öffnung f; ⟨fig⟩ Ventil nt; give ~ to Luft machen (+ dat) □ vt Luft machen (+ dat)

vent[2] n (in jacket) Schlitz m

ventilat|e /'ventɪleɪt/ vt belüften. ∼**ion** /-'leɪʃn/ n Belüftung f; (installation) Lüftung f. ∼**or** n Lüftungsvorrichtung f; (Med) Boatmungsgerät nt

ventriloquist /ven'trɪləkwɪst/ n Bauchredner m

venture /'ventʃə(r)/ n Unternehmung f □ vt wagen □ vi sich wagen

venue /'venjuː/ n Treffpunkt m; (for event) Veranstaltungsort m

veranda /və'rændə/ n Veranda f

verb /vɜːb/ n Verb nt. ∼**al** a, -ly adv mündlich; (Gram) verbal

verbatim /vɜː'beɪtɪm/ a & adv [wort]wörtlich

verbose /vɜː'bəʊs/ a weitschweifig

verdict /'vɜːdɪkt/ n Urteil nt

verge /vɜːdʒ/ n Rand m; be on the ∼ of doing sth im Begriff sein, etw zu tun □ vi ∼ on (fig) grenzen an (+ acc)

verger /'vɜːdʒə(r)/ n Küster m

verify /'verɪfaɪ/ vt (pt/pp -ied) überprüfen; (confirm) bestätigen

vermin /'vɜːmɪn/ n Ungeziefer nt

vermouth /'vɜːməθ/ n Wermut m

vernacular /və'nækjʊlə(r)/ n Landessprache f

versatil|e /'vɜːsətaɪl/ a vielseitig. ∼**ity** /-'tɪlətɪ/ n Vielseitigkeit f

verse /vɜːs/ n Strophe f; (of Bible) Vers m; (poetry) Lyrik f

version /'vɜːʃn/ n Version f; (translation) Übersetzung f; (model) Modell nt

versus /'vɜːsəs/ prep gegen (+ acc)

vertebra /'vɜːtɪbrə/ n (pl -brae /-briː/) (Anat) Wirbel m

vertical /'vɜːtɪkl/ a, -ly adv senkrecht □ n Senkrechte f

vertigo /'vɜːtɪgəʊ/ n (Med) Schwindel m

verve /vɜːv/ n Schwung m

very /'verɪ/ adv sehr; ∼ much sehr; (quantity) sehr viel; ∼ little sehr wenig; ∼ probably höchstwahrscheinlich; at the ∼ most allerhöchstens □ a (mere) bloß; the ∼ first der/die/das allererste; the ∼ thing genau das Richtige; at the ∼ end/beginning ganz am Ende/Anfang; only a ∼ little nur ein ganz kleines bisschen

vessel /'vesl/ n Schiff nt; (receptacle & Anat) Gefäß nt

vest /vest/ n [Unter]hemd nt; (Amer: waistcoat) Weste f □ vt ∼ sth in s.o. jdm etw verleihen; have a ∼ed interest in sth ein persönliches Interesse an etw (dat) haben

vestige /'vestɪdʒ/ n Spur f

vestment /'vestmənt/ n (Relig) Gewand nt

vestry /'vestrɪ/ n Sakristei f

vet /vet/ n Tierarzt m /-ärztin f □ vt (pt/pp vetted) überprüfen

veteran /'vetərən/ n Veteran m. ∼ **car** n Oldtimer m

veterinary /'vetərɪnərɪ/ a tierärztlich. ∼ **surgeon** n Tierarzt m /-ärztin f

veto /'viːtəʊ/ n (pl -es) Veto nt □ vt sein Veto einlegen gegen

vex /veks/ vt ärgern. ∼**ation** /-'seɪʃn/ n Ärger m. ∼**ed** a verärgert; ∼**ed question** viel diskutierte Frage f

VHF abbr (very high frequency) UKW

via /'vaɪə/ prep über (+ acc)

viable /'vaɪəbl/ a lebensfähig; (fig) realisierbar; (firm) rentabel

viaduct /'vaɪədʌkt/ n Viadukt nt

vibrant /'vaɪbrənt/ a (fig) lebhaft

vibrat|e /vaɪ'breɪt/ vi vibrieren. ∼**ion** /-'breɪʃn/ n Vibrieren nt

vicar /'vɪkə(r)/ n Pfarrer m. ∼**age** /-rɪdʒ/ n Pfarrhaus nt

vicarious /vɪ'keərɪəs/ a nachempfunden

vice¹ /vaɪs/ n Laster nt

vice² n (Techn) Schraubstock m

vice 'chairman n stellvertretender Vorsitzender m

vice 'president n Vizepräsident m

vice versa /vaɪs'vɜːsə/ adv umgekehrt

vicinity /vɪ'sɪnətɪ/ n Umgebung f; in the ∼ of in der Nähe von

vicious /'vɪʃəs/ a, -ly adv boshaft; (animal) bösartig. ∼ **circle** n Teufelskreis m

victim /'vɪktɪm/ n Opfer nt. ∼**ize** vt schikanieren

victor /'vɪktə(r)/ n Sieger m

victor|ious /vɪk'tɔːrɪəs/ a siegreich. ∼**y** /'vɪktərɪ/ n Sieg m

video /'vɪdɪəʊ/ n Video nt; (recorder) Videorecorder m □ attrib Video- □ vt [auf Videoband] aufnehmen

video: ∼ **cas'sette** n Videokassette f. ∼ **game** n Videospiel nt. ∼ 'nasty n Horrorvideo nt. ∼ **recorder** n Videorecorder m

vie /vaɪ/ vi (pres p vying) wetteifern

Vienn|a /vɪ'enə/ n Wien nt. ∼**ese** /vɪə-'niːz/ a Wiener

view /vjuː/ n Sicht f; (scene) Aussicht f, Blick m; (picture, opinion) Ansicht f; in my ∼ meiner Ansicht nach; in ∼ of angesichts (+ gen); keep/have sth in ∼ etw im Auge behalten/haben; be on ∼ besichtigt werden können □ vt sich (dat) ansehen; besichtigen ⟨house⟩; (consider) betrachten □ vi (TV) fernsehen. ∼**er** n (TV) Zuschauer(in) m(f); (Phot) Diabetrachter m

view: ∼**finder** n (Phot) Sucher m. ∼**point** n Standpunkt m

vigil /ˈvɪdʒɪl/ n Wache f

vigilan|ce /ˈvɪdʒɪləns/ n Wachsamkeit f.
~t a, -ly adv wachsam

vigorous /ˈvɪgərəs/ a, -ly adv kräftig; (fig)
heftig

vigour /ˈvɪgə(r)/ n Kraft f; (fig) Heftigkeit
f

vile /vaɪl/ a abscheulich

villa /ˈvɪlə/ n (for holidays) Ferienhaus nt

village /ˈvɪlɪdʒ/ n Dorf nt. ~r n
Dorfbewohner(in) m(f)

villain /ˈvɪlən/ n Schurke m; (in story)
Bösewicht m

vim /vɪm/ n (fam) Schwung m

vindicat|e /ˈvɪndɪkeɪt/ vt rechtfertigen.
~ion /-ˈkeɪʃn/ n Rechtfertigung f

vindictive /vɪnˈdɪktɪv/ a nachtragend

vine /vaɪn/ n Weinrebe f

vinegar /ˈvɪnɪgə(r)/ n Essig m

vineyard /ˈvɪnjəːd/ n Weinberg m

vintage /ˈvɪntɪdʒ/ a erlesen □ n (year)
Jahrgang m. ~ ˈcar n Oldtimer m

viola /vɪˈəʊlə/ n (Mus) Bratsche f

violat|e /ˈvaɪəleɪt/ vt verletzen; (break)
brechen; (disturb) stören; (defile)
schänden. ~ion /-ˈleɪʃn/ n Verletzung f;
Schändung f

violen|ce /ˈvaɪələns/ n Gewalt f; (fig) Hef-
tigkeit f. ~t a gewalttätig; (fig) heftig.
~tly adv brutal; (fig) heftig

violet /ˈvaɪələt/ a violett □ n (flower)
Veilchen nt

violin /vaɪəˈlɪn/ n Geige f, Violine f. ~ist
n Geiger(in) m(f)

VIP abbr (very important person) Pro-
minente(r) m/f

viper /ˈvaɪpə(r)/ n Kreuzotter f; (fig)
Schlange f

virgin /ˈvɜːdʒɪn/ a unberührt □ n Jungfrau f. ~ity /-ˈdʒɪnətɪ/ n Unschuld f

Virgo /ˈvɜːgəʊ/ n (Astr) Jungfrau f

viril|e /ˈvɪraɪl/ a männlich. ~ity /-ˈrɪlətɪ/
n Männlichkeit f

virtual /ˈvɜːtjʊəl/ a a ~ ... praktisch ein
... ~ly adv praktisch

virtue /ˈvɜːtjuː/ n Tugend f; (advantage)
Vorteil m; by or in ~e of auf Grund (+
gen)

virtuoso /vɜːtjʊˈəʊzəʊ/ n (pl -si /-zɪː/) Virtuose m

virtuous /ˈvɜːtjʊəs/ a tugendhaft

virulent /ˈvɪrʊlənt/ a bösartig; (poison)
stark; (fig) scharf

virus /ˈvaɪərəs/ n Virus nt

visa /ˈviːzə/ n Visum nt

vis-à-vis /viːzɑːˈviː/ adv & prep gegenüber
(+ dat)

viscous /ˈvɪskəs/ a dickflüssig

visibility /vɪzəˈbɪlətɪ/ n Sichtbarkeit f;
(Meteorol) Sichtweite f

visible /ˈvɪzəbl/ a, -bly adv sichtbar

vision /ˈvɪʒn/ n Vision f; (sight) Sehkraft
f; (foresight) Weitblick m

visit /ˈvɪzɪt/ n Besuch m □ vt besuchen;
besichtigen (town, building). ~ing hours
npl Besuchszeiten pl. ~or n Besucher(in)
m(f); (in hotel) Gast m; have ~ors Besuch
haben

visor /ˈvaɪzə(r)/ n Schirm m; (on helmet)
Visier nt; (Auto) [Sonnen]blende f

vista /ˈvɪstə/ n Aussicht f

visual /ˈvɪzjʊəl/ a, -ly adv visuell; ~ly
handicapped sehbehindert. ~ aids npl
Anschauungsmaterial nt. ~ disˈplay
unit n Bildschirmgerät nt

visualize /ˈvɪzjʊəlaɪz/ vt sich (dat) vorstellen

vital /ˈvaɪtl/ a unbedingt notwendig; (essential to life) lebenswichtig. ~ity
/vaɪˈtælətɪ/ n Vitalität f. ~ly /ˈvaɪtəlɪ/ adv
äußerst

vitamin /ˈvɪtəmɪn/ n Vitamin nt

vitreous /ˈvɪtrɪəs/ a glasartig; (enamel)
Glas-

vivaci|ous /vɪˈveɪʃəs/ a, -ly adv lebhaft.
~ty /-ˈvæsətɪ/ n Lebhaftigkeit f

vivid /ˈvɪvɪd/ a, -ly adv lebhaft; (description) lebendig

vixen /ˈvɪksn/ n Füchsin f

vocabulary /vəˈkæbjʊlərɪ/ n Wortschatz
m; (list) Vokabelverzeichnis nt; learn ~
Vokabeln lernen

vocal /ˈvəʊkl/ a, -ly adv stimmlich; (vociferous) lautstark. ~ cords npl Stimm-
bänder pl

vocalist /ˈvəʊkəlɪst/ n Sänger(in) m(f)

vocation /vəˈkeɪʃn/ n Berufung f. ~al a n
Berufs-

vociferous /vəˈsɪfərəs/ a lautstark

vodka /ˈvɒdkə/ n Wodka m

vogue /vəʊg/ n Mode f; in ~ in Mode

voice /vɔɪs/ n Stimme f □ vt zum Ausdruck
bringen

void /vɔɪd/ a leer; (not valid) ungültig; ~
of ohne □ n Leere f

volatile /ˈvɒlətaɪl/ a flüchtig; (person)
sprunghaft

volcanic /vɒlˈkænɪk/ a vulkanisch

volcano /vɒlˈkeɪnəʊ/ n Vulkan m

volition /vəˈlɪʃn/ n of one's own ~ aus
eigenem Willen

volley /ˈvɒlɪ/ n (of gunfire) Salve f;
(Tennis) Volley m

volt /vəʊlt/ n Volt nt. ~age /-ɪdʒ/ n (Electr)
Spannung f

voluble /'vɒljʊbl/ a, -bly adv redselig; (protest) wortreich

volume /'vɒljuːm/ n (book) Band m; (Geom) Rauminhalt m; (amount) Ausmaß nt; (Radio, TV) Lautstärke f. ~ control n Lautstärkeregler m

voluntary /'vɒləntərɪ/ a, -ily adv freiwillig

volunteer /vɒlən'tɪə(r)/ n Freiwillige(r) m/f □ vt anbieten; geben (information) □ vi sich freiwillig melden

voluptuous /və'lʌptjʊəs/ a sinnlich

vomit /'vɒmɪt/ n Erbrochene(s) nt □ vt erbrechen □ vi sich übergeben

voracious /və'reɪʃəs/ a gefräßig; (appetite) unbändig

vot|e /vəʊt/ n Stimme f; (ballot) Abstimmung f; (right) Wahlrecht nt; take a ~e on abstimmen über (+ acc) □ vi abstimmen; (in election) wählen □ vt ~e s.o. president jdn zum Präsidenten wählen. ~er n Wähler(in) m(f)

vouch /vaʊtʃ/ vi ~ for sich verbürgen für. ~er n Gutschein m

vow /vaʊ/ n Gelöbnis nt; (Relig) Gelübde nt □ vt geloben

vowel /'vaʊəl/ n Vokal m

voyage /'vɔɪɪdʒ/ n Seereise f; (in space) Reise f, Flug m

vulgar /'vʌlɡə(r)/ a vulgär, ordinär. ~ity /-'ɡærətɪ/ n Vulgarität f

vulnerable /'vʌlnərəbl/ a verwundbar

vulture /'vʌltʃə(r)/ n Geier m

vying /'vaɪɪŋ/ see vie

W

wad /wɒd/ n Bausch m; (bundle) Bündel nt. ~ding n Wattierung f

waddle /'wɒdl/ vi watscheln

wade /weɪd/ vi waten; ~ through (fam) sich durchackern durch (book)

wafer /'weɪfə(r)/ n Waffel f; (Relig) Hostie f

waffle[1] /'wɒfl/ vi (fam) schwafeln

waffle[2] n (Culin) Waffel f

waft /wɒft/ vt/i wehen

wag /wæɡ/ v (pt/pp wagged) □ vt wedeln mit; ~ one's finger at s.o. jdm mit dem Finger drohen □ vi wedeln

wage[1] /weɪdʒ/ vt führen

wage[2] n, & ~s pl Lohn m. ~ packet n Lohntüte f

wager /'weɪdʒə(r)/ n Wette f

waggle /'wæɡl/ vt wackeln mit □ vi wackeln

wagon /'wæɡən/ n Wagen m; (Rail) Waggon m

wail /weɪl/ n [klagender] Schrei m □ vi heulen; (lament) klagen

waist /weɪst/ n Taille f. ~coat /'weɪskəʊt/ n Weste f. ~line n Taille f

wait /weɪt/ n Wartezeit f; lie in ~ for auflauern (+ dat) □ vi warten (for auf + acc); (at table) servieren; ~ on bedienen □ vt ~ one's turn warten, bis man an der Reihe ist

waiter /'weɪtə(r)/ n Kellner m; ~! Herr Ober!

waiting: ~-list n Warteliste f. ~-room n Warteraum m; (doctor's) Wartezimmer nt

waitress /'weɪtrɪs/ n Kellnerin f

waive /weɪv/ vt verzichten auf (+ acc)

wake[1] /weɪk/ n Totenwache f □ v (pt woke, pp woken) ~ [up] □ vt [auf]wecken □ vi aufwachen

wake[2] n (Naut) Kielwasser nt; in the ~ of im Gefolge (+ gen)

waken /'weɪkn/ vt [auf]wecken □ vi aufwachen

Wales /weɪlz/ n Wales nt

walk /wɔːk/ n Spaziergang m; (gait) Gang m; (path) Weg m; go for a ~ spazieren gehen □ vi gehen; (not ride) laufen, zu Fuß gehen; (ramble) wandern; learn to ~ laufen lernen □ vt ausführen (dog). ~ out □ vi hinausgehen; (workers:) in den Streik treten; ~ out on s.o. jdn verlassen

walker /'wɔːkə(r)/ n Spaziergänger(in) m(f); (rambler) Wanderer m/Wanderin f

walking /'wɔːkɪŋ/ n Gehen nt; (rambling) Wandern nt. ~-stick n Spazierstock m

walk: ~-out n Streik m. ~-over n (fig) leichter Sieg m

wall /wɔːl/ n Wand f; (external) Mauer f; go to the ~ (fam) eingehen; drive s.o. up the ~ (fam) jdn auf die Palme bringen □ vt ~ up zumauern

wallet /'wɒlɪt/ n Brieftasche f

'wallflower n Goldlack m

wallop /'wɒləp/ n (fam) Schlag m □ vt (pt/pp walloped) (fam) schlagen

wallow /'wɒləʊ/ vi sich wälzen; (fig) schwelgen

'wallpaper n Tapete f □ vt tapezieren

walnut /'wɔːlnʌt/ n Walnuss f

waltz /wɔːlts/ n Walzer m □ vi Walzer tanzen; come ~ing up (fam) angetanzt kommen

wan /wɒn/ a bleich

wand /wɒnd/ n Zauberstab m

wander /'wɒndə(r)/ vi umherwandern, (fam) bummeln; (fig: digress) abschweifen. ~ about vi umherwandern. ~lust n Fernweh nt

wane /weɪn/ n be on the ~ schwinden; ⟨moon:⟩ abnehmen □ vi schwinden; abnehmen

wangle /'wæŋgl/ vt (fam) organisieren

want /wɒnt/ n Mangel m (of an + dat); (hardship) Not f; (desire) Bedürfnis nt □ vt wollen; (need) brauchen; ~ [to have] sth etw haben wollen; ~ to do sth etw tun wollen; we ~ to stay wir wollen bleiben; I ~ you to go ich will, dass du gehst; it ~s painting es müsste gestrichen werden; you ~ to learn to swim du solltest schwimmen lernen □ vi he doesn't ~ for anything ihm fehlt es an nichts. ~ed a gesucht. ~ing a be ~ing fehlen; he is ~ing in ihm fehlt es an (+ dat)

wanton /'wɒntən/ a, -ly adv mutwillig

war /wɔː(r)/ n Krieg m; be at ~ sich im Krieg befinden

ward /wɔːd/ n [Kranken]saal m; (unit) Station f; (of town) Wahlbezirk m; (child) Mündel nt □ vt ~ off abwehren

warden /'wɔːdn/ n Heimleiter(in) m(f); (of youth hostel) Herbergsvater m; (supervisor) Aufseher(in) m(f)

warder /'wɔːdə(r)/ n Wärter(in) m(f)

wardrobe /'wɔːdrəʊb/ n Kleiderschrank m; (clothes) Garderobe f

warehouse /'weəhaʊs/ n Lager nt; (building) Lagerhaus nt

wares /weəz/ npl Waren pl

war: ~fare n Krieg m. ~head n Sprengkopf m. ~like a kriegerisch

warm /wɔːm/ a (-er, -est), -ly adv warm; ⟨welcome⟩ herzlich; I am ~ mir ist warm □ vt wärmen. ~ up vt aufwärmen □ vi warm werden; (Sport) sich aufwärmen. ~hearted a warmherzig

warmth /wɔːmθ/ n Wärme f

warn /wɔːn/ vt warnen (of vor + dat). ~ing n Warnung f; (advance notice) Vorwarnung f; (caution) Verwarnung f

warp /wɔːp/ vt verbiegen □ vi sich verziehen

'**war-path** n on the ~ auf dem Kriegspfad

warrant /'wɒrənt/ n (for arrest) Haftbefehl m; (for search) Durchsuchungsbefehl m □ vt (justify) rechtfertigen; (guarantee) garantieren

warranty /'wɒrənti/ n Garantie f

warrior /'wɒriə(r)/ n Krieger m

'**warship** n Kriegsschiff nt

wart /wɔːt/ n Warze f

'**wartime** n Kriegszeit f

wary /'weəri/ a (-ier, -iest), -ily adv vorsichtig; (suspicious) misstrauisch

was /wɒz/ see be

wash /wɒʃ/ n Wäsche f; (Naut) Wellen pl; have a ~ sich waschen □ vt waschen; spülen ⟨dishes⟩; aufwischen ⟨floor⟩; (flow over) bespülen; ~ one's hands sich (dat) die Hände waschen □ vi sich waschen; ⟨fabric:⟩ sich waschen lassen. ~ out vt auswaschen; ausspülen ⟨mouth⟩. ~ up vt abwaschen, spülen □ vi abwaschen; (Amer) sich waschen

washable /'wɒʃəbl/ a waschbar

wash: ~basin n Waschbecken nt. ~cloth n (Amer) Waschlappen m

washed 'out a (faded) verwaschen; (tired) abgespannt

washer /'wɒʃə(r)/ n (Techn) Dichtungsring m; (machine) Waschmaschine f

washing /'wɒʃɪŋ/ n Wäsche f. ~machine n Waschmaschine f. ~powder n Waschpulver nt. ~-up n Abwasch m; do the ~-up abwaschen, spülen. ~-'up liquid n Spülmittel nt

wash: ~out n Pleite f; (person) Niete f. ~room n Waschraum m

wasp /wɒsp/ n Wespe f

wastage /'weɪstɪdʒ/ n Schwund m

waste /weɪst/ n Verschwendung f; (rubbish) Abfall m; ~s pl Öde f; ~ of time Zeitverschwendung f □ a (product) Abfall-; lay ~ verwüsten □ vt verschwenden □ vi ~ away immer mehr abmagern

waste: ~-di'sposal unit n Müllzerkleinerer m. ~ful a verschwenderisch. ~land n Ödland nt. ~ 'paper n Altpapier nt. ~'paper basket n Papierkorb m

watch /wɒtʃ/ n Wache f; (timepiece) [Armband]uhr f; be on the ~ aufpassen □ vt beobachten; sich (dat) ansehen ⟨film, match⟩; (be careful of, look after) achten auf (+ acc). ~ television fernsehen □ vi zusehen. ~ out vi Ausschau halten (for nach); (be careful) aufpassen

watch: ~dog n Wachhund m. ~ful a, -ly adv wachsam. ~maker n Uhrmacher m. ~man n Wachmann m. ~-strap n Uhrarmband nt. ~tower n Wachturm m. ~word n Parole f

water /'wɔːtə(r)/ n Wasser nt; ~s pl Gewässer pl □ vt gießen ⟨garden, plant⟩; (dilute) verdünnen; (give drink to) tränken □ vi ⟨eyes:⟩ tränen; my mouth was ~ing mir lief das Wasser im Munde zusammen. ~ down vt verwässern

water: ~colour n Wasserfarbe f; (painting) Aquarell nt. ~cress n Brunnenkresse f. ~fall n Wasserfall m '**watering-can** n Gießkanne f

water: ~-lily n Seerose f. ~logged a be ~logged ⟨ground:⟩ unter Wasser stehen. ~-main n Hauptwasserleitung f. ~-mark n Wasserzeichen nt. ~ polo n Wasserball m. ~-power n Wasserkraft f. ~proof a wasserdicht. ~shed n Wasserscheide f; ⟨fig⟩ Wendepunkt m. ~-skiing n Wasserskilaufen nt. ~tight a wasserdicht. ~way n Wasserstraße f

watery /'wɔːtəri/ a wässrig

watt /wɒt/ n Watt nt

wave /weɪv/ n Welle f; ⟨gesture⟩ Handbewegung f; ⟨as greeting⟩ Winken nt ◻ vt winken mit; ⟨brandish⟩ schwingen; ⟨threateningly⟩ drohen mit; wellen ⟨hair⟩; ~ one's hand winken ◻ vi winken ⟨to dat⟩; ⟨flag:⟩ wehen. ~length n Wellenlänge f

waver /'weɪvə(r)/ vi schwanken

wavy /'weɪvi/ a wellig

wax[1] /wæks/ vi ⟨moon:⟩ zunehmen; ⟨fig: become⟩ werden

wax[2] n Wachs nt; ⟨in ear⟩ Schmalz nt ◻ vt wachsen. ~works n Wachsfigurenkabinett nt

way /weɪ/ n Weg m; ⟨direction⟩ Richtung f; ⟨respect⟩ Hinsicht f; ⟨manner⟩ Art f; ⟨method⟩ Art und Weise f; ~s pl Gewohnheiten pl; in the ~ im Weg; on the ~ auf dem Weg ⟨to nach/zu⟩; ⟨under way⟩ unterwegs; a little/long ~ ein kleines/ganzes Stück; a long ~ off weit weg; this ~ hierher; ⟨like this⟩ so; which ~ in welche Richtung; ⟨how⟩ wie; by the ~ übrigens; in some ~s in gewisser Hinsicht; either ~ so oder so; in this ~ auf diese Weise; in a ~ in gewisser Weise; in a bad ~ ⟨person⟩ in schlechter Verfassung; lead the ~ vorausgehen; make ~ Platz machen ⟨for dat⟩; 'give ~' ⟨Auto⟩ 'Vorfahrt beachten'; go out of one's ~ ⟨fig⟩ sich ⟨dat⟩ besondere Mühe geben ⟨to zu⟩; get one's [own] ~ seinen Willen durchsetzen ◻ adv weit; ~ behind weit zurück. ~ in n Eingang m

way·lay vt ⟨pt/pp -laid⟩ überfallen; ⟨fam: intercept⟩ abfangen

way 'out n Ausgang m; ⟨fig⟩ Ausweg m

way-'out a ⟨fam⟩ verrückt

wayward /'weɪwəd/ a eigenwillig

WC abbr WC nt

we /wiː/ pron wir

weak /wiːk/ a ⟨-er, -est⟩ -ly adv schwach; ⟨liquid⟩ dünn. ~en vt schwächen ◻ vi schwächer werden. ~ling n Schwächling m. ~ness n Schwäche f

wealth /welθ/ n Reichtum m; ⟨fig⟩ Fülle f ⟨of an + dat⟩. ~y a ⟨-ier, -iest⟩ reich

wean /wiːn/ vt entwöhnen

weapon /'wepən/ n Waffe f

wear /weə(r)/ n ⟨clothing⟩ Kleidung f; ~ and tear Abnutzung f, Verschleiß m ◻ v ⟨pt wore, pp worn⟩ ◻ vt tragen; ⟨damage⟩ abnutzen; ~ a hole in sth etw durchwetzen; what shall I ~? was soll ich anziehen? ◻ vi sich abnutzen; ⟨last⟩ halten. ~ off vi abgehen; ⟨effect:⟩ nachlassen. ~ out vt abnutzen; ⟨exhaust⟩ erschöpfen ◻ vi sich abnutzen

wearable /'weərəbl/ a tragbar

weary /'wɪəri/ a ⟨-ier, -iest⟩ -ily adv müde ◻ v ⟨pt/pp wearied⟩ ◻ vt ermüden ◻ vi ~ of sth etw ⟨gen⟩ überdrüssig werden

weasel /'wiːzl/ n Wiesel nt

weather /'weðə(r)/ n Wetter nt; in this ~ bei diesem Wetter; under the ~ ⟨fam⟩ nicht ganz auf dem Posten ◻ vt abwettern ⟨storm⟩; ⟨fig⟩ überstehen

weather: ~-beaten a verwittert; wettergegerbt ⟨face⟩. ~cock n Wetterhahn m. ~ forecast n Wettervorhersage f. ~-vane n Wetterfahne f

weave[1] /wiːv/ vi ⟨pt/pp weaved⟩ sich schlängeln ⟨through durch⟩

weave[2] n ⟨Tex⟩ Bindung f ◻ vt ⟨pt wove, pp woven⟩ weben; ⟨plait⟩ flechten; ⟨fig⟩ einflechten ⟨in in + acc⟩. ~r n Weber m

web /web/ n Netz nt. ~bed feet npl Schwimmfüße pl

wed /wed/ vt/i ⟨pt/pp wedded⟩ heiraten. ~ding n Hochzeit f; ⟨ceremony⟩ Trauung f

wedding: ~ day n Hochzeitstag m. ~ dress n Hochzeitskleid nt. ~-ring n Ehering m, Trauring m

wedge /wedʒ/ n Keil m; ⟨of cheese⟩ [keilförmiges] Stück nt ◻ vt festklemmen

wedlock /'wedlɒk/ n ⟨liter⟩ Ehe f; in/out of ~ ehelich/unehelich

Wednesday /'wenzdeɪ/ n Mittwoch m

wee /wiː/ a ⟨fam⟩ klein ◻ vi Pipi machen

weed /wiːd/ n & ~s pl Unkraut nt ◻ vt/i jäten. ~ out vt ⟨fig⟩ aussieben

'**weed-killer** n Unkrautvertilgungsmittel nt

weedy /'wiːdi/ a ⟨fam⟩ spillerig

week /wiːk/ n Woche f. ~day n Wochentag m. ~end n Wochenende nt

weekly /'wiːkli/ a & adv wöchentlich ◻ n Wochenzeitschrift f

weep /wiːp/ vi ⟨pt/pp wept⟩ weinen. ~ing 'willow n Trauerweide f

weigh /weɪ/ vt/i wiegen; ~ anchor den Anker lichten. ~ down vt ⟨fig⟩ niederdrücken. ~ up vt ⟨fig⟩ abwägen

weight /weɪt/ n Gewicht nt; put on/lose ~ zunehmen/abnehmen. ~ing n ⟨allowance⟩ Zulage f

weight: ~lessness n Schwerelosigkeit f.
~-lifting n Gewichtheben nt

weighty /'weɪtɪ/ a (-ier, -iest) schwer; (*important*) gewichtig

weir /wɪə(r)/ n Wehr nt

weird /wɪəd/ a (-er, -est) unheimlich; (*bizarre*) bizarr

welcome /'welkəm/ a willkommen; you're ~! nichts zu danken! you're ~ to have it das können Sie gerne haben □ n Willkommen nt □ vt begrüßen

weld /weld/ vt schweißen; ~er n Schweißer m

welfare /'welfeə(r)/ n Wohl nt; (*Admin*) Fürsorge f. W~ State n Wohlfahrtsstaat m

well[1] /wel/ n Brunnen m; (*oil* ~) Quelle f; (*of staircase*) Treppenhaus nt

well[2] adv (better, best) gut; as ~ auch; as ~ as (*in addition*) sowohl ... als auch; ~ done! gut gemacht! □ a gesund; he is not ~ es geht ihm nicht gut; get ~ soon! gute Besserung! □ int nun, na

well: ~-behaved a artig. ~-being n Wohl nt. ~-bred a wohlerzogen. ~-heeled a (*fam*) gut betucht

wellingtons /'welɪŋtənz/ npl Gummistiefel pl

well: ~-known a bekannt. ~-meaning a wohlmeinend. ~-meant a gut gemeint. ~-off a wohlhabend; be ~-off gut dran sein. ~-read a belesen. ~-to-do a wohlhabend

Welsh /welʃ/ a walisisch □ n (*Lang*) Walisisch nt; the ~ pl die Waliser. ~ man n Waliser m. ~ rabbit n überbackenes Käsebrot nt

went /went/ see go

wept /wept/ see weep

were /wɜː(r)/ see be

west /west/ n Westen m; to the ~ of westlich von □ a West-, west- □ adv nach Westen; go ~ (*fam*) flöten gehen. ~erly a westlich. ~ern a westlich □ n Western m

West: ~ Germany n Westdeutschland nt. ~ Indian a westindisch □ n Westinder(in) m(f). ~ Indies /-'ɪndɪz/ npl Westindische Inseln pl

'westward[s] /-wəd[z]/ adv nach Westen

wet /wet/ a (wetter, wettest) nass; (*fam: person*) weichlich, lasch; '~ paint' 'frisch gestrichen' □ vt (pt/pp wet or wetted) nass machen. ~ 'blanket n Spaßverderber m

whack /wæk/ n (*fam*) Schlag m □ vt (*fam*) schlagen. ~ed a (*fam*) kaputt

whale /weɪl/ n Wal m; have a ~ of a time (*fam*) sich toll amüsieren

wharf /wɔːf/ n Kai m

what /wɒt/ pron & int was; ~ for? wozu? ~ is it like? wie ist es? ~ is your name? wie ist Ihr Name? ~ is the weather like? wie ist das Wetter? ~'s he talking about? wovon redet er? □ a welche(r,s); ~ kind of a was für ein(e); at ~ time? um wie viel Uhr?

what'ever a [egal] welche(r,s) □ pron was ... auch; ~ is it? was ist das bloß? ~ he does was er auch tut; ~ happens was auch geschieht; nothing ~ überhaupt nichts

whatso'ever pron & a ≈ whatever

wheat /wiːt/ n Weizen m

wheedle /'wiːdl/ vt gut zureden (+ dat); ~ sth out of s.o. jdm etw ablocken

wheel /wiːl/ n Rad nt; (*pottery*) Töpferscheibe f; (*steering* ~) Lenkrad nt; at the ~ am Steuer □ vt welche(r,s); schieben □ vi kehrtmachen; (*circle*) kreisen

wheel: ~barrow n Schubkarre f. ~chair n Rollstuhl m. ~clamp n Parkkralle f

wheeze /wiːz/ vi keuchen

when /wen/ adv wann; the day ~ der Tag, an dem □ conj wenn; (*in the past*) als; (*although*) wo ... doch; ~ swimming/ reading beim Schwimmen/Lesen

whence /wens/ adv (*liter*) woher

when'ever conj & adv [immer] wenn; (*at whatever time*) wann immer; ~ did it happen? wann ist das bloß passiert?

where /weə(r)/ adv & conj wo; ~ [to] wohin; ~ [from] woher

whereabouts[1] /weərə'baʊts/ adv wo

'whereabouts[2] n Verbleib m; (*of person*) Aufenthaltsort m

where'as conj während; (*in contrast*) wohingegen

where'by adv wodurch

whereu'pon adv worauf[hin]

wher'ever conj & adv wo immer; (*to whatever place*) wohin immer; (*from whatever place*) woher immer; (*everywhere*) überall wo; ~ is he? wo ist er bloß? ~ possible wenn irgend möglich

whet /wet/ vt (pt/pp whetted) wetzen; anregen (*appetite*)

whether /'weðə(r)/ conj ob

which /wɪtʃ/ a & pron welche(r,s); ~ one welche(r,s) □ rel pron der/die/das, (*pl*) die; (*after clause*) was; after ~ wonach; on ~ worauf

which'ever a & pron [egal] welche(r,s); ~ it is was es auch ist

whiff /wɪf/ n Hauch m

while /waɪl/ n Weile f; a long ~ lange; be worth ~ sich lohnen; its worth my ~ es lohnt sich für mich □ conj während; (*as*

long as) solange; (*although*) obgleich □ *vt*
~ away sich (*dat*) vertreiben

whilst /waɪlst/ *conj* während

whim /wɪm/ *n* Laune *f*

whimper /'wɪmpə(r)/ *vi* wimmern; (*dog:*)
winseln

whimsical /'wɪmzɪkl/ *a* skurril

whine /waɪn/ *n* Winseln *nt* □ *vi* winseln

whip /wɪp/ *n* Peitsche *f*; (*Pol*) Einpeitscher
m □ *vt* (*pt/pp* whipped) peitschen; (*Culin*)
schlagen; (*snatch*) reißen; (*fam: steal*)
klauen. ~ up *vt* (*incite*) anheizen; (*fam*)
schnell hinzaubern (*meal*). ~ped 'cream
n Schlagsahne *f*

whirl /wɜːl/ *n* Wirbel *m*; I am in a ~ mir
schwirrt der Kopf □ *vt/i* wirbeln. ~pool
n Strudel *m*. ~wind *n* Wirbelwind *m*

whirr /wɜː(r)/ *vi* surren

whisk /wɪsk/ *n* (*Culin*) Schneebesen *m* □ *vt*
(*Culin*) schlagen. ~ away *vt* wegreißen

whisker /'wɪskə(r)/ *n* Schnurrhaar *nt*; ~s
pl (*on man's cheek*) Backenbart *m*

whisky /'wɪskɪ/ *n* Whisky *m*

whisper /'wɪspə(r)/ *n* Flüstern *nt*;
(*rumour*) Gerücht *nt*; in a ~ im Flüsterton
□ *vt/i* flüstern

whistle /'wɪsl/ *n* Pfiff *m*; (*instrument*)
Pfeife *f* □ *vt/i* pfeifen

white /waɪt/ *a* (-r, -st) weiß □ *n* Weiß *nt*;
(*of egg*) Eiweiß *nt*; (*person*) Weiße(r) *m/f*

white-: ~ 'coffee *n* Kaffee *m* mit Milch. ~-
'collar worker *n* Angestellte(r) *m*. ~ 'lie
n Notlüge *f*

whiten /'waɪtn/ *vt* weiß machen □ *vi* weiß
werden

whiteness /'waɪtnɪs/ *n* Weiß *nt*

'whitewash *n* Tünche *f*; (*fig*) Schönfärberei *f* □ *vt* tünchen

Whitsun /'wɪtsn/ *n* Pfingsten *nt*

whittle /'wɪtl/ *vt* ~ down reduzieren;
kürzen (*list*)

whiz[z] /wɪz/ *vi* (*pt/pp* whizzed) zischen.
~-kid *n* (*fam*) Senkrechtstarter *m*

who /huː/ *pron* wer; (*acc*) wen; (*dat*) wem
□ *rel pron* der/die/das, (*pl*) die

who'ever *pron* wer [immer]; ~ he is wer
er auch ist; ~ is it? wer ist das bloß?

whole /həʊl/ *a* ganz; (*truth*) voll □ *n*
Ganze(s) *nt*; as a ~ als Ganzes; on the ~
im Großen und Ganzen; the ~ lot alle;
(*everything*) alles; the ~ of Germany
ganz Deutschland; the ~ time die ganze
Zeit

whole-: ~food *n* Vollwertkost *f*. ~-
'hearted *a* rückhaltlos. ~meal *a*
Vollkorn-

'wholesale *a* Großhandels- □ *adv* en gros;
(*fig*) in Bausch und Bogen. ~r *n* Groß-
händler *m*

wholesome /'həʊlsəm/ *a* gesund

wholly /'həʊlɪ/ *adv* völlig

whom /huːm/ *pron* wen; to ~ wem □ *rel
pron* den/die/das, (*pl*) die; (*dat*) dem/der/
dem, (*pl*) denen

whooping cough /'huːpɪŋ-/ *n*
Keuchhusten *m*

whopping /'wɒpɪŋ/ *a* (*fam*) Riesen-

whore /hɔː(r)/ *n* Hure *f*

whose /huːz/ *pron* wessen; ~ is that? wem
gehört das? □ *rel pron* dessen/
deren/dessen, (*pl*) deren

why /waɪ/ *adv* warum; (*for what purpose*)
wozu; that's ~ darum □ *int* na

wick /wɪk/ *n* Docht *m*

wicked /'wɪkɪd/ *a* böse; (*mischievous*)
frech, boshaft

wicker /'wɪkə(r)/ *n* Korbgeflecht *nt*
□ *attrib* Korb-

wide /waɪd/ *a* (-r, -st) weit; (*broad*) breit;
(*fig*) groß; be ~ (*far from target*) daneben-
gehen □ *adv* weit; (*off target*) daneben; ~
awake hellwach; far and ~ weit und
breit. ~ly *adv* weit; (*known, accepted*)
weithin; (*differ*) stark

widen /'waɪdn/ *vt* verbreitern; (*fig*) erweitern □ *vi* sich verbreitern

'widespread *a* weit verbreitet

widow /'wɪdəʊ/ *n* Witwe *f*. ~ed *a* verwitwet. ~er *n* Witwer *m*

width /wɪdθ/ *n* Weite *f*; (*breadth*) Breite *f*

wield /wiːld/ *vt* schwingen; ausüben
(*power*)

wife /waɪf/ *n* (*pl* wives) [Ehe]frau *f*

wig /wɪg/ *n* Perücke *f*

wiggle /'wɪgl/ *vi* wackeln □ *vt* wackeln mit

wild /waɪld/ *a* (-er, -est), -ly *adv* wild; (*animal*) wild lebend; (*flower*) wild wachsend;
(*furious*) wütend; be ~ about (*keen on*)
wild sein auf (+ *acc*) □ *adv* wild; run ~
frei herumlaufen □ *n* in the ~ wild; the
~s *pl* die Wildnis *f*

'wildcat strike *n* wilder Streik *m*

wilderness /'wɪldənɪs/ *n* Wildnis *f*; (*desert*) Wüste *f*

wild-: ~-'goose chase *n* aussichtslose Suche *f*. ~life *n* Tierwelt *f*

wilful /'wɪlfl/ *a*, -ly *adv* mutwillig; (*self-
willed*) eigenwillig

will¹ /wɪl/ *v aux* wollen; (*forming future
tense*) werden; he ~ arrive tomorrow er
wird morgen kommen; ~ you go? gehst
du? you ~ be back soon, won't you? du
kommst doch bald wieder, nicht? he ~ be
there, won't he? er wird doch da sein?
she ~ be there by now sie wird jetzt
schon da sein; ~ you be quiet! willst du
wohl ruhig sein! ~ you have some wine?

möchten Sie Wein? the engine won't start der Motor will nicht anspringen

will² *n* Wille *m*; (*document*) Testament *nt*

willing /'wɪlɪŋ/ *a* willig; (*eager*) bereitwillig; be ~ bereit sein. **~ly** *adv* bereitwillig; (*gladly*) gern. **~ness** *n* Bereitwilligkeit *f*

willow /'wɪləʊ/ *n* Weide *f*

'will-power *n* Willenskraft *f*

willy-'nilly *adv* wohl oder übel

wilt /wɪlt/ *vi* welk werden, welken

wily /'waɪlɪ/ *a* (-ier, -iest) listig

wimp /wɪmp/ *n* Schwächling *m*

win /wɪn/ *n* Sieg *m*; have a ~ gewinnen □ *v* (*pt/pp* won; *pres p* winning) □ *vi* gewinnen; bekommen (*scholarship*) □ *vi* gewinnen; (*in battle*) siegen. ~ **over** *vt* auf seine Seite bringen

wince /wɪns/ *vi* zusammenzucken

winch /wɪntʃ/ *n* Winde *f* □ *vt* ~ up hochwinden

wind¹ /wɪnd/ *n* Wind *m*; (*breath*) Atem *m*; (*fam: flatulence*) Blähungen *pl*; have the ~ up (*fam*) Angst haben □ *vt* ~ s.o. jdm den Atem nehmen

wind² /waɪnd/ *v* (*pt/pp* wound) □ *vt* (*wrap*) wickeln; (*move by turning*) kurbeln; aufziehen (*clock*) □ *vi* (*road:*) sich winden. ~ **up** *vt* aufziehen (*clock*); schließen (*proceedings*)

wind /wɪnd/: **~fall** *n* unerwarteter Glücksfall *m*; **~falls** *pl* (*fruit*) Fallobst *nt*. ~ **instrument** *n* Blasinstrument *nt*. **~mill** *n* Windmühle *f*

window /'wɪndəʊ/ *n* Fenster *nt*; (*of shop*) Schaufenster *nt*

window: **~-box** *n* Blumenkasten *m*. **~-cleaner** *n* Fensterputzer *m*. **~-dresser** *n* Schaufensterdekorateur(in) *m(f)*. **~-dressing** *n* Schaufensterdekoration *f*; (*fig*) Schönfärberei *f*. **~-pane** *n* Fensterscheibe *f*. **~-shopping** *n* Schaufensterbummel *m*. **~-sill** *n* Fensterbrett *nt*

'windpipe *n* Luftröhre *f*

'windscreen *n*, (*Amer*) **'windshield** *n* Windschutzscheibe *f*. ~ **washer** *n* Scheibenwaschanlage *f*. **~-wiper** *n* Scheibenwischer *m*

wind: ~ **surfing** *n* Windsurfen *nt*. **~swept** *a* windgepeitscht; (*person*) zersaust

windy /'wɪndɪ/ *a* (-ier, -iest) windig; be ~ (*fam*) Angst haben

wine /waɪn/ *n* Wein *m*

wine: **~-bar** *n* Weinstube *f*. **~glass** *n* Weinglas *nt*. **~-list** *n* Weinkarte *f*

winery /'waɪnərɪ/ *n* (*Amer*) Weingut *nt*

'wine-tasting *n* Weinprobe *f*

wing /wɪŋ/ *n* Flügel *m*; (*Auto*) Kotflügel *m*; **~s** *pl* (*Theat*) Kulissen *pl*

wink /wɪŋk/ *n* Zwinkern *nt*; not sleep a ~ kein Auge zutun □ *vi* zwinkern; (*light:*) blinken

winner /'wɪnə(r)/ *n* Gewinner(in) *m(f)*; (*Sport*) Sieger(in) *m(f)*

winning /'wɪnɪŋ/ *a* siegreich; (*smile*) gewinnend. **~-post** *n* Zielpfosten *m*. **~s** *npl* Gewinn *m*

winter /'wɪntə(r)/ *n* Winter *m*. **~ry** *a* winterlich

wipe /waɪp/ *n* give sth a ~ etw abwischen □ *vt* abwischen; aufwischen (*floor*); (*dry*) abtrocknen. ~ **off** *vt* abwischen; (*erase*) auslöschen. ~ **out** *vt* (*cancel*) löschen; (*destroy*) ausrotten. ~ **up** *vt* aufwischen; abtrocknen (*dishes*)

wire /'waɪə(r)/ *n* Draht *m*. **~-haired** *a* rauhaarig

wireless /'waɪəlɪs/ *n* Radio *nt*

wire 'netting *n* Maschendraht *m*

wiring /'waɪərɪŋ/ *n* [elektrische] Leitungen *pl*

wiry /'waɪərɪ/ *a* (-ier, -iest) drahtig

wisdom /'wɪzdəm/ *n* Weisheit *f*; (*prudence*) Klugheit *f*. ~ **tooth** *n* Weisheitszahn *m*

wise /waɪz/ *a* (-r, -st), **-ly** *adv* weise; (*prudent*) klug

wish /wɪʃ/ *n* Wunsch *m* □ *vt* wünschen; ~ s.o. well jdm alles Gute wünschen; I ~ you could stay ich wünschte, du könntest hier bleiben □ *vi* sich (*dat*) etwas wünschen. **~ful** *a* **~ful thinking** Wunschdenken *nt*

wishy-washy /'wɪʃɪwɒʃɪ/ *a* labberig; (*colour*) verwaschen; (*person*) lasch

wisp /wɪsp/ *n* Büschel *nt*; (*of hair*) Strähne *f*; (*of smoke*) Fahne *f*

wisteria /wɪs'tɪərɪə/ *n* Glyzinie *f*

wistful /'wɪstfl/ *a*, **-ly** *adv* wehmütig

wit /wɪt/ *n* Geist *m*, Witz *m*; (*intelligence*) Verstand *m*; (*person*) geistreicher Mensch *m*; be at one's ~s' end sich (*dat*) keinen Rat mehr wissen; scared out of one's ~s zu Tode erschrocken

witch /wɪtʃ/ *n* Hexe *f*. **~craft** *n* Hexerei *f*. **~-hunt** *n* Hexenjagd *f*

with /wɪð/ *prep* mit (+ *dat*); ~ **fear/cold** vor Angst/Kälte; ~ **it** damit; I'm going ~ you ich gehe mit; take it ~ you nimm es mit; I haven't got it ~ me ich habe es nicht bei mir; I'm not ~ you (*fam*) ich komme nicht mit

with'draw *v* (*pt* -drew, *pp* -drawn) □ *vt* zurückziehen; abheben (*money*) □ *vi* sich zurückziehen. **~al** *n* Zurückziehen *nt*; (*of money*) Abhebung *f*; (*from drugs*) Entzug *m*. **~al symptoms** *npl* Entzugserscheinungen *pl*

with'drawn *see* withdraw □ *a* ⟨*person*⟩ verschlossen

wither /'wɪðə(r)/ *vi* [ver]welken

with'hold *vt* (*pt/pp* -held) vorenthalten (from s.o. jdm)

with'in *prep* innerhalb (+ *gen*); ~ the law im Rahmen des Gesetzes □ *adv* innen

with'out *prep* ohne (+ *acc*); ~ my noticing it ohne dass ich es merkte

with'stand *vt* (*pt/pp* -stood) standhalten (+ *dat*)

witness /'wɪtnɪs/ *n* Zeuge *m*/ Zeugin *f*; ⟨*evidence*⟩ Zeugnis *nt* □ *vt* Zeuge/Zeugin sein (+ *gen*); bestätigen ⟨*signature*⟩. ~box *n*, (*Amer*) ~stand *n* Zeugenstand *m*

witticism /'wɪtɪsɪzm/ *n* geistreicher Ausspruch *m*

wittingly /'wɪtɪŋlɪ/ *adv* wissentlich

witty /'wɪtɪ/ *a* (-ier, -iest) witzig, geistreich

wives /waɪvz/ *see* wife

wizard /'wɪzəd/ *n* Zauberer *m*. ~ry *n* Zauberei *f*

wizened /'wɪznd/ *a* verhutzelt

wobb|le /'wɒbl/ *vi* wackeln. ~ly *a* wackelig

woe /wəʊ/ *n* (*liter*) Jammer *m*; ~ is me! wehe mir!

woke, woken /wəʊk, 'wəʊkn/ *see* wake[1]

wolf /wʊlf/ *n* (*pl* wolves /wʊlvz/) Wolf *m* □ *vt* ~ [down] hinunterschlingen

woman /'wʊmən/ *n* (*pl* women) Frau *f*. ~izer *n* Schürzenjäger *m*. ~ly *a* fraulich

womb /wu:m/ *n* Gebärmutter *f*

women /'wɪmɪn/ *npl see* woman; W~'s Libber /'lɪbə(r)/ *n* Frauenrechtlerin *f*. W~'s Liberation *n* Frauenbewegung *f*

won /wʌn/ *see* win

wonder /'wʌndə(r)/ *n* Wunder *nt*; (*surprise*) Staunen *nt* □ *vt/i* sich fragen; (*be surprised*) sich wundern; I ~ da frage ich mich; I ~ whether she is ill ob sie wohl krank ist? ~ful *a*, -ly *adv* wunderbar

won't /wəʊnt/ = will not

woo /wu:/ *vt* (*liter*) werben um; (*fig*) umwerben

wood /wʊd/ *n* Holz *nt*; (*forest*) Wald *m*; touch ~! unberufen!

wood: ~cut *n* Holzschnitt *m*. ~ed /-ɪd/ *a* bewaldet. ~en *a* Holz-; (*fig*) hölzern. ~pecker *n* Specht *m*. ~wind *n* Holzbläser *pl*. ~work *n* (*wooden parts*) Holzteile *pl*; (*craft*) Tischlerei *f*. ~worm *n* Holzwurm *m*. ~y *a* holzig

wool /wʊl/ *n* Wolle *f* □ *attrib* Woll-. ~len *a* wollen. ~lens *npl* Wollsachen *pl*

woolly /'wʊlɪ/ *a* (-ier, -iest) wollig; (*fig*) unklar

word /wɜːd/ *n* Wort *nt*; (*news*) Nachricht *f*; by ~ of mouth mündlich; have a ~ with sprechen mit; have ~s einen Wortwechsel haben. ~ing *n* Wortlaut *m*. ~ processor *n* Textverarbeitungssystem *nt*

wore /wɔː(r)/ *see* wear

work /wɜːk/ *n* Arbeit *f*; (*Art, Literature*) Werk *nt*; ~s *pl* (*factory, mechanism*) Werk *nt*; at ~ bei der Arbeit; out of ~ arbeitslos □ *vi* arbeiten; (*machine, system:*) funktionieren; (*have effect*) wirken; (*study*) lernen; it won't ~ (*fig*) es klappt nicht □ *vt* arbeiten lassen; bedienen ⟨*machine*⟩; betätigen ⟨*lever*⟩; ~ one's way through sth sich durch etw hindurcharbeiten. ~ off *vt* abarbeiten. ~ out *vt* ausrechnen; (*solve*) lösen □ *vi* gut gehen, (*fam*) klappen. ~ up *vt* aufbauen; sich (*dat*) holen ⟨*appetite*⟩; get ~ed up sich aufregen

workable /'wɜːkəbl/ *a* (*feasible*) durchführbar

workaholic /wɜːkə'hɒlɪk/ *n* arbeitswütiger Mensch *m*

worker /'wɜːkə(r)/ *n* Arbeiter(in) *m*(*f*)

working /'wɜːkɪŋ/ *a* berufstätig; ⟨*day, clothes*⟩ Arbeits-; be in ~ order funktionieren. ~ class *n* Arbeiterklasse *f*. ~class *a* Arbeiter-; be ~-class zur Arbeiterklasse gehören

work: ~man *n* Arbeiter *m*; (*craftsman*) Handwerker *m*. ~manship *n* Arbeit *f*. ~out *n* [Fitness]training *nt*. ~shop *n* Werkstatt *f*

world /wɜːld/ *n* Welt *f*; in the ~ auf der Welt; a ~ of difference ein himmelweiter Unterschied; think the ~ of s.o. große Stücke auf jdn halten. ~ly *a* weltlich; ⟨*person*⟩ weltlich gesinnt. ~-wide *a* & *adv* /-'-'-/ weltweit

worm /wɜːm/ *n* Wurm *m* □ *vt* ~ one's way into s.o.'s confidence sich in jds Vertrauen einschleichen. ~eaten *a* wurmstichig

worn /wɔːn/ *see* wear □ *a* abgetragen. ~out *a* abgetragen; ⟨*carpet*⟩ abgenutzt; ⟨*person*⟩ erschöpft

worried /'wʌrɪd/ *a* besorgt

worry /'wʌrɪ/ *n* Sorge *f* □ *v* (*pt/pp* worried) □ *vt* beunruhigen, Sorgen machen (+ *dat*); (*bother*) stören □ *vi* sich beunruhigen, sich (*dat*) Sorgen machen. ~ing *a* beunruhigend

worse /wɜːs/ *a* & *adv* schlechter; (*more serious*) schlimmer □ *n* Schlechtere(s) *nt*; Schlimmere(s) *nt*

worsen /'wɜːsn/ *vt* verschlechtern □ *vi* sich verschlechtern

worship /'wɜːʃɪp/ *n* Anbetung *f*; (*service*) Gottesdienst *m*; Your/His W ~ Euer/

Seine Ehren □ v (pt/pp -shipped) □ vt anbeten □ vi am Gottesdienst teilnehmen

worst /wɜ:st/ a schlechteste(r,s); (most
serious) schlimmste(r,s) □ adv am
schlechtesten; am schlimmsten □ n the
~ das Schlimmste; get the ~ of it den
Kürzeren ziehen

worsted /'wʊstɪd/ n Kammgarn m

worth /wɜ:θ/ n Wert m; £10's ~ of petrol
Benzin für £10 □ a be ~ £5 £5 wert sein;
be ~ it (fig) sich lohnen. ~less a wertlos.
~while a lohnend

worthy /'wɜ:ðɪ/ a würdig

would /wʊd/ v aux I ~ do it ich würde es
tun, ich täte es; ~ you go? würdest du
gehen? he said he ~n't er sagte, er würde
es nicht tun; what ~ you like? was
möchten Sie?

wound¹ /wu:nd/ n Wunde f □ vt verwun-
den

wound² /waʊnd/ see wind²

wove, woven /waʊv, 'waʊvn/ see weave²

wrangle /'ræŋgl/ n Streit m □ vi sich
streiten

wrap /ræp/ n Umhang m □ vt (pt/pp
wrapped) ~ [up] wickeln; einpacken
⟨present⟩ □ vi ~ up warmly sich warm
einpacken; be ~ped up in (fig) aufgehen
in (+ dat). ~per n Hülle f. ~ping n Verpackung f. ~ping paper n Einwickelpapier
nt

wrath /rɒθ/ n Zorn m

wreak /ri:k/ vt ~ havoc Verwüstungen
anrichten

wreath /ri:θ/ n (pl ~s /-ðz/) Kranz m

wreck /rek/ n Wrack nt □ vt zerstören;
zunichte machen ⟨plans⟩; zerrütten ⟨mar-
riage⟩. ~age n /-ɪdʒ/ n Wrackteile pl; (fig)
Trümmer pl

wren /ren/ n Zaunkönig m

wrench /rentʃ/ n Ruck m; (tool) Schraubenschlüssel m; be a ~ (fig) weh tun □ vt
reißen; ~sth from s.o. jdm etw entreißen

wrest /rest/ vt entwinden (from s.o. jdm)

wrestl|e /'resl/ vi ringen. ~er n Ringer m.
~ing n Ringen nt

wretch /retʃ/ n Kreatur f. ~ed /-ɪd/ a
elend; (very bad) erbärmlich

wriggle /'rɪgl/ n Zappeln nt □ vi zappeln;
(move forward) sich schlängeln; ~ out of
sth (fam) sich vor etw (dat) drücken

wring /rɪŋ/ vt (pt/pp wrung) wringen; (~
out) auswringen; umdrehen ⟨neck⟩; ringen
⟨hands⟩; be ~ing wet tropfnass sein

wrinkle /'rɪŋkl/ n Falte f; (on skin) Runzel
f □ vt kräuseln □ vi sich kräuseln, sich
falten. ~d a runzlig

wrist /rɪst/ n Handgelenk nt. ~-watch n
Armbanduhr f

writ /rɪt/ n (Jur) Verfügung f

write /raɪt/ vt/i (pt wrote, pp written, pres
p writing) schreiben. ~ down vt aufschr-
reiben. ~ off vt abschreiben; zu Schrott
fahren ⟨car⟩

'write-off n ≈ Totalschaden m

writer /'raɪtə(r)/ n Schreiber(in) m(f); (author) Schriftsteller(in) m(f)

'write-up n Bericht m; (review) Kritik f

writhe /raɪð/ vi sich winden

writing /'raɪtɪŋ/ n Schreiben nt; (hand-
writing) Schrift f; in ~ schriftlich. ~-
paper n Schreibpapier nt

written /'rɪtn/ see write

wrong /rɒŋ/ a, -ly adv falsch; (morally)
unrecht; (not just) ungerecht; be ~ nicht
stimmen; ⟨person:⟩ Unrecht haben;
what's ~? was ist los? □ adv falsch; go ~
⟨person:⟩ etwas falsch machen; ⟨machine:⟩
kaputtgehen; ⟨plan:⟩ schief gehen □ n Unrecht nt □ vt Unrecht tun (+ dat). ~ful a
ungerechtfertigt. ~fully adv ⟨accuse⟩ zu
Unrecht

wrote /raʊt/ see write

wrought 'iron /rɔ:t-/ n Schmiedeeisen
nt □ attrib schmiedeeisern

wrung /rʌŋ/ see wring

wry /raɪ/ a (-er, -est) ironisch; ⟨humour⟩
trocken

X

xerox (P) /'zɪərɒks/ vt fotokopieren

Xmas /'krɪsməs, 'eksməs/ n (fam) Weihnachten nt

X-ray /'eks-/ n (picture) Röntgenaufnahme
f; ~s pl Röntgenstrahlen pl; have an ~
geröntgt werden □ vt röntgen;
durchleuchten ⟨luggage⟩

Y

yacht /jɒt/ n Jacht f; (for racing) Segelboot
nt. ~ing n Segeln nt

yank /jæŋk/ vt (fam) reißen

Yank n (fam) Amerikaner(in) m(f), (fam)
Ami m

yap /jæp/ vi (pt/pp yapped) ⟨dog:⟩ kläffen

yard¹ /jɑ:d/ n Hof m; (for storage) Lager
nt

yard[2] *n* Yard *nt* (= 0,91 m). ∼stick *n* (*fig*) Maßstab *m*

yarn /jɑːn/ *n* Garn *nt*; (*fam: tale*) Geschichte *f*

yawn /jɔːn/ *n* Gähnen *nt* □ *vi* gähnen. ∼ing *a* gähnend

year /jɪə(r)/ *n* Jahr *nt*; (*of wine*) Jahrgang *m*; for ∼s jahrelang. ∼book *n* Jahrbuch *nt*. ∼ly *a & adv* jährlich

yearn /jɜːn/ *vi* sich sehnen (for nach). ∼ing *n* Sehnsucht *f*

yeast /jiːst/ *n* Hefe *f*

yell /jel/ *n* Schrei *m* □ *vi* schreien

yellow /'jeləʊ/ *a* gelb □ *n* Gelb *nt*. ∼ish *a* gelblich

yelp /jelp/ *vi* jaulen

yen /jen/ *n* Wunsch *m* (for nach)

yes /jes/ *adv* ja; (*contradicting*) doch □ *n* Ja *nt*

yesterday /'jestədeɪ/ *n & adv* gestern; ∼'s paper die gestrige Zeitung; the day before ∼ vorgestern

yet /jet/ *adv* noch; (*in question*) schon; (*nevertheless*) doch; as ∼ bisher; not ∼ noch nicht; the best ∼ das bisher beste □ *conj* doch

yew /juː/ *n* Eibe *f*

Yiddish /'jɪdɪʃ/ *n* Jiddisch *nt*

yield /jiːld/ *n* Ertrag *m* □ *vt* bringen; abwerfen (*profit*) □ *vi* nachgeben; (*Amer, Auto*) die Vorfahrt beachten

yodel /'jəʊdl/ *vi* (*pt/pp* yodelled) jodeln

yoga /'jəʊgə/ *n* Yoga *m*

yoghurt /'jɒgət/ *n* Joghurt *m*

yoke /jəʊk/ *n* Joch *nt*; (*of garment*) Passe *f*

yokel /'jəʊkl/ *n* Bauerntölpel *m*

yolk /jəʊk/ *n* Dotter *m*, Eigelb *nt*

yonder /'jɒndə(r)/ *adv* (*liter*) dort drüben

you /juː/ *pron* du; (*acc*) dich; (*dat*) dir; (*pl*) ihr; (*acc, dat*) euch; (*formal*) (*nom & acc, sg & pl*) Sie; (*dat, sg & pl*) Ihnen; (*one*) man; (*acc*) einen; (*dat*) einem; all of ∼ ihr/Sie alle; I know ∼ ich kenne dich/euch/Sie; I'll give ∼ the money ich gebe dir/euch/Ihnen das Geld; it does ∼ good es tut einem gut; it's bad for ∼ es ist ungesund

young /jʌŋ/ *a* (-er /-gə(r)/, -est /-gɪst/) jung □ *npl* (*animals*) Junge *pl*; the ∼ die

Jugend *f*. ∼ster *n* Jugendliche(r) *m/f*; (*child*) Kleine(r) *m/f*

your /jɔː(r)/ *a* dein; (*pl*) euer; (*formal*) Ihr

yours /jɔːz/ *poss pron* deine(r), deins; (*pl*) eure(r), euers; (*formal, sg & pl*) Ihre(r), Ihr[e]s; a friend of ∼ ein Freund von dir/Ihnen/euch; that is ∼ das gehört dir/Ihnen/euch

your'self *pron* (*pl* -selves) selbst; (*refl*) dich; (*dat*) dir; (*pl*) euch; (*formal*) sich; by ∼ allein

youth /juːθ/ *n* (*pl* youths /-ðːz/) Jugend *f*; (*boy*) Jugendliche(r) *m*. ∼ful *a* jugendlich. ∼ hostel *n* Jugendherberge *f*

Yugoslav /'juːgəslɑːv/ *a* jugoslawisch. ∼ia /-'slɑːvɪə/ *n* Jugoslawien *nt*

Z

zany /'zeɪnɪ/ *a* (-ier, -iest) närrisch, verrückt

zeal /ziːl/ *n* Eifer *m*

zealous /'zeləs/ *a*, -ly *adv* eifrig

zebra /'zebrə/ *n* Zebra *nt*. ∼ 'crossing *n* Zebrastreifen *m*

zenith /'zenɪθ/ *n* Zenit *m*; (*fig*) Gipfel *m*

zero /'zɪərəʊ/ *n* Null *f*

zest /zest/ *n* Begeisterung *f*

zigzag /'zɪgzæg/ *n* Zickzack *m* □ *vi* (*pt/pp* -zagged) im Zickzack laufen; (*in vehicle*) fahren

zinc /zɪŋk/ *n* Zink *nt*

zip /zɪp/ *n* ∼ [fastener] Reißverschluss *m* □ *vt* ∼ [up] den Reißverschluss zuziehen an (+ *dat*)

'Zip code *n* (*Amer*) Postleitzahl *f*

zipper /'zɪpə(r)/ *n* Reißverschluss *m*

zither /'zɪðə(r)/ *n* Zither *f*

zodiac /'zəʊdɪæk/ *n* Tierkreis *m*

zombie /'zɒmbɪ/ *n* (*fam*) like a ∼ ganz benommen

zone /zəʊn/ *n* Zone *f*

zoo /zuː/ *n* Zoo *m*

zoological /zəʊə'lɒdʒɪkl/ *a* zoologisch

zoolog|ist /zəʊ'ɒlədʒɪst/ *n* Zoologe *m* /-gin *f*. ∼y Zoologie *f*

zoom /zuːm/ *vi* sausen. ∼ lens *n* Zoomobjektiv *nt*

Phonetic symbols used for German words

a	Hand	hant		ŋ	lang	laŋ
aː	Bahn	baːn		o	Moral	moˈraːl
ɐ	Ober	ˈoːbɐ		oː	Boot	boːt
ɐ̯	Uhr	uːɐ̯		o̯	Foyer	fo̯aˈjeː
ã	Conférencier	kõferãˈsi̯e		õ	Konkurs	kõˈkʊrs
ãː	Abonnement	abɔnəˈmãː		õː	Ballon	baˈlõː
ai̯	weit	vai̯t		ɔ	Post	pɔst
au̯	Haut	hau̯t		ø	Ökonom	økoˈnoːm
b	Ball	bal		øː	Öl	øːl
ç	ich	ɪç		œ	göttlich	ˈɡœtlɪç
d	dann	dan		ɔy	heute	ˈhɔytə
dʒ	Gin	dʒɪn		p	Pakt	pakt
e	Metall	meˈtal		r	Rast	rast
eː	Beet	beːt		s	Hast	hast
ɛ	mästen	ˈmɛstən		ʃ	Schal	ʃaːl
ɛː	wählen	ˈvɛːlən		t	Tal	taːl
ɛ̃ː	Cousin	kuˈzɛ̃ː		ts	Zahl	tsaːl
ə	Nase	ˈnaːzə		tʃ	Couch	kau̯tʃ
f	Faß	fas		u	kulant	kuˈlant
ɡ	Gast	ɡast		uː	Hut	huːt
h	haben	ˈhaːbən		u̯	aktuell	akˈtu̯ɛl
i	Rivale	riˈvaːlə		ʊ	Pult	pʊlt
iː	viel	fiːl		v	was	vas
i̯	Aktion	akˈtsi̯oːn		x	Bach	bax
ɪ	Birke	ˈbɪrkə		y	Physik	fyˈziːk
j	ja	jaː		yː	Rübe	ˈryːbə
k	kalt	kalt		ỹ	Nuance	ˈnỹãːsə
l	Last	last		ʏ	Fülle	ˈfʏlə
m	Mast	mast		z	Nase	ˈnaːzə
n	Naht	naːt		ʒ	Regime	reˈʒiːm

ʔ	Glottal stop, e.g. Koordination /koʔɔrdinaˈtsi̯oːn/.
ː	Length sign after a vowel, e.g. Chrom /kroːm/.
ˈ	Stress mark before stressed syllable, e.g. Balkon /balˈkõː/.

Die für das Englische verwendeten Zeichen der Lautschrift

ɑː	barn	bɑːn	l	lot	lɒt
ã	nuance	'njuːãs	m	mat	mæt
æ	fat	fæt	n	not	nɒt
æ̃	lingerie	'læ̃ʒərɪ	ŋ	sing	sɪŋ
aɪ	fine	fam	ɒ	got	gɒt
aʊ	now	naʊ	ɔː	paw	pɔː
b	bat	bæt	ɔɪ	boil	bɔɪl
d	dog	dɒg	p	pet	pet
dʒ	jam	dʒæm	r	rat	ræt
e	met	met	s	sip	sɪp
eɪ	fate	feɪt	ʃ	ship	ʃɪp
eə	fairy	'feərɪ	t	tip	tɪp
əʊ	goat	gəʊt	tʃ	chin	tʃɪn
ə	ago	ə'geʊ	θ	thin	θɪn
ɜː	fur	fɜː(r)	ð	the	ðə
f	fat	fæt	uː	boot	buːt
g	good	gʊd	ʊ	book	bʊk
h	hat	hæt	ʊə	tourism	'tʊərɪzm
ɪ	bit, happy	bɪt, 'hæpɪ	ʌ	dug	dʌg
ɪə	near	nɪə(r)	v	van	væn
iː	meet	miːt	w	win	wɪn
j	yet	jet	z	zip	zɪp
k	kit	kɪt	ʒ	vision	'viʒn

ː   bezeichnet Länge des vorhergehenden Vokals, z. B. boot [buːt].

ˈ   Betonung, steht unmittelbar vor einer betonten Silbe, z. B. ago [ə'geʊ].

(r) Ein „r" in runden Klammern wird nur gesprochen, wenn im Textzusammenhang ein Vokal unmittelbar folgt, z. B. fire /'faɪə(r); fire at /'faɪər æt/.

Guide to German pronunciation

Consonants are pronounced as in English with the following exceptions:

b	as	p	
d	as	t	*at the end of a word or syllable*
g	as	k	

ch		as in Scottish lo<u>ch</u> *after a, o, u, au*
		like an exaggerated h as in <u>h</u>uge *after i, e, ä, ö, ü, eu, ei*

-chs	as	x	(as in bo<u>x</u>)
-ig	as	-ich /ɪç/	*when a suffix*
j	as	y	(as in <u>y</u>es)

ps		the p is pronounced
pn		

qu	as	k+v	

s	as	z	(as in <u>z</u>ero) *at the beginning of a word*
	as	s	(as in bu<u>s</u>) *at the end of a word or syllable, before a consonant, or when doubled*

sch	as	sh	

sp	as	shp	*at the beginning of a word*
st	as	sht	

v	as	f	(as in <u>f</u>or)
	as	v	(as in <u>v</u>ery) *within a word*

w	as	v	(as in <u>v</u>ery)

z	as	ts	

Vowels are approximately as follows:

a	short	as	u	(as in b<u>u</u>t)
	long	as	a	(as in c<u>a</u>r)
e	short	as	e	(as in p<u>e</u>n)
	long	as	a	(as in p<u>a</u>per)
i	short	as	i	(as in b<u>i</u>t)
	long	as	ee	(as in qu<u>ee</u>n)
o	short	as	o	(as in h<u>o</u>t)
	long	as	o	(as in p<u>o</u>pe)
u	short	as	oo	(as in f<u>oo</u>t)
	long	as	oo	(as in b<u>oo</u>t)

Vowels are always short before a double consonant, and long when followed by an h or when double

| ie | is pronounced ee | | (as in k<u>ee</u>p) |

Diphthongs

au		as	ow	(as in h<u>ow</u>)
ei ai		as	y	(as in m<u>y</u>)
eu äu		as	oy	(as in b<u>oy</u>)

German irregular verbs

1st, 2nd and 3rd person present are given after the infinitive, and past subjunctive after the past indicative, where there is a change of vowel or any other irregularity.

Compound verbs are only given if they do not take the same forms as the corresponding simple verb, e.g. *befehlen*, or if there is no corresponding simple verb, e.g. *bewegen*.

An asterisk (*) indicates a verb which is also conjugated regularly.

Infinitive Infinitiv	Past Tense Präteritum	Past Participle 2. Partizip
abwägen	wog (wöge) ab	abgewogen
ausbedingen	bedang (bedänge) aus	ausbedungen
*backen (du bäckst, er bäckt)	buk (büke)	gebacken
befehlen (du befiehlst, er befiehlt)	befahl (beföhle, befähle)	befohlen
beginnen	begann (begänne)	begonnen
beißen (du/er beißt)	biss (bisse)	gebissen
bergen (du birgst, er birgt)	barg (bärge)	geborgen
bersten (du/er birst)	barst (bärste)	geborsten
bewegen²	bewog (bewöge)	bewogen
biegen	bog (böge)	gebogen
bieten	bot (böte)	geboten
binden	band (bände)	gebunden
bitten	bat (bäte)	gebeten
blasen (du/er bläst)	blies	geblasen
bleiben	blieb	geblieben
*bleichen	blich	geblichen
braten (du brätst, er brät)	briet	gebraten
brechen (du brichst, er bricht)	brach (bräche)	gebrochen
brennen	brannte (brennte)	gebrannt
bringen	brachte (brächte)	gebracht
denken	dachte (dächte)	gedacht
dreschen (du drischst, er drischt)	drosch (drösche)	gedroschen

Infinitive	Past Tense	Past Participle
Infinitiv	Präteritum	2. Partizip
dringen	drang (dränge)	gedrungen
dürfen (ich/er darf, du darfst)	durfte (dürfte)	gedurft
empfehlen (du empfiehlst, er empfiehlt)	empfahl (empföhle)	empfohlen
erlöschen (du erlischst, er erlischt)	erlosch (erlösche)	erloschen
*erschallen	erscholl (erschölle)	erschollen
*erschrecken (du erschrickst, er erschrickt)	erschrak (erschräke)	erschrocken
erwägen	erwog (erwöge)	erwogen
essen (du/er isst)	aß (äße)	gegessen
fahren (du fährst, er fährt)	fuhr (führe)	gefahren
fallen (du fällst, er fällt)	fiel	gefallen
fangen (du fängst, er fängt)	fing	gefangen
fechten (du fichtst, er ficht)	focht (föchte)	gefochten
finden	fand (fände)	gefunden
flechten (du flichtst, er flicht)	flocht (flöchte)	geflochten
fliegen	flog (flöge)	geflogen
fliehen	floh (flöhe)	geflohen
fließen (du/er fließt)	floss (flösse)	geflossen
fressen (du/er frisst)	fraß (fräße)	gefressen
frieren	fror (fröre)	gefroren
*gären	gor (göre)	gegoren
gebären (du gebierst, sie gebiert)	gebar (gebäre)	geboren
geben (du gibst, er gibt)	gab (gäbe)	gegeben
gedeihen	gedieh	gediehen
gehen	ging	gegangen
gelingen	gelang (gelänge)	gelungen
gelten (du giltst, er gilt)	galt (gölte, gälte)	gegolten
genesen (du/er genest)	genas (genäse)	genesen
genießen (du/er genießt)	genoss (genösse)	genossen
geschehen (es geschieht)	geschah (geschähe)	geschehen
gewinnen	gewann (gewonne, gewänne)	gewonnen
gießen (du/er gießt)	goss (gösse)	gegossen
gleichen	glich	geglichen

Infinitive Infinitiv	Past Tense Präteritum	Past Participle 2. Partizip
gleiten	glitt	geglitten
glimmen	glomm (glömme)	geglommen
graben (du gräbst, er gräbt)	grub (grübe)	gegraben
greifen	griff	gegriffen
haben (du hast, er hat)	hatte (hätte)	gehabt
halten (du hältst, er hält)	hielt	gehalten
hängen²	hing	gehangen
hauen	haute	gehauen
heben	hob (höbe)	gehoben
heißen (du/er heißt)	hieß	geheißen
helfen (du hilfst, er hilft)	half (hülfe)	geholfen
kennen	kannte (kennte)	gekannt
klingen	klang (klänge)	geklungen
kneifen	kniff	gekniffen
kommen	kam (käme)	gekommen
können (ich/er kann, du kannst)	konnte (könnte)	gekonnt
kriechen	kroch (kröche)	gekrochen
laden (du lädst, er lädt)	lud (lüde)	geladen
lassen (du/er lässt)	ließ	gelassen
laufen (du läufst, er läuft)	lief	gelaufen
leiden	litt	gelitten
leihen	lieh	geliehen
lesen (du/er liest)	las (läse)	gelesen
liegen	lag (läge)	gelegen
lügen	log (löge)	gelogen
mahlen	mahlte	gemahlen
meiden	mied	gemieden
melken	molk (mölke)	gemolken
messen (du/er misst)	maß (mäße)	gemessen
misslingen	misslang (misslänge)	misslungen
mögen (ich/er mag, du magst)	mochte (möchte)	gemocht
müssen (ich/er muss, du musst)	musste (müsste)	gemusst
nehmen (du nimmst, er nimmt)	nahm (nähme)	genommen
nennen	nannte (nennte)	genannt
pfeifen	pfiff	gepfiffen
preisen (du/er preist)	pries	gepriesen
quellen (du quillst, er quillt)	quoll (quölle)	gequollen

Infinitive Infinitiv	Past Tense Präteritum	Past Participle 2. Partizip
raten (du rätst, er rät)	riet	geraten
reiben	rieb	gerieben
reißen (du/er reißt)	riss	gerissen
reiten	ritt	geritten
rennen	rannte (rennte)	gerannt
riechen	roch (röche)	gerochen
ringen	rang (ränge)	gerungen
rinnen	rann (ränne)	geronnen
rufen	rief	gerufen
*salzen (du/er salzt)	salzte	gesalzen
saufen (du säufst, er säuft)	soff (söffe)	gesoffen
*saugen	sog (söge)	gesogen
schaffen[1]	schuf (schüfe)	geschaffen
scheiden	schied	geschieden
scheinen	schien	geschienen
scheißen (du/er scheißt)	schiss	geschissen
schelten (du schiltst, er schilt)	schalt (schölte)	gescholten
scheren[1]	schor (schöre)	geschoren
schieben	schob (schöbe)	geschoben
schießen (du/er schießt)	schoss (schösse)	geschossen
schinden	schindete	geschunden
schlafen (du schläfst, er schläft)	schlief	geschlafen
schlagen (du schlägst, er schlägt)	schlug (schlüge)	geschlagen
schleichen	schlich	geschlichen
schleifen[2]	schliff	geschliffen
schließen (du/er schließt)	schloss (schlösse)	geschlossen
schlingen	schlang (schlänge)	geschlungen
schmeißen (du/er schmeißt)	schmiss (schmisse)	geschmissen
schmelzen (du/er schmilzt)	schmolz (schmölze)	geschmolzen
schneiden	schnitt	geschnitten
*schrecken (du schrickst, er schrickt)	schrak (schräke)	geschreckt
schreiben	schrieb	geschrieben
schreien	schrie	geschrie[e]n
schreiten	schritt	geschritten
schweigen	schwieg	geschwiegen
schwellen (du schwillst, er schwillt)	schwoll (schwölle)	geschwollen

Infinitive	Past Tense	Past Participle
Infinitiv	Präteritum	2. Partizip
schwimmen	schwamm (schwömme)	geschwommen
schwinden	schwand (schwände)	geschwunden
schwingen	schwang (schwänge)	geschwungen
schwören	schwor (schwüre)	geschworen
sehen (du siehst, er sieht)	sah (sähe)	gesehen
sein (ich bin, du bist, er ist, wir sind, ihr seid, sie sind)	war (wäre)	gewesen
senden[1]	sandte (sendete)	gesandt
sieden	sott (sötte)	gesotten
singen	sang (sänge)	gesungen
sinken	sank (sänke)	gesunken
sinnen	sann (sänne)	gesonnen
sitzen (du/er sitzt)	saß (säße)	gesessen
sollen (ich/er soll, du sollst)	sollte	gesollt
*spalten	spaltete	gespalten
speien	spie	gespie[e]n
spinnen	spann (spönne, spänne)	gesponnen
sprechen (du sprichst, er spricht)	sprach (spräche)	gesprochen
sprießen (du/er sprießt)	spross (sprösse)	gesprossen
springen	sprang (spränge)	gesprungen
stechen (du stichst, er sticht)	stach (stäche)	gestochen
stehen	stand (stünde, stände)	gestanden
stehlen (du stiehlst, er stiehlt)	stahl (stähle)	gestohlen
steigen	stieg	gestiegen
sterben (du stirbst, er stirbt)	starb (stürbe)	gestorben
stinken	stank (stänke)	gestunken
stoßen (du/er stößt)	stieß	gestoßen
streichen	strich	gestrichen
streiten	stritt	gestritten
tragen (du trägst, er trägt)	trug (trüge)	getragen
treffen (du triffst, er trifft)	traf (träfe)	getroffen
treiben	trieb	getrieben
treten (du trittst, er tritt)	trat (träte)	getreten
*triefen	troff (tröffe)	getroffen

Infinitive Infinitiv	Past Tense Präteritum	Past Participle 2. Partizip
trinken	trank (tränke)	getrunken
trügen	trog (tröge)	getrogen
tun (du tust, er tut)	tat (täte)	getan
verderben (du verdirbst, er verdirbt)	verdarb (verdürbe)	verdorben
vergessen (du/er vergisst)	vergaß (vergäße)	vergessen
verlieren	verlor (verlöre)	verloren
verschleißen (du/er verschleißt)	verschliss	verschlissen
verzeihen	verzieh	verziehen
wachsen[1] (du/er wächst)	wuchs (wüchse)	gewachsen
waschen (du wäschst, er wäscht)	wusch (wüsche)	gewaschen
weichen[2]	wich	gewichen
weisen (du/er weist)	wies	gewiesen
*wenden[2]	wandte (wendete)	gewandt
werben (du wirbst, er wirbt)	warb (würbe)	geworben
werden (du wirst, er wird)	wurde (würde)	geworden
werfen (du wirfst, er wirft)	warf (würfe)	geworfen
wiegen[1]	wog (wöge)	gewogen
winden	wand (wände)	gewunden
wissen (ich/er weiß, du weißt)	wusste (wüsste)	gewusst
wollen (ich/er will, du willst)	wollte	gewollt
wringen	wrang (wränge)	gewrungen
ziehen	zog (zöge)	gezogen
zwingen	zwang (zwänge)	gezwungen